ALBION A–Z

IMPORTANT CORRECTION

On page 152 we have wrongly referred to the death of Tim McCoy, and in the acknowledgements on page 8 to the "late" Tim McCoy.

We are very happy to report that Tim McCoy is, in fact, still resident in Woodingdean.

We very much regret a serious error that has caused great distress to Tim McCoy, his family, friends and colleagues. We apologise sincerely for this mistake and for the offence it has caused.

Tim Carder and Roger Harris

ALBION A–Z

A Who's Who of

BRIGHTON & HOVE ALBION F.C.

Tim Carder & Roger Harris

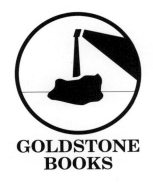

GOLDSTONE
BOOKS

First published in Great Britain by Goldstone Books, 1997

ISBN 0 9521337 1 7

Printed by FotoDirect Ltd
Unit A2, Enterprise Estate
Crowhurst Road
Brighton, BN1 8AF

Goldstone Books
113 Surrenden Road
Brighton, BN1 6WB

Contents

Introduction

It gives us enormous pleasure to publish this second book on the history of the Albion, a companion and complementary volume to the highly successful *Seagulls! The Story of Brighton & Hove Albion F.C.* We believe the two together must form *the* most comprehensive work ever on the history of a football club.

It also sees the culmination of a project that began in earnest way back in 1980. The Albion were struggling even then, but at the bottom of Division One (now the Premiership) rather than at the bottom of the Football League!

Inspired by stories of the exploits of men such as 'Bullet' Jones, Jack Doran, 'Tug' Wilson, Potter Smith and Stan Willemse, we set out – independently at first – to document the history of the football club for Brighton and Hove, a significant but previously overlooked part of our community. A chance meeting in Brighton Reference Library one day led to a long-lasting and fruitful collaboration.

In 1993 we published *Seagulls!*, the first comprehensive history of the club to contain all the Albion's teams and results over the years, together with a season-by-season history and many historic photographs.

Albion A–Z concentrates on the players and managers of the club, and contains a biography of everyone who has worn the famous blue-and-white shirt in a first-team competitive game. Naturally, each biography represents a personal opinion of one or other of the authors *to the end of 1996–97*, together with the factual information that makes up the detail of a football career. Many names in this volume will be familiar to readers, whose opinions of those players may well differ from those expressed but are just as valid. We have usually tried to concentrate on the positive aspects of each player's game where appropriate.

There are also many players contained herein who will not be familiar to the reader. Many of them were unknown to us, but extensive research and interviewing has revealed the nature of many of these now-forgotten men. Some remain a mystery, and the authors would welcome any comments or information on such players. Whether familiar or not, we hope that this work will provide an insight into the men who have represented our football club over the last 96 years.

There are a wealth of statistics and records, and as many players as possible are illustrated with photographs. A good many of these are of poor quality, perhaps enlarged from a poor original, but we believe it better to print *any* image of these long-forgotten men for the sake of posterity than omit them. In the main section (*Albion Players*) we have illustrated over 91% of the 829 players. In all there are 891 illustrations in this book. The time it has taken to compile this number of photos prompts us to ask readers *never* to throw away any memoribilia that may be of interest to current or future Albion historians.

Of course, from a sales point of view, we could hardly have chosen a worse time to publish. Attendances, not surprisingly, are at an all-time low as the club is forced to play at Gillingham, but there is a new board in place and a new spirit of co-operation with *one* council that appears to realise how the twin towns need the Albion as much as the Albion needs Brighton and Hove.

When *Seagulls!* was published in 1993 the club was in the middle of the shenanigans in the High Court that eventually led to the takeover by Bill Archer and Greg Stanley.. In our introduction then we welcomed the eventual granting of planning permission for retail stores on the Goldstone and the club's positive noises on securing a new ground. Like all other supporters, little did we suspect what was to happen. What a waste the last few years have been – apart from increasing fraternity among fans – but what a wealth of material for chroniclers of the club!

We stated then that 'Sussex without Brighton & Hove Albion is unthinkable.' Well the unthinkable has happened. Perhaps more correctly we should have said 'Brighton & Hove Albion without Sussex is unsustainable.' We also referred to the 1992–93 season as probably the most traumatic ever, but it now pales into insignificance against 1996–97, probably the most eventful, emotional and, at times, distressing campaign ever endured by supporters of *any* club.

The Albion *will* survive providing a swift return is made to the Brighton and Hove area, even if only to a temporary facility. In the early days of the century, when Brighton United folded to be followed soon after by the demise of Brighton & Hove Rangers, it was men of character such as John Jackson that saw the cause of professional football in Brighton and Hove finally reach fruition in the formation of the Albion in June 1901. It now needs men – and women – of similar disposition to resolve the current situation to the satisfaction of all concerned and ensure the long-term future of the 'Seagulls'. Let us all hope that the Albion are playing in a splendid new local stadium in time for their centenary in 2001.

Meanwhile, the club needs all the help it can get, and we hope that this book will assist in its own small way – by renewing enthusiasm amongst its readers and by contributing to the Albion's coffers.

Whether you read *Albion A–Z* from cover to cover, or dip in here and there to read about your favourite players, we hope that you enjoy it – and remember what a significant part Brighton & Hove Albion Football Club still has to play in this community.

Tim Carder and Roger Harris
November 1997

We welcome comments on *Albion A–Z* and its predecessor, *Seagulls!* If you have any information that will add to the knowledge of the history of the club – perhaps a photograph of a player that we have so far been unable to trace, or the whereabouts of a former player – then please write to Goldstone Books, 113 Surrenden Road, Brighton BN1 6WB. We are interested in *any* memoribilia relating to the Albion. You may also send e-mail to *timc@mistral.co.uk* or use the Internet web site at *http://www3.mistral.co.uk/timc* to make observations.

Acknowledgements

We would like to thank the numerous individuals and organisations who have helped along the long road to the successful conclusion of this project.

A special mention should be reserved for the Association of Football Statisticians and its membership, without whose inspiration this work would not have been possible. Many members of the Association have already compiled comprehensive volumes on their own particular clubs which have paved the way for this book. The existence of such splendid works greatly facilitated much of the gathering of information on players' careers. We acknowledge the debt we owe these historians and statisticians, and the companies that have published their research. Indeed, we invite historians of other clubs to use the information contained herein in the same spirit, for the further extension of the history of our national game.

There are, of course, many other books of equal excellence by authors not in the A.F.S. which have also proved invaluable, and we salute the compilers of them.

Major sources of information on Albion careers include the absolutely invaluable newspapers of the Southern Publishing Company, in particular the now-defunct *Sussex Daily News* and the *Evening Argus*.

Other major sources include: numerous football clubs; the records of the Football League and the Football Association; the Office of Population Censuses and Surveys (St Catherine's House) for their registers of births, deaths and marriages; the Public Record Office at Kew; Companies House; the British Library (Newspaper Division) at Colindale; the East Sussex Record Office at Lewes and its West Sussex counterpart at Chichester; and the reference libraries of Brighton, Hove, Hastings and Worthing.

Once again our Scottish correspondent, Nigel Bishop, has made a major contribution with a good deal of research at the equivalent bodies north of the border, as well as helping greatly with his in-depth knowledge of the Albion in the 1960s.

Other unexpected sources have included the archives of Lancing College, Ardingly College, Sidney Sussex College (Cambridge) and Jesus College (Oxford)

It is also most appropriate to express our appreciation for the many web-site maintainers around the world, most of them amateurs, for providing a wealth of information, particularly on those foreign players who are often hard to keep track of. The Internet provides a readily available means of following football events and careers in all continents of the world.

Among many ex-Albion players to have helped considerably with their own and others' careers, the following stand out: Jack Mansell, for his tremendous memory of his colleagues at the Goldstone Ground and for his scrapbooks; David Adekola; Harry Baldwin; Nicky Bissett; Walter Borthwick; Des Broomfield; Gary Brown, Dave Busby; Les Champelovier; Glyn Collins; Jeff Darey; Denis Foreman; Reg Fox; Dennis Gordon; Peter Harburn; Stan Hickman; Roy Jennings; Stewart Kerr; Dave Macciochi; the late Tim McCoy; Paddy McIlvenny; the late Ernie Marriott; Stuart Munday; Ashley Neal; Derek Neate; Dave Ridley; Adrian Thorne; Christer Warren; Jess Willard; Stan Willemse; Glen Wilson; the late Harold Winnard (formerly Harold Sly).

Other individuals who we would also like to thank for their assistance include: Danny Bloor, Terry Booth, Mrs D. Bowley, Gary Chalk, Mike Davage, Gerry Desmond, Leigh Edwards, Paul Hebdon, Trefor Jones, Tony Millard, Tim Parsons, Michael Sharpe, Paul Taylor, Ian Thomson, Liam Ward, Mrs H. Watts and Christine Woolgar.

Many thanks are due to XPS Limited, xerographic printers of Portslade, for the use of equipment, and to the staff of our main printers, FotoDirect Ltd, for their co-operation and advice.

We are sure there have been many others along the way. The omission of anyone from the above reflects only on the size of the task undertaken, not on their contribution. To them and all those mentioned we are eternally grateful.

Illustrations

We are indebted once again to the *Evening Argus* for permission to use many photgraphs from their extensive library, and we would like to express our appreciation of the photographers employed by the Southern Publishing Company over the years.

Thanks are also due to Brighton & Hove Albion F.C. itself for permission to use official club photographs and also the seagull logo.

Brighton & Hove Libraries must also be gratefully acknowledged for their co-operation over the use of photographs from their collection from the old *Brighton & Hove Herald* newspaper.

We must also give a very special mention to Dave Ticehurst for providing a good many photographs, particularly in the early years. His own book, *Brighton and Hove Albion: A Portrait in Old Picture Postcards* (ISBN 1 85770 070 8, £5.95), is still available and is a must for anyone interested in the Albion.

The compilation of photographs for this work has been a lengthy task, so it is difficult to express our thanks adequately to the following: Rose Ticehurst, Stuart Ashby, Mark Steer, John Wells, Pete Henry, Dave Damen, Lancing Football Club and Sawbridgeworth Town Football Club.

We would also like to thank Stewart Weir for permission to use a number of his photgraphs, and express our congratulations on his superb *More Than 90 Minutes: Two Extraordinary Years in the Life of a Football Club* (ISBN 0 9531214 0 2) which chronicles, in pictures, the unprecedented events of the 1995–96 and 1996–97 seasons.

The publishers have been unable to trace the copyright holders of many of the illustrations used and offer sincere apologies to anyone whose rights may have been infringed. Any photographer or other copyright holder is cordially invited to contact the publishers in writing, providing proof of copyright.

Brief History of Brighton & Hove Albion F.C.

For a detailed history the reader is referred to Seagulls! The Story of Brighton & Hove Albion F.C. *by the same authors ISBN 0 9521337 0 9*

In November 1897 the first professional football club in Brighton and Hove, Brighton United, was formed. It competed in the Southern League at the County Cricket Ground in Hove from 1898, but the gates were poor and the club folded in 1900 before the end of its second season.

Some enthusiasts then formed Brighton & Hove Rangers, an amateur club which played to the north of Brighton at Withdean. Rangers managed some excellent results against good opposition and secured a place in the Southern League for 1901–02, but then they too were forced to disband.

John Jackson, the former manager of United, organised a meeting on 24 June 1901 at the Seven Stars Hotel (now O'Sullivans bar) in Ship Street at which a new, third club was formed. Brighton & Hove United took up the now-defunct Rangers' place in the Southern League, but, because of complaints by Hove F.C., the name was soon changed to Brighton & Hove Albion.

Run semi-professionally, the infant club beat Shoreham 2–0 in its first game on 7 September 1901 on a pitch off Dyke Road. The first competitive fixture, played at the County Ground, saw Albion defeat Brighton Athletic 6–2 in the preliminary round of the F.A. Cup.

Playing in 'fisherman's-blue' shirts and white 'knickers', the team challenged for promotion from the Second Division but fell away to finish third in their first season. A number of games were also played at Hove F.C.'s Goldstone Ground, and from 1902 the two clubs shared the arena.

In 1902–03, Albion finished joint champions with Fulham and won promotion in a test match against Watford, with winger Ben Garfield scoring four times in a 5–3 win. The first season in Division One of the Southern League was a struggle, the club being forced to seek re-election, but 1904 was a notable year: a limited company was formed to maintain progress; Hove vacated the Goldstone leaving Albion as sole tenants; and the club adopted a new strip of blue-and-white stripes.

League form was erratic over the next few seasons, but Albion reached the F.A. Cup's competition proper for the first time in 1905–06, losing narrowly to Middlesbrough in round two. In 1908, Preston North End from the Football League's First Division were beaten and Liverpool were taken to a replay. The latter tie attracted a record crowd of 12,000 to the Goldstone.

In 1909–10, however, Albion won the Southern League championship. Jack Robson, manager since 1908, had assembled an excellent side with the meanest defence in the club's history. Men such as Bob 'Pom Pom' Whiting, Joe Leeming, Billy Booth, Bert Longstaff, Bill 'Bullet' Jones and Charlie Webb (who, in March 1909, had become Albion's first international) were outstanding in a superb season. Just sixteen players were used as the club also annexed the Southern Charity Cup.

Winning the title qualified Albion for the F.A. Charity Shield, which was then played for by the champions of the Football and Southern Leagues. On 5 September 1910, Albion defeated Aston Villa 1–0 at Stamford Bridge, the goal being scored by Webb. As the team returned to an ecstatic reception at Brighton, the club was dubbed 'Champions of England'.

League form declined slowly until 1915, when the club closed down during the First World War, but in the F.A. Cup there were some notable triumphs, the best result being a 1–0 win over First Division Oldham Athletic in 1914. Towards the end of the war Charlie Webb, who was a prisoner of the Germans at the time, was appointed manager, and he remained at the helm until 1947.

Albion struggled when normal fare was resumed in 1919, but in 1920 the Southern League's First Division was absorbed by the Football League as the Third Division (South). The club's first game in the new section was a 2–0 defeat at Southend. Over the next nineteen seasons Albion usually finished in the top half, but challenged for promotion (limited to one club) only in the late 1930s.

Some excellent players passed through the Goldstone between the wars, though, and Tommy Cook, who scored 123 goals for the club, became the first Brighton player to be capped by England. Other notable performers were forwards Tug Wilson (who played in 566 matches), Bobby Farrell, Bert Stephens and Potter Smith; half-backs Reg Wilkinson, Dave Walker, Wally Little and Paul Mooney; and full-back Jack Jenkins (who won eight caps for Wales).

The greatest triumphs were reserved for the F.A. Cup: First Division sides Oldham Athletic, Sheffield United, Everton, Grimsby Town, Portsmouth, Leicester City and Chelsea were all defeated.

The best Cup run came in 1932–33. The club competed in the qualifying rounds (because the secretary had neglected to apply for exemption) and thrashed the local amateur sides. In the first round proper Albion defeated Crystal Palace, then beat Wrexham, Chelsea and Bradford (P.A.) to set up a fifth-round tie with West Ham United. A record Hove crowd of 32,310 watched a 2–2 draw, but the 'Hammers' won the replay to end the Sussex interest after nine ties and eleven matches!

The club endured great financial difficulties during the Second World War, and only a takeover by the board of the greyhound stadium saved the day in 1940. On Christmas Day 1940, Albion lost 18–0 at Norwich City with a team that had to be partly made up with spectators!

In 1948, Albion sought re-election to the Football League for the only time. Nevertheless, attendances rose rapidly and the Goldstone's League record was broken four times in nine months. Under managers Don Welsh and Billy Lane the club's fortunes improved, and there were a number of near misses in the battle for promotion. In 1955–56, Albion scored 112 goals but finished only second.

Promotion and the championship were finally achieved in 1957–58, when Watford were beaten 6–0 in the final game with Adrian Thorne, a local 20-year-old, scoring five goals. Although the team lost 9–0 at Middlesbrough in their first-ever Second Division game, huge crowds flocked to the Goldstone as they improved to finish in twelfth place. On 27 December 1958 an all-time record crowd of 36,747 attended the 3–0 win over Fulham.

After four seasons of struggle in Division Two, Albion were relegated in 1962, then fell straight through the Third Division into Division Four. Under Archie Macaulay, and inspired by former England centre-forward Bobby Smith, the team won the championship in 1964–65 by defeating Darlington in their final match before a crowd of 31,423 at Hove.

In 1971–72, Albion, under Pat Saward, won promotion to Division Two largely because of outstanding away form, but were promptly relegated following thirteen consecutive defeats. Saward was replaced by the outspoken Brian Clough, but the club was then humiliated at home by the amateurs of

Walton & Hersham (4–0 in the F.A. Cup) and Bristol Rovers (8–2 in the League). Things soon improved and the drop was avoided, but Clough left for Leeds United leaving his assistant Peter Taylor in charge.

Albion came close to promotion in 1975–76 and acquired the nickname 'Seagulls', but Taylor then rejoined his former colleague at Nottingham Forest. New manager Alan Mullery steered the club to second place the following season with star forward Peter Ward scoring a club-record 36 goals, ably supported by men such as Brian Horton, Peter O'Sullivan, Eric Steele, Graham Cross, Chris Cattlin and Ian Mellor. In the Second Division in 1977–78 the team missed out on another promotion only on goal difference, and fans turned up in unprecedented numbers to witness the attempt; the average gate was 25,264.

The following season Albion won their last game 3–1 at Newcastle to finish second and earn a place in Division One. Their first game in the top flight was on 18 August 1979, a 4–0 home defeat by Arsenal, and the 'Seagulls' struggled at the bottom of the table until a win at the home of European champions Nottingham Forest restored confidence; they finished sixteenth.

In 1980–81, Albion avoided relegation by winning their last four games, but Mullery resigned and was replaced by Mike Bailey. In finishing thirteenth in 1981–82, Albion's football became very negative and, with the club struggling the following season, Bailey was replaced by Jimmy Melia. Although the 'Seagulls' finished bottom, they reached the F.A. Cup final with wins over Newcastle United, Manchester City, Liverpool, Norwich City and Sheffield Wednesday.

In the Wembley final, Albion drew 2–2 with Manchester United with goals from Gordon Smith and Gary Stevens, and nearly clinched the Cup in the last minute of extra time when Smith's close-range shot was saved. United won the replay convincingly, 4–0.

Following relegation Albion sold stars such as Steve Foster, Gary Stevens and Michael Robinson, and Chris Cattlin replaced Melia as manager. In 1984–85 he took the 'Seagulls' close to promotion, and to the last eight of the F.A. Cup the following season, but was then sacked amid outcry among supporters. Alan Mullery returned but was quickly dismissed to be replaced by Barry Lloyd. Relegation soon followed, but the club bounced straight back in 1987–88 on the back of Garry Nelson's 32 goals, and made it to the Division Two play-off final in 1990–91. However, Notts County won 3–1 at Wembley and the 'Seagulls' were relegated the following season.

But the glory years of the late 1970s and early '80s had taken their toll. Unrealistic salaries led to debts which grew and grew. Abysmal financial management allowed the club to get into such a state that winding-up orders were sought for unpaid tax. The club's position was so dire that fellow directors were happy to transfer their shares to Bill Archer and Greg Stanley in 1993, who brought in a new loan to pay off the immediate debts. In came the former M.P. for Eastbourne, David Bellotti, as chief executive, while manager Barry Lloyd was quickly replaced by Liam Brady, bringing about renewed enthusiasm among supporters.

In 1995, though, it was revealed that Archer, Stanley and Bellotti had agreed to sell the Goldstone Ground to developers, even though there were no acceptable plans to relocate the club to a new stadium. That action, and subsequent events, precipitated a bitter 'war'. With the club refusing to lease back the ground, the 1995–96 season culminated in a pitch invasion by desperate supporters which saw the goals wrecked and the game against York City abandoned. Three days later the board finally agreed to lease the Goldstone for another year. Meanwhile, Albion were relegated to the bottom division for the first time for over 30 years.

Brady, who had felt unable to continue as manager, fronted a takeover consortium, but majority owner Bill Archer rejected any approach, an attitude which prompted another pitch invasion in October 1996 that led to the deduction of two points. Home games were played in a malevolent atmosphere until Bellotti was finally driven from the ground in December 1996. With the club already bottom of the League and facing relegation to the Conference, manager Jimmy Case was replaced by Steve Gritt who immediately set about rekindling team spirit with discipline and organisation.

Following appeals by fans, the F.A. finally introduced both sides to mediators for prolonged talks. Supporters themselves continued an inspired campaign that culminated in 'Fans United' on 8 February 1997, a unique event in the history of the game. From that moment Albion followers started to believe in their team again, and Albion, through outstanding home form, managed to catch their fellow strugglers.

Against expectations, the mediators secured an agreement for the future of the club in March 1997 which was announced the following month. Fittingly, Albion said goodbye to the Goldstone Ground, their home since 1902, with a win over Doncaster Rovers to move off the bottom of the table. Probably the most important game ever in the club's 96-year history, the showdown at Hereford was drawn, a result which saved Albion and instead relegated the home side to the Conference as they had scored fewer goals.

At the end of a turbulent summer, which saw Albion survive a motion to expel them from the Football League, the club found themselves playing at Gillingham, Kent, but on 2 September 1997 a new board, led by Dick Knight and backed by stadium constructors Alfred McAlpine Ltd, took over the club. A 'battle' had been won but the 'war', which will only end when the Albion are playing in a permanent stadium in Brighton or Hove, is far from over.

Major Honours

Southern League Division Two Champions	1903
Southern League Champions	1910
Southern Professional Charity Cup Winners	1910
F.A. Charity Shield winners	1910
Football League Div.3 (South) champions	1958
Football League Div.4 champions	1964
Football League Div.3 runners-up (promoted)	1972, 1977, 1988
Football League Div.2 runners-up (promoted)	1979
F.A. Cup finalists	1983
Football League Div.2 Play-Off finalists	1991

League Record

Southern League Division Two	1901–03
Southern League Division One	1903–20
Football League Division Three (South) (wartime 1939–46)	1920–58
Football League Division Two	1958–62
Football League Division Three	1962–63
Football League Division Four	1963–65
Football League Division Three	1965–72
Football League Division Two	1972–73
Football League Division Three	1973–77
Football League Division Two	1977–79
Football League Division One	1979–83
Football League Division Two	1983–87
Football League Division Three	1987–88
Football League Division Two (N.B. Divisions renumbered 1992)	1988–96
Football League Division Three	1997–

Albion Players

This section contains biographical details of the 829 men who have played in first-team competitive matches for the Albion from 1901 until 1997, except for those who appeared only in wartime games between 1939 and 1946 (see *Albion Wartime Players*). Friendly matches, local competitions and mini-tournaments are not included. Note that transfer fees are largely derived from the Press.

For the purposes of this volume, first-team competitive matches are defined as those played in the following competitions only (because the first eleven would normally be fielded):

- Football League (**FL**) 1920–39 & 1946–97, but *not* including three abandoned matches (16.9.1968, 1.1.1977 & 27.4.1996) or the three matches played in the aborted 1939–40 season. The competition has been known as the Canon League (1983–86), Today League (1986–87), Barclays League (1987–93), Endsleigh Insurance League (1993–96) and Nationwide Football League (1996–date).
- Football (Barclays) League Division Two Play-offs (**Play-offs**) 1991
- Football Association Challenge Cup (**FAC**) 1901–1939 & 1945–97, *including all* qualifying ties. The match on 16.1.1908 was abandoned in extra time with the score at 2–1, but was deemed to be a 1–1 draw, the full-time score; the extra-time goal (scored by Jack Hall) has *not* been counted here. The 1945–46 competition **is** included.
- Football League Cup (**FLC**) 1960–97. The competition has been known as the Milk Cup (1982–86), Littlewoods Challenge Cup (1986–90), Rumbelows League Cup (1990–92) and the Coca-Cola Cup (1992–date)

- Football League Full Members Cup (**FMC**) 1985–87 & 1988–92. The competition has been known as the Simod Cup (1987–89) and the Zenith Data Systems Cup (1989–92)
- Football League Associate Members Cup (**AMC**) 1987–88 and its continuation, the Football League Trophy, 1992–97. The competition has been known as the Freight Rover Trophy (1984–88), Sherpa Van Trophy (1988–89), Leyland Daf Cup (1989–91), Autoglass Trophy (1991–94) and the Auto Windscreens Shield (1994–date).
- Football League Division Three Southern Section Challenge Cup, commonly known as the Southern Section Cup (**SSC**) 1933–39. Note that the 1938–39 tournament *is* included even though it was never completed.
- Southern League (**SL**) 1901–15 & 1919–20, but *not* including the reserves in Division Two in 1904–05 & 1907–08, or the abandoned game on 18.1.1908
- Southern League Test Match (**Test**) 1903
- Football Association Charity Shield (**FACS**) 1910
- United League (**UL**) 1905–07, but *not* including the abandoned match on 2.10.1905.
- Western League (**WL**) 1907–09, but *not* including the abandoned match on 11.11.1907.
- Western League Championship Match and replay (**WL Ch.**) 1909
- Southern Football Alliance (**SA**) 1912–14
- Southern Professional Charity Cup (**SCC**) 1907–15, *including* those matches in 1912–13 & 1913–14 played by the reserves.
- South Eastern League (**SEL**) 1902–03 *only*, regarded as a first-team competition that season but contested mainly by the reserves thereafter.

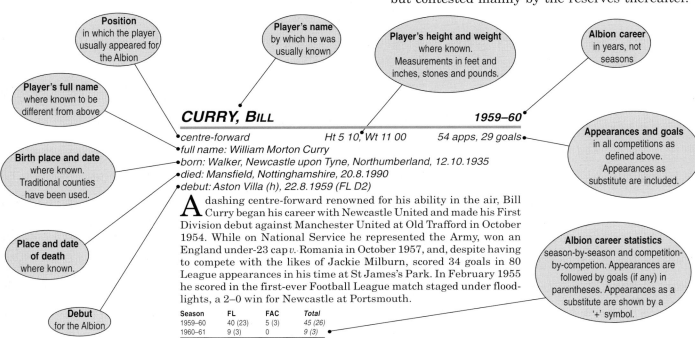

CURRY, BILL   *1959–60*

centre-forward   Ht 5 10, Wt 11 00   *54 apps, 29 goals*
full name: William Morton Curry
born: Walker, Newcastle upon Tyne, Northumberland, 12.10.1935
died: Mansfield, Nottinghamshire, 20.8.1990
debut: Aston Villa (h), 22.8.1959 (FL D2)

A dashing centre-forward renowned for his ability in the air, Bill Curry began his career with Newcastle United and made his First Division debut against Manchester United at Old Trafford in October 1954. While on National Service he represented the Army, won an England under-23 cap v. Romania in October 1957, and, despite having to compete with the likes of Jackie Milburn, scored 34 goals in 80 League appearances in his time at St James's Park. In February 1955 he scored in the first-ever Football League match staged under floodlights, a 2–0 win for Newcastle at Portsmouth.

Ovals (annotations):
- Position: in which the player usually appeared for the Albion
- Player's name: by which he was usually known
- Player's height and weight: where known. Measurements in feet and inches, stones and pounds.
- Albion career: in years, not seasons
- Player's full name: where known to be different from above
- Appearances and goals: in all competitions as defined above. Appearances as substitute are included.
- Birth place and date: where known. Traditional counties have been used.
- Place and date of death: where known.
- Albion career statistics: season-by-season and competition-by-competion. Appearances are followed by goals (if any) in parentheses. Appearances as a substitute are shown by a '+' symbol.
- Debut: for the Albion

Season	FL	FAC	Total
1959–60	40 (23)	5 (3)	45 (26)
1960–61	9 (3)	0	9 (3)
Total	49 (26)	5 (3)	54 (29)

ABBIS, KEITH — 1957–61

left-half — Ht 5 11, Wt 11 07 — 19 apps, 3 goals
full name: Keith Douglas Abbis
born: Hatfield, Hertfordshire, 26.4.1932
debut: Rotherham United (a), 7.11.1959 (FL D2)

After joining the Albion as a professional in October 1957, Keith Abbis had to wait over two years to make his first-team debut but then played only intermittently over the following fourteen months. His best run in the side came at the end of 1959–60 when he made ten consecutive appearances, performing well as Albion lost just twice to pull clear of the Second Division relegation zone.

Keith was released in May 1961 and joined Southern League Chelmsford City, subsequently playing for Romford and Brentwood Town. Before his days as a professional at the Goldstone, Keith had played as an amateur for Hitchin Town and Wycombe Wanderers

Season	FL	Total
1959–60	17 (3)	17 (3)
1960–61	2	2
Total	19 (3)	19 (3)

ADDINALL, BERT — 1953–54

centre-forward — Ht 5 11, Wt 12 00 — 63 apps, 33 goals
full name: Albert William Addinall
born: Marylebone, London, 30.1.1921
debut: Torquay United (a), 17.1.1953 (FL D3(S))

Although he enjoyed only a brief career at Hove, Bert Addinall quickly won a place in the hearts of Goldstone fans with his strength in the air and his penchant for scoring spectacular goals. With a record of 33 goals in 63 games, "Our Albert's" strike-rate compares with the best in the club's history, and he is one of only two players – the other is Arthur Attwood – to have scored in five or more consecutive games on two occasions.

As a schoolboy Bert represented both Middlesex and London, and first appeared for Queen's Park Rangers in the early stages of the Second World War. During the hostilities he served firstly in Air Raid Precautions, then with the Army as a driver in the Royal Army Surgical Corps before qualifying as a sergeant P.T. instructor. In 1946 he played for the Army against its Belgian counterparts.

Bert's post-war record with Rangers – 59 goals from 149 Football League games – was excellent by any standard, and after ten years at Loftus Road he was rewarded with a richly-deserved testimonial from the West London club

In January 1953, at the age of 31, Bert arrived at the Goldstone together with his Rangers colleague Harry Gilberg, in exchange for Albion's Ron Higgins and a four-figure sum. The following season, 1953–54, he led the club's goalscorers with 22 goals as Albion made a vain bid for the championship of the Third Division (South).

Bert moved on to Crystal Palace in July 1954, but his career was curtailed by injury after just a handful of games and he became a taxi-driver in London while also turning out for the Kent League side Snowdown Colliery until 1957. In 1965, Bert became landlord of the Ferry Inn, Shoreham, for a spell, after which he returned to his cab.

Season	FL	FAC	Total
1952–53	19 (11)	0	19 (11)
1953–54	41 (20)	3 (2)	44 (22)
Total	60 (31)	3 (2)	63 (33)

ADEKOLA, DAVID — 1996

forward — Ht 5 11, Wt 12 02 — 1 app
full name: David Adeoulu Adekola
born: Lagos, Nigeria, 18.5.1968
debut: Cambridge United (h), 12.10.1996 (FL D3)

A Nigerian international striker, David Adekola gained a reputation in the Football League as a fast and direct forward with Bury, whom he joined in January 1993 after two years with the French club AS Cannes. His eight goals

from sixteen games helped the 'Shakers' into the 1993 Division Three play-offs, but a losing semi-final proved to be the pinnacle of his career in England. In February 1994 he moved on loan to Exeter City, and played a single game for AFC Bournemouth following his release from Gigg Lane in 1994. David followed that with trials for Wigan Athletic and Hereford United, plus games for Conference sides Halifax Town (March 1995) and Bath City (April 1995). He gained a Somerset Premier Cup winner's medal with the latter club.

During the 1995–96 season the pacy African played in five games for Cambridge United, and scored their consolation against the Albion in a 4–1 home defeat in the Football League Trophy (Auto Windscreens Shield) before dropping into the Isthmian League with Bishop's Stortford. But in December 1995 he was signed by the German Second Division club Preussen Koln, managed by the ex-England forward Tony Woodcock, and scored ten goals in seventeen matches. David returned to England in December 1996 when Jimmy Case gave him a trial. The 28-year-old did little to impress on his only first-team appearance before being substituted, though, and his stay in Sussex, which was also hampered by injury, lasted only a month before he rejoined Bishop's Stortford.

Before arriving in Europe, David had played for the Julius Berger club in Lagos, Nigeria, winning one League championship and two winner's medals in the Cup. He played for the under-21s in a tournament in Chile in 1987 and was top scorer in the African national junior championships, but although he developed into a full international he failed to make the Nigerian squad for the 1994 World Cup in the U.S.A. and never subsequently figured again.

Season	FL	Total
1996–97	1	1
Total	1	1

AKINBIYI, ADE — 1994–95

forward — Ht 6 1, Wt 12 08 — 7 apps, 4 goals
full name: Adeola Peter Akinbiyi
born: Hackney, London, 10.10.1974
debut: Brentford (a), 26.11.1994 (FL D2)

Ade Akinbiyi arrived at the Goldstone on loan in November 1994 to provide greater fire-power in a side that had not won for eleven matches. Although his first game ended in defeat, the big striker – very much in the mould of former Albion favourite Michael Robinson – contributed a great deal to a big improvement in the club's performances with four goals. The 20-year-old's other six games resulted in three wins and three draws, and his forward somersault to celebrate a goal thrilled the fans.

Ade had represented the Inner London Schools while attending Hackney Free School, and joined Norwich City as a trainee in July 1991. Turning professional in February 1993, he made his senior debut in City's celebrated – and ultimately triumphant – UEFA Cup tie against Bayern Munich in November 1993. Later in 1993–94, Ade had a four-match loan period with Hereford United during which he scored twice, but he failed to break into the "Canaries'" forward line on a regular basis and moved to Gillingham for a record £250,000 fee in January 1997, where his powerful running, agility in the box and fierce shooting quickly earned him the plaudits of the Priestfield crowd.

Season	FL	Total
1994–95	7 (4)	7 (4)
Total	7 (4)	7 (4)

ALLAN, DEREK   1996–

central defender   Ht 6 0, Wt 12 01   42 apps
full name: Derek Thomas Allan
born: Irvine, Ayrshire, Scotland, 24.12.1974
debut: Swindon Town (a), 3.4.1996 (FL D2)

Capable of playing as a full-back or central defender, Derek Allan initially joined the Albion on loan from Southampton in March 1996, but signed permanently during the summer. The 21-year-old Scot had little experience behind him and initially appeared error-prone, but a season of League football knocked the raw edges off his game and he earned the respect of the Goldstone crowd during 1996–97 with his all-out effort and determined tackling. Brave and tenacious, he won the *Evening Argus*'s award for the season's most consistent performer despite suffering a series of injuries.

As a youngster Derek turned out for Ayr United Boys' Club before joining the senior club, and went on to make five Scottish League appearances in the no.5 shirt at the age of eighteen in February and March 1993. He was obviously a lad of some potential for, shortly afterwards, Southampton paid £70,000 for his signature and gave him his Premiership debut at the end of the season. It was, however, the only senior appearance Derek was to make at The Dell. Plagued by injury and hernia problems, he was released in May 1996 to join up with the Albion on a permanent basis.

Season	FL	FLC	AMC	Total
1995–96	8	0		8
1996–97	31	2	1	34
Total	39	2	1	42

ALLEN, A.   1903

left-back   1 app
debut: Grays United (a), 25.4.1903 (SEL)

Allen was a trialist of unknown origin who replaced Jock Caldwell at left-back for the final South Eastern League match of the club's second season, 1902–03. With a lucrative friendly against Brentford being played on the same day at the Goldstone and the crucial Southern League test match to decide promotion due two days later, Albion fielded a much-weakened team at Grays and were resoundingly beaten 5–0.

Season	SEL	Total
1902–03	1	1
Total	1	1

ALLSOPP, TOMMY   1905–07

outside-left   103 apps, 11 goals
full name: Thomas Charlesworth Allsopp
born: Leicester, Leicestershire, 18.12.1880
died: Norwich, Norfolk, 7.3.1919
debut: Millwall (h), 2.9.1905 (SL D1)

In his two seasons at the Goldstone, Tommy Allsopp missed just 8 games out of 111, and his consistency was a big factor in the great improvement of 1906–07 which saw Albion finish third in the Southern League's First Division. Although a big man for a winger, he showed a fair turn of speed and provided a good many chances for centre-forward Jack Hall.

Tommy had joined his home-town club, Leicester Fosse, as an eighteen-year-old in August 1899, and was quickly drafted into the first team. 'Although still a youth, Allsopp is undoubtedly a player of great ability, and with a little more experience should develop into a first-class man,' ran a report in the sporting Press. A regular in Fosse's Second Division side until May 1902, he then moved into the Southern League with Luton Town and enjoyed two fine seasons at Kenilworth Road, but returned to Leicester in May 1904 where he brought his total of League and Cup appearances for Fosse up to 70 before being released to join the Albion during the 1905 close season. After two excellent years at the Goldstone, Tommy moved on to Norwich City in May 1907 (together with his left-wing partner Wally Smith) and saw out his career with 23 goals from 124 Southern League and F.A. Cup outings. Also a professional cricketer, he represented both Leicestershire and Norfolk as a slow left-arm bowler.

Having survived wartime duties with the Labour Battalion in France, during which he attained the rank of sergeant, Tommy contracted influenza on the way home and subsequently died at the age of 38 while licensee of the City Arms in Norwich. He was buried with military honours in Norwich Cemetery.

Season	SL	FAC	UL	Total
1905–06	34 (4)	5	14 (3)	53 (7)
1906–07	38 (3)	1	11 (1)	50 (4)
Total	72 (7)	6	25 (4)	103 (11)

ANDREWS, PHIL   1993–97

forward   Ht 5 11, Wt 11 00   36 apps, 1 goal
full name: Philip Donald Andrews
born: Andover, Hampshire, 14.9.1976
debut: Cambridge United (a), 9.4.1994 (FL D2)

Lively and willing, Phil Andrews has been a natural goalscorer since his days with the Basingstoke Town and Fleet Town youth teams. Associated with the Albion for some years since being spotted

by youth development officer Ted Streeter, the Hampshire youngster partnered his future Brighton colleague Simon Fox up front for Fleet and helped his side to a league-and-cup double. Although he trained with Crystal Palace for a time, Phil arrived at the Goldstone as a trainee in 1993 to play a big part in the youth team's successful runs in both the F.A. Youth Cup and

Southern Junior Floodlit Cup that season, scoring a number of vital goals. The exuberant seventeen-year-old played for an F.A. XI *v.* Combined Services at Aldershot in March 1994, and was rewarded with his senior debut the following month.

Showing a nice touch in and around the box, Phil signed a professional contract towards the end 1994–95, but struggled to find the net in the senior side where his appearances came largely as a substitute. Transfer-listed by Jimmy Case in November 1996, he was given another chance by new manager Steve Gritt and headed his first senior goal at Torquay, but he was released at the end of the season to link up once again with Case at Bashley in the Southern League.

Season	FL	FAC	FLC	AMC	Total
1993–94	1+4	0	0	0	1+4
1994–95	0+5	0+1	0+1	0+1	0+8
1995–96	0+8	1+1	1+1	1+1	3+11
1996–97	1+6 (1)	0+1	0	0+1	1+8 (1)
Total	2+23 (1)	1+3	1+2	1+3	5+31 (1)

ANSELL, George — 1930–33

inside-forward   Ht 5 10, Wt 11 07   *7 apps, 2 goals*
full name: George Thomas Leonard Ansell
born: Worthing, Sussex, 28.11.1909
died: Stafford, Staffordshire, 7.10.1988
debut: Gillingham (a), 13.4.1932 (FL D3(S))

A pupil at Steyning Grammar School before going up to Jesus College, Oxford, in 1927, George Ansell graduated in Classics four years later and gained soccer 'Blues' for the university in the three successive seasons 1928–31. During his time at Oxford he played for the famed Corinthians and also assisted his home-town club, Worthing, in the Sussex County League; in 1929 he scored both goals in a 2–0 win over Southwick in the Sussex Senior Cup final. In 1930, George signed amateur forms for the Albion, joined the paid ranks in August 1931, and appeared in all three inside-forward positions in seven first-team outings.

After two years as a professional he left the game in April 1933 to take up a post as a teacher in Scarborough, but returned in the latter part of 1935–36 to play four League matches for Norwich City. George subsequently taught at Kimbolton School in Huntingdonshire for many years, playing football locally for Kimbolton Town and Eynesbury Rovers into his 40s. On retiring from the teaching profession in 1969, he lived in Stafford until his death.

Season	FL	FAC*	Total
1931–32	1	0	1
1932–33*	5 (1)	1 (1)	6 (2)
Total	6 (1)	1 (1)	7 (2)

Note: Ansell's one appearance and goal in the 1932–33 F.A. Cup came in the qualifying competition.

ANTHONY, Walter — 1905–08

outside-right   Ht 5 8, Wt 11 06   *119 apps, 13 goals*
born: Basford, Nottingham, Nottinghamshire, 21.11.1879
died: Basford, Nottingham, Nottinghamshire, 26.1.1950
debut: Swindon Town (a), 20.9.1905 (UL)

A tricky little ball-player, noted for the accuracy of his crosses with either foot, Walter Anthony developed both his physique and his

game at the Goldstone to become a fine player. He rarely missed a game, and produced such sparkling displays in his third season with the club that he was sold for a big fee.

Walter began his career in Derbyshire junior soccer with Osmaston before progressing to Heanor Town in February 1899. His form with the Midland Leaguers attracted nearby Nottingham Forest and in February 1903 he was offered a professional engagement by the Football League giants at the age of 23, but he was considered too frail to compete in the hurly-burly of senior football and failed to fulfil his early promise, making just six First Division appearances before his release to join the Albion in May 1905.

Having impressed during the three F.A. Cup matches with Preston North End in January 1908, the 28-year-old winger was transferred to Blackburn Rovers the following month as the main part of a triple deal which also saw the departure of Dick Wombwell and Joe Lumley for Ewood Park. Walter went on to make 149 League appearances for the First Division side and won a League championship medal in 1911–12. In May 1914 he dropped into the Lancashire Combination with Stalybridge Celtic. Walter was the younger brother of the Nottinghamshire cricketers George and Henry Anthony.

Season	SL	FAC	UL	WL	SCC	Total
1905–06	24 (3)	5	6 (1)	0	0	35 (4)
1906–07	35 (4)	1	12 (3)	0	0	48 (7)
1907–08	21 (1)	5	0	8 (1)	2	36 (2)
Total	80 (8)	11	18 (4)	8 (1)	2	119 (13)

ARCHER, Arthur — 1907–08

right-back   Ht 5 9, Wt 12 07   *39 apps*
born: Ashby-de-la-Zouch, Leicestershire, 1877
debut: Norwich City (a), 7.9.1907 (SL D1)

A much-travelled player on his arrival at the Goldstone in May 1907, Arthur Archer brought a great deal of experience to the Albion defence, but the side struggled and his career in Sussex lasted just one season. The Leicestershire-born full-back started out in local minor football with Burton St Edmunds, Tutbury Hamton and Swadlincote Town before joining Burton Wanderers in August 1894 for their first season as a Football League club. In July 1897 he was transferred to Small Heath (later renamed Birmingham) for a £50 fee and went on to make 170 League and Cup appearances in five seasons, being ever-present in their Division Two promotion side of 1900–01.

Arthur moved into the Southern League with New Brompton (later Gillingham) in March 1902, and was released in August 1903 to join Queen's Park Rangers. During his time with New Brompton and Q.P.R., the stocky full-back also turned out occasionally – and somewhat oddly – for Tottenham Hotspur in the London League, a secondary competition played in midweek. In August 1905, together with his future Goldstone colleague Duncan Ronaldson, Arthur followed his

Rangers team-mate John Bowman to Norwich City on the latter's appointment as player-manager of the newly professionalised club, and enjoyed two fine seasons with the 'Canaries' before joining the Albion. A big man in stature and in heart, he was extremely popular during his only season on the South Coast. A contemporary report stated that he was 'a rough-and-ready player with untiring energy and an effective style.'

On leaving Hove in August 1908, Arthur rounded off his playing days with a season at Millwall before setting out on a new career coaching football on the Continent. Two years in Germany were followed by a spell in Belgium with Ghent until the outbreak of the Great War, during which he served in the Army. Arthur returned to Ghent in 1920, and subsequently had a year in Italy and two years in Belgium before becoming trainer with Watford (managed by his old Albion team-mate Harry Kent) in 1924.

Season	SL	FAC	WL	SCC	Total
1907–08	28	5	2	4	39
Total	28	5	2	4	39

ARMSTRONG, ARTHUR   1909–10

outside-right   *3 apps*
full name: Arthur Singleton Armstrong
born: Southwell, Nottinghamshire, 1887
died: Wolverhampton, Staffordshire, 13.8.1962
debut: Plymouth Argyle (a), 16.10.1909 (SL D1)

Recruited by First Division Derby County from the Bakewell club in October 1906, Arthur Armstrong played in the last two matches of the "Rams'" 1906–07 relegation campaign and their first two games in Division Two, but then drifted into non-League football with Heanor United. In June 1909, Jack Robson signed the wingman for the Albion, but he was also unable to make the grade at the Goldstone and played just twice in the 1909–10 Southern League championship campaign in the absence of George Featherstone. Arthur departed for Pontypridd in May 1910 and later played for Loughborough Corinthians and Heanor Town. In his youth he was an acrobat with Sanger's Circus, and worked as a telegraphist for the Great Northern Railway on retiring from football.

Season	SL	SCC	Total
1909–10	2	1	3
Total	2	1	3

ARMSTRONG, DAVE   1968–70

outside-left   *45 apps, 6 goals*
full name: David Thomas Armstrong
born: Mile End, Poplar, London, 9.11.1942
debut: Gillingham (a), 14.9.1968 (FL D3)

Chiefly remembered for phenomenal pace, Dave Armstrong made his name in Isthmian League football with Barking and Ilford, and was selected for the Great Britain Olympic qualifying squad in 1965 while playing for Hornchurch in the Athenian League. The 23-year-old winger preferred to turn professional, though, and signed for Millwall in December 1965. In nearly three years at The Den he made just 20 League appearances (6 as substitute), and came to the Goldstone in September 1968 when Archie Macaulay paid a £5,000 fee. A slimly-built winger, Dave was left-footed to a fault and made most of his appearances in the no.11 shirt, but he also played a number of games on the right during his two seasons with the club. Released at the end of the 1969–70 season, he moved into the Southern League with Dover together with his team-mate Ken

Blackburn, and later played for Wimbledon. Dave was also a great boxing enthusiast.

Season	FL	FAC	Total
1968–69	27+2 (6)	0	27+2 (6)
1969–70	11+4	1	12+4
Total	38+6 (6)	1	39+6 (6)

ARMSTRONG, GERRY   1986–89

centre-forward   *Ht 5 11, Wt 13 02*   *55 apps, 7 goals*
full name: Gerard Joseph Armstrong
born: Belfast, Co. Antrim, Northern Ireland, 23.5.1954
debut: Portsmouth (h), 23.8.1986 (FL D2)

Although unable to reproduce his best form at the Goldstone towards the end of his professional career, Gerry Armstrong was a most experienced international and contributed a great deal to the club, both as an ideal man for the substitute's bench and as a coach to the reserves. Between 1977 and 1986 the powerfully-built striker played in 63 matches for Northern Ireland, scored twelve goals, and starred in the 1982 World Cup finals in Spain where his strong running and goalscoring exploits won him the accolade of 'British Player of the Tournament'.

Gerry's career began as a part-time professional with Bangor in the Irish League – he worked for the Northern Ireland housing executive – but took off in November 1975 when he was signed by Tottenham Hotspur. With ten goals in 84 League appearances behind him, the Ulsterman was transferred to Watford for £250,000 in 1980, but he found his opportunities limited in a successful side – he also suffered a broken leg – and consequently scored only twelve goals in 76 League appearances, 26 of them as substitute. Nevertheless, he helped the 'Hornets' to promotion to the First Division in 1981–82 and to runner's-up spot the following term. Following his adventures in Spain, Gerry signed for Real Mallorca in 1983, but after two seasons on the holiday island he returned to England with West Bromwich Albion. He made eight appearances for the

'Throstles', then moved to Chesterfield on loan before signing permanently for the Derbyshire Third Division club.

In June 1986, Gerry was brought to Hove by Alan Mullery as a foil for Dean Saunders and Terry Connor, but had scored only two goals by January and was loaned to Millwall for two months. On his return Gerry took to coaching the youth team and looked set for a new career, but 34-year-old's days with the Albion were numbered when, after being sent off during a Sussex Senior Cup tie at Southwick in January 1989, he was involved in a skirmish with a spectator which resulted in court proceedings. Although his action was completely out of character, Gerry resigned from the club and turned to non-League football as player-coach of Crawley Town, but a year later, in February 1990, he left the Southern League club following a grossly exaggerated confrontation with abusive spectators. Thereafter he played for Glenavon, Waterford, Bromley, Southwick and Worthing United, and acted as a scout for Watford while taking a post as sports-and-leisure manager at the Newman School, Hove.

In November 1991 he became player-manager of Worthing and immediately revitalised the 'Rebels', leading them to the Isthmian League Division Two title in 1993, but resigned from his position the same year following his appointment as assistant to the new Northern Ireland manager Bryan Hamilton. He did, however, have a few more games for Southwick at the end of 1994–95. Later working as a representative for a sportswear company and as a pundit on Ulster radio, Gerry continues to play football in the Sussex Sunday League. In April 1996 he became the first-ever full-time coach and development officer of the Sussex County Football Association, while continuing his role with the Northern Ireland team, and in June 1997 he took over the post of manager of the Sussex representative side.

Season	FL	FLC	FMC	AMC	Total
1986–87	27+4 (4)	2	1	0	30+4 (4)
1987–88	0+11 (1)	1	0	0+2 (1)	1+13 (2)
1988–89	3+2 (1)	0+1	1	0	4+3 (1)
Total	30+17 (6)	3+1	2	0+2 (1)	35+20 (7)

ASPDEN, TOMMY   1904–05

outside-right   *7 apps*
full name: Thomas Eccles Aspden
born: Liverpool, Lancashire, 1881
debut: New Brompton (a), 3.9.1904 (SL D1)

Having appeared in Burnley's Second Division team on 29 occasions during the previous season, Tommy Aspden came to the South Coast with a good reputation in May 1904 and was initially preferred on the right flank, but he soon lost his place to Tommy White and, after failing to fit in at the Goldstone, moved on to an unknown non-League destination in May 1905. Before joining Burnley in August 1903, Tommy had played for Preston North End's reserve team and for Kettering Town in the Southern League.

Season	SL	Total
1904–05	7	7
Total	7	7

ATHERTON, JACK   1938–39

inside-left   *Ht 5 10, Wt 12 00*   *10 apps, 2 goals*
full name: John James Atherton
born: Preston, Lancashire, 1917
debut: Port Vale (a), 3.12.1938 (FL D3(S))

Costing £250 in May 1938, Jack Atherton arrived at the Goldstone from Preston North End, having joined the Deepdale staff at the age of sixteen in May 1934. His opportunities with his home-town club were limited, though, and he made their First Division side on just four occasions in four seasons. He couldn't win a regular place on the South Coast with the Albion either, despite scoring a brace of goals against Notts County in only his third outing.

Jack didn't play senior football during the war years, but Albion retained his registration until May 1947 when he was put on the transfer list. There were no offers and Jack never again appeared in the Football League.

Season	FL	SSC	Total
1938–39	9 (2)	1	10 (2)
Total	9 (2)	1	10 (2)

ATKINSON, JIMMY   1908–09

left-half   *Ht 5 10, Wt 11 09*   *46 apps, 1 goal*
full name: James Atkinson
born: Manchester, Lancashire, c. 1886
debut: Southampton (h), 2.9.1908 (SL D1)

Jimmy Atkinson started out in Manchester League football with Newton Heath Athletic at the age of fifteen, and was playing for Sale Holmefield when he enjoyed a fruitless trial with Manchester United. In March 1905 the young inside-forward was offered terms by Bolton Wanderers, and went on to score on his First Division debut twelve months later, in an excellent 5–2 win at Birmingham. Later transformed into a half-back, he stayed at Burnden Park for more than three years, but appeared in just two more League games before being released to join the Albion during the summer of 1908.

First choice at left-half throughout 1908–09, Jimmy turned in some sterling performances but was released at the end of the season. Subsequently engaged by Exeter City, he appeared in 44 League and Cup matches during 1909–10, but when the 'Grecians' found themselves unable to pay summer wages to retained players he was released to join Barrow-in-Furness in the Lancashire Combination. Gentlemanly in demeanour, Jimmy was said to have been on the big side for a wing-half, weighing in at nearly 12 stone, but he appeared to be much lighter.

Season	SL	FAC	WL	WL Ch.	SCC	Total
1908–09	32 (1)	1	8	2	3	46 (1)
Total	32 (1)	1	8	2	3	46 (1)

ATTWOOD, ARTHUR   1931–35

centre-forward   *Ht 5 9, Wt 11 03*   *104 apps, 75 goals*
full name: Arthur Albert Attwood
born: Walsall, Staffordshire, 1.12.1901
died: Hove, Sussex, 6.12.1974
debut: Fulham (h), 7.11.1931 (FL D3(S))

Something of a late developer, Arthur Attwood was 26 when he set out on his Football League career with Walsall, yet he went on to become a most remarkable goalscorer, hitting 95 goals in just 155 League games for his four clubs. Indeed, with 75 goals in 104 games, he set the best strike-rate of any Albion forward with 50 goals or more, and twice scored in eight consecutive games. The Walsall-born forward also scored six goals against Shoreham in the F.A. Cup to set a new Albion record (albeit a debatable one in the qualifying competition after club secretary Albert Underwood famously forgot to apply to the F.A. for exemption).

After serving with the Shropshire Regiment in the Army of Occupation on the Rhine, Arthur worked and played football for the L.M.S. Railway in Walsall on his release before joining the local League team as a professional in January 1928. Thirteen goals in fourteen Third Division appearances prompted Everton to sign him in February 1929, but with the great Dixie Dean leading the Goodison attack Arthur had only three outings in the first team before moving to Bristol Rovers in May 1930, where he scored 29 goals in 55 games.

On joining the Albion in November 1931 he got off to a terrific start: after missing out on his debut, he then notched fourteen goals in the next eight games and finished the season as top scorer with 29 goals from 30 matches. The following season he hit the net 35 times to set a new club record, but it was a somewhat dubious total as it included eleven goals from the four F.A. Cup qualifying ties. Although rather on the small side for a centre-forward, Arthur made up for the lack of inches with dynamic speed and effort, and maintained his performances until hit by a series of injuries in 1933–34.

Struck down by appendicitis in February 1934, the 32-year-old lost his place to the equally dynamic Buster Brown and moved on to Northfleet United in August 1935, assisting them to the Kent League championship in the following two seasons. In 1937, Arthur was reinstated as an amateur to play for Hove in the Sussex County League while working locally as a bus-conductor. He served with the R.A.F. throughout the war and guested on the right wing for Leicester City in a 2–1 defeat at Charlton in September 1945 at the age of 43. Even in 1950 he was still occasionally turning out for Hove.

Season	FL	FAC*	SSC	Total
1931–32	27 (25)	3 (4)	0	30 (29)
1932–33*	33 (20)	10 (15)	0	43 (35)
1933–34	21 (9)	3	1 (1)	25 (10)
1934–35	6 (1)	0	0	6 (1)
Total	87 (55)	16 (19)	1 (1)	104 (75)

Note: Four appearances and eleven goals of Attwood's 1932–33 F.A. Cup total came in the qualifying competition.

AULT, ALFRED   1913

centre-forward   *1 app, 1 goal*
born: Ashbourne, Derbyshire, 1892
debut: Brentford (h), 19.2.1913 (SA)

An amateur trialist from Ashbourne Town of the Matlock & District League, Alfred Ault was invited to the Goldstone along with his team-mate Sid Kitchen to play in the Southern Alliance match with Brentford in February 1913. Although both players scored in a 3–2 victory, neither was offered terms.

Season	SA	Total
1912–13	1 (1)	1 (1)
Total	1 (1)	1 (1)

15 players who won European club competitions

Player	Competition	Club	Year
Beal, Phil	UEFA Cup	Tottenham Hotspur	1972
Boyle, John	Cup-Winners' Cup	Chelsea	1971
Case, Jimmy	European Cup	Liverpool	1977, 1978, 1981
	UEFA Cup	Liverpool	1976
Chivers, Martin	UEFA Cup	Tottenham Hotspur	1972
Corrigan, Joe	Cup-Winners' Cup	Manchester City	1970
Dear, Brian	Cup-Winners' Cup	West Ham United	1965
Iovan, Stefan	European Cup	Steaua Bucharest	1986
Kinnear, Joe	UEFA Cup	Tottenham Hotspur	1972
Lawrenson, Mark	European Cup	Liverpool	1984
Mortimer, Dennis	European Cup	Aston Villa	1982
Osman, Russell	UEFA Cup	Ipswich Town	1981
Robinson, Michael	European Cup	Liverpool	1984
Rougvie, Doug	Cup-Winners' Cup	Aberdeen	1983
Smith, Bobby	Cup-Winners' Cup	Tottenham Hotspur	1963
Stevens, Gary	UEFA Cup	Tottenham Hotspur	1984

BADMINTON, ROGER   1966–68

right-back   *2 apps*
full name: Roger Geoffrey Badminton
born: Portsmouth, Hampshire, 15.9.1947
debut: Doncaster Rovers (a), 16.5.1967 (FL D3)

Roger Badminton was an outstanding young footballer, winning England schoolboy honours and playing for Albion's reserve team while still at school in Havant. In March 1966 he joined the Goldstone staff as an amateur and turned professional the following July, but the young full-back then suffered a catalogue of serious knee and hip injuries, and his early progress came to a halt. Indeed, his senior career came to an end when he was carried off after only six minutes of his second game. Following an operation to remove a troublesome appendix, Roger quit the first-class game in October 1968 just a few weeks after his 21st birthday. He subsequently became an assistant manager in a Northampton meat-packing factory.

Season	FL	FLC	Total
1966–67	1	0	1
1967–68	0	1	1
Total	1	1	2

BAILEY, CRAIG   1961–63

centre-forward   *5 apps, 2 goals*
full name: William Craig Bailey
born: Airdrie, Lanarkshire, Scotland, 6.7.1944
debut: Swindon Town (a), 11.9.1962 (FL D3)

Signed in December 1961 from Scottish junior club Kirkintilloch Rob Roy, seventeen-year-old Craig Bailey was considered an excellent prospect by manager George Curtis who travelled to Scotland by air to obtain his signature. The youngster's arrival, though, coincided with the club's rapid decline from the Second Division to the Fourth and he had little opportunity to shine in a struggling side. In March 1963, Southern League Cambridge United paid £900 for Craig's services, but he returned to Scotland in March 1964 to play for Motherwell.

Season	FL	FLC	Total
1962–63	4 (1)	1 (1)	5 (2)
Total	4 (1)	1 (1)	5 (2)

BAIRD, IAN   1996–

centre-forward   *Ht 6 0, Wt 12 09*   *40 apps, 13 goals*
full name: Ian James Baird
born: Rotherham, Yorkshire, 1.4.1964
debut: Chester City (h), 17.8.1996 (FL D3)

Strong, willing and determined, Ian Baird has plundered over 150 senior goals for ten clubs during a varied career which has seen him involved in transfers worth nearly £2 million, but he has also gained a reputation as one of the most fiery players in the Football League. Sent off a number of times, the powerful forward has felt the wrath of both the football and judicial authorities on occasion, but has also helped bring success to many of his clubs. Indeed, his crucial goals during 1996–97 played a big part in keeping the Albion in the Football League.

An England Schools representative, Ian became an apprentice with Southampton and signed as a professional in April 1982, but made only 22 First Division appearances for the 'Saints' before joining Leeds United for £75,000 in March 1985. (He also had loan-spells at Cardiff City and Newcastle United.) It was at Elland Road that the

strapping forward really built his reputation as a formidable striker and target-man. In 85 Second Division games he scored 33 goals, but the Yorkshire club lost out in the 1987 play-offs to Charlton Athletic and Ian moved to Portsmouth, newly promoted to Division One, for £285,000. He was not a great success in the struggling 'Pompey' side, though, and returned to Leeds in March 1988 for a cut-price £120,000.

During 1989–90, Ian played in 24 matches and scored four goals as Leeds won the Second Division championship, but was sold to Middlesbrough in January 1990 for £500,000 before the triumphant end of the season. While never a prolific scorer, he kept up a respectable record on Teesside until moving to Scotland with Heart of Midlothian for £400,000 in the summer of 1991. Leading the Edinburgh side to runner's-up spot in the Scottish League, Ian scored in their subsequent victory over Slavia Prague in the UEFA Cup before going out to Belgian side Standard Liege. After two successful years north of the border, the 29-year-old forward joined Bristol City in the 1993 close season for £295,000, but a punctured lung inhibited his appearances at Ashton Gate and he moved to Plymouth Argyle on a 'free' in 1995, where he turned out in midfield on quite a number of occasions. The 'Pilgrims' won promotion to Division Two in 1995–96, but Ian played no part in the final run-in nor in the play-offs.

Instead he signed for the Albion in July 1996 for a £35,000 fee, and led the forwards for most of the season, playing many games as captain. While his competitive style won him few favours with opponents or referees, it did establish him as a favourite of the home crowd, and his thirteen goals provided a vital lifeline. Although lacking the pace of his younger days, Ian was still able to latch onto a good number of crosses, but his temperament let him down again on the emotional last-ever game at the Goldstone Ground when he was sent off against Doncaster Rovers for fighting.

While proving a handful for most goalkeepers, Ian has also been on the receiving end himself. During his spell at Hearts he was required to play a game against Aberdeen in goal, a match which was lost 3–2.

Season	FL	FAC	FLC	AMC	Total
1996–97	34+1 (13)	1+1	2	1	38+2 (13)
Total	34+1 (13)	1+1	2	1	38+2 (13)

BAKER, BERT   1901–06

outside-right   20 apps, 6 goals
full name: Herbert Reginald Baker
born: Brighton, Sussex, 1879
died: Brighton, Sussex, 23.9.1953
debut: Brighton Athletic (h), 21.9.1901 (FAC Prelim.)

Bert Baker was a wonderful servant of the game at all levels locally. As well as being a prominent amateur player, he served as secretary to the Brighton, Hove & District Schools F.A. from 1902 to 1945 and then became its president; his 50 years in office were marked by a match between Brighton Boys and London Boys at the Goldstone

on 26 September 1951. He also worked in the Albion club office for many years following his retirement from teaching until his death at the age of 74.

A pupil of Brighton's Hanover Terrace School, Bert trained as a schoolmaster at St Mark's College, Chelsea, and returned to his home town to teach at the Circus Street and Stanford Road schools for many years. He played for the Preston Park-based North End Rangers in the East Sussex Senior League, and was on the books of Brighton Havelock when he was enlisted to assist Brighton United during the 1899–1900 season.

After United folded Bert turned out for North End Rangers' ambitious successors Brighton & Hove Rangers, and subsequently joined the Albion in the summer of 1901 for their opening season. Blessed with natural pace, Bert made a telling contribution down the right flank and had the honour of scoring the club's first-ever competitive goal, one of a hat-trick in a 6–2 F.A. Cup victory over Brighton Athletic. He later had a spell with Clapton and was on Notts County's staff for a while (although he didn't appear in the first eleven), but remained an amateur throughout his playing career.

Season	SL	FAC	Total
1901–02	9 (2)	4 (3)	13 (5)
1902–03	4 (1)	3	7 (1)
Total	13 (3)	7 (3)	20 (6)

BAKER, CHARLIE   1960–64

goalkeeper   87 apps
full name: Charles Joseph Baker
born: Turners Hill, Sussex, 6.1.1936
debut: Notts County (a), 20.10.1960 (FLC R2)

Despite being Albion's last line of defence for eighteen months, Charlie Baker remained a part-time professional throughout his four-and-a-half years at the Goldstone while also working for the Bell

Precision engineering company in Crawley. The young 'keeper had played for Turners Hill and Horsham while learning his trade as an apprentice toolmaker, and then joined the R.A.F. on National Service, playing football for the Coastal Command against the Combined Services in Gibraltar.

One of Charlie's officers recommended him to the Albion and he signed on as a part-timer in January 1960. The following October the 24-year-old goalkeeper took over from Dave Hollins, and retained the job throughout the 1961–62 season despite the club's relegation from the Second Division. In 1962–63, Charlie made thirteen League appearances as Bert McGonigal's deputy, and spent the following season in the reserves before leaving for Aldershot on a free transfer in July 1964. After 28 League appearances at the Recreation Ground, Charlie was released to join Crawley Town for a brief period, and later had a spell as manager of A.P.V. Athletic in the Sussex County League. His brother David was also on Albion's books as a junior in 1961.

Season	FL	FAC	FLC	Total
1960–61	27	3	1	31
1961–62	41	1	1	43
1962–63	13	0	0	13
Total	81	4	2	87

BALDWIN, HARRY   1939–52

goalkeeper   Ht 5 9, Wt 12 03   215 apps
born: Saltley, Birmingham, Warwickshire, 17.7.1920
debut: Bristol Rovers (h), 8.9.1945 (wartime)*
peacetime debut: Romford (h), 17.11.1945 (FAC R1 Lg1)*

Although Harry Baldwin was on the short side for a goalkeeper, he proved to be a wonderfully consistent performer for the Albion, reaching his peak during 1947–48 when he saved seven penalties out of nine, including an incredible run of five in succession. His first appearances for the club came in 1939 when, as a nineteen-year-old, he played in the first three League games of the aborted Division Three (South) competition, but it was another six years before he appeared between the Brighton posts again. The war could easily have ruined a promising career, but he returned in 1945 to play well over 200 times for the first team.

As a schoolboy Harry represented Erdington (Birmingham), and joined Birmingham League side Sutton Town at the age of fifteen where he quickly attracted the attention of nearby West Bromwich Albion. On joining the 'Throstles' in May 1937, he made rapid progress:

after playing for the youth team on Good Friday 1938, he was promoted to the reserves the following day and made his First Division debut as a seventeen-year-old amateur on Easter Monday, in an extraordinary 4–3 home win over local rivals Birmingham in front of more than 34,000 spectators. Retaining his position for the remainder of the 1937–38 campaign, he was offered professional terms in April but fractured a collar bone early the following season and never regained his first-team spot.

Released in May 1939, Harry came to the Goldstone on the recommendation of the former West Brom. and England inside-forward Eddie Sandford, a nephew of Brighton's assistant trainer Bill 'Bullet' Jones. During the war he served in the Royal Navy, representing the Devonport Division against the R.A.F. South Western Command, and guested for Nottingham Forest, Northampton Town, Worcester City and Redditch Town. In 1945 he returned to Hove to play in every match of the first post-war F.A. Cup tournament, and then competed with Jack Ball for the goalie's jersey over six seasons. In 1950–51 the pair enjoyed a joint testimonial before Harry moved on in 1952 after thirteen war-interrupted years at the Goldstone.

Taking up a position with the British Timken engineering company in Northampton, he turned out for Kettering Town in the Southern League, but returned to the Football League with Walsall in December 1953. After applying in vain for the vacant managerial post at Peterborough United, Harry joined Wellington Town in the Cheshire League, but decided to call it a day in 1956 after sustaining severe head injuries during an F.A. Cup tie with Bilston. Having successfully operated in the Birmingham machine-tools industry for many years – he ran two companies – Harry now lives in retirement in Kenilworth, keeping a weather-eye on the results of both Albions.

Season	FL	FAC	Wartime	Total
1939–40*	0	0	0	0
1945–46	0	10	32	42
1946–47	10	0	0	10
1947–48	26	2	0	28
1948–49	40	1	0	41
1949–50	37	1	0	38
1950–51	33	4	0	37
1951–52	18	1	0	19
Total	164	19	32	215

Note: Baldwin's first game for the Albion was Bristol City (h), 2.9.1939 (FL D3(S)), but this game was deleted from the record when the Football League Third Division (South) was aborted on the outbreak of war.

BALL, JACK   1940–53

goalkeeper   Ht 6 1, Wt 11 07   164 apps
full name: John Albert Ball
born: Brighton, Sussex, 16.7.1923
debut: Queen's Park Rangers (a), 13.12.1941 (wartime)
peacetime debut: Norwich City (a), 5.10.1946 (FL D3(S))

While many players had their careers wrecked by the Second World War, Jack Ball's positively flourished during the seven emergency seasons of the conflict. Thrust into first-team action at the age of eighteen in 1941, the Brighton-born goalkeeper went on to serve the club for another thirteen years and enjoyed a benefit in 1950–51. Blessed with a wonderful pair of hands, he was also a more-than-useful performer at cricket, golf, snooker and billiards.

The young Jack represented Brighton Boys while attending the Brighton Intermediate School, and had played for Vernon Athletic in the Brighton League when he joined the Albion staff as an amateur in 1940. After making his first-team debut in December 1941, when regular goalie Gordon Mee moved to the left wing to accommodate him, Jack made his next appearance at Clapton Orient somewhat curiously on the left flank himself. Nevertheless, the tall, slim custodian impressed the management sufficiently to become a regular between the posts in 1942–43 – at the age of just

nineteen – and signed as a professional in February 1943, the first of Albion's wartime junior side to do so. A month later he was called into the R.A.F., but continued to play for the club throughout the war years whenever his duties allowed.

When things returned to normal in 1946 manager Charlie Webb selected Jack as the first choice between the posts, but the 23-year-old no.1 suffered a broken wrist in November 1947, allowing Harry Baldwin to take over, and the two men then became great rivals for the honour of guarding Albion's net. The pair shared a benefit and enjoyed two testimonial games: one against an All-Star XI in September 1950, and a second versus Liverpool in April 1951, both of which attracted good attendances.

Baldwin left the club in 1952, and Jack, who lost his place to Harry Medhurst, followed the next year when he left for the Southern League and Hastings United. He took a leading role in United's wonderful F.A. Cup escapades during the 1950s: they reached the third round proper in 1953–54 (losing 3–0 at Norwich City after 3–3 draw) and 1954–55 (2–1 at Sheffield Wednesday); the second round in 1955–56 (4–1 at Northampton Town); and the first round in 1956–57 (4–0 at Ipswich Town). Jack remained at the Pilot Field until the early 1960s. A faithful servant of the Albion through bad times and good, he was a popular figure at the Goldstone and still resides in Hove.

Season	FL	FAC	Wartime	Total
1941–42	0	0	3	3
1942–43	0	0	29	29
1943–44	0	0	6	6
1944–45	0	0	4	4
1945–46	0	0	4	4
1946–47	32	1	0	33
1947–48	16	3	0	19
1948–49	2	0	0	2
1949–50	5	0	0	5
1950–51	13	0	0	13
1951–52	28	0	0	28
1952–53	17	1	0	18
Total	113	5	46	164

BAMFORD, HARRY　　　　　　　　　　　　*1946–47*

right-back　　　　　　　　　　　　　　　　　*8 apps*
full name: Harry F. E. Bamford
born: Kingston upon Thames, Surrey, 8.4.1914
died: Rochdale, Lancashire, 1949
debut: Aldershot (a), 18.9.1946 (FL D3(S))

Harry Bamford played for the Ealing Youth Club on leaving school, but didn't break into the senior ranks until the age of 26 when he played regularly for Aldershot in the wartime emergency competitions of 1940–41. He also appeared briefly for his local club, Brentford, with whom he was registered. Harry arrived at the Goldstone in June 1946 for the initial post-war season and, although normally a full-back, made his debut on the right wing. He also had an outing at centre-forward in his eight first-team appearances, but was released in May 1947 and died two years later at the age of 35.

Season	FL	Total
1946–47	8	8
Total	8	8

BARBER, STAN　　　　　　　　　　　　　*1934–35*

left-half　　　　*Ht 5 10, Wt 11 12*　　　　*1 app*
full name: Stanley Barber
born: Wallsend, Northumberland, 28.5.1908
died: Newcastle upon Tyne, Northumberland, 18.4.1984
debut: Southend United (a), 26.9.1934 (SSC R1 rep)

Having joined Newcastle United as a seventeen-year-old in September 1925, Stan Barber remained with the 'Magpies' for three years, but had only one outing in the First Division, a 5–1 reverse at Burnley toward the end of 1927–28. In June 1928 he was transferred to Bristol City for £500 and appeared in 23 Second Division matches before moving to Exeter City in a direct swap for Alec Sheffield in June 1930.

It was at the other St James's Park that the Geordie half-back enjoyed the best spell of his career, gaining great popularity with his whole-hearted approach to the game. Over four seasons the strongly-built favourite scored ten goals in 127 League and Cup matches, but latterly suffered a breakdown in health and was released in May 1934 when he was recruited by the Albion. Stan's sole first-team appearance for Brighton came in a Southern Section Cup replay with Southend United, the only game that regular left-half Dave Walker missed during the 1934–35 season, and in 1935, after playing in a variety of positions for the reserves, he hung up his boots and returned to his native Tyneside.

Season	SSC	Total
1934–35	1	1
Total	1	1

BARHAM, MARK　　　　　　　　　　　　　*1989–92*

outside-right　　*Ht 5 7, Wt 11 00*　　*88 apps, 13 goals*
full name: Mark Francis Barham
born: Folkestone, Kent, 12.7.1962
debut: Oxford United (h), 30.12.1989 (FL D2)

Spotted playing for Folkestone Town at the age of fourteen by Norwich City, Mark Barham became an apprentice at Carrow Road and signed as a professional in April 1980. Making rapid progress, he went on to play 177 League games for the 'Canaries' and earned two England caps on the tour of Australia in 1983, but his blossoming

career met with a serious setback in December 1983 when he wrenched a knee at Tottenham. Out of the City side for ten months, he came back to gain a League Cup winner's medal in 1985 and a Second Division championship medal the following year, but never really rediscovered his early form and moved to Huddersfield Town in July 1987 for a £100,000 fee. Unfortunately, Mark failed to make an impression as the 'Terriers' were relegated to the Third Division, and after a trial period with Crystal Palace he joined Middlesbrough in November 1988 where he played in four League matches before leaving the club after just eight months.

When West Bromwich Albion released him after a handful of games, the former England man came to the Goldstone on trial in December 1989. Given a last opportunity to re-establish himself by Barry Lloyd, Mark responded admirably and went on to serve the Albion for two-and-a-half seasons. Although not especially quick, he was clever on the ball and helped the club to the 1991 Second Division play-off final with some excellent service for the main strikers, Mike Small and John Byrne. In May 1992, following relegation, he was released (although he remained to play in the pre-season friendlies) and joined Shrewsbury Town on a free transfer in September.

However, his career was again marred by injury and in February 1993 he joined Southwick in the Sussex County League in an effort to regain fitness. Mark subsequently played for the Kitchee club in Hong Kong, and signed for ambitious Sittingbourne in the Southern League upon his return to England. In the summer of 1994 he rejoined Southwick, but then ruptured a tendon and moved back to Norwich to work in the family construction business. In September 1996, Mark became manager of Fakenham Town in the Eastern Counties League.

Season	FL	Play-offs	FAC	FLC	FMC	Total
1989–90	16+1 (2)	0	2 (1)	0	0	18+1 (3)
1990–91	32 (4)	3 (1)	3 (2)	1	3	42 (7)
1991–92	22+2 (2)	0	0	2	1 (1)	25+2 (3)
Total	70+3 (8)	3 (1)	5 (3)	3	4 (1)	85+3 (13)

BARKER, CLEM　　　　　　　　　　　　　*1901–02*

centre-forward　　　　　　　　　　*8 apps, 8 goals*
full name: Charles John Barker
born: London, 1880
debut: Brighton Athletic (h), 21.9.1901 (FAC Prelim.)

A lightly-built centre-forward with a good turn of speed, 'Clem' Barker was playing for Hove when he signed professional forms for the Albion at the age of 21 just before the start of the club's initial season in July 1901. He scored the club's first-ever goal – in a 2–0 friendly win over Shoreham at the Dyke Road Field on 7 September 1901 – and went on to register eight goals in his eight competitive games of the season, but things rapidly turned sour. Branded as something of a troublemaker, he was once suspended by the F.A. for misconduct – a rare punishment in those days – and, together with Frank McAvoy, was involved in a violent row with manager John Jackson in February 1902. The pair never played for the club again and the situation

deteriorated to such an extent that they were convicted of threatening behaviour towards Jackson the following August after an incident involving the manager's wife at his Hove beer-house, the Farm Tavern. Clem was bound over to keep the peace and returned to local football.

Season	SL	FAC	Total
1901–02	5 (4)	3 (4)	8 (8)
Total	5 (4)	3 (4)	8 (8)

BARKER, Don — 1946–47

inside-forward   Ht 5 11, Wt 12 08   14 apps, 4 goals
full name: Donald Barker
born: Long Eaton, Derbyshire, 17.6.1911
died: Derby, Derbyshire, 1979
debut: Port Vale (h), 31.8.1946 (FL D3(S))

While playing for Johnson & Barnes F.C. in the Nottingham Alliance, Don Barker had an unsuccessful trial with Notts County but was then offered terms by Bradford (Park Avenue) in January 1934. After 55 Second Division appearances for the Yorkshire club, he was transferred to Millwall in January 1937, featured in the "Dockers'" Southern Section championship side of 1937–38, and starred in their first season back in the Second Division. Don played little football during the war years, but Charlie Webb paid £400 in July 1946 to bring the 35-year-old forward to the Goldstone Ground (although the chronic post-war lack of housing in Sussex meant he was forced to travel to matches from his Midlands home). He started the 1946–47 campaign as a regular in the team, appearing in both inside-forward berths and later having two outings at centre-half, but Don's best years were behind him and he retired at the end of the season. As a youngster, Don had been an excellent cricketer and sprinter.

Season	FL	Total
1946–47	14 (4)	14 (4)
Total	14 (4)	14 (4)

BATES, Don — 1950–62

right-half   Ht 6 3   21 apps, 1 goal
full name: Donald Lawson Bates
born: Hove, Sussex, 10.5.1933
debut: Walsall (a), 12.10.1957 (FL D3(S))

With 21 years on the County Ground staff, Don Bates was perhaps better known as a Sussex county cricketer, taking 880 first-class wickets and winning his county cap in August 1957, but he also enjoyed a twelve-year career at the Goldstone, most of which was spent in the reserves or 'A' team. Nevertheless, he made an important

contribution to the Albion's cause as all his 21 first-team appearances came in the run-in to promotion in 1958 when he took over the right-half berth from Steve Burtenshaw in January.

Don attended Hove Grammar School, where he played football for Brighton Boys and Sussex Schools, and made his first-class debut for Sussex C.C.C. as a teenaged fast-bowler in 1950. The following November, after a brief spell with Lewes, he signed as a forward for the Albion and served for five seasons in the Metropolitan League and

Football Combination sides upon his demob from National Service in November 1953. After his brief spell of first-team glory in 1958, Don returned to the reserves until 1962 when he left for a cricket-coaching post in South Africa at the age of 29. In 1968 he enjoyed a benefit with Sussex, and a testimonial football match was played involving his former colleagues from the promotion side. Don subsequently had a spell as player-manager with Steyning Town in the Sussex County League and taught P.E. at special schools. Thereafter he ran a launderette business in Brighton.

Season	FL	Total
1957–58	21 (1)	21 (1)
Total	21 (1)	21 (1)

BATEY, Ginger — 1913–15

centre-forward/half-back   Ht 5 11, Wt 12 00   40 apps, 4 goals
full name: Jasper Matthews Batey
born: Tyne Dock, South Shields, Co. Durham, 7.7.1891
died: in action, France, 23.10.1916
debut: Southampton (h), 3.9.1913 (SL D1)

After impressing the Albion management with a hat-trick for Portsmouth's reserves against the Brighton 'Lambs' on Boxing Day 1912, 'Ginger' Batey – nicknamed for the popular ginger beer

of the time – came to the Goldstone as a centre-forward the following May. An enthusiastic and popular player, he had scored 26 goals for 'Pompey' during 1912–13 – although only two of them came in the Southern League – but was soon converted into a half-back of some class after joining the Albion. Having made the first team sporadically in his first season with the club, he then became the regular left-half in 1914–15 until enlisting with the Footballers' Battalion of the Middlesex Regiment in February when he was lost to the club.

Ginger met his death at the age of 25 while serving as a messenger with the Army Cyclist Corps, and is buried in the Cambrin Military Cemetery in France. Before signing for Portsmouth in November 1912 he had worked as a postman while playing for South Shields in the North Eastern League and for Coventry City reserves.

Season	SL	FAC	SA	SCC	Total
1913–14	10	0	9 (3)	0	19 (3)
1914–15	19 (1)	1	0	1	21 (1)
Total	29 (1)	1	9 (3)	1	40 (4)

BAXTER, Bobby — 1961–67

left-back   Ht 5 8, Wt 10 07   220 apps, 7 goals
full name: Robert Denholm Baxter
born: Redcar, Yorkshire, 4.2.1937
debut: Preston North End, 25.11.1961 (FL D2)

Wonderfully consistent and versatile, Bobby Baxter played mainly at left-back for the Albion, but also turned out at left-half, inside-left and on the left wing in six seasons at the Goldstone. The son of Bob Baxter, Middlesbrough's Scottish international of the 1930s, young Bobby was playing for the Scottish junior club Bo'ness United when he joined Darlington in November 1959. At this stage in his career he was a forward and scored 30 goals in 67 League appearances for the 'Quakers', but after coming to Hove in August 1961 – with

Dennis Windross making the reverse journey – he soon slotted in at no.3.

Although Albion were relegated from Division Two to Division Four in his first two seasons in Sussex, Bobby was one of the few successes, a determined player who was a regular as the club regained a place in Division Three and for two seasons thereafter. Transferred to Torquay United in July 1967, he appeared in 62 League games for the Devon side before returning to Darlington in July 1969. By the time he was released a year later Bobby had 366 League appearances under his belt. After settling in Torquay, he played for Plymouth City for a short time before serving a five-year stint in the South Western League as player-manager of Bodmin Town where he turned out for the last time at the age of 39.

Season	FL	FAC	FLC	Total
1961–62	22	1	0	23
1962–63	38 (4)	1	1	40 (4)
1963–64	11 (2)	0	3 (1)	14 (3)
1964–65	39	1	0	40
1965–66	41	3	3	47
1966–67	44	6	6	56
Total	195 (6)	12	13 (1)	220 (7)

BEAL, PHIL
1975–77

midfield   Ht 5 10, Wt 11 09   12 apps
full name: Phillip Beal
born: Godstone, Surrey, 8.1.1945
debut: Rotherham United (h), 16.8.1975 (FL D3)

Phil Beal enjoyed a wonderful career with Tottenham Hotspur after signing professional forms in January 1962. The former Surrey Schools representative went on to make 420 League and Cup appearances for Spurs; gained England youth honours in 1963; played in winning League Cup final sides in 1971 and 1973; and won a UEFA Cup medal in 1972 when Tottenham defeated Wolves over two legs.

In July 1975, after fifteen years of excellent service at White Hart Lane, the fair-haired full-back arrived at the Goldstone at the age of 30 on a free transfer. Although he started the 1975–76 season as a first-team midfielder, Phil was unable to hold down a place in the Albion side and departed for the United States in February 1977 for spells with Los Angeles Aztecs and Memphis Rogues. On returning to England he played for Chelmsford City in the Southern League; had a four-match sojourn with Crewe Alexandra from August 1979; and subsequently played for Oxford City and Woking. Now the manager of a car-hire firm in West Drayton, Middlesex, Phil was a tenacious, hard-working defender who maintained a high level of performance over almost two decades.

Season	FL	FLC	Total
1975–76	8+1	1	9+1
1976–77	1	1	2
Total	9+1	2	11+1

BEALE, BOB
1905–08

goalkeeper   Ht 5 10, Wt 11 00   21 apps
full name: Robert Hughes Beale
born: Maidstone, Kent, 8.1.1884
died: Dymchurch, Kent, 5.10.1950
debut: Crystal Palace (h), 11.10.1905 (UL)

The son of a Maidstone town councillor, Bob Beale joined the Albion from Maidstone United as a promising young goalkeeper during the summer of 1905 and stayed for three seasons, but he made only 21 first-team appearances, being deprived of a more regular place by the excellence of, firstly, Mark Mellors and then Hugh MacDonald. Undeterred, he left the Goldstone and went on to become a custodian of the highest class himself.

Bob departed for Norwich in May 1908 and gave the Norfolk club fine service for four years, making 105 Southern League appearances. In May 1912 he joined Manchester United for a £275 fee and was a regular in their First Division side until the outbreak of war, totalling 112 League and Cup matches. He was also selected to represent the Football League v. Scottish League at Hampden Park in March 1913, and played for The North v. England in the international trial match at Roker Park in January 1914.

After guesting for Arsenal in their first wartime campaign, Bob joined Southern League side Gillingham in July 1919 before returning to Maidstone United in the Kent League for two seasons 1920–22, but his Football League registration was retained by Manchester United and he occasionally assisted their reserve team until 1921, travelling north from his Maidstone home. His son Walter, also a goalkeeper, played for Tunbridge Wells Rangers against the Albion in the F.A. Cup in 1937, and was on Manchester United's books in 1938–39.

Season	SL	UL	WL	Total
1905–06	3	8	0	11
1907–08	7	0	3	10
Total	10	8	3	21

BEAMISH, KEN
1972–74

centre-forward   Ht 6 0, Wt 12 06   99 apps, 28 goals
full name: Kenneth George Beamish
born: Bebington, Cheshire, 25.8.1947
debut: Oldham Athletic (h), 15.3.1972 (FL D3)

Fondly remembered for scoring some spectacular winning goals during the 1971–72 Third Division promotion campaign, Ken Beamish quickly became an Albion hero. Tall and lean, he packed a powerful shot, and scored a total of 159 goals in 553 League games for six clubs with his all-action, 'run-till-he-drops' style.

After playing for Cheshire and Liverpool County at youth level, Ken joined Tranmere Rovers as a junior but also qualified as a draughtsman before turning professional in July 1966. By March 1972 he had 49 goals from 176 League matches to his name, a record which prompted Albion manager Pat Saward to bring him to the Goldstone for £25,000 plus Alan Duffy, the highest fee the club had paid at the time. Bolstering an already potent forward line for the remaining months of a tense promotion battle, Ken scored six times in fourteen games, and finished the following campaign as top scorer as Albion were immediately relegated. He led the way again in 1973–74, but left the Goldstone in May 1974 following the recruitment of Fred Binney and moved on to Blackburn Rovers for a £26,000 fee (another club record at the time).

The Lancashire club won the Third Division championship in his first season, but after two years Ken moved on to Port Vale in September 1976 and then to Bury in September 1978. He returned to Tranmere in November 1979, and signed for Swindon Town in May 1981 where he turned to coaching before taking the managerial post in March 1983. According to Garry Nelson (q.v.) in his book *Left Foot Forward*, Ken was exceptional at man-management, but his time in charge at the Fourth Division club lasted only fifteen months. He subsequently took the post of commercial manager at Blackburn Rovers where he has remained for some years.

Season	FL	FAC	FLC	Total
1971–72	12+2 (6)	0	0	12+2 (6)
1972–73	31+7 (9)	1	1 (1)	33+7 (10)
1973–74	43+1 (12)	0	1	44+1 (12)
Total	86+10 (27)	1	2 (1)	89+10 (28)

BEDFORD, Ginger   1924–25

half-back	Ht 5 11, Wt 11 01	17 apps

full name: Sidney George Bedford
born: Northampton, Northamptonshire, 1897
died: Northampton, Northamptonshire, 18.9.1958
debut: Watford (h), 1.11.1924 (FL D3(S))

'Ginger' Bedford joined his local club, Northampton Town, in November 1920, and made his debut four months later in a 2–1 defeat at Swindon towards the end of the "Cobblers'" initial season in the newly created Third Division. With 72 League games under his belt, he joined the Albion in May 1924 and turned out at left-back, right-half and centre-half in his seventeen appearances for the club, but was released at the end of the 1924–25 season, joining Luton Town in June. The tall, powerfully-built defender met with little success at Kenilworth Road, appearing in just one Third Division game before returning to his home county in 1926 with Rushden Town, whom he assisted to the championship of the Northamptonshire League in 1926–27.

Season	FL	FAC	Total
1924–25	14	3	17
Total	14	3	17

BEECH, George   1914–20 & 1924–26

centre/inside-forward	Ht 5 8, Wt 11 00	8 apps

born: Sheffield, Yorkshire, 1892
died: Bevendean Hospital, Brighton, Sussex, 4.1.1964
debut: Plymouth Argyle (a), 2.9.1914 (SL D1)

Although he played in just eight senior games for the Albion, George Beech had a long association with the club and local sport generally. As a youngster he represented Sheffield Schools at both football and athletics, and signed for Sheffield Wednesday – for whom his father had also played – from Attercliffe Sports Club in May 1911. He never won a first-team spot with the 'Owls', though, and arrived in Hove in April 1914 as part of the deal which took David Parkes to Sheffield.

BEECH - BRIGHTON+HOVE ALBION F.C. 1923-24.

A forward at this stage of his career, George made great use of his pace – he had been a professional sprinter in his youth – and made four Southern League appearances in 1914–15 before serving with the Footballers' Battalion during the First World War. He had two more games when things returned to normal in 1919–20, but nearly all his time with the club was spent in the reserves until he departed for the Welsh League club Bridgend during 1920–21.

At the end of his first campaign in Wales, the Yorkshireman signed for the Southern League side Ebbw Vale and scored both goals for the Monmouthshire side in a 2–1 friendly win over Albion in March 1922 before returning to the Goldstone Ground two years later, in 1924.

George made two appearances at left-back in the Football League side and was then appointed assistant trainer while still playing for the 'Lambs'; two years later he became head trainer. On leaving the Albion in 1929 he took over the Lord Clyde pub in Queen's Road, Brighton, and later qualified as a masseur. From 1948 to 1952 he held the trainer's post with the Brighton Tigers ice-hockey club, and ran the Battle of Trafalgar pub in Guildford Road, Brighton, for some considerable time.

Season	FL	SL	Total
1914–15	0	4	4
1919–20	0	2	2
1924–25	2	0	2
Total	2	6	8

BEENEY, Mark   1991–93

goalkeeper	Ht 6 4, Wt 13 00	88 apps

full name: Mark Raymond Beeney
born: Pembury, Kent, 30.12.1967
debut: Oxford United (h), 20.4.1991 (FL D2)

Mark Beeney made the most vital save of any goalkeeper in the history of the Albion: his sale to Premier League side Leeds United in April 1993 rescued the club from imminent financial ruin. It was a rapid rise to the top for the Kent-born player who turned out as a central-defender for Ringlestone Colts while at school in Maidstone. In fact he didn't take up goalkeeping until joining Gillingham on schoolboy forms at the age of fourteen.

After completing an apprenticeship, Mark signed professional forms in 1986 but made just two Third Division appearances for the 'Gills' before moving on loan to Maidstone United where his career really took off. After signing permanently, he went on

to appear in around 250 matches for the 'Stones', enjoying an outstanding season in 1988–89 as United won the Conference championship and, with it, promotion to the Football League. He also gained an England semi-professional cap when he came on as a substitute against Italy in La Spezia. Although Mark retained the no.1 jersey for most of Maidstone's initial Fourth Division campaign, he lost his place in March 1990 and moved to Aldershot for a seven-match loan period.

In March 1991 he arrived at the Goldstone as cover for Perry Digweed for a £30,000 fee as Albion launched a determined effort to reach the Second Division play-offs, and had a good run in the side the following season. In 1992–93 he took over as first choice and had a superb season, developing into an excellent and commanding goalkeeper. For such a big man, his reactions and shot-stopping were superb.

On 20 April 1993, with Albion absolutely desperate for money to stave off a winding-up petition, Mark was sold to the reigning Football League champions Leeds United for an initial £350,000 fee, cash which enabled the club to pay off a large portion of its debt to the Inland Revenue and allowed the court case the following day to be dismissed. As part of the deal Leeds were to pay Albion an additional £5,000 for each of his first 50 appearances, but Mark has found it difficult to break into the first team at Elland Road, and by the end of the 1996–97 season he had only 41 appearances to his name. Nevertheless, with the total fee paid by Leeds standing at £555,000, he is second only to Mark Lawrenson (at £900,000) as the most expensive player ever sold by the Albion.

In 1996, Mark was looking to make a lucrative move to South Korea, but was frustrated by his manager, Howard Wilkinson, who demanded a fee of £300,000 and the deal was cancelled. It was not the goalkeeper's first flirtation with other countries. In April 1994 he was nearly selected for the Republic of Ireland international team, only to be informed that having an Irish great-great-grandfather was not sufficient!

Season	FL	FAC	FLC	FMC	AMC	Total
1990–91	2	0	0	0	0	2
1991–92	24+1	2	2	2	0	30+1
1992–93	42	5	4	0	4	55
Total	68+1	7	6	2	4	87+1

BELL, WILLIE   1969–70

left-back   Ht 5 10, Wt 11 11   *52 apps, 1 goal*
full name: William John Bell
born: Johnstone, Renfrewshire, Scotland, 3.9.1937
debut: Walsall (h), 9.8.1969 (FL D3)

Having played a big part in the early development of Don Revie's great Leeds United side, Scottish international Willie Bell had a wealth of experience when he joined his former Leeds team-mate Freddie Goodwin as Albion's player-coach, but his time at the Goldstone Ground ended after just one season when he left somewhat acrimoniously, following his manager to Birmingham.

After joining Glasgow amateurs Queen's Park from Neilston Juniors in 1957, Willie played at left-half in two amateur internationals before turning professional with Leeds in July 1960 where he was converted into a left-back. In 1964 the Yorkshire side were Second Division champions, lost in the F.A. Cup final to Liverpool the following year, and were runners-up to Dynamo Zagreb in the Fairs Cup (now UEFA Cup) in 1967; Willie played his part on all three occasions, and also appeared for the full Scotland side twice in 1966, against Portugal and Brazil.

After 243 games at Elland Road, the Scottish defender lost his place to future England star Terry Cooper and was transferred to Leicester City in September 1967 for a £45,000 fee. In July 1969, at the age of 31, Willie arrived at the Goldstone to join his former colleague Freddie Goodwin for the latter's first full season as manager,

and turned in some excellent performances in the no.3 shirt. Indeed, his experience and hard-tackling contributed greatly to a defence which conceded just 43 League goals as Albion very nearly gained promotion. That near-success encouraged Birmingham City to offer Goodwin the manager's post at St Andrews, and Willie followed him onto the City coaching staff. He was, however, still registered as a Brighton player and Birmingham were subsequently fined £5,000 for an illegal approach.

On Goodwin's dismissal in September 1975, Willie was appointed manager of the First Division club, and retained the post for two years. In December 1977 he took over the hot seat at Lincoln City, but resigned after ten months and departed for Colorado, U.S.A., where he became football coach to a religious group known as The Campus Crusade for Christ.

Season	FL	FAC	FLC	Total
1969–70	44 (1)	5	3	52 (1)
Total	44 (1)	5	3	52 (1)

BELLAMY, WALTER   1935–36

outside-left   Ht 5 8, Wt 11 00   *3 apps*
full name: Walter Richard Bellamy
born: Tottenham, Middlesex, 6.11.1904
died: Hadley Wood, Middlesex, 19.10.1978
debut: Queen's Park Rangers (a), 12.9.1935 (FL D3(S))

A prominent amateur in his early days, Walter Bellamy played for the Amateurs *v.* Professionals in two F.A. Charity Shield

contests, represented Middlesex, and won two England amateur international caps against Ireland in 1926 and 1927. The Tottenham-born winger made his name in the Isthmian League with Ilford, Tufnell Park and Dulwich Hamlet, and caught the eye of the Spurs management who signed him as a professional in February 1927. Playing mainly as a reserve, he remained at White Hart Lane for more than eight years, but did appear in 73 League and Cup games before being released to join the Albion in September 1935. A speedy, direct outside-left, Walter acted as deputy to Bert Stephens throughout 1935–36 but was released at the end of the campaign. He later played for New Camp F.C. while serving in Gibraltar during the early part of the war, and ran a heating-oil business in London for many years. Walter died in 1978 at the age of 73 while playing golf.

Season	FL	Total
1935–36	3	3
Total	3	3

BENCE, PAUL   1965–68

defender   Ht 5 9, Wt 11 00   *1 app*
full name: Paul Ian Bence
born: Littlehampton, Sussex, 21.12.1948
debut: Walsall (a), 11.5.1968 (FL D3)

After skippering Sussex Schools and training with the Albion while at Andrew Cairns School in Littlehampton, Paul Bence joined the Goldstone staff as an apprentice in October 1965 and was offered professional terms in May 1967. His senior career with the club was somewhat brief, though, lasting just thirteen minutes when he came on as substitute in the last game of the 1967–68 campaign at Walsall. Already on the free transfer list, Paul departed for Reading a month later where he made thirteen League appearances before joining Brentford on a free transfer in July 1970.

It was at Griffin Park that Paul finally found his niche in football. Developing into a versatile player, he appeared in every outfield position in 244 League games over nearly seven seasons. Prominent

in the "Bees'" Fourth Division promotion campaign of 1971–72, he was Player of the Season the following term and went on to skipper the side, his sterling performances and passing ability making him a great favourite of the Brentford faithful. After a five-match loan period with Torquay United in December 1976 and January 1977, he was released the following March and moved into non-League football as player-coach to Wokingham Town. Paul later managed the Isthmian League club, and subsequently held a similar post with Wycombe Wanderers in the Alliance Premier League (1984–86). He now works as an area salesman for a major brewery in Abingdon.

Season	FL	Total
1967–68	0+1	0+1
Total	0+1	0+1

BENNETT, KEN   1950–53

inside/centre-forward   107 apps, 41 goals
full name: Kenneth Edgar Bennett
born: Wood Green, Middlesex, 2.10.1921
died: Rochford, Essex, December 1994
debut: Torquay United (h), 19.8.1950 (FL D3(S))

A well-built, craggy-featured character, Ken Bennett scored at better than a goal every third game for the Albion over three seasons, and was top scorer in 1952–53. His first experience of adult football came with Wood Green Town where his father was trainer. After joining Tottenham Hotspur's ground staff, he signed as a professional at the age of nineteen in 1940 and turned out briefly for Spurs in the wartime leagues while serving with the Royal Artillery. During the 1945–46 transitional season he guested extensively for Southend United and was officially transferred in June 1946, going on to net sixteen goals in 54 League and Cup outings for the Essex club over the next two years. In June 1948, Ken moved on to Bournemouth but dropped into the Southern League with Guildford City a year later.

Even so, when Don Welsh brought the 28-year-old forward to the Goldstone in June 1950 he arrived with a good reputation, and performed capably in the middle of the front line as the club maintained a respectable position in the Third Division (South). Ken proved a good poacher in front of the net, with many of his goals coming via knock-downs from his colleagues, but he perhaps lacked the battling qualities, enthusiasm and craft necessary in a high-calibre centre-forward. In March 1952, during a 5–1 win over Walsall, he had the opportunity of a hat-trick when full-back Jack Mansell, who had already once scored from the spot, made way for him to take a penalty. Ironically, Ken's shot was saved and Mansell himself netted the rebound!

Ken departed for Crystal Palace in July 1953 in exchange for his namesake Ron Bennett, but returned to the Southern League with Tonbridge later in the season, and subsequently played for Headington United (which became Oxford United), Plessey F.C. and Clacton Town. His elder brother Les enjoyed an outstanding career with Spurs and West Ham United, and was player-manager of Clacton Town at the time Ken played for them. On hanging up his boots the younger Bennett initially worked as a storeman with the Plessey company in Ilford, but later became a grocer in Walthamstow until retiring.

Season	FL	FAC	Total
1950–51	29 (8)	2 (1)	31 (9)
1951–52	42 (18)	1 (1)	43 (19)
1952–53	30 (11)	3 (2)	33 (13)
Total	101 (37)	6 (4)	107 (41)

BENNETT, RON   1953–54

outside-right   Ht 5 8, Wt 11 01   3 apps
full name: Ronald Bennett
born: Barwell, Leicestershire, 8.5.1927
debut: Leyton Orient (h), 26.8.1953 (FL D3(S))

Ron Bennett first appeared for Wolverhampton Wanderers as a teenager towards the end of the Second World War, and remained on the Molineux staff until his transfer to Portsmouth in July 1948. His first game for 'Pompey' came in their second successive League championship season of 1949–50, but, with England international Jack Froggatt in possession of the left-wing berth, Ron's first-team outings were thin on the ground. Moving to Crystal Palace in January 1952, he came to the Goldstone in July 1953 when Ken Bennett made the reverse journey. Ron appeared down the right flank at Hove but was again deprived of a regular place, this time by Dennis Gordon, and in May 1954 he was released to join Margate in the Kent League. He subsequently played for Southern League Tonbridge.

Season	FL	Total
1953–54	3	3
Total	3	3

BENTLEY, HARRY   1920–22

defender   Ht 5 8, Wt 11 00   70 apps
born: Sheffield, Yorkshire
debut: Southend United (a), 28.8.1920 (FL D3(S))

Signed for a big fee in 1920, Harry Bentley proved to be a shrewd acquisition for the Albion and his experience was invaluable during the club's first season in the Football League's newly formed Third Division. Having joined Sheffield Wednesday from the local Heeley Friends club in May 1910, he had to wait four years to make his League debut, a 2–0 defeat at Oldham in April 1914, but then, having established himself in the First Division side, he lost four years to war service with the Royal Field Artillery (although he did appear occasionally for Wednesday during the conflict). On returning to Hillsborough for the start

H. BENTLEY

BRIGHTON & H.A.

of the 1919–20 season, Harry totalled 52 League and Cup appearances before joining the Albion for £250 in May 1920. In two seasons at the Goldstone he appeared in every defensive position except centre-half as the club initially struggled in the new competition, and in August 1922 the versatile defender was sold to Swindon Town for £350, a useful profit. Harry then saw out his League career with eleven appearances spread over the next two seasons.

Season	FL	FAC	Total
1920–21	40	3	43
1921–22	24	3	27
Total	64	6	70

BERRY, GREG   1995

midfield/striker	Ht 5 11, Wt 12 00	6 apps, 2 goals

full name: Gregory John Berry
born: Grays, Essex, 5.3.1971
debut: Wrexham (a), 26.8.1995 (FL D2)

Normally a hard-working, left-sided midfielder, Greg Berry scored the Albion's first goal for three games on his debut at Wrexham and was thereafter played mainly as an out-and-out striker. His other goal for the club secured the first away win of the 1995–96 campaign at Bristol City.

Born in Grays, Greg stated out with his local Essex Senior League side, East Thurrock United, and signed for Leyton Orient at the age of eighteen in July 1989. The £2,000 fee was a record for the Essex junior club, but was greatly increased when, after scoring 20 goals in 104 League and Cup games for the Third Division side, he was transferred to Premier League side Wimbledon in August 1992 for £250,000, ten per cent of which was due to his original club. He made just eight appearances for the 'Dons', though, and left for Millwall in March 1994 for £200,000.

Hampered by injury in his time at The Den, Greg had scored four goals in 21 First Division outings before arriving in Hove. After proving useful in his month on the South Coast, he left the Albion scene rather sadly on a stretcher, carried off after sustaining ankle ligament damage at Bournemouth. In March 1996, Greg rejoined Leyton Orient on loan, making seven appearances before returning to The Den where he was given a free transfer at the end of 1996–97.

Season	FL	Total
1995–96	6 (2)	6 (2)
Total	6 (2)	6 (2)

BERRY, LES   1986–87

full-back	Ht 6 2, Wt 11 13	28 apps

full name: Leslie Dennis Berry
born: Plumstead, Woolwich, London, 4.5.1956
debut: Portsmouth (h), 23.8.1986 (FL D2)

Discovered playing Sunday football in the Welling area of Kent, Les Berry initially signed amateur forms for Charlton Athletic before turning professional in March 1974. Tall and lanky, he proved to be an excellent find and went on to play in 396 League and Cup games for the 'Valiants'. In May 1984 he enjoyed a testimonial match against Arsenal, but appeared just seven times when Charlton won promotion to Division One in 1985–86 and was granted a free transfer at the end of the campaign. Les arrived at the Goldstone in August 1986, but his best days appeared to be behind him and by January he had lost his place in a struggling side.

In March 1987, though, he enjoyed a new lease of life by returning to Kent on loan with Gillingham (where his father was a director). Les played in all subsequent games as the 'Gills' narrowly missed out on promotion to Division Two in the play-offs, and remained at Priestfield the following term before joining Maidstone United in the Conference during the summer of 1988. Making 40 appearances in the side which won Football League status in 1989, he continued playing for the 'Stones' in Division Four for almost two seasons until returning to the Conference with Welling United in March 1991. Les retired from the game in 1992 and now works as an assistant to after-dinner speaker Bob 'The Cat' Bevan.

Season	FL	FAC	FLC	FMC	Total
1986–87	22+1	2	2	1	27+1
Total	22+1	2	2	1	27+1

BERTOLINI, JACK   1958–66

right-half	Ht 5 9, Wt 11 10	279 apps, 14 goals

full name: John Bertolini
born: Alloa, Clackmannanshire, Scotland, 21.3.1934
debut: Middlesbrough (a), 23.8.1958 (FL D2)

Signed by Billy Lane in July 1958 to strengthen the half-back line for Albion's first season in the Second Division, Jack Bertolini proved to be an outstanding acquisition. Consistency personified, he enjoyed a run of 193 consecutive appearances, by far the greatest number of any outfield player until bettered by Peter O'Sullivan in 1974. Indeed, the amiable half-back was ever-present for the three seasons 1959–62 as the club struggled in the Second Division, and again in 1962–63 in the Third.

Born in Alloa of Italian ancestry – his grandfather came from Italy – Jack played for Tullibody Secondary School and Sauchie Thistle Juveniles before moving up to the East of Scotland Junior League with Alva Albion Rangers in August 1951. Playing at outside-right, the young Scot quickly attracted inquiries from senior clubs and he had a trial in Falkirk's reserves in November 1951. Jack also received offers from Bristol City and Alloa, but a week later he signed for Stirling Albion. Preston North End were the next side to show an interest, but after two seasons at Annfield Park he was transferred to Workington in January 1953 and spent his first three years in Cumberland as a part-timer while working as a pipe-fitter at the Solway Colliery.

Jack performed for a number of managers in five-and-a-half years with the 'Reds', including Bill Shankly and Joe Harvey, and it was Harvey who converted him into a wing-half. After scoring 35 goals in 181 League appearances at Borough Park, he looked set to rejoin Shankly at Huddersfield Town, but his wife took an instant shine to the South Coast when Albion showed an interest after seeing him play for the Third Division (North) against the Southern Section in 1958, and the

24-year-old duly signed for Brighton with reserve-team player Roy Tennant making the reverse journey.

One of those players who never seem to have an off day, the quietly-spoken Scot was the model professional and a rock in the Albion side during traumatic times. Although he made most of his appearances at right-half, he also had spells in the no.2 shirt as well. After losing his place during the club's Fourth Division days, Jack was turning out for the reserves in October 1965 when he was stretchered off with knee-ligament damage and advised not to play again. For some time thereafter he worked in the Goldstone office and assisted with coaching the youngsters, and in November 1967 he received a joint benefit with coach Cyril Hodges. In 1970–71, Jack managed Sussex County League side Whitehawk, and took charge of Sussex Sunday League Premier Division side Fishersgate in 1973–75. Jack still lives in Mile Oak, Portslade, and has worked in the truck- and van-hire business for many years.

Season	FL	FAC	FLC	Total
1958–59	30	1	0	31
1959–60	42 (3)	5	0	47 (3)
1960–61	42 (2)	3 (1)	2	47 (3)
1961–62	42 (1)	1	1	44 (1)
1962–63	46 (2)	1	1	48 (2)
1963–64	30 (4)	1	2 (1)	33 (5)
1964–65	24	1	2	27
1965–66	2	0	0	2
Total	258 (12)	13 (1)	8 (1)	279 (14)

BEST, JACK   1919–20

outside-left   Ht 5 7, Wt 11 00   17 apps, 2 goals
born: Birmingham, Warwickshire, c. 1896
debut: Brentford (a), 30.8.1919 (SL D1)

Jack Best arrived at the Goldstone at the age of 23 in July 1919 having played twelve games for Birmingham during the 1916–17 and 1917–18 wartime seasons. Initially first-choice left-winger in Albion's last season in the Southern League, he found it difficult to settle on the South Coast and, having lost his place to Tom Brown in January, returned to his Midlands home in March for 'family reasons'. Jack had also guested for Coventry City during the war years.

Season	SL	Total
1919–20	17 (2)	17 (2)
Total	17 (2)	17 (2)

BILEY, ALAN   1985–86

forward   Ht 5 8, Wt 11 11   40 apps, 9 goals
full name: Alan Paul Biley
born: Leighton Buzzard, Bedfordshire, 26.2.1957
debut: Barnsley (a), 13.3.1985 (FL D2)

An instinctive, will-o'-the-wisp striker, Alan Biley started out as an apprentice with Luton Town, but it was after joining Cambridge United in July 1975 that he came to prominence. In four-and-a-half years at the Abbey Stadium, as the "U's" won promotion from the Fourth Division to the Second in consecutive seasons 1976–78, he hit 74 Football League goals in 165 games, still a club

record. Inevitably his scoring feats attracted a number of bigger clubs, and in January 1980 he was transferred to First Division Derby County for £300,000. An instant hit at the Baseball Ground, Alan finished the season as top scorer with nine goals – including two against the Albion – from eighteen games, but was unable to prevent the 'Rams' being relegated. After moving to Everton for £350,000 in July 1981, he registered just three goals before being loaned to Stoke City in March 1982.

Five months later, in August 1982, Portsmouth invested £100,000 for the lively 25-year-old's

services and he responded by quickly regaining his intuitive scoring touch. Alan scored 51 times in 105 League games at Fratton Park, including 22 as 'Pompey' carried off the Third Division title in 1982–83. However, after two years with Portsmouth, Alan became unsettled, asked for a transfer, and arrived at the Goldstone in March 1985 for £50,000.

Unable to re-capture his best form in Hove, he looked set for a move to New York Express in 1986, but the American side were unable to complete the $19,000 transfer, and when he returned to the Goldstone in November he was immediately loaned to his former club, Cambridge United. When his contract was paid up in May 1987, Alan moved abroad to enjoy spells with Twente Enschede (Holland), Brest (France) and Panionios (Greece), and also had a brief trial period with Huddersfield Town. He subsequently played for Havant in the Wessex League and later became manager of the Eastern Counties League club Ely City while running a sports promotion agency. Alan now runs a gymnasium in Biggleswade, Bedfordshire, but still turns out occasionally for nearby Potton United in the United Counties League.

Season	FL	FAC	FLC	Total
1984–85	12+1 (4)	0	0	12+1 (4)
1985–86	22 (4)	0+2	2+1 (1)	24+3 (5)
Total	34+1 (8)	0+2	2+1 (1)	36+4 (9)

BINNEY, FRED   1974–77

centre-forward   Ht 5 10, Wt 11 07   85 apps, 44 goals
full name: Frederick Edward Binney
born: Plymouth, Devon, 12.8.1946
debut: Crystal Palace (h), 17.8.1974 (FL D3)

Remarkable speed off the mark and an uncanny instinct for the net enabled Fred Binney to score a packet of goals in the lower divisions. A career record of 180 goals from 379 League matches speaks volumes, and his performances for the Albion – 44 goals in 85 games – only added to his reputation.

Fred came into the pro game in October 1966, signing for Torquay United from Launceston and becoming a regular scorer in the reserves at Plainmoor, but his career really took off during a loan-spell with Exeter City in February 1969 when he netted eleven goals in seventeen games. Signed permanently in March 1970, the Plymouth-born forward enjoyed four prolific years in the Fourth Division with the 'Grecians' and finished the 1972–73 season as the League's leading marksman with 28 goals (jointly with West Ham United's 'Pop' Robson).

In May 1974, Albion manager Brian Clough paid £25,000, plus John Templeman and Lammie Robertson, for the 27-year-old striker's services. It was a major investment for the club at the time, but it was a deal which paid dividends. Topping the Goldstone scoring charts in his first season, Fred repeated the feat in the near-promotion campaign of 1975–76 with 27 goals, but he was too similar in style to the emerging Peter Ward and lost his place in September 1976 to Ian Mellor. He never played for the first team again, and after spending the summer of 1977 with St Louis in the U.S.A he left the Goldstone for Plymouth Argyle on a free transfer in October 1977. A fine playing career was rounded off at Hereford United, where he moved into coaching, looking after the youth team at Edgar Street until 1982. After a spell in Malaysia, he returned to Exeter City as a coach in 1985–86.

Always willing to go in where it hurts, Fred will be remembered by many supporters for his bravery when he returned to the fray against Third Division leaders Hereford United at the Goldstone in December 1975 swathed in bandages following a nasty head-wound.

Season	FL	FAC	FLC	Total
1974–75	24+2 (9)	3 (3)	3 (1)	30+2 (13)
1975–76	38 (23)	3 (3)	2 (1)	43 (27)
1976–77	6 (3)	0	4 (1)	10 (4)
Total	68+2 (35)	6 (6)	9 (3)	83+2 (44)

BIRDSALL, George 1913

centre-forward *1 app*
born: Saxton, Yorkshire, 30.9.1891
debut: Reading (h), 10.4.1913 (SCC R2 rep)

George Birdsall was a former Newcastle United triallist who was playing for Brompton in the Northallerton League when he arrived in Hove for his one Albion first-team game. He then returned to Brompton before joining the Army during the First World War. In 1919 he turned out for Harpenden Town, and went on to join Derby County in March 1921, for whom he made eight League appearances.

Season	SCC	Total
1912–13	1	1
Total	1	1

BISSET, Tommy 1952–62

right-back/centre-forward Ht 6 0, Wt 12 00 *123 apps, 5 goals*
full name: Thomas Alexander Bisset
born: Croydon, Surrey, 21.3.1932
debut: Walsall (a), 6.4.1953 (FL D3(S))

Older Albion fans will remember Tommy Bisset as a tall, leggy full-back, but he joined the club as a forward and played seven times in the no.9 shirt before switching to right-back during 1955–56.

A representative of Croydon and Surrey Schools, he played junior football in Croydon before being called into the Army on National Service. After serving with the Royal Signals in Eritrea, where he represented the Eritrean League *v.* Sudan, Tommy signed for the Athenian League side Redhill upon his demob from the Forces, but soon joined Albion as a 20-year-old amateur centre-forward in December 1952.

A month later he signed professional forms and played in his first League match at Walsall in April 1953, but it was not until switching to the no.2 shirt in September 1955 that he had an extended run in the team. After returning to the reserves the following season, Tommy acted as a deputy full-back until the club won promotion in 1958.

More than half his 115 League appearances came in the Second Division, but in 1960–61 he lost his place to Doz Little and departed for Southern League Guildford City at the end of the campaign. He subsequently played for Yiewsley (soon to become Hillingdon Borough), Haywards Heath as player-coach, and Southwick. Tommy ran his own decorating business in the Brighton area on his retirement. His uncle was the remarkable Bob Thomson, who enjoyed a splendid career as a centre-forward with Chelsea and Charlton Athletic despite having sight in only one eye.

Season	FL	FAC	Total
1952–53	1	0	1
1953–54	3 (1)	1	4 (1)
1954–55	1	0	1
1955–56	43	1	44
1956–57	6 (2)	0	6 (2)
1957–58	3	0	3
1958–59	28	1	29
1959–60	22	5	27
1960–61	8 (2)	0	8 (2)
Total	115 (5)	8	123 (5)

BISSETT, Nicky 1988–95

central defender Ht 6 2, Wt 12 10 *124 apps, 8 goals*
full name: Nicholas Bissett
born: Fulham, London, 5.4.1964
debut: Bradford City (a), 9.11.1988 (FMC R1)

Nicky Bissett must surely have been one of the unluckiest players ever to appear for the Albion. Despite performing reliably when called upon, he remained a fringe member of the first team for five years because of continual battles against injury since first damaging an ankle in December 1989.

Once employed as a gas-servicing engineer, Nicky joined the Isthmian League side Hornchurch as a full-back after being recommended by a local park-keeper. Subsequently offered a trial by Fulham, the lanky Londoner was unable to take the necessary time off work, but continued to climb the non-League ladder, firstly with Walthamstow Avenue, then with Dagenham – for whom he played over 100 games – and finally with Barnet, whom he joined in March 1988 for £20,000, then a record fee between non-League clubs. Nicky had made just sixteen appearances for the Conference side when Albion manager Barry Lloyd paid a large fee (which eventually reached £115,000) for his signature in September 1988.

After a delay caused by jury service, the 24-year-old defender initially played in the reserves, but came into the first team in December and, following Larry May's retirement, became first-choice centre-half. Dominant in the air, he won much acclaim with some solid displays after adjusting to the pace of the Football League – Lloyd was reputed to have rejected an offer of £250,000 for his new star – but suffered a badly-broken leg at Swindon in April 1990 which kept him out of action for almost a year.

Nicky came back at the end of the 1990–91 season to help the club reach the Second Division play-off final at Wembley, but fractured the leg again in February 1993 and suffered a serious knee injury in November 1994. Although his dedication to the cause greatly impressed manager Liam Brady – he would cycle in from his Worthing home to strengthen his legs – Nicky was forced to call it a day as far as the professional game was concerned in the close season of 1995 at the age of 31 — a sad day for all involved. He then signed for Crawley Town, managed by his former team-mate Colin Pates, but played only one game before joining County League side Stamco. However, Nicky found himself unable to compete sufficiently because of his knee and quickly retired from football completely, subsequently moving to his wife's home city of York to become a postman.

Season	FL	Play-offs	FAC	FLC	FMC	AMC	Total
1988–89	16	0	0	0	1	0	17
1989–90	28+1 (5)	0	0	2	1	0	31+1 (5)
1990–91	3	3	0	0	0	0	6
1991–92	11+2 (1)	0	2	1	1	0	15+2 (1)
1992–93	12	0	4	1	0	2	19
1993–94	12 (1)	0	0	3	0	0	15 (1)
1994–95	12 (1)	0	0	4	0	2	18 (1)
Total	94+3 (8)	3	6	11	3	4	121+3 (8)

BLACKBURN, Ken 1968–70

centre-forward *1 app, 1 goal*
full name: Kenneth Alan Blackburn
born: Wembley, Middlesex, 13.5.1951
debut: Shrewsbury Town (a), 12.3.1969 (FL D3)

Ken Blackburn was a sturdily-built forward who scored in his only Football League appearance. Outstanding as a schoolboy sportsman, he had represented South-West England as a prop-forward at rugby and had also played soccer for Gloucester Schools. In January 1968, after playing for Cheltenham Town's youth team, Ken joined

the Albion as an apprentice, and was promoted to the first team at Shrewsbury in March 1969 in the absence of Alex Dawson. The seventeen-year-old no.9 scrambled the ball into the net for a last-minute winner in a 2–1 victory and signed professional forms two months later, but after spending the following season in the reserves he was released in May 1970 and joined Dover in the Southern League. Ken later moved back to the county of his youth with Gloucester City.

Season	FL	Total
1968–69	1 (1)	1 (1)
Total	1 (1)	1 (1)

Football League club the following year, in the newly formed Third Division, before retiring in 1922 at the age of 38.

Season	SL	FAC	FACS	SCC	Total
1909–10	42	1	0	4	47
1910–11	34	3	1	3	41
Total	76	4	1	7	88

13 players who worked in coal mines

Player	Player
Bertolini, Jack	McAteer, Tom
Booth, Billy	Martin, Ted
Brown, Buster	Mooney, Paul
Burton, Billy	Sykes, Albert
Hodge, Billy	Willis, George
Ison, Ernie	Wilson, Ernie
Kirkwood, Dan	

BLACKMAN, FRED   1909–11

right-back   Ht 5 10, Wt 12 07   88 apps
full name: Frederick Ernest Blackman
born: Kennington, Lambeth, London, 8.2.1884
debut: Portsmouth (a), 1.9.1909 (SL D1)

'Wonderfully quick on his feet; sure kick with either foot; fearless tackler.' So ran a description of Fred Blackman in a 1910 edition of *Athletic News*, a most apt commentary on an outstanding player who played a large part in Albion's magnificent successes of 1910 and who very nearly won England honours. A cabinet-maker by trade, the Kennington-born full-back arrived in Sussex in May 1907 to join the recently professionalised Hastings & St Leonards United club; he had played for Woolwich Arsenal but failed to make the first team. The young full-back spent two successful seasons at the Central Ground – the second as skipper – and played a leading role in the "Chopbacks'" excellent F.A. Cup runs when they reached the first round proper (equivalent to today's third round) in 1907–08 (losing 1–0 to Portsmouth) and 1908–09 (losing 2–0 at Blackpool).

Fred's impressive performances with the East Sussex club encouraged Brighton manager Jack Robson to secure his services in May 1909. An instant success at the Goldstone, he appeared in every match as Albion carried off the Southern League championship in his first season with a goals-against total that remains a record for the club (for a season of 42 or more matches). The Southern League recognised Fred as the best in the business, choosing him for their representative side against the Football League on two occasions in 1910: a 2–2 draw at Chelsea and an excellent 3–2 victory at Tottenham. The following term, in January 1911, the 26-year-old was selected for the England international trial match at Tottenham, but his side lost 4–1.

Fred's superb form naturally attracted the attention of the big Football League clubs, and in May

F. BLACKMAN.

1911 he was transferred to Huddersfield Town for a big fee of £300. After 92 Second Division appearances in nearly three years at Leeds Road he moved to Leeds City in February 1914, but returned south during the First World War to assist Fulham in the emergency London Combination tournament. In 1919 he returned to the Southern League with Queen's Park Rangers, and played in their first match as a

BLUNDEN, BERTIE   1901–02

utility forward   7 apps, 2 goals
full name: Bertie Victor J. Blunden
born: Brighton, Sussex, 1881
debut: Shepherd's Bush (h), 25.1.1902 (SL D2)

One of the talented local amateurs who assisted Albion during their initial campaign, 1901–02, Bertie Blunden impressed the management in a friendly with Richmond Association in January 1902, and held his place for all but two of the nine remaining Southern League fixtures that season, scoring two goals. He moved on to play for St Albans in the South Eastern League in 1902–03.

Season	SL	Total
1901–02	7 (2)	7 (2)
Total	7 (2)	7 (2)

BOLLINGTON, JACK   1920–21

right-half   Ht 5 9, Wt 10 12   16 apps
full name: John Edward Bollington
born: Belper, Derbyshire, 1892
debut: Merthyr Town (a), 6.9.1920 (FL D3(S))

Jack Bollington's professional career came to a most unfortunate and abrupt end when, in January 1921, his leg was broken in an F.A. Cup tie against Cardiff City. The sound of the fracture was said to have reverberated around the Goldstone to such an extent that several people in the large crowd fainted.

As a junior Jack had played for Sunderland, and also turned out for non-League Walsall before joining Southern League side Southend United in 1919. Playing at right-half for the 'Shrimpers' in a Third Division match against the Albion in September 1920, he

BOLLINGTON · BRIGHTON + HOVE ALBION F.C · 1920 · 21.

so impressed Charlie Webb that the Brighton manager obtained his signature the following day and played him against Merthyr Town 24 hours later. Jack's terrible accident came in just his sixteenth appearance for the club, and Albion and Cardiff played a testimonial match for his benefit in November 1921. On retiring he spent some time coaching in Holland with Haarlem F.C.

Season	FL	FAC	Total
1920–21	14	2	16
Total	14	2	16

BOORN, ALAN — 1971–74

midfield   Ht 5 6, Wt 9 12   *2 apps*
born: Folkestone, Kent, 11.4.1953
debut: Blackpool (h), 30.12.1972 (FL D2)

After skippering the Kent Schools and Kent Boys' Clubs teams as a lad, Alan Boorn joined Folkestone Town as an amateur, and captained the England amateur youth team in 1971. He then had a brief spell with Coventry City, but arrived at the Goldstone in May 1971 as a promising, eighteen-year-old midfielder. Turning professional in December 1972, he made his first-team debut the same month in the absence of Bert Murray, but was unfortunate to appear in the middle of Albion's record 13-match losing streak and could do little in his two games to stop the rot. During the 1973–74 season.

Ian was loaned to Canterbury City and Tonbridge, and was released by the Albion at the end of the season to join Canterbury on a permanent basis. He subsequently played for Horsham, Dartford and Dover before returning to his first club, Folkestone Town.

Season	FL	Total
1972–73	2	2
Total	2	2

BOOTH, BILLY — 1908–20

right-half   Ht 5 10, Wt 12 00   *369 apps, 12 goals*
full name: William Booth
born: Sheffield, Yorkshire, 9.5.1886
died: Brighton, Sussex, 1963
debut: Southampton (h), 2.9.1908 (SL D1)

One of the finest half-backs ever to wear an Albion shirt, Billy Booth was a star of the best side to grace the Goldstone Ground for nearly 80 years. Playing a big part in the club's early 'golden age' – Southern League championship, Southern Charity Cup and F.A. Charity Shield in 1910 – the former collier was the first Brighton player to appear in more than 100 consecutive first-team games. In fact, his magnificent run only came to an end because of representative duty with the Southern League XI. In twelve years with the club, four of which were lost to the Great War, Billy played 369 matches, a total beaten only by Bert Longstaff during the Southern League era.

The Yorkshire-born half-back played for his local Thorpe Hesley Parish Church club before joining Sheffield United in 1905 for three seasons. He played in one First Division match for the 'Blades', but then refused the offer of a new contract and arrived at the Goldstone Ground in May 1908 at the age of 22. (In fact, Sheffield United retained his Football League registration until 1920, when they valued him at £50.)

Billy quickly endeared himself to the Hove fans with his non-stop, energetic style, and remained the driving-force of the side until 1920. His tremendous consistency earned him two England trial matches in 1912–13 – The South *v.* England at White Hart Lane, and England *v.* The North at Manchester City's Hyde Road ground – which prompted his selection as travelling reserve for the international match with Ireland in Belfast. He also represented the Southern League on seven occasions during the period 1910–14, against the Football League, Scottish League and Irish League.

A wonderful servant of the Albion, Billy was granted a testimonial in March 1914 and skippered the side in 1914–15. During the Great War he served with the Footballers' Battalion, but returned to captain the side again in the first post-war Southern League campaign.

In 1920, Albion became founder members of the Football League's Third Division, but Billy was now 34 and returned to his native Yorkshire with Castleford Town in the Midland League. However, he came back to Sussex to assist Worthing briefly during the 1925–26 season and, having married a local girl, then lived in Brighton until his death at the age of 76. His son, Sammy Booth (q.v.), also played for the Albion.

Season	SL	FAC	FACS	WL	WL Ch.	SA	SCC	Total
1908–09	39	1	0	10 (1)	2	0	3 (1)	55 (2)
1909–10	42	1	0	0	0	0	4	47
1910–11	38 (1)	3	1	0	0	0	5	47 (1)
1911–12	36 (3)	1	0	0	0	0	3	40 (3)
1912–13	36 (1)	3	0	0	0	11 (1)	0	50 (2)
1913–14	38 (2)	4 (1)	0	0	0	8	1	51 (3)
1914–15	36 (1)	3	0	0	0	0	1	40 (1)
1919–20	38	1	0	0	0	0	0	39
Total	303 (8)	17 (1)	1	10 (1)	2	19 (1)	17 (1)	369 (12)

BOOTH, SAMMY — 1938–39 & 1947–49

centre-half/inside-forward   Ht 6 1, Wt 12 10   *29 apps, 7 goals*
full name: William Samuel Booth
born: Hove, Sussex, 7.7.1920
died: Eastbourne, Sussex, 18.2.1990
debut: Bournemouth & B.A. (h), 30.8.1947 (FL D3(S))

The son of Billy Booth (q.v.), Sammy Booth lost the chance to emulate the exceptional career of his father when the Second World War interrupted his progress. Having played for Brighton Boys in 1934–35, the Hove-born youngster turned out for Hove Penguins and first appeared for Albion's reserve team as a seventeen-year-old amateur in April 1938. He went on to sign professional forms for the club, but was transferred to Port Vale in February 1939 and moved to Cardiff City two months later where he played in the three matches of the aborted 1939–40 Third Division.

Sammy's football career then suffered from the wartime hiatus until he returned to Ninian Park, but he found it impossible to break into the Cardiff side and returned to the Goldstone in August 1947. An honest but basic player, he made a great contribution to team morale during a wretched campaign which saw the club forced to apply for re-election; the life and soul of the dressing-room, Sammy was the club's comedian, a real character who enlivened every training session. Initially played as a centre-half, he later moved up front to appear in all three inside-forward positions, but a

fractured collar-bone suffered in February 1948 effectively ended his Albion career, and he played in just eight more League games before being released to join Hastings United in May 1949.

Sammy spent four seasons as a player at the Pilot Field, followed by two as trainer, and was granted a testimonial match in March 1955 in which United beat an Albion XI 3–2. Particularly remembered for his long-legged, short-stridden running-gait, he coached in South Africa for some time and lived in Eastbourne – where his house was called 'Goldstone' – for many years until his death.

Season	FL	FAC	Total
1947–48	20 (5)	1 (1)	21 (6)
1948–49	8 (1)	0	8 (1)
Total	28 (6)	1 (1)	29 (7)

BORTHWICK, WALTER   1967

inside-right   Ht 5 11   1 app
full name: Walter Ross Borthwick
born: Edinburgh, Midlothian, Scotland, 4.4.1948
debut: Doncaster Rovers (a), 16.5.1967 (FL D3)

Although he has enjoyed a long and successful career north of the border, Walter Borthwick's experience of English football was brief, lasting just one game. Having joined Morton as a youngster, he arrived at the Goldstone on a month's trial in May 1967 upon the recommendation of the former Glasgow Rangers and Scotland skipper George Young, a good friend of Albion manager Archie Macaulay. Given a run-out in the final game of the season, a 1–1 draw against Doncaster Rovers, the nineteen-year-old was offered terms but preferred to return to Scotland for a two-month trial with Dundee United.

He was not taken on at Tannadice, though, and instead joined East Fife in September 1967, a move which proved an outstanding success. 'East Fife never made a better signing,' ran one commentary on his seven seasons in Methil. Always giving 100 per cent effort, Walter was a model player, an energetic and versatile half-back or midfielder who appeared in a number of positions for the 'Fifers'. A star of the side which won promotion to Division One of the Scottish League in 1970–71, he moved to St Mirren in August 1974 and was a regular at Love Street until he joined St Johnstone in November 1976. Walter returned to St Mirren briefly in July 1977, and two months later joined his final club, Dunfermline Athletic, where he was to become player-coach.

With around 300 Scottish League appearances – and one Football League game – to his name, he joined Heart of Midlothian in 1981 as coach and retained the position until 1991 when he moved to Arbroath as manager. However, he was in charge at Gayfield Park for only a few months at the start of the 1991–92 season before returning to Dunfermline Athletic for two years as the club's community officer. Walter is now the Scottish F.A.'s development officer for the south of Scotland.

Season	FL	Total
1966–67	1	1
Total	1	1

BOULTON, BILL   1903–04

left-back   6 apps
full name: William Boulton
born: Bedwellty, Monmouthshire, Wales, 1882
debut: Wellingborough Town (a), 5.9.1903 (SL D1)

Bill Boulton spent one season with the Albion: 1903–04, the club's first in Division One of the Southern League. The 21-year-old full-back was described as 'an admirable player, equally clever with head and feet', but his appearances were limited because of the consistency of both Duncan Cameron and Jock Caldwell. Bill had played for Aberdare before his arrival at the Goldstone and returned to minor football on his release in May 1904.

Season	SL	Total
1903–04	6	6
Total	6	6

BOWDEN, OSSIE   1937–38

inside-left   Ht 5 9, Wt 10 10   1 app
full name: Oswald Bowden
born: Byker, Newcastle upon Tyne, Northumberland, 7.9.1912
died: Newcastle upon Tyne, Northumberland, 20.5.1977
debut: Bristol City (h), 6.11.1937 (FL D3(S))

In a nine-year professional career dogged by injury and illness, Ossie Bowden made fewer than 30 first-team appearances for his four clubs. He was developed as an amateur by Newcastle Swifts, Newcastle United's nursery club, but signed as a pro–fessional for Derby County in May 1930 and played in ten First Division matches in five years at the Baseball Ground. Ossie moved to Nottingham Forest in June 1935 where he again failed to win a regular place – he scored three times in fourteen Second Division matches – and in May 1937 Charlie Webb brought him to the Goldstone for the not inconsiderable fee of £400. He enjoyed just one outing in the absence of Jimmy Cargill, however, and was released at the end of the season to join Southampton on a free transfer. After two games for the 'Saints' in 1938–39, Ossie was released, and the outbreak of war shortly afterwards effectively brought his senior career to an end.

Season	FL	Total
1937–38	1	1
Total	1	1

BOYLE, JOHN   1973

midfield   Ht 5 8, Wt 11 10   10 apps
born: Motherwell, Lanarkshire, Scotland, 25.12.1946
debut: Grimsby Town (a), 22.9.1973 (FL D3)

John Boyle began his career in unusual fashion when, while on holiday in London, he arrived at Stamford Bridge unannounced to ask for a trial and impressed the Chelsea management sufficiently to be taken on the staff. He went on to play for Scotland at youth level and signed professional forms in August 1964, becoming a part of the successful Chelsea side which won the Football League Cup in 1965, lost in the 1967 F.A. Cup final to Tottenham Hotspur, and won the European Cup Winners' Cup against Real Madrid in 1971.

The hard-working midfielder first came to the attention of Albion fans when he was sent off for kicking Wally Gould in the celebrated F.A. Cup tie between the teams in February 1967, but found himself on loan at the Goldstone for two months in the autumn of 1973 in an attempt to bolster the struggling Brighton midfield. After 198 League games for Chelsea, John was transferred to Orient in December 1973 where he saw out his League career. He subsequently played in the U.S.A. and for Dulwich Hamlet, and was manager of the Southern League side Dartford in 1978–79.

Season	FL	Total
1973–74	10	10
Total	10	10

BRADFORD, JACK   *1923–25*

inside-left	*Ht 5 9, Wt 11 12*	*3 apps*

full name: John William Bradford
born: Pegg's Green, Leicestershire, 6.11.1903
debut: Watford (a), 7.3.1925 (FL D3(S))

Jack Bradford worked on his father's farm as a lad while playing for the local Pegg's Green Victoria club, but was recommended to Birmingham by his elder brother Joe, a future England inside-forward, and joined him on the St Andrews staff as an amateur in March 1922. Having played only reserve-team football for Birmingham, the nineteen-year-old signed for the Albion in August 1923 but again had to be content with second-eleven fare until given his chance in the League side in March 1925 in the absence of Jimmy Hopkins. He did not impress, though, and having played just three first-team games he left for Preston North End on a free transfer in June 1925. Once again his chances were restricted and in August 1926 he was transferred to Walsall where his career finally took off.

BRADFORD · B·H ALBION F.C.1923·24

A stalwart at Fellows Park for over ten years, Jack was appointed player-coach to the 'Saddlers' in 1934 and made his 300th League appearance at the Goldstone in February 1937. As well as having an England international relative in brother Joe, Jack had another in his cousin, Leicester City's Hughie Adcock.

Season	FL	Total
1924–25	3	3
Total	3	3

BRAND, BILL   *1919–20*

left-half		*2 apps*

full name: William J. Brand
born: London, c. 1892
debut: Southampton (a), 14.2.1920 (SL D1)

Although born in London, Bill Brand was a local man who joined the Albion in 1919 after twelve years' service as a regular soldier. He made a brace of Southern League appearances when Gunner Higham was absent through injury, but was released in May 1920 after one season with the club and, having been reinstated as an amateur, departed for an unknown non-League destination.

Season	SL	Total
1919–20	2	2
Total	2	2

BREMNER, KEVIN   *1987–90*

striker	*Ht 5 9, Wt 12 05*	*141 apps, 40 goals*

full name: Kevin Johnston Bremner
born: Banff, Banffshire, Scotland, 7.10.1957
debut: York City (h), 15.8.1987 (FL D3)

Although he was by no means the surest striker ever to play for the Albion, there was never any doubting Kevin Bremner's commitment to the cause. A real battler, the Banff-born forward always gave maximum effort and was never afraid to go in where it hurts. He was rewarded with a career total of 136 goals from 444 games in both the Football League and Scottish League.

One of a handful of Albion professionals to have come out of the north of Scotland, Kevin started out with his local club in Banff, the Highland League side Deveronvale, for whom he played part-time while working as an auctioneer's clerk. In October 1980 he moved

into the Football League with Colchester United following a brief trial, and became a regular in the forward line at Layer Road for two years. During the 1982–83 campaign Kevin had the unusual experience of playing for five clubs when, after starting out in Colchester's line-up, he had loan spells with Birmingham City, Wrexham and Plymouth Argyle before joining Millwall for £25,000 in February 1983. Life with the 'Lions' proved fruitful, and he scored 33 goals in 96 League outings before being transferred to Reading in August 1985 for a £36,000 fee. Helping the Berkshire side to promotion in his first season, Kevin maintained his form at Elm Park with a goal every third game. It was form which caught the eye of Barry Lloyd, especially as he hit the back of the Brighton net three times in 1986–87.

The Albion manager paid £65,000 for the Scottish striker's signature in July 1987 to form a new striking partnership with Garry Nelson, an arrangement which paid immediate dividends as the club won its place back in the Second Division at the first attempt. Kevin himself hit thirteen goals, but his unselfish running contributed a good deal to his partner's exceptional total of 32. Top scorer during 1989–90, Kevin was very much a form player – he could be very good or very bad – and lost favour with the crowd for a while, but he bounced back with a hat-trick against Birmingham City on New Year' Eve 1988 and remained one of the principal strikers until leaving to become player-coach at Peterborough United in July 1990.

After moving back to Scotland with Dundee in September 1991, Kevin scored six goals in 24 appearances in their First Division championship season of 1991–92. He then had a loan-spell with Shrewsbury Town in March 1992, but returned to the Highland League as player-manager of Brora Rangers until leaving the Sutherland club in the summer of 1994. Kevin's career then turned full-circle when he rejoined his first club, Deveronvale, as player-manager, but a year later, in 1995, he became youth-team manager at Gillingham.

The possessor of abundant energy, he played in all four divisions of the Football League and figured in three Third Division promotion sides: Millwall 1984–85, Reading 1985–86, and Albion 1987–88; and a Fourth Division promotion campaign with Peterborough in the 1990–91 season. His elder brother, Des, is a former Scottish international.

Season	FL	FAC	FLC	AMC	Total
1987–88	42+2 (8)	4 (1)	1	4 (4)	51+2 (13)
1988–89	41 (15)	1	0	0	42 (15)
1989–90	42+1 (12)	2	1	0	45+1 (12)
Total	125+3 (35)	7 (1)	2	4 (4)	138+3 (40)

BRENNAN, JIMMY   *1908–09*

outside-right	*Ht 5 9, Wt 12 00*	*18 apps, 3 goals*

full name: James Francis Brennan
born: Templemore, Co. Tipperary, Ireland, 10.9.1884
debut: Croydon Common (h), 16.9.1908 (WL D1 'A')

A good all-round athlete who won many prizes for running and jumping, Jimmy Brennan also excelled at cricket and tennis, but his football career came to a sad end. The fleet-footed winger skippered Prior Park College, Bath, for three years before becoming a shipping clerk in Liverpool, where he assisted the Valkyrie and Africa Royal clubs. After turning professional with Bury in May 1907,

Jimmy made the "Shakers'" First Division side just once, in a 2–0 defeat by Sheffield Wednesday at Gigg Lane (in a line-up which included Brighton's future skipper Joe Leeming), and was released to join the Albion in May 1908.

Although he retained the right-wing spot for the first half of 1908–09, he then fell foul of the management for breaching his contractual obligation to keep himself fit; the 24-year-old Irishman was known to be very fond of a drink and in February 1909 was warned by the F.A. as to his future conduct. Eventually suspended *sine die* by the club, Jimmy appealed to the F.A. and the ban was commuted to six weeks, but he was released at the end of the season and returned to minor football.

Season	SL	WL	Total
1908–09	10 (1)	8 (2)	18 (3)
Total	10 (1)	8 (2)	18 (3)

BRENNAN, PADDY   1948–52

wing-half	Ht 5 8, Wt 11 07	47 apps

full name: Patrick Joseph Brennan
born: Dublin, Co. Dublin, Irish Free State, 1.3.1924
died: Hove, Sussex, 11.1.1991
debug: Reading (h), 20.11.1948 (FL D3(S))

Paddy Brennan's first senior club was the League of Ireland outfit Shelbourne in his home city of Dublin, but his fine form attracted the attention of the Albion scouts and he was brought to the Goldstone as a 24-year-old in August 1948. Although he had to wait until November to make his Football League debut, the talented Irishman then came to be regarded by commentators as one of the cleverest players on the staff, second only perhaps to Johnny McNichol.

A most popular player as well as something of a joker, Paddy became first-choice left-half during the 1949–50 campaign but lacked consistency. After losing his place the following season to the emerging Glen Wilson, he remained in the reserves until May 1952 when he was transfer-listed and departed for Yeovil Town. In November 1952 he came up against the Albion as Yeovil skipper in an F.A. Cup first-round tie, but the Somerset side were beaten 4–1 on their own infamous slope. On leaving Yeovil, Paddy played for Weymouth and Dover, and was appointed player-coach of Hove Town in the Sussex County League in 1957. For some 30 years he worked as an ambulance officer in Hove.

Season	FL	FAC	Total
1948–49	8	1	9
1949–50	29	1	30
1950–51	8	0	8
Total	45	2	47

BRETT, FRANK   1930–35 & 1936

full-back/centre-half	Ht 5 11, Wt 12 00	143 apps

full name: Frank Bernard Brett
born: Stirchley, Birmingham, Warwickshire, 10.3.1899
died: Chichester, Sussex, 21.7.1988
debut: Exeter City (h), 6.9.1930 (FL D3(S))

Frank Brett was 31 when he joined the Albion, but he went on to make 143 appearances for the club, firstly as a left-back, then as a dominating centre-half. His finest hour came in the club's F.A. Cup

third-round tie with Chelsea in January 1933, when his wonderful display completely snuffed out the threat of the immortal Hughie Gallacher and enabled Albion to defeat the First Division side 2–1.

Having worked for Cadbury's, the chocolate company, on leaving school, Frank joined the Army on the outbreak of the Great War and served on the Western Front as a gunner with the Royal Field Artillery. His football career began on his demob in 1918 when he joined Birmingham League side Redditch, and a year later he signed for Aston Villa as an amateur. Albion's former manager Jack Robson then took him to Manchester United as a professional in March 1921, but it was amid some confusion over his registration for, when the details had been sorted out, United were fined ten guineas for infringing the rules. Nevertheless, the young full-back went on to make ten appearances in the First Division side before returning to Villa Park in August 1922 as part of the deal which took England centre-half Frank Barson to Old Trafford.

Frank failed to win a first-team place with Villa, however, and was transferred to Northampton Town in May 1923 where he played in well over 200 Third Division (South) games in seven seasons and skippered the team with distinction. Signing for the Albion on a free transfer in May 1930, the veteran defender was made captain and became the dominant personality of the side for three years with his rock-steady play and determined tackling. In December 1932, when Paul Mooney was injured, he moved from left-back to centre-half with great success, but made way for the recovered Mooney the following season and moved into the Southern League with Tunbridge Wells Rangers in September 1935. The following August he returned to the Albion to assist briefly in the reserves, but after finally leaving the Goldstone in October 1936, Frank concentrated on running his coal-merchant's business in Westbourne Street, Hove, and later became a bookmaker in partnership with Ernie 'Tug' Wilson (q.v.). He continued playing football with Hove in the Sussex County League until the Second World War.

Season	FL	FAC*	Total
1930–31	40	2	42
1931–32	37	3	40
1932–33*	33	7	40
1933–34	13	0	13
1934–35	8	0	8
Total	131	12	143

Note: Three of Brett's F.A. Cup appearances came in the qualifying competition of 1932–33.

BRIDGE, MICK   1913–14

wing-half	2 apps

full name: Michael Bridge
debut: Newport County (a), 16.10.1913 (SA)

Mick Bridge was a youngster from Turton F.C., the home-town club of Albion skipper Joe Leeming, who was signed as a professional by Brighton during the close season of 1913. He was given very little opportunity to impress during his one season at the Goldstone Ground, though, making the midweek Southern Alliance side on just two occasions and playing only sporadically for the second eleven.

Season	SA	Total
1913–14	2	2
Total	2	2

BRIDGES, BARRY — 1972–74

striker   Ht 5 10, Wt 11 11   71 apps, 14 goals
full name: Barry John Bridges
born: Horsford, Norfolk, 29.4.1941
debut: Aston Villa (a), 2.9.1972 (FL D2)

Exceptional speed coupled with excellent control and a fierce shot brought Barry Bridges a fair amount of success in a seventeen-year career as a professional. One of the most prolific goalscorers in the country at his peak, the Norfolk-born forward won four England caps and finished with a career tally of 190 goals from 474 League matches.

Barry had played for Norwich Boys and appeared five times for England Schools before joining Chelsea's ground staff in 1956 where he won further honours: England youth caps in 1957–58 and an F.A. Youth Cup runner's-up medal in 1958. On turning professional in May 1958 he went on to score 80 goals in 176 League appearances for the Londoners, winning a League Cup trophy in 1965 and representing the Football League the same season. In April 1965 he was rewarded with his first England appearance, against Scotland at Wembley, and gained three more caps that year as Alf Ramsey experimented with his team for the 1966 World Cup. Playing at centre-forward, he scored once, in a 1–1 draw against Yugoslavia in Belgrade.

Capable of latching onto the slimmest of chances with his pace, Barry starred in Tommy Docherty's emerging Chelsea side, but, following a breach of club discipline and the emergence of the prodigious Peter Osgood, he was transferred to Birmingham City for £55,000 in May 1966 where he scored 47 times in 104 League and Cup matches. In August 1968, Barry moved on to Queen's Park Rangers, but was unable to rediscover his best form and joined Millwall in September 1970. Two years later Pat Saward splashed out a club-record £29,000 fee to bring the experienced forward to the Goldstone as replacement for Kit Napier. Barry was 31 when he joined the club and his career foundered somewhat as Albion made an immediate return to Division Three; scoring just fourteen times in 71 games, he could not always hold down a first-team place and was released in May 1974 to join the Highlands Park club of Johannesburg.

Remaining in South Africa until December 1975, he then returned to Sussex and had a few games with Bexhill Town in the County League. Barry ran Eastbourne's New Wilmington Hotel for some time in partnership with his wife's parents, but he subsequently had a spell as player-manager with St Patrick's Athletic in the League of Ireland, followed by stints as manager with Sligo Rovers and then with Dereham Town, King's Lynn and Horsford in his native county.

Season	FL	FAC	FLC	Total
1972–73	25+8 (4)	1	1	27+8 (4)
1973–74	31+2 (10)	2	1	34+2 (10)
Total	56+10 (14)	3	2	61+10 (14)

BRILEY, LES — 1991–92

midfield   Ht 5 6, Wt 11 00   17 apps
full name: Leslie Briley
born: Lambeth, London, 1.10.1956
debut: Watford (h), 14.9.1991 (FL D2)

Les Briley arrived at the Goldstone at the age of 35 with 506 League appearances under his belt, but he was not a great success in a poor Albion side and was released after just one season.

A South London Schools representative, Les enjoyed an apprenticeship with Chelsea and signed professional forms in 1974, but failed to make the senior side before joining Hereford United in

1976 for their only season in Division Two. Following United's swift return to the Third Division, the tenacious midfielder was transferred to Wimbledon for £18,000 in February 1978 towards the end of their first campaign in the Football League. After 61 League appearances for the 'Dons', including 26 in 1978–79 when they won promotion to Division Three, Les joined Aldershot for £43,000 in March 1980 where he turned out in 157 Fourth Division games, but it was his next move, to Millwall in May 1984 in exchange for Andy Massey, that proved the best of his career.

In seven seasons at The Den, Les became a great favourite of the "Lions'" fans as he skippered the side and played a major role in the club's advance from the Third Division to the First. Released in September 1991, he had 227 League games for Millwall behind him but must have thought his playing days were over.

However, Albion manager Barry Lloyd, an old Hereford team-mate, offered him a place on the Goldstone staff as a standby midfield player for the 1991–92 season. Les hustled and bustled in the centre of the pitch in his seventeen games, but could do little to prevent relegation to the new Second Division. Released in May 1992, he moved into the Conference as player-coach of Slough Town. In October 1993 he was made player-manager, but remained in the post only until the end of the season as the 'Rebels' were relegated.

Season	FL	FMC	Total
1991–92	11+4	2	13+4
Total	11+4	2	13+4

BROADHEAD, ARNOLD — 1921–24

inside-forward   Ht 5 5, Wt 10 00   8 apps, 2 goals
born: Darnall, Sheffield, Yorkshire, 1900
debut: Newport County (a), 26.2.1921 (FL D3(S))

Arnold Broadhead signed for the Albion from a Sheffield junior club in February 1921 and scored on his first-team debut the same week. Taken on as a professional a month later, he turned in some splendid performances for the 'Lambs' but failed to reproduce his reserve-team form in the League side. His consistent displays in the second eleven earned him a place in the Southern League's representative team against the Central League in March 1922, when he scored the consolation goal in a 5–1 reverse at Wolverhampton. In March 1924 he moved on to Swindon Town, but appeared just once in their Third Division side before forsaking the first-class game a year later at the age of 25.

Arnold then took employment as a bus-conductor and married a girl from Hove; Jack Burnham (q.v.) was best man at their wedding.

Season	FL	Total
1920–21	5 (2)	5 (2)
1921–22	3	3
Total	8 (2)	8 (2)

BROMAGE, RUSSEL   1990–92

left-back   Ht 5 11, Wt 11 05   *2 apps*
born: Blurton, Stoke-on-Trent, Staffordshire, 9.11.1959
debut: Barnsley (a), 25.8.1990 (FL D2)

Signed by Barry Lloyd on a free transfer from Bristol City as cover for injured left-back Ian Chapman, Russel Bromage was a very experienced defender with 395 League games to his name, but he played just twice for the

Albion's senior team. He made his name with Port Vale, for whom he signed professional forms in November 1977 after an apprenticeship. Initially a midfielder, it was in the no.3 shirt that he found his niche and he went on to make 347 League appearances for Vale over ten years, scoring thirteen times. Twice, in 1983–83 and 1985–86, he featured heavily in Fourth Division promotion successes for the Potteries club, and was Player of the Season in 1980–81.

In October 1983, Russel had a two-match loan-period at Oldham, but, after receiving a testimonial, left Vale Park in August 1987 when he was transferred to Bristol City. He added another 46 League games to his total in three seasons at Ashton Gate before joining the Albion in August 1990, but spent most of his two years at the Goldstone in the reserves; he also had a three-match loan-spell with Maidstone United in January 1991.

On his release in 1992, Russel joined Southwick as player-coach and subsequently became player-manager. In January 1995, however, he was suspended by the Sussex County League side for four games after being sent off, and resigned from his post the following month, moving to nearby Lancing as a player. Moving further along the coast, he spent 1995–96 as manager of Littlehampton Town, but was dismissed at the end of a disappointing season and joined Shoreham where he became player-coach. In the summer of 1997 he was appointed joint manager with his former Albion colleague John Byrne. Russel has a window-cleaning business in Shoreham but spends his summers coaching youngsters in the United States.

Season	FL	FLC	Total
1990–91	1	1	2
Total	1	1	2

BROMLEY, BRIAN   1971–73

midfield   Ht 5 8, Wt 11 10   *55 apps, 3 goals*
born: Burnley, Lancashire, 20.3.1946
debut: Chesterfield (h), 27.11.1971 (FL D3)

An experienced and influential midfielder for the Albion, Brian Bromley will be remembered as one of the key players who steered the club to promotion success in 1971–72. His senior career began with Bolton Wanderers, for whom he made his First Division debut as a sixteen-year-old apprentice. In July 1963 he signed as a professional, won England youth honours the following year, and went on to make 184 League and Cup appearances for the 'Trotters' before joining Portsmouth for £25,000 in November 1968. However, a serious knee condition hampered his career at Fratton Park, and after three years with the Hampshire side he came to the Goldstone in November 1971 for two months on loan.

One of Pat Saward's many temporary signings, Brian was enlisted to maintain the push for promotion following the departure of another loan man, Bertie Lutton, and had a profound influence on the side. Cool, strong and determined, he proved an inspiration and, although he went back to 'Pompey' in January, he soon returned to Hove on a

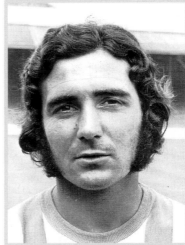

permanent basis for £14,000 and was installed as skipper for the successful run-in to promotion. A powerhouse in the middle of the park, he inspired all around him with his non-stop running.

The following season, 1972–73, was horrendous for everyone connected with the club, though, and Brian was no exception; he made just nineteen appearances as Albion made a swift return to the Third Division, and was transferred to Reading in September 1973. After a brief loan-spell at Darlington early in 1975, he was released by Reading in May 1975 to join Wigan Athletic, then in the Northern Premier League. Brian subsequently returned to Hampshire and spent several seasons with Waterlooville in the Southern League.

Season	FL	FAC	FLC	Total
1971–72	28+1 (3)	2	0	30+1 (3)
1972–73	17+2	1	1	19+2
1973–74	2	0	1	3
Total	47+3 (3)	3	2	52+3 (3)

BROOMFIELD, DES   1938–48

half-back   Ht 5 8, Wt 11 04   *26 apps, 1 goal*
full name: Desmond Stretton Broomfield
born: Hove, Sussex, 6.10.1921
debut: Southampton (h), 30.12.1939 (wartime)
peacetime debut: Port Vale (h), 31.8.1946 (FL D3(S))

A pupil at Shoreham Grammar School, Des Broomfield arrived at the Goldstone as a sixteen-year-old amateur in 1938 and appeared briefly for the club during the war, making his entry into the senior team in a farcical 9–4 defeat of Southampton in December 1939. He spent most of the war years in the R.A.F., attaining commissioned rank, but returned to the Albion in 1946 upon his release from the Forces, and made his peacetime debut as an amateur on the right wing in the initial post-war League fixture. Signed as a part-time professional in January 1947, Des subse-

quently played in both wing-half berths before being released to join Hastings United during the close season of 1948. He later signed for Shoreham, where he played a major role in the "Musselmen's" County League championship successes of 1951–52 and 1952–53. Des now lives in retirement in Portslade.

Season	FL	FAC	Wartime	Total
1939–40	0	0	2	2
1945–46	0	0	2 (1)	2 (1)
1946–47	18	0	0	18
1947–48	2	2	0	4
Total	20	2	4 (1)	26 (1)

BROPHY, HARRY   1936–38

centre-half   Ht 6 0, Wt 12 00   *1 app*
full name: Henry Frank Brophy
born: Leicester, Leicestershire, 22.10.1916
debut: Crystal Palace (a), 30.9.1936 (SSC R1)

In a long and varied career, Harry Brophy had an outstanding start: he skippered Islington to the English Schools Trophy in 1931; represented London and Middlesex Boys; joined the Arsenal ground

staff at the age of fifteen from where he was farmed out to Margate, their nursery club; and turned professional for the 'Gunners' at the age of seventeen. Yet despite his early promise, Harry failed to fulfil his potential at the highest level and arrived at the Goldstone in September 1936 where he was destined to play just one first-team game, a Southern Section Cup game against Crystal Palace. While playing for the reserves in December 1936, the unfortunate defender broke a leg which set his career back even further. Released in May 1938, he was given another opportunity by Southampton. 'Broph' considered that he hadn't been given a fair deal by the Albion and proved his point by playing 37 Second Division games for the 'Saints' in 1938–39.

Upon the outbreak of war Harry joined the police force, but soon signed up with the Merchant Navy and took part in the Dunkirk evacuation; yet he still found time to guest for Bradford (Park Avenue), Crystal Palace, Fulham and Huddersfield Town. After the war he played for Nuneaton Town in 1945 before emigrating to Australia, where he turned out for the Corinthian club in Queensland in 1949 before setting out on a coaching career: with Queensland and Australia (1952–56); as manager of Mauritius (1957–59); coach to Hakoah Sports (Melbourne, 1961); coach to Hellenic (Brisbane, 1961); and manager-coach to FC Prague (Sydney, 1962). Harry later returned to England and now lives in Bedford. Also a capable cricketer, he was on the ground staff of Surrey C.C.C. as a fast-bowler in 1936.

Season	SSC	Total
1936–37	1	1
Total	1	1

BROUGHTON, F.   1902–03

utility player   *9 apps*
debut: Southall (h), 13.9.1902 (SL D2)

Brought to the Goldstone from Brentford in August 1902, Broughton played at centre-half in the Albion's opening fixture of the 1902–03 season, a 4–2 home win over Southall which turned out to be his only outing in the Southern League side. He went on to appear in all the half-back positions and at both inside- and outside-right in the subsidiary South Eastern League matches, but he was released at the end of the season.

Season	SL	SEL	Total
1902–03	1	8	9
Total	1	8	9

BROWN, ALAN   1958–62

centre-forward   Ht 6 2, Wt 14 00   *8 apps, 2 goals*
born: Lewes, Sussex, 11.12.1937
debut: Bury (a), 12.9.1961 (FLC R1)

Alan Brown was one of six football-playing brothers, three of whom – Alan, Irvin (q.v.) and Stan (q.v.) – were on the Goldstone staff at various times. A massively-built forward, he had played local soccer with Lewes St Mary's and Portslade before turning professional with Brighton in September 1958 following a recommendation by his sports-officer while serving with the Army in Gibraltar. Making his first-team debut in a League Cup first-round tie at Bury in September 1961, Alan

played in a further seven League matches, scoring two goals, before leaving for Exeter City in January 1962. His stay in the West Country was a brief one, though, as he returned to Sussex later in the year to sign for Hastings United in the Southern League. Alan later played for Margate, Dover and Crawley Town, and now works as a landscape gardener in the Lewes area.

Season	FL	FLC	Total
1961–62	7 (2)	1	8 (2)
Total	7 (2)	1	8 (2)

BROWN, BILL   1913–14

centre-forward   *19 apps, 10 goals*
full name: William Brown
born: Swalwell, Whickham, Co. Durham, c. 1890
debut: Cardiff City (a), 26.2.1913 (SA)

Bill Brown joined the Albion from the Northern Combination club Lintz Institute at the age of 22 in February 1913, and was given a run in the first team towards the end of the season, scoring three goals in ten games in the minor competitions. On Bullet Jones's return from Birmingham the following term, however, Bill's role became that of a reserve, despite scoring two hat-tricks in the Southern Alliance. He was also a regular scorer for the reserves and hit another two hat-tricks in the South Eastern League, but he was released in May 1914 and returned to minor football.

Season	SL	SA	SCC	Total
1912–13	5	3 (2)	2 (1)	10 (3)
1913–14	1	7 (7)	1	9 (7)
Total	6	10 (9)	3 (1)	19 (10)

BROWN, BUSTER   1934–37

centre-forward   Ht 5 10, Wt 12 00   *66 apps, 45 goals*
full name: Oliver Maurice Brown
born: Burton upon Trent, Staffordshire, 10.10.1908
died: London, 1953
debut: Gillingham (a), 31.3.1934 (FL D3(S))

For a period of just over a year, Oliver Brown – known to one and all as 'Buster' – was one of the most prolific marksmen ever seen at the Goldstone Ground and carved his own niche in Albion folklore. Signed in March 1934 as a replacement for Arthur Attwood, the regular centre-forward who had been struck down with a bout of appendicitis, he scored an amazing total of fifteen goals in the remaining fixtures of the season – including two hat-tricks – in one of the most intense bursts of goalscoring in the long history of the club. Incredibly, Buster ended the campaign as top scorer, five goals ahead of Attwood, yet he played in only ten games!

A product of Burton junior football, Buster worked down the local pit until joining Birmingham League side Burton Town. His goalscoring prowess was soon recognised by Nottingham Forest who obtained his signature in February 1930, but after learning his trade in the reserves he was transferred to Norwich City in December 1931. Buster quickly made a name for himself with the 'Canaries', scoring 33 goals in 51 Third Division outings. It was form which prompted Second Division West Ham United to sign him in June 1933 but, with England international Vic Watson leading the attack, he had to be content in the reserves until he arrived at the Goldstone nine months later to write his name into the record books.

In 1934–35, following the death of his wife, the burly 25-year-old missed pre-season training but still repeated the top-scoring feat with 26 League and Cup goals. That proved to be the end of his success at the Goldstone, though. Replaced by Alec Law the following season, he made just ten more first-team appearances before leaving the club and the first-class game in 1937 (though he appeared briefly as a guest player for West Ham during the war). Buster later worked in the prison service in London until his death at the age of 44.

A typical centre-forward of his era – big, beefy and bustling – when he was dropped by the Albion it was stated that he was 'too slow', but with a career record of 79 goals from 121 outings Buster didn't do too badly! His brother Ambrose was a professional with Chesterfield, Portsmouth and Wrexham.

Season	FL	FAC	SSC	Total
1933–34	8 (11)	0	2 (4)	10 (15)
1934–35	40 (23)	3 (2)	3 (1)	46 (26)
1935–36	9 (4)	0	0	9 (4)
1936–37	1	0	0	1
Total	58 (38)	3 (2)	5 (5)	66 (45)

BROWN, FREDDIE   1923–24

inside-right/centre-forward   Ht 5 7, Wt 11 07   19 apps, 3 goals
full name: Frederick Brown
born: Gainsborough, Lincolnshire
debut: Northampton Town (a), 25.8.1923 (FL D3(S))

Freddie Brown started out in the Midland League with his home-town club Gainsborough Trinity, but was working at Hadfield's Steel & Armaments works in Sheffield when he first appeared for Sheffield United in the wartime regional league in January 1916.

BROWN - BRIGHTON-HOVE ALBION F.C. 1923-24.

After playing fairly regularly for the 'Blades' throughout the latter part of the conflict, he was officially signed in August 1919 and won a place in the First Division side during the two seasons following the war, scoring seven goals in 36 matches, but then spent a couple of seasons in the reserves (making a single additional first-team appearance) before arriving at the Goldstone on a free transfer in August 1923.

Freddie led Albion's attack in the opening eight games of the season before losing his place to Tommy Cook, but when Andy Neil was transferred to Arsenal in March he came back into the team at inside-right. Given a free transfer at the end of the 1923–24 campaign, he left for Gillingham in August, and in three seasons at Priestfield scored 27 goals in 95 Third Division outings; in 1925–26 he was top scorer with fifteen goals. In June 1927, Freddie's career turned full cycle when he returned to Gainsborough Trinity. His elder brother, Arthur, played for Sheffield United, Sunderland, Fulham, Middlesbrough and England before the Great War.

Season	FL	Total
1923–24	19 (3)	19 (3)
Total	19 (3)	19 (3)

BROWN, GARY   1962–65

half-back   Ht 6 1, Wt 12 03   1 app
full name: Gary John Brown
born: Lewes, Sussex, 22.7.1946
debut: Luton Town (a), 1.9.1965 (FLC R1)

One of the local Brown clan, Gary Brown was a cousin of Irvin, Alan and Stan Brown (q.v.), the Lewes-born brothers who all had spells on the Albion staff. After two years as a junior, he signed professional forms at the age of eighteen in 1964 but had just one outing with the seniors, in place of Norman Gall at centre-half in a 1–1 League Cup draw at Luton in September 1965. Four months

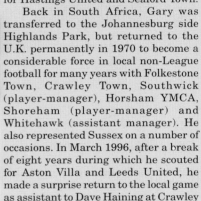

later he departed for South Africa to play for Durban City, but returned to England in 1967 to have a trial with Charlton Athletic, and also turned out for Hastings United and Seaford Town.

Back in South Africa, Gary was transferred to the Johannesburg side Highlands Park, but returned to the U.K. permanently in 1970 to become a considerable force in local non-League football for many years with Folkestone Town, Crawley Town, Southwick (player-manager), Horsham YMCA, Shoreham (player-manager) and Whitehawk (assistant manager). He also represented Sussex on a number of occasions. In March 1996, after a break of eight years during which he scouted for Aston Villa and Leeds United, he made a surprise return to the local game as assistant to Dave Haining at Crawley Town, but the position lasted only seven months. Gary runs his own contract curtain-manufacturing business, while his son Steve is a defender with Charlton Athletic.

Season	FLC	Total
1965–66	1	1
Total	1	1

BROWN, IRVIN   1951–58

centre-half   Ht 6 3, Wt 12 04   3 apps
born: Lewes, Sussex, 20.9.1935
debut: Northampton Town (a), 9.11.1957 (FL D3(S))

Irvin Brown was the eldest of Albion's three Lewes-born Brown brothers, and joined the ground staff as a sixteen-year-old in September 1951 having represented East Sussex Schools and the Lewes St Mary's club. Signed as a professional in October 1952, he served a long apprenticeship with the 'A' team and reserves before making the League side for the match at Northampton in November 1957, but as understudy to the consistent Ken Whitfield his chances were few, and in September 1958 he was transferred to Bournemouth for £2,000. Irvin met with greater success at Dean Court and appeared in 65 Third Division matches before joining Poole Town in the Southern League in 1962. Later playing for Hamworthy, he still lives in Poole, working as a carpenter.

Season	FL	Total
1957–58	3	3
Total	3	3

BROWN, KEVAN   1987–88

right-back   Ht 5 9, Wt 11 08   65 apps
full name: Kevan Barry Brown
born: Andover, Hampshire, 2.1.1966
debut: Birmingham City (a), 14.2.1987 (FL D2)

The son of former Southampton and Wrexham forward Peter Brown, Kevan Brown was on Southampton's books as a schoolboy and, after initial rejection, joined the 'Saints' as a trainee and graduated to full professional.

He failed to make the first team, though, and came to the Goldstone on loan in February 1987, with Barry Lloyd signing him for £7,500 the following month. Quiet and steady, Kevan appeared regularly until suffering a serious injury in March 1988 which necessitated the signing of Gary Chivers.

When he recovered, the 22-year-old full-back was never able to oust the experienced Chivers and was transferred to Aldershot for £12,000 in November 1988 where, in almost four seasons, he clocked up 146 League appearances before the ill-fated 'Shots' folded in March 1992. After a brief trial at Portsmouth, Kevan joined Woking the following summer on their elevation to the Conference and won the Player of the Season award in his first year with the club. Having blossomed into one of the most reliable defenders in non-League football, he won further recognition with the *Non-League Club Directory* Player of the Season award for 1994–95; regular appearances for the England semi-professional side and F.A. representative teams; and success in the F.A. Trophy finals of 1994, 1995 and 1997, the latter triumphs as skipper. By day Kevan teaches football at a school in Winchester.

In March 1997, Kevan unwittingly caused a Woking game to be abandoned when he fell into a two-foot deep hole that suddenly opened up in the Kingfield pitch!

Season	FL	FAC	FLC	AMC	Total
1986–87	15	0	0	0	15
1987–88	35	4	2	5	46
1988–89	2+1	0	1	0	3+1
Total	52+1	4	3	5	64+1

BROWN, MICK   1973–74

central defender   Ht 5 9, Wt 11 08   8 apps, 1 goal
full name: Michael John Leslie Brown
born: Swansea, Glamorgan, Wales, 27.9.1951
debut: Rochdale (a), 25.8.1973 (FL D3)

A Welsh schoolboy international, Mick Brown was an apprentice and professional with Crystal Palace for more than four years, but didn't appear in their League side and was released to join the Albion on a free transfer in June 1973. He failed to make an impression, though, and was soon on the move, signing for Brentford on loan for a month in September, but was recalled early by manager Pat Saward during an injury crisis.

Mick stayed at the Goldstone under Brian Clough and Peter Taylor until May 1974 when he was dismissed following damage to windows at the ground while celebrating Pat Hilton's birthday

rather too enthusiastically. On leaving the club Mick played in South Africa for the Johannesburg side Highlands Park.

Season	FL	Total
1973–74	5+3 (1)	5+3 (1)
Total	5+3 (1)	5+3 (1)

BROWN, SAM   1931–32

left-back   Ht 5 7, Wt 11 00   4 apps
born: Glasgow, Lanarkshire, Scotland, c. 1901
debut: Queen's Park Rangers (a), 3.10.1931 (FL D3(S))

Sam Brown's first club of note was Rutherglen Glencairn, but in 1922 he joined the Scottish First Division side Third Lanark. His seven seasons with the Glasgow club included loan-spells with the Stirling-based Second Division side King's Park (April 1923) and also with East Stirlingshire (September 1928), but in May 1929 he was signed by Bournemouth. The robust defender was a regular in the "Cherries'" first team for two seasons, amassing 58 Third Division (South) appearances, but on joining the Albion in May 1931 he found life more difficult. The form of skipper Frank Brett condemned him to a season in the reserves, and he left for Chester. In November 1932,

Sam joined Swindon Town where he appeared just twice before leaving the Football League arena.

Season	FL	Total
1931–32	4	4
Total	4	4

BROWN, STAN   1972

midfield   Ht 5 7, Wt 11 03   9 apps
full name: Stanley Brown
born: Lewes, Sussex, 15.9.1941
debut: Huddersfield Town (a), 14.10.1972 (FL D2)

The youngest of Albion's three Brown brothers, Stan Brown didn't play for the club until nearing the end of his career. Fulham stole a march on Brighton when they took the Sussex Schools skipper onto their ground staff as a fifteen-year-old, and signed him as a professional in May 1959. In a distinguished, fifteen-year stint with the Londoners, the diminutive midfield dynamo played 397 League and Cup games, many of them in the First Division, but arrived in Hove in October 1972 at the age of 31 for two months on loan in an attempt to bolster the midfield. It was not a good time to be at the Goldstone, though; only one of his nine matches was won, and his last five games coincided with the beginning of a club-record, thirteen-match losing streak.

On his return to Craven Cottage he was transferred to Colchester United in December 1972 where he finished his Football League career. Stan subsequently turned out for Wimbledon and Margate in the

Southern League, and represented Sussex while appearing for Haywards Heath (player-manager 1974–77), Ringmer, Southwick and Burgess Hill Town in the County League. He continued to play into his 40s, and now runs soccer-coaching schools in the Lewes area while working for a car-sales company.

Season	FL	Total
1972–73	9	9
Total	9	9

BROWN, TOM   1920–21

outside-left   Ht 5 9, Wt 11 07   30 apps, 1 goal
full name: Thomas Henry Brown
born: Darlington, Co. Durham, c. 1897
debut: Plymouth Argyle (h), 24.1.1920 (SL D1)

A product of Houghton le Skerne School, Tom Brown guested briefly for Portsmouth during the Great War, and also played for the Close Works club in Darlington before joining the 'Pompey' staff as

an amateur during the 1919 close season. Portsmouth won the Southern League championship in 1919–20, but Tom appeared in only five matches – although never on a losing side – before November and returned to his native county to play for Spennymoor United in the North Eastern League.

In January 1920, Charlie Webb signed the 22-year-old winger as a professional and drafted him straight into Albion's Southern League team where he took over the left-wing duties from Jack Best. Albion became founder members of the Football League's Third Division in 1920 and Tom remained first choice on the left flank for the initial two months of the season, but then relinquished his place to Zach March. He helped the reserves win the championship of the reorganised Southern League's English Section and finish runners-up in the South Eastern League, but at the end of the season he was released and joined Cardiff City on a free transfer in August 1921. Tom subsequently played for Bristol City (May 1922), South Shields (June 1923) and Luton Town (May 1924), but performed only a fringe role with each before dropping into the Western League with Poole Town in 1925.

Season	FL	SL	Total
1919–20	0	16 (1)	16 (1)
1920–21	14	0	14
Total	14	16 (1)	30 (1)

BUCKLEY, CHRIS   1905–06

right-half   Ht 5 9, Wt 10 10   32 apps, 3 goals
full name: Christopher Sebastian Buckley
born: Barton-on-Irwell, Eccles, Lancashire, 9.11.1886
died: Birmingham, Warwickshire, January 1973
debut: Crystal Palace (h), 11.10.1905 (UL)

One of the youngest players to appear for the Albion before the Second World War, Chris Buckley joined the Goldstone staff at the age of eighteen in May 1905 after playing in Manchester junior circles with the Catholic Collegiate Institute and Ship Canal clubs, and gaining experience in Manchester City's reserves. Arriving in Hove at the same time as his elder brother Frank (q.v.), the young Lancastrian made his first-team debut in October 1905 a month before his nineteenth birthday and was prominent in the club's excellent F.A. Cup run that season. He developed rapidly in the right-half slot, so much so that he was transferred to First Division giants Aston Villa in May 1906 after just one season.

Chris went on to play in 144 League and Cup games for Villa, and won a League championship medal in 1910; he subsequently played in the side defeated by the Albion for the F.A. Charity Shield in September 1910. Having also represented the Football League on two occasions, he joined Arsenal in July 1914 where he remained until 1921, playing in 56 League matches as well as appearing regularly during the early part of the First World War (when he also guested briefly for Birmingham). On leaving Arsenal, Chris continued in non-League football until a broken leg put paid to his playing days. After turning to farming in Redditch, he later became a successful businessman in Manchester and was invited to join Aston Villa's reconstructed board in 1936 after the Midlanders had been sensationally relegated to Division Two for the first time. Indeed, he was chairman from 1955 until 1967.

Season	SL	FAC	UL	Total
1905–06	19 (1)	4	9 (2)	32 (3)
Total	19 (1)	4	9 (2)	32 (3)

BUCKLEY, FRANK   1905–06

half-back   Ht 6 0, Wt 12 09   34 apps, 2 goals
full name: Franklin Charles Buckley
born: Urmston, Lancashire, 9.11.1882
died: Walsall, Staffordshire, 22.12.1964
debut: Millwall (h), 2.9.1905 (SL D1)

Better known as a manager either side of the Second World War, Frank Buckley was also an excellent half-back of the old school, a forceful, attacking player who went on to play for England. Usually known as 'Major' Buckley in his latter years, Frank began his Army career as a boy in 1898 and saw service in the South African Boer War. His professional football career began with Aston Villa reserves, but took off when he joined the Albion in May 1905 at the age of 22 together with his younger brother Chris (q.v.).

More or less a regular at either centre- or left-half, Frank was a busy player and a skilled tackler, but spent just one season at the Goldstone before signing for Manchester United in June 1906 for their first campaign back in Division One. In September 1907 he moved to neighbouring Manchester City and on to Birmingham in July 1909 before joining Derby County in May 1911. In three seasons with the 'Rams', Frank won a Second Division championship medal and an England cap against Ireland in 1914 at centre-half in a 3–0 defeat at Middlesbrough. Moving on to Bradford City for £1,000 in May 1914, he re-enlisted with the Army on the outbreak of war and was commissioned as a lieutenant. Later attaining the rank of major – the title he retained for the rest of his life – he commanded the newly formed Footballers' Battalion and served with great distinction. Twice mentioned in despatches, he was badly injured on the Somme.

Following the restoration of peace, Frank was appointed secretary-manager of Norwich City in March 1919 – where he also made a single appearance in the Southern League team – before taking a position as a commercial traveller at the end of the 1919–20 season, but in 1923 he returned to the game as manager of Blackpool, and took a similar post with Wolverhampton Wanderers in 1927.

It was at Molineux that Major Buckley gained a reputation as one of the finest managers of his era, leading Wolves to the Second Division championship in 1932 and building an excellent side which finished runners-up in the First Division in 1937–38 and 1938–39. Notable for a number of gifted young players, the team became known as the 'Buckley Babes' and earned a reputation for tireless and exciting play. Prior to the 1939 F.A. Cup final, which Wolves unexpectedly lost to Portsmouth, the Major was rumoured to have recommended a potion based on monkey glands to his players, but it was later revealed to have been a publicity stunt dreamed up by the manager!

A strict disciplinarian – he was known as 'The Martinet of Molineux' – Major Buckley remained with Wolves until 1944. He later had spells in charge at Notts County (1944–46), Hull City (1946–48), Leeds United (1948–53) and Walsall (1953–55) before retiring. In 1941 he was presented with a Football League long-service award.

Season	SL	FAC	UL	Total
1905–06	25 (2)	1	8	34 (2)
Total	25 (2)	1	8	34 (2)

BULL, GARRY   1995

striker   Ht 5 8, Wt 11 07   *11 apps, 4 goals*
full name: Garry William Bull
born: Tipton, Staffordshire, 12.6.1966
debut: Bradford City (h), 19.8.1995 (FL D2)

With 84 goals from 156 Conference and Fourth Division games for Barnet, Garry Bull exhibited the same prolific goalscoring traits as his cousin, England international Steve Bull, but struggled to find his scoring touch in higher company. He began his career as a midfielder, joining Southampton in October 1986 from the Sutton Coldfield-based Paget Rangers (then in the Southern League), but failed to make the "Saints'" first team. In March 1988 he signed for Cambridge United, but hit the net only four times in nineteen games during a twelve-month stay with the Fourth Division side before dropping down to the Conference with Barnet for a fee of £2,000.

Scoring on his debut for the 'Bees', Garry blossomed into a superb poacher of goals, and was leading scorer in the Conference with 30 goals from just 33 games when the Underhill side won the competition in 1990–91 to earn promotion to the Football League. Maintaining his form in the Fourth Division, Garry scored 20 times as an ever-present during 1991–92 and seventeen the following term. However, the club's financial troubles resulted in him being granted a free transfer, and in July 1993 he joined Nottingham Forest on their relegation to Division One.

Upset by an early injury at the City Ground, Garry played only eleven times as Forest finished second, and moved to Birmingham City on loan in September 1994. Teaming up with his former Barnet manager Barry Fry, he rediscovered his goalscoring touch with seven goals in eleven games for the prospective champions of Division Two and Fry was apparently ready to offer £250,000 for his former star, but the deal was said to have been blocked by the City board and he returned to Nottingham to make just one

Premiership appearance in 1994–95 when he scored his first goal for the club.

In August 1995, Garry came to the Goldstone on loan to boost the Albion strike-force. At his best when playing off a big target man, he was unable to find his finest form as leader of the attack, and returned to the City Ground in October with four goals to his name from eleven appearances. In December he rejoined Birmingham City on a free transfer, but moved on to York City the following March as part of deal which took Paul Barnes to St Andrews, and hit the net regularly for his new club. Indeed, he scored in the rearranged fixture at the Goldstone at the end of the season, a game York won 3–1 to confirm their escape from relegation.

Season	FL	AMC	Total
1995–96	10 (2)	1 (2)	11 (4)
Total	10 (2)	1 (2)	11 (4)

BUNTING, JOHN   1924–25

goalkeeper   Ht 6 2, Wt 11 09   *8 apps*
full name: John Baden Bunting
born: Bingham, Nottinghamshire, 1900
debut: Gillingham (h), 20.9.1924 (FL D3(S))

Brought to the Goldstone from Midland League Boston United as cover for Walter Cook in August 1924, John Bunting had previously played for Grantham, Leicester City reserves and Nottingham Forest reserves. The experienced Cook was initially preferred beneath the bar, but Albion made a poor start to the 1924–25 campaign, conceding ten goals in the opening four matches and dropping into the lower half of the Southern Section, and the young deputy was soon given an opportunity to display his wares. John responded by keeping a clean sheet in his first two appearances as Albion set out on a fine sequence of four wins and a draw to climb to second spot, but two defeats followed and he returned to the 'Lambs'. At the end of the season he was given a free transfer and

returned to the Midland League with Mansfield Town.

Something of a dandy, John preferred to travel to away games dressed impeccably in a grey suit, black Homburg, grey spats and gloves, carrying a silver-mounted ebony cane and with his kit in a Gladstone bag!

Season	FL	Total
1924–25	8	8
Total	8	8

BURNETT, DENNIS   1975–77

central defender   Ht 5 11, Wt 11 12   *51 apps, 1 goal*
full name: Dennis Henry Burnett
born: Bermondsey, London, 27.9.1944
debut: Port Vale (a), 6.9.1975 (FL D3)

Impressing all at the Goldstone with his cool, skilful play, Dennis Burnett played only 51 games for the Albion but proved a valuable acquisition at the start of the club's golden age. His considerable experience from the higher divisions contributed a great deal to the transformation of the team from Third Division strugglers to candidates for a place in Division Two in 1975–76.

The young Dennis joined West Ham United's ground staff after representing North-West Kent Schools, and signed professional forms in October 1962. The following year he won an F.A. Youth Cup medal, and went on to play in the "Hammers'" losing League Cup final side of 1966. After 50 First Division appearances, he moved to nearby Millwall for £15,000 in August 1967 and became something of an institution in the "Lions'" defence, playing 257 League games before a £60,000 transfer took him to Hull City in October 1973.

Dennis returned to The Den in March 1975 on a month's loan, and joined the Albion the following August on a free transfer. Quickly settling into the team alongside Andy Rollings, he also skippered the side for a spell as Albion finished fourth, but his opportunities diminished when Graham Cross arrived at the Goldstone and his contract was mutually terminated in February 1977.

On leaving Hove, Dennis moved to the U.S.A. with St Louis (with whom he had played during the summer of 1975) and then had a short spell in Dublin with Shamrock Rovers before taking the player-manager's post with the Norwegian club Haugur. After leading them to the second round of the European Cup-Winners' Cup in 1980–81, he returned to Brighton in 1982 to run a decorating business while playing locally for Eastbourne United, Horsham and Saltdean United (as player-manager). After spells as coach to Haywards Heath and Ringmer, he became assistant manager at Lancing in 1994 before rejoining Saltdean as coach in the 1995 close season, guiding them to the County League Division Two title in 1996.

Season	FL	FAC	FLC	Total
1975–76	36	3	0	39
1976–77	5+3 (1)	0	4	9+3 (1)
Total	41+3 (1)	3	4	48+3 (1)

BURNETT, JIMMY
1907–08

inside-forward   Ht 5 10, Wt 12 00   31 apps, 5 goals
full name: James J. Burnett
born: Aberdeen, Aberdeenshire, Scotland
debut: Norwich City (a), 7.9.1907 (SL D1)

After playing junior football in his native city for Victoria United (signed August 1895) and Aberdeen (July 1897), Jimmy Burnett set out on a senior career with Portsmouth in 1902. The *Athletic News* commented: 'A fine physique, speed, cleverness and pluck are the attributes of this promising young forward,' but despite scoring twelve goals in just sixteen Southern League and F.A. Cup appearances in two seasons, he met with only moderate success at Fratton Park and returned to Scotland in the summer of 1904 for a season with Dundee.

Jimmy was only a fringe member of the team at Dens Park, though, and signed for Grimsby Town in May 1905 where his career took a turn for the better as he scored eleven goals in 52 Second Division outings. In May 1907 he was released to join the Goldstone staff along with team-mate Tom Morris, but despite being a regular in Albion's Southern League team for the first three months of the 1907–08 season, Jimmy subsequently appeared only sporadically. In May 1908 he was one of four players to join ex-Albion manager Frank Scott-Walford at Leeds City, where he remained until leaving the first-class game in 1910.

Jimmy's football career bore remarkable similarities to that of Tom Rodger (q.v.). They were at Dundee together as youngsters; were team-mates at Grimsby and the Goldstone; and both left for Leeds City in May 1908.

Season	SL	FAC	WL	SCC	Total
1907–08	16 (2)	5	8 (2)	2 (1)	31 (5)
Total	16 (2)	5	8 (2)	2 (1)	31 (5)

Players' birthplaces

The most prolific towns and cities for producing Albion players.
(Note: London is split into separate boroughs. Wartime players are not included.)

Town or City	County	No. of Players
Brighton	Sussex	30
Glasgow	Lanarkshire	24
Birmingham	Warwickshire	15
Dublin	Co. Dublin	14
Hove	Sussex	13
Liverpool	Lancashire	12
Manchester	Lancashire	10
Sheffield	Yorkshire	10
Dundee	Angus	9
Newcastle upon Tyne	Northumberland	9
Belfast	Co. Antrim	8
Shoreham-by-Sea	Sussex	8
West Ham	Essex	8
Leicester	Leicestershire	7
Edinburgh	Midlothian	6
Hackney	London	6
Nottingham	Nottinghamshire	6
Sunderland	Co. Durham	6
Hammersmith	London	5
Lambeth	London	5
Stoke-on-Trent	Staffordshire	5
Aberdare	Glamorgan	4
Blackburn	Lancashire	4
Cuckfield	Sussex	4
Derby	Derbyshire	4
East Ham	Essex	4
Fulham	London	4
Islington	London	4
Lewes	Sussex	4
Middlesbrough	Yorkshire	4
Motherwell	Lanarkshire	4
Portsmouth	Hampshire	4
Southampton	Hampshire	4
Swansea	Glamorgan	4
Wallsend	Northumberland	4
Wishaw	Lanarkshire	4

BURNHAM, JACK
1920–21

left-back   Ht 5 11, Wt 12 08   1 app
full name: John Robert Burnham
born: Sunderland, Co. Durham, 1896
debut: Reading (a), 9.10.1920 (FL D3(S))

Recommended by Albion's former goalkeeper Bill Crinson when he was secretary of the Sunderland Comrades club, Jack Burnham signed as a professional for Brighton in March 1920 but couldn't compete with regular left-backs Wally Little and Jim Rutherford. Consequently, he made just one first-team appearance for the club before joining Queen's Park Rangers on a free transfer in August 1921 where he met with greater success.

After two years in London with Rangers, Jack returned to his native North-East in July 1923 with Durham City in the Third Division (North), where he remained for four seasons before moving into non-League football with West Stanley and Jarrow.

Season	FL	Total
1920–21	1	1
Total	1	1

BURNS, Tony   1966–69

goalkeeper   Ht 6 0, Wt 12 11   67 apps
full name: Anthony John Burns
born: Edenbridge, Kent, 27.3.1944
debut: Mansfield Town (a), 10.9.1966 (FL D3)

Tall, fair-haired and handsome, Tony Burns regularly figured in the *Football League Revue*'s list of the ten best-looking footballers nominated by female readers. But he was certainly more than just a pretty face; he was also a very competent goalkeeper who, with some excellent handling, was able to keep the equally safe Brian Powney from between the Albion posts on many occasions.

Tony represented South-West Kent while at school in Edenbridge, and played as an amateur for Tonbridge in the Southern League and for Crystal Palace before signing as a professional for Arsenal in March 1963 at the age of nineteen. It was a stiff challenge for the young goalkeeper to contend with Jim Furnell and Bob Wilson at Highbury, but he had made the First Division team on 31 occasions when Albion manager Archie Macaulay signed him for a bargain £2,000 in July 1966. Tony vied with Brian Powney as Albion's last line of defence during his near-three seasons at the Goldstone, but was released in March 1969 to join Charlton Athletic where he made just ten League appearances.

In 1970, following a couple of months back at Tonbridge, he left for a three-year spell with Durban City in South Africa, but returned to England in October 1973 at the age of 29 to sign for Crystal Palace where he clocked up another 90 Football League games. Tony spent January 1977 on loan to Brentford, and subsequently played for Memphis Rogues in the U.S.A. (summer 1978), Plymouth Argyle (August 1978), and Dartford and Hastings United in the Southern League before hanging up his gloves in 1980 when he became manager at Tonbridge. In 1982 he moved ten miles north to take the reins at Gravesend & Northfleet, but returned to Tonbridge in 1989 for a second brief spell in charge.

Tony had the then unusual experience for a goalkeeper of being selected as Albion's substitute for the Third Division fixture at Reading on 18 October 1968 – only one sub. was allowed at the time – when Norman Gall was injured at the eleventh hour, but in the event he was not called upon.

Season	FL	FAC	FLC	Total
1966–67	12	5	1	18
1967–68	27	0	2	29
1968–69	15	2	3	20
Total	54	7	6	67

BURTENSHAW, Steve   1951–67

wing-half   Ht 6 0, Wt 11 12   252 apps, 3 goals
full name: Stephen Burtenshaw
born: Portslade-by-Sea, Sussex, 23.11.1935
debut: Exeter City (a), 11.4.1953 (FL D3(S))

In a sixteen-year career with the Albion, Portslade-born Steve Burtenshaw played 252 games as a solid half-back, but it will be as a coach and manager away from the Goldstone Ground that he will best be remembered, especially at Arsenal with whom he was associated for many years.

Coming from a well-known local football-playing family – his elder brothers Charlie (see *Albion Wartime Players*) and Bill were both professionals with Luton Town and Gillingham – Steve was a dominating schoolboy player, skippering both Brighton and Sussex Boys, and having a trial for the England schoolboy team while a pupil at Portslade County Secondary School. In August 1951 he joined the Albion ground staff, and won an F.A. County Youth Cup winner's medal in 1952 when Sussex beat the Liverpool Association 3–1 over two legs.

Signed as a professional in November 1952, he made his first-team debut five months later as a seventeen-year-old, but took several seasons to establish himself in the team because of National Service with the Army (during which he served in Germany and gained representative honours). Indeed, although he played in 28 League matches – mainly at right-half – in Albion's 1957–58 promotion campaign, Steve lost his place to Jack Bertolini the following term and it was only when he switched to left-half in 1960 that he became a first-team regular for four seasons.

Nevertheless, he was a superb club man and was granted a testimonial in November 1963. The following year Steve was appointed assistant coach, and played his last League match in December 1966, over thirteen years after his first. After helping in the reserves until December 1967, he then began a long association with Arsenal as reserve-team coach. In 1971 he took over as chief coach when Don Howe left Highbury, but resigned in September 1973, subsequently becoming Queen's Park Rangers coach (October 1973); Sheffield Wednesday manager (January 1974); Everton coach (summer 1976); Queen's Park Rangers manager (August 1978); Arsenal youth-team coach (February 1982) and caretaker manager (March 1986) before settling in as chief scout the following month.

In 1995, Steve became the subject of a Premiership inquiry into the 'bung' allegations surrounding his former manager George Graham, and was dismissed from his position at Highbury in August 1996 when Graham's successor, Bruce Rioch, was sacked. The experienced 60-year-old then became chief scout at Queen's Park Rangers the following month.

Season	FL	FAC	FLC	Total
1952–53	2	0	0	2
1953–54	15	0	0	15
1956–57	25	0	0	25
1957–58	28	3	0	31
1958–59	13 (1)	0	0	13 (1)
1959–60	1	1	0	2
1960–61	37	3	2	42
1961–62	42	1	1	44
1962–63	36 (1)	1	1	38 (1)
1963–64	33 (1)	1	1	35 (1)
1964–65	2	0	0	2
1965–66	2	0	0	2
1966–67	1	0	0	1
Total	237 (3)	10	5	252 (3)

BURTON, Billy   1936–37

right-back   Ht 5 10, Wt 12 00   7 apps
full name: John William Burton
born: Shirebrook, Derbyshire, 1.4.1908
died: Mansfield, Nottinghamshire, 17.8.1975
debut: Millwall (h), 19.9.1936 (FL D3(S))

Billy Burton came through the junior ranks with Mansfield Woodhouse Albion, Woodhouse Comrades and Sutton Junction, and was signed by Nottingham Forest in November 1929. In nearly seven years with Forest he made just 35 League appearances, giving loyal service in the reserves before arriving at the Goldstone in June 1936 where he had to play second-fiddle to regular right-back Ernie King during the 1936–37 campaign. Billy was released at the end of the season and returned to Nottinghamshire to work and play football for Bilsthorpe Colliery.

Season	FL	SSC	Total
1936–37	6	1	7
Total	6	1	7

BUSBY, DAVE   1973–75

striker   Ht 5 10, Wt 11 08   4 apps
full name: David Everett Busby
born: Paddington, London, 27.7.1956
debut: Shrewsbury Town (h), 20.10.1973 (FL D3)

The first black player to appear in Albion's first team, Dave Busby was born in London but went to school in Sussex at Heathfield, where one of his fellow pupils was Frank Bruno, the future world heavyweight boxing champion. After playing as a junior for Heathfield United, the promising young striker came under the wing of Albion stalwarts Glen and Joe Wilson, and joined the Goldstone staff as an apprentice when he left school in 1973. Making his senior debut at the age of seventeen – then the second-youngest player for the club in peacetime – the speedy forward signed as a professional in August 1974 and continued to score regularly for the reserves, but he enjoyed only a handful of first-team appearances before being given a free transfer in May 1975.

After a spell working in a greengrocer's shop, Dave qualified as a car mechanic before taking up football again with Worthing in the Isthmian League. While at Woodside Road he represented Sussex, scoring twice for the county against an Albion XI in October 1978. Blackpool offered the 22-year-old a trial in February 1979 and he stayed with the club until the end of the season, but he didn't appear for the senior side before his release at the end of the season. Dave moved on to Barrow for the following campaign where he scored a hat-trick in a friendly against his erstwhile team-mates from Bloomfield Road, but after a year with the Alliance Premier League club he returned nearer home when Southern League side Gravesend & Northfleet paid £3,500 for his signature.

Two seasons later, after a possible transfer to Bournemouth had fallen through, he moved on to Tooting & Mitcham United for a couple of years, but was back in Sussex with Littlehampton Town in 1983. After leaving the Sussex County League side in 1985, Dave played local football in the London area. He now works as a maintenance controller for a Surrey-based car-rental firm, but still plays for the company football team.

Season	FL	FLC	Total
1973–74	0+1	0	0+1
1974–75	1+1	0+1	1+2
Total	1+2	0+1	1+3

BUTLIN, BARRY   1975

forward   Ht 5 11, Wt 10 04   5 apps, 2 goals
full name: Barry Desmond Butlin
born: Rosliston, Derbyshire, 9.11.1949
debut: Colchester United (a), 20.9.1975 (FL D3)

Barry Butlin's varied career began with Derby County, for whom he signed professional forms in January 1967 at the age of seventeen and went on to play nine League and Cup games, winning a Texaco Cup medal in 1972. The young striker met with greater success during a long loan-spell at Notts County from January 1969 where he scored thirteen goals in 30 League games. This run of form resulted in a £50,000 transfer to Luton Town in November 1972 (their record fee at the time) where he was top scorer with seventeen goals in their Second Division promotion campaign of 1973–74. In October 1974, Barry joined Nottingham Forest for £120,000,

but he managed only seventeen goals in 74 League outings at the City Ground and arrived at the Goldstone on a month's loan in September 1975 when Peter Taylor, his former boss at Derby, sought to augment the forward line for a promotion bid.

Barry won instant popularity in his short time at Hove when he scored the only goal of the game to give Albion victory over arch rivals Crystal Palace in only his second appearance, but he returned to Nottingham after five games and had another loan-spell with Reading in January 1977 before joining Peterborough United for £20,000 in August 1977. He remained with the 'Posh' for two years until moving to Sheffield United, his final Football League club, where he made 53 League appearances and scored twelve goals.

Season	FL	Total
1975–76	5 (2)	5 (2)
Total	5 (2)	5 (2)

BYRNE, JOHN   1990–91, 1993 & 1995–96

striker   Ht 6 0, Wt 12 04   110 apps, 28 goals
full name: John Frederick Byrne
born: Wythenshawe, Cheshire, 1.2.1961
debut: Charlton Athletic (h), 15.9.1990 (FL D2)

Albion manager Barry Lloyd completed an excellent piece of business in September 1990 when he signed John Byrne from the French club Le Havre for £125,000. In a comparatively short time at the Goldstone the skilful striker became one of the club's most popular players of the '90s, and it was a sad day when he was sold on at considerable profit. Yet he returned to Hove on loan in 1993, and joined the club again in 1995 to become the first Albion player to make senior appearances in three separate spells.

John's professional career began when he was recommended to York City by a Manchester taxi driver. Taken on as an apprentice, he signed pro forms in January 1979 and went on to score 55 goals in 175 League matches, including 27 as City ran away with the Fourth Division championship in 1983–84. That feat caught the attention of Queen's Park Rangers, and he joined the First Division outfit for a fee of £100,000 in October 1984. Quickly gaining the first of 23 caps for the Republic of Ireland (his father was Irish), the energetic forward won a League Cup runner's-up medal in 1986 and scored 30 goals in 126 League matches in an excellent four-year spell at Loftus Road, before departing for the Continent during the close season of 1988. Although he was leading scorer in his first season with the French Second Division side, his fortunes tumbled after breaking a leg and a prospective move to Sunderland fell through.

So desperate was John to return to England that he applied to every First and Second Division club, yet, despite being a member of the Republic's squad for the 1990 World Cup finals, only Blackburn Rovers and Albion showed interest. Thus it was that he arrived at the Goldstone to form a tremendous spearhead with Mike Small as the club forced its way into the Division Two play-offs. John soon added to his collection of international caps and quickly impressed the Goldstone fans with his whole-hearted displays. While never a prolific scorer of goals since his York days, he used his skill and football brain to great effect, and would bring his colleagues into the play either by holding the ball up or with a deft touch. In October 1991, though, Sunderland came up with a £225,000 fee in October 1991 which hard-up Albion could not ignore, and John departed for the North-East. As Brighton's fortunes tumbled, their former striker was a huge success at Roker – causing Albion fans to resent his transfer even more – and scored in every round as the Wearsiders progressed to the 1992 F.A. Cup final only to lose 2–0 to Liverpool. In October 1992, though, he was transferred to Millwall for £250,000 where injuries prevented him from making an impression.

In March 1993, John made a brief return to the Goldstone on loan for the remainder of the season, but moved on to Oxford United – where he rejoined his former York and Sunderland manager Dennis Smith – in November 1993 for an undisclosed fee. However, having kept his home in nearby Shoreham, he returned to Hove for a third spell in February 1995 – on a free transfer for personal reasons – as an immediate replacement for Kurt Nogan. Dogged by injury and never able to recover the form which endeared him to the fans in his first spell at the Goldstone, John was released at the end of 1995–96 and joined Crawley Town in the Southern League. His stay at Town Mead lasted only a few months, though, and he joined County League side Shoreham in March 1997, becoming joint manager with his former Albion team-mate Russel Bromage in the summer.

Season	FL	Play-offs	FAC	FLC	FMC	AMC	Total
1990–91	34+4 (9)	0+1	2 (2)	0	2	0	38+5 (11)
1991–92	13 (5)	0	0	2 (2)	0	0	15 (7)
1992–93	5+2 (2)	0	0	0	0	0	5+2 (2)
1994–95	14 (4)	0	0	0	0	0	14 (4)
1995–96	15+10 (2)	0	3 (2)	1+1	0	0+1	19+12 (4)
Total	81+16 (22)	0+1	5 (4)	3+1 (2)	2	0+1	91+19 (28)

BYRNE, PAUL — 1995

midfield — Ht 5 11, Wt 13 00 — *8 apps, 1 goal*
full name: Paul Peter Byrne
born: Dublin, Co. Dublin, Republic of Ireland, 30.6.1972
debut: Wrexham (h), 11.3.1995 (FL D2)

Although he can overdo it sometimes, Paul Byrne is at his best running at opponents with the ball to set up chances for his strikers, a role he performed all too briefly with the Albion. A Republic of Ireland international at schoolboy and youth levels, the skilful midfielder was associated with Arsenal from the age of 14, but joined Oxford United as a trainee from Dublin junior side Bluebell United. After six League appearances in three years as a professional, he was released in September 1991 to join Irish League side Bangor where he enjoyed great success. In 1992–93, Paul was voted Northern Ireland's Player of the Year at the age of 20 by his fellow players and by the football writers, and culminated a tremendous season with the winning goal in a second replay against local rivals Ards to win the Irish Cup for the County Down side for the first time ever.

It was only a matter of time before a big English or Scottish club took an interest, and in May 1993 Celtic manager Liam Brady signed Paul for £70,000. Although he was included in the full Republic squad against Russia in March 1994, Paul didn't make a great impact at Parkhead and played just 31 League and Cup games, scoring three times. After trials with Bolton Wanderers and Watford, he came to Hove in March 1995 as Brady, then manager at the Goldstone, sought an extra cutting edge from midfield. He remained until the end of the season and scored a memorable 40-yard goal at Rotherham, but there was never a real probability that he would become a permanent member of the staff. Instead, Paul returned to Celtic, but then joined First Division Southend United for £80,000 in August 1995 where he has become an influential member of the side.

Season	FL	Total
1994–95	8 (1)	8 (1)
Total	8 (1)	8 (1)

CALDWELL, JOCK — 1901–05

left-back — Ht 5 9, Wt 12 08 — *65 apps, 15 goals*
full name: John Caldwell
born: Shawwood, Ayrshire, Scotland, 28.11.1874
debut: Brighton Athletic (h), 21.9.1901 (FAC Prelim.)

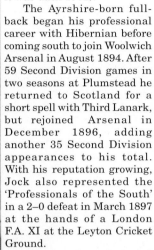

One of the great successes of Albion's earliest days, Jock Caldwell was a robust defender with a prodigious kick who became the club's first penalty expert: thirteen of his fifteen goals came from the spot (or line, as it was until 1902).

The Ayrshire-born full-back began his professional career with Hibernian before coming south to join Woolwich Arsenal in August 1894. After 59 Second Division games in two seasons at Plumstead he returned to Scotland for a short spell with Third Lanark, but rejoined Arsenal in December 1896, adding another 35 Second Division appearances to his total. With his reputation growing, Jock also represented the 'Professionals of the South' in a 2–0 defeat in March 1897 at the hands of a London F.A. XI at the Leyton Cricket Ground.

In May 1898, Jock was one of the first players to be recruited by the newly formed Brighton United and played in 45 of the ill-fated club's 49 competitive matches in its initial season, but then returned to Scotland again to play for the Ayrshire junior side Galston. In 1901 the 26-year-old was tempted back to Hove to join the Albion on its formation, and became an essential member of the team until May 1904. During the 1902–03 promotion campaign Jock was the club captain, but his last season at the Goldstone, 1904–05, was spent entirely in the reserves.

Season	SL	Test	FAC	SEL	Total
1901–02	16 (5)	0	4	0	20 (5)
1902–03	10 (5)	1	5 (3)	18 (2)	34 (10)
1903–04	11	0	0	0	11
Total	37 (10)	1	9 (3)	18 (2)	65 (15)

CALLOW, J. W. — 1902

goalkeeper/winger — *3 apps*
debut: Maidenhead (h), 1.2.1902 (SL D2)

A versatile amateur who gave prominent service to the Burgess Hill club over a number of years, Callow appeared in three different positions – including goalkeeper – in his three Southern League outings during Albion's first season, 1901–02. He also played cricket for Sussex Colts.

Season	SL	Total
1901–02	3	3
Total	3	3

CAMERON, DUNCAN — 1903–04

full-back — *20 apps*
born: Glasgow, Lanarkshire, Scotland, c. 1881
debut: Brentford (a), 10.10.1903 (SL D1)

An early Press report described Duncan Cameron as 'young, tall and speedy; he should develop into a first-class back.' One of many newcomers signed in the summer of 1903 to strengthen the team on Albion's promotion to the Southern League First Division, he became a regular member of the side after initially playing in the reserves, and alternated between the two full-back berths until March

1904. Duncan then returned to Clyde, the club he had joined as a professional in October 1902, and helped the 'Bully Wee' to carry off the Scottish Division Two championship flag the following season. He subsequently played for non-league Montrose (signed February 1905) and the First Division club Port Glasgow Athletic (October 1907).

Season	SL	FAC	Total
1903–04	19	1	20
Total	19	1	20

CAMPBELL, GREG   1987

forward   Ht 5 11, Wt 11 05   2 apps
full name: Gregory Robert Campbell
born: Portsmouth, Hampshire, 13.7.1965
debut: Derby County (h), 7.3.1987 (FL D2)

The son of former Fulham, Portsmouth and Chelsea manager Bobby Campbell, Greg Campbell was on Manchester United's books as a lad before becoming an apprentice with West Ham United in July 1981, but he enjoyed little success in his professional career. Usually played as a conventional target man, he made the "Hammers'" League side just five times in nearly six years at Upton Park, and came to the Goldstone in February 1987 on a month's loan to make two appearances as substitute.

In the summer of 1987, Greg joined the Dutch club Sparta Rotterdam, but returned to England with Plymouth Argyle in November 1988 where he scored six goals in 35 Second Division outings before joining Northampton Town on a free transfer during the 1990 close season. Following the appointment of administrators to run the financially stricken 'Cobblers' in 1991–92, Greg was made redundant in April 1992 along with eight of his team-mates and manager Theo Foley.

Season	FL	Total
1986–87	0+2	0+2
Total	0+2	0+2

CARGILL, JIMMY   1936–39

forward   70 apps, 20 goals
full name: James Cargill
born: Arbroath, Angus, Scotland, 20.11.1914
debut: Gillingham (a), 29.8.1936 (FL D3(S))

Jimmy Cargill was a versatile player whose 70 appearances for the Albion were evenly – and unusually – divided between the right-wing and inside-left berths. After winning schoolboy honours at Arbroath High School, he progressed into junior football with Arbroath Roselea and Arbroath Woodside before joining Second Division Nottingham Forest as a professional in August 1934 at the age of nineteen. Two weeks later he made his League debut, a sensational derby game against Notts County at Meadow Lane which Forest won 5–3, but in two seasons at the City Ground he made the first team on just eleven occasions before transferring to the Albion in June 1936.

The 21-year-old Scot rendered excellent service at the Goldstone for three seasons, then moved on to Barrow in the Third Division (North) in June 1939 where he played only once before the war brought regular football to a close. Jimmy continued to play for the Lancashire club in the regional emergency competitions throughout the 1939–40 season, but it then closed down for the duration, bringing his senior career to a premature end.

Season	FL	FAC	SSC	Total
1936–37	30 (8)	0	1	31 (8)
1937–38	22 (7)	1	0	23 (7)
1938–39	14 (4)	1	1 (1)	16 (5)
Total	66 (19)	2	2 (1)	70 (20)

CAROLAN, JOE   1960–62

left-back   Ht 5 9, Wt 11 04.   36 apps
full name: Joseph Francis Carolan
born: Dublin, Co. Dublin, Eire, 8.9.1937
debut: Sunderland (h), 10.12.1960 (FL D2)

One of many excellent young players to emerge from the Dublin junior club Home Farm, Joe Carolan was discovered playing as a half-back for the Leinster League team by Manchester United scout Billy Behan, and joined the Old Trafford professional staff in February 1956. He appeared in United's F.A. Youth Cup-winning side that season, but was then successfully converted into a left-back by Matt Busby and went on to win caps for the Republic against Chile and Sweden early in 1960.

After 66 First Division appearances, Joe came to the Goldstone in December 1960 for a fee of around £13,000, one of three signings manager Billy Lane made in a matter of weeks to bolster the struggle against relegation from the Second Division. The Irishman took over the left-back slot from Doz Little and immediately added some poise to a creaking defence as Albion avoided the drop, but he soon lost favour with new manager George Curtis the following season and left for Tonbridge in the Southern League in July 1962 where he skippered the team with great success for six years. Joe then played for Canterbury City (1968–69) and Sheppey United (player-manager 1969–70) before rejoining Tonbridge as player-manager (1970–71).

At his best a cool, dominating defender, Joe was just 24 when he left the Football League arena, but he reckoned he was financially better off as a part-timer while plying his trade as a window-cleaner. His sons, Ian and Neil, both played for Tonbridge in the 1980s.

Season	FL	FAC	Total
1960–61	22	3	25
1961–62	11	0	11
Total	33	3	36

CARRUTHERS, JACK   1926–34

half-back/centre-forward   Ht 5 8, Wt 11 00   27 apps, 9 goals
full name: John Walter Carruthers
born: Fulham, London, 29.11.1901
died: Brighton, Sussex, November 1947
debut: Coventry City (a), 5.1.1929 (FL D3(S))

Jack Carruthers enjoyed only a brief career as a professional and had just one extended spell in the Albion team, but he made quite an impact as a stop-gap centre-forward, scoring eight times in twelve matches in 1930–31, and hit a hat-trick against Bristol Rovers at the Goldstone on Boxing Day.

Born and brought up in Fulham, Jack attended St Thomas's School and represented the West London Schools v. East London at the age of eleven. The youngster helped his father in the family greengrocery business, but enlisted with the Army in 1919, and remained in uniform for six years before coming to Brighton in 1925 to find employment

initially with the Southdown bus company and then on the Corporation's trams. Playing his football for his works' teams – Southdown Athletic and Brighton Tramways – and also for Eastbourne, Jack gained an excellent reputation and assisted the Albion reserves for the first time in March 1926. Capable of playing well in any position, he was generally regarded as a half-back and made his League debut as an amateur in January 1929. The following year he was signed as a professional, and had his moment of glory in 1930–31 when, after two games at wing-half, he was given his chance as leader of the attack in the absence of Geordie Nicol.

Jack was released in May 1934 and returned to the Brighton Tramways club. On the outbreak of war in 1939 he re-enlisted with the Army and saw hectic service in the London blitz with the 53rd Anti-Aircraft Battery; he later served in India, Burma and Assam. Demobbed in 1945, Jack returned to Brighton to work as a chromium-plater but died in November 1947 at the age of 46. A collection was made on behalf of his family at the F.A. Cup replay with Hartlepools United in December.

Season	FL	FAC*	Total
1928–29	3	0	3
1930–31	13 (8)	1	14 (8)
1932–33*	7 (1)	3	10 (1)
Total	23 (9)	4	27 (9)

Note: Two of Carruthers' F.A. Cup appearances of 1932–33 came in the qualifying competition.

CARTER, WILLIAM   1913–15

centre-half   *1 app*
born: Brighton, Sussex, 1893
debut: Newport County (h), 2.10.1913 (SA)

William Carter was a member of the Brighton-based Vernon Athletic club and assisted the Albion as an amateur during the two seasons before the Great War. He made the first team on just one occasion, at centre-half – in the absence of David Parkes – in a home defeat by Newport County in the Southern Alliance, but had been a centre-forward with Vernon and was a key figure in their team which carried off the championship of the West Sussex Senior League and the Royal Irish Rifles Charity Cup in 1911–12.  William returned to the Goldstone after the war to assist the reserves briefly during the 1919–20 season.

Season	SA	Total
1913–14	1	1
Total	1	1

CASE, JIMMY   1981–85 & 1993–95

midfield   Ht 5 9, Wt 12 08   *183 apps, 15 goals*
full name: James Robert Case
born: Liverpool, Lancashire, 18.5.1954
debut: West Ham United (a), 29.8.1981 (FL D1)

Famed throughout the League for his tough tackling, fearsome shooting and professional dedication in 22 wonderful years as a player, Jimmy Case won the respect of everyone involved in the

game and proved a popular acquisition at every club with which he was involved. With eight seasons at Liverpool – at the pinnacle of their success – behind him, Jimmy is also the most bemedalled player ever to turn out for the Albion. After a rocky start to his Goldstone career, he blossomed into one of the most influential players of recent times, and many fans were upset when he was sold after nearly four years at the club. He was supposed to be coming to the end of his playing days; yet, almost unbelievably, he returned to Hove nearly nine years later as player-coach and became the first 40-year-old to appear for the club in peacetime. Having finally hung up his boots in 1995, the affable 'Scouser' was quickly thrust back into the limelight as successor to Liam Brady in the Goldstone 'hot seat', but his year-long reign during the most traumatic period in the club's history proved to be in direct contrast to his illustrious playing career.

As a talented youngster, Jimmy actually came to Albion's attention as early as 1971 when director Mike Bamber watched him play for the South Liverpool club, but manager Pat Saward's attempt to sign him proved fruitless. Working as an electrician, he had already been rejected by Burnley but joined Liverpool in May 1973 – initially as a semi-professional while completing his electrical apprenticeship – and went on to win four League championship medals, three European Cup winner's medals, a UEFA Cup winner's medal and a League Cup winner's trophy. He also scored a superb goal in the 1977 F.A. Cup final defeat by Manchester United. Curiously, though, he made just one representative appearance while at Anfield, for the England under-23 side.

Following the emergence of Sammy Lee, Jimmy's first-team outings became fewer and he was transferred to the Albion for £350,000 in August 1981 to add thrust to the midfield, but it was not until the following season that he fulfilled those hopes. Under fellow Liverpudlian Jimmy Melia, the pin-point passing and powerful shooting for which Jimmy was renowned flourished, especially in the great F.A. Cup run of 1983; he scored goals in the fourth, fifth (the winner at Liverpool!) and sixth rounds as well as the semi-final as the club reached Wembley for the first time. Despite rumours to the contrary, Jimmy remained at the Goldstone following relegation from Division One and emerged as the club's most effective player. He was made captain in February 1984 and was voted Player of the Season for 1983–84.

In March 1985, with Albion challenging for promotion back to the First Division, manager Chris Cattlin decided that the 30-year-old midfielder was nearing the end of his career and sold him to Southampton for just £30,000. The transfer was a complete surprise to one and all, but Albion's loss was the "Saints'" gain as Jimmy went on to perform admirably for another six seasons in the top flight, scoring ten goals in 215 League outings and skippering the talented Southampton side. He also won a second representative honour, playing for the Football League against the Irish League in the latter's centenary match in November 1990. In the summer of 1991, following speculation that he might be appointed manager, Jimmy was released by the new incumbent, Ian Branfoot, and joined AFC Bournemouth for the 1991–92 season. He moved on to Halifax Town as player-coach the following term, and, after a spell with Wrexham, spent the summer of 1993 playing for the British Wanneroo club in Australia.

Having played a single game for Darlington at the beginning of 1993–94, Jimmy finally appeared to have pulled the curtain down on his League career when he moved into the Southern League with Sittingbourne in November 1993, but after just four appearances, and at the age of 39, he made a welcome return to the Goldstone in December 1993 as player-coach under new manager Liam Brady. 'He was the best signing I ever made,' Brady was later to comment. Although he immediately became the club's oldest-ever player in peacetime, Jimmy brought much-needed passing ability and experience to the midfield, and played a large part in turning the club's fortunes around during the first half of 1994. He also brought his total of League appearances to over 600, and in October 1994 a crowd of 15,645 saw Albion take on Liverpool to swell the popular player's testimonial fund by around £75,000.

As he struggled to keep clear of injury in 1994–95, Jimmy concentrated on his role as coach and reserve-team manager, and his first-team appearances became more sporadic. Following two games as substitute in 1995–96, he finally called it a day at the age of 41 after suffering an alarming but ultimately minor neck injury in a reserve game.

Less than two weeks later, on 21 November 1995, he stepped into the breach as manager following the resignation of Brady to face his

most severe challenge ever. Jimmy, though, remained optimistic and phlegmatic. When questioned about the pressures of his new job, he retorted: 'My electrician's exam was much tougher than this!', but, with the Goldstone Ground sold, the club was engulfed in the most dire crisis in its history. Despite his enthusiasm for the cause, not even Jimmy Case could prevent relegation to the lowest section of the League for the first time since the early '60s as morale reached rock-bottom.

Although allowed to pay out transfer fees unheard of in recent Albion history, Jimmy was unable to stop the club plummetwing to the bottom of the League. The former playing hero initially enjoyed popular support while the board took the 'flak', but he eventually became a target for the discontented masses as the team displayed only a lack of organisation, tactics and enthusiasm during the awful autumn of 1996. While trying to stay aloof from the off-field problems, Jimmy admitted that they were affecting both him and his players, but refused to quit. Seemingly unable to do anything to turn the club's playing fortunes around, he was sacked from the most unwelcome job in football in December 1996 with Albion nine points adrift at the bottom.

It was an ignominious way for a once-popular hero to leave the Goldstone, and most supporters will prefer to remember Jimmy in happier times. After a little scouting in the meantime, he returned to managership with Southern League side Bashley Town in May 1997, a few miles from his Hampshire home.

Season	FL	FAC	FLC	Total
1981–82	33 (3)	2 (1)	3	38 (4)
1982–83	35 (3)	8 (4)	1	44 (7)
1983–84	35 (4)	1+1	2	38+1 (4)
1984–85	21+3	2	2	25+3
1993–94	21	0	0	21
1994–95	9	0	2	11
1995–96	0+2	0	0	0+2
Total	154+5 (10)	13+1 (5)	10	177+6 (15)

CASSIDY, BILL   1962–67

left-half/inside-left   *Ht 5 10, Wt 12 00*   *129 apps, 30 goals*
full name: William Pitt Cassidy
born: Hamilton, Lanarkshire, Scotland, 4.10.1940
died: 1995
debut: Coventry City (h), 1.12.1962 (FL D3)

One of the great Goldstone characters of the 1960s, Bill Cassidy was not only a dressing-room joker but also a highly versatile footballer who wore the nos.3, 6, 7, 8, 9 and 10 shirts in his five seasons with the Albion. On the staff of Glasgow Rangers as a youngster, Bill joined Rotherham United on a free transfer in August 1961. When

Albion manager George Curtis paid around £6,000 for his services in November 1962, the big, hard-running Scot was initially played at left-half, but proved himself a true utility player and served the club well in all departments.

Immediately showing a willingness to go for goal, he scored some crucial goals as Albion won the Fourth Division championship in 1964–65, a season in which he will be especially remembered for his determined approach to the game. On leaving the Goldstone Ground in July 1967, Bill went on to appear in three successive Southern League championship sides: with Chelmsford City in 1967–68, and with their fierce rivals Cambridge United in 1968–69 and 1969–70 (for whom he hit 56 goals in 120 games). He also had a summer spell in the United States with the Detroit Cougars.

Bill remained with Cambridge on their election to the Football League in 1970, and notched six goals in 31 outings in their initial Fourth Division campaign. He then returned to the Southern League with Kettering Town (First Division North champions 1971–72) and Ramsgate Athletic, and then had a spell as player-manager with Ross County in the Scottish Highland League. Sadly, Bill suffered a serious illness at the age of 42 and fell upon hard times, including a spell as a guest of Her Majesty, before passing on at the age of 54.

Season	FL	FAC	FLC	Total
1962–63	25	0	0	25
1963–64	29 (6)	1	2	32 (6)
1964–65	24 (10)	0	0	24 (10)
1965–66	24+4 (7)	1 (2)	3 (2)	28+4 (11)
1966–67	11+1 (2)	1	3 (1)	15+1 (3)
Total	113+5 (25)	3 (2)	8 (3)	124+5 (30)

CATTLIN, CHRIS   1976–80

full-back   *Ht 5 11, Wt 12 05*   *114 apps, 2 goals*
full name: Christopher John Cattlin
born: Milnrow, Lancashire, 25.6.1946
debut: Southend United (a), 14.8.1976 (FLC R1 Lg1)

Chris Cattlin joined the Albion towards the end of his playing career as a tough-tackling full-back, but still made a large contribution to the club's enormous success in the late 1970s at the height of 'Seagull mania'. Yet it is as a manager that he will be best remembered. After a gap of three years Chris rejoined the Goldstone staff, quickly taking over the 'hot seat', and nearly led Albion back to the First Division. He enjoyed a comparatively successful time at the helm, striking up a good rapport with the Hove crowd, and his dismissal caused shock-waves amongst supporters. Indeed, many would pinpoint his sacking as the final nail in the coffin of the club's chances during the 1980s.

Something of an all-round sportsman, Chris represented the

Ashton-under-Lyne schools at rugby and cricket as well as soccer. His football career began in Burnley's youth team, but in August 1964 he signed as a professional for Huddersfield Town and within six months, at the age of eighteen, was a regular in their Second Division side. In March 1968, Chris was transferred to Coventry City for £80,000, a record fee for a full-back at the time, and went on to play for the 'Sky Blues' for more than eight years, winning two England under-23 caps in 1969 and playing a total of 217 First Division games.

In June 1976, in one of his last deals for the club, Albion manager Peter Taylor signed Chris on a free transfer, and the experienced 30-year-old performed solidly in both full-back berths as the 'Seagulls' rose from the Third Division to the First. On retiring at the end of the 1979–80 campaign – and bolstered by the proceeds of a testimonial match, Albion v. Coventry City, in August 1977 – Chris then concentrated on running a Brighton Rock shop on the sea-front, but in July 1983, with Albion relegated back to the Second Division, he was appointed first-

team coach by chairman Mike Bamber — without the knowledge of manager Jimmy Melia. It was a move which led to a great deal of friction. Gradually it became apparent that the coach was taking charge of team selection and tactics, and when Melia felt obliged to quit in October 1983, Chris was almost immediately appointed as his successor.

Something of a disciplinarian, he quickly introduced a stricter regime and sold a number of star players. A shrewd judge of talent, he brought in his own men and the policy almost paid dividends the following season as Albion finished just one win from a return to the First Division. In 1985–86 he took the side to the quarter-finals of the F.A. Cup for only the second time ever.

For Chris, being manager of Brighton & Hove Albion was a matter of pride; he intimated that he did not *need* the job on a number of occasions. In April 1986 though, following a very disappointing end to the season, he was sacked after two-and-a-half years in charge and replaced by former manager Alan Mullery. It was a dismissal which alienated a good many supporters and caused a great deal of discontent among the rest. Indeed, a number of demonstrations were staged following his departure, and throughout the next seven-and-a-half years, with Mullery and then Barry Lloyd in charge, there were often calls from a vociferous minority for Chris's return; but, as a successful businessman, he has had little involvement in the game since. He did, however, fight a long legal battle with the club over allegations of gross misconduct, a matter which was eventually settled in his favour out of court.

Season	FL	FAC	FLC	Total
1976–77	37 (1)	3	5	45 (1)
1977–78	31	1	6 (1)	38 (1)
1978–79	27	1	2	30
1979–80	0	0	1	1
Total	95 (1)	5	14 (1)	114 (2)

CAVEN, JOE   1962

centre-forward   Ht 5 9, Wt 11 00   10 apps
full name: John Brown Caven
born: Kirkintilloch, Dunbartonshire, Scotland, 11.10.1936
debut: Luton Town (a), 3.3.1962 (FL D2)

With Brighton struggling for Second Division survival in February 1962, manager George Curtis laid out a four-figure fee for Airdrie centre-forward John Caven. A proven goalscorer over four seasons with the Lanarkshire club, the stocky little Scot was seen as Albion's saviour but he was on a hiding to nothing. There was no lack of effort on the part of 'Joe' – as he was always known during his time at the Goldstone – but in a poor side he was given virtually no service and failed to register a single goal in nine appearances.

After Albion's inevitable drop into Division Three, Joe was sought by Falkirk, Queen of the South and Morton, but was eventually

transferred to Raith Rovers in November 1962. After signing for Morton a year later, he remained at Cappielow Park for some time, playing a prominent part as the Greenock club ran away with the Division Two title in 1963–64. Joe, who had joined Airdrie from Bellshill Athletic in 1957, scored a hatful of goals in Scottish football, but his spell at the Goldstone was an unhappy experience.

Season	FL	Total
1961–62	9	9
1962–63	1	1
Total	10	10

CHAMBERLAIN, BERT   1926–29

left-back   Ht 5 11, Wt 12 07   9 apps
full name: Hubert George Chamberlain
born: Langley, Birmingham, Warwickshire, 10.11.1899
debut: Gillingham (a), 29.10.1927 (FL D3(S))

Bert Chamberlain's lengthy career was spent almost entirely as a reserve-team player. After joining West Bromwich Albion from Cradley Heath in April 1922, he made just four League appearances in four seasons, but won Central League championship medals with the reserves in 1922–23 and 1923–24, and was capped at junior level against Scotland in 1925. When he came to the Goldstone in August 1926, Bert was deprived of a place by Irish international Jack Curran, but consistently turned in good performances for the 'Lambs' and captained the Southern League champ-ionship side in 1927. Bert left the Albion for Southern League side Dartford in May 1929, but was reinstated as an amateur in 1933 to play for Shoreham in the Sussex County League, later becoming their coach.

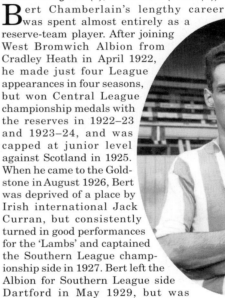

Season	FL	Total
1927–28	4	4
1928–29	5	5
Total	9	9

CHAMBERLAIN, MARK   1994–95

winger   Ht 5 9, Wt 10 07   24 apps, 3 goals
full name: Mark Valentine Chamberlain
born: Stoke-on-Trent, Staffordshire, 19.11.1961
debut: Plymouth Argyle (h), 20.8.1994 (FL D2)

After making an explosive entry into the First Division with his home-town club – he was chosen for the full England squad after just six games in the top flight – Stoke City winger Mark Chamberlain was soon dubbed 'the black Stanley Matthews', but was never quite able to live up to that illustrious sobriquet.

Having played for England Schools, Mark joined his brother Neville – who himself had a trial with Albion in the late 1970s – on the Port Vale staff and made his League debut in the Fourth Division in August 1978 at the age of seventeen. After four years of excellent crossing and trickery down the Vale wing, he made the short journey to Stoke City's Victoria Ground in the summer of 1982 for a £100,000 fee and quickly graduated to the under-21 and full international sides. Making his first full England appearance in December 1982, when he came on as a substitute to score in a 9–0 win over Luxembourg,

Mark went on to gain eight caps. He made the starting line-up on five consecutive occasions in the summer of 1984, and also won four caps at under-21 level.

In September 1985, 23-year-old Mark joined Sheffield Wednesday for £300,000 but was never able to establish himself in the first team; indeed, he made 34 of his 66 League appearances at Hillsborough as a substitute. In 1988 he dropped a division, signing for Portsmouth for £200,000, and scored 20 goals in 167 League games for the Hampshire side. After recovering from a hernia operation in the summer of 1994, Mark was offered a place on the coaching staff at Fratton Park, but he preferred to continue as a player and arrived at the Goldstone on trial in August.

Making a rapid impression by scoring on his debut, the former England international was rewarded with a contract but struggled thereafter to produce his old form and, after winning a Sussex Senior Cup medal with the reserves, was released at the end of the season. Mark then had trials at Airdrieonians and Exeter City, and subsequently joined the St James's Park staff on a short-term contract. Such were the financial restraints at the Third Division club that a supporters' trust paid his wages for a while, but he quickly established himself in the side, mainly as a right-back, and earned himself a longer contract. In April 1997, Mark left the Devon club to take the post of player-manager at Fareham Town in the Southern League.

Season	FL	FAC	FLC	AMC	Total
1994–95	12+7 (2)	1	3 (1)	1	17+7 (3)
Total	12+7 (2)	1	3 (1)	1	17+7 (3)

CHAMPELOVIER, LES　　　　　　1956–58

inside-right　　　　　　　　　　　　　　　　*1 app*
full name: Leslie William Champelovier
born: Kensington, London, 23.4.1933
debut: Aldershot (a), 2.10.1957 (FL D3(S))

Despite being an accomplished amateur international forward, Les Champelovier made just one appearance in the Football League, in a 3–2 win for the Albion at Aldershot. His football career began

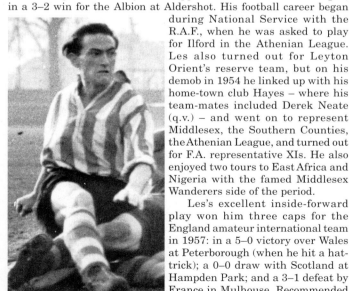

during National Service with the R.A.F., when he was asked to play for Ilford in the Athenian League. Les also turned out for Leyton Orient's reserve team, but on his demob in 1954 he linked up with his home-town club Hayes – where his team-mates included Derek Neate (q.v.) – and went on to represent Middlesex, the Southern Counties, the Athenian League, and turned out for F.A. representative XIs. He also enjoyed two tours to East Africa and Nigeria with the famed Middlesex Wanderers side of the period.

Les's excellent inside-forward play won him three caps for the England amateur international team in 1957: in a 5–0 victory over Wales at Peterborough (when he hit a hat-trick); a 0–0 draw with Scotland at Hampden Park; and a 3–1 defeat by France in Mulhouse. Recommended to the Albion by scout Charlie Faulkner, Les was first invited to assist the reserves as an amateur in October 1956, and made his one first-team appearance as a deputy for the injured Albert Mundy in October 1957 in the Third Division

(South) championship campaign. He continued to play for Hayes until 1962 when he moved to Harlow Town in the Delphian League, but was forced to quit senior football a year later with a recurring knee injury. Les continued to play in Essex junior soccer for two years before turning to coaching youngsters. He still lives in Harlow where he worked as a draughtsman in the electronics industry for many years.

Season	FL	Total
1957–58	1	1
Total	1	1

CHANNON, VIC　　　　　　　　1921–24

outside-left　　　　　　　　　　　　　　　　*2 apps*
full name: Hubert Victor Channon
born: Hove, Sussex, 1899
debut: Brentford (a), 14.4.1922 (FL D3(S))

One of the finest local amateurs of the inter-war period, Vic Channon enjoyed an illustrious career in Sussex senior football. His triumphs make impressive reading:

> R.U.R. Cup winners
> 　*(Vernon Athletic 1921–22)*
> Senior Cup finalists
> 　*(Shoreham 1924–25)*
> R.U.R. Cup winners
> 　*(Horsham 1930–31)*
> County League champions
> 　*(Horsham 1931–32)*
> R.U.R. Cup winners
> 　*(Horsham 1931–32)*
> County League champions
> 　*(Horsham 1932–33)*
> R.U.R. Cup finalists
> 　*(Horsham 1932–33)*

Vic assisted the Albion in the early 1920s and made his two first-team appearances in consecutive games in April 1922 when Zach March was injured. Rejoicing in the nickname 'Cuckoo', he also won his county colours and had a spell with Tunbridge Wells Rangers in the Southern League.

Season	FL	Total
1921–22	2	2
Total	2	2

CHAPMAN, GEORGE　　　　　　1946–48

inside-left　　　*Ht 5 9, Wt 11 07*　　*48 apps, 14 goals*
full name: George W. Chapman
born: Linton, Derbyshire, 8.10.1920
debut: Crystal Palace (a), 11.9.1946 (FL D3(S))

George Chapman joined West Bromwich Albion from the Donisthorpe club at the age of eighteen in November 1938, but had to wait eight years to make his first appearance in the regular Football League — with Brighton. He did play in a few games in the emergency competitions for the 'Throstles' in the early part of the war, but joined the Goldstone staff for £500 following a trial period in July 1946. George was the club's regular inside-left in 1946–47, the first season of resumed 'normal' fare, and finished as leading scorer with the modest total of ten goals, including a

splendid hat-trick in a 5–0 home defeat of Mansfield Town. In 1947–48 he made fifteen appearances before losing favour with new manager Don Welsh following the signing of George Willis and Eric Lancelotte in February, and was released at the end of the season when he moved into the Southern League with Tonbridge.

Season	FL	FAC	Total
1946–47	32 (10)	1	33 (10)
1947–48	11 (2)	4 (2)	15 (4)
Total	43 (12)	5 (2)	48 (14)

CHAPMAN, IAN   1986–96

left-back/midfield   Ht 5 9, Wt 12 09   *331 apps, 16 goals*
full name: Ian Russell Chapman
born: Brighton, Sussex, 31.5.1970
debut: Birmingham City (a), 14.2.1987 (FL D2)

Few players please a crowd more than a local boy who 'makes good', and no Brighton-born player 'made better' with the Albion than Ian Chapman. Indeed, of players born throughout Sussex, only Bert Longstaff and Brian Powney played more games for the club.

Ian burst onto the scene in February 1987 when, amid a welter of publicity, he became the first graduate of the F.A.'s National School of Excellence at Lilleshall to play in the Football League. Standing in at left-back for Chris Hutchings, he also, at the age of sixteen,

became the Albion's youngest-ever peacetime player, a record he held until April 1994 and the debut of Simon Fox. With five games under his belt before his seventeenth birthday, Ian remained mainly in the reserves until 1989 when Keith Dublin moved into the centre of defence. Quickly becoming a popular member of the side, he retained his place until injury and a loss of form saw him out of the side during 1990–91 when he requested a transfer. However, he fought his way back into the team and had a regular spot at either left-back or on the left side of midfield thereafter.

At his best when coming forward in the no.3 shirt, Ian has a crunching tackle and a cracking shot, and has scored a number of spectacular goals. Even when below par he gives total effort, a tenacious and committed player. The son of a former Whitehawk player, he learnt his football in the "Hawks'" junior team while attending the Rudyard Kipling and Longhill Schools in Woodingdean, and played for Brighton and Sussex Boys before moving to the F.A. School for two years of intensive coaching. After playing for England Schools while at Lilleshall, he signed as an apprentice for the Albion in 1986 and became the longest-serving player on the Goldstone staff in 1992. On Sundays he enjoys coaching the Downs Hotel side from Woodingdean in the Sussex Sunday League.

In April 1996, Ian was surprisingly released by manager Jimmy Case. Two weeks later he won the fans' vote as Player of the Season. After a close-season trial with Portsmouth, the 26-year-old full-back joined newly promoted Gillingham but appeared only intermittently in their Second Division side during 1996–97.

Season	FL	Play-offs	FAC	FLC	FMC	AMC	Total
1986–87	5	0	0	0	0	0	5
1988–89	18+1	0	0	0	0	0	18+1
1989–90	41+1 (1)	0	2	2	1	0	46+1 (1)
1990–91	15+8	0+2	0+2	1+1	1+2	0	17+15
1991–92	35+2 (2)	0	2 (2)	2	1	0	40+2 (4)
1992–93	32+2 (1)	0	4	4	0	3	43+2 (1)
1993–94	45 (3)	0	1	3	0	1	50 (3)
1994–95	38+2 (4)	0	1	5	0	1	45+2 (4)
1995–96	36 (3)	0	2	1+1	0	4	43+1 (3)
Total	265+16 (14)	0+2	12+2 (2)	18+2	3+2	9	307+24 (16)

CHASE, CHARLIE   1940–46

right-half/inside-right   *26 apps, 3 goals*
full name: Charles Thomas Chase
born: Patcham, Brighton, Sussex, 31.1.1924
debut: Watford (h), 1.6.1940 (wartime)
peacetime debut: Romford (h), 17.11.1945 (FAC R1 Lg1)

One of five youngsters drafted into the senior side for a wartime match against Watford at the Goldstone in June 1940, Charlie Chase appeared sporadically for the Albion when his service duties permitted, but after the war ended he was transferred to Watford and never played in the regular Football League for his local club. He did, however, make four appearances in the 1945–46 F.A. Cup competition.

Charlie attended the Stanford Road (Brighton) and Patcham schools, and represented both Brighton Boys – in three successive years – and Sussex Schools. As he grew he progressed to the Downs Athletic and Southwick clubs, and in 1940 became one of the first lads to be recruited for the newly formed Albion junior team. Three weeks after the side's first match, the sixteen-year-old made his surprise first-team debut – in a 2–2 draw – and went on to clock up nineteen appearances for the seniors before enlisting with the Royal Sussex Regiment in May 1942. One of those games was the memorable 18–0 defeat at Norwich on Christmas Day 1940, but a happier experience came when he helped the juniors to victory in the Sussex Wartime League Cup and the R.U.R. Charity Cup in 1943, and he also gained youth honours for Sussex before being posted abroad.

Following service in Egypt and Palestine, Charlie volunteered for the Parachute Regiment and saw action in France where, at Breville, he was wounded shortly after D-Day in 1944 and was subsequently invalided out of the Army in May 1945. Fortunately he recovered sufficiently to sign professional forms with the Albion in December 1945. Nine months later he left for Watford, and signed for Crystal Palace on a free transfer in July 1948 where he played in 55 League matches before leaving the first-class game prematurely in 1950. Charlie ran a tobacconist's shop in Islingword Road, Brighton, for some time, and was later employed as groundsman at Brighton College for many years before taking up a similar post at Oxford University. He now lives in retirement in Patcham.

Season	FAC	Wartime	Total
1939–40	0	2	2
1940–41	0	13	13
1941–42	0	4 (1)	4 (1)
1945–46	4 (2)	3	7 (2)
Total	4 (2)	22 (1)	26 (3)

CHEETHAM, JACK   1925–27

inside-right   Ht 5 8, Wt 11 00   *8 apps*
full name: John Cheetham
born: Wishaw, Lanarkshire, Scotland, 25.3.1904
died: Manchester, Lancashire, 16.10.1987
debut: Plymouth Argyle (a), 13.2.1926 (FL D3(S))

Jack Cheetham arrived at the Goldstone as a trialist from the Scottish Second Division club Broxburn United in October 1925 with the reputation of a highly promising inside-forward. Signed two months later, he then failed to live up to expectations; all his first-team appearances came in the latter part of the 1925–26 season, and he was consigned to the 'Lambs' for the whole of the following campaign.

Placed on the free-transfer list at the end of 1926–27, Jack had an unsuccessful trial with West Ham United before dropping into non-League football with Eccles Borough and Hurst, but he returned to the League fold in January 1929 with Swansea Town and scored eleven goals in 25 Second Division outings until August 1930, when he resumed his non-League wanderings with Connah's Quay, Ashton National and Hyde United. In just over two seasons in the Cheshire League with the Hyde club Jack is reputed to have scored 160 goals, and was rewarded with a move to Accrington Stanley in the Third Division (North) in May 1933. He was leading scorer for Stanley in 1933–34 with fifteen goals in 39 League games, but was released at the end of the season and had a couple of years with Stalybridge Celtic before ending his career with a spell at Witton Albion.

Season	FL	Total
1925–26	8	8
Total	8	8

CHIVERS, GARY   1988–93

defender   *Ht 5 11, Wt 11 05*   *252 apps, 16 goals*
full name: Gary Paul Stephen Chivers
born: Stockwell, Lambeth, London, 15.5.1960
debut: Grimsby Town (h), 19.3.1988 (FL D3)

Brought to the Goldstone in 1988 to deputise for the injured Kevan Brown, Gary Chivers rapidly became an indispensable member of the Albion team, a classy, reliable performer who clocked up over 250 appearances for the club. Born a Chelsea supporter in south London, he represented the London Schools and graduated through an apprenticeship with his favourite club to sign professional forms at the age of eighteen in July 1978. In seven years as a pro at Stamford Bridge, Gary played in 133 League games, both in defence and midfield, before moving to Swansea City in August 1983. Injuries limited his chances at the Vetch Field, however, and in February 1984 he returned to London with Queen's Park Rangers where his career regained momentum. Gary had 60 First Division outings and played in the UEFA Cup while at Loftus Road, but in October 1987 he left

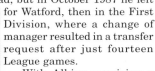

for Watford, then in the First Division, where a change of manager resulted in a transfer request after just fourteen League games.

With Albion requiring a new right-back in March 1988 to maintain their promotion bid, Barry Lloyd paid £40,000 for Gary's signature and his new acquisition performed admirably as the club finished runners-up in Division Three. After an indifferent spell the following season, the versatile Londoner soon won the fans over with his reliable and consistent displays, and went on to skipper the side on many occasions. Particularly good at reading a game and snuffing out danger before it arose, Gary could also score goals when needed, and his total of eleven in the no. 2 or 3 shirts is the best figure – excluding penalties – of any Albion full-back. In September 1991 he started a match at Millwall in goal following a pre-match injury to Perry Digweed, and kept a clean sheet for eight minutes until he was replaced by substitute 'keeper Mark Beeney.

Granted a testimonial in August 1992 in lieu of a signing-on fee – after just over four years at the Goldstone – Gary was released in May 1993, largely in an attempt to reduce the wage bill, and spent the summer in Oslo with the Norwegian League club Lyn, but he returned to England to join AFC Bournemouth in November 1993, making his home debut in the "Cherries'" 4–2 F.A. Cup win over the Albion. In August 1994 he appeared to be on the point of joining Scarborough as player-coach, but before he could reach Yorkshire the club dismissed manager Steve Wicks and Gary went back to Bournemouth. In January 1995 he returned to Sussex with the ambitious Hastings-based County League club Stamco (while also

running Chelsea's under-13 team), and took over as Worthing player-manager in September 1996, but he left Woodside Road after just three months following a dispute with the board. Gary then became a chauffeur with ambitions to become a London taxi-driver.

While Gary was with the Albion, it was reported that Malta were interested in having him in their national side – his father was born on the Mediterranean isle – but nothing came of it.

Season	FL	Play-offs	FAC	FLC	FMC	AMC	Total
1987–88	10	0	0	0	0	0	10
1988–89	46 (6)	0	1	2	1	0	50 (6)
1989–90	41 (3)	0	2	2	1	0	46 (3)
1990–91	39 (4)	0	3	2	2	0	49 (4)
1991–92	36+2 (1)	0	1	2	2 (1)	0	41+2 (2)
1992–93	43	0	5	4	0	2 (1)	54 (1)
Total	215+2 (14)	3	12	12	6 (1)	2 (1)	250+2 (16)

CHIVERS, MARTIN   1979–80

centre-forward   *Ht 6 2, Wt 13 07*   *6 apps, 1 goal*
full name: Martin Harcourt Chivers
born: Southampton, Hampshire, 27.4.1945
debut: Notts County (h), 31.3.1979 (FL D2)

The most prolific goalscorer ever to sign for the Albion, Martin Chivers was a superbly-built striker who, in a professional career of over seventeen years, hit 220 League goals at very nearly one every other game, an excellent strike-rate. He hit just the one for Brighton, but many supporters will remember the classic header that helped the team win a vital point at Orient in April 1979.

After playing for Hampshire Schools, Martin began his career in 1962 as an amateur with Southampton. He signed as a professional at the age of seventeen, and went on to enjoy a tremendous time at The Dell, scoring 97 goals in 174 League matches and helping the club into the First Division for the first time in 1965–66 with 30 goals. In January 1968, Martin joined Tottenham Hotspur in a player-exchange deal rated at £125,000, a British record at the time, and was a huge success, scoring 118 goals in 278 League appearances and helping the

club to a UEFA Cup triumph and two League Cup final victories. Martin also scored thirteen times in 24 games for England, won seventeen under-23 caps, and represented the Football League. After eight glorious years at White Hart Lane he moved to Switzerland with Servette, and helped them to a Swiss Cup triumph before returning to the Football League with Norwich City in July 1978.

In March 1979, following a suspension for Teddy Maybank, Alan Mullery paid £15,000 for the 33-year-old as a stop-gap centre-forward to maintain Second Division Albion's successful promotion bid. After six appearances for Brighton, Martin did some scouting for the club before becoming player-manager with Dorchester Town in the Southern League. He then enjoyed a short spell with the Norwegian club Vard and had two months with Barnet before a knee operation ended his career. Since retiring, Martin has concentrated on running a hotel in Potters Bar while making occasional broadcasts as a radio pundit.

Season	FL	FLC	Total
1978–79	3 (1)	0	3 (1)
1979–80	1+1	1	2+1
Total	4+1 (1)	1	5+1 (1)

CLARE, EDWIN   1905–06

right-back   *Ht 6 0, Wt 12 06*   *28 apps*
full name: William Edwin Clare
born: Basford, Nottingham, Nottinghamshire, 1883
debut: Millwall (h), 2.9.1905 (SL D1)

The son of a Nottingham coal-mining contractor, Edwin Clare joined Notts County in April 1904 and made his first-team debut in the last game of the 1903–04 season. After appearing in five more First

Division matches the following term, he was released to join Albion in May 1905 at the age of 21, and was ever-present in the Southern League team until Christmas when he lost his place to Tom Turner. Edwin subsequently appeared only in the United League side and was released in May 1906, but he didn't play senior football again. Soon after leaving the Gold-stone he married a Hove girl and lived in Brunswick Terrace, but he quickly returned to his native Midlands and joined Mansfield Wesley (forerunners of Mansfield Town) playing in the Notts & District League. He also performed the duties of best man at the wedding of ex-Albion man Mickey Good. Edwin was also a professional cricketer and was on the Nottinghamshire ground staff for some time.

Season	SL	FAC	UL	Total
1905–06	15	1	12	28
Total	15	1	12	28

CLARK, PAUL   1977–82

midfield/defender   Ht 5 10, Wt 12 05   93 apps, 9 goals
full name: Paul Peterson Clark
born: South Benfleet, Essex, 14.9.1958
debut: Tottenham Hotspur (a), 19.11.1977 (FL D2)

Renowned at the Goldstone for his bone-jarring tackles, fierce shooting and all-round swashbuckling style, Paul Clark quickly earned the nickname 'Tank' and was a great success in the side which took the Second Division by storm in 1977–78 and 1978–79. But although he enjoyed some terrific times with the Albion, it was with his local team, Southend United, that he spent most of his professional career.

After playing for Basildon, Essex and England Schools, Paul joined the 'Shrimpers' as an apprentice and turned professional in July 1976. A month later he made his first-team debut as a seventeen-year-old substitute in a League Cup tie against the Albion, and gained England youth honours the same season. In November 1977, Alan Mullery paid a £30,000 fee plus Gerry Fell for the promising youngster, and Paul was more-or-less a regular in the Brighton side over the next two seasons as Albion won promotion to the top flight.

Paul's powerful, never-say-die displays made him a great favourite at the Goldstone. In February 1979 he was selected for the England under-21 squad, but the game was called off and he was not chosen

again. At the end of the campaign the Viking-like midfielder proved his versatility by moving into the centre of defence when required, but after appearing in the First Division side for a few months he became something of a forgotten man after rejecting a move to Portsmouth. Loaned to Reading in October 1981, he returned to Southend on a free transfer in August 1982 and went on to make 276 League appearances for them.

Paul enjoyed two spells as player-manager before Dave Webb's reappointment in 1988, and was granted a testimonial in February 1990, Arsenal providing the opposition at Roots Hall. In 1990–91 he missed just six games as the 'Shrimpers' won promotion to the Second Division for the first time in their history, but in the summer he moved across the Thames estuary to Gillingham on a free transfer and made 90 League appearances before being released at the end of 1993–94. Paul then moved into the Southern League with Chelmsford City, but joined Cambridge United as assistant manager in 1995, making two appearances during 1995–96. In November 1996 he enjoyed one game

as caretaker manager, but then linked up with his former Cambridge boss, Tommy Taylor, at Leyton Orient. Shortly afterwards Paul also signed playing forms for the Isthmian League side Billericay Town.

Season	FL	FAC	FLC	Total
1977–78	26 (3)	2	0	28 (3)
1978–79	28+5 (4)	0+1	3+1	31+7 (4)
1979–80	7+4 (2)	0	5	12+4 (2)
1980–81	8+1	2	0	10+1
Total	69+10 (9)	4+1	8+1	81+12 (9)

CLARKE, BILLY   1935–36

right-half   Ht 5 8, Wt 11 01   1 app
full name: William Vincent Clarke
born: Newport, Monmouthshire, Wales, 17.1.1911
died: Newport, Monmouthshire, Wales, 16.9.1970
debut: Bristol Rovers (h), 18.4.1936 (FL D3(S))

Billy Clarke joined his home-town club, Newport County, in 1929 and was signed as a professional in November 1930. In 1930–31 he was on the fringe of the first team, but came to the fore the following season in the Southern League – County were voted out of the Football League in 1931 – until moving to Charlton Athletic in April 1932. He

failed to make the League side in his short stay at The Valley, though, and returned to Newport in August 1932 following their election back to the Third Division (South). After 46 League games in his two spells at Somerton Park, Billy signed for Portsmouth in July 1934, but made just one appearance, in a 3–2 First Division win at Wolves, before moving along the coast to the Goldstone in May 1935.

Again employed as a reserve, he had just one first-team outing when Len Darling was out with an injury. Billy signed for Aldershot in May 1936, and subsequently played for Crewe Alexandra (signed August 1937), Hereford Town, Accrington Stanley (one month trial in August 1938) and Rhyl before the outbreak of war in 1939. In 1945–46, the last of the wartime emergency seasons, he appeared briefly back at Newport, and subsequently joined Ebbw Vale where he played into his 40s.

Season	FL	Total
1935–36	1	1
Total	1	1

CLARKE, JEFF   1984

central defender   Ht 6 0, Wt 13 08   5 apps
full name: Jeffrey Derrick Clarke
born: Hemsworth, Yorkshire, 18.1.1954
debut: Carlisle United (a), 25.8.1984 (FL D2)

A robust and accomplished defender who came to the Goldstone on loan in August 1984, Jeff Clarke proved a great success in his five games for the Albion, but the club's inability to afford a paltry £20,000 fee shocked supporters and was one of the first signs of the financial troubles to come.

Jeff was an England schoolboy international who started as a junior with Manchester City and signed as a professional in January 1972. He enjoyed thirteen League outings for City before moving

to Sunderland in June 1975 as part of the deal which took England centre-half Dave Watson to Maine Road. Over the next seven years, Jeff made 181 League appearances for the 'Rokerites' and won a Second Division championship medal in 1976. In July 1982 he moved up the road to Newcastle United on a free transfer, and it was while out of the side at St James's Park that he came to the Goldstone on loan in August 1984.

On returning to Newcastle, the 30-year-old defender reclaimed a place in the "Magpies'" line-up and went on to play a further 71 League games before being released. During the summer of 1987, Jeff joined the Turkish side MKE Ankaragucu, but returned to the North-East in February 1988 with Whitley Bay before taking the post of Newcastle's Football in the Community officer. In 1993 he became a member of the club's coaching staff, but left St James's Park in June 1997 following a shake-up by new manager Kenny Dalglish.

Season	FL	FLC	Total
1984–85	4	1	5
Total	4	1	5

CLARKE, NOBBY   1955–58

inside-left   Ht 5 8, Wt 11 02   *2 apps*
full name: Donald Leslie Clarke
born: Poole, Dorset, 29.6.1931
debut: Aldershot (h), 3.9.1955 (FL D3(S))

Like his Albion contemporaries Peter Harburn and Malcolm Stephens, 'Nobby' Clarke saw service in the Royal Navy, but was unable to match their success at the Goldstone. After leaving the

Forces he signed for Cardiff City in August 1954, but never made their First Division side and came to Hove the following May. Although he showed abundant skills in the reserves, Nobby was never given a real opportunity in the Albion first team and remained in the shadow of Denis Foreman until joining Guildford City on a free transfer in February 1958. He subsequently played for Sittingbourne before emigrating to New Zealand in 1963, where he played for the North Shore club among others. On returning to the U.K. in 1966, Nobby worked as a window-cleaner in Reading.

Season	FL	Total
1955–56	2	2
Total	2	2

CLARKE, RAY   1979–80

striker   Ht 5 10, Wt 11 06   *33 apps, 9 goals*
full name: Raymond Charles Clarke
born: Hackney, London, 25.9.1952
debut: Arsenal (a), 3.11.1979 (FL D1)

Although he spent just nine months in Hove and was transferred at the end of Albion's first campaign in Division One, Ray Clarke played a big part in the club's successful fight to avoid relegation from the top flight in 1979–80. A more-than-useful target man, he arrived at the Goldstone Ground via an unusual route. After playing for Islington, London and Middlesex Schools, Ray was taken on as an apprentice by Tottenham Hotspur and signed professional forms in October 1969, but, after gaining an F.A. Youth Cup winner's medal and playing for the England youth team, he made just a single appearance in the First Division as substitute before joining Swindon Town in June 1973.

It wasn't until signing for Mansfield Town for £5,000 in August 1974 that he made his name, though. In 1974–75, Ray scored 28 goals as the 'Stags' won the Fourth Division championship, and followed

up with 24 the following term as the Nottinghamshire club enjoyed a truly remarkable escape from relegation. These stirring exploits won the attention of Dutch side Sparta Rotterdam, and in July 1976 he moved to Holland for £80,000. Two years with Sparta were followed by an outstanding season with Ajax in 1978–79 in which Ray scored 38 goals as the Amsterdam giants completed the Dutch League-and-Cup double. He then had a brief spell in Belgium with Bruges before signing for the Albion in October 1979 for £175,000.

The 27-year-old Londoner joined the 'Seagulls' at a low ebb but did his bit to turn the club's fortunes around, scoring nine goals and proving an effective partner for the more prolific Peter Ward. It was, therefore, something of a surprise when he was sold to Newcastle United for £175,000 (an Albion record at the time) in July 1980, but manager Alan Mullery was determined to reconstruct his side. Unfortunately, after just fourteen League appearances for the 'Magpies', Ray's career came to a premature end because of injury and he moved to East Anglia on his retirement from the game. He now runs a hotel in the Isle of Man.

Season	FL	FAC	FLC	Total
1979–80	30 (8)	2 (1)	1	33 (9)
Total	30 (8)	2 (1)	1	33 (9)

CLARKSON, DAVE   1991–92

midfield   Ht 5 9, Wt 10 00   *15 apps*
full name: David James Clarkson
born: Preston, Lancashire, 1.2.1968
debut: Sunderland (a), 5.10.1991 (FL D2)

An enthusiastic and popular player in his short time at the Goldstone, Dave Clarkson was born in Lancashire, but was brought up in Tasmania to where his parents had emigrated when he was a youngster. A good all-round sportsman, Dave spent two years at the Australian Institute of Sport and graduated to play for Brisbane Lions and Adelaide City before joining the Melbourne club Sunshine George Cross in 1989. After an unsuccessful trial with Newcastle United he went back to Australia, but returned to England in April 1991 on trial with the Albion. After appearing with the reserves in the latter stages of the 1990–91 season, the young midfielder was signed for a £5,000 fee (which would have risen to £30,000 after 20

first-team appearances) and quickly forced his way to the fringe of the senior eleven.

Dave made the starting line-up for the first time in an F.A. Cup tie with Crawley Town, and impressed everyone with his work-rate combined with a fair measure of skill. The eager 24-year-old moved back to Australia on completing his contract in May 1992, but then, apparently concerned by the Albion's somewhat uncertain financial future, failed to return to Hove, joining the 'Aussie' side Heidelberg United instead. His erstwhile club down under, Sunshine George Cross, subsequently launched a winding-up petition against the Albion for payment of the £25,000 balance on the transfer fee, but the High Court dismissed the claim in February 1993 as he had appeared in only fifteen senior matches (although he was non-playing substitute on twelve other occasions). Late in 1994, Dave was playing in Hong Kong, but he was back in Australia two years later playing for South Melbourne.

Season	FL	FAC	Total
1991–92	4+9	2	6+9
Total	4+9	2	6+9

CLAYTON, RONNIE 1958–60

inside-right Ht 5 9, Wt 11 00 *14 apps, 3 goals*
full name: Ronald Clayton
born: Kingston upon Hull, Yorkshire, 18.1.1937
debut: Grimsby Town (h), 10.9.1958 (FL D2)

Ronnie Clayton's signature was sought by both Hull City and Grimsby Town on his release from service with the R.A.F., but he preferred to join Hereford United in the Southern League because his wife came from that area. In January 1958, together with his Hereford team-mate Freddie Jones, he signed for Arsenal, but the pair never made the London side's first team and arrived together at the Goldstone the following September for a combined fee of £5,000. Slightly-built but hard to dispossess, Ronnie had a memorable debut in a 2–0 home win over Grimsby Town, impressing everyone with his deft ball-play, but a puzzling loss of form and a fractured ankle curtailed his first-team appearances, and in May 1960 he returned the Southern League with Hastings United. He subsequently played for Rugby Town and Hinckley Athletic before rejoining his first club, Hereford United.

Season	FL	Total
1958–59	8 (1)	8 (1)
1959–60	6 (2)	6 (2)
Total	14 (3)	14 (3)

CLELLAND, DAVE 1948–49

outside-right Ht 6 0, Wt 12 06 *8 apps, 1 goal*
full name: David Clelland
born: Netherburn, Lanarkshire, Scotland, 18.3.1924
debut: Bournemouth & B.A. (a), 3.1.1948 (FL D3(S))

In a career which spanned four clubs, Dave Clelland totalled just 26 League games. It began with Arsenal, for whom he signed in

August 1946 following his demob from the Army, but Dave had still to make his first appearance in the Football League when Albion secured his transfer in January 1948. It came on the day after his arrival in Hove, in a 4–1 reverse at Bournemouth, but after a short run in the team he lost his place to Jess Willard and spent a considerable time in the reserves.

Released in May 1949, Dave had trials with Ipswich Town and Crystal Palace, but joined Weymouth in the Southern League in October 1949 where he remained until signing for Scunthorpe United in July 1950

at the age of 26 for their first season in the Football League. On hanging up his boots, he joined the Metropolitan Police. Fast and strong, Dave had been an all-round athlete during his Army days.

Season	FL	Total
1947–48	8 (1)	8 (1)
Total	8 (1)	8 (1)

COCHRANE, JOHNNY 1961–63

inside/outside-right Ht 5 6, Wt 10 00 *15 apps, 3 goals*
full name: John James Cochrane
born: Belfast, Co. Antrim, Northern Ireland, 11.5.1944
debut: Newcastle United (h), 10.3.1962 (FL D2)

Signed as a seventeen-year-old from Glentoran in October 1961, Johnny Cochrane made a huge impression in his first game for the Albion, scoring a magnificent goal in a 4–1 win over Hamilton Academical in a friendly match at the Goldstone. His League debut was a very different experience, though, a 4–0 home defeat at the hands of Newcastle United. Johnny began the 1962–63 season by scoring both goals in a 2–2 draw at Queen's Park Rangers in the opening fixture and appeared in the first twelve League matches, but he lost his place when Jimmy Collins was recruited from Spurs and never appeared subsequently, and at the end of the season the slightly-built winger was released. In August 1963 he had a month on trial with Exeter City and played in two Fourth Division matches before returning to the Irish League with Ards.

Season	FL	FLC	Total
1961–62	2	0	2
1962–63	12 (3)	1	13 (3)
Total	14 (3)	1	15 (3)

CODNER, ROBERT 1988–95

midfield Ht 5 11, Wt 11 08 *315 apps, 47 goals*
full name: Robert Andrew George Codner
born: Walthamstow, Essex, 23.1.1965
debut: AFC Bournemouth (h), 10.9.1988 (FL D2)

One word was always used when describing Robert Codner: enigmatic. It was entirely appropriate, for the gifted midfielder could often be extremely good or woefully bad. Over his seven seasons at the Goldstone the plusses tended to outweigh the minuses, but supporters remained divided on his contribution right up to the time he left the club.

Raised in Leytonstone, Robert played for Essex Boys and was on Orient's books as a schoolboy. He went on to play for Spurs' youth team, but preferred to continue his college career and didn't enter the game full-time until 1983, when he joined Leicester City as an eighteen-year-old professional after being spotted playing for a Sunday side called Trojans. In his trial at Filbert Street young Robert scored a hat-trick, but in nearly two years with City he never made the first team and was eventually released.

Following an unsuccessful trial with Colchester United, and somewhat disillusioned with the game, Robert took a break from football to work on a building site – while continuing his business studies – before joining Dagenham in the Alliance Premier League. Some five months later he moved on to Barnet, where he was selected for the England semi-professional team in a 2–0 win over Wales at Rhyl in 1988. It was also while at Underhill that he became involved in the financial world, working in the City for a large insurance company. One of his stated ambitions during his Goldstone career was to become a millionaire, and for some time he would travel back to the City after training.

After 141 games and nineteen goals for the 'Bees', Robert was about to sign for Wimbledon in August 1988 when Millwall offered him a trial in a pre-season friendly against the Albion. Barry Lloyd had seen him play on several occasions while watching his Barnet – and future Brighton – colleague Nicky Bissett, and his performance in this match persuaded the Albion manager to outbid Millwall's £100,000 offer in September 1988, just a week after signing Bissett; the fee involved eventually reached £115,000. Robert immediately showed huge promise; his surging runs from midfield and incisive passing quickly made him an important cog in the Albion engine room. He was also a good finisher and went on to score nearly half a century of goals for the club. But a loss of form and apparent lack of appetite on occasion turned some fans against him and led to a number of contractual problems. Late in 1992, during a period of suspension, he spent a week training with Dundee, but a £100,000 bid by the Scottish club was rejected.

Despite the problems, Robert was more-or-less an automatic choice under Barry Lloyd, and in 1993 he was given the captaincy for a short time because of injuries. However, further disruption to his career came in December 1993 when he was gaoled for driving offences. Three weeks in Lewes Prison appeared to re-focus his mind on the game as he emerged to regain his place under Liam Brady and show more consistent form, but he was dropped early in 1995, placed on the transfer list, and released at the end of the season.

Robert then had trials with Birmingham City and Luton Town before joining First Division Reading in September 1995 on a short-term contract, playing a handful of games. In January 1996 he played one game for Crawley Town and had a brief spell with Woking before joining Ilkeston Town in the Southern League the following month. In March he played briefly for Peterborough United, but then returned to his former stamping-ground of Barnet, by then in the Third Division of the Football League. After twelve months Robert left for Southend United in March 1997 where he played four League games before linking up with Stevenage Borough in the Conference for 1997–98.

Season	FL	Play-offs	FAC	FLC	FMC	AMC	Total
1988–89	22+6 (1)	0	0	0	1	0	23+6 (1)
1989–90	45 (9)	0	2 (1)	2	1	0	50 (10)
1990–91	42 (8)	3 (2)	2	2	3 (1)	0	52 (11)
1991–92	44+1 (6)	0	0+1	2 (1)	2	0	48+2 (7)
1992–93	43 (3)	0	5 (2)	4	0	3+1	55+1 (5)
1993–94	40 (8)	0	1	4	0	2	47 (8)
1994–95	21+2 (4)	0	1 (1)	4+2	0	1	27+4 (5)
Total	257+9 (39)	3 (2)	11+1 (4)	18+2 (1)	7 (1)	6+1	302+13 (47)

29 players who have run pubs

Player	Player
Addinall, Bert	Lawrenson, Mark
Allsopp, Tommy	MacDonald, Hugh
Beech, George	Mooney, Paul
Dear, Brian	Moore, Jimmy
Doran, Jack	Murray, Bert
Dutton, Harry	Robertson, Tom
Edmonds, Eddie	Ryan, Gerry
Farrell, Bobby	Sayer, Peter
Garbutt, Ray	Steele, Eric
Good, Mickey	Tennant, Des
Gould, Wally	Willemse, Stan
Hall, Jack	Wilson, Glen
Harburn, Peter	Woodhouse, Jack
Jenkins, Jack	Yates, Billy
Kent, Harry	

COHEN, JACOB   1980–81

left-back   Ht 5 8, Wt 11 10   6 apps
born: Israel, 25.9.1956
debut: Stoke City (a), 18.10.1980 (FL D1)

Having first played for Israel in December 1976, Jacob Cohen was a seasoned international defender when he arrived at the Goldstone on trial from Maccabi Tel Aviv in August 1980 (following the signing of his compatriot Moshe Gariani). Recommended by former Albion favourite Jack Mansell, manager of the Israeli national team, Jacob was watched by chief scout Jimmy Melia playing for his country in Sweden and was signed for a £40,000 fee in October 1980. Neither player made a great impact at the Goldstone, though, and Jacob was included in the First Division line-up on just three occasions – also coming on as a substitute three times – in the absence of Gary Williams. Indeed, he made the starting eleven of his national side more often than his club side, winning four Israeli caps (out of a total of sixteen international appearances) during his brief stay in Hove. Fast and courageous, Jacob returned to Israel with Bethsheba F.C. on the conclusion of the 1980–81 season, although Albion retained his Football League registration for 1981–82.

Season	FL	Total
1980–81	3+3	3+3
Total	3+3	3+3

COLCLOUGH, EPHRAIM   1901–02

inside-left   7 apps, 3 goals
born: Stoke-on-Trent, Staffordshire, 1875
died: Stoke-on-Trent, Staffordshire, 1914
debut: Brighton Athletic (h), 21.9.1901 (FAC Prelim.)

Considered quite a catch on his arrival from Watford for the Albion's first-ever season in August 1901, Ephraim Colclough never showed his top form at the County Ground and left the club for an unknown non-League destination before the end of the campaign. Before joining Watford in July 1900, he had appeared in Stoke's First Division team on three occasions, having signed as a professional for the 'Potters' from local junior football in January 1899.

Season	SL	FAC	Total
1901–02	3 (1)	4 (2)	7 (3)
Total	3 (1)	4 (2)	7 (3)

COLEMAN, JIMMY   1909–12 & 1915

inside-forward   50 apps, 7 goals
full name: James Henry Coleman
born: Hastings, Sussex, 22.8.1886
debut: Coventry City (a), 22.1.1910 (SL D1)

'With the ball at his feet, he is a tricky individual', ran a contemporary description of Jimmy Coleman, who played for the Rock-a-Nore club in the East Sussex Senior League before turning professional with Hastings & St Leonards United in 1907. He came to the fore in United's runs to the first round of the F.A. Cup in 1907–08 and 1908–09 (along with Billy Lamb, Fred Blackman and Bill Perkins, q.v.), and joined Albion's staff in May 1909.

Jimmy made his first-team debut in January 1910 during Albion's Southern League championship season. It was the perfect time for a new man to come into the team, and it wasn't until his 22nd appearance, in November 1911, that he figured on the losing side! Released to join the newly formed Southern League club Swansea Town during the summer of 1912, Jimmy gained a Welsh Cup winner's medal in his first season at the Vetch Field, but returned to the Goldstone in February 1915 to assist the Albion in the latter stages of their final season before the wartime shutdown. After the war he was reinstated as an amateur and played for Hastings & St Leonards in the newly created Sussex County League into the mid 1920s, gaining numerous local honours.

Season	SL	FACS	SCC	Total
1909–10	11 (1)	0	1 (1)	12 (2)
1910–11	24 (5)	1	1	26 (5)
1911–12	3	0	0	3
1914–15	9	0	0	9
Total	47 (6)	1	2 (1)	50 (7)

COLES, DAVID   1989

goalkeeper   *Ht 5 10, Wt 12 00*   *1 app*
full name: David Andrew Coles
born: Wandsworth, London, 15.6.1964
debut: Shrewsbury Town (a), 11.3.1989 (FL D2)

In a chequered career, David Coles has been associated with eight League clubs but played regularly for just one, Aldershot. His first side was Birmingham City, for whom he signed as a professional in April 1982 after an apprenticeship, but he failed to make the first team at St Andrews and was transferred to Mansfield Town in March 1983 at the start of a nomadic career in the lower divisions. After just three games for the 'Stags', he joined Aldershot in August 1984 to make 120 League appearances, but was loaned to Newport County in January 1988, one of five goalkeepers employed by the Welsh club in its last Football League campaign. Released by Aldershot at the end of the 1987–88 season, Dave then had a spell with the HJK club of Helsinki, assisting them to the Finnish championship, before returning to England for brief engagements with Colchester United and then Crystal Palace.

In February 1989 the Londoner arrived at the Goldstone as cover for John Keeley when the regular deputy, Perry Digweed, was quite seriously injured, and he played in one match, a 1–1 draw at Shrewsbury when Keeley's neck glands swelled up, before being released in May 1989. On leaving the Albion, Dave rejoined Aldershot where he added a further 30 Fourth Division matches to his total before moving to Fulham on a free transfer in the close season of 1991. His stay at Craven Cottage was a brief one, though, as he joined Crawley Town in November

1991 for an even shorter spell before moving on to Yeovil Town the following month. Now a social worker by profession, Dave made over 100 appearances for the Conference club before moving to Gloucester City in the Southern League in the summer of 1994.

Season	FL	Total
1988–89	1	1
Total	1	1

COLES, DONALD   1901–04

right-back/centre-forward   *25 apps, 2 goals*
full name: Donald Stratton C. Coles
born: Plymouth, Devon, 29.7.1879
debut: Fulham (h), 31.11.1901 (SL D2)

One of a number of amazingly versatile local players who assisted Albion in the club's formative years, Donald Coles was the son of a Notting Hill dentist but was educated in Sussex at Ardingly College. His early football was played with Burgess Hill and Brighton Athletic, during which time he represented Sussex, and after appearing briefly for Brighton & Hove Rangers during 1900–01 he joined the Albion as an amateur. Donald played regularly in the club's first season, 1901–02, and turned out at right-back, left-half and centre-forward.

His performances earned him a three-month spell with Leicester Fosse early in the following season, but he played only a single first-team match for the Midlands club, a 5–0 Second Division defeat at Chesterfield in September, before returning to the Albion and turning professional.

Although he was the regular right-back as Albion won their way to the Southern League's test match, Donald missed out on that final triumph and spent the following season in the reserves. In 1904 he applied for reinstatement as an amateur, but the F.A. refused permission until the following year when he went on to play briefly for St Leonards United (in their only season as a professional outfit before amalgamating with the Hastings & St Leonards club).

Season	SL	SEL	Total
1901–02	13 (2)	0	13 (2)
1902–03	5	7	12
Total	18 (2)	7	25 (2)

COLLINS, GLYN   1966

goalkeeper   *2 apps*
born: Hereford, Herefordshire, 18.1.1946
debut: Oldham Athletic (a), 18.5.1966 (FL D3)

After playing for Hereford United's reserves and for Abergavenny in the Welsh League, Glyn Collins turned down an apprenticeship with West Bromwich Albion in 1963 to play for the Gloucestershire club Cinderford Town in the West Midlands League. A typesetter by trade, he was recommended to Brighton by scout Jock Rogers, who had been on the staff at The Hawthorns. Glyn arrived in Hove as a 20-year-old amateur in February 1966. Two months later, with Albion safely in mid table, he had two Third Division outings in place of Brian Powney and performed adequately, but he was released at the end of the season to join Worcester City in the Southern League for a couple of years. He also enjoyed a loan-spell with Bromsgrove Rovers and a season with Merthyr Tydfil in the Southern League before rejoining Cinderford. Glyn then played for a number of local clubs while earning his living in printing and engineering.

Season	FL	Total
1965–66	2	2
Total	2	2

COLLINS, JIMMY   1962–67

inside-forward   Ht 5 9, Wt 12 00   *221 apps, 48 goals*
full name: James Collins
born: Sorn, Ayrshire, Scotland, 21.12.1937
debut: Carlisle United (a), 2.10.1962 (FL D3)

The Albion play-maker for several seasons in the mid 1960s, Jimmy Collins was signed by George Curtis for £9,000. It was the beleaguered manager's most astute move in his time with the club as the 24-year-old inside-forward demonstrated unhurried, constructive skills in a poor side which was relegated to the Fourth Division. When Archie Macaulay took over in April 1963 he regarded Jimmy as the general of the team, and the little Scot rarely missed a game over the next three seasons, playing his part superbly in the 1964–65 Fourth Division championship campaign – initially as skipper – with seventeen goals.

Born in Ayrshire, Jimmy started with the Lugar Boys' Club and Lugar Boswell Thistle, for whom he played on the losing side in the 1956 Scottish Junior Cup final before a Hampden Park crowd of 64,702. He also won two Scottish junior caps that year. Shortly afterwards, in June 1956, Tottenham Hotspur paid £1,000 to bring the teenager to London as a part-time professional while he completed both his National Service in the Army and an apprenticeship as a bricklayer. Although a talented performer, Jimmy lived in the shadow of the legendary John White in his six years at White Hart Lane and consequently made the First Division team only twice, but he was rewarded with a benefit after five years on the staff.

A natural ball-player, Jimmy arrived at the Goldstone in October 1962 and went on to play 221 games, scoring 48 goals from his inside-forward role. Although later employed as a sweeper with considerable success, he eventually became concerned for his future at the club and, having asked for a transfer in January 1967, moved into the Southern League at the end of the season with Wimbledon. After four years at Plough Lane, Jimmy subsequently played for Stevenage, Southwick (including a spell as manager), Shoreham and Saltdean United, and turned out occasionally for Corals in the Sussex Sunday League into his 50s while working in the building trade.

Season	FL	FAC	FLC	Total
1962–63	34 (4)	1	0	35 (4)
1963–64	46 (12)	1	3	50 (12)
1964–65	45 (17)	1	2	48 (17)
1965–66	40 (8)	3 (1)	2	45 (9)
1966–67	34+2 (3)	1	6 (3)	41+2 (6)
Total	199+2 (44)	7 (1)	13 (3)	219+2 (48)

COLLINS, NED   1901–02

right-back   *8 apps*
full name: Edwin Alfred Collins
born: Shoreham-by-Sea, Sussex, 1870
debut: Brighton Athletic (h), 21.9.1901 (FAC Prelim.)

Ned Collins, the most prominent of the local players who appeared for both Brighton United and the Albion, played for the excellent Southwick side of the 1890s and appeared in four successive Sussex Senior Cup finals for them, gaining a winner's medal at the fourth attempt in 1897. He also accumulated numerous other local honours and won his county colours in 1895–96.

Ned was recruited as a professional by Brighton United in 1899–1900, the second season of the club's brief existence, but had been reinstated as an amateur by the time he played for the Albion during their opening season. In fact he turned out for a strengthened Shoreham team which lost 2–0 to the Albion in the latter's first-ever match (played on 7 September 1901 at Dyke Road Field), but then played in the new club's first competitive game, an F.A. Cup tie with Brighton Athletic. Ned subsequently played for Southwick Swifts and Shoreham where he was still turning out in 1910 at the age of 40.

Season	SL	FAC	Total
1901–02	4	4	8
Total	4	4	8

CONNELLY, EDDIE   1949–50

inside-left   Ht 5 8   *7 apps, 1 goal*
full name: Edward Connelly
born: Dumbarton, Dunbartonshire, Scotland, 9.12.1916
died: Luton, Bedfordshire, 16.2.1990
debut: Notts County (h), 22.10.1949 (FL D3(S))

Newcastle United paid £90 for Eddie Connelly's services in March 1935 when he was playing for the Fife club Rosslyn Juniors and a great future was predicted for him, but, despite showing tremendous skills, he never quite fulfilled his potential and was transferred to Luton Town for £2,100 in March 1938. After 50 League matches and sixteen goals in just over a season for the 'Hatters', Eddie joined West Bromwich Albion in August 1939 and continued to play for the 'Throstles' in the early part of the war while also guesting for Luton and for Dunfermline Athletic.

He returned to West Bromwich for 1945–46, but then rejoined Luton in April 1946 to make an additional 38 League appearances before moving to Leyton Orient in June 1948. On his arrival in Hove in October 1949, the 32-year-old was past his best and retired at the end of the campaign after making seven first-team appearances. A splendid little ball manipulator, though quick to lose his cool at times, Eddie was suspended *sine die* in November 1940 after being sent off twice while playing for West Brom., but the ban was lifted in October 1941.

Season	FL	FAC	Total
1949–50	6 (1)	1	7 (1)
Total	6 (1)	1	7 (1)

CONNOR, NAT   1909–10

inside-forward   *11 apps, 4 goals*
full name: Nathaniel Connor
born: Johnstone, Renfrewshire, Scotland, 2.7.1882
died: Elderslie, Renfrewshire, Scotland, 30.5.1952
debut: Watford (a), 18.9.1909 (SL D1)

Nat Connor came to the Goldstone in May 1909 and, though never a regular in the team, made a significant contribution to the Southern League championship effort of 1909–10 as stand-in for the recognised forwards. He appeared in all three inside-forward berths, scoring on his debut in a 2–1 win at Watford, and netted four times in eleven outings.

Before his arrival on the South Coast, Nat had been a veritable journeyman, seldom remaining anywhere for long. In turn, he played for junior club Johnstone (signed January 1902), his home-town side; Port Glasgow Athletic (March 1903), where he made 30 First Division appearances; Celtic (January 1905), as a trialist; Abercorn in the Scottish Second Division (February 1905); Johnstone again (August 1905); Abercorn again (October 1905); Arthurlie, also in the Scottish

Second Division (July 1906); Johnstone again (August 1907); and, for a very brief spell, Clyde (May 1909).

On his release from the Albion in July 1910, Nat returned north of the border for a fourth stint with Johnstone. An engine- and machine-tool-fitter by trade, he died at the age of 69 from lung cancer.

Season	SL	FAC	SCC	Total
1909–10	9 (4)	1	1	11 (4)
Total	9 (4)	1	1	11 (4)

CONNOR, TERRY   1983–87

striker   Ht 5 7, Wt 10 00   174 apps, 59 goals
full name: Terence Fitzroy Connor
born: Leeds, Yorkshire, 9.11.1962
debut: Aston Villa (h), 26.3.1983 (FL D1)

It took Terry Connor some time to win Albion fans over, but his persistence and tenacity eventually paid off, and a sterling performance in the 7–0 hammering of Charlton Athletic in October 1983 finally convinced the Goldstone crowd that the bustling striker was a good acquisition. After that he never looked back, and remained one of the club's principal strikers for three seasons.

An energetic forward who always gave maximum effort, Terry represented both Leeds and West Riding Schools before joining Leeds United as an apprentice in May 1979. Signed as a professional six months later at the age of seventeen, he scored on his First Division debut the following week and went on to hit nineteen goals in 96 League games for the Elland Road club, a promising start to his career. He also won a European Youth Championship winner's medal in 1980 with England.

In March 1983, Terry arrived at the Goldstone from the Second Division club in direct exchange for Andy Ritchie, a deal which was valued at £500,000, the club-record amount that Albion had paid Manchester United for Ritchie. Although he came to Hove as the 'Seagulls' were facing their first F.A. Cup semi-final, the 20-year-old striker was cup-tied and unable to play. He was, therefore, in and out of the team – which was also relegated – and struggled to find his form until the following October when, as mentioned above, he played a large part in the thrashing of Charlton Athletic. With his confidence boosted, Terry became a consistent goal-netter for the club, scoring exactly 50 Second Division goals and ended up top scorer on three occasions. In November 1986 he played as an over-age member of England's under-21 side and scored a superb goal in a 1–1 draw with Yugoslavia at Peterborough.

Terry won the Player of the Season award in 1986–87, but Albion were relegated and their leading scorer was transferred to Portsmouth, newly promoted to the First Division, in July 1987 for a fee of £200,000. However, he was plagued by injury at Fratton Park, making just 48 League appearances in three seasons, and moved on to Swansea City in August 1990 for £150,000. As skipper of the 'Swans' he lifted the Welsh Cup after a 2–0 win over Wrexham at Cardiff Arms Park in May 1991. Four months later he joined Bristol City for £192,000, but had the misfortune to break a leg at Ashton Gate and, on regaining fitness, was loaned back to Swansea in November 1992. In the summer of 1993, Terry joined Yeovil Town and made fourteen Conference appearances without scoring before joining Calne Town

in the Great Mills Western League in January 1994 as player-manager. He also became involved with Swindon Town's community scheme, and then took a similar post with Bristol Rovers, also coaching at their school of excellence. Terry subsequently became Rovers' reserve-team manager in 1995 but left the following year. In the summer of 1997 he returned to Bristol City as coach.

Season	FL	FAC	FLC	Total
1982–83	5+2 (1)	0	0	5+2 (1)
1983–84	40 (13)	3 (2)	3 (2)	46 (17)
1984–85	37+1 (14)	0+1	2 (2)	39+2 (16)
1985–86	33 (14)	5 (2)	0	38 (16)
1986–87	38 (9)	2	2	42 (9)
Total	153+3 (51)	10+1 (4)	7 (4)	170+4 (59)

CONWAY, MICK   1972–75

winger   Ht 5 7, Wt 10 03   2 apps, 1 goal
full name: Michael Denis Conway
born: Sheffield, Yorkshire, 11.3.1956
debut: Nottingham Forest (h), 28.4.1973 (FL D2)

Spotted playing for Westdene against the Albion youth team in the Sussex Sunday Minor Cup final of 1972, Mick Conway was taken on as an apprentice at the Goldstone the following September. The former Brighton and Sussex Schools representative progressed rapidly, and was given his big chance by manager Pat Saward in the final game of the 1972–73 Second Division season after it had become certain that Albion would be relegated. At the age of just 17 years 48 days, Mick became the club's youngest-ever player in a peacetime League match – until Ian Chapman played in 1987 – and celebrated with the equalising goal in a 2–2 draw.

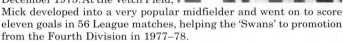

In September 1973 the young winger was included in England's youth squad and signed as a professional twelve months later, but he made only one further appearance in the Albion first team before being transferred to Swansea City for £3,000 in December 1975. At the Vetch Field, Mick developed into a very popular midfielder and went on to score eleven goals in 56 League matches, helping the 'Swans' to promotion from the Fourth Division in 1977–78.

However, the season did not end happily for the 22-year-old Yorkshireman, for he was badly hurt in a car crash in April 1978 and suffered injuries which eventually forced him to retire from the professional game; Albion took their newly promoted First Division side to Swansea for his testimonial in May 1979. Mick subsequently returned to the Brighton area and turned out for his old club, Westdene. In the early 1990s he was believed to be a mature student at college in London.

Season	FL	Total
1972–73	1 (1)	1 (1)
1973–74	0+1	0+1
Total	1+1 (1)	1+1 (1)

COOK, TOMMY   1921–29

centre-forward   Ht 5 9, Wt 11 04   209 apps, 123 goals
full name: Thomas Edwin Reed Cook
born: Cuckfield, Sussex, 5.2.1901
died: Brighton, Sussex, 15.1.1950
debut: Queen's Park Rangers (a), 23.9.1922 (FL D3(S))

In 1995 a new Albion 'fanzine' appeared: *The Tommy Cook Report*. The title, in its own small way, paid tribute to one of the greatest players ever to have graced the Goldstone turf. In short, Tommy Cook remains an Albion legend. A true son of Sussex and a real *Boys' Own* sporting hero, he scored 123 goals for the Albion, played centre-forward for England, and was a notable batsman for Sussex C.C.C.

T. COOK · B + H ALBION F.C · 1925 + 6
WEARING HIS ENGLISH INTERNATIONAL CAP + JERSEY

Born in Cuckfield, Tommy attended the York Place School in Brighton before joining the Royal Navy towards the end of the Great War in 1917 at the age of sixteen. Serving on the mine-sweeper *H.M.S. Glow Worm*, he won a medal for gallantry when he dived into Archangel harbour in northern Russia to rescue a ship-mate. When shore-leave permitted he would turn out occasionally for the wartime amateur football club Brighton & Hove, but on his release Tommy was employed by the Southdown bus company and played for Cuckfield before signing for the Albion as an amateur in August 1921.

After playing for the reserves throughout 1921–22 – as a half-back as well as in the forward line – he made his first-team debut as a 21-year-old inside-left in September 1922 and turned professional four days later, but it was on switching to centre-forward that he began to build his reputation as a goalscorer. For seven seasons the name Cook appeared regularly on the goal-sheet, and he topped the list in 1923–24, 1924–25 and 1927–28. He scored eight hat-tricks, a club record, and his total of 123 League and Cup goals is 24 more than the next best figure of any Albion player in peacetime.

Known for his 'trade mark' of fetching the ball from the net each time he scored, Tommy was a constructive leader who packed a sure shot and inspired the less-able colleagues around him. On 25 February 1925, his prolific scoring feats won him the ultimate accolade: leading the England attack in a 2–1 defeat of Wales at Swansea. It was a rare honour for a Third Division player, and an even rarer one for an Albion man. Indeed, he remained the club's only England cap until Peter Ward joined him in May 1980.

Granted a benefit in March 1927 (which realised £437), Albion's ace marksman left for a cricket-coaching post in South Africa on the conclusion of the 1929 cricket season, but returned to England the following September, signing for Northfleet in the Southern League. In October 1931 he returned to the Football League with Bristol Rovers, and scored 21 goals in 42 League appearances before retiring in 1933 at the age of 32. Four years later he emigrated to South Africa where, in addition to his cricket-coaching duties, he ran the Prince Alfred Hotel in Simonstown.

When the Second World War broke out Tommy enlisted with the Royal South African Air Force. In 1943 he was the only survivor from a plane which crashed on take-off and spent months recovering in hospital, but he never overcame the mental scars caused by the tragedy and suffered regular nightmares and fits of depression thereafter.

Nevertheless, the former Albion star returned to England in May 1947 to answer the call from the club's directors when they appointed him manager, with the veteran Charlie Webb moving 'upstairs' as general manager. It was a bold effort to restore the Albion's pre-war fortunes, but Tommy's time at the helm, in difficult circumstances, proved to be less than happy or successful. The club continued to struggle and sank towards the re-election zone in the Third Division (South) with just three wins from seventeen games. In November there was an unprecedented demonstration on the pitch by around 500 supporters following a 4–0 home defeat, and eleven days later, after just seven months in charge, he left the club to make way for Don Welsh.

Sadly, Tommy's health deteriorated further after he left the Goldstone, and he died in tragic circumstances in 1950, taking his own life at the age of 48. But nothing can diminish the memory of an all-time great.

While a great Sussex football hero, Tommy's cricket feats for the county from 1922 until 1937 were almost as splendid as those of his soccer career. Indeed, he always preferred the summer game and gave it precedence over his football commitments, obliging him to miss the opening and closing Albion matches each season. In sixteen years with Sussex he scored 20,198 runs at an average of 30·22 and registered 32 centuries (including three double hundreds), with a top score of 278 *v.* Hampshire at Hove in June 1930. He hit over 1,000 runs in a season on ten occasions, with a highest aggregate of 2,132 (average 54·66) in 1934, and his natural athleticism helped make him an excellent fielder. An outstanding all-round sportsman, Tommy played in an England cricket trial at Old Trafford in 1932 and was unfortunate not to represent his country at the summer game as well as at football.

Season	FL	FAC	Total
1922–23	18 (6)	5 (3)	23 (9)
1923–24	33 (25)	4 (3)	37 (28)
1924–25	33 (18)	3	36 (18)
1925–26	9 (8)	1	10 (8)
1926–27	36 (21)	3 (2)	39 (23)
1927–28	37 (25)	2 (1)	39 (26)
1928–29	24 (11)	1	25 (11)
Total	190 (114)	19 (9)	209 (123)

COOK, WALTER   1924–26

goalkeeper   Ht 5 10, Wt 11 00   55 apps
full name: Walter Charles Cook
born: Castleford, Yorkshire, 1893
died: Harrogate, Yorkshire, 1973
debut: Brentford (a), 30.8.1924 (FL D3(S))

A well-built goalkeeper who came to the Goldstone at the end of a somewhat chequered career, Walter Cook began his football life as an amateur with Leeds City in the 1918–19 wartime season, and graduated into a professional with the ill-fated club. In October 1919, City were expelled from the Football League and disbanded by the

COOK (W) B+HOVE ALBION GOALKEEPER
1924-25

F.A. for making illegal payments to players. As a consequence, the City players became the subject of a celebrated auction at the Metropole Hotel, Leeds, with each player sold as one 'lot'. In Walter's case, Castleford Town, his home-town club, were the successful bidders, and he went on to impress in their excellent F.A. Cup run during 1919–20 when the Midland League club reached the second round – then the last 32 – only to be beaten narrowly 3–2 by First Division Bradford (Park Avenue).

In May 1920, Third Division founder-members Plymouth Argyle gave Walter another chance to make the grade, but in four seasons at Home Park he had to live in the shadow of the remarkably consistent Fred Craig and consequently made the first team on just seven occasions. After joining the Albion for a £400 fee in August 1924 his prospects were much brighter and he was first choice between the posts for the ensuing season, but Walter then had to share the duties with the emerging Stan Webb in 1925–26 before leaving the first-class game in May 1926 at the age of 33.

Season	FL	FAC	Total
1924–25	34	3	*37*
1925–26	18	0	*18*
Total	*52*	*3*	*55*

COOMBER, George   1913–25

half-back   272 apps, 6 goals
full name: George Stephen Comber*
born: West Hoathly, Sussex, 19.1.1890
died: Hove, Sussex, 6.3.1960
debut: Newport County (a), 16.10.1913 (SA)

One of the finest servants the club has ever been lucky enough to employ, George Coomber was an amiable character whose generosity was reflected over the years by his assistance of several of his former Albion colleagues when they fell on hard times. But he was also a fine player, and was the rock on which the Brighton half-back line was built in the uncertain period after the Great War.

Born in Sussex at West Hoathly, George attended St Martin's School in Lewes Road, Brighton, but took up an apprenticeship in the glass-blowing industry in London where he played his football for Tufnell Park. A tall half-back, he was chosen for the Middlesex representative side and had a trial period with Tottenham Hotspur,

G. COOMBER
166 BRIGHTON & H.A.

but returned to Sussex in the summer of 1913 to sign as an amateur for the Albion. After turning professional in April 1914, George soon established himself in the first team and missed only four games during 1914–15, the last season before the club closed down for the duration of the Great War.

While serving in the Army, George guested fairly regularly for Watford (and, briefly, for Spurs), but returned to the Goldstone in 1919. Now a mature Albion stalwart, he reached his peak when the club was elected to the new Third Division of the Football League in 1920 and attracted the attention of a number of First Division clubs.

An elegant player who rarely missed a match, George skippered the side with distinction from December 1922 until an injury, suffered during a match at Southend in October 1924, forced his retirement at the age of 34. There was a dispute over his compensation and he took the club to court over the matter, but it emerged that it was the insurance company which had refused payment – as he had played for the reserves subsequent to recovery – and George and the Albion parted company on good terms. In April 1923 he received £480 from a benefit match and used the money to help establish a construction firm in Portslade upon his retirement. In fact, the company carried out a good deal of gratuitous work at the Goldstone and operated for many years after his death (until 1982 in fact, run by his nephews).

Season	FL	SL	FAC	SA	SCC	Total
1913–14	0	7	0	9	1	*17*
1914–15	0	35 (2)	2	0	1	*38 (2)*
1919–20	0	33 (2)	1	0	0	*34 (2)*
1920–21	33	0	3 (1)	0	0	*36 (1)*
1921–22	40	0	3	0	0	*43*
1922–23	41	0	5	0	0	*46*
1923–24	42 (1)	0	4	0	0	*46 (1)*
1924–25	12	0	0	0	0	*12*
Total	*168 (1)*	*75 (4)*	*18 (1)*	*9*	*2*	*272 (6)*

Note: George's surname was really 'Comber', but he was referred to as 'Coomber' throughout his football career and for the sake of continuity that name has been retained in this volume. His construction business was 'George Comber & Co. Ltd'.

COOPER, Geoff   1987–89

left-wing/midfield   Ht 5 10, Wt 11 00   9 apps
full name: Geoffrey Victor Cooper
born: Kingston upon Thames, Surrey, 27.12.1960
debut: Southend United (h), 20.1.1988 (AMC R1)

A late starter in the Football League, Geoff Cooper was 27 and working as an insurance agent when Albion signed him as a wide-playing midfielder from Bognor Regis Town for £4,000 following a short trial period in December 1987. Although he had had a trial with Portsmouth as a youth in 1976, Geoff's career really began in the Sussex County League with Chichester-based Portfield from where he also had a few games for Bognor's reserves, but he then worked for a building company – and played football – in Saudi Arabia.

On his return to England, Geoff became an essential member of the highly successful Bognor team that won the Sussex Senior Cup on five successive occasions and embarked on a number of exciting F.A. Cup runs in the 1980s. In nine years with the 'Rocks', he played over 400 games and represented the Isthmian League. However, his Albion career never really came off and he departed for Barnet on a free transfer in June 1989 where he was converted into a left-back of considerable ability, assisting the club to the Conference title and promotion to the Football League in 1991.

The success continued, and Geoff played his part as the 'Bees' won promotion to Division Two in 1993, although he also had loan spells with Bognor, Farnborough Town, Welling United and Wycombe Wanderers (twice); indeed, he assisted Wycombe during their run-in to the Conference championship of 1993, and also appeared in the team which won the F.A. Trophy that season. Despite Barnet's financial troubles in 1993–94, Geoff remained at Underhill and was appointed the club's community development officer in May 1994. However, after one more League appearance he emigrated to New Zealand and had a spell in Hong Kong before returning to Sussex once more to link up again with Bognor in 1996.

Season	FL	FAC	AMC	Total
1987–88	0+2	0	0+1	*0+3*
1988–89	2+3	1	0	*3+3*
Total	*2+5*	*1*	*0+1*	*3+6*

COOPER, Jim   1962–65

winger   Ht 5 9, Wt 11 00   45 apps, 8 goals
full name: James Thomson Cooper
born: Glasgow, Lanarkshire, Scotland, 28.12.1939
debut: Crystal Palace (a), 1.9.1962 (FL D3)

Capable of playing down either flank, Jim Cooper was a schoolboy sprint champion who possessed an exceptional turn of speed. Arriving at the Goldstone as a trialist from Airdrieonians in 1962, he was signed in August that year but never really established himself in a struggling side that had just been relegated from the Second Division and was to end the season heading for the Fourth. Put on the transfer list in January 1964, the Scottish winger looked set to join Chesterfield, but the move fell through.

Jim then remained at the Goldstone for a third season, playing in the reserves, before joining Hartlepools United in July 1965. A year later the 26-year-old followed the well-worn path, so popular at the time, to South Africa where he played for Addington and Cape Town City.

Season	FL	FAC	FLC	Total
1962–63	20 (2)	1 (1)	0	21 (3)
1963–64	21 (4)	1	2 (1)	24 (5)
Total	41 (6)	2 (1)	2 (1)	45 (8)

CORRIGAN, JOE   1983–85

goalkeeper   Ht 6 4, Wt 15 09   42 apps
full name: Thomas Joseph Corrigan
born: Manchester, Lancashire, 18.11.1948
debut: Carlisle United (h), 17.9.1983 (FL D2)

A massively-built goalkeeper who brought his considerable skills to the Goldstone at the tail-end of a long and distinguished career, Joe Corrigan ranks among Manchester City's all-time greats, yet he was initially regarded as something of a comical character by the Maine Road fans. He won them over through sheer hard work, dedication and bravery, and went on to play 592 League and Cup games in seventeen years with the club. Joe appeared in City's victorious League Cup final sides of 1970 and 1976; in the team which won the European Cup-Winners' Cup in 1970; represented the Football League in 1977; won caps at under-21, under-23, and B-international levels; and played nine times for the full England side from 1976 to 1982, finishing on the losing side just once.

Joe joined City as an amateur from Sale F.C. in 1966, signed professional forms in January 1967, and, after breaking into the first team, went on to guard the net at Maine Road until March 1983 when he joined Seattle Sounders in the U.S.A. However, the West Coast club folded in the summer and the 34-year-old 'keeper returned to England with the Albion in September 1983, immediately taking over from Perry Digweed. He missed just one game during the remainder of 1983–84, but lost his place to Graham Moseley at the outset of the following campaign and moved to Norwich City on loan in September and then to Stoke City in November.

It was while turning out for Stoke that Joe picked up the injury – a problem which was aggravated in the Brighton reserves when a disc in his neck burst – which eventually led to his retirement in 1985 at the age of 36, but not before he had won a tribunal decision against the Albion following a disagreement with manager Chris Cattlin over his right to talk to the Press. Having been involved in a haulage business in Prestbury, Cheshire, for some time, Joe applied for the Albion managership in May 1986. Always keen to move back into the game, he has coached the goalkeepers at a number of clubs, and was appointed full-time goalkeeping coach at Liverpool in October 1994.

Season	FL	FAC	FLC	Total
1983–84	36	3	3	42
Total	36	3	3	42

COTTERILL, STEVE   1992

forward   Ht 6 1, Wt 12 05   11 apps, 4 goals
full name: Stephen John Cotterill
born: Cheltenham, Gloucestershire, 20.7.1964
debut: Leyton Orient (a), 15.8.1992 (FL D2)

A useful striker whose career was curtailed by persistent injury, Steve Cotterill attended a rugby-playing school in Cheltenham but also nurtured a soccer career with the Cheltenham Town youth team. After taking employment with a firm of timber merchants, he broke into Town's first team in 1984–85, the season the

Gloucestershire side won the Southern League championship, and made a handful of appearances in the Alliance Premier League – and the renamed Conference – before moving back into the Southern League in 1987 with Worcestershire side Alvechurch.

A year later he joined another Southern League side, Burton Albion, for £4,000, and hit 23 goals in the League and League Cup in 1988–89, form which tempted Wimbledon to try him in the First Division. Signed for a combined fee of £60,000 with his striking partner John Gayle in February 1989, Steve scored on his debut, but went on to make just seventeen League appearances in more than four seasons, scoring six times. A severe knee injury kept him out for fourteen months, and it was on his recovery that he came to the Goldstone on two months' loan in August 1992 to form a promising strike-force with fellow loan player Paul Moulden.

Unfortunately, Albion had little chance of mustering the resources to buy the brave, hard-working forward. Instead, he returned to Wimbledon, asked for a transfer, and joined AFC Bournemouth for £80,000 in July 1993. Steve ended the 1993–94 season as the "Cherries'" leading scorer, but he then suffered further injury problems. When his Football League career was prematurely ended during 1994–95 because of knee ligament damage, the unlucky goal-getter became player-manager of Sligo Rovers in the League of Ireland, but he returned to England in 1996 to make a guest appearance for Dorchester Town. Steve then turned out briefly for Cirencester Town in December 1996 before joining up again with Cheltenham Town. In January 1997 he was appointed caretaker manager, guiding his home-town side to second place in the Southern League and promotion to the Conference, and had his position confirmed during the summer.

Season	FL	Total
1992–93	11 (4)	11 (4)
Total	11 (4)	11 (4)

COUGHLAN, DEREK   1993–96

central defender   Ht 6 4, Wt 13 04   1 app
full name: Derek James Coughlan
born: Cork, Co. Cork, Republic of Ireland, 2.1.1977
debut: Oxford United (h), 12.3.1996 (FL D2)

Derek Coughlan's first-team career with the Albion lasted just 65 minutes before he was substituted during a home defeat by Oxford United. The nineteen-year-old, who had been drafted for his debut because of injuries and suspensions, performed his duties in a youthful back-four admirably, but made way for the experienced John Byrne as Albion tried to rescue something from a game they were desperate to win.

The young Irishman had joined the club as a trainee in 1993 direct from school, and turned professional two years later in 1995. His first involvement with the senior side actually came in October 1994 when, at the age of seventeen, he was named as reserve goalkeeper against Rotherham United in the absence of Nicky Rust's regular backup, Mark Ormerod; fortunately he was not called upon. Released at the end of 1995–96, Derek returned to Ireland to play for Cork City and was included in the national under-21 squad in April 1997.

Season	FL	Total
1995–96	1	1
Total	1	1

CRAVEN, W.   1902

inside-left   *1 app*
debut: St Albans Amateurs (a), 18.10.1902 (SEL)

Craven was a player of unknown credentials who was pressed into service when Albion were forced to play two first-team fixtures on the same day, an F.A. Cup qualifying tie at Shoreham and a South Eastern League match at St Albans on 18 October 1902. Both matches resulted in victory but Craven was not called upon again.

Season	SEL	Total
1902–03	1	1
Total	1	1

CRINSON, BILL   1909–13

goalkeeper   *Ht 6 0, Wt 12 08*   *13 apps*
full name: William James Crinson
born: Sunderland, Co. Durham, 1883
debut: Swindon Town (n), 24.4.1911 (SCC F)

Bill Crinson was the eternal reserve: in a senior career spanning some six years with Sheffield Wednesday and the Albion he made just nine League appearances. Bill joined Wednesday from the

Wearside League champions Southwick in May 1906, and, after four senior outings in two seasons on the Owlerton staff, played for the newly formed Huddersfield Town club in the North Eastern League. In June 1909 he joined the Albion, only to live in the considerable shadow of Bob 'Pom Pom' Whiting for four years, making just thirteen first-team appearances until, in September 1913, he returned to the North Eastern League with Sunderland Rovers. Bill became secretary of Sunderland Comrades F.C. after the Great War and also scouted for the Albion on occasion.

Season	SL	SA	SCC	Total
1910–11	1	0	2	3
1912–13	4	3	3	10
Total	5	3	5	13

CROSS, GRAHAM   1976–77

central defender   *Ht 6 0, Wt 13 00*   *56 apps, 4 goals*
full name: Graham Frederick Cross
born: Leicester, Leicestershire, 15.11.1943
debut: Southend United (a), 14.8.1976 (FLC R1 Lg1)

Although his Albion career lasted just one season, Graham Cross left a great impression on the club's supporters. The experienced centre-back brought a touch of class to the defence with his coolness and skill, and he never missed a match as Albion swept to promotion from the Third Division.

Graham spent most of his career with Leicester City, for whom he signed as a professional in November 1960, and in sixteen years at Filbert Street played in 599 League and Cup games, a club record. He also gained a League Cup winner's trophy in 1964 and a runner's-up medal the following year; was twice a losing finalist in the F.A.

Cup, in 1963 and 1969; made eleven appearances in England's under-23 side; and assisted City to the Second Division title in 1970–71. By 1975, though, his career at Filbert Street was drawing to a close, and towards the end of 1975–76 he had a twelve-match loan spell with Chesterfield. In June 1976, Peter Taylor brought the highly capable defender to the Goldstone on a free transfer, one of his last signings for the club.

Although he had had a superb season – apart from two separate, nail-biting occasions when he took two attempts to score from the penalty spot – Graham was now 33 and, with Albion building for the future, he was transferred to Preston North End in July 1977 along with Harry Wilson plus £50,000 in exchange for left-back Gary Williams. In 1977–78 he made 40 appearances as North End were promoted to the Second Division. Graham then had a spell with Enderby Town in the Southern League, but returned to the Football League in March 1979 for three months with struggling Lincoln City, after which he coached and managed Hinckley Athletic. Also an all-rounder with Leicestershire C.C.C., Graham later took to running a post-office near Leicester, but was convicted of offences concerned with the business and served time as a guest of Her Majesty.

Season	FL	FAC	FLC	Total
1976–77	46 (3)	3	7 (1)	56 (4)
Total	46 (3)	3	7 (1)	56 (4)

CROWTHER, STAN   1961

left-half   *Ht 6 1, Wt 12 06*   *4 apps*
full name: Stanley Crowther
born: Bilston, Staffordshire, 3.9.1935
debut: Plymouth Argyle (h), 31.3.1961 (FL D2)

In an incident-packed League career which lasted just five years, Stan Crowther played in two F.A. Cup finals and won three under-23 caps, but he endured a miserable time at the Goldstone and was eventually sacked.

On leaving school Stan had a spell on the West Bromwich Albion ground staff while playing for the local Erdington Albion club, but he then threw in his lot with Bilston Town in the West Midlands League. In August 1955 he was recruited by Aston Villa and went on to play in the side that beat Manchester United in the 1957 F.A. Cup final.

The following season he was selected three times for the England under-23s, but his career then took a dramatic turn. In February 1958, Stan was one of the first players signed by Manchester United in the wake of the Munich air-disaster, and a couple of months later the fair-haired wing-half played in his second successive F.A. final. (He received special permission from the F.A. to play in the Cup as he had already appeared for Villa that season.) This time, though, he picked up only

a runner's-up medal as United lost 2–0 to Bolton Wanderers. In December 1958, Stan was transferred to Chelsea for £10,000 where he made 51 League appearances, but then came to the Albion for just £3,000 in March 1961, Billy Lane's last major signing for the club.

With more than 100 First Division appearances under his belt, the strapping 25-year-old was a considerable capture for Second Division Brighton, but after just four League outings he was sensationally sacked in October 1961 by new manager George Curtis when he refused to turn out for the 'A' team in a Metropolitan League fixture. Stan appealed to the Football League but they backed the club, and so he joined Rugby Town in December 1961 where he assisted the Southern League side to promotion to the Premier Division before ending his career with Hednesford Town in 1963. A hard-tackling, attacking wing-half, Stan was just 26 when he dropped into non-League football.

Season	FL	Total
1960–61	4	4
Total	4	4

CRUMP, FRED   1908–09

inside-forward   20 apps, 5 goals
full name: Frederick Crump
debut: West Ham United (h), 5.9.1908 (SL D1)

A very experienced player by the time he arrived at the Goldstone in May 1908, Fred Crump began his career in the Birmingham League with Stourbridge before joining the senior ranks with Derby County in June 1899. He subsequently played for Glossop (signed May 1900), Northampton Town (close season 1902), and Stockport County (August 1905) where he hit 33 goals in 59 Second Division matches, but found life more difficult on the South Coast. Fred figured in all three inside-forward positions for the Albion during the 1908–09 Southern League campaign, but netted just five goals in 20 appearances and was released in August 1909 to return to the Birmingham League with Walsall.

Season	SL	WL	SCC	Total
1908–09	11 (2)	8 (3)	1	20 (5)
Total	11 (2)	8 (3)	1	20 (5)

CRUMPLIN, JOHN   1987–93 & 1993–95

right-wing/right-back   Ht 5 8, Wt 11 10   245 apps, 9 goals
full name: John Leslie Crumplin
born: Bath, Somerset, 26.5.1967
debut: Ipswich Town (h), 21.3.1987 (FL D2)

John Crumplin was one of those players who could either be very good or woefully bad. When he first came to the Goldstone the majority of his performances were fitful to say the least; but in his latter years the good times far outweighed the bad performances and he became a great favourite of the Goldstone crowd, a 'Football Genius' to many. It was an accolade which was initially used in irony, but such were his sterling performances and never-say-die effort that it was latterly used as a tongue-in-cheek tribute to a popular player.

Born in Bath – where his father was stationed on Army duty – John was initially raised in Singapore and came to Sussex at the age of eight when his family settled in Walberton. A West Sussex Schools representative, he signed schoolboy forms for Southampton, but faded from the scene after breaking a leg and subsequently joined Bognor Regis Town. The young defender made his first-team debut at the age of sixteen and represented Sussex at youth level before joining Portsmouth as a trainee. It was at Fratton Park that he first came to Albion's notice in October 1984 while turning out at centre-half for "Pompey's" reserves. In an extraordinary incident involving Hans Kraay, John was injured as the result of a foul by Brighton's controversial Dutchman – for which the latter was sent off – and,

while receiving treatment, was kicked by the disgraced Kraay as he trooped off the pitch!

Nevertheless, John was eventually released and returned to Bognor. In his second spell at Nyewood Lane he was converted into a right-winger and, while working as a bricklayer, was given an opportunity with the Albion by Barry Lloyd. The trial was a success and he was taken on as a professional in March 1987 for a fee which eventually rose to £6,000; Albion also played a friendly with the 'Rocks' as part of the deal.

The 20-year-old winger had 26 League outings in 1987–88 as Albion won promotion to Division Two, but often became a focus of the crowd's frustration. After three hesitant years on the staff it seemed that John's career was going nowhere, but a tremendous performance at Bournemouth in December 1989, when he came on as a substitute full-back, restored his confidence and he finally won the fans over with a series of whole-hearted performances in the no.2 shirt. Although still prone to the occasional lapse, he proved himself a reliable, hard-working player capable of playing in a variety of positions, a versatility which caused him to be chosen as substitute on more occasions that any other Albion man.

It was a big surprise when he was released in May 1993, but, after close-season trials with Partick Thistle and Hull City, he was offered a new contract by Lloyd and rejoined the club in August. After performing well in 1993–94, John was subsequently transfer-listed in September 1994 by new manager Liam Brady and joined Woking in the Conference in March 1995, going on to win a medal in the "Cards'" successful defence of the F.A. Trophy in May. However, problems with his wages – Woking supporters were funding his appearances towards the end of the season – saw him take up a trial with Portsmouth again in the close season before returning to the Kingfield. In the summer of 1996, 'Crumps' returned to Sussex with Crawley Town, but made only a handful of appearances before knee-ligament trouble side-lined him. John subsequently became assistant manager and was in temporary charge for one match, a Sussex Senior Cup tie against the Albion reserves in November 1996, but was released by the new manager at the end of the season. He then became manager of County League side Selsey.

An excellent crosser of the ball, John scored direct from a corner for Albion reserves in the Roy Haydon Memorial Trophy match in August 1988, but proved it was no fluke when he repeated the feat for the first team in April 1994 at Wrexham – despite falling over as he delivered the cross!

Season	FL	FAC	FLC	FMC	AMC	Total
1986–87	5	0	0	0	0	5
1987–88	19+7 (2)	3	1+1	0	3 (1)	26+8 (3)
1988–89	7+5	0	0	0	0	7+5
1989–90	14+11 (2)	0	1	1	0	16+11 (2)
1990–91	45+1	3	2	3	0	53+1
1991–92	27+2	2	1	2	0	32+2
1992–93	27+5 (1)	3+1 (1)	3	0	3	36+6 (2)
1993–94	29+3 (2)	0+1	1+2	0	1	31+6 (2)
Total	173+34 (7)	11+2 (1)	9+3	6	7 (1)	206+39 (9)

CURBISHLEY, ALAN   1987–90

midfield   Ht 5 11, Wt 11 10   132 apps, 15 goals
full name: Llewellyn Charles Curbishley
born: Forest Gate, East Ham, Essex, 8.11.1957
debut: Chesterfield (a), 22.8.1987 (FL D3)

A product of the West Ham United soccer 'academy', 'Alan' Curbishley was schooled well in the art of football at Upton Park and went on to enjoy an excellent career as an inventive midfielder. Since becoming a manager, he has continued to use his shrewd football brain with some success.

Alan won England Schools honours before becoming an apprentice with the 'Hammers', and had also gained a number of youth caps by the time he signed as a professional in July 1975. He made his League debut at the age of seventeen, the First Division side's youngest-ever player, and graduated to the England under-21 squad in February 1979. Five months later Alan moved to Birmingham for £275,000 to enjoy his best years as a midfield play-maker. He helped the 'Blues' to promotion back to the First Division in his first season at St Andrews, and won his only under-21 cap in November 1980, in a 5–0 victory over Switzerland.

Able to control a game on his day, Alan was now considered worthy of inclusion in the England 'B' squad during preparations for the 1982 World Cup, but he then had the misfortune to break his kneecap and never featured again. Transferred to Aston Villa for £100,000 in March 1983, he made another 36 First Division appearances before moving into Division Two with Charlton Athletic at Christmas 1984, then helped the 'Valiants' to promotion to Division One in 1985–86. Albion manager Barry Lloyd first bid for the experienced midfielder in March 1987, but was unable to meet the £50,000 asking price. The following August, though, he landed the 29-year-old for £32,500 after prolonged negotiations and installed his new acquisition as the midfield brains behind Albion's Third Division promotion-winning side.

During the 1989–90 campaign Alan inherited the captaincy in the absence of Steve Gatting, but returned to Charlton in June 1990 as player-coach. In July 1991, following Lennie Lawrence's departure for Middlesbrough, Alan was appointed joint team manager with Steve Gritt (the future Albion manager), an unusual arrangement but an apparently successful one as the 'Valiants' came close to promotion; he also made a further 28 League appearances in his second spell at The Valley. In June 1995 he became sole manager and led Charlton to the Division One play-offs in 1996.

Season	FL	FAC	FLC	FMC	AMC	Total
1987–88	34 (6)	3	1	0	4	42 (6)
1988–89	32+5 (6)	1 (1)	1	1	0	35+5 (7)
1989–90	45 (1)	2 (1)	2	1	0	50 (2)
Total	111+5 (13)	6 (2)	4	2	4	127+5 (15)

CURRAN, JACK   1925–30

full-back   Ht 5 8, Wt 11 00   *193 apps*
full name: John Joseph Curran
born: Belfast, Co. Antrim, Ireland, 1898
debut: Norwich City (a), 14.9.1925 (FL D3(S))

Jack Curran built an excellent reputation as a full-back in Ireland and Wales, and was an outstanding member of the Albion side which finished outside of the top five just once in the Third Division (South) in the late 1920s. Signed by the Irish League club Glenavon in 1920 from a Lurgan youth team called Queen's Park, Jack gained an Irish Cup runner's-up medal in his first season, added another in 1921–22, and won his first cap for Ireland against Wales in April 1922. He also represented the Irish League on two occasions before moving to Wales with Pontypridd, where he gained two more caps, against England and

Scotland, and played for the Welsh League representative side on two occasions.

After his spell in the Principality, Jack returned to Glenavon where he won a fourth cap and again played for the Irish League before joining the Albion in July 1925. A solid defensive full-back, he quickly struck up a splendid partnership with Welsh international left-back Jack Jenkins at the Goldstone, and served the club admirably for five years, but left Sussex under a disciplinary cloud early in the 1930–31 season. Jack subsequently returned to Ulster to join the Belfast club Linfield in December 1930, where he won further domestic honours before hanging up his boots.

Season	FL	FAC	Total
1925–26	31	2	33
1926–27	41	3	44
1927–28	37	2	39
1928–29	25	0	25
1929–30	42	6	48
1930–31	4	0	4
Total	180	13	193

CURRY, BILL   1959–60

centre-forward   Ht 5 10, Wt 11 00   *54 apps, 29 goals*
full name: William Morton Curry
born: Walker, Newcastle upon Tyne, Northumberland, 12.10.1935
died: Mansfield, Nottinghamshire, 20.8.1990
debut: Aston Villa (h), 22.8.1959 (FL D2)

A dashing centre-forward renowned for his ability in the air, Bill Curry began his career with Newcastle United and made his First Division debut against Manchester United at Old Trafford in October 1954. While on National Service he represented the Army, won an England under-23 cap v. Romania in October 1957, and, despite having to compete with the likes of Jackie Milburn, scored 34 goals in 80 League appearances in his time at St James's Park. In February 1955 he scored in the first-ever Football League match staged under flood-lights, a 2–0 win for Newcastle at Portsmouth.

It was no surprise, therefore, that it took an Albion record fee of £13,000 to bring Bill to the Goldstone in 1959 for the club's second campaign in Division Two. Although not particularly big for a no.9, he responded superbly, running at defences and leading the attack in typically belligerent style. Bill scored 26 goals in his first season – including three hat-tricks – but became unsettled the following season and, after requesting a transfer, moved to Derby County for £12,000 in September 1960 where he spent almost five years, scoring 63 goals in 148 Second Division games before signing for nearby Mansfield Town in March 1965.

Bill enjoyed a terrific start at Field Mill and scored fifteen goals in his first sixteen games, including two hat-tricks and a four-goal haul. After nearly three years in Nottinghamshire he transferred a dozen miles up the road to Chesterfield, his last League club. In January 1969, Bill joined Boston United on loan for two months before becoming coach to Worksop Town, but returned to Boston in February 1971 as manager and guided the Lincolnshire club to the Northern Premier League title twice and to the League Cup twice. In May 1976 he left York Street, and became manager at Sutton Town a year later, a post he held for nine years until May 1986.

Blessed with good acceleration and anticipation, Bill found the net regularly throughout his career, and a record of 178 goals from 394 League games speaks for itself.

Season	FL	FAC	Total
1959–60	40 (23)	5 (3)	45 (26)
1960–61	9 (3)	0	9 (3)
Total	49 (26)	5 (3)	54 (29)

17 players who won the F.A. Cup

Player	Club	Year
Crowther, Stan	Aston Villa	1957
Downs, Dickie	Barnsley	1912
Jones, Herbert	Blackburn Rovers	1928
Kinnear, Joe	Tottenham Hotspur	1967
Lawrenson, Mark	Liverpool	1986
Leeming, Joe	Bury	1900, 1903
Little, Doz	Manchester City	1956
Mellors, Mark	Bradford City	1911
Moore, Jimmy	Barnsley	1912
Nelson, Sammy	Arsenal	1979
Saunders, Dean	Liverpool	1992
Smith, Bobby	Tottenham Hotspur	1961, 1962
Stapleton, Frank	Arsenal	1979
	Manchester United	1983, 1985
Wilson, Alex	Arsenal	1936
Wragg, Billy	Nottingham Forest	1898
Young, Eric	Wimbledon	1988
Young, Willie	Arsenal	1979

Liverpool at Anfield in March 1908, and was released at the end of that season to join Pendlebury in the Manchester League. In October 1908 he signed for the Albion and was immediately drafted into the first team, but found it difficult to compete with the experienced full-backs already on the staff – Joe Leeming, Tom Stewart and Tom Turner – and therefore failed to gain a regular place. Ted was released from the Goldstone Ground in May 1909 and returned to non-League football. He had a spell with Pontypridd just before the Great War, but resurfaced in Brighton in 1922 playing for Vernon Athletic in the Sussex County League.

Season	SL	WL	SCC	Total
1908–09	6	7	2	15
Total	6	7	2	15

DALTON, GEORGE   1967–70

left-back   *Ht 5 9, Wt 11 08*   *28 apps*
born: West Moor, Newcastle upon Tyne, Northumberland, 4.9.1941
debut: Swindon Town (a), 19.8.1967 (FL D3)

One of the unluckiest players ever to pull on an Albion shirt, George Dalton was considered a future England prospect when he suffered a severe leg fracture while playing for Newcastle United in 1964. Signed as a seventeen-year-old wing-half in November 1958, he had switched to left-back on winning a first-team place and went on to gain wide respect as a solid no.3, but the broken leg effectively ended his career at St James's Park and he arrived at the Goldstone in June 1967 on a free transfer after 85 League games for the 'Magpies'.

However, after establishing himself as an Albion first-choice, George was unfortunate enough to break his leg in the same two places in a match against Oxford United at Hove in January 1968. Subsequently out of action for twelve months, he never played in the Football League again. The Geordie defender appeared for the reserves while coaching the juniors during 1969–70 and studied physiotherapy, but when manager Freddie Goodwin left for Birmingham City in May 1970 he took George with him as trainer. Albion complained to the F.A. that he was still their player, but it was decided that he had been given a free transfer and no action was taken. George remained at St Andrews until 1976 when he took the physio's job with Coventry City, a position he has held ever since.

Season	FL	FAC	FLC	Total
1967–68	24	2	2	28
Total	24	2	2	28

DALTON, TED   1908–09

right-back   *15 apps*
full name: Edward Dalton
born: Manchester, Lancashire
debut: Reading (a), 7.10.1908 (WL D1 'A')

In three years with Manchester United, Ted Dalton made just one appearance in the First Division side, an amazing 7–4 defeat by

DANIELS, HARRY   1948–50

wing-half   *Ht 5 9, Wt 11 00*   *33 apps*
full name: Harry Augustus George Daniels
born: Kensington, London, 25.6.1920
debut: Bournemouth & B.A. (a), 25.9.1948 (FL D3(S))

Although he was wounded during the North Africa campaign of the Second World War, Harry Daniels was a member of the Royal Artillery's football team which won the Army Cup twice in successive seasons during the war. He was, at the time, a professional with Queen's Park Rangers, the club he had signed for in 1940 as an amateur from Kensington Sports. Having joined the paid ranks in 1943, Harry remained at Loftus Road as a reserve-team player for the first post-war seasons, and made just seven appearances in Rangers' Third Division (South) championship side of 1947–48 before arriving at the Goldstone Ground for a fee of £2,000 in August 1948.

Never one to get worked up at events on or off the pitch, the 28-year-old wing-half was nicknamed the 'Silent Knight' by his colleagues at Hove because of his quietly-spoken nature, He proved to be a good passer of the ball, though. In his first season with the Albion, Harry clocked up 28 League games, but he was dropped by manager Don Welsh the following term and left for York City in July 1950 where he ended his League career with five Third Division (North) matches. He subsequently played for Dover in the Kent League.

Season	FL	FAC	Total
1948–49	28	1	29
1949–50	4	0	4
Total	32	1	33

DAREY, JEFF   1957–61

centre-forward   *Ht 5 9, Wt 11 00*   *11 apps, 2 goals*
full name: Jeffrey Arthur Darey
born: Hammersmith, London, 26.2.1934
debut: Crystal Palace (h), 22.4.1957 (FL D3(S))

After completing his National Service with the Royal Engineers in Germany, Jeff Darey made his name in Isthmian League football with Wimbledon. He represented Surrey and the London F.A., and was honoured with four England amateur caps (v. Scotland, Wales, France and Northern Ireland) in 1955 before switching his allegiance to the reigning Athenian League champions Hendon the following year. It was while playing for the Middlesex club that Jeff signed amateur forms for Chelsea, but he then moved to Brighton for family reasons and soon linked up with the Albion, signing as a part-time professional in March 1957 while working in the printing trade.

A spirited leader of the attack, Jeff made his Football League debut in the absence of Peter Harburn a month later, in a 1–1 draw with Crystal Palace, and scored in a dramatic match with Reading at the Goldstone five days later when, with the score 3–3 at the interval, Albion bagged another five to run out 8–3 winners.

Jeff remained at the Goldstone for four years, but with Harburn and Adrian Thorne also vying for the no.9 shirt he had to wait until Albion had been promoted to the Second Division in 1958 before reappearing in the first team. Subsequently placed on the transfer list when the club was forced to economise, he left for Southern League side Guildford City in January 1961, a path followed by a clutch of Albion men at the time. Jeff later played for Swiss Cottage in the Sussex Sunday League and still lives in Hangleton, Hove. Indeed, he reckons that moving home to the Sussex coast was one of the best decisions he ever made.

Season	FL	FLC	Total
1956–57	2 (1)	0	2 (1)
1958–59	2	0	2
1959–60	3	0	3
1960–61	3 (1)	1	4 (1)
Total	10 (2)	1	11 (2)

DARLING, LEN   1933–48

wing-half   Ht 5 7, Wt 12 03   341 apps, 14 goals
full name: Henry Leonard Darling
born: Gillingham, Kent, 9.8.1911
died: Felixstowe, Suffolk, 6.2.1958
debut: Aldershot (a), 14.10.1933 (FL D3(S))

In the course of his fifteen-year career with the Albion, Len Darling became a tremendous favourite of the Goldstone fans who loved his all-out effort and robust style. A stalwart of the club during the Second World War, the popular wing-half made 341 appearances, a total which would surely have been higher but for the seven years of emergency competition.

Born and bred in the Medway Towns, Len began his career with Colchester Town and Tufnell Park, but then returned home with Chatham. A Kent county representative, he signed for Gillingham in May 1932, but after just one season he arrived at the Goldstone in August 1933 to establish himself as a first-team regular in 1934–35, in a dynamic and forceful wing-half role.

On the outbreak of war in 1939, Len joined the A.R.P. Ambulance Service, but continued to turn out for the Albion throughout the conflict and played in 113 matches, a good number of them at centre-forward. He also guested for Bournemouth in 1945–46.

A regular member of the side when normality returned to football in 1946, Len retired in April 1947 to qualify as a school-teacher under the Government's post-war training scheme. However, with Albion struggling during 1947–48, he made a come-back, and played a further 21 League games before finally turning to his new profession at the age of 36.

Len was also a qualified F.A. coach and had trained a number of local schools both before and after the war. During the 1938–39 season he coached Crawley Town

while turning out for the Albion in the Third Division, and coached the England youth team in 1947–48.

Season	FL	FAC	SSC	Wartime	Total
1933–34	9	0	0	0	9
1934–35	37 (1)	3	3	0	43 (1)
1935–36	30	5 (1)	2	0	37 (1)
1936–37	19 (1)	0	0	0	19 (1)
1937–38	23	4	1	0	28
1938–39	33	1	0	0	34
1939–40	0	0	0	35 (1)	35 (1)
1940–41	0	0	0	26	26
1941–42	0	0	0	4	4
1942–43	0	0	0	12 (3)	12 (3)
1943–44	0	0	0	13	13
1945–46	0	8	0	23 (3)	31 (3)
1946–47	27 (3)	1 (1)	0	0	28 (4)
1947–48	21	1	0	0	22
Total	199 (5)	23 (2)	6	113 (7)	341 (14)

DAVIE, JOCK   1936–46

centre-forward   Ht 5 9, Wt 11 04   191 apps, 120 goals
full name: John Davie
born: Dunfermline, Fife, Scotland, 19.2.1913
debut: Gillingham (a), 29.8.1936 (FL D3(S))

Jock Davie's total of 120 goals for the Albion in first-team competitions puts him third on the club's all-time list. Although 62 were scored in the peculiar conditions of wartime, it nevertheless demonstrates the scoring-power of the beefy Scot, and he holds the record, along with Tommy Cook, for the most hat-tricks: eight. He led his line in dashing style and was known to complain bitterly if the ball wasn't played to him in the manner which he preferred.

Jock's arrival at the Goldstone in May 1936 was preceded by spells with Hibernian, Dundee (trial), Torquay United (trial), and at Margate where, during a six-month stay, he reputedly scored 50 goals in all matches as the Kent club carried off the Southern League title in 1935–36. The 23-year-old centre-forward continued his feats in Sussex and was most unfortunate that his best years coincided with the war. He was particularly prolific in the F.A. Cup, in which he netted eighteen goals in fourteen games; they included one four-goal haul and two hat-tricks.

When war broke out in 1939, Jock enlisted with the Police Reserve Force and was later an Army P.T. instructor, reaching the rank of sergeant. One of the most prolific guest players in the country, he appeared for no fewer than nineteen other clubs*, and scored a hat-trick *against* the Albion in August 1941 while playing for Queen's Park Rangers. In August 1946, at the resumption of peacetime football, 33-year-old Jock was released to join Stockton

in the North Eastern League, but he returned to the Football League in December 1946 for a brief spell with Barnsley before finishing his career with Kidderminster Harriers.

Season	FL	FAC	SSC	Wartime	Total
1936–37	24 (13)	1 (1)	1	0	26 (14)
1937–38	38 (17)	4 (7)	0	0	42 (24)
1938–39	27 (9)	1	1 (1)	0	29 (10)
1939–40	0	0	0	34 (22)	34 (22)
1940–41	0	0	0	6 (2)	6 (2)
1941–42	0	0	0	26 (27)	26 (27)
1942–43	0	0	0	8 (5)	8 (5)
1943–44	0	0	0	2 (2)	2 (2)
1945–46	0	8 (10)	0	10 (4)	18 (14)
Total	89 (39)	14 (18)	2 (1)	86 (62)	191 (120)

Note: Davie made wartime guest appearances for Aldershot, Brentford, Charlton Athletic, Chesterfield, Clapton Orient, Crystal Palace, Fulham, Leeds United, Manchester United, Mansfield Town, Millwall, Nottingham Forest, Notts County, Portsmouth, Queen's Park Rangers, Reading, Southampton, Sunderland and Tottenham Hotspur.

DAVIES, KEN   1948–50

outside-left   Ht 5 6, Wt 9 10   36 apps, 5 goals
full name: Kenneth Davies
born: Doncaster, Yorkshire, 20.9.1923
debut: Swindon Town (h), 21.8.1948 (FL D3(S))

A schoolboy product of the Balby district of Doncaster, Ken Davies joined Wolverhampton Wanderers from Oswin Club Old Boys and then spent some time back in Yorkshire with their nursery club,

Wath Wanderers. From 1943 he appeared fairly frequently in Wolves' wartime line-ups, but was transferred to Walsall for £600 in June 1946 and played in 28 Third Division (South) matches in two seasons at Fellows Park before coming to the Goldstone for a £250 fee in May 1948.

Brave, skilful, and a fine crosser of the ball, Ken also had his fair share of pace and a fierce shot. He was initially first choice at outside-left, but lost his place to Mickey Kavanagh in December and subsequently appeared only sporadically until leaving for Chippenham Town in the Western League on the conclusion of the 1949–50 campaign.

Season	FL	Total
1948–49	14 (1)	14 (1)
1949–50	22 (4)	22 (4)
Total	36 (5)	36 (5)

DAVIES, PETER   1965–66

right-half   Ht 5 9, Wt 10 08   8 apps
born: Llanelli, Carmarthenshire, Wales, 8.3.1936
debut: Hull City (h), 28.8.1965 (FL D3)

Despite attending a rugby-playing school, Peter Davies went on to play football for Llanelli, his home-town club, in the Southern League before signing as a professional for Arsenal at the age of 21 in December 1957. However, he failed to make the League team at Highbury and it was generally felt that his talent was wasted in the reserves. In March 1959 came his big break when he moved back to Wales with Swansea Town as part of the record transfer deal which took Mel Charles to Arsenal.

In six years at the Vetch Field, Peter played in 133 League games and won a Welsh Cup medal in 1961, but after arriving at the Goldstone on a free transfer in July 1965 he again failed to make his mark. Although he had a brief run in the side early in 1965–66, Peter returned to South Wales after just seven months in January 1966 in order to revive his clothing business, joining Southern League Merthyr Tydfil. However, he was soon on the move again, leaving for South Africa later that year to play for the Germiston club.

Season	FL	FLC	Total
1965–66	6	2	8
Total	6	2	8

DAWSON, ALEX   1968–71

centre-forward   Ht 5 10, Wt 13 10   65 apps, 29 goals
full name: Alexander Downie Dawson
born: Aberdeen, Aberdeenshire, Scotland, 21.2.1940
debut: Swindon Town (a), 14.12.1968 (FL D3)

One of the last of the big, bustling, old-fashioned centre-forwards, Alex Dawson was a superb goalscorer throughout his career, plundering 212 goals from 393 Football League outings. In his early days in the First Division, the strapping, dark-haired Scot was celebrated enough to earn the label 'The Black Prince of Football'.

Although born in Aberdeen, Alex went to school in Hull – where his father worked on the trawlers – and played for England Schools before joining Manchester United as a youngster. A member of a later class of 'Busby Babes', he graduated through the Old Trafford junior teams – appearing in two F.A. Youth Cup-winning sides – to sign as a professional in April 1957, and made his First Division debut the same month at the age of seventeen, scoring in a 2–0 home win over Burnley.

Alex established himself in United's attack following the 1958 Munich air-disaster, and scored a hat-trick in the F.A. Cup semi-final replay (5–3 v. Fulham at Highbury) as the decimated club won its way to Wembley just three months after the tragedy. He picked up only a runner's-up medal in a 2–0 defeat by Bolton Wanderers, though. After 54 goals in 93 League and Cup matches for United, Alex joined Preston North End for £18,000 in October 1961, where he netted 114 goals in 197 League appearances and collected a second F.A. Cup runner's-up medal in 1963–64, scoring a goal as the Second Division club lost 3–2 to West Ham United.

In March 1967, Alex moved on to Bury, and in December 1968 became Freddie Goodwin's first acquisition on taking the managerial post at the Goldstone. Costing around £9,000, the experienced 28-year-old was drafted straight into Albion's relegation-threatened Third Division side and didn't let his former Manchester United team-mate down as he scored seventeen goals in 23 matches to lift the team into the top half of the table. With his all-action, buccaneering style, Alex became a huge favourite with the Goldstone fans, the scourge of many a goalkeeper, and remained first-choice centre-forward until losing his place under Pat Saward in 1970–71.

Loaned to Brentford in September 1970, he scored six goals in ten outings for the 'Bees' who were keen to sign him permanently, but Albion's asking-price was too high and the deal fell through. Alex made just two more appearances in Albion's League team and left for Corby Town in the summer of 1971 where he top-scored for two seasons, but was then forced to retire with a knee problem, becoming trainer of the Southern League club. He subsequently played local junior football with Corby Locos and now lives in Rothwell, Northamptonshire, working in a Kettering plastics factory.

Season	FL	FAC	FLC	Total
1968–69	23 (17)	0	0	23 (17)
1969–70	28+3 (9)	5 (2)	3 (1)	36+3 (12)
1970–71	2+1	0	0	2+1
Total	53+4 (26)	5 (2)	3 (1)	61+4 (29)

DAY, ALBERT   1938–46

centre-forward   Ht 5 10, Wt 12 00   17 apps, 8 goals
born: Camberwell, London, 7.3.1918
died: Brighton, Sussex, January 1983
debut: Bournemouth & B.A. (a), 28.10.1939 (wartime)
peacetime debut: Romford (a), 24.11.1945 (FAC R1 Lg2)

Albert Day was signed by Albion manager Charlie Webb shortly after scoring a hat-trick for the victorious Hastings & St Leonards side in the Sussex Senior Cup final of April 1938, and played for the reserves until the outbreak of the war. The former Sussex representative appeared occasionally for Brighton throughout the conflict, and also guested for Lincoln City and Reading while serving as an Army physical training instructor. In 1945–46 he represented Albion at Romford in the F.A. Cup, his only first-team appearance in a peace-time competition for the club, and also had a lengthy spell as a guest with Ipswich Town where his performances resulted in a permanent move to Portman Road in May 1946.

In three seasons at Ipswich he scored 25 goals in 63 League games, but was transferred to Watford in August 1949 where he made just four appearances before being released. After playing for Folkestone and Ashford in the Kent League, Albert was reinstated as an amateur to play briefly for Sussex County League Crawley Town in September 1955 before retiring.

Season	FAC	Wartime	Total
1939–40	0	3	3
1941–42	0	1 (2)	1 (2)
1942–43	0	2	2
1944–45	0	4 (4)	4 (4)
1945–46	1	6 (2)	7 (2)
Total	1	16 (8)	17 (8)

DEAR, BRIAN   1967

inside-forward   *7 apps, 5 goals*
full name: Brian Charles Dear
born: Plaistow, West Ham, Essex, 18.9.1943
debut: Workington (a), 17.3.1967 (FL D3)

Brian Dear enjoyed a wonderful career as a young player for West Ham United, but eventually lost his way and drifted out of the first-class game at the age of just 27. After playing for both East Ham and England as a schoolboy, he joined the "Hammers'" staff at the age of fifteen and signed as a professional in December 1960. A voracious goalscorer, Brian netted 39 times in 85 League and Cup outings at Upton Park, including five in a 20-minute spell against West Bromwich Albion in April 1965. He also won a European Cup-Winners' Cup medal in 1965 and gained a League Cup runner's-up trophy in 1966.

By March 1967, however, Brian, who had a continual weight

problem throughout his career, had lost his first-team place and came to the Goldstone on loan, the club's first such player under the Football League's new regulations. Although he impressed by scoring five times in seven matches, he was considered too expensive at £20,000 and returned to West Ham. In February 1969 he moved to Fulham, and then to Millwall five months later, but on being released from a short stay at The Den, Brian was unemployed and playing for Woodford Town when Ron Greenwood offered him a second chance with West Ham in October 1970.

Sadly, there was no happy ending. In January

1971 he was one five members of the "Hammers'" staff found drinking in a night-club a few hours before an F.A. Cup tie with Blackpool. West Ham lost 4–0, and Brian was subsequently dismissed after just four League games in his second spell with the club. (The other four culprits, including Bobby Moore and Jimmy Greaves, received only heavy fines.) In September 1971 he rejoined Woodford Town. Brian is now a steward at a social club in Southend-on-Sea, having worked as a publican in Essex for several years, and occasionally helps out in the hospitality suites at Upton Park.

Season	FL	Total
1966–67	7 (5)	7 (5)
Total	7 (5)	7 (5)

DENNETT, J. W.   1903–04

left-back   *2 apps*
debut: Kettering Town (h), 14.11.1903 (SL D1)

Dennett gained a good deal of experience in Army football, but was playing for Burgess Hill in the Mid Sussex Senior League when he joined the Albion as a part-time professional during the 1903–04 season. In 1904 his reinstatement as an amateur was deferred by the F.A., but it was subsequently approved and he went on to play for Burgess Hill again for a number of years.

Season	SL	Total
1903–04	2	2
Total	2	2

DENNISON, BOB   1924–25

inside-right   Ht 5 9, Wt 11 05   *28 apps, 13 goals*
full name: Robert Dennison
born: Arnold, Nottinghamshire, 6.10.1900
died: Norwich, Norfolk, 24.6.1973
debut: Brentford (a), 30.8.1924 (FL D3(S))

Bob Dennison was a free-scoring inside-forward who, in a career of 247 League games, hit 84 goals, a creditable total at better than one every third appearance. One of a family of ten children, he joined Norwich City from Arnold St Mary's, a Nottinghamshire junior club, in August 1920 for the "Canaries'" first season in the newly created Third Division. In four seasons with City, Bob netted 38 times in 126 League and Cup appearances, form which prompted Albion manager Charlie Webb to entice him to the Goldstone Ground in August 1924.

Keeping up his impressive scoring-rate, the 23-year-old forward hit thirteen goals – including two hat-tricks – in his first nineteen appearances for the Albion, but had failed to score for nine games when he was replaced by £650 record signing Sam Jennings in March 1925 and consigned to the reserves. Allowed to join First Division giants Manchester City on a free transfer in May, Bob scored four goals in seven games at Maine Road, then signed for Clapton Orient in August 1926. With 28 goals in 70 League outings over three seasons for the Second Division side behind him, Bob moved on to Chesterfield in the Third Division (North) in July 1929, but left the Football League ranks at the end of the 1929–30 season to return to East Anglia for four years with Yarmouth Town.

Season	FL	FAC	Total
1924–25	25 (10)	3 (3)	28 (13)
Total	25 (10)	3 (3)	28 (13)

DEXTER, CHARLIE　　　　　　　1914–15

left-back　　　　　　　　　　　　　*36 apps*
full name: Charles Dexter
born: Shardlow, Derbyshire, 1889
died: in action, 1916
debut: Plymouth Argyle (a), 2.9.1914 (SL D1)

Charlie Dexter set out on a professional football career in April 1911 when he joined Sheffield Wednesday from Ilkeston Town at the age of 21, but he had little chance of breaking into Wednesday's star-studded First Division side and was confined to the reserves until he was freed to join Portsmouth in the Southern League during the close season of 1912. Acting as deputy to the renowned amateur-international left-back Arthur Knight (who gained full England honours after the war), Charlie made the Southern League team on just fourteen occasions at Fratton Park before moving along the South Coast to join the Albion in April 1914. (His transfer came just a couple of weeks after completing a seven-day suspension for being sent off while playing in a match at Northampton. He is reputed to have been only the second player in "Pompey's" history to receive marching orders.)

Charlie's career blossomed at the Goldstone and he was first-choice left-back in 1914–15, but the season was dominated by the First World War. After enlisting – along with the majority of his Albion colleagues – with the Footballers' Battalion, he returned to his Midlands home when the club closed down in 1915, but lost his life the following year while serving with the Warwickshire Regiment.

Season	SL	FAC	Total
1914–15	33	3	36
Total	33	3	36

DICKOV, PAUL　　　　　　　　　1994

forward　　　　Ht 5 5, Wt 11 09　　*8 apps, 5 goals*
born: Glasgow, Lanarkshire, Scotland, 1.11.1972
debut: Exeter City (a), 26.3.1994 (FL D2)

Paul Dickov grew up a Celtic supporter in a football-mad family, the son of Polish parents; his father was a schoolboy with Rangers, while brothers Steve (Stenhousemuir) and Allan (various clubs) also attracted attention. In 1989 he first came to prominence, scoring for Scotland in the World Under-16 Championship final before a 51,000 crowd at Hampden Park (the Scots lost on penalties to Saudi Arabia), but was then tempted south by Arsenal who took him on as a trainee.

Paul made good progress at Highbury, gaining Scottish Youth honours and winning four under-21 caps, but found it difficult to break into the Arsenal first team. Having made his League debut as a substitute in March 1993, he scored in his first full match a few weeks later, against Spurs, but amassed only a handful of appearances for the 'Gunners' despite scoring prolifically in the reserves. Indeed, Paul scored the winning goal against

Albion's reserve side a month before arriving on loan at the Goldstone in March 1994. (Earlier in the same season he had a three-month spell on loan at Luton Town, where he scored just once in fifteen League games.)

The diminutive Scot quickly endeared himself to the Hove crowd with his tenacious, fiery play, and he played a large part in securing the club's position in Division Two with five goals in his month at the Goldstone. On his return to Highbury, Paul won a place on the bench in Arsenal's successful European Cup Winners' Cup final side, but was not called upon and continued to play a deputy role to the club's principal strikers until he signed for Manchester City for £1 million in August 1996.

Season	FL	Total
1993–94	8 (5)	8 (5)
Total	8 (5)	8 (5)

DIGWEED, PERRY　　　　　　　1981–93

goalkeeper　　Ht 6 0, Wt 11 04　　*201 apps*
full name: Perry Michael Digweed
born: Chelsea, London, 26.10.1959
debut: West Bromwich Albion (a), 17.1.1981 (FL D1)

Perry Digweed's Albion career was a roller-coaster ride of highs and lows, so much so that after loan spells with four other clubs he went on to be voted best player as the team fought its way to Wembley. He left Sussex with only 201 League and Cup appearances to his name after more than twelve years on the Goldstone staff, but he rarely let the club down.

Once a worker at Covent Garden fruit and vegetable market, Perry played for West London Schools before joining Fulham as an apprentice in 1976, and had had just fifteen first-team outings for the 'Cottagers' when he signed for Albion manager Alan Mullery in January 1981 for £150,000. It was a staggering sum for an inexperienced 21-year-old goalkeeper, but he immediately took over from the then-suspect Graham Moseley and, having brought an instant improvement to Albion's net-minding, retained his place for the remainder of the season as the club escaped relegation from the First Division.

Moseley then fought back to regain his place, and Perry had to play second-fiddle to Moseley and a succession of other goalkeepers over the next decade or so. He was first choice in the two years 1985–87, but then had to wait until the 1990s before re-establishing himself between the posts.

Although certainly a brave and competent 'keeper, especially in his latter years, luck was definitely not on Perry's side. Three times he was selected for the England under-21 squad, only to withdraw on each occasion because of club commitments or injury. Indeed, he was plagued by injury, and a ruptured urethra suffered during a match with West Bromwich Albion in September 1988 briefly threatened his life. Amazingly, it was his first appearance for sixteen months (although he was due to play two games earlier but no one remembered to inform him!) and the new injury kept him out of the reckoning for a further seventeen months, but he regained a regular place following John Keeley's departure for Oldham and performed heroically during the 1990–91 campaign when he won the Player of the Season award as Albion made it to the Division Two play-off final.

Over the years Perry had loan periods as cover at West Bromwich Albion (October 1983), Charlton Athletic (January 1985), Newcastle United (December 1987) and Wimbledon (March 1993), but didn't make a first-team appearance with any. He did, however, play three First Division games for Chelsea in February 1988. Perry enjoyed a testimonial season in 1991–92, but was released in May 1993 and, following a pre-season trial with Luton Town, joined Wimbledon in the Premiership as understudy to Hans Segers. Without playing a first-team game for the 'Dons', he joined Watford in January 1994 after a month on loan at Vicarage Road, but was released at the end of the 1994–95 season after 31 appearances. Perry has since worked as a personal assistant to a well-known horse-racing family.

Season	FL	Play-offs	FAC	FLC	FMC	Total
1980–81	15	0	0	0	0	15
1981–82	12	0	0	0	0	12
1982–83	15	0	1	0	0	16
1983–84	4	0	0	0	0	4
1985–86	33	0	5	2	1	41
1986–87	22	0	0	2	1	25
1988–89	1	0	0	0	0	1
1989–90	11	0	0	0	0	11
1990–91	42	3	3	1	3	52
1991–92	20	0	0	0	0	20
1992–93	4	0	0	0	0	4
Total	179	3	9	5	5	201

DILLON, JOHN   1962–63

outside-left   *22 apps, 3 goals*
born: Coatbridge, Lanarkshire, Scotland, 9.11.1942
debut: Queen's Park Rangers (a), 18.8.1962 (FL D3)

A product of Scottish junior football, John Dillon signed professional forms for Sunderland at the age of seventeen in November 1959 and made his Second Division debut in a 1–0 defeat at Middlesbrough in September 1960. After 22 first team outings at Roker Park, the fleet-footed winger signed for Albion manager George Curtis, his former coach at Sunderland, in June 1962 as part of the club's new youth policy, and was drafted straight into the League eleven. John found it difficult to settle on the South Coast, though, and in November asked for a transfer which he subsequently withdrew, but he struggled to make his mark as Curtis's inexperienced side was relegated to Division Four. Leaving for Crewe Alexandra in July 1963, John returned to Scotland with his home-town club Albion Rovers in July 1964 where he met with some success for five seasons.

Season	FL	FAC	Total
1962–63	21 (3)	1	22 (3)
Total	21 (3)	1	22 (3)

DIXON, TOMMY   1958–60

centre/inside-forward   Ht 6 0, Wt 11 10   *36 apps, 12 goals*
full name: Thomas Charles Dixon
born: Newcastle upon Tyne, Northumberland, 8.6.1929
debut: Sheffield Wednesday (h), 11.10.1958 (FL D2)

A tall, clever forward, particularly good in the air, Tommy Dixon maintained an excellent strike-rate throughout his career with 136 goals in 312 League appearances, a high percentage of which were scored with his head. He began as an amateur on the books of Newcastle United, but signed for West Ham United in February 1951 at the age of 21 and, having broken into the first-team at Upton Park, was leading scorer in 1953–54 with nineteen goals. The following season, though, he lost his place, and was transferred to Reading in March 1955 where he enhanced his reputation over three years, topping the scoring charts in 1956–57 and 1957–58 with 28 and 24 goals respectively.

In October 1958, Billy Lane signed the 29-year-old forward to bolster Albion's flagging attack in their initial Second Division campaign, and he responded with ten goals in 30 League games as the club staved off the very real possibility of relegation after a

disastrous start. However, Tommy was unable to hold down a place in 1959–60 and was put on the transfer list as the club sought to make economies. He left for Workington in July 1960, and moved on to Barrow in October 1961 where he saw out his Football League career with 23 goals in 62 Fourth Division outings.

Season	FL	FAC	Total
1958–59	30 (10)	1	31 (10)
1959–60	5 (2)	0	5 (2)
Total	35 (12)	1	36 (12)

DOBSON, COLIN   1972

midfield   Ht 5 7, Wt 10 06   *4 apps*
born: Eston, Yorkshire, 9.5.1940
debut: Bristol Rovers (a), 22.1.1972 (FL D3)

Colin Dobson was a skilled midfielder who finished his apprenticeship in the shipbuilding industry on Teesside before signing as a full-time professional for Sheffield Wednesday in 1961, by which time he had been on the staff for five years. In a further five years at Hillsborough he scored 52 goals in 193 League and Cup appearances; represented the Football League *v.* England in the F.A. Centenary/Football League 75th Anniversary match at Highbury in 1963; and played for England's under-23 team on two occasions.

In August 1966 the talented Yorkshireman moved on to Huddersfield Town to become a prominent member of the team which carried off the Second Division title in 1969–70, but arrived at the Goldstone on loan in January 1972 to help the Albion in their bid for promotion from Division Three. However, Colin's contribution to the Brighton cause was quickly and unfortunately curtailed when he suffered a broken leg in his fourth outing, and he returned to Huddersfield.

In July 1972 he signed for Bristol Rovers, and went on to appear in 62 League games for Rovers, including the 8–2 embarrassment of the Albion at the Goldstone in December 1973. Colin also took to coaching at Eastville, and subsequently coached Coventry City's youth team. From 1983 to 1985 he was assistant to his former Bristol Rovers team-mate John Rudge at Port Vale, then had a spell in the Middle East as national coach to Bahrain and to the Rayyan club in the United Arab Emirates. In 1986–87, Colin was reserve-team coach at Aston Villa, and became coach at Gillingham under Keith Burkinshaw in 1988. At the start of the 1996–97 season he was assisting Port Vale.

Season	FL	Total
1971–72	2+2	2+2
Total	2+2	2+2

DODD, GEORGE   1913–14

utility forward   *19 apps, 2 goals*
full name: George Francis Dodd
born: Wallasey, Cheshire, 1882
debut: West Ham United (h), 13.12.1913 (SL D1)

A player of wide experience with more than 100 First Division matches to his name, George Dodd arrived in Hove in December 1913 with a nomadic reputation, having played for Wallasey Town, Stockport County (signed August 1905), Lancashire Combination side Workington (close season 1907), Notts County (December 1907),

Chelsea (May 1911) and Millwall (May 1913). A versatile front man, he appeared in all five forward positions in his nineteen games for the Albion, but was released in May 1914 and spent the following season with Darlington in the North Eastern League before war brought about the cessation of normal football.

After helping out one of his former clubs, Chelsea, in the wartime London Combination in 1916–17, George joined Luton Town in October 1919 for the last season of the old-format Southern League before leaving for Welsh club Treherbert in May 1920. He returned to the Football League fold with Charlton Athletic on their elevation to the Third Division (South) the following summer, but made just one senior appearance at the age of 39 before being released to join the Kent League club Catford Southend as secretary-manager in July 1924.

George scored the first League goal ever conceded by Chelsea, the only goal of the match when he made his debut for Stockport County at Edgeley Park on the opening day of the 1905–06 season. Seven years later he was playing *for* Chelsea and helping the 'Pensioners' regain First Division status as runners-up to Second Division champions Derby County on goal average.

Season	SL	FAC	Total
1913–14	17 (2)	2	19 (2)
Total	17 (2)	2	19 (2)

DOLLMAN, FRANK   1902

utility player   *2 apps*
full name: Francis Thomas Dollman
born: Brighton, Sussex, 1877
debut: Maidenhead (h), 1.2.1902 (SL D2)

An itinerant local amateur, Frank Dollman played for the Brighton Hornets, Hove and Brighton Athletic clubs, and won his county colours in 1899–1900 before joining Brighton & Hove Rangers in 1900. One of the newly formed club's leading players, he missed just one of their thirteen competitive matches playing as either an inside-forward or a half-back. On Rangers' demise Frank returned to Hove F.C. and was a member of the team that played Clapton on 7 September 1901 at the Goldstone Ground, the first-ever football match staged at the venue. Later that season he assisted the Albion on two occasions in the club's first campaign, turning out at inside-left and centre-half. Frank was also a champion swimmer and diver with the Hove Swimming Club.

Season	SL	Total
1901–02	2	2
Total	2	2

DONNELLY, PETER   1962–65

forward   Ht 6 0, Wt 11 06   *59 apps, 13 goals*
born: Kingston upon Hull, Yorkshire, 22.9.1936
debut: Queen's Park Rangers (a), 18.8.1962 (FL D3)

Something of an all-round sportsman, Peter Donnelly was an excellent club-cricketer, and became the Army's light-heavy and heavyweight boxing champion during his National Service. He embarked on a Football League career at the age of seventeen in March 1954 when he signed professional forms for Doncaster Rovers, and played six League games in four years for the Yorkshire club before moving to Scunthorpe United in July 1958. The Hull-born forward met with greater success in Lincolnshire, scoring nineteen goals in 39 Second Division outings, and in June 1960 he joined First Division Cardiff City in exchange for Joe Bonson, going on to hit the net eight times in 30 League games before a £5,000 move to Swansea Town in October 1961.

After nine months at the Vetch Field, the rugged forward arrived in Hove in July 1962 when George Curtis paid £7,000 for his services. Peter was bought to bolster relegated Albion's attack for their first campaign back in the Third Division, but the campaign proved a complete disaster for the club. Even so, the 26-year-old had a fair season, topping the goalscorers with 11 goals out of a modest total of 58 as Albion sank to the obscurity of Division Four. Strong and experienced but left-footed almost to a fault, he appeared in three forward positions and missed just one League game all season, but lost his place the following term after damaging a knee early on.

The outset of the 1964–65 season saw Peter in dispute with the club over financial terms, and he had just three first-team outings before joining Bradford City for a £500 fee in March 1965. Three weeks later he wreaked revenge on his former club by scoring twice in a 4–1 defeat of Albion at Valley Parade, temporarily denting Brighton's promotion hopes. On leaving City after just thirteen League appearances he played for Margate in the Southern League for several seasons, and later appeared with Canterbury City.

Season	FL	FAC	FLC	Total
1962–63	45 (11)	1	0	46 (11)
1963–64	8 (2)	0	2	10 (2)
1964–65	3	0	0	3
Total	56 (13)	1	2	59 (13)

DORAN, JACK   1920–22

forward   Ht 5 9, Wt 11 07   *85 apps, 55 goals*
full name: John Francis Doran, M.M.
born: Belfast, Co. Antrim, Ireland, 3.1.1896
died: Sunderland, Co. Durham, 7.1.1940
debut: Swansea Town (h), 6.3.1920 (SL D1)

In a comparatively short stay at the Goldstone Ground, Jack became one of the most prolific forwards ever to play for the club, a goalscoring machine who was adored by the fans. On joining the Albion from Norwich City in March 1920, the burly Ulsterman scored ten goals in the ten remaining games to gain the rare distinction of being top scorer for two clubs in the same season, but his career really took off when the Football League's Third Division became reality the following summer.

In 1920–21 he led the way with 22 goals, and made an extraordinary start to the 1921–22 season by netting the first twelve – and sixteen of the first seventeen – goals registered by the Albion; they included home and away hat-tricks against Exeter City, and a five-goal haul at the Goldstone against Northampton Town (four goals in eight minutes).

Such outstanding form – 55 goals in just 85 games – made the football world sit up and take notice. Jack was rewarded with Irish caps against England (twice) and Wales in 1920, '21 and '22, only the second

J. DORAN.

Albion player to become an international, and joined First Division Manchester City for £1,050 in August 1922, but it proved to be a bad move and his time in Hove was undoubtedly the pinnacle of his career.

Although he was only 24 years of age on his arrival in Hove, Jack had had an interesting life before his move to Sussex. Born in Belfast, he migrated as a youngster with his family to the north-east of England and went on to represent the Northumberland Schools *v.* County Durham. In 1912–13, at the age of sixteen, he was on Gillingham's books, but young Jack was released without making the first team to join Pontypridd where, somewhat strangely, he played for a Billy Meredith XI against a South Wales representative side three weeks before his seventeenth birthday in what was billed as a Welsh international trial match!

The 1914–15 season saw him playing for Coventry City, but he soon enlisted with the Footballers' Battalion of the Middlesex Regiment (commanded by former Albion half-back Frank Buckley) and served with great distinction. Indeed, in 1916, at the age of 20, he was awarded the Military Medal for his bravery on the Somme while serving with the 7th Battalion.

In the latter part of the war Jack guested for Brentford and Newcastle United, and in 1919 Major Buckley (q.v.), his former C.O. who had recently been installed as manager of Norwich City, took him on the "Canaries'" staff. The Irishman's valour was also reflected in his performances as leader of the attack, and he scored eighteen goals for the Norfolk club before Charlie Webb brought him to the Goldstone in an inspired move.

After astounding everyone with his feats for Brighton, Jack had only three games – scoring one goal – for Manchester City before the management tried to convert him into a centre-half. Understandably, he never settled at Maine Road and moved on to Crewe Alexandra in January 1924 before drifting into Southern League football with Mid Rhondda at the end of the season. A short period in south Wales was followed by a return to Ireland with Shelbourne in December 1924, where he appeared in the Dublin-based club's losing F.A. of I. Cup final side that season, but in August 1925 he re-crossed the Irish Sea to see out his career with two years in the Midland League with Boston Town. In the 1930s he was reported to be the manager of League of Ireland club Waterford.

Always a larger-than-life figure, Jack became a publican in the North-East on retiring, but died from the effects of tuberculosis in 1940 just four days after his 44th birthday. The popular Irishman's name lives on in Albion folklore, though, and will always feature prominently when the club's greatest goalscorers are discussed.

Season	FL	SL	FAC	Total
1919–20	0	10 (10)	0	10 (10)
1920–21	40 (21)	0	2 (1)	42 (22)
1921–22	31 (23)	0	2	33 (23)
Total	71 (44)	10 (10)	4 (1)	85 (55)

DOUGAL, DAVE   1908

outside-right   14 apps, 1 goal
full name: David Wishart Dougal
born: Dundee, Angus, Scotland, 22.3.1882
died: Dundee, Angus, Scotland, 5.3.1837
debut: Crystal Palace (h), 29.2.1908 (SL D1)

Dave Dougal's career began when he joined Dundee Hibernian, a junior side in his home city, in August 1902 and stepped up to senior football with Dundee in May 1903. After nearly two seasons playing for the Scottish First Division club, he saw service with the reserve teams of Preston North End and Grimsby Town, but failed to make an impression until joining Clapton Orient in August 1905; he played in every forward position except inside-left as Orient finished bottom of Division Two in their first season as a Football League club.

By the time he moved into the Southern League with Reading during the close season of 1907, Dave had made 50

League appearances for the struggling London club, and added a further 20 for the 'Biscuitmen' before Frank Scott-Walford brought him to the Goldstone – together with fellow Dundonian Tom Rodger – in February 1908. The 25-year-old winger missed only one Southern League match during the remainder of the 1907–08 campaign, but in June 1908 he joined the migration to Leeds City where Walford had recently become manager. Dave remained at Elland Road for two seasons, scoring twice in 25 Second Division outings, before returning to Scotland with Montrose in November 1910. He worked in the confectionery trade for many years after leaving the game.

Season	SL	Total
1907–08	14 (1)	14 (1)
Total	14 (1)	14 (1)

DOVEY, ALAN   1971–73

goalkeeper   Ht 6 0, Wt 11 12   8 apps
full name: Alan Raymond Dovey
born: Stepney, London, 18.7.1952
debut: Bristol Rovers (a), 1.5.1971 (FL D3)

After playing for Thurrock Schools, Alan Dovey joined Chelsea as an apprentice and signed as a professional at the age of seventeen in October 1969, but, with goalkeepers of the calibre of Peter Bonetti, Tommy Hughes and John Phillips (the latter two also going on to play for the Albion) on the staff, he understandably failed to make an appearance in the senior side and came to the Goldstone on loan in March 1971 as cover for Brian Powney. Subsequently signed for a £1,000 fee in July, Alan was drafted into the first team for the last two matches of the 1970–71 campaign to give him experience, but in two years with the club he was always a capable understudy to the consistent Powney. Placed on the transfer list in March 1973, he decided to leave the Football League scene at the end of the season to

pursue a career in insurance, but continued to play locally with lengthy spells at Southwick and Worthing, and represented Sussex on several occasions. Alan later spent a considerable time with Peacehaven & Telscombe in the Sussex County League.

Season	FL	FLC	Total
1970–71	2	0	2
1971–72	2	1	3
1972–73	2	1	3
Total	6	2	8

DOWNS, DICKIE   1924–25

right-back   Ht 5 7, Wt 12 00   16 apps
full name: John Thomas Downs*
born: Middridge, Co. Durham, 13.8.1886
died: Durham, Co. Durham, 24.3.1949
debut: Brentford (a), 30.8.1924 (FL D3(S))

One of the game's great characters in the immediate pre- and post-Great War periods, 'Dickie' Downs was reputed to be the innovator of the sliding tackle and was dubbed the 'India-Rubber Man'. His style of play and distinctive legs also made him one of the era's most popular players. Born in County Durham, he started out with local clubs Crook and Shildon in the Northern League, and signed professional forms for Barnsley in May 1908 where he went on to become a huge favourite. He played in two F.A. Cup finals for the Second Division club: on the losing side against Newcastle United in 1910, but a winner against West Bromwich Albion in 1912 in a remarkable run which saw six replays, including the final.

Dickie also represented the Football League on two occasions and spent a total of twelve war-interrupted years at Oakwell, making 305 League and Cup appearances, but in March 1920 he joined

Everton for £3,000. It was a massive sum for a 33-year-old, but he continued to excel and was capped by England against Ireland in October 1920. By the time he arrived at the Goldstone in August 1924, Dickie was 38, but appeared regularly at right-back until an injury in December enforced his retirement. His football obituary ran: 'Dickie Downs had legs like oak trees, except that they were a trifle bowed; he was given to fly-kick volleys and flying tackles.' After hanging up his boots he coached on the Continent for several years.

Season	FL	Total
1924–25	16	16
Total	16	16

Note: Dickie is referred to as 'Richard W. Downs' in many publications, but his birth and death registrations at St Catherine's House confirm the above data. A glance at his forenames may suggest how he became known as Dickie!

DOWNSBOROUGH, PETER   1973

goalkeeper   Ht 5 10, Wt 13 02   3 apps
born: Halifax, Yorkshire, 13.9.1943
debut: Plymouth Argyle (a), 8.9.1973 (FL D3)

A goalkeeper of vast experience, Peter Downsborough came to the Albion on loan in August 1973 as a temporary replacement for the injured Brian Powney and played in three games. The loan-spell came towards the end of a long and successful career guarding the net, but he actually started out as a centre-forward for Halifax and West Riding Schools. In fact, it was only in an emergency that he took over between the posts, but he then stayed there for the rest of his football days.

Peter signed as a professional for Halifax Town in September 1960, but moved to Swindon Town after 148 League games at The Shay, helping the Wiltshire side to promotion from Division Three in 1968–69 and to a memorable League Cup final success over Arsenal at Wembley the same season. A popular figure at the County Ground for eight years, he was loaned to Bradford City in November 1973 shortly after his spell at the Goldstone, and signed permanently six weeks later at the age of 30. Peter then took his career total to 651 League games before retiring in 1978. Now a builder in Halifax, he was renowned for constructing his own house while turning out for Bradford City.

Season	FL	Total
1973–74	3	3
Total	3	3

DUBLIN, KEITH   1987–90

defender   Ht 5 11, Wt 11 09   151 apps, 6 goals
full name: Keith Barry Lennox Dublin
born: High Wycombe, Buckinghamshire, 29.1.1966
debut: York City (h), 15.8.1987 (FL D3)

With 51 League games for Chelsea behind him, Keith Dublin was a promising 21-year-old when he joined the Albion. Three years in Hove knocked the raw edges off the young full-back's play, and he

blossomed into a fine central-defender before moving on for a considerable profit.

A member of the High Wycombe team which carried off the English Schools Trophy in 1981, Keith was an associate schoolboy of Watford, but became an apprentice with Chelsea for whom he signed professional forms in October 1983. Making his League debut as an eighteen-year-old in the penultimate match of Chelsea's 1983–84 Division Two championship campaign, he also won six England under-19 youth caps and went on to compete for the left-back spot with another future Brighton player, Doug Rougvie, but was persuaded to come to the Goldstone by Albion coach Martin Hinshelwood, formerly at Chelsea himself.

After signing in August 1987 for a fee which reached £50,000, Keith played at left-back in every match as Albion returned to the Second Division at the first attempt, but moved into the middle of the back four in February 1989 and developed into a central-defender of some class. Strong in the tackle, capable in the air and a good reader of the game, he was voted Player of the Season in 1989–90, but, with ambitions of furthering his career with another club, he was sold to Watford in July 1990 for a fee of £275,000. Keith was a regular in the "Hornets'" side until the summer of 1994 when he moved to fellow First Division side Southend United in a player-exchange deal. Once again he established himself as a first-class defender, and he has now clocked up more than 100 League appearances for a club for the third time.

Season	FL	FAC	FLC	FMC	AMC	Total
1987–88	46 (5)	4	2	0	5	57 (5)
1988–89	43	1	1	1	0	46
1989–90	43	2 (1)	2	1	0	48 (1)
Total	132 (5)	7 (1)	5	2	5	151 (6)

DUCKWORTH, JOE   1930–32

goalkeeper   Ht 5 10, Wt 12 04   40 apps
full name: Joseph Duckworth
born: Blackburn, Lancashire, 29.4.1898
debut: Clapton Orient (a), 7.3.1931 (FL D3(S))

Joe Duckworth attended Moss Street School in Blackburn and was playing for Accrington Stanley in the Lancashire Combination when he signed for First Division Blackburn Rovers as a seventeen-year-old amateur in April 1915. Although he was offered professional terms after the war in August 1919, Joe failed to make the grade in the top flight and appeared in just seven League and Cup matches before joining Aberdare Athletic in July 1921 on their election to the Football League. In three seasons with the Welsh club he appeared in 84 Third Division games, but was transferred to Reading in June 1924 where he missed just one League match in his first four seasons.

Unspectacular but ever-reliable, Joe played a prominent role in the Berkshire side's Southern Section

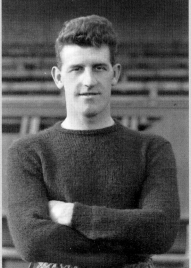

championship success of 1925–26, during which he was ever-present, and clocked up 202 League appearances in six consistent years at Elm Park before being released to join the Albion in June 1930 at the age of 32. Although on the small side for a goalkeeper, his bravery was beyond question, and he turned in some excellent performances while sharing the custodial role with Stan Webb for two seasons. Joe departed for York City on a free transfer in July 1932 where he saw out his career with seven appearances during the 1932–33 season, bringing his career total to 335 in all four sections of the Football League.

Season	FL	FAC	Total
1930–31	12	0	12
1931–32	25	3	28
Total	37	3	40

DUFFY, ALAN   1970–72

forward   Ht 5 6, Wt 10 06   *54 apps, 8 goals*
born: West Stanley, Co. Durham, 20.12.1949
debut: Bradford City (h), 17.1.1970 (FL D3)

Energetic, bustling and direct, Alan Duffy never really lived up to the early promise he showed when he was capped by England at youth level. An apprentice with Newcastle United, whom he joined from school, the young forward signed as a pro in March 1967 to become a regular scorer in the "Magpies'" Central League side, but he had made the first team on just four occasions when Freddie Goodwin paid £10,000 to bring him to the Goldstone in January 1970.

The stocky striker was an instant success in Albion's Third Division side, scoring after just eleven minutes of his debut, and retained the no.8 shirt for the remainder of the season as Albion just missed out on promotion, but an injury suffered early the following term sidelined him for some time and he was later tried unsuccessfully in a midfield role. In 1971–72 he played his part in the club's promotion success, but only as a substitute; he was called upon nine times in the first part of the season.

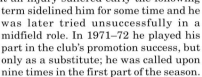

Somewhat hot-headed, Alan fell foul of officialdom on several occasions during his two years at the Goldstone, the most serious of which came in January 1972 when he was suspended for six weeks after a post-match incident with the Walsall goalkeeper. On another memorable occasion, in a goal-less draw with Preston North End in February 1971, Kit Napier was preparing to re-take a penalty when Alan ran in and blasted the ball against the crossbar, much to the anger of his team-mates, manager Pat Saward, and a near-10,000 Goldstone crowd!

In March 1972, Saward used his standby forward as part of the deal for Tranmere Rovers' Ken Beamish. Alan then remained at Prenton Park until August 1973 when he moved back to the North-East with Darlington, but after making 24 Fourth Division appearances during 1973–74 he was not retained and dropped into the Northern League with Evenwood Town and Consett. Alan's grandfather was a professional with Leeds United in the 1920s.

Season	FL	FAC	FLC	Total
1969–70	20 (6)	0	0	20 (6)
1970–71	14+7 (2)	0	1	15+7 (2)
1971–72	0+9	0+2	1	1+11
Total	34+16 (8)	0+2	2	36+18 (8)

DUGNOLLE, JACK   1933–38 & 1946–48

half-back   Ht 5 9, Wt 11 02   *74 apps*
full name: John Henry Dugnolle
born: Peshawar, North-West Frontier, India (now Pakistan), 24.3.1914
died: Worthing, Sussex, 31.8.1977
debut: Bristol Rovers (a), 2.11.1935 (FL D3(S))

When young Jack Dugnolle signed for the Albion there was a good deal of excitement, the prospect of a local lad playing for the club creating much interest, but it was not until after the war that he

became a regular in the League team, by which time he was a veteran. He was actually born in the North-West Frontier Province of British India – now in Pakistan – where his father was a subaltern in the Royal Sussex Regiment, but came to prominence at the Connaught Road School in Hove when he played for the Brighton Boys team which reached the final of the English Schools Trophy in 1928 only to lose to North Staffordshire. After winning a host of honours at schoolboy level, Jack graduated into the Sussex County League with Hove and Southwick, and it was while with the 'Wickers' that he first assisted Albion's reserve team as an amateur in February 1933.

Signed as a professional in October 1934, Jack made the first team on just seven occasions in the following four seasons and was released to join Southern League Tunbridge Wells Rangers in September 1938, but within six months he had returned to the Football League with Second Division Plymouth Argyle. The war brought a temporary halt to his career – although he played for Argyle and guested for Albion occasionally – but Jack rejoined the Goldstone staff in August 1946 at the age of 32 and played in all three half-back positions before retiring in 1948. He then remained with the club as coach to the newly formed 'A' team and often played alongside the youngsters. In 1951, Jack joined Horsham as a player and won a Metropolitan League championship medal in his first season at Queen Street, but on hanging up his boots for the last time he became coach, and later manager, of Worthing. After retiring he wrote a coaching manual, *Soccer Simplified*, and scouted for several League clubs.

Season	FL	FAC	Wartime	Total
1935–36	2	0	0	2
1936–37	1	0	0	1
1937–38	4	0	0	4
1941–42	0	0	1	1
1945–46	0	0	1	1
1946–47	32	1	0	33
1947–48	27	5	0	32
Total	66	6	2	74

DUNCLIFFE, JOHN   1963–68

left-back   Ht 5 8, Wt 10 00   *22 apps*
full name: Michael John Duncliffe
born: Brighton, Sussex, 17.9.1947
debut: Watford (h), 27.3.1967 (FL D3)

John Duncliffe showed a considerable amount of talent as a youngster, but enjoyed only limited success at the Goldstone and had to move away from his home town to achieve his potential. A pupil of St Joseph's and Fitzherbert Schools, Brighton, John skippered Brighton Boys as a centre-forward and was subsequently taken on Albion's staff as a junior. Reported to have been 'as complete a little footballer as the Brighton Boys side has produced for several years', John was also captain and star goalscorer for the Brighton Braves 'grice-hockey' team (that is 'skating' on grass).

It was as a defender that he made his name, though, signing professional forms at the age of eighteen in September 1965 and playing at left-back in the reserves before making his entrance into the League team when Bobby Baxter was out with an injury toward the end of the 1966–67 season.

The following term he won a regular place in the side when George Dalton broke his leg in late January and turned in some useful performances, but at the end of the season he was given a free transfer by manager Archie Macaulay and signed for Grimsby Town in June along with Mike Hickman.

John was a regular in the "Mariners'" Fourth Division side for two seasons, and appeared in 72 League matches before leaving for Peterborough United on a free transfer in June 1970. In three seasons with the 'Posh' he missed only eighteen League games and was often played as a central defender, but in May 1973 he was a victim of a big clear-out at London Road and dropped into the Southern League with Cambridge City. John later played for Wisbech Town.

Season	FL	Total
1966–67	2	2
1967–68	20	20
Total	22	22

DUTTON, HARRY   1929–33

left-half   Ht 5 7, Wt 11 00   104 apps, 5 goals
full name: Henry Robert Dutton
born: Edmonton, Middlesex, 16.1.1898
died: Enfield, Middlesex, 1972
debut: Crystal Palace (a), 19.10.1929 (FL D3(S))

A real 90-minute player who always gave maximum effort, Harry Dutton arrived at the Goldstone in 1929 and quickly made the left-half berth his own, missing just a handful of games until making way for Potter Smith in February 1932. After representing Edmonton Schools as a lad, the young Harry impressed the West Bromwich Albion scouts with his cleverness when playing for Tufnell Park in the Isthmian League. Joining the 'Throstles' in May 1921, he remained at The Hawthorns for six years but played in only 57 First Division matches.

DUTTON - BRIGHTON & HOVE ALBION - 1929-30.

A regular member of the reserve team, Harry won three Central League championship medals before joining fellow Division One side Bury in March 1927, and, on coming to Hove in October 1929 in his early 30s, had almost 100 First Division appearances to his name. He was a regular in the Albion side for two-and-a-half years, and remained at the Goldstone until retiring in 1933 when he was granted a permit to play for Shoreham in the Sussex County League. On leaving the Albion, Harry became mine host of the Devonshire Arms in Carlton Hill, Brighton.

Season	FL	FAC	Total
1929–30	32 (3)	6 (1)	38 (4)
1930–31	38	2	40
1931–32	23 (1)	3	26 (1)
Total	93 (4)	11 (1)	104 (5)

EACOCK, FRED   1919–20

inside-left   13 apps, 3 goals
full name: Frederick John Eacock
born: Highworth, Wiltshire, 1898
debut: Merthyr Town (h), 6.9.1919 (SL D1)

Fred Eacock was a member of a well-known local football-playing family, three of whom were on Albion's books at various times (see also "Eacock, Jack"). During the Great War he served with the Sussex Volunteer Regiment, and came to the fore as a footballer with Brighton & Hove F.C., an amateur club formed in 1915 following the closure of the Albion and which continued for the duration of the conflict.

When normal conditions were restored in 1919, Fred joined Albion as an amateur, but he also turned out for the newly formed Brighton & Hove Amateurs club (along with Teddy Elliott and Reg Phillips, q.v.) when not required at the Goldstone. After three short runs in the Southern League side, he was not signed on when the club was elected to the Football League's new Third Division in 1920. Fred later played for Southwick and Tunbridge Wells Rangers.

Season	SL	Total
1919–20	13 (3)	13 (3)
Total	13 (3)	13 (3)

EACOCK, JACK   1908–10

inside-right   1 app
full name: John Henry Eacock
born: Brighton, Sussex, 1889
debut: Northampton Town (a), 2.4.1910 (SL D1)

A member of a local football-playing clan (see also "Eacock, Fred"), Jack Eacock both grew up and went to school in Hanover Terrace, Brighton, and turned out for the town's schools representative side

before signing for the Albion as a nineteen-year-old amateur in May 1908. His arrival at the Goldstone came shortly after he appeared for Brighton Helmston in the Sussex Senior Cup final; the West Sussex Senior League side losing 3–1 to Worthing. He had also represented Sussex v. Essex at Hastings, a performance which earned him a trial with professional side Hastings & St Leonards United.

When not required by Albion, Jack turned out for Shoreham, but he was subsequently offered professional terms at the Goldstone and was a regular in the reserves for two seasons. He made just one senior appearance, as deputy for the injured Jimmy Coleman in a 1–1 draw at Northampton during the 1909–10 Southern League championship campaign. Released in May 1910, Jack returned to local football but was briefly recalled to assist the reserves during the 1913–14 season.

Season	SL	Total
1909–10	1	1
Total	1	1

EDMONDS, EDDIE   1922–29

utility player   Ht 5 9, Wt 11 06   14 apps
full name: Alfred John Edmonds
born: Brighton, Sussex, 16.10.1902
died: Bury, Lancashire, March 1942
debut: Bournemouth & B.A. (a), 24.2.1926 (FL D3(S))

Educated at St Luke's Terrace School, Brighton, 'Eddie' Edmonds gained fame in the post-Great War period as 'one of the smartest dribblers in Sussex' while playing for the Brighton-based sides Vernon Athletic and Allen West in the Sussex County League. In 1922–23 he won a County League championship medal with Vernon, and also won his Sussex county colours. Eddie turned out for Albion's reserve team as early as 1922, but didn't join the Goldstone staff as a professional until July 1925.

A highly versatile player, he appeared in the three half-back berths, at centre-forward and at inside-right in his fourteen outings with the first eleven. On leaving the Albion in August 1929, he played in turn for Clapton Orient, Bury (June 1932) and Mansfield Town (June 1934) before retiring from the Football League in 1935 to become a publican in Bury. He went on to play as a part-time professional with Manchester North End in the Manchester League.

Season	FL	Total
1925–26	5	5
1926–27	1	1
1928–29	8	8
Total	14	14

EDWARDS, ALISTAIR   1989–90

striker   *Ht 6 1, Wt 12 06*   *1 app*
full name: Alistair Martin Edwards
born: Whyalla, South Australia, 21.6.1968
debut: Leeds United (a), 16.12.1989 (FL D2)

Alistair Edwards has enjoyed only limited success in Britain in three separate spells, but he has a host of honours from Australia, his homeland, and is now the holder of more than 30 international caps. Blessed with considerable pace for a tall man, Alistair was recognised as a goalscorer at an early age: he played for the Australian youth team and moved to Canberra to learn his trade at the élite Australian Institute of Sport. In 1987 he came to the attention of British clubs during the World Youth Tournament in Chile with performances which earned him a two-year contract with Glasgow Rangers, but he left Ibrox six months early because of homesickness.

On his return down under, Alistair played for the Sydney Olympic club, represented the Australian under-21 side, and was voted

Australian under-20 Player of the Year in 1988. Arriving at the Goldstone on trial in November 1989, the 21-year-old Aussie impressed Barry Lloyd sufficiently for a deal to be arranged at a fee of £25,000 and he was taken on as a non-contract player until the transaction could be finalised, but it was then discovered that he had a pelvic condition which cast doubt on his future health and the transfer fell through. Nevertheless, he stayed on to make his Football League debut at Leeds in the absence of Kevin Bremner before returning to Australia.

Taking up his place with Sydney Olympic again, Alistair graduated to the full-international side, but moved into the flourishing Malaysian League in 1990 with Singapore, who reached the Cup final that season. One of the leading goalscorers throughout his time in Malaysia, he also played for Johor (Cup winners 1991) before returning to Singapore, then moved to Selangor. But the lure of England proved too great for the Aussie and he undertook a successful trial with Millwall in January 1995. Rewarded with a contract, Alistair found his opportunities somewhat limited at The Den and made just four League appearances for the 'Lions' before moving to Hong Kong. He then moved back to Sydney in 1996 and to Sarawak in Malaysia.

Season	FL	Total
1989–90	1	1
Total	1	1

EDWARDS, LEN   1954–55

right-half   *6 apps*
full name: Leonard Owen Edwards
born: Wrexham, Denbighshire, Wales, 30.5.1930
debut: Norwich City (h), 16.10.1954 (FL D3(S))

A tall, red-headed wing-half, Len Edwards joined Sheffield Wednesday in January 1951 and became a regular in their Central League side, but he made the first eleven just twice, appearing in two games of the Yorkshire club's Second Division championship campaign of 1951–52. In March 1954, Len signed for the Albion and made his debut at centre-forward, but his primary role was as a deputy to Harry Gilberg at right-half. He met with greater success after moving to Crewe Alexandra in the Third Division (North) in December 1955, where he made 40 League appearances before leaving the first-class game.

Season	FL	Total
1954–55	6	6
Total	6	6

EDWARDS, MATTHEW   1992–94

utility forward   *Ht 5 10, Wt 11 00*   *78 apps, 8 goals*
full name: Matthew David Edwards
born: Hammersmith, London, 15.6.1971
debut: Colchester United (a), 18.8.1992 (FLC R1 Lg1)

Although born in Hammersmith, Matthew Edwards arrived on the South Coast with his family at an early age. From the age of nine he played for Saltdean Tigers and he trained with the Albion at thirteen, but the family then moved to Surrey and the youngster was playing for Elmbridge Borough schools when he was recommended

to Tottenham Hotspur. Signing for Spurs as an associate schoolboy, he was then taken on as an apprentice and became a full professional, but he never played for the first team at White Hart Lane and made his Football League debut during a loan-spell with Reading in March 1991.

Matty also had a loan period with Peterborough United, but realised his time with Spurs was up when manager Peter Shreeves forgot his name! Arriving at the Goldstone on a free transfer in July 1992, he was played mainly in a wide role but was also occasionally as a principal striker, scoring some memorable goals in cup matches against Manchester United and Portsmouth. However, despite his keenness and effort, Matthew was unable to maintain the consistency required at Division Two level and was released at the end of 1993–94 to join Kettering Town in the Conference.

Unfortunately, he missed the entire 1994–95 season because of a serious leg injury, and moved to Walton & Hersham on loan early in 1995–96. In December 1995, Matthew signed for the Surrey side, but was transferred to Enfield the following March.

Season	FL	FAC	FLC	AMC	Total
1992–93	24+9 (2)	3+1 (1)	4 (1)	3	34+10 (4)
1993–94	25+2 (4)	1	4	2	32+2 (4)
Total	49+11 (6)	4+1 (1)	8 (1)	5	66+12 (8)

EDWARDS, SEAN   1984–87

full-back   Ht 5 9, Wt 11 07   *1 app*
full name: Sean William Edwards
born: Hastings, Sussex, 29.10.1967
debut: Crystal Palace (a), 16.10.1985 (FMC Prelim.)

Sean Edwards joined Albion's staff as an apprentice in 1984 direct from school in Bexhill. Developing his game in the reserves, he was chosen for an F.A. Colts XI v. Public Schools XI in March 1985, and was included in the squad for the Full Members Cup tie at Crystal Palace seven months later, making what was to be his only first-team appearance when he came on as a late substitute for the injured Chris Hutchings. Three weeks later he was signed as a professional.

Continuing in the Combination side for two seasons, Sean was released in May 1987 and joined Crawley Town in the Southern League. The young full-back's form at Town Mead was impressive and he became the focus of enquiries from several Football League clubs, but a shoulder injury kept him out of the game for a considerable time. Returning to the side for 1990–91, he went on to gain a Sussex Senior Cup winner's medal, but was transferred to Hythe Town for a £5,000 fee in August 1991. Sean later played for Kitchee and Instant-Dict during a three-year spell in Hong Kong, but came back to Sussex in the summer of 1996 to re-sign briefly for Crawley and then Horsham.

Season	FMC	Total
1985–86	0+1	0+1
Total	0+1	0+1

EDWARDS, W. G.   1906

inside-right   *1 app*
debut: Clapton Orient (h), 31.1.1906 (UL)

Edwards was a trialist who played in the United League fixture with Clapton Orient at the Goldstone in January 1906, which ended in a goal-less draw. He also had a couple of outings in the reserve team but was not signed.

Season	UL	Total
1905–06	1	1
Total	1	1

EGAN, HARRY   1934–36

inside-left   Ht 5 10, Wt 11 05   *23 apps, 11 goals*
born: Tibshelf, Derbyshire, 23.2.1912
died: Chesterfield, Derbyshire, 1979
debut: Newport County (a), 22.2.1934 (SSC R2)

One of several young players recruited by the Albion from the Nottinghamshire area in the 1930s, Harry Egan was signed from Sutton Town for £100 in January 1934 to fill in for the injured Potter Smith. Scoring twice on his League debut, he quickly made a name for himself and within two months Sunderland offered a four-figure fee for the 22-year-old's services, but Albion refused to release him. Nevertheless, when Smith recovered Harry was relegated to the reserves, and played in only six more League matches for the club during the next two seasons before moving on to Southend United in June 1936 and then to Aldershot the following May.

Gaining a regular first-team spot at the Recreation Ground, he played in 59 Third Division (South) matches and scored nineteen goals, form which persuaded Cardiff City to invest £1,500 for his transfer in December 1938, and he made seventeen appearances for the Welsh side until the outbreak of war. During the conflict Harry guested for Aldershot, Chesterfield, Derby County, Mansfield Town, Nottingham Forest and Swindon Town before retiring from the professional game. His father, William, played for Wales v. Scotland in 1892.

Season	FL	SSC	Total
1933–34	13 (7)	3 (2)	16 (9)
1934–35	2 (1)	1 (1)	3 (2)
1935–36	4	0	4
Total	19 (8)	4 (3)	23 (11)

ELLIOTT, MARK   1977–79

winger   Ht 5 9, Wt 11 00   *3 apps*
full name: Richard Mark Elliott
born: Rhondda, Glamorgan, Wales, 20.3.1959
debut: Shrewsbury Town (h), 15.3.1977 (FL D3)

A toolmaker by trade, Mark Elliott was a winger from Pen-y-graig in the Rhondda Valley with Boys' Club representative honours to his name, and was playing for Ton Pentre when he was recommended to Albion by John Stead, his trainer and occasional scout for Brighton. Following a successful trial, the seventeen-year-old signed for the club in February 1977 and made three League appearances shortly afterwards. In September 1977 he was selected for the Welsh youth squad, but never figured in the Brighton first team again and moved to Cardiff City on a free transfer in September 1979. After seven League outings at Ninian Park, and four during a loan-spell with AFC Bournemouth in January 1980, Mark made a brief return to Ton Pentre before enjoying a less-than-successful trial with Aldershot. He completed his League career with eleven games as a non-contract player at Wimbledon towards the end of the 1981–82 season before dropping into the Isthmian League with Walton & Hersham in 1982–83.

In 1983 the 24-year-old Welshman returned to Glamorgan permanently, settling in Tonyrefail where he turned out for the local side in the Welsh League for ten seasons and now runs a catering business.

Season	FL	Total
1976–77	3	3
Total	3	3

ELLIOTT, TEDDY   1907–15

outside-right   *6 apps, 2 goals*
full name: Edward Henry Elliott
born: Brighton, Sussex, 1887
debut: Crystal Palace (a), 2.12.1908 (WL D1 'A')

A prominent figure on the local scene for many years, Teddy Elliott joined the Albion as a 20-year-old amateur from Southwick in August 1907 and was subsequently offered professional terms. A regular in the reserve team for four seasons, he appeared in every forward position plus all the half-back berths, but was usually regarded as a winger as, despite his short and stocky build, he possessed a remarkable turn of speed and a fair degree of skill. Indeed,

he won both the 60-yard sprint and the football-dribbling race at the club's 1907 sports day.

Teddy clocked up around 100 matches for the 'Lambs' and scored twice on his debut in the Southern League side, a 5–0 win over Bristol Rovers at the Goldstone in December 1908, but played just six first-team games before being released in May 1911. Initially refused reinstatement as an amateur, he was granted permission in 1912 and subsequently rejoined Southwick, where he played a major role in the "Wickers'" Sussex Senior Cup triumph of 1913 and went on to gain numerous county honours. He also continued to assist the Albion reserves occasionally up to 1915.

After returning unscathed from wartime service with the Royal Engineers, Teddy resumed his football career and gained further local honours: a Royal Irish Rifles Cup winner's medal with Brighton & Hove Amateurs in 1920, and a County League championship and R.U.R. Cup medal with the Brighton-based Vernon Athletic in 1923 at the age of 36. He was still turning out for the Brighton & Hove Gas Company's club in the Brighton, Hove & District League into his 40s.

Season	SL	WL	Total
1908–09	5 (2)	1	6 (2)
Total	5 (2)	1	6 (2)

ELLIS, SYD — 1957–59

full-back | Ht 5 9, Wt 11 03 | 44 apps
full name: Sydney Carey Ellis
born: Charlton, Greenwich, London, 16.8.1931
debut: Crystal Palace (a), 23.11.1957 (FL D3(S))

Syd Ellis's Albion career started encouragingly – he took over the no.3 shirt from Roy Jennings a third of the way into the 1957–58 campaign and played his part in clinching the Third Division (South) championship – but went rapidly downhill the following season when he lost out in a defensive re-shuffle as manager Billy Lane sought to stem a flood of Second Division goals. Thus he was never able to fulfil the promise he had shown in his early days when he won an England under-23 cap.

A London Schools representative, Syd was educated at the Charlton Central School and played for Greenwich United as a youngster. He was also on Crystal Palace's books as an amateur, but in May 1949 he signed professional forms for his local club, Charlton Athletic. On demob from National Service with the R.A.O.C. he was

loaned to Southern League side Tonbridge to gain experience, and returned to The Valley to earn a reputation as a classy full-back. Making his First Division debut against Middlesbrough in September 1953, an 8–1 win for Charlton, he played for the England under-23s against Italy in January 1954.

After 48 League games for the 'Valiants', Syd arrived at the Goldstone for £2,000 in November 1957 and was drafted straight into the championship-winning team. However, with Albion conceding 90 goals – the worst total ever – in the Second Division in 1958–59, the 27-year-old full-back was unable to hold his place (although he did return at right-back towards the end of the season) and subsequently signed for Southern League Guildford City in August 1959. Employed in the advertising business after leaving the professional game, he returned to The Valley in the mid 1960s to coach the youth team.

Syd's football career bore amazing similarities to that of Eric Gill. Club-mates at Charlton, they were in the same unit on National

Service; were both farmed out to Tonbridge; both came to the Goldstone; and both ended up with Guildford City!

Season	FL	FAC	Total
1957–58	25	2	27
1958–59	17	0	17
Total	42	2	44

EVANS, TOM — 1921–22

right-half | Ht 5 7, Wt 10 07 | 5 apps
full name: Thomas Eli Evans
born: Dudley, Worcestershire, 1896
debut: Swindon Town (a), 1.4.1922 (FL D3(S))

Tom Evans appeared briefly for Birmingham during the 1917–18 wartime season, and signed for the 'Blues' in June 1919 from Cradley St Luke's. During the 1919–20 season he played in six Second Division matches, five of which ended in victory, but then spent the following campaign in the reserves before being released to join the Albion in August 1921. With long-serving Jack Woodhouse occupying the right-half berth, Tom's opportunity didn't arrive until the following April when he played in five successive matches during Woodhouse's absence due to an injury, but he was released at the end of the 1921–22 season and returned to the Midlands to join Cradley Heath on their elevation to the Birmingham League.

Season	FL	Total
1921–22	5	5
Total	5	5

EVERITT, MIKE — 1968–70

left-back/midfield | Ht 5 10, Wt 12 07 | 31 apps, 1 goal
full name: Michael Dennis Everitt
born: Weeley, Essex, 16.1.1941
debut: Mansfield Town (h), 10.8.1968 (FL D3)

After playing for Clacton and Essex Boys, Mike Everitt joined Arsenal's ground staff on leaving school, signed professional forms in February 1958, and remained at Highbury for a further three years, but he made the First Division team on just nine occasions. In February 1961 he joined Northampton Town where he met with greater success, appearing in 207 League matches as the 'Cobblers' won promotion from the Fourth Division to the First in five seasons (his team-mates including future Albion players Derek Leck and Charlie Livesey).

While at the County Ground, Mike was loaned to a New York club, but was transferred to Plymouth Argyle for £12,000 in March 1967 and came to the Goldstone in July 1968 for £2,500, one of manager Archie Macaulay's last signings. Although he had a lengthy run in the team during his first season at the Goldstone, Mike was never a regular choice and spent most of the time in the second string before being released in May 1970 at the age of 29.

On leaving the club he had a spell as player-manager with Plymouth City, and in April 1971 became player-manager at Wimbledon. After two years at Plough Lane, in which the 'Dons' finished in the middle of the Southern League's Premier Division, Mike took over the reins at Fourth Division Brentford in August 1973, but after two seasons at Griffin

Park he was replaced by John Docherty and moved on to Leicester City as coach under his former Arsenal colleague Jimmy Bloomfield until 1977.

Season	FL	FAC	FLC	Total
1968–69	18 (1)	3	1	22 (1)
1969–70	6+3	0	0	6+3
Total	24+3 (1)	3	1	28+3 (1)

38 players who managed Football/Premier League clubs

Player	Club	Period
Beamish, Ken	Swindon Town	1983–84
Bell, Willie	Birmingham City	1975–77
Buckley, Frank	Blackpool	1923–27
	Wolverhampton Wanderers	1927–44
	Notts County	1944–46
	Hull City	1946–48
	Leeds United	1948–53
	Walsall	1953–55
Burtenshaw, Steve	Sheffield Wednesday	1974–75
	Queen's Park Rangers	1978–79
Case, Jimmy	Brighton & Hove Albion	1995–96
Cattlin, Chris	Brighton & Hove Albion	1983–86
Clark, Paul	Southend United	1987–88
Cook, Tommy	Brighton & Hove Albion	1947
Curbishley, Alan	Charlton Athletic	1991–
Everitt, Mike	Brentford	1973–75
Fisher, Albert	Notts County	1913–27
Gregory, John	Portsmouth	1989–90
	Wycombe Wanderers	1996–
Horton, Brian	Hull City	1984–88
	Oxford United	1988–93
	Manchester City	1993–95
	Huddersfield Town	1995–
Hughes, Tommy	Hereford United	1982–83
Jennings, Sam	Rochdale	1937–38
Jones, Les	Scunthorpe United	1950–51
Kent, Harry	Watford	1910–26
Kinnear, Joe	Wimbledon	1992–
Lawrenson, Mark	Oxford United	1988
	Peterborough United	1989–90
McEwan, Bily	Sheffield United	1986–88
	Rotherham United	1988–91
	Darlington	1992–93
McGrath, John	Port Vale	1979–83
	Chester City	1984
	Preston North End	1986–90
	Halifax Town	1991–92
McHale, Ray	Scarborough	1989–93, 1994–95
McNeill, Ian	Wigan Athletic	1976–81
	Shrewsbury	1987–90
Mansell, Jack	Rotherham United	1965–67
	Reading	1969–71
Martin, Neil	Walsall	1981–82
Moore, John	Luton Town	1986–87
Napier, John	Bradford City	1978
Osman, Russell	Bristol City	1993–94
	Cardiff City	1996–
Sexton, Dave	Leyton Orient	1965
	Chelsea	1967–74
	Queen's Park Rangers	1974–77
	Manchester United	1977–81
	Coventry City	1981–83
Sirrell, Jimmy	Brentford	1967–69
	Notts County	1969–75, 1978–87
	Sheffield United	1975–77
Smillie, Neil	Gillingham	1995
Smith, Bobby	Bury	1973–77
	Port Vale	1977–78
	Swindon Town	1978–80
	Newport County	1985–86
Smith, Dave	Mansfield Town	1974–76
	Southend United	1976–83
	Plymouth Argyle	1984–88
	Torquay United	1989–91
Stapleton, Frank	Bradford City	1991–94
Webb, Charlie	Brighton & Hove Albion	1919–47
Wilkinson, Howard	Notts County	1982–83
	Sheffield Wednesday	1983–88
	Leeds United	1988–96
Wilson, Danny	Barnsley	1994–
Wilson, Glen	Exeter City	1960–62
Worthington, Frank	Tranmere Rovers	1985–87

EYRES, Jack — 1931–32

inside-left — Ht 5 8, Wt 11 00 — *11 apps, 3 goals*
full name: John Eyres
born: Lostock Gralam, Cheshire, 20.3.1899
died: Gainsborough, Lincolnshire, 2.10.1975
debut: Bristol Rovers (a), 6.2.1932 (FL D3(S))

After developing his skills in the Cheshire League with Nantwich and Witton Albion, Jack Eyres joined Stoke in June 1922 at the age of 23 and went on to play 66 League games in seven years at the Victoria Ground. In 1926–27 his twelve goals helped the 'Potters' win the Third Division (North) championship. Two years later, in May 1929, he moved on to Walsall where, in 1930–31, he finished top of the scoring charts with sixteen goals. Three of them came at Hove in a 3–3 draw, the final match at the Goldstone that season, and two weeks later Albion manager Charlie Webb secured the 32-year-old's transfer.

Much was expected of the new signing who had 37 goals to his name in 89 games for Walsall, but the continual excellence of Potter Smith at inside-left kept him out of the side until late in the season when he scored three goals in eleven games for the club. Jack left for Bristol Rovers in May 1932 and scored twelve goals in 64 Southern Section matches in two seasons at Eastville before moving to York City in July 1934, his final Football League club. After thirteen goals from 37 League appearances as captain, he moved into the Midland League as player-coach with Gainsborough Trinity. Jack was also a keen angler and a skilful bowls player.

Season	FL	Total
1931–32	11 (3)	11 (3)
Total	11 (3)	11 (3)

FARRELL, Bobby — 1928–42

outside-right — Ht 5 7, Wt 10 08 — *466 apps, 95 goals*
full name: Robert Farrell
born: Dundee, Angus, Scotland, 1.1.1906
died: Hove, Sussex, 17.1.1971
debut: Norwich City (a), 22.9.1928 (FL D3(S))

One of the greatest characters ever to grace an Albion shirt, Bobby Farrell was the comedian of the team in the 1930s, but he was also a fine footballer: his total of 466 games puts him fourth in the club's all-time list, while he stands fifth in the roll of leading scorers with 95 goals. A fixture in the side for ten years, Bobby was a huge favourite of the Goldstone crowd, and his abundant energy and tricky play down the right flank endeared him to a generation of supporters.

Bobby started out in junior football with Dundee North End and joined Dundee as a 20-year-old in August 1926, but came south to Portsmouth on a month's trial in 1928. Fortunately – for Brighton – the ebullient little Scot was not signed and came along the coast to join the Albion at the age of 22 in September 1928, winning a regular spot shortly after his arrival. Perhaps inclined to hang on to the ball a little too long initially, he soon matured into a first-rate winger and rarely missed a game for the next decade, There was a time, early in the 1936–37 campaign, when he lost form after being moved to the inside-left berth against his will and became the target of senseless barracking, but he rapidly regained popularity on returning to his usual position on the right flank and continued to turn in terrific performances until giving way to Stan Hurst in 1938–39.

Bobby retired at the end of that season to become landlord of the Adur Hotel on Hove sea-front, but returned to assist the club in the wartime competitions until 1941 having joined the R.A.F. in December 1940. After playing his last Albion game at the age of 35, he maintained a keen interest in the club right to the end and seldom missed a home game. Also a fine cricketer, he acted as twelfth man and baggage manager to the Sussex C.C.C. from 1933 to 1939. At the time of his death in 1971, Bobby was landlord of the Nevill Hotel in Hove. His funeral at the Downs Crematorium was attended by club chairman Tom Whiting together with many fans and former players.

Season	FL	FAC*	SSC	Wartime	Total
1928–29	32 (4)	1	0	0	33 (4)
1929–30	37 (6)	5 (1)	0	0	42 (7)
1930–31	38 (5)	2	0	0	40 (5)
1931–32	38 (8)	3 (2)	0	0	41 (10)
1932–33*	41 (10)	11 (6)	0	0	52 (16)
1933–34	41 (6)	3 (1)	4	0	48 (7)
1934–35	36 (5)	3 (1)	3	0	42 (6)
1935–36	35 (6)	5 (4)	1 (1)	0	41 (11)
1936–37	35 (7)	1	1	0	37 (7)
1937–38	39 (3)	4 (2)	1	0	44 (5)
1938–39	10 (6)	0	0	0	10 (6)
1939–40	0	0	0	28 (11)	28 (11)
1940–41	0	0	0	8	8
Total	382 (66)	38 (17)	10 (1)	36 (11)	466 (95)

Note: Four appearances and five goals of Farrell's 1932–33 F.A. Cup total came in the qualifying competition.

FARRELL, PADDY   1901–04

right-half   Ht 5 9, Wt 11 04   51 apps, 1 goal
full name: Patrick Farrell
born: Legoniel, Belfast, Co. Antrim, Ireland, c. 1871
died: Hove, Sussex, 1950
debut: Brighton Athletic (h), 21.9.1901 (FAC Prelim.)

The first full international to play for the Albion, Paddy Farrell was one of the stars of the club's early years and played in every game of the first season, 1901–02. Born in Belfast, he began his senior career with Distillery and helped the club to an Irish League-and-Cup double in 1895–96. He spent the following season in Scotland with Celtic, playing mainly a reserve role, but had the somewhat dubious honour of making the first team for a first-round Scottish Cup tie in which the famed Glasgow club were sensationally beaten 4–2 by non-League Arthurlie.

In May 1897, Paddy came south to join Second Division Woolwich Arsenal, and arrived in Sussex twelve months later, one of the first players to be recruited by the newly formed Brighton United club. The fleet-footed Irishman remained at the County Ground throughout United's brief existence, appearing in 57 competitive matches, but returned to Belfast with Distillery when the club folded in the spring of 1900.

It was then that he won Irish caps against Scotland and Wales, and also represented the Irish League v. Scottish League during the 1900–01 season, but when the Albion were formed in the summer of 1901 he returned to Hove to play for the new club until his retirement in May 1904.

Paddy lived in Westbourne Street, Hove, for many years until his death at the age of 79. One of his sons, Cyril, starred locally with Southwick and Hastings & St Leonards between the wars.

Season	SL	Test	FAC	SEL	Total
1901–02	16	0	4	0	20
1902–03	7	1	5	13 (1)	26 (1)
1903–04	4	0	1	0	5
Total	27	1	10	13 (1)	51 (1)

FARRINGTON, MARK   1991–94

forward   Ht 5 10, Wt 11 12   33 apps, 4 goals
full name: Mark Anthony Farrington
born: Liverpool, Lancashire, 15.6.1965
debut: Watford (h), 14.9.1991 (FL D2)

As Albion's fortunes started to tumble in 1991, Mark Farrington became one of the main targets for the Goldstone crowd's frustration. Signed by manager Barry Lloyd for £60,000, he was beset by injury problems throughout his career in Sussex, never looked fully fit, and proved incapable of filling the considerable vacancy left by erstwhile striker Mike Small. Indeed, the unfortunate Liverpudlian almost personified the crisis in which the club found itself.

While attending Hillfoot School in Liverpool and playing for the Allerton youth side, Mark was an associate schoolboy with Everton and became an apprentice at the age of sixteen. He started off well at Goodison, scoring four goals in the F.A. Youth Cup final of 1983 when the Everton youngsters lost out to Norwich City over two legs and a replay. It was a performance remembered well in Norfolk, for when he was released by the Merseyside club without making a first-team appearance in May 1983, Norwich snapped him up, but in two seasons with the 'Canaries' he produced only a couple of goals from fourteen First Division appearances and had a ten-match loan-spell with Cambridge United from March 1985.

Mark left for Cardiff City on a free transfer during the summer of 1985 and scored three goals in 31 League appearances for the Welsh side before being released for a breach of club discipline. With a fruitless trial at Portsmouth behind him, the 21-year-old forward set out on a career on the Continent in 1986 and had better luck, playing in turn for Willem II (Netherlands), Racing Genk (Belgium) and Fortuna Sittard (Netherlands). It was with the Fortuna club that Mark enjoyed the most fruitful part of his career: he scored a hat-trick against PSV Eindhoven and hit four goals against Volendam, a performance which persuaded Hertha Berlin (West Germany) to sign him up, but he spent just eight months with the German club before moving to Feyenoord (Netherlands) after scoring twice in a trial match for the Dutch side. However, a change of coach caused problems for the nomadic striker and he was unable to claim a place in the Rotterdam-based club's first team.

In March 1991, Mark came to the Goldstone on trial and scored inside ten seconds on his first appearance for the reserves, but it wasn't until August that he was signed. The fee for the 26-year-old was scheduled to rise to £100,000 after an agreed number of appearances – a sizeable sum for a cash-strapped club to pay for a player of little pedigree – but he was plagued by injuries and failed to show any form whatsoever at the Goldstone.

After nearly three barren years in Hove he was released in May 1994, the same month he captained the reserves to a Sussex Senior Cup final triumph against Peacehaven & Telscombe. Mark turned down offers from Hereford United (where he made one League appearance as a substitute) and Walsall, and was playing in Hong Kong late in 1994. In 1995–96 he returned to England with Runcorn, where he played in five Conference games, before moving on to Telford United for an even shorter spell in February 1996. He has also played football in Norway.

Season	FL	FLC	FMC	AMC	Total
1991–92	8+6 (1)	0+2	2	0	10+8 (1)
1992–93	3+5 (2)	0	0	0	3+5 (2)
1993–94	4+2 (1)	0	0	1	5+2 (1)
Total	15+13 (4)	0+2	2	1	18+15 (4)

FASHANU, JUSTIN   1985–86

striker   Ht 6 1, Wt 12 07   20 apps, 2 goals
full name: Justinus Soni Fashanu
born: Hackney, London, 19.2.1961
debut: Grimsby Town (h), 17.8.1985 (FL D2)

One of the most controversial players of recent years, Justin Fashanu commanded some huge fees during his career, but was never able to reproduce the form that catapulted him to fame as a teenager with Norwich City. Because of some notorious clashes with Albion players before he joined the club, he was never very popular with the Goldstone fans, and a lack of form during his time in Sussex – just two goals in 20 games – did little to help his cause. Unable to fulfil his early potential, he was eventually overtaken by his younger brother John, the former England international and TV presenter.

The son of African parents, Justin was cared for by Dr Barnado's before being fostered by a Norfolk family. The strapping youngster was an outstanding schoolboy boxer and worked as a steel-erector before joining Norwich as an apprentice, but then enjoyed a rapid rise to fame as an aggressive centre-forward after signing as a professional in December 1978. A record of 40 goals – many of them quite spectacular – in 103 League and Cup games for the 'Canaries' earned him England honours at youth, under-21 (eleven caps in total) and B levels, and established him as one of the most exciting prospects in the Football League.

After a summer in Australia playing for Adelaide City in 1980, Justin was transferred to Nottingham Forest for £1 million in August

1981 at the age of 20, but his time at the City Ground under Brian Clough was little short of disastrous and he was loaned to Southampton for two months at the beginning of the 1982–83 season. Still considered a prospect, he scored a goal in England's 5–4 aggregate triumph over West Germany in the final of the 1982 European under-21 championship while on the staff at The Dell. In December 1982, though, Forest sold their unhappy striker to Notts County for just £150,000, and he scored 20 goals in 64 League games at Meadow Lane before arriving at the Goldstone in June 1985 for a £115,000 fee.

There were, however, already doubts about Justin's fitness when he came to Hove and an exploratory operation on his left knee sidelined him for a month. On his return, though, it was the *right* knee that became a problem, and after four months at a rehabilitation centre he was forced to retire in July 1986 at the age of 25. Following a long legal battle over insurance, Justin's contract was eventually paid up in January 1987. It appeared to be a sad end to a career which had at one time promised so much, but he was determined not to give in and fought his way back to fitness in America, later playing for Los Angeles Heat and Edmonton Brickmen in the North American Soccer League.

In October 1989, after an absence of three years, Justin made a return to the Football League with two substitute appearances for First Division Manchester City. He then had further trials with West Ham United (November 1989), Ipswich Town (February 1990), Leyton Orient (March 1990) and Newcastle United (October 1991), and played non-League football for Southall and Leatherhead. It was at this time that the Hackney-born forward 'came out' and protested against discrimination within the game because of his sexual preferences, but he then joined Torquay United in December 1991 and became player/assistant manager in June 1992. Justin resigned in January 1993 and joined Airdrieonians in the Scottish League Premier Division.

The controversial striker then played very briefly for the Swedish club Trelleborg before joining Heart of Midlothian during the close

season of 1993, but left Tynecastle under a cloud following adverse newspaper publicity in February 1994. Two months later Justin was coaching in the U.S.A., and signed for the Wellington-based Miramar Rangers in October 1996 to become the highest-paid player in New Zealand. In 1997 he was turning out for Atlanta Ruckus in the United States' A-League.

Season	FL	FAC	FLC	Total
1985–86	16 (2)	3	1	20 (2)
Total	16 (2)	3	1	20 (2)

FEARON, RON   1988

goalkeeper   Ht 6 0, Wt 11 12   7 apps
full name: Ronald Thomas Fearon
born: Romford, Essex, 19.11.1960
debut: Swindon Town (a), 24.9.1988 (FL D2)

Once an apprentice with Queen's Park Rangers, Ron Fearon was playing for Dover in the Southern League when he joined Reading in February 1980. It proved a good move for the Essex-born 'keeper, who went on to make 67 League and Cup appearances for the 'Royals' before moving to California with the San Diego Sockers in 1983. On his return to England he rejoined Dover, then moved to Sutton United where he was selected as a reserve for the England semi-professional team. It was while with Sutton that Ron first caught the eye of Albion manger Barry Lloyd, but it was with Ipswich Town in August 1987 that he returned to the Football League fold after a five-year absence.

In September 1988, with the Goldstone in the grip of a goalkeeping injury crisis, the confident 27-year-old arrived in Hove on loan and quickly won the admiration of the crowd, but he was recalled to Portman Road five weeks later and a request for a further loan-period was refused. Ron made just 28 League appearances for Ipswich, but the Suffolk club retained his registration for some years.

Over the next few seasons he played for Wichita Wings in the U.S. Major Indoor Soccer League from 1989 to 1991; joined Leyton Orient for a trial period in November 1991; spent time at Heart of Midlothian during 1991–92 (but could not shift the consistent Henry Smith); played for Berlin in the German Second Division in 1992–93; had a one-match loan-spell with Walsall in February 1993; played for Sutton United, Billericay Town and Grays Athletic in the Isthmian League; and spent some of the 1993–94 campaign on the Southend United staff without appearing in the first team.

In September 1995 he re-signed for Third Division Leyton Orient as reserve goalkeeper, and made eighteen League appearances before joining Columbus Crew for the inaugural season of the U.S. Major Soccer League in 1996. During 1996–97, Ron played for Chelmsford City in the Southern League before moving to Dover Athletic in the Conference.

Season	FL	Total
1988–89	7	7
Total	7	7

FEATHERSTONE, GEORGE   1909–10

inside-right   22 apps, 9 goals
born: Middlesbrough, Yorkshire, 1885
debut: Portsmouth (a), 1.9.1909 (SL D1)

Sheffield United recognised the potential of 22-year-old George Featherstone in February 1908 when they signed him as a professional from Stockton a couple of months before the County Durham side clinched their second successive Northern League championship. Born in neighbouring Middlesbrough, the young forward had enjoyed a successful spell with Stockton, reaching the Amateur Cup final in 1907 when he picked up a runner's-up medal in a 2–1 defeat by Clapton at Stamford Bridge.

With eleven goals from 29 First Division outings for the 'Blades' to his name, George was a fine prospect when Albion signed him on a free transfer in the summer of 1909, and he became an essential member of the Southern League championship side of 1909–10. Although dogged by injury, he formed a splendid understanding with Bert Longstaff down the right wing, but left the Goldstone Ground at the end of the season and returned to junior football. A tall, elegant inside-forward, George maintained a good scoring-rate throughout his brief professional career.

Season	SL	SCC	Total
1909–10	21 (8)	1 (1)	22 (9)
Total	21 (8)	1 (1)	22 (9)

FEEBERY, Jack   1921–24

full-back   Ht 6 0, Wt 12 00   67 apps, 3 goals
full name: John Henry Feebery*
born: Hucknall, Nottinghamshire, 10.5.1888
died: Nottingham, Nottinghamshire, 1960
debut: Southend United (h), 27.8.1921 (FL D3(S))

It was a misunderstanding between the Exeter City chairman and his manager Arthur Chadwick, who was on a scouting mission in Manchester, which resulted in Jack Feebery being put on the free-transfer list in August 1921. Albion manager Charlie Webb quickly stepped in, signing burly full-back before the mistake could be rectified, and promptly made the experienced defender his skipper. Exeter's loss was Brighton's gain, and the 33-year-old went on to play

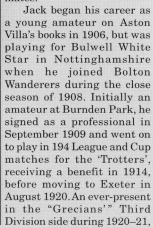

in every match during his first season at the Goldstone, an inspiration to his team-mates.

Jack began his career as a young amateur on Aston Villa's books in 1906, but was playing for Bulwell White Star in Nottinghamshire when he joined Bolton Wanderers during the close season of 1908. Initially an amateur at Burnden Park, he signed as a professional in September 1909 and went on to play in 194 League and Cup matches for the 'Trotters', receiving a benefit in 1914, before moving to Exeter in August 1920. An ever-present in the "Grecians'" Third Division side during 1920–21, he made his unexpected entrance at the Goldstone the following season and spent three years in Hove. Granted a free transfer in 1924, the 36-year-old moved into the Southern League with the South Wales club Mid Rhondda.

Jack's younger brothers were also professional footballers: Albert played for Coventry City and Crystal Palace, while Harold was with Derby County, Bolton Wanderers and Mansfield Town.

Season	FL	FAC	Total
1921–22	42 (1)	3	45 (1)
1922–23	17 (2)	2	19 (2)
1923–24	3	0	3
Total	62 (3)	5	67 (3)

Note: Jack is referred to as 'Feebury' in some documents and publications, but his real name was 'Feebery'.

FELL, Gerry   1974–77

winger/midfield   Ht 5 11, Wt 11 09   91 apps, 20 goals
full name: Gerald Charles Fell
born: Newark, Nottinghamshire, 1.3.1951
debut: Colchester United (h), 25.1.1975 (FL D3)

The sight of Gerry Fell striding down the right flank to deliver a cross or fire in a thunderbolt shot was a sight that gave pleasure to many Albion fans. Unusually tall for a winger, the former bank clerk from Nottinghamshire was a schoolboy high-jump and 800 metres champion, and possessed devastating pace. Gerry's football career began with Stamford, but after playing well against Long Eaton United in an F.A. Cup tie, he was signed by the latter club. In 1974, Brian Daykin, the former manager of the Midland Counties League side, became assistant to Peter Taylor at the Goldstone and persuaded his boss to give his former winger a trial. The lanky 23-year-old proved a success and left his job to sign as a professional for the Albion in November 1974.

For most of his time at Hove, Gerry vied with Tony Towner for the right-wing berth, but he still made 23 League appearances in the 1976–77 Third Division promotion campaign, scoring four goals. In November 1977 he left for Southend United as part of the deal which brought Paul Clark to Brighton, and played in 45 League matches at Roots Hall before moving to Torquay United in July 1980. After five games on loan at York City in March 1982, Gerry returned to the Brighton area and played for Whitehawk for six years while working in the insurance industry. He skippered the 'Hawks' to the Sussex County League title in 1983–84, and also led the Sussex representative team.

Season	FL	FAC	FLC	Total
1974–75	20 (5)	0	0	20 (5)
1975–76	25+4 (7)	3 (1)	0+1	28+5 (8)
1976–77	19+4 (4)	0+1	3+1	22+6 (4)
1977–78	1+6 (3)	0	1+2	2+8 (3)
Total	65+14 (19)	3+1 (1)	4+4	72+19 (20)

FERGUSON, Mick   1984–86

striker   Ht 6 1, Wt 12 08   21 apps, 7 goals
full name: Michael John Ferguson
born: Newcastle upon Tyne, Northumberland, 3.10.1954
debut: Birmingham City (h), 6.10.1984 (FL D2)

Mick Ferguson will be remembered by many Albion fans as a largely ineffective centre-forward, but his overall tally of 84 goals from 207 League appearances for five clubs, mainly in the top flight, bears testimony to an otherwise successful career. Although he represented Newcastle as a schoolboy, Mick became an apprentice with Coventry City and signed as a professional in December 1971. He then had to wait three years to make the first team, but went on to form a powerful partnership up front with Ian Wallace, scoring 51 goals in 127 First Division games for the 'Sky Blues' before Everton paid £280,000 for his transfer in August 1981.

The tall striker struggled to make the senior team at Goodison Park, though, scoring just once in seven outings before moving to Birmingham City on loan in November 1982. Eight goals in 20 League matches during the remainder of the 1982–83 season persuaded City to pay £60,000 for his services in June, but a series of injuries kept him out of the side and he returned to Coventry on loan in March 1984.

In September 1984, Mick arrived at the Goldstone as part of the deal for Mark Jones, the Albion full-back moving to Birmingham, but

he struggled to make an impact at Hove and took a good deal of criticism from the fans who expected great things from him. Powerful in the air, he scored seven goals in 21 outings, but five of them came from just eight games during his one successful spell early in 1985–86. In March 1986, at the age of 31, he moved on to Colchester United and scored seven times in ten Fourth Division matches during the remainder of the season. On his release from Layer Road in May 1987, Mick played for Wealdstone in the Football Conference, after which he returned to his native North-East as Sunderland's community football officer until 1996.

Season	FL	FAC	FLC	Total
1984–85	8 (1)	0	1	9 (1)
1985–86	9 (5)	1	2 (1)	12 (6)
Total	17 (6)	1	3 (1)	21 (7)

FERRIER, JOHN 1946–47

centre-forward 1 app, 1 goal
born: Edinburgh, Midlothian, Scotland, 6.10.1927
debut: Torquay United (a), 21.12.1946 (FL D3(S))

John Ferrier came to the Goldstone Ground as a nineteen-year-old amateur in July 1946, and was one of no fewer than eight players tried out at centre-forward during the first post-war season. Signed as a professional in October, he made his debut at Torquay – when Frank Hindley became stranded on a difficult rail journey from his home in the Midlands – and scored in a 3–1 defeat, but it proved to be his only first-team outing and he was released at the end of the season.

On leaving the Albion, John drove a taxi in Brighton for some time before returning to Scotland where he subsequently played for the Glasgow junior club Ashfield (signed April 1948) and for Clyde (June 1953). In May 1956 he was transferred to Exeter City, and played in 32 senior matches at left-back at St James's Park before joining Yeovil Town in the Southern League on a free transfer in May 1957.

Season	FL	Total
1946–47	1 (1)	1 (1)
Total	1 (1)	1 (1)

FFENNELL, EDGAR 1901–03

outside-left 1 app
full name: Edgar Molineux Ffennell
born: Cuckfield, Sussex, 1877
debut: Hitchin Town (a), 18.4.1903 (SEL)

Edgar Ffennell's family owned a wine-merchant's business in Western Road, Brighton, and were also shareholders in Brighton United, the first professional football club in the area. Indeed, Edgar himself turned out as an amateur for United's reserves on occasion. He also appeared with Brighton Hornets, Brighton Athletic and Brighton & Hove Rangers, and was Albion's outside-left in their first-ever game, a 2–0 friendly win over Shoreham in September 1901. Edgar assisted the first-team in April 1902 in the absence of Ben

Garfield, and contributed to a 1–0 win at Hitchin Town in the South Eastern League.

Season	SEL	Total
1902–03	1	1
Total	1	1

FISHER, ALBERT 1905–06

inside-right Ht 5 8, Wt 11 04 20 apps, 8 goals
full name: Albert William Fisher
born: Birmingham, Warwickshire, February 1881
died: Nottingham, Nottinghamshire, 4.12.1937
debut: Millwall (h), 2.9.1905 (SL D1)

An exceptionally swift inside-forward – he was the Aston Villa 150-yard sprint champion of 1902 – Albert Fisher played his early football in Birmingham junior circles with Ashbury Richmond (Handsworth & District League champions 1900–01) and Soho Caledonians (Small Heath & District League champions 1901–02) before joining Villa as a professional in August 1902. Three months later he made his First Division debut in a 4–2 defeat of Bolton Wanderers at Villa Park, but, with so many great players on the staff, it proved to be his only outing in the first team.

Albert enjoyed by far the most successful part of his career following his transfer to Bristol City in August 1903, where he partnered another future Albion player, Dick Wombwell, on the left flank and scored 21 goals in 50 Second Division matches, but his sojourn at Ashton Gate lasted only two seasons and he was released in May 1905 to be quickly snapped up by the Albion management.

Unfortunately, the 24-year-old's subsequent career then took a downward trend. He failed to reproduce his Bristol City form at the Goldstone and was employed as deputy for Proctor Hall during his only season on the South Coast. A move to Manchester City followed in June 1906, but again he failed to make an impact, appearing in just five First Division matches. City released Albert at the end of the 1906–07 season, but he was soon recruited by the newly formed Bradford (Park Avenue) club and played in the Yorkshire side's first-ever match which, somewhat strangely, was in the Southern League. He was not a success, though, and moved on to Coventry City during the summer of 1908 on their election to the Southern League.

After an equally modest season at Highfield Road, Albert joined Merthyr Town and was subsequently installed as player-manager, leading the Welsh club to the Southern League Division Two title in 1912. A year later he took over as manager of Notts County and led the 'Magpies' twice to the Second Division championship before leaving the post in 1927.

Season	SL	UL	Total
1905–06	8	12 (8)	20 (8)
Total	8	12 (8)	20 (8)

FITCH, BARRY 1961–64

left-back Ht 5 7, Wt 10 07 1 app
full name: Barry Edward Fitch
born: Brighton, Sussex, 19.11.1943
debut: Oxford United (a), 18.9.1963 (FL D4)

A former Brighton Boys representative, Barry Fitch joined the Albion as a junior and was signed as a professional in November 1961, but had to wait almost two years to make what was to be his only appearance in the first eleven. A poor start to the 1963–64 Fourth

Division campaign, coupled with injuries to Bill Cassidy and Jack Bertolini, gave Barry his opportunity at left-back, and he helped the side to a fine 3–1 win at Oxford.

Released in March 1964 to join Western League Salisbury (along with colleague Phil Gilbert), the Brighton-born defender became something of an institution with the Wiltshire side and remained with them for nine years as they entered the Southern League. Barry later turned out for Basingstoke Town and Frome Town, but returned to Salisbury in 1975 for a second, three-year spell to take his appearances there to a club-record total of 713. He ended his playing days with Cowes on the Isle of Wight and then West End near Southampton.

Season	FL	Total
1963–64	1	1
Total	1	1

FITCHIE, TOM   1907

inside-left   *1 app*
full name: Thomas Tindal Fitchie
born: Edinburgh, Midlothian, Scotland, 11.12.1881
died: Wandsworth, London, 17.10.1947
debut: Brentford (h), 2.10.1907 (WL)

One of the leading amateurs of his day, Tom Fitchie was noted for his terrific dribbling skills and played in four full internationals for Scotland. Although Scottish by birth, he spent his early days in London and, after representing South London Schools, played for West Norwood over a number of years; he also appeared once for Tottenham Hotspur in the Southern League during the 1901–02 season. Tom subsequently played extensively for Woolwich Arsenal and Queen's Park (Glasgow), during which time he gained his Scottish caps, and also appeared with London Caledonians, Norwich City, Glossop and Fulham.

As an amateur Tom was a free agent, and guested as such for the Albion in a goal-less Western League match with Brentford in October 1907.

Season	WL	Total
1907–08	1	1
Total	1	1

FLANNERY, TOM   1912–13

inside-forward   *Ht 5 8, Wt 11 07*   *14 apps, 9 goals*
full name: Thomas Flannery
born: Liverpool, Lancashire, 1890
debut: Southampton (a), 2.10.1912 (SA)

Having previously played for the Staffordshire side Leek, Tom Flannery was signed from the Potteries club Hanley Swifts at the age of 22 in May 1912, and scored prolifically for the Albion reserves. During 1912–13 he netted 24 goals from 30 outings for the 'Lambs', and played a big part in the club's run to the Southern Charity Cup final – contested mainly by the second eleven that season – with five goals in six matches; indeed, he scored a hat-trick in a 3–1 win over Reading in a second-round replay at the Goldstone.

In February 1913, Tom made his debut for the Southern League side and scored a second-half equaliser in a 1–1 draw at Southampton.

He was unfortunate, though, to have to compete with the likes of Charlie Webb, Bobby Simpson and Billy Miller for the two inside-forward berths and was consequently unable to sustain a decent run in the first team. In May 1913, Tom was released from the Albion staff to join Chester in the Lancashire Combination.

Season	SL	SA	SCC	Total
1912–13	5 (2)	3 (2)	6 (5)	14 (9)
Total	5 (2)	3 (2)	6 (5)	14 (9)

FLATTS, MARK   1993–94

utility forward   *Ht 5 6, Wt 9 08*   *10 apps, 1 goal*
full name: Mark Michael Flatts
born: Haringey, Middlesex, 14.10.1972
debut: Cambridge United (h), 1.1.1994 (FL D2)

Although he made his League debut for Arsenal in September 1992, Mark Flatts made just a handful of appearances for the 'Gunners' and enjoyed more productive spells on loan to other clubs. A representative of both Haringey and Middlesex schools, the diminutive winger spent two years at the F.A.'s National School of Excellence and joined the Highbury staff as a trainee upon his graduation from Lilleshall. He went on to win England youth honours, but found it almost impossible to break into the first team and was loaned to Cambridge United for five matches in October 1993.

With ten League games for Arsenal behind him, Mark arrived at the Goldstone on a temporary basis in January 1994 under new manager Liam Brady. The 21-year-old quickly impressed with his ball-skills and pace, and was also used as a striker during his two months in Sussex, but, having played his part in securing the Albion's position in Division Two, he returned to Highbury to remain on the fringe of the first team. In March 1995 he joined Bristol City on loan, playing six games, and a year later joined Grimsby Town on a similar arrangement with a view to a permanent transfer. However, although he impressed initially, Mark returned to London in disgrace, having missed training and two reserve games at Blundell Park without permission. Released by Arsenal during the summer of 1996, he joined the Italian side Torino on trial, but quickly returned to England with Manchester City in September and then Watford. He failed to make an impression at either club and moved on to Kettering Town where he made two Conference appearances.

Season	FL	Total
1993–94	9+1 (1)	9+1 (1)
Total	9+1 (1)	9+1 (1)

FLOOD, PAUL   1967–71

forward   *Ht 5 8, Wt 10 09*   *41 apps, 8 goals*
full name: Paul Anthony Flood
born: Dublin, Co. Dublin, Eire, 29.6.1948
debut: Colchester United (h), 23.8.1967 (FLC R1)

An international for the Republic of Ireland at schoolboy, youth and amateur levels, Paul Flood played for the Bohemians club of Dublin and had a spell with Coventry City before arriving in Hove in June 1967. (He also won an All-Ireland Gaelic football medal.) The Dublin-born forward remained with the Albion for four seasons, mainly as a fringe player, but had a good run in the team in the first half of the 1968–69 campaign when he also turned out at left-back on occasion.

On being given a free transfer in May 1971, Paul moved into the Southern League for a lengthy spell with Tonbridge, and subsequently enjoyed a distinguished career with a number of local clubs: he saw service with Eastbourne United, Horsham, Southwick, Worthing, Shoreham, and Peacehaven & Telscombe at various times, during which he represented Sussex. In the early 1990s, Paul was playing alongside his son in Worthing's reserve team, and turned out in the Sussex Sunday League for many years. He now works in the insurance industry.

Season	FL	FAC	FLC	Total
1967–68	11+3 (3)	0	0+1 (1)	11+4 (4)
1968–69	17 (3)	2	3	22 (3)
1970–71	4 (1)	0	0	4 (1)
Total	32+3 (7)	2	3+1 (1)	37+4 (8)

FORD, G. W. 1910–12

inside-right 1 app
debut: Queen's Park Rangers (a), 4.3.1911 (SL D1)

Ford was a talented amateur from the Isthmian League club Dulwich Hamlet who assisted the Albion occasionally over two seasons, 1910–12. He made three appearances for the 'Lambs', scoring in each match, and had one outing in the Southern League side, a goal-less draw at Queen's Park Rangers. In 1912–13 he was turning out for the Brighton-based club Vernon Athletic in the West Sussex Senior League.

Season	SL	Total
1910–11	1	1
Total	1	1

FOREMAN, Denis 1952–62

inside/outside-left Ht 5 8, Wt 10 07 219 apps, 69 goals
full name: Denis Joseph Foreman
born: Cape Town, South Africa, 1.2.1933
debut: Aldershot (h), 25.10.1952 (FL D3(S))

Whether wearing the no.10 shirt or no.11, Denis Foreman performed admirably for more than 200 games down the Albion left during the 1950s and contributed much to the splendid entertainment that was produced at the Goldstone during that era. With his natural ball-control and distribution, the popular little South African created many goal opportunities for his colleagues while maintaining a good scoring-rate himself with 69 goals from 219 appearances.

A product of the Hibernian club of Cape Town, Denis was working for the Post Office in his native city when Leeds United and Glasgow Celtic both made overtures for his signature, but the deals fell through. Instead, he came to the Goldstone as a nineteen-year-old trialist in February 1952 on the recommendation of his compatriot Dirk Kemp, the former Liverpool goalkeeper who had guested for the Albion during the Second World War. Denis performed well during his trial period, and, after signing professional forms in March 1952, broke into the League side at outside-left the following October to the exclusion of Frankie Howard, the winger with whom he was to form a great partnership.

Equally at home at either inside- or outside-left, he gave fine service to the club for ten years. In 1954, Denis was selected for an F.A. XI v. Oxford University, and played for a team of

'Anglo-Springboks' v. Scotland at Ibrox in March 1956. He was also an essential member of Albion's 1957–58 Southern Section championship side, netting ten goals in 37 matches, but an injury early the following season kept him out for a long spell. Denis's first-team outings subsequently diminished and he was released in the summer of 1962 to join Hastings United for a season in the Southern League. That was followed by spells as player-coach with Wigmore Athletic and Steyning Town in the Sussex County League.

Denis was also a fine cricketer, and played for Western Province in South Africa in 1951–52, and for Sussex as a middle-order batsman from 1952 to 1967 (capped 1966). His highest score in 130 matches for Sussex was 104 v. Nottinghamshire at Hove in July 1967. The following year he was appointed sports master at Seaford College, Petworth, and has held a similar post at Shoreham College since 1974.

On his arrival at Southampton docks in 1952, Denis was carrying three cricket bats, departure gifts from his pals in Cape Town, when he was greeted by a concerned Billy Lane. The Albion manager hastily inquired of the young South African: 'You do realise that we're a *football* club?'

Season	FL	FAC	Total
1952–53	17 (6)	0	17 (6)
1953–54	34 (8)	0	34 (8)
1954–55	25 (8)	2 (1)	27 (9)
1955–56	40 (12)	2 (3)	42 (15)
1956–57	45 (16)	2	47 (16)
1957–58	37 (10)	2 (2)	39 (12)
1958–59	3 (1)	0	3 (1)
1959–60	4 (2)	0	4 (2)
1960–61	6	0	6
Total	211 (63)	8 (6)	219 (69)

FORSTER, Derek 1974–76

goalkeeper Ht 5 9, Wt 11 02 3 apps
born: Newcastle upon Tyne, Northumberland, 19.2.1949
debut: Walsall (a), 1.10.1974 (FL D3)

On 22 August 1964, Sunderland apprentice Derek Forster became the youngest player ever to appear in the old First Division when he stood in for the injured Jim Montgomery in a 3–3 draw against Leicester City at the tender age of 15 years 185 days. Three months later he kept goal for the England Schoolboys team! Signed as a professional in December 1965, he was a member of Sunderland's F.A. Youth Cup-winning side in 1967, but failed to realise his early promise and made just eighteen League appearances in eight years at Roker.

Released to join Third Division Charlton Athletic on a free transfer in July 1973, Derek played second fiddle to John Dunn at The Valley until joining Albion on a free transfer in July 1974 as cover for Peter Grummitt. He made his first-team debut in a 6–0 defeat at Walsall in October 1974, but made just two more appearances and was suspended by the club for a week at one stage for a breach of discipline. In May 1976, Derek was released, thereby bringing his League career to a close, and in 1980–81 he was back in Sunderland, playing for Roker F.C. in the Wearside League.

Season	FL	Total
1974–75	3	3
Total	3	3

FOSTER 1906

inside-right 1 app
debut: New Brompton (a), 2.4.1906 (UL)

Foster was a trialist who had one outing in April 1906. He partnered Joe Lumley on the right in place of regular inside-forward Proctor Hall, but he failed to impress as Albion lost 2–0 at New Brompton.

Season	UL	Total
1905–06	1	1
Total	1	1

FOSTER, STEVE   1979–84 & 1992–96

centre-half   *Ht 6 2, Wt 13 07*   *332 apps, 15 goals*
full name: Stephen Brian Foster
born: Portsmouth, Hampshire, 24.9.1957
debut: Cambridge United (h), 28.8.1979 (FLC R2 Lg1)

Steve Foster presided over the Albion defence for four years in Division One before continuing a successful career away from Sussex, but returned eight years later to oversee the back line in less happy times. In more than 300 appearances for the club, the veteran defender rarely had a bad game, and was the dominant personality in the side whenever he played, an inspirational skipper. One of only three Albion players to gain full-international caps for England and a veteran of 669 League games, Steve was one of the game's best-known defenders of recent years, especially with his distinctive white headband 'trademark', a legacy of 30 stitches in his forehead.

Yet, as a youngster, Steve played as a striker for Portsmouth and Hampshire Schools, when he also trained with Southampton. He wasn't offered an apprenticeship at The Dell, though, and instead joined Portsmouth as a trainee forward, making his senior debut at the age of seventeen and signing professional forms in October 1975. A year later he was tried at centre-half during an injury crisis and was an immediate success, so much so that he retained "Pompey's" no.5 shirt until signing for the Albion in July 1979 for the club's first campaign in the First Division. The fee was £150,000 in a deal which proved to be a bargain for the 'Seagulls'.

With Andy Rollings injured early on in the season, 'Fozzie' came into the side and held his place; he had thereby appeared in

all four divisions of the Football League by the age of 21. Although he came to the Goldstone with something of a 'wild man' reputation, he matured rapidly, and quickly made the centre-half role his own. Indeed, he was voted Player of the Season at the end of his first campaign, and went on to play in all but twelve games of Albion's four-year spell among the élite. Although not the most skilful of defenders, Steve was the foundation upon which Albion's defence was built, a true Brighton rock. Dominant in the air, he also timed his tackling superbly and led the side by example after being made captain in 1981. Constantly encouraging or berating his colleagues as necessary, he would always try to coax the best out of them.

In April 1980, 'Fozzie' won his first international honour, coming on as a sub. for the England under-21s in East Germany. He earned a full cap against Northern Ireland at Wembley in February 1982, and after winning a second cap in a friendly against the Netherlands he was included in the England squad for the 1982 World Cup finals in Spain, playing in the 1–0 defeat of Kuwait. In fact, England won all three of the matches in which he played without conceding a goal.

Steve gave an heroic performance in the 1983 F.A. semi-final against Sheffield Wednesday, but he missed the club's first-ever visit to Wembley when he was suspended for the final. Albion tried in vain to overturn the F.A. ban in the courts, but the first game with Manchester United was drawn and he returned to the side for the

replay. United won the second match 4–0; cruelly, their fans taunted the Albion skipper with choruses of 'Stevie Foster, what a difference you have made!' In fact, with Chris Ramsey injured, bringing him back into the side was the only option.

In October 1983, Chris Cattlin took over from Jimmy Melia as manager and two strong personalities clashed. Consequently, the burly centre-half departed for Aston Villa in March 1984 in a player-plus-cash deal rated at £200,000, but he made just fifteen League appearances at Villa Park before signing for Luton Town in November 1984 for £150,000. Steve was a great success at Kenilworth Road and figured in 163 First Division matches, skippering the 'Hatters' to a League Cup triumph in 1988. He was later appointed player/assistant manager, but in July 1989 'Fozzie' forsake any immediate thoughts of management by signing for Oxford United, managed by his former Albion colleague Brian Horton, for £175,000.

An essential member of United's team until he sustained a bad injury in November 1991, Steve achieved the rare distinction of clocking up more than 100 appearances for four different clubs, but was released in 1992 with the intention of retiring. Still living in Hove – as he had since 1979 – he approached Albion boss Barry Lloyd to ask if he could train with the club to maintain his fitness. As the pre-season warm-up progressed, though, it became apparent that the club's former star was the answer to current defensive problems, and his retirement was postponed.

Once again 'Fozzie' proved an inspiration and, at the age of 35, was chosen as Player of the Season by the fans for a second time. He remained the lynchpin of the Albion defence for two more seasons, but missed much of 1995–96 because of injury and, he alleges, club 'politics'. At the end of the season he announced his retirement to concentrate on his insurance business for footballers (which was inspired by an injury to Albion trainee Billy Logan). Always ready to voice his opinions, Steve revealed that Albion's off-the-field problems influenced his decision, and spoke out against the way the club was being run. Ironically, his testimonial against Sheffield Wednesday was postponed until the start of 1996–97 because of damage caused during the pitch invasion protesting against the board in April 1996.

Season	FL	FAC	FLC	AMC	Total
1979–80	38 (1)	2	5	0	45 (1)
1980–81	42 (1)	2	3 (2)	0	47 (3)
1981–82	40 (2)	3	3	0	46 (2)
1982–83	35+1 (1)	6	2	0	43+1 (1)
1983–84	16 (1)	3	0	0	19 (1)
1992–93	35 (4)	3	4	2	44 (4)
1993–94	34 (2)	1	0	1	36 (2)
1994–95	38	0	5	0	43
1995–96	8 (1)	0	0	0	8 (1)
Total	286+1 (13)	20	22 (2)	3	331+1 (15)

FOX, MARK   1992–97

midfield   *Ht 5 11, Wt 10 11*   *26 apps, 1 goal*
full name: Mark Stephen Fox
born: Basingstoke, Hampshire, 17.11.1975
debut: Bristol Rovers (a), 23.2.1994 (FL D2)

While studying at Brighton Hill Community School, Mark Fox represented Basingstoke Schools and was associated with both Portsmouth and Crystal Palace, but it was with the Albion that he chose to pursue a professional career. After turning out for Basingstoke Town as a youngster, he was spotted playing for Fleet Town in the North Hampshire League by Albion youth development officer Ted Streeter and signed for the club as a 15-year-old schoolboy. Joining the Goldstone staff as a trainee in 1992, he worked his way through the ranks, made his League debut in February 1994, and became a full pro two months later, but never made the breakthrough into regular first-team action.

Transfer-listed by Jimmy Case in November 1996, Mark was released at the end of the season by new manager Steve Gritt but linked up again with Case when he signed for Southern League Bashley for 1997–98. In 1993 the slightly-built midfielder was joined on the staff by his younger brother Simon (q.v.).

Season	FL	AMC	Total
1993–94	4+8	0	4+8
1994–95	4+5 (1)	1	5+5 (1)
1995–96	0+2	0	0+2
1996–97	0+2	0	0+2
Total	8+15 (1)	1	9+17 (1)

FOX, REG   1952–56

full-back   Ht 5 8, Wt 12 00   *23 apps*
full name: Reginald Allan Fox
born: Edmonton, Middlesex, 16.10.1929
debut: Bournemouth & B.A. (a), 1.10.1952 (FL D3(S))

Reg Fox represented both Edmonton and Middlesex Boys while at St James's School, and went on to play for Spurs' juniors and the Isthmian League club Tufnell Park. After his call-up for National Service with the Royal Signals, the young full-back played in numerous regimental representative matches and was also selected for the British Army. While stationed at Dover he was invited for a trial with Fulham, and became a professional at Craven Cottage in December 1949 on his demob at the age of 20.

Reg developed his game in the "Cottagers'" reserve team, and was recruited by Albion manager Billy Lane in October 1952. Seen as a replacement for the popular Jack Mansell (who had been

transferred to Cardiff City), the stocky defender was drafted straight into Albion's League side but had to share the left-back berth with Maurice McLafferty during the remainder of the 1952–53 season. Equally capable of playing at right-back, Reg remained at the Goldstone for almost four years, but competition for places in Albion's excellent side of the mid '50s was fierce, and with the likes of Des Tennant and Jimmy Langley to contend with his opportunities were limited. In August 1956 he went to Mansfield Town for a month's trial, but the 'Stags' offered only £500 for his services while Albion demanded £750, and so the deal fell through. A month later he signed for Southern League side Hastings United on a free transfer, and subsequently played for Folkestone and Lewes. Reg settled in Brighton and now lives in the Woodingdean district of the town.

Season	FL	FAC	Total
1952–53	11	2	13
1953–54	4	0	4
1954–55	4	1	5
1955–56	1	0	1
Total	20	3	23

FOX, SIMON   1993–97

forward   Ht 5 10, Wt 10 02   *24 apps*
full name: Simon Michael Fox
born: Basingstoke, Hampshire 28.8.1977
debut: Fulham (h), 23.4.1994 (FL D2)

On 23 April 1994, at the age of 16 years 238 days, Simon Fox became the youngest player ever to appear for the Albion in the Football League in peacetime, beating the record set by Ian Chapman seven years earlier. Eleven months later at York, in his second senior game, Simon was joined on the pitch by his elder brother Mark (q.v.), the first pair of brothers to play together for the club since the Rutherfords in 1921. Tall and lean, Simon has a fiery temperament and has run into trouble with referees on a number of occasions.

Both of Albion's Fox 'cubs' were discovered by scout Ted Streeter. Originally a defender, Simon followed his brother from Basingstoke Town to Fleet Town (together with Phil Andrews, q.v.) and, despite having been associated with Portsmouth, signed school-boy forms for Brighton. The Hampshire-born striker became a trainee in 1993 and was a prominent member of the excellent youth side of 1993–94. In March 1994 he was selected for an F.A. XI *v.* Combined Services at Aldershot. Simon's two goals clinched the Sussex Senior Cup for the reserves against Bognor Regis Town in May 1995 and he signed a professional contract shortly after, but he was unable to find the net on his limited first-team opportunities. Transfer-listed by Jimmy Case in November 1996, he was initially retained by new manager Steve Gritt at the end of the season, but was then released because of budgetary restraints imposed by chief executive David Bellotti and signed for Hastings Town in July 1997.

Season	FL	FLC	AMC	Total
1993–94	0+1	0	0	0+1
1994–95	1+1	0	0	1+1
1995–96	0+6	0+1	0+1	0+8
1996–97	5+7	0	1	6+7
Total	6+15	0+1	1+1	7+17

FRANKS, KEN   1962–63

outside-left   *1 app*
full name: Kenneth Franks
born: Motherwell, Lanarkshire, Scotland, 24.4.1944
debut: Bristol City (a), 26.12.1962 (FL D3)

Signed by manager George Curtis as part of his commitment to youth, eighteen-year-old Ken Franks joined the Albion from the Scottish junior club Blantyre Victoria in June 1962 just a few weeks after his team-mate David James made the same move, but the youngster's time at the Goldstone lasted less than a season. Indeed, if Allan Jackson hadn't missed a train connection when travelling from his Bury home for the Boxing Day fixture at Bristol City, Ken would probably never have appeared in Albion's League team at all. The match resulted in a fine 2–1 victory, but the young Scot subsequently returned to the

reserves. Curtis was released from the managerial post at the Goldstone in February 1963 and took over at Stevenage Town; his protégé followed him on a free transfer shortly afterwards.

Season	FL	Total
1962–63	1	1
Total	1	1

FULLER, EDDIE   1921–27, 1929–31 & 1932–33

half-back/centre-forward   Ht 5 8, Wt 10 05   *78 apps, 20 goals*
full name: Edward William Fuller
born: Staines, Middlesex, 1900
debut: Merthyr Town (h), 4.2.1922 (FL D3(S))

Recruited from the Isthmian League club London Caledonians in February 1921, Eddie Fuller joined the Albion as a wing-half,

but when Jack Doran was injured in February 1922 he was tried out at centre-forward with considerable success and retained the berth in the 1922–23 season following Doran's transfer to Manchester City. Eddie finished the season as top scorer with thirteen goals, but, with the emergence of Tommy Cook, he reverted to wing-half and in May 1927 was released to join Watford on a free transfer.

After two seasons at Vicarage Road, Eddie returned to the Goldstone in September 1929 to play a reserve-team role and made just two senior appearances. During 1931–32 he took a break from football, but rejoined the Albion in August 1932 for a third spell, playing for the 'Lambs' until 1933 when he quit the professional game. Eddie went on to play for Worthing, gaining winner's medals in the Sussex County League, R.U.R. Cup and Sussex Senior Cup in the two seasons 1933–35.

Season	FL	FAC	Total
1921–22	9 (1)	0	9 (1)
1922–23	34 (13)	2	36 (13)
1923–24	5	0	5
1924–25	16	2	18
1925–26	8 (6)	0	8 (6)
1929–30	2	0	2
Total	74 (20)	4	78 (20)

FUNNELL, Simon   1990–95

forward   Ht 6 0, Wt 12 08   35 apps, 2 goals
full name: Simon Paul Funnell
born: Shoreham-by-Sea, Sussex, 8.8.1974
debut: Ipswich Town (a), 2.5.1992 (FL D2)

A product of the King's Manor School in Shoreham, Simon Funnell scored a hatful of goals for the Albion reserves and youth team, but was unable to translate his prowess to the level of the Second Division. The Brighton Boys representative actually spent two years as an associated schoolboy with Southampton, but he was turning out for the Shoreham-based side Adur Athletic, for which he played from the age of ten, when he was invited to the Goldstone Ground for a trial in 1990 and impressed sufficiently to be taken on as a trainee.

After a fine run in the reserves, the young striker was included in the first-team pool towards the end of the 1991–92 season and had his first outing as a late substitute for Raphael Meade in the last game of the campaign, a defeat at Ipswich which saw Albion relegated. Two days later he won a Sussex Senior Cup medal as the reserves overcame Langney Sports 1–0 in the Goldstone final, and subsequently signed a professional contract. Simon had a decent run in the first team in 1993–94 and scored his first senior goals, but remained a fringe player. He won a second Senior Cup medal in May 1994, but was loaned to County League side Shoreham in January 1995 and was released at the end of the season.

At the beginning of 1995–96 he joined Isthmian Leaguers Worthing but swiftly returned to Shoreham, forsaking any hopes of a professional career to earn a living as a furniture polisher. Simon's prolific goalscoring for his home-town club was rewarded with a Sussex County League Cup winner's medal in April 1996, but he followed the Middle Road management back to Worthing the following season.

Season	FL	FAC	FLC	AMC	Total
1991–92	0+1	0	0	0	0+1
1992–93	0+2	0+1	2+1	0	2+4
1993–94	14+10 (2)	0	1	0	15+10 (2)
1994–95	0+1	0	0+1	0+1	0+3
Total	14+14 (2)	0+1	3+2	0+1	17+18 (2)

FUSCHILLO, Paul   1974–75

defender   Ht 5 10, Wt 11 08   17 apps, 1 goal
full name: Paul Michael Fuschillo
born: Islington, London, 20.10.1948
debut: Wrexham (h), 27.2.1974 (FL D3)

Paul Fuschillo enjoyed a splendid early career as an amateur, but his involvement in the professional game was brief and largely unproductive. While studying for an economics degree at Newcastle University, the young Londoner captained the English Universities XI in 1969–70, and, following his graduation, was an amateur on Arsenal's staff before going up to Oxford University where he played in the 1971 Varsity match. A talented defender, he also played for Wycombe Wanderers in the Isthmian League, and won an England amateur cap against France in February 1971.

Paul was also a member of the Great Britain team which attempted to qualify for the 1972 Olympics, but when the side was eliminated he signed as a professional for Blackpool in July 1971 and went on to make eleven League appearances in nearly three years at Bloomfield Road. In February 1974, Albion's management duo of Brian Clough and Peter Taylor signed the 25-year-old in a £15,000 joint deal with his team-mate Billy McEwan, and he quickly impressed with his skilful displays at full-back and in the centre of the defence. After just ten games for the club Paul was made skipper, but he then suffered a series of knee injuries which restricted his appearances and was released at the end of the 1974–75 season.

Season	FL	Total
1973–74	13	13
1974–75	4 (1)	4 (1)
Total	17 (1)	17 (1)

Players' star signs
Not including wartime players

Star Sign	Dates	No. of Players
Aries	21 March - 19 April	46
Taurus	20 April - 20 May	61
Gemini	21 May - 21 June	46
Cancer	22 June - 22 July	49
Leo	23 July - 22 August	38
Virgo	23 August - 22 September	49
Libra	23 September - 23 October	66
Scorpio	24 October - 22 November	54
Sagittarius	23 November - 21 December	45
Capricorn	22 December - 20 January	62
Aquarius	21 January - 19 February	50
Pisces	20 February - 20 March	49

GABBIADINI, RICARDO   1990

forward   Ht 6 0, Wt 13 05   *1 app*
born: Newport, Monmouthshire, Wales, 11.3.1970
debut: Portsmouth (a), 16.4.1990 (FL D2)

One of the nomads of the modern game, Ricardo Gabbiadini has travelled the length and breadth of the country – and beyond – playing for a host of clubs in the lower divisions and minor leagues. The younger brother of the more successful Marco Gabbiadini, Rikki started out as a trainee with York City and made his sole appearance  as such when he came on as a substitute in a 3–0 defeat at Preston in January 1988. The following year he moved to Sunderland – his more successful brother had already made the same journey – but failed to make his mark at Roker and was loaned out to Blackpool (September 1989) and Grimsby Town (October 1989). It was as a loan player that he arrived at the Goldstone in March 1990, but he never looked likely to create an impression, making just a fourteen-minute appearance as substitute for Kevin Bremner in a 3–0 defeat at Portsmouth.

After returning to Sunderland at the end of the season, Rikki subsequently had a two-match loan period with Crewe Alexandra in October 1990 before joining Hartlepool United in March 1991. Twelve months later he moved on to Scarborough, and in September 1992 joined Carlisle United where he enjoyed his most successful period with three goals in eighteen League matches during 1992–93. On his release from Brunton Park he had a three-match spell with Frickley Athletic in the Northern Premier League, and has since played for Chesterfield, Sligo Rovers in the League of Ireland, Denaby United, Gainsborough Trinity, Goole Town and Ossett Albion. In 1995, Ricardo joined Bradford (Park Avenue) where he has at last found his niche.

Season	FL	Total
1989–90	0+1	0+1
Total	0+1	0+1

GALL, MARK   1991–92

striker   Ht 5 10, Wt 12 00   *33 apps, 14 goals*
full name: Mark Ian Gall
born: Brixton, Lambeth, London, 14.5.1963
debut: Swindon Town (h), 26.10.1991 (FL D2)

Although he could not prevent the Albion being relegated, Mark Gall lifted the gloom considerably at the Goldstone in 1991–92 and was voted Player of the Season at the end of his first campaign. It was most unfortunate, therefore, that the talented Londoner should  be forced to retire the following season without playing a first-team game.

Mark graduated to the Football League via Greenwich Borough and Maidstone United, joining the 'Stones' in January 1989 for £2,000 while they were in the Conference. The burly forward formed a formidable striking partnership with Steve Butler which carried the club to the Conference championship, and he played in Maidstone's first-ever Football League match in August 1989. Blessed with a fair share of on-the-ball skills, Mark first attracted Albion

manager Barry Lloyd while in the Conference, but the asking-price of £125,000 was too much. Lloyd eventually got his man for £45,000 in October 1991 immediately following the departure of John Byrne from the Goldstone, and the pacy forward amply rewarded his new manager's faith with tremendous enthusiasm in a struggling team.

Although he could sometimes be a little too tricky on the ball for his own good, Mark made an immediate impression with the fans, but a knee injury from early in his career caused problems that proved insurmountable despite a number of operations in the close season, and, after just 20 more minutes of reserve football in November 1992, Mark was forced to hang up his boots the following month at the age of 29. He subsequently worked in the family baking business.

Season	FL	FAC	FMC	Total
1991–92	30+1 (13)	1 (1)	1	32+1 (14)
Total	30+1 (13)	1 (1)	1	32+1 (14)

GALL, NORMAN   1962–74

defender   Ht 5 9, Wt 11 05   *488 apps, 4 goals*
full name: Norman Albert Gall
born: Wallsend, Northumberland, 30.9.1942
debut: Watford (a), 29.9.1962 (FL D3)

For eleven years Norman Gall was Albion's 'Mr Reliable', a consistent defender either in the centre of the back line or at full-back, and his total of 488 appearances puts him third on the all-time Albion list. Yet, initially, he was a most unpopular selection when drafted into the side by George Curtis in preference to the long-serving and popular skipper Roy Jennings, and was dropped after only three games. It proved only a minor setback for the 20-year-old Geordie.

Norman was signed from Gateshead in March 1962, where he had played as an amateur while serving an apprenticeship as a marine engineer, and soon established himself as first-choice pivot. His career really blossomed during the 1964–65 Fourth Division championship campaign – he missed  just two games and formed a terrific half-back line with Dave Turner and either Jack Bertolini or the unfortunate Barrie Rees – and he was virtually an automatic choice for the next nine years or so. Capable of playing in the middle of the back-four or in either full-back berth – he also played as a stop-gap centre-forward in November 1968 – Norman instilled great confidence with his calm displays and was voted Player of the Season in 1971 and 1974, the first man to win the accolade twice. He scored only four goals in 488 games, but one of them was a memorable 25-yard header at Torquay in 1970.

Ever-present throughout the tremendous 1971–72 Division Three promotion campaign, he fell out with manager Pat Saward after a heavy defeat at Millwall the following season and was subsequently placed on the transfer-list, but he won his place back and was appointed captain by new boss Brian Clough in December 1973. Having received benefit matches in tandem with goalkeeper Brian Powney in May 1971 and May 1972, Norman was released at the end of the 1973–74 season at the age of 31. He then spent three seasons with Horsham in the Isthmian League, followed by spells with Eastbourne United and Southwick. Norman has also coached Worthing's youth team and co-managed their reserves.

Season	FL	FAC	FLC	Total
1962–63	5	0	0	5
1963–64	41	1	3	45
1964–65	44 (1)	1	2	47 (1)
1965–66	43	3	2	48
1966–67	45 (1)	6	6	57 (1)
1967–68	31+1	1	1	33+1
1968–69	28+7 (1)	1+1	2	31+8 (1)
1969–70	32+3 (1)	5	0	37+3 (1)
1970–71	43+1	3	1	47+1
1971–72	46	3	2	51
1972–73	32+1	0	1	33+1
1973–74	37	2	1	40
Total	427+13 (4)	26+1	21	474+14 (4)

GALLACHER, BERNARD — 1991–93

left-back   Ht 5 9, Wt 11 00   50 apps, 1 goal
born: Johnstone, Renfrewshire, Scotland, 22.3.1967
debut: Blackburn Rovers (a), 2.11.1991 (FL D2)

Bernard Gallacher was a Perthshire Schools representative who joined Aston Villa as a sixteen-year-old trainee and signed pro forms on his eighteenth birthday in March 1985. After making his debut at Old Trafford in the last game of the 1986–87 campaign, which saw Villa relegated to Division Two, he missed just one match the following season as Villa returned to the top flight at the first attempt, but a loss of form and a knee injury curtailed his subsequent outings. After a month on loan at Blackburn Rovers from November 1990 he was released in May 1991.

Following an unfruitful, two-match spell at Doncaster Rovers, Bernard arrived at the Goldstone for a trial in October 1991 and was soon drafted into the League team. Indeed, he quickly impressed with his cool displays and made the no.3 shirt his own; he was given a contract and also skippered the side in the absence of Dean Wilkins and Gary Chivers. Bernard lost out to Ian Chapman the following season, though, and made only occasional appearances before being released in May 1993, when he returned to the Midlands on a non-contract basis with Northampton Town and made five League appearances towards the end of the 1993–94 season. During the next campaign he turned out for Conference side Bromsgrove Rovers on a non-contract basis, and then played some football in Hong Kong.

Season	FL	FAC	FMC	AMC	Total
1991–92	31 (1)	2	1	0	34 (1)
1992–93	14	1	0	1	16
Total	45 (1)	3	1	1	50 (1)

GARBUTT, RAY — 1951–52

centre-forward   32 apps, 17 goals
full name: Raymond Hardiman Garbutt
born: Middlesbrough, Yorkshire, 9.5.1925
died: Middlestone Moor, Spennymoor, Co. Durham, 2.11.1994
debut: Northampton Town (a), 27.3.1951 (FL D3(S))

Ray Garbutt joined his home-town team, Middlesbrough, as a young amateur, but his early progress was hindered by the war. In fact he saw hectic service as a Navy gunner on tank-landing craft – he survived the sinking of his vessel during the D-Day landings – and in North Africa, and subsequently in Burma, Malaya, Sumatra and Singapore. Yet he also found time to play representative football against Tommy Walker's (of Hearts and Scotland fame) touring side on two occasions in India.

On his return to 'civvy street' Ray was playing for South Bank East End on Teesside when he was spotted by a Manchester City scout, and joined the paid ranks at Maine Road in September 1947. Still only 22, he played for City's Central League side during 1947–48, but was released to join Spennymoor United in the North Eastern League. Two years later, in May 1950, Watford offered him a second opportunity to break into the Football League and the Yorkshireman responded by scoring eight goals in 22 Third Division (South) matches during the 1950–51 campaign.

In March 1951, Ray came to Hove in a direct swap for Albion's Cyril Thompson and set out on the most successful phase of his career, averaging more than a goal every other game – mostly in the no.9 shirt but also occasionally on the left wing – in a 20-month stay at the Goldstone. An honest workhorse in the front line, he perhaps lacked the power and finesse to maintain a permanent place, and was transferred to Workington in November for around £5,000. A disagreement regarding his share of the transfer fee blighted Ray's time in Cumberland, though, and after scoring twice in eight Third Division (North) outings he quit the game – although Workington retained his registration for six years.

Ray subsequently became steward of a working men's club in Spennymoor and later entered the licensed trade, but then spent 29 years with G.E.C. as a fitter until his retirement in 1990. Seldom found far from a golf course, he won the County Durham Seniors title on one occasion and took part in the Senior Open Championship.

Season	FL	Total
1950–51	9 (4)	9 (4)
1951–52	23 (13)	23 (13)
Total	32 (17)	32 (17)

GARDINER, J. J. — 1901–06

goalkeeper   7 apps
born: c. 1882
debut: Southall (a), 15.2.1902 (SL D2)

A former pupil of Brighton Grammar School, Gardiner was a Brighton Hornets player who was one of five goalkeepers fielded during Albion's first season, 1901–02. He continued to assist the reserves as an amateur on the odd occasion until 1905, and also played for Burgess Hill, Brighton Amateurs and Worthing. A prominent member of Brighton Rugby Club, he also refereed local soccer matches.

Gardiner was heavily involved in raising funds for the struggling professionals. In 1906 he was vice-president of the Albion's Summer Wage Fund committee, and it was proposed that he would become a director the same year after promising to take up shares in the club, but his appointment never came about..

Season	SL	SEL	Total
1901–02	4	0	4
1902–03	1	2	3
Total	5	2	7

GARDNER, ANDY — 1904–05

outside-left   Ht 5 8, Wt 11 07   28 apps, 13 goals
full name: Andrew Gardner
born: Milton, Glasgow, Lanarkshire, Scotland, 17.4.1877
debut: New Brompton (a), 3.9.1904 (SL D1)

A ndy Gardner played for Kilbarchan Victoria while at school, and graduated to the Renfrewshire village's senior team before joining Clyde at the age of eighteen in 1895, but after six years in the Scottish League he decided to try his hand in England and played for five different clubs over the next five seasons. The first was newly promoted Grimsby Town, who recruited Andy in May 1901 for their first season in Division One, and he missed just three games as the 'Mariners' narrowly avoided relegation.

Transferred to Newcastle United in May 1902, the Scots winger found life harder with the star-studded 'Magpies' and made the first team only nine times before signing for Bolton Wanderers in May 1903. The Second Division club were F.A. Cup runners-up that season, but Andy didn't figure in the Cup run and had only eight League outings before his release to join Albion in the Southern League during the summer of 1904.

Although troubled with injuries, he proved to be a fleet-footed sharpshooter at the Goldstone; he scored on his debut, a 2–2 draw at New Brompton, and maintained an excellent scoring-rate during the

1904–05 campaign. Nevertheless, he was one of those released at the end of the season when wholesale changes were made, and moved on to Queen's Park Rangers where his career foundered, probably because of further injury problems; he made only five Southern League appearances for Rangers before departing from the first-class scene on the completion of the 1905–06 season. Andy played for Carlisle United in the North Eastern League in 1907–08, then returned to Scotland with the junior side Johnstone in April 1908 before rejoining Carlisle in January 1909.

Season	SL	FAC	Total
1904–05	23 (10)	5 (3)	28 (13)
Total	23 (10)	5 (3)	28 (13)

GARFIELD, BEN   1902–05

outside-left   Ht 5 7, Wt 11 04   64 apps, 29 goals
full name: Benjamin Walter Garfield
born: Higham Ferrers, Northamptonshire, August 1872
debut: Southall (h), 13.9.1902 (SL D2)

One of the great characters – and most notable players – of Brighton's early years, Ben Garfield had played for England only four years before arriving in Hove and was a major capture for the infant club. The slight winger began his career in his native Northamptonshire with Finedon and Kettering Town, and was introduced to the Football League by Burton Wanderers in June 1894 where he scored 27 goals in 59 Second Division matches over two seasons. Such form earned him a transfer to First Division West Bromwich Albion in May 1896, and he went on to become a most popular and famous performer with the 'Throstles', scoring 38 goals in 117 League and Cup games over six years. It was an excellent return for a winger in any era, and Ben was rewarded with an England cap in March 1898 in a 3–2 defeat of Ireland in Belfast.

Although he suffered a number of injuries during his time with West Brom., it still caused a minor sensation when he was released to join Brighton in August 1902 amid competition from more illustrious clubs. At 30 years of age, Ben made quite an impact at the Goldstone with some sparkling displays, the finest of which was undoubtedly his four-goal performance in the 5–3 defeat of Watford in the test match that clinched promotion to the Southern League's First Division in April 1903. A real bundle of energy, he gave total commitment, but the injury problems continued and his appearances became fewer. In May 1905, Ben was released and moved to Tunbridge Wells Rangers, but was soon forced to retire. He subsequently fell on hard times, and a smoking-concert at the George Inn, Hove, raised the not inconsiderable sum of £13 8s. 6d for his benefit.

Season	SL	Test	FAC	SEL	Total
1902–03	7 (4)	1 (4)	5 (5)	18 (7)	31 (20)
1903–04	23 (7)	0	1	0	24 (7)
1904–05	8 (2)	0	1	0	9 (2)
Total	38 (13)	1 (4)	7 (5)	18 (7)	64 (29)

GARIANI, MOSHE   1980–81

midfield   Ht 5 7, Wt 10 00   1 app
born: Tiberias, Israel, 18.6.1957
debut: Southampton (a), 6.9.1980 (FL D1)

In an international career which began in April 1978, Moshe Gariani represented his country eleven times, three of which came during his brief spell on the South Coast of England. The slightly-built

22-year-old came to Albion's attention in the friendly match against the Israeli national side, managed by former Goldstone favourite Jack Mansell, in February 1980. Having scored sixteen goals from midfield for his club side, Maccabi Nethanya, in their 1979–80 championship season, he came to Brighton for £40,000 in May 1980. (Albion also played a friendly against Maccabi at the Goldstone as part of the deal, when Moshe was captain for the night.) However, Moshe had scant opportunity to show his skill and passing ability to the Hove crowd, and made just one appearance in Albion's First Division side, as a substitute for seventeen minutes at Southampton. In August 1981 he was transferred to Tel Aviv in his native country for a small fee.

Season	FL	Total
1980–81	0+1	0+1
Total	0+1	0+1

GATTING, STEVE   1981–91

defender/midfield   Ht 5 11, Wt 11 11   369 apps, 21 goals
full name: Steven Paul Gatting
born: Park Royal, Willesden, Middlesex, 29.5.1959
debut: Everton (a), 12.9.1981 (FL D1)

A fine defender at the Goldstone for almost a decade, Steve Gatting had his fair share of contretemps with the management and a number of injury problems, but always came back to reclaim his place and set an example to others with his cool, unhurried style. Yet he came to the club as a midfielder – most of his 58 League appearances for Arsenal were in midfield – and he was only drafted into the defence following an eleventh-hour injury to Gary Stevens as Albion prepared for a First Division game at Everton.

A fine all-round sportsman, Steve could have chosen a career in cricket after playing for the Middlesex 2nd XI, but preferred football and signed as an Arsenal apprentice. The former Brent and Middlesex Schools representative became a full professional in February 1977, but had to compete with the likes of Liam Brady and Graham Rix in the "Gunners'" midfield, and was offered to the Albion in 1981 in a player-plus-cash deal for Mark Lawrenson which fell through. New manager Mike Bailey maintained an interest in him, though, and paid £200,000 for the classy performer in September 1981.

Having impressed in his new defensive role, the 22-year-old

retained the position for the rest of the 1981–82 season. When Jimmy Melia took over the reins the following season, he was played in midfield and at left-back, but reverted to central defence for the 1983 F.A. Cup final in the absence of Steve Foster and had a storming game alongside Gary Stevens. In the replay he was switched to right-back, a most uncomfortable position for a decidedly left-footed player and a decision which may have had a big effect on the final result.

From that point Steve's Goldstone career consisted very much of highs and lows. He suffered a severe pelvic strain in 1984 which side-lined him for thirteen months, and in July

1987 it seemed his time in Hove was up when he was placed on the free-transfer list, but he fought his way back and played in every match as the team won back its place in Division Two, taking over the captaincy from Doug Rougvie in March 1988. Plagued with a series of injuries over the next few seasons, the long-serving defender was granted a testimonial match in August 1990 when Arsenal provided the opposition.

Steve's last game for the Albion was the 1991 Division Two play-off final and he left on a free transfer for Charlton Athletic in August. Sixty-four League appearances for the 'Valiants' brought his career tally to 441, and on his release in May 1993 he joined the ambitious Hastings-based club Stamco on their promotion to the First Division of the Sussex County League (he had previously coached them while playing for Charlton). The experienced defender subsequently played a major role in the club's rapid rise to the Premier Division of the Southern League as St Leonards Stamcroft. Steve also coaches cricket and soccer in local schools, and is a regular in the Sussex Cricket League with Preston Nomads. Cricket, in fact, runs in the family: his elder brother, Mike Gatting, is the Middlesex and former England cricket captain.

Season	FL	Play-offs	FAC	FLC	FMC	AMC	Total
1981–82	39 (3)	0	3	3 (1)	0	0	45 (4)
1982–83	40 (4)	0	7	2	0	0	49 (4)
1983–84	35 (4)	0	3	3	0	0	41 (4)
1984–85	8	0	0	1	0	0	9
1985–86	14+3	0	1	0	0	0	15+3
1986–87	40 (1)	0	2	2	1	0	45 (1)
1987–88	46 (3)	0	4	1	0	5 (1)	56 (4)
1988–89	29 (3)	0	1	2	1	0	33 (3)
1989–90	19	0	2	0	0	0	21
1990–91	43 (1)	3	3	0	3	0	52 (1)
Total	313+3 (19)	3	26	14 (1)	5	5 (1)	366+3 (21)

GEARD, GLEN   1976–81 & 1983

midfield   Ht 5 7, Wt 10 03   *1 app*
full name: Glen John Harris Geard
born: Malta, 25.2.1960
debut: Arsenal (a), 13.11.1979 (FLC R4 rep)

Although he played one senior game for the Albion, Glen Geard was better known as a talented and successful player for numerous local clubs, but will always be remembered for the fiery

temperament which landed him in trouble with the authorities on many occasions. Born in Malta but raised in Bevendean, he played for both Brighton and Sussex Boys, and had a trial for the England Schools side. A prodigious talent, he played for the Albion youth side at the age of thirteen in 1973, won a first-team place with Lewes in the Athenian League as a sixteen-year-old, and, after trials with several League clubs, arrived at the Goldstone as an apprentice in October 1976.

Having impressed with the reserves he was taken on as a professional in February 1978, but, after making his debut at Highbury, he fell foul of manager Alan Mullery because of his poor disciplinary record. Released in March 1981, Glen returned to Lewes but was given a second chance at the Goldstone by Jimmy Melia in 1983 which he failed to make the most of. Glen subsequently represented Sussex on many occasions during spells with Horsham, Whitehawk, Eastbourne United, Worthing, Southwick, Shoreham, Crawley Town, Lewes (again), and Littlehampton Town. His final move was a return to Shoreham as player/assistant manager, but an injury forced him to retire in August 1994.

On hanging up his boots Glen retained his managerial role at Middle Road, but followed his boss, Sammy Donnelly, to nearby Worthing in the autumn of 1996 to help keep the 'Rebels' in the Isthmian League Division One when relegation had look a certainty.

In fact he also shook off the effects of his injuries to turn out for Whitehawk again during the season.

Season	FLC	Total
1979–80	1	1
Total	1	1

GEDDES, GAVIN   1993–94

left-wing   Ht 5 10, Wt 11 08   *15 apps, 2 goals*
full name: Gavin John Geddes
born: Brighton, Sussex, 7.10.1972
debut: Bristol Rovers (h), 1.9.1993 (FL D2)

Gavin Geddes attended Blatchington Mill School in Hove, where he represented Brighton Boys, and played for Hove Park Colts and Saltdean Tigers; he also trained with the Albion. His adult career began with Lewes; he then played for County League side Shoreham before moving along the coast to Wick in 1992. Employed by a pharmaceutical company in Hove, Gavin came to prominence the following season, 1992–93, when he scored 22 League goals as the Littlehampton-based club finished third in the County League, and scored in their Sussex Senior Cup triumph

over Oakwood at the Goldstone the same season.

Rated as one of the county's most promising players, the wiry, fair-haired forward represented Sussex, but was on the verge of moving to Australia when he was given an extended trial by the Albion and forced his way into the first team as a left-winger. Although he showed an ability to beat his man, he was never quite able to sustain his form in the higher grade and was released by new manager Liam Brady in February 1994.

Gavin subsequently had a brief trial with AFC Bournemouth and a similar spell with Slough Town before joining Crawley Town in March 1994. A year later he joined Worthing on loan to the end of the season, but then returned to Town Mead. In February 1996, Gavin joined Sussex County League Division Two promotion hopefuls Saltdean United on a dual registration with Crawley, and also had a brief spell on loan with Horsham in March 1997.

Season	FL	FAC	FLC	AMC	Total
1993–94	7+5 (1)	1	0+1	1 (1)	9+6 (2)
Total	7+5 (1)	1	0+1	1 (1)	9+6 (2)

GILBERG, HARRY   1953–56

right-half/inside-forward   Ht 5 8, Wt 11 00   *72 apps, 5 goals*
born: Tottenham, Middlesex, 27.6.1923
died: Torquay, Devon, 16.9.1994
debut: Torquay United (a), 17.1.1953 (FL D3(S))

Having represented Tottenham and Middlesex as a schoolboy, Harry Gilberg joined Tottenham Hotspur's ground staff in 1937 and signed as an amateur in May 1939, before being farmed out to both Walthamstow Avenue and Northfleet United for experience. During the war he served as air crew, completing more than 30 operational flights and attaining the rank of warrant officer. In September 1944, Harry was signed as a professional by Spurs, and in the last two seasons of wartime emergency fare he made guest appearances for both Charlton Athletic and Southend United, but he played only a reserve-team role at White Hart Lane when things returned to normal in 1946, making just three senior appearances.

After requesting a transfer, Harry crossed the capital to join Queen's Park Rangers in August 1951 and missed only two games as Rangers were relegated from Division Two in his first season. In January 1953 he was brought to the Goldstone by Billy Lane, along with his Rangers team-mate Bert Addinall, in an effort to solve a lack of penetration in attack; Lane had been keen to sign him (as assistant manager) for Brentford before the war but the opportunity never arose. Although he did well in the remaining games of the season, Harry suffered a knee injury in the opening fixture of the 1953–54 campaign and had an operation to remove the cartilage in October, but he was restored to the side the following season and played in 39 League games as an excellent, attacking wing-half. However, the knee problems wouldn't go away and brought about his enforced retirement in 1956. In 1994, Harry was living in Broxbourne, Hertfordshire, when he collapsed and died on holiday in Torquay.

Season	FL	FAC	Total
1952–53	19 (2)	0	19 (2)
1953–54	6 (1)	0	6 (1)
1954–55	39	5 (2)	44 (2)
1955–56	3	0	3
Total	67 (3)	5 (2)	72 (5)

GILBERT, PHIL   1962–64

inside-forward   Ht 5 10, Wt 11 04   6 apps, 3 goals
full name: Philip Leonard Gilbert
born: Minster, Kent, 11.9.1944
debut: Derby County (a), 28.4.1962 (FL D2)

Seventeen-year-old Phil Gilbert was signed by George Curtis from Southern League Ramsgate Athletic in January 1962 and made his Football League debut the following April, one of three teenagers drafted in for the last game of the 1961-62 campaign after Albion had been relegated to Division Three. The young forward's six appearances were spread over three seasons, but he bagged three goals from both inside-forward berths before being released to join Salisbury in the Western League – together with Albion team-mate Barry Fitch – in March 1964. Like Fitch, Phil went on to serve the Wiltshire club admirably. He stayed on after they were elected to the Southern League in 1968, playing a variety of roles and amassing over 300 appearances in eight years.

Season	FL	Total
1961–62	1	1
1962–63	4 (3)	4 (3)
1963–64	1	1
Total	6 (3)	6 (3)

GILGUN, PAT   1925–26

inside/centre-forward   Ht 5 8, Wt 11 04   4 apps, 3 goals
full name: Patrick Gilgun
born: Shotts, Lanarkshire, Scotland, 30.12.1901
died: Carfin, Lanarkshire, Scotland, 26.9.1981
debut: Southend United (a), 10.10.1925 (FL D3(S))

Affectionately known as 'Scruffy' by Albion fans because of his somewhat unkempt appearance, Pat Gilgun was one of a number of Brighton players to have scored a host of goals for the reserves but received little opportunity to demonstrate that ability in the first team. His career effectively began in January 1924 when he joined Celtic from Law Scotia F.C., but he was immediately loaned to Vale of Leven to gain experience. On his return to Celtic Park, Pat appeared in three League games before moving to East Stirlingshire on loan for the 1924–25 season.

In May 1925 the stocky little Scot came south in company with his 'Shire team-mate Paul Mooney, but, unlike Mooney and despite scoring 23 goals for the reserves in 1925–26, he failed to make his mark at the Goldstone Ground. Pat's chance came in October 1925 when, with injury ruling out Tommy Cook, he appeared in all three inside-forward positions and scored three goals, but he was then consigned back to the 'Lambs'. In August 1926 he moved to Norwich City on a free transfer, but again struggled to make the first team and appeared in only twelve League matches before being released to join Southern League side Sittingbourne in July 1927. Pat was subsequently employed by Lloyd's Paper Mill in Sittingbourne and played for the works' team, but he then returned to Lanarkshire where he was a steelworker for many years.

Season	FL	FAC	Total
1925–26	3 (3)	1	4 (3)
Total	3 (3)	1	4 (3)

GILHOOLY, PADDY   1904–05

inside-right   Ht 5 7, Wt 11 07   16 apps, 5 goals
full name: Patrick Gilhooly
born: Draffan, Lanarkshire, Scotland, 6.7.1876
died: Cleland, Lanarkshire, Scotland, 20.2.1907
debut: New Brompton (a), 3.9.1904 (SL D1)

A thoroughly outgoing character, Paddy Gilhooly was a typical Scottish ball-player and gained great popularity wherever he went, but he never adapted to the rigours of the game south of the border. Having come through the junior ranks with Vale of Avon Juveniles, Larkhall Thistle and Cambuslang Hibs, Paddy joined Celtic in October 1896 and quickly made his name as a goalscoring utility forward, the 'darling' of the Celtic Park crowd. He was, though, also something of an enigma, often accused of being selfish and undisciplined. In 1897–98 he won a Scottish League championship medal as the 'Celts' annexed the title without losing a match, and represented the Scottish League v. Football League at Villa Park the same season. Scoring seventeen goals in 46 Scottish League games, Paddy caught the eye of the Sheffield United management and in September 1900 he joined the Bramall Lane staff, but he was not a great success in the English First Division and was released to join Tottenham Hotspur in the Southern League in September 1901.

Paddy first came to the notice of Albion supporters in September 1902 when he scored a hat-trick in Spurs' reserves' 3–1 defeat of the Brighton first team in the South Eastern League. Twenty months later, in May 1904 – and after just eighteen Southern League appearances in three years at White Hart Lane – he was brought to the Goldstone. Despite being described as 'possessing fine control over the ball and a good shot', Paddy failed to consolidate his position with the Albion and was released in May 1905 when he returned to Scotland. Within two years of departing, he died at his Cleland home following surgery in Glasgow for an unnamed illness at the age of 31.

Season	SL	FAC	Total
1904–05	15 (5)	1	16 (5)
Total	15 (5)	1	16 (5)

GILL, ERIC   1952–60

goalkeeper   Ht 5 10, Wt 11 10   296 apps
full name: Eric Norman Gill
born: Camden, London, 3.11.1930
debut: Leyton Orient (h), 20.9.1952 (FL D3(S))

For five years, from 21 February 1953 to 22 February 1958, Eric Gill appeared between the Albion posts in 247 consecutive matches – 231 Football League and 16 F.A. Cup – to set a new club record and equal the best for a goalkeeper then held by Ted Ditchburn of Spurs. (In fact, he passed the previous Albion best, 175 games by another goalkeeper, Billy Hayes, in September 1956.) The following week he turned up at Brighton Station to travel with the team for the match at Coventry, but was obviously ill and reluctantly sent home. Always an immaculate figure, he was understandably a great favourite with the fans and was presented with a silver salver to commemorate his 200th successive game.

Eric played at centre-forward as a schoolboy, but then joined Charlton Athletic in February 1948 as a seventeen-year-old goalkeeper. During National Service with the R.A.O.C. he represented the Army, but at The Valley he had to contend with the legendary Sam Bartram and made only one first-team appearance. On his demob he was loaned to Tonbridge in the Southern League.

In June 1952, Albion manager Billy Lane brought Eric to Hove for £400 amid competition from Gillingham and Cardiff City, and the 21-year-old 'keeper quickly established himself as an automatic choice. Although not particularly tall for a goalie, he was near faultless in his handling and guarded the Albion net throughout the mid '50s, one of the club's more prosperous eras. In 1957–58 he played a big part in the Third Division (South) championship success, but an injury sustained during training the following term meant that he was never quite the same player again. Eric left for Guildford City in June 1960, a route taken by several ex-Albion players of the period, and clocked up 225 Southern League appearances in six years with the Surrey club.

While with the Albion, Eric took over the Perrimay Hotel in Charlotte Street, Brighton, and later ran Simpson's Hotel in Marine Parade. He still lives in the Brighton area and is prominent on the bowls scene, having won his Sussex colours in August 1995. His son Steve played for England Schools at football and was on West Ham United's books as a youngster.

Season	FL	FAC	Total
1952–53	17	0	17
1953–54	46	4	50
1954–55	46	5	51
1955–56	46	2	48
1956–57	46	2	48
1957–58	43	3	46
1958–59	27	0	27
1959–60	9	0	9
Total	280	16	296

GILLIVER, ALAN   1969–71

striker   Ht 6 1, Wt 13 00   68 apps, 24 goals
full name: Alan Henry Gilliver
born: Swallownest, Yorkshire, 3.8.1944
debut: Walsall (h), 9.8.1969 (FL D3)

A widely travelled striker, Alan Gilliver began his career with Huddersfield Town on leaving school and signed as a professional in August 1961, going on to net 22 goals in 46 League appearances for the Second Division club before joining Blackburn Rovers in June 1966. The fee was said to be £30,000, but it soon became apparent that the player was suffering from a slipped disc and the Football League subsequently ordered Huddersfield to return £18,000 to Blackburn as medical records were not made available at the time of the transaction. The affair led to a medical examination becoming a requirement in all transfer deals.

In May 1968 the Yorkshireman returned to his native county with Rotherham United, but was recruited by Albion manager Freddie Goodwin on a free transfer in July 1969 as a replacement for Charlie Livesey and did well in his first season, top-scoring with sixteen goals in League and Cup as Albion came close to gaining promotion to Division Two. The following season, though, he had notched only eight goals before new manager Pat Saward sold him in February 1971 to Lincoln City for a fee of around £10,000. Alan later played for Bradford City (June 1972), where he enjoyed his most productive period with 30 goals in 70 League outings; Stockport County (June 1974); Baltimore Comets in the U.S.A. (May 1975); Boston United (September 1975); Buxton, on loan (March 1976); Gainsborough Trinity (August 1976); and had a second, brief spell as a non-contract player with Bradford City during 1978–79.

Having finished his career with a total of 95 goals from 297 Football League appearances, Alan later returned to Valley Parade, first as security officer, then as commercial manager and stadium manager. Also an excellent cricketer, he had a trial for Yorkshire C.C.C. as a batsman and played in the Lancashire League. He also appeared for the Sussex second XI during the summer of 1970.

Season	FL	FAC	FLC	Total
1969–70	31+1 (12)	5 (2)	3 (2)	39+1 (16)
1970–71	23+2 (7)	2 (1)	1	26+2 (8)
Total	54+3 (19)	7 (3)	4 (2)	65+3 (24)

GIPP, DAVID   1984–89

forward   Ht 5 7, Wt 9 12   6 apps
full name: David Thomas Gipp
born: Forest Gate, East Ham, Essex, 13.7.1969
debut: Blackburn Rovers (a), 25.4.1987 (FL D2)

A prolific scorer for the Albion reserve and youth teams, David Gipp received scant opportunity to demonstrate his undoubted natural talents in the first team. Unable to fulfil that early promise, he has now drifted around the non-League scene for a number of years. Spotted by George Petchey playing Sunday football for Tiger F.C. in South Woodford, the young striker was coached by Petchey on day-release from school and also trained with Arsenal, Watford and West Ham United. However, he impressed Chris Cattlin while playing for a London XI against Albion's youth side, and was taken onto the staff at the Goldstone where his mentor, Petchey, had also become assistant manager.

David made his reserve-team debut at the age of fifteen and signed professional forms on his seventeenth birthday in July 1986. With a low centre of gravity, the young striker was like lightning in the box and scored a hatful of opportunist goals. Selected for training with the England under-17 squad in 1985, he looked assured of a successful senior career when he made his League debut in April 1987 and almost scored with his very first touch. However, he had to compete with much more experienced men in the front line and was never given a decent run in the first team. Consequently, in July 1989 he was released after just six senior appearances to join Barnet at the age of 20.

David has since played for Wycombe Wanderers (on loan), Chelmsford City (on loan), Wealdstone, Chesham United, Harrow Borough, Chelmsford City (for a second spell), Braintree Town, Southwick, Aveley, Chesham United again, and St Albans, but returned to Sussex in the 1995 close season to take up a trial with Worthing. He then rejoined Braintree Town.

Season	FL	FLC	Total
1986–87	0+3	0	0+3
1987–88	1+1	1	2+1
Total	1+4	1	2+4

GOFFEY, BERT — 1937–42

inside-forward   Ht 5 9, Wt 12 00   60 apps, 10 goals
full name: Herbert Henry Goffey
born: Sundridge, Kent, 9.5.1911
debut: Swindon Town (h), 4.12.1937 (FL D3(S))

Bert Goffey came through the junior ranks with Sevenoaks, Higham Ferrers Town and Northampton Nomads, and had trial periods with Northampton Town and Bristol Rovers before joining Norwich City as an amateur in December 1934. After turning professional in May 1935, he scored nine goals in 32 Second Division matches for the 'Canaries' over the next two seasons, and came to the Goldstone in June 1937 when Charlie Webb laid out a sizeable fee for his transfer. Nevertheless, Bert was confined to a reserve-team role for the first three months of the 1937–38 campaign, but a series of excellent performances in early December then saw him gain favour over Jimmy Cargill. Finding the net on his debut, a 3–1 defeat of Swindon Town at the Goldstone, he came into the side during a terrific run of eleven games undefeated which saw Albion soar from the lower reaches to fifth place in the Southern Section, and established himself at inside-left for the rest of the season as the club pushed for promotion to the Second Division.

Bert's appearances were eventually divided between the two inside-forward positions, but on one occasion he was selected at centre-half in an emergency. The 28-year-old's career was effectively brought to an end by the war, but he did turn out for the Albion on the rare occasions that service as an Army P.T. instructor afforded up to 1942. Fortunate to be among those evacuated from the Dunkirk beaches in 1940, Bert now lives in retirement in Northampton where he worked on the railway for some considerable time.

Season	FL	FAC	SSC	Wartime	Total
1937–38	24 (2)	3	0	0	27 (2)
1938–39	28 (7)	0	1	0	29 (7)
1939–40	0	0	0	1 (1)	1 (1)
1940–41	0	0	0	1	1
1941–42	0	0	0	2	2
Total	52 (9)	3	1	4 (1)	60 (10)

GOOCH, A. G. — 1902

utility player   3 apps, 1 goal
debut: Bedford Queen's Engineering Works (a), 27.9.1902 (SEL)

Recruited from Dartford United during the close season of 1902, Gooch played in both full-back berths and at inside-right in his three outings for Albion's South Eastern League team, scoring the only goal in a 1–0 win at St Albans in his last appearance. In 1907–08 he was reinstated as an amateur by the F.A.

Season	SEL	Total
1902–03	3 (1)	3 (1)
Total	3 (1)	3 (1)

GOOD, MICKEY — 1904–05

centre-half   29 apps, 6 goals
full name: Michael Lee Harrington Sullivan Good*
born: Cork, Co. Cork, Ireland, 1873
died: Luton, Bedfordshire, 21.1.1959
debut: New Brompton (a), 3.9.1904 (SL D1)

The lynchpin of Albion's defence during 1904–05, Mickey Good was the son of a Lanarkshire coal-miner, and started out with junior side Airdrie Hill before signing for Scottish League side Airdrieonians in August 1895. Having attracted the attention of Small Heath (later Birmingham), he joined the 'Heathens' in December 1896 and spent nearly three years with the Second Division club, but was never a regular in the first team and was released to join Southern League Watford in August 1899. Two seasons in Hertfordshire were followed by spells with Preston North End (signed June 1901), Bristol City (August 1902) and Reading (close season 1903) before he arrived at the Goldstone in May 1904.

A popular personality both on and off the field, Mickey was a dominant figure in his only season in Hove and even led the attack on one occasion, but, at the age of 31, he wasn't retained at the end of the season. Soon after leaving the club he married the daughter of the landlord of Hove's Neptune Inn – Edwin Clare performed the duties of best man – and the couple took over the Flowing Tide in Cannon Street (the site of which now, alas, lies under the Brighton Centre).

During 1905–06, Mickey played for Southern United, a professional club based at Nunhead in south-east London, and was given permission to train at the Goldstone, but he fell out with the South Eastern League side in March 1906 in a dispute over his wages. The club subsequently defied an F.A. order to pay him which led to an inquiry into its management and ultimately to its demise. Later living in the Luton area, Mickey was a welcome guest at the Goldstone in 1957, by which time he had lost his sight, but he passed away two years later at the age of 85.

Season	SL	FAC	Total
1904–05	25 (5)	4 (1)	29 (6)
Total	25 (5)	4 (1)	29 (6)

Note: Good was born with the surname Sullivan but changed it early in life.

GOODCHILD, JOHNNY — 1961–66

forward   Ht 5 8, Wt 10 07   176 apps, 46 goals
full name: John Goodchild
born: Littletown, Co. Durham, 2.1.1939
debut: Scunthorpe United (a), 19.8.1961 (FL D2)

With 21 goals from 44 League outings with Sunderland behind him, Johnny Goodchild was an excellent capture for the Albion

when he signed in May 1961, and he scored twice in his first game, a 3–3 draw at Scunthorpe United.

The versatile forward had joined Sunderland as an amateur from the nearby Ludworth Juniors club, signed as a professional in September 1956, and scored on his First Division debut, a 3–2 win against Leicester City at Roker Park in September 1957.

Johnny's spindly frame housed a tough character and he became a regular at the Goldstone Ground for five seasons, but he struggled to settle initially as the club plummeted from the Second Division to the Fourth over the next two seasons and appeared in every forward position. However, on resuming his preferred left-wing role he was a revelation, and had a superb season in 1964–65 as Albion carried off the Fourth Division championship; he missed just three games and scored ten goals. In June 1966 the 27-year-old forward left for York City, and moved nearer his native heath for a short spell with Darlington in July 1967 before retiring from League football.

Season	FL	FAC	FLC	Total
1961–62	34 (10)	1	0	35 (10)
1962–63	31 (7)	1	1	33 (7)
1963–64	42 (14)	1	2 (1)	45 (15)
1964–65	43 (10)	1	2	46 (10)
1965–66	12+1 (3)	3 (1)	1	16+1 (4)
Total	162+1 (44)	7 (1)	6 (1)	175+1 (46)

GOODEVE, KEN   1973–74

central defender   Ht 5 10, Wt 10 10   6 apps
full name: Kenneth George Alfred Goodeve
born: Manchester, Lancashire, 3.9.1950
debut: Tranmere Rovers (a), 8.12.1973 (FL D3)

Ken Goodeve was an apprentice at Manchester United and was taken on as a professional at the age of seventeen in September 1967, but he had little chance of making the first team and was transferred to Luton Town in April 1970. After fifteen League games in over three years at Kenilworth Road, Ken became Brian Clough's first permanent signing for the Albion in December 1973. The new manager forked out £20,000 for his services, but the 23-year-old defender played just six matches for the club before moving to Watford for £10,000 in June 1974 where he was a regular for two seasons. Ken subsequently played for Hitchin Town, Buckingham Town, Bedford Town and Wootton Blue Cross.

Season	FL	Total
1973–74	5+1	5+1
Total	5+1	5+1

GOODWIN, FRED   1911–13

outside-left   63 apps, 16 goals
full name: Frederick Goodwin
born: Leek, Staffordshire, 1887
debut: Coventry City (h), 9.9.1911 (SL D1)

One of several players recruited from the Leek United club in the period immediately before the First World War, Fred Goodwin signed for the Albion during the summer of 1911 and formed a formidable left-wing partnership with Charlie Webb during his first season at the Goldstone Ground. However, his form

deteriorated the following term, mainly because of injury problems, and he was subsequently transferred to West Ham United in April 1913, but within a few weeks he had moved on to Exeter City without appearing in the "Hammers'" Southern League side. Fred remained with the 'Grecians' until 1915, netting five goals in 40 Southern League outings, but his career was cut short by wounds received during the war.

Season	SL	FAC	SA	SCC	Total
1911–12	36 (10)	1	0	2	39 (10)
1912–13	13 (2)	2	7 (3)	2 (1)	24 (6)
Total	49 (12)	3	7 (3)	4 (1)	63 (16)

GOODWIN, IAN   1970–74

central defender/midfield   Ht 5 11, Wt 12 11   60 apps
full name: Ian David Goodwin
born: Irlam, Lancashire, 14.11.1950
debut: Doncaster Rovers (a), 29.9.1970 (FL D3)

The selection of Ian Goodwin ahead of club captain John Napier for the last twelve matches of the 1971–72 Third Division campaign was a big surprise, but Pat Saward's decision was vindicated as Albion remained unbeaten to finish second to Aston Villa. It was the strapping defender's finest hour, for the following season proved to be disastrous for both him and the club.

Ian played for Stretford and Lancashire Schools, and was an apprentice at both Oldham Athletic and Coventry City before signing professional forms with the latter club in August 1970. He made just four League appearances at Highfield Road, though, and was brought to the Goldstone on loan for two months in September 1970 by Saward, who had been his coach at Coventry. The loan was extended to four months and, after returning to City, he was signed permanently in March 1971 on a 'free'.

Ian didn't figure much initially, mainly because of knee trouble, but made his dramatic re-entry in March 1972 and played his part in the promotion success. In 1972–73, though, Albion fell straight back into Division Three and Ian missed most of the term with further knee problems. After an operation he was installed as captain in the hope that his stirring physical presence would prove inspirational, but it was to no avail and the injuries continued to hamper him. In January 1974 his contract was cancelled and the 23-year-old returned to the Midlands on a personnel management course while assisting Nuneaton Borough. Ian was later employed by Rolls-Royce.

Season	FL	FAC	FLC	Total
1970–71	19+1	2	0	21+1
1971–72	13+1	0	0	13+1
1972–73	14	1	1	16
1973–74	6+2	0	0	6+2
Total	52+4	3	1	56+4

GOORD, GEORGE   1923–26

centre-forward   1 app, 1 goal
full name: George William Goord
born: Brighton, Sussex, 1897
died: Southend, Essex, 3.5.1961
debut: Luton Town (a), 17.10.1925 (FL D3(S))

George Goord gained an R.U.R. Cup winner's medal with the Brighton-based club Vernon Athletic in 1923, and assisted Albion's reserve team on several occasions between 1923 and 1925 along with a number of his Vernon team-mates. He also represented Sussex and played for the Civil Service club in the Isthmian League. In October 1925, George had his only first-team outing for the Albion, scoring the opening goal in a 3–3 draw at Luton. On the strength that performance he was signed as a professional two days later, but wasn't retained at the end of 1925–26 and returned to non-League football.

Season	FL	Total
1925–26	1 (1)	1 (1)
Total	1 (1)	1 (1)

GORDON, DENNIS   1952–61

outside-right   Ht 5 11, Wt 11 07   293 apps, 64 goals
full name: Dennis William Gordon
born: Wolverhampton, Staffordshire, 7.6.1924
debut: Exeter City (h), 24.9.1952 (FL D3(S))

Known affectionately as 'Flash', Dennis Gordon provided superb entertainment down the Albion right and was an essential member of the side which thrilled so many people throughout the 1950s. The popular winger had an ability to worm his way out of tight situations, and he monopolised the no.7 shirt for five seasons, missing just nine League games between 1953 and 1958.

A pupil of Southfield Secondary School in Oxford, Dennis played senior football for Headington United (later Oxford United) from the age of fourteen before joining the R.A.F. in 1942. He saw service with Bomber Command in India, but also played football and rugby for R.A.F. Bombay and the Combined Services, and guested for Lincoln City while stationed at Coningsby towards the end of the war. On his

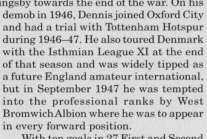

demob in 1946, Dennis joined Oxford City and had a trial with Tottenham Hotspur during 1946–47. He also toured Denmark with the Isthmian League XI at the end of that season and was widely tipped as a future England amateur international, but in September 1947 he was tempted into the professional ranks by West Bromwich Albion where he was to appear in every forward position.

With ten goals in 27 First and Second Division matches for the 'Throstles', Dennis was a considerable acquisition for Brighton when Billy Lane paid £3,500 for his transfer in July 1952. Although he started out at the Goldstone in the no.9 shirt, it was as a typical, old-fashioned winger that he thrilled the Hove crowds with his pace and dribbling skills for nearly a decade. In the Third Division (South) championship campaign of 1957–58, Dennis bagged twelve goals, but he found himself vying for the no.7 berth with Mike Tiddy during Albion's first two seasons in Division Two, and in May 1961, at the age of 36, he was released to join Guildford City in the Southern League. Two years later he moved on to Tunbridge Wells Rangers (where he played alongside his son Mike, who had previously appeared in Albion's reserve team) before finally hanging up his boots in May 1966, a month short of his 42nd birthday.

Employed in Brighton Corporation's Housing Department on leaving the Albion, Dennis retired in 1982 following an operation. Happily, he recovered fully and still leads an active life in Hove.

After a West Bromwich defeat of Blackpool at The Hawthorns in April 1950, the *Birmingham Sports Mail* proclaimed, 'On the night, Flash Gordon was faster than Stan Mortensen and cleverer than Stanley Matthews' — praise indeed!

Season	FL	FAC	Total
1952–53	18 (4)	0	18 (4)
1953–54	45 (10)	4 (1)	49 (11)
1954–55	43 (14)	5 (1)	48 (15)
1955–56	46 (9)	2	48 (9)
1956–57	44 (6)	2	46 (6)
1957–58	43 (12)	3	46 (12)
1958–59	17 (2)	0	17 (2)
1959–60	18 (5)	0	18 (5)
1960–61	3	0	3
Total	277 (62)	16 (2)	293 (64)

GORDON, LES   1928–30

left-half   Ht 5 9, Wt 11 08   18 apps
full name: Leslie William Gordon
born: Barking, Essex, 13.7.1903
debut: Charlton Athletic (a), 26.1.1929 (FL D3(S))

Les Gordon played for Grimsby Rovers before becoming a professional with Sheffield United in May 1923, but in two seasons at Bramall Lane he never appeared in the First Division side and was released to join Crystal Palace in August 1925, where he again failed to break into the first team. In May 1927, Les was playing for Shirebrook in the Midland League when he joined Nottingham Forest, and played his first Football League match the following October, a 2–0 Second Division defeat of Hull City, but his stay at the City Ground was brief, and he had made just one more first-team appearance when he was released to return to Shirebrook before the end of the season.

In August 1928, Les came south to join the Albion staff and inherited the left-half berth from long-serving Wally Little in the latter half of 1928–29. The following season he played in the reserves until he had the misfortune to break a leg on 11 December in a Southern League game at Bournemouth, an injury which ended his Football League career at the age of 26. Les then disappeared from the scene only to resurface in October 1936 when he applied for a permit to play as an amateur for the Cleethorpes Buses works' team.

Season	FL	Total
1928–29	18	18
Total	18	18

GOTSMANOV, SERGEI   1990

forward   Ht 5 8, Wt 11 01   16 apps, 4 goals
full name: Sergei Anatolovich Gotsmanov
born: Minsk, U.S.S.R.(now Belarus), 27.3.1959
debut: Sunderland (a), 24.2.1990 (FL D2)

Soviet international midfielder Sergei Gotsmanov came to the Goldstone on trial from Dinamo Minsk in February 1990 and shone like a beacon for the last two months of the season in a poor Albion side, playing a great part in keeping the club in the Second Division. Speaking no English on his arrival in Hove, Sergei had a couple of games in the reserves before becoming only the second Soviet player to appear in the Football League when he came on as a substitute at Sunderland. Although he was played out of position as a striker because of an injury to Garry Nelson, the skilled Belarussian quickly endeared himself to the Goldstone crowd with a goal and a star performance on his full debut, and everyone concerned with the club hoped that his services might be secured on a permanent basis.

It was not to be, though. In August 1990, Southampton

came up with a £150,000 fee (to Dinamo) and wages that the Albion could not match, but Sergei's spell at The Dell was not a great success and he was released in May 1991 to join the German club Halle. He subsequently returned to his former club Dinamo Minsk, (Belarussian League champions in 1992, '93 and '94, Cup winners '92 and '94) and became a regular international for Belarus, his national side following the dissolution of the Soviet Union. From 1994 he played for Dinamo's reserve side, known as Dinamo-93 Minsk and also playing in the Belarussian League, but moved into the U.S. Indoor Soccer League in 1996 with Minnesota Thunder.

Sergei had started out at the age of eight with the Dinamo junior team Trudavay, and progressed to the senior squad at seventeen. After a year on compulsory military service, during which he played for the local club while stationed in the Belarussian town of Brest, he went on to play over 350 games for Dinamo from 1979 and won 31 caps for the U.S.S.R.'s national team. In June 1984, Sergei scored in the Soviets' 2–0 defeat of England at Wembley, and appeared in the side which lost 2–0 to the Netherlands in the 1988 European Championship final in Munich. His wife Olga is the Belarussian national gymnastics coach.

Season	FL	Total
1989–90	14+2 (4)	14+2 (4)
Total	14+2 (4)	14+2 (4)

GOTTS, JIM
1946–47

outside-right
2 apps
full name: James A. Gotts
born: Seaton Deleval, Northumberland, 17.1.1917
debut: Torquay United (a), 21.12.1946 (FL D3(S))

Jim Gotts played for Ashington in the North Eastern League before the outbreak of war in 1939, but then disappeared from the football scene until resurfacing in Brentford's ranks during the 1945–46 transitional season. After scoring one goal in four outings for the 'Bees', he was recruited by Albion manager Charlie Webb in June 1946 for the return of regular League football, but a pre-season injury limited his opportunities. A lively winger, Jim was one of seven players to appear down the right flank during the difficult 1946–47 campaign, but, at the late age of 29, there was little prospect of a career in the Football League and he departed from the first-class game on his release in May 1947.

Season	FL	Total
1946–47	2	2
Total	2	2

GOUGH, ARTHUR
1925–28

centre-forward
10 apps, 4 goals
full name: Arthur Victor Gough
born: Cirencester, Gloucestershire, 20.1.1900
died: South Cerney, Gloucestershire, 17.7.1975
debut: Merthyr Town (h), 7.11.1925 (FL D3(S))

With well over 100 goals to his name in just three years at the Goldstone, Arthur Gough was one of the most prolific marksmen ever to wear an Albion shirt, yet he was never able to establish himself in the first team and spent almost all his time in the reserves. One of eleven children, Arthur began adult life as an apprentice hairdresser, but volunteered for the Army at the age of seventeen and saw service on the Somme as a despatch rider. On returning to the Cotswolds he took a number of jobs – one as a rabbit-trapper on the large country estates nearby – while playing football for the amateur Swindon Victoria side from where, in October 1923, he graduated to Bristol Rovers to spend two years in their reserve team.

Following a brief trial at the Goldstone, the 25-year-old turned professional with the Albion in September 1925 where, for three seasons, he had to contend with Tommy Cook for a place in the side. The England international centre-forward missed most of the 1925–26 season through injury and no fewer than six players were tried as leader of the attack in his absence. 'Goughy' was given his chance in the autumn of 1925 and responded with two goals in six games, but he then returned to the 'Lambs' and his first-team opportunities were

GOUGH · BRIGHTON & HOVE ALBION · 1925-26 ·

subsequently thinly spread; after two goals in three games in April 1926, he made just one more appearance in the following two seasons as Cook resumed his regular role.

In the reserves, though, Arthur was sensational. In 1926–27 he hit 60 goals in the Southern League and London Combination – the second eleven played 74 game that season – and bagged nine hat-tricks in his time at the Goldstone, thrilling spectators with his speedy, bustling approach. In May 1928 he moved to Walsall on a free transfer, where he netted four goals in sixteen Southern Section games during 1928–29, and then joined Merthyr Town in July 1929 where he ended his senior career with four goals from ten appearances as the hapless Welsh club conceded 135 goals to finish bottom of the Third Division (South).

When Merthyr were voted out of the Football League, Arthur retired from the professional ranks and returned to Gloucestershire to resume his former occupation as a gent's hairdresser while playing for a number of local amateur sides. For fourteen years he was superintendent of the Cirencester open-air swimming-pool before becoming a bookmaker, an occupation he pursued until his retirement in 1970. Also a keen cricketer for the Cirencester club, Arthur is believed to be a great-uncle of Scottish international Richard Gough. His brother Mac played for Queen's Park Rangers.

Season	FL	FAC	Total
1925–26	8 (4)	1	9 (4)
1926–27	1	0	1
Total	9 (4)	1	10 (4)

GOULD, WALLY
1964–68

winger
Ht 5 8, Wt 10 09
193 apps, 46 goals
full name: Walter Gould
born: Rawmarsh, Yorkshire, 25.9.1938
debut: Stockport County (a), 11.1.1964 (FL D4)

A fixture in the Albion team for four years, Wally Gould was a brilliant little ball-playing winger with a fair degree of pace, and played a major part in the Fourth Division championship effort of 1964–65 when he missed only three games and topped the scorers with 21 goals.

As a lad in Rawmarsh, Wally represented Rother Valley Schools and became a junior with Rotherham United while working as an apprentice electrician, an occupation which caused him the loss of several fingers. During his time at Millmoor he was loaned to Rawmarsh Welfare, but in March 1958 he signed as a professional down the road with Sheffield United.

After just five Second Division appearances in nearly three years at Bramall Lane, Wally moved on to York City in February 1961 where his career really took off. With 25 goals from 120 Fourth Division appearances, the 23-year-old winger signed for the Albion in January 1964 for £4,000 and quickly impressed the Goldstone fans. For four years he maintained a consistent level of performance and seldom missed a match, creating many an

99

opportunity with his direct style while also scoring a good number of goals himself, but in February 1968, much to the reluctance of the club, he was released to pursue a highly successful career in South African football.

After starting with Durban United, Wally moved on to the Cape Town club Hellenic in October 1968 as player/assistant manager under former England striker 'Budgie' Byrne, and then became player-manager with East London United. During a spell back in England in 1973–74 he played for Folkestone in the Southern League, and, on returning to the U.K. permanently in 1975, again appeared in the Southern League with Chelmsford City before taking to running a pub. However, after just a few weeks as a licensee, he was offered a coaching job with Stoke City and was appointed assistant to manager Alan Durban in 1979, remaining in the post until Durban was replaced by Richie Barker in 1981.

Season	FL	FAC	FLC	Total
1963–64	18 (3)	0	0	18 (3)
1964–65	43 (21)	1	2	46 (21)
1965–66	41 (10)	3 (1)	3	47 (11)
1966–67	42 (9)	6	6	54 (9)
1967–68	22+2 (2)	2	2	26+2 (2)
Total	166+2 (45)	12 (1)	13	191+2 (46)

GOULDING   1902

inside-left   *1 app*
debut: Luton Town (res.) (a), 6.12.1902 (SEL)

Goulding was a trialist who played in the South Eastern League fixture at Luton in December 1902, but he failed to impress as Albion went down 3–0.

Season	SEL	Total
1902–03	1	1
Total	1	1

GOVIER, STEVE   1974

central defender   *Ht 6 0, Wt 12 00*   *16 apps, 1 goal*
full name: Stephen Govier
born: Watford, Hertfordshire, 6.4.1952
debut: Crystal Palace (h), 17.8.1974 (FL D3)

Brought to the Goldstone Ground in April 1974 together with his Norwich City team-mate Andy Rollings for a combined fee of £25,000, Steve Govier enjoyed – unlike his colleague – only a brief stay on the South Coast. Having joined the 'Canaries' as a 15-year-old amateur, he graduated through an apprenticeship to sign professional forms at Carrow Road in July 1969. The former Watford Schools

representative went on to play in 30 League and Cup games for City, appearing briefly in their Second Division championship side during 1971–72, but he spent most of his time in the reserves, clocking up 183 outings for the Norwich second eleven.

Following his arrival in Hove as part of Brian Clough and Peter Taylor's reconstruction of the Albion, Steve was a regular at the heart of the defence at the outset of the 1974–75 Third Division campaign, but he then picked up an injury, lost his place to Graham Winstanley, and was transferred to Grimsby Town in December for £16,000, the largest fee received by the club at the time. Unfortunately, a severe ligament injury cut short the lanky defender's career at Blundell Park after just 24 League games, and he was forced to quit the game completely in May 1977 at the age of 25. In 1990 he returned to football in Norfolk as manager of the Anglian Combination club Coltishall, and three years later took the reins at Wymondham Town in the same competition.

Season	FL	FLC	Total
1974–75	12 (1)	4	16 (1)
Total	12 (1)	4	16 (1)

GRAHAM, JOHN   1905

centre-forward   *1 app*
full name: John Lang Graham
born: Dalry, Ayrshire, Scotland, 7.8.1881
died: Saltcoats, Ayrshire, Scotland, 15.5.1965
debut: Southampton (h), 14.10.1905 (SL D1)

John Graham came to Hove as a trialist in October 1905 with a reputation as an experienced centre-forward. Although described in the Press as a Scottish international, he had, in fact, represented the Scottish *League* against the Irish League in February 1901.

John set out on his pro career with Kilmarnock, whom he joined from the local Rugby XI club in June 1900 shortly after losing in the Scottish Junior Cup final. Fourteen goals from 37 games earned the young forward his representative honour, but in May 1902 he came south to try his luck with Bristol Rovers. A year later he returned to Scotland with Celtic, but failed to make his mark and, after appearing just four times in 1903–04, was released to sign for Millwall at the end of the campaign.

John's career continued to decline with the 'Dockers' for whom he made only one appearance in the Southern League side before moving briefly into the Lancashire Combination with Accrington Stanley in April 1905. The following September saw him on Alloa Athletic's books, but he was not a success and a few weeks later he arrived at the Goldstone to endure a miserable time. After appearing in one Southern League fixture, once for the reserves and once in a friendly match, John faded into obscurity and his departure failed to solicit any public comment. In March 1906 he resurfaced in his native Ayrshire when he joined the junior club Kilwinning Eglinton. On hanging up his boots John worked as a miner, but later worked for ICI as an explosives operative for many years.

Season	SL	Total
1905–06	1	1
Total	1	1

GRANT, ALAN   1956–60

left-half   *Ht 5 9, Wt 11 10*   *1 app*
full name: Alan James Grant
born: Havant, Hampshire, 6.1.1935
debut: Plymouth Argyle (a), 24.11.1956 (FL D3(S))

When Billy Lane signed Alan Grant from Gosport Borough Athletic as an amateur in February 1956, Albion undertook to play a fund-raising match with the Hampshire League side; and when he turned professional two months later the club made a handsome donation to Borough's bank account. Alan remained at the Goldstone Ground for more than four years, but broke into the

League side just once, when the team was reshuffled in the absence of Frankie Howard at Plymouth Argyle in November 1956, a game which ended in a 2–0 defeat.

Although his regular spot was at half-back, he also played in goal for the reserves on many occasions in the Football Combination before moving to Exeter City in June 1960, but regular first-team football was again out of reach and he made only five League and Cup appearances, all in the 1960–61 season. Alan subsequently played for Eastbourne United, Lewes, Tunbridge Wells, Bedford Town and Salisbury at various times. During his National Service he represented the R.A.F.

Season	FL	Total
1956–57	1	1
Total	1	1

GRANT, JIMMY — 1946–47

outside-left   1 app
full name: James Grant
born: Scotland
debut: Bristol Rovers (a), 7.12.1946 (FL D3(S))

Having served with the R.A.F. in the Middle East during the war, Jimmy Grant arrived at the Goldstone as a trialist in 1946 and, after scoring twice in the reserves' 8–0 Football Combination win over Aldershot on 30 November, was signed on amateur forms. When Wally Hanlon was badly concussed in a Cup-tie at Norwich the following week and subsequently hospitalised, manager Charlie Webb didn't hesitate in giving the Scot his chance on the left wing, but, despite having a reasonable game in a goal-less draw at Bristol Rovers, he never appeared in the League team again and was released in May 1947. Jimmy later played for Eastbourne, where he gained an R.U.R. Cup winner's medal in 1950 and a Sussex Senior Cup runner's-up medal the following year, and also represented the county.

Season	FL	Total
1946–47	1	1
Total	1	1

GRAYER, S. — 1903

inside/outside-right   2 apps
debut: Brentford (res.) (a), 21.3.1903 (SEL)

Grayer was a trialist who played in Albion's South Eastern League team toward the end of the 1902–03 season. His two outings resulted in a 3–0 win at Brentford and a 4–0 home defeat of Bedford Queen's Engineering Works.

Season	SEL	Total
1902–03	2	2
Total	2	2

GREALISH, TONY — 1981–84

midfield   Ht 5 7, Wt 11 07   121 apps, 8 goals
full name: Anthony Patrick Grealish
born: Paddington, London, 21.9.1956
debut: West Ham United (a), 29.8.1981 (FL D1)

Tony Grealish, the man who captained Albion in the 1983 F.A. Cup final, was an accomplished midfield performer when he joined the club in 1981, but had to endure a good deal of criticism from the terraces before winning over the Goldstone fans with some sterling displays. It was always going to be hard for the player who replaced the hugely popular Brian Horton, but Tony had a fine pedigree for the job. The son of a Galway publican, he was raised in London and represented for West London Schools, but was playing Sunday football for Beaumont F.C. on Hackney Marshes when he was discovered by Orient manager George Petchey. After an apprenticeship, he signed as a professional in July 1974 and went on to make 171 League appearances for the "O's", but he never forgot his Irish roots and turned down the chance of an England youth cap to play for the Republic of Ireland.

In fact, Tony won seven full caps at Brisbane Road before moving to Luton Town for £150,000 in August 1979, and was a seasoned international with 23 appearances for the Republic behind him when Mike Bailey paid more than £100,000 for the combative 24-year-old in July 1981. The following October he was presented with a silver salver to mark his 25th cap, and six months later had the honour of captaining his country for the first time, the only Albion player ever to so do. After a rocky first campaign, Tony found his form in 1982–83 and took over the captaincy for the Cup final in the absence of Steve Foster; he emerged from the Wembley tunnel wearing a white headband in sympathy for his suspended colleague.

Less than a year later, though, in March 1984, he joined an exodus of highly-paid players from the Goldstone following the club's relegation and signed for West Bromwich Albion for £95,000. Tony won the last of 44 caps at The Hawthorns before moving to Manchester City in January 1987 after three months on loan at Maine Road. He subsequently had a brief spell with Salgueiros in Portugal before

joining Rotherham United on a free transfer in August 1987 where he made 110 League appearances over three seasons. Two more League appearances as player-coach with Walsall brought his career total to 571, and in the summer of 1992 he moved into the Conference with newly promoted Bromsgrove Rovers. (In August 1992 he played for the West Bromwich Albion All Stars team which won the Umbro Veterans Trophy at Wembley.)

While working in the insurance business, Tony then had spells with Moor Green, Halesowen Harriers, Sutton Coldfield Town and Evesham United (player-coach) before returning to Bromsgrove as coach at the start of the 1994–95 season. In September 1994, following the resignation of Bobby Hope, he took over as caretaker manager; two months later he was appointed to the post permanently, having also had to turn out as a player once more, but was dismissed in March 1995. Tony now works in the scrap-metal business.

Season	FL	FAC	FLC	Total
1981–82	34+3 (1)	3	2 (1)	39+3 (2)
1982–83	38 (2)	8	2 (1)	48 (3)
1983–84	23+2 (3)	3	3	29+2 (3)
Total	95+5 (6)	14	7 (2)	116+5 (8)

GREEN, FREDDIE — 1938–48

full-back   Ht 5 8, Wt 11 05   35 apps
full name: Frederick Zeanes Green
born: Chesterfield, Derbyshire, 9.9.1916
debut: Watford (h), 26.4.1939 (FL D3(S))

Freddie Green was described as 'a fearless tackler' and 'kicked a good length ball', then the basic elements of good full-back play. He set out on a professional career in June 1935 at the age of eighteen when he joined Torquay United from Sheffield junior club Mosborough Trinity, and had 86 League matches under his belt by the time he arrived at the Goldstone Ground three years later.

Freddie was confined to the reserves during the 1938–39 season, but made the first eleven for the final two games as deputy for the injured Ernie Marriott. Lost to the first-class game throughout the war, he missed what should have been the best years of his career, but returned to Hove towards the end of the 1945–46 transitional season and went on to play in a further 24 Southern Section matches before his release in May 1948.

In the immediate post-war period Freddie often hitch-hiked to Hove from his Torquay home on Friday and spent the night in the old, primitive West Stand before turning out on the Saturday. In the 1980s he was living close to Torquay United's Plainmoor ground.

Season	FL	Wartime	Total
1938–39	2	0	2
1945–46	0	9	9
1946–47	21	0	21
1947–48	3	0	3
Total	26	9	35

GREGORY, JOHN   1979–81

right-back/midfield   Ht 6 1, Wt 11 00   81 apps, 7 goals
full name: John Charles Gregory
born: Scunthorpe, Lincolnshire, 11.5.1954
debut: Arsenal (h), 18.8.1979 (FL D1)

One of a handful of players to have won international caps after leaving the Goldstone, John Gregory was a highly versatile footballer who brought a good deal of experience and 'steel' to the Albion side, both in defence and midfield. Signed for a club-record fee in 1979, he played a large part in the "Seagulls'" survival in the First Division during his two seasons in Hove.

The son of a professional footballer of the same name, John was born in Scunthorpe when his father was turning out for the local club, but was brought up in St Neots where he represented Huntingdonshire, Cambridgeshire and the Eastern Counties Schools. After joining Northampton Town as an apprentice, he signed as a professional in May 1972 and went on to make 187 League

appearances for the 'Cobblers', mainly in defence, but on joining Aston Villa in June 1977 he demonstrated his versatility by playing a variety of roles in defence, midfield and up front. In July 1979, Alan Mullery splashed out a record sum of £250,000 to bring the 25-year-old to Hove and played him at right-back, but towards the end of the 1980–81 season John was moved to midfield and responded with four vital goals as the club escaped relegation by the skin of its teeth.

An uncompromising tackler, he attracted the attention of Queen's Park Rangers manager Terry Venables and moved to Loftus Road for £300,000 in June 1981, a sum which Albion found hard to resist. The classy performer proved a great success with Rangers, playing in the losing F.A. Cup final side of 1982 and winning a Division Two championship medal the following season. He also won six caps for England before moving to Third Division Derby County for a £100,000 fee in November 1985, where he was an essential part of the "Rams'" rapid rise to Division One. In July 1988 he joined Portsmouth as player-coach and was later appointed assistant manager, but after taking over as manager in January 1989 he was dismissed twelve months later. John then signed for Plymouth Argyle as a player and temporarily took charge of the team after the dismissal of Ken Brown, but brought his playing career to an end with a seven-match spell at Bolton Wanderers from March 1990.

With the experience of 598 League games behind him, John moved back into coaching in the summer of 1991 with Leicester City, where his former Villa team-mate Brian Little had recently been appointed manager, but having assisted the 'Foxes' into the Premiership in 1994 he accompanied Little back to Aston Villa in November 1994. After nearly two years at Villa Park, John was appointed manager of Wycombe Wanderers in October 1996.

Season	FL	FAC	FLC	Total
1979–80	33	1	3	37
1980–81	39 (7)	2	3	44 (7)
Total	72 (7)	3	6	81 (7)

GREGORY, JULIUS   1906–08

left-back   87 apps, 2 goals
born: Stockport, Cheshire, 1881
died: in action, 1916
debut: Leyton (a), 1.9.1906 (SL D1)

Although he was a regular and effective performer over two seasons with the Albion, Julius Gregory endured a torrid time at the Goldstone Ground. The robust full-back proved to be a little 'over-enthusiastic', and was strongly censured by the F.A. in November 1906 for charging a Northampton Town player 'with undue violence', an episode which led to an unfortunate crowd incident at half-time; Northampton were subsequently ordered to post warning-notices and

to provide better protection for players on their way to the dressing-rooms. Eleven months later, in October 1907, he was suspended for a month following misconduct in a stormy 3–2 defeat at Southampton. This time Albion were ordered to caution their travelling followers –

many of whom had made the journey by paddle-steamer, the *S.S. Brighton Queen* – for their 'unseemly demonstration'.

Born in Stockport, Julius had signed professional forms for Bury in September 1903 at the age of 22, and played in fourteen First Division matches in two seasons with the 'Shakers' before moving to Manchester City in May 1905. Although he made the first team on just three occasions during 1905–06, City were reluctant to release him, but Julius chose to leave Hyde Road for Hove in June 1906 (no transfer fees were required for Football League players joining Southern League clubs at the time). The first-choice left-back for two seasons – apart from his suspension – Julius was released from the Goldstone in May 1908 and moved on to Luton Town where he made 26 Southern League appearances during the 1908–09 campaign, the last of his senior career. Julius died in action while serving as a private with the Royal Fusiliers in 1916.

Season	SL	FAC	UL	WL	SCC	Total
1906–07	36	1	11 (2)	0	0	48 (2)
1907–08	28	0	0	8	3	39
Total	64	1	11 (2)	8	3	87 (2)

GRIERSON, TOM   1908–09

outside-right   7 apps, 1 goal
full name: Thomas William Grierson
born: Sunderland, Co. Durham, 1885
debut: Southampton (a), 7.9.1908 (SL D1)

Spotted playing for Seaham White Star in the Wearside League, Tom Grierson was recruited by the Albion at the age of 23 during the close season of 1908. During the following campaign he played a reserve-team role and performed well, heading the South Eastern League team's scorers with sixteen goals. Although normally an inside-left, Tom appeared mainly on the right-wing in the few first-team outings that came his way, but he wasn't retained

at the end of the season and returned to the North-East.

Season	SL	WL	SCC	Total
1908–09	5 (1)	1	1	7 (1)
Total	5 (1)	1	1	7 (1)

GROVES, FREDDIE   1921–24

outside-right   Ht 5 8, Wt 11 00   60 apps, 2 goals
full name: Frederick William Groves
born: Shadwell, London, 13.1.1891
debut: Southend United (h), 27.8.1921 (FL D3(S))

Freddie Groves joined Woolwich Arsenal from Barnet Alston in August 1912 and made his debut in their Second Division side as an amateur. In October 1913, shortly after the "Gunners'" historic move from Plumstead to Highbury, he signed professional forms and became a regular in the renamed Arsenal team during the First World War, totalling 125 appearances in four seasons of regional football.

With six goals from 50 First Division matches to his name following the restoration of peace, Freddie was quite a notable player when he joined the Albion for a club-record £500 fee in August 1921. Although generally regarded as a right-winger, he appeared in every forward position in his three years at the Goldstone. For two seasons he vied with Jack Nightingale for the outside-right berth, but Nightingale made the position his own in 1923–24 and 33-year-old Freddie departed for Charlton Athletic on a free transfer in June 1924. On retiring from the first-class game in 1925 he married a Brighton lass and worked as a docker. Freddie subsequently played for Dartford in the Southern League.

Season	FL	FAC	Total
1921–22	23 (1)	2	25 (1)
1922–23	26	5	31
1923–24	4 (1)	0	4 (1)
Total	53 (2)	7	60 (2)

GROVES, HENRY   1919–20

inside-right   Ht 5 7, Wt 11 00   5 apps
full name: Henry George Groves
born: London, 1898
debut: Brentford (a), 30.8.1919 (SL D1)

Henry Groves appeared briefly for Arsenal in each of the four seasons of regional football during the First World War, netting twice in nineteen outings. When the situation returned to normal in 1919, he was recruited by the Albion and played in the initial post-war Southern League fixture, but he soon lost his place and, with injury and a resultant loss of form curtailing his appearances, was released at the end of the 1919–20 season. In November 1922, Henry was reinstated as an amateur to play for Chelmsford.

Season	SL	Total
1919–20	5	5
Total	5	5

GRUMMITT, PETER   1973–77

goalkeeper   Ht 5 11, Wt 11 01   158 apps
full name: Peter Malcolm Grummitt
born: Bourne, Lincolnshire, 19.8.1942
debut: Tranmere Rovers (a), 8.12.1973 (FL D3)

Possibly the finest goalkeeper ever to play for the Albion, Peter Grummitt combined superb handling, bravery and excellent reflexes with the experience of 434 League games when he arrived at the Goldstone Ground in December 1973. His performances played a major part in the transformation of the club's fortunes: from Third Division strugglers to promotion contenders at the start of its most successful era.

After starting out with Bourne Town, Peter signed for Nottingham Forest in May 1960 and, in a ten-year career at the City Ground, won three England under-23 caps, represented the Football League, and made 313 First Division appearances. In January 1970 he was transferred to Sheffield Wednesday where he added 121 League games to his total, and toured Australia with an F.A. XI in 1971.

Brian Clough and Peter Taylor brought the 31-year-old to the Goldstone on loan in December 1973 and, with Albion having just lost 8–2 at home to Bristol Rovers, immediately selected him for first-team duties. Signed permanently for a bargain £7,000 fee the following month, Peter was the first-choice goalkeeper for the next three seasons, delighting the Goldstone crowds with his agility and clean handling, but his Football League career came to an abrupt end because of a knee injury sustained in a match against Tranmere Rovers in March 1977 which was compounded by an arthritic hip.

By December, Peter had to admit that the battle to regain full fitness had failed, but he played in his own benefit match in May 1978 and used the proceeds to buy a newsagent's shop in Queen's Road, Brighton. He also had a very brief spell as manager of Lewes and as youth-team coach at Worthing, but Peter then dusted off his gloves to play part-time football, firstly for Dover and then for Worthing with whom he gained representative honours for Sussex, before returning to the Nottingham area.

Season	FL	FAC	FLC	Total
1973–74	16	0	0	16
1974–75	43	3	4	50
1975–76	46	3	2	51
1976–77	31	3	7	41
Total	136	9	13	158

GURINOVICH, IGOR   1990–91

forward   6 apps, 2 goals
full name: Igor Nikolaivich Gurinovich
born: Minsk, U.S.S.R. (now Belarus), 5.3.1960
debut: Oldham Athletic (a), 1.12.1990 (FL D2)

Following closely in the footsteps of Sergei Gotsmanov, Igor Gurinovich failed to make the same impression as his compatriot when his English career was cut short by a failure to gain a work permit.

A graduate of the Institute of Culture in Minsk, he went on to join the Dinamo Minsk club and represented the Soviet youth team. In 1980 he played for the U.S.S.R. side which won the bronze medal at the Moscow Olympics, and gained one cap at full international level against West Germany in March 1984.

Brought to the Goldstone on loan at the age of 30 in November 1990, Igor impressed both Barry Lloyd and the fans in his six outings in the first team, and everyone at the Goldstone was keen to see him permanently on the staff. A fee of £50,000 was agreed with Dinamo, but the deal collapsed when the Home Office, after consultation with the P.F.A., refused his application as he was not a current international.

On leaving Hove, Igor played in Cyprus and then for the Veres Rivne side which finished at the foot of the Ukrainian First Division in 1993, but he then returned to Minsk with the Torpedo club. He also played three times for the Belarussian national side in their vain struggle to qualify for Euro '96, scoring once in a 4–2 defeat by the Czech Republic. In 1994–95, Igor scored four goals in thirteen games towards the end of the season for Linzer ASK, but the club, despite finishing sixth in the top division of the Austrian League, ended the campaign in receivership and he left at the end of the season. By 1997 he was back in Minsk, playing for Ataka-Aura in UEFA's Inter-Toto Cup.

Season	FL	FAC	FMC	Total
1990–91	3+1 (1)	1 (1)	1	5+1 (2)
Total	3+1 (1)	1 (1)	1	5+1 (2)

GUTTRIDGE, RON — 1948–50

full-back   Ht 5 10, Wt 11 04   17 apps

full name: Ronald Guttridge
born: Prescot, Lancashire, 28.4.1916
debut: Swindon Town (h), 21.8.1948 (FL D3(S))

Ron Guttridge joined Aston Villa from the Prescot Cables club of the Lancashire Combination in March 1937, but never made the League side before the outbreak of war. During the hostilities he played for Villa, made 50 guest appearances for Liverpool, and had spells with

Notts County and Nottingham Forest, but was 30 years of age when he made his peacetime debut for Villa in the First Division during the 1946–47 season. Ron was unable to hold a place in the side at Villa Park, though, and joined the Albion in June 1948 when manager Don Welsh paid £500 for his transfer. The quietly-spoken veteran remained at the Goldstone for two seasons, but, after a run of nine games at the start of the 1948–49 campaign, he struggled to make the team and in May 1950 was released to join Hastings United in the Southern League.

Season	FL	Total
1948–49	10	10
1949–50	7	7
Total	17	17

HACKING, BOB — 1947–48

inside-forward   22 apps, 3 goals

full name: Robert Edward Hacking
born: Blackburn, Lancashire, 30.3.1918
debut: Bournemouth & B.A. (h), 30.8.1947 (FL D3(S))

Bob Hacking was a product of Blackburn Technical School and a Lancashire county representative who joined Blackburn Rovers as an amateur in September 1942. During the war he served in the Royal Air Force and made guest appearances for Arsenal and Luton Town, and it was for the 'Hatters' that he signed as a professional in April 1947 at the late age of 29. Four months later, after just one appearance at Kenilworth Road, Bob was recruited by Albion manager Tommy Cook who paid a hefty £500 for his signature.

The Lancastrian inside-forward alternated between the left and right berths until February 1948 when, in a disastrous re-election

campaign, he lost his place as new boss Don Welsh went on a £7,000 spending spree in a desperate bid to bring about an improvement. In August 1948, Bob left for Southport and went on to play in 181 Third Division (North) matches, mainly as a half-back. In six seasons at Haig Avenue he gained a reputation as an excellent ball-player, and became a great favourite with the fans before moving into the Lancashire Combination for a season with Lancaster City. On hanging up his boots Bob became a market-gardener, and now lives in retirement in the Southport area.

Season	FL	FAC	Total
1947–48	17 (2)	5 (1)	22 (3)
Total	17 (2)	5 (1)	22 (3)

HAIG-BROWN, ALAN — 1903–05

outside-right   3 apps

full name: Alan Roderick Haig-Brown
born: Charterhouse School, Godalming, Surrey, 6.9.1877
died: in action near Bapaume, France, 25.3.1918
debut: West Ham United (a), 31.10.1903 (FAC Q3)

Alan Haig-Brown was one of those remarkable gentleman amateurs that abounded in English sport around the turn of the century. The youngest son of the headmaster of Charterhouse School, he was educated at Charterhouse and at Pembroke College, Cambridge (where he achieved an M.A.), and played for the Old Carthusians, Cambridge University (Blues 1898 and 18'99) and the Corinthians. He also represented Pembroke College at athletics and cricket.

A soldier and a scholar, 'Haigers' was appointed to the teaching staff of Lancing College in 1899, and also commanded the school's Cadet Corps and Officer Training Corps from 1906 until 1915 when he enlisted with the Army. During this period the fleet-footed winger assisted both Worthing and Shoreham in the West Sussex Senior League, and gained a Senior Cup runner's-up medal with the latter side in 1906. He also represented Sussex – winning his colours in 1900–01 – and played occasionally for Albion's reserves over several seasons, but made just three appearances in the first-team. As a talented amateur the football world was his oyster: he also appeared briefly for Tottenham Hotspur in the Southern League and for Clapton Orient in the Football League.

Alan was also a writer of some note: he made contributions to *The Times* and other newspapers; had more than a thousand poems and articles published; and was the author of three books, *Sporting Sonnets*, *My Game Book* and *The O.T.C. in the Great War*.

'Haigers' attained the rank of lieutenant-colonel during the conflict, commanding the 23rd Battalion of the Middlesex Regiment, and was twice mentioned in dispatches in addition to being awarded the Distinguished Service Order for his bravery. Sadly, he was one of thousands of men who lost their lives in the Second Battle of the Somme, but his obituaries in *The Times* and Lancing College's Magazine reflected both the devotion of the troops under his command and that of his former pupils and colleagues.

Season	FAC	UL	Total
1903–04	1	0	1
1905–06	0	2	2
Total	1	2	3

18 players who won the Football League Cup

Player	Club	Year
Barham, Mark	Norwich City	1985
Beal, Phil	Tottenham Hotspur	1971, 1973
Boyle, John	Chelsea	1965
Bridges, Barry	Chelsea	1965
Case, Jimmy	Liverpool	1981
Chivers, Martin	Tottenham Hotspur	1971, 1973
Corrigan, Joe	Manchester City	1970, 1976
Cross, Graham	Leicester City	1964
Downsborough, Peter	Swindon Town	1969
Foster, Steve	Luton Town	1988
Kinnear, Joe	Tottenham Hotspur	1971, 1973
Langley, Jimmy	Queen's Park Rangers	1967
Lawrenson, Mark	Liverpool	1982, 1983, 1984
Mortimer, Dennis	Aston Villa	1977
Robinson, Michael	Liverpool	1984
Saunders, Dean	Aston Villa	1994
Sidebottom, Geoff	Aston Villa	1961
Wilson, Danny	Luton Town	1988
	Sheffield Wednesday	1991

HALL, ERNIE   *1937–39*

| centre-half | Ht 5 10 | 4 apps |

full name: Ernest Hall
born: Crawcrook, Co. Durham, 6.8.1916
debut: Gillingham (a), 29.9.1937 (SSC R1)

Newcastle United paid £10 for seventeen-year-old Ernie Hall's signature in September 1933 when he was playing for the West Wylam club, but in three-and-a-half years at St James's Park he had little opportunity to shine, making the League side on just two occasions. In May 1937 he joined the Albion, but again his chances were somewhat limited and, after acting as understudy to Jack Stevens for two seasons, Ernie left for Stoke City just before the outbreak of war in September 1939.

Season	FL	SSC	Total
1937–38	3	1	4
Total	3	1	4

HALL, FRETWELL   *1920–21*

| right-half | Ht 5 11, Wt 12 07 | 12 apps |

born: Wortley, Yorkshire, 1892
debut: Southend United (a), 28.8.1920 (FL D3(S))

Fretwell Hall played for South Shields and Goole Town before enlisting with the Army on the outbreak of the Great War. He saw active service with the Veterinary Corps in the Balkans, but came through unscathed to join Norwich City in August 1919, where he played in 30 matches during the last season of the old Southern League. In June 1920 the dapper wing-half was brought to the Goldstone Ground for Albion's initial Football League campaign and played at right-half in the inaugural match, but with Jack Bollington and George Coomber also in contention for the right-half berth he totalled only twelve appearances and saw out most of the season with the reserves.

F. HALL

The 'Lambs' won the Southern League's English Section title in 1920–21 and were also runners-up in the South Eastern League; Fretwell was chosen to represent the latter's representative side on 29 March against the champions, Portsmouth reserves. Two months later he was released and returned to his native Yorkshire with Halifax Town in June for their opening season in the newly formed Third Division (North) where he was later joined by his brother Ellis. After 51 League appearances in two seasons at The Shay, Fretwell returned to the Southern League with Torquay United (1923–24) and Peterborough & Fletton United (1924–25).

Fretwell was the youngest of four football-playing brothers. His eldest brother, Ben, made 269 League and Cup appearances for Derby County before the First World War, and also played for Grimsby Town and Leicester Fosse before being appointed manager of Bristol Rovers in 1920; Harry played for Huddersfield Town; and Ellis for Hull City, Hastings & St Leonards United, Stoke, Huddersfield Town, Hamilton Academical, Millwall and Halifax Town.

Season	FL	Total
1920–21	12	12
Total	12	12

HALL, JACK   *1908–09*

| outside-right | Ht 5 10, Wt 12 00 | 27 apps, 3 goals |

full name: John Edward Hall
born: South Shields, Co. Durham, 1881
debut: Southampton (h), 2.9.1908 (SL D1)

Although he made a total of 27 senior appearances for the Albion, all in the 1908–09 season, Jack Hall was never a regular in the side. In fact, he shared the right-wing spot with Jimmy Brennan and Tom Grierson, and his appearances came in several short spells. Jack played for the junior clubs Harton Star and Kingston Villa in his native County Durham, but joined the Albion from Barnsley during the close season of 1908 after three years with the Yorkshire club, in which he scored fourteen goals in 74 Second Division games.

After leaving the Goldstone in May 1909, Jack played for Rochdale in the Lancashire Combination and then for South Shields, his home-town club, in the North Eastern League until February 1911 when he signed for Preston North End. (The F.A. subsequently ordered Preston to pay Albion a £5 fee for his transfer as the club still held his registration.) Jack scored three times in eighteen First Division outings at Deepdale, but was released to return to the Southern League with Pontypridd in May 1912. A year later he rejoined South Shields where he saw out his playing days.

Jack went on to enjoy a successful coaching career in Holland after the First World War, holding posts with Feyenoord (1926–30), P.S.V. Eindhoven (1930–35), V.U.C. (1935–38) and Feyenoord again (1940).

Season	SL	FAC	WL	WL Ch.	SCC	Total
1908–09	20 (3)	1	3	1	2	27 (3)
Total	20 (3)	1	3	1	2	27 (3)

HALL, JACK   *1906–08*

| centre-forward | Ht 5 11, Wt 13 03 | 93 apps, 54 goals |

full name: John Henry Hall
born: Hucknall, Nottinghamshire, 3.7.1883
died: Birmingham, Warwickshire, 20.2.1949
debut: Leyton (a), 1.9.1906 (SL D1)

'Wonderfully accurate near the net and knows how to keep a quintette together.' So ran a contemporary description of Jack Hall, a prolific centre-forward who hit 138 goals in 291 Football League and Southern League matches for his five clubs. The Hucknall-born goal-getter was top scorer in his two seasons at the Goldstone Ground and was the first player to score more than 50 goals for the Albion. Indeed, he held the club's aggregate scoring record for more than four years until it was overtaken by Bert Longstaff in December 1911.

Jack started out with his local boys' club and progressed into the Midland League with Newark. The quietly-spoken forward had a trial with nearby Nottingham Forest, but in October 1904 he joined Stoke and went on to score eighteen goals in 53 First Division matches for the 'Potters' before joining the Albion in May 1906.

Mixing zeal with brains, Jack led the forwards in dashing style and his form at the Goldstone was quite outstanding. The acquisition of such a capable goalscorer transformed a team which had just escaped relegation the previous season into one which finished third in the Southern League's First Division. In his first season he netted 28 goals in all competitions, setting a club record of 22 League goals in the process, and hit another 26 the following term. Such prolific scoring attracted the Middlesbrough scouts, and when the First Division club came up with a £700 fee in April 1908 the 24-year-old moved to Ayresome Park. (In fact, there was a maximum transfer fee of £350 at the time, but the big clubs got around the problem by buying two players, one they wanted and one they didn't – a 'make-weight'. Thus Jack was accompanied to Yorkshire by Harry Kent, 'Boro paying the maximum £350 for both men.) However, the F.A. fined Middlesbrough £100 after Stoke protested that they still held the player's Football League registration.

In his two seasons at Ayresome Park, Jack twice finished as top scorer (ahead of the legendary Steve Bloomer) with a total of 30 goals from 59 League games, but in June 1910 he was transferred to Leicester Fosse in the Second Division where he remained for just six months before moving on to Birmingham in December. In five successful years at St Andrews he netted 47 goals in 97 Second Division matches up to the First World War before being forced out of the first-class game with a series of injuries. Jack moved into the licensed trade on his retirement as a professional, but also turned out for his home-town club, Hucknall Town. For many years until his death in 1949 he was landlord of the Small Heath Tavern, just a short distance from St Andrews.

Season	SL	FAC*	UL	WL	SCC	Total
1906–07	37 (22)	1	9 (6)	0	0	47 (28)
1907–08*	30 (16)	5 (2)	0	7 (5)	4 (3)	46 (26)
Total	67 (38)	6 (2)	9 (6)	7 (5)	4 (3)	93 (54)

Note: Hall's goal in the F.A. Cup tie at Preston North End (16.1.1908) has not been included as it was scored in extra-time which was not completed because of bad light. The F.A. deemed the match to be a 1–1 draw, the score at the end of 90 minutes.

HALL, PROCTOR   1905–06

inside-right   Ht 5 8, Wt 10 08   40 apps, 8 goals
born: Blackburn, Lancashire, 1883
debut: Leyton (h), 6.9.1905 (UL)

A diminutive, ball-playing inside-forward, Proctor Hall was one of Frank Scott-Walford's first acquisitions on his appointment as Albion manager in 1905, but, like many players of that era, his stay lasted just one season. His first major club was Manchester United, whom he joined in September 1903 from Oswaldtwistle Rovers of the Lancashire Combination, but he had only eight appearances in the first team before being released to join the Goldstone staff in 1905.

Although he was Albion's regular inside-right during 1905–06, Proctor left for Aston Villa at the end of the season, but failed to make the senior team in a very short stay at Villa Park and was transferred to Second Division Bradford City in October 1906. Six goals from 28 Second Division outings for the Yorkshire club were followed by spells with Luton Town (signed May 1907), Chesterfield (January 1908), and Hyde in the Lancashire Combination (close season 1909). During the summer of 1912, Proctor was recruited by the newly formed Newport County and was ever-present in their first season in the Southern League's Second Division, after which he moved on to another Welsh Southern League club, Mardy.

Season	SL	FAC	UL	Total
1905–06	27 (7)	5 (1)	8	40 (8)
Total	27 (7)	5 (1)	8	40 (8)

HAMMOND, HARRY   1903 & 1906–07

right-half   1 app
full name: Harry Edward Hammond
born: Hove, Sussex, 1882
debut: Grays United (a), 25.4.1903 (SEL)

Harry Hammond appeared in Albion's final South Eastern League match of the 1902–03 season, a 5–0 defeat at Grays United when a number of trialists were given a run-out while the first-teamers took on Brentford in a friendly. A prominent member of the Hove Park club which carried off the Sussex Junior Cup in 1905 and the Mid Sussex Senior League title in 1904–05 and 1905–06, Harry signed for the Albion as an amateur again in 1906–07 and played regularly for the reserves, but in February 1907 Hove Park complained to the F.A. that an illegal approach had been made to the player. Albion, however, made a successful counter-claim that Hove Park had fielded Harry without giving them the required notice, and the Association's commission of inquiry fined the amateur club £1. (Amateurs could play for any club of their choice, but F.A. rules required that 48 hours' notice should be given to their previous club.)

Season	SEL	Total
1902–03	1	1
Total	1	1

HANLON, WALLY   1946–48

outside-left   Ht 5 7, Wt 10 01   78 apps, 4 goals
full name: Walter Hanlon
born: Glasgow, Lanarkshire, Scotland, 23.9.1919
debut: Port Vale (h), 31.8.1946 (FL D3(S))

A slimline left-winger with clever ball-control and the ability to beat a man on a sixpence, Wally Hanlon joined Clyde in April 1945 for the last emergency season and came south in August 1946. Quickly impressing all at the Goldstone with his touch-line skills, he missed just twelve matches in two seasons with the Albion — all through injury. In May 1948, Wally was transferred to Bournemouth, but after just one season at Dean Court he moved on to Crystal Palace in July 1949 where he became a great favourite over the next six years. In April 1954 he received a testimonial, a strong London XI taking on Palace for his benefit. After leaving Selhurst Park, Wally played for Sudbury Town.

Season	FL	FAC	Total
1946–47	41 (4)	1	42 (4)
1947–48	31	5	36
Total	72 (4)	6	78 (4)

HANNAM, DAVE   1959–63

outside-right   Ht 5 7, Wt 10 07   6 apps, 2 goals
full name: David Vincent Hannam
born: Islington, London, 10.5.1944
debut: Portsmouth (h), 25.9.1962 (FLC R2)

A Sussex representative at youth level while an Albion junior, Dave Hannam was signed as a professional a few weeks after his seventeenth birthday in June 1961 having spent two years on the ground staff. A fast and determined little winger, he made excellent

progress in the reserves, but on breaking into the League team in 1962–63 he struggled to impress – like several other youngsters thrown in at the deep end that season – in a very poor side which was relegated to Division Four.

Dave failed to survive new manager Archie Macaulay's end-of-season clear-out and joined Tunbridge Wells Rangers in the Southern League. In the summer of 1964 he played for Slavia in the Victoria State League in Australia, and then had spells with Crawley Town and Hastings United before becoming a key member of the excellent Southwick team of the late 1960s and early '70s, where he won a County League championship and gained a Sussex Senior Cup medal. Dave suffered two serious leg-breaks while at Old Barn Way and retired from the game, but he later had a spell as coach with Shoreham. He is now in business in Florida, U.S.A.

Season	FL	FLC	Total
1962–63	5 (2)	1	6 (2)
Total	5 (2)	1	6 (2)

HARBURN, Peter   1951–52 & 1955–58

centre-forward   Ht 6 1, Wt 12 07   *133 apps, 65 goals*
full name: Peter Arthur Patrick Harburn
born: Finsbury, London, 18.6.1931
debut: Gillingham (a), 8.4.1955 (FL D3(S))

One of the chief entertainers at the Goldstone in the mid '50s, Peter Harburn was a big, powerful centre-forward who scored a hatful of goals as Albion battled for promotion to the Second Division. The ex-sailor's best season was his first full campaign, 1955–56, when he scored in eight consecutive games and hit 27 goals, but he finished top scorer just once, in the successful 1957–58 promotion campaign when he and Dave Sexton bagged 20 goals apiece.

Peter had been an amateur on Brentford's ground staff in 1946, but he joined the Royal Navy as a Boy Seaman a year later and was soon representing the Senior Service. In 1949–50 he turned out for Uxbridge in the Corinthian League, and the following season appeared in both the Portsmouth and Albion reserve teams, but it wasn't until 1955 that he joined Brighton on a permanent basis together with his fellow sailor Malcolm Stephens.

Making his Football League debut in a 1–1 draw at Gillingham in April 1955, Peter initially played in the Albion first team as an

amateur. In February 1956 he was named in the Great Britain squad for the Melbourne Olympics, but just two days earlier he had signed professional forms for the club having bought himself out of the Navy, and therefore had to decline the invitation. It was a tremendous disappointment to miss out on the trip to Australia and he received a letter of apology from the Football Association, but it did little to damage his career at the Goldstone Ground as he went on to lead an excellent attack in dynamic fashion. The enthusiastic no.9 was selected to represent the Third Division's Southern Section against the Northern Section at Brunton Park, Carlisle, in March 1958 and bagged the only goal of the game.

Almost inevitably, Peter's form caught the attention of bigger clubs, and he was transferred to First Division Everton for £8,000 in August 1958; coming just before Albion's debut in the Second Division, it was a tremendous blow to supporters. The move was not a success, though, and he scored just once in four appearances before moving on to Second Division Scunthorpe United five months later in January 1959. Despite scoring in the first minute of his debut for the Lincolnshire side, his stay was again brief, and in October 1959 he signed for Workington where he scored 23 times in 67 outings before leaving the first-class game in 1961.

Peter went on to play in the Southern League for Chelmsford City, Stevenage Town and Wisbech Town, and subsequently became coach and manager at Chelmsford. He was mine-host of the Bird in Hand pub in Chelmsford for some time, and was still playing in Essex junior football for Longmeads F.C. as a goalkeeper in 1984. Indeed, he was voted Player of the Season five years after his son had gained the same distinction! Peter subsequently worked as a salesman in the motor trade and lives in Great Baddow near Chelmsford.

Season	FL	FAC	Total
1954–55	7 (3)	0	7 (3)
1955–56	41 (23)	2 (4)	43 (27)
1956–57	36 (15)	2	38 (15)
1957–58	42 (20)	3	45 (20)
Total	126 (61)	7 (4)	133 (65)

HARDING, F.   1905–06

centre-half   *1 app*
debut: Clapton Orient (h), 31.1.1906 (UL)

Harding was recruited by the Albion during the summer of 1905 from Swindon Town where he had been a reserve-team player. He performed a similar role with the Albion and made a solitary first-team appearance in a goal-less United League match with Clapton Orient at the Goldstone Ground, but he was released in May 1906.

Season	UL	Total
1905–06	1	1
Total	1	1

HARDMAN, J.   1902–04

half-back   *21 apps, 1 goal*
debut: Brighton Amateurs (h), 4.10.1902 (FAC Q1)

Hardman was an aptly named half-back who was serving as a guardsman when he was spotted by the Albion. Signed in September 1902, he appeared in four different positions in the Southern League team before leaving the club in May 1904. A tall, dominating defender, particularly strong in the air, Hardman scored on his Southern League debut, a 5–0 home win over Chesham Town.

Season	SL	Test	FAC	SEL	Total
1902–03	3 (1)	1	3	11	18 (1)
1903–04	3	0	0	0	3
Total	6 (1)	1	3	11	21 (1)

HARKER, Frank   1905–06

inside-left   *1 app*
full name: Frank Miles Harker
born: Hove, Sussex, 1884
debut: Leyton (h), 12.12.1906 (UL)

Frank Harker was a member of the Hove team which appeared in successive Sussex Senior Cup finals, losing to Shoreham in 1906 but defeating Eastbourne after a replay in 1907, and also represented Sussex. He assisted Albion occasionally over a three-season period, and made a solitary appearance in the first eleven as a late stand-in for Wally Smith in a 1–1 United League draw with Leyton at the Goldstone in December 1906.

Season	UL	Total
1906–07	1	1
Total	1	1

HARLAND, LOHMANN   1902–03

left-half   28 apps, 2 goals
full name: Alfred Harland
born: Southwick, Sussex, 1873
debut: Southall (h), 13.9.1902 (SL D2)

One of Brighton United's trio of Southwick players – the others were Ned Collins and Jimmy Paige – Alfred Harland was usually known by the nickname 'Lohmann', probably after the famed Surrey and England bowler of the period, George Lohmann, as he was also a splendid cricketer with Southwick and Sussex Colts. Indeed, a newspaper article referred to Lohmann Harland in 1945 as "the best cricketer/footballer the 'Little Wickers' have ever produced." Together with his two future United colleagues, Lohmann appeared in four successive Sussex Senior Cup finals for Southwick in the 1890s but won on just one occasion, in 1897.

A Sussex representative (colours 1895–96), he joined Brighton United as a professional during the club's final season, 1899–1900, but was later reinstated as an amateur to play for Southwick Swifts. Lohmann made a guest appearance in a friendly for the Albion in their first season, 1901–02, and joined the club during the close season of 1902 to become a regular member of the side which won the Southern League's Second Division title jointly with Fulham. However, he missed out in the promotion-clinching test match and, after playing for the reserves, returned to local football.

Season	SL	FAC	SEL	Total
1902–03	9	5 (2)	14	28 (2)
Total	9	5 (2)	14	28 (2)

HARRISON, JACK   1931–34

outside-left   Ht 5 8, Wt 10 07   5 apps, 3 goals
full name: John Richard Harrison
born: Rhyl, Flintshire, Wales, 1908
debut: Coventry City (a), 29.4.1933 (FL D3(S))

Exceptionally fast and the possessor of a 'cannon-ball' shot in his left foot, Jack Harrison was a notable boxer and athlete at his school. He was also a fair footballer and won Welsh junior international honours with Llandudno Junction. After joining his home-town club, Rhyl Athletic, the young winger signed for Manchester City in February 1929, but made only two First Division appearances before transferring to Sheffield United in June 1930.

After a year in Yorkshire, Jack arrived at the Goldstone in August 1931, but a month into the season he broke his collar-bone in the reserves and was out for the rest of the term. It was not until April 1933 that he made his first-team debut, but, like a number of other reserve left-wingers of the period, he found it impossible to dislodge Ernie 'Tug' Wilson. When he was released in 1934, Jack forsook the first-class game to resume his trade as a plumber.

Season	FL	Total
1932–33	2 (2)	2 (2)
1933–34	3 (1)	3 (1)
Total	5 (3)	5 (3)

HASSELL, TOMMY   1950–51

inside-left   52 apps, 19 goals
full name: Thomas William Hassell
born: Stoneham, Southampton, Hampshire, 5.4.1919
died: Hove, Sussex, April 1984
debut: Luton Town (a), 2.10.1943 (wartime)
peacetime debut: Bristol Rovers (h), 16.9.1950 (FL D3(S))

A wartime guest who later joined the Albion on a permanent basis, Tommy Hassell represented Eastleigh and Hampshire at schoolboy level, and progressed to the Hampshire League with Romsey Town and Southern Railway (Eastleigh). Joining Southampton as an amateur in 1939, he signed pro forms in February 1940, soon after the outbreak of the Second World War, and scored 26 goals in 112 wartime matches for the 'Saints' while also playing for Chelsea, Luton Town and Millwall.

Tommy made 39 guest appearances for the Albion over a three-season period before joining Aldershot in May 1946, but came to the Goldstone as a part-time professional in August 1950 at the age of 31 after 113 League games at the Recreation Ground. A small, quiet ball-player, Tommy turned in some useful performances for the Albion, but his best years had already been lost to the war and he left for Kent League side Folkestone in June 1951. He later played for Lewes, Bexhill Town and Newhaven in the Sussex County League, and returned to the Goldstone as an assistant trainer from 1964 to 1967. For many years until his death in 1984, Tommy worked as a fitter in the British Rail workshops at Brighton.

Season	FL	FAC	Wartime	Total
1943–44	0	0	23 (11)	23 (11)
1944–45	0	0	7 (1)	7 (1)
1945–46	0	0	9 (3)	9 (3)
1950–51	11 (4)	2	0	13 (4)
Total	11 (4)	2	39 (15)	52 (19)

HASTINGS, BILL   1909–12

outside-left   100 apps, 15 goals
full name: William Hastings
born: West Hartlepool, Co. Durham, 1888
debut: Portsmouth (a), 1.9.1909 (SL D1)

After arriving at the Goldstone from Northern League side West Hartlepool during the summer of 1909, Bill Hastings missed just one game as Albion won the Southern League championship and Southern Charity Cup in 1909–10, and was absent for only two the following season when the club lifted the F.A. Charity Shield. Although occasionally appearing on the right flank, he was at his most effective on the left and provided excellent service for the main goalscorers, Bill 'Bullet' Jones and Charlie Webb. Indeed, Bill was a crucial part of the finest team assembled at Hove in over 75 years.

In February 1912, Second Division Birmingham paid £100 for his signature, and he remained at St Andrews until September 1914 before moving to Watford, where he won a second Southern League championship medal in 1914–15. During the Great War, Bill served with the Royal Flying Corps, and played for Hartlepools United in the North Eastern League when peace resumed.

Season	SL	FAC	FACS	SCC	Total
1909–10	41 (4)	1	0	4 (1)	46 (5)
1910–11	37 (6)	2	1	5 (2)	45 (8)
1911–12	7 (1)	0	0	2 (1)	9 (2)
Total	85 (11)	3	1	11 (4)	100 (15)

HAWLEY, FRED   1925–26

centre-half   Ht 5 10, Wt 12 00   *39 apps, 4 goals*
full name: Frederick Hawley
born: Alvaston, Derby, Derbyshire, 28.10.1890
debut: Newport County (a), 29.8.1925 (FL D3(S))

In a lengthy professional career, Fred Hawley accumulated 306 League appearances, and, but for the four-year break caused by the First World War, may well have established himself in the top flight for many years. The well-built pivot joined Sheffield United from Ripley Town for a £70 fee in December 1912 and made his debut for the 'Blades' at centre-forward in a 4–1 victory over Derby County at Bramall Lane, but he quickly reverted to the centre-half berth and had made 57 First Division appearances before the wartime hiatus in 1915. Working in a Coventry munitions factory throughout the hostilities, he guested at various times for Coventry City, Birmingham, Derby County and both Nottingham clubs in the wartime regional competitions.

Fred was officially transferred to Coventry City in May 1919 for the considerable sum of £350 on their election to the Second Division of the Football League, but was soon on the move when Birmingham paid £250 for his services in January 1920. After a brief spell back at Coventry towards the end of the 1919–20 season, he joined Swindon Town in May 1920 for their first campaign in the newly formed Third Division, and remained in Wiltshire until March 1923 when he was recruited by Bristol City to strengthen their defence for the run-in to the championship of the Third Division (South) that season.

In June 1925, Albion paid £350 for the experienced defender, a massive outlay for a 34-year-old at the time, and he held the centre-half spot throughout the 1925–26 season, forming a splendid understanding with wing-halves Reg Wilkinson and Wally Little. Fred was released to join Queen's Park Rangers in May 1926, his last club before moving into non-League football with Loughborough Corinthians two years later.

F. HAWLEY - BRIGHTON & HOVE ALBION · 1925 · 25 ·

Season	FL	FAC	Total
1925–26	37 (4)	2	39 (4)
Total	37 (4)	2	39 (4)

HAWORTH, JACK   1909–12

left-half   *99 apps, 9 goals*
full name: John Houghton Haworth
born: Bolton, Lancashire, 1887
debut: Norwich City (a), 7.10.1909 (SL D1)

In January 1910, with Albion challenging for the Southern League title, manager Jack Robson drafted Jack Haworth, who had made three appearances as a deputy half-back, into the first team as a stop-gap centre-forward in place of the suspended Bill 'Bullet' Jones. The experiment lasted just two matches – a 3–0 victory over Brentford and a home defeat by Southampton in the F.A. Cup – before Robson

swapped Haworth and regular left-half Harry Middleton. This latter move proved an outstanding success, and the 22-year-old wing-half from Bolton made the position his own as the club lost only one more game in sweeping to the title.

Jack was playing for Turton in the Lancashire Combination when he was recommended by Albion skipper Joe Leeming, himself a native of Turton, and he arrived at the Goldstone in the close season of 1909. A fixture in an exceptional side for two years, he played in the team which won F.A. Charity Shield in September 1910, and missed just one game before First Division Middlesbrough splashed out a big fee of £600 on him in February 1912. Jack was converted into a right-back at Ayresome Park and remained with the First Division club until the First World War brought about a closure of regular football in 1915, which effectively ended his career after 64 League and Cup outings for the Yorkshire side.

Season	SL	FAC	FACS	SCC	Total
1909–10	20 (2)	1	0	4 (1)	25 (3)
1910–11	37 (5)	3	1	5	46 (5)
1911–12	24	1 (1)	0	3	28 (1)
Total	81 (7)	5 (1)	1	12 (1)	99 (9)

HAYES, BILLY   1919–24

goalkeeper   Ht 6 0, Wt 12 00   *225 apps*
full name: Thomas William Hayes
born: Eccleston, Lancashire, 28.5.1895
debut: Brentford (a), 30.8.1919 (SL D1)

Billy Hayes was a remarkably consistent goalkeeper who, having joined the Goldstone staff in August 1919 at the age of 24, missed just one game in five seasons with the Albion and made 175 consecutive appearances, a club record which stood until it was surpassed by Eric Gill in September 1956. He presided over the meanest defence since the club joined the Football League – conceding just 34 goals in 1922–23 (equalled in 1984–85) – and kept his goal intact for seven consecutive games in December 1923 and January 1924, still the best performance by any Albion goalkeeper.

Born in Eccleston, Lancashire, Billy became a professional at nearby Preston North End at the age of seventeen in 1912, but

was loaned to Chorley in the Lancashire Combination for the 1913–14 campaign before making his debut for Preston in the side which won promotion to the First Division in 1914–15. That was the last season before the First World War brought about a four-year break in regular League football, and on the resumption of normality in 1919 he arrived in Sussex.

After being ever-present in the Albion first team's final campaign in the Southern League, Billy played in their first-ever Football

W. HAYES. BRIGHTON & HOVE ALBION F.C. 1920–21

League game in August 1920 and went on to establish his impressive record. In June 1924 he was somewhat surprisingly released and left for Southend United where he was again ever-present in his first season. After two years with the Essex side, he headed back north in June 1926 for a season with Accrington Stanley, and then, in the summer of 1927, moved to Stockport County where he added another sixteen League appearances to bring his career total in the Football League and Southern League to 328 games. Billy subsequently lined up for Winsford United, Burscough Rangers, Stalybridge Celtic and Bacup Borough before hanging up his gloves. His son, Sam Hayes, was an amateur goalkeeper with Blackburn Rovers and Accrington Stanley.

Season	FL	SL	FAC	Total
1919–20	0	42	1	43
1920–21	41	0	3	44
1921–22	42	0	3	45
1922–23	42	0	5	47
1923–24	42	0	4	46
Total	167	42	16	225

HEALER, ERNIE
1963–64

inside-left 3 apps, 1 goal
full name: Ernest Healer
born: Birtley, Co. Durham, 13.11.1941
debut: Workington (a), 14.12.1963 (FL D4)

Ernie Healer, who had been on Darlington's staff as a youngster, arrived at the Goldstone in October 1963 on a free transfer from Berwick Rangers. Archie Macaulay's first signing for the Albion, the 22-year-old inside-forward made three successive appearances in the absence of Bill Cassidy in December 1963, performing up front alongside Keith Webber and showing some promise, but he injured an ankle after giving his side a half-time lead in a 2–1 home defeat by Exeter City on Boxing Day and never played for the first team again. Ernie was released at the end of the season and moved into the Southern League with Crawley Town, where he had the misfortune to break a leg on two occasions in 1965.

Season	FL	Total
1963–64	3 (1)	3 (1)
Total	3 (1)	3 (1)

HENDERSON, BILLY
1919–20

wing-half Ht 5 10, Wt 13 00 2 apps
full name: William Henderson
born: Whitburn, Co. Durham, 5.1.1900
died: South Shields, Co. Durham, 18.1.1934
debut: Merthyr Town (a), 17.1.1920 (SL D1)

Billy Henderson came to the Goldstone as a promising half-back from Wearside League club Whitburn in November 1919 and made his Southern League debut two months later at the age of 20. However, with the vastly experienced pre-war middle line of Billy Booth, George Coomber and Gunner Higham still in possession, his opportunities were rare, and when Albion became one of the founder members of the Third Division in 1920 he was released to join Aberdare Athletic in the Southern League.

The following year the Welsh club were elected to the Football League,

and such was Billy's form that he signed for Second Division West Ham United in March 1922. His career positively blossomed at Upton Park, and in 1923 he played at right-back in the "Hammers'" team which lost 2–0 to Bolton Wanderers in the historic first F.A. Cup final at the new Wembley Stadium. Billy made 183 League and Cup appearances for West Ham and remained with the club until hanging up his boots in 1928, but six years later he died from the effects of tuberculosis at the age of 34.

Season	SL	Total
1919–20	2	2
Total	2	2

HENDERSON, CROSBY
1911–12

right-back Ht 5 9, Wt 11 06 13 apps
full name: Crosby Gray Henderson
born: South Hylton, Co. Durham, 12.5.1885
died: Sunderland, Co. Durham, 27.4.1970
debut: Brentford (h), 6.9.1911 (SL D1)

Recruited by Newcastle United from Wearside League club Hylton Star in May 1906, Crosby Henderson continued to ply his trade as a fitter in a Sunderland shipyard in his two seasons at St James's Park, but failed to make the United first team and was transferred to Grimsby Town in May 1908. At Blundell Park, Crosby enjoyed much greater success and became the regular left-back. After 65 Second Division appearances for the 'Mariners', he moved to Birmingham in May 1910, but, after playing in the first six games of the season, he languished in the reserves until being released in May 1911. The 26-year-old full-back then came to the Goldstone and was given a run at right-back in

Albion's Southern League team, but failed to fulfil expectations and lost his place to Ralph Routledge in December 1911. Released at the end of the season, Crosby departed for Luton Town, his last senior club.

Season	SL	SCC	Total
1911–12	12	1	13
Total	12	1	13

HENDERSON, STEWART
1965–73

right-back Ht 5 6, Wt 10 11 226 apps, 1 goal
full name: James Stewart Henderson
born: Bridge of Allan, Stirlingshire, Scotland, 5.6.1947
debut: Shrewsbury Town (a), 6.5.1966 (FL D3)

Solid and tenacious, Stewart Henderson was an unspectacular but reliable full-back who always gave total effort. Voted Player of the Season by Goldstone supporters in 1969–70, he clocked up well over 200 appearances for the Albion but missed out on the run-in to the club's greatest triumph in his time at Hove: promotion to the Second Division in 1972.

Having represented Stirlingshire as a schoolboy, Stewart won three caps for Scotland Schools before joining the Chelsea ground staff at the age of seventeen, but he failed to progress at Stamford Bridge. Arriving at the Goldstone Ground on trial in July 1965, the young defender impressed manager Archie Macaulay who offered him terms the following October. After breaking into the first team towards the end of the 1965–66 campaign, Stewart shared the right-back slot with Jimmy Magill the following term before making the no.2 shirt virtually his own in 1968. In August 1968 he scored his only senior goal for the club, in a 6–0 win over Oldham Athletic.

Ever-present during the 1971–72 promotion campaign until March, Stewart was then sensationally dropped by manager Pat Saward for the last twelve games to make way for new forward Ken Beamish; Bert Murray took over the right-back berth. The following term Stewart made just three senior appearances before joining Reading on a free transfer in June 1973.

It proved a splendid move for the quietly-spoken Scot who remained at Elm Park for eighteen years. In that time he amassed a further 166 League appearances and skippered the team, then took over as trainer before ending his playing days in 1983. Stewart subsequently became assistant manager and then youth development officer, and retained the post of coach until 1991. He later scouted for his former Reading manager Ian Branfoot during the latter's time in charge at Southampton.

Season	FL	FAC	FLC	Total
1965–66	4	0	0	4
1966–67	24	0	4	28
1967–68	13	0	0	13
1968–69	40 (1)	3	3	46 (1)
1969–70	45	5	3	53
1970–71	36	3	1	40
1971–72	34	3	2	39
1972–73	2	0	1	3
Total	198 (1)	14	14	226 (1)

HENNIGAN, MIKE   1964–65

centre-half   *Ht 5 11, Wt 11 06*   *4 apps*
full name: Michael Hennigan
born: Thrybergh, Yorkshire, 20.12.1942
debut: Barrow (h), 22.8.1964 (FL D4)

Best known for his backroom role at Leeds United, Mike Hennigan enjoyed only a very limited playing career which began as an amateur with Huddersfield Town. From there he joined his local club, Rotherham United, and signed for Sheffield Wednesday as a professional in March 1961, but he failed to make their First Division side and was transferred to Southampton in June 1962. In two years at The Dell he had just three Second Division outings as a deputy for Tony Knapp, and in July 1964 was brought to the Goldstone by Archie Macaulay. Drafted straight into the first team, Mike had the misfortune to break an elbow in only the second match of Albion's Fourth Division championship season, a recurrence of an injury suffered with the 'Saints' four months earlier, and did not reappear until late in the campaign, by which time Norman Gall was re-established as pivot.

Released at the end of the season, he left for South Africa – together with team-mate Andy McQuarrie – to play for Durban United, and also played for Bloemfontein before returning to England with Stevenage Town, but he went 'down under' again in 1970 with Marconi Fairfield in Australia. After coaching in the Sheffield area from 1971, Mike rejoined Sheffield Wednesday as youth-team coach in 1984 under former Albion player Howard Wilkinson, and followed his boss to Leeds United in 1989 where he became assistant manager. During their time at Elland Road, Leeds lifted the Division Two title in 1990, won the last Football League championship before the advent of the Premier League in 1992, and reached the 1996 League Cup final, but Mike left the Yorkshire club when Wilkinson was sacked in September 1996.

Season	FL	Total
1964–65	4	4
Total	4	4

HICKMAN, MIKE   1964–68

utility player   *Ht 5 10, Wt 11 03*   *18 apps, 1 goal*
full name: Michael Frederick Thomas Hickman
born: Elstead, Surrey, 2.10.1946
debut: Oxford United (a), 23.10.1965 (FL D3)

Mike Hickman never quite made it as an Albion player, but showed what he was really capable of in a long spell with Grimsby Town, during which he played in 253 League games scoring 48 goals. Born in Surrey, he came to the Goldstone as a junior and was offered professional terms at the age of eighteen in June 1965. Initially a centre-forward, Mike was soon converted to wing-half, but never gained a regular place in the first team during his three seasons with the club and left for Grimsby on a free transfer in June 1968.

Albion's loss was definitely the "Mariners'" gain as Mike established himself as a constructive rather than prolific forward for the Lincolnshire club over the next seven years. In 1971–72 he starred in their Fourth Division championship side, and helped to consolidate Grimsby's position in Division Three before moving to Blackburn Rovers for £10,000 in February 1975, whom he immediately assisted to the Third Division title.

Eight months later, though, Mike joined Torquay United for £2,500 where he ended his Football League career with seventeen Fourth Division appearances before taking a coaching post with the Devon club. Later emigrating to Australia, he returned after more than ten years 'down under' to take the post of youth-team coach with Reading. In December 1994, Mike followed his manager Mark McGhee to Leicester City as reserve-team coach, and, in similarly controversial circumstances, moved with him again to Wolverhampton Wanderers a year later.

Season	FL	FAC	FLC	Total
1965–66	0+1	0	0	0+1
1966–67	5	0	0	5
1967–68	7+2	2 (1)	1	10+2 (1)
Total	12+3	2 (1)	1	15+3 (1)

HIGGINS, RON   1951–53

centre-forward   *8 apps*
full name: Ronald Valentine Higgins
born: Silvertown, East Ham, Essex, 14.2.1923
debut: Southend United (h), 5.1.1952 (FL D3(S))

A fitter in a London shipyard, Ron Higgins turned out regularly for the Green & Siley Weir works' team, but also appeared in two League matches as an amateur for Leyton Orient during 1949–50 before joining Tonbridge in the Southern League. The Essex-born forward developed into a prolific goalscorer with the Kent club, becoming the subject of competition from a number of League teams, and in December 1951 Albion secured the 28-year-old's signature as a part-timer.

During his fifteen months at the Goldstone, Ron retained his fitter's job and trained at Upton Park with West Ham United. He showed a great deal of enthusiasm as leader of the attack, but didn't enjoy the best of luck and played in just eight matches, failing to register a goal. In January 1953, Ron left for Queen's Park Rangers as part of the transaction which brought Bert Addinall and Harry Gilberg to the Goldstone, and returned to the non-League scene with Canterbury City in May 1954.

Season	FL	Total
1951–52	8	8
Total	8	8

HIGHAM, GUNNER   1907–20

left-half   Ht 5 9, Wt 12 07   *159 apps, 1 goal*
full name: Thomas Edwin Higham
born: Daventry, Northamptonshire, 22.12.1887
debut: Leyton (a), 6.1.1908 (WL D1 'A')

'Gunner' Higham initially played for Albion's reserves as a nineteen-year-old amateur in 1907, but his early appearances were restricted because of his duties with the 18th Brigade, Royal Field Artillery, stationed at Preston Barracks in Brighton — hence the nickname by which he was always known. Chosen to represent both the Brighton and Sussex Football Associations on a number of occasions, he was a superbly-built footballer who, on his release from the service in January 1909, signed as an Albion professional.

Towards the end of 1911–12, Gunner established himself in the first team, and went on to become a great favourite with the supporters. He also earned for himself an excellent reputation at left-half and was chosen for the Southern League's representative side which defeated the Irish League 4–1 in Dublin on 11 October 1913. Two days later he played in the eleven which lost 5–0 to the Scottish League in Glasgow.

A first-team regular throughout 1912–13 and 1913–14, Gunner was, as a reservist, the first Brighton player called to the colours on the outbreak of the Great War in 1914 and consequently missed the whole of the last season (1914–15) before the club's four-year shutdown. Within a matter of weeks of being called up he was serving in France, but kept supporters back home informed of the situation on the Front with a series of letters to the club which were published in the local Press.

Despite being gassed in the fighting at Mons, Gunner was able to guest briefly for Watford during the war, but returned to the Goldstone in one piece when the hostilities ended to resume his role in a classic half-back line: Billy Booth, George Coomber and Gunner Higham. In April 1920 he was granted a benefit match, and a crowd of 10,500 at the Southern League fixture with Newport County contributed £605 3s. to his welfare. The sum was a record for the Southern League at the time, allowing the popular stalwart, who was now 32, to retire from the game a satisfied man when he was released at the end of the season.

Season	SL	FAC	WL	SA	Total
1907–08	5	0	1	0	6
1908–09	0	0	3	0	3
1911–12	15	0	0	0	15
1912–13	37	3 (1)	0	14	54 (1)
1913–14	35	4	0	9	48
1919–20	32	1	0	0	33
Total	124	8 (1)	4	23	159 (1)

HILL, W.   1902

inside-right   *6 apps, 1 goal*
debut: Chesham Town (h), 1.3.1902 (SL D2)

One of three trialists given an opportunity by the Albion in February 1902, Hill was turning out for Cuckfield at the time, but had arrived in Sussex from the Midlands where he was reputed to have played as an amateur for Wellingborough Town's Southern League team. With Albion seeking to strengthen their forward line in a vain bid to win the championship of the Southern League's Second Division in their first season, Hill's initial outing came in a 7–1 friendly win over Southampton Wanderers (the club's first match at the Goldstone Ground) and he retained his place for the next four Southern League fixtures. The first, a 4–0 defeat of Chesham Town, was Albion's first competitive game on the ground which became home.

The local Press claimed that 'The executive have unearthed a clever inside-right', but, after appearing briefly towards the start of the 1902–03 season, Hill faded from the scene and returned to the Cuckfield club, where he remained for some years. He represented the Mid Sussex League on several occasions in their annual fixtures with the East and West Sussex Leagues.

Season	SL	SEL	Total
1901–02	4	0	4
1902–03	1	1 (1)	2 (1)
Total	5	1 (1)	6 (1)

HILTON, PAT   1973–74

forward/midfield   Ht 5 8, Wt 10 00   *22 apps, 2 goals*
full name: Patrick John Hilton
born: Aylesham, Kent, 1.5.1954
debut: Luton Town (h), 10.2.1973 (FL D2)

Although he played rugby at Dover Grammar School, Pat Hilton also played soccer for Aylesham Youth Club and went on, at the age of 15, to become the youngest player ever to appear in a Southern League match for Folkestone Town. The young forward started to attract interest from League clubs, and after a trial with Coventry City he enjoyed a spell as an apprentice with West Bromwich Albion before returning to Kent with Canterbury.

In February 1973, Pat signed for Brighton at the age of 18. A week later, with the club on a record, thirteen-match losing streak, he and fellow youngster Tony Towner were thrown in at the deep end for their League debuts against Luton Town, a game which Albion won 2–0. Pat, though, never established himself like Towner, and after playing in nineteen games as a striker the following season he was dismissed at the end of the campaign – along with Mick Brown and Terry Norton – for damaging windows at the Goldstone while celebrating his 20th birthday rather too well.

On leaving the Albion, Pat joined Blackburn Rovers and appeared on sixteen occasions as they carried off the Third Division title in 1975, but he moved back to his native Kent with Gillingham in September 1975. At the end of 1976–77 he enjoyed a thirteen-match loan spell with Aldershot, and then moved to Southport for whom he made 27 League appearances during the 1977–78 season, their last as a Football League club. Pat subsequently returned to the Southern League with Folkestone Town and went on to play for Dover, Canterbury, Folkestone Town for a third spell, Thanet United, and Hythe. In 1990 he rejoined Gillingham as a player, and was appointed youth-team manager for a time in October 1991. Pat later worked for British Telecom and on the Channel Tunnel project in Kent.

Season	FL	FAC	Total
1972–73	3	0	3
1973–74	15+2 (2)	2	17+2 (2)
Total	18+2 (2)	2	20+2 (2)

HINDLEY, FRANK   1939–47

centre-forward   Ht 5 10, Wt 12 00   *16 apps, 6 goals*
full name: Frank C. Hindley
born: Worksop, Nottinghamshire, 2.11.1915
debut: Romford (h), 17.11.1945 (FAC R1 Lg1)*

Frank Hindley's sixteen appearances for the Albion came in the immediate post-war period, but he actually joined the club from Nottingham Forest in May 1939 and played in two of the three matches of the aborted 1939–40 Third Division (South) season, games which were deleted from the official record. Signed by Forest as a professional from Netherton United in December 1937, he had enjoyed only limited first-team experience before his arrival at Hove. When war was declared Frank joined the Sherwood Foresters, and received a bullet wound in a shoulder in May 1940 while serving in North Africa. The Worksop-born forward guested for Forest and Mansfield Town during the emergency period, and played a few games for the Albion in the 1945-46 transitional season.

When peace was finally restored Frank led the Brighton attack in fine style, impressing with his dash and vigour. He would travel to matches from his Midlands home, a difficult situation exacerbated by the unreliability of post-war public transport, and in May 1947, at the age of 32, he was released to retire from the game. His son, Peter Hindley, starred for Nottingham Forest in the 1960s and '70s.

Season	FL	FAC	Wartime	Total
1945–46	0	3 (1)	2	5 (1)
1946–47	10 (4)	1 (1)	0	11 (5)
Total	10 (4)	4 (2)	2	16 (6)

Note: Hindley's first game for the Albion was Port Vale (h), 26.8.1939 (FL D3(S)), but this game was deleted from the record when the Football League Third Division (South) was aborted on the outbreak of war.

HIPKIN, Reg   1948–49

wing-half/centre-forward   Ht 5 9, Wt 11 00   *15 apps, 1 goal*
full name: Reginald Willimont Hipkin
born: Syderstone, Norfolk, 31.12.1921
debut: Bristol City (a), 6.3.1948 (FL D3(S))

When Don Welsh took over as Albion manager in 1947, he quickly brought in new players to strengthen the staff. Among them was Reg Hipkin, signed from Welsh's former club Charlton Athletic in February 1948 for £1,750. Reg had played for Fakenham Town as a schoolboy and had a trial with Aston Villa, but joined his local club Norwich City at the age of sixteen in 1938 to work, like many a hopeful youngster, in the club office. A year later he was transferred to Wolverhampton Wanderers, but the war interrupted his career and, after a few guest appearances for Watford, Chelsea and Hartlepools United, he joined Charlton on a free transfer in September 1946.

After two games in the First Division, Reg arrived at the Goldstone and played in fifteen League games, but his career was brought to a premature end when he sustained a knee injury at Bristol Rovers in November 1948; a collection on his behalf was made during the match with Newport County at the Goldstone in January 1950. Shortly after leaving the club Reg was appointed player-coach of Littlehampton Town in the Sussex County League, and later worked as an engineer in Gillingham.

Season	FL	Total
1947–48	10	10
1948–49	5 (1)	5 (1)
Total	15 (1)	15 (1)

HOBSON, Gary   1996–

central defender/left-back   Ht 6 1, Wt 12 10   *52 apps, 1 goal*
born: North Ferriby, Yorkshire, 12.11.1972
debut: Rotherham United (h), 30.3.1996 (FL D2)

Although he was only 23 on his arrival at the Goldstone, Gary Hobson brought valuable experience and poise to the centre of the Albion defence when he signed for £60,000 in March 1996. A trainee with his local League side, Hull City, on leaving school, he made four League appearances at left-back in April 1991 (with the 'Tigers' bottom of the old Division Two) before graduating to full

pro status shortly afterwards in July. Over the next two seasons Gary played sporadically in the senior side, but established himself in the no.3 shirt during the 1993–94 season before switching to the middle the following term. He went on to amass more than 160 senior appearances for the club (and one goal in the F.A. Cup) to become a great favourite at Boothferry Park.

With City struggling at the foot of the Second Division – along with the Albion – throughout the 1995–96 campaign, it was something of a surprise when Jimmy Case brought Gary to Hove just before the transfer deadline, especially as the 'Seagulls' had hammered the Yorkshire side 4–0 less than two weeks earlier. Nevertheless, he appeared to be a good acquisition and immediately impressed with his ability to pass the ball out of defence. A solid but deceptively quick performer, he was one of the few players to emerge from the near-disastrous 1996–97 season in Division Three with much credit, often playing as the senior partner in an inexperienced back-four. During the campaign Gary also opened his scoring account in the Football League, powering home a header in the 5–0 'Fans United' win over Hartlepool United – his 177th League appearance.

Season	FL	FAC	FLC	AMC	Total
1995–96	9	0	0	0	9
1996–97	35+2 (1)	2	2	2	41+2 (1)
Total	44+2 (1)	2	2	2	50+2 (1)

HODGE, Billy   1912–14

right-back   *33 apps*
full name: William McDowall Hodge
born: Skares, Ayrshire, Scotland, 15.5.1885
died: Skares Row, Ayrshire, Scotland, 6.6.1960
debut: Croydon Common (h), 9.10.1912 (SA)

Billy Hodge arrived in Hove from Ayr United during the summer of 1912, and got his chance when Ralph Routledge was forced to quit the game early in the 1912–13 campaign. Capable of filling either full-back berth, the robust Scot had a good run in the first team until giving way to Frank Spencer in January, but played in all six matches of the excellent Southern Charity Cup run when Albion, fielding mainly a reserve side, went all the way to the final only to be beaten 4–1 after extra time by Queen's Park Rangers at The Den. Billy made only occasional appearances in the first team the following season and played his final game for the reserves in January 1914, after which he moved back to Scotland.

He joined the Ayrshire junior club Galston in September, and made the short journey to Lanemark in February 1915 before disappearing from the scene when the First World War brought chaos to organised football. Billy later worked as a colliery pump attendant.

Season	SL	SA	SCC	Total
1912–13	13	8	6	27
1913–14	1	5	0	6
Total	14	13	6	33

9 players who gained university degrees

Player	Player
Ansell, George	Sommer, Juergen
Fuschillo, Paul	Stille, Giles
Haig-Brown, Alan	Suddaby, Peter
Meola, Tony	Wilkinson, Howard
Paterson, Henry	

HODGE, ERIC   1956–59

left-back   Ht 6 0, Wt 12 00   4 apps
full name: Eric Richard Carew Hodge
born: Cape Town, South Africa, 3.4.1933
debut: Aldershot (a), 2.10.1957 (FL D3(S))

Eric Hodge arrived in England from Cape Town in October 1956 to join the Albion on a part-time basis, and went on to impress in a variety of positions with the reserves. During the 1957–58 promotion campaign the 24-year-old South African made four first-team appearances as stand-in for Roy Jennings at left-back, and remained at the Goldstone until July 1959 when he moved on to Aldershot. Eric later played for Haywards Heath, but on returning to South Africa in February 1962 he joined Durban United and became a successful businessman in the construction industry. Also a fine cricketer, he skippered the Brighton & Hove club in 1960 and was on Sussex C.C.C.'s staff as a medium-pace bowler. During his stay in the U.K., Eric worked as a draughtsman with a Brighton engineering company.

Season	FL	Total
1957–58	4	4
Total	4	4

HODGES, CYRIL   1946–47

centre-forward   28 apps, 18 goals
full name: Cyril Leslie Hodges
born: Hackney, London, 18.9.1919
died: Brighton, Sussex, September 1979
debut: Crystal Palace (a), 9.2.1944 (wartime)
peacetime debut: Reading (h), 19.10.1946 (FL D3(S))

A well-known figure at the Goldstone for many years as a player, trainer and coach, Cyril Hodges enjoyed an all-too-brief playing career which was disrupted by the war and terminated by injury.

A Hackney, Middlesex and London Schools representative, Cyril  started out with Eton Manor in the London League before signing amateur forms for Arsenal in February 1944. Wartime duties as a P.T. instructor with the Duke of Cornwall's Light Infantry curtailed his football activities, but he still managed a few games for the 'Gunners' and also for Sunderland towards the end of the period. He also made nineteen guest appearances for the Albion during 1944–45 and scored nineteen goals, including two *against* Arsenal and four in a 6–2 win over Millwall.

In April 1945, Cyril turned professional and played on the left wing in the first League match staged at Highbury after the war, but he was soon on the move and signed for

Brighton in October 1946. It was hoped that the 27-year-old centre-forward would reproduce the form of his guest days, but his career came to an end after less than a year with the club when a serious knee injury enforced his retirement from the professional game.

Cyril joined Haywards Heath as player-coach on leaving the Goldstone and helped them to the Sussex County League title in successive seasons, 1949–50 and 1950–51. He later coached Hove White Rovers, but rejoined Albion as assistant trainer in 1957, becoming trainer-coach in 1963 and senior coach in 1967. After receiving a joint benefit with Jack Bertolini in November 1967, he resigned from his post in December 1968 shortly after Freddie Goodwin took over as manager.

Season	FL	Wartime	Total
1944–45	0	19 (15)	19 (15)
1946–47	9 (3)	0	9 (3)
Total	9 (3)	19 (15)	28 (18)

HOLLEY, GEORGE   1919–20

inside-forward   Ht 5 10, Wt 12 07   13 apps, 5 goals
born: Seaham Harbour, Co. Durham, 25.11.1885
died: Wolverhampton, Staffordshire, 27.8.1942
debut: Brentford (a), 30.8.1919 (SL D1)

Although in the autumn of his career when he arrived at the Goldstone, George Holley was undoubtedly Albion's most notable player of the Southern League era. One of the greatest inside-forwards in the land in the years leading up to the First World War, he had ten England caps and a League championship medal to his name. Renowned as a ball-artist, he could often leave opponents mesmerised, but backed his considerable skills up with wonderful consistency.

It was with Sunderland that George rose to fame. He signed professional forms for the First Division club from Seaham White Star at the age of eighteen in November 1904, and went on to score 154 goals in 315 League and Cup games up to 1915. In 1908–09 he was capped for the first time by England, and toured South Africa with the F.A. in 1910. In 1913 he gained his championship medal and played in team beaten 1–0 by Aston Villa in the F.A. Cup final, the 'Rokerites' thus missing the elusive 'double' by a narrow margin. He also represented the Football League on five occasions.

During the Great War, George guested for Fulham, and joined the Albion for a club-record £200 fee in July 1919. Although, at the age of 33, he was past his best, the ex-England man still  proved a great attraction for the fans, but, unfortunately for all concerned, his appearances were restricted by a serious leg injury and in March 1920 he was forced to call it a day after just thirteen games. He returned to Sunderland as a member of the coaching staff and later held the trainer's posts at Wolverhampton Wanderers and Barnsley. After suffering ill-health for six years, George died in his adopted Wolverhampton at the age of 56. His son, Tom Holley, starred for Barnsley and Leeds United either side of the Second World War.

Season	SL	FAC	Total
1919–20	12 (5)	1	13 (5)
Total	12 (5)	1	13 (5)

HOLLINS, DAVE   1956–61

goalkeeper   Ht 6 0, Wt 11 102   73 apps
full name: David Michael Hollins
born: Bangor, Caernarfonshire, Wales, 4.2.1938
debut: Coventry City (a), 1.3.1958 (FL D3(S))

Signed from Merrow F.C. of Guildford in October 1956, Dave Hollins had the unenviable task of understudying Albion goalkeeper Eric

Gill, who was then in the middle of his club-record run of 247 consecutive appearances. His chance finally came in March 1958, in the Third Division (South) championship season, when Gill was taken ill before the journey to Coventry. The 20-year-old stand-in performed well and Albion remained unbeaten in his three games before the more experienced man returned, but it will be for his *fourth* appearance that Dave may be best remembered.

That extraordinary match in August 1958 was the club's debut in the Second Division, a tough fixture at Middlesbrough. With Gill again unavailable, the young Welshman was on the receiving end of a 9–0 thrashing, the heaviest peacetime defeat in Albion history. It did little to dent his confidence, though, and in September 1959 he took over as the no.1 'keeper. Two months later he won a Welsh under-23 cap in a 1–1 draw with Scotland at Wrexham, and added a second against England in February 1961. The following month, with Charlie Baker guarding the Albion net, Dave was sold to Newcastle United for £11,000, and he went on to spend six years at St James's Park, winning eleven caps at senior level for his country.

On leaving Tyneside, Dave played in turn for Mansfield Town (February 1967), Nottingham Forest (on loan March 1970), Aldershot (July 1970) and Portsmouth (on loan April 1971), notching up a grand total of 312 Football League appearances in the process. Dave left the first-class game for Southern League Romford in July 1971, and now runs a decorating business. He also enjoys playing bowls for the London Welsh club.

Dave is a member of the famous Hollins football-playing clan. His father Bill was a goalkeeper on Wolverhampton Wanderers books in the 1920s; older brother Roy was on Albion's staff and played for the reserves in the mid '50s; and younger brother John won fame with Chelsea, Queen's Park Rangers, Arsenal and England.

Season	FL	FAC	FLC	Total
1957–58	3	0	0	3
1958–59	15	1	0	16
1959–60	33	5	0	38
1960–61	15	0	1	16
Total	66	6	1	73

HOPKINS, JIMMY   1923–29

inside-left   Ht 5 7, Wt 10 00   233 apps, 75 goals
full name: James Hopkins
born: Ballymoney, Co. Antrim, Ireland, 12.7.1899
died: Guildford, Surrey, 22.6.1943
debut: Watford (a), 10.2.1923 (FL D3(S))

Jimmy Hopkins became a fixture in the Albion side almost from the moment he arrived in Hove as a 23-year-old in January 1923. Scoring within 60 seconds of his debut for the reserves, the young Ulsterman soon took over the inside-left role in the first team, becoming an essential member of the side which finished consistently highly in the Third Division (South) during the mid 1920s. Although slightly built, he possessed an exceptional turn of speed, and such was his impressive form that he won a place in the Irish team which drew 0–0 with England in Belfast in October 1925, the third Albion man of the period to win an international cap.

Jimmy had started out with Willowfield United on leaving school, but then joined the junior club Belfast United run by former Brighton United favourite Toby Mercer. Two good seasons with them prompted Mercer to recommend him to Arsenal, and he joined the Highbury staff in September 1919. The will-o'-the-wisp inside-forward had to wait until March 1921 to make his First Division debut, scoring in a 4–3 win at West Bromwich Albion, but illness, coupled with the plethora of inside-forward talent available, meant that he had only 21 League outings to his name when he arrived at the Goldstone Ground.

While giving great support to centre-forwards such as Tommy Cook and Sam Jennings, Jimmy also weighed in with an average of more than ten goals a season himself; his total of 75 goals – including three hat-tricks – puts him well up the list of all-time Albion scorers. After missing only a handful of games through injury in six years at the Goldstone Ground, Jimmy was released in May 1929 to join non-League Aldershot whom he assisted to the Southern League championship in 1929–30. He remained with the Hampshire club until its election to the Football League in 1932, when he retired at the age of 32.

- HOPKINS - B+H.ALBION.F.C. 1923-24 -

Season	FL	FAC	Total
1922–23	17 (5)	0	17 (5)
1923–24	42 (19)	4 (1)	46 (20)
1924–25	36 (11)	3 (2)	39 (13)
1925–26	39 (9)	2	41 (9)
1926–27	21 (8)	1	22 (8)
1927–28	38 (13)	2	40 (13)
1928–29	27 (7)	1	28 (7)
Total	220 (72)	13 (3)	233 (75)

HOPKINS, MEL   1964–67

full-back   Ht 5 11, Wt 11 07   62 apps, 2 goals
full name: Melvyn Hopkins
born: Ystrad, Rhondda, Glamorgan, Wales, 7.11.1934
debut: Notts County (h), 10.10.1964 (FL D4)

A vastly experienced full-back when he signed for the Albion in 1964, Mel Hopkins enjoyed an excellent career with Tottenham Hotspur and Wales, but was unfortunate to miss out on his club's greatest triumphs. After joining Spurs from the Ystrad Boys' Club in the Rhondda Valley, he turned professional in May 1952, made his Division One debut during 1952–53, and established himself in the splendid Tottenham team of the era two seasons later. Mel went on to make 219 First Division appearances in his time at White Hart Lane, and was particularly noted for his attacking sorties.

In April 1956 the Welsh defender won his first full cap when he took over the no.3 shirt from the great Alf Sherwood against Northern Ireland, and he became a fixture in the international side, playing in all five matches of the 1958 World Cup finals in Sweden when the gallant Welshmen lost 1–0 to Brazil in the quarter-finals. However, after suffering a broken nose in 1959, his first-team opportunities

with Tottenham diminished and he played no part in the side that won the 'double' in 1960–61 or in the F.A. Cup-winning team the following season. He did, however, remain an automatic choice for Wales until 1963.

In October 1964, 29-year-old Mel signed for the Albion for £5,000 just eighteen months after he had won his 34th and final cap, and he joined his former Spurs colleagues Bobby Smith and Jimmy Collins on the club's triumphant march to the Fourth Division championship that season. Things took a downward turn the following term, though, and Mel requested a transfer in February 1966, but he remained at the Goldstone until July 1967 when he left for Canterbury City. After a spell in the Irish League with Ballymena United, the experienced Welshman joined Bradford (P.A.) in January 1969 and played 30 Fourth Division games as the club finished bottom of the Football League two seasons running and were voted out in favour of Cambridge United.

Mel was still living in Sussex while at Park Avenue and found his appearances restricted because the club couldn't afford his rail fares, so he signed for Wimbledon in the Southern League. He subsequently scouted for Derby County (managed by another former Spurs team-mate, Dave Mackay); was a leader at Shoreham Boys' Club; and played briefly for Lancing in the Sussex County League. He still lives in Shoreham, working as a sports officer and coach for Horsham District Council.

Season	FL	FAC	FLC	Total
1964–65	34 (1)	1	0	35 (1)
1965–66	22+1 (1)	0	2	24+1 (1)
1966–67	1	0	1	2
Total	57+1 (2)	1	3	61+1 (2)

HORSCROFT, GRANT   1987–88

centre-half   *Ht 6 4, Wt 14 00*   *2 apps*
born: Fletching, Sussex, 30.7.1961
debut: Bristol Rovers (a), 19.12.1987 (FL D3)

One of the most massive players ever to don an Albion shirt, Grant Horscroft has been a dominating player in Sussex football for some years, but enjoyed only a brief career as a full-time professional at the Goldstone. The giant defender started out with Ringmer in the Sussex County League, and graduated to the Isthmian League with

Lewes where he also won Sussex Senior Cup honours. He had a trial at Wimbledon and enjoyed a loan period with Sutton United while with Lewes, but was working in an Uckfield warehouse when manager Barry Lloyd offered him a trial with the Albion in March 1987 that proved a success.

The 26-year-old defender signed for a £2,000 fee the following month and made two senior appearances when regular centre-half Doug Rougvie was under suspension. In his normal reserve-team capacity, Grant had the honour of being the first Albion skipper to lift the Sussex Senior Cup – in its peace-time format – when the second eleven defeated his former club, Lewes, in the 1988 final. After being released to rejoin Lewes in September 1988, he brought his number of appearances to well over 500 and also had spells as assistant and caretaker manager, but returned to his original club, Ringmer, when the "Rooks'" side broke up because of financial problems in January 1993. Together with members of his sizeable family, Grant also forms the backbone of the Fletching cricket team.

Season	FL	Total
1987–88	2	2
Total	2	2

HORTON, BRIAN   1976–81

midfield   *Ht 5 10, Wt 11 04*   *252 apps, 41 goals*
born: Hednesford, Staffordshire, 4.2.1949
debut: Preston North End (a), 13.3.1976 (FL D3)

Captain of the Albion for five years during the late 1970s and early '80s, the club's most successful spell ever, Brian 'Nobby' Horton remains one of the best-loved footballers ever to grace the Goldstone turf. Indeed, his popularity can be gauged by the fact that he was voted Player of the Season in 1976–77 despite the outstanding feats of 36-goal Peter Ward. A hard-working, combative dynamo in midfield,

he never gave less than total effort and was an inspiration to all those around him. Able to defend and tackle with the best, Brian created many an opening for his forwards while also posing a considerable threat himself; he scored 41 goals – 17 of them penalties – in 252 games for the club.

Since hanging up his boots, the former Birmingham and Staffordshire Schools representative has gone on to enjoy a lengthy career as a manager, yet his early days were anything but successful. Released by Walsall after two years as an apprentice, he drifted into non-League football with Hednesford Town while working in the building trade. After four years with the West Midlands Regional League club, Brian was taken on by Port Vale in July 1970 and became a fixture in their Third Division side, continually impressing with his powerful midfield displays.

In March 1976, after 236 League matches and 33 goals for Vale, the 27-year-old midfielder was signed for the Albion by Peter Taylor for a giveaway £27,000, a deal which caused outrage amongst Vale supporters and the Potteries Press. Taking over the engine-room role of skipper Ernie Machin, Brian himself took over the captaincy after just a handful of games and led the team superbly for the next five years. Renowned for his non-stop talking, berating and encouragement on the pitch – of colleagues and officials – he was an inspiration to his team-mates both with his leadership and his play. Steve Foster (q.v.) called him – as a compliment – 'a professional moaner for 90 minutes'.

After leading the Albion to promotion in 1977, Brian topped the club's list of League scorers as the 'Seagulls' fought their way into the First Division two years later. After two seasons in the top flight, though, he found his time at the Goldstone to be up when Mike Bailey took over as manager, and moved on to Luton Town in August 1981. The success continued as he captained the 'Hatters' to the Division Two title in the first of three seasons at Kenilworth Road. In May 1984, Brian moved into management as player-manager of Hull City; he guided the 'Tigers' to promotion from the Third Division in 1984–85, and to sixth place in Division Two the following term when he made his last appearance as a player just a few weeks before his 38th birthday. Rewarded with a place on the City board, he was, however, sacked in April 1988 after a poor run of results and joined Oxford United as assistant to his former Goldstone colleague Mark Lawrenson.

In October 1988, Brian inherited the managerial role on Lawrenson's dismissal, but oversaw five rather indifferent years at the Manor Ground. He was, therefore, something of a surprise choice to take over the hot-seat at Manchester City in the Premiership in August 1993, a post from which he was sacked in May 1995. A month later he took charge of First Division Huddersfield Town, and managed a Football League XI against the Italian League Serie B in November 1995.

A late starter in the Football League at the age of 21, Brian still totalled 689 League and Cup matches and scored 88 goals during a seventeen-year career. Many Albion supporters believed that one day he would return to the Goldstone as manager, but the right circumstances have never quite come about. He will, therefore, be forever remembered as the best captain the club ever had, his only rival perhaps being Joe Leeming.

Season	FL	FAC	FLC	Total
1975–76	11	0	0	11
1976–77	45 (9)	3	6 (3)	54 (12)
1977–78	42 (8)	2 (1)	6 (2)	50 (11)
1978–79	39+1 (11)	1	4	44+1 (11)
1979–80	42 (4)	2	5 (1)	49 (5)
1980–81	38 (1)	2 (1)	3	43 (2)
Total	217+1 (33)	10 (2)	24 (6)	251+1 (41)

HOUGHTON, F. — 1912

inside-right — *1 app*
debut: Croydon Common (a), 13.11.1912 (SA)

An amateur trialist from the Birmingham area, Houghton was given an opportunity to impress in the Southern Alliance match at Croydon Common in November 1912, but the Albion went down 2–1 and nothing more was heard of him.

Season	SA	Total
1912–13	1	1
Total	1	1

HOWARD, FRANKIE — 1949–59

outside-left — Ht 5 6, Wt 10 07 — *219 apps, 31 goals*
full name: Francis Henry Howard
born: Acton, Middlesex, 30.1.1931
debut: Millwall (a), 4.9.1950 (FL D3(S))

After 40 years of service for the Albion, it was a sad day in November 1993 when 62-year-old Frankie Howard was made redundant – somewhat acrimoniously – as part of a drastic economy programme. As a player the little left-winger graced the Goldstone pitch for ten years, and as groundsman he looked after the same turf with loving care for more than 28 years.

A former Acton Boys representative, Frankie first came to Hove as a teenage trialist from Guildford City and was offered professional terms in May 1950. A chunky little player with an impish sense of humour, he was one of the fastest players ever to have appeared in Albion's colours, having been a noted sprinter for Polytechnic Harriers in his youth; yet, oddly, he was rejected for National Service because of flat feet! His early career at the Goldstone came in fits and starts, but in 1954–55 he became a regular in the side and formed a splendid partnership with Denis Foreman down the left wing.

Frankie was at his best during the 1957–58 promotion season, missing only five games, but in March 1959 he tore knee ligaments while playing for the reserves which resulted in his retirement nine months later at the age of 28. A place was found for him on the staff, and in 1962 he was appointed groundsman; he also enjoyed a testimonial match in November. Shortly afterwards Frankie took a job in the building industry, but returned to the Goldstone as groundsman in September 1965. He was rewarded with two more testimonials, in 1975 and 1988–89, and contributed considerably to the game locally over the years in his associations with Wigmore Athletic, Lower Bevendean and the Sussex intermediate representative team.

Season	FL	FAC	Total
1950–51	6	0	6
1951–52	26 (2)	0	26 (2)
1952–53	18 (2)	3 (2)	21 (4)
1953–54	12 (1)	4 (1)	16 (2)
1954–55	36 (8)	5 (1)	41 (9)
1955–56	27 (4)	2 (1)	29 (5)
1956–57	27 (6)	2	29 (6)
1957–58	41 (2)	3	44 (2)
1958–59	7 (1)	0	7 (1)
Total	200 (26)	19 (5)	219 (31)

HOWELL, GRAHAM — 1972–74

right-back — Ht 5 8, Wt 10 13 — *46 apps*
full name: Graham Frank Howell
born: Salford, Lancashire, 18.2.1951
debut: Sunderland (h), 26.8.1972 (FL D2)

A representative of both Altrincham and Sale Schools, Graham Howell was taken onto the Manchester City ground staff and signed as a professional at the age of seventeen in October 1968, but his experience at Maine Road was confined to the City reserves. In

June 1971 the young full-back joined Bradford City and quickly became a regular, missing just three games during 1971–72 as the Yorkshire side finished bottom of the Third Division.

After a season at Valley Parade, Graham came south to the Goldstone for £17,500 in August 1972 and was drafted straight into Albion's newly promoted team, but, as at Bradford, he was unfortunate to join a club at what was to become a low point in its history. Playing mainly at right-back (although he also appeared in midfield), the 21-year-old Lancastrian went on to make 36 appearances as Albion were unceremoniously relegated straight back to the Third Division, and had another ten games in 1973–74, but he was released at the end of the season, joining Cambridge United in July 1974. After 71 Fourth Division outings in two seasons at the Abbey Stadium, Graham departed from the Football League scene.

Season	FL	FAC	FLC	Total
1972–73	32+3	1	0	33+3
1973–74	8+1	0	1	9+1
Total	40+4	1	1	42+4

HOWELL, RONNIE — 1973–74

midfield — Ht 5 8, Wt 10 00 — *30 apps, 9 goals*
full name: Ronald Roger Howell
born: Tottenham, Middlesex, 22.5.1949
debut: Charlton Athletic (h), 29.8.1973 (FLC R1)

Ronnie Howell had just one season at the Goldstone Ground, but may be remembered for scoring a hat-trick at Charlton in January 1974 and for being sent off at Wrexham two months later. A junior with Millwall, Ronnie signed professional forms in March 1967 and made fourteen Second Division appearances for the 'Lions' before moving to Cambridge United in September 1970 for their first season in the Football League. After a dozen games at the Abbey Stadium, he dropped into the Southern League with Kettering Town, but in July 1972 Swindon Town offered him another opportunity of Second Division fare and the midfielder played in 25 matches during 1972–73. Signed on a free transfer by Pat Saward in July 1973, Ronnie made 30 intermittent appearances in midfield for a struggling Albion side, and enjoyed his finest moment in January 1974 when he scored three times – one of them a penalty – in a 4–0 win at The Valley against Charlton Athletic. He was, though, one of a number of victims of manager Brian Clough's massive clear-out at the end of the season and left

for Tooting & Mitcham United in the Isthmian League. Ronnie subsequently enjoyed a fair degree of success in non-League football with Leytonstone, Enfield, Dagenham, and as player-coach at Barnet.

Season	FL	FAC	FLC	Total
1973–74	26+1 (9)	2	1	29+1 (9)
Total	26+1 (9)	2	1	29+1 (9)

HOWES, ARTHUR 1902–04

goalkeeper   Ht 5 11, Wt 13 00   49 apps
born: Leicester, Leicestershire, 1876
debut: Tottenham Hotspur (res.) (h), 24.9.1902 (SEL)

Arthur Howes first crossed paths with his future Albion manager, John Jackson, in September 1896 when, at the age of 20, he joined his local club Leicester Fosse where Jackson was trainer. After a run of twelve Second Division outings at Filbert Street, the well-built goalkeeper moved to Reading in November 1897 for a short spell in the Southern League, but returned to Fosse during the following close season. In May 1899, a year after his appointment as manager of Brighton United, Jackson brought Arthur to the South Coast after he had been 'the best Fosse man on the field' in a friendly match between the two clubs a few months earlier; but, although he played in the first four games of 1899–1900, he had to be content with being understudy to Tom Spicer for much of the season.

When the United club folded in March 1900 the burly custodian migrated to Scotland to play for Dundee, but in September 1902 Jackson once again obtained his services, this time for the Albion. Arthur shared the goalkeeping duties with Squire Whitehurst in his first season with the club, but then missed only one game in 1903–04, Albion's first season in the First Division of the Southern League. Released at the end of the campaign, he left for Queen's Park Rangers to amass a further 53 Southern League and F.A. Cup appearances until 1907 when he disappeared from the first-class game.

Season	SL	FAC	SEL	Total
1902–03	2	3	10	15
1903–04	33	1	0	34
Total	35	4	10	49

HOWLETT, GARY 1982–84

midfield   Ht 5 8, Wt 10 04   37 apps, 2 goals
full name: Gary Patrick Howlett
born: Dublin, Co. Dublin, Republic of Ireland, 2.4.1963
debut: Liverpool (h), 22.3.1983 (FL D1)

In just his eleventh senior match, Gary Howlett delivered the delightful cross from which Gordon Smith scored Albion's opening goal of the 1983 F.A. Cup final against Manchester United. It was an incredible rise to fame for the 20-year-old Dubliner who had made his League debut just two months earlier, scoring in a 2–2 draw with Liverpool at Hove. Sadly, his fall from prominence was equally rapid: after subsequently struggling to make the Albion side, he left the Goldstone after 37 senior games to spend the rest of his career in relative obscurity in the lower divisions and in the League of Ireland.

A junior with the Home Farm club of Dublin, Gary had trials with both Liverpool and Manchester United, but it was Coventry City who took him on, and Gary won an Irish youth cap while at Highfield Road. He failed to make the City first team, though, and was released in May 1982 to arrive at the Goldstone on trial. Rewarded with a contract by

manager Mike Bailey, Gary made his First Division debut in place of Gerry Ryan in March 1983, and returned to the side when Ryan was injured, holding his place to the end of the season as Albion tumbled to relegation but also made it to Wembley. In June 1983 the slightly-built midfielder won four under-21 caps – scoring one goal – at the Toulon tournament in France, and, although appearing only sporadically in Albion's League team, was selected for the full Republic of Ireland squad in May 1984. During the summer of 1984 he came on as a substitute against China in Sapporo, Japan, to win his only full cap.

Gary continued to display his delicate skills at the start of the 1984–85 season, but in December he was transferred to AFC Bournemouth for a £15,000 fee, much to the chagrin of many Goldstone fans. After 60 League games for the 'Cherries', including 23 during their 1986–87 Third Division championship campaign, Gary had loan spells with Aldershot and Chester City before joining York City in January 1988. A regular at Bootham Crescent for more than three seasons – with thirteen goals from 101 league appearances – he was released in February 1991 and returned to his native land with Shelbourne where he met with immediate success.

Gary represented the League of Ireland v. Irish League in November 1991, and assisted the 'Shels' to the 1991–92 League championship. In 1995–96 he played for the Dublin-based club in their somewhat unsuccessful UEFA Cup campaign, but thereafter suffered a series of injuries and moved on loan to the Belfast-based Irish League side Crusaders for two months late in 1996. Still playing a major role in the Shelbourne midfield, Gary also earns his living with Aer Lingus at Dublin Airport.

Season	FL	FAC	FLC	Total
1982–83	9 (1)	3	0	12 (1)
1983–84	15+2	0	2	17+2
1984–85	6 (1)	0	0	6 (1)
Total	30+2 (2)	3	2	35+2 (2)

HOYLAND, FRED 1924–26

outside-right   Ht 5 6, Wt 11 00   5 apps
full name: Frederick Hoyland
born: Pontefract, Yorkshire, 1898
debut: Southend United (h), 28.2.1925 (FL D3(S))

Diminutive right-winger Fred Hoyland broke into senior football with Swansea Town in February 1920, joining the Vetch Field staff during their last campaign as a Southern League club, but he didn't make the first eleven until the 'Swans' joined the newly created Football League Division Three the following season. After just nine League appearances for the Welsh side in two seasons, Fred was transferred to Second Division Bury for a £75 fee in May 1922, but he wasn't a great success at Gigg Lane either and quickly drifted into non-League football for a brief spell with Glossop until joining Birmingham in August 1923. After playing in six First Division matches for the 'Blues' during 1923–24, Charlie Webb secured his

F. HOYLAND - BRIGHTON + HOVE ALBION - 1925-26.

services for the Albion in August 1924. Fred remained at the Goldstone for two seasons but, with Jack Nightingale occupying the outside-right berth to great effect, he had little chance of a run in the Third Division team and left the Football League circuit on his release in May 1926.

Season	FL	Total
1924–25	4	4
1925–26	1	1
Total	5	5

HUDSON, Colin   1961–62

outside-left   Ht 5 6, Wt 11 00   1 app
full name: Colin Arthur Richard Hudson
born: Undy, Monmouthshire, Wales, 5.10.1935
debut: Bristol Rovers (a), 26.12.1961 (FL D2)

Colin Hudson gained a fine reputation in Wales before joining the Albion in June 1961. After playing for Undy and Chepstow Town, he signed for Newport County as an amateur, turned professional in April 1954, and went on to score 21 goals in 81 League appearances after making his debut while on National Service with the R.A.F. In July 1957, Colin was transferred to Cardiff City in exchange for three players, and his direct, never-say-die style made him very popular with the Ninian Park fans; but, despite gaining a Welsh Cup winner's medal in 1959 and assisting the 'Bluebirds' back to the First Division in 1959–60, he was never an automatic choice. On coming to the Goldstone, Colin made Albion's first team on just one occasion before rejoining Newport County for a £2,000 fee in June 1962. A year later he moved to Worcester City in the Southern League, and subsequently played for Barry Town, Bath City, Barry Town again , and Cwmbran Town.

Season	FL	Total
1961–62	1	1
Total	1	1

HUGHES, Darren   1986–87

midfield/left-back   Ht 5 11, Wt 10 11   29 apps, 2 goals
full name: Darren John Hughes
born: Prescot, Lancashire, 6.10.1965
debut: Birmingham City (h), 1.10.1986 (FMC R1)

Darren Hughes was one of the first Albion acquisitions made with money from the club's new Lifeline scheme when he was signed for £30,000 in 1986, but it appeared to be good money squandered as he was sold on thirteen months later for a greatly reduced fee without making much of an impact in Sussex. An apprentice with Everton, Darren signed professional forms at Goodison in July 1982 and made his First Division debut a couple of months after his eighteenth birthday. He appeared in Everton's F.A. Youth Cup-winning side of 1984, but had made the first team only three times before being released to join Shrewsbury Town during the summer of 1985.

With 37 Second Division games for the 'Shrews' under his belt, the 20-year-old Lancastrian was signed by Albion manager Alan Mullery in September 1986. Darren never really settled into a regular position at the Goldstone, though – he was played at left-back, in midfield, and occasionally as a striker in a relegation side – and he joined Port Vale on loan in September 1987.

The association became permanent a month later for £5,000, a deal which proved a bargain for the Potteries club as Darren missed only two games as an attacking left-back during their Third Division promotion campaign of 1988–89. He went on to make 222 appearances for Vale, but a bad leg injury in July 1992 severely disrupted his career and his contract was subsequently cancelled during 1994–95. The 29-year-old spent the tail-end of the season and the first part of

1995–96 with Northampton Town, but subsequently joined Exeter City in November 1995 to play against the Albion once again in the Third Division during 1996–97.

Season	FL	FAC	FMC	Total
1986–87	26 (2)	2	1	29 (2)
Total	26 (2)	2	1	29 (2)

HUGHES, Tommy   1973

goalkeeper   Ht 6 1, Wt 12 04   3 apps
full name: Thomas Alexander Hughes
born: Dalmuir, Clydebank, Dunbartonshire, Scotland, 11.7.1947
debut: Luton Town (h), 10.2.1973 (FL D2)

After starting out with Clydebank Juniors, Tommy Hughes joined Chelsea as a professional in July 1965, but he had to be content with understudying Peter Bonetti and consequently made just eleven League appearances in a six-year stay at Stamford Bridge. Nevertheless, he was capped twice by Scotland at under-23 level before signing for Third Division Aston Villa for £12,500 in May 1971. Tommy

played sixteen times in 1971–72 as Villa pipped Albion for the Third Division championship, but then lost his place to Jim Cumbes and came to the Goldstone on loan for a month in February 1973 when Albion were struggling at the foot of Division Two. Although manager Pat Saward was keen to make the arrangement permanent, Albion could not meet Villa's asking-price and the 25-year-old Scot returned to the Midlands only to be transferred to Hereford United for £15,000 in August 1973. Voted Player of the Season in his first term at Edgar Street, Tommy appeared in the side which carried off the Third Division title in fine style in 1975–76. After 240 League outings for Hereford he hung up his gloves in 1982, but then had a traumatic spell as manager when the club finished at the bottom of Division Four in 1982–83.

Season	FL	Total
1972–73	3	3
Total	3	3

HULME, Arthur   1902–09

full-back/right-half   174 apps, 7 goals
full name: Joseph Arthur Hulme
born: Leek, Staffordshire, 18.12.1877
died: in action, Geudecourt, France, 3.10.1916
debut: Southall (h), 13.9.1902 (SL D2)

One of the great characters in the Albion's early history, and the club's first long-serving professional, Arthur Hulme combined a jovial personality with honest endeavour, making him a great favourite over the course of seven years. Although very sturdily built, Arthur started out in Staffordshire junior soccer as an inside-forward, and signed for Lincoln City at the age of nineteen in June 1897. Despite scoring ten goals in 29 outings for the struggling Second Division club during 1897–98, he was released at the end of the season and spent the rest of his career in the Southern League.

His first stop was Gravesend United, whom he joined during the summer of 1898, and in May 1901 he moved on to Bristol Rovers from where he was recruited by the infant Albion in August 1902. By this time Arthur had been transformed into a utility defender and was highly influential in the

successful push for promotion in his first season at Hove. Remaining at the Goldstone for seven seasons, he was team captain in 1905–06, and in November 1907 became the first Albion player to be granted a benefit match. He retired in May 1909 to become trainer of his home-town club, Leek United, from where he recommended several young players to Brighton. In 1914, Arthur enlisted with the Royal Sussex Regiment on the outbreak of war, but lost his life on the Somme while serving as a corporal with the 7th Battalion.

Season	SL	Test	FAC	UL	WL	SEL	SCC	Total
1902–03	9	1	5	0	0	17 (1)	0	32 (1)
1903–04	32	0	1	0	0	0	0	33
1904–05	11	0	1	0	0	0	0	12
1905–06	25	0	5 (1)	10 (1)	0	0	0	40 (2)
1906–07	21	0	0	11 (1)	0	0	0	32 (1)
1907–08	13 (2)	0	0	0	8 (1)	0	2	23 (3)
1908–09	1	0	0	0	1	0	0	2
Total	112 (2)	1	12 (1)	21 (2)	9 (1)	17 (1)	2	174 (7)

HULSE, BEN   1904–05

centre-forward   Ht 5 11, Wt 12 04   30 apps, 10 goals
full name: Benjamin Daniel Hulse
born: Liverpool, Lancashire, 1875
died: Liverpool, Lancashire, 30.5.1950
debut: New Brompton (a), 3.9.1904 (SL D1)

An experienced goalscorer when he joined the Albion towards the end of a fine career in May 1904, Ben Hulse stayed, like so many players of the era, for just one season with the club. In his younger days Ben was said to have 'taken to the game like a duck takes to water', and entered the professional ranks at the early age of fifteen with Liverpool South End (initially in the Liverpool & District League, then the prestigious Lancashire League). Crossing the Mersey to play for Rock Ferry, he gained a Liverpool & District Cup winner's medal when the newly formed Cheshire club defeated Everton's reserves.

Subsequently recruited by another new club, New Brighton Tower, in April 1897, Ben found his registration annulled in May because Tower were not affiliated to the F.A. at the time, and he was quickly snapped up by First Division Blackburn Rovers. In three seasons at Ewood Park the strapping inside-forward notched 21 goals in 85 League games before he was transferred, in a curious irony, back to New Brighton Tower in August 1900. By this time the ambitious Wirral club had progressed to the Football League, and Ben finished 1900–01 as top scorer with fourteen goals from 31 Second Division outings.

Tower, however, folded through lack of support just before the opening of the 1901–02 season, and in September Ben joined Millwall in the Southern League. In three seasons with the 'Dockers' at North Greenwich the robust Liverpudlian was converted into a centre-forward and maintained an excellent scoring-rate, bagging 35 goals from 60 League games. In 1903 he captained the side to an F.A. Cup semi-final defeat by Derby County. The following year Ben arrived at the Goldstone and struggled initially to find the net, yet his ability to orchestrate the forward line was much admired and he was installed as skipper for a spell. At the end of the season he left both the club and the first-class game at the age of 29.

Season	SL	FAC	Total
1904–05	26 (7)	4 (3)	30 (10)
Total	26 (7)	4 (3)	30 (10)

HUMPHREY, JOHN   1997–

right-back   Ht 5 10, Wt 11 04   11 apps
born: Paddington, London, 31.1.1961
debut: Northampton Town (h), 4.3.1997 (FL D3)

When manager Steve Gritt sought to shore up the Albion defence in the desperate fight against relegation from the Football

League in 1996–97, he turned to his former Charlton Athletic room-mate, John Humphrey. Although just turned 36, the experienced full-back proved a calm addition to a fallible rearguard. Indeed, Albion lost just three of his eleven games to complete an almost miraculous escape from the dreaded drop.

Although born in London, John completed an apprenticeship with Wolves and signed professional forms in February 1979. Over the next six seasons he made 149 League appearances as the club divided its time between the top two divisions. Ever-present as Wolves finished runners-up to Q.P.R. in the Second Division in 1983, John also played in every game when the club was relegated to Division Three for the first time in more than 60 years in 1985. Sold to Charlton Athletic for £60,000 in July 1985, the 24-year-old defender proved a bargain buy for the London side which immediately won promotion to the First Division in 1986. John was consistency personified during the "Valiants'" exile at Selhurst Park, and was voted Player of the Season three seasons running, 1987–90. In 1987 he played in the losing Full Members Cup side at Wembley against Blackburn Rovers, but was sold to Crystal Palace for £400,000 following Charlton's relegation in 1990.

John spent five more seasons at Selhurst, this time gaining a winner's medal from the Full Members (ZDS) Cup in 1991, and a Football League championship medal as Palace won a place in the Premiership in 1994. But he also suffered two relegations from the top flight, played in two losing League Cup semi-finals, and spent time on loan at Reading in December 1993. In 1995, John returned on a 'free' to Charlton, by then back at The Valley, but he moved on after just one season to Gillingham.

Calm and unassuming, and with the experience of three promotions and six relegations behind him, John was Steve Gritt's first signing in January 1997 and proved just the man for the crisis. Although occasionally turned by a skilled winger, he often recovered admirably and covered well for his less experienced colleagues. There was speculation that, as the holder of a full badge, he might become reserve-team coach, but because of budgetary cuts required by Albion's chief executive, David Bellotti, John had to be released at the end of the season, a poor reward for a steadfast professional. However, he was quickly reinstated and given a contract following a change of heart in the Albion boardroom.

Season	FL	Total
1996–97	11	11
Total	11	11

HUMPHRIES, BOB   1956–57

inside-right   10 apps, 2 goals
full name: Robert Humphries
born: Hindhead, Surrey, 4.7.1933
died: Spain, 1988
debut: Newport County (a), 10.11.1956 (FL D3(S))

Once an amateur on Tottenham Hotspur's books, Bob Humphries joined Sheffield United as a professional in December 1955, but failed to make the first team at Bramall Lane and arrived at the Goldstone in November 1956. Playing largely as understudy to Albert Mundy, he made ten appearances before moving on to Millwall nine months later in August 1957. Bob remained at The Den for three seasons until June 1960 when he joined Hastings United in the Southern League, and later played for Cambridge United, Hastings United for a second spell, and Tunbridge Wells Rangers. In 1966 he took over as player-manager of Bognor Regis Town in the Sussex County League for two years. Bob was killed in a car crash in Spain at the age of 54.

Season	FL	Total
1956–57	10 (2)	10 (2)
Total	10 (2)	10 (2)

HURST, STAN   *1937–39*

winger   Ht 5 8, Wt 11 00   *34 apps, 11 goals*
full name: Stanley Charles Hurst
born: Newton St Cyres, Devon, 21.6.1911
died: Crediton, Devon, 28.5.1993
debut: Bristol Rovers (h), 9.10.1937 (FL D3(S))

Despite playing rugby at Crediton Grammar School, Stan Hurst turned to soccer with his works' team, Jackson's United, and with the village sides Newton Poppleford and Tipton St John before signing as an amateur for Exeter City in August 1932. The young forward represented both Devon and an F.A. XI *v.* Royal Navy, and had already made his Football League debut by the time he joined the paid ranks in December 1932. Stan became a regular in the "Grecians'" attack for three seasons. Appearing in all the forward positions, he scored 28 goals in 112 League and Cup games before transferring to Watford in August 1936 where he again met with some success, hitting twelve goals in 29 Southern Section outings.

Stan impressed the Goldstone fans after joining the Albion for a £125 fee in June 1937, but he was soon returned to the reserves, a situation which puzzled supporters. In fact he had to wait until the 1938–39 season before getting an extended run in the team at outside-right, but in June 1939 he departed for Aldershot where he made his final appearance in the last wartime emergency season, 1945–46, before returning to his home patch with Crediton United. In 1993, Stan collapsed and died while playing golf at the age of 81.

Season	FL	FAC	Total
1937–38	8 (3)	0	8 (3)
1938–39	25 (8)	1	26 (8)
Total	33 (11)	1	34 (11)

HUTCHINGS, CHRIS   *1983–87*

full-back/midfield   Ht 5 10, Wt 11 00   *175 apps, 6 goals*
full name: Christopher Hutchings
born: Winchester, Hampshire, 5.7.1957
debut: Barnsley (a), 26.11.1983 (FL D2)

Chris Hutchings' introduction to the Albion was bizarre to say the least. Playing at left-back for Chelsea in the infamous Goldstone match of September 1983, when hundreds of so-called supporters of the London side ran riot at the final whistle, he was arrested for swearing at a policeman who told him to leave the pitch and subsequently fined £250 by Hove magistrates. By the time he appeared in court, though, he was turning out in the no.3 shirt for the Albion, having signed for £50,000 in November 1983.

Chris started out as an apprentice with Southend United, but left the game as a youngster and worked as a bricklayer in the London area while turning out for Southall and then Harrow Borough in the Isthmian League. Chelsea paid Harrow £15,000 for his services in July 1980 and he immediately

repaid them by scoring the winning goal at Cardiff on his debut in midfield. Converted to left-back the following season, he went on to play in 87 Second Division matches for the Londoners before coming to the Goldstone, where he soon became a fixture in the defence.

Equally reliable on either flank, Chris held his place in the back line until 1987 and the acquisition of Keith Dublin. Placed on the transfer list, he was expected to join Aldershot, but then fought his way back into the side as a tough-tackling midfielder and was offered a new contract. In December 1987, though, Huddersfield Town came in with terms which he couldn't ignore and he moved to Yorkshire for a £28,000 fee. After 110 Third Division outings and ten goals for the 'Terriers', Chris moved on to Walsall during the summer of 1990, and joined Rotherham United on a free transfer in July 1991, assisting the 'Millers' to runner's-up spot in Division Four in his first season at Millmoor. On hanging up his boots at the end of 1993–94 he joined the Yorkshire club's coaching staff for the following season, and played for Droylsden before joining Bradford City in a similar capacity in the autumn of 1995. In January 1996, Chris was appointed first-team coach at Valley Parade, but he left the club at the end of the season.

Season	FL	FAC	FLC	FMC	AMC	Total
1983–84	26 (1)	3	0	0	0	29 (1)
1984–85	42 (1)	2 (1)	2	0	0	46 (2)
1985–86	29 (1)	3	1	1+1	0	34+1 (1)
1986–87	36	2	2	1	0	41
1987–88	20 (1)	1	2 (1)	0	1	24 (2)
Total	153 (4)	11 (1)	7 (1)	2+1	1	174+1 (6)

HYDE, LEN   *1903–04*

winger   Ht 5 8, Wt 12 00   *29 apps, 4 goals*
full name: Leonard Joseph Hyde
born: Birmingham, Warwickshire, 6.5.1876
died: Birmingham, Warwickshire, 30.12.1932
debut: Wellingborough Town (a), 5.9.1903 (SL D1)

Len Hyde's career can best be described as 'nomadic'. After playing for Harborne in the Birmingham Junior League, he joined Kidderminster Harriers in 1896 and went on to play for Grimsby Town (signed April 1897), Bristol St George's (January 1898), Wellingborough Town (close season 1898), Tottenham Hotspur (May 1899) and Wellingborough for a second spell (April 1902). Signed by the Albion in July 1903 for the club's initial season in the Southern League's First Division, Len performed with great skill and aplomb down either wing. A tricky ball-player with exceptional pace, he played in 29 League games before leaving for Doncaster Rovers in August 1904 on their re-election to the Football League. He missed just two matches as Rovers finished bottom of the League and were swiftly voted out again.

Season	SL	Total
1903–04	29 (4)	29 (4)
Total	29 (4)	29 (4)

INNES, BOB   *1905–06*

right-half   Ht 5 9, Wt 11 00   *29 apps, 1 goal*
full name: Robert Innes
born: Lanark, Lanarkshire, Scotland, 23.7.1878
debut: Millwall (h), 2.9.1905 (SL D1)

Scotsman Bob Innes followed a path taken by a host of his fellow countrymen in search of employment: to the Royal Ordnance Factory in Woolwich. In 1895, at the age of seventeen, he started

playing for the works' Southern League team, and went on to gain a reputation as a 'clever and capable right-half' with Gravesend United (1896–98) and New Brompton (1898–1901) while still employed at the Woolwich factory. Bob represented the Southern League *v.* London F.A. in a 3–3 draw at Millwall in February 1899, and was tempted into professionalism with First Division Notts County in May 1901 for whom he made an immediate impact, becoming a regular member of the side for two seasons before moving across the Trent to Nottingham Forest in September 1903.

With more than 80 First Division outings to his name, Bob became an Albion player in May 1905 and was ever-present in the team up to Christmas, but, after losing his place to Chris Buckley, he subsequently appeared in five United League fixtures only before being released to join Swindon Town in June 1906. Bob remained with the Wiltshire club until his retirement from the first-class game in 1909.

Season	SL	FAC	UL	Total
1905–06	15 (1)	1	13	29 (1)
Total	15 (1)	1	13	29 (1)

IOVAN, STEFAN — 1991–92

defender   Ht 6 1, Wt 12 06   10 apps
born: Bucharest, Romania, 23.8.1960
debut: Portsmouth (a), 16.4.1991 (FL D2)

Stefan Iovan was the first Romanian to appear in the Football League, and the only player in history to gain winner's medals in both the European Cup and the Sussex Senior Cup! Possibly the most experienced man ever to play for the Albion, he arrived in Sussex with the highest of pedigrees, having played more than 300 games for Steaua Bucharest, the champions of Romania on five successive occasions from 1984 to 1989 and his only previous club. Capable of playing in all defensive positions, Stefan appeared in two European

Cup finals for Steaua: in 1986 when he skippered the side to victory over Barcelona on penalties; and in 1989 when they lost 4–0 to AC Milan. He also won 34 caps for his country and played in the Romanians' six qualifying matches for the 1990 World Cup, but didn't make the side for the final series in Italy.

In August 1990, when Albion undertook a trip to Bucharest for a pre-season tournament, the tall, sturdy defender made a big impression on manager Barry Lloyd. Overtures were made for his transfer as early as November, but objections from the P.F.A. delayed proceedings and it wasn't until April 1991 that Stefan finally arrived at the Goldstone for £60,000 in time to play in the Division Two play-offs. The following season, though, he was rather curiously given little chance to show his considerable talents – perhaps because he was used to the sweeper system rather than the traditional English back-four – and spent most of his time languishing in the reserves, helping them to a 1–0 Sussex Senior Cup final victory over Langney Sports.

At the end of the season Stefan was released after just ten senior games for the Albion, and subsequently joined a club in Crete before returning to play for Rapid Bucharest in his native country.

Season	FL	Play-offs	FMC	Total
1990–91	0+2	3	0	3+2
1991–92	4	0	1	5
Total	4+2	3	1	8+2

IRVINE, WILLIE — 1971–72

centre-forward   Ht 5 10, Wt 11 04   76 apps, 29 goals
full name: William John Irvine
born: Carrickfergus, Co. Antrim, Northern Ireland, 18.6.1943
debut: Fulham (h), 10.3.1971 (FL D3)

Willie Irvine will be remembered for helping to revitalise the Albion in the early 1970s; particularly for scoring sixteen League goals as the club unexpectedly won promotion to Division Two in 1971–72; and especially for scoring a quite superb, team-worked goal against Aston Villa in March 1972 that was a runner-up in the BBC's Goal of the Season competition.

One of a crop of talented youngsters developed at Burnley in the early 1960s, Willie won Northern Ireland schoolboy honours and joined the Lancashire club straight from school. After signing as a professional in June 1960, he won his first full cap in April 1963 before he had even made his League debut, but then got off to a terrific start in Division One, scoring in his first game and a hitting a hat-trick in his second. Willie forged a great partnership with Andy Lochead and scored 78 goals in 125 League appearances at Turf Moor, including 29 in 1965–66 as Burnley finished third in the First Division. He also won seventeen caps for Northern Ireland while with the 'Clarets' to add to three at under-23 level, and appeared in the same Irish side as his elder brother Bobby (Linfield and Stoke City goalkeeper) on three occasions.

In January 1967, though, the Ulsterman broke his leg at Everton, and after recovering was transferred to Preston North End in March 1968 for £45,000. Three years later, in March 1971, Willie came to the Goldstone as one of Pat Saward's many loan players and, after scoring on his debut against Fulham, signed permanently for a bargain £7,000 fee in July 1971. The experienced striker played a major part in Albion's Third Division promotion campaign the following season, and his form won him three more caps to bring his total to 23, but in 1972–73, with Albion struggling in vain for Second Division survival, he played in only eleven League matches before being transferred to Halifax Town in December in a deal which brought Lammie Robertson to the Goldstone. Twelve months later he joined Great Harwood in the Northern Premier League and started a business in Burnley, where he now runs a local youth side.

Though on the small side for a centre-forward, Willie was quick off the mark and finished his career with the excellent record of 133 goals from 285 League outings, predominantly in the First Division. He also starred for the Northern Ireland side in the BBC TV series 'Quiz Ball' while at the Goldstone.

Season	FL	FAC	FLC	Total
1970–71	14 (6)	0	0	14 (6)
1971–72	41+3 (16)	3 (1)	2	46+3 (17)
1972–73	11 (5)	0	2 (1)	13 (6)
Total	66+3 (27)	3 (1)	4 (1)	73+3 (29)

ISAAC, BOB — 1987–90

central defender   Ht 5 11, Wt 12 07   33 apps
full name: Robert Charles Isaac
born: Hackney, London, 30.11.1965
debut: Oldham Athletic (h), 21.2.1987 (FL D2)

As a Chelsea apprentice, Bob Isaac won four caps for the England under-19 team in 1985, but missed out on the 'Little World Cup' when he was recalled to Stamford Bridge for first-team duty. In March 1985 he made his First Division debut in the absence of Colin Pates (who also later came to Brighton), a 3–1 win at Watford, but he had made just nine outings in the League team before joining the Albion in February 1987 for a fee which reached £50,000. An inexperienced but promising defender, Bob made a vital contribution to the Third Division promotion run-in in 1987–88 when he replaced Doug Rougvie, but was extremely unfortunate with injuries, being side-lined for more than a year with a knee problem which required several operations.

Sadly, in August 1990, he was forced to call it a day at the age of just 24, and now works as a personal assistant to a well-known horse-racing family.

Season	FL	FLC	Total
1986–87	11	0	11
1987–88	10	1	11
1988–89	9	2	11
Total	30	3	33

ISHERWOOD, Bob   1908–09

outside-left   *2 apps*
full name: Robert Isherwood
born: Leigh, Lancashire, 1888
debut: Leyton (h), 14.10.1908 (WL D1 'A')

Bob Isherwood was brought to the Goldstone Ground from the Lancashire club Radcliffe Wednesday during the close season of 1908 and was offered professional terms. He played regularly for the reserves but made the first team just twice, appearing in consecutive Western League matches in October 1908 in the absence of the injured Joe Jee. On the completion of the 1908–09 season Bob was not retained and returned to minor football.

Season	WL	Total
1908–09	2	2
Total	2	2

ISON, Ernie   1924–31

outside-left   *Ht 5 6, Wt 10 12*   *16 apps*
full name: Ernest Ison
born: Hartshill, Warwickshire, 12.6.1903
died: Burntwood, Staffordshire, 26.10.1983
debut: Southend United (h), 21.4.1926 (FL D3(S))

Well over 60 years since he left the Goldstone, Ernie Ison still holds an unenviable Albion club record. Between 1924 and 1931, the former collier made over 300 appearances for the reserves, a total barely approached by anyone else; yet he played just sixteen times for the first team. The reason for Ernie's lengthy spell in the 'Lambs' was the consistent form of the venerable Ernie 'Tug' Wilson, who made more senior appearances for the club than any other player.

The 21-year-old winger arrived at the Goldstone in August 1924 from Nuneaton where he had played as a part-time professional in the Birmingham League. Despite taking on one of the most unenviable tasks in football as understudy to the irremovable Wilson, he gave uncomplaining service, and his skills and loyalty made him a popular figure with the fans in an era when the second string attracted large attendances. There can be little doubt that he would have achieved first-team football elsewhere had he not elected to remain with the Albion.

Often known as 'Rabbit' because of his speed and distinctive gait, the unlucky Ernie enjoyed a joint benefit with Reg Smith and Reg Wilkinson in April 1930 after five years with the club, and was released to join Southport in June 1931 where he figured in ten Third Division (North) matches before moving on to Watford in August 1932. In the latter part of his career, though, Ernie suffered with cartilage problems and made just three appearances for the 'Brewers' before dropping into the Kent League with Ramsgate Athletic in May 1933. Employed in the building industry during his time in Kent, he returned to his native Hartshill during the Second World War where he was employed in a munitions factory. When peace was restored Ernie became a surface hand at Ansley Colliery, and subsequently worked in a Nuneaton factory until his retirement.

Season	FL	Total
1925–26	2	2
1926–27	4	4
1928–29	6	6
1929–30	1	1
1930–31	3	3
Total	16	16

JACKSON, Allan   1962–64

inside-left   *Ht 5 10, Wt 11 07*   *22 apps, 5 goals*
born: Newhall, Derbyshire, 22.8.1938
debut: Coventry City (h), 1.12.1962 (FL D3)

In November 1962, with Albion battling against relegation, manager George Curtis signed Allan Jackson and Bill Cassidy in an unsuccessful bid to halt the slide into Division Four. The fee for Jackson was £8,000, and the 24-year-old forward went some way to justifying it with five goals from fifteen outings during the remainder of a calamitous campaign. The following season, though, he fell out of favour with new manager Archie Macaulay, and made only a further seven appearances before being placed on the transfer list in January 1964. At the end of the season he returned to his native Derbyshire with Southern League Burton Albion.

A staunch Methodist and youth leader who declined to play in fixtures on religious holidays, Allan had entered the professional game with Wolverhampton Wanderers on his seventeenth birthday in August 1955. He had to compete with the likes of Dennis Wilshaw, Peter Broadbent and Bobby Mason for the inside-left berth, though, and had little opportunity to impress in four seasons on the Molineux staff. Nevertheless, he made two appearances in both of Wolves' League championship successes of 1957–58 and 1958–59. After moving on to Bury in June 1959, Allan's talents were given wider scope in the lower company. He scored 43 times in

124 League matches for the 'Shakers' and was leading marksman with 24 goals when they carried off the Third Division title by a six-point margin in 1960–61. That was the peak of his success, though, and he was just 26 when he left the Football League arena after seventeen months at the Goldstone.

Season	FL	FLC	Total
1962–63	15 (5)	0	15 (5)
1963–64	6	1	7
Total	21 (5)	1	22 (5)

JACOBS, STEVE 1984–86

midfield/defender   Ht 5 8, Wt 12 02   61 apps, 4 goals
full name: Steve Douglas Jacobs
born: West Ham, Essex, 5.7.1961
debut: Carlisle United (a), 25.8.1984 (FL D2)

Renowned for his combative play, Steve Jacobs gained something of a 'hard man' reputation while making 101 First Division appearances for Coventry City. In fact, he first came to the notice of the Brighton fans when he was sent off in tandem with Albion's Chris Ramsey at the Goldstone in April 1983. A Newham and Essex Schools representative, Steve graduated from an apprenticeship with the 'Sky Blues' to sign as a professional in November 1978. After a hesitant start he won a regular place in the City side under Dave Sexton, but lost favour when Bobby Gould took over the reins at Highfield Road in 1983.

In June 1984, Sexton, a former Albion player, recommended him to Brighton manager Chris Cattlin, and the 22-year-old midfielder arrived at the Goldstone on a free transfer. Adding a necessary degree of 'steel' to the side, Steve was sent off on three occasions during his two seasons with the club, but also proved an effective performer both in midfield and at full-back. He maintained a place in the side during much of the 1985–86 campaign, but will be particularly remembered for his magnificent contribution as a substitute at Peterborough which secured a home replay for Albion in the fifth round of the F.A. Cup. At the end of the season, though, he was released by new manager Alan Mullery, much to the surprise of most supporters. Indeed, many Albion fans pointed to the lack of a midfield ball-winner such as Jacobs as one reason for the tame relegation suffered by the club the following season.

The tough-tackling East Ender joined Charlton Athletic on a monthly-contract basis, but enjoyed just one outing in the "Valiants'" first team before moving on to Gillingham in January 1986. After seven Third Division appearances for the 'Gills', Steve then disappeared from the first-class scene at the age of 25.

Season	FL	FAC	FLC	FMC	Total
1984–85	18 (2)	2	2	0	22 (2)
1985–86	29+1 (1)	3+1 (1)	3	2	37+2 (2)
Total	47+1 (3)	5+1 (1)	5	2	59+2 (4)

JAMES, DAI 1926–29

inside/outside-right   Ht 5 7, Wt 11 00   32 apps, 9 goals
full name: David James
born: Aberdare, Glamorgan, Wales, 16.11.1899
debut: Brentford (h), 15.1.1927 (FL D3(S))

Recruited by his home-town club, Aberdare Athletic, in June 1921 for their inaugural season in the Football League, Dai James went on to give excellent service at Herbert Street for more than five seasons. In 170 Southern Section appearances for the Glamorgan side, he occupied all the half-back and forward positions at various times, and it cost Albion the then considerable sum of £375 to secure his transfer in December 1926.

Dai's role at the Goldstone became primarily that of a reserve, although he did appear in 26 League games during the 1927–28 campaign. A series of injuries sidelined him for lengthy periods, but he continued to prove his versatility by performing in a variety of forward berths during a two-and-a-half season spell with the club. In May 1929 the stocky little Welshman was released and departed for non-League football.

Season	FL	FAC	Total
1926–27	2	0	2
1927–28	26 (8)	2 (1)	28 (9)
1928–29	2	0	2
Total	30 (8)	2 (1)	32 (9)

JAMES, DAVID 1962–63

outside-right   6 apps
born: Cambuslang, Lanarkshire, Scotland, 2.12.1942
debut: Queen's Park Rangers (a), 18.8.1962 (FL D3)

Signed by George Curtis from the Lanarkshire junior club Blantyre Victoria in May 1962, David James was drafted straight into Albion's first team and impressed on his debut, a 2–2 draw at Queen's Park Rangers in the opening fixture of the 1962–63 season. The nineteen-year-old winger, dubbed one of "Curtis's Cubs" as the manager pursued a policy based on youth, retained the outside-right spot as Albion enjoyed a good start to the campaign, but lost his place as the team soon began to plunge into the lower reaches. No fewer than nine players appeared in the no.7 shirt that season, but David was not recalled and, after bagging a hat-trick in his last game for the reserves, he left for Southern League Cambridge United in April 1963 three weeks after fellow Scottish youngster Craig Bailey had taken the same route.

Season	FL	FLC	Total
1962–63	5	1	6
Total	5	1	6

JAMES, TONY 1939–49

utility player   Ht 5 8, Wt 11 02   74 apps, 22 goals
full name: Thomas Anthony George James
born: Llanwonno, Mountain Ash, Glamorgan, Wales, 16.9.1919
debut: Norwich City (a), 5.10.1946 (FL D3(S))

Tony James signed for the Albion as a nineteen-year-old right-winger from Southern League Folkestone in May 1939, but little was seen of him at the Goldstone Ground until he returned from his wartime duties in 1946. The dynamic Welshman played for the Army's Middle Eastern touring side (known as The Wanderers) during the war years, and became very much a utility player with the Albion when things returned to a peacetime format, appearing in four different positions during the 1946–47 campaign . Described as 'a good tackler with skilful distribution', he settled into his preferred attacking right-half role the following season when he finished as the club's leading scorer with fourteen goals in the League and F.A. Cup.

During his third season at Hove, though, Tony's career was beset by injuries and he departed for Bristol Rovers in June 1949 where he remained for two seasons. However, the injury problems continued, and he made only 21 League appearances before returning to the Southern League with Bath City in 1951. On retiring from the game Tony ran a ladies' hairdressing salon in Bristol. Also a fine cricketer, he 'took nets' with Sussex during his time at Hove.

Season	FL	FAC	Total
1946–47	23 (8)	0	23 (8)
1947–48	42 (12)	5 (2)	47 (14)
1948–49	4	0	4
Total	69 (20)	5 (2)	74 (22)

JASPER, DALE 1986–88

midfield   Ht 6 0, Wt 11 07   60 apps, 8 goals
full name: Dale William Jasper
born: Croydon, Surrey, 14.1.1964
debut: Portsmouth (h), 23.8.1986 (FL D2)

Dale Jasper listed his football ambition in the Albion programme as 'Winning the Sussex Senior Cup'. In May 1988 the joke backfired on the wiry midfielder when, having been out of first-team reckoning for several weeks, he was in the reserves' side which lifted the Cup for the first time — just a few days before he was released!

Looking somewhat fragile in the hurly-burly of an English midfield, Dale undoubtedly possessed skill but was never quite able to establish himself in the Albion side. Outstanding as a schoolboy, he skippered both Croydon and Surrey Schools, and led the Croydon team which lost to Bristol in the English Schools Trophy final of 1979. By this time Dale was on Chelsea's books and became an apprentice. The former Chelsea star Alan Hudson considered the versatile youngster one of the best prospects at Stamford Bridge, but, after signing as a professional in January 1981, he made the League team on just ten occasions and was released to join the Albion on a free transfer in May 1986 at the age of 22.

After 60 senior games for Brighton, Dale moved on to Crewe Alexandra in July 1988 where he played in 39 matches in his first season as the 'Railwaymen' gained promotion to Division Three. He went on to total 111 League games for the Cheshire side, but was released in 1992 and turned out for Crawley Town in the Southern League in 1992–93. Dale then returned to his home county of Surrey with Kingstonian, and he remains with the Isthmian League side. He did not, however, feature in the team which defeated Albion in F.A. Cup first round in November 1994.

Season	FL	FAC	FLC	FMC	AMC	Total
1986–87	32+3 (2)	1 (1)	2	1	0	36+3 (3)
1987–88	12+2 (4)	1+1	0+1	0	3+1 (1)	16+5 (5)
Total	44+5 (6)	2+1 (1)	2+1	1	3+1 (1)	52+8 (8)

JEE, JOE 1908–09

outside-left   44 apps, 7 goals
full name: Joseph William Jee
born: Chorlton-cum-Hardy, Lancashire, 1883
debut: Southampton (h), 2.9.1908 (SL D1)

Signed as a professional by Bolton Wanderers in April 1906, 23-year-old Joe Jee made six First Division appearances for his

first senior club during 1907–08, but failed to live up to expectations at Burnden Park and was released to join the Albion in May 1908. He turned in some excellent performances down Albion's left wing, missing only seven Southern League matches during 1908–09, and it came as something of a surprise when he was not retained at the end of the season. Returning north to join Midland League Huddersfield Town, Joe became a great favourite with the Leeds Road crowd when they were admitted to the Football League in 1910, netting 34 goals in 171 League appearances. Retained by the Yorkshire club until October 1919, he was awarded £150 in lieu of a benefit match and transferred across the Pennines to non-League Nelson for £50.

Season	SL	FAC	WL	WL Ch.	SCC	Total
1908–09	31 (5)	1	9 (2)	1	2	44 (7)
Total	31 (5)	1	9 (2)	1	2	44 (7)

JENKINS, JACK 1922–29

full-back   Ht 5 9, Wt 11 08   231 apps, 4 goals
full name: John Jenkins
born: Gwersyllt, Denbighshire, Wales, 20.3.1892
died: Brighton, Sussex, 16.4.1946
debut: Norwich City (h), 26.8.1922 (FL D3(S))

Although he didn't break into the Football League scene until he was 30, Jack Jenkins went on to enjoy a most distinguished career and held the record as the most-capped Albion player for 55 years. A sturdily-built defender, he inspired the team with his confidence and coolness in either full-back berth for seven years, and was captain in 1925–26.

Jack started out with Mold Town in his native north Wales in 1907 before moving south a year later to join Mardy in the Southern League. In December 1912, at the age of 20, he played for Billy Meredith's XI v. South Wales in an international trial match at Ninian Park, but it was to be another eleven years before he made his first appearance for his country. The thoughtful Welshman moved on to Pontypridd in 1914, and guested for Portsmouth and Cardiff City during the Great War before rejoining Mardy in 1919, but in 1920 he rejoined Pontypridd. The Southern League club's inside-

JENKINS · B+H · ALBION F.C.
WEARING HIS WELSH INTERNATIONAL CAP + JERSEY.

forward at the time was former Albion player Fred Osborne, and he recommended his team-mate to Brighton manager Charlie Webb. Thus Jack arrived at the Goldstone in August 1922 despite considerable competition from Leeds United.

In his first season Jack played in every League match as the Albion defence conceded just 34 goals, a record for the club in the Football League (equalled in 1984–85). During his second League campaign he won his first Welsh cap in a 2–0 win over Scotland at Cardiff in February 1924, and went on to play against England and Ireland as the Principality carried off the Home International Championship that season. In all he played eight times for Wales, a total which stood as a club record until surpassed by Mark Lawrenson in April 1980.

After his retirement in 1929, Jack ran the Waggon & Horses pub in Brighton's Church Street for some time, and in December 1932 was reinstated as an amateur to play for the Brighton Hotels side in the local midweek league. At the time of his death in 1946, after a long illness, he was living in Whitehawk Road, Brighton. Always the gentleman, Jack was a credit to the game of football.

Season	FL	FAC	Total
1922–23	42	3	45
1923–24	35	4	39
1924–25	40	3	43
1925–26	38	2	40
1926–27	13	0	13
1927–28	28 (3)	2	30 (3)
1928–29	20 (1)	1	21 (1)
Total	216 (4)	15	231 (4)

JENNINGS, Roy   1952–64

full-back/centre-half   Ht 6 1, Wt 12 10   297 apps, 22 goals
full name: Roy Thomas Edward Jennings
born: Swindon, Wiltshire, 31.12.1931
debut: Watford (h), 31.1.1953 (FL D3(S))

Fondly remembered by older supporters as the king-pin of the Albion side in the late 1950s and early '60s, Roy Jennings in fact took several years to find his true vocation. The strapping defender's first six years at the Goldstone were spent as a full-back, but he was a revelation when switched to the centre-half berth in place of Ken Whitfield – just like the man he replaced had been when he made a similar move – and went on to skipper the club from 1960 until 1964.

Roy represented Wiltshire as a youth and also won England honours at that level in 1950. On the books of Swindon Town and Southampton as an amateur, he did his National Service in the R.A.F. and signed for the Albion as a professional in May 1952 upon the recommendation of chief scout Ted Nash, the former Swindon goalkeeper. Initially appearing sporadically in both full-back positions with limited success, Roy made around 60 League appearances before his dramatic switch at Christmas 1958 during Albion's first season in Division Two. The hard-as-nails defender thereafter made the position his own and became a great favourite, despite the club falling

from the Second Division into the Fourth. Dominant in the air and strong in the tackle, he missed just nine games over the next four-and-a-half seasons until 1963–64 when he moved to left-back to allow the young Norman Gall into the side.

Indeed, a measure of his popularity at the Goldstone had come in September 1962 when manager George Curtis dropped him in favour of Gall; the decision resulted in angry crowd demonstrations and a swift reinstatement. Also a penalty specialist, Roy scored thirteen times from the spot before his release to join Crawley Town on a free transfer in 1964. After four years at Town Mead he was appointed player-manager until his retirement in 1970. Now a magistrate and a partner in a financial consultancy, Roy lives in the Gossops Green area of Crawley.

Season	FL	FAC	FLC	Total
1952–53	6	0	0	6
1953–54	4	0	0	4
1955–56	2	1	0	3
1956–57	29 (3)	0	0	29 (3)
1957–58	17 (1)	1	0	18 (1)
1958–59	26	1	0	27
1959–60	42 (2)	5	0	47 (2)
1960–61	40 (5)	3	2	45 (5)
1961–62	40 (4)	1	1	42 (4)
1962–63	41 (7)	1	1	43 (7)
1963–64	29	1	3	33
Total	276 (22)	14	7	297 (22)

JENNINGS, Sam   1925–28

inside-right/centre-forward   Ht 5 11, Wt 11 04   115 apps, 63 goals
full name: Samuel Jennings
born: Cinder Hill, Nottingham, Nottinghamshire, 16.4.1898
died: Robertsbridge, Sussex, 26.8.1944
debut: Northampton Town (h), 14.3.1925 (FL D3(S))

One of the surest strikers ever to play for the Albion, Sam Jennings enjoyed a long career with numerous clubs. At the Goldstone he demonstrated his considerable prowess in 1926–27 by out-scoring the immortal Tommy Cook, a rare feat indeed.

Born in Nottinghamshire, Sam played for the Highlands Vale Boys' Club before enlisting with the Coldstream Guards on the outbreak of war in 1914. The Army soon discovered that he was under age, however, and he went to work in a munitions factory until rejoining the Coldstreams in 1916. During this period Sam guested for Notts County and Tottenham Hotspur, but joined Basford United in his native county when the armistice was signed. In May 1919 he was recruited by Southern League Norwich City (along with his elder brother Billy, who had played for Notts County before the war) and impressed First Division Middlesbrough enough for them to pay £2,250

S. JENNINGS · BRIGHTON · HOVE ALBION · 1925·26.

for his signature in April 1920, a massive sum at the time. Illness marred Sam's progress at Ayresome Park, though, and after just ten League outings he was transferred to Reading in June 1921 where his career regained momentum. In three seasons at Elm Park he netted 45 goals in 110 Third Division outings, form which saw him return to the top flight with West Ham United in June 1924.

In March 1925, Albion manager Charlie Webb paid a club-record £650 fee for the versatile forward, money which proved well spent: Sam bagged a hat-trick in only his third match and, whether at inside-right or centre-forward, continued to score goals in abundance. In 1925–26 he topped the list with 20 goals and did so again in 1926–27 with 27, but, despite scoring 63 goals at better than one every other game, he lost favour with the fickle Goldstone fans during his third full season and departed for Second Division Nottingham Forest for

Players' countries of birth	
Not including wartime players	
Country	**No. of Players**
England	568
Scotland	118
Wales	36
Republic of Ireland (4 born before partition of Ireland)	20
Northern Ireland (4 born before partition of Ireland)	15
U.S.A.	3
Belarus (then part of U.S.S.R.)	2
Israel	2
Malta	2
South Africa	2
Australia	1
Channel Islands	1
Germany (then West Germany)	1
India	1
Netherlands	1
New Zealand	1
Nigeria	1
Pakistan (then part of Indian Empire)	1
Romania	1
Singapore	1
Zimbabwe (then Rhodesia)	1

an undisclosed fee in May 1928. Twelve months later he moved on to Port Vale and led scoring list with 24 goals as the Potteries side carried off the championship of the Third Division (North) in his first season at Hanley. January 1932 saw him sign for Burnley for a brief spell, where he brought his League goals total to a splendid 185 from 361 appearances.

Ever the wanderer, Sam went on to play for Marseilles in the French League, then coached in Switzerland, and with Wisbech Town and Glentoran, prior to his appointment as manager of Rochdale in October 1937, a position he held until the following year. Sam suffered two bouts of pneumonia during his spells with Norwich City and Middlesbrough which made him prone to chills, and he died at the age of 46 after a long stay at the Robertsbridge Sanatorium in eastern Sussex.

Season	FL	FAC	Total
1924–25	11 (8)	0	11 (8)
1925–26	41 (20)	1	42 (20)
1926–27	41 (25)	2 (2)	43 (27)
1927–28	17 (8)	2	19 (8)
Total	110 (61)	5 (2)	115 (63)

JEPSON, BERT   1933–35

outside-right   Ht 5 8, Wt 10 07   54 apps, 11 goals
full name: Albert Edward Jepson
born: Glass Houghton, Castleford, Yorkshire, 9.5.1902
died: Binfield, Berkshire, 18.12.1981
debut: Southend United (a), 28.10.1933 (FL D3(S))

Bert Jepson played for Frickley Colliery in the Midland League as a youngster and joined the Huddersfield Town staff in May 1927, but, with so many great players available at Leeds Road, he was never in contention for a first-team place and was released to join Southampton in August 1928. His obvious skills were given more scope at The Dell, and he scored eighteen goals in 95 League and Cup matches during a four-year stay. In June 1932 the Yorkshire winger moved to Fulham on a free transfer and spent a season in their reserve team before coming to the Goldstone in August 1933.

In two years with the Albion, Bert shared the right-wing spot with Stan Thompson, but retired from the professional game in 1935. Taking employment with the Belgravia Dairy, he managed their outlet in Applesham Avenue, Hangleton, for almost 20 years and assisted their football club to the Sussex Intermediate Cup in 1936. In 1951, at the age of 48, Bert was still playing locally for Hove, and also coached the then Sussex County League club.

Season	FL	FAC	SSC	Total
1933–34	15 (2)	0	4	19 (2)
1934–35	30 (6)	3 (1)	2 (2)	35 (9)
Total	45 (8)	3 (1)	6 (2)	54 (11)

JEST, SYD   1961–64

full-back   Ht 5 10, Wt 11 04   12 apps
full name: Sydney Thomas Jest
born: Ramsgate, Kent, 4.6.1943
debut: Derby County (h), 9.12.1961 (FL D2)

Syd Jest was one of the young players signed by George Curtis as part of his unsuccessful youth scheme. Joining the Albion as an eighteen-year-old full-back from Southern League Ramsgate Athletic in December 1961, he was plunged straight into Second Division duty in the absence of Bob McNicol in a 2–1 home defeat by Derby County. Although he retained the right-back berth for the following match,

Syd made the bulk of his twelve appearances in 1962–63 as Albion tumbled into the Fourth Division. Having played for the reserves throughout the following term, he was released in May 1964 and returned to Kent to play, in turn, for the Southern League clubs Gravesend & Northfleet, Margate, and Ramsgate Athletic. Syd later turned out for Sheppey United in the Kent League.

Season	FL	Total
1961–62	2	2
1962–63	10	10
Total	12	12

JOHNSON, MICK   1955–57

centre-forward   2 apps
full name: Michael W. Johnson
born: York, Yorkshire, 4.10.1933
debut: Queen's Park Rangers (h), 1.12.1956 (FL D3(S))

Signed by Newcastle United as a youngster in April 1951, Mick Johnson was released after three years on the St James's Park staff in June 1954 without appearing in the League team. He went on to play for Blyth Spartans in the North Eastern League, and joined the Albion as a 22-year-old in December 1955, spending a year in the reserves before making his two first-team appearances at centre-forward in the absence of Peter Harburn. In fact, Mick was very much a left-footed player, which limited his options as a centre-forward, and he was far better-suited to his more usual left-wing role. During the summer of 1957 he signed for Gloucester City on a free transfer, but returned to the League in August 1958 with Fulham. In a four-season stint at Craven Cottage, Mick played in just 27 League and

Cup matches, despite scoring twice against Charlton Athletic on his debut, and moved on to Doncaster Rovers in July 1962. Mick finished his League career with a dozen games for Barrow, signing in March 1963.

Season	FL	Total
1956–57	2	2
Total	2	2

JOHNSON, ROSS   1992–

defender   Ht 6 0, Wt 12 04   59 apps
full name: Ross Yorke-Johnson
born: Brighton, Sussex, 2.1.1976
debut: Reading (h), 20.10.1993 (AMC Group)

Although transfer-listed in November 1996 by Albion manager Jimmy Case, Ross Johnson proved himself towards the end of a traumatic season when he took over from more experienced men as the club clawed its way to safety. The Brighton-born defender was rewarded with another contract from new manager Steve Gritt.

Educated at the Hertford Road and Dorothy Stringer Schools in Brighton, Ross played for Hollingbury Hawks, both Brighton and Sussex Boys, and trained with the Albion at the Worthing school of excellence before joining the club as a trainee in 1992. In fact he also spent a week training with Everton who offered to take him on as an associate schoolboy, but Ross preferred to sign for his local side. In October 1993 he made his senior debut as a seventeen-year-old in an Associate Members (Autoglass) Cup match with Reading and performed creditably alongside the experienced Steve Foster, who was more than twice the youngster's age.

Captain of the excellent youth team of 1993–94, Ross was offered a three-year contract in April 1994, just a few days before making his League debut at full-back against Cambridge United, but his first-team opportunities were limited until November 1995 when he impressed alongside Paul McCarthy in the absence of the injured Foster and Russell Osman. Ross proved to be the find of the season as he matured rapidly into a regular member of the senior side. His form fell off towards the end of a campaign which saw Albion relegated to the bottom section of the League, and he struggled in the early part of 1996–97, but the 21-year-old came back well in the New Year and proved an inspiration as he fought successfully to keep his home-town club in the League, winning several 'man-of-the-match' nominations. Although he still needs to knock some raw edges off his game and improve his distribution, few players at the Albion have a bigger heart than Ross.

Season	FL	FAC	FLC	AMC	Total
1993–94	1+1	0	0	1	2+1
1995–96	19+1	2	0	2	23+1
1996–97	21+8	0	0+1	1+1	22+10
Total	41+10	2	0+1	4+1	47+12

JOHNSTON, RON   1950–51

inside-left   1 app
full name: Ronald Johnston
born: Port Dundas, Glasgow, Lanarkshire, Scotland, 3.4.1921
debut: Plymouth Argyle (h), 18.11.1950 (FL D3(S))

Ron Johnston's formative football years coincided with the Second World War, but, when peace arrived, Rochdale gave him his chance in the Third Division (North), signing him as a professional in November 1947 at the late age of 26. After scoring seven goals in seventeen fixtures during the remainder of the season, he was transferred to Exeter City in June 1948, but met with only moderate success at St James's Park and was released in 1949 to join Weymouth in the Southern League.

Ron began the 1950–51 season with Headington United (later to become Oxford United), but in November 1950 Don Welsh obtained his signature for the Albion. The Scottish inside-forward played in just one League game while at the Goldstone Ground, though, a humiliating 6–0 home defeat at the hands of Plymouth Argyle a few days after his arrival, and he returned to non-League football at the end of the season when he was given a free transfer.

Season	FL	Total
1950–51	1	1
Total	1	1

JONES, ABE   1922–23

inside-right/centre-forward   Ht 5 7, Wt 11 04   6 apps, 1 goal
full name: Abel Jones
born: Birmingham, Warwickshire, 1898
debut: Norwich City (h), 26.8.1922 (FL D3(S))

Abe Jones was the son of a former West Bromwich Albion professional of the same name, and nephew of Brighton's legendary shooting star Bill 'Bullet' Jones. Abe junior attended

Birmingham's Bratt Street School, and had progressed to the local Sandwell club when he joined Birmingham in August 1919. Despite scoring twice on his debut in April 1920, he made the League team just twice more before moving to Reading in August 1921.

Brought to Hove in June 1922, Abe played at inside-right at the start of the season, but was then tried in the problem centre-forward spot with little joy. He was dropped after six games, never appeared in the first team again, and was released in May 1923 for a season with Merthyr Town before finishing his League career with a short spell at Stoke City.

Season	FL	Total
1922–23	6 (1)	6 (1)
Total	6 (1)	6 (1)

JONES, BULLET   1909–12 & 1913–20

centre-forward   Ht 5 5   179 apps, 69 goals
full name: William Henry Jones
born: Tipton, Staffordshire, 24.3.1881
died: Hove, Sussex, 15.3.1948
debut: Portsmouth (a), 1.9.1909 (SL D1)

One of the legendary heroes of Albion history, Bill Jones – usually known as 'Bullet' – stood just 5' 5" but walked tall at the Goldstone for 38 years: from May 1909, when he joined the club as a 28-year-old centre-forward, until 1947. Idolised by the fans during his playing days, Bullet hung up his boots at the age of 39 in 1920, but continued to serve the club, first as a scout, then as assistant trainer and, during the Second World War, as head groundsman. In fact, he occasionally turned out for the reserves until 1927, and was still thrilling the crowds in charity matches in the 1930s. The nickname 'Bullet' adds to the folklore and was conferred upon him for his thunderous shooting-power, but when he started out in the Midlands he was known as 'The Tipton Slasher'.

After spells with Smethwick Town and Halesowen, Bill signed professional forms for Small Heath (which soon became Birmingham) in August 1901, and scored 80 goals in 197 League and Cup games over eight fruitful seasons with the club. In 1902–03 he helped the side win promotion to Division One, represented the Football League v. Irish League in October 1904, and came close to winning a full cap when he appeared for the North v. South in an international trial match at Stamford Bridge in February 1907.

Bill arrived in Hove in May 1909 and quickly became a firm favourite with his cheery personality, bandy legs and on-field antics. Despite a two-month suspension during the 1909–10 Southern League championship campaign – he was sent off for clashing with both the Norwich City goalkeeper and his replacement, and also 'sauced' the referee – he topped the scoring list with 22 goals, and repeated the feat with 19 the following season. In January 1912, Birmingham signed Bullet for a second time for a fee of £300 and he scored 22 goals in 53 Second Division outings, forming an excellent partnership up front with another former Albion marksman, Jack Hall. Much to the delight of Albion supporters, though, their 32-year-old favourite returned to the

Goldstone in November 1913 and topped the scoring list again during 1914–15. In fact, his form won him another representative appearance, this time for the Southern League in a 1–1 draw with the Scottish League at Millwall in October 1914.

During the Great War, Bill served with the Footballer's Battalion of the Middlesex Regiment and also turned out for Luton Town, but he returned to the Goldstone for the resumption in 1919 and bowed out of first-team action on 20 December 1919 at the age of 38, the oldest player ever to appear for the club at the time. His son, Les, played for the club briefly during the Second World War and managed the wartime junior side (see *Albion Wartime Players Who's Who*).

Sadly, Bill died in tragic circumstances. After retiring as Albion groundsman on his wife's death in 1947, he subsequently suffered a nervous breakdown and passed away at Hove General Hospital in March 1948 at the age of 66, having been found in a gas-filled room at his home in Sackville Road.

Season	SL	FAC	FACS	SCC	Total
1909–10	34 (20)	0	0	3 (2)	37 (22)
1910–11	35 (17)	3 (2)	1	5	44 (19)
1911–12	16 (5)	1	0	2	19 (5)
1913–14	23 (5)	3 (1)	0	0	26 (6)
1914–15	35 (12)	3 (1)	0	1	39 (13)
1919–20	13 (4)	1	0	0	14 (4)
Total	156 (63)	11 (4)	1	11 (2)	179 (69)

JONES, FREDDIE   1958–60

outside-left   Ht 5 7, Wt 10 07   76 apps, 15 goals
full name: Frederick George Jones
born: Caerphilly, Glamorgan, Wales, 11.1.1938
debut: Cardiff City (h), 13.9.1958 (FL D2)

Freddie Jones joined Arsenal in January 1958 together with his Hereford United team-mate Ronnie Clayton, and came to the Goldstone eight months later, again with Clayton, in a deal which cost the Albion £5,000. Of the two it was Clayton who initially caught the eye, but he quickly faded from the scene and it was the 20-year-old Welshman who made a lasting impression. A nippy left-winger with tricky ball skills, Freddie was a regular and popular face in Brighton's Second Division side for two seasons, and won a Welsh under-23 cap against Scotland in November 1959 (together with 'keeper Dave Hollins).

Following the acquisition of Bobby Laverick in June 1960, though, Freddie lost his place and, after asking for a transfer, moved on to Swindon Town for a small fee in December 1960 where he gained further under-23 honours. In July 1961 he was exchanged for Grimsby Town's Ralph Hunt, and went on to play a major role in the "Mariners'" promotion to the Second Division with eight goals from 41 appearances in his first season at Blundell Park. Reading paid £3,000 for his transfer in July 1963, but in August 1964 he gave up League football at the age of 26 and returned to the Southern League with his old club, Hereford United.

Season	FL	FAC	FLC	Total
1958–59	35 (9)	1	0	36 (9)
1959–60	29 (4)	5 (1)	0	34 (5)
1960–61	5 (1)	0	1	6 (1)
Total	69 (14)	6 (1)	1	76 (15)

JONES, HERBERT   1934–35

left-back   Ht 5 8, Wt 10 04   43 apps
full name: Herbert Jones
born: Blackpool, Lancashire, 3.12.1896
died: Fleetwood, Lancashire, 11.9.1973
debut: Bristol Rovers (h), 25.8.1934 (FL D3(S))

In a long and distinguished career, Herbert Jones proved to be very much a defensive full-back, so much so that he failed to score a single goal in his 378 Football League appearances. He was also a master of positioning, and snuffed out many a promising attack with timely interceptions.

Herbert's career began with the South Shore Strollers in Blackpool and then, in 1920, in the Lancashire Combination with Fleetwood before he was signed by Blackpool in May 1922 at the age of 25.

After 94 League matches at Bloomfield Road, Herbert made the move which brought him national recognition: to Blackburn Rovers in December 1925 where he played in the victorious F.A. Cup final side of 1928 and made 247 First Division appearances in eight-and-a-half years. His distinctive bald pate became a feature at football grounds all over the country, and in April 1927 he won the first of six caps for England. He also represented the Football League on three occasions.

Herbert was 37 when he came to Hove in June 1934 and was appointed captain, but at the end of the season he returned to the Fleetwood club. An engineer by trade, he was of a studious disposition which was reflected in his displays on the pitch, although he was also blessed with a fair degree of pace. During the Great War, Herbert was injured at Ypres while serving with a Lancashire regiment.

Season	FL	FAC	SSC	Total
1934–35	37	3	3	43
Total	37	3	3	43

JONES, JIMMY   1922–24

outside-left   19 apps, 3 goals
full name: James Willie Jones
born: Warsop, Nottinghamshire, 1896
debut: Norwich City (h), 26.8.1922 (FL D3(S))

Jimmy Jones came to the Goldstone from the Central Alliance club Alfreton Town in August 1922 and was drafted straight into the first team, but he did have a limited amount of League experience already. Having started out with Welbeck Colliery in 1914, he signed for Notts County in 1919 and made ten First Division appearances during 1919–20. He spent the following season in the reserves, though, and after an unsuccessful trial with Midland League Mansfield Town in May 1921 he threw in his lot with Alfreton.

During 1922–23, Albion's left-wing duties were shared by Jimmy and the young Tug Wilson, but the following term Wilson made the position his own and his rival was forced to kick his heels in the reserves. Released in May 1924, Jimmy returned to the Midland League with Mansfield Town on a free transfer, but shortly after the opening of the 1924–25 campaign he joined Crystal Palace and played four games as they were relegated from Division Two that season. He then had a spell with Worksop Town before rejoining Welbeck Colliery.

J-JONES · BRIGHTON + HOVE ALBION F.C · 1923-24

Season	FL	FAC	Total
1922–23	16 (3)	2	18 (3)
1923–24	1	0	1
Total	17 (3)	2	19 (3)

JONES, LES   1948–50

inside-forward	Ht 5 8, Wt 11 06	3 apps

full name: Leslie Jenkin Jones
born: Aberdare, Glamorgan, Wales, 1.7.1911
died: Llanfyrnach, Pembrokeshire, Wales, 11.1.1981
debut: Southend United (a), 2.10.1948 (FL D3(S))

One of several inside-forwards signed by Arsenal manager George Allison in the late 1930s in an effort to fill the gap left by the retirement of the great Alex James, Les Jones performed a difficult task well, scoring three goals in 28 matches in 1937–38 as the 'Gunners' clinched their fifth championship in eight years.

Les began as a youngster with his local Aberdare Athletic club while working in his father's butcher's shop. Cardiff City offered him professional terms in August 1928, and he began to make his name as a skilful schemer who could also score goals, winning the first of eleven caps for Wales in May 1933 against France. The following January he was transferred to Coventry City for a large fee and scored 20 goals as City carried off the Third Division (South) title in 1935–36. After attracting scouts from all the leading clubs, 26-year-old Les joined Arsenal in November 1937 and played his part in their continuing success with his incisive passing, but the war effectively ended his career at Highbury. After assisting a whole host of clubs* in the emergency competitions and adding five wartime caps to his

collection, he returned to Wales with Swansea Town in June 1946 where he made two League appearances, and in August 1947 was appointed player-manager of Southern League Barry Town.

Twelve months later Les was recruited by Albion manager Don Welsh chiefly as a scout, but also on a part-time playing basis; he would train at the Vetch Field and travel to matches from his Swansea home. At the age of 37, though, he made only three League appearances before his appointment as manager of Scunthorpe United on their election to the Football League in 1950, a position he held until the following year. He subsequently held a coaching post with Stockport County, was secretary of the British Timken company's social club in Northampton, and had a second spell as manager of Barry Town. In view of the limited number of games he played at the Goldstone, Les's biggest contribution to the Albion was probably the introduction of his young Barry team-mate, Des Tennant.

Season	FL	Total
1948–49	3	3
Total	3	3

Note: The clubs for which Jones made guest appearances during the war were: Coventry City, Fulham, Leicester City, Lincoln City, Manchester City, Mansfield Town, Nottingham Forest, Notts County, Sheffield Wednesday, Southampton, Swansea Town and West Ham United.

JONES, MARK   1984

right-back	Ht 5 8, Wt 10 12	9 apps

full name: Mark Anthony Waldron Jones
born: Warley, Staffordshire, 22.10.1961
debut: Grimsby Town (h), 7.4.1984 (FL D2)

Spotted playing for Warley Schools, Mark Jones was taken on as an apprentice by Aston Villa and, after signing as a professional in July 1979 and appearing in the F.A. Youth Cup-winning side of 1980, was fortunate to be with the club at a peak in its fortunes. Despite making just 24 League appearances for Villa, he played in the European Cup, won a European Super Cup medal in January 1983, and was a member of the team which lost to the Uruguayan club Penarol in the World Club Championship in Tokyo in December 1983.

Mark was valued at £50,000 when he arrived at the Goldstone in March 1984 as part of the deal which took Steve Foster to Villa Park, but the 22-year-old full-back had little time to show his worth with the Albion and played in only nine games before moving to

Birmingham City in September 1984 as the heavier part of a player-plus-cash deal involving Mick Ferguson. In March 1987, Mark signed for Shrewsbury Town after a period on loan, but moved on to Hereford United three months later where he enjoyed the best part of his career. A regular in the United side for four seasons, he made 157 Fourth Division appearances and gained a Welsh Cup winner's medal in 1990, but was released from the Edgar Street staff in May 1991 and dropped into the Southern League with Worcester City. After loan periods with Hednesford Town and Redditch United, Mark was voted Player of the Season by the Worcester fans in 1992–93, but moved on to Conference side Merthyr Tydfil during the summer of 1993 for a single season.

Season	FL	Total
1983–84	6	6
1984–85	3	3
Total	9	9

JOYNES, DICK   1905–08

utility forward	Ht 5 9, Wt 12 00	112 apps, 22 goals

full name: Richard Albert Joynes
born: Nottinghamshire, c. 1880
debut: Leyton (h), 6.9.1905 (UL)

Signed as a 24-year-old winger from Midland League Newark in May 1905, Dick Joynes went on to appear in all the forward positions during his three seasons with the Albion, but was not a great goalscorer and hit the net only ten times in 70 Southern League matches. He began his career with Newark, but in December 1901 he signed for nearby Notts County and was a regular in their First Division side for almost two years, scoring three goals in 46 appearances. Released in May 1903, Dick returned to his original club for two years before coming to Sussex. He gained a fine reputation as a utility forward at the Goldstone, making chances for the main goalscorers, and in May 1908 signed for his former Albion boss Frank Scott-Walford at Leeds City shortly after

the latter's appointment as manager. Dick then saw out his senior career at Elland Road with 22 Second Division outings over two seasons.

Season	SL	FAC	UL	WL	SCC	Total
1905–06	31 (4)	5 (1)	11 (4)	0	0	47 (9)
1906–07	11 (4)	0	11 (6)	0	0	22 (10)
1907–08	28 (2)	3 (1)	0	9	3	43 (3)
Total	70 (10)	8 (2)	22 (10)	9	3	112 (22)

KAVANAGH, MICKY   1948–50

inside/outside-left	Ht 5 5, Wt 10 05	27 apps, 7 goals

full name: Michael Kavanagh
born: Dublin, Co. Dublin, Irish Free State, 31.12.1927
debut: Bristol Rovers (a), 13.11.1948 (FL D3(S))

Like many Irish professional players, Micky Kavanagh attended a non-soccer playing school, St Lawrence O'Toole's in Dublin, where he won medals for hurling and Gaelic football. At the age of fourteen he started playing the association game with the Stella Maris Boys' Club and adapted quickly, progressing through Johnville F.C. to the minors of the senior club Bohemians. With ambitions of becoming a

professional, the sixteen-year-old Dubliner accepted the offer of a trial with Hull City and, armed with the obligatory passport of the time, made the arduous wartime journey by sea and rail only to arrive at Hull's Paragon Station in the early hours with no one to meet him. Fortunately, a friendly bobby allowed him to spend the night in a police box!

Mick played for City's colts team under the watchful eye of manager Major Frank Buckley (a former Albion half-back) until 1946 when, somewhat disillusioned, he returned to Dublin. Playing junior football for Clonliffe Celtic, he was subsequently spotted by Albion trainer Sam Cowan who was checking on another player. After his previous unhappy experience Mick initially turned down the offer of a month's trial, but later had a change of heart and impressed manager Don Welsh sufficiently to be offered a contract in February 1948. A wee forward with a twinkling-toes style, he made his debut on the left wing, but later appeared in both inside-forward positions and looked set for a fine future.

However, the energetic young Irishman's career was cruelly terminated after just two-and-a-half years when severed ligaments in his left knee enforced his retirement at the age of 22, an injury that bothers him to this day. Mick then assisted his Albion colleague Jack Mansell as coach to Littlehampton Town, and became manager/coach of the Sussex County League club for eight years until 1960, receiving a benefit in 1957 when the 'Marigolds' took on an Albion XI. He also had a spell as manager of Fishersgate Midway in the Worthing League in the early '60s. Mick worked as a lathe operator for the Brighton engineering company C.V.A. for many years, and still resides in the Hangleton district of Hove.

Season	FL	FAC	Total
1948–49	12 (3)	1	13 (3)
1949–50	14 (4)	0	14 (4)
Total	26 (7)	1	27 (7)

KEELEY, JOHN — 1986–90

goalkeeper — Ht 6 0, Wt 12 03 — *160 apps*
full name: John Henry Keeley
born: Plaistow, West Ham, Essex, 27.7.1961
debut: Ipswich Town (a), 11.10.1986 (FL D2)

One of the greatest bargains in Albion history, John Keeley cost the club just £1,500 and was sold for £240,000. In between he made 160 appearances as a reliable, agile and sometimes brilliant goalkeeper, and played a major role in the promotion campaign of 1987–88 when he appeared in every game.

As a schoolboy John trained with his local club, West Ham United, and played for the South-East Essex representative side, but joined Southend United as an apprentice where he made his first-team debut in a friendly against the Albion in August 1978. Despite making 76 League and Cup appearances for the 'Shrimpers', John often had to live in the shadow of Mervyn Cawston and quit the Essex club in December 1984 following a disagreement with manager Bobby Moore. After taking to driving a taxi on Canvey Island,

he played part-time football for Maldon Town and Chelmsford City until he was spotted by Albion scout Terry Gill.

Signed after a brief trial in August 1986, John quickly impressed the Goldstone fans with his safe handling and sharp reflexes when regular 'keeper Perry Digweed was injured. Greatly helped by weekly coaching under former England man Peter Bonetti, he developed rapidly and starred in the successful 1987–88 Third Division promotion campaign. The following season his consistent excellence was rewarded when he was voted Player of the Season.

After four splendid years at the Goldstone, the 29-year-old departed for Oldham Athletic in August 1990 for the big fee which Albion couldn't refuse, but his career sadly foundered at Boundary Park where he was forced to play second fiddle to the remarkably consistent John Hallworth, and he made the League side just twice in three seasons. After loan spells with Oxford United (November 1991), Reading (February 1992) and Chester City (August 1992 and November 1992), John returned to his native Essex with Colchester United on a free transfer during the summer of 1993, but his time at Layer Road was soon marred by a broken ankle and in March 1994 he returned to his former club Chelmsford City. However, John played just two matches before he was sold to Stockport County, and went on to assist the Division Two side to the play-off final at Wembley at the end of the season.

In February 1995 he moved to Peterborough United on a free transfer, but the arrangement was rapidly terminated after just three games following an abusive reaction from the London Road fans. John then returned to Chelmsford City and took to driving his cab on Canvey Island once again. Early in 1995–96 he joined the local Isthmian League side, a move which unexpectedly thrust him into the national spotlight when Canvey Island met Albion in the F.A. Cup first round and forced a replay. Receiving a rapturous welcome from Brighton supporters in both matches, John acknowledged that his time at the Goldstone was by far the happiest and most successful of his career. He returned to Sussex for the 1997–98 season with Worthing.

Season	FL	FAC	FLC	FMC	AMC	Total
1986–87	20	2	0	0	0	22
1987–88	46	4	2	0	5	57
1988–89	37	1	2	1	0	41
1989–90	35	2	2	1	0	40
Total	138	9	6	2	5	160

KEENE, DOUG — 1950–53

winger — Ht 5 7, Wt 10 07 — *65 apps, 10 goals*
full name: Douglas Charles Keene
born: Hendon, Middlesex, 30.8.1928
died: Kirkcaldy, Fife, Scotland, 21.1.1986
debut: Torquay United (h), 19.8.1950 (FL D3(S))

A Hendon Schools representative, Doug Keene played two games as an amateur for Brentford during the final wartime season, but after National Service overseas with the King's Own Yorkshire Light Infantry he joined Guildford City in the Southern League. The young winger enjoyed some success with the Surrey side, so much so that his manager, Billy Lane, recommended him to his old boss at Brentford. Thus Doug returned to Griffin Park, signing professional forms in September 1947 just a couple of weeks after his nineteenth birthday.

After performing well in the "Bees'" reserves, and playing in thirteen Second Division matches, he was transferred to the Albion in June 1950 two months after his former boss, Lane, had been appointed assistant to

manager Don Welsh. Doug's versatility enabled him to play down either flank at the Goldstone, and an ability to cross the ball accurately with either foot provided many opportunities in front of goal. Indeed, in November 1950 he scored direct from a corner against Southend United.

In July 1953, on the completion of three seasons at Hove, he was transferred to Colchester United for £1,000 and appeared regularly during the 1953–54 campaign. Doug then returned to the Southern League with Dartford, and after ending his playing days moved to Scotland. He was working as a postman in Kirkcaldy at the time of his death from a heart-attack.

Season	FL	FAC	Total
1950–51	33 (6)	2	35 (6)
1951–52	15 (2)	1	16 (2)
1952–53	13 (2)	1	14 (2)
Total	61 (10)	4	65 (10)

KELLY, JOHN   1926

goalkeeper   Ht 5 9, Wt 12 00   2 apps
born: Wishaw, Lanarkshire, Scotland, 4.5.1902
debut: Charlton Athletic (a), 17.4.1926 (FL D3(S))

After starting out with Wishaw Y.M.C.A. and Vale of Fleet, John Kelly joined Scottish First Division side Motherwell in May 1923, but dropped into the short-lived Third Division of the Scottish League in September 1925 with Peebles Rovers. In March 1926, with Walter Cook sidelined through injury, John was brought to the Goldstone to provide cover for Stan Webb between the posts and proved a capable deputy. He appeared in consecutive matches in April, but was released at the end of the season, joining Gillingham on a free transfer in September 1926.

John's subsequent travels were many and varied: Crystal Palace (June 1927); Thames in the Southern League (July 1928); Nithsdale Wanderers, a junior club based in Sanquhar, Dumfriesshire (close season 1929); Glasgow Celtic (August 1929); Nithsdale Wanderers (on loan later in 1929–30); and Carlisle United (May 1930) where he enjoyed the most successful part of his itinerant career with 77 Third Division (North) appearances in three seasons before finishing with short spells at Coleraine in the Irish League and back at Motherwell. Also a professional boxer at one time, John was a sparring partner of the British and European welterweight champion Tommy Milligan. While with Carlisle he shared digs with a young Bill Shankly, later the legendary Liverpool manager.

Season	FL	Total
1925–26	2	2
Total	2	2

KELLY, WILLIE   1904–05

right-half   Ht 5 10, Wt 12 00   3 apps
full name: William Kelly
born: Kirkintilloch, Dunbartonshire, Scotland, 27.3.1880
debut: Northampton Town (h), 10.9.1904 (SL D1)

One of a number of Albion players recruited from Notts County during the first decade of the century, Willie Kelly was described as 'a perfect glutton for work who can stay for hours', but he was not a conspicuous success at the Goldstone and left after just three games in the senior side. In his native Scotland, Willie had won two junior international caps with Hamilton Academical (signed August 1898) before coming south to join the newly professional and renamed West

Ham United club in 1900 (they had previously operated as an amateur outfit for five years under the title of Thames Ironworks).

In and out of the "Hammers'" Southern League team for three seasons, Willie amassed 32 appearances before signing for Notts County in May 1903. The well-built wing-half made his First Division debut in a 3–2 win over Newcastle United at Trent Bridge, but made the first team only once more before being released in May 1904 to join the Albion. He appeared in all three half-back berths in the reserves at the Goldstone, but played in just three first-team matches at right-half, and was released at the end of 1904–05 when he returned to Scotland to play in turn for the junior clubs Bathgate (July 1905) and Maxwelltown Volunteers (September 1906).

Season	SL	Total
1904–05	3	3
Total	3	3

KENNEDY, ANDY   1992–94

forward   Ht 6 2, Wt 13 00   56 apps, 16 goals
full name: Andrew John Kennedy
born: Stirling, Stirlingshire, Scotland, 8.10.1964
debut: Manchester United (h), 23.9.1992 (FLC R2 Lg1)

Although often used alongside the prolific Kurt Nogan in his time with the Albion, Andy Kennedy did little to endear himself to the home crowd. Strongly built with a good touch and a proven scoring record, he could have formed an excellent partnership with the lethal Nogan, but an apparent lackadaisical attitude and shortage of commitment severely inhibited his success at the Goldstone Ground, and it was no surprise when he was released by manager Liam Brady.

Spotted by Rangers scout Davie Provan when playing as a winger for Sauchie Thistle, Andy was taken on as an apprentice by the Glasgow giants. Later converted into a striker, he gained Scotland youth honours and signed professional forms in 1982, but after fifteen League appearances at Ibrox – he also enjoyed a loan-spell in Hong Kong with Seiko F.C. – he was deemed surplus to requirements and transferred to Birmingham City for £50,000 in March 1985. Andy led the line in 1985–86, scoring six goals as City were relegated from the First Division, but had little joy the following term and spent the last two months on loan to Sheffield United.

In June 1988, Blackburn Rovers bought Andy for £50,000 and the lanky Scot went on to enjoy the most successful part of his career, hitting 23 League goals in 59 outings as Rovers twice made it to the Division Two play-offs. Two goals against the Albion in November 1988 and another in May 1990 alerted Brighton manager Barry Lloyd, but in the summer of 1990 Andy was exchanged for Watford's Lee Richardson. He was not a great success at Vicarage Road, though, and made just 25 League appearances in two seasons. After a short loan spell with Bolton Wanderers in October 1991, he arrived at the Goldstone in July 1992 and made his Albion debut in a League Cup tie against Manchester United on his recovery from injury.

Andy hit sixteen goals in 47 starts, a not unreasonable return, but his shortcomings meant he was in and out of the team in his two years with the club. After gaining a Sussex Senior Cup winner's medal with the reserves in May 1994, he was released and joined Gillingham in September, but by December he was playing in Hong Kong. Andy then performed briefly in Ireland and Scotland, and also for Witton Albion before returning to the Brighton area in October 1995 to assist Steve Foster (q.v.) in his insurance business. The Scot has since played for Isthmian Leaguers Hendon, but will probably best be remembered nationally for salacious tabloid publlicity while dating a Page Three model and for his reputation as 'Mad Dog' Kennedy.

Season	FL	FAC	FLC	AMC	Total
1992–93	26+4 (8)	5 (2)	2	2+1 (1)	35+5 (11)
1993–94	8+4 (2)	1 (2)	3 (1)	0	12+4 (5)
Total	34+8 (10)	6 (4)	5 (1)	2+1 (1)	47+9 (16)

KENNEDY, JIMMY   1905–06

left-half   Ht 6 0, Wt 12 04   22 apps, 3 goals
full name: James John Kennedy
born: Dundee, Angus, Scotland, 8.5.1883
died: Glasgow, Lanarkshire, Scotland, 20.7.1947
debut: Millwall (h), 2.9.1905 (SL D1)

Jimmy Kennedy was a youngster with Glasgow Celtic when Albion obtained his signature in May 1905, but he had to understudy regulars Frank Buckley and Harry Kent at the Goldstone and consequently left for Leeds City in June 1906 after one season. The Scottish half-back developed into a fine player at Elland Road and remained with the club for three seasons, but in August 1909 he was transferred to Stockport County and moved on to Tottenham Hotspur seven months later. Unfortunately, Jimmy broke a shoulder blade within a few weeks of the move and subsequently struggled to win a place in Spurs' First Division side, making just thirteen League appearances in two-and-a-half seasons at White Hart Lane.

In April 1912 he returned to the Southern League with Swindon Town, and joined Norwich City in July 1913 before signing for Watford manager Harry Kent, his former Albion team-mate, for a fee of £75 in December 1913; he subsequently skippered the 'Brewers' to the Southern League championship in 1914–15. Following the resumption of normal football after the First World War, Jimmy was transferred to Gillingham for a £25 fee in December 1919 and became trainer at the Kent club for two years on retiring in May 1920. When he died in 1947, 64-year-old Jimmy was trainer at Partick Thistle.

Season	SL	FAC	UL	Total
1905–06	11 (1)	4 (1)	7 (1)	22 (3)
Total	11 (1)	4 (1)	7 (1)	22 (3)

KENNEDY, WILLIE   1905–06

centre-forward   11 apps
full name: William Kennedy
born: Scotland
debut: Millwall (h), 2.9.1905 (SL D1)

Having played for Renton and Clyde as a youngster in Scotland, Willie Kennedy was transferred to Second Division Bradford City in March 1905, but spent only a couple of months in the Yorkshire club's reserves before he was released to join the Albion in May. Though adaptable enough to appear anywhere in attack, Willie didn't fit in with the scheme of things at the Goldstone. He was given an opportunity to impress at

the outset of the 1905–06 campaign, but played mainly for the reserves before returning to the Football League with Stockport County at the end of the season. The little Scot appeared in eighteen Second Division matches for County in 1906–07, but on the completion of that season he left Edgeley Park and returned to Scotland with the junior club Stenhousemuir in August 1907.

Season	SL	UL	Total
1905–06	6	5	11
Total	6	5	11

KENT, HARRY   1905–08

half-back   Ht 6 0, Wt 12 00   151 apps, 16 goals
full name: Henry Kent
born: Foleshill, Warwickshire, 22.10.1879
died: Watford, Hertfordshire, 22.12.1948
debut: Leyton (h), 6.9.1905 (UL)

'A hard-running, worrying player, and a strong tackler', Harry Kent was a mainstay at the Goldstone for three seasons in the 1900s and missed just six Southern League matches. Quickly establishing himself as a classy performer on his arrival, he was equally at home in any of the half-back positions but considered at his best in the middle of the line. Also a considerable threat in the opposition penalty-area, he scored sixteen goals in 151 appearances.

Born in Warwickshire, Harry played for Notts County's reserves as an eighteen-year-old amateur, but turned professional with Heanor Town in the Midland Counties League in September 1900, from where he graduated into the Midland League with Ilkeston Town. After three seasons in the same competition with Newark, he arrived at the Goldstone in May 1905 together with his team-mate Dickie Joynes. Skippering the side in 1906–07 – when Albion unexpectedly finished in third place – and 1907–08, Harry left Hove in April 1908 when he was joined Middlesbrough as a 'make-weight' in the deal for Jack Hall, the Brighton centre-forward. (There was a maximum transfer fee of £350 at the time, but the wealthier clubs got around it by signing two players, the one they wanted for plus one they did not. Thus Middlesbrough paid £350 for each player, effectively a £700 fee for Hall.)

Harry played just six games at Ayresome Park before returning to the Southern League with Watford in August 1909. A year later he was appointed player-manager of the Hertfordshire club and, after hanging up his boots, led the 'Brewers' to the Southern League title in 1914–15. He remained in charge for sixteen years until his resignation in 1926, making him the longest-serving boss in Watford's history. From 1922 until his death in 1948, Harry was licensee of the Wellington Arms in Watford, and was buried near to the football ground in the Vicarage Road cemetery.

Season	SL	FAC	UL	WL	SCC	Total
1905–06	32 (3)	5	12 (4)	0	0	49 (7)
1906–07	37 (7)	1	10 (1)	0	0	48 (8)
1907–08	35 (1)	5	0	10	4	54 (1)
Total	104 (11)	11	22 (5)	10	4	151 (16)

KEOWN, MARTIN   1985

full-back/central defender   Ht 6 1, Wt 12 04   27 apps, 3 goals
full name: Martin Raymond Keown
born: Oxford, Oxfordshire, 24.7.1966
debut: Manchester City (a), 23.2.1985 (FL D2)

Eighteen-year-old Martin Keown arrived at the Goldstone on loan from Arsenal without a single League appearance to his name, but he quickly established himself as a redoubtable player and it was

no surprise to the Hove public that he went on to greater things. Indeed, he has won full caps for England and earned a reputation as the best man-marker in the Premiership, with an uncanny ability to read a game.

Raised in Oxford by Irish parents, Martin was actually playing as a centre-forward for Oxford Schools when he was spotted an Arsenal scout, and subsequently became an apprentice at Highbury. After winning England youth honours, the young defender signed professional forms in February 1984 and arrived in Sussex a year later, initially as deputy for the suspended Eric Young and Hans Kraay. Quickly showing his ability at either full-back or in central defence, Martin was named the Division Two Young Player of the Month for March 1985 and, with his loan period extended to the end of the season, became a regular in the side as the Albion nearly made it back to the First Division. Again he played for Brighton for three months at the start of the following season, and on returning to Highbury made his long-awaited Arsenal debut, retaining his place for the rest of the season. In June 1986, Aston Villa paid £200,000 for his signature and the long-legged defender went on to make 112 League appearances at Villa Park, increasing his reputation sufficiently – he won eight under-21 caps – to be transferred to Everton for £750,000 in August 1989.

It was at Goodison that Martin enjoyed the best phase of his career. Having also represented England at 'B' international level, a series of outstanding performances at the heart of the Everton defence resulted in a first outing in the England senior team against France at Wembley in February 1992, and he retained his place for the dismal European Championship campaign in Sweden the following summer. In February 1993, with nine full caps to his name, Martin sensationally returned to Highbury when George Graham splashed out £2 million for his former player in an effort to improve an already impressive defence. Although he found it difficult to hold down a place in a star-studded back-four, Martin has established himself in the side either as cover for injured players or in a specialist marking role, and has gone on to amass fifteen full caps (by the summer of 1997). In May 1995 he broke his nose in the final of the European Cup Winner's Cup as Arsenal lost out to Real Zaragoza.

Season	FL	FLC	FMC	Total
1984–85	16	0	0	16
1985–86	5+2 (1)	2 (1)	2 (1)	9+2 (3)
Total	21+2 (1)	2 (1)	2 (1)	25+2 (3)

KERR, STEWART   1994

goalkeeper   Ht 6 2, Wt 13 00   2 apps
full name: James Stewart R. Kerr
born: Lanark, Lanarkshire, Scotland, 13.11.1974
debut: AFC Bournemouth (a), 2.11.1994 (FL D2)

Stewart Kerr arrived at the Goldstone on loan in November 1994 when both Nicky Rust and Mark Ormerod were injured, and performed creditably, despite conceding three goals in his second appearance. The two games the young 'keeper played for the Albion were in fact the first League games of his career, for, despite having won eight under-21 caps for Scotland and two at under-18 level, he had yet to make a first-team appearance for Celtic. A graduate of the

famed Celtic Boys' Club, Stewart became a trainee in April 1991 and was signed as a professional for the Glasgow giants by Albion manager Liam Brady in May 1993 when he was in charge at Parkhead. He won his first under-21 cap the same month in the Toulon tournament in France and looks set for a fine future in Scotland. After returning to Celtic he continued to play for the under-21s, but finally made the breakthrough into regular first-team football during 1996–97.

Season	FL	Total
1994–95	2	2
Total	2	2

KING, EDDIE   1901–02

centre-half/centre-forward   3 apps
full name: Edgar George King
born: Tunbridge Wells, Kent, 1876
died: Yarmouth, Isle of Wight, 1945
debut: Chesham Town (h), 1.3.1902 (SL D2)

A very successful player in local circles, Eddie King appeared in six Sussex Senior Cup finals, gaining winner's medals with Eastbourne Swifts (1898), Eastbourne (1899 and 1903) and Eastbourne Old Town (1905). In 1901–02, while playing for St Leonards, he assisted the Albion as an amateur in the club's first season, making his initial appearance in a 4–0 win over Chesham Town (the first Southern League match staged at the Goldstone Ground). Eddie represented the county on numerous occasions (awarded colours in 1896–97), and was also a fine cricketer, scoring numerous runs for Eastbourne and the Sussex Colts.

Season	SL	Total
1901–02	3	3
Total	3	3

KING, ERNIE   1931–38

full-back   Ht 6 2, Wt 13 00   217 apps
full name: Ernest William King
born: Brockley, Lewisham, London, 25.11.1907
debut: Fulham (a), 19.3.1932 (FL D3(S))

A giant full-back, fond of the sliding tackle, Ernie King took fourteen months to establish himself in the Albion first team, but once in he could not be shifted and was a fixture for five years.

The young defender won representative honours for Dorset while playing for Wyke Sports, and was tempted into the Southern League by Weymouth where his form attracted the attention of West Bromwich Albion. Introduced to The Hawthorns as an amateur in June 1928, Ernie signed as a pro in April 1929 and had two seasons in the "Throstles'" Central League team before Charlie Webb obtained his transfer for Brighton in September 1931. Equally at home on either side, Ernie established an excellent partnership with right-back Harry Marsden, then moved into that berth himself with, firstly, Herbert Jones and then Ted Martin at left-back. A regular from 1932 until October 1937 when he sustained the

injury which eventually forced him out of the game, he was granted a benefit match in May 1938 against First Division Bolton Wanderers. Ernie later ran a hotel in Weymouth for many years.

Season	FL	FAC	SSC	Total
1931–32	1	0	0	1
1932–33	28	7	0	35
1933–34	34	3	5	42
1934–35	41	3	3	47
1935–36	39	5	2	46
1936–37	34	1	0	35
1937–38	9	1	1	11
Total	186	20	11	217

KING, P. 1902

inside-right 1 app
debut: West Hampstead (a), 5.4.1902 (SL D2)

One of several trialists on view in the 7–1 friendly victory over Southampton Wanderers in February 1902, Albion's first match on the Goldstone Ground, King made his Southern League debut in the last game of the 1901–02 season, a 3–1 defeat at West Hampstead, but was not retained.

Season	SL	Total
1901–02	1	1
Total	1	1

KINNEAR, JOE 1975–76

right-back Ht 5 8, Wt 11 06 18 apps, 1 goal
full name: Joseph Patrick Kinnear
born: Dublin, Co. Dublin, Eire, 27.12.1946
debut: Cardiff City (h), 30.8.1975 (FL D3)

Now best-known as the manager of Premiership side Wimbledon, Joe Kinnear enjoyed a lengthy career with Tottenham Hotspur. Although never one of the star names at White Hart Lane, he was a consistent performer and amassed 258 League and Cup appearances for the First Division side, winning a host of honours at club and international level.

Although born in Dublin, the young Joe was raised in Watford and represented both town and county as a schoolboy. In August 1963, while playing in the Athenian League for St Albans City, he joined Tottenham and signed as a professional in February 1965. Over the next decade he gained an F.A. Cup winner's medal in 1967; League Cup winner's trophies in 1971 and 1973; a UEFA Cup winner's medal in 1972; and represented the Republic of Ireland 25 times. In August 1975, after twelve years at White Hart Lane, the 28-year-old full-back signed for Albion manager Peter Taylor for £5,000 to strengthen a useful squad, but he was released from his contract a year later after making just eighteen appearances. The tough-tackling defender did, however, win another cap while in Sussex, and received a deferred testimonial with a benefit match at the Goldstone Ground between Albion and Tottenham.

Joe subsequently joined Woodford Town and became player-manager, thus beginning a second career as a manager and coach. After a spell as a player with Dunstable, he went to Nepal briefly as prospective manager of the national team in 1985 before coaching in Sharjah for two years. After further coaching in Malaysia, Joe returned to England in December 1987 as assistant manager to his former Tottenham colleague Dave Mackay at Doncaster Rovers. In March 1989 he succeeded Mackay in an acting capacity, but was dismissed after only a few weeks following a poor run.

When Ray Harford took the reins at First Division Wimbledon in 1990, Joe joined the "Dons'" coaching staff, and when Harford's successor, Peter Withe, was dismissed in January 1992, he took over in a caretaker role. Subsequently given the position on a permanent basis, he has successfully maintained the club's unlikely position among the élite of the English game and, with his relaxed attitude, continued to promote Wimbledon's 'Crazy Gang' image. In January 1996, Joe was interviewed for the post of manager of the Republic of Ireland team but subsequently withdrew his application.

Season	FL	FAC	Total
1975–76	15+1 (1)	1+1	16+2 (1)
Total	15+1 (1)	1+1	16+2 (1)

KIRKWOOD, DAN 1928–33

inside-right Ht 5 11, Wt 12 00 181 apps, 82 goals
full name: Daniel Kirkwood
born: Dalserf, Lanarkshire, Scotland, 24.12.1900
died: Stonehouse, Lanarkshire, Scotland, 20.10.1977
debut: Luton Town (a), 25.8.1928 (FL D3(S))

A big man with a powerful shot, Dan Kirkwood scored 82 goals for the Albion in 181 games, a superb performance for an inside-forward. Top scorer in 1928–29 with 21 goals, he helped form the most prolific strike-force in the club's history the following season when he and Hugh Vallance scored 63 goals between them. But in addition to his excellent strike-rate, the talented Scot also prompted the best attacks and created many a chance for his colleagues.

Dan began his career with Ashgill Y.M.C.A. on leaving school, and first signed as a professional for Airdrieonians in April 1923. Transferred to Glasgow Rangers in August 1924 (where his older brother Andy was already on the staff), he had to understudy the great Andy Cunningham in his time at Ibrox and consequently moved on loan twice to St Johnstone, in October 1925 and April 1926. In November 1926 he moved to Sheffield Wednesday, but again found his opportunities restricted and played in only eighteen League matches.

However, one of his senior appearances came in the third-round F.A. Cup tie between Wednesday and the Albion in January 1927. The bulky Scot impressed Brighton manager Charlie Webb with his intelligent play and shooting ability, and in August 1928 Webb paid £500 for Dan's signature amid competition from Aston Villa and Huddersfield Town; his judgement was rewarded with a superb return over five seasons. As well as being a tremendous goalscorer, he was also the brains of the forward line: on the slow side but superbly constructive.

Dan remained at Hove for more than five years until an injury resulted in him being given a free transfer to Luton Town in October 1933, but he stayed at Kenilworth Road for only a few weeks before finishing his League career with Swindon Town. Also an excellent bowls player, Dan won a county championship in his native Scotland. After hanging up his boots he was employed as a collier for the rest of his working days, and died in Stonehouse Hospital at the age of 76.

Season	FL	FAC*	Total
1928–29	40 (20)	1 (1)	41 (21)
1929–30	40 (28)	6 (3)	46 (31)
1930–31	36 (13)	2	38 (13)
1931–32	41 (12)	3 (2)	44 (14)
1932–33*	11 (1)	1 (2)	12 (3)
Total	168 (74)	13 (8)	181 (82)

Note: One appearance and two goals of Kirkwood's 1932–33 F.A. Cup total came in the qualifying competition.

KITCHEN, SID 1913

inside-left 1 app, 1 goal
full name: Sidney Kitchen
born: Retford, Nottinghamshire, 1893
debut: Brentford (h), 19.2.1913 (SA)

One of two amateur trialists from Ashbourne Town of the Matlock & District League (the other was Alf Ault), Sid Kitchen scored the winner against Brentford on his debut but was not offered terms.

Season	SA	Total
1912–13	1 (1)	1 (1)
Total	1 (1)	1 (1)

KITTO, DICK   1906–07

inside-left   1 app
full name: Richard Henry Kitto
born: Portsea, Portsmouth, Hampshire, 1882
debut: Clapton Orient (h), 31.1.1906 (UL)

Dick Kitto arrived from Portsmouth in the summer of 1905 along with newly appointed trainer Joe Clayton and acted as Joe's assistant for four seasons, but he was also registered as a player and occasionally turned out in an emergency in a variety of positions for the reserves. In January 1906, Dick made a single appearance in the first eleven, filling in for the absent Billy Yates in a goalless United League match with Clapton Orient. On leaving the Goldstone in May 1909 he became trainer of Albion's Southern League rivals Croydon Common, and took up a similar post with Southend United a year later.

Season	UL	Total
1905–06	1	1
Total	1	1

KNIGHT, PETER   1956–57 & 1964–66

winger   Ht 5 8, Wt 11 00   11 apps, 1 goal
full name: Peter Richard Knight
born: Brighton, Sussex, 12.11.1939
debut: Bradford (P.A.) (h), 18.1.1964 (FL D4)

Peter Knight was the most naturally-gifted local player of his generation. He had it all: speed, balance, terrific ball-control and a good shot in both feet; everything, in fact, but the right mental approach. A product of the Carden and Patcham Schools in Brighton, Peter graduated into the Sussex County League with Hove White  Rovers and was on Albion's books as an amateur at the age of seventeen, but despite showing great promise in the 'A' team he was released. After numerous outstanding performances for Brighton North End, Newhaven and Lewes, the Brighton-born winger was given a second chance at the Albion by Archie Macaulay. Signed as a professional in January 1964 at the age of 25, he made his debut three days later and, with his abundance of skills, should have established himself in the team, but an apparent lack of dedication and an easy-going manner failed to impress the manager and he was released to join Hastings United in the Southern League in the summer of 1966.

After little more than a season at the Pilot Field, Peter fell foul of the management after failing to turn up for a game at Ramsgate and returned to the local scene, doing the rounds of the local clubs including Littlehampton Town and Newhaven. He also represented Sussex on several occasions, and continued to play in the Sussex Sunday and Midweek Leagues into his 40s. Peter worked for a Brighton-based brewery for several years.

Season	FL	FLC	Total
1963–64	2	0	2
1964–65	3 (1)	0	3 (1)
1965–66	4+1	1	5+1
Total	9+1 (1)	1	10+1 (1)

KRAAY, HANS   1983–85

midfield/defender   Ht 5 11, Wt 11 12   23 apps, 3 goals
born: Utrecht, Netherlands, 22.12.1959
debut: Fulham (h), 27.12.1983 (FL D2)

The first Continental player to appear in Albion's first team during peacetime, Hans Kraay was also one of the most controversial figures ever to represent the club. He arrived at the Goldstone on trial quietly enough in November 1983 and was signed permanently three months later, but when news of a lengthy suspension by his home association leaked out he was labelled 'The Dirtiest Player in Europe' by the tabloid Press.

The combative Dutchman started out with AZ '67 Alkmaar and Excelsior Rotterdam in Holland, and also played for San Jose Earthquakes and Edmonton Drillers in the North American Soccer League. In 1982–83 he was voted Player of the Season for NAC Breda back in the Netherlands, and it was while with them that he pushed a referee over at the end of a match, a misdemeanour which earned him his lengthy ban. Albion manager Chris Cattlin was undeterred by Hans's reputation, though; more impressed by the commitment of his Dutch import, he persevered with him to some effect. Playing both in defence and midfield for the Albion, Hans's unbounded enthusiasm won much admiration, especially his 'pogo' antics in front of opposition goalkeepers at corner-kicks which caused many North Standers to emulate him; but he will be chiefly remembered for his reckless tackling and petulance. An incident involving the then Portsmouth player John Crumplin (q.v.) demonstrates the case in point.

In February 1985, shortly after Cattlin had described him as 'the finest professional I have known', 25-year-old Hans had a public contretemps with his manager after flinging his shirt to the ground on being substituted. He soon regained a place in the team, though, and was a regular in the side as Albion nearly won promotion back to Division One. However, after being sent off twice while at the Goldstone and cautioned on numerous occasions, his poor disciplinary record eventually became unacceptable and he was released in September 1985.

Hans returned to his homeland with Molenbeek and, subsequently, RKC Wallwijk, De Graafschap and the Ijmuiden-based Telstar (his suspension had been cut in the Dutch courts during his time in England). While playing for the Albion, he also worked as a freelance journalist, writing articles on the English game for Dutch magazines, and has since appeared as a presenter on Dutch television. Still playing in the Dutch League at the age of 36, he now turns out for Den Bosch. His father, also Hans, managed Feyenoord, Ajax and PSV Eindhoven at various times.

Season	FL	Total
1983–84	2+3	2+3
1984–85	17+1 (3)	17+1 (3)
Total	19+4 (3)	19+4 (3)

KYDD, DAVID   1963–66

right-half   Ht 5 9, Wt 10 12   3 apps, 1 goal
full name: David Richard Kydd
born: Penge, Kent, 22.12.1945
debut: Ipswich Town (h), 21.9.1965 (FLC R2)

A rugby player at school, David Kydd was not particularly involved in the round-ball game until he joined Beckenham League side Cater Rovers as a youth. His form and potential soon attracted the attentions of an Albion scout, and young David was offered a place on the Goldstone ground staff by manager George Curtis. Although he joined the club as a centre-forward and packed a tremendous shot in both feet, it was at right-half that he made his three first-team appearances. Having signed pro forms in September 1963, David had to wait two years to make his senior debut, but was rewarded for his patience with Albion's consolation goal in a 2–1 League Cup defeat by Second Division Ipswich Town at the Goldstone.

The nineteen-year-old was retained for the following two Third Division fixtures, but then returned to the reserves. Possessed of a fiery temper, which resulted in a number of dismissals during his time at the Goldstone, David was released to join Southern League Chelmsford City in March 1966, and subsequently played for Margate and Dartford. Ironically, Albion had turned down an offer from Swindon Town in March 1964, stating that they would not let the youngster go at any price.

Season	FL	FLC	Total
1965–66	2	1 (1)	3 (1)
Total	2	1 (1)	3 (1)

LAMB, BILLY   1902–04

centre-half   *39 apps, 3 goals*
full name: William Charles H. H. Lamb
born: Woolwich, London, 1877
debut: Luton Town (res.) (h), 17.9.1902 (SEL)

Billy Lamb made his name with both the Hastings & St Leonards and St Leonards clubs in the East Sussex Senior League, and was recruited by the Albion as a professional in October 1902. A tall

man, particularly strong in the air, he was first-choice centre-half during the Southern League promotion campaign of 1902–03 and appeared briefly the following term, but left the club for Tunbridge Wells Rangers in May 1904. After first skippering the Kent side, he then became player-manager, but in 1906 he returned to former pastures with the professional Hastings & St Leonards United club in the Second Division of the Southern League. Billy skippered Hastings to the first round – now equivalent to round three – of the F.A. Cup in both 1906–07 (when they were beaten 3–1 at Norwich) and 1907–08 (losing 1–0 at home to Portsmouth) before rejoining Tunbridge Wells Rangers in May 1908. Also a first-rate cricketer, he held professional engagements with several northern clubs including Hartlepool and Ashton-under-Lyne.

Season	SL	Test	FAC	SEL	Total
1902–03	8 (1)	1	5	17 (2)	31 (3)
1903–04	8	0	0	0	8
Total	16 (1)	1	5	17 (2)	39 (3)

LAMBERT, MARTIN   1982–85 & 1989

forward   Ht 5 10, Wt 11 05   *5 apps*
full name: Martin Clive Lambert
born: Southampton, Hampshire, 24.9.1965
debut: Leeds United (a), 29.8.1983 (FL D2)

An outstanding schoolboy footballer, Martin Lambert represented both Southampton and England Schools, and once scored four goals in a match for Southampton against Brighton Boys. It was a

feat that obviously registered with the Albion, though, for in January 1981 he signed as an associate schoolboy. Graduating to an apprenticeship, Martin continued his excellent progress with appearances for the England youth team in 1983, a professional contract in August 1983, and a first-team debut the same month, but that proved to be the pinnacle of his career in England.

When Chris Cattlin took over as manager at the Goldstone later that year, the lanky striker, with sixteen goals for England at school and youth levels, was tried at centre-half because of a glut of strikers on the books. The experiment failed, and Martin was released at the end of the 1984–85 season to join Torquay United on a free transfer where he made six League appearances. A brief trial period with Exeter City followed before he returned to Sussex with Worthing in November 1985. A month later he took great delight in scoring twice to knock Albion's reserves out of the Sussex Senior Cup, but then pursued a more successful career on the Continent, hitting more than 50 goals in 90 matches in spells with Volendam (Netherlands), Union (Belgium) and Sedan (France).

In July 1989, Barry Lloyd brought Martin back to the Goldstone as a reserve striker on a free transfer, but he made just two substitute appearances before moving to Wycombe Wanderers in the Conference in November 1989 for a £15,000 fee where he scored five times in nineteen League games. Since that time he has had spells with Bognor Regis Town (loan), Worthing, Crawley Town, Worthing again, Chertsey Town and Saltdean United. Sadly, Martin Lambert's career proved a classic example of an exceptional schoolboy footballer who failed to fulfil his potential.

Season	FL	FLC	Total
1983–84	2+1	0	2+1
1989–90	0+1	0+1	0+2
Total	2+2	0+1	2+3

LANCELOTTE, ERIC   1948–50

inside-forward   Ht 5 11, Wt 11 06   *62 apps, 15 goals*
full name: Eric Charles Lancelotte
born: India, 26.2.1917
debut: Watford (a), 21.2.1942 (wartime)
peacetime debut: Bristol City (a), 6.3.1948 (FL D3(S))

Eric Lancelotte guested briefly for the Albion during the 1941–42 wartime season while registered with Charlton Athletic, but didn't appear in a Brighton side again until he signed for a club-record fee of £3,250 in February 1948, one of several deals conducted by new manager Don Welsh in a vain effort to avoid the necessity of having to apply for re-election to the Third Division (South).

Although born in India, Eric grew up very much a 'cockney' in south-east London. After representing Woolwich Schools, he played for Romford in the Athenian League, and was taken on as a professional by Charlton in May 1935 having served on the ground staff for almost two seasons. He went on to spend a war-interrupted thirteen years at The Valley and played in 40 First Division matches before his arrival at the Goldstone. (During the conflict he also played in India and Burma with a Forces' touring side.)

An elaborate ball-player, Eric remained at the Goldstone for two-and-a-half years – despite the failure of 1947–48 – and gave good service to the club. Considered to be the brains of the team – at least until the advent of Johnny McNichol – he was not a prolific goalscorer himself, but made numerous chances for his fellow forwards, often with lengthy dribbles. Distinctive on the pitch with his sloping shoulders and peculiar nodding run, Eric lost the no.8 shirt to McNichol in 1949–50 and, having played just twice since November, asked for a transfer in May 1950. Joining Chippenham Town in the Western League, he returned to Sussex with Hastings United in February 1951, and subsequently played for both Ashford and Folkestone. In 1955, Eric became assistant manager of the Bexleyheath & Welling club.

Season	FL	FAC	Wartime	Total
1941–42	0	0	1 (1)	1 (1)
1947–48	14	0	0	14
1948–49	32 (8)	1	0	33 (8)
1949–50	14 (6)	0	0	14 (6)
Total	60 (14)	1	1 (1)	62 (15)

LANGLEY, Ernie   1905–07 & 1908–09

centre-forward   1 app
full name: Ernest George Langley
born: Hove, Sussex, 1888
debut: Watford (h), 28.10.1905 (UL)

Ernie Langley was a Sussex County player who first appeared in Albion's ranks during 1905–06, the season that his club, Hove Park, carried off the Mid Sussex Senior League title. The youngster made his one appearance in Albion's first team as a seventeen-year-old amateur, in a United League

home defeat by Watford, before he was registered as a professional in December 1906. Upon the completion of the 1906–07 season, though, Ernie was released and had an unsuccessful trial with Croydon Common on their election to the Southern League, but subsequently rejoined the Goldstone staff in March 1908 and assisted the reserve team in a variety of forward positions. Later reinstated as an amateur, he played for Shoreham and Southwick, starring on the right wing as the 'Little Wickers' completed the treble of Sussex Senior Cup, Royal Irish Rifles Charity Cup and West Sussex Senior League in 1910–11. The highlight of Ernie's time with the Albion came in January 1907 when he scored a hat-trick for the reserves in a 3–3 draw with Chelsea's second string at the Goldstone.

Season	UL	Total
1905–06	1	1
Total	1	1

11 players who worked as teachers

Player	Player
Baker, Bert	Suddaby, Peter
Darling, Len	Thorne, Adrian
Foreman, Denis	Wilcock, George
Haig-Brown, Alan	Wilkinson, Howard
Morgan, Sammy	Williams, D.
Redfern, Bob	

LANGLEY, Jimmy   1953–57

left-back   Ht 5 8, Wt 11 07   178 apps, 16 goals
full name: Ernest James Langley
born: Kilburn, Willesden, Middlesex, 7.2.1929
debut: Queen's Park Rangers (a), 19.8.1953 (FL D3(S))

One of Albion's all-time 'greats', Jimmy Langley was adored by the large Goldstone crowds of the mid '50s, and many a tear was shed when he inevitably moved on to bigger and better things after nearly four years in Hove. Nicknamed 'Rubber Legs' because of his superb tackling, he was a wholehearted player who thrilled spectators with lengthy dashes and dribbles up the field long before the 'overlapping full-back' had been thought of. Indeed, many of his admirers were of the opinion that his abilities were wasted at full-back.

Jimmy started out as an amateur in Middlesex, appearing for Yiewsley at the age of fifteen, and went on to play for Hayes, Hounslow Town, Uxbridge and Brentford. While serving with the Royal Army Medical Corps at Crookham (where he gained Hampshire representative honours), the young defender came to the attention of Guildford City manager Billy Lane and he joined the Southern League club in August 1948. After four years in Surrey, Jimmy was transferred to Second Division Leeds United in June 1952 and was tried on the left wing, but had reverted to left-back by the time Lane, then manager of the Albion, signed the 24-year-old for a second time after protracted negotiations in July 1953.

Immediately winning a regular place in the no.3 shirt, Jimmy missed just five games in his time at Hove and skippered the team for more than two years. In 1955–56, Albion's 'nearly season', he played a big part in the side which finished runners-up with a record number of goals scored and points gained. As well as tackling and dribbling, other features of his game were speed of recovery, usually with a perfectly timed tackle when seemingly beaten, and a prodigiously long throw-in which was as effective as a corner-kick. In March 1955, Jimmy became one of only two Albion players – the other was Peter Ward – to be chosen for the England B team, playing in a 1–1 draw with West Germany at Sheffield, and went on to gain a further two B-international caps while with the club. In fact, he came very close to gaining a full cap when he was selected as travelling reserve against Northern Ireland in October 1956. In addition, he played for the Football League – Albion's only representative ever – in a 3–2 win over the Irish League at Newcastle in October 1956; turned out for the Football Association against the Forces' representative sides on several occasions; toured the West Indies in 1955 and South Africa in 1956 with the F.A.; and twice played for the Third Division (South) against the Northern Section.

It was only a matter of time before one of the bigger clubs came after him, and in February 1957 Fulham paid £12,000 for the Langley signature. Forming a great partnership with right-back George Cohen, Jimmy enhanced his reputation at Craven Cottage and gained three full caps in 1957–58, against Scotland, Portugal – when he missed a penalty – and Yugoslavia. He did, however, score from the spot for the London side that lost in the first-ever Inter Cities Fairs' Cup final (precursor of the UEFA Cup) to a Barcelona XI over two legs. Prominent in Fulham's promotion campaign during 1958–59, the ever-popular Jimmy made his first return visit to Hove on 27 December 1958. With the 'Cottagers' vying for the leadership of Division Two in Albion's first-ever season of Second Division fare, the game attracted a crowd of 36,747, a new Goldstone record which was never beaten.

In July 1965, after eight years at Craven Cottage, Jimmy moved to Queen's Park Rangers where he gained further success at the age of 38 with a Third Division championship medal and a League Cup winner's trophy in 1966–67. The following season he was released to take the player-manager's post at Hillingdon Borough, and he led the Southern League club to Wembley in 1971 when they lost to Telford

United in the F.A. Trophy final, after which he hung up his well-worn boots at the age of 42. Following his retirement Jimmy became trainer-coach at Crystal Palace, but subsequently had three more spells as boss at Hillingdon. He still lives in Uxbridge and is vice-president of the new Hillingdon Borough club, also helping to coach the Middlesex Sunday League XI.

Always keen to go forward, Jimmy's attacking tendency was manifestly reflected in a career tally of 57 goals from 585 League appearances, an admirable ratio for a full-back. A hugely popular player at each of his clubs, he was also an avid collector of — well, almost anything (but especially cigarette cards), and he gained a reputation as something of a 'magpie' amongst his Albion colleagues. Also superstitious, Jimmy had to tap the left-hand post with each boot before the kick-off of every game.

Season	FL	FAC	Total
1953–54	46 (1)	4	50 (1)
1954–55	45 (3)	4	49 (3)
1955–56	44 (7)	2 (1)	46 (8)
1956–57	31 (3)	2 (1)	33 (4)
Total	166 (14)	12 (2)	178 (16)

LANHAM, CHARLIE   1902

inside-right   *1 app*
full name: Charles Hamilton Lanham
born: Dorking, Surrey, 20.12.1877
died: Battersea, London, 8.10.1953
debut: Tottenham Hotspur (a), 27.10.1902 (SEL)

Signed as an eighteen-year-old professional by Tottenham Hotspur in August 1896 for their first campaign in the Southern League, Charlie Lanham remained with the club for fifteen months, latterly as a reinstated amateur. On leaving Spurs in December 1897 as a free agent he went on to do the rounds of the metropolitan Southern League clubs, initially joining Millwall and subsequently moving on to Southall where he first came to the attention of Albion manager John Jackson with impressive displays in the two fixtures against the Middlesex club during 1901–02. The speedy inside-forward was recruited by Jackson in August 1902, but made just one appearance, ironically at Tottenham in a 3–0 South Eastern League defeat. Charlie went on to play in turn for West Hampstead, Shepherd's Bush and Brentford.

Season	SEL	Total
1902–03	1	1
Total	1	1

LAVERICK, BOBBY   1960–62

inside/outside-left   *Ht 5 9, Wt 11 07*   *69 apps, 22 goals*
full name: Robert Laverick
born: Castle Eden, Co. Durham, 11.6.1938
debut: Leyton Orient (a), 31.8.1960 (FL D2)

A representative of Durham Schools, Bobby Laverick also had a trial for England while at Trimdon Grange School before joining the Chelsea ground staff in 1953 at the age of fifteen. A year later he played for the England youth team against Holland and a career in the Chelsea first team seemed assured, but after signing as a pro in June 1955 he made just seven League appearances in three-and-a-half years at Stamford Bridge (although two years were spent on National Service with the R.A.M.C.). A move to Everton in February 1959 provided greater opportunity, and Bobby scored six goals in 22 First Division outings before Billy Lane signed him for the Albion in June 1960.

Seen as a considerable capture for the club, he remained at the Goldstone for two seasons and, whether at inside- or outside-left, scored regularly as the team struggled to maintain its hard-earned Second Division status. However, when relegation became a reality under new boss George Curtis, he was one of many experienced players released and moved on to Coventry City in July 1962. The chunky winger's time at Highfield Road was not a great success, though, and he played in only four Third Division matches before dropping out of the Football League at the age of 24. Bobby then went on to enjoy a long and fruitful career in senior non-League circles with Nuneaton Borough, Corby Town, King's Lynn, South Shields, Ashford Town, Ramsgate Athletic, Tonbridge and Ashford Town for a second time, before becoming player-manager of the Kent League club Snowdown Colliery in 1972. He now resides in Ashford, Kent.

Season	FL	FAC	FLC	Total
1960–61	31 (10)	3 (1)	1 (1)	35 (12)
1961–62	32 (10)	1	1	34 (10)
Total	63 (20)	4 (1)	2 (1)	69 (22)

LAW, ALEC   1935–39

centre-forward   *Ht 5 9, Wt 10 07*   *74 apps, 40 goals*
full name: Alexander Law
born: Bathgate, West Lothian, Scotland, 28.4.1910
debut: Torquay United (h), 31.8.1935 (FL D3(S))

The unfortunate Alec Law broke a collar-bone on three occasions during an injury-prone career and also suffered a fractured leg while playing for the Albion against Crystal Palace in April 1936. Yet, despite the setbacks, he maintained a highly creditable scoring-rate, and his record of 40 goals in just 74 games compares with the best in Albion history. Although born in West Lothian, Alec came to prominence in the Lanarkshire League with Fauldhouse United and went on to sign for First Division Sheffield Wednesday. In three seasons at Hillsborough, the Scottish centre-forward had just nine League outings, scoring four goals, and came south to join the Albion in June 1935.

Bringing the best out of his wingers with raking passes to either flank, Alec was an accomplished leader of the attack, and his speed off the mark enabled him to score at better than a goal every other game for Albion. In his first season he led the scorers with 27 goals from 39 games, including two hat-tricks and a four-goal haul at home to Notts County, but then his season was abruptly ended by the broken leg. Sadly, he was never the same player again, and on his recovery he was forced to play second fiddle to Jock Davie. Moving to Chester in the Third Division (North) in June 1939, Alec found his career effectively ended by the outbreak of war at the age of 29.

Season	FL	FAC	SSC	Total
1935–36	32 (23)	5 (4)	2	39 (27)
1936–37	18 (7)	0	0	18 (7)
1937–38	1	0	1	2
1938–39	15 (6)	0	0	15 (6)
Total	66 (36)	5 (4)	3	74 (40)

LAWRENSON, MARK   1977–81

central defender   *Ht 5 10, Wt 10 10*   *174 apps, 7 goals*
full name: Mark Thomas Lawrenson
born: Preston, Lancashire, 2.6.1957
debut: Cambridge United (a), 13.8.1977 (FLC R1 Lg1)

Probably the most accomplished footballer ever to grace an Albion shirt, Mark Lawrenson was a world-class defender who had barely a single bad game in four years with the club. Quite simply, he had it all. As well as an uncanny ability to read a game, he was strong in the tackle, excellent in the air, precise in his distribution, and could bring the ball forward with tremendous, often devastating, effect. How many other central defenders could run the length of the pitch with the ball to score a classic solo goal, as he did against Wolves in January 1979? Playing a major part in Albion's efforts to reach the First Division – he was Player of the Season in the 1978–79 promotion season – Mark again performed wonders to keep the club in the top flight. When he finally left the Goldstone for Liverpool it was no surprise that he fetched the then enormous sum of £900,000, still the highest fee ever for a Brighton player.

The son of former Preston North End and Southport player Tom Lawrenson, Mark was born close to Preston's Deepdale ground and was something of an all-round sportsman, representing Preston and Lancashire Schools at both football and cricket. Indeed, he had a trial with Lancashire C.C.C. who were prepared to take him on, but after playing football for the Blackpool nursery team Bispham he signed as a professional for Preston in August 1974. Making his senior debut at the age of seventeen, Mark went on to play 73 League games for the 'Lilywhites' and won his first cap for the Republic of Ireland – his mother was born there – in April 1977. Three months later, despite fierce competition from Liverpool, he joined the Albion when chairman Mike Bamber personally flew to Benidorm in Spain to clinch the signature of the on-holiday defender for the rather precise figure of £111,111, Brighton's first six-figure purchase.

It proved to be an outstanding piece of business as Mark immediately impressed and became an automatic choice as the club

fought its way into the top flight. He did, however, miss the crucial last three games of 1978–79 with a broken arm, and sustained another serious injury early in the club's first campaign in Division One. Showing his versatility, he returned to the side in midfield, playing a major role in his first game back, the famous November 1979 defeat of European champions Nottingham Forest which gave Albion the will to survive amongst the élite. Mark also established himself in the Republic of Ireland side, and amassed a total of fourteen caps while at the Goldstone, a record for the

club at the time. In the summer of 1980, he signed a ten-year contract and enjoyed another outstanding season as the side escaped relegation by a narrow margin.

By now Mark was universally recognised as one of the cleverest defenders in the country, and the pressure from the biggest clubs proved too great for Albion to resist. Both Liverpool and Manchester United made firm enquiries for Brighton star, but while manager Alan Mullery agreed a deal with United boss Ron Atkinson, chairman Mike Bamber arranged a transfer to Liverpool, a situation which went some way to producing the rift which ended with Mullery leaving the Goldstone. Mark, in fact, was made club captain in the wake of Brian Horton's departure, but never got the chance to lead the Albion in a League game as Mike Bailey, Mullery's successor, completed the deal with Liverpool in August 1981. The massive fee of £900,000 for the 24-year-old, which was also a Liverpool club record at the time, would be equivalent to around £7 million in 1997.

In almost seven years of continual success at Anfield, Mark won nearly every honour possible at club level: five League championships, one European Cup, one F.A. Cup, and three League Cups. With 240 League games for the 'Reds' to his name, he also brought his tally of international caps for the Republic of Ireland up to 38 and ensured his place in history as one of the very best defenders in the English game in recent years.

In March 1988, at the age of 30, an Achilles' tendon problem forced his retirement, but he was almost immediately appointed manager of Oxford United, a First Division side already destined for relegation. However, Mark's incumbency at the Manor Ground ended in acrimony after just seven months when he was dismissed for making adverse comments about the sale of star striker Dean Saunders, a deal conducted by the Maxwell family, owners of the club. Replaced as manager by his former Albion colleague Brian Horton, whom he had appointed as his assistant, Mark then played a few matches for Thame United in the South Midlands League and had two games for Barnet in the Conference before moving to the U.S.A. as player-coach of Tampa Bay Rowdies. In August 1989 he took the manager's post at Peterborough United, but resigned after fourteen months in the job. Since that time he has dusted off his boots to play for Corby Town (Southern League), Chesham Town (Isthmian League), Moreton Town (Hellenic League) and Oxford City (Isthmian League).

With his autobiography published in March 1988, Mark took to running the Eagle Tavern at Great Coxwell in Oxfordshire while providing expert comment on television and radio. In October 1996 he was invited to become defensive coach at Newcastle United in the Premiership, but he left at the end of the season following a shake-up by new manager Kenny Dalglish.

Having proved himself a truly outstanding defender at the highest level, both with the Albion and after he left the Goldstone, there is no doubt that he ranks among the very greatest of the club's all-time 'greats'.

Season	FL	FAC	FLC	Total
1977–78	40 (1)	2	6	48 (1)
1978–79	39 (2)	1 (1)	4 (1)	44 (4)
1979–80	33 (1)	2	2	37 (1)
1980–81	40 (1)	2	3	45 (1)
Total	152 (5)	7 (1)	15 (1)	174 (7)

LAWSON, HECTOR 1928–29

left-half/inside-left   Ht 5 8, Wt 11 00   7 apps
full name: Hector Stewart Ramsay Lawson
born: Shettleston, Glasgow, Lanarkshire, Scotland, 21.5.1896
died: Dundee, Angus, Scotland, 3.5.1971
debut: Watford (a), 1.12.1928 (FL D3(S))

Hector Lawson's football career really took off in August 1916 when he joined Glasgow Rangers as a 20-year-old left-winger from the nearby Shettleston junior club. Most of his near-eight years at Ibrox were spent in the shadow of the 'Wee Blue Devil', the peerless Scottish international Alan Morton, though, and he had loan-spells with Vale of Leven (April 1920), Third Lanark (October 1921) and Clyde (March 1923) before the reigning Football League champions Liverpool were tempted to pay £1,000 for his services in January 1924. Hector maintained a regular place during the remainder of the 1923–24 campaign, but the follow-

ing term he largely missed out and returned to Scotland with Airdrieonians for a £500 fee in August 1925. A year later he moved on to Aberdeen where he appeared in 24 Scottish League games over a two-season period and was converted into a left-half.

On arriving at the Goldstone in August 1928, the much-travelled Scot was reaching the veteran stage. He had a three-match run at left-half as stand-in for Wally Little and four games at inside-left when Jimmy Hopkins was indisposed, but never looked likely to displace either for any length of time. Released in May 1929, Hector was recruited by Newport County in August where he met with greater success, making 57 League appearances and coaching the reserve team before departing for Ireland to play for Shamrock Rovers in August 1931. He subsequently worked as a plate-layer on the railways and died in a Dundee hospital shortly before his 75th birthday in 1971.

Season	FL	Total
1928–29	7	7
Total	7	7

LAWTON, NOBBY 1967–71

midfield   Ht 5 9, Wt 11 07   127 apps, 16 goals
full name: Norbert Lawton
born: Manchester, Lancashire, 25.3.1940
debut: Leyton Orient (a), 23.9.1967 (FL D3)

Albion's midfield general for three-and-a-half seasons, Nobby Lawton came to the Goldstone with an enviable pedigree. Once a 'Busby Babe', he was a product of Manchester schools football and joined the Manchester United ground staff as a junior. After gaining an F.A. Youth Cup winner's medal in 1957 (in the same line-up as his future Albion colleague Alex Dawson), he signed professional forms in April 1958 but, despite the upheavals caused by the Munich air-disaster a few weeks earlier, had to wait until April 1960 before making his First Division debut. The majority of Nobby's 36 League appearances for United came in the 1961–62 season and he spent most of his six years at Old Trafford in the Central League, but Preston North End came up with a £20,000 fee for his services in March 1963 and he was duly installed as skipper at Deepdale.

In his first full season with the club, the 24-year-old Mancunian had the honour of leading his team out at Wembley for the F.A. Cup final (again in the same line-up as Dawson), but the Second Division side lost 3–2 to West Ham United in an exciting game. Nobby scored 22 goals in 143 League appearances for Preston, and in September 1967 Albion manager Archie Macaulay laid out a £10,000 fee to bring him to the Goldstone. The classy midfielder soon inherited the captaincy of Brighton's Third Division side and served on the team-selection committee for two matches in November 1968 before the appointment of Freddie Goodwin as manager. Nobby's experience was a big factor in the ensuing improvement, and he played a major part in the exciting but ultimately unsuccessful 1969–70 promotion campaign.

However, he lost his place during 1970–71 and requested a transfer. Leaving for Lincoln City on a 'free' in February 1971 (in a deal which also took Alan Gilliver to Sincil Bank), Nobby made just 20 more League appearances before a knee injury ended his career; he was subsequently granted a benefit match. While at the Goldstone, Nobby served on the executive committee of the Professional Footballers Association. He may also be remembered for an astonishing, 40-yard goal against Shrewsbury Town at the Goldstone in February 1969 (the visiting 'keeper was future Albion player John Phillips).

Season	FL	FAC	FLC	Total
1967–68	22 (2)	1	0	23 (2)
1968–69	34 (4)	2 (1)	3 (1)	39 (6)
1969–70	39 (2)	4 (1)	3	46 (3)
1970–71	17 (4)	2 (1)	0	19 (5)
Total	112 (12)	9 (3)	6 (1)	127 (16)

LEACH, GEORGE 1904–05 & 1909

centre-forward   Ht 6 0, Wt 13 07   5 apps, 1 goal
born: Malta, 18.7.1881
died: Rawtenstall, Lancashire, 10.1.1945
debut: Brentford (h), 8.10.1904 (SL D1)

An accomplished all-round sportsman, George Leach was best-known as a prominent professional cricketer, scoring 5,870 runs (highest score 113 n.o.) and taking 413 wickets (average 27·91) for Sussex between 1903 and 1914. A massive, old-style centre-forward, he played for the Eastbourne team which won the Sussex Senior Cup in 1899 (defeating Hastings & St Leonards 3–0 at the County Ground, Hove), and then saw service overseas as a bombardier with the Royal Artillery. George subsequently played for both Hailsham and Eastbourne Old Town in the East Sussex Senior League, during which time he represented Sussex at football, and joined the Albion in August 1904. Although he spent the majority of the 1904–05 season playing

in a variety of defensive positions for the reserves, he made his two Southern League appearances in his more familiar role as leader of the attack in the absence of skipper Ben Hulse.

George moved on to Tottenham Hotspur at the end of the season where he had just two outings in the Southern League in two years before being released to join Tunbridge Wells Rangers in April 1907. On returning to the Goldstone in March 1909 he appeared in the first eleven on just three more occasions and was released at the end of the season. After leaving Sussex County Cricket Club in 1914, George continued to play the summer game as a professional in the Lancashire League.

Season	SL	SCC	Total
1904–05	2	0	2
1908–09	2	1 (1)	3 (1)
Total	4	1 (1)	5 (1)

LEADBETTER, JIMMY 1952–55

inside-forward   Ht 5 10, Wt 11 00   115 apps, 33 goals
full name: James Hunter Leadbetter
born: Edinburgh, Midlothian, Scotland, 15.7.1928
debut: Crystal Palace (h), 23.8.1952 (FL D3(S))

Although nobody was ever going to replace Johnny McNichol adequately when he left for Chelsea in 1952, Jimmy Leadbetter did a fair job. The lanky Scot was relatively inexperienced on his arrival in Hove, but had excellent ball-control and maintained a good scoring-rate with 33 goals from 115 appearances as an inside-forward, playing a large role in the club gaining runner's-up spot in the Third Division (South) in 1953–54.

Born and raised in Edinburgh, Jimmy attended Tynecastle School, served as a gunner with the Royal Artillery in Gibraltar, and represented the Combined Services at football. After he returned to Scotland, his form with Armadale Thistle and Edinburgh Thistle attracted the attention of Chelsea, and in July 1949 he signed professional forms for the London club. Learning his trade in the reserves, Jimmy spent three years at Stamford Bridge in which he made just three First Division appearances as deputy for England international inside-forward Roy Bentley. Arriving at the Goldstone in August 1952 as part of the deal for McNichol, Jimmy enjoyed a fine debut, scoring the first goal in a 4–1 victory over Crystal Palace.

A regular for three seasons, he proved to be made from the typical Scottish mould, a thoughtful ball-player who made numerous openings for his centre-forward as well as being unafraid to have a go himself — just as McNichol had been.

Although he was a success at the Goldstone, it was after his transfer to Ipswich Town in June 1955 that Jimmy really showed his worth. Played in a deep-lying left-wing role by manager Alf Ramsey, he enjoyed a prominent part in the Suffolk side's incredible run of success in the late 1950s and early '60s as they finished top of the Third Division (South) in 1956–57, won the Second Division title in 1960–61, and gained the Football League championship the following season. Indeed, he missed just one game during the latter two successes, and amassed 344 League appearances for the club. He also gained a reputation as a penalty-kick specialist.

On leaving Ipswich after a decade of service in 1965, Jimmy became player-manager of Sudbury Town in the Eastern Counties League for five years. A motor-mechanic by trade, he then returned to Scotland to join his father's garage business, and later worked in the distribution department of the *Edinburgh Evening News*. He now lives in retirement in Edinburgh and actively pursues his other great sporting love: golf.

Season	FL	FAC	Total
1952–53	34 (10)	2	36 (10)
1953–54	43 (15)	3 (2)	46 (17)
1954–55	30 (4)	3 (2)	33 (6)
Total	107 (29)	8 (4)	115 (33)

LEAMON, FRED   1949–50

centre-forward   Ht 5 8, Wt 11 09   11 apps, 4 goals
full name: Frederick William Leamon
born: Jersey, Channel Islands, 11.5.1919
died: London, 27.8.1981
debut: Reading (a), 14.9.1949 (FL D3(S))

A late starter in the Football League after wartime service as a Royal Marine commando, Fred Leamon played for Bath City before joining Newport County at the age of 26 in January 1946.

Netting twelve goals in sixteen games during the remainder of the season, he appeared in the opening matches of the 1946–47 campaign, County's sole season as a Second Division club, but signed for Bristol Rovers in October 1946. The sturdily-built Channel Islander scored 21 goals in 43 League games in two-and-a-half seasons at Eastville before Don Welsh brought him to Hove on a free transfer in July 1949.

Although not especially tall for a centre-forward, Fred was an excellent header of the ball and a real comedian in the dressing-room, but he spent just one season with the Albion and his only extended run in the team came in December following the transfer of Cliff Pinchbeck to Port Vale. Released in May 1950, he joined the exodus – Jock Sim, Ken Davies and Eric Lancelotte also made the same move – to Western League side Chippenham Town. Fred lived in Chepstow for many years and represented Wales at bowls many times. He died from a heart-attack suffered while acting as a security man to a BBC TV unit covering the wedding of Prince Charles and Lady Diana Spencer in 1981.

Season	FL	Total
1949–50	11 (4)	11 (4)
Total	11 (4)	11 (4)

LECK, DEREK   1965–67

right-half   Ht 6 0, Wt 12 00   33 apps
full name: Derek Alan Leck
born: Northbourne, Kent, 8.2.1937
debut: Southend United (h), 27.11.1965 (FL D3)

D erek Leck joined Millwall as an eighteen-year-old inside-forward in May 1955 having previously played for the Leyton Youth Club, but in three seasons as a professional at The Den he made just eight League appearances and in June 1958 was transferred to Northampton Town for a modest £350. The deal proved an outstanding success for both club and player as Derek was transformed into a stylish wing-half during his seven years at the County Ground, accumulating 46 goals from 247 League outings in all four divisions as the 'Cobblers' sensationally moved from the Fourth Division to the First in just five seasons. Ever-present in 1964–65, he and his future Albion team-mate Charlie Livesey played a big part in clinching a place for Northampton in Division One.

That summer he turned down a move back into the Third Division with Albion, but manager Archie Macaulay persisted and eventually got his man in November 1965 when Derek signed for a £6,000 fee. Seen as the answer to the problem no.4 spot, he performed well during

the remainder of the 1965–66 campaign, but suffered an Achilles' tendon injury the following term which seriously reduced his effectiveness, and at the end of the season he was released to join Hastings United in the Southern League. A year later he moved on to Crawley Town where he enjoyed three fine seasons. After leaving the Goldstone, Derek worked as a storekeeper in a Portslade factory for some time.

Season	FL	FAC	FLC	Total
1965–66	21	2	0	23
1966–67	8+1	0	1	9+1
Total	29+1	2	1	32+1

LEE, BARNEY   1902–03

inside-right   Ht 5 8, Wt 11 00   19 apps, 9 goals
full name: Bernard James Lee
born: Alloa, Clackmannanshire, Scotland, 5.3.1873
debut: Southall (h), 13.9.1902 (SL D2)

B arney Lee started his senior career in August 1893 when he joined Leith Athletic in the Scottish First Division. Selected to represent Edinburgh *v.* Glasgow in an inter-city fixture, his reputation soon attracted the attention of the Bury management who secured his services in September 1894. In his first season at Gigg Lane the 'Shakers' carried off the championship of the Second Division in rare style, eleven points clear of runners-up Notts County, and Barney mustered twelve goals from 22 appearances, but the following season he appeared only twice in the loftier company and was released to join Second Division Newcastle United in May 1896. A barren time at St James's Park – he failed to make the first team – was followed by a spell at Nelson and a period out of the game because of a family illness, but in February 1899 he joined the Scottish junior club Bo'ness.

Barney moved on to the Stirling-based King's Park club in September 1900, from where he was recruited by the Albion in August 1902. The 29-year-old Scot played a considerable part in Albion's promotion to the Southern League's top flight in 1902–03, appearing in all the forward positions and bagging a hat-trick against Brighton Amateurs in an F.A. Cup qualifying tie, but he was released at the end of the season and returned to the Scottish junior scene with Broxburn.

Season	SL	FAC	SEL	Total
1902–03	8 (2)	3 (7)	8	19 (9)
Total	8 (2)	3 (7)	8	19 (9)

LEEMING, JOE   1908–14

full-back   Ht 5 10, Wt 12 00   238 apps
full name: Joseph Leeming
born: Turton, Lancashire, 1877
died: Turton, Lancashire, 30.4.1962
debut: Southampton (h), 2.9.1908 (SL D1)

O nly Brian Horton can rival Joe Leeming as the Albion's most successful skipper ever. After arriving at the Goldstone in 1908, the burly full-back assumed the captaincy the following season and, in its first golden era, led the club to the Southern League championship and the Southern Charity Cup. The following September, as Albion made it a 'treble', Joe received the F.A. Charity Shield from Charles Crump, vice-president of the Football Association, following the historic 1–0 victory over Aston Villa at Stamford Bridge, one of the club's greatest-ever achievements.

Young Joe went to work in the spinning-room of the Edgworth Spinning Company at the age of ten, but football was always the highlight of his life, and he got his first big chance at sixteen when he joined the local Turton club playing in the prestigious Lancashire Combination. After serving for two seasons in the reserves, he spent three years in the first eleven, earning the princely sum of 3s. 6d. (17·5p) per week.

Prophetically described in an early Press report as 'A nicely-built young fellow, with skill and judgement behind him and a great future in front of him,' Joe set out on an outstanding professional career when he joined Bury in January 1898. (His brother Albert was also on the Bury playing staff for a time.) He made his senior debut in a 1–0 derby win over great rivals Blackburn Rovers on the last day of the 1897–98 season and soon caught the eye of the selectors, being chosen to represent the Football League in a 3–1 defeat of the Irish League at Bolton in November 1899. In ten years with the 'Shakers', Joe proved his worth by appearing in eight different positions in 255 First Division matches, and starred in their two F.A. Cup final successes: at centre-half in 1900 when Southampton were beaten 4–0;

and at inside-left in the 6–0 thrashing of Derby County in 1903, when he scored two second-half goals in what is still the record score for an F.A. Cup final.

In May 1908 the experienced 31-year-old was attracted to Hove by Albion's new manager, Jack Robson. Although reputed to be on the slow side, Joe more than compensated for any lack of pace with exceptional positional play and wielded a huge influence on the team for six seasons. After appearing in every match of the Southern League championship success of 1909–10, he was selected for the F.A.'s summer tour of South Africa and played in one of the unofficial international matches. Granted a benefit match (which realised £118) as reward for five years' service in April 1914, Joe left the Goldstone the following month for Chorley in the Lancashire Combination.

On the completion of the 1914–15 campaign the 38-year-old veteran hung up his boots and took up wartime employment at a munitions factory established in the Quarlton Vale mill in Turton. When peace was restored in 1918 he moved to the neighbouring Know mill where he worked as a machinist in the finishing department until his retirement in 1948. Joe lost a leg to a gangrenous infection in 1952, but remained active and maintained an avid interest in the happenings at Gigg Lane until his death at 85. Now, more than 80 years after leaving the Albion he still holds one club record: the most games, 238, of any outfield player without scoring a goal!

Season	SL	FAC	FACS	WL	WL Ch.	SA	SCC	Total
1908–09	32	1	0	6	2	0	2	43
1909–10	42	1	0	0	0	0	4	47
1910–11	33	3	1	0	0	0	2	39
1911–12	27	1	0	0	0	0	2	30
1912–13	34	3	0	0	0	8	0	45
1913–14	25	4	0	0	0	4	1	34
Total	193	13	1	6	2	12	11	238

LEGGETT, Peter   1965–66

winger   4 apps
full name: Peter Robert Leggett
born: Newton-le-Willows, Lancashire, 16.12.1943
debut: Hull City (h), 28.8.1965 (FL D3)

Peter Leggett's early school-days were spent in West Germany where his father was serving in the Army, but he was attending Swanage Grammar School when spotted by Southern League Weymouth. In May 1962, at the age of nineteen, Peter moved into the senior ranks with Swindon Town and appeared in fifteen Second Division matches before joining Albion's staff on a free transfer in July 1965. Although capable of playing down either wing, he found his opportunities limited with Wally Gould and Johnny Goodchild in possession of the outside berths and was released to join Chelmsford City in the Southern League in March 1966.

Peter was a great success with the Essex club, and it was something of a surprise when he was sold to Cambridge United in 1968 for the two clubs were then bitter rivals in the Southern League.

Something of a George Best 'look-alike' at the Abbey Stadium, he figured in United's championship side of 1969, but rejoined the Football League circuit with Lincoln City in January 1970. Peter failed to make the "Imps'" first-team, though, and when Cambridge United were elected to the Football League during the summer of 1970 he returned to net three goals in 21 matches during their first League campaign. In May 1971 he was released and drifted back into non-League football.

Season	FL	FLC	Total
1965–66	2+1	1	3+1
Total	2+1	1	3+1

LEWIS, Allen   1975–77

left-back   Ht 5 9, Wt 10 06   3 apps
full name: Allen Trevor Lewis
born: Oxford, Oxfordshire, 19.8.1954
debut: Colchester United (h), 25.1.1975 (FL D3)

Allen Lewis won a European Youth Championship winner's medal with England in 1971–72 while an apprentice with Derby County, and added another the following season, but his promising career never reached the expected heights. Signed as a professional in May 1972, he made just two League appearances for the 'Rams' and spent two months on loan at Peterborough in March and April 1974. After

three games on loan with the Albion early in 1975, manager Peter Taylor, who had been assistant manager at Derby, signed Allen in March for around £7,000, but his new acquisition was destined never to play another senior match for the club. Indeed, he was one of six players suspended by the management in September 1975 following a disgraceful performance by the reserves and was placed on the transfer list. The following April, Allen had an unsuccessful trial with Sheffield Wednesday, and it was not until July 1977 that he finally left the Goldstone for Reading on a free transfer. In the most successful part of his senior career, Allen made 149 League appearances in midfield over five seasons and won a Fourth Division championship medal in 1978–79. After being released from Elm Park he joined Southern League Witney Town in July 1982.

Season	FL	Total
1974–75	3	3
Total	3	3

LEWIS, George   1948–49

centre-forward   Ht 6 0, Wt 12 08   25 apps, 8 goals
full name: Thomas George Lewis
born: Troedrhiwfuwch, Glamorgan, Wales, 20.10.1913
died: Hemel Hempstead, Hertfordshire, 6.8.1981
debut: Swindon Town (h), 21.8.1948 (FL D3(S))

A robust, well-built centre-forward, George Lewis joined Watford from the New Tredegar Buds club in 1933 as an amateur full-back, but was soon appearing up front. Offered professional terms in May 1934, he remained on the fringe of the first team at Vicarage Road until the outbreak of war in 1939, netting eleven goals in just 25 Third Division (South) outings. An Army P.T. instructor for the duration of the conflict, George scored over 100 goals for Watford in the wartime emergency competitions, a performance which saw Southampton pay a four-figure fee for his services in July 1946. Joint top-scorer for the 'Saints' with fifteen goals in 1946–47, he lost his touch the following season and was replaced by Charlie Wayman.

With Albion finishing bottom of the Third Division (South) in 1948, manager Don Welsh had to bring in new blood and paid £1,100 for George's services in June 1948. The first-choice centre-forward during 1948–49, he missed out through injury on occasion, but scored a goal every third League game and showed considerable enthusiasm until his release at the end of the campaign. The 35-year-old Welshman then departed for Dartford where, after calling it a day as a player, he became groundsman to the Southern League club. George's brother Jim also played for Watford.

Season	FL	FAC	Total
1948–49	24 (8)	1	25 (8)
Total	24 (8)	1	25 (8)

LEWIS, JACK   1906–07

inside-right   43 apps, 12 goals
full name: John Richard Lewis
born: Aberystwyth, Cardiganshire, Wales, 1882
died: Burton upon Trent, Staffordshire, 12.9.1954
debut: Leyton (a), 1.9.1906 (SL D1)

Although born in Wales, Jack Lewis learned his football in Birmingham junior circles before joining Bristol Rovers at the age of seventeen in September 1899. He figured prominently in their first season in the Southern League with five goals from 25 games, but was released to join Portsmouth in May 1900. A season at Fratton

Park was followed by a switch to the Football League with Burton United in August 1901 where he remained for three years, scoring 24 goals in 74 Second Division outings.

In August 1904, Jack rejoined Bristol Rovers and assisted them to the Southern League championship during the ensuing campaign. His form at Eastville over two seasons saw him become the first-ever Rovers player to gain international recognition when he was chosen to represent Wales in a 1–0 defeat by England at Cardiff Arms Park in March 1906. Two months later he came to the Goldstone as an inside-right, and missed just 10 of the 53 competitive matches during 1906–07, but in April 1907 he completed a full tour of the South Coast clubs by joining Southern League rivals Southampton.

On transferring to Croydon Common in September 1908, Jack met with considerable success, helping the Selhurst-based side to the Southern League Second Division title and netting 40 goals in 61 competitive matches during 1908–09 before rejoining Burton United (by then a Southern League Division Two club) in August 1909. Despite being somewhat on the small side, Jack enjoyed a good deal of success against the predominantly big defences of the period, averaging more than a goal every third game throughout his career.

Season	SL	FAC	UL	Total
1906–07	32 (8)	1	10 (4)	43 (12)
Total	32 (8)	1	10 (4)	43 (12)

LEY, GEORGE   1972–74

left-back   Ht 5 9, Wt 11 12   51 apps
full name: Oliver Albert George Ley
born: Exminster, Devon, 7.4.1946
debut: Oxford United (h), 23.9.1972 (FL D2)

Although George Ley was an amateur with Hitchin Town as a youngster and had a trial with Arsenal, it was in his native Devon that he turned professional, signing as a left-winger for Exeter City in September 1963. (He shared digs in Exeter with former Albion favourite Adrian Thorne.) After 104 League and Cup games for City, George joined Portsmouth in May 1967, but he was now ensconced in a left-back role and became a firm favourite of the Fratton Park crowd, making 184 League appearances.

A cultured defender with a ferocious left-foot shot, he joined Albion in September 1972 for a £25,000 fee, but could do little to stop a struggling side from falling straight back into the Third Division. In December 1973 he lost his place to new signing Harry Wilson, and moved on to Gillingham in August 1974 where he spent almost two years before leaving for the U.S.A. to play for Dallas Tornado during the summer of 1976. George subsequently had a spell with St Patrick's Athletic in the League of Ireland.

Season	FL	FAC	FLC	Total
1972–73	31	1	0	32
1973–74	16	2	1	19
Total	47	3	1	51

LIDDELL, JOHN   1947–48

inside-left   4 apps, 1 goal
debut: Queen's Park Rangers (h), 29.3.1947 (FL D3(S))

John Liddell joined Clapton Orient in 1944 and played regularly in the last two-and-a-half seasons of wartime fare. Having guested briefly for Bolton Wanderers during 1943–44, he was transferred to the 'Trotters' in September 1946, but spent just seven months in the reserves at Burnden Park before Charlie Webb brought him to the Goldstone Ground in March 1947. Drafted into Albion's league team as deputy for George Chapman just three days after his arrival, John played in four consecutive matches but failed to make the most of the opportunity and was released to join Southern League Gravesend & Northfleet in September 1947. In June 1948 he was recruited by the newly formed Hastings United club and appeared in its first-ever fixture, a 2–1 Southern League win at Tonbridge.

Season	FL	Total
1946–47	4 (1)	4 (1)
Total	4 (1)	4 (1)

LITTLE, DOZ   1958–61

left-back   Ht 5 8, Wt 11 00   91 apps
full name: Roy Little
born: Manchester, Lancashire, 1.6.1931
debut: Scunthorpe United (a), 18.10.1958 (FL D2)

Roy Little – known to all as 'Doz' – gave little thought to becoming a professional footballer at the rugby-playing Central Grammar School in Manchester and took employment in the textile trade at the age of seventeen, but he was signed as an amateur by Manchester City while playing for the local Geenwood Victoria club. In 1948 he was called into the R.A.F. on National Service (during which he represented the Maintenance Command team), but returned to Maine Road as a professional in August 1949 and went on to enjoy nine tremendous years as an integral part of the excellent City side of the

1950s. The skilful defender appeared in consecutive F.A. Cup finals – in 1955 when City lost 3–1 to Newcastle United and in 1956 when Birmingham City were defeated 3–1 – but after losing his first-team place he sought a transfer and arrived at the Goldstone in October 1958 for a £6,500 fee.

The 27-year-old Mancunian's experience proved invaluable during Albion's early days in the Second Division, and he was a regular in the no.3 shirt for nearly three years before moving on to Crystal Palace in May 1961. At the end of the 1961–62 campaign Doz left Selhurst Park to take the post of player-manager with Southern League Dover, a position he retained for a number of years.

Season	FL	FAC	FLC	Total
1958–59	30	1	0	31
1959–60	38	5	0	43
1960–61	15	0	2	17
Total	83	6	2	91

LITTLE, WALLY   1919–29

left-back/left-half   Ht 5 8, Wt 11 04   *332 apps, 36 goals*
full name: Walter James Little
born: Southall, Middlesex, 10.11.1897
died: Exeter, Devon, 15.8.1976
debut: Bristol Rovers (h), 20.9.1919 (SL D1)

After switching from left-back to left-half at the start of the 1921–22 season, Wally Little became a fixture in the Albion side. Over the next seven-and-a-half years he turned in consistently excellent displays and missed only a handful of games, becoming a great favourite of the Goldstone crowd. His small stature, bandy legs

and tenacious, no-frills style endeared him to the Hove fans, while he also became the club's penalty expert. Indeed, he put away no fewer than 26 spot-kicks in his Albion career, the highest total in the club's history.

Wally arrived at the Goldstone Ground on trial in August 1919 and impressed the management in a reserve fixture against Reading sufficiently to be signed at the age of 21 upon his demob from the Army the following month. Playing at left-back in the club's first-ever Football League match in 1920, he went on to give outstanding service and was awarded a benefit in March 1925. After a sparkling, ten-year Goldstone career, Wally moved on to Clapton Orient on a free transfer in May 1929 where he clocked up a further 24 League matches before hanging up his boots a year later.

Ironically, the penalty ace had to *face* a spot-kick in May 1922. Wally went into goal following an injury to Sid Townsend in a reserve-team friendly but neglected to inform the referee of the change. To the delight of the spectators he then saved the consequent penalty!

Season	FL	SL	FAC	Total
1919–20	0	23	0	23
1920–21	16	0	1	17
1921–22	28 (5)	0	3 (1)	31 (6)
1922–23	41 (4)	0	5	46 (4)
1923–24	35 (3)	0	4 (2)	39 (5)
1924–25	42 (5)	0	3	45 (5)
1925–26	36 (8)	0	2 (1)	38 (9)
1926–27	37 (5)	0	3	40 (5)
1927–28	31 (1)	0	2	33 (1)
1928–29	19 (1)	0	1	20 (1)
Total	285 (32)	23	24 (4)	332 (36)

LIVESEY, CHARLIE   1965–69

centre/inside-forward   Ht 5 11, Wt 11 00   *146 apps, 37 goals*
full name: Charles Edward Livesey
born: West Ham, Essex, 6.2.1938
debut: Peterborough United (a), 18.9.1965 (FL D3)

With a rate of one goal every four games, Charlie Livesey was not a great goalscorer for the Albion, but he was certainly one of the cleverest forwards to play for the club since the Second World War. In fact, his ability was such that England manager Alf Ramsey had him watched just a few months before the World Cup finals in January 1966 — with Brighton mid-table in the Third Division! He appeared in all four divisions of the Football League during a lengthy career and registered 106 goals in 329 League games, but never quite achieved the success that his rich talent deserved.

Born in West Ham, Charlie started out with the local Custom House club as a lad and had a trial with Wolves, but it was with Southampton that he turned professional in March 1956. He had to wait until the 1958–59 campaign to break into the "Saints'" Third Division team, but, having been given the chance, he grabbed it with both hands, scoring four goals in a 6–1 defeat of Hull City in only his fourth appearance. Such form attracted the attention of Chelsea and he was valued at £15,000 when exchanged for Cliff Huxford in May 1959. Charlie went straight into the First Division side at Stamford Bridge and in two seasons scored eighteen goals in 42 League and Cup games, vying for the no.9 shirt with Ron Tindall, but in August 1961 he was sold to Gillingham for £5,000 where he was leading scorer

with fifteen goals in his only full season with the struggling Fourth Division club. After moving on to Watford for £6,000 in October 1962, he was transferred to Northampton Town for £17,000 in August 1964, a good move for both club and player as he helped the 'Cobblers' to promotion to the First Division in 1964–65.

In September 1965 the 27-year-old forward joined his sixth club when Albion manager Archie Macaulay brought him to the South Coast for a fee of around £7,000 to bolster the attack for the challenge of the Third Division. A powerful runner with keen anticipation, Charlie quickly won many admirers among the Goldstone crowd and was acknowledged as the club's most talented player. Initially played as leader of the attack, the skilful forward subsequently operated in an inside role and was more-or-less a regular for four years. On the expiry of his contract in April 1969 he was released by new manager Freddie Goodwin and ended up in the Southern League with Crawley Town. Twelve months later he gained a good deal of satisfaction when his new side beat Albion's first team in the final of the Sussex Professional Cup.

Season	FL	FAC	FLC	Total
1965–66	27 (11)	3 (3)	0	30 (14)
1966–67	38 (6)	0+1 (1)	6 (2)	44+1 (9)
1967–68	40 (7)	1+1	2 (1)	43+1 (8)
1968–69	19+2 (4)	3 (1)	3 (1)	25+2 (6)
Total	124+2 (28)	7+2 (5)	11 (4)	142+4 (37)

LIVINGSTONE, ARCHIE   1904–05

left-half   31 apps, 1 goal
full name: Archibald Lang Livingstone
born: Kilpatrick, Dunbartonshire, Scotland, 30.8.1872
debut: New Brompton (a), 3.9.1904 (SL D1)

'A left-half of exceptional pertinacity and resource', Archie Livingstone played for junior clubs Greenock and Glasgow Whitefield while working as a fitter's apprentice, and had six games for Third Lanark reserves, but turned professional with Burnley. Joining the First Division club in March 1893, the 20-year-old Scot enjoyed seven seasons at Turf Moor, although he missed the 1896–97 campaign when Burnley were relegated. The Lancashire club bounced straight back, carrying off the Second Division title the following term when Archie missed just nine games, but after 169 League appearances he left Burnley in September 1900 for nearby Nelson in the Lancashire League. A year later he was enticed back to the Football League by the newly formed Burton United club, and in three

seasons he appeared in 72 Second Division matches.

A ferocious tackler who was equally capable in the air, Archie was brought to Hove in May 1904 as Albion made sweeping changes to shore up the club's status as a Southern League First Division outfit, and his experience proved invaluable. The *Sussex Daily News* wrote, 'Tenacity is one of Livingstone's chief traits; fast on his feet and a very difficult customer to get past, while no believer in indulgence in football embroidery or in playing to the gallery.' In fact, his tenacity led to trouble in March 1904 when he was sent off for fighting against Hitchin Town and subsequently suspended for a month.

When Norwich City turned professional and were elected to the Southern League during 1905, the swarthy wing-half was one of their first recruits, and he went on to make 109 League appearances for the 'Canaries' up to 1910 when he was appointed manager of their reserve team. Granted a benefit match in April 1911, Archie became player-manager of Peterborough City in August 1912 and remained in charge of the South Eastern League club after retiring as a player. His brother George, three years his junior, enjoyed a long and fruitful career with Dumbarton, Hearts, Sunderland, Celtic, Liverpool, Manchester City, Glasgow Rangers, Manchester United and Scotland.

Season	SL	FAC	Total
1904–05	26	5 (1)	31 (1)
Total	26	5 (1)	31 (1)

LLOYD, ARTHUR   1908–09

left-half   13 apps
born: Smethwick, Staffordshire, 1881
died: Birmingham, Warwickshire, 1945
debut: Plymouth Argyle (a), 12.9.1908 (SL D1)

Arthur Lloyd joined Wolverhampton Wanderers from the Birmingham League club Halesowen in December 1905, and made his First Division debut three days later in a 1–1 draw at Molineux against Sheffield United. A regular in the Wolves half-back line for two-and-a-half seasons, Arthur scored four times in 79 league matches but was released to join the Albion in May 1908. He should have been a considerable acquisition for the club, yet was unable to hold a place in team and was forced to play second-fiddle to Jimmy Robertson at left-half. Arthur's time at the Goldstone was a big disappointment

to management and supporters alike, and in April 1909 he was released to join Barrow-in-Furness in the Lancashire Combination.

Season	SL	WL	SCC	Total
1908–09	10	2	1	13
Total	10	2	1	13

LONGDON, BILLY   1939–46

half-back/outside-right   Ht 5 9, Wt 11 00   110 apps, 4 goals
full name: Charles William Longdon
born: Clowne, Derbyshire, 6.5.1917
debut: Aldershot (h), 21.10.1939 (wartime)
peacetime debut: Romford (h), 17.11.1945 (FAC R1 Lg1)

As Billy Longdon's career at the Goldstone corresponded almost exactly with the Second World War emergency period, his appearances were confined to nine games in the 1945–46 F.A. Cup competition and 101 in the regional wartime competitions. In seven years with the Albion he never made an appearance in the regular Football League.

An amateur with Mansfield Town's reserves in 1937–38, Billy moved on to Southern League Folkestone, but signed for Brentford in January 1939 and played for their reserves for the rest of the season. At the end of the campaign he arrived in Hove, but war broke out the following September and the Derbyshire-born half-back enlisted with the Metropolitan Police Reserve and subsequently joined the R.A.F. He also turned out for the Albion whenever available, though, and guested for another eight clubs*. Although usually a half-back, Billy enjoyed a long run in the no. 7 shirt during 1945–46, but he was transferred to Bourne-mouth at the end of the

campaign. After nine appearances in his one season at Dean Court, he moved north to Rochdale in July 1947 where he had just two first-team outings before moving into the Southern League with Tonbridge a year later.

In the Spartan days of early post-war Britain, Billy would often travel down to the Goldstone from his Midlands home on a Friday evening and sleep in the old West Stand. In a nation then dominated by shortages, he also had the reputation of being able to lay his hands on almost anything. Indeed, he managed the impossible: obtaining a brand-new football for Harry Baldwin's son's birthday!

Season	FAC	Wartime	Total
1939–40	0	20	20
1940–41	0	2	2
1941–42	0	12	12
1942–43	0	29	29
1943–44	0	13 (1)	13 (1)
1944–45	0	1	1
1945–46	9 (2)	24 (1)	33 (3)
Total	9 (2)	101 (2)	110 (4)

Note: The clubs for which Longdon guested during the war were Bournemouth & Boscombe Athletic, Bristol City, Chesterfield, Liverpool, Mansfield Town, New Brighton, Southport and Swansea Town.

LONGHURST, G. R.   1913

outside-right   1 app
debut: Southampton (h), 29.1.1913 (SCC R1 rep)

An amateur trialist from Ardingly of the Mid Sussex League, Longhurst was drafted into Albion's team for the Southern Charity Cup first-round replay with Southampton in January 1913, when manager Jack Robson fielded what was essentially a reserve eleven because of an F.A. Cup tie with Everton three days later. The

'Lambs' performed heroics in walloping a strong 'Saints' side 4–1 and went on to reach the final, but nothing more was seen of Longhurst.

Season	SCC	Total
1912–13	1	1
Total	1	1

LONGLAND, JOHNNY   1954–56

left-half   *3 apps*

full name: John Longland
born: Southampton, Hampshire, 24.9.1932
debut: Watford (h), 27.11.1954 (FL D3(S))

Johnny Longland played for Winchester City as a youngster, and was recommended to the Albion by an Army officer while serving with the R.A.M.C. in Hong Kong. After impressing sufficiently in a trial to be signed as a professional in May 1954, he made his first League appearance as a 22-year-old half-back the following November, a 3–1 win over Watford at the Goldstone, but then had to be content with a supporting role to Glen Wilson at left-half and received few opportunities. Released in May 1956, Johnny departed for non-League soccer and had a spell as player-coach with Lewes in the Sussex County League from December 1958.

Season	FL	Total
1954–55	3	3
Total	3	3

LONGSTAFF, BERT   1906–22

outside/inside-right   Ht 5 8, Wt 11 00   *443 apps, 86 goals*

full name: Albert Edward Longstaff
born: Shoreham-by-Sea, Sussex, 9.10.1885
died: Brighton, Sussex, July 1970
debut: Crystal Palace (a), 7.11.1906 (UL)

Bert Longstaff was the most successful locally-born player ever to wear an Albion strip. For ten years (interrupted by a four-year break during the Great War) he was a fixture in the side and was, naturally, a tremendous favourite of the Goldstone crowds. The Shoreham-born forward was also the only player to hold both the records for aggregate appearances (for 21 years) and goals (on-and-off for nine years) with 86 goals from 443 matches.

A bright future was predicted for the young Bert when he first played for Shoreham in the West Sussex Senior League at the age of

seventeen in 1902–03, but an approach from Tottenham Hotspur was rejected because his mother wanted him to remain at home. Having impressed both the Sussex selectors and the Albion management while assisting his Shoreham side to a 'treble' in 1905–06 – Sussex Senior Cup, Royal Irish Rifles Charity Cup and West Sussex League championship – he played for the Albion as an amateur from November 1906 before signing as a pro in October 1907. He soon established himself in the first team and missed few games until 1921.

In his early days with the club Bert appeared at inside-right, but soon found his best position on the right-wing from where he delivered many a telling cross for the inside forwards. While consistently turning in excellent performances for many years, he was considered to be at his peak in the momentous year of 1910 when Albion annexed the Southern League title, the F.A. Charity Shield and Southern Charity Cup. Chosen to represent the Southern League against both the Football League and Irish League in October 1914, he was, however, forced to cry off through injury, and the First World War put paid to any further opportunity of representative honours.

In 1920, when Albion joined the Football League, Bert was nearly 35, yet he retained his speed and terrific ball-control to make 38 appearances in that initial Third Division campaign. In May 1922 the ever-popular stalwart left the Goldstone and was reinstated as an amateur two years later to play for his first club, Shoreham, in the Sussex County League. Indeed, he appeared in the "Musselmen's" side beaten 2–1 by Southwick in the 1925 Sussex Senior Cup final.

A tinsmith by trade, Bert was a partner in a motor-engineering business in Gloucester Road, Brighton, from 1920 to 1933, and subsequently became an employee of the Worthing-based engineering company Paine-Manwaring. He received two benefits with the Albion, in 1913 and 1923 (a year after he left the club), and coached in local schools during the 1930s. Bert lived in Freshfield Road, Brighton, for more than 40 years until his death at the age of 84. His brother, Harvey Longstaff (q.v.), also played for the Albion.

Season	FL	SL	FAC	FACS	UL	WL	WL Ch.	SA	SCC	Total
1906–07	0	1	0	0	4 (1)	0	0	0	0	5 (1)
1907–08	0	28 (10)	0	0	0	7 (4)	0	0	3	38 (14)
1908–09	0	39 (15)	1	0	0	9 (4)	2	0	2	53 (19)
1909–10	0	39 (14)	1	0	0	0	0	0	4 (2)	44 (16)
1910–11	0	35 (3)	3	1	0	0	0	0	5 (1)	44 (4)
1911–12	0	30 (2)	1	0	0	0	0	0	2	33 (2)
1912–13	0	36 (2)	3	0	0	0	0	14 (3)	1	54 (5)
1913–14	0	37 (5)	4	0	0	0	0	12 (7)	0	53 (12)
1914–15	0	31 (5)	3 (1)	0	0	0	0	0	1	35 (6)
1919–20	0	39 (3)	1	0	0	0	0	0	0	40 (3)
1920–21	38 (4)	0	3	0	0	0	0	0	0	41 (4)
1921–22	3	0	0	0	0	0	0	0	0	3
Total	41 (4)	315 (59)	20 (1)	1	4 (1)	16 (8)	2	26 (10)	18 (3)	443 (86)

LONGSTAFF, HARVEY   1909–13

centre-forward   *9 apps, 4 goals*

full name: Harvey Leopold Longstaff
born: Shoreham-by-Sea, Sussex, 1892
debut: Luton Town (a), 16.10.1912 (SA)

The younger brother of Bert Longstaff (q.v.), Harvey Longstaff made a name for himself locally with Steyning, Shoreham and Worthing in the West Sussex Senior League, and also with the Brighton-based club St Margaret's Athletic in the Mid Sussex Senior League. He assisted Albion's reserve team as an amateur as early as 1909, but wasn't signed as a professional until 1912. Harvey got his opportunity soon after Jimmy Smith's departure for Bradford (Park Avenue), but failed to solve the problem centre-forward spot and, after missing the entire 1913–14 season owing to a 'painter's colic', was transferred to Southend United in July 1914. He ran a tobacconist's shop in Lewes Road, Brighton, after the First World War.

Season	SL	SA	SCC	Total
1912–13	5 (2)	1	3 (2)	9 (4)
Total	5 (2)	1	3 (2)	9 (4)

LOWE, HARRY   1913–14

inside-right   Ht 5 9, Wt 10 07   8 apps, 5 goals
full name: Horace Lowe
born: Hayfield, Derbyshire, 1890
died: Camden Town, London, 15.7.1966
debut: Newport County (h), 2.10.1913 (SA)

Harry Lowe came to the Goldstone as a 23-year-old trialist from Northwich Victoria in August 1913 and was offered a professional engagement shortly afterwards. Despite scoring four goals in five Southern Alliance matches, he didn't make the Southern League side until April 1914 when he scored in a 4–2 home win over Merthyr Town, but a month later he was transferred to Tottenham Hotspur where his debut in the First Division came in an amazing 7–5 defeat at Middlesbrough in February 1915. Switching to the half-back line after the Great War, Harry's spell at White Hart Lane stretched to thirteen years but mainly as a reserve-team player as he made only 72 League and Cup appearances. In May 1927 he was released to join Fulham, but retired after just three games and took to coaching in Spain where he became manager of the Barcelona-based club Deportiva Espanol until 1935. Returning to England just before the outbreak of civil war in Spain, he subsequently managed the touring Islington Corinthians side before rejoining Spurs as reserve-team coach in 1938.

Season	SL	SA	SCC	Total
1913–14	2 (1)	5 (4)	1	8 (5)
Total	2 (1)	5 (4)	1	8 (5)

LUMBERG, ALBERT   1933–34

full-back   Ht 5 5, Wt 10 09   21 apps
born: Connah's Quay, Flintshire, Wales, 20.5.1901
died: Rhuddlan, Flintshire, Wales, 16.2.1986
debut: Queen's Park Rangers (a), 26.8.1933 (FL D3(S))

A great deal was expected of 32-year-old Albert Lumberg, a Welsh international full-back, when he signed for the Albion from Wolverhampton Wanderers in June 1933 for a fee of £250, but injury, together with a difference of opinion with the management following his omission from an F.A. Cup tie, reduced his effectiveness. Albert started out in north Wales with the Connah's Quay and Mold clubs, and then spent six seasons with nearby Wrexham where he won three international caps, gained a Welsh Cup winner's medal in 1925, and toured Canada with a Welsh F.A. side in 1929. After transferring to Wolves for £650 in May 1930, he added a fourth cap to his tally before arriving at the Goldstone. Albert appeared in both full-back berths during his season with the Albion, but was not retained in May 1934 and moved on to Stockport County. He then had brief spells with Clapton Orient (signed February 1935), Lytham, New Brighton (from November 1935),

Winsford United, and as player-manager with the Irish club Newry. He also ran the line in the Ireland–Wales match of 1938.

Season	FL	Total
1933–34	21	21
Total	21	21

LUMLEY, JOE   1905–08 & 1909–12

half-back   Ht 5 11, Wt 12 00   52 apps, 2 goals
full name: Joseph Lumley
born: Birtley, Co. Durham, 1882
debut: Leyton (h), 6.9.1905 (UL)

Joe Lumley started his professional career with Sheffield United in October 1904 and played for the "Blades'" reserves for the remainder of that season, but in May 1905 he was released to join the Albion. The 22-year-old Geordie was a forward on his arrival at the Goldstone and figured mainly in the midweek United League side during his first season with the club, but on switching to half-back he enjoyed more success and had a lengthy run in the Southern League team during 1906-07. Joe was transferred to Blackburn Rovers in February 1908, as a make-weight in a triple deal which also took Walter Anthony and Dick Wombwell to Ewood Park, but he failed to make Rovers' senior team and returned to the Goldstone in May 1909 where he remained a useful reserve for three more seasons. The possessor of exceptional pace, Joe was Albion's 100-yard sprint champion of 1906.

Season	SL	FAC	UL	WL	SCC	Total
1905–06	2	0	10 (1)	0	0	12 (1)
1906–07	18	1	9 (1)	0	0	28 (1)
1907–08	0	0	0	4	0	4
1910–11	3	0	0	0	2	5
1911–12	2	0	0	0	1	3
Total	25	1	19 (2)	4	3	52 (2)

LUTTON, BERTIE   1971–73

forward   Ht 5 10, Wt 10 09   30 apps, 4 goals
full name: Robert John Lutton
born: Banbridge, Co. Down, Northern Ireland, 13.7.1950
debut: Aston Villa (a), 11.9.1971 (FL D3)

A junior with Wolverhampton Wanderers, Bertie Lutton signed professional forms at Molineux in September 1967, and went on to make 21 First Division appearances in the famous gold shirt, both as a forward and in defence. In September 1969 he played his part in Wolves' 3–2 victory in the celebrated League Cup tie at the Goldstone, and had won two caps for Northern Ireland before joining the Albion on two months' loan in September 1971.

Despite returning to Molineux at the end of his loan period, Bertie impressed Brighton manager Pat Saward sufficiently for him to pay £5,000 for his services in March 1972. The Ulsterman made seventeen appearances in Albion's 1971–72 promotion season and scored some crucial goals, but the following term found him languishing in the reserves and he was loaned to First Division West Ham United in January 1973. After protracted negotiations the 'Hammers' came up with £12,000 for his transfer, but, despite adding four more caps to his collection (making him the first ever West Ham player to be capped by Northern Ireland), he made just twelve League appearances at Upton Park. On his release in October 1974, Bertie had a brief spell with Horsham in the Isthmian League before later emigrating to Australia.

Season	FL	FLC	Total
1971–72	11+6 (4)	0	11+6 (4)
1972–73	7+5	1	8+5
Total	18+11 (4)	1	19+11 (4)

LYON, BERTIE   1904–05

utility player	Ht 5 7, Wt 12 00	34 apps, 5 goals

full name: Herbert Ernest Saxon Bertie Cordey Lyon
born: Mosbrough, Derbyshire, c. 1877
debut: Wellingborough Town (a), 17.9.1904 (SL D1)

If Bertie Lyon lacked anything, it certainly wasn't Christian names! Although born in north Derbyshire, he was brought up in the south of the county at Church Gresley and played for Gresley Rovers as a centre-half from the age of sixteen. Having assisted Rovers to the championship of the Derbyshire Senior League, the young pivot graduated to the Football League when he was transferred to Leicester Fosse for £50 in January 1899, and began to earn a reputation as a utility player. After just over a season at Filbert Street he moved on to Nelson in the Lancashire League where he played as a centre-forward with great success, plundering over 100 goals in a single season.

Word of his exploits enticed Southern League Watford to sign him during the summer of 1901. Bertie subsequently enjoyed further spells in the Southern League with Reading (close season 1902) and West

Ham United (close season 1903) before his arrival at the Goldstone in May 1904. The nomadic utility man appeared in five different positions during his year with the Albion, mainly in the forward line, and, despite initially struggling to acclimatise to his new surroundings, came to be regarded as one of the most reliable players in the team once he had settled in.

Nevertheless, Bertie continued his annual migrations when he left for Swindon Town in May 1905, and subsequently played for Carlisle United in the North Eastern League (May 1906), Swindon Town for a second spell (May 1907), Blackpool back in the Football League (June 1908, for a £35 fee to Leicester) and Walsall. An incredibly adaptable footballer, Bertie was even selected as goalkeeper on one occasion during his time with Leicester.

Season	SL	FAC	Total
1904–05	29 (5)	5	34 (5)
Total	29 (5)	5	34 (5)

McALLISTER, BILLY   1921–25

inside-forward/right-half	95 apps, 6 goals

full name: William McAllister
born: Glasgow, Lanarkshire, Scotland, c. 1900
debut: Charlton Athletic (a), 22.10.1921 (FL D3(S))

While reminiscing in 1947, Albion manager Charlie Webb referred to Billy McAllister as 'a brilliant ball-player but prone to frequent hot-headed lapses,' a description which was entirely accurate. When the volatile Glaswegian was signed from Southern League Ebbw Vale in October 1921, Albion played a friendly match with the Welsh club later that season as part of the transaction, but Billy threw a clod of earth into the crowd following an altercation with several spectators and had to be escorted to the dressing-room at the final whistle. Later that evening the fans caught up with him in a local restaurant and further ugly scenes developed. The troubles were most probably a carry-over from the match at nearby Newport County two

McALLISTER - BRIGHTON + HOVE F.C. 1923-24.

days earlier when he had been sent off for misconduct, resulting in a one-month suspension.

Billy set out on a professional career in August 1919 when he joined the Dunbartonshire junior club Renton, but he was soon on the move, being recruited by First Division St Mirren twelve months later. Opportunities proved few at Love Street, though, and after a loan-spell with nearby Johnstone (April 1921) he migrated to South Wales with Ebbw Vale during the summer of 1921.

An inside-forward on his arrival at the Goldstone, Billy was immediately drafted into the first team, but then suffered a loss of form and had to be content with a backup role to Andy Neil and Tommy Cook throughout the 1922–23 season. In January 1923 he represented the Southern League (in which Albion's reserves competed) in their 3–0 defeat of the Central League at Coventry. The following season, though, Billy returned to the first team at right-half and performed his task well for fifteen months until he was dropped just before the busy Christmas programme of 1924.

Having fallen out with manager Webb, the impetuous Scot requested a transfer and signed for Middlesbrough for a sizeable fee in February 1925. After 33 Second Division outings for his new side Billy moved on to Queen's Park Rangers in October 1926, where he appeared in 26 Southern Section matches before returning to his native Scotland with Raith Rovers in November 1927. After almost two seasons at Starks Park he was transferred to Heart of Midlothian in May 1929.

Season	FL	FAC	Total
1921–22	21 (3)	0	21 (3)
1922–23	8 (1)	2	10 (1)
1923–24	41 (2)	4	45 (2)
1924–25	19	0	19
Total	89 (6)	6	95 (6)

McATEER, TOM   1903–04

centre-half	Ht 5 10, Wt 12 07	34 apps, 6 goals

full name: Thomas McAteer
born: Glasgow, Lanarkshire, Scotland, 8.8.1878
debut: Wellingborough Town (a), 5.9.1903 (SL D1)

One of a number of experienced players brought in by manager John Jackson as Albion faced the challenge of the Southern League's First Division for the first time, Tom McAteer was described in the Press as 'A grand centre-half of the fearless type, with a very safe tackle and grand placing.' Beginning his adult life as a coal-miner, Tom played football for Stirlingshire junior sides Kilsyth Wanderers and Smithston Hibernian before signing for Bolton Wanderers in November 1898. He went on to appear in 59 League matches, assisting the 'Trotters' to promotion to the First Division in 1899–1900, but was released to join West Ham United in the Southern League in May 1902.

The burly Scot failed to live up to his reputation with the 'Hammers', though, and was snapped up by the Albion during the close season of 1903. Installed as skipper at the Goldstone, Tom missed only just game during 1903–04, but returned to Scotland with Dundee in May 1904. Tom subsequently had spells with Clyde (August 1906) and then with Northern League side Carlisle United (1907–08) before rejoining Clyde in February 1908. Two years later, in 1910, he skippered the 'Bully Wee' to the Scottish Cup final where they were beaten 2–1 by his former club, Dundee, after two replays.

Following a transfer to Celtic in May 1910, though, he went one better, scoring a tremendous last-minute goal as the 'Celts' beat Hamilton Academical 2–0 at Ibrox Park in the final of 1911. In two seasons at Celtic Park, Tom appeared in 28 League and Cup games before dropping into junior football with Wishaw Thistle in 1912. He subsequently returned to the Scottish League with spells at Albion Rovers (November 1912) and Abercorn (July 1913), and had a very brief period with Broxburn United before joining the Army on the outbreak of World War One. Tom served with the 3rd Battalion of the Cameron Highlanders and was badly wounded in 1915, but he survived the bloody conflict to return to the pit at Kilsyth.

Season	SL	FAC	Total
1903–04	33 (6)	1	34 (6)
Total	33 (6)	1	34 (6)

McAVOY, FRANK 1901–02

utility player 15 apps, 9 goals
full name: Francis McAvoy
born: Saltpans, Ayr, Ayrshire, Scotland, 16.11.1875
debut: Brighton Athletic (h), 21.9.1901 (FAC Prelim.)

Frank McAvoy was playing for the Scottish junior club Ayr when he joined Woolwich Arsenal in May 1895, and in three good seasons at the Manor Ground he proved his versatility by appearing in seven different positions in 44 Football League outings. However, he was suspended by the 'Gunners' in March 1898 and signed for Brighton United in May. Frank played at centre-half for the newly formed professional outfit, and made 69 competitive appearances (a total equalled only by Willie McArthur) before the club folded in March 1900. Shortly afterwards he left for Gravesend United, but when Brighton & Hove Albion were formed a year later he was brought

back to the South Coast and installed as captain.

Playing as a forward or half-back, Frank was the leading goalscorer in that initial 1901–02 season, but in late February things turned sour. Following a blazing row with John Jackson at Christmas, he was involved in another incident with the manager which resulted in the latter being set upon and knocked to the ground; Frank never played for the club again. With Jackson apparently living in constant fear of injury from the fiery Scot, the situation came to a head in August 1902 when, together with his ex-Albion colleague Clem Barker, Frank arrived at Jackson's Hove pub, the Farm Tavern in Farm Road. Fortunately the manager was in Lewes at the time, but the pair were subsequently convicted of using threatening behaviour towards him in an incident with Mrs Jackson. Bound over to keep the peace for six months, Frank joined Watford in September 1902 where he remained for one season before returning north of the border to play for First Division St Mirren (signed October 1903) and then for his original club, Ayr, who by then had progressed to the Second Division of the Scottish League (September 1904).

Season	SL	FAC	Total
1901–02	11 (6)	4 (3)	15 (9)
Total	11 (6)	4 (3)	15 (9)

71 players with full international caps
*won caps with Albion. Wartime players not included. Figures to June 1997.

Player	Country	Period	No. of Caps
Adekola, David	Nigeria	?	?
Armstrong, Gerry	Northern Ireland	1977–86	63
Barham, Mark	England	1983	2
Bell, Willie	Scotland	1966	2
Bridges, Barry	England	1965	4
Buckley, Frank	England	1914	1
Byrne, John*	Republic of Ireland	1985–93	23
Carolan, Joe	Republic of Ireland	1960	2
Chamberlain, Mark	England	1982–84	8
Chivers, Martin	England	1971–73	24
Cohen, Jacob*	Israel	1976– c. 82	16
Cook, Tommy *	England	1925	1
Corrigan, Joe	England	1976–82	9
Curran, Jack	Ireland	1922–23	4
Doran, Jack*	Ireland	1920–22	3
Downs, Dickie	England	1920	1
Edwards, Alistair	Australia	c. 1991–	>30
Farrell, Paddy	Ireland	1901	2
Foster, Steve*	England	1982	3
Garfield, Ben	England	1898	1
Gariani, Moshe*	Israel	1978– c. 82	11
Gotsmanov, Sergei	USSR	c.1984–89	31
	Belarus	c.1992–94	?
Grealish, Tony*	Republic of Ireland	1976–85	45
Gregory, John	England	1983–84	6
Gurinovich, Igor	USSR	1984	1
	Belarus	c.1994–95	c. 3
Holley, George	England	1909–13	10
Hollins, Dave	Wales	1962–66	11
Hopkins, Jimmy*	Ireland	1925	1
Hopkins, Mel	Wales	1956–62	34
Howlett, Gary*	Republic of Ireland	1984	1
Iovan, Stefan	Romania	c. 1985–89	34
Irvine, Willie*	Northern Ireland	1963–72	23
Jenkins, Jack*	Wales	1924–26	8
Jones, Herbert	England	1927–28	6
Jones, Les	Wales	1933–38	11
Keown, Martin	England	1992–	15
Kinnear, Joe*	Republic of Ireland	1967–75	26
Langley, Jimmy	England	1958	3
Lawrenson, Mark*	Republic of Ireland	1977–87	38
Lewis, Jack	Wales	1906	1
Lumberg, Albert	Wales	1929–31	4
Lutton, Bertie	Northern Ireland	1970–73	6
Magill, Jimmy*	Northern Ireland	1961–66	26
Martin, Neil	Scotland	1965	3
Meola, Tony	USA	1988–94	90
Moorhead, George	Ireland	1923–29	3
Morgan, Sammy*	Northern Ireland	1972–78	18
Napier, John	Northern Ireland	1966	1
Nelson, Sammy*	Northern Ireland	1970–82	51
O'Regan, Kieran*	Republic of Ireland	1983–85	4
Osman, Russell	England	1980–83	11
O'Sullivan, Peter*	Wales	1973–78	3
Penney, Steve*	Northern Ireland	1984–88	17
Reed, Billy	Wales	1954	2
Richards, Billy	Wales	1932	1
Robinson, John	Wales	1995–	8
Robinson, Mike*	Republic of Ireland	1980–86	24
Rougvie, Doug	Scotland	1983	1
Ryan, Gerry*	Republic of Ireland	1978–84	18
Saunders, Dean*	Wales	1986–	58
Sayer, Peter	Wales	1977	7
Smith, Bobby	England	1960–63	15
Sommer, Jeurgen	USA	1994–	6
Stapleton, Frank	Republic of Ireland	1976–90	71
Stevens, Gary	England	1984–86	7
Thomas, Mickey*	Wales	1976–86	51
Ward, Peter*	England	1980	1
Webb, Charlie*	Ireland	1909–11	3
Wilson, Danny*	Northern Ireland	1986–92	24
Worthington, Frank	England	1974	8
Young, Eric	Wales	1990–95	21

McCAIRNS, TOM   1903–04

centre-forward   Ht 5 9, Wt 11 10   17 apps, 5 goals
full name: Thomas McCairns
born: Dinsdale, Co. Durham, 22.12.1873
died: Willesden, Middlesex, 1932
debut: Reading (h), 28.12.1903 (SL D1)

A contemporary report had it that Tom McCairns was 'wonderfully fast considering his weight, and has few equals in keeping his head in front of goal.' Those qualities enabled him to score a host of goals for Grimsby Town, but he finished his career as a journeyman forward and the Goldstone Ground was just a brief stop on a whirlwind tour of nine clubs in seven years.

After assisting Middlesbrough Ironopolis to the championship of the Northern League in 1890–91, Tom spent two seasons with Whitby

before joining Second Division Grimsby in September 1893. In five seasons with the 'Mariners' he scored 86 goals in 137 League games, including six in a 7–1 win over Leicester Fosse in April 1896, and was the club's leading marksman three times. Such form won him a place as leader of the Football League's attack in a 2–2 draw with the Irish League at the Victoria Ground, Stoke, in November 1895.

When he left the Lincolnshire side at the end of 1897–98, Tom played for Bristol Rovers (signed May 1898), Notts County (May 1899), Lincoln City (November 1899), Barnsley (June 1901), Wellingborough Town (May 1902), Queen's Park Rangers (May 1903), Brighton & Hove Albion (December 1903), Southern United (May 1904) and Kettering Town. In May 1909 he made an unsuccessful application to the F.A. for the reinstatement of his amateur status to enable him to play for an unnamed London club.

Season	SL	Total
1903–04	17 (5)	17 (5)
Total	17 (5)	17 (5)

McCARTHY, PAUL   1988–96

central defender   Ht 6 0, Wt 13 06   217 apps, 8 goals
full name: Paul Jason McCarthy
born: Cork, Co. Cork, Republic of Ireland, 4.8.1971
debut: Bradford City (h), 17.3.1990 (FL D2)

H aving won ten caps for the Republic of Ireland at under-21 level, one of the biggest disappointments of Paul McCarthy's career must be his failure to make a full international appearance. It certainly hasn't been for want of trying for, after becoming an Albion regular in 1992, he blossomed into one of the team's few reliable and consistent performers as the club's fortunes tumbled. Indeed, it was the lack of stability at the Goldstone Ground that persuaded him he would be better off elsewhere, and it was a sad day for Albion supporters when he decided to join Wycombe Wanderers amid the turmoil of the 1996 close season.

Paul played hurling and Gaelic football (representing Cork Schools at the latter game) at school, but also played soccer for the local Rockmount club where he gained a number of caps at various age levels. In fact it was while he was a member of the Irish under-16 squad that he attracted the attention of Albion scout Ted Streeter, and was brought to the Goldstone as a trainee in July 1988; the fee to Rockmount was a couple of match balls! Having gone on to win further caps at under-17 and youth levels, Paul signed as a full professional in April 1989 and made his first-team debut in March 1990, coming on as a substitute forward late in the game to create the winning goal in a 2–1 win over Bradford City.

Over the next few seasons injuries and contractual disputes led to him being in-and-out of the side – in December 1991 he had a trial with Scottish Premier Division club Airdrieonians – but the return of veteran Steve Foster in 1992 brought out the best in the young

Irishman and he developed into a sound central defender. Nominated more than once as Barclays Young Eagle of the Month for the region, Paul won his first cap for the Republic's under-21 team in a game against England in November 1990 and subsequently skippered the side from November 1992. In November 1993 he was named Republic of Ireland Under-21 Player of the Year, and was third in the 1993–94 Albion Player of the Season award.

Continuing to mature in the absence of Foster, Paul took over the captaincy from his erstwhile partner and performed bravely as Albion battled vainly against relegation during 1995–96. Indeed, he may well have won the Player of the Season award had he not been injured for the last two months of the campaign; he eventually came second to Ian Chapman in the annual poll of supporters.

Strong in the air and deceptively quick, Paul turned down several offers of a new contract and signed for Wycombe in the summer of 1996, looking for the security that was sadly missing at the Albion. The fee, settled by a tribunal, was £100,000, and he quickly established himself in the Second Division side.

Season	FL	FAC	FLC	FMC	AMC	Total
1989–90	2+1	0	0	0	0	2+1
1990–91	21	3	2	3	0	29
1991–92	20	1	0	0	0	21
1992–93	30	3	2	0	4	39
1993–94	37 (3)	1	1	0	1	40 (3)
1994–95	37 (2)	1	4 (1)	0	2	44 (3)
1995–96	33 (1)	4	2	0	2 (1)	41 (2)
Total	180+1 (6)	13	11 (1)	3	9	216+1 (8)

McCARTHY, TOM   1935–36

centre-half   Ht 5 8, Wt 12 06   2 apps
full name: Thomas A. McCarthy
born: Dundee, Angus, Scotland
debut: Luton Town (a), 19.10.1935 (FL D3(S))

H aving joined Dundee as a professional from Lochee United in July 1928, Tom McCarthy was farmed out to nearby Montrose twice during the 1928–29 season in order to gain experience. On

returning to Dens Park he became a regular at centre-half in the First Division side for five seasons prior to his transfer to the Goldstone in June 1935. The experienced Scot was quite a catch for the Albion, but he made the first team just twice in 1935–36 in the absence of regular centre-half Jack Stevens. The possessor of an unusual build for a pivot – just 5' 8" tall but weighing nearly 12½ stone – Tom appeared in every defensive position except goalkeeper for the reserves, but was released in May 1936 and returned to his native city to link up with Dundee United.

Season	FL	SSC	Total
1935–36	1	1	2
Total	1	1	2

MACCIOCHI, DAVE　　　　　　　　1992–93

midfield　　　　　　　　　　　　　　　　　　2 apps
full name: David Andrew Macciochi
born: Harlow, Essex, 14.1.1972
debut: Stoke City (a), 16.9.1992 (FL D2)

A Harlow Schools representative, Dave Macciochi was spotted by Leyton Orient scout Pat Holland and spent a couple of months at the club's centre of excellence. After following Holland to Queen's Park Rangers, the Essex youngster became a trainee at Loftus Road and signed professional forms in 1990, but he failed to make Rangers' League side and spent the summer of 1992 on loan with the Norwegian Premier League strugglers Sogndal. Released on his return to London, Dave had a brief trial with Millwall and arrived at the Goldstone early in 1992–93 for three months.

Few Albion fans were to see him in action, though, as he was released in January 1993 after making just two appearances in the senior side as a substitute, both away from home. On leaving Hove, Dave dropped into non-League football with fleeting spells at Kingstonian, Dulwich Hamlet and Whyteleafe before settling in with Bishop's Stortford in October 1993, whom he assisted to the Isthmian League Division One title that season. A quick, left-sided midfielder or winger with a penchant for free-kicks, he moved on to Sawbridgeworth Town in 1994 and remains on their books, but plays most of his football for local side Tateley while concentrating on his cafe business.

Season	FL	Total
1992–93	0+2	0+2
Total	0+2	0+2

McCOY, TIM　　　　　　　1940–41 & 1951–54

centre-half　　　　　　Ht 6 0, Wt 12 00　　　　124 apps
full name: Wilfred McCoy
born: Birmingham, Warwickshire, 4.3.1921
died: Brighton, Sussex, 1993
debut: Portsmouth (a), 5.10.1940 (wartime)
peacetime debut: Colchester United (h), 13.1.1951 (FL D3(S))

A lways known by his nickname (after the celebrated Hollywood cowboy), 'Tim' McCoy lost his formative years to the war, his experience being a classic example of the conflict spoiling a potentially excellent career. Nevertheless, he enjoyed a useful if all-too-brief spell as a professional footballer.

In 1939, Tim was playing in Birmingham junior football when Bolton Wanderers offered him a trial, but he was called into the Army before the opportunity came to fruition. Posted to Preston Barracks in Brighton a year later, he became the first captain of Albion's newly formed junior side and also played seven times for the senior team in the 1940–41 emergency competitions, making his debut as a nineteen-year-old. He also played overseas in brigade football during the hostilities.

When peace returned he was approached by several First Division clubs, and was recommended to Portsmouth by an Army sports officer.

Offered terms in August 1946 after a trial at Fratton Park, Tim had hoped to remain in Brighton and played in Albion's pre-season public trial match at the Goldstone. However, to the astonishment of the local Press, he was not taken on and so signed for 'Pompey' the following week. Making eighteen First Division appearances as deputy to Reg Flewin, he moved on to Northampton Town in December 1948, but after almost three years with the 'Cobblers', the 29-year-old finally returned to the Goldstone when manager Don Welsh obtained his signature in January 1951.

Tim proved a first-class stopper and played a major part in the unsuccessful promotion effort of 1951–52. Although he lacked mobility on the ground, he made up for it with his bravery in the air, and always played his heart out for his team. A fixture in the no.5 shirt until September 1953 when Alex South took over as pivot, he left for Southern League Tonbridge in May 1954 and subsequently played for Dover. In 1958 he became player-coach at East Grinstead. When Tim left the Albion he became the Brighton area representative of the Hoover company, and lived locally in Woodingdean.

Season	FL	FAC	Wartime	Total
1940–41	0	0	7	7
1950–51	22	1	0	23
1951–52	42	1	0	43
1952–53	36	2	0	38
1953–54	12	1	0	13
Total	112	5	7	124

McCURLEY, KEVIN　　　　　　　1948–51

outside-right/centre-forward　Ht 5 10, Wt 12 00　　21 apps, 9 goals
born: Consett, Co. Durham, 2.4.1926
debut: Newport County (a), 2.4.1949 (FL D3(S))

T hough born and bred in the North-East, Kevin McCurley was living in Worthing (and had turned out for the local club in the Sussex County League) when he joined the Albion as a professional in September 1948. Developing rapidly in his first season with the club, he progressed through the 'A' team and reserves to make his League debut on his 23rd birthday in April 1949, but subsequently received scant opportunity to prove himself in the side. A good athlete and strong runner, he showed great promise and was particularly powerful in the air, but was placed on the transfer list at the end of the 1950–51 season.

Kevin's raw potential was recognised by his former Albion manager Don Welsh, who snapped him up shortly after taking the reins at Liverpool, but his protégé failed to make the League side at Anfield, and was transferred to Colchester United in March 1952. Scoring 91 goals in 224 League appearances at Layer Road, he was an unqualified success and a thorn in Albion's flesh on more than the odd occasion. After eight years with the Essex club, Kevin was transferred to Oldham Athletic in June 1960, but dislocated a knee on his debut and, at the age of 34, never played another Football League match.

He subsequently joined Southern League Tonbridge and in 1961–62 broke the club's goals-in-a-season record with 40 goals; yet, amazingly, the Kent club were relegated from the Premier Division. Kevin later played for Ramsgate Athletic and Canterbury City before ending his career with Snowdown Colliery in the Kent League.

Season	FL	Total
1948–49	7 (5)	7 (5)
1949–50	3 (1)	3 (1)
1950–51	11 (3)	11 (3)
Total	21 (9)	21 (9)

MacDONALD, HUGH · 1906–08

goalkeeper　　Ht 6 2, Wt 15 06　　102 apps
full name: Hugh Lachlan MacDonald
born: Kilwinning, Ayrshire, Scotland, 1884
died: Plumstead, Woolwich, London, 27.8.1920
debut: Leyton (a), 1.9.1906 (SL D1)

Over 6 feet tall and weighing in at more than 15 stone, goalkeeper Hugh MacDonald was a huge man, but his ground work was near faultless and he enjoyed an excellent two years in Sussex. After doing the rounds of the Ayrshire junior clubs as a youngster, Hugh joined Woolwich Arsenal in January 1905, but was released to join the Goldstone staff in the summer of 1906 when Frank Scott-Walford signed him as a replacement for Mark Mellors. The massive Scot immediately impressed with some tremendous performances and was ever-present in his first season at Hove. In fact, his form was so good that the Arsenal management realised they had made a mistake in releasing him and re-signed the Scot in May 1908.

Hugh remained at the Manor Ground for the next two seasons, but was transferred to Oldham Athletic in July 1910 on their promotion to the First Division. The 'Latics' finished seventh in their initial season in the top flight and Hugh appeared in every game, but he lost favour and fell foul of the management the following term after refusing to travel for a reserve-team fixture. Soon on the move, he joined Bradford (P.A.) in December 1911, but twelve months later returned to Woolwich Arsenal for a third spell when he brought his total of League and Cup appearances for the 'Gunners' up to 103 before a transfer to Fulham in November 1913. Hugh subsequently returned to the Southern League with Bristol Rovers in February 1914, but on retiring became a publican in Plumstead where he died at the age of just 35.

Season	SL	FAC	UL	WL	SCC	Total
1906–07	38	1	14	0	0	53
1907–08	31	5	0	9	4	49
Total	69	6	14	9	4	102

McDONALD, MURDO · 1930–31

outside-right　　Ht 5 7, Wt 11 00　　10 apps, 1 goal
full name: Murdoch McDonald
born: Redding, Stirlingshire, Scotland, 1.7.1901
died: Falkirk, Stirlingshire, Scotland, 22.12.1934
debut: Exeter City (a), 15.3.1930 (FL D3(S))

Murdo McDonald's career began with the Scottish junior clubs Grange Rovers (based in Grangemouth) and St Ninian's Thistle (Stirling), but in April 1921, at the age of 20, he crossed the Firth of Forth to become a professional with Cowdenbeath. Eighteen months later, in October 1922, he signed for Bo'ness, another Second Division club, and quickly came to the forefront. Impressing several leading Scottish and English clubs with his form, Murdo joined Rangers in April 1923 for a substantial fee. The Glasgow giants walked off with the League championship in 1923–24, but with the huge amount of international talent on the Ibrox staff the young inside-forward performed only a fringe role and was released to rejoin Bo'ness in May 1925.

In July 1926 the Bo'ness manager, Andrew Wylie, took the reins at Reading on the elevation to the Second Division, and took his star player to Elm Park with him. Murdo made 65 League appearances, scoring thirteen goals, for the 'Biscuitmen' before signing for the Albion for £500 in March 1930. Capable of filling any of the forward positions, he was initially recruited to fill the breach left by the injured Bobby Farrell at outside-right, but on Farrell's recovery he was employed mainly in the reserves at inside-right or right-half during his fifteen months at the Goldstone.

Murdo departed for an unknown Irish side in May 1931, but returned to Bo'ness in January 1933 only for the West Lothian club to go out of business four months later. At this point the 33-year-old Scot hung up his boots to concentrate on his haulage contracting business in Polmont, Stirlingshire, where he also became a prominent member of the local golf club. In November 1934, Murdo married a school-mistress from nearby Maddiston but tragedy quickly struck. After returning from his honeymoon he was loading a lorry in Glasgow when a bathtub shifted, trapping one of his fingers. Blood-poisoning set in, and two weeks later he passed away in the Falkirk & District Royal Infirmary.

Season	FL	Total
1929–30	6	6
1930–31	4 (1)	4 (1)
Total	10 (1)	10 (1)

McDONALD, PAUL · 1996–

winger　　Ht 5 7, Wt 9 05　　56 apps
full name: Paul Thomas McDonald
born: Motherwell, Lanarkshire, Scotland, 20.4.1968
debut: Crewe Alexandra (h), 17.2.1996 (FL D2)

A great success over seven seasons for Hamilton Academical, Paul McDonald has struggled at times to reproduce his best form south of the border, but often shone during Albion's traumatic 1996–97 season, never more so than in the 5–0 'Fans United' defeat of Hartlepool United that proved such a turning-point.

A product of Merry Street Boys' Club, the diminutive winger signed as a professional for the 'Accies' at the age of eighteen in June 1986, and made his debut soon after in the Scottish Premier Division against Hibernian. It was a bad season for the Lanarkshire side as they finished bottom of the section and tried out 41 players in the process, but they bounced straight back as champions in 1987–88

with Paul enjoying 18 League outings. History, however, repeated itself and the 'Accies' were again relegated as the speedy young no.11 established himself in the side. Over the next four seasons Paul became a great favourite at Douglas Park as Hamilton won the Scottish League Challenge Cup (the B&Q Cup for non-Premier Division sides) in 1991–92 and 1992–93 while maintaining a healthy position in Division One. He also weighed in with a good number of goals – he was a regular penalty taker – and was joint leading scorer with fourteen strikes in 1993–94.

After 242 outings and 31 goals for Hamilton, Paul moved into the English Premiership with Southampton for a £75,000 fee in June 1993, but he rarely got a look-in. Out for several months with torn ligaments during his first season with the 'Saints', he enjoyed just four outings as substitute in more than two-and-a-half years at The Dell and became increasingly frustrated after playing consistently well in the reserves. In October

1995 he joined Burnley on loan and played in a 3–0 victory over the Albion, but moved along the South Coast to the Goldstone in February 1996 when Jimmy Case paid an initial £40,000 fee scheduled to rise to £75,000.

Immediately impressing with his trickery and incisiveness, Paul was unfortunate to sustain a stress fracture of his ankle at Wycombe in just his fifth game for the club, but blossomed down Albion's left flank the following season when he made more appearances than anyone else. It was a traumatic time to be at the Goldstone – the ground's last season – but the crowd quickly took to the wee Scots winger who, while lacking in consistency, never wanted for effort. His starring performance at 'Fans United', when he made four of the five goals, should earn him a place in Albion folklore for many years to come.

Season	FL	FAC	FLC	AMC	Total
1995–96	5	0	0	0	5
1996–97	40+5 (4)	2	2	2 (1)	46+5 (5)
Total	45+5 (4)	2	2	2 (1)	51+5 (5)

McDONALD, WILLIE   1906–08

left-half   *99 apps, 1 goal*
full name: William McDonald
born: Scotland, c. 1883
debut: Leyton (a), 1.9.1906 (SL D1)

In April 1904, while playing for the junior side Nithsdale Wanderers (based in Sanquhar, Dumfriesshire), Willie McDonald signed for Kilmarnock and went on to become a regular for the Ayrshire club, making 51 first-team appearances in two years. He made a brief

return to the junior ranks on loan with Lanemark and back at Nithsdale in April 1906, but was recruited by the Albion the following month. Described as 'a brainy and intelligent wing-half who feeds his forwards with precision and adroitness,' Willie was a great success at the Goldstone for two seasons, missing only a handful of games through injury. In July 1908, as a number of players followed ex-Albion manager Frank Scott-Walford, he joined the exodus to Leeds City, but had only fourteen Second Division outings at Elland Road before returning to Scotland with his former club Nithsdale Wanderers in August 1909. Willie subsequently rejoined Lanemark in November 1909 where he remained until 1915. His brother John also played for Kilmarnock.

Season	SL	FAC	UL	WL	SCC	Total
1906–07	32	1	12 (1)	0	0	45 (1)
1907–08	36	5	0	9	4	54
Total	68	6	12 (1)	9	4	99 (1)

McDOUGALD, JUNIOR   1994–96

striker   *Ht 5 11, Wt 12 06*   *95 apps, 22 goals*
full name: David Eugene Junior McDougald
born: Big Spring, Texas, U.S.A., 12.1.1975
debut: Swansea City (a), 13.8.1994 (FL D2)

The son of a U.S. airman (also David) and an English mother, Junior McDougald was born in Texas but came to England as a baby to be brought up in Huntingdonshire. Showing great promise as a youngster, Junior was associated with Tottenham Hotspur from the age of nine and had trials with a number of other top clubs. He attended Spurs' school of excellence, then moved to the national school at Lilleshall where he played for England at under-15 and under-16 level. However, Junior failed to make the first team at White Hart Lane in his one year as a pro. and was released at the end of 1993–94. In fact he scored for Watford reserves against the Albion in April 1994 and had the chance to join the Vicarage Road staff, but opted for Brighton during the summer and became a regular in the forward line.

A member of the growing Christians in Sport movement, the nineteen-year-old striker impressed with his pace, running and commitment, but lost his form in a struggling side and rarely looked to be the answer to the supporters' prayers. Despite top-scoring in his two seasons on the South Coast, Junior looked to have lost all confidence during the bitter 1995–96 relegation campaign and made a hash of many clear opportunities. In March 1996 he was allowed to join Chesterfield on a month's loan where he scored three times in nine games, but returned to the Goldstone for the final League game of the season. Although offered a new deal to remain with the club, Junior preferred the prospect of Second Division football and signed for Rotherham United in July 1996 for the surprisingly large sum of £50,000, but he suffered injury problems as the 'Millers' were relegated to the Third Division and scored just twice in sixteen starts.

Season	FL	FAC	FLC	AMC	Total
1994–95	37+4 (10)	1	6 (2)	2 (1)	46+4 (13)
1995–96	34+3 (4)	3 (3)	1	4 (2)	42+3 (9)
Total	71+7 (14)	4 (3)	7 (2)	6 (3)	88+7 (22)

MACE, STAN   1927–28

centre-half   *Ht 5 10, Wt 11 07*   *5 apps*
full name: Robert Stanley Mace
born: Grimsby, Lincolnshire, 2.12.1895
debut: Bournemouth & B.A. (h), 27.12.1927 (FL D3(S))

Stan Mace made a late entry into the professional ranks at the age of 26, signing for Sheffield United in March 1922 for £100 after joining the 'Blades' from Grimsby Rovers as an amateur a month

earlier. He went on to give fine service in the Central League side for more than five years, but made the First Division side on just four occasions. Nevertheless, his loyalty was rewarded with a testimonial match which realised the considerable sum of £350. Brought to the Goldstone for a £150 fee in August 1927, Stan acted as deputy to Paul Mooney at centre-half but was not retained at the end of the 1927–28 campaign and departed from the first-class scene. On leaving the game Stan became a postmaster in the Dore district of Sheffield. During the Great War he had served with the Sportsmen's Battalion of the Royal Fusiliers.

Season	FL	Total
1927–28	5	5
Total	5	5

McEWAN, BILLY   1974

midfield   *Ht 5 10, Wt 11 02*   *28 apps, 3 goals*
full name: William McGowan Johnston McEwan
born: Cleland, Lanarkshire, Scotland, 20.6.1951
debut: Wrexham (h), 27.2.1974 (FL D3)

After 362 games in both the English and Scottish Football Leagues, Billy McEwan was well-equipped for the managerial and coaching career he has pursued since hanging up his boots in 1984.

His first professional club was Hibernian, whom he joined as an apprentice from Pumpherston Juniors. He went on to make 61 League appearances for the Edinburgh side before moving south to Blackpool in May 1973, but came further south still nine months later in February 1974 when he signed for the Albion. The Brighton managerial duo of Brian Clough and Peter Taylor had been interested in the Scottish midfielder during their days at Derby, and signed him in a deal worth £15,000 that also brought Paul Fuschillo to the South Coast.

Although he made only 28 appearances for the club, Billy showed the leadership and determination qualities which would help see him into management and was installed as skipper towards the end of his spell at the Goldstone. In November 1974 the 23-year-old left for Chesterfield (together with Ronnie Welch in the deal which brought Ken Tiler to Hove), but then had spells with Mansfield Town (January 1977), where he won a Third Division championship medal in 1976–77; Peterborough United (November 1977); and Rotherham United (July 1979).

In 1984, Billy joined the coaching staff at Rotherham. He later moved to nearby Sheffield United as youth-team coach, and when Ian Porterfield left for Aberdeen in April 1986 he took over the reins at Bramall Lane, but resigned in January 1988 with the 'Blades' destined for relegation to Division Three. Three months later he returned to Rotherham as manager and remained with 'Millers' until January 1991, guiding them to the Fourth Division championship in 1989. Billy later became assistant to another former Albion player, Scarborough manager Ray McHale, but left the Yorkshire club in April 1992 because of financial cut-backs. A few weeks later he was appointed manager of Darlington, but with the 'Quakers' bottom of the Football League he resigned in October 1993. The following month Billy was appointed to the coaching staff of Derby County, and was coach to the 'Rams' when they won promotion to the F.A. Premiership in 1995–96.

Season	FL	FLC	Total
1973–74	15 (3)	0	15 (3)
1974–75	12	1	13
Total	27 (3)	1	28 (3)

McGARRIGLE, KEVIN   1993–97

central defender   *Ht 5 11, Wt 11 05*   *52 apps, 1 goal*
born: Newcastle upon Tyne, Northumberland, 9.4.1977
debut: Port Vale (h), 7.5.1994 (FL D2)

Seventeen-year-old Kevin McGarrigle made his senior debut in the last game of 1993–94 when veteran Steve Foster had to pull out through injury. Coming just a few weeks after being offered a three-year professional contract, it was a great thrill for the talented youngster from North Shields who was still in his first year as a trainee.

A product of the famed Wallsend Boys Club, the lanky Geordie joined the Albion in 1993 after trials with numerous clubs, and played a big part in the successful youth team of 1993–94. Looking set for an excellent career, Kevin played

for an F.A. XI *v.* Combined Services at Aldershot in March 1994, and became a regular in a five-man defence towards the end of the 1994–95 season, looking very composed for one so young. He started the following campaign in midfield, but both the club and its brightest prospect struggled to find their best form and he was used mainly as a standby defender thereafter. As he was overtaken in the first-team stakes by Ross Johnson, Kevin's appearances became even more sporadic, and he was released by Steve Gritt to join, firstly, Spennymoor United and then Blyth Spartans for 1997–98.

Season	FL	FAC	FLC	AMC	Total
1993–94	1	0	0	0	1
1994–95	16+1	0	0	0	16+1
1995–96	8+6 (1)	0	2	1+1	11+7 (1)
1996–97	9+4	2	0	0+1	11+5
Total	34+11 (1)	2	2	1+2	39+13 (1)

McGHIE, JOE   1909–13

centre-half   *156 apps, 3 goals*
full name: Joseph McGhie
born: Kilbirnie, Ayrshire, Scotland, 22.3.1884
died: Largs, Ayrshire, Scotland, 9.9.1976
debut: Portsmouth (a), 1.9.1909 (SL D1)

Joe McGhie's four seasons at the Goldstone corresponded with the greatest successes of Albion's early years, a connection that was no mere coincidence. Although not particularly tall, the talented Scot developed into an outstanding pivot at Hove and played a leading role in the 1909–10 Southern League championship campaign – he missed only one game – and the subsequent victory over Aston Villa in the F.A. Charity Shield. Together with Billy Booth and Jack Haworth (and later Gunner Higham), he formed one of the club's best-ever half-back lines.

Joe began his career with Vale of Garnock Strollers in the North Ayrshire League, and had won caps as a Scottish junior international when he was signed by Sunderland in May 1906 amid competition from several leading clubs including Celtic and Bradford City. After 41 First Division matches at Roker Park, he moved to Sheffield United in April 1908 for £250, but failed to reproduce his form at Bramall Lane and was released to join the Albion during the summer of 1909 at the age of 25. For four years he was never rivalled for the centre-half spot, but in May 1913 he refused the terms offered and left

for Stalybridge Celtic in the Central League. A devout church-goer, Joe returned to his native Ayrshire on his retirement from the game and became a pillar of the local community for many years. He was regularly to be seen riding his bicycle around the countryside up to his death at the age of 92.

Season	SL	FAC	FACS	SA	SCC	Total
1909–10	41 (1)	1	0	0	2	44 (1)
1910–11	32	3	1	0	0	36
1911–12	32 (2)	0	0	0	3	35 (2)
1912–13	28	3	0	9	1	41
Total	133 (3)	7	1	9	6	156 (3)

McGONIGAL, BERT   1962–66

goalkeeper   *Ht 6 0, Wt 11 00*   *62 apps*
full name: Robert Edwin McGonigal
born: Cookstown, Co. Tyrone, Northern Ireland, 2.5.1942
debut: Queen's Park Rangers (a), 18.8.1962 (FL D3)

Bert McGonigal started out as a centre-half and was selected as such for the Northern Ireland trials, but it was as a goalkeeper that he went on to win schoolboy honours for his country. A joiner by trade, he was playing for Glentoran as a part-time professional when he came to the Goldstone in February 1962 at the age of nineteen, initially to share the goalkeeping duties with Charlie Baker and then with the emerging Brian Powney. However, Bert's appearances were cut short by a serious injury sustained during the course of a fiery 2–0 home win over Darlington in December 1963 which kept him out for the rest of the season. Following his recovery the young 'keeper played a supporting role to Powney for almost two seasons before being released to join Cape Town City in February 1966 at the age of 23.

Bert went on to enjoy a highly successful spell back in Ulster with Linfield, during which he was chosen to represent the Irish League against both the Football League and the League of Ireland; gained an Irish Cup runner's-up medal in 1967–68 and an Irish League championship medal the following season; and appeared in the 1969–70 European Cup for the Belfast-based club. Though capable of brilliant displays with his keen positional sense and bravery, Bert was occasionally prone to disconcerting errors and never fully inspired confidence in Albion supporters.

Season	FL	FAC	FLC	Total
1962–63	25	1	1	27
1963–64	21	1	2	24
1964–65	5	0	0	5
1965–66	6	0	0	6
Total	57	2	3	62

McGRATH, DEREK   1988–1992

midfield   Ht 5 5, Wt 10 01   7 apps
full name: Derek Brendan Joseph McGrath
born: Dublin, Co. Dublin, Republic of Ireland, 24.1.1972
debut: Oxford United (a), 25.4.1990 (FL D2)

A product of the Hillcrest Juniors club of Dublin, Derek McGrath had a fruitless trial with Oldham Athletic at the age of fourteen, but progressed to the Republic of Ireland's under-15 and under-16 representative sides before signing for the Albion in February 1988, one of a clutch of young Irishmen on the club's books. He signed pro

forms in December 1989 and developed his game in the reserves as a fiery, hard-tackling midfielder while also playing for his country's youth team. After making his League debut in April 1990 at the age of eighteen Derek became a fringe member of the first-team squad and won his first under-21 cap in May 1990, in a 1–1 draw with Malta.

However, a pelvic problem hindered his progress and in January 1992 he was released after just seven first-team appearances as the club sought to cut its wage-bill. After returning to Ireland the same month, Derek straightaway joined Shamrock Rovers, the country's most successful club, and, having had an fruitless trial with Nottingham Forest in 1992–93, remains an essential element of the Dubliners' side. In 1994, Rovers won the League championship, and he subsequently played in their brief 1994–95 UEFA Cup campaign. Derek's father, Joe McGrath, was national director of coaching with the F.A. of Ireland for several years.

Season	FL	FAC	Total
1989–90	1	0	1
1990–91	1+4	0+1	1+5
Total	2+4	0+1	2+5

McGRATH, JOHN   1972

central defender   Ht 6 0, Wt 12 07   3 apps
full name: John Thomas McGrath
born: Manchester, Lancashire, 23.8.1938
debut: Middlesbrough (h), 2.12.1972 (FL D2)

Despite joining Bolton Wanderers as an amateur from Miles Platting Swifts, it was with Bury that John McGrath signed as a professional in October 1955, and he went on to play 148 League games for the 'Shakers'. In February 1961 the rugged, uncompromising defender was sold to Newcastle United – for a £24,000 fee plus Bob Stokoe – and his career blossomed. At St James's Park, John added 170 League games to his total, quickly gained representative honours as an England under-23 international, and assisted the 'Magpies' to the Second Division title in 1964–65. In February 1968, Southampton paid £30,000 for his transfer and he went on to clock up a further 168 League matches, representing the Football League against the Scottish League on one occasion.

While at The Dell, John came to the Albion on loan in December 1972, in an unsuccessful attempt by manager Pat Saward to limit the worst run of results in the club's history. After hanging up his boots in 1973, John became a coach and youth-team manager at The Dell, but took the manager's post at Port Vale in December 1979 where he remained for three years, leading the Staffordshire side to promotion from Division Four in 1982–83. In January 1984 he was appointed manager at Chester City, and in July 1986 took over the reins at Preston North End, guiding the Fourth Division side to promotion in 1986–87. John remained at Deepdale until resigning in February 1990, but returned to management in October 1991 at Halifax Town where he developed something of a reputation as a football wit. However, with the Yorkshire side near the bottom of the new Third Division and unable to find money for new players, he resigned in December 1992 during the club's last season in the Football League.

Season	FL	Total
1972–73	3	3
Total	3	3

McHALE, RAY   1980–81

midfield   Ht 5 9, Wt 12 06   13 apps
full name: Raymond McHale
born: Sheffield, Yorkshire, 12.8.1950
debut: Wolverhampton Wanderers (h), 16.8.1980 (FL D1)

Ray McHale set out on his career a little later than most modern players, signing as a full pro for Chesterfield at the age of 21 in September 1971 after playing as a part-timer. Born in Sheffield, Ray had represented both the city's and Yorkshire's schools at cricket before taking an apprenticeship as a plasterer, but also played football for the Hillsborough Boys' Club and for Huddersfield Town's youth team.

After 124 Third Division games in three years for the 'Spireites', he joined Halifax Town in October 1974 for two years before moving on to Swindon Town in September 1976, where he became a popular and influential figure over four seasons. With 33 goals in 173 League games for the Wiltshire side, Ray added to his reputation as a classy and consistent midfielder, and was given an opportunity at a higher level when he joined First Division Albion in May 1980 in a £100,000 deal (Andy Rollings and £25,000 making the reverse journey).

However, the leap from the Third Division to the First proved too great, and after just thirteen games he signed for Barnsley for £60,000 in March 1981. Ray was soon on the move again, though, with spells at Sheffield United (August 1982), Bury (on loan February 1983), Swansea City (January 1985) and Rochdale (summer 1986) before joining Scarborough in 1987 for their Football League debut.

Ray scored in Scarborough's first-ever Football League match, and appeared in 25 Fourth Division games that season. On leaving Seamer Road he played for Goole Town and Guiseley (the latter as player-manager), but returned to Scarborough as assistant manager in January 1989. The following November he was promoted to manager, but was dismissed in April 1993, after which he returned to Guiseley as manager and led the Yorkshire club to a treble of Northern Premier League Division One championship, Division One Cup and President's Cup in 1993–94. However, in December 1994 he joined Scarborough for the third time, remaining as manager until March 1995 when he was appointed assistant to Mitch Cook.

In a seventeen-year playing career, Ray amassed 598 League appearances for ten clubs, scoring 88 goals and turning out in all four divisions of the Football League. He didn't enjoy the best of times at the Goldstone, though, and perhaps his most memorable involvement with the Albion came in the celebrated fixture on New Year's Day 1977, a game which was abandoned after 67 minutes because of the pitch conditions. He scored twice in Swindon's 4–0 'victory' that had to be replayed.

Season	FL	FLC	Total
1980–81	9+2	2	11+2
Total	9+2	2	11+2

MACHIN, ERNIE — 1974–76

midfield — Ht 5 8, Wt 11 00 — 72 apps, 1 goal
full name: Ernest Machin
born: Little Hulton, Lancashire, 26.4.1944
debut: Reading (h), 28.8.1974 (FLC R1)

A dominating midfielder with each of his three Football League clubs, Ernie Machin began his career in the Lancashire Combination with Nelson before joining Third Division Coventry City in March 1962. Despite repeated cartilage problems, he was an integral part of the City side which won rapid promotion to the First Division by 1967, and totalled 286 appearances for the 'Sky Blues', many as skipper, before joining Plymouth Argyle in December 1972.

Albion manager Peter Taylor laid out a £30,000 fee for the 30-year-old's experience in August 1974 and immediately installed him as team captain. While asserting himself in 1975–76 as the engine-room of the side, Ernie never quite settled in at the Goldstone – he still lived in Coventry and trained in the Midlands – and was

replaced after 72 appearances by Brian Horton in March 1976 as the club strove – in vain – for promotion. Released at the start of the following campaign at his own request, Ernie returned to Coventry City for a spell as youth-team coach, but then left the game and now works as a delivery driver in Coventry.

In October 1972, Ernie won an important test-case against the F.A. Following a sending-off, he was cleared by a disciplinary committee on the evidence of a television recording, but was then suspended for another offence the committee had spotted on the film — without being charged or being given the chance to offer a defence. The High Court adjudged this to be against the principles of natural justice, and the case led to the establishment of the disciplinary points system.

Season	FL	FAC	FLC	Total
1974–75	28	0	3	31
1975–76	36 (1)	3	2	41 (1)
Total	64 (1)	3	5	72 (1)

McILVENNY, PADDY — 1951–55

right-half — Ht 5 7, Wt 10 08 — 66 apps, 5 goals
full name: Patrick Denis McIlvenny
born: Belfast, Co. Antrim, Northern Ireland, 11.9.1924
debut: Bristol Rovers (h), 5.4.1952 (FL D3(S))

Paddy McIlvenny came from a football-playing family: his father was an Irish international centre-forward with Distillery, Cardiff City, Sheffield Wednesday and Shelbourne, and his brother Bob went on to play for Oldham Athletic, Bury, Southport and Barrow. Paddy himself had a spell as an amateur with Belfast Distillery, but crossed the Irish Sea together with Bob to join the excellent Merthyr Tydfil side which won the Southern League championship in three successive seasons in the late 1940s and the Welsh Cup in 1949. Inevitably the Ulsterman's form came to the attention of nearby Cardiff City who took him on as a pro in May 1950, but he had failed to win a place in their Second Division team before arriving in Hove in July 1951.

An excellent, ball-playing half-back, Paddy understudied Jess Willard in his first season with the club, but the following term he won a regular place in the side, occasionally appearing at inside-right.

However, a broken leg in March 1954 limited his subsequent outings, resulting in a free transfer to Aldershot in December 1955 after he had refused the terms offered by the Albion management. Paddy later moved into the Southern League with Hastings United (where he skippered the side that lost 2–1 to Notts County in the F.A. Cup in 1959) and Dover before taking over as manager of Southwick in the Sussex County League in 1961. On retiring from the game Paddy started a building and decorating business in the town, and also pursued his other sporting love, golf; he captained

the Sussex representative team and, among many other local honours, won the Sussex Seniors championship in 1985, 1986, 1987 and 1993.

Season	FL	FAC	Total
1951–52	1	0	1
1952–53	39 (5)	3	42 (5)
1953–54	18	3	21
1954–55	2	0	2
Total	60 (5)	6	66 (5)

MACKAY, TOMMY — 1925–26

inside-left — Ht 5 8, Wt 10 08 — 1 app
full name: Thomas Mackay
born: Wishaw, Lanarkshire, Scotland
debut: Queen's Park Rangers (h), 24.10.1925 (FL D3(S))

Discovered playing for Wishaw in the Lanarkshire League, where he won fame as a Scotland junior internationalist, Tommy Mackay signed for St Mirren in June 1924 in the face of much competition, and arrived in Hove in July 1925. He had little chance of breaking into an excellent Albion front line, though, and spent most of his time in the reserves; he made just one first-team appearance when Jimmy Hopkins was on Ireland duty. Given a free transfer in May 1926, Tommy returned to Scotland.

Season	FL	Total
1925–26	1	1
Total	1	1

McKENNA, BRIAN 1989–91

goalkeeper Ht 6 0, Wt 13 12 1 app
full name: Brian Francis Joseph McKenna
born: Dublin, Co. Dublin, Republic of Ireland, 30.1.1972
debut: Middlesbrough (h), 27.10.1990 (FL D2)

A regular in Albion's Combination team for two seasons, Brian McKenna made his first-team debut at the age of eighteen in the absence of Perry Digweed and was on receiving the end of a 4–2

home defeat by Middlesbrough. The youngster's obvious nervousness on his big day did little to help his cause, but he was often left exposed by a very poor defensive display.

Discovered playing for the famed Home Farm club in his native city, the Dublin-born goalkeeper had trials with Manchester United and Derby County before coming to the Goldstone. After receiving specialist coaching under former England 'keeper Peter Bonetti, Brian signed professional forms in July 1989 and represented the Republic of Ireland at youth level on numerous occasions, but was released in June 1991 a few

months after Mark Beeney was acquired as reserve goalkeeper. Brian returned to his native country with the University College club in Dublin, and progressed to the national under-21 side. He later moved to Limerick City and had an unsuccessful trial with Bristol City in March 1994. Brian now plays for Dublin-based St Patrick's Athletic.

Season	FL	Total
1990–91	1	1
Total	1	1

McLAFFERTY, MAURICE 1952–54

left-back Ht 5 10, Wt 11 07 22 apps
born: Baillieston, Lanarkshire, Scotland, 7.8.1922
debut: Aldershot (h), 25.10.1952 (FL D3(S))

Maurice McLafferty played for St Mirren after leaving Our Lady's High School in Glasgow, and in 1946 represented the R.A.F. against an F.A. XI. In August 1951 he joined Sheffield United after a month on trial, and had made eighteen Second Division appearances for the 'Blades' when he arrived at the Goldstone for a £1,000 fee in July 1952. The 29-year-old Scot started out in the reserves,

but, following Jack Mansell's transfer to Cardiff City in October 1952, he vied for the left-back spot with Reg Fox and made all his 22 first-team appearances in 1952–53 as a calm and thoughtful performer. When Jimmy Langley joined the staff the following season, Maurice faded from the scene and moved into the Southern League with Dartford in August 1954. He later played for Hastings United, captaining the team to the F.A. Cup first round in 1956, and was player-coach at Newhaven in the Sussex County League for a spell. Maurice worked in

Albion's fund-raising office for some time in the 1960s, and was steward at the Champion House Club in Southwick until his retirement. He now concentrates his energies on another sport: bowls.

Season	FL	FAC	Total
1952–53	21	1	22
Total	21	1	22

McKENNA, HAROLD 1924–25

centre-half Ht 5 11, Wt 11 12 8 apps
born: Yoker, Glasgow, Lanarkshire, Scotland
debut: Southampton (a), 31.1.1925 (FAC R2)

Harold McKenna was signed from the Scottish First Division club Third Lanark in November 1924 in the hope that he would prove a satisfactory replacement for George Coomber, who had received the injury that brought about his retirement a few weeks earlier. Having played for St Mirren (signed June 1919) and Glasgow Rangers (August 1921) before his transfer to Third Lanark in February 1922, Harold was an experienced centre-half upon his arrival at the Goldstone Ground, but he failed to fulfil the club's expectations. Making his debut in a 1–0 defeat at Southampton in a second round F.A. Cup tie, Harold enjoyed a seven-match run in the League side towards the end of 1924–25, but eventually lost his place to Eddie Fuller and returned to the reserves. In September 1925 he moved back to Scotland to join Alloa on a free transfer.

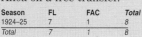

Season	FL	FAC	Total
1924–25	7	1	8
Total	7	1	8

McLEOD, BOB 1947–48

inside-right 1 app
full name: Robert Boyd McLeod
born: Govanhill, Glasgow, Lanarkshire, Scotland, 22.1.1919
debut: Exeter City (h), 15.11.1947 (FL D3(S))

Bob McLeod was a native of Glasgow who began his career with the Aberdeen works side A. Hall & Co. in August 1946, but was playing for an unidentified Glaswegian junior club when he was brought to the Goldstone in November 1947. A two-footed inside-forward, his initial form was impressive and he was drafted into the League side just two weeks after his arrival, but he rapidly faded from the scene and returned to Scotland.

Season	FL	Total
1947–48	1	1
Total	1	1

McNAB, NEIL 1980–83

midfield Ht 5 7, Wt 10 10 115 apps, 5 goals
born: Greenock, Renfrewshire, Scotland, 4.6.1957
debut: Southampton (a), 9.2.1980 (FL D1)

In a League career that lasted more than 20 years in both England and Scotland, Neil McNab never quite achieved the success that his precocious talent had promised, yet he was an influential and inventive midfielder wherever he played. Something of a football prodigy, he won schoolboy honours with Greenock and Scotland, and signed as a professional for his home-town club, Morton, at the age of just fourteen. By making his senior debut in a 5–0 win over Partick Thistle on 14 April 1973 at the age of 15 years 314 days, he is reputed to have been the youngest outfield player ever to appear in the Scottish League.

Neil went on to play for the Scotland youth team, and in February 1974 joined Tottenham Hotspur for £40,000; curiously, though, he was too young to be a professional in England and spent four months on the ground staff as an amateur until his seventeenth birthday. However, the unusual status did not prevent the talented youngster from making his Spurs debut at the age of sixteen, and he went on to play 72 League games in nearly five years at White Hart Lane, gaining a Scotland under-21 cap against Wales in February 1978. He also gained an F.A. Youth Cup winner's medal. In 1978 he was named in the preliminary Scottish squad for the World Cup finals but was omitted from the final 22.

Neil's Tottenham career came to an end with the arrival of the Argentine World Cup-winning stars Osvaldo Ardiles and Ricardo Villa, and in November 1978 he was transferred to Bolton Wanderers for a £250,000 fee. Sixteen months later, in February 1980, Alan Mullery paid £230,000 for the 22-year-old's signature and the little Scot became

an influential figure in First Division Albion's midfield for three years. While rarely posing a direct threat himself – four of his five goals came from penalty kicks – Neil's promptings created many an opportunity for the Brighton strike-force as the club fought to establish itself in the First Division, but his fiery temper led to a number of disciplinary problems. In October 1980 he was suspended for four matches and fined £500 for pushing the referee in a match with Norwich City, and received a similar fine and a two-match ban in February 1982 after fighting with Southampton's Alan Ball in an exhibition 5-a-side match at the Brighton Centre.

In September 1982, after turning down a loan-spell arranged by manager Mike Bailey with Second Division Newcastle United as 'insulting', Neil launched a bitter attack on the club hierarchy and demanded a transfer, despite having five years of a six-year contract to run. When Jimmy Melia took charge in December 1982 he was dropped and moved to Leeds United on a month's loan, but the hard-up Second Division side could ill afford the £65,000 asking-price and he returned to the Goldstone. Playing just one more game for Brighton, he had another loan spell with Portsmouth in March 1983, and was sold to Manchester City in July 1983 for a giveaway £30,000.

It was money well spent by the Maine Road club for Neil went on to play 221 League games for City, assisting them to promotion to Division One in both 1984–85 and 1988–89; he also appeared at Wembley in the losing Full Members Cup final side of 1985–86. In January 1990, Neil joined ambitious Tranmere Rovers for a club-record £125,000 fee and used his experience to good effect in their rapid climb to the Second Division; he also appeared in Rovers' victorious Associate Members (Leyland Daf) Cup final side of 1990. In January 1992, at the age of 34, Neil joined Huddersfield Town on loan and played in eleven matches for the 'Terriers'. Released by Tranmere at the end of 1992–93, he then had brief spells with Ayr United, Darlington and League of Ireland side Derry City before returning to England with Witton Albion in the Conference. Neil then took the post of youth-team coach at Manchester City, but was dismissed in May 1997.

Season	FL	FAC	FLC	Total
1979–80	15+1	0	0	15+1
1980–81	33 (1)	2	2	37 (1)
1981–82	38+2 (3)	3 (1)	3	44+2 (4)
1982–83	14	0	2	16
Total	100+3 (4)	5 (1)	7	112+3 (5)

McNAUGHTON, JOCK   1936–46

left-back   Ht 5 11, Wt 11 00   *14 apps*
full name: John McNaughton
born: Perth, Perthshire, Scotland, 19.1.1912
died: Almondbank, Perthshire, Scotland, 27.6.1986
debut: Newport County (a), 10.9.1936 (FL D3(S))

Jock McNaughton joined Nottingham Forest from Perth Roselea in 1934, and had made fifteen Second Division appearances before coming to the Goldstone during the summer of 1936. However, in the three seasons leading up to the Second World War he had to fight with the consistent Ted Martin for the left-back spot and consequently enjoyed just seven outings in the first eleven. Jock served as an Army P.T. instructor during the conflict and was among those evacuated from the Dunkirk beaches in 1940. He appeared fleetingly in the wartime emergency competitions for the Albion, but didn't resume his career when things returned to normal in 1946 and became a lorry driver in his native Perth.

Season	FL	SSC	Wartime	Total
1936–37	3	0	0	3
1937–38	0	1	0	1
1938–39	3	0	0	3
1940–41	0	0	6	6
1945–46	0	0	1	1
Total	6	1	7	14

McNEIL, MATT   1953–56

half-back   Ht 6 2, Wt 12 05   *60 apps*
full name: Matthew Alexander McNeil
born: Glasgow, Lanarkshire, Scotland, 28.7.1927
died: Glasgow, Lanarkshire, Scotland, 22.4.1977
debut: Queen's Park Rangers (a), 19.8.1953 (FL D3(S))

Signed for a club-record fee, Matt McNeil proved a great disappointment with the Albion and was never able to establish himself in the first team. Although he made 60 appearances for the club, they were spread over three seasons, and only in 1954–55 did he manage to put together a useful run of 31 games.

A 'bean-pole' half-back with a commanding presence, Matt signed for Hibernian in his native Scotland in April 1947 before joining Newcastle United for a £6,400 fee in December 1949. He found it difficult to break into a powerful side, though, and had made only

nine First Division appearances when he was transferred to Second Division Barnsley for £10,500 in August 1951. Matt remained at Oakwell for two years, playing in 69 League games, but the 'Colliers' were relegated to the Third Division (North) in his second season and he signed for the Albion for a record £7,000 fee in August 1953 after a short trial period.

The lofty Scot played in the opening nine fixtures of the 1953–54 campaign, but then lost his place at right-half to Paddy McIlvenny and made only one more appearance as fast-improving Albion finished runners-up to Ipswich Town in the Third Division (South). Matt appeared in all three half-back berths in his limited spells in the first eleven, but, following the conversion of Ken Whitfield into a classy pivot in March 1955, his chances of regaining a place were reduced and he was transferred to rivals Norwich City for £3,000 in March 1956, thus bringing the total spent on his transfers to nearly £27,000. In just over a season at Carrow Road he made 44 league appearances, but was released in July 1957 for an unfruitful spell in the Southern League with Cambridge United. Matt ran a newsagent's business in Norwich before returning to Scotland where he subsequently worked as a sales representative in Kirkintilloch. He later fell victim to cancer and died in Glasgow's Stobhill Hospital at the age of 49.

Season	FL	FAC	Total
1953–54	10	0	10
1954–55	29	5	34
1955–56	14	2	16
Total	53	7	60

McNEILL, IAN   1959–62

inside-forward   Ht 5 7, Wt 10 08   128 apps, 13 goals
full name: Ian McKeand McNeill
born: Baillieston, Glasgow, Lanarkshire, Scotland, 24.2.1932
debut: Lincoln City (h), 21.3.1959 (FL D2)

The brains behind Albion's Second Division side for three years, Ian McNeill was a thoughtful, creative inside-forward who went on to enjoy a successful career in management. The young Glaswegian played in Boys' Brigade football and represented Scotland at youth level after leaving school in Baillieston. A promising career beckoned and Ian received offers from Wolves, Everton and Barnsley, but he preferred to join Aberdeen in 1950. Two of his six years with the club

were spent in Kenya on National Service with the Army, though, and he was regarded as a reserve-team player before signing for Leicester City in March 1956. It was just what the 24-year-old Scot needed, and he became an essential member of City's Second Division championship side in his first full season, 1956–57.

In March 1959, Billy Lane paid £7,000 for Ian's services and he proved an excellent acquisition for Second Division Albion. A wee ball-player in the typically Scottish mould, Ian was also strong in the tackle and had a good burst of speed. He quickly became the play-maker as the team fought to remain in Division Two, and it came as a big surprise when he was put on the transfer list by manager George Curtis at the end of the 1961–62 campaign when Albion were finally relegated. Joining Southend United in July for just £3,000, he returned to Scotland a year later as player-coach of Ross County in the Highland League, and in 1964 played for Dover before rejoining Ross.

Ian subsequently had two spells as manager of Wigan Athletic, in 1968–70 and 1976–81 (separated by a period in charge of Northwich Victoria), and steered the Lancashire club into the Football League in 1978. On leaving Springfield Park in 1981 he was appointed assistant manager at Chelsea, and remained in the post until December 1987 when he took the manager's job with Shrewsbury Town. In April 1990 he joined Millwall as assistant to new manager Bruce Rioch but left the job after just a few months. He linked up again with Rioch at Bolton Wanderers, but left the post of chief scout in November 1996.

Season	FL	FAC	FLC	Total
1958–59	7 (2)	0	0	7 (2)
1959–60	35 (5)	5	0	40 (5)
1960–61	38 (4)	3 (1)	2	43 (5)
1961–62	36 (1)	1	1	38 (1)
Total	116 (12)	9 (1)	3	128 (13)

McNICHOL, JOHNNY   1948–52

inside-forward   Ht 5 10, Wt 11 07   165 apps, 39 goals
full name: John McNichol
born: Kilmarnock, Ayrshire, Scotland, 20.8.1925
debut: Swindon Town (h), 21.8.1948 (FL D3(S))

One of the most influential players ever to have donned a Brighton & Hove Albion shirt, Johnny McNichol was the brains of the side during the late 1940s and early '50s, and was universally admired by all those that saw his thoughtful play. Indeed, long-serving supporters are of the general opinion that the talented Scot was the finest inside-forward to have played for the club since the Second World War. While celebrated as a football craftsman and visionary, he also backed his skills and perception up with a fierce shot and eye for goal, scoring at an admirable rate of almost a goal every fourth game.

Born in Kilmarnock, Johnny played for his local schools' representative side and graduated into Ayrshire junior football with Hurlford United. During the war he served as a mechanic in the Fleet

Air Arm and guested for Inverness Caledonian. He also joined Newcastle United as an amateur, turning professional on his demob in August 1946 upon his 21st birthday. In 1947–48, Johnny was a member of the United reserve team which won the Central League championship, but, feeling he was worthy of first-team football elsewhere, he turned down the terms offered at the end of the season.

He was right, of course. Fortunately for the Albion, manager Don Welsh was successful with a club-record bid of £5,000 in August 1948, and Johnny came to the Goldstone Ground to serve the club admirably for four seasons. Having played a major role in the vast improvement of 1948–49, he topped the scoring charts in both of the following seasons, and was captain in 1951–52 when the club launched an unsuccessful promotion attempt under new manager Billy Lane.

It was obvious that his talent was wasted in the Third Division, though, and a move to a First Division side was considered virtually inevitable. Having reputedly turned down Manchester City, Everton and Huddersfield Town, Johnny chose Chelsea in August 1952 and became manager Ted Drake's first signing at Stamford Bridge. The fee, £12,000 plus inside-forward Jimmy Leadbetter, was a sizeable one at the time and more than double the previous record for an Albion player, but it proved an excellent investment as Johnny appeared in 202 League and Cup games for the 'Pensioners', and was the inspiration behind the team which took the League championship to 'The Bridge' for the first and only time in 1955.

After nearly six years at Chelsea, during which he was unfortunate not to win a Scottish cap, Johnny moved to Crystal Palace in March 1958 for a five-year spell, skippering the team to promotion from Division Four in 1960–61 and clocking up a further 205 League and Cup appearances, mainly at right-back or at right-half. In 1963 he became player-manager of the struggling Tunbridge Wells Rangers club in the Southern League for four years, and, on retiring, spent twelve years in Palace's fund-raising department at Selhurst Park. Johnny then served in a similar capacity at the Goldstone from 1979 until 1992, during which time he introduced the 'Wishbone' scratch-cards. Still fondly remembered by supporters of a certain age, he now lives in retirement in Saltdean.

Season	FL	FAC	Total
1948–49	33 (2)	1	34 (2)
1949–50	38 (9)	1	39 (9)
1950–51	46 (12)	4 (2)	50 (14)
1951–52	41 (14)	1	42 (14)
Total	158 (37)	7 (2)	165 (39)

McNICOL, Bob — 1959–62

right-back   Ht 5 11, Wt 12 00   99 apps, 1 goal
full name: Robert Hugh McNicol
born: Cumbernauld, Dunbartonshire, Scotland, 13.2.1933
died: Tenerife, Canary Islands, Spain, 25.4.1980
debut: Aston Villa (h), 22.8.1959 (FL D2)

Bob McNicol scored just one goal in 99 appearances for the Albion, but it was one of the most famous strikes in the club's history. The 27-year-old Scot will always be remembered for his spectacular, 35-yard goal in the F.A. Cup fourth-round tie with Burnley at the Goldstone in January 1961 which helped Albion take the reigning Football League champions to a replay.

Initially a carpenter by trade, Bob began his soccer career in Dunbartonshire with Vale of Leven and gained a Scottish Junior Cup winner's medal in 1953 when Annbank United were beaten 1–0 in front of a 56,000 Hampden Park crowd. With Hibernian, Airdrieonians and Raith Rovers all vying for his signature, the hard-tackling full-back joined Stirling Albion in July 1953 and continued to turn out for them during National Service with the R.A.F. at Dunfermline; he also skippered the Coastal Command representative team. After three years at Annfield Park, Bob was transferred to Accrington Stanley for £750 in May 1956 and went on to appear in 147 consecutive League and Cup games for the ill-fated Lancashire outfit. Once while at Peel Park, in March 1959, he was selected as goalkeeper, but finished on the wrong end of a 5–2 defeat at Bournemouth! In fact it was a broken toe suffered while guarding the net that caused his impressive run of consecutive matches to come to an end.

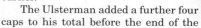

In June 1959, Bob was brought to the South Coast by Albion manager Billy Lane for a £4,700 fee, but his time at the Goldstone was unsettled. Although he was ever-present during the 1960–61 Second Division campaign, he twice requested a transfer and remained on the list for six months from September 1961. After an appeal to the Football League, Albion's £2,500 price tag was deemed to be too extravagant and he left for Gravesend & Northfleet on a free transfer in July 1962.

Bob was particularly impressive during the Kent club's excellent F.A. Cup run of 1962–63. Before going out to Second Division Sunderland in a fourth-round replay, the Southern Leaguers had won 1–0 at Carlisle United in the third, and in October 1963 the 'Cumbrians' offered him a two-month trial. Making one appearance in United's Fourth Division promotion team, he was not kept on at Brunton Park, and joined Stalybridge Celtic in the Cheshire League. Bob subsequently became a newsagent in Church, Lancashire, but later worked for his family's haulage business. In 1980 he was living near Huddersfield when he and his family were killed in an air-crash in Tenerife.

Season	FL	FAC	FLC	Total
1959–60	24	0	0	24
1960–61	42	3 (1)	2	47 (1)
1961–62	27	0	1	28
Total	93	3 (1)	3	99 (1)

McQUARRIE, Andy — 1964–65

inside-right/centre-forward   Ht 6 0, Wt 12 00   3 apps, 1 goal
full name: Andrew McQuarrie
born: Glasgow, Lanarkshire, Scotland, 2.10.1939
debut: Hartlepools United (a), 29.8.1964 (FL D4)

A Scottish junior internationalist with Largs Thistle before joining Albion Rovers in 1961, Andy McQuarrie gained a good reputation as a goalscorer in his only full season with the Coatbridge club. In

November 1962, Chesterfield were tempted to pay £3,000 for his signature, and he netted twelve goals in 38 Fourth Division matches at the Recreation Ground. Albion manager Archie Macaulay brought Andy to the Goldstone Ground in July 1964 for the club's second season as a Fourth Division side, but, with the likes of Bobby Smith, Jack Smith, Jimmy Collins and Bill Cassidy occupying the central berths, he made little impression and was released at the end of the campaign when, together with his team-mate Mike Hennigan, he followed the trail to South Africa to play for Durban United. Andy subsequently had a lengthy spell with Cape Town City, and later played in the Southern League for Gloucester City and Worcester City.

Shortly after his arrival at the Goldstone, Andy saved a 13-year-old girl from drowning in the sea off Hove. Due to play for the reserves that evening, he was mildly reprimanded for breaking club rules which forbade swimming on match days!

Season	FL	FLC	Total
1964–65	2 (1)	1	3 (1)
Total	2 (1)	1	3 (1)

MAGILL, Jimmy — 1965–68

right-back   Ht 5 10, Wt 12 04   56 apps, 1 goal
full name: Edward James Magill
born: Carrickfergus, Co. Antrim, Northern Ireland, 17.5.1939
debut: Swansea Town (h), 30.10.1965 (FL D3)

With 21 full caps for Northern Ireland (and one at under-23 level), Jimmy Magill was a seasoned international when he joined Albion for around £6,000 in October 1965; Archie Macaulay signed the 26-year-old Arsenal defender as the club struggled in the Third Division relegation zone. After joining the Highbury staff from the Ulster club Portadown in May 1959, he had 131 League and Cup games for the 'Gunners' under his belt, and his experience and steadiness at right-back played a big part in helping Albion avoid the drop. Less than two weeks after arriving on the South Coast, Jimmy played in Northern Ireland's 2–1 defeat by England at Wembley to become Albion's first full international since Jack Jenkins played for Wales 39 years earlier.

The Ulsterman added a further four caps to his total before the end of the 1965–66 season, but the following term proved disastrous for the popular full-back as he suffered a series of bad knee injuries which kept him out of the Albion side for long periods and caused him to miss two more internationals. Jimmy subsequently became unsettled and requested a transfer, but there were no offers and further injury problems brought about his premature retirement from the game in October 1968.

A qualified F.A. coach, he left for a career in Denmark – his wife was Danish – as coach to Viborg in January 1969, and subsequently coached FC 1909 Odense and FC Fredrikshaven.

Season	FL	FAC	FLC	Total
1965–66	28	3	0	31
1966–67	15	1	2	18
1967–68	7 (1)	0	0	7 (1)
Total	50 (1)	4	2	56 (1)

MANSELL, JACK   1949–52

left-back   Ht 5 8, Wt 10 03   122 apps, 11 goals
full name: John Mansell
born: Salford, Lancashire, 22.8.1927
debut: Southend United (h), 26.2.1949 (FL D3(S))

Better known as a coach and manager in latter years, Jack Mansell was also a fine left-back and won a host of honours on moving into the First Division for a big fee after 122 appearances for the Albion. His football career took him around the world, but it began in Salford, where he graduated through Salford Boys and Salford Youth Club to an amateur on the Manchester United staff. Greatly influenced by his former teacher, ex-West Bromwich Albion forward Arthur Gale, Jack became an apprentice engineer with Salford Corporation Transport, but was then called up for National Service. He represented the Army and played for the Klagenfurt club while stationed in Austria.

Early in 1949, Jack came to Hove for a lengthy trial period as a winger and made his first-team debut on the left wing against Southend United in February before turning pro in March, but it was on switching to left-back the following season – a move first mooted by Jack Dugnolle in the 'A' team – that he quickly developed into a cultured defender, becoming a regular in the no.3 shirt during 1950–51. Blessed with good pace, Jack was a hard tackler and possessed a fierce shot; he scored eleven goals for the first eleven, four of which came from the penalty spot. Always interested in the tactical side of the game, he earned his preliminary F.A. coaching badge in 1951 and his full badge the following year. He coached County League side Littlehampton while playing for the Albion and also held regular coaching schools at the King Alfred in Hove.

It was always going to be difficult to hold on to a player of his class, and when Cardiff City came up with a £15,000 offer the 25-year-old joined the First Division side in October 1952. Jack didn't enjoy the best of times at Ninian Park, though. He played for the Welsh League XI against the Irish League in September 1953, but requested a transfer and joined Portsmouth two months later for £23,000 where he met with great success. While at Fratton Park, Jack won two England B caps, represented the Football League on two occasions, and was selected for two F.A. tours of South Africa. He also played in the first-ever Football League game staged under floodlights, a 2–0 home defeat by Newcastle United in 1956.

In May 1957, Jack coached Natal's provincial side to Curry Cup success in South Africa. Sadly, his League career was effectively ended by a bout of appendicitis, and in February 1958 he was released by Portsmouth to take the player-manager's job with Eastbourne United, the start of an illustrious career in management. Having steered the Sussex side to Metropolitan League Cup and Sussex Senior Cup

triumphs with an early use of the 4–2–4 system, Jack took the helm of the Amsterdam side Blau Witt in August 1961 on the recommendation of England coach Walter Winterbottom – with whom he had worked as a staff coach at Lilleshall – and led them to third place in the Dutch League.

His subsequent travels filled several passports: coach to Sheffield Wednesday (1962); manager of Telstar (Ijmuiden, Netherlands, 1963); Rotherham United manager (1965); manager of Boston Beacons (U.S.A., 1967); manager of Reading (1969); coach at Queen's Park Rangers (1971, for three weeks); manager of Heracles (Salonika, Greece, 1971); manager of Galatasaray (Istanbul, Turkey, 1973); national coach to Bahrain (1975); manager of the Israeli national team (1980); and manager of Haifa (Israel).

Jack very nearly became manager at the Goldstone, but the job was given to George Curtis just ahead of him in 1961; he was an applicant again in 1963 when Archie Macaulay was the successful candidate. Now living in contented retirement in Seaford – at the 33rd house of his adult life – Jack was also a keen cricketer, keeping wicket for Sussex Club & Ground, and was instrumental in introducing the young Denis Foreman (q.v.) to the County Ground.

Season	FL	FAC	Total
1948–49	9 (1)	0	9 (1)
1949–50	11	1	12
1950–51	39 (1)	4 (2)	43 (3)
1951–52	46 (6)	1	47 (6)
1952–53	11 (1)	0	11 (1)
Total	116 (9)	6 (2)	122 (11)

MANSFIELD, W.   1901–03

centre-forward   2 apps
debut: Wycombe Wanderers (a), 1.4.1902 (SL D2)

Mansfield was a Derby County reserve-team player who arrived on the South Coast with a good reputation to play for the amateur Brighton & Hove Rangers side in March 1901, one of their several recruits from the Midlands. He had just two competitive outings with Rangers, the final and replay of the Brighton Challenge Shield (losing 3–2 to Brighton Athletic at the County Ground), but then remained in Sussex to assist the newly formed Albion as an amateur from 1901 to 1903. Mansfield made just two first-team appearances before leaving the area.

Season	SL	SEL	Total
1901–02	1	0	1
1902–03	0	1	1
Total	1	1	2

MARCH, ZACH   1913–22

outside-left   Ht 5 8, Wt 11 00   97 apps, 9 goals
full name: George Zillwood March
born: Bosham, Sussex, 25.10.1892
died: Bognor Regis, Sussex, 18.9.1994
debut: Croydon Common (h), 19.11.1913 (SA)

Although he played for the Albion either side of the First World War, it was not until the 1990s that 'Zach'* March achieved fame nationally. Sixty years or so after he last wore a pair of football boots in anger, the little winger from Bosham was identified as the oldest surviving ex-professional footballer in the country, and became something of a celebrity before passing away at his Bognor rest home in 1994 just a few weeks before his 102nd birthday.

Discovered playing for Bosham in the West Sussex League, Zach signed amateur forms for the Albion in 1913 and became a professional the

Z. MARCH BRIGHTON + HOVE ALBION F.C. 1920-21

7 players who worked on the buses

Player	Player
Attwood, Arthur	Gordon, Les
Broadhead, Albert	Thompson, Cyril
Carruthers, Jack	Williams, Reg
Cook, Tommy	

following year. Although he made his Southern League debut in April 1914, he didn't win a regular first-team place until the club joined the Third Division in 1920; indeed, he played on the left wing in Albion's first Football League match. A nippy little player – he was an Army sprint champion – Zach left for Portsmouth in May 1922, a club he had appeared for briefly in wartime football while serving with the 4th Battalion of the Royal Sussex Regiment, but made their Third Division team on just four occasions and was not retained in May 1923.

Forsaking the first-class game he joined Chichester City, and skippered the Sussex County League side to successive Sussex Senior Cup finals, lifting the trophy in 1926 when they defeated Eastbourne 5–1 at the Dripping Pan, Lewes. Zach was subsequently presented with an oak occasional table in recognition of his services to the West Sussex club. On retiring from the game he ran the family building firm, based in School Lane, Bosham, for many years.

Season	FL	SL	FAC	SA	SCC	Total
1913–14	0	2	0	4 (1)	0	6 (1)
1914–15	0	15 (2)	0	0	1	16 (2)
1919–20	0	12 (4)	1	0	0	13 (4)
1920–21	24	0	3 (2)	0	0	27 (2)
1921–22	32	0	3	0	0	35
Total	56	29 (6)	7 (2)	4 (1)	1	97 (9)

Note: March acquired the nickname 'Zach' at an early age when his boyhood friends assumed the initial Z stood for Zachariah; he was known by this name throughout his football career. 'Zillwood' was, in fact, his paternal grandmother's name.

MARLOWE, RICKY   1974–76

forward   Ht 6 0, Wt 11 04   29 apps, 7 goals
full name: Richard Ronald Marlowe
born: Edinburgh, Midlothian, Scotland, 10.8.1950
debut: Crystal Palace (h), 17.8.1974 (FL D3)

After starting out with the Bonnyrigg Rose club in Midlothian, Ricky Marlowe spent five months under Brian Clough and Peter Taylor at Derby County, but did not make an appearance in the first team before his transfer to Shrewsbury Town in December 1973 after a month on loan. He first came to the attention of Albion fans in unfortunate circumstances, colliding accidentally with Peter Grummitt in March 1974 and causing the pelvic injury that was to keep the Brighton goalkeeper out for the rest of the season. Four months later Ricky signed for the aforementioned Taylor, by then manager at the Goldstone Ground, and came to Hove principally as a backup striker for regular forwards Fred Binney and Ian Mellor.

Blessed with exceptional pace, Ricky proved quite a sight in full stride with his long, blond locks flowing behind him, but his finishing did not match his speed and he was in and out of the first team during 1974–75. In January 1976 he had two games on loan with Aldershot, and was also experimented with at full-back in Albion's reserves, but he was released in May 1976 to join Wimbledon on a free transfer. Ricky assisted the 'Dons' to the Southern League championship in his first season, on the strength of which they made a successful bid for Football League status, but he left the club during the summer before their debut season of first-class fare began. Ricky was also a keen breeder of greyhounds, perhaps appropriate for one whose most notable asset was his speed.

Season	FL	FAC	FLC	Total
1974–75	24+1 (5)	0+1	2+1 (2)	26+3 (7)
Total	24+1 (5)	0+1	2+1 (2)	26+3 (7)

MARRIOTT, ERNIE   1933–49

right-back   Ht 5 9, Wt 12 02   246 apps, 3 goals
full name: Ernest Marriott
born: Sutton-in-Ashfield, Nottinghamshire, 25.1.1913
died: Hove, Sussex, 6.9.1989
debut: Gillingham (h), 13.4.1935 (FL D3(S))

Ideally built for a full-back, Ernie Marriott was a favourite at Hove for sixteen years, but his time at the Goldstone coincided with the Second World War and his appearances were restricted to 246, 66 of which came during the seven years of emergency competition. One of a number of veterans to return when hostilities ended, he played a big part in steering the Albion through the uncertain years that followed as football struggled to return to normality.

Ernie was playing for the Nottinghamshire side Sutton Junction when he was recommended to the Albion by a Midlands football agent and given a trial with the reserves in April 1933. Signed on amateur forms – because Albion couldn't afford another professional at the time – he returned to Sutton for eight months until being offered pro terms in January 1934. The 21-year-old defender made his first-team debut three months later, but then served a lengthy apprenticeship with the reserves – making more than 120 appearances in the London Combination – before making the right-back berth his own in 1937–38. Ernie missed just two games in 1938–39 as Albion finished third in Division Three (South), but joined the R.A.S.C. shortly after war broke out and later transferred to the Worcestershire Regiment, turning out for Glentoran while stationed in Northern Ireland.

The war took a hefty chunk out of Ernie's football career, but he turned out for the Albion when available, and returned to the Goldstone in 1946 at the age of 33. Skippering the team in 1947–48, he shared a joint testimonial with four other players the following season, but was released in May 1949 to join Tonbridge in the Southern League. Having attended the first F.A. coaching course at Lilleshall, he joined Eastbourne United as player-coach in August 1951 and subsequently returned to the Goldstone as reserve-team coach for two seasons from 1952. Ernie married a local girl in 1937 (Jack Dugnolle performed the duties of best man) and lived in the Hangleton area of Hove for many years until his death in 1989.

Season	FL	FAC	SSC	Wartime	Total
1934–35	6	0	0	0	6
1935–36	8	0	0	0	8
1936–37	4	0	0	0	4
1937–38	33 (1)	4	0	0	37 (1)
1938–39	40	1 (1)	1	0	42 (1)
1939–40	0	0	0	27 (1)	27 (1)
1940–41	0	0	0	2	2
1941–42	0	0	0	4	4
1942–43	0	0	0	3	3
1943–44	0	0	0	15	15
1944–45	0	0	0	1	1
1945–46	0	5	0	14	19
1946–47	36	1	0	0	37
1947–48	36	5	0	0	41
Total	163 (1)	16 (1)	1	66 (1)	246 (3)

MARSDEN, HARRY   1929–34

right-back   Ht 5 8, Wt 11 00   191 apps
full name: Henry Marsden
born: Bentley, Yorkshire, 1902
debut: Gillingham (h), 26.10.1929 (FL D3(S))

Although he played as a left-winger at school, it was as a right-back that Harry Marsden appeared for the Albion with great success, making 191 appearances and missing only a handful of games

through injury. Following an amateur career with Bentley Colliery, Doncaster Rovers and Wombwell (during which time he worked as a cinema projectionist), he turned professional with Nottingham Forest in May 1925 at the age of 23, but appeared in just fourteen Second Division matches in nearly four years at the City Ground before being released to join the Albion in July 1929.

Starting out in the 'Lambs', Harry took over the right-back spot in the first team from Reg Smith in October and went on to prove himself a magnificent defender, retaining his place in the side for five years and striking up good partnerships with left-backs Jack Curran, Frank Brett and Ernie King. In July 1934 he was given a free transfer and left for Gillingham, but returned to his native county to assist York City's reserve team in August 1935.

Season	FL	FAC*	SSC	Total
1929–30	29	6	0	35
1930–31	28	0	0	28
1931–32	42	3	0	45
1932–33*	36	11	0	47
1933–34	29	3	4	36
Total	164	23	4	191

Note: Four of Marsden's 1932–33 F.A. Cup appearances came in the qualifying competition.

MARTIN, DAVE   1997

midfield   *Ht 6 1, Wt 13 02*   *1 app*
born: East Ham, Essex, 25.4.1963
debut: Scunthorpe United (a), 5.4.1997 (FL D3)

Although his Albion career lasted just 79 minutes, Dave Martin extended his influence far beyond the minimal time he spent on the pitch. Renowned as a dressing-room joker, the 33-year-old was brought to the club on loan by Steve Gritt in the hope that his experience, determination and clowning would have a positive influence on his temporary colleagues. The results speak for themselves: just two defeats from the last seven games as Albion pulled off an amazing escape from relegation to the Conference.

Dave began his career at Millwall, with whom he completed an apprenticeship before he turned professional in May 1980. He also won an F.A. Youth Cup winner's medal and England Youth honours before going on to make 163 appearances for the 'Lions'. In 1983 he gained a winners' medal in the Football League Trophy, but moved to Wimbledon in September 1984 for £35,000. The tough midfielder spent just two seasons at Plough Lane, making fifteen appearances as the 'Dons' won promotion to Division One in 1986. Released on a free transfer, he was snapped up by Southend United where he was to spend seven years. Although suffering relegation once, the Essex side won promotion three times in five seasons with Dave playing a major part on each occasion, especially during 1990–91 when he weighed in with an impressive eleven goals as United earned a place in the First Division for the first time in their history.

During 1991–92, though, Dave spent time on loan to Colchester United during their run-in to the Conference title, and also appeared in their winning F.A. Trophy side. In 1993 he finally left Roots Hall for Bristol City, but missed much of his second season with the 'Robins' through injury and played seven games on loan at Northampton Town in February and March 1995. His next stop was Gillingham, where he made 31 appearances as the Kent side won promotion to the Second Division. During 1996–97 he spent a short time with Leyton Orient before rejoining Northampton.

Arriving in Hove just before the transfer deadline in March 1997, Dave looked a basic player, lacking the skill and composure of many of his colleagues, but in a long career in the lower division he has made up for any lack of ability with his motivational and battling qualities.

Season	FL		Total
1996–97	1		1
Total	1		1

MARTIN, JACK   1908–09

centre-forward   *Ht 6 0, Wt 12 07*   *52 apps, 25 goals*
full name: John Martin
born: South Shields, Co. Durham, c. 1885
debut: Southampton (h), 2.9.1908 (SL D1)

A big, bustling centre-forward, Jack Martin found the net consistently for each of his four senior clubs, and scored a total of 97 goals in 229 Football League and Southern League outings. After starting out with Tyne Dock and Kingston Villa, the strapping six-footer signed for Lincoln City in May 1904 where his scoring exploits – 30 goals from 65 Second Division games – were soon noted by Blackburn Rovers who took him into the First Division in May 1906. In two seasons at Ewood Park, Jack scored 27 goals in 62 League and Cup matches, but, amazingly, he was accused of playing too deep and was released to join the Albion in May 1908. He missed just three Southern League games during the 1908–09 season and hit 25 goals in all competitions, including a burst of ten goals in six games in March and April, but he was released again the following month for reasons unknown and moved on to Millwall where, in two seasons, he was once more the leading scorer until he dropped out of the first-class game in May 1911.

Season	SL	FAC	WL	WL Ch.	SCC	Total
1908–09	37 (18)	1	10 (4)	2 (2)	2 (1)	52 (25)
Total	37 (18)	1	10 (4)	2 (2)	2 (1)	52 (25)

MARTIN, NEIL   1975–76

forward   *Ht 6 0, Wt 11 03*   *22 apps, 9 goals*
born: Tranent, East Lothian, Scotland, 20.10.1940
debut: Rotherham United (h), 16.8.1975 (FL D3)

One of the foremost strikers of his day, Neil Martin scored more than 200 goals during his professional career, and cost over £200,000 in transfers. His first senior club was Alloa, whom he joined at the age of eighteen from Tranent Juniors. After a stint with Queen of the South, during which he scored 33 goals in 61 League games, Neil was transferred to Hibernian for £6,000 in July 1963 and built a reputation as an ace marksman with 53 goals in just 65 League matches; he also won a Scottish under-23 cap, had two games for the Scottish League XI, and played twice for the full international team.

In October 1965, Sunderland splashed out £50,000 for Neil's signature and the lanky Scot maintained his remarkable scoring record in the English First Division with 38 goals from 86 outings, also gaining a third cap. A move to Coventry City for £90,000 followed in February 1968, and then to Nottingham Forest for £66,000 in February 1971. Neil remained at the City Ground until July 1975 when he was released by Brian Clough to sign for his former partner, Albion manager Peter Taylor, on a free transfer.

Approaching 35 years of age on his arrival at the Goldstone, Neil was very much a stop-gap partner for Fred Binney but responded with an admirable nine goals from eighteen full appearances. However, after losing his place to new signing Sammy Morgan he fell out with the management and was freed to join arch rivals Crystal Palace in March 1976. Neil later tried his luck in Ireland with St Patrick's Athletic and, after a spell in the U.S.A., became assistant manager of the Arabic Sporting Club in Kuwait under Dave Mackay. In 1981–82 he was appointed general manager at Walsall, after which he returned to Kuwait in a coaching capacity.

Season	FL	FAC	FLC	Total
1975–76	13+4 (8)	3 (1)	2	18+4 (9)
Total	13+4 (8)	3 (1)	2	18+4 (9)

MARTIN, TED   1932–46

left-back   Ht 5 8, Wt 11 00   *237 apps, 4 goals*
full name: Edward Martin
born: Greasley, Nottinghamshire, 15.5.1910
died: Selston, Nottinghamshire, January 1990
debut: Bournemouth & B.A. (h), 5.11.1932 (FL D3(S))

One of a large number of players signed by Albion from the Nottinghamshire area between the wars, Ted Martin made four League appearances in his first season on the South Coast and then had to wait two-and-a-half years for his next, but when he regained a first-team place in September 1935 he subsequently made the left-back slot his own until the outbreak of war in 1939.

Ted started out with Selston Amateurs in the Nottinghamshire League at the age of sixteen and progressed into the Derbyshire Senior League with Heanor Town. He had a trial with West Bromwich Albion during 1931–32 but wasn't offered terms, and joined the professional staff at the Goldstone in September 1932 following a month on trial. Though small in stature for a full-back, he proved as reliable as the biggest and the best, and was ever-present in the 1937–38 Football League season as the club came close to promotion. In April 1939, Albion beat Second Division West Ham United 2–0 in a benefit for the stalwart full-back.

Ted served with the Army in Europe during the war but appeared for the Albion whenever duties allowed, and also guested briefly for Portsmouth and Bournemouth. His last first-team match for the Albion was against Walthamstow Avenue in the F.A. Cup tournament of 1945–46, but he turned out for the reserves the following season until an injury forced his retirement at the age of 36. After leaving the club Ted worked in the electrical department of Pye Hill Colliery for many years.

Season	FL	FAC*	SSC	Wartime	Total
1932–33*	4	1	0	0	5
1933–34	0	0	1	0	1
1935–36	37	5	2	0	44
1936–37	37	1	1	0	39
1937–38	42 (4)	3	0	0	45 (4)
1938–39	35	1	1	0	37
1939–40	0	0	0	33	33
1940–41	0	0	0	16	16
1941–42	0	0	0	5	5
1943–44	0	0	0	6	6
1944–45	0	0	0	3	3
1945–46	0	1	0	2	3
Total	155 (4)	12	5	65	237 (4)

Note: Martin's 1932–33 F.A. Cup appearance came in the qualifying competition.

MASKELL, CRAIG   1996–

forward   Ht 5 10, Wt 11 04   *58 apps, 20 goals*
full name: Craig Dell Maskell
born: Aldershot, Hampshire, 10.4.1968
debut: Brentford (h), 2.3.1996 (FL D2)

With well over 100 League goals to his name, Craig Maskell has proved a regular sharpshooter wherever he has played — except in the top flight. Starting out in his native county as an apprentice with Southampton, the young striker signed professional forms in April 1986 and made his First Division debut as an eighteen-year-old just four days later. He scored his first goal in his second game, but struggled to gain a place in the "Saints'" senior side thereafter and moved to Swindon Town on loan in March 1987 (but made no appearances at the County Ground).

Craig's big break came when he was transferred to Huddersfield Town in the Third Division for £20,000 in May 1988. At Leeds Road he blossomed into a renowned goalscorer, and in his first season he was second only to Steve Bull in the country with 28 League goals. In 1989–90 he was again Town's leading scorer with 21 goals from all competitions, but returned nearer his native patch in the summer of 1990 when he joined Reading, also in Division Three, for £250,000 to equal the Berkshire club's transfer record. In two seasons at Elm Park, Craig hit 26 League goals and led the scorers in 1991–92, but moved on to Swindon Town in 1992 for a £225,000 fee.

Once again, the talented striker led the list in his first season at the County Ground with 23 goals as the Wiltshire side won its way into the Premiership via the play-offs; he scored in each semi-final leg, and also in the memorable 4–3 victory over Leicester City at Wembley. He was also rewarded with selection for the Football League representative XI, scoring twice in a 3–1 victory over the Italian League Serie B at Ashton Gate in October 1992. However, Craig made way for new strikers Andy Mutch and Jan-Aage Fjortoft as the 'Robins' struggled in the Premiership, and he enjoyed only fourteen League outings, scoring three times.

Nevertheless, his first club, Southampton, were prepared to offer him a second chance and signed him for a fee of £250,000 in February 1994. Scoring on his return to The Dell against Liverpool, Craig netted plenty of goals for the "Saints'" reserves, but struggled to make the first team and moved to Bristol City on loan in January 1996.

In March 1996, Albion manager Jimmy Case, looking for an experienced goalscorer, paid £40,000 (rising to £100,000) for the 27-year-old striker. While neither especially fast or strong, Craig has been a poacher of goals throughout his career but struggled along with the rest of the team as the club tumbled to relegation, despite impressing with a couple of spectacular curling strikes from his 'educated' left foot.

But you can rarely keep a proven goalscorer down, and in 1996–97 he finished top scorer for the Albion with sixteen goals, a respectable total considering the club finished next to bottom of Division Three. While appearing as dispirited as anyone with the state of the club during the first half of the season, Craig blossomed under new manager Steve Gritt and hit a hat-trick in the memorable 'Fans United' defeat of Hartlepool United. No one present will forget the 28-year-old's gesture at the end of the match: kissing the match-ball and throwing it into the packed North Stand. On the day fans of all clubs united to demand their football back, Craig Maskell ensured they got it!

Season	FL	FAC	FLC	AMC	Total
1995–96	15 (4)	0	0	0	15 (4)
1996–97	37 (14)	2 (1)	2	2 (1)	43 (16)
Total	52 (18)	2 (1)	2	2 (1)	58 (20)

MASON, TOMMY 1974–76

midfield Ht 5 3, Wt 10 04 28 apps, 2 goals
full name: Thomas Herbert Andrew Mason
born: Buxton, Derbyshire, 20.2.1953
debut: AFC Bournemouth (a), 21.9.1974 (FL D3)

A pint-sized bundle of energy, Tommy Mason joined Derby County as an apprentice when he left school. He failed to make a single senior appearance in three years with the 'Rams', though, but must have made an impression on County's assistant manager Peter Taylor for, when the latter became Albion manager, he signed the enthusiastic midfielder in a joint deal with Jim Walker worth £25,000 in September 1974. Tommy totalled 28 games for the club, but he was not a great success in a struggling side and was released in May 1976 to join Horsham in the Isthmian League. He had an unsuccessful trial period with Portsmouth in October 1977, during which he appeared against Albion's reserves, and later played for Carshalton Athletic.

Season	FL	FAC	Total
1974–75	23+2 (2)	3	26+2 (2)
Total	23+2 (2)	3	26+2 (2)

MASSIMO, FRANCO 1984–87

forward 2 apps
born: Horsham, Sussex, 23.9.1968
debut: Shrewsbury Town (h), 12.4.1986 (FL D2)

R aised in Horsham by Italian parents, Franco Massimo's principal asset was sheer speed: he set a new record when winning the Sussex Schools 100-metre title and came fourth in the national championships. In 1984 he first appeared in Albion's youth team, and within a year, while still an associate schoolboy, was playing for the reserves. Franco became an apprentice in May 1985 and made his solitary League appearance in April 1986, coming on as a second-half substitute for Alan Biley. The following season he signed as a

non-contract professional, but a chronic inflammation of his pelvic bones, which seriously inhibited his running, cruelly forced the young speedster to take a rest from the game, effectively ending his professional career. The unfortunate Franco was released to become something of a nomad, playing locally for Southwick, Crawley Town (for whom he scored a hat-trick on his debut), Worthing, Horsham, Dorking, Three Bridges, Steyning Town and Horsham Y.M.C.A. He later joined Storrington where he was appointed joint manager with his brother Tony, but resigned in June 1994 after two seasons in charge of the Sussex County League club.

Season	FL	FLC	Total
1985–86	0+1	0	0+1
1986–87	0	0+1	0+1
Total	0+1	0+1	0+2

MATTHEWS, CHARLIE 1912–14

right-half 12 apps, 1 goal
full name: Charles Matthews
born: Newhaven, Sussex, 1889
died: in action, France, 19.8.1916
debut: Bristol Rovers (a), 20.4.1912 (SL D1)

C harlie Matthews played for Horsham in the West Sussex Senior League and had represented Sussex before joining the Albion in December 1911. After playing what turned out to be his only Southern League game as an amateur at Bristol Rovers, the Newhaven-born half-back was offered a professional engagement in September 1912, but his subsequent first-team outings were confined to the subsidiary Southern Alliance and Southern Charity Cup competitions. A regular in the reserves for two seasons until answering the call to arms in 1914, Charlie lost his life on the Somme while serving as a private with the Royal Sussex Regiment, one of almost 2,000 men of the 2nd Battalion lost during the Great War.

Season	SL	SA	SCC	Total
1911–12	1	0	0	1
1912–13	0	3	5 (1)	8 (1)
1913–14	0	3	0	3
Total	1	6	5 (1)	12 (1)

MAY, LARRY 1988–89

centre-half Ht 6 1, Wt 12 00 25 apps, 3 goals
full name: Lawrence Charles May
born: Sutton Coldfield, Warwickshire, 26.12.1958
debut: Leeds United (h), 1.10.1988 (FL D2)

A dominating central defender for his four League clubs, Larry May started out as a Leicester City apprentice and turned professional in September 1976. In seven seasons as a pro at Filbert Street, he made 187 League appearances and appeared in two Second Division promotion sides, being ever-present as City carried off the championship of Division Two in 1979–80. He also spent the summer of 1978 playing for the New England Teamen in the North American Soccer League. In August 1983, Larry was transferred to Barnsley for £110,000, then a record for the Yorkshire club, but moved eleven miles down the A61 to Hillsborough in February 1987 to make 31 First Division appearances for Sheffield Wednesday.

With Albion in dire trouble at the foot of Division Two in September 1988 – the first eight games were lost – Barry Lloyd looked to the commanding 29-year-old for salvation and persuaded him, after prolonged negotiation, to come to the Goldstone for £200,000. It was a wise move: Larry had an immediate steadying effect as Albion defeated Leeds United 2–1, and brought some much-needed experience into the heart of the defence. Strong in the air and on the ground, he played a major role as the club fought its way to the safety of nineteenth place. Unfortunately, his Goldstone career was brought

to a premature close after just 25 outings because of a bad knee injury sustained in a collision with team-mate Paul Wood against Manchester City in April 1989.

Already the holder of a full F.A. coaching badge, Larry joined Albion's backroom staff as reserve-team coach (and occasionally turned out for the second eleven in emergencies). Helping to nurture the club's promising youngsters in the early 1990s, he was a popular member of staff, but was a victim of a drastic economy drive in November 1993 which was considered necessary to safeguard the very existence of the Albion. Larry then assisted with coaching at the North Sussex Football Academy near Horsham and with Ringmer in the Sussex County League before joining Portsmouth as youth-team coach in February 1995, but he left Fratton Park early in 1997 to concentrate on soccer schools for youngsters and became involved in the Crawley Town/Crawley Borough Council Football in the Community scheme.

Season	FL	FAC	Total
1988–89	24 (3)	1	25 (3)
Total	24 (3)	1	25 (3)

MAYBANK, TEDDY   1977–79

forward   Ht 5 10, Wt 10 12   73 apps, 18 goals
full name: Edward Glen Maybank
born: Lambeth, London, 11.10.1956
debut: Blackburn Rovers (h), 26.11.1977 (FL D2)

Teddy Maybank first appeared at the Goldstone in September 1971 when he played for South London Schools against Brighton Boys, and he seemed set for a fine career when he signed as a professional for Chelsea in February 1974 following an apprenticeship. The fair-haired forward went on to score six goals in 28 First Division matches for the London side, but, following a successful loan-spell with nearby Fulham in November 1976 (in which he netted three times in four games), Teddy joined the 'Cottagers' for £65,000 in March 1977.

Just eight months later, in November 1977, Albion manager Alan Mullery offered a staggering £238,000 for his services. It was a huge fee for Brighton, more than twice the previous record, but Teddy, playing a traditional centre-forward role in place of the popular Ian Mellor, got off to a cracking start by scoring in his first two

matches. The Goldstone fans, perhaps justifiably, expected wonders, but the huge fee proved to be a millstone around Teddy's neck as things started to go wrong and the supporters started to criticise him. While lacking the skill expected of a record buy, he was also dogged with cartilage problems and missed the climax to the 1977–78 campaign, but started 35 of the 42 League matches the successful following season when Albion won promotion to Division One. Indeed, he had the honour of scoring the club's first-ever goal in the top flight, but played in only eleven First Division games before being dropped in favour of new acquisition Ray Clarke.

Teddy then fell out with his manager and returned to Fulham, where he had been a great favourite, for £150,000 in December 1979. He was soon on the move again, though, leaving for PSV Eindhoven in August 1980, but was forced to retire from the professional game because of a bad injury after only a handful of matches in the Netherlands. On his subsequent return to the Brighton area he played briefly for Whitehawk, Shoreham and Wick in the Sussex County League.

One of the most heavily criticised players of recent years, Teddy enjoyed his finest hour at the Goldstone on Boxing Day 1978 when he scored a hat-trick against Cardiff City, a feat which helped stem some of the abuse. Still living locally, he ran a squash-court repair business until 1996 and turned out for Corals in the Sussex Sunday League for many years. Teddy also appeared as a contestant on the television show 'Blind Date'.

Season	FL	FAC	FLC	Total
1977–78	16 (4)	1	0	17 (4)
1978–79	35+2 (10)	1	4 (1)	40+2 (11)
1979–80	11 (2)	0	3 (1)	14 (3)
Total	62+2 (16)	2	7 (2)	71+2 (18)

MAYO, KERRY   1995–

midfield   Ht 5 10, Wt 13 01   27 apps
born: Cuckfield, Sussex, 21.9.1977
debut: Carlisle United (h), 23.11.1996 (FL D3)

Kerry Mayo nearly went down in Albion history as the man who lost the club's Football League status. Fortunately, his own goal in the relegation decider at Hereford was equalised by Robbie Reinelt and the day ended happily for the nineteen-year-old midfielder from Peacehaven.

Yet few people at the start of the season would have predicted that Kerry would be involved with the first team at the death. After playing for Brighton and Sussex Schools, and attending the club's Worthing School of Excellence, he completed a two-year apprenticeship at the Goldstone but was given only a six-month professional contract in 1996. However, he forced his way into the side as Jason Peake fell from favour in November, and the flame-haired youngster rapidly won praise for his enthusiasm, tackling and stamina. Able to play in midfield and at full-back, Kerry was rewarded with a new contract and established himself as a first-team regular, enjoying a rousing climax to his first campaign and, at times, looking like a future Albion captain.

Season	FL	FAC	AMC	Total
1996–97	22+2	0+1	1+1	23+4
Total	22+2	0+1	1+1	23+4

MEADE, RAPHAEL   1991–92 & 1994

striker   Ht 5 10, Wt 11 09   49 apps, 12 goals
full name: Raphael Joseph Meade
born: Islington, London, 22.11.1962
debut: Wolverhampton Wanderers (h), 31.8.1991 (FL D2)

Raphael Meade enjoyed the classic career of a young Arsenal player: Islington Boys while at Tollington Park School, then schoolboy forms and an apprenticeship with the Highbury club before signing as a professional in June 1980. Although competition was fierce for the striking roles, young Raphael appeared in 41 First Division matches (16 as substitute) and registered a highly creditable tally of fourteen goals, but he left north London under a cloud and moved to the Continent in the summer of 1985 with Sporting Lisbon.

After three years and 25 League games in Portugal, Raphael sought to resume his British career and joined Dundee United in the summer of 1988, scoring four goals in eleven Scottish Premier Division matches before moving on to Luton Town in March 1989. The well-built striker then pursued a somewhat nomadic career: after a single appearance in Albion's reserve team (March 1990), he had a trial with Ipswich Town (also March 1990); a five-match, non-contract spell with Plymouth Argyle (from February 1991); an outing with Millwall's reserves; and a sojourn in Denmark with OB Odense.

In August 1991, Raph returned to the Goldstone as a free agent and was signed on a short-term contract following an impressive display in the reserves. He was soon called up for the first team and retained his place, scoring twelve times as Albion were tamely relegated. Although capable of great skill and spectacular goals, he was unable to produce the goods consistently and it was no surprise when he was freed in May 1992 (but remained to play in the pre-season friendlies).

Raphael then turned out for Fulham reserves early in 1992–93, and in March 1993 went to Hong Kong to play for the Ernest Borel club. On returning to the U.K. he joined Dover Athletic, but returned to the Goldstone in January 1994 to help out the reserves, scoring the only goal against Peacehaven & Telscombe in the Sussex Senior Cup final. In 1994–95 he made a further three League appearances as substitute before being released in November 1994, but continued to train with the club and play for the reserves when required until joining Southwick in the County League for a brief spell. Raphael moved on to Crawley Town in January 1995 where he top-scored the following term, but he was freed late in 1996 to spend the rest of the 1996–97 season with Sittingbourne before being released once more.

Season	FL	FAC	FLC	FMC	Total
1991–92	35+5 (9)	2 (2)	2 (1)	2	41+5 (12)
1994–95	0+3	0	0	0	0+3
Total	35+8 (9)	2 (2)	2 (1)	2	41+8 (12)

MEDHURST, Harry   1952–53

goalkeeper   14 apps
full name: Harry Edward P. Medhurst
born: Byfleet, Surrey, 5.2.1916
died: Woking, Surrey, 8.4.1984
debut: Coventry City (a), 15.11.1952 (FL D3(S))

An amateur with Woking in the Isthmian League for three years, Harry Medhurst turned professional with West Ham United in November 1936 and remained at Upton Park for ten years. Making his debut in December 1938, he turned out regularly for the 'Hammers' during the war while serving as a physical training instructor with the Essex Regiment and Royal Artillery, and also guested briefly for Sheffield Wednesday in the emergency competitions. In December 1946, Harry was exchanged for Chelsea's Joe Payne and went on to become tremendously popular at 'The Bridge', appearing in 157 League and Cup games. After six years with the 'Pensioners' he arrived at the Goldstone in November 1952 at the age of 36 and performed well for fourteen games before giving way to Eric Gill. At the end of the season Harry hung up his gloves and returned to Chelsea where he served as assistant trainer, head trainer and physio (a post also held by

his son Norman 1983–88) until his retirement in 1975. Harry was also a good enough batsman to appear in the Surrey second eleven.

Season	FL	FAC	Total
1952–53	12	2	14
Total	12	2	14

MEE, Gordon   1934–45

goalkeeper   Ht 5 11, Wt 11 10   134 apps
born: Belper, Derbyshire, 13.5.1913
died: Hove, Sussex, 9.1.1975
debut: Queen's Park Rangers (a), 12.9.1935 (FL D3(S))

A fine all-round sportsman who also excelled at swimming, cricket, golf, tennis, athletics and bowls, Gordon Mee started out with the Pottery Wesleyans club in Belper before progressing to Matlock Town in the Central Combination. Arriving in Hove as a trialist in December 1934, he was offered professional terms a month later, but, with the consistent Charlie Thomson wearing the jersey, his chances of a first-team place were limited in the five seasons before the war. Nevertheless, Gordon rendered loyal service and made around 160 appearances in the reserves in addition to 41 League outings. Indeed, Albion were fortunate to have a player of his ability as second-string goalkeeper.

When hostilities commenced he joined the Police Reserve, but continued to play regularly for the club in the initial three seasons of emergency fare – occasionally performing an outfield role – before his duties took him away from the area. Gordon totalled 93 appearances for the Albion during the war before moving to Watford in October 1945, where he was first choice between the posts before retiring on the completion of the final season of wartime competition in 1946.

Season	FL	Wartime	Total
1935–36	7	0	7
1936–37	3	0	3
1937–38	15	0	15
1938–39	16	0	16
1939–40	0	25	25
1940–41	0	27	27
1941–42	0	33	33
1942–43	0	5	5
1943–44	0	3	3
Total	41	93	134

MELLON, Jimmy   1926–27

right-half   Ht 5 9, Wt 11 07   1 app
full name: James Mellon
born: Kelvinside, Glasgow, Lanarkshire, Scotland, 22.12.1902
debut: Norwich City (h), 6.10.1926 (FL D3(S))

Jimmy Mellon joined Hibernian from Uddingston Juniors in June 1924 and spent two seasons at Easter Road before coming to the Goldstone in August 1926. The 23-year-old right-half made his Albion debut as a stand-in for Reg Wilkinson in a 3–2 victory over Norwich City in October, but it was to be his only first-team appearance as the popular Wilkinson didn't miss another match that season. Jimmy performed consistently well in the reserves, but had no realistic chance of displacing Wilkinson and was released at the end of the season when he is believed to have returned to Scotland.

Season	FL	Total
1926–27	1	1
Total	1	1

MELLOR, IAN — 1974–78

forward   Ht 6 1, Wt 10 12   150 apps, 35 goals
born: Wythenshawe, Cheshire, 19.2.1950
debut: Crystal Palace (h), 17.8.1974 (FL D3)

After a rocky start to his Albion career, Ian Mellor proved to be the perfect foil for the record-breaking Peter Ward during the unforgettable 1976–77 promotion campaign, contributing twelve goals to the cause himself. Although he was subsequently replaced as the club battled to win a second successive promotion, he remained a very popular figure at the Goldstone and has returned on several occasions to appear in testimonial matches.

Nicknamed 'Spider' by the Hove crowd because of his long legs, Ian was working as a postman and playing for Wythenshawe Amateurs when he joined the staff at Manchester City, signing as a professional in December 1969. After 40 First Division appearances at Maine Road he was transferred to Norwich City in March 1973 for £65,000 and had scored nine goals in 43 League and Cup outings on the left wing when Brian Clough and Peter Taylor paid a club-record £40,000 for him in May 1974.

Displaying delicate ball-skills for such a lanky player, Ian scored five goals in his first game for the Albion, an end-of-season friendly in Majorca, and followed up by netting the winner against Crystal Palace on his League debut, but he failed to settle – he was suspended by the club and made available for transfer – until a burst of six goals in eleven games during 1975–76 saw him re-established in the first team. The following season he was paired with Peter Ward and the new strike-force took Albion to promotion.

Now firmly established as a crowd favourite, Ian started the following Second Division campaign in the no.9 shirt but lost his place to the new record signing, Teddy Maybank, in November 1977 and made only one more appearance before leaving the Goldstone to join Chester in February 1978 for £30,000. After 40 League games at Sealand Road he moved on to Sheffield Wednesday in June 1979 where he added a further 70 League outings to his total before joining Bradford City on a free transfer in May 1982. Ian finished his career with spells at Tsun Wan (Hong Kong), Worksop, Matlock Town and Gainsborough Trinity while working as an agent for the Puma sportswear company. He now works as the Manchester-based commercial executive with the Professional Footballers' Association.

Season	FL	FAC	FLC	Total
1974–75	26+2 (6)	3 (1)	4	33+2 (7)
1975–76	33+1 (9)	3	1+1	37+2 (9)
1976–77	41+2 (12)	3 (2)	3+2 (1)	47+4 (15)
1977–78	16+1 (4)	1+1	6	23+2 (4)
Total	116+6 (31)	10+1 (3)	14+3 (1)	140+10 (35)

MELLORS, MARK — 1904–06

goalkeeper   Ht 6 1, Wt 13 02   83 apps
born: Old Basford, Nottingham, Nottinghamshire, 30.4.1880
died: Wharfedale, Yorkshire, 20.3.1961
debut: New Brompton (a), 3.9.1904 (SL D1)

One of several splendid goalkeepers to serve the Albion in their early days, Mark Mellors missed just five games in two years of Southern League competition after arriving at the Goldstone from Notts County in May 1904. A huge man, he had a trial with Nottingham Forest while playing for Carrington in the Nottinghamshire Amateur League, but was not offered terms and threw in his lot with Bulwell United until he was signed as an amateur by Notts County in November 1902.

Soon turning professional, he had made nine First Division appearances for County before signing for the Albion in 1904 at the age of 24. Blessed with a quiet and gentlemanly disposition, Mark

was popular with players and fans alike, and when he married in 1905 the supporters opened a fund to buy him a wedding gift. His wonderful displays attracted several Football League clubs, and in May 1906 he was transferred to Sheffield United for a £100 fee (paid to Notts County as they still held his Football League registration).

Competition was fierce at Bramall Lane, though, and with the admirable Joe Lievesley a fixture between the posts Mark's opportunities were limited to a single First Division appearance in three years with the 'Blades'. In April 1909 he was transferred to Bradford City for £350 where he remained until the outbreak of the Great War, gaining an F.A. Cup winner's medal in 1911 when City surprisingly beat red-hot favourites Newcastle United in a replay; the goalkeeper performed heroically, frustrating the famed United forwards in both matches. Following his retirement Mark became a businessman in Bradford.

Season	SL	FAC	UL	Total
1904–05	32	5	0	37
1905–06	31	5	10	46
Total	63	10	10	83

MENDHAM, C. J. — 1901–02

outside-right   5 apps, 7 goals
debut: Brighton Athletic (h), 21.9.1901 (FAC Prelim.)

Signed in July 1901, Mendham was one of the Albion's first professionals and is believed to have arrived from Glossop. He netted seven goals in his five League and Cup outings in 1901–02, including two goals on three occasions, but had to be make do with being Bert Baker's deputy on the right wing during much of that first season and departed before the end of the campaign.

Season	SL	FAC	Total
1901–02	3 (4)	2 (3)	5 (7)
Total	3 (4)	2 (3)	5 (7)

MEOLA, TONY — 1990

goalkeeper   Ht 6 1, Wt 14 09   2 apps
full name: Antonio Michael Meola
born: Belleville, New Jersey, U.S.A., 21.2.1969
debut: Wolverhampton Wanderers (h), 1.9.1990 (FL D2)

U.S.A. international goalkeeper Tony Meola arrived at the Goldstone in August 1990 shortly after appearing in the World Cup final series in Italy, and filled in unconventionally but successfully when regular 'keeper Perry Digweed was unexpectedly sidelined. Raised by Italian parents – his father Vincent played in the Italian League with Avellino in the early 1960s – in the New Jersey town of Kearny, a hot-bed of soccer in an otherwise 'unconverted' nation, Tony was voted All-American goalkeeper by a national magazine while at the local high school. He went on to star for both the University of Virginia (where he won the Hermann Trophy for best college player and also played baseball) and the Missouri Athletic Club, and after

starring for the U.S.A. in the World Under-20 Championships in Chile in 1987, won his first full cap in June 1988 at the age of nineteen, a 1–0 defeat by Ecuador in Albuquerque. Having left college early to pursue a professional career, Tony was drafted as a centre-field by the New York Yankees and had to choose between baseball and soccer; he plumped for the latter and established himself as the American no.1 late in 1989 to play a major part in the States' successful qualification for Italia '90.

After conceding eight goals in the U.S.A.'s three games in the finals, it looked as though the extrovert American was about to join Sporting Lisbon, but instead he chose England to further his career. After a brief sojourn at the Goldstone, Tony moved on to Watford for an unsuccessful trial – he played in just one ZDS Full Members Cup match – before returning to his native land with Fort Lauderdale Strikers. However, following the collapse of organised leagues in the U.S.A., he played his football only with the national squad preparing for the 1994 World Cup and was outstanding in his country's 2–0 defeat of England in June 1993; he also spent time acting and appeared in a film, *The Desperate Trail*.

In 1994, Tony captained the U.S.A. in the World Cup finals and performed well as the hosts reached the quarter-finals, winning his 90th cap, but as soon as the tournament had finished he signed for the New York Jets American football team as a punter. With hopes high for a continuing upsurge of interest in American soccer, it was a bitter blow for the best-known player in the States to 'defect', but he was soon released by the Jets. In 1995 he led the Long Island Rough Riders to the championship of the U.S. Indoor Soccer League, before joining the New York/New Jersey MetroStars for the inaugural 1996 season of the Major Soccer League.

Season	FL	FLC	Total
1990–91	1	1	2
Total	1	1	2

Aberdeen in 1920 where he enjoyed the most successful part of his career with 126 League and Cup outings over a three-season spell. In June 1923 he returned to England for a season with Southend United, appearing in 30 Third Division (South) matches, after which he was released to join Dumbarton in September 1924.

Season	SL	FAC	SA	SCC	Total
1912–13	1	1	3 (1)	5	10 (1)
Total	1	1	3 (1)	5	10 (1)

MIDDLETON, Harry   1909–11

left-half   38 apps, 5 goals
full name: Henry Middleton
born: Newcastle upon Tyne, Northumberland
debut: Portsmouth (a), 1.9.1909 (SL D1)

Harry Middleton was playing for the County Durham club Hamsterley when he signed amateur forms for Newcastle United in July 1906. Offered professional terms the following February, he

played only a reserve-team role at St James's Park for three seasons before being released to join the Albion in May 1909. Drafted straight into the first team at left-half, Harry made a major contribution to the Southern League championship campaign of 1909–10, especially when moved up front in January to take over from the suspended 'Bullet' Jones; he scored some crucial goals in the run-in to the title. However, the Geordie half-back lost his place to Jack Haworth the following term and moved on to Watford (managed by former Albion skipper Harry Kent) in February 1911. On leaving the Hertfordshire side in June 1912, Harry joined Darlington and assisted the 'Quakers' to the North Eastern League championship in 1912–13. In August 1913 he moved on to Blyth Spartans, but was not a great success and was released in January 1914.

Season	SL	FAC	SCC	Total
1909–10	33 (5)	1	4	38 (5)
Total	33 (5)	1	4	38 (5)

MIDDLETON, Billy   1912–13

outside-right   10 apps, 1 goal
full name: William Middleton
born: Hetton-le-Hole, Co. Durham
debut: Croydon Common (h), 9.10.1912 (SA)

Billy Middleton arrived at the Goldstone from North Eastern League side Newcastle City during the summer of 1912 with

the reputation of a promising young winger, but, despite playing consistently well in the reserves, he appeared in the Southern League side just once. He did, however, play in the excellent goal-less draw with First Division Everton in the second round of the F.A. Cup, and also appeared in the final of the Southern Charity Cup in which the Albion side – mostly reserves – were defeated 4–1 after extra time by Queen's Park Rangers. Released in May 1913, Billy migrated to Scotland to join Ayr United, and was transferred to

MILLAR, Arthur   1904–05

wing-half   Ht 5 10, Wt 13 00   36 apps, 1 goal
full name: Arthur Thomson Millar
born: Rossie Island, Montrose, Angus, Scotland, 26.1.1877
debut: Wellingborough Town (a), 17.9.1904 (SL D1)

Arthur Millar played for his local club, Montrose, from the age of sixteen and carved out a name for himself so rapidly that he was signed by Millwall Athletic during the summer of 1896 at the age of nineteen. The well-built Scot enjoyed an excellent five-year stint at East Ferry Road (the club were then playing at Millwall on the Isle of Dogs) and mustered well over 100 Southern League appearances. In his time with the 'Dockers', which included a second spell in 1903–04, the club won the Southern League, the United League (twice), the Southern District Combination, the London League and the Southern Charity Cup. In September 1900 he was rewarded for his considerable contribution with a benefit match against Tottenham Hotspur.

Arthur joined Midland giants Aston Villa in April 1901 – he had been an inspirational skipper when Millwall defeated Villa in an F.A. Cup quarter-final second replay in March 1900 – but life proved more difficult in the First Division and he played in only ten League matches before returning to Millwall in May 1903 after a period on loan. Arriving at the Goldstone in May 1904, he alternated between the two wing-half berths during his one season on the South Coast and proved particularly adept at breaking up opposing combinations. A hard, resolute defender, Arthur left the Albion in May 1905 and is thought to have returned to Scotland.

Season	SL	FAC	Total
1904–05	31	5 (1)	36 (1)
Total	31	5 (1)	36 (1)

MILLARD, A.   1903

inside-right   *1 app*
debut: West Ham United (a), 21.2.1903 (SEL)

Millard was one of the numerous amateurs who were given trials during the 1902–03 season, playing in the South Eastern League fixture at West Ham which ended in a crushing 5–0 defeat. He obviously failed to impress as his services were not subsequently called upon.

Season	SEL	Total
1902–03	1	1
Total	1	1

MILLER, ALLY   1962

outside-left   Ht 5 8, Wt 10 12   *1 app*
full name: James Alistair Williamson Miller
born: Govan, Glasgow, Lanarkshire, Scotland, 24.1.1936
debut: Derby County (a), 28.4.1962 (FL D2)

Ally Miller began his senior career in the Scottish League with the Glasgow club Third Lanark, but was transferred to St Mirren in 1956 for whom he went on to score over 55 goals in 160 Scottish League outings. The highlight of a six-year spell in Paisley came when he scored the second goal in a 3–1 defeat of Aberdeen in the 1959 Scottish Cup final. In April 1962, Ally arrived at the Goldstone on trial and played in the last Second Division game of the season, but he failed to impress in a relegated side. Three weeks later he joined Norwich City for two seasons before moving back into the Scottish League with Berwick Rangers, Dumbarton and Hamilton Academical.

Season	FL	Total
1961–62	1	1
Total	1	1

MILLER, BILL   1910–22

inside-forward   *112 apps, 52 goals*
full name: William Miller
born: Alnwick, Northumberland, 1890
debut: Watford (a), 10.9.1910 (SL D1)

Signed from Ryhope Villa of the Wearside League at the age of 20 during the summer of 1910, Bill 'Dusty' Miller remained at the Goldstone for a war-interrupted twelve years. Yet, despite his quite outstanding scoring feats, he was never considered a first-team regular. He never let the side down, scoring 52 goals in 112 first-team games, but was invariably dropped when someone else came on the scene. But such was his scoring prowess that he bagged more than 190 goals in all matches – including the reserves – for the Albion, a total bettered only by Bert Stephens in the club's history.

Top-scorer for the first team with 20 goals in 1913–14 (despite playing in only 31 of the 59 competitive matches), Bill scored prolifically for the second eleven, particularly in 1911–12 when he netted 36 times (including two four-goal hauls and two hat-tricks) as the 'Lambs' finished the season as runners-up to Chelsea in the South Eastern League. Selected for the South Eastern League representative side on three occasions, Bill guested briefly for Watford during the First World War, and played on into the Third Division era until his release in May 1922 when he was granted a permit to play for Hove; he later appeared for Redhill and Shoreham (although Redhill were fined £1 by the F.A. for fielding Bill when his permit allowed him to play only for Hove). A year after leaving the Goldstone he was granted a benefit match, a joint affair with Bert Longstaff. Bill married a local girl in 1913 – goalkeeper Bob Whiting performed the duties of best man – and settled in the Brighton area. During the Great War he guested briefly for Arsenal and Portsmouth while serving with the Army.

Season	FL	SL	FAC	SA	SCC	Total
1910–11	0	4 (1)	0	0	0	4 (1)
1911–12	0	2	0	0	0	2
1912–13	0	19 (7)	1	6 (5)	3	29 (12)
1913–14	0	21 (13)	4 (1)	6 (6)	0	31 (20)
1914–15	0	17 (10)	0	0	1	18 (10)
1919–20	0	21 (9)	0	0	0	21 (9)
1920–21	7	0	0	0	0	7
Total	7	84 (40)	5 (1)	12 (11)	4	112 (52)

MINTON, JEFF   1994–

midfield   Ht 5 6, Wt 11 10   *121 apps, 16 goals*
full name: Jeffrey Simon Thompson-Minton
born: Hackney, London, 28.12.1973
debut: Swansea City (a), 13.8.1994 (FL D2)

Although standing just 5' 6" tall, Jeff Minton more than makes up for his lack of height with his work-rate, eagerness to get forward, and spring-heeled ability to win the ball in the air. Since arriving at the Goldstone Ground in 1994, he has yet to produce the consistency which would make him outstanding, but he has shown great potential and could mature into the finished article before long.

Having represented Hackney and Tower Hamlets at schools level, Jeff joined his favourite club, Tottenham Hotspur, as a trainee in July 1990 at the age of sixteen. A graduate of the F.A.'s National School of Excellence at Lilleshall, he won youth caps for England and turned pro in February 1992. Two months later he scored on his first-team debut against Everton and retained his place for the last game of the season. He also came on as a substitute in a League Cup tie, but that proved to be the limit of his senior football with Spurs, and after suffering a bad knee injury in 1993–94 he was released at the end of the season.

With a number of other clubs keen to sign him, Jeff chose Brighton principally because of the reputation of manager Liam Brady and quickly established himself in the side. During both the 1995 and 1996 close seasons he delayed signing new deals, but there was no further outside interest and on both occasions he signed on the dotted line. Packing a good shot into both feet, the stocky little midfielder led the club's League scorers during the 1995–96 relegation campaign and looked set to retain a big influence as the most constructive player in the team. Despite falling out with new manager Steve Gritt and asking for a transfer, he forced his way back into the team towards the end of 1996–97 as Albion successfully held on to their Football League status.

Season	FL	FAC	FLC	AMC	Total
1994–95	37+2 (5)	1	5	1	44+2 (5)
1995–96	37+2 (8)	4	1	3	45+2 (8)
1996–97	22+3 (3)	1	2	0	25+3 (3)
Total	96+7 (16)	6	8	4	114+7 (16)

MITCHELL, F.   1901–03

left-half   *20 apps, 1 goal*
debut: Shepherd's Bush (a), 28.9.1901 (SL D2)

Mitchell played in all but one of Albion's Southern League matches during the club's first-ever season, 1901–02, but played only briefly in the South Eastern League team the following season. A local amateur, he had previously turned out for the Preston Park-based North End Rangers and for Brighton & Hove Rangers. In fact, he played in twelve of Brighton & Hove Rangers' thirteen competitive matches during their one and only season, 1900–01, gaining runner's-up medals in the Sussex Senior Cup and Brighton Challenge Shield.

Season	SL	FAC	SEL	Total
1901–02	15 (1)	3	0	18 (1)
1902–03	0	0	2	2
Total	15 (1)	3	2	20 (1)

MOCHAN, CHARLIE   1905–06

left-back   Ht 5 9, Wt 11 10   *8 apps*
full name: Charles Mochan
born: Glasgow, Lanarkshire, Scotland, 8.6.1879
debut: Millwall (h), 2.9.1905 (SL D1)

Charlie Mochan was a Scottish junior internationalist with the Glasgow League club Strathclyde before joining Grimsby Town in November 1904 (where his team-mates included the future Albion trainers Alf Nelmes and Fred Coles). Having appeared in the "Mariners'" Second Division side on twelve occasions during 1904–05, he was released the following summer to join the Albion, but his time at the Goldstone was not a great success; in fact, none of his eight senior matches were won. After appearing at left-back in the opening two Southern League fixtures of the campaign, Charlie

was dropped in favour of the more experienced Arthur Hulme. He made six additional first-team appearances in the United League side during the remainder of the 1905–06 season, but at the end of it he was released and returned to Scotland to join the junior club Renton in December 1906.

Season	SL	UL	Total
1905–06	2	6	8
Total	2	6	8

MOFFATT, BILLY   1930–32

right-back/wing-half   Ht 5 8, Wt 11 00   *23 apps*
full name: William John Moffatt
born: Bellshill, Lanarkshire, Scotland, 30.6.1897
died: Southsea, Hampshire, 17.10.1952
debut: Exeter City (h), 6.9.1930 (FL D3(S))

Billy Moffatt was an adaptable character who, after signing from Portsmouth in May 1930, was employed as a standby player by the Albion; he appeared at right-back and in both wing-half berths during his first season with the club. 'Pompey' had plucked him from Bo'ness, where he had given sterling service for five seasons in the Scottish Second Division, in May 1925, and he quickly settled in at Fratton Park, playing in every match as the Hampshire club were promoted to Division One in 1926–27. With 138 appearances for Portsmouth to his name, he arrived at the Goldstone Ground at the age of 32, but after two years the veteran defender was released in May 1932 and moved into non-League football. He later made one appearance for Portsmouth during the wartime emergency competitions while well into his 40s.

Season	FL	FAC	Total
1930–31	18	2	20
1931–32	3	0	3
Total	21	2	23

MOFFATT, JOHNNY   1951–53

outside-right   *2 apps*
full name: John Black Moffatt
born: Greenock, Renfrewshire, Scotland, 22.12.1929
debut: Ipswich Town (h), 14.2.1953 (FL D3(S))

Johnny Moffatt played for Glasgow Boys and represented Greenock at intermediate level. After completing national service with the King's Own Scottish Borderers, he played for Bedley Juniors before joining the renowned Scottish junior club Bellshill Athletic for the 1951–52 season, but was soon brought to the Goldstone as a trialist (along with team-mate John Dougan) and signed as a professional in December 1951. While impressing on either wing for the reserves, Johnny made Albion's League team on just two occasions in the absence of Billy Reed and was released in May 1953. He worked locally in the building trade for several years while playing for Little-hampton, and was chosen for the County League's representative side in 1958–59. Johnny later returned to Scotland.

Season	FL	Total
1952–53	2	2
Total	2	2

MOONEY, PAUL — 1925–36

centre-half   Ht 5 11, Wt 12 03   315 apps, 11 goals
born: Chapel, Lanarkshire, Scotland, 7.4.1901
died: Brighton, Sussex, 19.10.1980
debut: Queen's Park Rangers (h), 24.10.1925 (FL D3(S))

An unassuming, quietly-spoken Scot, Paul Mooney was a superb defensive centre-half, particularly noted for his ability in the air. Indeed, he was dubbed 'the man with the cast-iron head', and on one occasion, at Walsall in March 1928, headed a goal from the halfway line! An Albion regular for nine years, he clocked up 315 appearances for the club and formed part of a tremendous middle line with Reg Wilkinson and either Wally Little, Harry Dutton or Dave Walker.

On leaving school Paul followed his father down his local coal-mine, and joined East Stirlingshire as a part-time professional in November 1922. A regular in the 'Shire side for two-and-a-half years, he missed just four games and assisted them to promotion from the Scottish League Division Three in 1923–24. In July 1925, a few weeks after his 24th birthday, Paul joined Albion and quickly became an institution, the rock around which manager Charlie Webb built his teams. After nearly nine years, though, in December 1934, he was involved in an accidental collision of heads that resulted in the death of Gillingham centre-forward Simeon Raleigh and consequently lost some of his appetite for the game.

Nevertheless, Paul continued playing for the club until 1936, and then turned out as a permit player for the Brighton-based Vernon Athletic in the Sussex County League. From his retirement from the professional game until his death, he ran the Wellington Hotel in College Place, Brighton.

Although an excellent centre-half, Paul was certainly no goalkeeper. With Albion already 3–1 down in a London Combination game in December 1929, the unfortunate Scot took over between the posts following an injury to goalkeeper Jimmy Newton and proceeded to let in another seven goals as Chelsea ran out 10–1 winners!

Season	FL	FAC*	SSC	Total
1925–26	7	0	0	7
1926–27	40 (2)	3	0	43 (2)
1927–28	37 (3)	2	0	39 (3)
1928–29	29 (2)	1	0	30 (2)
1929–30	16	0	0	16
1930–31	41 (2)	2	0	43 (2)
1931–32	39	3	0	42
1932–33*	17	7	0	24
1933–34	29	3	5	37
1934–35	27 (1)	3	3 (1)	33 (2)
1935–36	1	0	0	1
Total	283 (10)	24	8 (1)	315 (11)

Note: Four of Mooney's 1932–33 F.A. Cup appearances came in the qualifying competition.

MOORE, BERNARD — 1942–48 & 1954–55

centre-forward   Ht 5 10, Wt 12 00   113 apps, 58 goals
full name: Bernard John Moore
born: Brighton, Sussex, 18.12.1923
debut: Clapton Orient (h), 26.12.1942 (wartime)
peacetime debut: Romford (h), 17.11.1945 (FAC R1 Lg1)

The one that got away! Bernard Moore was a product of the Brighton Intermediate School who, after representing Brighton Boys as a wing-half in 1937–38, joined the Albion staff in the early part of the war. Playing in the Albion junior side which won the Sussex

Wartime League Cup and R.U.R. Cup in 1942–43, he made his first-team debut the same season at the age of nineteen and became a regular in the side in 1944 as an inside-forward. After signing as a professional in September 1945, Bernard was the club's leading scorer in the final emergency season with 28 goals, but service in the Far East then curtailed his appearances and, on returning to Hove in 1947, he struggled to win a place in the team.

Released to join the infant Hastings United club for £200 in October 1948, Bernard was a revelation at the Pilot Field. In fact, his form with the Southern Leaguers was little short of astonishing, and in two-and-a-half seasons he notched 138 goals in 121 matches, an incredible record which tempted Luton Town to pay £4,500 for his transfer in January 1951. With United bottom of the Southern League, the fee (a record for a Southern League player at the time) saved the club from liquidation and resurrected his career.

In three years at Kenilworth Road, Bernard scored 31 goals in 73 Second Division games, a performance which prompted Albion manager Billy Lane to pay £3,000 to bring the erstwhile favourite back to the Goldstone after five-and-a-half years in exile. His arrival was heralded with great anticipation by the fans who remembered his long-range shooting prowess, and he did not disappoint, scoring a further eleven goals for the club in 34 matches, but he was past his best and was allowed to join Bedford Town in November 1955, just short of his 32nd birthday. Bernard played a great part in the Southern Leaguers' famous F.A. Cup run of 1955–56, scoring an 85th-minute equaliser to force a 2–2 draw with mighty Arsenal at Highbury before losing 2–1 in the third-round replay.

Season	FL	FAC	Wartime	Total
1942–43	0	0	1	1
1943–44	0	0	7 (4)	7 (4)
1944–45	0	0	28 (13)	28 (13)
1945–46	0	9 (1)	26 (27)	35 (28)
1947–48	8 (2)	0	0	8 (2)
1953–54	7 (2)	0	0	7 (2)
1954–55	22 (8)	5 (1)	0	27 (9)
Total	37 (12)	14 (2)	62 (44)	113 (58)

MOORE, JIMMY — 1922–23

inside-left   Ht 5 8, Wt 10 04   6 apps, 2 goals
full name: James Moore
born: Boldon, Co. Durham, 1.9.1891
died: December 1972
debut: Norwich City (h), 26.8.1922 (FL D3(S))

A team-mate of Albion's Dickie Downs at Barnsley before the First World War, Jimmy Moore played more than 100 League games for the 'Colliers' after turning out for Boldon Colliery, Ardsley and Nelson. Joining the Yorkshire side in August 1911, he went on to collect an F.A. Cup winner's medal in 1912 when the Second Division side beat West Bromwich Albion in a replay. Having guested for Southampton during the war while working as a carpenter in an Isle of Wight aircraft factory, Jimmy joined the Southern League club in May 1919 and stayed at The Dell for the "Saints'" first season in the Third Division, during which he was ever-present.

After returning to Yorkshire with Leeds United in May 1921, the 30-year-old inside-forward arrived in Hove in August 1922 to play in the first six matches of the campaign before losing his place to the young Tommy Cook. Thereafter, Jimmy failed to regain his place and left for Halifax Town in September 1923, later having spells with Queen's Park Rangers (August 1924) and Crewe Alexandra (June 1925) before moving to the Netherlands as coach to NAC Breda in 1927. On retiring from the game, Jimmy ran a pub in Barnsley and served on Barnsley's board of directors after the Second World War.

Season	FL	Total
1922–23	6 (2)	6 (2)
Total	6 (2)	6 (2)

MOORE, JOHN — 1972

central defender	Ht 5 11, Wt 12 04	5 apps

born: Harthill, Lanarkshire, Scotland, 21.12.1943
debut: Huddersfield Town (a), 14.10.1972 (FL D2)

After making just four Scottish League appearances for Motherwell, John Moore joined Luton Town on a free transfer in May 1965 in what proved a tremendous move, for he went on to play 272 League games for the 'Hatters' and was a member of the team which won promotion from Division Four to the Second in the late 1960s. In October 1972, with the departure of John Napier imminent, Albion manager Pat Saward took the Scottish defender on loan for a month and his experience helped the club to one of its best runs in a disastrous season – just one game was lost during his spell in Hove – but after five games he returned to Kenilworth Road and was released in August 1974 to join Northampton Town, his last League club.

John had a spell as manager of Dunstable Town, but returned to Luton in 1978 as coach. After eight years on the "Hatters'" backroom staff, he was promoted to manager in May 1986 following David Pleat's departure for Spurs, and took the club to its highest-ever position of seventh in the First Division. However, he resigned in June 1987 because of the high-profile exposure endured by a top-flight manager, becoming assistant manager once again. In December 1995, while youth-team coach, he was put in joint temporary charge again for a short time until the advent of Lennie Lawrence, then became club coach once again.

Season	FL	Total
1972–73	5	5
Total	5	5

MOORHEAD, GEORGE — 1922

centre-half	Ht 5 11, Wt 11 06	1 app

born: New Zealand, 1896
died: Belfast, Co. Antrim, Northern Ireland, 1976
debut: Norwich City (h), 26.8.1922 (FL D3(S))

George Moorhead served with the Royal Irish Rifles during the Great War and signed for Southampton on his release in 1920, but, after nine games during their initial season in the Football League, his registration was cancelled by the F.A. and a twelve-month suspension was imposed on him for irregularities when he joined the 'Saints'. Following this unhappy hiatus, George resumed his career with the Albion in August 1922, but was unable to win a

regular place in the League team and left after just four months to join Linfield in the Irish League.

If his time in England was somewhat unfortunate, George's subsequent career in Irish football was a huge success. Capped for Ireland v. Scotland in 1923, 1928 and 1929, he also represented the Irish League on nine occasions and gained an Irish Cup winner's medal with Linfield in 1923. He spent the 1924–25 season with Glenavon, after which he returned to Linfield. George also had a brief spell in the Scottish League with Heart of Midlothian from November 1926.

Season	FL	Total
1922–23	1	1
Total	1	1

MOORHOUSE, BEN — 1919–20

winger		4 apps

full name: Benjamin Moorhouse
born: Oldham, Lancashire, c. 1897
debut: Swindon Town (a), 22.11.1919 (SL D1)

Ben Moorhouse played for Stalybridge Celtic in the Lancashire Combination before joining the Army in 1915, and arrived at the Goldstone as a trialist on his demob in November 1919. Having impressed in the reserves' 3–1 South Eastern League victory over Reading, the Lancastrian winger was included in the ailing Southern League side the following week. Capable of playing down either flank, Ben retained his place for four consecutive matches, but was then confined to the 'Lambs' until his release into junior football in May 1920.

Season	SL	Total
1919–20	4	4
Total	4	4

MORGAN, SAMMY — 1975–77

forward	Ht 6 1, Wt 11 00	37 apps, 8 goals

full name: Samuel John Morgan
born: Belfast, Co. Antrim, Northern Ireland, 3.12.1946
debut: Gillingham (a), 27.12.1975 (FL D3)

As brave and uncompromising a centre-forward as any defender could wish to meet, Sammy Morgan became a regular in the Northern Ireland international side during the 1970s after starting out with the Gorleston club of Great Yarmouth where he grew up. In July 1970 he signed as a professional with Third Division Port Vale, and went on to score 24 goals in 113 League games for the Burslem side. Winning his first cap in February 1972 in a 1–1 draw with Spain, Sammy added six more during his spell with Vale before Aston Villa paid £25,000 for his signature in August 1973.

Although he helped his club to promotion from the Second Division in 1974–75, Sammy scored just nine times in more than two years at Villa Park and was transferred to the Albion for £30,000 in December 1975 after pro-longed negotiations. The rugged striker scored seven goals during the remainder of that term, but, after recovering from a badly fractured cheek-bone at the beginning of 1976–77, he became almost a permanent fixture as substitute as the team won promotion from Division Three. Perhaps his most memorable performance was at Crystal Palace in an F.A. Cup replay when he came on for the injured Andy Rollings and gave a heroic display at centre-half.

Sammy was transferred to Cambridge United for £15,000 in August 1977 and made 37 League appearances in his only season at the Abbey Stadium, helping the club into Division Two for the first time. He then moved to the Netherlands with Sparta Rotterdam and Groningen, and also played in the U.S.A. before returning to Great Yarmouth in 1980 to become a school-teacher. A qualified F.A. coach,

24 players with relatives who also played for the Albion

* played wartime matches for Albion only

Players	Relationship
Booth, Billy & Sammy	Father & son
Brown, Irvin & Alan & Stan (& Gary)	3 brothers (and 1 cousin)
Buckley, Frank & Chris	Brothers
Burtenshaw, Steve & Charlie*	Brothers
Eacock, Fred & Jack	?
Eastham, George* & Harry*	Brothers
Fox, Mark & Simon	Brothers
Jones, Bullet & Les* (& Abe)	Father & son (& nephew)
Longstaff, Bert & Harvey	Brothers
Rutherford, Jack & Jim	Brothers
Wilson, Joe & Glen	Brothers

he became manager at Gorleston and returned to the Goldstone in December 1987 in his capacity as coach to the Great Yarmouth Schools team. Sammy won a total of eighteen caps (three goals) for Northern Ireland, two of which were gained while he was with the Albion.

Season	FL	FAC	Total
1975–76	18 (7)	0	18 (7)
1976–77	1+16 (1)	0+2	1+18 (1)
Total	19+16 (8)	0+2	19+18 (8)

MORRAD, FRANK   1948–51

full-back   Ht 5 9, Wt 12 10   *45 apps, 3 goals*
full name: Frank G. Morrad
born: Brentford, Middlesex, 28.2.1920
debut: Aldershot (h), 14.2.1948 (FL D3(S))

Frank Morrad joined his local club, Brentford, as an amateur at the age of sixteen in 1936, but was soon released and went on to play for Southall in the Athenian League until the outbreak of war. During the conflict he signed for Notts County and also guested for Arsenal, Clapton Orient and Crystal Palace, but when things returned to normal he played in just one League match at Meadow Lane before transferring to the renamed Leyton Orient in November 1946. Frank crossed the capital to join Fulham in August 1947, but could not find a place in the "Cottagers'" League team and was brought to the Goldstone as a trialist before the end of the season.

Signed permanently in February 1948 – as a part-timer while also working for a bookmaker – Frank normally played as an old-fashioned full-back and rarely ventured forward, but he also turned out at inside-left on occasion and had a run at centre-half in Albion's Third Division (South) side. A strong tackler with a fierce shot, the 28-year-old defender helped to steady the ship at a crucial time, and played his part in the great improvement of 1948–49 after the club had successfully applied for re-election.

At the end of 1950–51, Frank was transfer-listed and returned to the metropolitan area in August to end his Football League career with two seasons at Brentford, the club he had set out with, before dropping into the Southern League with Bedford Town in August 1953.

Season	FL	FAC	Total
1947–48	11	0	11
1948–49	16 (3)	0	16 (3)
1949–50	8	0	8
1950–51	8	2	10
Total	43 (3)	2	45 (3)

MORRIS, BILL   1949–51

outside-left   *31 apps, 4 goals*
full name: William Henry Morris
born: Swansea, Glamorgan, Wales, 28.9.1920
debut: Bristol City (h), 17.9.1949 (FL D3(S))

A Welsh schoolboy international from 1935, Bill Morris began his Football League career somewhat late in life because of the war, signing for his local club, Swansea Town, in May 1946 at the age of 25. In three seasons at the Vetch Field he made the first team on sixteen occasions, appearing briefly in their Third Division (South) championship side of 1948–49, before his transfer to the Goldstone in September 1949 for a substantial fee. Bill shared the no.11 shirt with Ken Davies during 1949–50 and impressed with his pace and control, but he was forced to play a reserve role to Doug Keene the following term (although he turned out at left-half for a five-match spell). In May 1951 he was released and moved into non-League football.

Season	FL	FAC	Total
1949–50	17 (3)	1	18 (3)
1950–51	11 (1)	2	13 (1)
Total	28 (4)	3	31 (4)

MORRIS, MARK   1996–

central defender   Ht 6 1, Wt 13 08   *14 apps, 1 goal*
full name: Mark John Morris
born: Carshalton, Surrey, 26.9.1962
debut: Hartlepool United (a), 2.11.1996 (FL D3)

Brought to the Goldstone with the Albion bottom of the Football League, Mark Morris made an immediate impact. Installed as captain in his very first game, the experienced 34-year-old scored the winning goal at Hartlepool to secure the club's only away win of the season.

Born in Carshalton, Mark became an apprentice with his local side, Wimbledon, turning professional in September 1980. In seven years as a professional at Plough Lane the strapping defender made nearly 200 appearances, earning himself a Fourth Division championship medal in 1983 and promotion on three other occasions. In 1985–86 he played fourteen League games on loan with Aldershot, but returned to Wimbledon for the following season which saw the "Dons'" debut in the First Division. In July 1987, Mark moved across the capital to join Watford in a £35,000 deal, but the Hertfordshire side lost their place in the top flight and he

moved on to Sheffield United for £175,000 in the summer of 1989. Once again Mark was a mainstay of a successful promotion effort in 1989–90, but he made only 14 League appearances for the 'Blades' in Division One before joining AFC Bournemouth for £100,000 in July 1991.

An automatic choice at Dean Court for nearly five years, Mark proved a strong and reliable defender, and was made club captain. In 1996–97, though, he lost favour, and on his return from a loan-spell with Gillingham he signed for the Albion on a free transfer in October 1996. His determination and motivational qualities were evident from the outset, and it was a great blow when he sustained an injury that kept him out of the side for four months. However, Mark regained his place for the final run-in and proved a tower of strength at a critical time.

Season	FL	FAC	Total
1996–97	11+1 (1)	2	13+1 (1)
Total	11+1 (1)	2	13+1 (1)

MORRIS, TOM   1907–09

centre-half   46 apps, 4 goals
full name: Thomas Henry Morris
born: Caistor, Lincolnshire, 1884
died: in action, World War One
debut: Norwich City (a), 7.9.1907 (SL D1)

A big, mobile centre-half, Tom Morris spent his early days with Haycroft Rovers and Grimsby Rovers before signing professional forms for Grimsby Town in February 1906. He did well at Blundell Park and played in 28 Second Division matches for the 'Mariners' in 1906–07, but was released in May 1907 to join the Albion. Tom was first-choice centre-half during 1907–08, but an injury in February 1908 forced him to miss the remainder of the season and he played second-fiddle to Joe Wilson the following term, making just seven more first-team appearances before joining former Albion manager Frank Scott-Walford at Leeds City in March 1909. After playing 109 League and Cup games at Elland Road up to May 1913, Tom was appointed player-coach of Scunthorpe & Lindsey United in the Midland League, but rejoined  Walford a year later after the former Leeds boss had taken over as manager of Coventry City. During the Great War, Tom guested with Wolverhampton Wanderers before losing his life at the Front.

Season	SL	FAC	WL	SCC	Total
1907–08	24 (1)	5	8 (1)	2	39 (2)
1908–09	5 (2)	1	1	0	7 (2)
Total	29 (3)	6	9 (1)	2	46 (4)

MORTIMER, DENNIS   1985–86

midfield   Ht 5 10, Wt 12 04   49 apps, 2 goals
full name: Dennis George Mortimer
born: Liverpool, Lancashire, 5.4.1952
debut: Grimsby Town (h), 17.8.1985 (FL D2)

This highly talented midfielder and superb leader was one of the most experienced men ever to play for the Albion. Unfortunate not to win a full England cap, Dennis Mortimer competed at the very highest levels for Aston Villa, and put his experience and intelligence to good use with the Albion in his one season at the Goldstone Ground.

Brought up in the Liverpool satellite town of Kirkby, Dennis represented the local schools before joining Coventry City as an apprentice. Signed as a professional in September 1969, he won a number of caps at youth level and went on to play in 193 First Division matches for the 'Sky Blues', also making six appearances for England's under-23s. In December 1975, Aston Villa paid £175,000 for Dennis's signature and he went on to enjoy nine very successful years at Villa Park. Gaining a League Cup winner's trophy in 1977, he also captained the England B team, and in 1980–81 led Villa to the League championship. The culminating moment of his playing career came the following year when he was presented with the European Cup in Rotterdam after Villa had beaten Bayern Munich 1–0.

Dennis had a short loan-spell with Sheffield United in December 1984, and enjoyed a well-deserved testimonial the following year. With half an eye on a coaching career, he was released on a free transfer by Villa and arrived at the Goldstone in August 1985 to play a big part in helping the club reach the F.A. Cup quarter-finals for only the second time. In August 1986, though, he preferred to return to the Midlands with Birmingham City, again on a free transfer, and moved into non-League circles a year later with, firstly, Kettering Town as player-coach and then Redditch United as player-manager.

Dennis was appointed Community Officer at West Bromwich Albion in August 1992, and subsequently became coach and assistant manager at The Hawthorns, but was dismissed along with his boss Keith Burkinshaw in October 1994 following a bad string of results.

Season	FL	FAC	FLC	FMC	Total
1985–86	40 (2)	4	3	2	49 (2)
Total	40 (2)	4	3	2	49 (2)

MOSELEY, GRAHAM   1977–86

goalkeeper   Ht 6 0, Wt 11 08   224 apps
born: Stretford, Lancashire, 16.11.1953
debut: Bristol Rovers (a), 18.4.1978 (FL D2)

The last line of defence during Albion's Division One days, Graham Moseley was dropped on a number of occasions but always managed to regain his place. His nine-year career on the South Coast took a number of unexpected turns, but his total of 224 appearances remains the highest of any Albion goalkeeper since Brian Powney in the early 1970s.

Like many a no.1, he came into the job almost by accident as the tallest lad in his school team, and went on to represent Stretford and Lancashire Schools before becoming an apprentice with Blackburn Rovers. After a year on the Ewood Park staff Graham was signed as a professional in September 1971 in order to gain an £18,000 fee from Derby County, and he was transferred to the 'Rams' the following day. The young 'keeper gained England youth honours and was chosen for the England under-23 squad during his time at the Baseball Ground, but was often kept out of the first team by Colin Boulton and had only 44 senior outings in six years with the club.

After spells on loan at Aston Villa (August 1974) and Walsall (October 1977), Graham was signed by manager Alan Mullery for £20,000 in November 1977 to compete with Eric Steele for the no.1 shirt at the Goldstone. Tall and lean, he was considered a better handler with Steele a superior shot-stopper, but both were excellent at their jobs. When Albion rose to join the élite for the first time ever in 1978–79, Graham made seventeen League appearances and followed up with 33 outings in the club's opening campaign in Division One. He was  somewhat accident-prone, though. Twice he was ruled out of contention following incidents with a hedge-trimmer in his garden and a glass window during a club holiday in Jersey. When Mullery finally acknowledged him as no.1 goalkeeper in October 1979, Graham fell sick, allowing Steele to make an unexpected final appearance between the Albion posts.

However, a succession of costly mistakes during 1980–81 – the dropping of crosses was a particular bugbear for a time – persuaded Mullery to bring in Perry Digweed and Graham was put up for transfer. He stayed with the club, though, shared the jersey with Digweed for two seasons, and played in the 1983 F.A. Cup final. In 1983–84 both 'keepers made room for Joe Corrigan and Graham was again placed on the transfer list, spending three weeks on loan at Ipswich Town in March 1984. His up-and-down Goldstone career then took another twist: left out of the 1984–85 pre-season team photo, he came into the side following an injury to Digweed and played in every match as Albion came close to returning to the First Division. His tremendous form earned him the supporters' vote as Player of the Season, the first goalkeeper to win the award.

After almost nine eventful years in Sussex, Graham joined Cardiff City on a free transfer in August 1986 where he added 38 League appearances to his tally before his career was cruelly terminated by injuries suffered in a car crash in January 1988. He was granted a benefit match, City *v.* West Ham United at Ninian Park, and Albion's F.A. Cup final side was re-assembled to meet Spurs at the Goldstone in April 1990 in support of his testimonial fund, an event which raised around £18,000 for the popular former 'keeper. Now living in Chepstow, Graham works as a postman.

Season	FL	FAC	FLC	FMC	Total
1977–78	4	0	0	0	4
1978–79	17	1	2	0	20
1979–80	33	2	4	0	39
1980–81	26	2	3	0	31
1981–82	30	3	3	0	36
1982–83	27	7	2	0	36
1983–84	1	0	0	0	1
1984–85	42	2	2	0	46
1985–86	9	0	1	1	11
Total	189	17	17	1	224

MOULDEN, PAUL   1992

forward   Ht 5 8, Wt 11 03   11 apps, 5 goals
full name: Paul Anthony Moulden
born: Farnworth, Lancashire, 6.9.1967
debut: Leyton Orient (a), 15.8.1992 (FL D2)

Paul Moulden's main claim to fame is his entry in the *Guinness Book of Records*: in 1981–82, as a fourteen-year-old forward, he hit 289 goals in 40 league games for Bolton Lads' Club, plus another 51 in other competitions to total 340 for the season! The son of Tony Moulden (a winger with Bury, Rochdale, Peterborough and Notts County), Paul's obvious scoring talents won him England Schools honours and an apprenticeship with Manchester City, where he won youth caps and an F.A. Youth Cup winner's medal in 1986. He progressed to the first team and top-scored with thirteen League goals when City won promotion to the First Division in 1988–89. It was something of a surprise, therefore, when he was sold to Second Division AFC Bournemouth for £160,000 the following August, but his stay at Dean Court lasted just eight months – he scored  fourteen times in 38 games – before Oldham Athletic bought him for £225,000 in March 1990.

Paul didn't enjoy his time at Boundary Park, though; he never held down a first-team place and an ankle injury in late 1991 seriously threatened his career. After spending the summer of 1992 with Molde in Norway, he came to the Goldstone on loan in August 1992 for two months to form an emergency strike-force with fellow 'loanee' Steve Cotterill. While maintaining a long and noble tradition as the team's practical joker, Paul was also quite a success on the pitch, scoring five times in eleven games with his trickery around the box, but

cash-strapped Albion were never in a position to buy him. Returning to Oldham reserves, he joined Birmingham City for £150,000 in March 1993, but, despite a good start, he did not figure in the scheme of things at St Andrews and was transferred to Huddersfield Town in March 1995. After just two games as a substitute, Paul was released at the end of the season and joined Rochdale in September 1995, but dropped out of the League scene the following summer when he signed for Accrington Stanley.

Season	FL	Total
1992–93	11 (5)	11 (5)
Total	11 (5)	11 (5)

MUIR, IAN   1984–85

forward   Ht 5 8, Wt 10 13   4 apps
full name: Ian James Muir
born: Coventry, Warwickshire, 5.5.1963
debut: Portsmouth (a), 31.3.1984 (FL D2)

Tranmere Rovers managed to do what five other clubs before them had failed to do: realise the phenomenal goal-scoring potential of Ian Muir. Such was the extent of their success that the Coventry-born striker now holds the all-time scoring record at Prenton Park.

Ian's potential was spotted at an early age, and he won England Schools caps before being taken on as an apprentice by Queen's Park Rangers. Signed as a professional in September 1980, he gained an England youth cap in October 1981 in a World Youth Championship third-place play-off against Romania. He scored twice on his Second Division debut, a 5–0 win over Cambridge United at Loftus Road, and a glittering career seemed assured, but he made Rangers' League side just once more before being loaned to Burnley in October 1982.

On his return to London, Ian continued in the reserves until he joined Birmingham City on a free transfer in August 1983, but he was again restricted to a role with the second string. Having scored fifteen goals for City's reserves, Chris Cattlin brought him to the Goldstone on another 'free' in February 1984 and he made his debut at Portsmouth in March, but with the established Albion team doing well the following season he was never really given the opportunity to shine and moved to Swindon Town on loan in January 1985.

One of the players restricting his chances at the Goldstone, Frank Worthington, was appointed player-manager at Tranmere in the summer of 1985 and took Ian to the Wirral on a free transfer shortly after. At this stage he had just two goals to his name from eleven League outings for five clubs, but he went on to play a massive part in Rovers' rapid rise up the League, scoring prolifically as the Prenton Park side won promotion to Division Three in 1989 and to Division Two in 1991. A superb poacher, his finishing skills also helped the club to a Wembley triumph in May 1990 when they defeated Bristol Rovers 2–1 in the final of the Associate Members (Leyland DAF) Cup competition. Indeed, his Tranmere total of 141 League goals would have been even higher but for a severe injury sustained in March 1991. Out for nearly a year, Ian was unable to regain a regular place after recovering and rejoined Birmingham City in the 1995 close season for a £125,000 fee. However, he made just one League appearance at St Andrews and spent September 1995 on loan with Darlington before joining the Sing Tao club in Hong Kong.

Season	FL	Total
1983–84	2	2
1984–85	1+1	1+1
Total	3+1	3+1

MULHALL, JOHN — 1924–25

inside-right — 2 apps
born: Dykehead, Lanarkshire, Scotland, 3.10.1902
debut: Reading (a), 6.12.1924 (FL D3(S))

John Mulhall was signed from the Lanarkshire side Dykehead for a £225 fee in November 1924 only three months after he had joined the Scottish Third Division club. The 22-year-old inside-right was drafted straight into Albion's League side in the absence of Bob Dennison, but he struggled to impress in goal-less draws with Reading and Swansea Town. On dropping into the reserves John scored five goals in his first two matches, but his game then deteriorated. The loss of form was attributed to acute home-sickness, and in August 1925 he returned to Scotland with Falkirk. In July 1926 he rejoined his home-town club, Dykehead.

Season	FL	Total
1924–25	2	2
Total	2	2

MULVANEY, JIM — 1950–51

right-back/centre-forward — Ht 6 0, Wt 12 07 — 10 apps
full name: James Mulvaney
born: Airdrie, Lanarkshire, Scotland, 27.4.1921
debut: Aldershot (a), 26.8.1950 (FL D3(S))

Jim Mulvaney joined Dumbarton in the early part of the Second World War, during which he served as an air-gunner with the R.A.F., and made his entry into the Football League on transferring to Luton Town in June 1948. After two moderate seasons at Kenilworth Road, he arrived at the Goldstone with Peter Walsh in August 1950 in exchange for Albion's skipper Jack Whent (Walsh never appeared in Albion's first team). Jim was a versatile player, appearing at right-back, outside-right and centre-forward, but could not find a regular niche and moved on to Bradford City in October 1951. Sixteen outings with City in 1951–52 were followed

by a month on trial at Halifax Town in November 1952, but he wasn't taken on and subsequently played for Bath City in the Southern League.

Season	FL	FAC	Total
1950–51	8	2	10
Total	8	2	10

MUNDAY, STUART — 1989–96

defender/midfield — Ht 5 11, Wt 11 00 — 117 apps, 5 goals
full name: Stuart Clifford Munday
born: Stratford, West Ham, Essex, 28.9.1972
debut: Plymouth Argyle (a), 22.2.1992 (FL D2)

Although much maligned for many wayward touch-line clearances during his time at the Goldstone, there was never any doubting Stuart Munday's commitment to the Albion cause. Making the vast majority of his 117 appearances in the no.2 shirt, the Essex-born youngster always looked a much better player in the centre of defence, but, with the likes of Steve Foster and Paul McCarthy to contend with, he had to make do with the full-back berth where he used his enthusiasm and pace to good effect. He was also used on occasion as a midfield ball-winner.

Raised in Shoeburyness, Stuart represented both Southend and Essex Schools, and attended Tottenham Hotspur's school of excellence at Dagenham while playing Sunday football for the Basildon club Hyde Rovers. In 1989, shortly after gaining a medal in the final of the English Schools Inter-County championship (Essex and West Midlands drawing 3–3), he arrived at the Goldstone as a trainee. Signing professional forms in July 1990, Stuart worked his way

through the youth and reserve teams, and made his first appearance in the League side in February 1992; the nineteen-year-old had a fine game in a 1–1 draw at Plymouth and retained the no.2 shirt for the rest of the season. Stuart's home debut was sensational, when he headed a late winner in a 3–2 defeat of Southend United, his local club, as Albion struggled desperately against relegation.

In the summer of 1995 he was lucky to survive a car crash, but his strong Christian faith helped him through a traumatic time. Unfortunately, 1995–96 was traumatic for all involved at the Goldstone and Stuart, deprived of regular outings, asked for a transfer. Released at the end of the season to join Conference side Dover Athletic, he went on to win recognition with an appearance in an F.A. representative side against the Isthmian League.

Stuart will probably be best remembered in Sussex for his five goals, all splendid efforts (especially his long-range scorer against Premiership side Leicester City) — and for those woeful clearances!

Season	FL	FAC	FLC	AMC	Total
1991–92	14 (1)	0	0	0	14 (1)
1992–93	7	1	0	3	11
1993–94	33+1 (1)	1	4	1	39+1 (1)
1994–95	18+13 (2)	0+1	2+1 (1)	2	22+15 (3)
1995–96	8+3	0+2	1	1	10+5
Total	80+17 (4)	2+3	7+1 (1)	7	96+21 (5)

MUNDEE, DENNY — 1995–

midfield — Ht 5 10, Wt 11 00 — 71 apps, 8 goals
full name: Denny William John Mundee
born: Swindon, Wiltshire, 10.10.1968
debut: Burnley (a), 21.10.1995 (FL D2)

Renowned for the versatility which has seen him occupy every position for his various clubs, Denny Mundee started out as an apprentice with Queen's Park Rangers where he even turned out as a goalkeeper for the reserves on one occasion. However, he was released without a senior appearance to his name and returned home to join Swindon Town in 1986, but enjoyed a similarly unsuccessful time at the County Ground.

Working in a Wiltshire scrap-yard, the teenager turned out as a forward for Southern League side Salisbury before signing up with AFC Bournemouth, for whom his elder brothers Brian and Barry had played, in March 1988. It took Denny some time to establish himself in the "Cherries'" line-up, and he had nine games on loan to Torquay United in the early part of 1989–90, but during 1991–92 he made the starting line-up on 28 occasions in the League – wearing six different shirts – and another 23 the following season – with seven different numbers!

After exactly 100 League outings at Dean Court, Denny joined Brentford on a free transfer and played as a full-back until, in an emergency, he was employed as a striker to some effect and scored thirteen goals inside three months during 1993–94, four of them penalties. Becoming a great favourite at Griffin Park, he hit a memorable hat-trick in a 4–3 home defeat by Bristol Rovers in January 1994, but spent the following season largely in midfield, and was released in 1995 after rejecting a new contract.

After leaving Brentford, Denny trained with Dorchester Town and was poised to play for the Southern League side when Albion manager Liam Brady offered him a monthly contract. Played initially as a forward, he subsequently moved out to the right side of midfield and held his place to the end of the season. Although he struggled to find consistency, Denny's ability to play anywhere ensured he remained in the first-team squad, and he enjoyed a much better second season at the Goldstone. Building a great rapport with Albion fans protesting against the actions of the club board in selling the ground, the 28-year-old enjoyed his best form since arriving in Hove before being cruelly sidelined by a back injury. The possessor of a celebrated 'shuffle' trick to beat opponents, Denny also has a fierce shot and a first-class record from the penalty-spot.

Season	FL	FAC	AMC	Total
1995–96	31+1 (3)	4	2 (1)	37+1 (4)
1996–97	27+2 (4)	2	2	31+2 (4)
Total	58+3 (7)	6	4 (1)	68+3 (8)

MUNDY, ALBERT   1953–58

inside-right/centre-forward   Ht 5 8, Wt 10 08   178 apps, 90 goals
full name: Albert Edward Mundy
born: Gosport, Hampshire, 12.5.1926
debut: Bristol City (h), 28.11.1953 (FL D3(S))

A prolific scorer for the Albion, Albert Mundy stands second only to the immortal Tommy Cook in the club's list of League scorers, and his rate – 87 goals from 165 League appearances – also compares with the best. Three times during the 1950s, a period of sustained entertainment at the Goldstone, 'Our Albert' headed the goalscorers, and he is one of only two players (the other is Bert Stephens) to score more than 20 goals in each of three successive seasons.

Albert arrived with a fine reputation from Portsmouth in November 1953, having joined the Fratton staff from Gosport Borough Athletic in 1951. An instant success at Hove, the 27-year-old forward rapidly became a great favourite and formed a splendid partnership with winger Dennis Gordon. Although he was an instinctive finisher, Albert was essentially an inside-forward and led the attack only on the odd occasion; his scoring consistency was thus all the more remarkable.

Despite contributing ten goals to Albion's Third Division (South) championship campaign in 1957–58, Albert lost his place to the recently signed Dave Sexton and left for Aldershot in February 1958, for whom he played 130 League games. In a match against Hartlepools United in October 1958, the ace striker registered a goal for Aldershot just six seconds after the start, a remarkable feat which remains a joint Football League record. Later switched to half-back, he left the 'Shots' in July 1961 to join the large ex-Albion contingent at Guildford City. After several seasons with the Southern Leaguers, Albert returned to his home-town as player-coach with Gosport Borough Athletic in the Hampshire League.

Season	FL	FAC	Total
1953–54	21 (11)	3	24 (11)
1954–55	41 (18)	5 (3)	46 (21)
1955–56	46 (28)	2	48 (28)
1956–57	34 (20)	2	36 (20)
1957–58	23 (10)	1	24 (10)
Total	165 (87)	13 (3)	178 (90)

MURFIN, CLARRIE   1936–38

outside-left   *1 app*
full name: Clarence Murfin
born: Barnsley, Yorkshire, 2.4.1909
debut: Walsall (h), 25.9.1937 (FL D3(S))

Clarrie Murfin enjoyed a chequered football career after joining Barnsley from the local West Ward club at the age of 21 in April 1930. Having played in 23 Second Division matches, he was released to join Midland League Scunthorpe & Lindsey United in August 1932, but returned to the first-class game the following July with Rochdale, where he scored seven goals in 26 Third Division (North) outings during 1933–34. This spell in Lancashire was followed by another season in the Midland League with Gainsborough Trinity, but his Football League career was again resurrected when Bradford (P.A.) obtained his signature in March 1935, although his time at Park Avenue was spent mostly in the reserves. Charlie Webb brought Clarrie to the Goldstone in June 1936, but, with Bert Stephens holding down the left-wing berth, he made just a single appearance in the first-team in two seasons and was released in May 1938.

Season	FL	Total
1937–38	1	1
Total	1	1

MURRAY, BERT   1971–73

utility player   Ht 5 8, Wt 11 07   109 apps, 26 goals
full name: Albert George Murray
born: Shoreditch, London, 22.9.1942
debut: Preston North End (h), 27.2.1971 (FL D3)

Forever remembered as 'The People's Player', Bert Murray was signed with cash from manager Pat Saward's Buy-a-Player Fund, an appeal which saw hundreds of fans participating in schemes to earn money for transfers. Happily, he lived up to his tag and was a hugely popular and effective player for the club, especially in the tremendously exciting Third Division promotion campaign of 1971–72 when he won the Player of the Season award.

Bert first arrived at the Goldstone in February 1971 on loan from Birmingham City and made an instant impression, but was on the point of joining Fulham when he unexpectedly signed for £10,000 early in March. A few days later, rather ironically, he played a large part in Albion's 3–2 win over second-placed Fulham, the first home victory for over two months, and continued to inspire the team which rose from 23rd place to a final position of 14th.

Bert's career began at Chelsea when he joined the Londoners directly from school in 1958 after playing for England Schoolboys. Signed as a professional in May 1961, he won England Youth honours and six caps at under-23 level, and went on to score 39 goals in 160 League appearances, appearing in virtually every position on the pitch. In 1965 he played in Chelsea's League Cup-winning side, but was transferred to Birmingham City for £25,000 in August 1966 under a cloud, having been disciplined along with a number of his colleagues (including Barry Bridges (q.v.), who was also sold to

Birmingham) for a breach of club rules. He went on to make a further 138 League appearances at St Andrews.

At the Goldstone, 28-year-old Bert appeared in midfield and on the right-wing where his excellent displays were rewarded with twelve goals in the aforementioned 1971–72 season. But it was in the home straight of that successful promotion campaign that the 'People's Player' proved just what an asset he was when Saward dramatically switched him to right-back to accommodate new forward Ken Beamish. The change proved a triumph for both the manager and his multi-talented player who, calm and capable, slotted into the no.2 shirt with considerable ease. In fact, Albion never lost once in the final twelve games of the season following the switch.

However, the following season proved disastrous for the Albion as the team dropped straight back to the Third Division. Bert was made team captain midway through the lamentable campaign and finished level with Beamish on nine League goals, but with wholesale changes being made he was loaned to Peterborough United in September 1973, signing for £6,000 the following month. During his time at London Road he made 123 League appearances and missed just four matches as the 'Posh' carried off the Fourth Division championship in 1973–74. On retiring from the professional game in 1977 the popular cockney entered the licensed trade, and is now landlord of The Bull at Market Deeping, Lincolnshire. In 1986, Bert was still playing junior soccer at the age of 43.

Season	FL	FAC	FLC	Total
1970–71	17 (4)	0	0	17 (4)
1971–72	44+1 (12)	3 (1)	2	49+1 (13)
1972–73	38+1 (9)	0	2	40+1 (9)
1973–74	0+1	0	0	0+1
Total	99+3 (25)	3 (1)	4	106+3 (26)

MYALL, STUART
1991–96

full-back/midfield   Ht 5 10, Wt 12 12   93 apps, 4 goals
full name: Stuart Thomas Myall
born: Eastbourne, Sussex, 12.11.1974
debut: West Bromwich Albion (a), 3.4.1993 (FL D2)

On the Albion's books from the age of eleven at the club's Eastbourne school of excellence, Stuart Myall went on to play in midfield for Sussex Schools and also represented the county at cricket. He was head boy at Cavendish School, while his father, Sid Myall, was a stalwart centre-half for Eastbourne Town and Sussex.

The youngster went on to play for the Littlehampton Town youth side, and also had an international trial before being arriving at the

Goldstone as a trainee in July 1991. Farmed out to Wokingham Town in the Isthmian League for experience during 1992–93, Stuart made his Albion first-team debut in April 1993 and signed a professional contract the same month. Looking set for a bright future as a full-back or midfielder, he gained a winner's medal in the Sussex Senior Cup with the reserves in May 1994, but injury and weight problems led to a drop in form and he was transfer-listed by manager Liam Brady in September 1994, only to have fruitless trials with AFC Bournemouth and Preston North End.

However, Stuart knuckled down, regained his fitness, and returned to the side on merit in November 1994, proving a revelation in the midfield anchor role. A neat passer of the ball, he retained his place for much of the remainder of the season, and also posed a considerable threat with his excellent long throw. Capable of playing in either full-back berth as well, he occupied a number of positions

during 1995–96 and was an important backup member of the squad, but at the end of the season he was surprisingly released by Jimmy Case, only to be snapped up by Second Division Brentford. Stuart struggled at Griffin Park, though, and moved to Hastings Town on a month's loan in December 1996 without making a single first-team appearance for Brentford.

Season	FL	FAC	FLC	AMC	Total
1992–93	7	0	0	0	7
1993–94	12+1	0	2	2	16+1
1994–95	23+4 (2)	0	0	0	23+4 (2)
1995–96	27+6 (2)	4	2	2+1	35+7 (2)
Total	69+11 (4)	4	4	4+1	81+12 (4)

NAPIER, JOHN
1967–72

centre-half   Ht 6 1, Wt 12 02   247 apps, 5 goals
full name: Robert John Napier
born: Lurgan, Co. Armagh, Northern Ireland, 23.9.1946
debut: Swindon Town (a), 19.8.1967 (FL D3)

A major force in the Albion rearguard for nearly five years, John Napier always gave total effort and missed just five League games from his arrival at the Goldstone in 1967 until he was unexpectedly dropped for the successful run-in to promotion in 1972. He won the club's first-ever Player of the Season award in 1969, and was captain for two years, leading the side with typical determination. Usually performing alongside Norman Gall as the 4–3–3 formation became fashionable, the dominating Ulsterman was a rock in a respectable Albion defence which conceded an average of only 51 League goals from 1967 to 1972.

After winning three caps for Northern Ireland as a schoolboy, John joined the Bolton Wanderers ground staff at the age of fifteen in 1962 and showed tremendous promise, signing as a professional on his seventeenth birthday. Eleven youth caps followed, including an appearance at Wembley in the 'Little World Cup' final of 1963 when he had the misfortune to score an own-goal in a 4–0 defeat by England. John's form with the 'Trotters' in Division Two came to the attention of the selectors and he was rewarded with an under-23 cap. In May 1966, at the age of nineteen, he appeared in the full Northern Ireland side which lost 2–0 to West Germany in Belfast. However, he was unable to maintain a first-team place at Burnden Park and arrived in Hove in August 1967 for a £25,000 fee, an Albion record at the time.

The lanky centre-half immediately became a fixture in the side and won a second under-23 cap in March 1968. In fact, he had been selected for the senior team a month earlier but had to pull out because Albion had a rearranged game the same evening. After skippering the club in 1970–71 and 1971–72, John missed the climax of the latter season when he was dropped by Pat Saward in favour of Ian Goodwin following a couple of bad results. He continued to play in the reserves without complaint, but was transferred to Bradford City for £10,000 in October 1972 where he played 107 Fourth Division games before joining Baltimore in the U.S.A. on a free transfer in May 1975.

On returning to England, John played for Mossley in the Northern Premier League before rejoining Bradford City on a non-contract basis during 1976–77. Appointed coach at Valley Parade in 1977, he took over as manager for eight months in 1978 but then left again for the U.S.A. where he was associated with the San Diego Jaws. John spent five years running a football-equipment store, and became involved in organising summer soccer-camps for youngsters in the States.

Season	FL	FAC	FLC	Total
1967–68	45 (1)	2	1	48 (1)
1968–69	46 (2)	3	3	52 (2)
1969–70	42 (1)	5	3	50 (1)
1970–71	46	3	1	50
1971–72	34 (1)	3	2	39 (1)
1972–73	5+1	0	2	7+1
Total	218+1 (5)	16	12	246+1 (5)

NAPIER, KIT   *1966–72*

forward   Ht 5 11, Wt 11 06   *291 apps, 99 goals*
full name: Christopher Robin Anthony Napier
born: Dunblane, Perthshire, Scotland, 26.9.1943
debut: Peterborough United (h), 1.10.1966 (FL D3)

A skilful ball-player in the Scottish tradition, Kit Napier enlivened many a Goldstone afternoon in the late 1960s and early '70s. While looking a little lazy at times, he would often break out of apparent indolence with a quick burst of pace or a sleight of foot to launch a raid on the opposing goal. Packing a fierce shot in both feet, he hit 99 goals in 291 matches for the Albion, a total exceeded in peacetime only by Tommy Cook, and played in all the forward positions – as a centre-forward, as a supporting striker, and as a winger – during his six years in Hove, becoming a great favourite. While excelling at all aspects of forward play, Kit has had no peer in one particular art: able to deliver beautifully flighted, inswinging corner-kicks from either flag right into the danger area, he scored directly with one such centre against Bury in December 1969.

With a considerable pedigree behind him – his grandfather was secretary of Falkirk; his father was on York City's books; Uncle Charlie was a Scottish international with Celtic, Derby County and Sheffield Wednesday; and Uncle George played for Kilmarnock, Cowdenbeath, East Stirlingshire and Airdrieonians – it was almost inevitable that Kit would become a footballer, and he signed as a professional for Blackpool in November 1960 after a spell on the ground staff. In three years at Bloomfield Road he made the First Division side only twice, though, and was transferred to nearby Preston North End for £2,000 in June 1963. A season at Deepdale brought only limited opportunity and just one Second Division appearance, and in July 1964 Kit dropped into the Third Division with Workington. His time

in Cumberland was considerably more successful with 25 goals from 58 League appearances, a record which tempted Newcastle United to try him in the First Division again for a fee of £18,000 in November 1965. Kit's debut came later that month in a 2–0 win over his former club, Blackpool, at St James's Park, but he failed to make much impression and made the "Magpies'" League side on just eight occasions.

Albion manager Archie Macaulay showed an interest in him during the summer of 1966, but it was the end of September when the slimly-built 23-year-old arrived at the Goldstone for a fee of £8,500 to score twice on his debut, a 5–2 home win over Peterborough United which was the first League victory of the season. That feat naturally won him instant popularity, but he sustained his performances for another six years and maintained his status with the crowd with his skill, bravery and, above all, goalscoring. Indeed, he is only Albion player in peacetime to have scored ten or more goals in each of six consecutive seasons.

In 1967–68, Kit equalled Albert Mundy's post-war record with 28 goals in League and Cup, a terrific achievement bearing in mind that Albion finished a mediocre season in mid table. (It was thought to be a new post-war record at the time and he was presented with a gold wrist-watch to commemorate the feat, but it in fact equalled the record set by Mundy in 1955–56.) The leading scorer in five of his six seasons at the Goldstone, Kit netted nineteen goals in 1971–72 when Albion were promoted to Division Two, but that successful campaign was to be his last with the club.

Not seeing eye-to-eye with manager Pat Saward, he was transferred to Third Division Blackburn Rovers for £15,000 in August 1972 where he hit ten goals in 54 Third Division outings over two seasons. Given a free transfer in May 1974, Kit left for South Africa to play for Durban United and has remained in that country ever since, working in the motor trade with some success.

His greying locks earned him the nickname 'The Silver Fox' in his new homeland.

Season	FL	FAC	FLC	Total
1966–67	30+2 (9)	6 (1)	2	38+2 (10)
1967–68	45 (24)	2 (1)	2 (3)	49 (28)
1968–69	43 (14)	3 (2)	3 (2)	49 (18)
1969–70	41+2 (10)	5	3 (1)	49+2 (11)
1970–71	43+2 (11)	3 (2)	0	46+2 (13)
1971–72	44 (16)	3 (3)	2	49 (19)
1972–73	3+1	0	1	4+1
Total	249+7 (84)	22 (9)	13 (6)	284+7 (99)

NASH, H.   *1912*

inside-left   *1 app*
debut: Southend United (h), 4.12.1912 (SA)

A trialist from the Troedyrhiw club based near Merthyr Tydfil, Nash played at inside-left in the Southern Alliance fixture against Southend United in December 1912 to the temporary exclusion of Charlie Webb. He performed well in a 4–0 victory but was not offered terms.

Season	SA	Total
1912–13	1	1
Total	1	1

NEAL, ASHLEY   *1996*

defender   Ht 6 0, Wt 11 10   *8 apps*
full name: Ashley James Neal
born: Liverpool, Lancashire, 16.12.1974
debut: Northampton Town (a), 28.9.1996 (FL D3)

T he son of Phil Neal, the former Liverpool and England full-back, Ashley Neal has a lot to live up to, but showed little sign of doing so during his month on loan at the Albion. Sadly, of the eight games he played, seven ended in defeat and one in a draw.

Ashley was in the Merseyside Schools side which lifted the English Schools Under-16 County Cup in 1990, and went on to become a trainee at Anfield, but his career was badly set back by an injury he recieved on tour with the club in South Africa. He also survived unscathed an incident where his car became an inferno.

When he arrived in Hove in September 1996, the 21-year-old defender was in his fourth year as a pro but had yet to make a senior appearance. After a trial in the reserves, he signed loan forms to make his League debut in a 3–0 defeat at  Northampton where he showed up well, but as team morale began to wither so did Ashley's form, and he made some crucial errors which turned the crowd against him. In the end it was a relief when he returned to Liverpool. Two months later, in December 1996, he signed for Huddersfield Town on a 'free', but quickly moved to Peterborough United after failing to make the Yorkshire club's first team.

Season	FL	Total
1996–97	8	8
Total	8	8

NEATE, DEREK   *1955–59*

outside-left   Ht 5 8, Wt 10 06   *24 apps, 6 goals*
full name: Derek George Stanbridge Neate
born: Uxbridge, Middlesex, 1.10.1927
debut: Leyton Orient (h), 18.4.1956 (FL D3(S))

A team-mate of Les Champelovier (q.v.) at Hayes, Derek Neate arrived at the Goldstone as an amateur from the Athenian League club in April 1955; he had impressed Albion manager Billy

Lane when playing alongside Brighton skipper Glen Wilson in a testimonial match at Griffin Park for the Brentford physio Jack Cartmell. Twelve months later he became a professional at the age of 28.

A speedy and clever little winger, Derek made his debut in a crucial match with Leyton Orient which Albion had to win to retain any thoughts of carrying off the Third Division (South) championship in 1955–56, but Orient earned a 1–1 draw in front of a 30,864 Goldstone crowd and went on to claim the title, a point ahead of the Albion. He remained with the club for four years, but was deprived of a regular place in the side by the consistency of Denis Foreman and Frankie Howard, although he enjoyed an impressive run in the latter half of the 1956–57 campaign. Given a free transfer in May 1959, Derek became player-coach with Bognor Regis Town in the Sussex County League for three seasons, and later had spells as manager of Southwick (1964–66), Worthing (1967–68) and Steyning Town (from 1968). He now lives in the Adur district of Sussex.

Season	FL	Total
1955–56	4	4
1956–57	20 (6)	20 (6)
Total	24 (6)	24 (6)

NEEDHAM, ARCHIE   1911–15

utility player   Ht 5 8, Wt 11 10   *131 apps, 14 goals*
born: Ecclesall, Yorkshire, 1881
died: Hove, Sussex, October 1950
debut: Stoke (a), 2.9.1911 (SL D1)

Archie Needham will go down in history as probably the greatest utility man the Albion have ever had. Appearing in every position except goalkeeper in the Southern League side during four seasons at the Goldstone, he was a capable performer wherever he played. The majority of his appearances were at right-back, right-wing or inside-right, but he also turned out on the left side on many occasions.

Archie made a name for himself as a lad when he represented Sheffield Schools, and was signed as a professional by Sheffield United at the age of nineteen in May 1901. Introduced to the First Division in a 3–1 home defeat by Middlesbrough in March 1903, he went on to score ten goals in fifteen League games at inside-left for the 'Blades'. In 1905, Archie joined Crystal Palace, newly elected to the Southern League, and rewarded manager Jack Robson's faith in him by hitting nineteen goals as Palace walked off with the Second Division championship. Remaining with the 'Glaziers' for four years, he made 104 appearances in the Southern League and F.A. Cup before reverting to the Football League with Glossop in May 1909.

One season with the Derbyshire Second Division club was followed by a transfer to Wolverhampton Wanderers in July 1910, but a year later Archie rejoined Jack Robson, by then in charge at the Goldstone, and proved an invaluable addition to the staff. Described as unorthodox, the versatile Yorkshireman started off at inside-right and made a swift impression, scoring nine goals – including two hat-tricks – in his first fourteen games. Towards the end of his first season he moved out to the wing, but then embarked on his play-anywhere role, going on to make 131 first-team appearances for the club before retiring in 1915.

Best man at Billy Booth's wedding in 1912, Archie served with the Footballers' Battalion during the Great War. On returning to the area he ran a haberdashery business in Boundary Road, Hove, while living in Hangleton Road for many years until his death at the age of 69. Between the wars he coached football in local schools.

Season	SL	FAC	SA	SCC	Total
1911–12	29 (8)	0	0	2 (3)	31 (11)
1912–13	32 (3)	2	14	0	48 (3)
1913–14	22	1	11	0	34
1914–15	15	3	0	0	18
Total	98 (11)	6	25	2 (3)	131 (14)

NEIL, ANDY   1920–24 & 1926–27

inside-forward   Ht 5 8, Wt 10 07   *185 apps, 30 goals*
full name: Andrew Neil
born: Crosshouse, Ayrshire, Scotland, 18.11.1892
died: Kilmarnock, Ayrshire, Scotland, 14.8.1941
debut: Crystal Palace (h), 25.12.1920 (FL D3(S))

One of the club's finest players during the 1920s, Andy Neil was an inventive inside-forward who, while not a great goalscorer himself, provided many an opportunity for his centre-forward, be it Jack Doran, Eddie Fuller or Tommy Cook. The 28-year-old Scot had a great influence on the team from the moment he joined the club in 1920 and dazzled with his wonderful ball-skills, so much so that Arsenal paid a big fee for him upon the recommendation of Albion manager Charlie Webb after just over three years in Hove.

Andy began his professional career with his local Scottish League club, Kilmarnock, at the age of 21 in January 1913, and made his debut in their First Division side in a 1–0 win at Motherwell three months later. During the First World War he assisted 'Killie', Clydebank and Third Lanark, and subsequently played for the Ayrshire junior sides Galston and Stevenston United before coming south to join the Albion in December 1920 in the club's first Football League season. Quickly establishing himself at inside-right, Andy was a fixture until March 1924 when he departed for Highbury for a £3,000 fee, an Albion record at the time.

When the innovative 'Gunners' introduced the 'policeman' centre-half system, it was Andy who was entrusted with the crucial roving inside-forward role (a job later perfected by the incomparable Alex James) upon the recommendation of skipper Charlie Buchan. Despite being described by Buchan as being 'as slow as the post', Andy had the ability to dictate the pace of a game and create chances for others. After 54 First Division games for Arsenal he returned to Hove at the age of 33 in March 1926, and continued to enthral Albion fans until moving to Queen's Park Rangers on a free transfer in May 1927, where he was converted into a wing-half and made over 100 Third Division appearances before retiring in 1930. A master-baker by trade, Andy died of a heart-attack at his Kilmarnock home at the age of 48.

Season	FL	FAC	Total
1920–21	18 (2)	3	21 (2)
1921–22	40 (3)	3	43 (3)
1922–23	42 (10)	5 (1)	47 (11)
1923–24	29 (7)	4 (1)	33 (8)
1925–26	12 (2)	0	12 (2)
1926–27	26 (4)	3	29 (4)
Total	167 (28)	18 (2)	185 (30)

NELSON, GARRY   *1987–91*

forward Ht 5 10, Wt 11 04   *166 apps, 59 goals*
full name: Garry Paul Nelson
born: Braintree, Essex, 16.1.1961
debut: York City (h), 15.8.1987 (FL D3)

One of Albion's great favourites of recent years, Garry Nelson quickly won the hearts of fans with a sustained display of skill, creativity, pace and expert finishing throughout the 1987–88 Third Division promotion campaign. Although unable to maintain his outstanding form in Division Two, the popular forward remained one of the principal strikers until 1990. Later to describe himself as a 'journeyman', he was – for one season at least – anything but as he acquired star-player status. His later criticism from afar of the hated Archer/Bellotti regime further endeared him to the club's supporters.

An Essex Schools representative, Garry had a trial with Colchester United as a youngster, but also turned out for Southend United in a reserve-team game against the Albion in November 1978, and joined the club as an eighteen-year-old professional the following July after gaining three A-levels; he turned down a place at Loughborough University to join the Roots Hall staff. Garry went on to play 129 League matches for the 'Shrimpers', mainly on the left wing, before moving to Swindon Town for £10,000 in August 1983. Two seasons at the County Ground were followed by a £15,000 move to Plymouth Argyle in July 1985, where he scored 20 goals in 74 appearances and helped the Devon side to promotion from Division Three in 1986.

In July 1987, Albion manager Barry Lloyd splashed out £72,500 to bring the 26-year-old to the Goldstone to form a new spearhead with Kevin Bremner. Played as an out-and-out striker for the first time in his career, Garry was an instant success and went on to score 32 goals for the season as Albion won promotion back to Division Two, a total bettered only by Peter Ward and Arthur Attwood in Albion history. Many of his goals were spectacular – a mazy dribble at Brentford in the F.A. Cup and a thunderbolt against Bristol City at the Goldstone perhaps stand out – and he ran away with the supporters' vote as Player of the Season. Garry was top scorer again with sixteen goals as the team struggled in the higher sphere the following season, but he hit just six goals in 1989–90 and subsequently struggled to make the side. After being loaned to Notts County for a month in November 1990, he was transferred to Charlton Athletic in August 1991 for a fee, set by a tribunal, of just £50,000. It proved a bargain for the Londoners as Garry continued to score goals – 37 in 185 League games – for another five years before joining Torquay United in the summer of 1996 as a player-coach. After just one season at Plainmoor he retired as a full-time player to take up a post as the London-based commercial executive of the P.F.A., but one game in the Southern League for St Leonards Stamcroft convinced him it was time to hang up his boots for good because of his dodgy knees.

Indeed, during his time at the Goldstone, Garry was the club's P.F.A. representative, a position which, as the players' spokesman, apparently led him into conflict with manager Barry Lloyd on more than one occasion. The 'feud' was revealed in his best-selling book *Left Foot Forward: A Year in the Life of a Journeyman Footballer* which was first published in September 1995 to critical acclaim. According to the author, the antagonism was fuelled by a transfer to AFC Bournemouth which fell through, and culminated in the manager informing him – at the Wembley urinals – that his services would not be required that day (for the 1991 Division Two play-off final). Having gained qualifications in business studies, finance and marketing during his playing days, Garry has also run his own picture-framing business and summer soccer-camps in the U.S.A.

Season	FL	Play-offs	FAC	FLC	FMC	AMC	Total
1987–88	42 (22)	0	4 (5)	1	0	5 (5)	52 (32)
1988–89	46 (15)	0	1	2	1 (1)	0	50 (16)
1989–90	32+1 (5)	0	2 (1)	2	1	0	37+1 (6)
1990–91	12+11 (5)	1	0	2	0	0	15+11 (5)
Total	132+12 (47)	1	7 (6)	7	2 (1)	5 (5)	154+12 (59)

NELSON, SAMMY   *1981–83*

left-back   Ht 5 10, Wt 11 00   *45 apps, 1 goal*
full name: Samuel Nelson
born: Belfast, Co. Antrim, Northern Ireland, 1.4.1949
debut: Huddersfield Town (h), 27.10.1981 (FLC R2 Lg2)

After joining the Arsenal ground staff as a young left-winger, Sammy Nelson signed professional forms at the age of seventeen in April 1966 and went on to enjoy a long and highly successful career at Highbury. The former Northern Ireland schoolboy international was soon converted into a left-back and went on to make 255 First Division appearances for the north London club. In 1966 he gained an F.A. Youth Cup winner's medal, and made his first-team debut in 1969–70, but he had to wait until 1975 and the departure of Bob McNab to Wolves before making the no.3 shirt his own.

In both 1978 and 1980, Sammy appeared on the losing side in the F.A. Cup final, but gained a coveted winner's medal in between when the 'Gunners' defeated Manchester United 3–2 in the 1979 final. He also appeared in the European Cup-Winners' Cup final of 1980, when Arsenal lost to Valencia in a penalty shoot-out in Brussels. He didn't always see eye-to-eye with the Highbury crowds, though, enjoying a relationship which resulted in an infamous lowering-of-the-shorts incident, but in November 1980 he was rewarded for fourteen years as a pro with a testimonial against Celtic. However, Kenny Sansom's arrival signalled the end of Sammy's days as a first-team force and he came to Hove in September 1981 when Mike Bailey paid a fee of around £30,000.

Taking over the no.3 shirt from Gary Williams, the experienced 32-year-old retained his place for the remainder of the 1981–82 campaign and spent the summer with the Northern Ireland World Cup team in Spain where he played in two games. After playing thirteen League matches at the outset of 1982–83, the tough-tackling full-back lost his place to Graham Pearce and took to coaching the reserves. His registration as a player was cancelled in April 1984 and he was appointed coach, but at the end of the year he resigned after a dispute with a number of senior players. He subsequently did some scouting for Arsenal and now commutes from his Brighton home to work for a finance company in London. In his heyday as one of the best left-backs in the Football League, Sammy won a total of 51 caps for Northern Ireland, the last four of which came while he was on Albion's books.

Season	FL	FAC	FLC	Total
1981–82	27 (1)	3	2	32 (1)
1982–83	13	0	0	13
Total	40 (1)	3	2	45 (1)

NEVINS, LAURIE   *1947–48*

winger   Ht 5 9, Wt 11 06   *5 apps*
full name: Laurence Nevins
born: Gateshead, Co. Durham, 2.7.1920
debut: Watford (a), 23.8.1947 (FL D3(S))

Discovered playing in the North Eastern League by Newcastle United, eighteen-year-old Laurie Nevins was taken on as an

amateur at St James's Park in May 1939 and turned pro in September 1940, but the war halted his progress although he still managed a few games for the 'Magpies' in the early days of the hostilities. Serving in the Royal Navy as a submariner, Laurie made guest appearances for Middlesbrough and Queen's Park Rangers before returning to Newcastle as a professional for 1946–47. After playing in the reserves, he became one of Tommy Cook's acquisitions during his short spell as Albion manager and arrived at the Goldstone in June 1947. Laurie turned out briefly on both wings before his release to join Hartlepools United in March 1948, his final League club.

Season	FL	Total
1947–48	5	5
Total	5	5

NEWMAN, Daren   1984–86

central defender   1 app
full name: Daren Lewis Newman
born: Brighton, Sussex, 14.8.1968
debut: Shrewsbury Town (h), 12.4.1986 (FL D2)

Having already appeared in the youth team, Daren Newman joined Albion as a trainee in January 1985 on leaving Newhaven's Tideway School and made rapid advances. The Brighton-born defender progressed to the fringe of the first-team squad in 1985–86, and was named as a sub. four times before making his one first-team appearance in the absence of Eric Young. Initially retained as a non-contract pro, he was released by new manager Alan Mullery in September 1986 to join Peacehaven & Telscombe in the Sussex County League.

Daren has since played for Southwick, Peacehaven for a second spell, and Newhaven, but in 1989 rejoined Peacehaven where, for four seasons, he was the driving-force of a formidable team which won many trophies and excelled in the F.A. Vase. He returned to Newhaven during the close season of 1993, but a year later joined Ringmer, and then moved back to Peacehaven. A competitive, dominating and – having lost most of his hair – distinctive figure in the midfield at Piddinghoe Avenue, Daren led  his club to further success and has also skippered the Sussex representative side. In 1996 he switched to Burgess Hill Town with whom he won another County League title.

Season	FL	Total
1985–86	1	1
Total	1	1

NEWTON, Jimmy   1929–30

goalkeeper   Ht 6 1, Wt 13 00   1 app
full name: James Newton
born: Horsforth, Yorkshire
debut: Clapton Orient (a), 3.5.1930 (FL D3(S))

Though English by birth, Jimmy Newton began his senior career with the famous Glasgow amateur club Queen's Park in June

1922, and assisted them to the Scottish Second Division championship in 1922–23 before turning professional with Bradford City in his native Yorkshire in June 1923. Having made the first team on just five occasions in two seasons at Valley Parade, Jimmy was released and moved on to Halifax Town in May 1925 where he enjoyed a much more successful time, missing only two Third Division (North) matches during the 1925–26 season. Nevertheless, he wasn't retained and joined Coventry City in June 1926. Ever-present with City in 1926–27, Jimmy remained at Highfield Road for three seasons, appearing in 70 Southern Section matches, but was confined to the reserves in 1928–29 and was freed to join the Albion at the end of the campaign. Acting as deputy to Stan Webb at the Goldstone, he had to wait until the final fixture of 1929–30 to make his debut for the first eleven, but it turned out to be his only first-team game for the club as, once again, he wasn't retained. He subsequently returned to Yorkshire and appeared as a permit player with the Otley and Burley Grove United clubs.

Season	FL	Total
1929–30	1	1
Total	1	1

NICHOLAS, Tony   1960–62

inside/centre-forward   Ht 5 10, Wt 12 00   70 apps, 23 goals
full name: Anthony Wallace Long Nicholas
born: West Ham, Essex, 16.4.1938
debut: Swansea Town (a), 5.11.1960 (FL D2)

After a spell on the Chelsea ground staff (together with his future Albion colleague Bobby Laverick), Tony Nicholas signed as a professional in May 1955 and was soon appearing in England's youth team. Showing tremendous promise, the Essex-born youngster made his First Division debut at the age of eighteen, and went on to score 21 goals in 63 League and Cup games for the London side before Billy Lane splashed out an Albion-record £15,000 fee for his services in November 1960.

Arriving at the Goldstone with a tremendous reputation, Tony impressed with his pace and shooting ability, and led the Albion's Second Division goal-scorers with thirteen goals from just 27 games in a struggling side. However, he had contractual problems the following term, and when Albion were relegated to Division Three in 1962 he became a victim of George Curtis's big clear-out.

Still only 24, Tony surprisingly dropped into the Southern League with Chelmsford City where he remained for three seasons before returning to the  Football League fold in June 1965 for a season with Leyton Orient. He subsequently did the rounds of the Southern League circuit with Dartford (1966–68), Cambridge United (Premier Division and Cup double winners 1968–69), Dartford for a second spell, Gravesend & Northfleet, and finally with Folkestone before calling it a day at the age of 35 in 1973.

Season	FL	FAC	FLC	Total
1960–61	27 (13)	3	0	30 (13)
1961–62	38 (9)	1	1 (1)	40 (10)
Total	65 (22)	4	1 (1)	70 (23)

NICOL, GEORDIE 1929–32

centre-forward Ht 5 8, Wt 11 08 *32 apps, 23 goals*
full name: George Nicol
born: Saltcoats, Ayrshire, Scotland, 14.12.1903
died: Saltcoats, Ayrshire, Scotland, 18.12.1968
debut: Bristol Rovers (a), 31.8.1929 (FL D3(S))

With nineteen goals from just 23 matches, including four in a 5–0 win over Gillingham at Christmas, Geordie Nicol led the Albion goalscorers in 1930–31 when the club finished fourth in the Third Division (South), but that was the height of the former pork-butcher's success in Hove. Given his chance when the prolific Hugh Vallance unexpectedly left the club in September 1930, he was unable to sustain his form the following season and returned to the reserves after just four games. The subsequent signing of Arthur Attwood ensured that he never made the first team again, and it was not until he moved to Kent that he was finally allowed to display his true worth.

The young Scot was working for the ham-curing firm Robertson & Co. and playing for Saltcoats Victoria when Manchester United signed him as a professional in January 1928. However, despite

netting twice in a 5–2 win over Leicester City on his first-team debut and scoring heavily for the reserves, he remained on the fringe of the First Division side and made just six appearances before requesting a transfer.

Arriving at the Goldstone in May 1929, the 25-year-old played in the opening matches of 1929–30, but was then forced to play a standby role as the amazing Vallance went on to set a new club scoring record. Having hit more than 40 goals for the 'Lambs', Geordie 'made hay' while the sun shone for him in 1930–31, but in 1932 he was released to try his luck in the Irish League with Belfast Distillery.

He soon returned to the Football League, though, joining Gillingham in September 1932 to make an immediate impact: with 28 goals in his first season he broke the club's scoring record despite missing the opening month of the campaign. Geordie remained at Priestfield until 1935, totalling 42 goals in 72 outings, but with the recession making it almost impossible to find employment he moved into the French League with Roubaix. On returning to his native Ayrshire in 1938, Geordie worked, firstly, for I.C.I. at Stevenston, then on the railways, and finally for the Ardrossan Harbour Board. Known later in life as 'Towser', he rather tragically died just four days after his 65th birthday as he collected his first pension.

Despite being on the short side for a centre-forward, Geordie was as hard as nails and accumulated 67 goals from a career tally of 111 League and Cup games, a formidable return. Yet, for all his toughness on the pitch, the ex-Manchester United man was devastated by the 1958 Munich air-disaster which almost wiped out his former club, and he showed no further interest in football until Celtic (whose Bobby Lennox was a distant relative) won the European Cup in 1967.

Season	FL	FAC	Total
1929–30	5 (3)	0	5 (3)
1930–31	22 (19)	1	23 (19)
1931–32	4 (1)	0	4 (1)
Total	31 (23)	1	32 (23)

NIGHTINGALE, JACK 1921–27

outside-right Ht 5 6, Wt 11 00 *195 apps, 33 goals*
full name: John Gladstone Nightingale
born: Oldbury, Worcestershire, 1899
died: Brighton, Sussex, 1967
debut: Exeter City (a), 31.8.1921 (FL D3(S))

One of the stalwarts of the 1920s, Jack Nightingale made 195 appearances on the Albion right and formed a terrific partnership with Andy Neil, the speed of the diminutive, fleet-footed winger

-NIGHTINGALE - B+H.ALBION.F.C.1923-24-

blending perfectly with the guile of the talented Scot. Playing a big part in the success of centre-forward Tommy Cook and others, he could also score himself, and, with fourteen goals to his name, was second-highest scorer in 1925–26 behind Sam Jennings.

Born in the Black Country, Jack played three Second Division matches for Wolves after joining the club in December 1919, but there was to be no future for him at Molineux and he was released in May 1920 to drop into the Birmingham League with Shrewsbury Town. However, his hopes of a Football League career were renewed in August 1921 when Albion paid £100 for his signature, and he shared the right-wing spot with Fred Groves for two seasons before making the position his own.

A regular for more than four years, Jack received a benefit in April 1927, a League fixture against Charlton Athletic which realised £338. After six seasons in Hove he moved back into the Birmingham League with his former club, Shrewsbury Town, for 1927–28. Albion, though, retained his Football League registration, and when he was put on the transfer list in May 1928 the club received inquiries from Brentford, Bristol Rovers and Bristol City, but he decided to leave the first-class game. Jack lived in Brighton for many years until his death at the age of 68.

Season	FL	FAC	Total
1921–22	20 (3)	1	21 (3)
1922–23	17 (2)	0	17 (2)
1923–24	38 (7)	4	42 (7)
1924–25	38 (3)	3	41 (3)
1925–26	41 (14)	2	43 (14)
1926–27	28 (4)	3	31 (4)
Total	182 (33)	13	195 (33)

NOGAN, KURT 1992–95

forward Ht 5 11, Wt 12 07 *120 apps, 60 goals*
born: Cardiff, Glamorgan, Wales, 9.9.1970
debut: Rotherham United (a), 17.10.1992 (FL D2)

With 60 goals in 120 games for the Albion, Kurt Nogan's strike-rate compares with the very best in the club's history. In fact, he scored those 60 goals in his first 100 games before enduring the barren 20-match run which saw him leave Hove under something of a cloud; but over a century of matches he hit the net at a rate which puts him up with the likes of Jack Doran, Tommy Cook and Arthur Attwood, three of the greatest goal-getters to have graced the Goldstone turf.

Yet few who saw the Welshman when he first arrived as a 22-year-old trialist would have envisaged his subsequent success. Looking at first a 'fish out of water', Kurt scored a freak goal – the ball rebounded off him from Bournemouth goalkeeper Vince Bartram's clearance – and his confidence soared. Despite appearing lazy at times, speed off the mark and excellent positioning saw him grab 22 goals in his first season and 26 the next, the first Albion player to score more than 20 times in consecutive seasons since Albert Mundy in 1954–57.

The younger brother of Grimsby Town striker Lee Nogan, Kurt represented Cardiff as a schoolboy and was playing Sunday football with his brother when the pair were invited for a trial with Luton Town. Lee was rejected, but Kurt joined the Kenilworth Road staff as an apprentice in 1986 where one of his chores was to clean ex-Albion skipper Steve Foster's boots! In January 1990 he made his League debut, scoring in a 2–2 draw at Liverpool, and scored again on his international debut, for the Welsh under-21 side against Poland in May 1990. Seven months later he won a second under-21 cap, in a

goal-less draw with England alongside his brother, Lee. However, Kurt scored just three times for the struggling 'Hatters' in 33 League games (16 of them as substitute) and was released in 1992 following the Bedfordshire club's relegation from the old First Division.

After an unsuccessful trial with Peterborough United – he played just one Anglo-Italian Cup fixture and a couple of reserve games – Kurt rejected an offer from Colchester United and was facing the prospect of unemployment when he was invited to the Goldstone by reserve-team coach Larry May in October 1992; he scored two goals in two reserve games to earn himself an initial three-month contract. Following his uncertain start, Kurt established himself in the Albion side with two goals against Burnley on Boxing Day and began his prolific scoring feats. On New Year's Day 1994 the quicksilver striker scored the first Albion hat-trick for three years and was the club's hottest property, forcing his way into the Welsh B-international squad and signing a two-and-a-half year contract. At the end of the campaign he was voted Player of the Season after hitting 26 goals in 48 games.

Kurt's last goal for the club was a sensational strike to seal a 3–0 aggregate victory over Premiership side Leicester City in the League Cup in October 1994. Apparently attracting interest from the likes of Liverpool, he then sadly underwent a dreadful goal-drought which caused him to become the butt of criticism from the terraces. In February 1995 he was the subject of an enquiry by Burnley (against whom he had scored five times in four matches), and signed for the then First Division club for £250,000 a few weeks later. At the time his departure was a great relief to all concerned, but the loss of the club's only regular goalscorer proved ultimately disastrous as no one could be found to replace him adequately.

Kurt's barren spell quickly ended at Turf Moor, and he ended 1995–96 as top scorer with 26 goals, inevitably netting against the Albion in a 3–0 home win. Named in the P.F.A.'s 'all-star team' for the section, he was also called up for the full Welsh international squad the same season, but the talented striker fell out with the Burnley management during 1996–97 and had a trial with Heart of Midlothian in February 1997. The following month Kurt moved to Preston North End for £150,000 plus a small sum dependent upon his appearances.

Season	FL	FAC	FLC	AMC	Total
1992–93	30 (20)	3+1	0	3 (2)	36+1 (22)
1993–94	41 (22)	1	4 (2)	2 (2)	48 (26)
1994–95	26 (7)	1	6 (5)	2	35 (12)
Total	97 (49)	5+1	10 (7)	7 (4)	119+1 (60)

O'BRIEN, JOE   1904–05

left-back   Ht 5 8, Wt 13 00   33 apps
full name: Joseph O'Brien
born: Shettleston, Glasgow, Lanarkshire, Scotland, 27.12.1875
debut: New Brompton (a), 3.9.1904 (SL D1)

'A tough, no-nonsense defender, strong as a horse and never tiring.' Joe O'Brien started out with Baillieston Thistle as a teenager before becoming a part-time professional with Clitheroe in the Lancashire League. In May 1896 he was tempted south to join Reading and had four fine seasons at Elm Park, being selected to represent the Southern League v. London F.A. in February 1899. In April 1900, Joe was transferred to Blackburn Rovers but, with the wealth of talent at Ewood Park, failed to command a place in the team and returned to Scotland in September 1901 for a season in the Northern League with Aberdeen. He signed for Swindon Town during the close season of 1902, and the following summer rejoined Reading for a

second spell. Arriving at the Goldstone in May 1904, Joe struck up a splendid understanding with skipper Tom Robertson at full-back during his only season with the Albion before returning to Swindon Town in May 1905. His second stint with the Wiltshire side lasted one season, after which he played in turn for Stalybridge Rovers and then Haslingden in the Lancashire Combination.

Season	SL	FAC	Total
1904–05	28	5	33
Total	28	5	33

O'DOWD, GREG   1988–92

defender   Ht 5 10, Wt 10 00   1 app
full name: Gregory Henry O'Dowd
born: Dublin, Co. Dublin, Republic of Ireland, 16.3.1973
debut: Middlesbrough (a), 21.3.1992 (FL D2)

Despite competition from Nottingham Forest, Greg O'Dowd signed as a trainee for the Albion in April 1988 from the League of Ireland First Division club Home Farm, a well-known Dublin nursery. One of a clutch of young Irishmen at the Goldstone under Barry Lloyd, he turned professional in October 1990 at the age of 17 and also appeared

in the Republic of Ireland youth team. In May 1992, six weeks after his only League appearance, Greg skippered the reserves to triumph in the Sussex Senior Cup final against Langney Sports, but was released later that week and returned to Ireland with Longford Town.

After one season with Longford, Greg moved to Dundalk and then joined Shamrock Rovers in January 1995. Eleven months and one goal later, the 22-year-old moved north of the border to sign for Coleraine, and was soon rewarded with an Irish League First Division championship medal, scoring nine times in eighteen games as a winger. In 1996–97, Coleraine were narrowly pipped for the Premier Division title and were also runners-up in the Ulster Cup, with Greg playing his part in both near-misses. His elder brother, Tony, plays in goal for Derry City and had a spell with Leeds United.

Season	FL	Total
1991–92	0+1	0+1
Total	0+1	0+1

OLIVER, GAVIN   1985

defender   Ht 5 11, Wt 13 10   17 apps
full name: Gavin Ronald Oliver
born: Felling, Co. Durham, 6.9.1962
debut: Grimsby Town (h), 17.8.1985 (FL D2)

Spotted by a Sheffield Wednesday scout while playing for a local boys' club, Gavin Oliver joined the 'Owls' as an associate schoolboy and later became an apprentice. Signed as a professional in August

9 players who played first-class cricket

Player	Player
Allsopp, Tommy	Cross, Graham
Bates, Don	Foreman, Denis
Brophy, Henry	Leach, George
Clare, Edwin	Suttle, Ken
Cook, Tommy	

1980, he remained at Hillsborough for more than six years but made just 20 League appearances. In January 1983 he joined Tranmere Rovers for an extended loan period, playing in seventeen Fourth Division matches, and it was in a similar situation that Gavin arrived at the Goldstone in August 1985. Playing in central defence and at full-back, his loan period was extended to three months and Chris Cattlin was keen to sign the accomplished defender permanently, but Wednesday's asking-price was too steep for Albion at the time and he returned to Sheffield. In November 1985, Gavin joined Bradford City for £25,000 and settled in well, clocking up 381 League and Cup appearances for the 'Bantams' at centre-half, right-back and in midfield. He was rewarded with a testimonial match against Leeds United in October 1994 before leaving Valley Parade the following summer.

Season	FL	FMC	Total
1985–86	15+1	1	16+1
Total	15+1	1	16+1

OLIVER, JIM   1965–68

forward Ht 5 11, Wt 11 07   50 apps, 6 goals
full name: James Robert Oliver
born: Maddiston, Stirlingshire, Scotland, 3.12.1941
debut: Aldershot (h), 13.3.1965 (FL D4)

Jim Oliver represented Scotland as a schoolboy, and graduated through the Woodburn Athletic and Linlithgow Rose clubs to Falkirk in the Scottish League, where he made his first team debut at the age of seventeen, scoring in a 5–1 win over Aberdeen. With 76 Scottish League outings behind him, Jim moved to Norwich City for £10,000 in August 1962 and scored fourteen goals in 40 Second Division appearances for the 'Canaries', including three in a 6–0 defeat of Stoke City in March 1963, but two broken legs suffered during the 1963–64 campaign ultimately restricted his opportunities at Carrow Road.

In March 1965, Archie Macaulay returned to his former club and paid £6,000 to bring the pacy forward to the Goldstone Ground, but,

although he appeared in all the forward positions, Jim was never able to establish himself as an Albion regular. When the substitute was introduced to League football for the first time in 1965–66, the Scot's versatility made him an ideal choice for the no.12 shirt and he made history by becoming Albion's first playing sub. when he came on for Bill Cassidy in the 80th minute of the 2–1 home defeat by Hull City on 28 August. A month after losing his place in November 1965 he requested a move, but remained with the club until February 1968 when he was transferred to Colchester United for £3,000.

Jim's debut for the Essex club came the day after his transfer, ironically in a goal-less draw at the Goldstone, and he was a regular in their line-up for just over two years with ten goals from 74 League matches. On his release at the end of the 1969–70 season, Jim moved into the Southern League with King's Lynn and subsequently played for Lowestoft Town (as

player-coach) and Gorleston Town before dropping into Norfolk junior football. He settled in Norwich and has worked as a sports-outfitter for many years.

Season	FL	FAC	FLC	Total
1964–65	5	0	0	5
1965–66	23+6 (3)	0	1	24+6 (3)
1966–67	6 (2)	5	1	12 (2)
1967–68	3 (1)	0	0	3 (1)
Total	37+6 (6)	5	2	44+6 (6)

O'RAWE, FRANK   1926–27

centre-half   Ht 5 9, Wt 11 07   1 app
full name: Francis O'Rawe
born: Uphall, West Lothian, Scotland, 20.12.1900
debut: Brentford (a), 28.8.1926 (FL D3(S))

Although born in Scotland, Frank O'Rawe always claimed Irish nationality, probably because of parental connections. Starting out as an inside-forward, he joined his local Scottish Second Division side, Bathgate, but it was after moving to Preston North End in September 1923 that he was converted into a centre-half. Frank was limited to just four outings in the First Division team at Deepdale, though, and moved on to Southend United in August 1924 where he met with greater success, making 58 League and Cup appearances in two seasons before Charlie Webb paid £450 for his signature in August 1926.

Despite the large fee, Frank failed to make an impression at the Goldstone. After playing in the opening fixture of the season, when Albion lost 4–0 at Brentford, he was displaced by Paul Mooney and never appeared in the senior side again. Released for a breach of contract toward the end of the 1926–27 campaign, he subsequently played for the Brighton-based Vernon Athletic club in the Sussex County League as a permit player. In 1933 he was turning out for the London works' side Whittaker Ellis.

Season	FL	Total
1926–27	1	1
Total	1	1

O'REGAN, KIERAN   1982–87

right-back/midfield   Ht 5 9, Wt 10 08   99 apps, 3 goals
born: Cork, Co. Cork, Republic of Ireland, 9.11.1963
debut: Norwich City (a), 14.5.1983 (FL D1)

Kieran O'Regan had to choose between soccer and Gaelic football as a lad in his native Cork. Wisely he opted for the association game and went on to enjoy a lengthy if unspectacular career as a professional in England. After joining the local Tramore Athletic club, he made such rapid progress that he was playing for the Republic's youth team in 1982. Spotted by Albion's former assistant coach Brian Eastick, the eighteen-year-old also impressed chief scout Jimmy Melia and arrived at the Goldstone for a trial period in September 1982.

Although he had doubts about his ability to make the grade, Kieran was persuaded to stay in Hove with Albion paying Tramore £10,000 for his signature in April 1983. The young full-back very nearly made a sensational debut when, with injury and suspension creating problems at the time of the F.A. Cup semi-final with Sheffield Wednesday in April 1983, he was selected as substitute. In the event he wasn't called upon, but he did play in the final League fixture of the season at Norwich –Albion's last in the First Division – and spent

the ensuing summer with the Republic's under-21 squad in France. When the 1983–84 campaign opened, the exuberant youngster was Albion's first-choice right-back, and in November he won the first of four full-international caps in the 8–0 defeat of Malta in Dublin.

Playing also in midfield, Kieran more than made up for any lack of skill with his enthusiasm, stamina and tackling, but remained only on the fringe of Albion's League team for the next three seasons. Following the club's relegation in May 1987, the 23-year-old Irishman signed for Swindon Town, but moved on to Huddersfield Town in August 1988 after 26 League appearances at the County Ground. It was at Leeds Road that Kieran found his niche, his terrier-like play perhaps finding an appropriate home with the 'Terriers'. Making well over 200 appearances in midfield, he assisted the Yorkshire side to the 1992 Third Division play-offs, and moved up a division a year later when West Bromwich Albion signed him for £25,000 in July 1993. After two seasons at The Hawthorns, Kieran returned to Yorkshire with Halifax Town in the summer of 1995. In February 1997, when skipper of the Conference side, he was appointed joint manager with the old Sunderland and Scotland star George Mulhall.

Season	FL	FAC	FLC	FMC	Total
1982–83	1	0	0	0	1
1983–84	30+1 (1)	0	3	0	33+1 (1)
1984–85	11+4	2	0	0	13+4
1985–86	6+9 (1)	0	1+1	1+1 (1)	8+11 (2)
1986–87	21+3	1	2	1	25+3
Total	69+17 (2)	3	6+1	2+1 (1)	80+19 (3)

O'REILLY, GARY   1984–87 & 1991–93

defender   Ht 5 11, Wt 12 00   123 apps, 6 goals
full name: Gary Miles O'Reilly
born: Isleworth, Middlesex, 21.3.1961
debut: Notts County (h), 28.8.1984 (FL D2)

Gary O'Reilly had an unusual football background: although his father played for the Bohemians club in Dublin, Gary himself was raised in Harlow, Essex; he played in the South East Counties League for both Arsenal and Spurs; and he represented Essex Boys and progressed to the England Schools side, but went on to play for the Eire youth team. While staying on at school to take 'A' levels, Gary turned out for Harlow Town's youth team and for Grays Athletic before signing professional forms for Tottenham Hotspur at the age of eighteen in September 1979.

Despite making 56 League and Cup appearances, mainly at left-back, he never really established himself in the Spurs first team in five seasons at White Hart Lane, though, and in August 1984 Albion manager Chris Cattlin paid £45,000 for the versatile defender. The 23-year-old initially played at right-back, but quickly found his niche in the middle of the back line and went on to form a fine partnership with Eric Young, a principal reason for Albion equalling

their fewest-goals-conceded record in the Football League in 1984–85, just 34. A good reader of the game, Gary covered his colleagues well, tackled strongly, and played solidly again the following term. He also made a considerable contribution behind the scenes with the Junior Seagulls and with a number of community projects.

In 1986–87, Gary suffered injury problems which restricted his appearances, but he had just made a come-back in the first eleven when, to the great surprise of Albion supporters, he was sold by Alan Mullery to Crystal Palace for a giveaway £40,000. It was the manager's last deal before his dismissal, but the club, falling deeper into financial difficulty, was desperate to generate cash to meet the wage-bill. The popular defender went on to play a large part in Palace's return to the First Division in 1989 and spent the summer with a Swedish club, but returned to Selhurst and appeared in the "Eagles'" losing F.A. Cup final side of 1990.

In 1990–91, Gary lost his first-team place and was loaned to Birmingham City in March, but rejoined the Albion in July 1991 on a free transfer. Although he made a further 31 League and Cup appearances, the 30-year-old never recaptured the form of his earlier spell with the club and retired in April 1993 following a series of unsuccessful knee operations, although he did turn out briefly for Bognor Regis Town in January 1994. Gary enjoyed a testimonial forum at Hove Town Hall in April 1994, and has concentrated on a broadcasting career since leaving the game, including a position as a presenter on Sky TV. He still lives locally and did much to support the fans' campaign against the Albion board during 1996–97.

Season	FL	FAC	FLC	FMC	Total
1984–85	36 (3)	2	2	0	40 (3)
1985–86	35	5	2	2	44
1986–87	7+1	0	0	0	7+1
1991–92	28 (3)	0	2	1	31 (3)
Total	106+1 (6)	7	6	3	122+1 (6)

ORMEROD, MARK   1992–

goalkeeper   Ht 6 0, Wt 11 05   22 apps
full name: Mark Ian Ormerod
born: Bournemouth, Hampshire, 5.2.1976
debut: Scarborough (h), 7.9.1996 (FL D3)

Shortly after signing as a trainee in 1992, sixteen-year-old Mark Ormerod was thrust into first-team action in friendlies against Wimbledon and Crystal Palace, but it was more than four years before he made his League debut. The wiry youngster had to be content with 82 games on the bench, playing second-fiddle to Nicky Rust, before donning the no.1 shirt in September 1996. Ironically, the only time Rust had been injured before that was when Mark himself was out with a broken hand.

Mark had been associated with AFC Bournemouth, his home-town club, as a school-boy, but when they dallied over offering him an apprenticeship in June 1992 Albion quickly stepped in. Becoming a full pro in 1994, he won a number of fans in the reserves who maintained that he was a better 'keeper than Rust. When finally given his chance, the former Bournemouth and Dorset Schools representative impressed with his clean handling and reactions, and also with his willingness to release the ball quickly to his forwards. In the latter half of 1996–97, Mark took over from the demoralised Rust as first choice, and, apart from two games, held his position to the end of the campaign which saw a dramatic escape from relegation to the Football Conference. When off-duty, Mark plays bass-guitar in a band, 'The Marlins'.

Season	FL	AMC	Total
1996–97	21	1	22
Total	21	1	22

OSBORNE, FRED   *1919–20*

inside-right   Ht 5 8, Wt 11 07   3 apps
full name: Frederick Osborne
born: Birmingham, Warwickshire, c. 1893
debut: Portsmouth (h), 24.9.1919 (SL D1)

Fred Osborne played for Worcester City in the Birmingham League immediately before the outbreak of the First World War, but his football activities were then largely curtailed by the host-ilities. He did, however, join Birmingham during the final wartime season, and also gues-ted briefly for Leicester Fosse, Lincoln City and Coventry City. One of Charlie Webb's first recruits on the former Albion forward's appointment as manager in 1919, 24-year-old Fred played three games in the club's last season in the Southern League, but failed to impress in a struggling side and was freed to join Western League Weymouth in May 1920. He later moved back to the Southern League with Ponty-pridd, and in 1922 made his

biggest contribution to Albion's cause by recommending the Welsh club's full-back, Jack Jenkins, to Webb.

Season	SL	Total
1919–20	3	3
Total	3	3

OSBORNE, JACK   *1927–29*

left-back   Ht 5 7, Wt 10 07   3 apps
full name: John Edward Osborne
born: Dundee, Angus, Scotland, 24.4.1902
died: Dundee, Angus, Scotland, 2.4.1968
debut: Swindon Town (h), 29.9.1928 (FL D3(S))

A joiner by trade, Jack Osborne joined Dundee United from local junior football in September 1924 and was one of three future Albion players – the others were Tommy Simpson and Willie Oswald – to figure in United's Second Division championship side in his first season at Tannadice. Transferred up the road to Forfar Athletic in May 1926, Jack spent just one season at Station Park before arriving at the Goldstone Ground, together with John Fox (who never appeared in the Albion first team), in September 1927 for an £80 fee.

Although he stayed with the club for two seasons, acting as a deputy to Jack Curran at left-back, Jack struggled to impress in the few first-team opportunities that came his way. In October 1929 he was released to return to Scotland with Brechin City, and subsequently became their player-secretary before moving to Montrose in 1935 and then Forfar Athletic in 1936.

Season	FL	Total
1928–29	3	3
Total	3	3

OSMAN, RUSSELL   *1995–96*

central defender   Ht 5 11, Wt 12 01   17 apps
full name: Russell Charles Osman
born: Repton, Derbyshire, 14.2.1959
debut: Cambridge United (a), 26.10.1995 (AMC group)

An automatic choice in the excellent Ipswich Town side of the late 1970s and early 80s, Russell Osman won a host of honours in a football career that only began when he took up the game at the age of fifteen. In fact, he played rugby at Burton Grammar School and captained the England Schools rugby XV. Joining Ipswich as an apprentice, the young defender won an F.A. Youth Cup winner's medal in 1975, signed professional forms in March 1976, and emulated his father, Rex (who was on Derby County's books in the early 1950s), by gaining England youth honours in 1977. Quickly establishing himself alongside Terry Butcher at the heart of the Portman Road defence, Russell went on to earn seven caps at under-21 level and also played for the England B team before making his full international debut against Australia in May 1980, the first of eleven appearances for England (seven of which were in partnership with his Ipswich colleague, Butcher).

It was generally felt that he disappointed with England, though, and it was Butcher who became the seasoned international. Nevertheless, Russell played his part as Ipswich continued to be a major force in the First Division and lifted the UEFA Cup in 1981. After 294 League appearances for the Suffolk side, he was transferred to Leicester City in July 1985 for £240,000 at the age of 26 where he again performed admirably, but City were relegated to the Second Division in his second season at Filbert Street. In 1987, Russell was installed as skipper, but moved back to the First Division with Southampton in June 1988 for £325,000 where he was a regular for two-and-a-half years.

In October 1991, the experienced defender joined Bristol City on loan and signed permanently the following month for a £60,000 fee. Becoming assis-tant to manager Denis Smith, Russell took over as caretaker manager in January 1993 as City struggled in Division One, taking the post permanently two months later. His appearances diminished as the 'Robins' continued to battle against relegation, though, and he was dismissed in November 1994 (although the club was still relegated). Joining Plymouth Argyle as an 'adviser' towards the end of the season, Russell was engaged in protracted litigation with Bristol City, and was still pursuing a claim for unfair dismissal in September 1995 when he arrived at the Goldstone on trial.

Signing the Albion on a non-contract basis, the 36-year-old hadn't appeared in League football for eighteen months; in his prime one of the coolest and most competent defenders in the country, he was now clearly past his best and did little to inspire confidence. In November, Russell settled his differences with his former club, but left Albion in February 1996 to join Cardiff City where he made fifteen appearances before being released at the end of the season. However, he returned to Ninian Park in November 1996 as manager of the Third Division side under Director of Football Kenny Hibbitt.

Although he has now faded from the national scene, Russell will be seen regularly for many years to come in the oft-repeated but critically *un*acclaimed film *Escape to Victory,* along with Michael Caine, Sylvester Stallone, a number of international star players, and many of his erstwhile team-mates at Ipswich.

Season	FL	FAC	AMC	Total
1995–96	11+1	2	3	16+1
Total	11+1	2	3	16+1

O'SULLIVAN, PETER — 1970–80 & 1980–81

outside-left/midfield   Ht 5 7, Wt 10 00   491 apps, 43 goals
full name: Peter Anthony O'Sullivan
born: Colwyn Bay, Denbighshire, Wales, 4.3.1951
debut: Torquay United (h), 15.8.1970 (FL D3)

One of Albion's all-time favourite sons, Peter O'Sullivan started out with the club as a winger, but matured into the brains of the team, a dominant influence in midfield for seven years who rarely missed a game. Indeed, 'Sully' played in 194 consecutive matches from 1970 until 1974, a record second only to that of goalkeeper Eric Gill, while his total of 491 first-team games has been bettered only by Ernie 'Tug' Wilson. Although his Albion career was full of ups and downs, the visionary Welshman always fought back to regain his place, and, together with his skipper Brian Horton, was the driving-force behind the club's rapid rise from the Third Division to the First in the late 1970s. It was no coincidence that his time at the Goldstone Ground included many of the club's finest hours. Seemingly able to thread the ball through the eye of a needle, 'Sully' also packed an explosive shot in his 'educated' left foot and hit a number of spectacular goals during eleven years in Hove.

Brought up in the Conwy valley, Peter played three times for the Welsh Schools, scoring on each occasion, before becoming an apprentice with Manchester United. Despite signing as a professional in March 1968, though, he was unable to break into the star-studded team at Old Trafford and joined the Albion on a free transfer in April 1970. Manager Freddie Goodwin's last transaction for the club, it was also surely one of the best deals in Brighton's history.

Ironically, Peter's long career at the Goldstone very nearly ended before it had really begun when, after just two appearances, he was listed at his own request after being dropped by new manager Pat Saward in favour of Howard Wilkinson. He was restored to the side within a couple of months, though, and rarely missed a game thereafter. Indeed, he showed such form that he won the first of six Welsh under-23 caps in January 1971, and attracted considerable interest from First Division clubs the following term as Albion won promotion to Division Two on a tidal wave of attacking football; he himself scored twelve times. The 1972–73 campaign was disastrous for the club, but Peter was called up for the Welsh squad and won his first full cap as a substitute against Scotland at Wrexham in March.

'Sully' started to operate in midfield in 1973–74, but was dropped by manager Peter Taylor in September 1974 and made available for transfer, bringing to an end his extraordinary run of 194 matches. Again, though, after an absence of seven games, he fought his way back into the side and developed into the chief play-maker over the next few seasons, adding two more full caps to his collection. A consistent performer in the 1976–77 promotion campaign, Peter got off to another bad start the following term in Division Two when he fell out with manager Alan Mullery and once again requested a transfer. Having made his peace, though, he regained his place and went on to enjoy probably his best season with the club, his promptings creating numerous opportunities for strikers Ian Mellor, Peter Ward, Teddy Maybank and Malcolm Poskett. Voted Player of the Season by supporters, he went on to miss just five games in 1978–79 when Albion finished in runner's-up spot in Division Two, thus ensuring that his testimonial season would coincide with the club's First Division debut. Among the many events organised for his benefit was a match with Southampton, 6,881 admirers raising around £10,000 towards his fund.

Presented with a silver tea-service and illuminated scroll on the occasion of his 400th League appearance, Peter was transferred to San Diego Sockers in April 1980 after playing in all but three games of Albion's first season in the top flight. After helping his new club reach the N.A.S.L. play-offs, it wasn't long before he was back at the Goldstone as Alan Mullery re-signed him in September 1980 to help stabilise a struggling side. His Albion career finally came to an end after eleven years when he was released to join Fulham in June 1981, and he was absent only once as the 'Cottagers' won promotion to the Second Division. The following season, 1982–83, he had loan spells at Charlton Athletic (October) and Reading (November) before leaving for a spell in Hong Kong. In August 1983 he joined Aldershot and made fourteen appearances in their Fourth Division side before departing from the Football League circuit, after 509 League games, in February 1984 when he signed for Maidstone United in the Alliance Premier League.

Peter subsequently returned to Sussex to do the rounds with Crawley Town, Worthing, Wick, Shoreham and Peacehaven, during which time he played for the county's representative side. In 1990–91, at the age of 40, he played a big part in helping Newhaven lift the County League Division Two title while working in the building industry.

Season	FL	FAC	FLC	Total
1970–71	35 (2)	3 (1)	1	39 (3)
1971–72	46 (10)	3 (2)	2	51 (12)
1972–73	42 (2)	1	2	45 (2)
1973–74	46 (4)	2	1	49 (4)
1974–75	39 (4)	3	4	46 (4)
1975–76	46 (7)	3	1	50 (7)
1976–77	43 (2)	3	7	53 (2)
1977–78	38 (4)	2	4	44 (4)
1978–79	37 (1)	1	4 (1)	42 (2)
1979–80	38+1 (1)	2	5	45+1 (1)
1980–81	22+2 (2)	2	0	24+2 (2)
Total	432+3 (39)	25 (3)	31 (1)	488+3 (43)

OSWALD, WILLIE — 1926–28

outside-right   Ht 5 8, Wt 11 07   14 apps, 2 goals
full name: William Oswald
born: Dundee, Angus, Scotland, 3.8.1900
debut: Watford (a), 12.3.1927 (FL D3(S))

Willie Oswald was playing for his local junior club, Dundee Celtic, when he was enticed south for a trial with Gillingham in March 1922. He signed professional forms in May, but after just one season at Priestfield he moved back to Scotland with St Johnstone. August 1924 saw his return to Dundee to play for United, where he won a Second Division championship medal in his first season, and he went on to score sixteen goals in 49 Scottish League games at Tannadice before coming to the Goldstone in August 1926. A reserve-team player with the Albion, Willie was deprived of a first-eleven place, firstly, by Jack Nightingale and then by his former Dundee United team-mate Tommy Simpson. Given a free transfer in May 1928, he is believed to have returned north of the border.

Season	FL	Total
1926–27	11 (1)	11 (1)
1927–28	3 (1)	3 (1)
Total	14 (2)	14 (2)

OWEN, F. — 1902–03

inside-forward — *4 apps*
debut: Queen's Park Rangers (a), 22.11.1902 (SEL)

A fringe member of Albion's team during 1902–03, Owen appeared in the South Eastern League side on four occasions, but failed to make the Southern League team which gained promotion to the First Division that season.

Season	SEL	Total
1902–03	4	4
Total	4	4

OWENS, LES — 1952–53

centre-forward — Ht 5 11, Wt 12 07 — *18 apps, 7 goals*
full name: Thomas Leslie Owens
born: Monkwearmouth, Sunderland, Co. Durham, 17.10.1919
died: Hellesdon, Norwich, Norfolk, 28.3.1974
debut: Crystal Palace (h), 23.8.1952 (FL D3(S))

Although he had a trial with Sunderland, Les Owens made his Football League debut as a teenager for First Division Charlton Athletic in September 1937 and showed great promise, but in February 1939 he dropped into the Third Division, signing for Doncaster Rovers for £1,000. During the war Les served with the 8th Army in Egypt, Sicily and Austria, but still managed to play a few games for Rovers, and also made guest appearances for Charlton and Coventry City. When normal service was resumed in 1946 the Sunderland-born forward returned to Doncaster, but moved on to Southport in December 1947, and subsequently played for Hartlepools United (July 1949), Norwich City (March 1950), and Reading (July 1951) for whom he scored a good number of goals in the reserves, before joining the Albion in June 1952.

Although he was 32 on his arrival at the Goldstone, Les was first-choice centre-forward until he broke several ribs during a match against Leyton Orient in September 1952, after which he appeared only briefly before losing his place to new recruit Bert Addinall. In August 1953 he left for Dartford in the Southern League, but suffered a broken leg after only a few weeks with the Kent side which brought about his retirement. He settled in Norwich and later had a seven-year stint (1960–67) as manager of the Hellesdon club. Les subsequently organised the Norwich City All Stars side which raised large sums of cash in aid of local charities. In 1974 he died of cancer at the age of 54. A superstitious character, Les would never don his boots until the very last moment before leaving the dressing room.

Season	FL	FAC	Total
1952–53	15 (4)	3 (3)	18 (7)
Total	15 (4)	3 (3)	18 (7)

OWERS, ADRIAN — 1987–91

midfield — Ht 5 8, Wt 10 02 — *43 apps, 4 goals*
full name: Adrian Richard Owers
born: Danbury, Essex, 26.2.1965
debut: Brentford (a), 26.3.1988 (FL D3)

A skilful midfielder who trained with Orient as a schoolboy, Adrian Owers had trials with both Tottenham Hotspur and Ipswich Town before joining Southend United as an apprentice at the age of sixteen, where he became a team-mate of future Albion colleagues John Keeley and Garry Nelson. After 27 League appearances for United, Adrian was released to join Southern League Chelmsford City as a part-timer

in 1985 while working as a clerk with Essex County Council, but was given an opportunity to resume his Football League career when Barry Lloyd paid £3,500 for his services in December 1987, plus another £4,000 after 20 appearances.

The 22-year-old from Essex impressed as a hard-shooting, constructive player in the latter stages of the 1987–88 Third Division promotion campaign, and was in and out of the side the following season, but he then suffered an Achilles' tendon injury and struggled to make the team. After a ten-match loan-spell at Gillingham from March 1991, Adrian was given a free transfer on the expiry of his contract at the end of the season. He then worked on the administrative staff of the Sussex Sunday League and appeared briefly for the ill-fated Maidstone United club during the last season of its existence before joining Redbridge Forest (now Dagenham & Redbridge) in the Conference in February 1992. In 1993 he made a welcome return to his former club, Chelmsford City, but came back to Sussex in March 1995 on loan to Worthing, whom he assisted to promotion to the Isthmian League Premier Division. Although it looked as though he was going to sign permanently for the 'Rebels', Adrian instead joined Southern League side Braintree Town in his home county during the 1995 close season while working in the banking industry.

Season	FL	FLC	FMC	Total
1987–88	9 (2)	0	0	9 (2)
1988–89	21+3 (2)	2	0+1	23+4 (2)
1989–90	0+4	0	0	0+4
1990–91	2+1	0	0	2+1
Total	32+8 (4)	2	0+1	34+9 (4)

PADDINGTON, ALBERT — 1903–04

left-half — Ht 5 8, Wt 11 10 — *32 apps*
full name: Albert Hillman Paddington
born: Bishopstoke, Hampshire, 30.6.1881
died: Portchester, Hampshire, 3.4.1932
debut: Wellingborough Town (a), 5.9.1903 (SL D1)

Albert Paddington was recruited from Southampton during the summer of 1903 to bolster Albion's defence after the club had gained promotion to Division One of the Southern League. Having skippered the reserves at The Dell, he maintained a regular place in the Brighton first eleven during 1903–04, missing just three games as the club struggled in the higher grade. Before joining Southampton in September 1899, Albert had played in turn for Basingstoke, Chandler's Ford and Eastleigh Athletic, and rejoined the last-mentioned club on leaving the Goldstone in May 1904.

Season	SL	FAC	Total
1903–04	31	1	32
Total	31	1	32

PARKER, J.   1912

left-back   *1 app*
debut: Luton Town (h), 8.4.1912 (SL D1)

An amateur trialist from Grangetown (near Sunderland), Parker played in a 1–0 Southern League defeat of Luton Town at the Goldstone in April 1912 but was not offered terms.

Season	SL	Total
1911–12	1	1
Total	1	1

PARKES, DAVID   1913–14

centre-half   *Ht 5 11, Wt 12 00*   *47 apps*
born: Lye, Worcestershire, 18.6.1892
debut: Southampton (a), 22.2.1913 (SL D1)

Although he played just 47 first-team games for the Albion after signing from the Staffordshire club Newcastle Town in January 1913, David Parkes quickly gained a reputation as a stylish centre-half and played a large part in the club's run to the last sixteen of the

F.A. Cup in 1913–14. Albion went out of the competition 3–0 at Sheffield Wednesday, but David's outstanding display caught the eyes of his hosts and a month later, in March 1914, the Yorkshire club paid a fee of £1,500 plus their reserve centre-forward, George Beech, for the 21-year-old. It was a huge sum at the time and an Albion record.

Soon after joining the Wednesday, David played for the Sheffield select XI in the prestigious annual fixture against Glasgow, and he remained at Hillsborough for a war-interrupted six years until May 1920 when he was transferred to Stoke for £150. He spent 1921–22 with Llanelli, then joined Rochdale in the Third Division (North) in June 1922, where he clocked up 210 League appearances and enjoyed a benefit before dropping into the Cheshire League with Macclesfield Town in 1928.

Season	SL	FAC	SA	SCC	Total
1912–13	6	0	2	5	13
1913–14	27	4	3	0	34
Total	33	4	5	5	47

PARLETT, FRANK   1910–14

left-back   *10 apps*
full name: Francis Thornton Parlett
born: Shoreham-by-Sea, Sussex, 1887
debut: Plymouth Argyle (h), 17.2.1912 (SL D1)

Frank Parlett was one of several fine players recruited from the Shoreham club in the early days of the Albion. Having started out in junior circles with Portslade, he graduated into the West Sussex Senior League with Steyning and Southwick before joining Shoreham in 1909. A Sussex representative, Frank first assisted Albion's reserves in 1910, but it was not until 1912 that he signed as a professional. Making his Southern League debut in February 1912 in a 1–0 home win over Plymouth Argyle, he had to wait until April 1914 for his next

outing. He did, however, maintain a place in the team – largely reserves – which reached the final of the Southern Professional Charity Cup in 1913 only to lose 4–1 to a strong Queen's Park Rangers side. Reinstated as an amateur in November 1919, Frank returned to Shoreham where he was still turning out in the late 1920s at the age of 40.

Season	SL	SA	SCC	Total
1911–12	1	0	0	1
1912–13	0	0	5	5
1913–14	3	1	0	4
Total	4	1	5	10

PARRIS, GEORGE   1995 & 1995–97

midfield   *Ht 5 9, Wt 13 00*   *88 apps, 5 goals*
full name: George Michael Parris
born: Ilford, Essex, 11.9.1964
debut: AFC Bournemouth (a), 11.2.1995 (FL D2)

Tough-tackling George Parris played mainly in midfield or as a striker for Redbridge, Essex, London and England Schools, but it was as a full-back that he came to prominence with his local League club, West Ham United, during the 1985–86 season when the 'Hammers' finished third in the First Division, their highest-ever League placing.

The former trainee was more-or-less a regular in the side over the next seven years, predominantly in the no.3 shirt, and he played his part as West Ham won promotion back to the top flight during 1991–92.

In March 1993, Birmingham City paid £150,000 for George, but he was unable to hold down a steady place in the struggling "Blues'" midfield following a series of injuries, and in 1994–95 he had three spells on loan: at Brentford (7 games), Bristol City (6 games), and, from February until the end of the season, at Brighton. Indeed, Albion manager Liam Brady – a former team-mate at Upton Park – had tried to obtain the services of the athletic Parris during the summer of 1994.

More of a combative midfield battler than a play-maker, George was offered terms by Brady at the end of the season when he was released by Birmingham, but housing problems prevented an immediate move. After a trial with Stoke City, he enjoyed a month in the Swedish League with Norrkoping, but returned to the Goldstone in September 1995 to become a fixture in the side, taking over the captaincy towards the end of the season when Paul McCarthy was injured.

While not the most skilful of players, George continued to use his greatest abilities – determination, stamina and spirit – to great effect in the engine-room of the side, but lost confidence during 1996–97, asked for a transfer, and was released at the end of the season. He subsequently joined Southend United on a non-contract basis for 1997–98. In April 1995, George enjoyed a belated testimonial granted by West Ham in a match against fellow Premiership side Ipswich Town.

Season	FL	FAC	FLC	AMC	Total
1994–95	18 (2)	0	0	0	18 (2)
1995–96	38 (2)	4	0	4	46 (2)
1996–97	17+1 (1)	2	2	2	23+1 (1)
Total	73+1 (5)	6	2	6	87+1 (5)

PARSONS, TED — 1903–05

half-back — 37 apps, 1 goal
full name: Edward Parsons
born: c. 1878
debut: Queen's Park Rangers (h), 12.12.1903 (SL D1)

Signed by Stoke from Stafford Rangers as a youngster in May 1897, Ted Parsons remained at the Victoria Ground for six years, but had made only 60 League appearances before joining the Albion in October 1903. Described as 'a player of the vigorous stamp', he was a valuable member of the staff, appearing in all three half-back positions during nearly two seasons at the Goldstone. After his release in May 1905, Ted disappeared from the senior game.

Season	SL	Total
1903–04	22	22
1904–05	15 (1)	15 (1)
Total	37 (1)	37 (1)

PATERSON, HENRY — 1914

right-back — 1 app
born: Hawick, Roxburghshire, Scotland, 1.5.1893
debut: Cardiff City (h), 1.4.1914 (SA)

Educated at Bridlington College, Henry Paterson went up to Sidney Sussex, Cambridge, where he gained a B.A. in 1914 and blues for football in 1913 and '14. The college annual commented, 'Kicks surely and an excellent length with either foot. Knows the game thoroughly and tackles with good judgement; uses his head well. Most enthusiastic, and should distinguish himself greatly at the game.'

Just two months after playing for the Light Blues' side that beat Oxford University 2–1, the young full-back was playing for Hove when he was drafted by the Albion for a Southern Alliance fixture with Cardiff City in April 1914. Albion won 4–0, and Henry impressed sufficiently to be given a couple more outings in the reserves. He joined the ranks of the Royal Field Artillery on the outbreak of war in 1914 and rose to the rank of lieutenant. Also a fine cricketer, Henry captained the Sidney Sussex College XI for two seasons.

Season	SA	Total
1913–14	1	1
Total	1	1

PATES, COLIN — 1991 & 1993–95

defender — Ht 6 0, Wt 13 00 — 81 apps
full name: Colin George Pates
born: Mitcham, Surrey, 10.8.1961
debut: Oldham Athletic (h), 2.3.1991 (FL D2)

In an eleven-year career with Chelsea, Colin Pates appeared in 281 League games, won a Second Division title in 1983–84 (when he was ever-present), and gained a Full Members Cup winner's medal in 1986. Born in Surrey, Colin joined the Londoners as a schoolboy and became an apprentice in July 1977. Four months after signing as a full professional in July 1979 he made his first-team debut, a 7–3 win at Orient, then played for the England team which won the UEFA Youth Championship in 1980, beating Poland 2–1 in the final.

Throughout the early 1980s, Colin was a stalwart at the heart of the Chelsea defence, but he lost his place in 1987–88 and left the following season for Charlton Athletic for a fee of £430,000, then a record for the 'Valiants'. After 38 First Division games for Charlton he moved to Arsenal for £500,000 in January 1990, but life at Highbury proved disappointing and first-team outings were few and far between.

In February 1991, with Albion in a central-defender injury crisis, Colin arrived at the Goldstone on loan and immediately impressed

with his cool, unhurried style, striking up a fine understanding with his former Chelsea teammate Gary Chivers as Albion made it to the Division Two play-off final. Arsenal's £350,000 valuation of Colin was far in excess of Albion's resources, though, and he returned to Highbury after the Wembley final, but after just 21 League games in three-and-a-half years for the 'Gunners' the experienced defender was released in 1993 and returned to Hove to play mainly at left-back.

However, in January 1995, Colin was forced to retire from the full-time game with a knee injury, but soon returned to the fray with Crawley Town, making an instant impression with his experience. Appointed player-manager at Town Mead in May 1995, he retired as a player because of a pelvic injury nine months later, but resigned as manager the same month following a poor run of results.

Season	FL	Play-offs	FAC	FLC	AMC	Total
1990–91	17	3	0	0	0	20
1993–94	34	0	1	3	0	38
1994–95	15+1	0	1	5	0+1	21+2
Total	66+1	3	2	8	0+1	79+2

PAYNE — 1903

left-half — 1 app
debut: Grays United (a), 25.4.1903 (SEL)

Payne was one of four trialists who played in the final South Eastern League fixture of the 1902–03 season, in which Albion fielded a much-weakened team because of a money-spinning home friendly with Brentford played by the first team the same day. Not surprisingly, Albion were trounced 5–0 at Grays and nothing further was seen of Payne.

Season	SEL	Total
1902–03	1	1
Total	1	1

PAYNE, JOHN — 1934–35

outside-left — Ht 5 7, Wt 10 02 — 9 apps, 1 goal
full name: John Frederick Payne
born: Southall, Middlesex, 3.6.1906
died: Bromley, Kent, 1981
debut: Bristol Rovers (h), 25.8.1934 (FL D3(S))

A swift-moving winger, capable of playing down either flank, John Payne joined the Botwell Mission club on leaving school, and graduated through Lyons Athletic to Southall in the Athenian League with whom he won Middlesex county honours. While at Southall he also appeared for West Ham United as an amateur and signed as a professional for the 'Hammers' in October 1926, but he enjoyed only four League appearances before transferring to Brentford in September 1929 where he began to make a name for himself.

Eighteen goals in 51 Southern Section matches persuaded Manchester City to give John a chance of First Division football in January 1931, but he struggled in the higher company and was released to join the Albion in August 1934 having made just four appearances in City's League side. John occupied the left-wing berth in the opening matches of the 1934–35 season, but lost his place to the ageless Ernie 'Tug' Wilson in late September and had only one more outing before leaving for Millwall in July 1935. In May 1936 he dropped into the Southern League with Yeovil & Petters United.

Season	FL	SSC	Total
1934–35	8 (1)	1	9 (1)
Total	8 (1)	1	9 (1)

PEAKE, JASON   1996–

midfield   Ht 5 9, Wt 11 05   *35 apps, 1 goal*
full name: Jason William Peake
born: Leicester, Leicestershire, 29.9.1971
debut: Chester City (h), 17.8.1996 (FL D3)

Billed as a classy midfielder with an 'educated' left foot which could spray passes all over the pitch, Jason Peake has yet to live up to the reputation which accompanied him to the Goldstone Ground in the summer of 1996. Helped little by having to commute from his home city of Leicester, a situation which led to a dispute with the club over relocation expenses, the 25-year-old asked for a transfer by March 1997. Ironically, he then scored his only first-team goal for the Albion, a spectacular 25-yard effort against Northampton Town, but the form which he had shown only in glimpses has continued to elude him.

A promising youngster, Jason played for the England youth side and took up an apprenticeship with Leicester City, where he went on to make ten appearances in the first team. During 1991–92 he played six Third Division games on loan for Hartlepool United before joining Halifax Town on a free transfer the following August. However, at the end of 1992–93 the Yorkshire side were relegated from the Football League. Jason was subsequently swapped for Rochdale's Alex Jones in March 1994 after scoring six goals from 27 Conference appearances.

It was at Spotland, where he also played as a left-back, that Jason built his reputation, and he was adored by the Rochdale fans. After 95 League games, though, he signed for the Albion for a fee, decided by a tribunal, of £80,000. That increased to £95,000 after 20 appearances, and was scheduled to rise to £120,000 after 40 games, but sadly Jason has managed only 35 thus far.

Season	FL	FAC	FLC	AMC	Total
1996–97	27+3 (1)	2	2	1	32+3 (1)
Total	27+3 (1)	2	2	1	32+3 (1)

PEARCE, GRAHAM   1982–86

left-back   Ht 5 9, Wt 11 00   *109 apps, 2 goals*
full name: Graham Charles Pearce
born: Hammersmith, London, 8.7.1959
debut: Ipswich Town (h), 28.8.1982 (FL D1)

A printer by trade, Graham Pearce was playing part-time football for Barnet in the Alliance Premier League when he impressed Albion manager Mike Bailey with two excellent performances in the F.A. Cup tie between the clubs in January 1982. Making his First Division debut in the opening game of 1982–83, Graham's fairy-tale introduction to top-level football saw him wearing the no.3 shirt for Brighton in the F.A. Cup final nine months later.

It was a rapid rise to fame for the left-back who had trials with Brentford and Queen's Park Rangers as a youngster but was not offered terms. After four years in the Southern League with Hillingdon Borough, where he represented Middlesex and toured with the Middlesex Wanderers, the stocky Londoner joined Barnet, but was on the transfer list at his own request when Albion paid a fee for him which reached £20,000. Albion's reserves also played a match at Barnet as part of the deal.

Graham initially competed for the left-back spot with Sammy Nelson and Steve Gatting, and spent most of the 1982–83 campaign in the reserves, but returned to the side when injuries and suspensions necessitated and made his dream appearances at Wembley as a 23-year-old in his first season as a full-time professional. The following term saw Graham as the regular left-back, but the signing of Chris Hutchings in November interrupted his first-team career until Hutchings was switched to the right. A good tackler but prone to the odd vital error, Graham was also employed in a sweeper role to some effect, but was released at the end of 1985–86.

After moving on to Gillingham, the competitive defender notched up another 65 League appearances before joining Brentford in October 1988, and then returned to Kent with Maidstone United during the summer of 1989. Graham played in 27 League games for the 'Stones' during their first season as a Fourth Division club before joining Isthmian League Enfield during the summer of 1990. A year later he was appointed manager of the Middlesex club while simultaneously holding a coaching post with Brentford, but was dismissed in December 1991 following a disagreement over playing policy. He then played for Kingstonian and Basingstoke Town while retaining his job as coach at Griffin Park until a change of manager in 1993. Graham now coaches in schools and colleges in the West London area as part of Brentford's community scheme, and has also turned out for Harrow Borough in the Isthmian League. In February 1996 he was appointed manager of Molesey but lasted less than two months in the post, and became assistant manager at Kingstonian in January 1997.

Season	FL	FAC	FLC	FMC	Total
1982–83	13+1	5	1	0	19+1
1983–84	18 (1)	0	3	0	21 (1)
1984–85	24	2	0	0	26
1985–86	32 (1)	5	3	2	42 (1)
Total	87+1 (2)	12	7	2	108+1 (2)

PENNEY, STEVE   1983–91

winger/midfield   Ht 5 9, Wt 10 04   *162 apps, 15 goals*
full name: Steven Alexander Penney
born: Ballymena, Co. Antrim, Northern Ireland, 16.1.1964
debut: Barnsley (a), 26.11.1983 (FL D2)

With seventeen caps for Northern Ireland, Steve Penney played in more international matches than any other player while on Albion's books, and his collection would surely have been greater but for the terrible injury problems which plagued the latter years of his career. Quite devastating down the wing in his early appearances for the club, it was a sad occasion when the amiable Ulsterman was forced to call it a day.

Having represented his country at youth level, Steve rejected the opportunity of an apprenticeship with Nottingham Forest in order to complete his education at Ballymena Academy (where he played rugby until he was fifteen). In fact, he joined Ballymena United while at school and had two seasons in the Irish League club's first team. After guesting for Linfield on a tour of the Netherlands, Steve came to Albion's attention when he was recommended to coach Sammy

Nelson by his former international colleague Jim Platt, the Ballymena goalkeeper. Invited to the Goldstone for a trial, the Ulster teenager was signed by Chris Cattlin for an initial £10,000 in November 1983 and drafted straight into the League side.

The speedy wing play of the nineteen-year-old took the Second Division by storm and Albion soon received inquiries from First Division clubs. Although he never quite performed as consistently again, Steve added to his reputation in 1984–85 and won his first full cap in a 3–0 defeat of Israel in Belfast in October 1984, thus raising the final amount due to Ballymena to £25,000. Having gained a regular place in the Northern Ireland side, the Albion winger played twice in the 1986 Mexico World Cup finals, but from that high point his career took an unfortunate turn. A series of injuries commenced in March 1987 with a hair-line fracture of an ankle, which was followed by serious knee problems necessitating surgery. Steve made a welcome return to first-team duty in March 1988, regained his international place, and appeared to be back to his best the following season despite a serious contractual dispute, but the knee problems recurred and he was lost from the reckoning for two years.

After a come-back in the reserves, Steve was given a free transfer toward the end of 1990–91 and joined Heart of Midlothian in July. After nine Scottish Premier Division appearances the unfortunate winger moved to Burnley on a free transfer in August 1992, but was forced to retire from the Football League at the age of 30 in February 1994 because of persistent knee problems after scoring three goals in eleven League outings for the Lancashire club. With his wife having qualified as an optician, Steve then returned to Ballymena to manage a franchise for a national chain of opticians.

Season	FL	FAC	FLC	FMC	AMC	Total
1983–84	22+3 (1)	3	0	0	0	25+3 (1)
1984–85	24+2 (4)	2	2	0	0	28+2 (4)
1985–86	30+7 (2)	5	2 (1)	1	0	38+7 (3)
1986–87	27 (3)	2	2	1	0	32 (3)
1987–88	13 (3)	0	1	0	0+1	14+1 (3)
1988–89	9+1 (1)	0	2	0	0	11+1 (1)
Total	125+13 (14)	12	9 (1)	2	0+1	148+14 (15)

PERKINS, BILL   1911

outside-left   *1 app*
full name: William Perkins
born: Ashford, Kent, 1883
debut: Millwall (h), 25.2.1911 (SL D1)

Born and bred in Ashford, Bill 'Waddles' Perkins and his elder brother Jack moved to Hastings early in life and went on to become stalwarts of the local game. Bill started out with St Leonards, and was a prominent member of the side which won the East Sussex Senior League championship in 1902–03; he also appeared in the Sussex Senior Cup final of 1904 when the 'Saints' were narrowly beaten 2–1 by Worthing. When the club turned professional as St Leonards United in 1905, Bill retained his amateur status, but joined the paid ranks the following year – while continuing to work as a painter and decorator – when United combined with Hastings & St Leonards to become Hastings & St Leonards United. He remained with them for the four seasons of their professional existence, competing in the Southern League Division Two, the South Eastern League and United League, and also played his part in the excellent F.A. Cup runs of 1906–07, 1907–08 and 1908–09 when the club

reached the first round proper (now equivalent to the third round) on each occasion, only to lose 3–1 at Norwich, 1–0 at home to Portsmouth, and 2–0 at Blackpool respectively.

On the demise of the Hastings club in 1910, Bill was recruited by the Albion and was a regular member of the reserve team throughout the 1910–11 season. His sole outing in the first eleven came in February 1911 in the rare absence of Bert Longstaff, a 3–2 victory over Millwall at the Goldstone, but he was released at the end of the season and returned to minor soccer.

Season	SL	Total
1910–11	1	1
Total	1	1

PHILBIN, JACK   1938–46

utility forward   Ht 5 7, Wt 10 08   *14 apps, 2 goals*
full name: John Philbin
born: Jarrow, Co. Durham, 1913
debut: Walsall (h), 27.8.1938 (FL D3(S))

Derby County discovered Jack Philbin playing for Washington Colliery and paid £150 for his services in December 1933 after just two games for the pit team, but he made the League side on just one occasion in three years at the Baseball Ground before moving to Torquay United in May 1936. Despite being a regular in the first team at Plainmoor, Jack found it difficult to break into the Albion side after arriving at the Goldstone in June 1938. Played on both wings and at inside-left in his six League outings for the club, the Geordie forward was unable to make any further progress because of the war, but he returned to Hove in 1946 and made eight further appearances during the 1945–46 transitional season before retiring from the senior game.

Season	FL	Wartime	Total
1938–39	6 (1)	0	6 (1)
1945–46	0	8 (1)	8 (1)
Total	6 (1)	8 (1)	14 (2)

PHILLIPS, JOHN   1980–81

goalkeeper   Ht 6 0, Wt 10 08   *1 app*
full name: Thomas John Seymour Phillips
born: Shrewsbury, Shropshire, 7.7.1951
debut: Crystal Palace (h), 27.12.1980 (FL D1)

It was almost inevitable that John Phillips became a footballer with Shrewsbury Town: his father Roy was a former centre-forward for the 'Shrews', while his grandfather Tommy Seymour was once a full-back for the club. Having represented both Shrewsbury and Shropshire Schools, John became an apprentice with the Third Division side and signed as a professional in November 1968. After 51 League appearances at Gay Meadow, the young goalkeeper was

transferred for £35,000 to Aston Villa in October 1969, but played in only fifteen Third Division matches for the fallen giants before joining Chelsea for £25,000 in August 1970. In nine years at Stamford Bridge he played second fiddle to Peter Bonetti, but still managed 125 League appearances, gained experience in Europe, and won four Welsh under-23 caps and four more at senior level.

After brief loan periods with Swansea City and Crewe Alexandra, the 28-year-old 'keeper was signed by the Albion for £15,000 in March 1980 as deputy for Graham Moseley, and made his sole appearance in a 3–2 Christmas-holiday win over Crystal Palace at the Goldstone the following season. With Perry Digweed having also joined the club, John left for Charlton Athletic on a free transfer in July 1981 and moved on to Crystal Palace in January 1983. On his release from Selhurst Park he played in Hong Kong, but returned to assist Palace's reserves in 1984. He now runs a motor-car business in Mitcham.

With just one senior game to his credit for the club, John may be best remembered by older Albion fans for conceding a 40-yard goal to Nobby Lawton at the Goldstone in February 1969 while playing as a seventeen-year-old for Shrewsbury.

Season	FL	Total
1980–81	1	1
Total	1	1

PHILLIPS, REG   1921–23

outside-left   Ht 6 0, Wt 11 00   3 apps
full name: Reginald Phillips
born: Hove, Sussex, c. 1900
died: Hove, Sussex, March 1924
debut: Southend United (a), 3.9.1921 (FL D3(S))

Reg Phillips first appeared on the local scene with the amateur Brighton & Hove club during the latter stages of the Great War, and played a major role when, as Brighton & Hove Amateurs, they

carried off the championship of the West Sussex Senior League and the Royal Irish Rifles Charity Cup in the initial post-war season, 1919–20. A Sussex representative at senior level, Reg was invited to assist Albion's reserve team as an amateur in February 1920, and was offered a professional engagement two months later. He helped the 'Lambs' to the Southern League title in 1921, and made his three first-team appearances early in the 1921–22 campaign; although he was normally a full-back, equally at home on the left or right, Reg somewhat oddly came into the side at outside-left in the absence of Zach March. After giving loyal service to the 'Lambs' until 1923 when he was sidelined through illness, Reg died in March 1924 aged just 23. A benefit match, Albion reserves v. Southampton, was arranged on 2 April with the proceeds donated to his family.

Season	FL	Total
1921–22	3	3
Total	3	3

PIGGIN, LIONEL   1912

left-back   2 apps
born: Nottingham, Nottinghamshire, 26.2.1891
died: Nottingham, Nottinghamshire, 1973
debut: Crystal Palace (h), 9.4.1912 (SL D1)

Lionel Piggin was a trialist from Peterborough City who appeared in two matches for the Albion at the end of the 1911–12 season, but, despite being on the winning side on both occasions, he wasn't signed and returned to the Peterborough club. After subsequently playing for Barrow-in-Furness in the Lancashire Combination, Lionel joined Swindon Town on a month's trial in August 1914 while working in the Wiltshire town, turning out in one Southern League fixture. He also appeared for Southampton, Bristol Rovers and the Southampton works' side Thorneycrofts in the wartime regional competitions. In 1919–20, Lionel was engaged by Brentford but he failed to make the Middlesex side's Southern League team.

Season	SL	Total
1911–12	2	2
Total	2	2

PINCHBECK, CLIFF   1949

centre-forward   14 apps, 5 goals
full name: Clifford Brian Pinchbeck
born: Cleethorpes, Lincolnshire, 20.1.1925
died: Cleethorpes, Lincolnshire, 2.11.1996
debut: Nottingham Forest (h), 20.8.1949 (FL D3(S))

A former England schoolboy international, Cliff Pinchbeck was playing in the Midland League for Scunthorpe & Lindsey United when Everton secured his services in December 1947, but he made their First Division side on only three occasions before joining the Albion in August 1949 for £2,000. Cliff impressed everyone with his dynamic qualities as leader of the attack, but his stay was brief: after a splendid performance in a 3–0 defeat at Port Vale on 29 October, he was signed by the Potteries outfit for £3,500 a fortnight later, giving Albion an excellent profit in just three months.

The Lincolnshire-born forward remained at Vale Park for two years, scoring 34 goals in 69 League outings, before being transferred to Northampton Town in December 1951, but his Football League career was ended by a broken ankle after three goals from three appearances. Cliff went on to play non-League football with Bath City and Salisbury City. During the war he had served in the infantry in the Middle East.

Season	FL	Total
1949–50	14 (5)	14 (5)
Total	14 (5)	14 (5)

PINDER, W.   1913

outside-right   1 app
debut: Southend United (a), 23.4.1913 (SA)

An amateur trialist from the north of England, Pinder partnered Jack Woodhouse on the right wing in the penultimate Southern Alliance fixture of the 1912–13 season at Southend. Albion, needing a win to retain any chance of winning the championship, won 1–0, but had to settle for the runner's-up spot behind Croydon Common. Nothing further was heard of Pinder.

Season	SA	Total
1912–13	1	1
Total	1	1

PIPER, STEVE   1970–78

defender/midfield   Ht 5 10, Wt 11 10   *190 apps, 9 goals*
full name: Stephen Paul Piper
born: Brighton, Sussex, 2.11.1953
debut: Burnley (h), 18.11.1972 (FL D2)

While never one of the stars of the successful Albion side of the mid 1970s, Steve Piper proved his worth as both a defender and a hard-tackling midfielder, and played in every game of the exhilarating 1976–77 promotion season. Indeed, he was one of the most successful locally-born players of modern times, making 190 appearances for the club.

Educated at Longhill School, Rottingdean, Steve played for both Brighton and Sussex Boys, had an England trial at the age of fourteen, and was one of two lads invited to meet the players at the Goldstone in 1968 by manager Freddie Goodwin. Turning out for Rottingdean and the Albion youth team, he signed as a full-time professional in September 1972 and made his first-team debut a couple of months later at the age of nineteen. It was a real baptism of fire, though: only one of his ten games during 1972–73 was won as the club was ignominiously relegated from the Second Division. Over the next three seasons Steve became a regular in the side, playing consistently in central defence although he occasionally turned out at right-back as well. In 1973–74 he was runner-up to Norman Gall in the Player of the Season poll.

In 1976 new manager Alan Mullery successfully played Steve as a ball-winner in midfield as Albion swept to promotion, but, having played in the opening fifteen games in Division Two, the unsung hero lost out to new signing Paul Clark and was put on the list at his own request. Portsmouth paid £20,000 for Steve's signature in February 1978, but his career at Fratton was effectively ended after just 29 League games when he sustained a bad knee injury nine months later.

It was initially thought that Steve would never play again, but following an operation he returned to "Pompey's" reserves before the knee broke down for a second time. Granted a testimonial match, Portsmouth *v.* Crystal Palace, he subsequently played in local football for Steyning Town, Worthing, Southwick, Littlehampton Town, Pagham (as player-manager) and Arundel. He also represented Sussex while working in the insurance industry. Since hanging up his boots, Steve has had brief spells as joint manager at Worthing and assistant manager at Littlehampton.

Season	FL	FAC	FLC	Total
1972–73	9	1	0	10
1973–74	34 (1)	2	0	36 (1)
1974–75	37 (1)	2	4	43 (1)
1975–76	19+2	1	2	22+2
1976–77	46 (4)	3	7	56 (4)
1977–78	15 (3)	0	6	21 (3)
Total	160+2 (9)	9	19	188+2 (9)

POINTON, JOE   1928–29

outside-right/centre-forward   Ht 5 11, Wt 11 00   *16 apps, 5 goals*
full name: Joseph Pointon
born: Leek, Staffordshire, 1905
died: Leek, Staffordshire, 1939
debut: Coventry City (h), 1.9.1928 (FL D3(S))

Joe Pointon started out with the Wesleyan and National clubs in his native Leek, but was playing for Congleton Town in the Cheshire League when he joined Port Vale as an eighteen-year-old amateur in April 1922. Subsequently signed as a professional, he had four years with Vale, mainly as a reserve, before moving on to Luton Town in May 1926. Joe scored eleven goals in 65 Southern Section outings for the 'Hatters' and was recruited by the Albion in July 1928, but he met with only moderate success at the Goldstone.

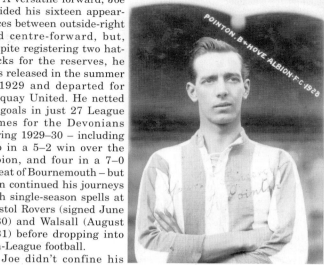

A versatile forward, Joe divided his sixteen appearances between outside-right and centre-forward, but, despite registering two hat-tricks for the reserves, he was released in the summer of 1929 and departed for Torquay United. He netted 22 goals in just 27 League games for the Devonians during 1929–30 – including two in a 5–2 win over the Albion, and four in a 7–0 defeat of Bournemouth – but soon continued his journeys with single-season spells at Bristol Rovers (signed June 1930) and Walsall (August 1931) before dropping into non-League football.

Joe didn't confine his prolific feats to the football pitch alone, though. When he died from the effects of tuberculosis at the age of 34, he left a widow and nine children, the eldest of which was reported as being just nine years old!

Season	FL	Total
1928–29	16 (5)	16 (5)
Total	16 (5)	16 (5)

PORTER, WILLIE   1907

outside-left   1 app
full name: William A. Porter
born: c. 1884
debut: Brentford (a), 16.10.1907 (WL)

Willie Porter was an amateur from the Isthmian League club London Caledonians who guested on the left-wing to the exclusion of Dick Wombwell in a 2–1 Western League defeat at Griffin Park in October 1907 (which was Brentford's long-serving winger Alex Underwood's benefit match). He had previously spent two seasons with Fulham (1901–03) during which he scored five goals in eleven Southern League and F.A. Cup appearances. In fact, his debut for the 'Cottagers' came in a 2–1 win over the infant Albion at Craven Cottage in March 1902, a defeat which effectively ended any Brighton hopes of winning the Southern League Division Two championship at the first attempt. As an amateur, Willie was a free agent and appeared in two matches for Chelsea during the first two seasons of their existence (1905–07). He went on to play for Ilford in the Isthmian League for several years.

Season	WL	Total
1907–08	1	1
Total	1	1

POSKETT, MALCOLM   1978–80

forward   Ht 6 0, Wt 11 02   *51 apps, 18 goals*
born: Middlesbrough, Yorkshire, 19.7.1953
debut: Hull City (a), 4.2.1978 (FL D2)

A lanky, ball-playing striker, Malcolm Poskett enjoyed a mixed career until he was plucked from the Fourth Division by the Albion as a stop-gap centre-forward, but he became a great favourite of the Goldstone crowd and enjoyed similar popularity at his numerous ports-of-call subsequently. A North Riding Schools representative, the young Malcolm started adult life as an apprentice plater on his native Teesside while playing for the South Bank club in the Northern League. In April 1973 he was taken on as a professional by Middlesbrough, but made just one appearance as a substitute before moving on to Hartlepool United in July 1974 where he failed to make the first team.

Forsaking the League ranks, Malcolm worked in the North Sea oil industry while turning out for Whitby Town, but in November 1976 he rejoined Hartlepool where a record of 20 goals in 51 Fourth Division matches persuaded Alan Mullery to pay £60,000 for his services in February 1978 as a replacement for the absent Teddy Maybank. Scoring in his first two games for the Albion, the 24-year-old Yorkshireman quickly won over the huge crowds, but, with Maybank and Peter Ward also contesting the two striking roles, it was Malcolm more often than not who was omitted and he asked for a transfer on several occasions. Nevertheless, he played an important part in the successful push for Division One in 1978–79 with ten goals from 29 League appearances, but on the club's elevation to the top flight he played in only three matches before a £120,000 transfer to Watford in January 1980.

After netting seventeen goals from 63 League outings at Vicarage Road, Malcolm was transferred to Carlisle United for £20,000 in August 1982 and hit 40 League goals in 110 matches, but then became something of a wanderer, playing in turn for Darlington (July 1985), Stockport County (January 1986), Hartlepool United (on loan March 1986), and Carlisle again (on loan August 1986, signed September) where he was installed as temporary manager when Harry Gregg was sacked in November 1987. Released in May 1988, he had a season with Morecambe in the HFS Loans Northern Premier League before hanging up his boots. After scoring 119 goals in a career total of 380 Football League appearances, Malcolm now works as a car-salesman in Carlisle.

Season	FL	FAC	FLC	Total
1977–78	11+2 (6)	0	0	11+2 (6)
1978–79	21+8 (10)	1	2+1	24+9 (10)
1979–80	1+2 (1)	0	2 (1)	3+2 (2)
Total	33+12 (17)	1	4+1 (1)	38+13 (18)

POTTS, ERIC   1977–78

winger/midfield   Ht 5 5, Wt 10 02   *41 apps, 7 goals*
full name: Eric Thomas Potts
born: Liverpool, Lancashire, 16.3.1950
debut: Cambridge United (a), 13.8.1977 (FLC R1 Lg1)

Forever remembered as Albion's 'supersub', Eric Potts earned the accolade against Sunderland in February 1978, coming on for Gary Williams with half an hour left to transform a 1–0 deficit into a 2–1 victory with two goals in the last two minutes. Liverpool-born Eric started with Old Holts F.C. on Merseyside and then turned out for New Brighton, Blackpool (as an amateur) and Oswestry Town before

joining Sheffield Wednesday for £3,000 in December 1969. The flame-haired little winger had more than seven years at Hillsborough, scoring 25 goals in 182 League and Cup games, and was voted Player of the Season in 1975–76. In June 1977, Alan Mullery brought Eric to the Goldstone for a £14,000 fee and he contested the no.7 shirt with Tony Towner throughout the 1977–78 campaign, contributing some vital goals. When not in the team he was usually sub.

Transferred to Preston North End for £37,000 in August 1978, Eric made 57 League appearances for the 'Lilywhites' before moving on to Burnley for £20,000 in September 1980. While at Turf Moor he assisted Burnley to the 1981–82 Third Division championship, then

joined Bury on a free transfer during the summer where he remained for two seasons before leaving the Football League scene. Eric subsequently played for Witton Albion and Clitheroe.

Season	FL	FAC	FLC	Total
1977–78	19+14 (5)	1+1 (1)	6 (1)	26+15 (7)
Total	19+14 (5)	1+1 (1)	6 (1)	26+15 (7)

POWNEY, BRIAN   1960–74

goalkeeper   Ht 5 9, Wt 10 12   *386 apps*
full name: Brian William Powney
born: Seaford, Sussex, 7.10.1944
debut: Derby County (a), 28.4.1962 (FL D2)

With 386 appearances for the club to his name, Brian Powney played in more matches than any other Albion goalkeeper, and achieved by far the highest total of games of any Sussex-born player since the club joined the Football League in 1920. Making up for a lack of inches with his courage and spring-heeled agility – he was a star gymnast at school – Brian inspired considerable confidence in his colleagues and supporters, and came close to winning an England under-23 cap. However, he never quite overcame a deficiency in goal-kicking power.

After representing East Sussex Schools, the Seaford-born no.1 played for Eastbourne United as a youth before joining Albion's ground staff in 1960. In September 1961 he was offered professional terms, and made his first-team debut as a seventeen-year-old in the final fixture of Albion's 1961–62 Second Division relegation season, impressing with several excellent saves. In his early days at the Goldstone, Brian was third-choice goalie behind Charlie Baker and Bert McGonigal, and had to wait until December 1963 for an extended run in the team following a bad injury to McGonigal.

The following season, though, as Albion won the Fourth Division title, Brian established himself as first choice between the posts, and, despite losing his place through lack of form or injury on occasion, was a regular face in the side for ten seasons. He saw off serious challenges from both Tony Burns and Geoff Sidebottom, and missed only two games when Albion finished runners-up to Aston Villa in Division Three in 1971–72. In 1971 and 1972, Brian enjoyed a joint testimonial with Norman Gall as reward for ten years as a senior with the club, but was released by manager Brian Clough in May 1974 following the signing of the vastly experienced Peter Grummitt.

After thirteen years as a professional, the 29-year-old goalkeeper then embarked on a second career as a midfielder in local senior football with Southwick whom, as player-manager, he led to the Sussex County League title and an appearance in the first round of the F.A. Cup during his first season. Brian also played for Bexhill Town and Eastbourne United before becoming manager at Newhaven in 1976; returned to his role between the posts for Peacehaven & Telscombe in 1980; and played for and managed several Sussex Sunday League sides. Now running a vending-machine business, he also managed his home-town club, Seaford Town, from 1987 until May 1991.

Season	FL	FAC	FLC	Total
1961–62	1	0	0	1
1962–63	8	0	0	8
1963–64	25	0	1	26
1964–65	41	1	2	44
1965–66	38	3	3	44
1966–67	33	1	5	39
1967–68	19	2	0	21
1968–69	22	1	0	23
1969–70	21	3	0	24
1970–71	35	3	1	39
1971–72	44	3	1	48
1972–73	37	1	1	39
1973–74	27	2	1	30
Total	351	20	15	386

PREST, TOMMY — 1935–37

inside-forward   Ht 5 8, Wt 10 06   *28 apps, 6 goals*
full name: Thomas Walsh Prest
born: Darwen, Lancashire, 4.2.1908
debut: Newport County (h), 28.9.1935 (FL D3(S))

PREST - BRIGHTON + HOVE ALBION.

Tommy Prest played for Tuckhole's F.C. in the Blackburn League on leaving St Cuthbert's School, but quickly progressed to a higher grade of football with his local side Darwen in the Lancashire Combination where his natural talent soon attracted the bigger clubs. In January 1930 the slightly-built forward signed for Burnley, and went on to score fifteen goals in 80 First and Second Division appearances over five seasons at Turf Moor before joining the Albion in June 1935.

Described as an individual ball-artist, Tommy occupied all the attacking positions except centre-forward in his two seasons at the Goldstone, although he was generally preferred at inside-left. Transferred to Aldershot in June 1937, he joined Rochdale in September 1938 for the last season before the outbreak of the Second World War. Tommy was also an accomplished club cricketer.

Season	FL	SSC	Total
1935–36	21 (3)	1 (1)	22 (4)
1936–37	6 (2)	0	6 (2)
Total	27 (5)	1 (1)	28 (6)

PRYCE, JACK — 1903–05

inside-right   *23 apps, 5 goals*
full name: John Pryce
born: Renton, Dunbartonshire, Scotland, 25.1.1874
debut: Plymouth Argyle (a), 19.12.1903 (SL D1)

An inside-forward of slight physique, Jack Pryce joined his home-town Scottish League side, Renton, in 1893 and played in their losing Scottish Cup final side of 1895. In May 1896 he was transferred to Hibernian and played his way to the fringe of the Scotland international team, being selected to play against Wales in 1897, but he missed the game through injury. In September 1898, Jack crossed the border to play for Glossop North End, and in six months with the Derbyshire club played a big part in their promotion to the First Division. Transferred to Sheffield Wednesday in March 1899, he missed only three games as the 'Owls' won the Second Division title in 1899–1900, but left Yorkshire in May 1901 to sign for Queen's Park Rangers in the Southern League. Jack was quite a catch for the Albion, newly promoted to Division One of the Southern League, in October 1903, but never quite fulfilled expectations in nearly two years at the Goldstone and left in May 1905 when he is thought to have returned to his native Scotland.

Season	SL	Total
1903–04	21 (5)	21 (5)
1904–05	2	2
Total	23 (5)	23 (5)

PUGH, JIMMY — 1919–20

left-back   Ht 5 7, Wt 12 00   *23 apps*
full name: James Pugh
born: Abertillery, Monmouthshire, Wales, 1894
debut: Brentford (a), 30.8.1919 (SL D1)

Jimmy Pugh guested for Clapton Orient, Coventry City and Luton Town during the Great War, and was recruited by the Albion when the situation returned to normal in 1919. At the outset of the 1919–20 season he won a regular slot at left-back, but then lost out to Wally Little and was released to join his home-town club, Abertillery, in May 1920. Manchester United gave Jimmy a second chance to make the grade when they laid out £250 for his transfer in April 1922, but the stocky Welshman failed to make the most of the opportunity, and appeared just twice in the first team before moving to Wrexham in July 1923 for £150. Jimmy retired from the first-class game in May 1925, having played in 40 League matches for the Third Division (North) side.

Season	SL	FAC	Total
1919–20	22	1	23
Total	22	1	23

RAMSEY, CHRIS — 1980–84

right-back   Ht 5 9, Wt 10 12   *37 apps*
full name: Christopher Leroy Ramsey
born: Birmingham, Warwickshire, 28.4.1962
debut: Crystal Palace (a), 18.4.1981 (FL D1)

A placid, laid-back character off the field, Chris Ramsey was a competitive, hard-tackling but occasionally reckless full-back with a short fuse who was dismissed five times during a relatively short career with the Albion — and on a number of occasions subsequently. Indeed, he missed the F.A. Cup semi-final because of suspension, but it was his injury in the final itself that perhaps cost Albion ultimate victory.

Although he played for the losing Islington team in the 1977 English Schools Trophy final and was associated with Arsenal, Chris began his football career as a youngster with Bristol City, but was released at the end of the 1979–80 season without playing a senior game. During the summer he applied to eight London clubs for a trial, but it was Albion who gave him another chance and the raw defender arrived in Hove in August 1980. After steady progress in the reserves, Chris was thrust into the limelight in April 1981 when, just before his nineteenth birthday, he was given his League debut during a run of four consecutive victories which kept Albion in the First Division.

The following season Mike Bailey took over as manager and the inexperienced full-back was consigned to the reserves once more. Indeed, he never made a single appearance while Bailey held the reins, and had a trial at Brentford while on the transfer list. However, when Jimmy Melia and George Aitken took over the hot seat in December 1982, Chris was immediately restored and retained his place for the remainder of the season, coming back from suspension to claim the no.2 shirt in the Cup final against Manchester United.

Sadly, he was injured in the second half when United's Norman Whiteside trod on his ankle, and was unable to intercept the cross which led to Frank Stapleton's equaliser before being substituted. He was also was forced to miss the replay which Albion lost 4–0.

From that high point Chris's career nose-dived as a series of knee problems sidelined him for some time, and he played just five more games before moving to Swindon Town on loan in August 1984. Quickly becoming a popular figure at the County Ground, he signed permanently on a free transfer in December 1984 and made exactly 100 League appearances for the Wiltshire club before moving to Southend United in August 1987, but his time at Roots Hall was not a success and his contract was cancelled by mutual consent in December 1988.

Since that time Chris has played and coached some football in Malta, and also coached in the United States. In addition he has worked in the property business and taken a course in food nutrition. Now the youth development officer at Leyton Orient, Chris also looks after the Newham Ladies team.

Season	FL	FAC	FLC	Total
1980–81	3	0	0	3
1982–83	23	6	0	29
1983–84	4	0	1	5
Total	30	6	1	37

RANDALL, OSSIE   1919–22

goalkeeper   Ht 5 11, Wt 11 06   1 app
full name: Oswald James Henry Randall
born: Thatcham, Berkshire, 13.8.1895
died: Thatcham, Berkshire, 26.6.1978
debut: Grimsby Town (h), 29.9.1920 (FL D3(S))

Having played for the Devonport Royal Naval Barracks, Plymouth Argyle and Reading during the First World War, Ossie Randall joined the Albion on his demob in August 1919 as a reserve goalkeeper, and displayed such form for the 'Lambs' that he was selected for the Southern League's representative team which was defeated 5–1 by the Central League at Wolverhampton in March 1922. Unfortunate to be at the Goldstone at the same time as the amazingly consistent Billy Hayes, Ossie made the first team just once in his three years at the Goldstone (the only game Hayes missed in five seasons). In August 1922 he was transferred to Swindon Town where, after a season in the reserves, he was finally given the opportunity of first-team football, appearing in 71 Third Division (South) matches before his release to join Exeter City in August 1926. After playing fourteen Third Division (South) matches for the 'Grecians', Ossie forsook League football in May 1927.

Season	FL	Total
1920–21	1	1
Total	1	1

READMAN, JOE   1927–28

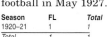

utility forward   Ht 5 10, Wt 12 00   6 apps
full name: Joseph Andrew Readman
born: West Hartlepool, Co. Durham, 20.11.1901
died: Ramsgate, Kent, 18.1.1973
debut: Torquay United (a), 1.10.1927 (FL D3(S))

Joe Readman was a junior with Bolton Wanderers before joining Bournemouth in May 1924 where, despite not being a regular in

the first team, he still gained a reputation as a goalscorer, netting 20 goals in 48 Southern Section matches. In August 1927, Charlie Webb obtained the burly forward's signature for the Albion and used him mainly as a reserve for the regular front line. During his eleven months at the Goldstone, Joe bagged 22 goals for the reserves and proved his versatility, appearing at inside-right, right-wing and centre-forward in his six outings for the first eleven. Transferred to Millwall in July 1928, he remained at The Den for three years before moving to Mansfield Town for £150 in July 1931. A month later Joe scored in a 3–2 win over Swindon Town, the "Stags'" first match as a Football League club, and totalled thirteen goals from 73 Third Division outings before dropping into non-League football with Ramsgate in August 1933 and then Ramsgate Press Wanderers.

Season	FL	Total
1927–28	6	6
Total	6	6

REDFERN, BOB   1947–48

outside-right   Ht 5 9, Wt 11 01   5 apps, 1 goal
full name: Robert Redfern
born: Crook, Co. Durham, 3.3.1918
debut: Watford (a), 23.8.1947 (FL D3(S))

Bob Redfern joined Wolverhampton Wanderers in May 1936 soon after his eighteenth birthday, but followed the well-worn path to Bournemouth in February 1937, a route taken by legions of young Wolves players in the '30s. The teenaged winger from County Durham spent ten years at Dean Court, including the seven-year break caused by the Second World War, and appeared in 89 peacetime League matches for the 'Cherries'. He also guested for Luton Town, York City, Crystal Palace and Fulham during the war. In August 1947, Bob became one of Tommy Cook's first signings for the Albion and was one of no fewer than ten players tried on the right wing during the 1947–48 re-election campaign. Released in May 1948, he subsequently worked as a school-teacher in Bournemouth and became secretary of Bournemouth Poppies F.C.

Season	FL	Total
1947–48	5 (1)	5 (1)
Total	5 (1)	5 (1)

REED, BILLY   1914–15

centre-forward/inside-left   Ht 5 8, Wt 11 00   21 apps, 9 goals
full name: William Featherstone Reed
born: Bishop Auckland, Co. Durham, 1893
debut: Southend United (h), 24.10.1914 (SL D1)

Brought to the Goldstone from the County Durham club Willington as a 20-year-old centre-forward in May 1914, Billy Reed was considered an excellent prospect having netted 32 goals for the Northern League champions during 1913–14. After scoring eight times for the reserves in three matches, the youngster earned a place in the South Eastern League's representative eleven against West Ham United (the reigning champions), and made his Southern League debut in the absence of Bill Miller at the end of October 1914. In the New Year of

1915, Billy established himself in the first eleven to end the season with an excellent return of nine goals from eighteen Southern League games, but it was to be Albion's last season for four years. The club closed down for the remainder of the First World War and Billy's budding football career foundered. He enlisted with the Footballers' Battalion of the Middlesex Regiment, along with the majority of Albion's staff, but lost an eye during the hostilities.

Season	SL	FAC	Total
1914–15	18 (9)	3	21 (9)
Total	18 (9)	3	21 (9)

Players' counties of birth

Players born in British Isles only. Not including wartime players.

County	Country	No. of Players
Sussex	England	86
Lancashire	England	55
Co. Durham	England	51
London	England	51
Lanarkshire	Scotland	50
Yorkshire	England	48
Staffordshire	England	25
Essex	England	24
Derbyshire	England	22
Glamorgan	Wales	21
Middlesex	England	21
Northumberland	England	21
Warwickshire	England	21
Nottinghamshire	England	20
Hampshire	England	18
Kent	England	17
Co. Dublin	Republic of Ireland	14
Co. Antrim	Northern Ireland	12
Ayrshire	Scotland	12
Surrey	England	12
Angus	Scotland	11
Leicestershire	England	11
Cheshire	England	9
Lincolnshire	England	9
Devon	England	7
Dunbartonshire	Scotland	7
Midlothian	Scotland	7
Renfrewshire	Scotland	7
Hertfordshire	England	5
Monmouthshire	Wales	5
Denbighshire	Wales	4
Stirlingshire	Scotland	4
Aberdeenshire	Scotland	3
Co. Cork	Republic of Ireland	3
Fife	Scotland	3
Flintshire	Wales	3
Norfolk	England	3
Northamptonshire	England	3
Oxfordshire	England	3
Perthshire	Scotland	3
Somerset	England	3
Suffolk	England	3
Wiltshire	England	3
Worcestershire	England	3
Berkshire	England	2
Clackmannan	Scotland	2
Cornwall	England	2
Dorset	England	2
Gloucestershire	England	2
West Lothian	Scotland	2
Co. Armagh	Northern Ireland	1
Banffshire	Scotland	1
Bedfordshire	England	1
Buckinghamshire	England	1
Caernarfonshire	Wales	1
Cambridgeshire	England	1
Cardiganshire	Wales	1
Carmarthenshire	Wales	1
Cumberland	England	1
Co. Down	Northern Ireland	1
East Lothian	Scotland	1
Herefordshire	England	1
Co. Kildare	Republic of Ireland	1
Roxburghshire	Scotland	1
Shropshire	England	1
Co. Tipperary	Republic of Ireland	1
Co. Tyrone	Northern Ireland	1

REED, BILLY   1948–53

outside-right   Ht 5 7, Wt 10 02   132 apps, 37 goals
full name: William George Reed
born: Ynyshir, Rhondda, Glamorgan, Wales, 25.1.1928
debut: Exeter City (a), 25.12.1948 (FL D3(S))

Billy Reed was one of the few players to gain international status after leaving the Goldstone. A fast-raiding winger, he proved a great success in his five seasons in Hove after an initial settling-in period, and developed an excellent understanding with Johnny McNichol down the right flank.

A Welsh schoolboy international, Billy played for Watts Town F.C. from the age of fourteen, and also represented the South Wales Federation of Boys' Clubs. In 1947 he won two caps against England at amateur level while playing for Rhondda Transport, before joining Cardiff City as a nineteen-year-old professional in July of that year.

After playing for the reserve team at Ninian Park, the young Welshman joined the Albion in August 1948 and contributed to the great improvement under Don Welsh. For a winger his scoring rate was tremendous, and he was joint top goalscorer on nineteen goals in 1951–52 when he played in every match.

Billy's time at the Goldstone Ground was not all plain-sailing, though, and after requesting a move on several occasions, his wish was fulfilled when he was transferred to Ipswich Town for £1,750 in July 1953.

It proved an excellent move. Billy went on to win two Third Division (South) championship medals at Portman Road (1953–54 and 1956–57), and also progressed to full international status (the first Ipswich player to do so) with caps against Yugoslavia and Scotland during 1954–55. After scoring 43 goals in 155 League appearances for the Suffolk club, he was transferred to Swansea Town in February 1958 for a £3,000 fee, but was forced into retirement after just eight matches. He subsequently played in minor football with Kaer Athletic, and worked as a local government officer in Swansea. Billy also coached local youngsters and did some scouting work for Dave Bowen, manager of the Welsh national side.

Season	FL	FAC	Total
1948–49	8	0	8
1949–50	21 (1)	0	21 (1)
1950–51	25 (6)	0	25 (6)
1951–52	46 (19)	1	47 (19)
1952–53	29 (10)	2 (1)	31 (11)
Total	129 (36)	3 (1)	132 (37)

REED, WALTER   1902

left-back   1 app
debut: St Albans Amateurs (a), 18.10.1902 (SEL)

Walter Reed was an amateur with Southall who played against the Albion at the Goldstone Ground in a 4–2 Southern League defeat for the Middlesex side in September 1902. The following month he was invited to guest for Brighton in a South Eastern League fixture at St Albans on a day when the club also had a qualifying F.A. Cup tie at Shoreham. Walter again played for Southall in the return Southern League fixture, an 8–0 victory for the Albion in February 1903.

Season	SEL	Total
1902–03	1	1
Total	1	1

REES, BARRIE   1965

right-half   12 apps, 1 goal
full name: Barrie Gwyn Rees
born: Rhyl, Flintshire, Wales, 4.2.1944
died: Nuneaton, Warwickshire, 27.3.1965
debut: Crewe Alexandra (h), 9.1.1965 (FL D4)

No Albion fan of the mid 1960s could ever forget the promising young player who was lost so tragically after making just twelve appearances in the Fourth Division championship season. Barrie Rees showed tremendous potential when he came into Albion's team on joining the club from Everton in January 1965.

Originally a centre-forward, he had represented Wales as a schoolboy before joining the Goodison ground staff where he signed professional forms in September 1961. After three appearances as leader of the attack and one at right-back for the First Division side, Barrie had been chosen as a reserve for the Welsh under-23 team before Archie Macaulay invested just under £10,000 for his services in January 1965.

Making his Albion debut at right-half in a 3–1 home defeat of Crewe Alexandra, the young Welshman quickly impressed, and his half-back partnership with Norman Gall and Dave Turner was seen as the backbone of the team for some time to come. After playing in a 3–1 defeat of Southport at the Goldstone Ground on the evening of 26 March 1965, which saw Albion move into second place, Barrie was driving to his parents' home in Rhyl when his Austin Mini was involved in a collision with a lorry on the A5 early the following morning, and he died at the Manor Hospital in Nuneaton just a few weeks after his 21st birthday. A tall, stylish player, Barrie was seen as a future full international and was a great loss to the club.

Season	FL	Total
1964–65	12 (1)	12 (1)
Total	12 (1)	12 (1)

REES, MAL   1949–50

inside-left   Ht 5 4   2 apps
full name: Maldwyn James Francis Rees
born: Neath, Glamorgan, Wales, 21.4.1924
debut: Newport County (a), 10.9.1949 (FL D3(S))

An amateur with Swansea Town, Mal Rees joined Norwich City in June 1946 for the initial post-war season and remained on the "Canaries'" books for three years, but had failed to make the League team at Carrow Road before arriving at the Goldstone Ground in September 1949. Recommended by his compatriot Les Jones, Albion's part-time player and scout, the tricky Welshman was pressed straight into first-team duty in a 1–0 win at Newport County in the absence of Eric Lancelotte, but had only one more chance to impress before being released to join Southern League Barry Town shortly afterwards. In July 1950, Jones, by then in charge of Scunthorpe & Lindsey United, took his protégé to Lincolnshire on his club's ascent from the Midland League to the Third Division (North). Mal scored one goal in eighteen appearances for Scunthorpe during that initial Football League season before drifting into minor football.

Season	FL	Total
1949–50	2	2
Total	2	2

REGAN, J.   1913

centre-half   1 app
debut: Croydon Common (h), 19.11.1913 (SA)

An amateur trialist from Newport, Isle of Wight, Regan was given a run-out at centre-half in a Southern Alliance fixture with Croydon Common at the Goldstone in November 1913, and presumably enjoyed the experience as Albion triumphed 5–0. Nothing more was seen of Regan, though.

Season	SA	Total
1913–14	1	1
Total	1	1

REINELT, ROBBIE   1997–

midfield/forward   Ht 5 10, Wt 12 07   12 apps, 3 goals
full name: Robert Squire Reinelt
born: Epping, Essex, 11.3.1974
debut: Carlisle United (a), 15.2.1997 (FL D3)

Robbie Reinelt scored probably the most important single goal in Albion's history, the equaliser at Hereford in May 1997. The 23-year-old had come on as a substitute just eight minutes earlier, but there was perhaps no better candidate to hit the goal that kept the club out of the Football Conference; for the enthusiastic midfielder-cum-striker had already suffered the trauma of playing for Aldershot when they went out of business, and was on Gillingham's books when they also enjoyed an escape from bottom place in the League at the expense of Halifax Town.

A trainee with Aldershot, Robbie went on to make sixteen appearances for the Hampshire side in the Football League before the club collapsed in March 1992, but he enjoyed just one victory with the 'Shots'. Returning to his home county, he had a trial for Colchester United and a game with Braintree Town, but then joined the Isthmian League Premier Division side Wivenhoe Town before signing for Gillingham in March 1993. However, he wasn't called upon as the Kent side just avoided the drop into non-League football.

In fact, Robbie made his Gillingham debut against the Albion in a Football League Cup tie in August 1993, scoring the only goal of the match. He went on to total eight goals from 67 games (20 of them as a substitute) until March 1995 when he was one half of an exchange deal with Colchester United's Steve Brown. Robbie impressed up front at Layer Road during

1995–96 but suffered from injury problems, and was transfer-listed the following summer following a disagreement with the management. Nevertheless, he netted against the Albion again in September 1996, but then adopted an almost permanent role on the subs' bench until Steve Gritt paid out £15,000 to bring him to Hove in February 1997.

Robbie's Albion debut lasted just 24 minutes when he broke his nose at Carlisle, but he came back to win the admiration of supporters with his running, control and determination, more than adequately filling the void left by skipper Ian Baird's suspension. Unlucky to be used only as a substitute at the famous showdown with Hereford, Robbie assured himself of eternal popularity with the club's followers by scoring that all-important goal that finally sealed a remarkable escape from the abyss.

Season	FL	Total
1996–97	7+5 (3)	7+5 (3)
Total	7+5 (3)	7+5 (3)

RICHARDS, BILLY   1935–37

outside-right   Ht 5 8, Wt 11 04   51 apps, 8 goals
full name: William Edward Richards
born: Abercanaid, Merthyr Tydfil, Glamorgan, Wales, 1905
died: Wolverhampton, Staffordshire, 30.9.1956
debut: Newport County (h), 28.9.1935 (FL D3(S))

A Welsh international winger, Billy Richards was noted for his speed and the accuracy of his crosses when he arrived at the Goldstone. A product of the South Wales coalfield, he started out in the Southern League with Mid Rhondda United and progressed to the Third Division with Merthyr Town where he made a single Southern Section appearance as an amateur in March 1926. Two months later he was recruited by Wolverhampton Wanderers, where he was soon joined by his younger brother and former Merthyr team-mate Dai who was to become one of the finest Welsh internationals of the inter-war years. Billy was offered professional terms at Molineux in August 1927, and made 31 Second Division appearances before joining Coventry City in March 1929 where he met with considerable success. The Welsh speedster scored twelve goals in 77 League outings for the Third Division side, but lost favour on the appointment of Harry Storer as manager and followed his former boss Jim McIntyre to Fulham for a £100 fee in June 1931.

After assisting the 'Cottagers' to the Third Division (South) championship in 1931–32, Billy was chosen to represent Wales in the 4–1 defeat of Ireland at Wrexham in December 1932. He arrived in Hove in May 1935 and was first choice on the right wing during the 1935–36 campaign, but injury and a loss of form saw him replaced by Bobby Farrell the following season, and he moved on to Bristol Rovers in May 1937 where he saw out his Football League career with four appearances during 1937–38 before dropping into the Southern League with Folkestone Town.

Season	FL	FAC	SSC	Total
1935–36	29 (7)	5	1	35 (7)
1936–37	15 (1)	1	0	16 (1)
Total	44 (8)	6	1	51 (8)

RIDLEY, DAVE   1946–47

centre-forward   5 apps
full name: David George Henry Ridley
born: Dinas, Pontypridd, Glamorgan, Wales, 15.12.1916
debut: Bournemouth & B.A. (a), 21.9.1946 (FL D3(S))

Dave Ridley played as an inside-forward in local football in Watford and for Bedford Town, but joined Millwall just before the end of the Second World War in January 1945 after seeing service with the Army. (He also guested briefly for Chelsea in that final wartime emergency season.) Although he scored for the 'Lions' in the F.A. Cup against Northampton Town, the 28-year-old Welshman enjoyed scant opportunity at The Den and signed for the Albion for a fee of £400 in July 1946. Injured in pre-season training, he was one of six players to wear the no.9 shirt in the first post-war campaign, but failed to impress in a poor side; in fact, of his five games, one was drawn and four were lost. Cartilage trouble prevented any further progress at the Goldstone, and Dave was released in May 1947, returning to Bedford for a couple of years when the knee recovered. He later moved back to South Wales where he played for Ton Pentre and Pembroke while working as a supervisor in a power-station. Dave later worked in Turkey and France before settling into retirement at Porth in the Rhondda Valley. His brother, Frankie, was a pro with Merthyr Town.

Season	FL	Total
1946–47	5	5
Total	5	5

RING, MIKE   1977–84

forward   Ht 5 10, Wt 10 06   6 apps
full name: Michael Paul Ring
born: Brighton, Sussex, 13.2.1961
debut: Huddersfield Town (a), 6.10.1981 (FLC R2 Lg1)

Born in Brighton and raised in Peacehaven, Mike Ring played for Brighton Boys, and was recommended to the Albion at the age of fourteen by former goalkeeper Peter Grummitt who was coaching at the local youth club. Joining the club as an apprentice, he turned professional in 1978 and made his first-team debut in 1981 at the age of 20. In April 1982, Mike joined Morton on loan to gain experience, and appeared in four League matches for the Scottish Premier Division side before returning to Hove. Over the next two seasons the young striker played for Albion's first team on just four occasions, though, and in 1983–84 he went on extended loan to Ballymena United where he gained an Irish Cup winner's medal.

On returning to the Goldstone, Mike was given a free transfer, but was then signed by his former Albion colleague Brian Horton, the manager of Hull City, during the summer of 1984. Scoring twice in 24 League outings for the 'Tigers', he spent a month on loan at Bolton Wanderers from March 1986 before joining Aldershot on a free transfer during the following close season. It was at the Recreation Ground that the frustrated forward enjoyed the best spell of a career which never really took off. He netted sixteen goals for the Hampshire side in 79 League games, but was released in 1989 and returned to Sussex for spells with Lewes, Farnborough Town, Crawley Town, Newhaven (assisting them to the County League Division Two title in 1990–91) and Peacehaven & Telscombe before hanging up his boots in 1993. Mike now works as a sales representative for a sports firm.

Season	FL	FLC	Total
1981–82	1	1	2
1982–83	0+1	0	0+1
1983–84	0+3	0	0+3
Total	1+4	1	2+4

RISDON, STAN   1936–48

utility player   Ht 5 11, Wt 12 00   251 apps, 13 goals
full name: Stanley William Risdon
born: Exeter, Devon, 13.8.1913
died: Hove, Sussex, 2.8.1979
debut: Crystal Palace (a), 30.9.1936 (SSC R1)

The greatest stalwart of Albion's wartime years, Stan Risdon made a total of 251 senior appearances for the club, but only 35 of them came in peacetime competition. Indeed, the versatile Devonian played in 216 matches out of 243 during seven seasons of regional competition, a remarkable feat. He skippered the team for most of the period, and even played in goal on two occasions.

Stan began his career with his local Tipton St John and St Mary's Majors clubs, and joined his home-town side, Exeter City, as an amateur inside-right in May 1933. After representing Devon, he was engaged as a professional in October 1933 and remained at St James's Park for three seasons, appearing in 35 Southern Section games and developing into a half-back before signing for the Albion in August 1936. Stan went on to play a variety of defensive roles at the Goldstone and also turned out at centre-forward on three occasions, but had had only 21 League outings before the outbreak of war in September 1939.

After his superb efforts for the club during the emergency, Stan was 33 by the time regular League football was reintroduced in 1946, but he remained at the Goldstone for two more seasons – bringing his total stay in Hove to twelve years – and received a well-deserved joint testimonial with four other long-serving players before signing for the newly formed Hastings United in 1948. He went on to serve the Southern League club with similar loyalty and was rewarded with another benefit match in 1954. Equally popular with his fellow players and fans alike, Stan was one of the most amiable characters ever to grace the Goldstone Ground.

Season	FL	FAC	SSC	Wartime	Total
1936–37	3	0	1	0	4
1937–38	17	0	1 (1)	0	18 (1)
1938–39	1	0	0	0	1
1939–40	0	0	0	25 (6)	25 (6)
1940–41	0	0	0	27 (2)	27 (2)
1941–42	0	0	0	34 (1)	34 (1)
1942–43	0	0	0	34 (2)	34 (2)
1943–44	0	0	0	35	35
1944–45	0	0	0	34 (1)	34 (1)
1945–46	0	9	0	27	36
1946–47	2	1	0	0	3
Total	23	10	2 (1)	216 (12)	251 (13)

RITCHIE, ANDY — 1980–83

forward   Ht 5 9, Wt 11 11   102 apps, 26 goals
full name: Andrew Timothy Ritchie
born: Manchester, Lancashire, 28.11.1960
debut: Aston Villa (a), 22.10.1980 (FL D1)

Costing £500,000, Andy Ritchie was the most expensive signing ever made by the Albion, but was never able to live up to the expectations that such a fee – and his own reputation as a youngster with Manchester United – demanded. Inevitably compared with his illustrious predecessor, Peter Ward, he never really won the affection of the Goldstone fans despite finishing top scorer in 1981–82 when the club reached its highest-ever position in the Football League, and he left Hove with a modest return of 26 goals from 102 games to his name.

A great future was predicted at an early age for the talented young forward with a considerable schoolboy pedigree behind him: representative appearances for Stockport, Greater Manchester and England Schools, not to mention playing cricket for Cheshire under-15s. Andy joined Manchester United as an apprentice on the recommendation of their former star Johnny Carey, and signed as a professional in December 1977. He made his First Division debut shortly after on Boxing Day, a 6–2 victory at Goodison Park just a month after his seventeenth birthday, and also played for the England youth team that season. Despite rave reviews at Old Trafford and a record of thirteen goals (including two hat-tricks) from 33 League

appearances, his chances in United's star-studded attack were restricted, and he signed for First Division Albion at the age of nineteen in October 1980 as a direct replacement for Ward.

It took Andy some time to settle, but his top-scoring feat in 1981–82 earned him the Player of the Season nomination, and he was chosen for the England under-21 team v. Poland in April 1982. Equipped with a powerful shot, he was a regular in the Albion side until October 1982 when the aforementioned Ward returned on loan in an attempt to boost both the

scoring-rate and the crowd figures, but soon came back into the team and played in four of Albion's F.A. Cup ties on the road to Wembley. With the club looking forward to its first semi-final, it was a big surprise when manager Jimmy Melia swapped him for Leeds United's Terry Connor in March 1983, but only because of the timing of the transaction.

Still just 22, Andy settled in well at Elland Road and matured into a solid striker over a four-year period, scoring 40 goals in 136 Second Division games. In August 1987 he moved to Oldham Athletic for £50,000 where he was to enjoy the best years of his career. Scoring 20 goals in his first season to lift the Player of the Season award, Andy impressed with his intelligent running and skill, and continued to score regularly for the 'Latics', finishing with 82 goals from 217 League appearances. In 1990 he made a great contribution to the club's runs to the League Cup final and the F.A. Cup semi-final, and performed equally well in the Second Division championship side of 1990–91.

In 1994, 33-year-old Andy unsuccessfully applied for the manager's post at Boundary Park, but was released in the summer of 1995 to join Scarborough in the Third Division. He ended 1995–96 as top scorer with a modest eight goals, but returned to Oldham in February 1997 as player/assistant manger.

Season	FL	FAC	FLC	Total
1980–81	23+3 (5)	2 (1)	0	25+3 (6)
1981–82	38+1 (13)	3	2 (1)	43+1 (14)
1982–83	21+3 (5)	4 (1)	1+1	26+4 (6)
Total	82+7 (23)	9 (2)	3+1 (1)	94+8 (26)

RITCHIE, GEORGE — 1919–21

inside-left   Ht 5 9, Wt 11 00   21 apps, 6 goals
full name: George Wight Ritchie
born: Liverpool, Lancashire, 1889
died: Manchester, Lancashire, 6.12.1960
debut: Crystal Palace (h), 25.12.1919 (SL D1)

George Ritchie played for Rossendale United and Chester in the Lancashire Combination, and had a spell in Preston North End's reserve team before joining Norwich City during the summer of 1913. A centre-forward at this point, he started out in the reserves, but subsequently switched to the inside-left role and became a regular in the "Canaries'" Southern League side during 1914–15, the last season before the close-down for the duration of the Great War. George guested briefly for Liverpool in 1915–16 before enlisting with the Grenadier Guards.

On his demob he returned to Norwich City as a trialist, but Albion's new manager Charlie Webb secured his signature in December 1919. The 30-year-old Liverpudlian made his debut in the 3–2 Goldstone defeat at the hands of Crystal Palace on Christmas Day, and retained the inside-left berth for the remainder of the season. In August 1920 he lined up at inside-right in Albion's first-ever Football League match, but quickly fell from favour and went

on instead to make a major contribution to the reserve team's championship of the Southern League's English Section that season. George was given a free transfer in May 1921 and moved on to Reading where he scored four goals in sixteen Third Division (South) matches before his release into non-League football in May 1922. Ironically, his last two outings with Reading came in consecutive fixtures against the Albion.

Season	FL	SL	Total
1919–20	0	18 (6)	18 (6)
1920–21	3	0	3
Total	3	18 (6)	21 (6)

ROBERTS, BILLY — 1903–05

inside-forward | Ht 5 8, Wt 11 09 | 73 apps, 17 goals
full name: John William Roberts
born: Liverpool, Lancashire, 1880
debut: Wellingborough Town (a), 5.9.1903 (SL D1)

'A wonderfully clever dribbler, and if his shooting were only on a par with his wizard-like manipulation of the ball with his feet, Billy Roberts would be indeed a great forward.' Thus was the 23-year-old Liverpudlian described by the *Sussex Daily News* during his first season at the Goldstone.

Billy was playing junior football with White Star Wanderers in Liverpool when, at the age of nineteen, he came to the notice of the Tottenham Hotspur management and joined the White Hart Lane staff in December 1899. He played in only three minor first-team games in just over two years with Spurs, though, and failed to break into their Southern League team. Consequently, he returned north with Stockport County in January 1902, but was then released three months later without having appeared in the first eleven and returned to the Southern League with Grays United. Having impressed in the two F.A. Cup ties against the Albion in November 1902, Billy was brought to the Goldstone the following summer and went on to enjoy by far the most successful part of his career.

Ever-present in 1903–04 when he finished leading scorer with a modest nine goals, he was particularly effective when paired in a left-wing duo with the experienced Ben Garfield in the latter part of the campaign as Albion struggled to survive in their initial season of top-flight Southern League fare. Retained for 1904–05, the skilful Liverpudlian was absent just once – in the last match of the season – and was again one of the successes of the side, but he was transferred to rivals Queen's Park Rangers in a double deal with his left-wing partner Andy Gardner in May 1905.

Billy found the net only once in 22 Southern League matches with Rangers and moved on to Preston North End in June 1906, but he failed to reproduce his impressive Albion form with either club. After just two outings in 1906–07 he was released by the First Division side and, following an unsuccessful trial with Leicester Fosse in November 1907, drifted into minor football.

Season	SL	FAC	Total
1903–04	34 (9)	1	35 (9)
1904–05	33 (6)	5 (2)	38 (8)
Total	67 (15)	6 (2)	73 (17)

ROBERTS, GORDON — 1949–51

outside-right | Ht 5 8, Wt 10 12 | 17 apps, 3 goals
full name: Douglas Gordon Roberts
born: Foleshill, Warwickshire, 30.5.1925
debut: Torquay United (a), 19.3.1949 (FL D3(S))

Gordon Roberts joined Wolverhampton Wanderers as a teenager in September 1942 and played briefly in wartime football. In 1945 he was transferred to Northampton Town and went on to score seven goals in 57 Third Division (South) games for the 'Cobblers' before coming to the Goldstone in March 1949, where he took over the right-wing slot from Des Tennant just three days after his arrival (with Tennant moving to right-back where he would later become a fixture). Fast and direct, Gordon retained his place in the side for the remainder of the 1948–49 campaign, but made only fleeting appearances over the following two seasons and was released to join Accrington Stanley in July 1951 where he enjoyed the most successful

part of his career. A regular in Stanley's Northern Section side during 1951–52, he became the first winger to register a Football League hat-trick for the club for almost fourteen years and scored eleven goals in 39 matches. In May 1952, Gordon dropped into the Southern League with Rugby Town, and worked as a draughtsman with the British Timken engineering company in Northampton for many years.

Season	FL	Total
1948–49	9 (3)	9 (3)
1949–50	8	8
Total	17 (3)	17 (3)

ROBERTS, J. — 1913

right-half | 1 app
debut: Newport County (h), 2.10.1913 (SA)

An amateur trialist from the north of England, Roberts was one of four young debutants who played in a 1–0 home defeat by Newport County in the opening fixture of Albion's triumphant Southern Alliance campaign of 1913–14, but was not heard of again.

Season	SA	Total
1913–14	1	1
Total	1	1

ROBERTSON, JIMMY — 1908–09

inside-forward | 37 apps, 10 goals
full name: James Robertson
born: Scotland
debut: Southampton (h), 2.9.1908 (SL D1)

Jimmy Robertson started out with the Scottish junior club Vale of Leven, but was playing for Belfast Distillery when he joined Blackburn Rovers in May 1905. A regular in the Lancashire club's line-up for three seasons, he scored 22 goals in 78 First Division outings before being released to join the Albion in May 1908. Jimmy played in a variety of positions at the Goldstone in 1908–09, although he usually partnered Joe Jee down the left flank. He played a big part in the Western League Division One Section 'A' championship success, but Albion struggled in the main competition, the Southern League, and only narrowly avoided relegation. As a result a number of players were released at

the end of the season and the burly Scot returned north of the border with his original club Vale of Leven (August 1909). He subsequently played for Falkirk from February 1911 until May 1914, and joined Dumbarton in May 1921.

Season	SL	FAC	WL	WL Ch.	SCC	Total
1908–09	23 (5)	1	9 (5)	2	2	37 (10)
Total	23 (5)	1	9 (5)	2	2	37 (10)

ROBERTSON, LAMMIE — 1972–74

forward/midfield | Ht 5 9, Wt 10 04 | 49 apps, 8 goals
full name: Archibald Lamond Robertson
born: Paisley, Renfrewshire, Scotland, 27.9.1947
debut: Queen's Park Rangers (h), 23.12.1972 (FL D2)

Lammie Robertson played his early football as a centre-half for the Glasgow junior club Drumchapel, but came south of the border at the age of nineteen to earn a living with Burnley in

September 1966. The lanky Scot failed to make an appearance in the League team at Turf Moor, though, and signed for nearby Bury on a free transfer in June 1968. Less than a year later, in February 1969, he was on the move again, across the Pennines to Halifax Town for £3,000, and it was at The Shay that he made his name by playing 149 League games, initially as a defender but later up front.

Albion manager Pat Saward made an unsuccessful bid for Lammie during the 1971–72 season, but landed the 25-year-old utility man in December 1972 for a £17,000 fee plus Willie Irvine. In a season and a half with the Albion, Lammie, playing mainly as a forward in a struggling team, scored eight goals, but made little lasting impression and was transferred to Exeter City in May 1974 as part of the deal which brought Fred Binney to Hove. By then a qualified F.A. coach, he made 133 League appearances for City before moving to the U.S.A. with Chicago Sting for the summer of 1976. On his return to St James's Park, Lammie missed just three games as Exeter won promotion to Division Three in 1976–77. He finished his Football League career with spells at Leicester City (September 1977), Peterborough United (August 1978) and Bradford City (January 1979), and subsequently played for Northwich Victoria (as player-manager) and Darwen.

Season	FL	FAC	FLC	Total
1972–73	15+1 (4)	0	0	15+1 (4)
1973–74	27+3 (4)	2	0+1	29+4 (4)
Total	42+4 (8)	2	0+1	44+5 (8)

ROBERTSON, TOM — 1904–06

right-back — Ht 5 10, Wt 12 04 — 31 apps, 1 goal
full name: Thomas Robertson
born: Newton Mearns, Renfrewshire, Scotland, c. 1875
debut: New Brompton (a), 3.9.1904 (SL D1)

One of the finest full-backs of his era, Tom Robertson was most unfortunate not to be chosen to represent his country. He came to the Goldstone in May 1904 from Southampton with a vast amount of experience behind him and was installed as captain, an appointment which met with universal approval. A contemporary biography stated that 'No more resolute player ever kicked a football; utterly fearless, his judgement in tackling is seldom at fault, and the very daring of his methods frequently saves the situation when skill alone would be of no avail.'

Tom began his career with Newton Thistle, but moved into senior football with the Scottish First Division club St Bernards at the age of nineteen in April 1894. Eight months later he crossed Edinburgh to join Hibernian where he gained a Scottish Cup runner's-up medal in 1896 (Hibs being beaten 3–1 by local rivals Hearts). In May 1897 the splendidly built full-back was transferred to Stoke, for whom he made 88 First Division appearances in three seasons, and represented the Anglo-Scots v. Home Scots at Cathkin Park, Glasgow, in March 1900 in what was effectively a trial match for the Scotland team. A month later Tom migrated to Liverpool, whom he assisted to the championship of the Football League in his first season, and the achievements continued when he moved on to Southampton in May 1902, the 'Saints' winning the Southern League title in both his seasons at The Dell.

With that amount of success under his belt, the 29-year-old Scot was quite a capture for the Albion in 1904, and his experience in the right-back berth helped the defence tighten considerably compared with the previous season. At the end of the campaign the popular defender retired to take over the tenancy of the Wick Inn in Western Road, Hove, where he remained until 1916, but he offered his services *gratis* to the club for the 1905–06 season and made brief appearances in the reserves.

Season	SL	FAC	Total
1904–05	26 (1)	5	31 (1)
Total	26 (1)	5	31 (1)

ROBINSON, G. L. — 1904–05

goalkeeper — 2 apps
debut: Bristol Rovers (a), 22.4.1905 (SL D1)

'A well-built young fellow who bids fair to be a goalkeeper of considerable ability.' Thus was Robinson described after impressing in his initial performances for the reserves on arriving at the Goldstone as an amateur in December 1904; he had previously played in the Middlesex area and appeared for Tottenham Hotspur in a friendly against the Albion three months earlier. Robinson got his first-team opportunity in the final two matches of the 1904–05 season when Mark Mellors was injured, but failed to live up to his predicted promise and conceded nine goals. In fact, the unfortunate goalkeeper became the central figure in the illegal payments scandal that rocked the club in the first half of 1905, when it was revealed that he had received wages before his registration as a professional (in the form of a £2 5s. payment for expenses 'considerably in excess' of what he had actually incurred). Although he was signed as a professional shortly afterwards, Robinson was suspended for three months by the Football Association and never played senior football again. (A number of directors were also suspended, while John Jackson, the former manager, received a censure.)

Season	SL	Total
1904–05	2	2
Total	2	2

ROBINSON, JOHN — 1987–92

winger — Ht 5 10, Wt 11 05 — 73 apps, 9 goals
full name: John Robert Campbell Robinson
born: Bulawayo, Rhodesia (Zimbabwe), 29.8.1971
debut: Portsmouth (a), 16.4.1990 (FL D2)

Although born in Rhodesia (now Zimbabwe) while his father was in the Army, John Robinson came to Sussex at the age of eight and is considered very much a local boy. It was, therefore, a great pity when he was sold to Charlton Athletic in 1992 for, as well as being a product of the county, he appeared to have a great future ahead of him. Blessed with deceptive pace and good ball-control, he has since confirmed that potential at The Valley by becoming a regular Welsh international.

A keen Albion fan as a lad, John attended Newhaven's Tideway School, and was a ball-boy at the Goldstone Ground when the 'Seagulls' beat Liverpool 2–0 in the F.A. Cup in January 1984. He went on to represent both Brighton and Sussex Schools, but Albion were somewhat fortunate to take him on as a trainee in 1987 after he had attended Southampton's school of excellence at Crawley and spent two years as an associate schoolboy on

Portsmouth's books. It was definitely those clubs' loss, though, as the young winger progressed through the juniors to the Combination team. In May 1988 he came on as a substitute in the Sussex Senior Cup final and turned the match for the Albion, the reserves defeating Lewes 3–0. Signed as a full professional in March 1989, John was farmed out to Crawley Town during 1989–90 to widen his experience and later that season made his Football League debut. In May 1991 he scored his first senior goal, a memorable winner at Millwall in the Division Two play-offs. A tenacious, determined and popular player, John become a regular in the side in 1991–92 and was voted Barclays Young Eagle for the South-East in October 1991.

In May 1992 he made his international debut for the Welsh under-21 side – his birth in Rhodesia allowed him to take his pick of the home countries – but, amid mounting speculation, the promising 21-year-old was sold to Charlton Athletic for £75,000 in September 1992 as financially-stricken Albion found it necessary to cash in on their saleable assets. (The sum was decided by a tribunal with Albion gaining a third of any future fee received by Charlton.) Although he started brightly at The Valley, John then hit a rocky patch, but blossomed in 1995–96 when his pinpoint crosses from either wing helped the 'Valiants' reach the Division One play-offs. With another four under-21 appearances to his name, he was rewarded with his first full cap for Wales late in the season, and by the summer of 1997 he had played in eight full internationals for his adopted country.

Season	FL	Play-offs	FAC	FLC	FMC	Total
1989–90	4+1	0	0	0	0	4+1
1990–91	11+4	2 (1)	0+1	1	0	14+5 (1)
1991–92	34+2 (6)	0	2	2 (1)	1 (1)	39+2 (8)
1992–93	6	0	0	2	0	8
Total	55+7 (6)	2 (1)	2+1	5 (1)	1 (1)	65+8 (9)

ROBINSON, MICHAEL   1980–83

centre-forward   Ht 6 1, Wt 13 07   *133 apps, 43 goals*
full name: Michael John Robinson
born: Leicester, Leicestershire, 12.7.1958
debut: Wolverhampton Wanderers (h), 16.8.1980 (FL D1)

For three years Michael Robinson led Albion's First Division line and scored more goals – 37 – for the club in the top flight than any other player, a feat which won him great popularity with the Goldstone crowds. Leading the attack in dashing style, the burly striker excited supporters with his power and determination, and was an overwhelming winner of the Player of the Season accolade in his first campaign on the South Coast. Although he went on to win a number of medals with Liverpool, his greatest feats in the game undoubtedly came with the Albion and he remains fondly in the memory of many Brighton fans.

Although born in Leicester, Michael was raised in Blackpool, represented the local schools, and became a target for a number of clubs, but chose to join nearby Preston North End rather than Coventry City with whom he had been associated as a schoolboy. Signing professional forms in July 1976, he scored twice in twelve League games during the next two seasons. In 1978–79, Michael scored thirteen times in 36 Second Division appearances for his newly promoted team and was obviously a player of potential, but in July 1979 he was sold to Manchester City for an unbelievable £756,000 fee, the second highest in the English game at the time; City manager Malcolm Allison's valuation of the virtually unknown 20-year-old shocked the football world and did much to fuel rapid inflation in the transfer market. Although he finished the 1979–80 season as top scorer at Maine Road with a modest eight League goals, Michael was unhappy at his new club and, after just one season, was brought to the Goldstone Ground in July 1980 for a more realistic £400,000 by Alan Mullery.

Relieved of the burden of that enormous fee, 'Robbo' was an instant success with the Albion and scored 22 goals in League and Cup in his first season, an outstanding return in a desperate struggle to avoid relegation. He also made his debut for the Republic of Ireland in October 1980 (on the strength of having an Irish grandmother) and went on to score four times in 24 internationals; he won thirteen caps while at the Goldstone. Thrilling the Albion fans with his buccaneering style, Michael had good pace and used his height and weight to great advantage.

It was not all plain sailing, though. He sought a transfer at the start of each of the following two seasons; had a long spell out through injury in 1981–82; and was hit by a metal object thrown from the North Stand in November 1981, an act of mindless hooliganism which prompted a critical outburst from the club's principal striker. His name was linked with several clubs, but Michael remained at the Goldstone to become one of the stars of the F.A. Cup final side in 1983, scoring three goals on the way to Wembley including the winner in the semi-final. Many supporters will remember his superb run in the last minute of extra time in the final, when he used his speed and physical presence to typical effect to set up the glorious chance to win the Cup which Gordon Smith was sadly unable to put away.

Albion were, of course, also relegated in 1983, and as the club found it necessary to off-load some of their higher-paid stars the 25-year-old centre-forward was transferred to Liverpool for £200,000 in August 1983. In his first season at Anfield, Michael won a League championship medal, a European Cup medal, and a League Cup medal, but he was never guaranteed a first-team place and joined Queen's Park Rangers in December 1984 for £100,000. In two years at Loftus Road, Michael appeared in another losing League Cup final side, but his scoring touch deserted him and he netted just six League goals before leaving for Spain and the Pamplona-based club Osasuna in January 1987.

Two years later, at the age of 30, 'Robbo' was forced into retirement with a knee injury and tore up his contract with Osasuna, a highly principled and unusual move. After a brief involvement in the air-freight business, Michael then began a new career as a sports presenter on Spanish television, a move which has proved most successful and lucrative. Indeed, the former Albion no.9 has developed into the biggest sporting star in the Spanish media, with his integrity and broken Spanish endearing him to the population of his adopted country.

Season	FL	FAC	FLC	Total
1980–81	42 (19)	2	3 (3)	47 (22)
1981–82	34+1 (11)	2	3	39+1 (11)
1982–83	35+1 (7)	8 (3)	2	45+1 (10)
Total	111+2 (37)	12 (3)	8 (3)	131+2 (43)

RODGER, TOM   1908

inside-left   Ht 5 7, Wt 11 10   *15 apps, 1 goal*
full name: Thomas Rodger
born: Dundee, Angus, Scotland, 9.6.1882
debut: Crystal Palace (h), 29.2.1908 (SL D1)

Tom Rodger started out with his home-town club, Dundee, in May 1903, but played only a reserve role at Dens Park until signing for Manchester United in April 1904. Again, though, he failed to break into the first team, and made the short journey to Preston North End in September 1904. The young Scot also struggled to make his mark at Deepdale, but he did play in five First Division games over two seasons before moving to Grimsby Town in August 1906. A right-winger on joining the 'Mariners', Tom was soon converted into an inside-forward and finished top scorer in 1906–07, but was nevertheless released to join Reading in the Southern League in June 1907.

In February 1908 he was recruited by Albion manager Frank Scott-Walford (along with his Reading team-mate Dave Dougal) and took over the problem inside-left berth for the remainder of the 1907–08 season, partnering Dick Joynes on the flank, but in May he joined the exodus to Leeds City a month after Walford had been appointed manager of the Yorkshire club. Having scored four goals in 25 Second Division matches during 1908-09, Tom left Elland Road and is believed to have returned to Scotland.

Curiously, his career bore amazing similarities to that of Dave Dougal (q.v.). They were both born in Dundee in 1882; they joined Dundee within eight days of each other in 1903; both went on to play for Preston North End, Grimsby Town and Reading; the pair joined Albion on the same day; and both departed for Leeds City during the close season of 1908!

Season	SL	Total
1907–08	15 (1)	15 (1)
Total	15 (1)	15 (1)

RODGERSON, TED 1920–22

inside-forward   Ht 5 8, Wt 11 07   *57 apps, 11 goals*
full name: Edward Rodgerson
born: Sunderland, Co. Durham, 1891
debut: Southend United (a), 28.8.1920 (FL D3(S))

Ted Rodgerson started his professional career at the age of 22 when Huddersfield Town signed him from Boldon Colliery in August 1913, but there was little chance of a place in the Second Division team for the inexperienced inside-forward and he was released to join Southend United in the Southern League in May 1914. During the war years Ted played no senior football, but in June 1919 he was transferred to Second Division Bury for a £10 fee, where he notched three goals in thirteen League appearances before Charlie Webb paid

£100 to bring him to the Goldstone in August 1920. Ted's debut was Albion's first match as a Football League club, and he missed only five games during that initial Third Division campaign. The following season he retained a place in the first team, but an injury suffered in the superb 1–0 F.A. Cup defeat of First Division Sheffield United in January 1922 effectively finished his career. After leaving the Goldstone, Ted had a brief spell with Clapton Orient from January 1923, but didn't appear in the League side. His brother Ralph played for Huddersfield Town, Leeds United and Dundee, while a second brother appeared in Albion's reservs during 1921–22.

Season	FL	FAC	Total
1920–21	37 (9)	3	40 (9)
1921–22	16 (2)	1	17 (2)
Total	53 (11)	4	57 (11)

RODON, CHRIS 1983–84

forward   Ht 5 11, Wt 12 00   *1 app*
full name: Christopher Peter Rodon
born: Swansea, Glamorgan, Wales, 9.6.1963
debut: Norwich City (a), 14.5.1983 (FL D1)

With 99 goals for Pontardawe Athletic over three seasons in the Welsh League to his name, Chris Rodon was a promising young striker who was working as a clerk at the Driver & Vehicle Licensing Centre in Swansea when he was invited to play in two games for Liverpool's reserves. He wasn't taken on at Anfield, though, and arrived at the Goldstone for a trial in January 1983. Albion's acting

managerial partnership of Jimmy Melia and George Aitken liked what they saw, gave Chris a two-year contract the same month – the fee to Pontardawe being £2,000 – and the nineteen-year-old forward made his League debut as a substitute for fifteen minutes in the club's final First Division game at Norwich in May. Included in the squad for the close-season tours of the U.S.A., Belgium and Holland, the young Welshman became homesick and returned to Glamorgan in August 1983 to play six games on loan for Second Division Cardiff City. In September 1983, after being suspended from his contract with the Albion, Chris announced that he would never play football again, but in 1987 he was turning out for Haverfordwest. His father, Peter, played for both Swansea Town and Bradford City.

Season	FL	Total
1982–83	0+1	0+1
Total	0+1	0+1

ROLLINGS, ANDY 1974–80 & 1986–87

centre-half   Ht 6 0, Wt 11 08   *192 apps, 12 goals*
full name: Andrew Nicholas Rollings
born: Portishead, Somerset, 14.12.1954
debut: Crystal Palace (h), 17.8.1974 (FL D3)

In five years as Albion's centre-half, Andy Rollings was a mainstay of the side which climbed from the depths of the Third Division all the way to the First. Improving greatly along the way, the young defender from the West Country became a dominating force at the heart of the Brighton defence, only to make way for Steve Foster once the club had reached the top.

Andy attended a rugby-playing school, but played soccer for his local Eastern Youth Club team and represented the Bristol boys' clubs. Norwich City soon spotted his potential and took him on as an apprentice, but, despite turning professional in December 1972 and playing in more than 100 games for the reserves, he had made the "Canaries'" League team on just four occasions when Brian Clough and Peter Taylor brought him to the Goldstone – together with his City team-mate Steve Govier – in April 1974 for a combined fee of £25,000.

Still just nineteen on his Albion debut, Andy found his time in Hove to be much more successful. The robust defender matured alongside the experience of Graham Winstanley, Dennis Burnett and Graham Cross over the next three years, and was firmly established as the club's first-choice centre-half in 1977–78 when Second Division Albion came so close to winning promotion for the second year in succession. Now playing alongside Mark Lawrenson, Andy, while never the fastest nor most skilful of defenders, proved to be an effective foil for the inspirational Lawrenson in the back-line, and was a vital cog in the side which won promotion to the top-flight in 1979. However, he was injured in his third Division One game, allowing Steve Foster to step up from the reserves, and was forced to act as the future England man's deputy thereafter. His penultimate

appearance in the first team was against his former club, Norwich City, in October 1979 but was an unhappy occasion: Andy's nose was broken in a clash with Justin Fashanu (an incident for which the City forward was never forgiven by the Hove crowd, even when he joined the Albion in 1985) before being dismissed during the second half.

In May 1980 the 25-year-old centre-half was valued at £75,000 when he left for Swindon Town in an exchange deal involving Ray McHale, but he made just twelve League appearances for the Wiltshire club before joining Portsmouth in August 1981. However, Andy suffered a serious knee injury at Fratton Park and left 'Pompey' on the completion of the 1982–83 campaign. He then had trials with Torquay United, Brentford and Aldershot during 1983–84, but finished the season with Maidstone United in the Alliance Premier League.

After leaving the Kent club, Andy played for Littlehampton Town, and gained a Sussex Senior Cup winner's medal with Steyning Town in 1986 before rejoining the Albion as a non-contract player in 1986–87, helping to develop the youngsters in the reserves. Since his release in May 1987 he has played locally for Southwick, Peacehaven & Telscombe, and has had a number of spells with both Shoreham and Newhaven, his current club, while running the Chalet Café in Preston Park, Brighton, for a number of years.

Season	FL	FAC	FLC	Total
1974–75	25	2	4 (1)	31 (1)
1975–76	36 (3)	2	0	38 (3)
1976–77	39 (4)	3	4	46 (4)
1977–78	24	1	4	29
1978–79	37 (3)	1	3	41 (3)
1979–80	7 (1)	0	0	7 (1)
Total	168 (11)	9	15 (1)	192 (12)

RONALDSON, Duncan   1907–08

inside/centre-forward   Ht 5 9, Wt 12 03   33 apps, 9 goals
full name: Duncan McKay Ronaldson
born: Glasgow, Lanarkshire, Scotland, 21.4.1879
died: Glasgow, Lanarkshire, Scotland, 20.9.1947
debut: Norwich City (a), 7.9.1907 (SL D1)

A Scottish junior internationalist with the Vale of Clyde and Rutherglen Glencairn clubs, Duncan Ronaldson was recommended to Queen's Park Rangers by their full-back George Newlands (a fellow Glaswegian and former Vale of Clyde player) and joined the London side in December 1900. Quickly gaining a reputation as an excellent forward with an eye for goal, he signed for First Division Grimsby Town in May 1901 and was a regular in the "Mariners'" team for two seasons.

However, after leaving Blundell Park he became something of a 'gypsy', playing in turn for First Division Bury (May 1903), then in the Southern League for Queen's Park Rangers (for a second spell May 1904), Norwich City (May 1905, for their initial season as a professional club, along with his Rangers colleague and future Albion favourite Arthur Archer), Brighton (May 1907, again with Archer), Southend United (May 1908) and Norwich City for a second spell (May 1909), before returning to Scotland with non-League Dunfermline Athletic in September 1910. A stocky ball-player with a rare turn of speed, Duncan occupied all three inside-forward positions during his one and only season in Hove. A tinsmith by trade, he died in his native Glasgow aged 68.

Season	SL	FAC	WL	SCC	Total
1907–08	19 (6)	2	9 (1)	3 (2)	33 (9)
Total	19 (6)	2	9 (1)	3 (2)	33 (9)

ROUGVIE, Doug   1987–88

centre-half   Ht 6 2, Wt 13 08   46 apps, 3 goals
full name: Douglas Rougvie
born: Ballingry, Fife, Scotland, 24.5.1956
debut: York City (h), 15.8.1987 (FL D3)

A rugged, hard-as-nails defender, Doug Rougvie won great popularity wherever he played for his uncompromising approach to the game, a style of play which earned him the nickname 'Doug the Thug'; yet he was a competent enough performer to play for Scotland and won a host of honours in his homeland. He could also be an inspirational leader, as he proved at the Goldstone Ground.

On Dunfermline Athletic's books as a schoolboy, Doug was playing for junior side Dunfermline United when he joined Aberdeen in 1972 at the age of sixteen. Farmed out to Rosemount, an Aberdeen junior club, for experience, he also completed his education in mechanical engineering before going on to appear in 308 League and Cup games for the 'Dons'. A great favourite at Pittodrie, he gained two Scottish League championship medals; three Scottish Cup winner's medals; a European Cup-Winners' Cup medal against Real Madrid in 1983; and made one appearance in a Scottish jersey, in a 2–0 defeat by Northern Ireland in 1983. Transferred unexpectedly to Chelsea in August 1984, Doug spent three seasons at Stamford Bridge and played in 90 League and Cup games, mainly at left-back (in competition

with his future Albion colleague Keith Dublin). In 1986 he added a Full Members Cup medal to his collection.

With the departure of Eric Young to Wimbledon imminent, Albion manager Barry Lloyd spent £50,000 in June 1987 to bring the hugely experienced 31-year-old to the Goldstone, and installed him as skipper following the departure of Danny Wilson. Although looking a little crude at times, Doug was a colossus at the heart of the defence as Albion gained immediate promotion back to the Second Division in 1987–88, but the season ended on a sour note when, after recovering from a bout of flu, he was replaced by Bob Isaac for the last few matches and requested a transfer. In September 1988 he moved on to Shrewsbury Town for £50,000, and joined Fulham five months later, but the following August he returned to Scotland with the club he had started out with as a lad, Dunfermline Athletic.

After 28 Premier Division outings for the 'Pars', Doug left for Montrose during the close season of 1990 and starred in the team which took the runner's-up spot in Division Two in his first season at Links Park. In December 1991 the 35-year-old defender was appointed manager, but left Montrose the following May and resumed as a player with Huntly in the Highland League, later to become manager. In 1993–94 he helped the Aberdeenshire club win the League and League Cup, and won a second championship the following season. In April 1995, Doug played for the Highland League XI which defeated an F.A. XI – effectively the England semi-pro side – 4–3 at St Albans.

Season	FL	FAC	FLC	AMC	Total
1987–88	35 (2)	4 (1)	2	5	46 (3)
Total	35 (2)	4 (1)	2	5	46 (3)

ROUTLEDGE, Ralph   1909–15

full-back   Ht 5 11, Wt 12 00   57 apps
born: Ryhope, Co. Durham, 1886
debut: Northampton Town (h), 26.11.1910 (SL D1)

A lbion recruited 22-year-old Ralph Routledge from the Wearside League club Ryhope Villa during the summer of 1909. It was an

investment which proved an excellent piece of business, for, on his day, Ralph came to be regarded as one of the best full-backs in the Southern League. Initially he had to develop his skills in the reserves, acting as a deputy for skipper Joe Leeming at left-back, before winning a regular place at right-back during the 1911–12 campaign. After playing in 31 of the 38 League matches of that season, the well-built full-back was dealt a cruel blow the following term when, in September 1912, he suffered a serious knee injury at Coventry, a devastating setback for both the club and the player. Forced to retire from the game for a time, he made a brief but unsuccessful come-back with the reserves, and was granted a testimonial (including the proceeds from a Southern Alliance fixture with Millwall in March 1913 which realised £51 9s. 3d.). However, after recuperating at his Sunderland home, Ralph made a second, more successful return to the Goldstone and played ten games for the first team in the 1914–15 season before enlisting with the Army. Despite guesting briefly for Watford during the war, he did not resume his career when peace was restored.

Season	SL	FAC	SCC	Total
1910–11	6	0	3	9
1911–12	31	1	2	34
1912–13	4	0	0	4
1914–15	9	0	1	10
Total	50	1	6	57

ROWE, ZEKE   1996

striker   Ht 5 10, Wt 11 08   9 apps, 3 goals
full name: Ezekiel Bartholomew Rowe
born: Stoke Newington, London, 30.10.1973
debut: Rotherham United (h), 30.3.1996 (FL D2)

Zeke Rowe spent two years as a trainee at Chelsea – he was the club's Young Player of the Season in 1991–92 – and four years as a professional from 1992, but he never once enjoyed an outing in the senior side at Stamford Bridge. Although slightly built, the young Londoner displayed both strength and mobility in the Chelsea reserves, but it was only when he joined Barnet on loan for two months in November 1993 that he made his League debut. Indeed, Zeke played for the 'Bees' against the Albion at the Goldstone in his twelve games on loan, during which he scored three times. In March 1996 he joined Swindon Town on trial to play in a couple of reserve games, and arrived in Hove on loan the same month to replace the disappointing Junior McDougald.

Showing good skills and pace up front, Zeke quickly impressed the Goldstone Ground crowds and scored three excellent goals in his nine games in a relegation-bound side. Released by Chelsea at the end of the season, it was hoped that the 22-year-old striker would sign for the Albion on a permanent basis, but he preferred to play in a higher standard of football and instead chose to join Peterborough United in the Second Division during the close season. Unfortunately

for Zeke he scored only three League goals as the 'Posh' were relegated in 1997, and made more appearances as a substitute than in the starting line-up.

Season	FL	Total
1995–96	9 (3)	9 (3)
Total	9 (3)	9 (3)

ROWELL, GARY   1986–88

midfield   Ht 5 10, Wt 11 03   14 apps
born: Seaham, Co. Durham, 6.6.1957
debut: Sunderland (a), 30.8.1986 (FL D2)

An accomplished attacking midfielder, Gary Rowell was worshipped by the fans on Wearside during a twelve-year career with Sunderland, but was sadly unable to reproduce his excellent form away from Roker Park. The son of John Rowell, the former Bournemouth, Wrexham and Aldershot forward, Gary played junior football in his native Seaham before joining the Roker staff as an apprentice in 1972. After turning professional in July 1974, the local youngster went on to become one of the club's greatest heroes of recent times, scoring 99 goals in nearly 300 League and Cup games. Top scorer in five of his ten seasons as a professional, he converted no fewer than 24 penalties and won an England under-21 cap in 1977.

However, all good things come to an end, and Gary's Sunderland career finished in 1984 following a dispute over the terms of his contract. He moved on to Norwich City, but his time at Carrow Road was wrecked by injury and twelve months later he returned to his native North-East with Middlesbrough. 'Boro, though, went into receivership during the 1986 close season and, with Ayresome Park padlocked, Gary was released to join the Albion in August 1986; Brighton manager Alan Mullery, in his second spell at the helm, thus finally signed a man he had pursued in the "Seagulls'" First Division days. The classy midfielder's debut came somewhat ironically at his spiritual home, Roker Park, but he was unable to establish himself in the Albion side until December, and then a toe injury suffered on 27 December effectively ended his career in Sussex. Making only three more appearances before his contract was paid up in February 1988, Gary joined Dundee on a month's contract and also had spells with Carlisle United (March 1988) and then Burnley (close season 1988), where he made nineteen appearances in the Fourth Division before he left the Football League arena.

Season	FL	FLC	FMC	Total
1986–87	8+2	0	0+1	8+3
1987–88	1+1	1	0	2+1
Total	9+3	1	0+1	10+4

RUGGIERO, JOHN   1977–79

midfield   Ht 5 10, Wt 11 05   12 apps, 2 goals
full name: John Salvatore Ruggiero
born: Blurton, Stoke-on-Trent, Staffordshire, 26.11.1954
debut: Cambridge United (a), 13.8.1977 (FLC R1 Lg1)

The son of Italian parents, John Ruggiero represented both Stoke and Staffordshire Boys, and had a trial for the England Schools team before joining Stoke City as an apprentice. Turning professional in May 1972, he played just nine League matches for the 'Potters' and was loaned out on three occasions: he spent the summer of 1973 in Zambia with Ndola United and eight months of 1975 in South Africa with Cape Town City where he assisted the club to a League-and-

Cup double; a somewhat less exotic port-of-call was Workington, where he had a three-match spell in January 1976.

Albion manager Alan Mullery paid £30,000 for John's signature in June 1977 to strengthen the side on its elevation to Division Two, and the 22-year-old midfielder scored on his League debut, coming on as sub-stitute and grabbing a late equaliser at Southampton. John found it difficult to gain a place in the team, however, and was loaned to Ports-mouth for a month in December 1977. After spending the 1978–79 campaign in the reserves, he left for Chester on a free transfer in April 1979 where he finished his League career with twelve Third Division outings. Though totalling only 38 League matches for his five English clubs, John appeared in all four divisions of the Football League.

Season	FL	FLC	Total
1977–78	4+4 (2)	4	8+4 (2)
Total	4+4 (2)	4	8+4 (2)

RULE, ARTHUR   1905

centre-forward   Ht 5 9, Wt 11 10   1 app
full name: Arthur George Rule
born: Isle of Sheppey, Kent, 10.12.1873
debut: Norwich City (h), 30.9.1905 (SL D1)

Famed for many years as the most dashing centre-forward in the county of Kent, Arthur Rule was an Admiralty civil servant by profession and appeared for a number of Southern League clubs as

his work took him to Whitehall and several other centres of naval activity; from 1893 to 1899 he played for his local club, Sheppey United, and also assisted New Brompton (now Gillingham), Tottenham Hotspur, Portsmouth, and the Isle of Wight club Ryde. In 1894–95 he bagged no fewer than 22 goals in just eleven games as New Brompton romped away with the Southern League Division Two title in their first season as a professional club. Registered as a professional by the Albion on 29 September 1905, he played in a 2–1 defeat of Norwich City at the Goldstone the following day which turned out to be his only appearance for the club. Arthur had represented the Thames & Medway Combination select XI against the United League in November 1898, when the latter side triumphed 4–2 at North-umberland Park, Tottenham.

Season	SL	Total
1905–06	1	1
Total	1	1

RUSHTON, GEORGE   1903–04

utility forward   Ht 5 9, Wt 11 00   22 apps, 4 goals
born: Stoke upon Trent, Staffordshire, 1880
debut: Swindon Town (h), 19.9.1903 (SL D1)

A formidable figure, happy in any of the forward positions, George Rushton signed for Burslem Port Vale from the Staffordshire junior club Leek Broughs in June 1901, and scored four goals from the right wing in nineteen Second Division matches during his first season with the Potteries club. He lost favour the following term, though, and had only two further outings before being released to join the Albion in May 1903. George enjoyed a successful time at the Goldstone, appearing in all the forward berths with the exception of outside-left, but left for the newly formed Hull City at the end of the 1903–04 season. A year later the 'Tigers' were elected to the Football League, and George netted fifteen goals in 29 League appearances, mainly as a centre-forward, before returning to the Southern League with Swindon Town in May 1907. During the close season of 1909 he was transferred to Brentford, but returned to Swindon in October 1909 without appearing in the "Bees'" Southern League team. George harvested fifteen goals from 62 League games in his two spells at Swindon, but dropped into the Midland League with Goole Town in 1912.

Season	SL	FAC	Total
1903–04	21 (4)	1	22 (4)
Total	21 (4)	1	22 (4)

RUSSELL, JOCK   1901–02

outside-left   Ht 5 5   17 apps, 3 goals
full name: John Russell
born: Carstairs, Lanarkshire, Scotland, 29.12.1872
died: Glasgow, Lanarkshire, Scotland, 10.8.1905
debut: Brighton Athletic (h), 21.9.1901 (FAC Prelim.)

One of several itinerant Scotsmen to play for the Albion in the club's formative years, Jock Russell started out with Wishaw Thistle and progressed into the Scottish League with Leith Athletic (close season 1892) and St Mirren (July 1895) before moving south to join Woolwich Arsenal in the English Second Division in June 1896. While at Plumstead he gained a reputation as the finest winger in the South, but was soon on the move, joining Bristol City in the Southern League during the summer of 1897. Three seasons in the West Country harvested 36 goals from 110 League and Cup outings, plus a representative appearance for the United League *v.* Thames & Medway Combination in March 1899. That success brought Jock a

move to Blackburn Rovers during the 1900 close season, but in September 1901 he arrived in Hove at the age of 28 for Albion's first-ever season.

The wee left-winger became one of the stars of the side, holding a regular place as the fledgling club narrowly missed promotion at the first attempt, but he left the club in May 1902 to return to the Scottish League for a season with Port Glasgow Athletic, fol-lowed by another with

Motherwell. In the summer of 1904, Jock joined Doncaster Rovers on their election to the Football League, but a year later the little Scot was working as a storekeeper on the railway in his native land when he died at the age of 32.

Season	SL	FAC	Total
1901–02	13 (2)	4 (1)	17 (3)
Total	13 (2)	4 (1)	17 (3)

RUST, NICKY   1993–

goalkeeper   Ht 6 0, Wt 13 01   192 apps
full name: Nicholas Charles Irwin Rust
born: Ely, Cambridgeshire, 25.9.1974
debut: Bradford City (a), 14.8.1993 (FL D2)

Still only in his early 20s, Nicky Rust has already made it into the top eight of Albion goalkeepers in terms of appearances. In his first three years at the Goldstone the promising ex-Arsenal trainee missed just two games, and equalled a club record in March 1995 by keeping five consecutive clean sheets in Football League games. But his form and confidence declined during the traumatic 1996–97 season such that he made way for his long-term understudy, Mark Ormerod,

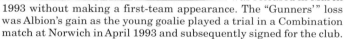

as the club fought desperately but successfully to retain its League status.

Nicky represented Cambridgeshire, East Anglia and England at schoolboy level, and attended the F.A.'s National School of Excellence after trials with a number of top clubs. On his graduation from Lilleshall, the young 'keeper joined Arsenal in 1991 where he won England youth honours, but, with an abundance of goalkeeping talent on the Highbury staff, he was released in March 1993 without making a first-team appearance. The "Gunners'" loss was Albion's gain as the young goalie played a trial in a Combination match at Norwich in April 1993 and subsequently signed for the club.

Although he was expecting only to be a reserve, the confident eighteen-year-old impressed manager Barry Lloyd sufficiently to be thrust into the position of no.1 'keeper and performed with great merit. While obviously still learning the game, he was the only ever-present in 1993–94, and was rewarded with a call-up as a standby for the England under-21 squad during the summer and again in August 1994. A good shot-stopper but still prone to the occasional misjudgement, Nicky has twice finished second in the Player of the Season poll as he continues to gain experience.

Season	FL	FAC	FLC	AMC	Total
1993–94	46	1	4	2	53
1994–95	44	1	6	2	53
1995–96	46	4	2	4	56
1996–97	25	2	2	1	30
Total	161	8	14	9	192

RUTHERFORD, JACK   1920–21

centre-half   Ht 6 1, Wt 13 00   29 apps, 2 goals
full name: John Rutherford
born: Bedlington, Northumberland, 1892
died: Morpeth, Northumberland, September 1930
debut: Southend United (h), 4.9.1920 (FL D3(S))

The young Jack Rutherford played for Ashington and Bedlington United before joining Tottenham Hotspur as a professional in December 1913, but, although he played in the wartime competitions

J. RUTHERFORD

for Spurs, he didn't make a regular Football League appearance and was transferred to Southern League Luton Town in July 1919. In August 1920 he was brought to the Goldstone for 'a big fee' as part of the effort to strengthen the team for its initial season in the Football League. The big North-Easterner, whose brother Jim (q.v.) was also on the staff, was installed as skipper, but missed the opening fixture through injury and was sidelined on several other occasions during the course of the season.

Though performing his task well, Jack left the club in May 1921 to play in the U.S.A., but, with the ship carrying him to his new career in the middle of the Atlantic Ocean, Cardiff City offered him terms by radio — probably making him the first player ever engaged in such a manner! Yet, after taking so much trouble to obtain his signature, it was ironic that the Welsh club couldn't find a place for him in their newly promoted First Division side, and he was transferred to Bristol Rovers for £350 in September 1922. Although reputedly receiving £7 a week at Eastville, Jack wasn't satisfied with the arrangement and in May 1923 he was released to join Mold in the Welsh National League. He subsequently enjoyed a spell in the Midland League with York City, but returned to the first-class game with Gillingham in November 1924 where he monopolised the centre-half berth for almost three seasons, totalling 84 Third Division (South) appearances before calling it a day in 1927. Three years later Jack sadly passed away after a long illness at the age of 38.

Season	FL	Total
1920–21	29 (2)	29 (2)
Total	29 (2)	29 (2)

RUTHERFORD, JIM   1920–21

left-back   29 apps
full name: James Rutherford
born: Bedlington, Northumberland, 1894
died: 1924
debut: Swansea Town (h), 27.11.1920 (FL D3(S))

Jim Rutherford joined his elder brother Jack (q.v.) on the Albion staff when he arrived as a trialist from Ashington of the Northern Alliance in August 1920. Registered as a professional in September, he spent the early part of the 1920–21 season in the reserves, but got his chance when Wally Little was indisposed in November and did so well that he retained the left-back spot for the rest of the season. After the arrival of Jack Feebery from Exeter during the summer of 1921, Jim resumed a reserve-team role for the entire 1921–22 season, and in September 1922 he left the Goldstone Ground to play and coach in the United States where he was reported to have died from an unknown cause two years later at the age of 32.

JIM RUTHERFORD

BRIGHTON & H. A.

Jim and Jack played fifteen times together, and were the last pair of brothers to play in the same Albion first team until Mark and Simon Fox both played at York in March 1995.

Season	FL	FAC	Total
1920–21	26	3	29
Total	26	3	29

RYAN, GERRY   1978–86

midfield/winger   Ht 5 10, Wt 10 12   *199 apps, 39 goals*
full name: Gerald* Joseph Ryan
born: Dublin, Co. Dublin, Republic of Ireland, 4.10.1955
debut: Stoke City (a), 27.9.1978 (FL D2)

A great favourite with Albion fans at the pinnacle of the club's success, Gerry Ryan mixed alternate doses of brilliance and mediocrity but was rarely dull. It was, therefore, a personal tragedy for many people when his career was ended so suddenly and cruelly by a broken leg, but the amiable Irishman took the setback with commendable restraint, and went on to become a successful publican before returning to the Goldstone as assistant manager in less happy times.

Yet the young Gerry didn't take up soccer seriously until the age of sixteen when he joined the Rangers club in Dublin. In fact, he had represented both his city and country at hurling as a schoolboy, and also played Gaelic football. Quickly taking to the association game, he joined League of Ireland club Bohemians – initially as an amateur, then as a part-time professional – and appeared in the team which won the F.A.I. Cup in 1976. Working as a clerical officer for Dublin Corporation, Gerry signed for Derby County in September 1977 and went on to make 30 League appearances for the 'Rams', earning his first international cap against Turkey in April 1978.

Albion manager Alan Mullery had competed for Gerry's signature when he joined Derby, but eventually got his man in September 1978 when he paid £80,000 for the 22-year-old forward, and was rewarded with instant success. Looking at home in the no.7 shirt, Gerry scored ten goals in his first season at the Goldstone, including the third goal in the final game at Newcastle which saw Albion promoted to the First Division for the first time. Few spectators present will have forgotten the mazy, 75-yard dribble with which he scored against Manchester City in December 1979, but he proved somewhat inconsistent and was in and out of the side throughout that debut season in the top-flight, coming on as substitute fifteen times. Capable of playing as a winger, in midfield, or as a striker, Gerry was an ideal substitute and made 52 appearances as such in total, thirteen more than any other Albion player. Indeed, he came on as substitute in the two F.A. Cup final matches with Manchester United in 1983, playing superbly at right-back in the first game after an injury to Chris Ramsey. (In fact, he would have been Michael Robinson's striking partner but for a hamstring injury prior to the semi-final which let in Gordon Smith.)

After nearly seven years at the Goldstone, Gerry was the victim of a disgraceful tackle by Henry Hughton at Crystal Palace in April 1985. His leg was broken in two places, and players and fans alike were both sickened and incensed by the incident. To his immense credit, though, the 29-year-old remained uninvolved in the subsequent recriminations even though it meant the end of his professional career. The occasionally brilliant Irishman received a benefit in August 1986 when a friendly with Spurs attracted the third-biggest gate of the season to the Goldstone, 10,759 admirers turning out on a balmy night to boost his fund.

Gerry, who won sixteen full caps with the Albion (he was the club's most-capped player until Steve Penney won his seventeenth in December 1988) became mine host of the Witch Inn at Lindfield on retiring. He played briefly for Hendon in 1988, being a friend of the Isthmian League club's chairman, but made a surprise return to the Goldstone in January 1994 as assistant to the new manager, his former Republic of Ireland team-mate Liam Brady. Indeed, he was influential in bringing Brady to the club. However, following the

manager's resignation in November 1995, Gerry, who was not on contract, was dismissed. Several months later he revealed some of the stories behind the pair's time at the club to the 'fanzine' *Gulls Eye*, including the fact that the management team took a cut in wages to finance a loan transfer. Having returned to his pub – for whom he also plays in the Sussex Sunday League Premier Division – Gerry now follows events at the Albion through his son, Darragh, who became a trainee in 1996.

Season	FL	FAC	FLC	Total
1978–79	34+1 (9)	1 (1)	0	35+1 (10)
1979–80	25+11 (5)	2 (1)	1+4	28+15 (6)
1980–81	2+8	0	1 (1)	3+8 (1)
1981–82	17+3 (1)	1+1	1+1	19+5 (1)
1982–83	16+10 (6)	2+2 (1)	0	18+12 (7)
1983–84	20+4 (6)	2+1 (1)	3 (1)	25+5 (8)
1984–85	17+5 (5)	2 (1)	0+1	19+6 (6)
Total	131+42 (32)	10+4 (5)	6+6 (2)	147+52 (39)

Note: Ryan was christened Gerald, but has always been known as Gerard by his family.

SALT, HAROLD   1921–22

inside-left   Ht 5 9, Wt 11 07   *6 apps, 2 goals*
born: Sheffield, Yorkshire
debut: Southend United (h), 27.8.1921 (FL D3(S))

Harold Salt had an amazingly chequered football career which took him to numerous clubs. Having appeared for Sheffield Wednesday in the last two seasons of regional football during the Great War, he was on the books of Ecclesfield United when recruited by the Albion in March 1921. The fair-haired Yorkshireman was a centre-half at this juncture and made his first-team debut as such, but was converted into an inside-forward during the 1921–22 season and had a run in the side toward the end of the campaign. With Andy Neil and Billy McAllister holding the inside berths, though, he had little chance of making the team on a regular basis and was released in May 1922 to join Mexborough back in his native county.

After a spell with Peterborough & Fletton United in the Southern Eastern League, Harold returned to the Football League with Queen's Park Rangers in May 1926 where he enjoyed only a moderate season before another sojourn in part-time football with Southern League side Grays Thurrock United. Then, in January 1928, Crystal Palace offered him yet another opportunity to make the grade and he set out on the most successful part of his career, assisting the 'Glaziers' to the runner's-up spot in the Third Division (South) in 1928–29 before transferring to Brentford in May 1929. In his first season at Griffin

Park the 'Bees' also took second place in the Southern Section, and he remained with the Middlesex club for three years before being released to join Walsall in May 1932, where he saw out his League career with ten Third Division (North) outings during 1932–33. In the summer of 1933, Harold joined Yeovil & Petter's United in the Southern League.

Season	FL	Total
1921–22	6 (2)	6 (2)
Total	6 (2)	6 (2)

SANDERS, ALLAN   1963–65

right-back   Ht 5 11, Wt 13 00   *86 apps*
born: Salford, Lancashire, 31.1.1934
debut: Southend United (h), 26.1.1963 (FL D3)

A strong and polished full-back, Allan Sanders cost the Albion £7,000 in January 1963, and used his experience to good effect, helping to steady the ship in troubled times: manager George Curtis

departed just two weeks later and the following season saw Brighton in the Fourth Division for the first time. The Salford-born defender began his professional career with Manchester City in August 1955, but had never played for the League team before he joined Everton on a free transfer in July 1956. Developing his game steadily at Goodison Park, Allan appeared in 56 First Division matches in just over three years before losing his place at right-back when Scottish international Alex Parker was signed from Falkirk. After moving on to Swansea Town for £6,000 in November 1959, he added a Welsh Cup medal and 92 Second Division appearances to his record before his arrival at the Goldstone Ground.

Allan's initial outing for the Albion was a 2–1 defeat of Arsenal in a friendly match at Hove, and he remained first-choice right-back for almost two years until the arrival of Mel Hopkins from Spurs effectively ended his career at the Goldstone. Following the completion of the 1964–65 campaign, Allan followed the popular trail to South Africa as player/assistant manager of Cape Town City and also coached in the Western Province. On returning to the U.K. he had a somewhat stormy season as manager of Worthing in 1968–69 before leaving the club the following October.

Season	FL	FAC	FLC	Total
1962–63	17	0	0	17
1963–64	41	1	2	44
1964–65	16	0	2	18
1965–66	6	0	1	7
Total	80	1	5	86

himself as one of the club's leading strikers. Indeed, he made his international debut in March 1986, and ended the season as leading scorer with nineteen goals to win the Player of the Season award. In the summer he toured Canada with Wales, but the following season was traumatic for both player and club: Albion were relegated to the Third Division and Dean went sixteen matches without a goal, scoring only six times in 35 outings. Manager Barry Lloyd dropped him in favour of local boy Richard Tiltman and, with the club in a dire financial position, accepted a £60,000 offer from First Division Oxford United in March 1987 much to the chagrin of supporters.

Dean added to a fine reputation at the Manor Ground with 22 goals from 59 League outings, a record which tempted Derby County to pay £1 million to bring him back into the First Division in October 1988 (and a transfer which led to the resignation of ex-Albion star Mark Lawrenson as Oxford manager). An immediate success at the Baseball Ground with six goals in his first five matches, he went on to establish himself on the international scene – he had won 58 caps by the summer of 1997 and scored 20 goals – and developed into one of the best strikers in the country, so much so that Liverpool splashed out a British record fee of £2·9 million for him in 1991. Top scorer at Anfield in 1991–92, 'Deano' gained an F.A. Cup winner's medal with the 'Reds', but moved on to Aston Villa for £2·3 million in September 1992 where he won a League Cup medal in 1994.

A great favourite at Villa Park – as, indeed, he has been at all his ports of call – Dean was nominated Player of the Season for 1994–95 but then made his fourth multi-million pound move, joining his former Liverpool manager Graeme Souness at the Turkish club Galatasaray for £2·35 million. Although he scored the winner in the 1996 Turkish Cup final, Dean returned to England with Nottingham Forest for £1·5 million in July 1996 at the age of 32.

Season	FL	FAC	FLC	FMC	Total
1985–86	39+3 (15)	5 (4)	2	2	48+3 (19)
1986–87	27+3 (6)	2	2	1	32+3 (6)
Total	66+6 (21)	7 (4)	4	3	80+6 (25)

SAUNDERS, DEAN   1985–87

forward   *Ht 5 8, Wt 10 06*   *86 apps, 25 goals*
full name: Dean Nicholas Saunders
born: Swansea, Glamorgan, Wales, 21.6.1964
debut: Grimsby Town (h), 17.8.1985 (FL D2)

To many Albion fans the sale of Dean Saunders, one of the most exciting players to grace the Goldstone turf in recent years, for just £60,000 epitomised the state of the club in the late 1980s. The lively Welshman combined good pace and explosive finishing with intelligent running and total commitment, and went on to become one of the best-known and most popular strikers in England. While never quite matching the scoring-rates of the very best, he has made his cut-price transfer look rather ridiculous as fees for him since he left the Goldstone have amounted to around £10 million.

Yet Albion themselves picked 'Deano' up for nothing, signing him in the summer of 1985 on a free transfer from Swansea City. The son of Roy Saunders, a former Liverpool and Swansea wing-half, Dean had represented Swansea Schools and joined his local club as an apprentice, signing pro forms in June 1982. Six months later he scored twice against Albion's reserves, and made his League debut the following season. In 1984–85 he scored nine goals in 30 Third Division matches to finish joint top scorer (and had a loan spell with Cardiff City in March), but was released at the end of the campaign, arriving in Hove in July 1985.

The 21-year-old quickly impressed with his speed and incisive style, and established

SAUNDERS, EDGAR   1922–23

centre-forward   *3 apps*
born: Birmingham, Warwickshire
debut: Norwich City (h), 26.8.1922 (FL D3(S))

Edgar Saunders joined the Albion in August 1922 having scored 40 goals for the Birmingham Tramways club in the Birmingham Combination the previous season. Despite 'possessing a shot like a rocket', he failed to impress the Goldstone management on leading the attack in the opening games of the 1922–23 campaign, but continued to play for the reserves until given a free transfer at the end of the season. Edgar left for Pontypridd in the Southern League but, after a season with the Welsh club, moved on to Peterborough & Fletton United, also in the Southern League. His elder brother 'Banjo' Saunders played for Nottingham Forest before the Great War.

Season	FL	FAC	Total
1922–23	2	1	3
Total	2	1	3

SAYER, PETER   1978–80

midfield   *Ht 5 7, Wt 10 02*   *64 apps, 6 goals*
full name: Peter Anthony Sayer
born: Cardiff, Glamorgan, Wales, 2.5.1955
debut: Sunderland (h), 25.2.1978 (FL D2)

A talented and industrious midfielder, Peter Sayer never quite lived up to expectations at the Goldstone. He greatly impressed the Hove crowd – and Brighton manager Alan Mullery – with a superb

display for Cardiff City in October 1977 (despite his side losing 4–0), and was signed for £100,000 four months later, but, although he showed good form at times, Peter was in and out of the Albion side for much of his spell in Sussex.

A representative of both Cardiff and Wales as a schoolboy, he joined Cardiff City as a professional at the age of eighteen in July 1973 and went on to make 82 League appearances at Ninian Park. In his five seasons with the club he gained further international honours at youth and under-21 levels, and helped City win the Welsh Cup in 1976. He also won seven full caps, the first of them in a 3–0 win over Czechoslovakia at Wrexham in March 1977.

The 22-year-old arrived at the Goldstone in February 1978 with Albion pushing for promotion to Division One for the first time. The following season Peter played in 32 League games as the club made it to the top, but after appearing in the first fourteen Division One matches in 1979–80 he was replaced by Mark Lawrenson in midfield and had only three more outings as substitute. Sold to Preston North End for £85,000 in August 1980, Peter made just 45 League appearances in four seasons at Deepdale and returned to Cardiff City on loan for a month in September 1981. Moving on to Chester City in the close season of 1984, he was released the following May and subsequently played for Chorley, Morecambe and Northwich Victoria. Peter now runs a public house in the Preston area.

Season	FL	FAC	FLC	Total
1977–78	6 (1)	0	0	6 (1)
1978–79	26+6 (5)	1	3	30+6 (5)
1979–80	14+3	0+1	4	18+4
Total	46+9 (6)	1+1	7	54+10 (6)

SCHOOLEY, HERBERT   1904–05 & 1906–07

right-half   1 app
born: Brighton, Sussex, 1883
debut: Leyton (a), 4.10.1906 (UL)

Herbert Schooley was a local player who was taken on as professional by the Albion and appeared fairly regularly for the 'Lambs' during 1904–05. In September 1905 he left for Tunbridge Wells Rangers, but returned to the Goldstone the following summer. Although predominantly a full-back, his  one first-team appearance was at right-half as deputy for Alex Smith in a 2–1 United League victory at Leyton during his second spell with the club.

Season	UL	Total
1906–07	1	1
Total	1	1

SCOTT, FRANK   1902–04

centre-forward   Ht 5 8, Wt 11 00   50 apps, 34 goals
born: Boultham, Lincoln, Lincolnshire, c. 1876
died: Lincoln, Lincolnshire, 3.7.1937
debut: Southall (h), 13.9.1902 (SL D2)

Arriving in Hove in 1902 for the club's second season, Frank Scott became Albion's first regular goalscorer, netting 34 goals in 50 outings over two years. Born just outside Lincoln, he joined Lincoln City from the local Adelaide club in October 1897 and scored eight goals in 45 Second Division matches as an inside-forward (playing alongside three future Albion stalwarts: Arthur Hulme, Tom McCairns

and Wally Smith). In May 1901 he moved into the Southern League with New Brompton (later Gillingham), then arrived in Hove in August 1902.

Switched to centre-forward, Frank was a great success at the Goldstone and played a major part in the club's victorious 1902–03 campaign when the championship of the Southern League's Second Division was shared with Fulham. In fact, he hit 46 goals in all first-team matches that term, including six in a friendly fixture with Hove and five in an 8–0 Southern League win at Southall. Frank met with less success against the stronger sides of Division One the following term, though, and lost his place to his former Lincoln team-mate Tom McCairns when the latter was signed from Queen's Park Rangers in December. Released in May 1904, Frank departed for an unknown non-League destination.

Season	SL	Test	FAC	SEL	Total
1902–03	10 (11)	1	5 (9)	20 (11)	36 (31)
1903–04	14 (3)	0	0	0	14 (3)
Total	24 (14)	1	5 (9)	20 (11)	50 (34)

SEAR   1902

centre-forward   2 apps, 1 goal
debut: Chesham Town (h), 1.3.1902 (SL D2)

Sear was one of three trialists drafted into Albion's team for the friendly match with Southampton Wanderers in February 1902 (the club's initial appearance on the Goldstone Ground) in an effort to improve the front line, but he had a mixed debut. Reported as 'doing absolutely nothing' in the first half, he had a much better second period and was retained for the Southern League game against Chesham Town a week later. A tall, tricky player from Luton, he was also rather slow and 'at times simply looks at the ball and makes no effort to gain possession.' Despite scoring one of the goals in a 4–0 win, Sear failed to impress the Albion supporters, and although he retained the centre-forward berth for the following match he was then released.

Season	SL	Total
1901–02	2 (1)	2 (1)
Total	2 (1)	2 (1)

SEXTON, DAVE   1957–59

inside/centre-forward   Ht 5 9, Wt 11 07   53 apps, 28 goals
full name: David James Sexton
born: Islington, London, 6.4.1930
debut: Aldershot (a), 2.10.1957 (FL D3(S))

While performing as a useful forward in the 1950s and early '60s, Dave Sexton won much greater acclaim as a manager and coach over the next 30 years or so, achieving his greatest successes at Chelsea in the early 1970s. The son of Archie Sexton, a contender for the British middleweight boxing crown in the 1930s, he became one of several West Ham players of the era who subsequently enjoyed success in the management field.

Dave started out with Southern League Chelmsford City on his demob from the Army in 1950 and signed for Luton Town in June 1951 before joining the 'Hammers' in March 1953. In just over three seasons at Upton Park he scored 29 goals in 77 League and Cup games before moving to Leyton Orient in June 1956. Dave was, therefore, a seasoned Second Division performer when Billy Lane brought him to the Goldstone for £3,000 in October 1957, and he played a big part in Albion's successful drive for promotion that term, scoring eighteen times in just 26 League games before injury ruled him out of the

climax to the season. Indeed, his impressive form won him a place in the Third Division's southern representative side *v.* Northern Section at Carlisle in March 1958. Blessed with excellent ball skills, Dave was the brains behind the attack and could control the pace of any game with the ease of his distribution, but he was also a fair goalscorer.

He appeared in all three inside-forward positions at the Goldstone, but was transferred to Crystal Palace in May 1959 following a less successful season in Division Two. He then suffered knee problems and was forced into retirement in January 1962 at the age of 31.

Shortly after leaving Selhurst Park, Dave was appointed assistant coach at Chelsea by the flamboyant new manager Tommy Docherty, the start of a tremendous new career for the quiet, thoughtful Londoner. Since that first coaching position he has served Orient (manager at the age of 34 in 1965), Fulham (coach), Arsenal (coach and assistant manager), Chelsea (taking over from Docherty as manager 1967–74, winning the F.A. Cup and European Cup Winners' Cup), Queen's Park Rangers (manager 1974–77), Manchester United (again successor to Docherty as manager 1977–81) and Coventry City (manager 1981–83). A resident of Hove for many years until his appointment at Old Trafford, he was later involved in the running of the F.A. School of Excellence at Lilleshall and also managed the England under-21 team until 1990. After a spell as national coach to Saudi Arabia he took a post on the Aston Villa staff from July 1992 until November 1994. In February 1994, at the age of 63, Dave was appointed England under-21 coach again, and remained a senior adviser when Glenn Hoddle took over from Terry Venables as England coach in 1996.

Season	FL	FAC	Total
1957–58	26 (18)	3 (2)	29 (20)
1958–59	23 (8)	1	24 (8)
Total	49 (26)	4 (2)	53 (28)

SEYMOUR, IAN   1971

goalkeeper   Ht 5 10, Wt 11 08   3 apps
full name: Ian Patrick Seymour
born: Edenbridge, Kent, 17.3.1948
debut: Barnsley (a), 6.2.1971 (FL D3)

One of Albion manager Pat Saward's many loan signings, Ian Seymour was brought in from Fulham for a month in February 1971 to ease a goalkeeping crisis when Brian Powney was out with a thigh injury and Geoff Sidebottom had been forced into retirement. First attracting the attention of Fulham while playing for Tonbridge in the Southern League, Ian joined the Craven Cottage staff for a £1,250 fee in August 1966. The Kent-born 'keeper went on to make 75 first-team appearances in six seasons for the London side, but was forced out of the first-class game soon after his Goldstone interlude by the effects of a broken leg and he returned to Tonbridge in July 1971 at the age of 24. He went on to serve the Kent club for a number of years and enjoyed a testimonial match in May 1975 against Fulham.

Season	FL	Total
1970–71	3	3
Total	3	3

SHANKS, DON   1981–83

right-back   Ht 5 11, Wt 10 08   54 apps
full name: Donald Shanks
born: Hammersmith, London, 2.10.1952
debut: West Ham United (a), 29.8.1981 (FL D1)

A Fulham apprentice who joined Luton Town at the age of seventeen in July 1970, Don Shanks represented England at youth level during his time at Kenilworth Road and had made 90 League appearances up to November 1974 when he was transferred to Queen's Park Rangers for a £35,000 fee. Helping Rangers to runner's-up spot in the First Division in 1975–76, he was released in 1981 after 180 League matches at Loftus Road and joined Albion on their pre-season tour of the Netherlands.

Proving a more-than-adequate replacement for the departed John Gregory, Don was quickly signed on a free transfer by manager Mike Bailey and went on to make 42 League and Cup appearances in the ensuing 1981–82 season, playing consistently well as Albion tightened up their First Division defence considerably to finish a respectable thirteenth. He appeared in twelve matches during the early part of 1982–83, but was dropped by Jimmy Melia and George Aitken in favour of Chris Ramsey when Bailey was dismissed in December 1982 and soon left for the Eastern club in Hong Kong. On returning to the U.K., Don joined Wimbledon on a non-contract basis and made one Third Division appearance in 1983–84 before leaving to play and coach in the United States. In 1991–92 he appeared briefly with the Maltese club Zurrieq.

While a useful footballer for Luton, Q.P.R. and the Albion, Don will also be remembered for his reputation as a playboy on the London gambling scene, and had a former Miss World, Mary Stavin, as his girlfriend. He now works for a well-known horse-racing family.

Season	FL	FAC	FLC	Total
1981–82	35+1	3	3	41+1
1982–83	10	0	2	12
Total	45+1	3	5	53+1

SHARP, ALF   1901

inside-forward   1 app
full name: Alfred Henry Sharp
born: Brighton, Sussex, 9.4.1876
died: Brighton, Sussex, 24.10.1948
debut: Shepherd's Bush (a), 28.9.1901 (SL D2)

Alf Sharp was the first local player to be offered professional terms by a Brighton club, signing for the short-lived Brighton United in March 1899 for the princely sum of 7*s.* 6*d.* (37·5p) per week plus 7*s.* 6*d.* per game. Born in Brighton, he played his early football on The Level with the junior clubs Eastern Rovers and Western Star, and progressed to the East Sussex Senior League with Brighton Hornets. In 1898 he joined another Preston Park club, North End Rangers, but then threw

his lot in with the local professionals (although he made his initial appearances for Brighton United as an amateur).

Following the club's demise in March 1900, Alf was reinstated as an amateur and joined the Brighton & Hove Rangers club which was formed out of North End Rangers in the wake of the professionals' collapse. He finished 1900–01 as leading scorer and played in the side which lost the Sussex Senior Cup final 3–1 to Eastbourne at the County Ground in March 1901. Following the formation of the Albion in June 1901, he played in the club's first-ever Southern League match, a 2–0 win at Shepherd's Bush, but declined to join the club on a permanent basis and returned to the East Sussex Senior League with Brighton Athletic. Alf subsequently worked at the railway engineering works in Brighton for many years.

Season	SL	Total
1901–02	1	1
Total	1	1

SHARPE, IVAN — 1911

winger   *2 apps*
full name: Ivan Gordon A. Sharpe
born: St Albans, Hertfordshire, 15.6.1889
died: Southport, Lancashire, 9.2.1968
debut: Coventry City (h), 4.2.11 (FAC R2)

Ivan Sharpe won renown in two fields: as a fine amateur footballer and also as an influential sports journalist. His profession took him to diverse parts of the country where he was often recruited by the local club, but he remained an amateur throughout a long and distinguished career with Watford (1907–08), Glossop (1908–11), Derby County (1911–13, assisting them to the Division Two championship in 1912) and Leeds City (1913–15). In 1920 he had a single match for the newly formed Leeds United to bring his senior career record to 45 goals from 219 League and Cup matches before hanging up his boots at the age of 31. Two of those games came in February 1911 when he guested for the Albion in two second-round F.A. Cup matches with Coventry City.

A fleet-of-foot winger – he was a member of Salford Harriers in his youth – Ivan gained eight amateur caps before the Great War and won a gold medal with Great Britain in the 1912 Stockholm Olympics, the same year he had a trial for the full England side. He also played on the Continent with the touring English Wanderers side, and briefly assisted the reserve teams of Nottingham Forest and Luton Town.

Yet, despite his achievements as a player, Ivan found greater fame as editor of *Athletic News* and as a sports commentator for the *Sunday Chronicle*, becoming president of the Football Writers' Association. In 1958 he was presented with a silver salver from that body for his services to the game, and was commissioned to write the 75th anniversary history of the Football League in 1963.

Season	FAC	Total
1910–11	2	2
Total	2	2

SHEPHERD, JOHNNY — 1958–60

inside/centre-forward   Ht 6 0, Wt 12 07   *45 apps, 19 goals*
full name: John Herbert Edwin Shepherd
born: Kensington, London, 29.5.1932
debut: Middlesbrough (a), 23.8.1958 (FL D2)

Johnny Shepherd burst onto the Football League scene in a spectacular way, hitting four goals for Millwall against Leyton Orient in his first match. It was a remarkable performance by the Kensington-born forward who, having worked in a leather factory, contracted polio while on National Service with the R.A.F. After recovering to play for the service's representative side on four occasions, he joined Millwall as an amateur and turned professional on his demob in October 1952. In five years as a pro at The Den, Johnny kept up an excellent rate with 78 goals from 166 League and Cup appearances, and in October 1957 he represented the Third Division (South) against the Northern Section.

In June 1958, John became Albion's first signing for their initial campaign in the Second Division. The burly 26-year-old made his debut in the disastrous 9–0 defeat at Middlesbrough, but the team slowly improved and he finished the season as leading scorer with seventeen goals. The following season, though, Johnny lost his place, and was transferred to Gillingham in February 1960 where he remained until joining Ashford Town in the Southern League during the summer of 1961. John subsequently played for Margate and Tunbridge Wells, and was appointed player-coach of Southwick in the Sussex County League in 1964; he later became manager and stayed at Old Barn Way for seven years. The former striker also took charge of the Sussex representative team and has been associated with the Albion's schoolboy and youth set-up since 1977, enjoying a testimonial dinner at Hove Town Hall in September 1993. For some considerable time now John has also been assistant manager at the Southwick Leisure Centre. His youngest son, Dominic, was an Albion trainee in 1995–96.

Season	FL	Total
1958–59	36 (17)	36 (17)
1959–60	9 (2)	9 (2)
Total	45 (19)	45 (19)

SHERIDAN, ALEX — 1970–72

full-back   Ht 5 11, Wt 10 12   *16 apps, 2 goals*
full name: Alexander Sheridan
born: Motherwell, Lanarkshire, Scotland, 19.7.1948
debut: Torquay United (h), 15.8.1970 (FL D3)

Alex Sheridan was a Scottish schools and youth internationalist who gained a fine reputation during four years with Queen's Park in the Scottish League, winning eight caps at amateur level. After a month on trial with the Albion, the 22-year-old defender was taken on as a professional in August 1970 and went straight into the first team, making sixteen appearances during 1970–71, but he spent the following season in the reserves and was released to join Southern League Maidstone United in June 1972. Alex worked in the architect's department of Maidstone Borough Council and studied for a degree in civil engineering while with the Kent club, but then returned to Sussex to work for West Sussex County Council and play for Hastings United and Crawley Town. An arthritic hip brought his playing days to an end at the age of 31, and he subsequently had a spell as manager of Shoreham in the Sussex County League before emigrating to Australia in 1988.

Season	FL	FLC	Total
1970–71	12+3 (2)	1	13+3 (2)
Total	12+3 (2)	1	13+3 (2)

SHORT, JIMMY   1933–35

inside-right/centre-forward   Ht 5 9, Wt 11 00   42 apps, 13 goals
full name: James William Short
born: Bedlington, Northumberland, 1909
debut: Bristol Rovers (h), 4.11.1933 (FL D3(S))

Jimmy Short started out in the North Eastern League with Jarrow before joining Sheffield Wednesday as a professional in November 1931, but his first two matches in Division One at the end of the 1931–32 season turned out to be his only outings for the "Owls'" first team before his transfer to the Albion in August 1933. After starting out in the London Combination team, the 23-year-old utility forward forced his way into the first eleven in early November and became a regular in the side, appearing in both inside-forward berths and at centre-forward during the 1933–34 campaign. Jimmy was retained for 1934–35, but his opportunities were fewer because of the consistency of Bobby Farrell and Potter Smith, and he was released in May 1935 to join Barrow in the

Third Division (North) where he made nine appearances before departing from the Football League.

Season	FL	FAC	SSC	Total
1933–34	25 (6)	2 (1)	3 (1)	30 (8)
1934–35	12 (5)	0	0	12 (5)
Total	37 (11)	2 (1)	3 (1)	42 (13)

SIDEBOTTOM, GEOFF   1969–71

goalkeeper   Ht 5 11, Wt 12 04   45 apps
full name: Geoffrey Sidebottom
born: Mapplewell, Yorkshire, 29.12.1936
debut: Stockport County (h), 11.1.1969 (FL D3)

Brave almost to a fault, Geoff Sidebottom performed his courageous goalkeeping feats throughout a sixteen-year professional career, but was eventually forced to retire because of the injuries he suffered. Playing for his village's youth side, he was given the opportunity to join Wolverhampton Wanderers at the age of seventeen in January 1954, but initially returned to Yorkshire with Wath Wanderers, Wolves' nursery club. Signed as a professional the following September, Geoff showed a good deal of promise at Molineux, but had to play a

supporting role to the incomparable Bert Williams and Malcolm Finlayson before making his debut in the 1958–59 championship season.

After clocking up 28 First Division appearances for Wolves, he joined Aston Villa for £15,000 in February 1961 and appeared in the second leg of the inaugural Football League Cup final that season, when Villa beat Rotherham United 3–2. Geoff made 70 First Division appearances in four years at Villa Park, and was transferred to Third Division Scunthorpe United in January 1965 where Freddie Goodwin had recently taken over as manager. After 59 League games for the Lincolnshire club he rejoined Goodwin, then in charge of New York Generals, and followed his mentor to the Goldstone on a free transfer in January 1969, two months after Goodwin's appointment as Albion manager.

The 32-year-old 'keeper immediately took over from Brian Powney and continued to share the jersey with Powney for two years, but he suffered severe concussion after saving at the feet of a Walsall forward in December 1969, and did further damage to his head when colliding

with a goal-post in a reserve match in October 1970. He made one more first-team appearance, but was advised to quit the game by neurologist Dr Roger Bannister, the former athlete. Hanging up his gloves in February 1971, Geoff was granted a testimonial in May 1972 with Goodwin's new club, Birmingham City, providing the opposition.

Season	FL	FAC	FLC	Total
1968–69	9	0	0	9
1969–70	25	2	3	30
1970–71	6	0	0	6
Total	40	2	3	45

SIM, JOHNNY   1946–50

centre-forward/left-half   Ht 5 9, Wt 11 02   35 apps, 7 goals
full name: John Sim
born: Glasgow, Lanarkshire, Scotland, 4.12.1922
debut: Leyton Orient (h), 16.11.1946 (FL D3(S))

An 'enthusiastic and dashing centre-forward', Johnny Sim (also known as Jock) was recruited from the Dunbartonshire junior club Kirkintilloch Rob Roy in October 1946 at the age of 23. After making his Albion first-team debut at home to Leyton Orient in November, he scored all five goals in the reserves' 5–3 win over Swansea Town on 7 December (including three in four minutes) and was immediately promoted back into the League team, keeping his place for much of the season.

Initially chosen to lead the attack, Johnny was a mature player for his age and not one to get over-excited by his early successes. Later played at left-half, he then fell victim to a number of injuries (including a fractured wrist and a broken collar-bone) and was thus unable to command a regular place in the League side

After four seasons at the Goldstone, Johnny was given a free transfer and moved on to Chippenham Town in the Western League in July 1950 (along with a trio of team-mates: Eric Lancelotte, Ken Davies and Fred Leamon). In March 1951 he signed for Plymouth Argyle, but did not appear in their Third Division team and soon returned to Chippenham. In 1959 he was playing for Calne in the Wiltshire League.

Johnny may not have been the greatest forward ever to put on an Albion shirt, but there was never any doubting his bravery or commitment to the cause. On 21 December 1946, despite being ruled out of the no.9 shirt for the reserves with a facial injury, he volunteered for goalkeeping duties in the Combination match against Bristol Rovers at the Goldstone Ground when Harry Baldwin was stranded on the railways; City won 2–1. Johnny was married on 20 December 1947; one hour later he led the Albion's forward-line in a 2–1 win over Hartlepools United in an F.A. Cup replay.

Season	FL	FAC	Total
1946–47	15 (5)	0	15 (5)
1947–48	6	3 (2)	9 (2)
1948–49	5	0	5
1949–50	6	0	6
Total	32 (5)	3 (2)	35 (7)

SIMMONDS, DANNY   1991–95

utility player   Ht 5 11, Wt 11 05   23 apps
full name: Daniel Brian Simmonds
born: Eastbourne, Sussex, 17.12.1974
debut: Exeter City (h), 2.10.1993 (FL D2)

A Sussex representative at both school and youth level, Danny Simmonds joined the Albion as a trainee on leaving school in 1991 and won a regular place in the reserves during 1992–93. Offered professional terms in April 1993 after two years with the club, the versatile, play-anywhere youngster made his Football League debut in October 1993 and performed usefully in his limited first-team outings. However, he was released at the end of the 1994–95 season

and joined Hastings Town in the Southern League after a brief trial with Portsmouth.

Danny won three Sussex Senior Cup medals with Albion reserves, in 1992, '94 and '95, and won a fourth with his new club in 1996 when he scored the only goal of the game against Crawley Town. In 1997 he was selected for the Great Britain side in the World Student Games. His father, Norman, played for Wimbledon in their Southern League days.

Season	FL	FLC	AMC	Total
1993–94	6+8	1	0+1	7+9
1994–95	2+2	0+1	2	4+3
Total	8+10	1+1	2+1	11+12

SIMPSON, BOBBY 1912–14

inside-forward 38 apps, 12 goals
full name: Robert Albert Simpson
born: Chorlton-cum-Hardy, Lancashire, 1888
debut: Bristol Rovers (h), 14.12.1912 (SL D1)

Although born in Lancashire, Bobby Simpson learned his football north of the border, joining Aberdeen from the local Westburn club in 1905 at the age of seventeen. In five years at Pittodrie he filled all the attacking positions at various times, and a record of 31 goals from 90 League and Cup games attracted the attention of a number of English clubs. Tempted south in May 1910, Bobby joined a band of Scottish players at Bradford (Park Avenue) and was a regular in their Second Division side for two seasons, netting nine times in 56 League and Cup appearances. In November 1912 he came to the Goldstone as part of the transaction that took Albion's prolific goalscorer Jimmy Smith to Bradford. The sale of Smith left a gap that was hard to fill, though, and as Albion tried a number of players at centre-forward Bobby performed well in an inside role. However, in October 1913 he sustained a broken leg in the last minute of a Southern Alliance game at Newport which brought his career to an end at the age of 25.

Season	SL	FAC	SA	Total
1912–13	22 (8)	3	2	27 (8)
1913–14	8 (3)	0	3 (1)	11 (4)
Total	30 (11)	3	5 (1)	38 (12)

SIMPSON, TOMMY 1927–28

outside-right Ht 5 7, Wt 10 07 30 apps, 6 goals
full name: Thomas Simpson
born: Dundee, Angus, Scotland, 1904
debut: Brentford (h), 27.8.1927 (FL D3(S))

Tommy Simpson started out in his native city with Dundee Osborne, but turned pro with Dundee United at the age of nineteen in 1923. In the four seasons 1923–27 he appeared in 101 Scottish League games and starred in the side that took the Second Division championship flag to Tannadice Park in 1924–25. Thus, when Charlie Webb laid out £250 to bring the clever little ball-player to Hove in June 1927, it caused an outcry in the Dundee newspapers. Tommy was initially preferred to Dai James on the right

flank at the Goldstone, but then formed a fine understanding with the equally diminutive Welshman when the latter switched to inside-right around Christmas. Yet, despite enjoying a successful season with the Albion, Tommy was released in May 1928 and returned to Scotland to sign for non-league Montrose the following December.

Season	FL	Total
1927–28	30 (6)	30 (6)
Total	30 (6)	30 (6)

SIRRELL, JIMMY 1951–54

inside-forward Ht 5 8, Wt 11 00 58 apps, 17 goals
full name: James Sirrell
born: Glasgow, Lanarkshire, Scotland, 2.2.1922
debut: Reading (a), 22.9.1951 (FL D3(S))

Jimmy Sirrell's playing career was less than spectacular, but he went on to enjoy a most successful time as a manager and has become almost a legend at Notts County where, in 1994, the new County Road stand was named after him. The Glasgow-born forward began his career with Renfrew Juniors while working as a coppersmith's apprentice. In 1939 he was associated with Chelsea, but spent the war working in shipyards in Cairo (Egypt) and Mombasa (Kenya) before joining Celtic in 1945. On the fringe of the first team for nearly four years, Jimmy netted four goals in 33 games for the Glasgow club before signing for Bradford (P.A.) in May 1949, but he failed to make his mark in a what turned out to be a relegation side and was subsequently brought to Hove by Billy Lane for a month on trial.

Signed in August 1951, Jimmy was a strong little player and, like so many of his countrymen, both thoughtful and skilful on the ball, but his lack of pace perhaps held him back. The canny Scot was also quite a comedian, the joker of the Albion's Third Division (South) side. Jimmy was in and out of the team for three seasons until he moved to Aldershot in August 1954. However, in 1956 his playing career was ended by sciatic nerve problems and he turned his attention to coaching at the age of 34.

Jimmy remained at the Recreation Ground as trainer and coach for a further nine years, then moved into management in 1967 with Brentford in the Fourth Division. Two years later he took over at Notts County where, apart from an eighteen-month interval at Sheffield United (1975–77) and a spell as general manager (1984–85), he remained in charge until 1987. Under Jimmy's shrewd guidance the 'Magpies' were transformed from Fourth Division also-rans into a First Division outfit, and he gained wide respect throughout football. He also served as a director with County from 1984 to 1987. After retiring from management Jimmy became chief scout at nearby Derby County, but returned to Meadow Lane in a similar role in 1994.

Season	FL	FAC	Total
1951–52	27 (7)	1	28 (7)
1952–53	9 (1)	0	9 (1)
1953–54	19 (8)	2 (1)	21 (9)
Total	55 (16)	3 (1)	58 (17)

SITFORD, TONY 1958–62

forward/full-back Ht 6 1, Wt 11 07 24 apps, 2 goals
full name: Jack Anthony Sitford
born: Crowborough, Sussex, 28.1.1940
debut: Notts County (a), 20.10.1960 (FLC R2)

Tony Sitford, a powerfully built six-footer from Crowborough, was an energetic leader of the attack, yet also displayed considerable aplomb as a defender. Having joined Albion's ground staff as a

teenager, he was signed as a professional in March 1959, and made his first-team debut in a Football League Cup tie at Notts County when the centre-forward berth had become something of a problem following the departure of Bill Curry early in the 1960–61 campaign. The following season the youngster was converted into a full-back, and, as Albion fought in vain to stave off relegation to the Third Division, had an extended run in the team before becoming a victim of manager George Curtis's big end-of-season clear-out.

Tony joined Gravesend & Northfleet in June 1962, the start of a splendid career in Kentish Southern League circles firstly as a player and later as a manager. In October 1963 he moved on to Dartford where he remained for almost six years and scored prolifically (in partnership with former Albion striker Tony Nicholas for two seasons). Voted Player of the Season in 1967–68, he returned to Gravesend & Northfleet in 1969 and managed the club with considerable success from 1974 to 1980, leading them to the Southern League Division One (South) title in 1974–75, the League Cup in 1978, and to fifth place in the inaugural Alliance Premier League in 1979–80. Tony was then associated with Maidstone United and managed Welling United before taking the helm at Kent League club Corinthian (based at Fawkham near Dartford) in 1987. Soon he became general manager of the Corinthian sports club which was developed by a local farming family on their own land.

Season	FL	FAC	FLC	Total
1960–61	2 (1)	0	1	3 (1)
1961–62	20 (1)	1	0	21 (1)
Total	22 (2)	1	1	24 (2)

SLY, HAROLD   1929–33

left-half   Ht 5 11, Wt 10 07   24 apps
born: Appley Bridge, Lancashire, 26.2.1904
debut: Bristol Rovers (a), 31.8.1929 (FL D3(S))

Born in Lancashire but raised in Birmingham, Harold Sly skippered his local schools representative team, and was recommended to Birmingham by the former Everton and England star Walter Abbott in March 1922; the eighteen-year-old was playing for the Rover Motor Company where he and Abbott were both

employees. Harold remained at St Andrews until 1925, playing as an amateur in the reserves, but was then released to join Tamworth Castle in the Birmingham Combination. In August 1927 he returned to the first-class game with Gillingham, and was transferred to the Albion in August 1929.

Harold's four seasons at the Goldstone were marred by knee problems and, after undergoing a cartilage operation, he was granted a free transfer in May 1933. Having received compensation for his injury – and therefore unable to play again professionally in England – he spent some time with F.C. de Sète in the French League, but enlisted with the R.A.F. in 1935 and served for a year with Hugh Vallance at Eastchurch where they both played for the R.A.F. representative team; they were, however, later omitted after complaints from a university side that the pair were former professionals. Harold changed his name to Winnard – his mother's maiden name – in 1942, and on leaving the Air Force in 1947 returned to the Brighton area where he practised as a chiropodist for many

years. For many years until his death he lived in Park View Road, just a goal-kick away from the Goldstone Ground.

Season	FL	FAC*	Total
1929–30	10	0	10
1930–31	1	0	1
1931–32	3	0	3
1932–33*	8	2	10
Total	22	2	24

Note: Sly's two F.A. Cup appearances came in the qualifying competition of 1932–33.

SMALL, MIKE   1990–91

striker   Ht 6 0, Wt 13 05   50 apps, 21 goals
full name: Michael Anthony Small
born: Selly Oak, Birmingham, Warwickshire, 2.3.1962
debut: Barnsley (a), 25.8.1990 (FL D2)

One of the most effective leaders of Albion's attack in recent years, Mike Small was a big man with deceptive ball-skills and an excellent football brain, yet enjoyed only a brief period of success in England. On leaving school he played for Bromsgrove Rovers before joining Luton Town in 1980 where, in three years, he gained England Youth honours, scoring three goals in the 1981 World Youth Championship in Australia. However, Mike made just four

appearances as substitute in the League team, and, after loan spells with Peterborough United and Hitchin Town, was released in 1983 to try his luck on the Continent. In a seven-year career in Europe, the powerfully-built striker played in turn for Go Ahead Eagles (in the Netherlands), Standard Liège (Belgium), Go Ahead for a second spell, Vitesse Arnhem (Netherlands), and subsequently spent two years in Greece with PAOK Salonika.

By this time Mike was 28 and looking to make his mark finally in the Football League. Offered a trial at the Goldstone Ground, he was signed for around £70,000 in August 1990 and proved a wonderful bargain, teaming up with John Byrne – who was signed a few weeks later – to form one of the most admired spearheads in the Second Division. With nineteen goals to his name by the middle of February he was unfortunate to suffer a severe injury and struggled to find his top form again, but the play-off semi-finals against Millwall brought out the best in Mike and his superb performances went a long way to seeing Albion into the final at Wembley. Twenty-one goals in the season attracted the attention of several leading sides, and with Albion desperately short of cash he was sold to West Ham United for a fee of £400,000 in August 1991; it was a good profit in one year but a severe blow to hopes of continuing the quest for promotion.

Mike's initial form at Upton Park was impressive, and he finished as top scorer in his first season with eighteen goals as the 'Hammers' were relegated from Division One, but he subsequently suffered from a back injury and was loaned to Wolves (September 1993) and Charlton Athletic (March 1994). Towards the end of 1993–94 he was released to play for the Swedish club B.K. Hacken. In October 1994 he joined Sligo Rovers and spent the rest of the campaign with the League of Ireland outfit, scoring eleven goals in 21 League games, but returned to Sussex in the summer of 1995 to train with Crawley Town while also training with Enfield. In November 1995, Mike signed for Littlehampton Town, then managed by his former Albion teammate Russel Bromage, but quickly moved up to the Conference with Stevenage Borough. In 1996 he joined nearby Baldock Town.

Season	FL	Play-offs	FAC	FLC	FMC	Total
1990–91	39 (15)	3 (1)	3 (2)	2 (1)	3 (2)	50 (21)
Total	39 (15)	3 (1)	3 (2)	2 (1)	3 (2)	50 (21)

SMALL, PETER   1957–59

utility forward   Ht 5 8, Wt 10 10   *8 apps, 3 goals*
full name: Peter Victor Small
born: Horsham, Sussex, 23.10.1924
debut: Gillingham (a), 24.8.1957 (FL D3(S))

Though Sussex-born and bred, Peter Small made his name as a professional footballer in the Midlands, and only returned to the county with the Albion late in his career. While attending Victory Road School he represented Horsham Schools and subsequently played for the local senior club. Serving with the R.A.S.C. from 1943, he took part in the victory parade in Berlin and then played for the German clubs Troisdorf and Neumünster in the immediate post-war period. An Army colleague, Hugh Billington of Luton Town, took Peter to Kenilworth Road for a trial, but he was set to join Crystal Palace when he received an eleventh-hour telegram from Luton and was signed as a pro in August 1947 at the age of 22. In almost three seasons with the 'Hatters' he met with only limited success, netting five goals in 28 Second Division games, and was transferred to Leicester City for £6,000 in February 1950, having impressed in a fifth-round F.A. Cup tie between the two sides the previous season.

Nicknamed 'The Horsham Flier' at Filbert Street, he figured prominently after a slow start as City carried off the Division Two championship and reached the sixth round of the Cup in 1953–54, but in September 1954 he moved on to nearby Nottingham Forest where he again appeared in a Second Division promotion side, in 1956–57. Peter was 32 when Billy Lane brought him to the Goldstone in July 1957, but he played the role of standby forward admirably during Albion's successful push for the Third Division (South) title in 1957–58. Dubbed 'Play Anywhere Peter', he retired in May 1959 and joined the club's coaching staff for a time.

Season	FL	Total
1957–58	8 (3)	8 (3)
Total	8 (3)	8 (3)

SMALL, SAMMY   1948–50

utility player   Ht 5 9, Wt 12 04   *40 apps*
full name: Samuel John Small
born: Birmingham, Warwickshire, 15.5.1912
debut: Leyton Orient (h), 27.3.1948 (FL D3(S))

A centre-forward for the greater part of his lengthy career, Sammy Small was an England junior international playing for Bromsgrove Rovers in the Birmingham Combination when Birmingham took him on as a professional in May 1934. For most of his time at St Andrews, Sammy played a reserve-team role, but on transferring to West Ham United in January 1937 he became a great favourite and scored 41 goals in 116 peacetime games. His eleven-year career at Upton Park spanned the war years and he turned out regularly in the emergency competitions, hitting 82 goals in 177 matches and

scoring the only goal to win the 1940 Football League (War) Cup final against Blackburn Rovers. He also guested for Birmingham and Coventry City toward the end of the conflict.

With Albion struggling desperately at the foot of the Third Division (South) during 1947–48, the experienced 35-year-old became one of Don Welsh's numerous mid-season signings in an unsuccessful attempt to avoid the need to apply for re-election. Showing his versatility in no fewer than eight positions from right-back to outside-left, Sammy joined the Goldstone staff in March 1948 and worked tremendously hard in his 40 outings. Stockily-built and distinctive with his balding pate, he was retained on a part-time basis for 1949–50, and made his last appearance in November 1949 at the age of 37 before retiring at the end of the season.

Season	FL	FAC	Total
1947–48	10	0	10
1948–49	27	1	28
1949–50	1	1	2
Total	38	2	40

SMART, FREDDIE   1909–15

outside-left   *18 apps, 1 goal*
full name: Frederick George Smart
born: Petworth, Sussex, 1887
debut: Southend United (a), 22.2.1911 (SL D1)

Having become the first captain of the reformed Southwick club at the age of nineteen in 1906, Freddie Smart served the 'Little Wickers' for many years and was a member of the excellent team which carried off both the West Sussex League championship and the Royal Irish Rifles Charity Cup in 1909 and 1911, as well as the Sussex Senior Cup in the latter year. He first appeared in Albion's reserve team in December 1909 and assisted the club until 1915. A speedy winger, at home on either flank, Freddie won a regular spot on the left wing in the Southern League side early in 1912–13, but made way for Fred Goodwin in November. He also represented Sussex on numerous occasions.

Season	SL	SA	SCC	Total
1910–11	1	0	0	1
1912–13	11 (1)	3	3	17 (1)
Total	12 (1)	3	3	18 (1)

SMILLIE, NEIL   1982–85

winger   Ht 5 6, Wt 10 07   *86 apps, 3 goals*
born: Barnsley, Yorkshire, 19.7.1958
debut: Ipswich Town (h), 28.8.1982 (FL D1)

Known to his colleagues as 'Specky' (because he wore spectacles off the pitch and contact lenses on it), Neil Smillie proved his worth as a capable winger in three seasons with the Albion, but was never quite able to hold down a regular place; yet he was an essential member of the side which won its way to the 1983 F.A. Cup final. The son of Ron Smillie, the former Barnsley and Lincoln City winger, Neil joined Crystal Palace as an apprentice from school and was signed as a professional in July 1974 on his seventeenth birthday, but his first-team opportunities were restricted and he made only 83 League appearances in eight seasons at Selhurst Park.

After a spell with Memphis in the U.S.A. and a three-match loan period at Brentford in January 1977, Neil was signed by Albion manager Mike Bailey in July 1982 in a player-exchange deal for Gary Williams, but he was largely omitted from the team until January 1983 when his trickery on the wing played a large part in the team's Cup success. Although the 24-year-old had an excellent final, he was in and out of the reckoning for the next two seasons before being transferred to Watford in June 1985 for the surprisingly large sum of £100,000.

After making just sixteen League appearances for the 'Hornets', Neil signed on loan for Reading in December 1986 before joining the Elm Park staff on a free transfer, and starred in the "Royals'" march

to Full Members (Simod) Cup honours at Wembley in 1987–88. In August 1988 he moved on to Brentford, again on a free transfer, and performed admirably, missing just two matches as the 'Bees' clinched the Third Division championship in 1992.

In the summer of 1993, Neil joined Third Division Gillingham as player-coach, and later became player/assistant manager. In February 1995 he was made caretaker manager by administrators appointed to run affairs at Priestfield, but left the club following the appointment of Tony Pulis in June to become the youth-team manager at Wycombe Wanderers. Once again he took on the role of caretaker manager for a brief time until the appointment of another ex-Albion man, John Gregory, in October 1996.

Season	FL	FAC	FLC	Total
1982–83	22+3	6+1 (1)	1	29+4 (1)
1983–84	25+1 (2)	2	1	28+1 (2)
1984–85	15+9	0	0	15+9
Total	62+13 (2)	8+1 (1)	2	72+14 (3)

SMITH, Albert   1901–03

inside-right   *16 apps, 6 goals*
full name: Albert John Smith
debut: West Hampstead (h), 26.10.1901 (SL D2)

Albert Smith played as a professional for Brighton United's reserve team in 1899–1900, but, following that club's demise, he was reinstated as an amateur in July 1900 – although his initial application was turned down – to play for Brighton & Hove Rangers. After playing in every competitive match for the newly formed amateur club, including the 3–1 defeat by Eastbourne in the final of the Sussex Senior Cup, Albert became one of the first players recruited by the infant Albion in 1901. He maintained a good scoring rate in his sixteen first-team appearances during the

initial two seasons, but was released in May 1903 and disappeared from the local scene.

Season	SL	Test	SEL	Total
1901–02	5 (2)	0	0	5 (2)
1902–03	2 (2)	1	8 (2)	11 (4)
Total	7 (4)	1	8 (2)	16 (6)

7 players who appeared in World Cup final stages

* appeared while with the Albion

Player	Country	Year
Armstrong, Gerry	Northern Ireland	1982, 1986
Foster, Steve*	England	1982
Hopkins, Mel	Wales	1958
Meola, Tony	USA	1990, 1994
Nelson, Sammy*	Northern Ireland	1982
Penney, Steve*	Northern Ireland	1986
Stevens, Gary	England	1986

SMITH, Alec   1906–07

right-half   *20 apps, 1 goal*
full name: Alexander Smith
debut: Leyton (a), 1.9.1906 (SL D1)

Signed by Frank Scott-Walford from Midland League Newark (along with his namesake Wally Smith) in July 1906, Alec Smith was more-or-less a regular in the side at right-half in the first half of the 1906–07 season, but fell completely out of favour in the New Year and spent the rest of the campaign in the reserves. Described as being 'a surer tackler than he is a placer', the burly wing-half was released in May 1907 and left for an unknown minor destination.

Season	SL	UL	Total
1906–07	12	8 (1)	20 (1)
Total	12	8 (1)	20 (1)

SMITH, Bobby   1964–65

centre-forward   Ht 6 0, Wt 12 11   *34 apps, 21 goals*
full name: Robert Alfred Smith
born: Lingdale, Yorkshire, 22.2.1933
debut: Barrow (h), 22.8.1964 (FL D4)

It caused a sensation in the world of football when 31-year-old Bobby Smith joined Fourth Division Albion for a modest £5,000 fee in May 1964. Possibly the biggest name ever to sign for the club, he had won his last England cap just six months earlier and had been an essential member of Tottenham's double-winning side of 1961. Indeed, such was the great man's reputation that a booklet featuring the highlights of a tremendous career was published to coincide with his arrival at the Goldstone, but during 1964–65 he only added to that reputation and was worshipped by Albion followers.

Brought up in the north of Yorkshire, Bobby started out with Redcar Boys' Club and Redcar United before joining the Chelsea ground staff in 1948. After signing as a professional in May 1950, he made his First Division debut at the age of seventeen and was reckoned to be one of the brightest prospects in the game, but he somehow lost his way at Stamford Bridge, suffering the weight problems which were to plague him, and finished with a record of 30 goals from 86 League and Cup games.

In December 1955, Bobby joined Tottenham Hotspur for £16,000 where his career really took off. Positively flourishing as leader of Spurs' star-studded attack, he equalled the club record of 36 League goals in 1957–58 (later eclipsed by Jimmy Greaves), and also played in the first Inter Cities Fairs' Cup (precursor of the UEFA Cup) final in 1958 for a London representative side which lost 8–2 on aggregate to a Barcelona XI. In 1958–59 he scored another 32 goals, but his greatest triumph came in 1961 when 'Super Spurs' became the first side this century to win the League-and-Cup 'double'; he hit 28 League goals and also scored in the F.A. Cup final. Bobby matured into a brave, robust scoring machine at Tottenham and made his England debut in October

1960. Scoring once in a 5–2 win over Northern Ireland, he went on to hit thirteen goals in a fifteen-game international career, including eight in his first five games. In 1962 he gained a second F.A. Cup winner's medal, scoring once in a 3–1 victory over Burnley, and helped Spurs to a European Cup-Winners' Cup triumph in May 1963.

With 208 goals in all competitions for Tottenham to his name, Bobby arrived at the Goldstone largely through the efforts of local bookmaker George Gunn. With Albion at a low ebb, the presence of the former England man brought back the missing crowds and the team responded by surging to the Fourth Division championship. Although he missed fifteen matches through injury, Bobby hit nineteen goals and led the line in excellent fashion with his traditional bustling centre-forward style. He was, though, also blessed with a deftness of touch which could release his fellow forwards, and no fewer than five other players also reached double figures thanks largely to his promptings. In July 1965, however, he reported for pre-season training weighing over 15 stone and was suspended for two weeks by manager Archie Macaulay for being unfit. A massively-built man at the best of times, he lost weight and returned to the team for a League Cup replay with Luton Town on 7 September, scoring in a 2–0 victory, but it was his last appearance for the club.

After falling out with Macaulay over the financial aspects of his articles for a Sunday newspaper, Bobby was transfer-listed and then sacked on 1 October 1965. Three days later he sensationally joined Hastings United in the Southern League; his first game at Ashford resulted in traffic chaos in the Kent town as the crowds flocked to see him perform. United's attendances doubled as Bobby, who was reputed to have been offered £50 a week, netted eleven goals in nineteen matches, but he was soon in trouble for failing to attend training-sessions and, following further absenteeism and suspensions, was dismissed in March 1967. Forsaking the game, he then took to driving a van for a living, but had a further brief spell in the Southern League with Banbury United, and, when Archie Macaulay resigned as Albion manager in October 1968, was among the many applicants for the vacant post.

Bobby has since suffered difficult times, owing mainly to the injuries he incurred in a rigorous, seventeen-year professional career, and his situation became something of an issue during the 1992 General Election campaign when it was revealed that he had been waiting two years for a hip-replacement operation. Only 19 of his 217 League goals came in his spell with the Albion, but Bobby made a welcome return to the Goldstone in March 1994 as a guest of the club for the match with York City and received a hero's welcome from the crowd. Indeed, to anyone who supported Albion in the mid 1960s, Bobby Smith was the ultimate hero.

Season	FL	FAC	FLC	Total
1964–65	31 (19)	1	1 (1)	33 (20)
1965–66	0	0	1 (1)	1 (1)
Total	31 (19)	1	2 (2)	34 (21)

SMITH, BOBBY   *1968–71*

wing-half/midfield   Ht 5 7, Wt 10 12   *85 apps, 2 goals*
full name: Robert William Smith
born: Prestbury, Cheshire, 14.3.1944
debut: Mansfield Town (h), 10.8.1968 (FL D3)

Following closely on the heels of his illustrious namesake, 'the other' Bobby Smith enjoyed a less-than-spectacular career as a player but continued in the game in managerial and coaching roles long after hanging up his boots. Though lightly-built, he was a tenacious character and clocked up 279 Football League appearances for his various clubs.

A promising England schoolboy international, he joined Manchester United as an apprentice in 1959, won two caps at youth level, and signed professional forms in April 1961 at the age of seventeen. However, despite making around 200 appearances in the reserves, he failed to make the United first team in four years as a pro, and was signed by his former Old Trafford colleague Freddie Goodwin, the Scunthorpe United manager, in March 1965. A regular in their Third Division side, he scored twelve goals in 82 League outings before moving to Grimsby Town for £8,000 in January 1967.

In June 1968 the 24-year-old wing-half became one of Archie Macaulay's last signings when he joined the Albion on a free transfer, but in three seasons at the Goldstone, largely under his former Scunthorpe boss Freddie Goodwin, Bobby never gained wide popularity with the supporters. Honest but limited, he asked for a transfer early in 1970–71, but remained with the club until June 1971 when he left for Chester on a free transfer. After just two League

appearances at Sealand Road, he was transferred on to Hartlepool in February 1972 after an extended loan-period.

In August 1973, Bobby set out on the next stage of his career when he was appointed player-coach at Bury; three months later he took over from Alan Brown as manager. Four years in charge at Gigg Lane were followed by spells at Port Vale (manager 1977–78), Swindon Town (manager 1978–80), Blackpool (coach 1981–82), Newport County (coach and later manager 1982–86), Cardiff City (coach 1988–90) and Hereford United (assistant manager 1990–91). In March 1991 he became assistant manager at Swansea City and enjoyed a testimonial against Manchester United in October 1995, the month he was appointed caretaker, but he left the post in December.

Season	FL	FAC	FLC	Total
1968–69	29+1 (1)	3	0	32+1 (1)
1969–70	22+1 (1)	0	3	25+1 (1)
1970–71	21+1	3	1	25+1
Total	72+3 (2)	6	4	82+3 (2)

SMITH, DAVE   *1961–62*

full-back   *16 apps*
full name: David Bowman Smith
born: Dundee, Angus, Scotland, 22.9.1933
debut: Scunthorpe United (a), 19.8.1961 (FL D2)

Better known as a manager than a player, it was only right that Dave Smith should enjoy a rewarding career after hanging up his boots for he endured a good deal of misfortune with injuries on the pitch. Having started out with the Scottish junior club Ashdale, Dave signed as a professional for Burnley in September 1950 but spent five years in the background before making his League debut in April 1955. He went on to make 100 League appearances over the next six years, but missed out completely during the First Division championship season of 1959–60. The versatile defender joined Albion in July 1961 and appeared in both full-back berths, but 1961–62 was not a good season to be at the Goldstone and, on the club's relegation to the Third Division, Dave was one of twelve players to be released. But it was a succession of broken legs that really blighted his playing career, and a fifth fracture, suffered shortly after joining Bristol City in July 1962, ended the Scottish defender's playing days.

On his enforced retirement the unfortunate 29-year-old looked to coaching – he had unsuccessfully applied for the managerial post at Southern League Romford while at Hove – and served on the backroom staffs at Burnley, Sheffield Wednesday (after a spell in Libya), Newcastle United and Arsenal. In 1974, Dave was appointed manager of Mansfield Town and led the 'Stags' to the Fourth Division title in 1975, but he left the club in 1976. He then took over at Southend United until 1983, winning promotion from Division Four in 1978 and the championship of the same division in 1981. Thereafter Dave managed Plymouth Argyle, winning promotion from Division Three in 1986; Dundee for seven months during 1988–89; and shaped the Torquay United side that was promoted to Division Three in 1991, although he resigned from his post in April.

Season	FL	FLC	Total
1961–62	15	1	16
Total	15	1	16

SMITH, GORDON   1980–84

midfield/forward   Ht 6 0, Wt 12 00   125 apps, 25 goals
full name: Gordon Duffield Smith
born: Kilwinning, Ayrshire, Scotland, 29.12.1954
debut: Wolves (h), 16.8.1980 (FL D1)

'And Smith *must* score!' Gordon Smith has gone down in history for the incident in the 1983 F.A. Cup final when, confronted only by Gary Bailey in the last minute of extra time, he shot against the Manchester United goalkeeper – who spread himself well – and thus failed to land the F.A. Cup (and a place in Europe) for the Albion. The famous phrase, uttered by BBC radio commentator Peter Jones, lived on in the title of an Albion 'fanzine' and a video of sporting 'howlers' in which Gordon himself talked at length about his nightmare miss. Yet it would be most unfair if the gifted Scot was remembered only for that gaffe. Described by manager Alan Mullery as 'the Trevor Brooking of Scottish football' when he paid £400,000 for the 25-year-old's signature in June 1980 (an Albion record at the time), Gordon was an intelligent, constructive player with undeniable skill on the ball, and was – that one incident excepted – a good finisher in his role as an attacking midfielder. But something, perhaps a lack of aggression and reluctance to use his physical attributes, often had the Goldstone Ground crowd very much divided on "Smithy's" merits.

As a precocious youngster he represented Ayrshire Schools, played regularly for Kilmarnock's reserves while still at school, and made his first-team debut for 'Killie' at the age of seventeen in August 1972. After 44 goals in 203 League and Cup games at Rugby Park, and four appearances in Scotland's under-23 team, Gordon joined Glasgow Rangers for £65,000 in August 1977 and won a host of honours in three seasons at Ibrox: a Scottish League championship, two Scottish Cups and two League Cups. He also played once for the Scottish under-21s.

The tall midfielder was an immediate success on arriving at the Goldstone in 1980: he scored on his debut, completed a nineteen-minute hat-trick at Coventry two months later, and finished second in the scoring list to Michael Robinson in his first season with the club. At his best when coming forward from the middle of the park, Gordon was played as an out-and-out striker by new manager Mike Bailey in January 1982, a situation which caused him to seek a transfer. Subsequently in and out of the side, he returned to Ibrox on loan in December 1982 and played in the Rangers side which was beaten 2–1 by Celtic in the Scottish League Cup final.

In the meantime, though, Bailey had left Hove and Gordon was welcomed back by Jimmy Melia, who used him as a striking partner for Michael Robinson following an injury to Gerry Ryan in March The Scot's contribution to the F.A. Cup run was substantial: it was Gordon who made the winner for Robinson in the semi-final, and it was he who opened the scoring at Wembley with a beautifully directed header before booking his place in football folklore.

Following the appointment of Chris Cattlin as manager, Gordon had little opportunity to impress and was transferred to Manchester City for £35,000 in March 1984, helping them to promotion to Division One in 1985. He subsequently played for Oldham Athletic (on loan January 1986, signed for £5,000 in February), Admira Wacker of Vienna (June 1986), F.C. Basle in Switzerland (August 1987), and Stirling Albion (August 1988) before retiring to pursue a business career. From 1991 to 1993, Gordon was assistant manager at St Mirren, but is now a financial adviser in Glasgow while also working as a pundit in the Scottish media.

Something of a crooner, Gordon sang a solo, 'When Seagulls are Flying', on the flip-side of Albion's 1983 Cup final record, 'The Boys in the Old Brighton Blue'. His grandfather, Mattha Smith, scored 116 goals in 439 matches for Kilmarnock between 1916 and 1931, and his father, William, was a Scotland junior internationalist with Ardeer Recreation. Gordon had the odd distinction of playing in major cup finals in two countries in the same season, but will always be remembered for that Wembley miss. His son, Grant, joined the Albion as a trainee in 1996, having taken up a trial suggested while his father was filming a video at the Goldstone Ground.

Season	FL	FAC	FLC	Total
1980–81	36+2 (10)	0+1	3	39+3 (10)
1981–82	24+3 (2)	1	2	27+3 (2)
1982–83	26+3 (6)	4 (1)	2	32+3 (7)
1983–84	11+4 (4)	0	1+2 (2)	12+6 (6)
Total	97+12 (22)	5+1 (1)	8+2 (2)	110+15 (25)

SMITH, JACK   1964–66

inside/centre-forward   Ht 5 11, Wt 12 00   96 apps, 36 goals
full name: John Smith
born: West Hartlepool, Co. Durham, 24.4.1936
debut: Stockport County (a), 11.1.1964 (FL D4)

A useful goalscorer for the Albion in both the Third Division and the Fourth, Jack Smith signed as a pro for his local club, Hartlepools United, in May 1953 and went on to hit 49 goals in 119 League games over seven seasons at the Victoria Ground, the last of which saw 'Pool finish bottom of the Fourth Division. Watford were impressed enough with Jack's form to pay £3,000 for his transfer in July 1960, but he enjoyed only limited success at Vicarage Road and moved on to Swindon Town in June 1961 where he netted 37 times in 97 League outings, including nineteen when the 'Railwaymen' were promoted to Division Two in 1962–63.

Manager Archie Macaulay signed the 27-year-old for around £6,000 in January 1964 to bolster Albion's promotion hopes, but it was the following term that the Fourth Division championship was won; Jack played an important role alongside Bobby Smith, registering eighteen goals. Although never quite as effective following the departure of his namesake, Jack remained a popular figure at Hove until departing for Notts County for £5,000 in September 1966. In three seasons at Meadow Lane he appeared in 78 Fourth Division matches before dropping into the Southern League with Margate. In 1971 he was appointed player-manager of Ramsgate Athletic, and subsequently had a spell as manager of Bath City. In 1979–80, Jack was coaching Portsmouth's youth team.

Season	FL	FAC	FLC	Total
1963–64	13 (6)	0	0	13 (6)
1964–65	35 (17)	1	2 (1)	38 (18)
1965–66	38 (10)	3 (2)	2	43 (12)
1966–67	2	0	0	2
Total	88 (33)	4 (2)	4 (1)	96 (36)

SMITH, JACK   1924–25

inside-forward   14 apps, 4 goals
full name: John William Smith
born: Derby, Derbyshire
debut: Brentford (a), 30.8.1924 (FL D3(S))

A lthough born in Derby, Jack Smith played for Scottish League side Third Lanark during the early part of the Great War, but

also guested extensively for Queen's Park Rangers in the last two wartime seasons, netting 21 goals in 37 London Combination appearances. In April 1919 he was officially transferred to Rangers and became a great favourite at Loftus Road for three seasons. An ever-present in the Southern League side during 1919–20, Jack also played in every match the following season when, with eighteen goals, he led the Q.P.R. scorers in their initial campaign as a Football League club. After scoring 45 goals in 122 League and Cup matches, he was transferred to Swansea Town in June 1922 for £250 where he continued to find the net on a regular basis. In his first season at the Vetch Field, Jack top-scored with 22 goals, and went on to total 36 in 67 League outings for the Welsh club before joining the Albion for a fee of £150 in August 1924.

While with both Q.P.R. and Swansea he had made a habit of scoring against the Albion – in December 1920 he hit a hat-trick into the Brighton net at Loftus Road – but, despite notching a brace on his debut, he met with less success at the Goldstone. With his time in Hove dogged by injuries, Jack was unable to win a regular place and was released in May 1925 when he left the first-class game.

Season	FL	Total
1924–25	14 (4)	14 (4)
Total	14 (4)	14 (4)

SMITH, JIMMY   1911–12

centre-forward   *65 apps, 40 goals*
full name: James Smith
born: Stafford, Staffordshire, c. 1889
died: in action on the Western Front, 1918
debut: Watford (h), 7.1.1911 (SL D1)

With a record of 40 goals for the Albion in just 65 first-team games, Jimmy Smith was the 'Peter Ward' (q.v.) of his day. Small in stature in an age of big, bustling centre-forwards, he was exceptionally quick off the mark and a terror in and around the penalty area. Plucked, like Ward, from the ranks of minor football, Jimmy had developed into a crack goalscorer with the Hanley P.S.A. club (62 goals in 1909–10) and had scored 20 goals for Hanley Swifts the following season before joining Albion at the age of 24 in January 1911. In fact, the Stafford-born striker went one better than Ward by scoring twice on his debut, a 5–0 win over Watford, and he soon became the natural successor to Bill 'Bullet' Jones as leader of the attack, enabling the club to sell the popular Jones for a handsome sum. In 1911–12, in his first full season, Jimmy netted 25 goals in 29 Southern League outings to establish a new club record, just as Ward did 65 years later; he bagged four hat-tricks, including all four goals in a 4–0 home win over Stoke, the club which had missed him on its own doorstep.

Naturally, the prolific forward's exploits attracted the attention of several Football League clubs, and in November 1912 he was sold to Bradford (Park Avenue) for a massive fee of £735 plus Bradford's Bobby Simpson, a new Albion record. Jimmy remained at Park Avenue until 1915 and notched up 60 goals in 100 appearances to bring his overall record to exactly 100 goals from 165 games, an impressive strike rate by any standard. Indeed, but for the First World War he would surely have improved greatly upon those excellent figures. Tragically, though, he lost his life in 1918 while serving on the Western Front, just a few weeks before he was due to return home to be married.

Season	SL	FAC	SA	SCC	Total
1910–11	14 (5)	2 (1)	0	1	17 (6)
1911–12	29 (25)	1	0	2 (2)	32 (27)
1912–13	13 (6)	0	3 (1)	0	16 (7)
Total	56 (36)	3 (1)	3 (1)	3 (2)	65 (40)

SMITH, PETER   1994–

right-back   Ht 6 0, Wt 12 01   *120 apps, 4 goals*
full name: Peter John Smith
born: Stone, Staffordshire, 12.7.1969
debut: Wycombe Wanderers (h), 17.8.1994 (FLC R1 Lg1)

With his distinctive appearance – extra-long legs and dreadlocks tied in a pony-tail – and his exceptional pace and commitment, Peter Smith became an instant favourite of the Goldstone fans when he was introduced to the League side in September 1994. It was a rapid rise from obscurity for the 25-year-old from the Black Country.

A former Stafford Schools represent-ative, he had attracted the attention of Coventry City while playing for numerous clubs in the Midlands – Lichfield, Tamworth, Alvechurch, Broms-grove Rovers, Willen-hall and Banbury United – as a forward and winger. After a spell in the building trade and then as a voluntary social work-er in New York, Peter returned to England to take up a position as a youth worker in Kent and turned out for the now-defunct

Kent League side Alma Swanley where he was converted into a defender.

Spotted by Albion's assistant manager Gerry Ryan in a charity match, Peter was undertaking an urban and environmental studies course at Greenwich University with a view to a career in community work at the time. Joining the Goldstone staff at the start of 1994–95, he impressed on the club's dismal Irish tour, scoring the only goal. Although obviously raw, Peter excited everyone with his speed, superb tackling and ability to bring the ball forward to some effect. Quickly rewarded with a contract – and dropping his course at Greenwich in favour of the Open University – he soon became a fixture in the first team, either at right-back or occasionally as a winger.

Indeed, such was his impact that he won the club's Player of the Season award in May 1995 at the end of his first season as a professional. Almost inevitably his form fell away thereafter, and he had to endure some criticism from supporters for his tactical naivety, but on his day he remains one of the most exciting players at the club.

Season	FL	FAC	FLC	AMC	Total
1994–95	35+3 (1)	1	4+1		41+4 (1)
1995–96	28+3 (1)	4 (1)	2	3+1	37+4 (2)
1996–97	26+4 (1)	0	2	2	30+4 (1)
Total	89+10 (3)	5 (1)	8+1	6+1	108+12 (4)

SMITH, POTTER   1929–37

inside-left/left-half   Ht 5 9, Wt 11 07   319 apps, 57 goals
full name: Thomas Potter Smith
born: Newcastle upon Tyne, Northumberland, July 1901
died: Brighton, Sussex, 1.9.1978
debut: Bristol Rovers (a), 31.8.1929 (FL D3(S))

Although he was 28 when he joined the Albion, Potter Smith remained at the club for eight years and came to be held in great affection. With superb skill on the ball and a tremendous appetite for work, he quickly established himself in the inside-left role vacated by Jimmy Hopkins and became a fixture during the 1930s, with only the occasional injury keeping him out. While not a great goalscorer himself, he still managed 57 goals from 319 Albion games, and played a big part in providing chances for the other inside men, particularly in his first season when Hugh Vallance and Dan Kirkwood together hit 63 goals.

A product of Newcastle junior football, Potter was working as a blacksmith and playing for St Peter's Albion in the Tyneside League when he joined Merthyr Town as a 20-year-old professional in May 1922. His early days were spent in transit: after just one season in Glamorgan he was transferred to Second Division Hull City in June 1923; returned to his native North-East with Hartlepools United in July 1924; and rejoined Merthyr in July 1925; but such was his form with the Third Division (South) side that First Division Cardiff City paid £750 for his services in March 1926. In three seasons at Ninian Park, Potter scored six goals in 43 League outings, gained a Welsh Cup winner's medal in 1928, and represented the Welsh League v. League of Ireland on two occasions, but he missed out on the 1927 F.A. Cup final when he went down with appendicitis.

Albion manager Charlie Webb obtained the dynamic Geordie's signature in June 1929 in what proved to be a shrewd transaction. Despite his wide experience, Potter had never been an automatic choice at any of his previous clubs, but was to serve Brighton splendidly, performing consistently at inside-left for six seasons and exerting a great influence on the team before switching to a half-back role in his last eighteen months with the club. Skipper in 1935–36 and 1936–37, he was released in September 1937 to join Crystal Palace, but didn't add to his career tally of 65 goals from 394 games in all four sections of the Football League before hanging up his boots.

On retiring, Potter settled in Hove and maintained a keen interest in Albion's fortunes until his death in 1978 at the age of 77. Indeed, such was his affection for the old place that his ashes were scattered over the Goldstone turf.

Season	FL	FAC*	SSC	Total
1929–30	37 (6)	6 (3)	0	43 (9)
1930–31	35 (5)	2 (2)	0	37 (7)
1931–32	42 (7)	3 (1)	0	45 (8)
1932–33*	41 (3)	11 (10)	0	52 (13)
1933–34	24 (5)	1	2	27 (5)
1934–35	36 (9)	3 (1)	2	41 (10)
1935–36	41 (4)	5	2	48 (4)
1936–37	25 (1)	1	0	26 (1)
Total	281 (40)	32 (17)	6	319 (57)

Note: Four appearances and eight goals of Smith's 1932–33 F.A. Cup total came in the qualifying competition of 1932–33.

SMITH, REG   1923–32

full-back   Ht 5 9, Wt 11 08   150 apps, 1 goal
full name: Redvers Smith
born: Rotherham, Yorkshire, 3.12.1901
debut: Swansea Town (h), 24.11.1923 (FL D3(S))

Although never an automatic choice, 'Reg' Smith rendered Albion fine service for eight seasons until an injury ended his

professional career. He arrived at the Goldstone as a young defender from Midland League Scunthorpe & Lindsey United in August 1923, but with Jack Jenkins and Jack Thompson holding down the full-back berths he initially had to be content with only the occasional first-team appearance. When injury forced Dickie Downs to hang up his boots in December 1924, Reg enjoyed a lengthy run at right-back, but with the arrival of Irish international Jack Curran he resumed a standby role. In his fourth season on the South Coast his opportunities became more frequent, and in 1929–30 he was installed as skipper until he lost his place because of an injury sustained at Crystal Palace in October.

It proved to be more than just a temporary set-back, though: the genial Yorkshireman subsequently enjoyed just two more outings in the League team (a record 8–2 victory at Merthyr and a 5–0 home win over Torquay) and made only fleeting appearances for the reserves before calling it a day in May 1931 at the age of 29. Reg received a joint testimonial with Ernie Ison and Reg Wilkinson in April 1930 when, as a result of the prevailing financial situation, the three stalwarts had to make do with the proceeds of collections at the Eastertide games. In July 1932 he was registered as a permit player with Sussex County League side Shoreham, and skippered the 'Musselmen' against the Albion in the F.A. Cup qualifying tie of October 1932 when the professionals triumphed 12–0.

Season	FL	FAC	Total
1923–24	12	0	12
1924–25	26	3	29
1925–26	16	0	16
1926–27	30	3	33
1927–28	15 (1)	0	15 (1)
1928–29	31	1	32
1929–30	13	0	13
Total	143 (1)	7	150 (1)

SMITH, W.   1903

right-half   1 app
debut: Hitchin Town (a), 18.4.1903, (SEL)

One of a number of amateur players from the Hove Park club who assisted the Albion in their South Eastern League matches during the 1902–03 season, Smith made his only appearance at right-half as a deputy for Paddy Farrell in a 1–0 win at Hitchin Town.

Season	SEL	Total
1902–03	1	1
Total	1	1

SMITH, WALLY   1906–07

inside-left   Ht 5 6, Wt 12 00   42 apps, 9 goals
full name: Walter Smith
born: Lincoln, Lincolnshire, 1874
died: Leigh-on-Sea, Essex, 14.11.1958
debut: Leyton (a), 1.9.1906 (SL D1)

Wally Smith played for the Lincoln clubs Blue Star and Grantham Avenue before joining Lincoln City at the age of 25 in January 1900. A regular in the "Imps'" forward line with 21 goals from 90 Second Division appearances, he was transferred to Small Heath (later Birmingham) for £350 in September 1903, but, despite the large fee, injury robbed him of a place in the "Heathens'" League side and he was released to join Newark in the Midland League in May 1904.

Wally came to Hove along with his Newark team-mate Alec Smith (no relation) in July 1906 amid competition from his former club, Lincoln City, and proved to be a model of consistency. A stocky inside-forward, he missed only two Southern League games in 1906–07 and won great popularity with the fans, but in May 1907 he left for Norwich City. On the completion of a less successful season with the 'Canaries' – three goals from eleven Southern League outings – he moved on to Southend United, but was released in 1909 and left the first-class arena. Wally spent 1909–10 playing for Lincoln Liberal Club F.C., but subsequently settled in Leigh-on-Sea where he worked as a brick-maker. He died in the Essex town at the age of 84.

Season	SL	FAC	UL	Total
1906–07	36 (5)	1 (1)	5 (3)	42 (9)
Total	36 (5)	1 (1)	5 (3)	42 (9)

SMITH, WILF   1974

full-back   Ht 5 10, Wt 11 03   5 apps
full name: Wilfred Samuel Smith
born: Neumünster, West Germany, 3.9.1946
debut: Grimsby Town (h), 16.10.1974 (FL D3)

Although born in West Germany, Wilf Smith was raised in Yorkshire, skippered Sheffield Boys, and played for England Schools before joining Sheffield Wednesday as an apprentice at the age of fifteen. After signing pro forms in September 1963, the young defender went on to play 233 games for the 'Owls', gaining England Youth honours and playing for the under-23s on six occasions. He also appeared three times for the Football League and, at the age of nineteen, played in the Wednesday's 1966 losing F.A. Cup final side.

In August 1970, Wilf was transferred to Coventry City for £100,000, a record fee for a full-back at the time, and added 135 League appearances to his total. While at Highfield Road he had loan periods with the Albion (October 1974) and Millwall (January 1975). In fact, Albion manager Peter Taylor was keen to sign the experienced 28-year-old, but the fee required by Coventry put paid to any deal. Wilf joined Bristol Rovers for £25,000 in February 1975, but moved on to Chesterfield in November 1976 where he brought his tally of League appearances to 432 before dropping into the Southern League with Atherstone Town in July 1977. On retiring from the game Wilf became a highly successful retailer in Yorkshire.

Season	FL	Total
1974–75	5	5
Total	5	5

SOMMER, JUERGEN   1991

goalkeeper   Ht 6 4, Wt 15 12   1 app
full name: Juergen Peterson Sommer
born: Manhattan, New York, U.S.A., 27.2.1969
debut: Cambridge United (a), 16.11.1991 (FL D2)

The son of a former SV Hamburg youngster who emigrated to the United States in the 1950s, Juergen Sommer was raised in Naples, Florida, and studied economics and German at Indiana State University. While playing for an American select eleven in Amsterdam, the giant goalkeeper caught the eye of a Luton Town scout and signed a two-year contract for the 'Hatters' following a trial in 1991. Juergen's football education continued with a secondment to Dunstable in the Southern League, and then with a month on loan at the Goldstone in November 1991 when regular 'keepers Mark Beeney and Perry Digweed were suspended and injured respectively. After playing for the Albion reserves in midweek, the 22-year-old made his Football League debut on the Saturday, performing splendidly in a goal-less draw with Second Division leaders Cambridge United. However, seventeen days later he had the misfortune to break his arm playing for Albion's reserves against his Luton Town colleagues on Dunstable's ground, a curious double irony.

After returning to Kenilworth Road and recovering from his injury, Juergen had further loan-spells with Torquay United (October 1992) and Conference sides Kettering Town (February 1993) and Wycombe Wanderers (March 1993), but took over as first-choice goalkeeper for Luton in 1993–94. Such was his progress that he won a place as third-choice goalkeeper in the U.S.A.'s 1994 World Cup squad, and gained his first cap when he came on as a substitute nine minutes from the end of the States' defeat by England at Wembley in September 1994. However, he later lost his place in the Luton side because of international duty and moved into the Premiership with Queen's Park Rangers for £600,000 at the end of August 1995. A good shot-stopper for such a huge man, Juergen came under some pressure as Rangers were relegated, but held his place. However, he was passed over for the U.S. Olympic squad in 1996 and has fallen behind in the international stakes.

Season	FL	Total
1991–92	1	1
Total	1	1

SOUTH, ALEX   1946–54

centre-half   Ht 6 0, Wt 11 07   85 apps, 4 goals
full name: Alexander William South
born: Brighton, Sussex, 7.7.1931
debut: Exeter City (h), 1.4.1950 (FL D3(S))

A member of a well-known Brighton football family – his brothers Billy and Eric were also associated with the Albion for short spells – Alex South was an impressive centre-half at Third Division level who went on to set a club record for appearances at Halifax, but he was unable to bring his obvious ability to bear in the highest grade.

Alex graduated in local football with Whitehawk School, the Boys' Brigade and Whitehawk Boys' Club; played for Brighton Boys; represented the England Boys' Clubs against Wales; and joined the Albion ground staff as a fifteen-year-old in 1946. The lanky

defender's career was then interrupted by National Service with the R.A.F., but he signed as a professional in March 1949 and made his League debut just over a year later at the age of eighteen. Alex had to be content with a second-fiddle role to Tim McCoy for three seasons, but took over the no.5 shirt early in the 1953–54 season – when Albion finished runners-up in the Third Division (South) – and impressed with his solid play, holding his place for twelve months before making way for record signing Matt McNeil.

In December 1954, ex-Albion manager Don Welsh signed his 23-year-old former defender for Liverpool with an eye to his future potential, but Alex was to play only seven League and Cup games at Anfield before moving on to Halifax Town in October 1956. The move across the Pennines proved a great success and he went on to enjoy 302 League outings, the most of any player at the time for the Yorkshire side. On his retirement in 1964, Alex joined the pools-promotion staff at Halifax and still resides in the town.

Season	FL	FAC	Total
1949–50	2	0	2
1950–51	12	0	12
1951–52	4	0	4
1952–53	20 (1)	0	20 (1)
1953–54	33 (2)	4	37 (2)
1954–55	10 (1)	0	10 (1)
Total	81 (4)	4	85 (4)

SPEARRITT, EDDIE   1969–74

utility player   Ht 5 9, Wt 11 09   232 apps, 25 goals
full name: Edward Alfred Spearritt
born: Lowestoft, Suffolk, 31.1.1947
debut: Crewe Alexandra (h), 25.1.1969 (FL D3)

One of the most consistent players to appear for the Albion in the early 1970s, Eddie Spearritt was also one of the most versatile and was equally at home either in midfield, as a central defender, or at left-back. Born in Lowestoft, he played representative football as a schoolboy for both his town and county, and had six months with Arsenal before joining the Ipswich Town staff as an apprentice. After

signing as a professional in February 1965, Eddie, playing mainly as a winger, scored thirteen times in 72 First and Second Division appearances, including seven goals from 20 outings when Ipswich won the championship of Division Two in 1967–68.

In January 1969, Albion manager Freddie Goodwin signed the 21-year-old for £20,000 and installed him on the left side of midfield. Having played a big part in the club's ultimately unsuccessful promotion push during 1969–70, Eddie was switched to left-back by new boss Pat Saward in February 1971, and proved so successful in the no.3 shirt that he was ever-present during the exceptional 1971–72 season when the club finished runners-up to Aston Villa in the Third Division. The possessor of a prodigious long-throw, he was one of the few players to come out of the calamitous 1972–73 campaign in Division Two with any credit – he wore five different numbers during the relegation battle – and won the Player of the Season nomination. At the start of 1973–74 he was made captain, but requested a transfer after being omitted by new manager Brian Clough in December, and left for Carlisle United on a free transfer in June 1974.

Having made fourteen appearances for the 'Cumbrians' in their only season in the First Division, Eddie played another seventeen games the following term before moving to Gillingham in August 1976. After a year at Priestfield he was released and emigrated to Australia where he played for Brisbane Lions until hanging up his boots in 1983. Remaining in Australia, Eddie tried his hand at football

management but then pursued a business career, becoming a manager with the L'Oreal cosmetics company in Brisbane.

Season	FL	FAC	FLC	Total
1968–69	18 (5)	0	0	18 (5)
1969–70	41+1 (4)	5	3 (1)	49+1 (5)
1970–71	38+4 (3)	2	1	41+4 (3)
1971–72	46 (3)	3 (1)	2 (1)	51 (5)
1972–73	39 (6)	1	2	42 (6)
1973–74	21+2 (1)	2	1	24+2 (1)
Total	203+7 (22)	13 (1)	9 (2)	225+7 (25)

SPENCER, FRANK   1912–20

full-back   Ht 5 6, Wt 12 07   142 apps
born: Willington, Co. Durham, c. 1890
debut: Watford (h), 21.9.1912 (SL D1)

Short and stocky, Frank Spencer proved to be a very strong defender with a fearsome tackle. Signed as a 22-year-old from the Parkside club of South Shields in May 1912, he soon won a place at right-back in Albion's Southern League side following the enforced retirement

of Ralph Routledge. Equally effective on the left flank, the burly defender alternated between the two full-back berths and was a regular in the side for three seasons before the club's closure during the First World War. Frank assisted both Blackpool and Watford briefly, but returned to the Goldstone on the resumption of normal service in 1919 and was first choice at right-back during Albion's last season in the Southern League. Released in May 1920 at the age of 30, he moved on to Abertillery Town in the Southern League's Welsh section together with his Albion colleague Jimmy Pugh. Frank still holds the Albion record of remaining undefeated in 24 successive (albeit sporadic) first-team appearances, from February to December 1913.

Season	SL	FAC	SA	SCC	Total
1912–13	13	3	8	1	25
1913–14	25	4	11	1	41
1914–15	34	3	0	1	38
1919–20	37	1	0	0	38
Total	109	11	19	3	142

SPOONER, BILLY   1913–14

outside-right   Ht 5 6, Wt 10 09   6 apps, 1 goal
full name: William Spooner
born: Cheadle, Staffordshire, 1889
debut: Exeter City (a), 8.11.1913 (SL D1)

Billy Spooner played non-League football in Staffordshire for Newcastle Town and Leek United before coming to the Goldstone in June 1913. The 23-year-old outside-right hardly missed a match for the reserves during the 1913–14 campaign, but made the Southern League team on just one occasion in the absence of centre-forward Billy Miller, a 4–1 defeat at Exeter when the forward line was shuffled to accommodate him on the right wing. After appearing in the Southern Alliance and Southern Charity Cup competitions, Billy returned to minor football

in May 1914, but resurfaced in 1916 to make 30 wartime appearances for Port Vale.

Season	SL	SA	SCC	Total
1913–14	1	4 (1)	1	6 (1)
Total	1	4 (1)	1	6 (1)

STANDING, JOHN   1961–62

right-back   Ht 5 8, Wt 10 12   10 apps
full name: John Robert Standing
born: Walberton, Sussex, 3.9.1943
debut: Derby County (a), 28.4.1962 (FL D2)

John Standing signed as a professional for the Albion at the age of eighteen in December 1961 after playing for Bognor Regis Town in the Sussex County League and for the Sussex youth side. Having made his League debut in the last game of the 1961–62 Second Division relegation campaign, he started the following season as first-choice right-back, part of George Curtis's effort to establish his new youth policy, but Albion fell rapidly to the bottom of Division Three and John lost his place in mid September. Three months later the nineteen-year-old defender was released to join Stevenage Town, and remained with the Hertfordshire club until 1968 when he returned to Sussex with Crawley Town. After two full seasons at Town Mead, John joined Hastings United in 1970, and in 1974 was appointed manager of Newhaven. Quiet and studious, he later had a short spell as boss of Haywards Heath in the County League.

Season	FL	Total
1961–62	1	1
1962–63	9	9
Total	10	10

STANLEY, TERRY   1969–72

midfield   Ht 5 7, Wt 9 12   23 apps
full name: Terence James Stanley
born: Brighton, Sussex, 2.1.1951
debut: Orient (h), 13.12.1969 (FL D3)

An outstanding schoolboy footballer for Coldean and Westlain Schools, Terry Stanley represented both Brighton and Sussex Boys, and joined Lewes in the Athenian League after playing for West Ham United's youth team. His form at the Dripping Pan prompted Albion manager Freddie Goodwin to give him an opportunity at the Goldstone, and his career continued with a runner's-up medal with Sussex in the F.A. County Youth Cup in May 1969. Having originally played as a winger, Terry was cast in a midfield role with the Albion, but never quite made the transition into the first-class game after signing as a full professional in November 1969. Although he remained with the club for three seasons, he made only 23 appearances, seven of those as a sub.

In May 1972, Terry was given a free transfer and moved on to Ramsgate Athletic in the Southern League, but he soon returned to Sussex to enjoy a long and successful career in local senior football, winning many honours with Horsham, Lewes, Burgess Hill Town, Worthing, Steyning Town, Southwick, and Peacehaven & Telscombe. He also played for the near-unbeatable Newick Rangers in the Sussex

Sunday League. In the latter half of 1977–78, Terry held the manager's position at Lewes until the arrival of former Albion goalkeeper Peter Grummitt as boss. His brother Mick was also a professional with the Albion but didn't make the first team.

Season	FL	FAC	Total
1969–70	4+3	0	4+3
1970–71	12+3	0+1	12+4
Total	16+6	0+1	16+7

STAPLETON, FRANK   1994

striker   Ht 6 0, Wt 13 01   2 apps
full name: Francis Anthony Stapleton
born: Dublin, Co. Dublin, Republic of Ireland, 10.7.1956
debut: AFC Bournemouth (a), 2.11.1994 (FL D2)

One of the most feared strikers in the country during the late 1970s and early '80s, Frank Stapleton netted 136 goals in 458 First Division appearances for three clubs and scored a record 20 goals for the Republic of Ireland in 70 internationals. But probably his greatest achievement was to appear in five F.A. Cup finals, gaining three winner's medals.

Frank, a schoolboy international, became one of several Irish youngsters on Arsenal's books when he joined the Highbury staff as an apprentice in 1972 at the age of sixteen. Turning professional in October 1973, he also won youth caps before making his Football League debut in March 1975, and soon became a fixture in the "Gunners'" forward line. He also became first-choice centre-forward for the Republic, winning his first cap in October 1976. Tall and lean, Frank was equally as strong in the air as with the ball at his feet, and, though never a prolific goalscorer, was as accomplished performer as a manager could wish for. He reached his first F.A. Cup final in 1978 only to lose out to Ipswich Town, but scored in the 3–2 win over Manchester United the following year. In 1980, however, he lost out again to West Ham United, and was in the Arsenal side which lost the European Cup Winners' Cup final on penalties to Valencia shortly after.

IRELAND

After nine years at Highbury, Frank moved to Manchester United for £900,000 in the summer of 1981 and, having lost out in the League Cup final to Liverpool in 1983, appeared in his fourth F.A. Cup final the same season, scoring the equaliser in the first game against the Albion; United won the replay 4–0. Two years later he won another F.A. Cup medal as United beat Everton 1–0. In the summer of 1987, Frank moved to the Continent with Ajax of Amsterdam, but played just four League games for the Dutch giants before returning to the First Division with Derby County in March 1988. The 1988–89 season was spent in France with Le Havre, and in June 1989 he joined Second Division Blackburn Rovers with whom he won his last two caps. After two seasons in Lancashire, Frank played one game for Aldershot in their final Football League season; turned out for Huddersfield Town in November 1991; and was appointed player-manager of Bradford City the following month. After just failing to lead the 'Bantams' into the Division Two play-offs in May 1994 he was dismissed.

In November 1994, at the age of 38, the vastly experienced Irishman arrived at the Goldstone to assist his former Arsenal and Ireland colleague Liam Brady, but it was a brief association, lasting just two games. Shortly after signing for the club Frank applied in vain for the vacant manager's post at Oldham Athletic – he had been training at Boundary Park since leaving Bradford – but was appointed reserve-team coach at Queen's Park Rangers a few days later by his former Old Trafford colleague Ray Wilkins. In February 1995 he resigned from his post at Loftus Road and took to scouting after finding it impossible to sell his home in Cheshire, but in January 1996 he was appointed head coach of the New England Revolution club in the new American Major Soccer League. However, Frank resigned following the club's failure to reach the play-offs that summer.

Season	FL	Total
1994–95	1+1	1+1
Total	1+1	1+1

STARKS, G. T.   1902

centre-forward   1 app
debut: St Albans Amateurs (a), 18.10.1902 (SEL)

Starks arrived from Southampton as a trialist in October 1902 and turned out in a South Eastern League fixture at St Albans when Albion were forced to play an F.A. Cup qualifying tie with Shoreham the same day. He wasn't taken on and disappeared from the local scene only to re-emerge some three years later in Hastings & St Leonards' pre-season public trial match in August 1905.

Season	SEL	Total
1902–03	1	1
Total	1	1

STEELE, ERIC   1977–79

goalkeeper   Ht 5 11, Wt 11 03   98 apps
full name: Eric Graham Steele
born: Wallsend, Northumberland, 14.5.1954
debut: Crystal Palace (a), 12.3.1977 (FL D3)

One of Albion's most popular players of recent years, Eric Steele struck up a wonderful rapport with the huge Goldstone crowds of the late 1970s and performed splendidly between the posts as the club surged into the First Division. Many supporters from behind the goals will remember, among other antics and in addition to any number of excellent saves, his Groucho Marx impersonation as he took his place under the bar; but he also contributed greatly to his adopted community, training as a P.E. teacher and doing much good work for the Chailey Heritage special school in particular.

An all-round sportsman who represented Northumberland schools at football, tennis and cricket, Eric had also played soccer for the England schoolboy side and was turning out for the famed Wallsend Boys' Club when he joined Newcastle United as an amateur. In July 1972 he signed professional forms, but never played a League match

for the 'Magpies' and was loaned to Peterborough United in December 1973. With the 'Posh' pushing successfully for promotion from Division Four the loan-period was extended to the end of the season, and Eric joined the London Road staff permanently in July 1974 for a £10,000 fee.

After 124 League games for Peterborough, the 22-year-old joined Albion for £19,000 as cover for Peter Grummitt in February 1977, and was elevated to first choice the following month when Grummitt was injured. As the club moved ever upward, Eric proved a reliable 'keeper behind a solid defence, instilling confidence with his superb reactions and competent handling. In 1978–79 he found himself competing fiercely with Graham Moseley for the no.1 jersey, but was between the posts more often than not, and had the satisfaction of playing in the team which

clinched promotion to the First Division by defeating Newcastle United 3–1 in front of his home-town crowd at St James's Park in May 1979.

However, Eric's career at the Goldstone came to a sudden end five months later when he indulged in a brief flurry of fisticuffs with full-back Gary Williams at Old Trafford. The embarrassing incident, in front of a 52,000 crowd, prompted manager Alan Mullery to put his errant 'keeper on the transfer-list and promote Moseley to no.1. As he prepared to leave Hove, Eric unexpectedly made one last appearance in the side when his great rival suddenly fell ill, but departed for Watford for £100,000 soon after, much to the disappointment of his many fans.

Because of the consistency of regular no.1 Steve Sherwood, Eric made only 51 League appearances in nearly five seasons at Vicarage Road, and had a seven-match loan-spell with Cardiff City in March 1983. In July 1984 he signed for Derby County, and assisted the 'Rams' to promotion from Division Three in 1985–86 and to the Division Two championship the following term. In August 1987 he moved on to Southend United, and was loaned to Mansfield Town in March 1988 for whom he made one last appearance at the Goldstone Ground.

On hanging up his gloves Eric became landlord of the Holly Bush Inn at Breedon on the Hill in Leicestershire, but later assisted both Notts County and Wolverhampton Wanderers briefly as cover during injury crises. He then turned to coaching goalkeepers full-time with a number of other clubs, while also working as a radio pundit in the Derby area.

Season	FL	FAC	FLC	Total
1976–77	15	0	0	15
1977–78	38	2	6	46
1978–79	25	0	2	27
1979–80	9	0	1	10
Total	87	2	9	98

STEELE, SIMON   1983–84

goalkeeper   Ht 6 0, Wt 11 00   1 app
full name: Simon Paul Steele
born: Southport, Lancashire, 29.2.1964
debut: Leeds United (a), 29.8.1983 (FL D2)

Simon Steele was an Everton apprentice who joined the Albion on a free transfer in May 1983 after being released from Goodison Park. With Graham Moseley on the transfer list and Perry Digweed injured, the nineteen-year-old 'keeper played in all three games on the pre-season trip to Majorca in August – he was particularly outstanding in the narrow defeat by Real Madrid – and made his League debut a week later with Moseley now injured and Digweed suspended. However, with the arrival of Joe Corrigan in September 1983, Albion had three experienced goalkeepers on the staff and there was no place for Simon.

After three Fourth Division games during a month's loan with Blackpool, he guested for Worthing in February 1984 and was released the following month to join Scunthorpe United as a non-contract trialist to play in the last five matches of the season. Simon has since played locally for Worthing, Bognor Regis Town (where he played a notable part in their F.A. Cup exploits against Football League opposition), Pagham, and Peacehaven & Telscombe before joining the Police Force. After three years in the constabulary, the Hove C.I.D. man returned to local senior football with Whitehawk in December 1993 before moving across town to join Withdean in 1996.

Season	FL	Total
1983–84	1	1
Total	1	1

STEMP, WAYNE · 1986–92

defender Ht 5 11, Wt 11 02 *4 apps*
full name: Wayne Darren Stemp
born: Plymouth, Devon, 9.9.1970
debut: Hull City (a), 28.10.1989 (FL D2)

Spotted playing for Staines Town in an F.A. Youth Cup match against the Albion juniors in November 1986, Wayne Stemp came to the Goldstone as a YTS trainee and impressed Barry Lloyd sufficiently to be offered professional terms in October 1988. He had played for Surrey Schools and Middlesex Boys' Clubs, and was associated with Brentford as a schoolboy, but they declined to offer him an apprenticeship. Wayne's first senior appearance for Albion came in a pre-season friendly against Shamrock Rovers in August 1989, and he made his League debut two months later in the absence of Gary Chivers. The young defender was a non-playing substitute in the Albion reserve team that won the Sussex Senior Cup in 1988, but did play in the side which again annexed the trophy in 1992. After loan periods to gain experience with Worthing, Bognor Regis Town and Farnborough Town, Wayne was released by the Albion in May 1992 and appeared with Woking, Staines Town and Bognor Regis Town before settling in again at Farnborough. In December 1996 he represented the F.A. against an Isthmian League XI.

Season	FL	Total
1989–90	2	2
1990–91	2	2
Total	4	4

STEPHENS, BERT · 1935–48

outside-left Ht 5 8, Wt 10 06 *366 apps, 174 goals*
full name: Herbert James Stephens
born: Gillingham, Kent, 13.5.1909
died: Thanet, Kent, September 1987
debut: Torquay United (h), 31.8.1935 (FL D3(S))

For thirteen years Bert Stephens scored goals for the Albion at a rate of virtually one every other game, an incredible feat of marksmanship and consistency which made him the most prolific goalscorer in the club's history; his record of 174 goals from 366 matches – including the wartime tournaments – is 51 more than the next best. When his tally in friendly and reserve-team matches is included as well, the total rises to around the 200 mark. Although a good many of those 174 goals were scored in the peculiar conditions of wartime emergency football – during which his appearances were restricted by service on fire duty – he had hit 87 goals before war broke out and may well have gone on to beat Tommy Cook's peacetime mark had the conflict not intervened. He remains one of only two players (the other being Albert Mundy) to have scored 20 goals in each of three consecutive seasons. Yet, while the records and figures themselves demand the utmost respect, perhaps the most impressive thing about Bert's prolific career was the fact that he was a left-winger!

Although born in Gillingham, Bert was raised in Ealing where he attended Southall County School and played for St Thomas's F.C. before graduating to the Ealing Association club in the Southern Amateur League. Working as a travelling salesman, the young winger appeared in Brentford's reserve team as an amateur and was subsequently signed as a professional in February 1931 at the age of 21. In four years at Griffin Park, Bert played in the highly successful reserve eleven that won the London Combination title in 1932 and 1933, but made the League side on only six occasions.

On his arrival at the Goldstone Ground in June 1935 the 26-year-old winger was initially played on the right while the venerable Ernie 'Tug' Wilson saw out his extraordinary Albion career on the other flank, but after seven games Bert was switched to his favourite wing and never looked back. He scored four times in four games after moving, and finished the season second only to Alec Law in the scoring charts. Playing a roving role, he had the knack of popping up in the right place at the right time, and went on to be leading scorer twice in the four seasons leading up to the Second World War, hitting two hat-tricks.

During the emergency Bert served with the National Fire Service and represented them in the Inter-Services Cup on several occasions, but he also continued to play for Albion whenever his duties allowed, scoring regularly and notching another four hat-tricks. He was played at centre-forward or inside-left on a handful of occasions during the emergency, but spent most of his time in the no.11 shirt until the resumption of regular League football in 1946. In his last two seasons with the club Bert played most of his games on the right flank with the younger Wally Hanlon on the left. No longer the devastating force he had been before the war, Bert played his last senior match in November 1947 at the age of 38 and hung up his boots the following year. During 1948 and 1949 he received a well-earned benefit in conjunction with fellow veterans Len Darling, Ernie Marriott, Stan Risdon and Joe Wilson.

Season	FL	FAC	SSC	Wartime	Total
1935–36	41 (19)	2 (2)	2	0	45 (21)
1936–37	41 (24)	1	1 (2)	0	43 (26)
1937–38	36 (22)	4 (1)	1	0	41 (23)
1938–39	40 (17)	1	1	0	42 (17)
1939–40	0	0	0	22 (14)	22 (14)
1940–41	0	0	0	16 (14)	16 (14)
1941–42	0	0	0	10 (3)	10 (3)
1942–43	0	0	0	29 (10)	29 (10)
1943–44	0	0	0	27 (11)	27 (11)
1944–45	0	0	0	28 (15)	28 (15)
1945–46	0	10 (5)	0	29 (11)	39 (16)
1946–47	20 (4)	1	0	0	21 (4)
1947–48	2	1	0	0	3
Total	180 (86)	20 (8)	5 (2)	161 (78)	366 (174)

STEPHENS, MALCOLM · 1955–57

inside-forward *29 apps, 14 goals*
full name: Malcolm Keith Stephens
born: Doncaster, Yorkshire, 17.2.1930
debut: Swindon Town (h), 26.3.1955 (FL D3(S))

Malcolm Stephens arrived at the Goldstone as an amateur early in 1955 along with his Royal Navy colleague Peter Harburn, and was chosen to represent Sussex in the Southern Counties Championship before signing as a professional in July 1955 at the age of 25. The stocky little inside-forward made his Football League debut before Harburn, but, unlike Peter, he was never able to command a regular spot despite an admirable scoring-rate. A clever ball-player, Malcolm was particularly impressive in the promotion bid of 1955–56 when he scored a number of crucial goals, but with Albert Mundy and Denis

Foreman dominating the inside-forward berths his opportunities diminished the following season and he was transferred to Rotherham United in July 1957. Twelve months later he made the short journey to join his home-town club Doncaster Rovers, where he saw out his senior career. As a result of his late entry into the Football League, Malcolm played in only 52 matches for his three clubs, yet totalled nineteen goals, an excellent return for an inside-forward.

Season	FL		Total	
1954–55	5 (1)		5 (1)	
1955–56	20 (13)		20 (13)	
1956–57	4		4	
Total	29 (14)		29 (14)	

STEVENS, GARY 1978–83

defender/midfield   Ht 6 0, Wt 11 05   152 apps, 3 goals
full name: Gary Andrews Stevens
born: Hillingdon, Middlesex, 30.3.1962
debut: Ipswich Town (h), 15.9.1979 (FL D1)

As one of only two players to progress right through the Albion ranks to full England honours – the other was Tommy Cook – Gary Stephens is remembered with great affection by Albion followers. Developing into one of the most complete defenders in the country, he became an integral part of the team that spent four years amongst the élite, reaching his peak in the 1983 F.A. Cup final, but that proved to be his last opportunity to shine for the Albion before moving on to great success elsewhere.

Yet Gary was nearly lost to the game even before his professional career had begun. Brought up in Bury St Edmunds, where he captained the Suffolk Schools, he signed for Ipswich Town as a schoolboy, but, with a surfeit of talented youngsters at Portman Road, he was released by manager Bobby Robson to join his local club, Bury Town.

Ipswich's loss was definitely Albion's gain, though, as Gary came to the Goldstone Ground as an apprentice in August 1978. Within a matter of months he was an established member of the reserve team, and greatly impressed in a pre-season tournament in Glasgow in August 1979 just before Albion's First Division debut. Manager Alan Mullery therefore had no qualms when he gave the seventeen-year-old his own debut – ironically in a 2–0 win over Ipswich – following an injury to star defender Mark Lawrenson in September 1979. Gary, who modelled his game to some extent on that of the exceptional Lawrenson, matured rapidly and signed as a full professional the following month. On Lawrenson's return he was played at full-back and in midfield, and registered his first goal in February 1980 — in a 1–1 draw at Ipswich!

Continuing to show his versatility by playing a variety of roles, Gary turned in any number of stylish performances and established himself in Albion's First Division side. There were numerous calls for him to be included in the England under-21 squad, and he eventually made his international debut in a 1–0 defeat of the Hungarian under-21s at Newcastle in April 1983. By that time Gary, playing in the no.6 shirt alongside Steve Foster, was one of the most consistent performers in the side and won the Player of the Season award for 1982–83, but he reserved perhaps his best display for the greatest stage of all, at Wembley in the F.A. Cup final against Manchester United. Denied the company of the suspended Foster, Gary performed heroically alongside Steve Gatting at the heart of the Albion defence and was voted Man of the Match. But in addition to his defensive duties, he also pushed up for a corner in the 86th minute and fired

home the goal which brought the scores level at 2–2. It was just his third goal for the club and his first of the season.

The replay, which was lost 4–0, proved to be his last game for Brighton, though. With Albion relegated, Tottenham Hotspur came in with a bid of £300,000, an offer neither the club nor the 21-year-old defender could ignore, and he left for White Hart Lane in June. Outstanding performances for Spurs resulted in a UEFA Cup winner's medal in his first season, seven more under-21 caps, and a first appearance for the full England side against Finland in October 1984. Gary went on to gain seven full caps (six as substitute) under Bobby Robson, the man who had rejected him as a boy, and was never on the losing side for England. He appeared twice in the 1986 World Cup finals in Mexico, against Morocco and Paraguay.

However, Gary's career was then marred by a series of injuries, and after almost seven years and 147 League appearances at White Hart Lane he joined Portsmouth on loan for ten weeks in January 1990, signing permanently for £250,000 in March. Further knee problems cut short his career, though, and in February 1992 he announced his retirement at the age of 29; testimonial events were subsequently organised on his behalf.

Still living in Sussex, Gary is now heavily involved in the media as a pundit and presenter on both radio and television, and in the world of sports promotion. Indeed, he is well-known as an astute businessman, having set up his promotions company at the age of 20 while with the Albion. In June 1993, Gary became manager of Petersfield Town in the Wessex League, but left after five months in charge because of the weight of his other commitments.

Season	FL	FAC	FLC	Total
1979–80	21+5 (1)	1	3	25+5 (1)
1980–81	33+1 (1)	2	1	36+1 (1)
1981–82	25+7	0+1	1+1	26+9
1982–83	41	8 (1)	1	50 (1)
Total	120+13 (2)	11+1 (1)	6+1	137+15 (3)

STEVENS, JACK 1934–43

centre-half   Ht 5 10, Wt 11 02   186 apps
full name: John Stevens
born: Broomhill, Northumberland, 1.2.1909
debut: Bristol Rovers (h), 25.8.1934 (FL D3(S))

A sure-footed and consistent defender, Jack Stevens was Albion's regular centre-half for three years from 1935 until 1938, a period in which the club twice came close to promotion. Having represented Northumberland as a schoolboy, Jack progressed through junior football before signing for the local Ashington club in the Third Division (North) at the age of eighteen in November 1927. After making the first team on two occasions during 1928–29 (Ashington's last season as a Football League club), he joined Manchester City in December 1929, but in three years at Maine Road failed to make the senior team and was released to join nearby Stockport County in October 1932. Earning a regular place at Edgeley Park, he made 66 League appearances and was ever-present during 1933–34 before coming to the Goldstone in June 1934 at the age of 25.

STEVENS · BRIGHTON + HOVE ALBION · 1934

Jack's initial appearances for the Albion were at right-back, but, following Paul Mooney's unfortunate decline late in the 1934–35 season, he was switched to centre-half and retained the spot for three seasons, missing just five League games. After making way for

Peter Trainor in 1938, he turned out regularly again in the initial season of regional wartime football (1939–40) before joining the Manchester Police Force.

In his youth, Jack was a professional sprinter, once winning the £70 first prize and gold medal in the Morpeth Spring Handicap. He also played cricket for Southwick during his time at the Goldstone.

Season	FL	FAC	SSC	Wartime	Total
1934–35	12	0	0	0	12
1935–36	40	5	1	0	46
1936–37	40	1	0	0	41
1937–38	39	4	0	0	43
1938–39	6	0	0	0	6
1939–40	0	0	0	37	37
1942–43	0	0	0	1	1
Total	137	10	1	38	186

STEVENS, NORMAN   1955–61

right-back   Ht 5 11, Wt 11 08   *1 app*
full name: Norman John Stevens
born: Shoreham-by-Sea, Sussex, 13.5.1938
debut: Stoke City (h), 18.4.1959 (FL D2)

Having appeared in the Albion's 'A' team, Norman Stevens was turning out for County League side Southwick when he joined the Goldstone staff in October 1955 at the age of seventeen. Although the promising defender went on to represent Sussex at youth level, he made just one senior appearance in six years with the club, as a stand-in for right-back Tommy Bisset during the 1958–59 season, the club's first as a Second Division side. On leaving the Goldstone in 1961, Norman did the rounds of the Southern League with Chelmsford City, Ashford Town and Tunbridge Wells, and subsequently rejoined Southwick. He now runs a painting and decorating business in the local area.

Season	FL	Total
1958–59	1	1
Total	1	1

STEWART, TOM   1908–09

full-back   *54 apps, 1 goal*
full name: Thomas Worley Stewart
born: Sunderland, Co. Durham, 1881
debut: Southampton (h), 2.9.1908 (SL D1)

Tom Stewart enjoyed only one campaign on the South Coast with the Albion, but proved to be an influential character, skippering the side and missing only one Southern League match as Albion fought desperately against the threat of relegation. His early successes came with the highly successful Sunderland-based side Royal Rovers which carried off the championship of the Wearside League in four consecutive seasons, 1900–04. Not surprisingly, he attracted the attention of the local senior club and joined the Sunderland staff as an amateur. Making his First Division debut as such in a 1–0 home win over Nottingham Forest, Tom was offered a professional engagement three weeks later in January 1905, and made four further first-team appearances before being released to join Portsmouth in May 1905. Competition for the two full-back berths was fierce at Fratton Park at the time, though; consequently, he failed to make the Southern League team and played just two games in the subsidiary competitions before returning to the Football League with Clapton Orient in August 1906. Meeting with greater scope at

Millfields Road, Tom played 50 League matches in two seasons as Orient struggled in the Second Division before Jack Robson enticed him to the Goldstone ground during the close season of 1908.

The wily defender played his part well at left-back and captain as Albion survived the very real threat of relegation, and had a storming game in the F.A. Cup against Manchester United when his timely tackles so frustrated Billy Meredith that the legendary 'Welsh Wizard' was sent off for lashing out at his tormentor. Released somewhat surprisingly at the end of the season, Tom moved on to Brentford, but departed from the first-class game without making a single appearance in the "Bees'" Southern League side.

Season	SL	FAC	WL	WL Ch.	SCC	Total
1908–09	39	1	10 (1)	2	2	54 (1)
Total	39	1	10 (1)	2	2	54 (1)

STILLE, GILES   1979–84

midfield   Ht 5 9, Wt 11 09   *29 apps, 4 goals*
full name: Giles Kevin Stille
born: Fulham, London, 10.11.1958
debut: Manchester City (h), 29.12.1979 (FL D1)

As a former pupil of Epsom College, a rugby-playing public school, Giles Stille had an unusual background for a professional footballer. While playing the handling game during the week, he nurtured his soccer skills in the local Sunday league with Clarion Sports, and graduated to the Isthmian League with Kingstonian, where, as a teenager, he was voted Player of the Season in 1977–78 and made a total of 82 appearances. On leaving school he studied social history at London University's Westfield College, and joined the Goldstone staff on a part-time basis in March 1979 while continuing his studies. Spotted by assistant manager Ken Craggs, he was signed for £3,000 amid a good deal of competition from other clubs.

Giles was still a part-timer when he made his First Division debut in December 1979, but had graduated and become a full-time professional by February 1981 when he made the starting line-up for the first time; he enjoyed a run of nine games and scored three times, but then returned to the reserves. A busy and tenacious little player, he remained on the fringe of the team for three seasons, a standby player for more senior midfielders, but rarely let the side down on his sporadic appearances. In 1982, Giles had to come to terms with the devastating news that he suffered from diabetes, a potentially debilitating illness for any sportsman, but he soldiered on bravely until February 1984 when he was cruelly struck by a chronic back injury that eventually brought about his retirement from League football the following December.

On leaving the Goldstone, Giles returned to Kingstonian and moved into mortgage-brokerage with former Albion winger Gerry Fell, but during the summer of 1985 he played for the Umea-based Tegs Sportklub in the Swedish Fourth Division. After returning to England he had a trial period with Sutton United, but signed for

Crawley Town in the Southern League where he remained for two seasons. In 1989, Giles returned to Sweden, and became manager of the Division Two side Tord in 1994.

Season	FL	FAC	Total
1979–80	0+1	0	0+1
1980–81	9+1 (3)	0	9+1 (3)
1981–82	3+2 (1)	0	3+2 (1)
1982–83	7+2	2	9+2
1983–84	1+1	0	1+1
Total	20+7 (4)	2	22+7 (4)

STORER, STUART   1995–

winger   Ht 5 11, Wt 12 13   93 apps, 10 goals
full name: Stuart John Storer
born: Harborough Magna, Warwickshire, 16.1.1967
debut: Birmingham City (a), 29.4.1995 (FL D2)

In March 1995, Stuart Storer did what no other Albion player had done for almost three-and-a-half years: he cost the club a transfer fee! The sum involved was a modest £15,000, but to the cash-strapped 'Seagulls' it was a considerable investment and great things were expected of the new man. Unfortunately he suffered an injury on his first day of training and only came into the team at the end of the season, but he made an immediate impact with a goal on his debut at Birmingham against one of his former clubs.

After playing for Rugby and Warwickshire Schools, Stuart trained with Wolves under manager Ian Greaves, but became a trainee with

Mansfield Town in 1983 when Greaves took over at Field Mill. He made his League debut in October 1983 at the age of sixteen, but lasted just one year with the Fourth Division club and played for Southern League side VS Rugby before continuing his apprenticeship with Birmingham City in 1984. The young winger graduated to the professional ranks at St Andrews, but played only a handful of games before being sold to Everton in March 1987.

Stuart didn't enjoy much success at Goodison either, and joined Wigan Athletic on loan in August 1987 where he made sixteen appearances. Leaving Everton after just nine months and without a senior outing to his name, he signed for Bolton Wanderers just before Christmas 1987 for £25,000 and finally established himself as a first-teamer, helping his new club to promotion from Division Four. At Burnden Park he made 165 appearances (38 of them as substitute) and scored fifteen goals, picking up an Associate Members (Sherpa Van) Cup winner's medal in 1989 and playing a second time at Wembley when Wanderers were defeated by Tranmere Rovers in the 1991 Division Two play-off final. In March 1993, Exeter City splashed out £25,000 for his signature, and he went on to make 92 appearances for the Devon side.

Albion manager Liam Brady first expressed interest in the right-wing speedster early in the 1994–95 season, but it was not until March 1995 that the deal was finally struck with cash from the sale of Kurt Nogan. Although renowned for his speed – he has run 100 metres in 10·4 seconds – the 28-year-old struggled against injury from the moment he arrived in Sussex and lost confidence, but he blossomed during the traumatic 1996–97 season when the Albion fought desperately against relegation to the Football Conference. Stuart started to produce the electrifying pace and crossing ability for which he was bought, and established himself as one of the most vital members of the squad. Also showing considerable determination and

commitment to the cause, his electric wing-play created numerous opportunities for the main strikers. Although perhaps lacking stamina at times, Stuart sustained his form through most of the season and was a key man in a truly remarkable escape from relegation. Indeed, he carved his own place in Albion folklore by netting the last-ever goal to be scored at the Goldstone Ground, in the 1–0 win over Doncaster Rovers on 26 April 1997 which lifted the club off the bottom of the Football League for the first time in almost seven months and set up the momentous climax at Hereford.

Season	FL	FAC	FLC	AMC	Total
1994–95	2 (1)	0	0	0	2 (1)
1995–96	28+10 (2)	1+1	2	3 (1)	34+11 (3)
1996–97	37+5 (6)	2	1+1	0	40+6 (6)
Total	67+15 (9)	3+1	3+1	3 (1)	76+17 (10)

STOTT, TOM   1911–12

centre-forward   2 apps, 1 goal
full name: Thomas Stott
born: Stockton-on-Tees, Co. Durham, 1888
debut: West Ham United (h), 26.4.1911 (SL D1)

Tom Stott came to Hove in April 1911 as a trialist from the Thornaby St Patrick club near Middlesbrough and scored three goals on his debut for the reserves, a 6–2 win over Swindon Town's second string. Four days later the young centre-forward found the net in a 3–0 Southern League eclipse of West Ham United at the Goldstone. During the 1911–12 season he scored 26 South Eastern League goals (including three hat-tricks) for the 'Lambs', but was kept out of the senior side by Bill 'Bullet' Jones and Jimmy Smith, and departed for Southend United in May 1912. Tom remained at Roots Hall until the outbreak of war in 1914.

Season	SL	SCC	Total
1910–11	1 (1)	1	2 (1)
Total	1 (1)	1	2 (1)

SUDDABY, PETER   1979–81

central defender   Ht 5 11, Wt 12 02   25 apps
born: Stockport, Cheshire, 23.12.1947
debut: Nottingham Forest (a), 17.11.1979 (FL D1)

When Peter Suddaby arrived at the Goldstone in November 1979, Albion were bottom of the First Division and seemingly doomed to relegation. Four months later they were more-or-less assured of retaining their status. It was no coincidence. The experienced defender had only 25 senior outings for Brighton, but played a huge part in transforming the club's fortunes. His effect on a previously wobbly defence was both profound and immediate. Indeed, his first game was the memorable victory over Nottingham Forest, the champions of Europe, which restored confidence to the whole club.

Born in Stockport but raised in Prestatyn, Peter attended St Asaph Grammar School and represented Flintshire Schools and the Welsh Grammar School XI as a centre-forward; he also played for several Welsh League clubs and for Rhyl in the Cheshire League while a sixth-former. By the time he left to study maths at the University of Wales in Swansea, Peter had been converted into a defender and went on to play for the British Universities representative side; he also turned out for the famous amateur club Skelmersdale. Looking to a career in teaching, he moved on to Oxford University's St Edmund Hall, winning a blue in the varsity match at Wembley in December 1969. He also played for Wycombe Wanderers, and won three England amateur international caps. After completing his studies in 1970, the talented and brainy defender turned professional with Blackpool at the age of 22 and gained an Anglo-Italian Cup winner's medal in his first season with the club. Peter went on to make 332 League appearances at Bloomfield Road, but in 1979 he was refused a new contract to take him up to a testimonial and joined the Albion on a free transfer.

Strong in the air and tenacious in the tackle, Peter was an inspiration for the rest of the season, but in May 1980 he slipped a disc. That was effectively the end of his Albion career and he was released in May 1981 without playing another first-team game. After six games on a non-contract basis for Wimbledon during 1981–82, he retired from the League ranks to teach mathematics at the American School in Uxbridge while playing and coaching with Hayes in the Isthmian League. In May 1986 he was persuaded to return to the professional game by Alan Mullery as chief coach at the Goldstone, and he remained with the club under Barry Lloyd following Mullery's dismissal in January 1987 until the end of the season when he resumed his teaching career. From August 1987 to January 1988 he managed Wycombe Wanderers in the Conference. Peter married singer Maureen Nolan, one of the Nolan Sisters.

Season	FL	FAC	Total
1979–80	21+2	2	23+2
Total	21+2	2	23+2

SULSTON, CECIL   1911–20

outside-right   *1 app*
full name: Cecil Edwin Sulston
born: Fulham, London, 1887
debut: West Ham United (h), 13.4.1912 (SL D1)

Cecil Sulston assisted the Albion as an amateur for nine years, from 1911 to 1920, but made the first team on just one occasion, a 2–0 home win over West Ham United when Archie Needham was indisposed. A much-honoured player locally, he appeared in turn for Brighton Amateurs, Hove (gaining a Sussex Senior Cup winner's medal in 1910) and Vernon Athletic (West Sussex Senior League champions and Royal Irish Rifles Charity Cup winners in 1912), then had a second spell with Brighton Amateurs before rejoining Vernon Athletic just before the First World War. Cecil also gained Sussex County colours and was still active on the local scene with Brighton Silverdale in the mid 1920s.

Season	SL	Total
1911–12	1	1
Total	1	1

SUTHERLAND, JIM   1901–03

centre-half   *20 apps, 1 goal*
full name: Amos James Sutherland
born: Brighton, Sussex, 1877
debut: Brighton Athletic, 21.9.1901 (FAC Prelim.)

Although, in the absence of Squire Whitehurst, he kept goal for the Albion in their first-ever Southern League match in September 1901 – and on two subsequent occasions – Jim Sutherland's normal role was at centre-half. The locally-born defender was playing for the Preston Park-based North End Rangers when he was first selected for Sussex, but he was then illegally approached by the new professional side Brighton United, an action for which United were admonished by an F.A. commission. However, he subsequently joined the offending club and appeared briefly as a professional during the season of United's liquidation, 1899–1900.

Jim was present at the inaugural meeting of the Brighton & Hove Rangers club which was subsequently formed from North End Rangers and the ashes of Brighton United in July 1900, and was reinstated as an amateur to become a regular for the new team, playing in every competitive match and winning his Sussex County colours during 1900–01. Jim joined the paid ranks again when the Albion were formed in 1901, and remained with the infant club for two seasons (although all his Southern League appearances came in the initial 1901–02 campaign).

Season	SL	FAC	SEL	Total
1901–02	15 (1)	4	0	19 (1)
1902–03	0	0	1	1
Total	15 (1)	4	1	20 (1)

SUTTLE, KEN   1949

outside-left   *Ht 5 6*   *3 apps*
full name: Kenneth George Suttle
born: Brook Green, Hammersmith, London, 25.8.1928
debut: Millwall (a), 5.9.1949 (FL D3(S))

Although best known for his remarkable cricket career with Sussex C.C.C., Ken Suttle was also a fine footballer for the Albion and in local non-League circles. Educated at Worthing High School, he played briefly for Albion's wartime junior team, but first appeared for Worthing in the local emergency competitions at the age of sixteen in 1944–45, and was a member of the victorious Worthing side in the 1946 Sussex Senior Cup final. In 1946–47 he represented Sussex, and had a year on the Chelsea ground staff before returning to the county with the Albion in July 1949. Blessed with good pace, Ken also possessed a fair shot, but his stay at the Goldstone was brief and after playing in three successive League matches in September 1949 he was released to join Chelmsford City in the Southern League. Ken later played for Betteshanger Colliery Welfare in the Kent League

and Tonbridge in the Southern League. For six years he was player-manager of Arundel, leading the excellent team which lifted the County League title in 1957–58 and 1958–59, and later played for Newhaven.

But it's for his quite outstanding career with the Sussex County Cricket Club that Ken will always be remembered. Between 1949 and 1971 the little left-hander became one of a select band of just five Sussex batsmen to have scored 30,000 first-class runs (30,225 at an average of 31·09). Awarded his county cap in 1952, he topped 1,000 runs in a season on seventeen occasions and, in a total of 49 centuries, scored hundreds against all the first-class counties; his top score was 204 n.o. against Kent in 1962. Yet, despite these admirable figures, the most amazing statistic is his all-time record run of 423 consecutive County Championship matches between 1954 and 1969, a staggering total unlikely ever to be eclipsed. Also a brilliant fielder, Ken was a member of the England touring side to the West Indies in 1953–54 and was unfortunate not to play test cricket. He later worked as a menswear salesman.

Season	FL	Total
1949–50	3	3
Total	3	3

SWEETMAN, GEORGE   1903–05

outside-left   1 app
born: Brighton, Sussex, 1882
debut: Grays United (a), 25.4.1903 (SEL)

A local amateur, George Sweetman appeared in the ranks of Brighton & Hove Rangers during the 1900–01 season, and assisted Albion in their final South Eastern League fixture of 1902–03, a 5–0 hiding at Grays United with what can best be described as an 'experimental' side while the 'real' first team played a lucrative friendly with Brentford. George turned out regularly for the reserves over the following two seasons, appearing in all the attacking positions except centre-forward, and was signed as a professional in August 1904, but he never appeared in the first team again.

Season	SEL	Total
1902–03	1	1
Total	1	1

SYKES, ALBERT   1926–28

left-half   Ht 5 8, Wt 11 00   16 apps
born: Shirebrook, Derbyshire, 29.9.1900
died: Rotherham, Yorkshire, 21.12.1994
debut: Brentford (h), 15.1.1927 (FL D3(S))

A lbert Sykes began his adult life as a coal miner in Yorkshire, but found diversion as a footballer with the Maltby Victoria and Maltby Main Colliery Welfare clubs. In November 1924, he left the pit altogether, entering the world of professional football when he signed for Birmingham. Making his senior debut in the final First Division fixture of 1924–25, a 1–0 victory at Notts County, he was subsequently confined to a reserve-team role at St Andrews and the game at Meadow Lane proved to be his only first-team outing. Joining the Albion in August 1926, Albert acted as Wally Little's deputy for two seasons and played the part admirably; in sixteen appearances he was on the losing side only twice. In June 1928 he was transferred to Lincoln City where he remained for three seasons, playing in 42 Third Division (North) matches before dropping into the Southern League with Peterborough & Fletton United in May 1931. Albert subsequently had a brief spell in Luton Town's reserve team, and in 1932–33 played for Grantham in the Midland League.

Season	FL	Total
1926–27	5	5
1927–28	11	11
Total	16	16

8 players who worked on the railways

Player	Player
Armstrong, Arthur	Sharp, Alf
Goffey, Bert	Thompson, Cyril
Hassell, Tommy	Upton, Nobby
Russell, Jock	Walker, Dave

TAWSE, BRIAN   1965–70

outside-left   Ht 5 6, Wt 10 00   114 apps, 16 goals
born: Ellon, Aberdeenshire, Scotland, 30.7.1945
debut: Watford (h), 27.12.1965 (FL D3)

B rian Tawse's goalscoring record as a lad was terrific and earned him a place on the Arsenal playing staff, the seventeen-year-old moving to Highbury in April 1963 from an Aberdeen youth club. He enjoyed good progress with the 'Gunners' and made his First Division debut on the right wing in November 1964. The wee Scot also appeared on the left flank, but, with the likes of George Armstrong and Jon Sammels to contend with, he managed just five first-team games before joining the Albion in December 1965 for around £8,000.

Immediately installed on the left in place of of Johnny Goodchild, the speedy little ball-player went on to enjoy a career of just over four years at Hove where he was dubbed 'Tiger'. Apart from the first half of 1966–67, Brian was more-or-less a regular for three years and attracted attention from a number of big clubs, but he lost favour under new manager Freddie Goodwin during 1968–69 and moved to Brentford in February 1970 for £2,500 at the age of 24. However, his stay at Griffin Park was brief as he emigrated to South Africa in 1971 after 21 Fourth Division games. Brian played for Durban United and worked as sales-manager with a car firm, later forming his own company, but returned to Hove in 1987 to continue working in the car-sales business. •

Season	FL	FAC	FLC	Total
1965–66	22 (6)	0	0	22 (6)
1966–67	22+1 (6)	5 (2)	1	28+1 (8)
1967–68	37+1 (2)	2	2	41+1 (2)
1968–69	14+3	2	0	16+3
1969–70	2	0	0	2
Total	97+5 (14)	9 (2)	3	109+5 (16)

TAYLOR, A. J.   1902–04

winger   16 apps, 5 goals
debut: Grays United (h), 20.12.1902 (SL D2)

R ecruited from Leyton in December 1902, Taylor played his part in Albion's Southern League promotion success that season, appearing on both wings. However, following the arrival of Len Hyde and George Rushton to strengthen the attack for the challenge of Division One, he spent the entire 1903–04 season in the reserve team and was then released. Taylor went on to play for Grays United in the South Eastern League after leaving the Goldstone but continued to train at Hove with his former team-mates.

Season	SL	Test	SEL	Total
1902–03	6 (2)	1	9 (3)	16 (5)
Total	6 (2)	1	9 (3)	16 (5)

TAYLOR, GEOFF   1948–49

outside-left   Ht 5 8, Wt 10 00   2 apps
full name: Geoffrey Arthur Taylor
born: Henstead, Suffolk, 22.1.1923
debut: Norwich City (a), 15.9.1948 (FL D3(S))

I n a career spanning five clubs, Geoff Taylor played in just ten Football League matches, two of which came with the Albion. A product of Norwich junior soccer, he served most of the war with the R.A.F. in the Middle East and signed for Norwich City in August 1946, but was released to join Reading in March 1947 and arrived at the Goldstone in August 1948. Geoff spent just over a year with the Albion, making his brace of appearances in the absence of Ken Davies, and left to join the French club Rennes as player-coach in December 1949. He returned to England with Bristol Rovers in September 1951, but made only three League appearances before leaving for Switzerland as player-coach with S.C. Bruhl in May 1952. A two-match spell with Queen's Park Rangers (signed November 1953) was followed by a permanent move to the Continent and a succession of player-coach posts, firstly at St Gallen in Switzerland, then in West Germany with VFR 07 Kirn, Soberheim, Idar Oberstein, VFL Veierbach, SV Bergen, FSV Schwarzerden and SV Bundenbach. Geoff finally hung up his boots in 1984 at the remarkable age of 61 and still lives in Germany.

Season	FL	Total
1948–49	2	2
Total	2	2

TAYLOR, JOE   1912

inside-right   *1 app*
full name: H. E. Taylor
debut: Cardiff City (h), 23.10.1912 (SA)

After playing for Worthing Old Boys, 'Joe' Taylor joined Worthing in 1905 and served them with great distinction for many years. In the eight seasons before the Great War he figured in five West Sussex Senior League championship sides (skippering two), won two Sussex Senior Cup medals, and played in three R.I.R. Cup-winning teams. A prolific goalscorer, Joe netted 52 times as a youngster in 1906–07 and represented the county on many occasions. Despite being hotly pursued by Hull City and enjoying a successful trial with Fulham – he scored the winning goal in a Southern Charity Cup tie – Joe initially signed amateur forms for the Albion in November 1908 and had one outing with the reserves that season, but in October 1912 he was invited to play in a Southern Alliance fixture with Cardiff City at the Goldstone, partnering Bert Longstaff on the right wing in a 4–1 victory. His father, also H. E. Taylor, was another stalwart of the Worthing club.

Season	SA	Total
1912–13	1	1
Total	1	1

TELFORD, J.   1902

goalkeeper   *1 app*
debut: Maidenhead (h), 1.2.1902 (SL D2)

When Albion's only professional goalkeeper, Squire Whitehurst, became indisposed early in 1902, the last line of defence became a major problem. Initially centre-half Jim Sutherland took over the unenviable task, but, with Albion pressing strongly for the championship of the Southern League Second Division, it was obviously not an ideal situation. The management therefore resorted to playing local amateurs between the posts. The first such player was Telford, a goalkeeper of unknown credentials whose only appearance came in a 2–1 home win over Maidenhead which maintained Albion's place at the top of the table.

Season	SL	Total
1901–02	1	1
Total	1	1

TEMPLEMAN, JOHN   1966–74

full-back/midfield   *Ht 5 11, Wt 11 07*   *255 apps, 18 goals*
full name: John Henry Templeman
born: Yapton, Sussex, 21.9.1947
debut: Queen's Park Rangers (h), 27.12.1966 (FL D3)

Sensationally thrust into the first team at the age of nineteen at Christmas 1966, John Templeman won instant popularity with Albion fans by shackling Rodney Marsh, the Queen's Park Rangers

forward who had terrorised the Brighton defence at Loftus Road just 24 hours earlier. Then Rangers had won 3–0, but, with John's major contribution, the return was drawn 2–2. Following that memorable debut, the blonde-haired youngster was a regular in the Albion side for seven years, and, despite missing most of the 1969–70 season under Freddie Goodwin, proved to be one of the most successful professional footballers to emerge from Sussex in recent years.

After playing for Arundel, John had, in fact, spent some time as a junior with Portsmouth, but arrived at the Goldstone following the disbandment of the reserve side at Fratton Park. Signed as a professional in July 1966, the lanky defender-cum-midfielder went on to serve the Albion admirably, and his consistent play and versatility twice earned him runner's-up position in the Player of the Season award: in 1968–69 when he wore six different numbers, and in the 1971–72 promotion season when he missed just one game and contributed seven goals from midfield. Renowned for his strong, intelligent running, John also possessed a thunderbolt shot and scored a number of spectacular goals. One of the few successes of the calamitous 1972–73 Second Division campaign, he left the Goldstone in May 1974 as Brian Clough and Peter Taylor continued their rebuilding of the squad, moving to Exeter City as part of the deal for Fred Binney.

John made 206 League appearances at St James's Park, and helped the 'Grecians' to second place in the Fourth Division in 1976–77 before moving to Swindon Town in July 1979. With 453 Football League outings to his name, he signed for Witney Town in the Southern League in November 1980 where he also managed a sports-centre for a while. After working in Saudi Arabia and coaching in Sweden for a couple of years, he returned to Sussex and was manager of County League side Arundel from June 1987 until September 1988. John was also a keen cricketer and turned out for the Arundel, Bognor and Pagham clubs at various times.

Season	FL	FAC	FLC	Total
1966–67	15+1	5	0	20+1
1967–68	32+2 (1)	2	2	36+2 (1)
1968–69	31 (3)	1	3 (1)	35 (4)
1969–70	2+1	1	0	3+1
1970–71	31+1 (2)	3	0+1	34+2 (2)
1971–72	44+1 (7)	3	2	49+1 (7)
1972–73	30+1 (2)	1	2	33+1 (2)
1973–74	34 (1)	2	1 (1)	37 (2)
Total	219+7 (16)	18	10+1 (2)	247+8 (18)

TENNANT, DES   1948–59

right-back/-half/-wing   *Ht 5 8, Wt 12 10*   *424 apps, 47 goals*
full name: Desmond Warren Tennant
born: Aberdare, Glamorgan, Wales, 17.10.1925
debut: Bristol City (a), 25.8.1948 (FL D3(S))

When the Barry Town player-manager, Les Jones, came to the Goldstone in 1948, he brought with him the Welsh side's 22-year-old utility player, Des Tennant. Although Jones's sojourn in Sussex was brief, his protégé was a huge success and went on to clock up 424 appearances, the seventh highest total in Albion history.

As a schoolboy, Des had excelled at both soccer and rugby, and had appeared briefly with Cardiff City towards the end of the war before joining Barry in the Southern League. He made his Albion debut at right-half early in 1948–49, and, although best remembered as a right-back, proved to be a versatile performer, turning out in the nos. 2, 4, 6, 7, 9 and 11 shirts at various times over the years. In fact, in his first season he played half his games on the right wing and ended the campaign as top scorer with eleven goals.

Weighing in at nearly 13 stone, the muscular Welshman possessed a fearsome tackle which made him the scourge of many a left-winger, and he soon earned the affectionate nickname of 'The Tank' He didn't actually settle into the no.2 berth until 1951, and even then he spent 1955–56 and 1956–57 largely at right-half. Indeed, he made more than 80 appearances as a half-back and around half that number as a winger. But, wherever he played, Des was an automatic choice for ten years, from 1948 to 1958, and was captain in 1950–51, 1952–53, and again in 1953–54 when Albion were runners-up in the Third Division (South). He was also Albion's penalty king, scoring 23 of his 47 goals from the spot, a record bettered only by Wally Little.

In May 1954, Des received a benefit when Second Division Brentford visited the Goldstone, around 3,500 fans turning out to pay their tribute. Four years later, after a decade of outstanding service to the club, he was presented with a writing-bureau. Des made 35 appearances during the 1957–58 Third Division (South) championship campaign, but, at the age of 33, he lost his place to Tommy Bisset the following term and retired in May 1959 to join the coaching staff. In 1962 he became chief scout and worked in the Goldstone office for a time before taking a post with the ambulance service. Des became landlord of the Allen Arms in Lewes Road, Brighton, in 1965, but returned to his native South Wales the following year where he still resides. His son, Warren, skippered Brighton Boys and was on Chelsea's staff as a youngster.

Season	FL	FAC	Total
1948–49	39 (10)	1 (1)	40 (11)
1949–50	40 (7)	1 (1)	41 (8)
1950–51	42 (2)	4 (1)	46 (3)
1951–52	42	1	43
1952–53	43 (5)	3 (1)	46 (6)
1953–54	38 (4)	4 (1)	42 (5)
1954–55	45 (5)	5 (2)	50 (7)
1955–56	42 (5)	0	42 (5)
1956–57	32 (2)	2	34 (2)
1957–58	35	3	38
1958–59	2	0	2
Total	400 (40)	24 (7)	424 (47)

THAIR, SID   1901–04

inside-forward   *49 apps, 19 goals*
full name: Sidney Frederick Thair
born: Camberwell, London, 1873
debut: Grays United (a), 4.1.1902 (SL D2)

Sid Thair was playing for the Brighton club Glengall Rovers in December 1901 when he was signed by the Albion. Quickly winning a regular place at inside-left, he was a fixture in the side for two years, and scored eighteen goals in 29 games during 1902–03, but lost his place midway through the 1903–04 season, the club's first in the Southern League's First Division, when the more experienced Jack Pryce was signed from Queen's Park Rangers. In May 1904 he was released to join Tunbridge Wells Rangers where he remained for two seasons, helping

the South Eastern League professionals to reach the first round proper of the F.A. Cup in 1905–06 (when Rangers held Norwich City to a 1–1 draw only to lose 5–0 on their own ground in the replay). Sid moved on to Hastings & St Leonards United during the summer of 1906 where he formed an excellent partnership with former Brighton United favourite Sid Hadden on the left wing, but returned to Tunbridge Wells Rangers in the close season of 1907 and continued playing until his 40th year.

Sid had the honour of scoring the Albion's first-ever goal at the Goldstone Ground, which was to become home to the club for 95 years, in a friendly against Southampton Wanderers on 22 February 1902 while their own pitch at the County Cricket Ground was occupied by a Sussex Senior Cup semi-final.

Season	SL	Test	FAC	SEL	Total
1901–02	9	0	0	0	9
1902–03	9 (5)	1 (1)	4 (4)	15 (8)	29 (18)
1903–04	10 (1)	0	1	0	11 (1)
Total	28 (6)	1 (1)	5 (4)	15 (8)	49 (19)

THOMAS, JACK   1910–11

inside-right   *3 apps, 1 goal*
full name: John William Thomas
born: Sacriston, Co. Durham, 1891
debut: Bristol Rovers (a), 24.12.1910 (SL D1)

Nineteen-year-old Jack Thomas joined the Albion during the summer of 1910 after impressing with Spennymoor United, champions of the North Eastern League in 1909–10, but, although he scored regularly for the reserves, he didn't enjoy the best of health during his time at the Goldstone and was unable to maintain a place in the first team. Transferred to Newcastle United for a £25 fee in June 1911, Jack appeared just once in their First Division side, in a 1–1 draw at Manchester City, before returning to Spennymoor United in May 1912.

Season	SL	SCC	Total
1910–11	1	2 (1)	3 (1)
Total	1	2 (1)	3 (1)

THOMAS, LYN   1947–49

centre-forward/outside-right   Ht 5 9, Wt 11 10   *14 apps, 4 goals*
full name: David S. Lyn Thomas
born: Port Talbot, Glamorgan, Wales, 19.9.1920
debut: Watford (a), 23.8.1947 (FL D3(S))

Lyn Thomas was a Welsh schoolboy international who won caps against England and Ireland, and played for Abergregon Juniors before joining Swansea Town in October 1942. During the war years he also guested for Wrexham, Blackpool, Accrington Stanley and Swindon Town, and was brought to the Goldstone Ground as a centre-forward in June 1947 in the hope that he could add some thrust to the attack.

Lyn began well and scored on his debut, a 3–2 win at Watford, but following two heavy defeats the 26-year-old Welshman was relegated to the reserves. A busy, bustling player, he later returned to the side at outside-right but struggled to impress as Albion sank to the bottom of the Third Division's Southern Section . In May 1949 he was given a free transfer and left for Folkestone in the Southern League.

Season	FL	FAC	Total
1947–48	13 (4)	1	14 (4)
Total	13 (4)	1	14 (4)

THOMAS, MICKEY   1981–82

midfield   Ht 5 6, Wt 10 06   23 apps, 1 goal
full name: Michael Reginald Thomas
born: Mochdre, Denbighshire, Wales, 7.7.1954
debut: Birmingham City (h), 7.11.1981 (FL D1)

One of the best-known Welsh internationals of modern times, Mickey Thomas will be remembered by Albion fans for what he *didn't* do rather than for his feats on the pitch. Continually beset by domestic problems – his wife couldn't settle on the South Coast – his spell in Sussex was little short of traumatic. In April 1982 he failed to appear for a match with Notts County, and went 'AWOL' at least three other times, so it was a great relief when he left the club after just nine months. An exciting and brilliant player on his day, he scored

77 goals in exactly 600 League games during a nomadic career, and won 51 full caps for Wales, five of which came during his unhappy spell with the Albion.

Mickey came to prominence with Wrexham, whom he joined as an amateur in 1969 after representing Clwyd & Conwy and North Wales Schools. In 1971 he became an apprentice, signed as a pro in April 1972, and went on to play a big part in the "Robins'" most successful era. Gaining Welsh Cup winner's medals in 1975 and 1978, he helped his side to the Third Division title in 1977–78. The tenacious little Welshman also represented his country at youth, under-21 and under-23 levels, and won his first full cap against West Germany in October 1976 in a 2–0 defeat in Cardiff.

His success as an attacking midfielder or winger attracted the attention of Manchester United, and he signed for them for £300,000 in November 1978. Mickey went on to enjoy 90 First Division outings at Old Trafford, playing in the side which lost the 1979 F.A. Cup final, but that proved to be the pinnacle of his career. After joining Everton in August 1981, in an exchange deal for John Gidman valued at £450,000, he started on a downward spiral which barely relented.

Mickey made just ten League appearances before joining the Albion three months later for a £350,000 fee, but his spell at Goodison was idyllic compared with his time in Hove. Never taken to by Sussex fans because of all the problems, the impish 28-year-old moved on in August 1982, joining Stoke City for £200,000. Mickey continued his wanderings for many years: he later turned out for Chelsea (January 1984), helping them to the 1983–84 Second Division title; West Bromwich Albion (September 1985), where he won his last cap; Derby County (on loan March 1986); Wichita Wings in the U.S.A. (August 1986); Shrewsbury Town (August 1988); Leeds United (August 1989); and Stoke City again (on loan March 1990, signed August 1990).

In August 1991, Mickey returned to Wrexham and enjoyed a last, brief moment of glory when he helped knock Arsenal out of the F.A. Cup, but he played his last League game in November 1992 at the age of 38 and was released in May 1993, joining Conwy United. However, amid a welter of publicity, he was gaoled two months later for passing counterfeit money. Mickey emerged from his cell nine months later to join the League of Wales side Inter Cardiff, assisting them in their brief 1994–95 UEFA Cup campaign, and became caretaker manager at Porthmadog in January 1995 for five months.

In July 1996, though, Wrexham announced that they would stage a benefit game for their erstwhile favourite who has fallen upon hard times since coming out of prison. But he retains a sense of humour as he tries to make a living on the after-dinner circuit: 'I'm surprised I haven't been offered a job in football, especially with all the money I could make!' In September 1997 a biography – *Mickey Thomas: Wild at Heart* – is to be published about an enduring character.

Season	FL	FAC	Total
1981–82	18+2	3 (1)	21+2 (1)
Total	18+2	3 (1)	21+2 (1)

THOMAS, REES   1949 & 1956–58

right-back   Ht 5 8, Wt 10 10   33 apps, 1 goal
born: Aberdare, Glamorgan, Wales, 3.1.1934
debut: Exeter City (h), 6.10.1956 (FL D3(S))

Rees Thomas was on Albion's ground staff as a fifteen-year-old in 1949, but he was subsequently released and joined Cardiff City in January 1951 where he remained for almost five years. However, the young Welshman failed to make the first team at Ninian Park and was loaned out to Torquay United for a brief period in August 1953 before being reintroduced to the Goldstone by manager Billy Lane in September 1956 at the age of 22. A week later he made his debut at left-back in the absence of Jimmy Langley, but it was on the right flank that he enjoyed a run in the side, retaining the no.2 shirt for most of the remainder of the 1956–57 season.

Early in 1957–58, Rees lost his place to his compatriot Des Tennant, and was transferred to Bournemouth & Boscombe Athletic in January 1958 where he became a regular first-teamer, clocking up 48 appearances in the "Cherries'" Third Division side. His form induced Portsmouth to give him an opportunity of Second Division football in July 1959, but 'Pompey' were relegated during his two seasons at Fratton Park and Rees was transferred to Aldershot in July 1961. Having played 103 Fourth Division games for the 'Shots', he left the first-class game in 1964.

Season	FL	FAC	Total
1956–57	23 (1)	2	25 (1)
1957–58	8	0	8
Total	31 (1)	2	33 (1)

THOMPSON, CYRIL   1950–51

centre-forward   Ht 5 9   45 apps, 16 goals
full name: Cyril Alfred Thompson
born: Southend-on-Sea, Essex, 18.12.1918
died: Folkestone, Kent, 1972
debut: Notts County (a), 11.3.1950 (FL D3(S))

Although his career at the Goldstone Ground lasted just twelve months, Cyril Thompson set an Albion record which has never been equalled. The 31-year-old centre-forward only scored sixteen goals for the club, but eight of them came in eight successive Football League matches during September and October 1950, a performance which no other player has been able to match in peacetime League competition.

The Essex-born forward was held prisoner by the Germans for much of the Second World War, but recovered his fitness sufficiently to join his local club, Southend United, as an amateur in July 1945 at the age of 26. After turning professional, he topped the "Shrimpers'" scoring charts in both 1946–47 and 1947–48, returning the highly creditable total of 41 goals from 70 League and Cup games. Such form earned him a transfer to First Division Derby County, but, with Jackie Stamps to contend with as leader of the attack, he struggled at the Baseball Ground and had played only sixteen League games for the 'Rams' when Don Welsh brought him to Hove in March 1950.

A basic centre-forward typical of his era, Cyril was strong and bustling in the box, and scored on his Albion debut. He enjoyed his incredible run of success early in the 1950–51 campaign, but then the scoring touch deserted him and in March 1951 he moved to

Watford in exchange for Ray Garbutt. Ending 1951–52 as top scorer with 22 goals, he netted 34 times in 78 League outings for the Hertfordshire side before leaving for Folkestone Town in July 1953. Cyril went on to score over 100 goals for the Kent League side and assisted them to a Kent Senior Cup and Senior Shield double in 1956–57. On hanging up his boots he became trainer at Folkestone, and also worked as an electrician on the railways for many years.

Season	FL	FAC	Total
1949–50	10 (4)	0	10 (4)
1950–51	31 (11)	4 (1)	35 (12)
Total	41 (15)	4 (1)	45 (16)

THOMPSON, JACK   1921–25

right-back   106 apps
full name: John George Thompson
born: Cramlington, Northumberland
debut: Southend United (h), 27.8.1921 (FL D3(S))

Jack Thompson joined Aston Villa in November 1919, but after an initial run in the first team he then had to act as deputy to the future England full-back Tommy Smart. In August 1921, with 26 First Division games behind him, he signed for Albion manager Charlie Webb and went on to give splendid service for three seasons.

Described as dashing, fearless and fleet of foot, Jack formed exceptional partnerships with left-backs Jack Feebery and Jack Jenkins, and played a big part in the superb defence of the period: Albion conceded just 34 goals in 1922–23, a club record for the Football League (equalled in 1984–85), and a miserly 37 the following term. However, in April 1924 he sustained an ankle injury in a match at Norwich which caused him to miss the whole of the 1924–25 season and brought about his retirement in May 1925. Granted a benefit match in March 1926 (when Albion drew 4–4 with Second Division Portsmouth), Jack worked locally as a bus driver for the Tillings company on  leaving the Goldstone. In August 1927 his amateur status was reinstated, allowing him to play for the Tillings football team in the Brighton, Hove & District League.

Season	FL	FAC	Total
1921–22	35	3	38
1922–23	25	5	30
1923–24	34	4	38
Total	94	12	106

THOMPSON, PAT   1951–55

inside-left   Ht 5 8, Wt 10 00   1 app
full name: Patrick Alfred Thompson
born: Exeter, Devon, 11.2.1932
debut: Bournemouth & B.A. (a), 10.3.1951 (FL D3(S))

Discovered by manager Don Welsh playing for the Exeter club Topsham, Pat Thompson signed as a professional for the Albion in January 1951 following a brief period on trial. The quiet, unassuming Devonian was completing his National Service with the Royal Navy at the time, but was quickly given an opportunity to impress when Ken Bennett was unable to play in a 2–2 draw at Bournemouth in March 1951. It turned out to be his only first-team appearance, but Pat performed admirably for the reserves over a lengthy period

and had a particularly brilliant game for a strong Albion XI v. Hastings United in a benefit match for United's former Goldstone favourite Sammy Booth at the Pilot Field in March 1955. Subsequently, when he was released at the end of the 1954–55 season, Pat was snapped up by the Southern League club.

Season	FL	Total
1950–51	1	1
Total	1	1

THOMPSON, STAN   1929–35

outside-right   Ht 5 4, Wt 9 08   73 apps, 20 goals
full name: Alfred Stanley Thompson
born: Durham, Co. Durham
debut: Barry Town (h), 14.12.1929 (FAC R2)

One of the shortest players ever to appear for the Albion, Stan Thompson packed a deceptively powerful shot into his size 4 boots and made up for any lack of inches with a big heart. As a lad he represented Deerness & District Schools, and was playing for a Durham junior club when Charlie Webb brought him to the Goldstone for a successful trial in October 1929. Stan made his senior debut just two months later, scoring once in a 4–1 F.A. Cup defeat of Barry Town, but his subsequent outings were infrequent until October 1932 when an injury to Dan Kirkwood caused a reshuffle of the forward-line to accommodate him on the right flank. The young winger proved a great asset with his exceptional pace, particularly in the marvellous F.A. Cup run of 1932–33, but he was never certain of a place in the side with the likes of Bobby Farrell and Bert Jepson to compete with.

After nearly six years in Hove, Stan was released in May 1935 and joined Hartlepools United in his native county, but returned south in September 1936 for a two-month trial period with Exeter City during which he played in three Third Division games. During the Second World War, Stan served in the Middle East with the R.A.F.

Season	FL	FAC*	SSC	Total
1929–30	0	1 (1)	0	1 (1)
1930–31	1	0	0	1
1931–32	4 (1)	0	0	4 (1)
1932–33*	31 (7)	9 (5)	0	40 (12)
1933–34	17 (4)	3	1	21 (4)
1934–35	5 (2)	0	1	6 (2)
Total	58 (14)	13 (6)	2	73 (20)

Note: Two appearances and four goals of Thompson's 1932–33 F.A. Cup total came in the qualifying competition.

THOMSON, CHARLIE   1934–39

goalkeeper   Ht 5 11, Wt 11 00   191 apps
full name: Charles Marshall Thomson
born: Perth, Perthshire, Scotland, 25.10.1905
debut: Bristol Rovers (h), 25.8.1934 (FL D3(S))

Charlie Thomson, Albion's last line of defence in the five seasons before the Second World War, was consistency personified and maintained a high level of performance until moving on in the summer of 1939. Having played for St Johnstone Y.M.C.A. and Alloa, the swarthy 28-year-old arrived at the Goldstone in June 1934 after five seasons on the Falkirk staff, and was seldom absent from the line-up as Albion came frustratingly close to clinching promotion from Division Three (South) on three occasions. Ever-present in his first season at Hove, Charlie greatly impressed the home crowd; indeed, the local Press once reported him as having given 'the finest display of goalkeeping seen at the Goldstone for many years.'

Following a move to Exeter in 1939, Charlie kept goal for the 'Grecians' in the three League fixtures of the aborted 1939–40 Third Division campaign, but on the outbreak of war he returned to Scotland with Dundee United where he appeared in the team beaten 1–0 by Glasgow Rangers in the Scottish War Cup final of May 1940. Joining Dundee in April 1945, he returned to Exeter the following November and played in their four FA Cup matches of the 1945–46 transitional season before rejoining Dundee, where he hung up his gloves shortly after at the age of 40. Charlie's son, Chick Thomson, won fame as a goal-keeper with Clyde, Chelsea and Nottingham Forest.

Season	FL	FAC	SSC	Total
1934–35	42	3	3	48
1935–36	35	5	2	42
1936–37	39	1	1	41
1937–38	27	4	1	32
1938–39	26	1	1	28
Total	169	14	8	191

THOMSON, NORMAN   1927–28

inside-right   Ht 5 8, Wt 11 00   11 apps, 5 goals
full name: Norman Shaw Thomson
born: Glasgow, Lanarkshire, Scotland, 20.2.1901
died: Ferring, Sussex, 6.6.1984
debut: Brentford (h), 27.8.1927 (FL D3(S))

After playing as a youngster for the renowned Glasgow junior club St Anthony's, Norman Thomson began his nomadic career as a professional footballer in 1921 when he joined Dumbarton. The first of many moves took him to Hibernian in May 1924, but he then migrated to England with Luton Town in August 1925 where his form – eight goals from 43 Third Division (South) matches – earned him a transfer to Clapton Orient in January 1927.

Norman's stay with the Second Division side proved brief, though, as Albion manager Charlie Webb obtained his services the following August, but, with inside-forwards of the calibre of Sam Jennings and Dai James already on the staff, his sojourn at the Goldstone was rather mixed. After playing in the opening two matches of 1927–28, he languished in the reserves until enjoying a late run in the first team as Albion improved tremendously to claim fourth place in the Southern Section. However, at the end of the season he failed to agree terms and moved on again to Walsall on a free transfer at the age of 27.

The Scottish inside-forward scored thirteen goals in 38 Southern Section games at Fellows Park in 1928–29, the most fruitful campaign of his career, but once again he moved on after just a year and joined Norwich City in July 1929 for a fee of £125. However, Norman developed knee trouble during his time with the 'Canaries', and he made just sixteen appearances before moving on to Brentford in August 1930 (where he made one appearance) and then to Swindon Town in August 1932 (three appearances). The knees worsened, though, and he quit the first-class game in 1933, although he continued to play in the Southern League with Folkestone for a short time.

Norman then started a motor-car business (which exists to this day, run by one of his sons) close to West Ham United's Upton Park ground, and lived in Sussex for many years until his death at the age of 83 in 1984. His wife was the sister of Albion's utility player Alf Edmonds, while another son, Ian, made his name as a pace-bowler for Sussex C.C.C. and England.

Season	FL	Total
1927–28	11 (5)	11 (5)
Total	11 (5)	11 (5)

THORNE, ADRIAN   1954–61

forward   Ht 5 8, Wt 11 00   84 apps, 44 goals
full name: Adrian Ernest Thorne
born: Hove, Sussex, 2.8.1937
debut: Southend United (a), 18.1.1958 (FL D3(S))

In only his seventh Football League match, 20-year-old Adrian Thorne carved a large niche for himself in Albion folklore when he scored five goals – including a hat-trick in the first ten minutes – in the celebrated 6–0 victory over Watford at the Goldstone in April 1958, a result which saw the club promoted to the Second Division for the first time after many years of near misses. One of only two players to score five goals for the club in a League match – the other was Jack Doran – that feat alone would have made him a great favourite of the Hove crowd, but the fact that he was a local boy made him even more popular.

Adrian attended the Brighton, Hove & Sussex Grammar School in Dyke Road, played for Brighton Boys, and graduated into the Sussex County League with Old Grammarians while still at school. He also repre-sented Sussex at youth level, and signed for the Albion on his seven-teenth birthday in August 1954. The young forward then had to wait over three years to break into the League team, and actually made his debut in January 1958 while stationed at Colch-ester on National Service with the Army. Stepping in for the absent Peter Harburn, he scored in his first game, and returned to the side when Dave Sexton was injured at

the end of the campaign to take his place in the record books.

A strong-running attacker, Adrian went on to appear in all the forward positions except right-wing, and maintained an average of a better than a goal every other game with 44 goals from 84 appearances. In 1960–61 he led the scorers with fourteen goals. Yet, despite possessing an undoubted natural flair for scoring goals, Adrian was never given a real opportunity to establish himself and was never allowed more than four months in the side at a time. After being replaced for the umpteenth time, he put in a transfer request and signed for fellow Second Division side Plymouth Argyle in June 1961 for a fee of £8,000.

Adrian scored only twice in eleven Second Division games at Home Park, though, and in December 1963 he joined nearby Exeter City where, ironically, he scored on his debut in the "Grecians'" 2–1 Boxing Day victory at the Goldstone. City clinched promotion to Division Three that season and Adrian went on to score nine goals in 41 League appearances before moving on to Leyton Orient in June 1965, his final League club. He later played for Cheltenham Town and Barnet, and is now a schoolteacher living in Twickenham.

Most pundits felt that the Albion management should have persevered with Adrian, a view shared by the majority of the club's followers at the time. But, whatever his achievements thereafter, he remains a hero to those who witnessed his extraordinary feat of April 1958.

Season	FL	FAC	FLC	Total
1957–58	7 (7)	0	0	7 (7)
1958–59	15 (10)	1	0	16 (10)
1959–60	27 (9)	5 (4)	0	32 (13)
1960–61	27 (12)	0	2 (2)	29 (14)
Total	76 (38)	6 (4)	2 (2)	84 (44)

TIDDY, MIKE   1958–62

outside-right   Ht 5 8, Wt 11 00   *146 apps, 12 goals*
full name: Michael Douglas Tiddy
born: Helston, Cornwall, 4.4.1929
debut: Leyton Orient (h), 25.10.1958 (FL D2)

With his distinctive grey-flashed hair, Mike Tiddy was a unmistakable character down the Albion right wing for nearly four seasons. Following a trial with Plymouth Argyle, he started out as a youngster with Torquay United, signing as a professional in November 1946, and made his League debut as a seventeen-year-old during the initial post-war season. After

National Service in the Army, Mike was transferred to Cardiff City in November 1950, and went on to win many admirers at Ninian Park where his superb wing-play established him in the first team for almost five years. After hitting nineteen goals in 145 League appearances, the Cornish flyer was transferred to Arsenal in September 1955 (along with his Cardiff team-mate Gordon Nutt), and continued to enhance his reputation with eight goals in 48 League games before Billy Lane secured his transfer for the Albion in October 1958.

Signed in an effort to strengthen a struggling side in its first season of Second Division fare, 29-year-old Mike made an instant impression at the Goldstone after taking over the right-wing spot from Dennis Gordon, and was a regular for four years although, as a Methodist lay-preacher, he declined to play on religious holidays at Easter and Christmas. In 1962 he returned to Cornwall for compassionate reasons, and was released in July to take the player-coach's position with Penzance in the South Western League. He subsequently became player-manager of Helston and then Falmouth Town, and ran the post-office at The Lizard after leaving Sussex. Mike's younger brother Terry was also on the Goldstone staff as a junior in 1959.

Season	FL	FAC	FLC	Total
1958–59	26 (3)	1	0	27 (3)
1959–60	31 (2)	5 (1)	0	36 (3)
1960–61	39 (3)	3	2	44 (3)
1961–62	37 (3)	1	1	39 (3)
Total	133 (11)	10 (1)	3	146 (12)

TILER, KEN   1974–79

right-back   Ht 5 11, Wt 10 13   *151 apps*
full name: Kenneth David Tiler
born: Sheffield, Yorkshire, 23.5.1950
debut: Hereford United (a), 16.11.1974 (FL D3)

One of the less-celebrated players of Albion's most successful era, Ken Tiler was a reliable defender who played his part in the successful promotion campaigns of 1976–77 and 1978–79. He was playing representative soccer for the Rotherham F.A. when he was spotted by the Chesterfield management, and joined the Saltergate staff as an amateur while completing his training as a turner. After signing professional forms in September 1970 at the age of 20, he made 139 League appearances for the 'Spireites' before Peter Taylor

signed him for Brighton in November 1974; Ken was rated at around £45,000 in an exchange deal involving Albion's Billy McEwan and Ronnie Welch.

Although he was first-choice right-back for three seasons as the club's fortunes soared, Ken often had to concede the no.2 shirt to Chris Cattlin in the Second Division and, after requesting a transfer, he joined Rotherham United for £15,000 in July 1979. After 46 League outings for the 'Millers', playing in a variety of positions, the lanky full-back joined Boston United in the Alliance Premier League in July 1981. Ken's son, Carl, is a centre-back with Sheffield United.

Season	FL	FAC	FLC	Total
1974–75	28	2	0	30
1975–76	30	2	2	34
1976–77	38	2	5	45
1977–78	17	0	6	23
1978–79	17	0	2	19
Total	130	6	15	151

TILTMAN, RICHARD   1986–88

forward   Ht 6 0, Wt 13 00   *16 apps, 1 goal*
full name: Richard George Tiltman
born: Shoreham-by-Sea, Sussex, 14.12.1960
debut: Sheffield United (a), 10.1.1987 (FAC R3)

Despite a prolific scoring record in local senior football, Richard Tiltman was unable to make the transition to League standard. Unfortunately, his Goldstone career coincided with a low point in the club's fortunes and he consequently became a target of the crowd's frustration.

After an unsuccessful trial with Arsenal as a youngster, Richard started out with Montague F.C. in the Worthing League and joined Sussex County League side Littlehampton Town in 1981, where his scoring feats soon won him selection for the Sussex representative side. In 1984 he stepped up into the Isthmian League with Worthing, and had a trial at Wimbledon in January 1985, but he joined Maidstone United in the Alliance Premier League the following summer for a fee of £4,000, then a record sum for the Worthing club. Richard suffered a number of injury problems in Kent, though, and returned to Worthing on loan in January 1986. He also had a similar spell with Crawley Town before spending the summer with the East Freemantle Tricolore club in Australia, but then returned to Maidstone.

In January 1987, ex-Worthing boss Barry Lloyd took over as Albion manager and signed his 26-year-old former star the same month following a brief trial in the reserves. After a few weeks on the staff Richard was played in preference to the popular Dean Saunders by Lloyd, a move which on its own turned the Brighton fans against the Shoreham-born forward, but he struggled throughout his time at the Goldstone and was released at the end of the 1987–88 season with just a single goal to his name.

Following a month on trial at Burnley, Richard returned to Sussex with Crawley Town and later moved on to Bognor Regis Town before leaving for Australia in April 1990 to play for the Perth Italia club. In December 1991, though, he linked up with Worthing again, assisting the 'Rebels' to promotion to the Isthmian League Premier Division in 1994–95 (although he was also loaned to Shoreham during the latter stages of the season when not required). In August 1995, Richard joined County League side Stamco, but re-signed for Worthing in March 1996.

Season	FL	FAC	FLC	Total
1986–87	9+3 (1)	0+2	0	9+5 (1)
1987–88	1	0	0+1	1+1
Total	10+3 (1)	0+2	0+1	10+6 (1)

TOWNER, TONY — 1970–78

winger — Ht 5 7, Wt 9 11 — 183 apps, 25 goals
full name: Antony James Towner
born: Brighton, Sussex, 2.5.1955
debut: Luton Town (h), 10.2.1973 (FL D2)

Following a miserable run of thirteen consecutive defeats in the middle of season 1972–73, Albion manager Pat Saward gave debuts to two youngsters, seventeen-year-old Tony Towner and eighteen-year-old Pat Hilton, and was rewarded with a 2–0 victory over Luton Town. Although Hilton quickly faded from the scene, Tony blew across the Goldstone turf like a breath of fresh air and held his place at outside-left for the rest of the season. It was the start of a long professional career for the winger from Bevendean which took him all over the country and encompassed 419 League games, but it was with his home-town club that he enjoyed most of his success.

A pupil at the Bevendean and Stanmer Schools, Tony played for Brighton Boys, and was turning out for Lower Bevendean when the Brighton League side's coach, Albion groundsman Frankie Howard, introduced him to the Goldstone. Taken on as an apprentice in December 1970, he made his invigorating debut as such before signing as a full professional in October 1972. Tony switched to the right flank in 1973–74, and enjoyed his best season the following term when he topped the League scorers with ten goals from 41 outings. Over the next three seasons 'Tiger', as he was affectionately dubbed the fans, vied with Gerry Fell and then Eric Potts for the no.7 shirt, but still played a significant part in the promotion success of 1976–77 and the near miss of following season. Having seen off

those rivals, though, the 23-year-old forward was forced to make way for Gerry Ryan in September 1978 and, having requested a move, left for Millwall the following month for a fee of £65,000, then an Albion record.

Although the 'Tiger' was a great success in the "Lions'" Den, cash-strapped Millwall sold their tenacious winger to Rotherham United in August 1980 along with John Seasman for £100,000, and he went on to spend three seasons at Millmoor (including a loan period at Sheffield United in March 1983). After moving to Wolverhampton Wanderers in August 1983, Tony then pursued a somewhat nomadic career with Charlton Athletic (September 1984), Rochdale (November 1985) and Cambridge United (April 1986) before moving into non-League football with Southern League side Gravesend & Northfleet in September 1986. He has since played for Fisher Athletic, Crawley Town (Sussex Senior Cup winners in 1990), Gravesend & Northfleet for a second spell, Crawley Town for a second spell (Sussex Senior Cup winners again in 1991), Lewes, Crawley Town yet again, Newhaven and Saltdean United (Sussex County League Division Two champions in 1996).

Now employed as a lorry-driver, Tony played his part in Crawley's famous run to the third round of the F.A. Cup in 1991–92, and came on as substitute in the 5–0 defeat by the Albion. He received a terrific reception from the large Hove crowd, a tremendous tribute to a very popular footballer thirteen years after he last graced the Goldstone turf for Brighton.

Season	FL	FAC	FLC	Total
1972–73	14 (2)	0	0	14 (2)
1973–74	20+3 (2)	0+1	0	20+4 (2)
1974–75	41 (10)	3	3	47 (10)
1975–76	28+1 (2)	0	2	30+1 (2)
1976–77	23 (6)	3	4	30 (6)
1977–78	23+3 (2)	2 (1)	0+2	25+5 (3)
1978–79	4+2	0	1	5+2
Total	153+9 (24)	8+1 (1)	10+2	171+12 (25)

TOWNLEY, JIMMY — 1928–30

inside-left — Ht 5 10, Wt 11 00 — 9 apps
full name: James Chadwick Townley
born: Blackburn, Lancashire, 2.5.1902
debut: Luton Town (a), 25.8.1928 (FL D3(S))

The son of the Blackburn Rovers and England winger William Townley, Jimmy Townley was born in Blackburn but spent most of his youth in Germany where his father held a coaching post. After playing for Hamburg Victoria and the Swiss club St Gallen, Jimmy returned to England in 1924 to try his hand in the Football League, firstly with Chelsea where he had an unfruitful trial, and then with Tottenham Hotspur for whom he signed professional forms in March 1925. His progress at White Hart Lane was hindered by a broken leg, however, and he made only three First Division appearances in just over three seasons.

In August 1928, Jimmy joined the Albion for a fee of £600, an enormous amount for the club at the time, but he failed to make an impression. Played at inside-left in the opening seven games of the 1928–29 season, he was dropped on Jimmy Hopkins' return from injury, and, after appearing at centre-forward in a couple of games later in the campaign, returned to the reserves before transferring to Clapton Orient in February 1930. After nineteen League outings with the Third Division (South) side, Jimmy was released in May 1931 and returned to Switzerland.

Season	FL	Total
1928–29	9	9
Total	9	9

TOWNSEND, ERIC — 1930–34

centre-forward — Ht 5 8, Wt 11 04 — 15 apps, 9 goals
full name: Eric Esme Townsend
born: Hove, Sussex, 14.2.1914
died: Hove, Sussex, 23.7.1976
debut: Clapton Orient (h), 12.9.1931 (FL D3(S))

An outstanding schoolboy footballer, Eric Townsend looked set for a great future in the game when, tragically, he was diagnosed as having a heart defect which forced him to retire from the professional ranks at the age of just nineteen. It was a tremendous blow for both Eric and the Albion, as he had already shown precocious talent with nine goals from just fifteen Third Division (South) outings and looked destined to become a rare goalscorer indeed. It was even more unfortunate as he was a Hove lad and had attracted a great deal of interest locally. The first seventeen-year-old to turn out for Brighton, Eric held the record as the club's youngest player in peacetime until Steve Burtenshaw first appeared in 1953.

A pupil at Connaught Road School, he won many schoolboy honours, including a runner's-up medal from the 1928 English Schools Trophy final when the local lads were defeated over two legs by North Staffordshire. Taken on as an amateur by the Albion in October 1930, Eric signed professional forms on his seventeenth birthday in February 1931 and scored on his debut the following September. Having returned to the reserves after three games, he continued learning his trade with the 'Lambs'. In 1932–33 he enjoyed eight outings in the first eleven and scored eight goals, but in October 1933 the sad diagnosis was made and Eric was advised to take a long break from the game.

The following year he left the Goldstone and drifted into non-League football with Shoreham in the Sussex County League, although he also had a two-month trial at Bournemouth. Eric later played for Hove and remained prominent on the local scene for a couple of seasons, but he never again played in the Football League. His father, Sid, played in goal for the Brighton-based Vernon Athletic in the County League and assisted Albion's reserve team on occasion from 1913 to 1923.

Season	FL	Total
1931–32	3 (1)	3 (1)
1932–33	8 (8)	8 (8)
1933–34	4	4
Total	15 (9)	15 (9)

TOWNSHEND, A. 1907–08

inside-left   2 apps
debut: Leyton (a), 6.1.1908 (WL)

Brought to the Goldstone as a young player from an unknown non-League source in November 1907, Townshend was only a fringe member of the reserve side, but appeared in a much-weakened first team which lost 6–1 at Leyton in a Western League fixture in January 1908. The game was played on the Monday afternoon preceding an F.A. Cup first-round tie with First Division Preston North End, and manager Frank Scott-Walford rested most of his regular side. Townshend enjoyed just one more outing in the Western League – again at Leyton and again a defeat.

Season	WL	Total
1907–08	1	1
1908–09	1	1
Total	2	2

TRAINOR, Peter 1938–48

centre-half   Ht 5 11, Wt 11 05   94 apps, 5 goals
born: Cockermouth, Cumberland, 2.3.1915
died: Whitehaven, Cumberland, 14.10.1979
debut: Walsall (h), 27.8.1938 (FL D3(S))

A strong and determined centre-half, Peter Trainor arrived at the Goldstone in May 1938, but then had his career severely curtailed by the war only to return after the emergency to become a rock in the Albion formation. Born in Cumberland, he started out with his local senior club, Workington, in the North Eastern League, and was taken on by Preston North End in August 1937, but had played only a reserve-team role at Deepdale before coming to Hove at the age of 23.

Peter immediately took over from the popular Jack Stevens and proved a commanding performer, but after that first season he managed just a couple of appearances for the Albion amid the hostilities. Returning to Hove at the age of 30 in 1945, he filled the no.5 shirt once again during the transitional 1945–46 season, and kept his place when the Football League returned to normal the following year. In October 1946, Peter was played as a stop-gap

centre-forward at the Goldstone against Notts County; remarkably, he scored a hat-trick, and scored another goal in two subsequent outings in the no.9 shirt. However, he lost his place the following season and, having reached the veteran stage, returned to non-league Workington in May 1948.

Peter should have made one more wartime appearance than he managed, for, in February 1941, he was due to play for the Albion at Arsenal, but no one told him that the 'Gunners' played their home games at White Hart Lane. When he turned up at Highbury he found it had been requisitioned as a first-aid post and air-raid patrol centre! Fortunately, Albion had a deputy in Blackburn Rovers' Jack Westby.

Season	FL	FAC	SSC	Wartime	Total
1938–39	34	1	1	0	36
1940–41	0	0	0	2	2
1945–46	0	4	0	15 (1)	19 (1)
1946–47	32 (4)	0	0	0	32 (4)
1947–48	5	0	0	0	5
Total	71 (4)	5	1	17 (1)	94 (5)

TRANTER, Wilf 1966–68

defender   Ht 5 9, Wt 12 00   57 apps, 1 goal
full name: Wilfred Tranter
born: Pendlebury, Lancashire, 5.3.1945
debut: Shrewsbury Town (a), 6.5.1966 (FL D3)

One of a latter crop of 'Busby Babes', Wilf Tranter graduated from apprentice to full pro with Manchester United in April 1963, but failed to make his mark and appeared just once in the star-studded First Division side, in March 1964 in a 2–0 win at West Ham United.

In May 1966, 21-year-old Wilf was released to join the Albion on a free transfer and proved to be a useful acquisition: capable of playing a variety of defensive roles, he appeared across the back four in his time with the club.

After 57 games he was given a free transfer to join the Baltimore Bays in the U.S.A. during the summer of 1968. In January 1969, Wilf signed for Fulham, but played only 23 first-team games over three years at Craven Cottage before moving into the Southern League with Dover in November 1972. (He also played for St Louis Stars in the States during the summer of 1972.) A qualified coach, Wilf became a member of the backroom staff at Swindon Town for a time, and was appointed manager of Southern League Witney Town in November 1980. In 1989 he was assistant manager at Hungerford Town. His brother, John, was briefly with the Albion in 1967–68.

Season	FL	FAC	FLC	Total
1965–66	3	0	0	3
1966–67	15	5	1	21
1967–68	28+1 (1)	1+1	2	31+2 (1)
Total	46+1 (1)	6+1	3	55+2 (1)

TRUSLER, Johnny 1954–56

centre-forward   1 app
full name: John William Trusler
born: Shoreham-by-Sea, Sussex, 7.6.1934
debut: Exeter City (a), 29.1.1955 (FL D3(S))

Johnny Trusler joined Albion's paid ranks from Sussex County League side Shoreham at the age of 20 in August 1954. A slightly-built centre-forward, he performed admirably in the reserve and 'A' teams, but made the senior side on just one occasion, in the absence of Bernard Moore in a 3–1 defeat at Exeter in January 1955. He left for the Kent League club Tunbridge Wells United in July 1956, but later returned to Shoreham where he remained prominent for some time before emigrating to Australia.

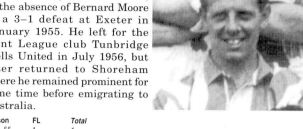

Season	FL	Total
1954–55	1	1
Total	1	1

TRUSSON, MIKE   1987–89

midfield   Ht 5 10, Wt 12 04   43 apps, 2 goals
full name: Michael Sydney Trusson
born: Northolt, Ealing, Middlesex, 26.5.1959
debut: Northampton Town (a), 5.12.1987 (FAC R2)

Mike Trusson made only a limited impact at the Goldstone, but he did enjoy a successful career as a journeyman in Yorkshire before coming to Sussex. After a fruitless trial with Chelsea, the Middlesex-born youngster was playing for a youth side in Somerset when he was taken on as an apprentice by Plymouth Argyle, and made his Football League debut as a trainee before signing professional forms in January 1977. Playing up front, Mike scored fifteen goals in 73 League games in four seasons at Home Park (which included a loan spell with Stoke City in December 1978) before moving to Sheffield United for £60,000 in July 1980.

While with the 'Blades' he won a Fourth Division championship medal in 1981–82 and appeared in 126 League matches before being exchanged for Rotherham United's Paul Stancliffe in December 1983. Three-and-a-half seasons and 124 League matches at Millmoor ended when a receiver was called in to handle the club's affairs. Mike was

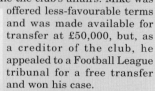

offered less-favourable terms and was made available for transfer at £50,000, but, as a creditor of the club, he appealed to a Football League tribunal for a free transfer and won his case.

Now able to negotiate his own conditions, he signed for the Albion in July 1987, but suffered persistent knee problems before making his debut five months later. Played as a tough-tackling midfielder, Mike was plagued with injuries while at the Goldstone and, unable to establish himself in the team, moved to Gillingham for a £20,000 fee in August 1989 where he brought his total of League appearances to 434 before further injuries cut short his career. In 1992 he was appointed youth-team coach at AFC Bournemouth and was promoted to head coach in January 1994, but lost his job in August 1994 when manager Tony Pulis was sacked and returned to Sussex with the ambitious Hastings-based club Stamco in the County League.

Mike had also retained an interest in Sussex with summer soccer schools for youngsters, and acted as a marketing consultant for the London theme restaurant 'Football Football'. In 1996 he was player-coach of Stamco, and played a big part in helping the club gain entry to the Southern League (as St Leonards Stamcroft) in the summer, but had to resign from his position in the spring of 1997 because of

his work commitments as a marketing executive for the Professional Footballers' Association.

Season	FL	FAC	FLC	AMC	Total
1987–88	13+2 (2)	3	0	2	18+2 (2)
1988–89	21+1	0	1	0	22+1
Total	34+3 (2)	3	1	2	40+3 (2)

TUCK, STUART   1991–

defender   Ht 5 11, Wt 11 02   82 apps
full name: Stuart Gary Tuck
born: Brighton, Sussex, 1.10.1974
debut: Fulham (a), 28.9.1993 (AMC Group)

Like his father, Keith, before him, Stuart Tuck made his first impact locally by playing for Brighton Boys, but unlike his dad he has gone on to become a professional with his local club. A pupil at St Luke's and Stanley Deason schools, Stuart played both in midfield and up front for the Queen's Park Jaguars and Bevendean Barcelona youth sides, and was associated with the Albion as a schoolboy. Receiving coaching at the club's school of excellence in Portslade, Stuart also went on to represent Sussex and earned an international trial, but by the time he joined the Albion staff as a trainee in 1991, the talented youngster had been converted into a defender. He skippered the youth team in 1992–93 and was awarded a professional contract after two years with the club.

Although Stuart first appeared on the bench in February 1993, he made his senior debut as an eighteen-year-old seven months later, one of a number of youngsters drafted into a struggling side, and subsequently impressed at both left-back and in central defence. In May 1994 he won a Sussex Senior Cup medal with Albion reserves, and blossomed during 1994–95 as a regular stand-in for the first-team when more-seasoned professionals were injured or suspended. A whole-hearted and tenacious defender, he looked set for a long run in the side during 1995–96, but then cruelly suffered from hernia and pelvic problems which kept him out of the reckoning for many months. Nevertheless, the continual improvement and promise of the Brighton-born youngster allowed Jimmy Case to release the long-serving Ian Chapman in the summer of 1996, and Stuart established himself as the regular left-back. While still needing to knock some raw edges off his game, he always gives total commitment and looks ready to develop further with greater experience.

Season	FL	FAC	FLC	AMC	Total
1993–94	5+6	0	1	1+1	7+7
1994–95	18+5	1	2	2	23+5
1995–96	7+1	0	2	1	10+1
1996–97	27	0	1	1	29
Total	57+12	1	6	5+1	69+13

TURNBULL, BILLY   1928–29

outside-right   Ht 5 6, Wt 11 00   5 apps
full name: William Turnbull
born: Blyth, Northumberland, c. 1900
debut: Luton Town (a), 25.8.1928 (FL D3(S))

Billy Turnbull's professional career spanned some twelve years and seven senior clubs, but he totalled only 85 Football League appearances and enjoyed his best times in his native Northumberland. After starting out with West Stanley in the North Eastern League,

the young winger joined Cardiff City in May 1922 but appeared just once in their First Division side before moving to Newport County in August 1924. Although he bagged 36 goals for the reserves at Somerton Park, Billy made the first team only six times – scoring four goals – during 1924–25 and returned to the North-East with Ashington at the end of the season to enjoy the most productive spell of his career. Ending the 1925–26 season as leading scorer for the Third Division (North) side with eighteen goals from 34 games, Billy attracted First Division Manchester City who paid £300 for his transfer in March 1926, but he failed to make the first team at Maine Road and was loaned out to Chesterfield for the 1927–28 season; he enjoyed a fair measure of success at Saltergate with ten goals from 29 Northern Section outings.

In August 1928, Charlie Webb brought the diminutive right-winger to the Goldstone. He played in Albion's opening two matches of the season, but, despite a further brief spell in the side in October, he was not a conspicuous success and was released in May 1929 to rejoin Ashington (who, by then, had returned to the North Eastern League). During the summer of 1932, Billy returned to the League ranks with Gateshead, and appeared in ten games in two seasons before joining Oldham Athletic, where he played only a reserve-team role.

Season	FL	Total
1928–29	5	5
Total	5	5

TURNER   1913

centre-forward   1 app
debut: Southend United (a), 23.4.1913 (SA)

Turner was a trialist from the north of England who led the Brighton attack in a crucial Southern Alliance fixture at Southend in April 1913. Albion triumphed by a goal to nil, but just lost out in the championship to Croydon Common. Nothing more was seen of Turner.

Season	SA	Total
1912–13	1	1
Total	1	1

14 players who won Football/Premier League championships

Football League 1888–1992, F.A. Premier League 1992–97.
Players made more than 10 appearances.

Player	Club	Date
Anthony, Walter	Blackburn Rovers	1912
Buckley, Chris	Aston Villa	1910
Case, Jimmy	Liverpool	1976, 1977, 1979, 1980
Holley, George	Sunderland	1913
Jones, Les	Arsenal	1938
Lawrenson, Mark	Liverpool	1982, 1983, 1984, 1986, 1988
Leadbetter, Jimmy	Ipswich Town	1962
McNichol, Johnny	Chelsea	1955
Mortimer, Dennis	Aston Villa	1981
Robertson, Tom	Liverpool	1901
Robinson, Michael	Liverpool	1984
Smith, Bobby	Tottenham Hotspur	1961
Willemse, Stan	Chelsea	1955
Wilson, Alex	Arsenal	1938

TURNER, DAVE   1963–72

half-back   Ht 5 10, Wt 11 12   338 apps, 34 goals
full name: David John Turner
born: Retford, Nottinghamshire, 7.9.1943
debut: Darlington (h), 7.12.1963 (FL D4)

For the best part of nine years Dave Turner was the driving force behind the Albion team, an unspectacular but essential player providing the power in the engine-room of the side. Although he arrived in Hove as a half-back, the dynamic Midlander proved a strong performer both in the back-four and in midfield as the pattern of the game evolved during the 1960s. Fast and direct, he went on to amass 338 games for the club, and appeared in two promotion sides.

As a youngster, Dave represented Nottinghamshire schools and had a couple of trials for England before he joined the Newcastle United ground staff straight from school. Signed as a professional in October 1960, he made his Second Division debut in April 1962 and gained an F.A. Youth Cup winner's medal the same year, but he made only one more appearance in the "Magpies'" first team before Archie Macaulay paid £4,500 for his transfer in December 1963.

The wholehearted 20-year-old was drafted straight into Albion's Fourth Division team and quickly made a name for himself with some sterling displays. Tremendously popular with team-mates and supporters alike, Dave missed just six matches as Albion carried off the Fourth Division championship in 1964–65, and was seldom missing from the line-up over the next five years until he started to suffer from injury problems, perhaps caused by his ferocious tackling. Described as 'imperious' on the ball, he also proved an inspirational skipper from the moment he was installed as captain at the age of 23 in the middle of the 1966–67 campaign.

Dave's last years at the club were plagued by knee problems and he was loaned to Portsmouth in December 1971, but he still managed nineteen games during the 1971–72 Division Three promotion campaign. At the end of the season he was granted a free transfer in recognition of his services and joined Blackburn Rovers in August 1972, but further cartilage problems brought about his retirement in 1974. Dave then had a spell as youth-team manager with Sheffield United, followed by a period as coach and assistant manager at Aldershot. On leaving the 'Shots' he spent ten years in Canada where he was chief coach to the Toronto Blizzards club, but returned to England in 1990 to rejoin the coaching staff at Aldershot for a time.

Season	FL	FAC	FLC	Total
1963–64	23 (2)	0	0	23 (2)
1964–65	40 (2)	1	2	43 (2)
1965–66	46 (5)	3 (1)	3	52 (6)
1966–67	45 (5)	6 (3)	5	56 (8)
1967–68	34+2 (2)	1	2	37+2 (2)
1968–69	35+1 (3)	2	3	40+1 (3)
1969–70	36 (5)	4	3	43 (5)
1970–71	18+1 (3)	0	1	19+1 (3)
1971–72	15+4 (3)	1	1	17+4 (3)
Total	292+8 (30)	18 (4)	20	330+8 (34)

TURNER, TOM   1905–09

full-back   136 apps
full name: Thomas Turner
born: Blantyre, Lanarkshire, Scotland, 8.2.1879
debut: Luton Town (a), 9.9.1905 (SL D1)

Although reputed to be on the slow side, Tom Turner made 136 appearances for the Albion, winning great respect as a full-back and becoming a firm favourite with the Hove fans, but he left the Goldstone Ground on the eve of some of the club's greatest triumphs.

Tom made his name with the famed Lanarkshire junior club Blantyre, and skippered Scotland in two of his four appearances in the junior international team. During the summer of 1905 the 25-year-old Scot was recruited by Frank Scott-Walford, and, although he initially failed to make an impact as Albion lost their opening three matches and struggled throughout the 1905–06 campaign, he came back at Christmas to establish himself as a regular in the side for three years. After four seasons at the Goldstone he was released in May 1909 and returned to Scotland. During the First World War, Tom served with the Cameron Highlanders.

Season	SL	FAC	UL	WL	SCC	Total
1905–06	23	4	7	0	0	34
1906–07	34	1	12	0	0	47
1907–08	21	5	0	10	2	38
1908–09	13	0	0	4	0	17
Total	91	10	19	14	2	136

TUSTIN, BILL   1908–09

goalkeeper   Ht 5 10, Wt 12 03   *4 apps*
full name: William Arthur Tustin
born: Birmingham, Warwickshire, 1882
debut: Southampton (h), 2.9.1908 (SL D1)

A brass-dresser by trade, Bill Tustin set out on an amateur football career with the Birmingham junior clubs Bournbrook and Soho Villa, and progressed to the Birmingham League with Stafford Rangers in 1904. During 1904–05 he came to prominence as Rangers lost 3–0 to Second Division Blackpool in an F.A. Cup sixth-qualifying-round replay after drawing 2–2 at Bloomfield Road; Bill saved an amazing four penalties out of five conceded over the two games. In June 1906 he moved into the Football League as an amateur with Glossop and was subsequently offered a professional engagement, but after 48 Second Division appearances in two seasons for the struggling Derbyshire club he became one of

new Albion manager Jack Robson's numerous recruits during the summer of 1908. Initially preferred to Bob Whiting between the posts, Bill lost his place to the big man after only three games and spent the remainder of 1908–09 in the reserves. On his release at the end of the season he disappeared from the scene, but a year later was reinstated as an amateur to play for an unnamed minor club.

Season	SL	WL	Total
1908–09	3	1	4
Total	3	1	4

TYLER, ALFIE   1913–15

outside-left   *69 apps, 1 goal*
full name: Alfred J. Tyler
born: East Grinstead, Sussex
debut: Southampton (a), 10.9.1913 (SL D1)

Alfie Tyler greatly impressed the Albion management while playing for East Grinstead in the Mid Sussex Senior League, and

particularly caught the eye in the 1912 Sussex Senior Cup final when the north Sussex club was beaten 4–1 by St Leonards Amateurs at the Goldstone Ground. Signed by the Albion in April 1913, the lively outside-left made an immediate impact and played in twelve first-team games as an amateur before being offered a professional engagement in October 1913.

Alfie was first-choice left-winger for the two seasons 1913–15, but then served with the Army throughout the Great War, initially with the Footballers' Battalion of the Middlesex Regiment. While stationed in the London area he guested briefly for Arsenal in each of the four seasons of wartime football, netting three goals in 24 outings in the various emergency competitions, and also for Watford. Albion closed down for the duration of the war and the long lay-off effectively ended Alfie's football career, although he played for Charlton Athletic during 1920–21, their last sea-

son in the Kent League before their election to Division Three (South).

Season	SL	FAC	SA	SCC	Total
1912–13	0	0	2	0	2
1913–14	24 (1)	2	11	1	38 (1)
1914–15	26	3	0	0	29
Total	50 (1)	5	13	1	69 (1)

UPTON, NOBBY   1958–66

half-back   Ht 5 10, Wt 11 00   *44 apps*
full name: Robin Patrick Upton
born: Lincoln, Lincolnshire, 9.11.1942
debut: Southend United (a), 3.11.1962 (FAC R1)

One of the most unfortunate players ever to play for the Albion, 'Nobby' Upton joined the Goldstone staff after skippering Lincoln Schools, and signed as a professional on his seventeenth birthday in November 1959. In his first season he won his Sussex colours at youth level, but had to wait three years for his first-team debut, an F.A. Cup tie at Southend. However, after three games as a wing-half, he underwent an operation on a damaged cartilage which kept him out for most of the remainder of the 1962–63 campaign. The following season Nobby had an extended run at centre-half, but in December 1964 he broke a leg in a reserve match at Leyton Orient. After recovering from this setback, the desperately unlucky 22-year-old broke his leg again in the 1965–66 pre-season and made just one appearance at the end of the campaign.

After a short trial at Torquay United in August 1966, Nobby played in the opening Albion fixture of the season, but it was his last first-team match and he left for Crawley Town on a free transfer three weeks later. In March 1968 he joined the exodus to South Africa to play for Durban

City, but has since returned to Hove and works as a railway inspector.

Season	FL	FAC	FLC	Total
1962–63	3	1	0	4
1963–64	25	0	1	26
1964–65	10	0	2	12
1965–66	1	0	0	1
1966–67	1	0	0	1
Total	40	1	3	44

VALLANCE, HUGH　　　　　　　　1929–30

centre-forward　　　　Ht 5 11, Wt 11 00　　50 apps, 34 goals
full name: Hugh Baird Vallance
born: Wolverhampton, Staffordshire, 14.6.1905
died: Birmingham, Warwickshire, 1973
debut: Swindon Town (h), 14.9.1929 (FL D3(S))

For 47 years, Hughie Vallance was a unique figure in Albion history: the only player to have scored 30 League goals in a season. Yet he arrived at the Goldstone with just one senior game to his name, and his career, while spectacular, was remarkably brief. He was, in truth, a one-season wonder.

Having served as a guardsman, Hugh began his football career as an amateur for Aston Villa in 1927, signing as a professional in January 1928, but had still to make the first team at Villa Park when he was transferred to Queen's Park Rangers four months later. Playing a reserve role at Loftus Road, the Wolverhampton-born forward had just one senior outing before joining the Albion in May 1929.

Hugh scored in his first game for the reserves, and was soon given

a chance in the first team following Geordie Nicol's failure to hit the net. The 24-year-old centre-forward grabbed his opportunity with both hands, scoring on his senior Albion debut, and quickly formed a deadly spearhead with inside-right Dan Kirkwood. By Christmas he had notched four hat-tricks as Albion rose to third place, and, with a sustained display of lethal finishing and power, went on to total 30 goals in just 37 Third Division (South) games, shattering the existing record of 25 League goals set by Jimmy Smith, Tommy Cook and Sam Jennings. He also scored twice in the club's run excellent run to the fifth round of the F.A. Cup. With Kirkwood only one behind his partner, the dynamic twin strike-force amassed an amazing 63 goals for the season.

Following this outstanding performance, though, Hugh's career took a rapid turn for the worse when, after just seven games – and two goals – of the 1930–31 season, he left the Goldstone Ground following a very serious misdemeanour, the details of which were not revealed. Moving into the Birmingham League with Worcester City, he signed for Evesham Town four months later, but returned to the South-East when he began the 1931–32 season with Tunbridge Wells Rangers. Hugh moved back into the Football League with Gillingham in December 1931 – Albion received a £500 fee – but, despite scoring seven goals in thirteen Third Division South appearances, he was released the following May to rejoin the non-League circuit with Kidderminster Harriers.

He didn't remain in Worcestershire for long, though, and was soon trying his luck on the other side of the English Channel, signing for the French club Nimes in September 1932. After a spell in Switzerland with Basle, Hugh's chequered football career ended with a second spell at Gillingham in 1934–35, during which he netted three goals in five outings. He then opted for a more secure profession when he joined the R.A.F. However, his club record for the Albion proved more durable, and wasn't bettered until four years after his death in 1973 when Peter Ward scored 32 Third Division goals in 1976–77.

Season	FL	FAC	Total
1929–30	37 (30)	6 (2)	43 (32)
1930–31	7 (2)	0	7 (2)
Total	44 (32)	6 (2)	50 (34)

VARCO, PERCY　　　　　　　　1932–33

centre-forward　　　　Ht 5 8, Wt 12 00　　　　1 app
full name: Percy Seymour Varco
born: Fowey, Cornwall, 17.4.1904
died: Fowey, Cornwall, 29.1.1982
debut: Coventry City (h), 17.12.1932 (FL D3(S))

Percy Varco looked to have a promising career ahead of him when Aston Villa paid Torquay United £200 for his signature in December 1923, but he played a reserve-team role for most of his time at Villa Park and was transferred to Queen's Park Rangers in June 1926. The Cornish centre-forward enjoyed limited success at Loftus Road, but, on moving to Norwich City in July 1927, he quickly became a great favourite, scoring 47 goals in only 65 League and Cup games and leading the line with great dash and daring. In February 1930 he moved back to the West Country with Exeter City and again performed wonders in the scoring department, hitting 46 goals in 90 League and Cup outings.

Great things were expected of 28-year-old Percy when he joined the Albion in June 1932, but he was plagued by injury and proved a big disappointment: he made the first team just once and managed only seven goals for the reserves. At the end of 1932–33 he was released and was granted for a permit to play as an amateur for St Austell in his native Cornwall. He went on to play for St Blazey and was coach to the Cornish F.A. in 1938–39. Percy later became a fish-merchant and had two terms as mayor of Fowey.

Season	FL	Total
1932–33	1	1
Total	1	1

VASEY, BOB　　　　　　　　1938–39

wing-half　　　　Ht 5 8, Wt 11 00　　16 apps, 1 goal
full name: Robert Henry Vasey
born: Annfield Plain, Co. Durham, 6.12.1907
debut: Notts County (a), 17.12.1938 (FL D3(S))

A late starter in senior football, Bob Vasey was playing for the County Durham side Consett when he had a trial with Nottingham Forest. Initially he declined Forest's terms, but then had a change of heart and signed for the Second Division club in January 1932 at the age of 24. The stocky wing-half made his Football League debut in a 3–1 home win over Spurs in August 1932, and remained at the City Ground for more than four years, totalling 23 League games before crossing the River Trent to join Notts County in June 1936. In 1936–37, Bob made 22 appearances as the 'Magpies' came desperately close to clinching the Third Division (South) championship, but played only five games the following season. Nevertheless, he impressed with a fine performance in County's 1–0 victory at the Goldstone, and after his release from Meadow Lane in May 1938 he was recruited by Albion manager Charlie Webb three months later. Bob broke into the

first team at right-half in the absence of Len Darling in December 1938. The 31-year-old also appeared at left-half and at left-back later in the campaign, but the war effectively brought his career to a close (although he guested briefly for Chester in 1941–42).

Season	FL	SSC	Total
1938–39	15 (1)	1	16 (1)
Total	15 (1)	1	16 (1)

VESSEY, TONY   1978–82

central defender   Ht 5 9, Wt 11 00   1 app
full name: Anthony William Vessey
born: Derby, Derbyshire, 28.11.1961
debut: Coventry City (h), 7.3.1981 (FL D1)

Spotted playing Sunday soccer in his native Derby, Tony Vessey joined the Albion as an apprentice and signed as a full professional in November 1979. He showed considerable promise under Alan Mullery and made his First Division debut as a nineteen-year-old in a 4–1 win over Coventry City, but new manager Mike Bailey put him on the transfer-list the following season and he departed for the Swedish Second Division club Vasalund in March 1982 with just a single senior game to his name.

On returning to Sussex the following October, Tony joined Steyning Town, and then enjoyed four seasons with the excellent Worthing side of the period. In 1987 he switched to Crawley Town where he was to give splendid service over the next few years. A fine reader of the game, he proved an inspirational skipper at Town Mead, clocking up more than 400 appearances, and led his side to a Sussex Senior Cup triumph in 1990. Twice voted Player of the Season, Tony returned to the Goldstone in 1992 when the Southern Leaguers were defeated 5–0 by the Albion in the third round of the F.A. Cup. In December 1994 he was appointed manager of the club following a short period as acting assistant manager, but felt it necessary to resign four months later – having led the 'Reds' to mid-table safety – because of his business commitments as an insurance consultant in Hove. Having hung up his boots because of injury problems, Tony then became reserve-team manager at Town Mead, but he still turned out in the occasional emergency and began to make more regular appearances again in 1996–97. In fact he signed for Burgess Hill Town on a dual registration and assisted them to the County League title. At the end of the season the 35-year-old was granted a benefit match by Crawley against Leyton Orient, the last-ever match staged at Town Mead, before retiring from the game.

Season	FL	Total
1980–81	1	1
Total	1	1

VICKERS, WILF   1947–48

centre-forward   5 apps, 1 goal
full name: Wilfred Vickers
born: Wakefield, Yorkshire, 3.8.1924
debut: Swindon Town (h), 17.9.1947 (FL D3(S))

Wilf Vickers was considered to be a centre-forward of some promise by the local Press when he joined the Albion from a junior club in September 1947, but his career never really took off. The 23-year-old Yorkshireman was unfortunate to arrive at the Goldstone as the club's fortunes reached their nadir. No fewer than eight players wore the

no.9 shirt during the calamitous 1947–48 campaign, and Wilf had little opportunity to impress as the team sank to the bottom of the Third Division (South), resulting in the ignominy of seeking re-election to the Football League for the first and only time. New manager Don Welsh failed to include him on his retained list in May 1948, and so Wilf moved on to West Bromwich Albion where he spent a season in the Central League team before moving to Exeter City for a £750 fee in June 1949. He remained at St James's Park for three years, but made the senior side on just fourteen occasions, scoring once, before returning to non-League football in 1952.

Season	FL	Total
1947–48	5 (1)	5 (1)
Total	5 (1)	5 (1)

VIRGO, JAMES   1995–97

left-back   Ht 5 10, Wt 12 10   2 apps, 1 goal
full name: James Robert Virgo
born: Brighton, Sussex, 21.12.1976
debut: Fulham (h), 22.8.1995 (FLC R1 Lg2)

Signed as a professional directly from school in 1995, James Virgo has an unusual background for a footballer. A youngster with the Hollingbury Hawks boys' team, he won the first sports scholarship to St Aubyn's Preparatory School in Rottingdean in 1987, and won a second scholarship to Ardingly College public school in 1991 (where former Albion forward Gerry Ryan helped with the coaching). The young full-back won a number of honours with his school, and also made a number of appearances in the Albion youth team and reserves while studying for his A-levels. In fact, he was named as a substitute for a Second Division game against Hull City in April 1995 but wasn't called upon.

Blessed with a powerful shot in his 'educated' left foot, James made his senior debut just a couple of weeks into his first professional season in August 1995. With the release of Ian Chapman at the end of 1995–96 he looked sure of greater involvement with the first-team squad, but Stuart Tuck and Kerry Mayo were both preferred in the no.3 shirt and James made just one more senior appearance before being released in May 1997 to try his luck with Sutton United. It was, however, a game the youngster will never forget. In sudden-death extra-time in the Associate Members Cup (Auto Windscreens Shield) he rifled a 'peach' of a free-kick into the Fulham net to seal an Albion win — truly a 'golden' goal!

Season	FLC	AMC	Total
1995–96	0+1	0	0+1
1996–97	0	1 (1)	1 (1)
Total	0+1	1 (1)	1+1 (1)

VITTY, JACK   1949–52

full-back   Ht 6 0, Wt 12 00   50 apps, 1 goal
full name: John Vitty
born: Windlestone, Co. Durham, 19.1.1923
debut: Notts County (h), 22.10.1949 (FL D3(S))

Jack Vitty served in the Royal Marines during the Second World War, and played briefly for South Shields and Boldon Villa on his demob before joining Charlton Athletic in November 1946. In nearly three years at The Valley he made only two appearances in the First Division side, but signed for the Albion in October 1949 when manager Don Welsh paid his former club £3,000 for the 26-year-old full-back. Plunged straight into first-team duty, Jack then shared the left-back berth with Jack Mansell for two seasons before switching to the right flank, but he couldn't contend with the form of regular no.2 Des

Tennant and asked for a transfer in the hope of finding regular first-team football. In July 1952 his ambition was fulfilled when he joined Workington, and the strapping six-footer went on to make 196 appearances in the Third Division (North), becoming skipper under manager Bill Shankly. In 1957 he returned to his roots with South Shields, and moved back to Boldon Villa three years later.

After leaving the full-time game Jack worked for British Steel in Jarrow, and then for a chemical company until 1980 when he had a five-year stint in Saudi Arabia. He now lives in retirement in Eaglescliffe, County Durham, and relaxes on the golf course. As a boy in South Shields, Jack played for the same school team as future England star Stan Mortensen. His younger brother Ron joined him at the Goldstone in 1951–52 after spells with Charlton Athletic, Hartlepools United and Bradford City, but didn't make the first team. Another brother, Jim, also had a spell on Charlton's staff.

Season	FL	FAC	Total
1949–50	28	1	29
1950–51	15	2	17
1951–52	4 (1)	0	4 (1)
Total	47 (1)	3	50 (1)

WADE, BRYAN   1990–92

forward   Ht 5 8, Wt 11 05   22 apps, 9 goals
full name: Bryan Alexander Wade
born: Bath, Somerset, 25.6.1963
debut: Middlesbrough (h), 27.10.1990 (FL D2)

Bryan Wade enjoyed only a brief Albion career, but he will always be remembered for one magnificent feat: scoring all four goals in a 4–2 win over Newcastle United at the Goldstone in January 1990, his first full home match.

The stocky little forward had enjoyed a chequered career before his arrival in Hove. Having started out with his home-town club, Bath City, in the Alliance Premier League, he joined nearby Trowbridge Town in the Southern League, and entered the Football League ranks in May 1985 with Swindon Town for whom he played 60 League games. Bryan's best season at the County Ground was 1985–86, when he scored ten times as the 'Robins' lifted the Fourth Division title, but in August 1988 he was transferred to Swansea City. Almost half of his 36 League appearances for the 'Swans' came as a substitute and he was plagued by injuries, but he gained a Welsh Cup winner's medal in 1989 when City beat Kidderminster Harriers 5–0 at the Vetch.

Released at the end of the 1989–90 campaign, Bryan had a short spell at with Haverfordwest, but in September 1990 Albion manager Barry Lloyd offered the 27-year-old a trial and he responded with a hat-trick in his first match for the reserves, a 5–0 win over Southampton. Offered a contract the following month, he suffered a hamstring injury which kept him on the sideline for several weeks, but, after one game as substitute, he scored on his full debut at Wolverhampton and entered the record books in the next game with his four-goal haul, the first by

an Albion player since Peter Ward over fourteen years earlier. Quick and willing, Bryan maintained a good scoring rate in the few opportunities that came his way, but his role was mainly that of a reserve – he hit three hat-tricks for the second XI – until his release following Albion's relegation to the new Second Division in May 1992. Forced to quit the full-time game because of a knee injury, he continued to play for Frome Town in the Western League in 1992–93, and returned to Trowbridge Town in the Southern League for 1993–94.

Season	FL	FAC	FMC	Total
1990–91	5+6 (6)	1	0+1	6+7 (6)
1991–92	7 (3)	1+1	0	8+1 (3)
Total	12+6 (9)	2+1	0+1	14+8 (9)

WAITES, GEORGE   1962–65

outside-right   Ht 5 9, Wt 11 00   24 apps, 1 goal
full name: George Edward Waites
born: Stepney, London, 12.3.1938
debut: Coventry City (h), 1.12.1962 (FL D3)

After playing in Norfolk junior football, George Waites enjoyed a stint in the Army and turned out for the Harwich & Parkeston club in the Eastern Counties League before joining Leyton Orient as an amateur in September 1958. Offered professional terms three months later, the cockney winger remained at Brisbane Road until January 1961 when he was exchanged for Norwich City's Errol Crossan in a bid to strengthen the "Canaries'" squad on their promotion to the Second Division. George proved quite a success at Carrow Road, scoring eleven goals in 40 League outings, but he moved back to Brisbane Road in July 1962, and five months later became one of George Curtis's signings during the calamitous season which saw the Albion relegated to Division Four.

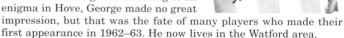

George cost Brighton £8,000, but he was unable to settle at the Goldstone and failed to win a regular place. One of five players given a free transfer at the end of 1963–64, he had a very brief spell with Millwall in April 1965 and then joined Gravesend & Northfleet in the Southern League. Something of an enigma in Hove, George made no great impression, but that was the fate of many players who made their first appearance in 1962–63. He now lives in the Watford area.

Season	FL	FLC	Total
1962–63	15 (1)	0	15 (1)
1963–64	8	1	9
Total	23 (1)	1	24 (1)

WAKE, TOM   1910–13

half-back   22 apps
full name: Thomas Wake
born: Richmond, Yorkshire
debut: Queen's Park Rangers (h), 29.10.1910 (SL D1)

Brought to the Goldstone from North Eastern League side Darlington during the summer of 1910, Tom Wake found his first-team opportunities limited by the consistency of regular centre-half Joe McGhie, but he turned in countless excellent displays for the reserves over two-and-a-half years, and his fine form for the 'Lambs' won him a place in the South Eastern League's representative side against the North Eastern League in 1911. Despite the lack of regular first-team football, Tom did turn out in all three half-back positions for the senior side and proved a capable deputy. Strangely, his one F.A. Cup appearance for the Albion came in the 2–1 first-round upset at Darlington in January 1912. During his third season with the club Tom suffered from a serious illness and was forced to retire in February 1913, although he subsequently played again for Darlington.

Season	SL	FAC	SA	SCC	Total
1910–11	10	0	0	5	15
1911–12	5	1	0	0	6
1912–13	0	0	1	0	1
Total	15	1	1	5	22

WALKER, BOB — 1962–63

right-half — *13 apps, 1 goal*
full name: Robert Walker
born: Wallsend, Northumberland, 23.7.1942
debut: Halifax Town (a), 15.9.1962 (FL D3)

Signed by Albion manager George Curtis from Northern Counties League side Gateshead in May 1962, Bob Walker deputised for Jack Bertolini in a pre-season friendly against Chelsea, but had to wait until Bertolini was switched to right-back in mid September before getting an extended run in the League side. However, when Syd Jest was drafted into the side at right-back, Bertolini reverted to right-half and the 20-year-old Geordie returned to reserve-team duties. In May 1963 he was given a free transfer and moved into the Southern League with Ashford, but joined Hartlepools United in the Fourth Division for a brief spell in August 1964 before returning to the Southern League with Margate. Bob resumed his Football League career with Bournemouth in January 1965, and signed for Colchester United on a free transfer in July 1967, where he made seventeen League appearances before drifting back into non-League football with Dover and Salisbury.

Season	FL	FLC	Total
1962–63	12 (1)	1	13 (1)
Total	12 (1)	1	13 (1)

WALKER, CLIVE — 1990–93

winger — Ht 5 7, Wt 11 09 — *130 apps, 12 goals*
born: Oxford, Oxfordshire, 26.5.1957
debut: Barnsley (a), 25.8.1990 (FL D2)

Although he was 33 when he joined the Albion, Clive Walker proved a great asset to the club after a rocky start and contributed a great deal over three seasons. With a wealth of experience behind him, the speedy winger was an essential member of the side which reached the Second Division play-off final in 1991, providing many an opportunity for strikers Mike Small and John Byrne as well as hitting some cracking goals himself.

An Oxford and England Schools representative, Clive became an apprentice with Chelsea and signed as a full professional in March 1975. In ten excellent years at 'The Bridge' (although he spent the summer of 1979 with Fort Lauderdale in U.S.A.), he scored 65 goals in 224 League and Cup appearances, a highly creditable strike-rate for a player who was predominantly a winger, but he also suffered a number of injuries which restricted his appearances towards the end of his time with the club. In July 1984 he moved to Sunderland for £75,000, but his first season in the North-East was somewhat mixed: his club was relegated to the Second Division, and also lost the League Cup final 1–0 to Norwich City with Clive missing a penalty. Signed by Queen's Park Rangers in December 1985, he failed to make an

impact at Loftus Road and was subsequently transferred to Fulham in October 1987, where he netted 29 times in 109 League outings; in 1989–90 he was top scorer with fifteen goals for the Third Division side.

Brighton manager Barry Lloyd paid £20,000 for the fleet-footed veteran in August 1990 and he went on to give the club a good return for its investment until he was released in May 1993. After trials with Swansea City and Slough Town, Clive subsequently joined Woking in the Conference where he was played as an out-and-out striker. Such was his success in the position that he top-scored for the Surrey side in his first season, 1993–94, and also helped them to F.A. Trophy triumphs at Wembley in 1994, 1995 and 1997. In 1994–95 he was voted Conference Player of the Season, and was awarded a testimonial against Chelsea in 1996. He also made an appearance for an F.A. representative eleven against the Isthmian League in December 1996, but was released at the end of the season.

Working as an antiques-buyer and also coaching at Queen's Park Rangers' centre of excellence while with Woking, Clive moved back into the game full-time as assistant to Eddie May at Brentford for 1997–98 after trials with Sutton United and Hastings Town.

Season	FL	Play-offs	FAC	FLC	FMC	AMC	Total
1990–91	44 (3)	3 (1)	3	2	3	0	55 (4)
1991–92	23 (2)	0	2 (1)	0	0+1	0	25+1 (3)
1992–93	36+2 (3)	0	4	4	0	3 (2)	47+2 (5)
Total	103+2 (8)	3 (1)	9 (1)	6	3+1	3 (2)	127+3 (12)

WALKER, DAVE — 1929–39

wing-half — Ht 5 8, Wt 11 00 — *349 apps, 30 goals*
full name: David Walker
born: Walsall, Staffordshire, 1908
debut: Northampton Town (a), 2.11.1929 (FL D3(S))

Once a clerk on the London, Midland & Scottish Railway, Dave Walker was one of a number of long-serving players who performed splendidly for the club in over 300 games between the wars. Yet he only established himself in the Albion first team when he switched positions and found his true vocation after more than three years at the Goldstone. A wholehearted performer, he then became an automatic choice until the outbreak of war.

Born in Walsall, Dave began his football career in the Midland Amateur League with Walsall Town and the L.M.S. Railway club, where he came to the attention of the Walsall management. Signed as a professional at the age of eighteen in September 1926, he scored seven goals in 20 League games as a forward for the 'Saddlers' before coming to Hove in August 1929. In his first three seasons with the Albion, Dave was a regular in the reserves and made just 36 first-team appearances, mainly as an inside-forward, but after being given a run at left-half in December 1932 he went on to make the position his own, linking up in a superb left-sided 'triangle' with Potter

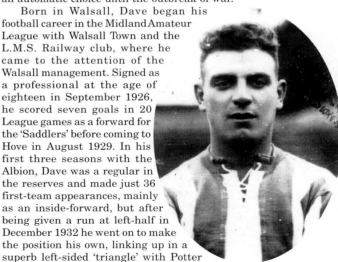

Smith and Tug Wilson. In fact, after adopting his new role Dave missed only fourteen games in the six-and-a-half seasons before the Second World War, and was a driving-force in the half-back line that made Albion such a formidable proposition in the Third Division (South) in the latter 1930s. A strongly-built player with a biting tackle, he took over the captaincy on the departure of Smith in 1937 and skippered the team until his retirement in May 1939. After eight years at the Goldstone, Dave was granted a testimonial match in April 1937, Albion drawing 1–1 with Second Division Southampton.

Season	FL	FAC*	SSC	Total
1929–30	6 (1)	0	0	6 (1)
1930–31	14 (7)	0	0	14 (7)
1931–32	15 (6)	0	0	15 (6)
1932–33*	36 (1)	10 (1)	0	46 (2)
1933–34	41 (2)	3 (1)	5	49 (3)
1934–35	42 (2)	3	2	47 (2)
1935–36	38 (3)	5	2	45 (3)
1936–37	40 (3)	1	1	42 (3)
1937–38	38 (2)	4	1	43 (2)
1938–39	40 (1)	1	1	42 (1)
Total	310 (28)	27 (2)	12	349 (30)

Note: Three of Walker's 1932–33 F.A. Cup appearances came in the qualifying competition.

WALKER, JIM — 1974–76

midfield	Ht 5 8, Wt 11 00	32 apps, 4 goals

full name: James McIntyre Walker
born: Northwich, Cheshire, 10.6.1947
debit: AFC Bournemouth (a), 21.9.1974 (FL D3)

Signed in September 1974 (in a £25,000 deal which also included his Derby County colleague Tommy Mason), Jim Walker made little impact at the Goldstone, a great disappointment to manager Peter Taylor who had been impressed by the midfielder while assistant to Brian Clough at the Baseball Ground. After starting out with his

home-town club, Northwich Victoria, in the Northern Premier League, Jim joined Derby in February 1968 and helped the 'Rams' to the Second Division title in his first full season. In March 1970 he had a ten-match loan spell at Hartlepool, but returned to Derby as a fringe player during the club's heady days as one of the most attractive sides in the country, and made six outings in their 1971–72 championship side.

His career on the South Coast never took off, though, and after being suspended along with six other players for a poor showing in a reserve-team game he was put on the transfer list and loaned to Peterborough United in October 1975. Jim joined the 'Posh' on a permanent basis for a £6,000 fee in February 1976, and the following November was transferred to Chester for whom he made 172 League appearances over almost six seasons, mostly at left-back. In 1982 he was appointed coach to the Middle Eastern club Al-Arabi, but returned to England in 1985 to join Blackburn Rovers as physiotherapist. Two years later Jim took a similar post with Aston Villa, a position he still holds.

Season	FL	FAC	FLC	Total
1974–75	23+4 (4)	3	0	26+4 (4)
1975–76	1	0	1	2
Total	24+4 (4)	3	1	28+4 (4)

WARD, ALF — 1904–05

outside-right	Ht 5 10, Wt 12 00	5 apps, 3 goals

full name: Alfred Ward
born: Eastwood, Nottinghamshire, 1883
died: Burton upon Trent, Staffordshire, August 1926
debut: Wellingborough Town (a), 17.9.1904 (SL D1)

Alf Ward joined Notts County from Clowne White Star in October 1903, and made seven First Division appearances during the remainder of the 1903–04 season before coming to the Goldstone in

May 1904. The 20-year-old winger bagged a hat-trick in his first game for the reserves, a 6–0 win over Wycombe Wanderers, and was quickly promoted to the senior team, but he failed to fulfil his early promise despite registering another three-goal haul in a 7–1 F.A. Cup defeat of Shoreham.

In May 1905, Alf departed for Aberdeen on their promotion to Division One of the Scottish League, and remained in the 'Granite City' for two seasons, scoring ten goals in 27 matches. He moved back to England with Bradford (Park Avenue) during the close season of 1907, when the newly formed Yorkshire outfit was admitted, somewhat bizarrely, to the Southern League after its bid to join the Football League had proved unsuccessful, and returned to the South Coast with Southampton in May 1908. After sustaining a knee injury on a close-season Continental tour, Alf made just four Southern League appearances for the 'Saints' before retiring at the end of the 1908–09 season.

Season	SL	FAC	Total
1904–05	3	2 (3)	5 (3)
Total	3	2 (3)	5 (3)

WARD, PETER — 1975–80 & 1982–83

forward	Ht 5 7, Wt 10 03	227 apps, 95 goals

full name: Peter David Ward
born: Lichfield, Staffordshire, 27.7.1955
debut: Hereford United (a), 27.3.1976 (FL D3)

Over the four seasons 1976–80, the average League gate at the Goldstone was more than 23,000. It was no coincidence that the leading scorer in each of those campaigns was Peter Ward. The quicksilver striker was the star of the show as Albion surged from the Third Division to the First, and his presence on the Goldstone turf brought thousands of fans flocking through the turnstiles. Quite simply, Peter Ward was magic, and probably gave more pleasure to more people in Sussex than anyone else in history!

Yet, at school in Derby he was considered too small to become a professional footballer and initially found employment as an apprentice engine-fitter with Rolls-Royce instead. Peter played his football for Borrowash Victoria in the Derby Combination, but soon stepped up to Southern League fare when he joined nearby Burton Albion. With a decent record of 21 goals from 50 games to his name, the young striker came to Brighton's attention when the Burton manager, Ken Guttridge, became coach at the Goldstone. Albion boss Peter Taylor first bid for 'Wardy' late in 1974, and landed his man in May 1975 for around £4,000. Quickly earning rave reviews in the reserves, Peter received his first opportunity in the senior side against promotion rivals Hereford United in March 1976. It turned out to be a dream debut for the 21-year-old: with his first touch in League football, he scored Albion's goal in a 1–1 draw after just 50 seconds — and all in front of the *Match of the Day* cameras!

The dream continued unabated for some time. With six goals from eight games as Albion just missed out on promotion in 1975–76, Peter demonstrated the skills and finishing which took the Third Division by storm the following term. Able to turn on a sixpence, he simply bemused opponents with his pacy dribbling, speed off the mark, and uncanny instinct for hitting the target. As Albion surged to promotion in 1976–77 on the back of his natural talent, 'Wardy' topped the national scoring charts with 36 goals in League and Cup, the only Brighton player ever to do so, and broke a club record which had lasted since the 1930s. In 1977–78, as Albion pushed for a second promotion, Peter came third in a national poll for country's most popular footballer, and his abilities were recognised on the international stage in September 1977 when he was selected for the England under-21s against Norway at Hove; he responded by scoring a hat-trick in a 6–0 win! Following that success he was named in the full England squad to play Luxemburg in October by Ron Greenwood, but failed to win even a place on the bench when the game was played.

After such an outstanding start, it was only natural that Peter suffered a comparative loss of form thereafter. Although he again led the scorers in 1978–79 as Albion made it to the First Division, the star striker had an indifferent season and asked for a transfer in the summer. Happily, the differences were settled on the eve of the club's debut in the top flight, but a moderate start to life in Division One prompted manager Alan Mullery to arrange a swap for Derby County's Gerry Daly in November 1979, a deal which Daly rejected. A few days later, though, Albion accepted a bid of £600,000 from Nottingham Forest (where his former Brighton boss Peter Taylor was assistant manager). The final decision was left to the player, but then Forest manager Brian Clough withdrew the offer and the deal fell through.

Coincidentally, bottom-of-the-table Albion were due at the City Ground, where European champions Forest were unbeaten for 51 matches, two days later. 'Wardy' positively sparkled in Albion's shock win, and suddenly the clouds lifted from both the club and its chief – but apparently unwanted – striker who went on to hit sixteen First Division goals for the season. In April, Peter gained a second under-21 cap, against East Germany, and the following month he came on as a sub. for the last eight minutes for England v. Australia in Sydney, only the second Albion player to win a full England cap – Tommy Cook was the first. He also equalled the shortest England career on record, that of West Ham United's Jimmy Barrett in 1928.

It was hoped that the rejuvenated goalscorer would strike up a successful partnership with expensive acquisition Michael Robinson in 1980–81, but, despite being selected for the England B squad against the U.S.A., Peter managed just two goals in fourteen games. When Forest renewed their interest in October 1980, the 25-year-old forward left the Goldstone for Nottingham, one side of a transfer triangle involving Forest's Gary Birtles and Manchester United's Andy Ritchie.

Valued at £450,000, the former Albion favourite found life at the City Ground rather difficult and was consigned to the reserves five months later. In and out of the League side, he was loaned to Seattle Sounders in March 1982 and enjoyed a tremendous season in the N.A.S.L., winning the national Player of the Year accolade as the Sounders finished runners-up in the Soccer Bowl. In October 1982 it appeared that he was to sign permanently for Seattle, but the deal was not finalised and instead he rejoined the Albion on loan.

Peter's return to his spiritual home immediately added around 8,000 to the Goldstone attendances, but after four months Brian Clough turned down a further extension to his loan and he returned to Nottingham. In November 1983, at the age of 28, Peter quit England and signed for Vancouver Whitecaps for £20,000. He subsequently played in the American indoor league for Cleveland Force and Tacoma Stars, and then moved back to Seattle before joining Tampa Bay Rowdies in June 1989; he also played in Baltimore and Wichita. In October 1990 he returned to England to play a few games for Hednesford Town in the Southern League, but then moved back to the States. For many years he ran a bar in Tampa, Florida, where he now coaches children and plays for a team called Rose & Crown in the local soccer league. Possibly the most popular player in the history of the club, Peter returned to play for the Albion just once more, teaming up with his old striking-partner Ian Mellor for Gerry Ryan's testimonial in August 1986. But for many supporters 'Wardy' will

always be around, occupying a special place in the hearts of those who witnessed his outstanding feats.

Season	FL	FAC	FLC	Total
1975–76	8 (6)	0	0	8 (6)
1976–77	46 (32)	3 (1)	7 (3)	56 (36)
1977–78	39 (14)	2 (1)	5 (2)	46 (17)
1978–79	27+5 (10)	0	3+1 (3)	30+6 (13)
1979–80	41+1 (16)	2	3 (2)	46+1 (18)
1980–81	11 (1)	0	3 (1)	14 (2)
1982–83	16 (2)	3 (1)	1	20 (3)
Total	188+6 (81)	10 (3)	22+1 (11)	220+7 (95)

WARD, W, 1903–04

inside/outside-right 3 apps, 5 goals
debut: Hitchin Town (h), 25.3.1903 (SEL)

A member of the Hove Park club, Ward appeared in the Albion's South Eastern League team towards the end of 1902–03 (when the first eleven competed in the tournament) and scored twice in a 9–1 victory over Hitchin Town on his debut. In his second appearance he scored a hat-trick against Bedford Queen's Engineering Works, and continued to play for the reserves on occasion until 1905.

Ward played a major role as Hove Park won the Mid Sussex Senior League title and the Brighton Challenge Shield in 1904–05, then switched his allegiance to Hove F.C. where he gained further success. He appeared in the side which lost the 1906 Sussex Senior Cup final, but gained a winner's medal the following year when Hove thrashed Eastbourne 4–0 at the Goldstone in a replay.

Season	SEL	Total
1902–03	3 (5)	3 (5)
Total	3 (5)	3 (5)

WARREN, CHRISTER 1996

forward Ht 5 10, Wt 11 04 3 apps
full name: Christer Simon Warren
born: Poole, Dorset, 10.10.1974
debut: Cambridge United (h), 12.10.1996 (FL D3)

Christer Warren arrived at the Goldstone on loan in October 1996 as Jimmy Case desperately sought a line-up to lift the Albion off the bottom of the Football League, but the frail-looking 22-year-old never looked like being the answer to the manager's prayers. Although he had one or two chances, he failed to hit the net and all three of the games in which he played were lost.

A Dorset county representative as a youngster, Christer came to prominence with the Cheltenham Town team which finished second in the Southern League three seasons running. During 1994–95 he had nine goals to his name when Southampton splashed out £60,000 for his services in March, a Cheltenham club record. He immediately returned to Whaddon Road on loan to the end of the season, but when he arrived at The Dell he found his chances severely limited and he has made the starting line-up on just two occasions. Christer came to Hove as a stand-in for the absent Ian Baird with a reputation as a pacy, direct forward, but his disappointing loan-spell was cut short by injury. After returning to the Southampton reserves he joined Fulham on loan in March 1997 where he scored once in eleven games.

Season	FL	Total
1996–97	3	3
Total	3	3

WATSON, HAROLD
1931–33

right-half   Ht 5 9, Wt 11 07   6 apps
born: Wath upon Dearne, Yorkshire, 23.3.1908
died: Staffordshire, 1982
debut: Thames (h), 26.3.1932 (FL D3(S))

After joining Stoke City as an eighteen-year-old half-back in August 1926, Harold Watson showed early promise and was a regular member of the reserve team that carried off the Central League title in 1927–28. His senior debut came at centre-half in a 5–1 defeat at Leeds United on Christmas Eve 1927, but he had only four Second Division games under his belt in five seasons when Albion signed him in July 1931.

Harold fared little better at the Goldstone where, although he was capable of filling any of the half-back berths, he was forced to play second fiddle to the likes of Reg Wilkinson, Paul Mooney and Harry Dutton. In his first season with the club, 1931–32, Harold made the League side just twice, and he had to continue his back-up role the following season when he played in a further four matches – none of which was won – before being released into non-League football in May 1933 at the age of 25.

Season	FL	Total
1931–32	2	2
1932–33	4	4
Total	6	6

WATSON, JIMMY
1945–46

left-back   Ht 5 10, Wt 12 07   20 apps, 2 goals
full name: William James Boyd Watson
born: Durham, Co. Durham, 1.1.1914
died: Bristol, Gloucestershire, 1979
debut: Aldershot (h), 3.11.1945 (wartime)
peacetime debut: Walthamstow Avenue (a), 8.12.1945 (FAC R2 Lg1)

Durham-born Jimmy Watson started out in the Scottish Central League with the St Anthony's club of Glasgow, but in his late teens he came south to Tunbridge Wells Rangers, and entered the Football League with Bristol Rovers in May 1933. After fourteen League matches he moved to Northampton Town in January 1934, and then on to Gillingham in August 1935. Playing as an inside-forward, Jimmy enjoyed his best times in a three-year spell at Priestfield; he hit 38 goals in 110 League games, and was the

leading scorer in 1936–37 and 1937–38. However, when the 'Gills' failed to gain re-election in 1938 he joined Notts County for £1,000, then re-signed for Bristol Rovers in July 1939.

War was to break out a few weeks later, though, and Jimmy guested for Blackpool and Bradford City. In 1945–46 he turned out at left-back for the Albion. Making his first appearance in win over Aldershot at Hove on 3 November, the ginger-haired North-Easterner was signed permanently four weeks later to enable him to play in the F.A. Cup tournament, which had been resurrected after an absence of six years (and was for registered players only). However, when things returned to normal in August 1946, Jimmy was 32 and didn't resume his Football League career.

Season	FAC	Wartime	Total
1945–46	6	14 (2)	20 (2)
Total	6	14 (2)	20 (2)

WEBB, CHARLIE
1908–15

inside-left   Ht 5 8, Wt 12 00   275 apps, 79 goals
full name: Charles Graham Webb
born: Curragh Camp, Co. Kildare, Ireland, 14.9.1886
died: Hove, Sussex, 13.6.1973
debut: West Ham United (a), 2.1.1909 (SL D1)

From 1919 until 1947, Charlie Webb was 'Mr Albion'. In that period of 28 years, he took charge of 1,215 matches, by far the greatest tenure of any Brighton manager, and won the respect of everyone in the world of football. Having already enjoyed an outstanding career as an inside-forward in 275 games before the First World War, he was involved at the Goldstone for a total of 40 years and undoubtedly ranks as one of the central figures in the club's history.

Born at The Curragh, a massive military camp to the south-west of Dublin, Charlie came from a line of Scottish soldiers – his father and grandfather both served in the Black Watch – and spent his childhood in Edinburgh Castle. In 1904, at the age of seventeen, he himself joined the Army and was posted to Ireland with the Essex Regiment, enabling him to turn out for the Bohemians club of Dublin.

Between tours of duty Charlie also played for Worthing with great success, and helped them to a 'treble' of Sussex Senior Cup, Royal Irish Rifles Cup and West Sussex Senior League in both 1904 and 1908. In March 1908 he had a trial with Glasgow Rangers, and was chosen to represent the Irish League v. Football League in October. The following month he won an Irish amateur cap, scoring the only goal in a 5–1 defeat by England.

In December 1908, Charlie was invited to assist the Albion and made his Southern League debut at West Ham a few days later, scoring in a 1–1 draw; but when the Army authorities discovered that he had appeared with a professional club, they banned him for twelve months and a subsequent F.A. inquiry fined Albion £5. Faced with the prospect of being unable to play football, Charlie immediately purchased his release from service and joined the Albion as an amateur, returning to the side in February 1909. A series of splendid displays soon attracted the attention of the Irish selectors, and the following month he became the first player to gain international honours while wearing the club's colours, winning full caps against Scotland and Wales.

In 1909–10 the 23-year-old inside-forward played in every League game, scoring nine goals as Albion won the Southern League championship and the Southern Charity Cup, and he scored the only goal in the F.A. Charity Shield triumph over Aston Villa the following September, one of the club's greatest-ever achievements. Still an amateur, he received a gold tie-pin for his efforts while his team-mates received money from a players' fund, but he subsequently signed professional forms. In March 1911 he won a third full cap, against Scotland, and represented the Southern League v. Football League in September 1912.

A superbly-built athlete, Charlie top-scored in 1912–13 and went on to score more Southern League goals (64) than any other Albion player, vying with Bert Longstaff for the club's all-time scoring record. However, his playing career was effectively brought to an end by a serious leg injury sustained during a match with Millwall at the Goldstone in November 1914, although he did play a few games towards the end of 1914–15.

When the Great War broke out, Charlie, as an ex-soldier, led the other Albion players in rifle-drill on the Goldstone pitch (initially with wooden replicas until the real items could be obtained). He then rejoined the Army and was commissioned as a second lieutenant with the King's Royal Rifle Corps, later reaching the rank of captain. In March 1918, though, Captain Webb was captured by the Germans in France and spent the remaining eight months of the war as a prisoner in Mainz. It was during this internment that Albion chairman Henry Miles offered him the position of manager at the Goldstone by post. Having duly accepted the proposition, the 32-year-old former player returned to Hove on his demob in June 1919 to begin the formidable task of rebuilding both the team and the ground.

His first action was to seek the advice of his former boss, Jack Robson, a move which demonstrated the shrewd mind of the new manager. With supporters rallying around to help re-establish the Albion, Charlie brought back a number of old favourites, signed some excellent new players who went on to serve the club splendidly, and by August all was ready for the big kick-off as football returned to normality. During the following season, Brighton's first in the Football League, he received a benefit and collected £495 15s. 11d. from the Third Division game with Watford on 23 April which attracted around 10,000 fans.

A keen judge of talent, he brought some excellent players to the Goldstone within a very limited budget over the next 20 years, and put together some fine teams which finished in the top five of the Third Division (South) on ten occasions. In fact he was offered the manager's job at Tottenham Hotspur, but turned it down, preferring to stay with the club he loved. Well respected by his players, who always referred to him as 'Mr Webb', he would sit in the directors' box continually puffing on a cigarette.

During the Second World War, Charlie was very much responsible for keeping the Albion running from day to day against, on occasion, seemingly impossible odds. He also served as an officer in the Home Guard. When the game returned to normal he remained in charge of the side, but in May 1947, at the age of 60, he made way for his former star, Tommy Cook, to run team affairs. Charlie continued as general manager, looking after administration, but retired from the Goldstone in 1948 when Don Welsh took over as secretary-manager.

Charlie passed away in 1973 at the age of 86, and a tree was planted in Hove Park to his memory by his daughter, Joyce. Always a gentleman in a very hard business, he won the respect and affection of the numerous players that passed through his care at the Goldstone, and gained admiration throughout the professional game which showed its appreciation with a long-service award. In September 1949 he enjoyed a second benefit, First Division Arsenal and Portsmouth playing in a testimonial match at the Goldstone before a gate of more than 13,000. The 'Gunners' presented him with a gold cigarette-case as a token of their esteem for one of the game's greatest servants.

Fortunately for historians of the club, Charlie was an excellent chronicler and kept many notes of his Albion dealings. He wrote a series of articles for the *Sussex Daily News* providing a revealing insight into life behind the scenes at the Goldstone in its early days.

Season	SL	FAC	FACS	WL	WL Ch.	SA	SCC	Total
1908–09	15 (5)	0	0	1	2	0	2	20 (5)
1909–10	42 (9)	1	0	0	0	0	3	46 (9)
1910–11	33 (14)	3	1 (1)	0	0	0	5 (1)	42 (16)
1911–12	38 (17)	1	0	0	0	0	3 (1)	42 (18)
1912–13	37 (10)	3 (1)	0	0	0	13 (2)	0	53 (13)
1913–14	36 (9)	4 (2)	0	0	0	13 (7)	1	54 (18)
1914–15	18	0	0	0	0	0	0	18
Total	219 (64)	12 (3)	1 (1)	1	2	26 (9)	14 (2)	275 (79)

WEBB, STAN   1924–35

goalkeeper   Ht 5 11, Wt 12 02   234 apps
full name: Sydney John Webb
born: Portslade-by-Sea, Sussex, 6.1.1906
died: Australia, January 1994
debut: Millwall (h), 14.10.1925 (FL D3(S))

'Stan' Webb, as he was always known, was a locally-born goalkeeper who proved a capable first-team custodian for over five years.

Indeed, he was the first local lad to play in 200 Football League games for the Albion.

In March 1924, Stan was working at the Brighton & Hove General Gas Company's works on the harbour arm at Portslade and playing football for Hove in the Sussex County League when he had a trial in the Albion reserves. Two months later he signed professional forms, but spent the 1924–25 season with Tunbridge Wells Rangers in the Southern League to gain experience. On returning to the Goldstone, Stan made his League debut at the age of nineteen and shared the goalkeeping jersey with Walter Cook, playing in 22 League matches during 1925–26, but he then served a lengthy apprenticeship in the reserves as understudy to 'Skilly' Williams until December 1928 when the 38-year-old veteran was injured. In 1931 he enjoyed a benefit, a joint affair with Paul Mooney, but also made way for Joe Duckworth before resuming his role between the posts to clock up 234 first-team appearances, a total second only to Bob Whiting for an Albion goalkeeper at the time.

In 1934, Stan lost his place to Charlie Thomson and spent a year in the reserves before returning to Tunbridge Wells Rangers in August 1935. A year later he joined Southwick where he remained until the war, gaining a Sussex Senior Cup winner's medal in 1937. Also a fine cricketer, he played for Sussex Club & Ground as a wicket-keeper for some years, and was baggage and travel manager – as well as travelling twelfth man – for several years for the Sussex C.C.C. In 1948, Stan emigrated to Australia where he remained until his death in 1994.

Season	FL	FAC*	SSC	Total
1925–26	22	2	0	24
1926–27	3	0	0	3
1928–29	22	0	0	22
1929–30	41	6	0	47
1930–31	30	2	0	32
1931–32	17	0	0	17
1932–33*	37	11	0	48
1933–34	33	3	5	41
Total	205	24	5	234

Note: Four of Webb's 1932–33 F.A. Cup appearances came in the qualifying competition.

WEBBER, KEITH   1963–64

forward   Ht 5 10, Wt 12 00   38 apps, 15 goals
full name: Keith James Webber
born: Cardiff, Glamorgan, Wales, 5.1.1943
died: Wrexham, Denbighshire, Wales, 1983
debut: Bournemouth & B.A. (h), 13.4.1963 (FL D3)

Keith Webber was a fair athlete – he was a Cardiff schools sprint champion – and also a talented rugby player – he played for Cardiff Boys and was a trialist for the national schools team – but it was to soccer that he turned with Southern League side Barry Town, where he was soon discovered by an Everton scout. Joining the Goodison staff at the age of seventeen in February 1960, Keith made his first-team debut eight months later, scoring in a 3–1 League Cup win over Walsall, but had only five more League and Cup outings for the 'Toffees'. Towards the end of 1962–63, Albion scout Des Tennant was checking on a Leeds United player in a reserve match, but was greatly impressed by the Everton centre-forward who scored a hat-trick, and a £9,000 fee brought Keith to Hove shortly afterwards in April 1963.

With his exceptional speed, all-out effort and regular goalscoring, the versatile 20-year-old was a good acquisition for the club and wore all the forward shirts from no.7 to no.11, but the arrival of Bobby Smith in the summer of 1964 put paid to his chances of first-team action and he moved on to Wrexham for £2,000 in September 1964. After two seasons back in Wales, he played in turn for Doncaster Rovers (July 1966, Fourth Division championship medal in 1969), Chester (June 1969) and Stockport County (July 1971). By the time he left the Football League for Morecambe in the Northern Premier League, Keith had 289 appearances to his name.

Season	FL	FAC	FLC	Total
1962–63	5 (1)	0	0	5 (1)
1963–64	29 (13)	1	2 (1)	32 (14)
1964–65	1	0	0	1
Total	35 (14)	1	2 (1)	38 (15)

WELCH, RONNIE   1973–74

midfield   Ht 5 6, Wt 10 07   *40 apps, 4 goals*
full name: Ronald Welch
born: Chesterfield, Derbyshire, 26.9.1952
debut: Aldershot (h), 26.12.1973 (FL D3)

A product of Burnley's famed youth scheme of the 1960s, Ronnie Welch joined the professional ranks at Turf Moor at the age of seventeen in October 1969, but had just one First Division appearance in four years with the 'Clarets' under his belt when he signed for new

Albion manager Brian Clough in December 1973. Arriving as part of a joint £70,000 package with Harry Wilson, Ronnie filled the no.4 shirt and briefly took over the captaincy when Norman Gall was absent in February as Clough made wholesale changes to improve the club's flagging fortunes. Again he led the side in April 1974, but his form suffered as he admitted the responsibility, at the age of just 21, was proving a burden. Although he was a regular in the side with nineteen appearances at the start of 1974–75, Ronnie left in November 1974 in a players-plus-cash deal for Chesterfield full-back Ken Tiler. After 24 Third Division outings for his home-town club, he was released in May 1977 and dropped into non-League football.

Season	FL	FLC	Total
1973–74	21 (2)	0	21 (2)
1974–75	14+1 (2)	4	18+1 (2)
Total	35+1 (4)	4	39+1 (4)

WEST, H. C.   1902–03

outside/inside-right   *10 apps, 4 goals*
debut: Tottenham Hotspur (res.) (h), 24.9.1902 (SEL)

An amateur from the Brighton Havelock club, West appeared either at outside- or inside-right for the Albion in ten first-team games during 1902–03 but, despite netting a hat-trick in a 14–2 F.A. Cup thrashing of Brighton Amateurs, he played in only one Southern League fixture, a 1–0 defeat at Fulham.

Season	SL	FAC	SEL	Total
1902–03	1	2 (3)	7 (1)	10 (4)
Total	1	2 (3)	7 (1)	10 (4)

WETTON, ALBERT   1951–53

utility player   *4 apps*
full name: Albert Smailes Wetton
born: Winlaton, Co. Durham, 23.10.1928
debut: Ipswich Town (h), 12.9.1951 (FL D3(S))

Although he was born in the North-East, Albert Wetton went to school in Enfield and played his early football with Cheshunt in

the London League. In October 1949 he joined his elder brother Ralph as a professional with Tottenham Hotspur, but failed to make the first team at White Hart Lane and signed for the Albion in June 1951 for a fee of £500.

The rugged 22-year-old was a forward on his arrival at the Goldstone, but during his second season with the club he also appeared at centre-half on two occasions, the first of which was the incredible F.A. Cup third-round tie at Barnsley when Albion, 3–0 up at the interval, lost 4–3! Making just four senior appearances, Albert played a reserve-team role in his two years or so in Hove and became quite a favourite with the sizeable crowds that watched the second eleven during the 1950s. Transferred to Crewe Alexandra for a small fee in October 1953, he made the Cheshire club's League side on just two occasions before moving into the Southern League with Gravesend & Northfleet in 1954. Albert subsequently played for Haywards Heath in their Metropolitan League days.

Season	FL	FAC	Total
1951–52	2	0	2
1952–53	1	1	2
Total	3	1	4

WHENT, JACK   1945–46 & 1947–50

half-back   Ht 5 10, Wt 11 00   *149 apps, 5 goals*
full name: John Richards Whent
born: Darlington, Co. Durham, 3.5.1920
debut: Chelsea (a), 21.4.1945 (wartime)
peacetime debut: Romford (a), 24.11.1945 (FAC R1 Lg2)

One of the stalwarts of the Albion side in the late 1940s, a period when the club was struggling to re-establish itself, Jack Whent was born in Darlington but spent most of his early years in North America; firstly in Vancouver, Canada, and then, from the age of thirteen, in Berkeley, California, where he played for Olympic F.C. and San Francisco Rovers. In 1942, Jack joined the Canadian Army and arrived in England the following year. He represented the Canadian Army in the Allied Cup competition, turned out for Spurs

as an inside-forward, and had a trial with Arsenal, but after recovering from a brush with a German bomb he was posted to Brighton in 1944 and recruited to assist the Albion junior team.

Signed as an amateur, Jack was promoted to the first-team in April 1945 and was a regular throughout the 1945–46 season, but moved back to Vancouver in 1946. While in Canada he met up with an Albion fan by the name of Cross who persuaded him to return to the Goldstone; Jack duly contacted the club and was taken on as a pro in August 1947 at the age of 27. A capable wing-half who occasionally turned out at inside-left, he later settled into the centre-half spot and skippered the team from 1948 to 1950. Although only of modest build and limited in his ball-skills, Jack was a solid, honest performer who led by example and rarely allowed an opposition forward to pass him. During his time at Hove he assisted Sam Cowan (see *Albion Wartime Players*) in coaching the Worthing team.

In August 1950, Jack was exchanged for Luton Town's Jim Mulvaney and Peter Walsh, but met with little success in the Second Division. He had a spell with Kettering Town in the Southern League before returning to Canada in 1953 where he linked up with the Westminster Royals club.

Season	FL	FAC	Wartime	Total
1944–45	0	0	3	3
1945–46	0	9	32 (1)	41 (1)
1947–48	21	2	0	23
1948–49	39	1	0	40
1949–50	41 (4)	1	0	42 (4)
Total	101 (4)	13	35 (1)	149 (5)

WHITE, TOM — 1904–06

outside-right — 35 apps, 3 goals
full name: Thomas Henry White
born: Tring, Hertfordshire, 12.11.1881
debut: Southampton (a), 1.10.1904 (SL D1)

Although born in Tring, Tom White was raised in nearby Chesham and played for the local Chesham Generals club for three seasons, during which time he represented the Berks & Bucks county association. After a spell in Essex with Grays United, the 22-year-old

winger signed for the Albion in March 1904 and became first choice on the right flank during 1904–05, but the following season he was ousted by Dick Joynes and the brilliant Walter Anthony, and was released to join Stockport County in May 1906. After appearing in 32 Second Division matches for County during 1906–07, Tom moved on to Carlisle United in the North Eastern League, but returned to the Southern League with Exeter City during the summer of 1908. The little outside-right played in the "Grecians'" first-ever match as a pro club, and made nineteen appearances in their initial season before joining his younger brother Charlie at Watford in August 1909.

Season	SL	FAC	UL	Total
1904–05	27 (1)	2 (2)	0	29 (3)
1905–06	2	0	4	6
Total	29 (1)	2 (2)	4	35 (3)

WHITEHOUSE, W. — 1914

centre-half — 1 app
debut: Portsmouth (h), 18.3.1914 (SA)

An amateur trialist from the Midlands, Whitehouse played in a 4–0 Southern Alliance victory over Portsmouth at the Goldstone in March 1914, and three days later turned out for the reserves in a 6–3 South Eastern League win over Croydon Common, but he was not subsequently engaged.

Season	SA	Total
1913–14	1	1
Total	1	1

WHITEHURST, SQUIRE — 1901–05

goalkeeper — 32 apps
born: Derby, Derbyshire, 1878
died: Manchester, Lancashire, 1944
debut: Brighton Athletic (h), 21.9.1901 (FAC Prelim.)

Squire Whitehurst, the Albion's first goalkeeper, was one of several players brought to the South Coast from the Midlands by the

Brighton & Hove Rangers club, and played in every competitive match for the Withdean-based amateurs during 1900–01, including the Sussex Senior Cup final defeat by Eastbourne. When Rangers folded, Squire was one of the first men to be engaged as a professional by the newly formed Brighton & Hove Albion in August 1901. The quaintly-named 'keeper served the club with some distinction for four seasons, two of them as first choice between the posts, but after Albion won promotion to the First Division of the Southern League in 1903 he was replaced by the more experienced Arthur Howes. In August 1908 he was re-signed as an amateur, but his services weren't called upon. A contemporary report described Squire as 'a wonderfully safe custodian'.

Season	SL	Test	FAC	SEL	Total
1901–02	7	0	4	0	11
1902–03	7	1	2	10	20
1903–04	1	0	0	0	1
Total	15	1	6	10	32

WHITFIELD, KEN — 1954–59

centre-half — Ht 5 11, Wt 11 10 — 182 apps, 4 goals
full name: Kenneth Whitfield
born: Durham, Co. Durham, 24.3.1930
debut: Millwall (a), 21.8.1954 (FL D3(S))

Signed as a centre-forward for an Albion record fee, Ken Whitfield only justified the big sum when he was switched to centre-half eight months after his arrival in Hove. It was a transformation which was little short of incredible; the constructive play of the Durham-born pivot contributed greatly to the entertaining fare presented at the Goldstone in the mid '50s, culminating in the championship of the Third Division (South) in 1958.

Having started out with Shildon Colliery in the Northern League, Ken was signed by Wolves as a professional at the age of seventeen in December 1947, but in almost six years he made only ten First Division appearances and was transferred to Manchester City for £13,000 in March 1953. In July 1954, Billy Lane paid £6,500 for the 24-year-old forward, but his initial performances were a great disappointment until his old boss at Molineux, Stan Cullis, recommended a switch to the no.5 shirt

where he had occasionally turned out for Wolves' reserves. Ken thereafter became the lynchpin of the Albion defence until he lost his place to Roy Jennings in December 1958, and he left for Queen's Park Rangers the following July where he ended his Football League days. He later had a spell as player-manager with Bideford Town in the Western League. Ken was also on the coaching staff at Luton Town for three years, and was assistant manager at Cardiff City from 1974 to 1978 under his former Queen's Park Rangers team-mate Jimmy Andrews.

Season	FL	FAC	Total
1954–55	22 (2)	0	22 (2)
1955–56	43 (1)	2	45 (1)
1956–57	45	2	47
1957–58	43	3	46
1958–59	22 (1)	0	22 (1)
Total	175 (4)	7	182 (4)

WHITING, BOB   1908–15

goalkeeper   Ht 6 0, Wt 12 00   320 apps
full name: Robert Whiting
born: West Ham, Essex, 6.1.1883
died: in action at Vimy Ridge, France, 28.4.1917
debut: Plymouth Argyle (a), 12.9.1908 (SL D1)

One of the finest goalkeepers ever to stand guard for the Albion, Bob Whiting was a giant of a man who delighted crowds throughout the Southern League with his prodigious kicking ability; he is once reputed to have cleared the opposition crossbar from his goal area! In honour of these ballistic exploits he was known throughout the game by the nickname 'Pom Pom', and participated in occasional goal-kicking competitions. Yet Bob was also a custodian of considerable ability and made 320 appearances for the club, a record total for an Albion goalkeeper until surpassed by Brian Powney in 1972. In 1909–10 he played in every game, conceding just 28 goals as Albion lifted the Southern League championship, an all-time low for the club (in a season of 42 or more matches).

R WHITING.

The following September he was between the posts when Brighton beat Football League champions Aston Villa 1–0 at Stamford Bridge for the F.A. Charity Shield, one of the club's greatest-ever triumphs.

Once a ship-builder, Bob played professionally for West Ham United reserves before joining the infant Tunbridge Wells Rangers club around 1904. Two years later he starred for the Kent club in an F.A. Cup tie against Norwich City, a display which persuaded Chelsea to sign him as their reserve 'keeper in April 1906 towards the end of their first campaign in the Football League. Thrust into the limelight at the start of 1906–07 following an injury to regular goalie Mick Byrne, Bob quickly made the position his own and played a big part in the promotion success that season. In two seasons at Stamford Bridge he made 52 League appearances before arriving at the Goldstone Ground at the age of 25 in the summer of 1908. Twice ever-present and missing only a handful of games during his time in Hove, 'Pom Pom' saw off three understudies and was an essential member of the team in the club's first 'golden era'.

As a reward for a wonderful, seven-year career in Hove, Bob was granted a benefit in October 1914, but it had to be postponed because of the poor wartime attendances. In fact, he enlisted with the Army on the outbreak of war and retired from the game in November 1914, but made a come-back the following February and remained the club's no.1 goalkeeper until it shut down in May 1915. Posted to France the following November as a private with the Footballers' Battalion, he was killed by enemy shell-fire while attending the wounded at Vimy Ridge. Aged just 34, his name lives on the memorial to the town's war dead in Hove Library, and in the roll-call of Albion's greatest players.

Season	SL	FAC	FACS	WL	WL Ch.	SA	SCC	Total
1908–09	37	1	0	11	2	0	3	54
1909–10	42	1	0	0	0	0	4	47
1910–11	37	3	1	0	0	0	3	44
1911–12	38	1	0	0	0	0	3	42
1912–13	34	3	0	0	0	13	3	53
1913–14	34	4	0	0	0	11	0	49
1914–15	31	0	0	0	0	0	0	31
Total	253	13	1	11	2	24	16	320

WHITINGTON, ERIC   1964–68

utility forward   Ht 6 1, Wt 12 06   41 apps, 12 goals
full name: Eric Richard Whitington
born: Brighton, Sussex, 18.9.1946
debut: Hull City (a), 5.2.1966 (FL D3)

Local-boy Eric Whitington was seen as a fine prospect, but he was never able to fulfil the potential he showed at Moulsecoomb and Westlain Schools, where he represented Brighton and Sussex Schools, and played in the final England Schools trial at Stockport in 1962. After signing for Arsenal during his last year at school, Eric was then taken on Chelsea's ground staff and went on to play for the England youth team in 1964, but he was released from Stamford Bridge in May 1964 to join the Albion.

Signed as a professional the following October, he made his Third Division debut at the age of nineteen in February 1966. In 1966–67 he was given a run up front and finished joint top-scorer on ten goals from 24 outings, but, despite the creditable scoring-rate, he was sometimes criticised for a lack of pace and was unable to maintain a regular place in the side.

Released in May 1968, Eric departed for South Africa to play for Highlands Park with some success, assisting the Johannesburg-based club to the national championship. On returning to England he had trials with Oxford United and Orient, and had talks with several other Football League clubs including the Albion, but joined Crawley Town in March 1971. For two years he scored prolifically for the Southern League side, and subsequently played for Folkestone, Eastbourne United and Horsham before seeing out his career with another spell at Crawley. His son, Craig, was on Albion's books as a schoolboy, and went on to play for Southwick, Worthing (where Eric was on the coaching staff), and Crawley Town before joining the League ranks, but was the subject of an F.A. ban for drug offences in 1996 while with Huddersfield Town.

Season	FL	FAC	FLC	Total
1965–66	0+1	0	0	0+1
1966–67	14+1 (6)	6 (4)	3	23+1 (10)
1967–68	12+4 (2)	0	0	12+4 (2)
Total	26+6 (8)	6 (4)	3	35+6 (12)

WHITTINGTON, DICK   1908–24

left-half   14 apps
full name: George Whittington
born: Hove, Sussex, 1885
died: Hove, Sussex, September 1947
debut: Southampton (h), 19.10.1912 (SL D1)

'Dick' Whittington was working as a labourer on Albion landlord John Clark's Goldstone Farm when he joined the football club's staff during the close season of 1908; he then remained with the Albion for 31 years! A strapping half-back, Dick appeared in the Southern League team just once as stand-in for Joe McGhie in October 1912. Although he also played a few games in the Southern Alliance and Southern Charity Cup, he was essentially a regular with the reserves and played his part admirably. On his return from war in 1919, Dick was appointed groundsman, but continued to assist the 'Lambs' in emergencies, bringing

his total of outings in the second string to around 200 when he played his final match in November 1924 at the age of 39. Dick then tended the Goldstone turf until the Second World War.

Season	SL	SA	SCC	Total
1912–13	1	3	5	9
1913–14	0	4	1	5
Total	1	7	6	14

WICKHAM, ALF   1902

outside-right   *1 app*
full name: Alfred William Wickham
born: Cuckfield, Sussex, 1880
debut: St Albans Amateurs (a), 18.10.1902 (SEL)

Alf Wickham was a member of Hurstpierpoint F.C., and was one of a number of local players recruited for a South Eastern League match at St Albans when Albion were forced to play an F.A. Cup tie with Shoreham the same day. It was his only appearance for the club.

Season	SEL	Total
1902–03	1	1
Total	1	1

WILCOCK, GEORGE   1913–15

goalkeeper   Ht 5 9, Wt 11 00   *21 apps*
full name: George Harrie Wilcock
born: Edinburgh, Midlothian, Scotland, 24.1.1890
died: Sheffield, Yorkshire, 1962
debut: Cardiff City (h), 15.11.1913 (SL D1)

George Wilcock turned to football after service with the Royal Field Artillery, playing for Bradford (P.A.) reserves and enjoying four League games with Barnsley before joining Goole Town in the Midland League as an amateur. He arrived in Hove in the summer of 1913 and was soon offered pro terms. The 23-year-old goalkeeper showed promise as Bob Whiting's deputy and had a run in the side on the big man's temporary retirement in 1914–15, but war service with his old unit brought a temporary halt to George's career.

Wounded at Loos in October 1915, he became an Army schoolmaster upon repatriation, but was spotted by Southampton while playing for a Land Forces XI v. Royal Navy at Plymouth, and joined the Hampshire club upon his demob in 1919. Making 20 appearances for the 'Saints' in the latter half of 1919–20, George greatly impressed the Preston North End management and joined the Deepdale staff in May 1920. However, after playing in the first seven Division One matches of 1920–21, he was dropped after a 6–0 hiding at Liverpool and joined Caerphilly in the Welsh National League. In July 1923, George obtained a permit to play as an amateur for Southampton Docks & Marine F.C.

Season	SL	FAC	SA	SCC	Total
1913–14	4	0	5	1	10
1914–15	7	3	0	1	11
Total	11	3	5	2	21

4 players who worked as policemen

Player	Player
Clelland, Dave	Stevens, Jack
Steele, Simon	Williams, Jack

WILKINS, DEAN   1983–84 & 1987–96

midfield   Ht 5 10, Wt 12 04   *375 apps, 31 goals*
full name: Dean Mark Wilkins
born: Hillingdon, Middlesex, 12.7.1962
debut: Middlesbrough (a), 10.12.1983 (FL D2)

Dean Wilkins had just eighteen League appearances under his belt when he left England for the Continent in 1984, but after three years in the Netherlands he returned considerably more experienced and played a large part at the Goldstone for nine years, appearing in more than 370 games and nearly leading the Albion back to the First Division in 1991. Although he often became the target of criticism from the terraces, the talented midfielder could transform a game when his vision and distribution came off. Equally, his outstanding free-kicks will long be remembered, especially the superb effort against Ipswich Town in May 1991 which famously clinched a place for the Albion in the Second Division play-offs.

A member of the Wilkins football dynasty, Dean is the younger brother of Ray (ex-England skipper), Graham (Chelsea and Brentford) and Steve (Brentford); and the son of George (Brentford, Bradford (P.A.), Nottingham Forest and Leeds United). As a schoolboy, he represented Middlesex and trained with Chelsea and Manchester United, but it was with Queen's Park Rangers that he served his apprenticeship, signing professional forms in May 1980. Originally a defender, he developed into a midfielder, but in three seasons at Loftus Road he made the starting line-up just twice.

In August 1983, Dean arrived at the Goldstone on a free transfer and appeared in the first-team three times, but was released after a loan-spell with Orient towards the end of the season. Recommended to PEC Zwolle in the Netherlands by his former Albion colleague Hans Kraay, he honed his skills during three seasons in the Dutch League. Although Zwolle finished bottom of the First Division in his first campaign, they regained their place the following season and finished 1986–87 in mid table.

In July 1987, Albion manager Barry Lloyd brought the 25-year-old back to the Goldstone for a £10,000 fee. After a rocky start to his second spell with the club, Dean played an important part in Albion's promotion back to the Second Division in 1987–88 and became an essential member of the side, making 123 consecutive appearances and captaining the team on many occasions. Although often criticised for his apparent lack of 'bite' and left-footed almost to a fault, there was no doubt that he was the chief play-maker in the side for several seasons and created countless goals with his imaginative passes. Beset by injury problems in his latter days, Dean enjoyed a testimonial season in 1995–96, his brother Ray bringing Queen's Park Rangers to the Goldstone for his benefit. At the end of the season, though, he was released, subsequently taking trials with Worthing and Torquay United. During 1996–97 he played for Worthing and Crawley Town before settling down with Bognor Regis Town.

Season	FL	Play-offs	FAC	FLC	FMC	AMC	Total
1983–84	2	0	1	0	0	0	3
1987–88	43+1 (3)	0	4	2	0	5 (2)	54+1 (5)
1988–89	42+1 (1)	0	1	2	1	0	46+1 (1)
1989–90	46 (6)	0	2	2 (1)	1	0	51 (7)
1990–91	46 (7)	3 (1)	3	2	3	0	57 (8)
1991–92	24+2	0	0+1	2	0	0	26+3
1992–93	32+3 (3)	0	5	4 (2)	0	4	45+3 (5)
1993–94	20+1 (2)	0	0	3	0	1	24+1 (2)
1994–95	11+3	0	0	3	0	0	14+3
1995–96	31+4 (3)	0	2+1	2	0	3	38+5 (3)
Total	297+15 (25)	3 (1)	18+2	22 (3)	5	13 (2)	358+17 (31)

WILKINS, JACK   1948–52

defender   Ht 5 10, Wt 12 00   47 apps, 2 goals
full name: Leonard Henry John Wilkins
born: Dublin, Co. Dublin, Ireland, 12.8.1920
debut: Swansea Town (a), 29.1.1949 (FL D3(S))

Born in Dublin but raised in London, Jack Wilkins was a sergeant in the Royal Electrical & Mechanical Engineers who represented the Army on many occasions and appeared briefly with Southampton in the last season of wartime football, 1945–46. Stationed at the Maresfield Camp near Uckfield, he also played for Guildford City's

Southern League side before joining the Albion as an amateur in October 1948, and made 27 League appearances before turning professional on his demob in July 1950, just a couple of weeks before his 30th birthday. Showing immense bravery in the air, the powerfully-built defender also impressed with his strong, calm play and divided his first–team outings between the right-back and centre-half berths, but he lacked mobility on the ground and spent his fourth season at Hove in the reserves.

Released in 1952, Jack returned to the Southern League with Bedford Town. He later served Haywards Heath for many years as player-coach, coach and manager, and skippered the team that beat Worthing 2–1 at the Goldstone in the 1958 Sussex Senior Cup final. An all-round sportsman, Jack was also a first-class hurdler in his Army days and played cricket for the Hove Montefiore club.

Season	FL	FAC	Total
1948–49	2	0	2
1949–50	25	0	25
1950–51	17 (2)	3	20 (2)
Total	44 (2)	3	47 (2)

WILKINSON, DARRON   1992–94

midfield   Ht 5 11, Wt 12 08   48 apps, 5 goals
full name: Darron Bromley Wilkinson
born: Reading, Berkshire, 24.11.1969
debut: Colchester United (h), 26.8.1992 (FLC R1 Lg2)

Darron Wilkinson joined the youth side of his local club, Wokingham Town, at the age of thirteen, and went on to represent Berks & Bucks both as a schoolboy and as an adult. He remained with the Isthmian League side for nine years, but was tracked by Albion manager Barry Lloyd for some time and came to the Goldstone in the close season of 1992 on a trial basis, taking time off from his job as a scaffolder. The trial was a success and the powerful 22-year-old was rewarded with a pro contract, a nominal fee being paid to his former club. An honest workhorse in midfield, Darron broke into the first team almost immediately when Dean Wilkins was suspended and held his place, but he was unable to sustain his best form into 1993–94 and was

released in May 1994 after gaining a Sussex Senior Cup winner's medal with the reserves. Late in 1994 he was playing football in Hong Kong. During the 1995–96 season Darron signed for Hayes and starred as the Middlesex side surged up the Isthmian League table to gain promotion to the Conference.

Season	FL	FAC	FLC	AMC	Total
1992–93	26+1 (3)	1+1	0+1	2 (2)	29+3 (5)
1993–94	8+3	0	2+1	2	12+4
Total	34+4 (3)	1+1	2+2	4 (2)	41+7 (5)

WILKINSON, HOWARD   1966–71

outside-right   Ht 5 9, Wt 11 12   147 apps, 19 goals
born: Netherthorpe, Sheffield, 13.11.1943
debut: Swindon Town (h), 20.8.1966 (FL D3)

Although his playing career was less than spectacular, Howard Wilkinson went on to become one of the most astute and successful managers in the modern game, a renowned and shrewd tactician. Even during his five years with the Albion, the fair-haired winger from Yorkshire was involved in coaching Brighton Boys, Sussex University and the Sussex County XI, and in 1968 he gained his full F.A. badge.

A Yorkshire and England Grammar Schools representative, Howard had trained with Sheffield United during his last year at school and played for Hallam F.C. before joining the ground staff at Sheffield Wednesday. He won England Youth honours while at Hillsborough and signed professional forms in June 1962, but had to wait until the 1964–65 campaign to make his First Division debut.

In July 1966 he arrived at the Goldstone with three goals and 22 League outings under his belt, and went on to make 147 appearances. Powerfully-built for a winger, Howard was blessed with good pace and could perform down either flank. However, he was injured in December 1966 and never quite established himself as an automatic choice thereafter. In fact, he was often selected as a substitute, and came off the bench on seventeen occasions. Given a free transfer in May 1971, he become player-coach with Boston United in the Northern Premier League.

It was at Boston that he had to choose between furthering his career in football or switching to teaching (having gained a degree in physical education from Sheffield University, and with a spell as a teacher at his former Abbeydale School behind him). His manager, Jim Smith, persuaded him to choose the former course, and when Smith left the Lincolnshire club Howard was put in charge; in his six years at Boston the club won the Northern Premier championship on four occasions. Howard also had a spell as manager of Mossley and, in addition to running the England semi-professional side, was appointed as the F.A.'s regional coach for the Sheffield area. In 1978 he was invited to assist Dave Sexton and Terry Venables in running the England under-21 side, and two years later was appointed coach at Notts County, later to become team manager under former Albion player Jimmy Sirrell. When Jack Charlton vacated the managerial hot seat at Sheffield Wednesday in 1983, Howard returned to his former club and became an instant success, leading the 'Owls' back to the First Division in his first season.

By the time he left for Leeds United in October 1988, Wednesday were established as a force in the top flight, but the challenge of restoring the fortunes at Elland Road proved irresistible and he led them to the Second Division championship in 1990. Two years later Leeds lifted the last Football League championship before the advent of the Premier League, and Howard was named Manager of the Season. In 1996 he led Leeds to the League Cup final. Known to be something of a disciplinarian, Howard remained one of the most respected managers in professional football until he was sacked in September 1996 following a series of poor results. Four months later he was appointed the first Technical Director of the Football Association, with an important role in the future development of coaching at all levels of the game.

Season	FL	FAC	FLC	Total
1966–67	31+1 (4)	1	6 (1)	38+1 (5)
1967–68	27+5 (7)	1	0	28+5 (7)
1968–69	32+3 (5)	2	3	37+3 (5)
1969–70	11+1 (1)	0+4	0	11+5 (1)
1970–71	15+3 (1)	1	0	16+3 (1)
Total	116+13 (18)	5+4	9 (1)	130+17 (19)

WILKINSON, REG   1924–34

right-half   Ht 5 8, Wt 10 09   396 apps, 16 goals
full name: Reginald George Wilkinson
born: Norwich, Norfolk, 26.3.1899
died: Norwich, Norfolk, 14.9.1946
debut: Watford (h), 1.11.1924 (FL D3(S))

For nearly ten years Reg Wilkinson's name was one of the first to be entered on Albion manager Charlie Webb's team-sheets. The polished half-back from Norwich made 396 appearances for the club, the eighth-best total ever, and once appeared in 115 consecutive games, a considerable achievement. His consistency was scantily rewarded when, together with fellow stalwarts Ernie Ison and Reg Smith, he received as a benefit the proceeds of collections at three Easter games in 1930 during a period of considerable financial uncertainty for the club.

Reg had started out with his local club, Norwich City, upon the completion of wartime duties with the King's Royal Rifle Corps in 1919. In August 1920 he was in the "Canaries'" first-ever Football League line-up, and gained a reputation as a stylish, attacking wing-half over the next three seasons, playing in 102 Third Division (South) matches. First Division Sunderland paid £250 for his transfer in June 1923, but he struggled to make the first team at Roker Park and spent most of the 1923–24 season in the reserves before coming to Hove in August 1924.

WILKINSON · BRIGHTON+HOVE ALBION F.C.

Starting out as a reserve at the Goldstone, Reg got his chance in December when Billy McAllister lost favour. After initially vying for the vacant right-half berth with Sid Bedford, he made the role his own and remained there until May 1934 when he retired at the age of 35. On leaving the Albion, Reg returned to Norfolk to work for the Norwich Electricity Works and turned out as a permit player for their football team for some ten years. Sadly, he collapsed and subsequently died while playing in a local league match at the age of 47.

Season	FL	FAC*	SSC	Total
1924–25	18	0	0	18
1925–26	36 (1)	2	0	38 (1)
1926–27	41	3	0	44
1927–28	42	2	0	44
1928–29	39 (2)	1	0	40 (2)
1929–30	40 (2)	6	0	46 (2)
1930–31	38	2	0	40
1931–32	39	3	0	42
1932–33*	34 (4)	8 (1)	0	42 (5)
1933–34	34 (5)	3 (1)	5	42 (6)
Total	361 (14)	30 (2)	5	396 (16)

Note: One of Wilkinson's 1932–33 F.A. Cup appearances came in the qualifying competition.

WILLARD, JESS   1946–53

forward/wing-half   Ht 5 9, Wt 11 12   202 apps, 24 goals
full name: Cecil Thomas Frederick Willard
born: Chichester, Sussex, 16.1.1924
debut: Queen's Park Rangers (h), 29.3.1947 (FL D3(S))

Always known as 'Jess' Willard (after the celebrated American heavyweight world boxing champion), this versatile player from Chichester might just as well have been called 'Mr Consistency'. Totally dependable in a variety of positions, he was one of the stalwarts who safely saw the Albion through the rocky period just after the Second World War to the stability and comparatively successful era of the early '50s.

Jess attended the Lancastrian Senior Boys' School in his home city, and represented Chichester, Sussex and the South of England Schools in 1938. During the war he played for an R.A.F. XI v. Army at Blackpool while training as air-crew, and also turned out for the European Sporting Club in Calcutta during a break in Far East operations. On his demob, Jess joined Chichester City in the Sussex County League where he soon came to the attention of the Sussex selectors, winning five county caps, and in November 1946 he was invited to the Goldstone for a trial with the reserves.

Noted for his non-stop running, he impressed sufficiently to be included in the first team soon after, and, with seven League outings as an amateur under his belt, signed as a 23-year-old professional in June 1947. Usually remembered as a dynamic, attacking wing-half, Jess actually joined the club as a forward and turned out in all numbers from 7 to 11 before settling into the no.4 shirt in February 1949. After five excellent seasons as a pro, he was granted a benefit match in May 1952, Albion beating Second Division Nottingham Forest 5–4 in front of a 6,000 Goldstone crowd. When Johnny McNichol departed for Chelsea in the 1952 close season, Jess inherited the captaincy, but an early injury kept him out of the side for most of the campaign and in July 1953 he was transferred to Crystal Palace for £1,150.

However, a cartilage injury curtailed his career at Selhurst, and after 46 League appearances for the 'Glaziers' he joined the backroom staff as trainer-coach. Jess remained with Palace for 20 years and played his part in the club's 1969 triumph when they gained First Division status for the first time. He subsequently had an eighteen-month spell as a coach at Brentford under former Albion player Mike Everitt, but now lives in retirement back in his home county at Turners Hill.

Season	FL	FAC	Total
1946–47	7 (2)	0	7 (2)
1947–48	29 (3)	5 (2)	34 (5)
1948–49	26 (1)	0	26 (1)
1949–50	32 (4)	1	33 (4)
1950–51	41 (8)	4	45 (8)
1951–52	45 (3)	1	46 (3)
1952–53	10 (1)	1	11 (1)
Total	190 (22)	12 (2)	202 (24)

WILLEMSE, STAN   1940 & 1946–49

left-back   Ht 5 11, Wt 13 00   110 apps, 6 goals
full name: Stanley Bernard Willemse
born: Hove, Sussex, 23.8.1924
debut: Southampton (a), 31.8.1940 (wartime)
peacetime debut: Aldershot (h), 26.1.1946 (FAC R4 Lg1)

Famed throughout the Football League for the ferocity of his tackling, Stan Willemse was one of the most successful footballers ever to emerge from Sussex. Having arrived at the Goldstone at the age of fifteen, the Hove-born youngster matured into one of the finest full-backs in the land and won considerable acclaim when he moved into the First Division. Although his uncompromising play earned

him the reputation of the 'dirtiest player in football', Stan won a host of honours to demonstrate that he possessed a good deal of quality in addition to his fearsome physical presence.

Educated at the West Hove and Knoll Schools, the promising young defender represented Brighton Boys, appeared in the same Sussex Schools team as Jess Willard and Charlie Chase, and played for The Rest *v.* England in an international trial match. Having progressed to Hove Penguins and Southwick, he was an early recruit of the Albion juniors, and in August 1940, just eight days after his sixteenth birthday, played his first senior match, a 3–1 defeat at Southampton in the Football League's emergency competition. After six games in the early part of the 1940–41 season, Stan joined the Royal Marine commando and trained as a P.T. instructor, attaining the rank of sergeant at the early age of nineteen. It meant he was lost to the club for the remainder of the war, but his career prospects survived despite a shrapnel wound suffered at Dunkirk, and in 1946 he returned to the Goldstone to appear at inside-left in the F.A. Cup ties of 1945–46.

Signed as a professional in June 1946, Stan took over the left-back spot from Freddie Green and soon made the berth his own. Extremely quick and with a no-frills approach to the game, the well-built defender was the scourge of many an outside-right and soon attracted the attention of the top clubs with some outstanding displays. In July 1949, Chelsea came up with a £6,000 offer that Albion could hardly refuse, and so Stan moved into the First Division where he was destined for great things. The fee was by far the largest received for a Brighton player at the time, and paid for the improvements made to the South Stand that summer; the 24-year-old duly inscribed his initials into the wet concrete footings and placed a coin alongside.

Stan went on to enjoy seven excellent seasons and 221 appearances at Stamford Bridge where his rugged style and enthusiasm won him the adulation of the fans and the dread of many a First Division winger. The great highlight undoubtedly came when he won a League championship medal in 1954–55, the only occasion Chelsea have lifted the title, but he also won individual honours by representing the Football League and being capped for the England B team. Indeed, he was probably denied full England honours only by the brilliance of the cultured Roger Byrne.

Stan travelled all over Europe with the touring London F.A. sides of the 1950s, and took part in the first floodlit game staged at Wembley Stadium, when London took on Frankfurt in an Inter Cities Fairs' Cup (precursor of the UEFA Cup) tie in 1955. In June 1956 he moved on to Leyton Orient on their elevation to the Second Division, but hung up his boots in May 1958. For some time thereafter Stan was landlord of The Eagle in Gloucester Road, Brighton. He later ran a betting-shop in Southwick and then worked as a security officer at London University, but now lives in retirement in Hove.

Season	FL	FAC	Wartime	Total
1940–41	0	0	5 (2)	5 (2)
1945–46	0	4 (1)	3	7 (1)
1946–47	21 (1)	1	0	22 (1)
1947–48	34	5	0	39
1948–49	36 (2)	1	0	37 (2)
Total	91 (3)	11 (1)	8 (2)	110 (6)

WILLIAMS, D. H.   1913

centre-forward   *2 apps, 1 goal*
debut: Portsmouth (h), 12.3.1913 (SA)

Williams was a master at the local Taunton House School who was given a trial in March 1913. Curiously, his only two outings

were both first-team matches. He scored on his debut, a 4–1 midweek defeat of Portsmouth at Fratton Park in the Southern Alliance, and played in a 1–0 Southern League win over Gillingham at the Goldstone three days later. However, despite two excellent victories, nothing more was seen of Williams.

Season	SL	SA	Total
1912–13	1	1 (1)	2 (1)
Total	1	1 (1)	2 (1)

WILLIAMS, Dave   1920–21

utility player   Ht 5 8, Wt 11 10   *31 apps, 5 goals*
full name: David H. Williams
born: Liverpool, Lancashire
debut: Gillingham (a), 28.2.1920 (SL D1)

Dave Williams started out in the Lancashire Combination with St Helen's Recreation, and progressed to the Football League with Glossop in September 1912. After making rapid progress with the Second Division side he was transferred to Notts County for an enormous £700 fee two months later, part of an unsuccessful attempt to keep the 'Magpies' in the First Division, but County then bounced straight back, lifting the Second Division title in 1914 with Dave contributing two goals from seven outings. On the outbreak of war he enlisted with the Army, and assisted Arsenal in 1916–17 while stationed in the London area. On his demob in July 1919 the Liverpool-born utility man joined Luton Town in the Southern League and netted five goals in 23 games during the first half of 1919–20.

In February 1920, Dave joined the Albion for £200, a big fee for a Southern League player at the time and equalling the Brighton record. Capable of turning in effective performances wherever selected to play, he scored on his debut at left-half, and went on to appear at right-half and in all the forward positions. Indeed, the constant switching of positions to cover for absent colleagues probably cost him a more regular place in the team, and he was largely confined to the reserves following the signing of Andy Neil in December 1920. Granted a free transfer in May 1921, Dave moved into the Kent League with Maidstone United.

Season	FL	SL	FAC	Total
1919–20	0	10 (3)	0	10 (3)
1920–21	20 (2)	0	1	21 (2)
Total	20 (2)	10 (3)	1	31 (5)

WILLIAMS, Gary   1977–82

left-back   Ht 5 10, Wt 11 00   *177 apps, 8 goals*
full name: Gary Peter Williams
born: Liverpool, Lancashire, 8.3.1954
debut: Cambridge United (a), 13.8.1977 (FLC R1 Lg1)

Consistency was the hallmark of Gary Williams' time with the Albion: he played in 146 games consecutively as the club won its way to the First Division and then established itself in the top flight. Tall and lean, the Liverpool-born defender had an unusual build for a full-back but still demonstrated the traditional skills of tough-tackling and competent clearing of his lines.

A junior tennis champion, Gary had trials with Liverpool and Coventry City, but left school to become a sewing-machine engineer while playing his football for Marine in the Cheshire County League.

Just over a year later, in April 1972, he signed professional forms as a forward for Preston North End following a month's trial, but was converted into a full-back early in 1975. The switch proved a great success as he went on to play in 112 League games for the 'Lilywhites', and in 1976–77 he was voted Player of the Season.

In July 1977, Albion, newly promoted to the Second Division, splashed out £50,000 plus defenders Harry Wilson and Graham Cross on the 23-year-old defender who quickly established himself in the no.3 shirt. Ever-present during the 1978–79 promotion campaign and also in the club's first-ever season in Division One, Gary enjoyed what was probably the highlight of his time at the Goldstone when he hit the spectacular long-range winner which gave Albion a 'double' over Nottingham Forest, the European champions, in March 1980. Another vital strike came in the last minute of a match at Sunderland in April 1981, a goal which kept Albion in with a chance – ultimately successful – of escaping relegation. Perhaps his worst moment was the time in October 1979 when he had a very public contretemps with his own goalkeeper, Eric Steele, following a misunderstanding in front of Manchester United's Stretford End.

In November 1981, Gary made way for the experienced Sammy Nelson, and was exchanged for Crystal Palace winger Neil Smillie in July 1982. However, his career at Selhurst Park was cut short by injury, and he was forced to retire after just ten League outings. During the summer of 1983, Gary had a couple of games with Saltdean United on tour in France and spent the 1983–84 season with Whitehawk in the County League, during which he represented Sussex. Granted a testimonial in May 1984 (Albion drawing 3–3 with an ex-Albion side), he used the proceeds to help establish a television and radio business in George Street, Brighton.

Season	FL	FAC	FLC	Total
1977–78	34	2	0+1	36+1
1978–79	42 (2)	1	4	47 (2)
1979–80	42 (2)	2	5	49 (2)
1980–81	26 (2)	0	3 (1)	29 (3)
1981–82	14 (1)	0	1	15 (1)
Total	158 (7)	5	13+1 (1)	176+1 (8)

WILLIAMS, JACK   1928–31

centre-half   Ht 6 0, Wt 12 00   48 apps, 1 goal
full name: Walter John Williams
born: Wolverhampton, Staffordshire
debut: Watford (a), 1.12.1928 (FL D3(S))

A towering figure at the heart of the defence, Jack Williams would, in the opinion of his Albion manager Charlie Webb, have developed into one of the best centre-halves in the country but for the injury problems which eventually forced his retirement. After joining his local club, Wolverhampton Wanderers, as an amateur in November 1925, Four months later Jack was offered a professional engagement four months later, but didn't make his Second Division debut until the opening match of the 1927–28 season. Although he held his place for the following two matches, he then

returned to the Central League side and was released to join Gillingham in August 1928.

Jack's stay at Priestfield was brief, though. After turning in an impressive display for the Kent side in their 3–1 defeat at the Goldstone on 27 October, he was signed by Charlie Webb the following week to compete with the popular Paul Mooney for the centre-half slot. In fact, he was selected as centre-forward on two occasions, but his blossoming career was interrupted by a serious injury sustained toward the end of his second season with the club, 1929–30. Jack attempted a come-back in the reserves during 1930–31, but it proved fruitless and the burly six-footer was forced to hang up his boots. In April 1932 a match was arranged for his benefit, Albion losing 2–0 to First Division Portsmouth. On leaving the game Jack joined the Brighton Police Force.

Season	FL	FAC	Total
1928–29	16	0	16
1929–30	26 (1)	6	32 (1)
Total	42 (1)	6	48 (1)

WILLIAMS, SKILLY   1926–29

goalkeeper   Ht 5 8, Wt 12 08   107 apps
full name: Reginald George Williams
born: Watford, Hertfordshire, 4.1.1890
died: Watford, Hertfordshire, 19.6.1959
debut: Brentford (a), 28.8.1926 (FL D3(S))

Reg Williams, usually known as 'Skilly', spent thirteen years with Watford, his home-town club, where he became something of a legend. By the time he arrived in Hove he was in his mid 30s, but he also contributed a great deal to the Albion. Originally employed as a kitchen assistant (hence the nickname, a slang term for a kind of broth) at Leavesden Mental Hospital, he joined the Watford staff in 1913. After gaining a regular place in the first team, Skilly then monopolised the goalkeeping jersey for twelve years and missed just fourteen League matches in eight peacetime seasons. In 1914–15 the stoutly-built goalkeeper was ever-present as the 'Brewers' lifted the Southern League championship. During the Great War he saw service with the Army and suffered shrapnel wounds on the Western Front (and also guested for West Ham United), but returned to Cassio Road, Watford, after the war to resume his place beneath the bar.

Having appeared in Watford's first-ever Football League match in 1920, Skilly took his aggregate of League and Cup appearances to 337 by May 1926 when Charlie Webb brought him to the Goldstone. With young Stan Webb still learning the game, the 36-year-old's experience proved invaluable to the Albion. In fact, he was installed as team captain for the three seasons before his retirement, the only goalkeeper ever to skipper the side on a regular basis. He played his last game at Brentford on Boxing Day 1928 just nine days short of his 39th birthday, and held the record as the oldest player to appear for the club in peacetime League football until Jimmy Case returned to the Goldstone in 1994.

After hanging up his gloves at the end of 1928–29, Skilly returned to Hertfordshire as a driver for the Watford National bus company, and obtained a permit to play as an amateur for their football team in August 1931. His son, also Reg, was a wing-half for Watford and Chelsea.

Season	FL	FAC	Total
1926–27	39	3	42
1927–28	42	2	44
1928–29	20	1	21
Total	101	6	107

WILLIAMSON   *1913*

inside-forward   *4 apps, 2 goals*
born: c. 1891
debut: Cardiff City (a), 26.2.1913 (SA)

A 21-year-old inside-forward from the Northern Combination side
Lintz Institute (from near Newcastle upon Tyne), Williamson
arrived at the Goldstone as a professional in February 1913 along
with his team-mate Bill Brown. He appeared in the reserves and a
number of minor first-team fixtures during the remainder of the
1912–13 campaign, scoring the only goal of the game at Cardiff in
the Southern Alliance on his first-team debut, but was released at
the end of the season.

Season	SA	SCC	Total
1912–13	2 (1)	2 (1)	4 (2)
Total	2 (1)	2 (1)	4 (2)

WILLIS, George   *1948–49*

inside-left   *Ht 5 8, Wt 11 00*   *28 apps, 13 goals*
born: Burnopfield, Co. Durham, 9.11.1926
debut: Bristol City (a), 6.3.1948 (FL D3(S))

B orn in County Durham but educated in Doncaster, George Willis
joined Wolverhampton Wanderers as a professional at the age
of seventeen in 1943 having spent some time with their Yorkshire
nursery team, Wath Wanderers. In the latter stages of the Second
World War he was conscripted as a 'Bevin Boy', working in a colliery,
but had still to make the first team at Molineux when he came to the
Goldstone in February 1948.

Signed for £1,000 shortly
after his release from the
pits, George was one of several players brought to Hove
by new manager Don Welsh
in a vain bid to avoid having
to apply for re-election.
While not particularly blessed with ball-skills, the
21-year-old was always
willing and covered a good
deal of the Goldstone pitch
with his hard running. Performing creditably during
the rest of that disastrous
1947–48 campaign, George
added considerable punch to
the attack and scored eight
goals in the remaining
fifteen matches. The following season, though, he was
only a fringe member of the first team, and left for Plymouth Argyle
in May 1949 where he stayed for nearly seven years without winning
a regular place. After fifteen goals in 56 League matches at Home
Park, George moved on to Exeter City in March 1956 where he ended
his Football League career with 26 Southern Section appearances
before joining Taunton Town in the Western League.

Season	FL	Total
1947–48	15 (8)	15 (8)
1948–49	13 (5)	13 (5)
Total	28 (13)	28 (13)

WILSON, Alex   *1947*

outside-right   *1 app*
full name: Alexander Wilson
born: Wishaw, Lanarkshire, Scotland, 29.10.1908
died: Boston, Massachusetts, U.S.A., April 1971
debut: Bristol Rovers (a), 13.9.1947 (FL D3(S))

A lex Wilson's one appearance for the Albion came completely out
of the blue. As club trainer, he was pressed into emergency service
on the right-wing in September 1947 against Bristol Rovers when
Jack Dugnolle failed to arrive for the Third Division (South) fixture

at Eastville. Although
Albion lost 4–1, he perf-
ormed creditably — for a
38-year-old former goal-
keeper!

Alex had won fame
before the war with
Morton and Arsenal, and
was a fringe member
of the "Gunners'" team
which won five League
championships during
the 1930s, picking up a
medal himself in
1937–38. He totalled 82
appearances for the club
as a 'steady rather than
spectacular' goalie, and
was between the posts in
1936 when Arsenal beat
Sheffield United 1–0 in
the F.A. Cup final. During
his time at Highbury, the
Scottish custodian trained as a masseur, and in 1939 he was appointed
physio to Kent County Cricket Club.

Alex continued to play for Arsenal during the early part of the
war and also turned out for St Mirren, but in November 1946 he
arrived at the Goldstone as trainer. In September 1952 he enjoyed a
testimonial match at Hove, an All-Star XI beating Arsenal 4–2, but
left the Albion the same year to become manager-coach at Worthing.
In 1953, Alex returned to the first-class scene as trainer to
Birmingham City, and subsequently held similar positions with
Sunderland and Blackpool. He moved to the United States as physio
to the Boston Beacons in 1967, and remained in that city until his
death in 1971. Alex's coaching methods were reported to have been
years ahead of their time, and he invented a number of revolutionary
training-aids including the 'Wilson Patented Ball-Slinger' (see photo).

Season	FL	Total
1947–48	1	1
Total	1	1

WILSON, Danny   *1983–87*

midfield   *Ht 5 6, Wt 11 04*   *155 apps, 39 goals*
full name: Daniel Joseph Wilson
born: Wigan, Lancashire, 1.1.1960
debut: Cardiff City (h), 3.12.1983 (FL D2)

D anny Wilson made an instant impression at the Goldstone by
scoring twice on his debut in December 1983. On loan from
Nottingham Forest at the time, the dynamic little midfielder signed
permanently the following month and became the driving-force behind
an Albion side that nearly won its way back to the top flight in 1985.
The enthusiasm and leadership he put to such good use as a player
in over 620 League games has now helped him to enjoy a successful
start to his managerial career.

The son of a Derry City part-timer, Danny was brought up in
Wigan and, although he signed schoolboy forms for Sunderland, joined
Wigan Athletic in the Northern Premier League before moving to Bury
in September 1977. Three seasons and 90 League appearances later
he was signed by ambitious Chesterfield in July 1980 for £100,000,
and was immediately rewarded with an Anglo-Scottish Cup winner's
medal. Inevitably he attracted interest from bigger clubs, and in
January 1983 Brian Clough took him to Nottingham Forest in
exchange for Calvin Plummer and Steve Kendal in a deal rated at
£100,000.

Played out of position as a winger at Forest, he made just ten
First Division appearances and joined Scunthorpe United on loan in
October 1983. At the end of November, Danny arrived at the Goldstone
on a similar basis to make his explosive entrance. With Jimmy Case
injured, Albion's play revolved around the loan man, and after
protracted negotiations manager Chris Cattlin signed the
inspirational 24-year-old for a fee of £45,000 in January 1984. A superb

passer of the ball, Danny took over the captaincy from Case during 1984–85 as Albion finished just three points away from a promotion place, but the following campaign saw the edge taken off his play by a series of injuries. Nevertheless, he made his debut for Northern Ireland – his mother was Irish – in December 1986, and won a further two caps before being sold to Luton Town for £150,000 in July 1987 following Albion's relegation to Division Three.

In three seasons at Kenilworth Road, Danny scored 24 times in 110 League outings and won a League Cup medal in 1988. In August 1990 he joined Sheffield Wednesday for a £200,000 fee, and enjoyed more success as the 'Owls' won promotion to the First Division and beat Manchester United in the League Cup final in his first season. He also brought his total of international caps up to 24, and appeared in the Wednesday sides which lost both the League Cup and F.A. Cup finals to Arsenal in 1993.

In August 1993, Danny moved to nearby Barnsley as assistant to manager Viv Anderson. The following May he took over as player-manager at Oakwell following Anderson's departure for Middlesbrough, and, against all the odds, guided his unfashionable team into the Premiership in 1997, winning many plaudits as one of the brightest young managers in the game.

Season	FL	FAC	FLC	FMC	Total
1983–84	26 (10)	3 (1)	0	0	29 (11)
1984–85	38 (5)	0	2	0	40 (5)
1985–86	33 (11)	5	3 (3)	2 (2)	43 (16)
1986–87	35+3 (7)	2	2	1	40+3 (7)
Total	132+3 (33)	10 (1)	7 (3)	3 (2)	152+3 (39)

WILSON, GLEN   1948–60

left-half   *Ht 5 9, Wt 11 10*   *436 apps, 28 goals*
full name: Glenton Edward Wilson
born: High Spen, Co. Durham, 2.7.1929
debut: Bournemouth & B.A. (a), 24.9.1949 (FL D3(S))

Like his elder brother Joe (q.v.), Glen Wilson spent half a lifetime in the cause of the Albion: twelve years as a highly respected and popular player, followed by eighteen years in a variety of roles from trainer and kit-man to caretaker manager. Wonderfully consistent, he proved an inspirational captain during the late 1950s when he led Albion to their first-ever promotion after 38 years in the Football League, and his total of 436 appearances has been exceeded by just five players.

Born into a hot-bed of football in County Durham, Glen enjoyed a highly successful soccer career at High Spen Senior School where he won England honours. In 1945 he joined Newcastle United as a sixteen-year-old amateur, but was then called into the Army on National Service, and it was while serving with the R.E.M.E. at Bordon Camp in Hampshire that he became an Albion player. Glen played in a friendly for nearby Farnham Town against Albion's 'A' team in 1948 and impressed Brighton player-coach Jack Dugnolle who recommended him to manager Don Welsh.

After playing for the 'A' team himself, the 20-year-old signed professional forms in September 1949 and made his first-team debut at inside-left a few days later, but his true vocation was as a left-half. Blessed with incredible stamina and a fierce tackle, Glen became an essential member of the side, the driving-force behind the team for ten seasons throughout the 1950s, and was widely regarded as the finest wing-half in the Third Division. Indeed, he represented the Southern Section against its northern counterpart on three occasions, and also played – rather curiously – for a Football Combination XI in an excellent 6–1 defeat of the Dutch national team in 1956. Glen was at his superb best during Albion's 1957–58 Third Division championship campaign, but later became the subject of bribery allegations regarding the Albion victory at Watford that helped clinch the title.

After two seasons in the Second Division, he was released to take the player-manager's post at Exeter City at the age of 30 in June 1960, but endured a miserable time at St James's Park: in his first season the hard-up 'Grecians' were forced to seek re-election, and he was dismissed towards the end of the following campaign in April 1962. Glen then returned to Brighton as landlord of the Flying Dutchman in Elm Grove, but joined the Albion backroom staff in 1966 and, apart from a two-year break, continued to serve the club faithfully until May 1986. In October 1973 he took charge of the team for two games between the sacking of Pat Saward and the appointment of Brian Clough.

Dismissed as part of an economy drive at the end of the 1985–86 season, Glen later became a porter at the University of Sussex, but it was a great pity that such a loyal servant of the club was forced to leave the Goldstone in such a shabby manner.

Season	FL	FAC	Total
1949–50	3	0	3
1950–51	34 (2)	2	36 (2)
1951–52	46	1	47
1952–53	36 (2)	3	39 (2)
1953–54	46 (2)	4	50 (2)
1954–55	44 (1)	5 (1)	49 (2)
1955–56	42 (4)	2	44 (4)
1956–57	44 (3)	2 (1)	46 (4)
1957–58	45 (2)	3	48 (2)
1958–59	42 (7)	1	43 (7)
1959–60	27 (2)	4 (1)	31 (3)
Total	409 (25)	27 (3)	436 (28)

WILSON, HARRY   1973–77

left-back   *Ht 5 9, Wt 10 12*   *146 apps, 4 goals*
born: Hetton-le-Hole, Co. Durham, 29.11.1953
debut: Aldershot (h), 26.12.1973 (FL D3)

Harry Wilson arrived at the Goldstone in December 1973 together with his Burnley team-mate Ronnie Welch for a combined fee of £70,000, but he proved to be a much more useful acquisition than his colleague and turned in consistent performances in the no.3 shirt for three years as Albion were transformed from Third Division strugglers into promotion candidates.

An England Schools international, Harry was an apprentice with Burnley before signing as a pro in December 1970, and also won England Youth caps while at Turf Moor. He had just ten League games under his belt when Brian Clough paid out the big fee, but he established himself as the regular left-back for the Albion until the arrival of Chris Cattlin in 1976. Transferred to Preston North End in July 1977 in the deal which brought Gary Williams to Hove, Harry suffered severe injuries in a car accident five months later and his League appearances at Deepdale were therefore restricted to just 42 in three seasons. He did, however, help the club to promotion to the Second Division in 1977–78 before joining Darlington on a free transfer in September 1980. After 85 Fourth Division outings for the 'Quakers', Harry moved on to Hartlepool United during the 1983 close season where he remained for a season before departing for the United States. After returning to the U.K., he had short spells as manager at Seaham Red Star and Whitby Town in the late '80s and early '90s before rejoining his first club, Burnley, as youth-team coach.

Season	FL	FAC	FLC	Total
1973–74	25	0	0	25
1974–75	42 (3)	3	4	49 (3)
1975–76	46 (1)	3	2	51 (1)
1976–77	17	1	3	21
Total	130 (4)	7	9	146 (4)

WILSON, JOE   1908–09

centre-half   Ht 5 11, Wt 11 04   *35 apps, 1 goal*
full name: Joseph Wilson
born: Westhoughton, Lancashire, 1884
debut: Southampton (h), 2.9.1908 (SL D1)

A tall, gangling figure, particularly impressive in the air, Joe Wilson was almost a legend at Millwall where he spent twelve years, many of them as skipper. The Lancashire-born defender's first League club was Blackburn Rovers, whom he joined for a fee of £125 in April 1905 after playing for Wigan County and Darwen in the Lancashire Combination. During three years at Ewood Park he enjoyed 43 First Division outings before joining the Albion staff in May 1908.

Joe had a fine season at the Goldstone, despite missing two months through injury, but in May 1909 he was transferred to Millwall where he was to become a huge favourite. Making 238 Southern League appearances for the 'Dockers', he represented the Southern League *v.* Scottish League in October 1910 and also played for a London XI *v.* Birmingham XI in October 1913. In September 1920, at the age of 36, Joe dropped into the Central League with Rochdale, and was appointed player-coach at Fleetwood in the Lancashire Combination the following summer.

Season	SL	WL	WL Ch.	SCC	Total
1908–09	25	6 (1)	2	2	35 (1)
Total	25	6 (1)	2	2	35 (1)

WILSON, JOE   1936–47

inside-right   Ht 5 6, Wt 10 07   *353 apps, 49 goals*
full name: Joseph Alexander Wilson
born: High Spen, Co. Durham, 28.3.1909
died: Brighton, Sussex, 3.4.1984
debut: Gillingham (a), 29.8.1936 (FL D3(S))

Joe Wilson's bald pate was a familiar sight at the Goldstone for 38 years, firstly as a player, then as assistant trainer, head trainer, caretaker manager and chief scout. Rarely has the club been served so faithfully by one man, and he was rewarded for his loyalty with three testimonials: in 1948–49, November 1961 and May 1974 — an extremely rare achievement. Because of his lack of hair there were many fans who thought the club had signed yet another veteran when he first joined the Albion staff. In fact, he was only 27 and remained on the playing staff for eleven years, making 353 senior appearances (178 of which came during the war). His younger brother Glen (q.v.) also served the club for many years, and the pair between them devoted 68 years to the Albion's cause.

Joe represented Durham as a left-back while at school in High Spen, and was discovered by Newcastle United while playing for Tanfield Lea in the North-West Durham League. Already thinning on top, he signed professional forms in September 1933 after five months as an amateur, and scored on his League debut, a 6–2 home win over Hull City on Christmas Day 1934.

After 30 League and Cup appearances for the 'Magpies', Joe signed for the Albion for a fee of £450 in May 1936 amid fierce competition from Cardiff City, and made an immediate impact. His awesome speed and skilful ball-play quickly won the admiration of the fans, and he

played a big part in making the club one of the strongest sides in the Third Division (South) in the three seasons before the war. Although usually an inside-right, he also appeared at right-half and outside-right to equal effect.

During the war he served in the Army as a physical training instructor, but still turned out regularly for the Albion and also made guest appearances for Aldershot, Fulham, Reading and Spurs. As one of the club's 'elder statesmen' during the emergency, Joe was a big influence on the many youngsters that were introduced to the side, never more so than when he arrived in Norwich at Christmas 1940 accompanied by just three juniors. The side was completed by a number of Norwich reserves and servicemen from the crowd, but Albion lost by a record score of 18–0. Manager Charlie Webb subsequently singled out his senior man for special praise, commending him for his never-say-die spirit.

After missing just three games of the 1946–47 post-war campaign, Joe decided to retire in May 1947 at the age of 38 and was appointed assistant trainer. On Alex Wilson's departure in 1952, he was promoted to head trainer and retained the post for eighteen years. Rarely seen on the bench without his beloved pipe, he amazed and delighted the Goldstone crowds throughout the '50s and '60s with his lightning sorties to bring solace to injured players. When George Curtis left the club in February 1963, Joe took over the managerial duties for nine games and immediately introduced a more attacking policy before making way for Archie Macaulay. In 1970 he was appointed chief scout, but retired in May 1974 at the age of 65.

Season	FL	FAC	SSC	Wartime	Total
1936–37	38 (7)	1	1	0	40 (7)
1937–38	42 (3)	4 (2)	1	0	47 (5)
1938–39	37 (5)	1	0	0	38 (5)
1939–40	0	0	0	22 (5)	22 (5)
1940–41	0	0	0	14 (2)	14 (2)
1941–42	0	0	0	28 (6)	28 (6)
1942–43	0	0	0	12 (2)	12 (2)
1943–44	0	0	0	32 (9)	32 (9)
1944–45	0	0	0	34 (6)	34 (6)
1945–46	0	10 (1)	0	36 (1)	46 (2)
1946–47	39	1	0	0	40
Total	156 (15)	17 (3)	2	178 (31)	353 (49)

WILSON, TUG   1922–36

outside-left   Ht 5 7, Wt 11 06   *566 apps, 71 goals*
full name: Ernest Wilson
born: Beighton, Yorkshire, 11.7.1899
died: Hove, Sussex, 27.12.1955
debut: Brentford (h), 21.10.1922 (FL D3(S))

Like Peter Pan, Ernie 'Tug' Wilson never seemed to grow old. For thirteen years the little winger from Yorkshire monopolised the left flank at the Goldstone, establishing a record number of appearances for the club, 566, that has never seriously been threatened since. Remarkable fitness and consistent, high-quality displays gave Tug the edge over any pretenders, while his deft feints and swerves, and his ability to cross a beautifully flighted centre with an 'educated' left foot, delighted the Albion crowds. Yet the young Ernie was rejected by Sheffield Wednesday in 1918 for being too small!

Educated at Swallow Nest School near Sheffield, he worked at Silverwood Colliery during the First World War, turning out for the works' team and also for Beighton Recreation. While playing for the Midland League club Denaby United, he had a trial with the Albion in May 1922, a Berks & Bucks Hospital Charity Cup match against Reading, and joined the club the following August. Once he had wrested the left-wing berth from Jimmy Jones early in 1922–23, Tug could not be shifted and went on to miss just 29 games over the next twelve seasons. While never a great scorer himself, he still weighed in with an average of more than six goals per season from 1925 onwards, and amassed 71 in fourteen years to put him high up in the all-time list of Albion goalscorers.

In 1935–36, Tug finally made way for Bert Stephens, and decided to retire at the age of 37 in May 1936. Immensely popular with the Goldstone fans, he qualified for two benefits with the club, in 1928 and 1933, which together netted him around £650. On leaving the professional game he was granted a permit to play for Vernon Athletic in the Sussex County League, and later became a bookmaker in partnership with his former Albion colleague Frank Brett. Also an above-average cricketer, he occasionally played for the Sussex second eleven. Sadly, Tug died in 1955 at the age of 56 while resident in Portland Road, Hove.

WILSON·BRIGHTON +HOVE ALBION F.C. 1923-24

Season	FL	FAC*	SSC	Total
1922–23	25 (2)	3	0	28 (2)
1923–24	41	4	0	45
1924–25	42	3	0	45
1925–26	40 (3)	2	0	42 (3)
1926–27	40 (4)	3	0	43 (4)
1927–28	42 (7)	2	0	44 (7)
1928–29	36 (4)	1	0	37 (4)
1929–30	41 (7)	6	0	47 (7)
1930–31	39 (6)	2	0	41 (6)
1931–32	41 (7)	3 (2)	0	44 (9)
1932–33*	40 (7)	11 (2)	0	51 (9)
1933–34	39 (8)	3	5	47 (8)
1934–35	35 (11)	3	2	40 (11)
1935–36	8 (1)	3	1	12 (1)
Total	509 (67)	49 (4)	8	566 (71)

Note: Four appearances and one goal of Wilson's 1932–33 F.A. Cup total came in the qualifying competition.

WINDROSS, DENNIS   1960–61

centre-forward   Ht 5 10, Wt 11 08   *21 apps, 4 goals*
born: Dunsdale, Yorkshire, 12.5.1938
died: Saltburn, Yorkshire, October 1989
debut: Lincoln City (a), 19.11.1960 (FL D2)

Dennis Windross joined Middlesbrough as an eighteen-year-old from the local Blackett Hutton club in May 1956, having played for Redcar Boys' Club and represented Redcar Schools as a centre-half. With Alan Peacock and the incredible Brian Clough also competing for the striking roles at Ayresome Park, he enjoyed very few opportunities for first-team football, but had scored once in four Second Division matches (and also topped the North Regional League scoring charts with 46 goals) when Albion manager Billy Lane brought him to the Goldstone for a fee approaching £1,000 in November 1960.

Dennis failed to fit in on the South Coast, though, and scored just twice in sixteen League games in the centre-forward role. The highlight of his short time with the Albion came in January 1961, in the fourth-round F.A. Cup tie against League champions Burnley, when he swept home a Mike Tiddy cross to put Albion 3–2 ahead in a memorable game that eventually ended 3–3. Dennis left for Darlington in June 1961 in exchange for Bobby Baxter, but, after 25 League appearances, moved on to Doncaster Rovers in June 1962 where he was converted into a wing-half and saw out his League career with an additional 51 games in the Fourth Division. At the time of his death in 1989, Dennis was a supervisor at Saltburn Leisure Centre.

Season	FL	FAC	Total
1960–61	18 (2)	3 (2)	21 (4)
Total	18 (2)	3 (2)	21 (4)

WINSTANLEY, GRAHAM   1974–79

central defender   Ht 5 11, Wt 11 03   *71 apps, 4 goals*
born: Croxdale, Co. Durham, 20.1.1948
debut: Gillingham (a), 26.10.1974 (FL D3)

Although he was mainly used as a standby player as the Albion swept from the Third Division into the First, Graham 'Tot' Winstanley – so called because he was the youngest of three brothers – played a big part in the club's success. Indeed, had it not been for his influential performances during 1974–75, Albion might well have found themselves in the Fourth Division rather than joining the élite. When the likes of Graham Cross, Dennis Burnett or Mark Lawrenson were injured or suspended, he proved a reliable, uncomplaining deputy who rarely let the side down.

After an apprenticeship with Newcastle United, Graham signed as a professional in December 1965, but made just seven First Division appearances before joining Carlisle United in August 1969 for a £7,000. He made 166 League appearances for the 'Cumbrians', assisting them into the First Division in 1973–74, but had been in the reserves for several months when Peter Taylor signed him on loan in October 1974 to bolster an Albion defence which had just conceded eighteen goals in six matches. The experienced 26-year-old was just the player to bring out the best in young Andy Rollings, and was signed permanently in November for just under £20,000. While on loan Graham even took over as skipper temporarily during Ernie Machin's absence, and was appointed club captain in August 1975. However, his fortunes took a turn for the worse shortly afterwards when he broke his nose, and a lengthy spell in the reserves followed.

In the four seasons 1975–79, Graham made just 39 senior appearances, but his fine attitude led to manager Alan Mullery describing him as the 'perfect professional'. Nevertheless, Graham understandably became concerned about his future, especially in February 1979 when Mullery refused to let him join Tranmere Rovers on loan, but in July 1979 he returned to Carlisle on a free transfer. After 33 Third Division outings during the 1979–80 season he retired as a player and joined the coaching staff at Brunton Park. In May 1982 he moved to Penrith as a player and subsequently became manager of the North West Counties League club.

Since retiring, Graham has enjoyed a varied business life in the Carlisle district. Beginning as a milkman, he subsequently spent two years as an insurance salesman followed by ten years as a partner in a building supplies firm. In more recent times he has worked for the Post Office and for the *Cumberland Times* newspaper.

Season	FL	FAC	FLC	Total
1974–75	29 (2)	3	0	32 (2)
1975–76	8+1	0	2	10+1
1976–77	4	0	0	4
1977–78	18 (2)	1	0	19 (2)
1978–79	4	0	1	5
Total	63+1 (4)	4	3	70+1 (4)

WISDEN, ALAN   1920–21

centre-forward   1 app
full name: Alan Leslie Wisden
born: Hastings, Sussex, 31.1.1896
died: Hastings, Sussex, 1978
debut: Luton Town (a), 23.10.1920 (FL D3(S))

A relative of John Wisden of *Cricketers' Almanack* fame, Alan Wisden came to the fore in the immediate post-Great War period with the Hastings-based club Rock-a-Nore. He arrived at the Goldstone in September 1920 and impressed with his performances in the reserves, but made only one appearance in the League team, as deputy for Jack Doran in a 3–2 defeat at Luton in October 1920. Still an amateur at the time, Alan signed as a professional the following month and turned out regularly for the second string, but was released in May 1921 and reinstated as an amateur to play for Hastings & St Leonards. He subsequently starred for the East Sussex club throughout the 1920s and represented the county (awarded colours in 1923–24). In line with his pedigree, Alan was also a brilliant cricketer for the Hastings club and, according to contemporary opinion, could have walked into the county team.

Season	FL	Total
1920–21	1	1
Total	1	1

WOFFINDEN, COLIN   1970–71

forward   4 apps, 1 goal
full name: Colin R. Woffinden
born: Hove, Sussex, 6.8.1947
debut: Gillingham (a), 14.11.1970 (FL D3)

Colin Woffinden was one of the most talented players produced by Sussex in recent times, but he made just four appearances as a substitute for the Albion and his greatest contribution to the club has been as a youth coach. Indeed, he did the club a considerable *disservice* in the 1970s by playing in the amateur Walton & Hersham side that humiliated Albion 4–0 at the Goldstone in the F.A. Cup in November 1973, and also in the Leatherhead side that won a third-round tie 1–0 at Hove the following season.

A Brighton Boys representative, Colin was associated with both the Albion and Tottenham Hotspur as a schoolboy, but graduated into local senior football with Worthing, Eastbourne United and Lewes in the Athenian League; he also had trials with the Albion, Lincoln City and Crawley Town during this period. While working as a tiler he had another six-month trial at the Goldstone from October 1970, and it was during this spell that the 23-year-old amateur played in the first team.

From Lewes, Colin moved on to bigger things with Sutton United and was selected for the England amateur squad in 1971–72, but he was often played out of position at Sutton and returned to Eastbourne United. In 1972–73 he won the F.A. Amateur Cup with Isthmian League club Walton & Hersham before joining Leatherhead. Colin's other clubs included Tooting & Mitcham United and Dorking. He also captained the Sussex representative side, although his appearances for his county were restricted by his being on contract for much of his latter career. After further spells with Lewes and Southwick, Colin was manager at Burgess Hill Town for a while, and also coached Lewes. For some years he has assisted with the Albion's youth and schoolboy schemes, and co-wrote *The Guinness Book of Skilful Soccer*.

Season	FL	FAC	Total
1970–71	0+3	0+1 (1)	0+4 (1)
Total	0+3	0+1 (1)	0+4 (1)

WOMBWELL, DICK   1907–08

inside/outside-left   Ht 5 6, Wt 12 00   35 apps, 7 goals
full name: Richard Wombwell
born: Nottingham, Nottinghamshire, 1877
debut: Norwich City (a), 7.9.1907 (SL D1)

Another of football's wanderers, Dick Wombwell was playing for Ilkeston Town in the Midland League when he signed for Derby County in May 1899. Partnering the immortal Steve Bloomer on the right wing, the Nottingham-born forward had 85 outings in the "Rams'" First Division side before transferring to Bristol City (where his team-mates included future Albion players Albert Fisher and Mickey Good) in August 1902. After almost three seasons with City, Dick signed for Manchester United in March 1905 and was a member of the side which won promotion to the First Division in 1905–06, but, following drastic changes in the playing staff during the following season, he moved north of the border in January 1907 for a fee of well over £500 to play for Heart of Midlothian. In a short stay in Edinburgh he appeared in the team beaten 3–0 by Celtic in the Scottish Cup final of 1907, his partner on the left wing being former Albion player Billy Yates.

Dick arrived at the Goldstone in the summer of 1907 and produced some outstanding performances, particularly in the memorable F.A. Cup run which saw Albion beat First Division Preston North End and take Liverpool to a replay. In February 1908, just two weeks after the second Liverpool match, First Division Blackburn Rovers signed him along with Joe Lumley and their main target, Walter Anthony, but his career turned full circle a year later when he returned to Ilkeston. A provider rather than a goalscorer, Dick netted 44 goals in his career total of 268 League appearances.

Season	SL	FAC	WL	SCC	Total
1907–08	19 (3)	5 (1)	9 (3)	2	35 (7)
Total	19 (3)	5 (1)	9 (3)	2	35 (7)

WOOD, PAUL   1987–90

forward   Ht 5 9, Wt 11 03   105 apps, 8 goals
full name: Paul Anthony Wood
born: Middlesbrough, Yorkshire, 1.11.1964
debut: Fulham (h), 29.8.1987 (FL D3)

After helping the Middlesbrough Schools to victory in the 1980 English Schools Trophy final, Paul Wood had a disastrous trial with Leeds United in which he suffered a broken leg, but he was subsequently taken on as an apprentice by Portsmouth and made his first-team debut in January 1984. However, his career at Fratton Park was restricted by a pelvic injury and he never really established himself in the side, 22 of his 47 League appearances coming as a sub.

With his principal strikers, Kevin Bremner and Garry Nelson, both injured in August 1987, Albion manager Barry Lloyd signed the 22-year-old forward for a transfer fee which eventually reached £80,000, and his new acquisition played in 31

League matches during the successful 1987–88 Third Division promotion campaign. Skilful and speedy, Paul was an exciting player on the ball, but his scoring rate – just eight goals from 105 outings – left something to be desired (although he was not usually played as an out-and-out striker). Having lost his place to new acquisition Mark Barham in December 1989, Paul joined Sheffield United two months later for a £90,000 fee and was drafted straight into the team which clinched promotion to the First Division. Ironically, he scored in a 2–2 draw at the Goldstone only a month after his transfer.

He struggled to make the team in the higher company, however, and was loaned to AFC Bournemouth in January 1991 where he stayed for the rest of the season. Paul returned to Dean Court for a further loan spell after the start of 1991–92 and was eventually signed for £40,000 in November, the fee being paid by a local businessman. After eighteen goals from 99 League outings for the 'Cherries', he returned to Portsmouth on loan in February 1994 and re-signed for his first club the following month for £40,000, but he has again been dogged by injury problems which have restricted his appearances.

Season	FL	FAC	FLC	FMC	AMC	Total
1987–88	26+5 (4)	1+1	0	0	3	30+6 (4)
1988–89	27+8 (1)	1	2	1	0	31+8 (1)
1989–90	24+2 (3)	0+1	2	1	0	27+3 (3)
Total	77+15 (8)	2+2	4	2	3	88+17 (8)

WOODHAMS, WILF — 1902

right-back — *2 apps*

full name: Wilfred Harold Woodhams
born: Eastbourne, Sussex, 1882
debut: Southall (h), 8.2.1902 (SL D2)

Wilf Woodhams was on the books of East Sussex Senior League club Brighton Athletic when Albion called on his services during the 1901–02 season, and he gave a good account of himself in his two Southern League outings. A Sussex representative, he played in the county's prestigious fixture against the Corinthians at the County Ground in April 1902 when the famed gentleman amateurs ran out comfortable 7–1 winners. Wilf was also prominent in local cricket.

Season	SL	Total
1901–02	2	2
Total	2	2

WOODHOUSE, JACK — 1912–24

right-half — *241 apps, 22 goals*

full name: John Woodhouse
born: Smethwick, Staffordshire
debut: Plymouth Argyle (h), 15.2.1913 (SL D1)

With 76 appearances for the Albion before the Great War, and another 165 afterwards, Jack Woodhouse's total of 241 games would surely have been far higher but for the four-year interruption. An adaptable and highly consistent performer, he appeared in seven different positions over the years, from right-back to inside-left, but was generally regarded as a wing-half. In a long career with the club he played in both the Southern League and the Football League eras, and only left the Goldstone Ground in 1924 because manager Charlie Webb would not agree to him running a public house while still an active player.

Jack was signed from the Staffordshire club Cheddleton Asylum in August 1912, and established himself in the Southern League side towards the end of the season, initially at inside-right but then as a half-back

in 1914–15. After returning from war duties with the Middlesex Regiment (he also guested briefly for Watford in the emergency competitions), he enjoyed an excellent season in 1919–20 and was selected for the F.A.'s tour of South Africa the following summer when he played in one of the unofficial international matches. Ever-present during Albion's initial season as a Football League club, Jack skippered the team in the very first Third Division fixture in the absence of Jack Rutherford. In September 1921 he represented the Southern League *v.* Welsh League, a somewhat curious selection as the Southern League was competed for by Albion reserves by that time and he was very much a regular in the first eleven. Jack made his final League appearances in August 1923 before giving way to Billy McAllister, and hung up his boots at the end of the season to take over the Alexandra Inn (now the Harbour View) on the coast road at Portslade for some 30 years.

Season	FL	SL	FAC	SA	SCC	Total
1912–13	0	8 (4)	0	9 (4)	3	20 (8)
1913–14	0	15 (2)	0	11 (2)	0	26 (4)
1914–15	0	26 (3)	3	0	1	30 (3)
1919–20	0	36 (7)	1	0	0	37 (7)
1920–21	42	0	3	0	0	45
1921–22	37	0	3	0	0	40
1922–23	36	0	5	0	0	41
1923–24	2	0	0	0	0	2
Total	117	85 (16)	15	20 (6)	4	241 (22)

WOOLGAR, PHIL — 1966–67

goalkeeper — *1 app*

full name: Phillip R.J. Woolgar
born: Worthing, Sussex, 24.9.1948
debut: Doncaster Rovers (a), 16.5.1967 (FL D3)

Phil Woolgar first appeared in the Sussex County League with Wigmore Athletic (now Worthing United) in 1965, and played for the Albion youth and reserve teams in 1966–67, winning a Sussex Professional Cup medal against Hastings United. In May 1967 he was drafted for the final League fixture of the season in the absence of Brian Powney and Tony Burns, a grand experience for an eighteen-year-old amateur. Having performed his task well in a 1–1 draw at Doncaster, Phil continued to assist the reserves on occasion and remained prominent locally with Lancing for many years. In 1984 he was turning out for Littlehampton at the age of 35, and still lives in Worthing. His father, Bob, appeared as a goalie in Albion's wartime junior team.

Season	FL	Total
1966–67	1	1
Total	1	1

WOOLVEN, HAROLD — 1906–07

forward — *3 apps, 2 goals*

full name: Harold Ernest Woolven
born: East Preston, Sussex, 1884
debut: Leyton (a), 4.10.1906 (UL)

A great servant of the Littlehampton club in the early years of the century, Harold Woolven played for the county and the West Sussex League representative teams on many occasions. He assisted the Albion as an amateur during 1906–07 and appeared in three first-team fixtures in the United League, each of which ended in victory. Harold scored twice in the second half to snatch a 4–3 win over Norwich City at the Goldstone in his second outing. He went on to play for Lewes before the outbreak of war in 1914.

Season	UL	Total
1906–07	3 (2)	3 (2)
Total	3 (2)	3 (2)

The most popular players' forenames

Names by which players were usually known, including nicknames. Excludes wartime players.

Name		Name		Name		Name	
Jack	39	Craig	2	Mel	1	Roger	1
Bill/Billy	31	Cyril	2	Moshe	1	Ross	1
Jim/Jimmy	31	Dean	2	Murdo	1	Roy	1
John/Johnny	31	Des	2	Nat	1	Sean	1
Tom/Tommy	27	Doug	2	Ned	1	Sergei	1
David/Dave	22	Duncan	2	Percy	1	Squire	1
George	21	Edgar	2	Perry	1	Stefan	1
Bob/Bobby	20	Gavin	2	Potter	1	Tim	1
Harold/Harry	20	Ginger	2	Proctor	1	Tug	1
Joe	16	Glen	2	Ralph	1	Vic	1
Michael/Mike/Mick/Micky/Mickey	16	Henry	2	Raphael	1	Wayne	1
Alan/Allan/Allen	15	Herbert	2	Rees	1	Zach	1
Peter	15	Hugh	2	Ricardo	1	Zeke	1
Frank/Frankie	14	Malcolm	2				
Fred/Freddie	14	Matthew/Matt	2				
Mark	13	Nicky	2				
Bert/Bertie	12	Ossie	2				
Paul	12	Richard/Ricky	2				
Gary/Garry	10	Robert/Robbie	2				
Steve	10	Russell/Russel	2				
Arthur	9	Abe	1				
Charlie	9	Ade	1				
Ken	9	Arnold	1				
Stan	9	Ashley	1				
Walter/Wally	9	Barney	1				
William/Willie	9	Bradley	1				
Albert	8	Bullet	1				
Eric	8	Buster	1				
Ron/Ronnie	8	Cecil	1				
Tony	8	Christer	1				
Brian/Bryan	7	Clarrie	1				
Ernie	7	Clem	1				
Ian	7	Cliff	1				
Alec/Alex	6	Clive	1				
Alfred/Alf/Alfie	6	Crosby	1				
Andy	6	Dai	1				
Derek	6	Dale	1				
Geoff/Jeff	6	Denny	1				
Les	6	Doz	1				
Reg	6	Edwin	1				
Sam/Sammy	6	Ephraim	1				
Stewart/Stuart	6	Franco	1				
Ted/Teddy	6	Fretwell	1				
Barrie/Barry	5	Geordie	1				
Chris	5	Giles	1				
Denis/Dennis	5	Glyn	1				
Dick/Dickie	5	Grant	1				
Eddie	5	Gunner	1				
Graham	5	Hans	1				
Colin	4	Harvey	1				
Donald/Don	4	Hector	1				
Jock	4	Howard	1				
Kevin/Kevan	4	Igor	1				
Paddy	4	Irvin	1				
Phil	4	Ivan	1				
Sid/Syd	4	Jacob	1				
Wilf	4	James	1				
Alistair/Ally	3	Jason	1				
Ben	3	Jess	1				
Dan/Danny	3	Juergen	1				
Daren/Darren/Darron	3	Julius	1				
Gerry	3	Junior	1				
Gordon	3	Justin	1				
Greg	3	Kerry	1				
Keith	3	Kieran	1				
Len	3	Kit	1				
Martin	3	Kurt	1				
Neil	3	Lammie	1				
Nobby	3	Larry	1				
Norman	3	Laurie	1				
Pat	3	Lee	1				
Ray	3	Leon	1				
Simon	3	Lionel	1				
Terry	3	Lohmann	1				
Adrian	2	Lyn	1				
Archie	2	Mal	1				
Bernard	2	Maurice	1				

WORTHINGTON, FRANK   1984–85

forward   Ht 5 11, Wt 11 09   35 apps, 8 goals
full name: Frank Stewart Worthington
born: Halifax, Yorkshire, 23.11.1948
debut: Carlisle United (a), 25.8.1984 (FL D2)

One of the game's great characters for more than 20 years, Frank Worthington enjoyed just one season at the Goldstone as he became something of a travelling showman during the latter part of his career, but he will be remembered by supporters of all clubs for playing the game with a certain *joie de vivre*. Indeed, his attitude to life can perhaps be summed up by this quotation: 'I've squandered fortunes on booze, birds and gambling — it's better than wasting it!' But Frank would never have survived so long without also being a superlative footballer, and it was as a skilful, free-scoring centre-forward that he will go down in the record books.

One of three brothers to play League football – the others were Dave and Bob – Frank had represented Halifax Schools and played for Ripponden United before turning professional with Huddersfield Town in November 1966. In 1969–70 he helped the 'Terriers' to the Second Division championship, and had also won two England under-23 caps before joining Leicester City for £80,000 in August 1972. Frank's career peaked at Filbert Street, with an appearance for the Football League XI and eight full caps (scoring two goals) for England in 1974, but it was far from finished. Next stop was Bolton Wanderers for £90,000 in October 1977 after a month on loan, where he again assisted his club to the Division Two title in 1977–78 and finished as leading scorer in the First Division with 24 goals the following season. The summer of 1979 found Frank playing for Philadelphia Fury, but on returning to Burnden Park he was transferred to Birmingham City for a £150,000 fee in November 1979 where he appeared in his third Division Two promotion side in 1979–80 before returning to the U.S.A. with Tampa Bay Rowdies for the summer. In March 1982, City exchanged Frank for Leeds United's Byron Stevenson, but he was soon on the move again with spells at Sunderland (December 1982) and Southampton (June 1983).

On the completion of the 1983–84 season he toured with Manchester United, but it was Albion manager Chris Cattlin who captured the 35-year-old crowd-pleaser on a free transfer in May 1984 (the pair had been team-mates and good friends in their early days with Huddersfield Town). Frank entertained the Goldstone fans for just the one season, which almost saw the club regain its place in the top flight, but he left lasting memories of his flamboyant ball-skills. At the end of the campaign he was offered a further one-year contract, but preferred to join Tranmere Rovers as player-manager. When an administrator took over the financial reins at Prenton Park, though, he was dismissed as manager, but remained with the Birkenhead club until February 1987 when he became player-coach at Preston North End.

In March 1988, Frank signed for Stockport County after a four-month loan period and took his total of Football League appearances to 757, the twelfth-highest in history. After leaving Edgeley Park he continued his nomadic wanderings with Cape Town Spurs (player-coach), Chorley, Stalybridge Celtic, Galway United, Weymouth, Radcliffe Borough, Guiseley and Preston North End (coach). In 1990–91 he was player-manager of Hinckley Town in the Southern League, but when former Albion player John McGrath became manager of Halifax Town in October 1991, Frank was appointed coach to his home-town club for a time.

Now a star of the after-dinner circuit, he still turns out in charity matches and other events, and will play wherever anyone will give him a game. In a sparkling professional career spanning eleven League clubs and 22 years, Frank scored 236 goals in 757 Football League outings and was granted a benefit match by the P.F.A. in 1991. In 1994 his autobiography was published: *One Hump or Two? The Frank Worthington Story.*

Season	FL	FAC	FLC	Total
1984–85	27+4 (7)	2	1+1 (1)	30+5 (8)
Total	27+4 (7)	2	1+1 (1)	30+5 (8)

WOSAHLO, BRADLEY 1991–94

forward   Ht 5 10, Wt 11 06   2 apps
full name: Bradley Edward Wosahlo
born: Ipswich, Suffolk, 14.2.1975
debut: Colchester United (h), 26.8.1992 (FLC R1 Lg2)

The son of erstwhile Ipswich Town professional Roger Wosahlo, Bradley Wosahlo signed schoolboy forms for his father's former club, represented Suffolk Schools while head boy at East Bergholt High School, and had a trial with West Bromwich Albion, but joined Brighton in January 1991 as a trainee. He made his first-team debut as a seventeen-year-old in August 1992 and was awarded a professional contract in April 1993, but had little opportunity to impress in the side, making just one further appearance, and was released in May 1994 to join Rotherham United on a trial basis.

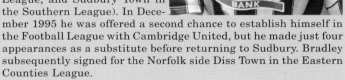

Bradley, who won a Sussex Senior Cup winner's medal with the Albion reserves in May 1992, went on to play for Woodbridge Town in the Eastern Counties League, and Sudbury Town in the Southern League). In December 1995 he was offered a second chance to establish himself in the Football League with Cambridge United, but he made just four appearances as a substitute before returning to Sudbury. Bradley subsequently signed for the Norfolk side Diss Town in the Eastern Counties League.

Season	FL	FLC	Total
1992–93	0	0+1	0+1
1993–94	1	0	1
Total	1	0+1	1+1

WRAGG, BILLY 1905–06

left-back   Ht 6 0, Wt 13 04   10 apps
full name: William Wragg
born: Hinckley, Leicestershire, 1876
debut: Norwich City (h), 30.9.1905 (SL D1)

Billy Wragg joined the Albion from Doncaster Rovers in September 1905 towards the end of a somewhat chequered career. The strapping defender had started out with his local club, Hinckley, before joining Nottingham Forest as a professional in April 1896. Two years later he appeared at left-half in Forest's F.A. Cup final triumph over Derby County, but finished the match as a passenger on the wing

having suffered an injury in the first half. Transferred to Leicester Fosse the following March, he made 49 appearances for the Second Division club before losing his place early in the 1900–01 season.

Billy's career then took a downward trend, most probably because of injury problems. In January 1901 he moved on to Small Heath (forerunners of Birmingham), but played in just one Second Division match before joining Watford seven months later. Again he failed to win a regular place, and spent the 1902–03 season in the Midland League with his former club, Hinckley. Billy returned to the Football League with Chesterfield in August 1903 and made 21 Second Division appearances before spending 1904–05 with Accrington Stanley in the Lancashire Combination.

Billy then had a brief spell with Doncaster Rovers in the Midland League before coming to Hove in September 1905. Considering his experience and colourful pedigree, his arrival was greeted with surprisingly little publicity, but he was never able to win a regular place in the Albion team. He performed in a variety of defensive roles, mainly in the reserves, but was released at the age of 30 at the end of 1905–06 and departed for an unknown destination in minor football. In 1908, Billy was reported to be performing on the stage of the *London Coliseum* in 'The Great Football Sketch', along with a number of prominent professional and former professional footballers.

Season	SL	UL	Total
1905–06	4	6	10
Total	4	6	10

WRIGHT, BARRIE 1969–70

left-back/midfield   Ht 5 10, Wt 11 07   10 apps
born: Bradford, Yorkshire, 6.11.1945
debut: Plymouth Argyle (a), 4.1.1969 (FL D3)

Barrie Wright represented Yorkshire Boys and skippered the England Schools team before joining Leeds United as an apprentice, but his senior career never fulfilled the early promise. After signing as a professional in November 1962 he won England Youth honours, but enjoyed just eight League and Cup appearances for a Leeds team which was just embarking on the greatest era in the club's history. Barrie spent the summer of 1964 with New York Rangers, and made his final appearance for Leeds in a League Cup tie in October 1965 as stand-in for Norman Hunter before returning to the U.S.A. for a stint with New York Generals.

His manager in New York was his former Leeds colleague Freddie Goodwin, and when Goodwin became Albion's boss he wasted little time in signing Barrie and his team-mate Geoff Sidebottom, and they arrived at the Goldstone in January 1969. However, the 23-year-old defender made little impression in Sussex and left for Hartlepool in September 1970, where he drifted out of the Football League at the age of 26 without making a first-team appearance.

Season	FL	Total
1968–69	5+1	5+1
1969–70	3+1	3+1
Total	8+2	8+2

WRIGHT, JOE   1932–34

goalkeeper	Ht 5 10, Wt 13 07	14 apps

full name: Joseph Wright
born: Gateshead, Co. Durham, 1907
died: Newton Abbott, Devon, 20.11.1936
debut: Queen's Park Rangers (a), 26.12.1932 (FL D3(S))

Joe Wright made the transition from the obscurity of the North Eastern League to the First Division of the Football League virtually overnight when he joined Leicester City from Birtley F.C. at the age of 22 in late April 1929. Making his debut in a 4–1 home win over Manchester United at the start of following season, the Geordie 'keeper made fifteen First Division appearances during the 1929–30 campaign, but his last game was a remarkable 6–6 home draw with Arsenal and he was put on the transfer list a week later, moving on to Torquay United in July.

Joe was first-choice goalkeeper at Plainmoor for two years until Albion manager Charlie Webb secured his transfer in July 1932, and he proved an admirable deputy for Stan Webb. A stockily-built custodian, he enjoyed few opportunities during his first season at the Goldstone, but was then preferred to Webb at the beginning of the 1933–34 campaign only to return to the reserves in late September as Albion got off to a poor start. Given a free transfer in May 1934, Joe subsequently suffered from poor health and died sixteen months later at the age of 29.

Season	FL	Total
1932–33	5	5
1933–34	9	9
Total	14	14

WRIGHT, STEVE   1923–24

left-half	Ht 5 7, Wt 11 03	4 apps

full name: Stephen Wright
born: Leicester, Leicestershire, 1893
died: Leicester, Leicestershire, 15.10.1959
debut: Northampton Town (a), 25.8.1923 (FL D3(S))

Steve Wright represented Leicestershire Schools and had experience with the Bohemians club of Dublin before the outbreak of the First World War in 1914. During the hostilities he saw service with the Leicestershire Regiment and the R.A.M.C., but when the war ended he joined Bolton Wanderers in May 1919 on his demob. A centre-half at this point in his career, Steve made his debut in a 3–1 defeat of Chelsea at Burnden Park in September 1920, but remained on the fringe of the "Trotters'" First Division side for three seasons and had accumulated just ten appearances when he was sold to Norwich City for £750 in July 1922. His first outing in a "Canaries'"

shirt came in a goal-less draw against the Albion at the Goldstone, and he was a regular at left-half in City's struggling Third Division (South) side with 36 appearances throughout the 1922–23 season.

During the summer of 1923, Steve unsuccessfully applied for the vacant player-manager post at Kent League Chatham Town, and in August was recruited by Albion manager Charlie Webb, but, after figuring in the opening matches of the 1923–24 campaign, the diminutive wing-half was struck down with injuries and in May announced his retirement at the age of 31. Steve later had spells as a trainer with Lincoln City and Ipswich Town during the 1930s.

WRIGHT · BRIGHTON + HOVE ALBION F.C. 1923–24

Season	FL	Total
1923–24	4	4
Total	4	4

YATES, BILLY   1905–06

inside-left	Ht 5 9, Wt 11 04	51 apps, 9 goals

full name: William Yates
born: Birmingham, Warwickshire, c. 1883
debut: Millwall (h), 2.9.1905 (SL D1)

Billy Yates played his early football in Birmingham junior circles with the Witton Shell Shop and Erdington clubs, and was taken on by Aston Villa in March 1903, but he had yet to make the First Division line-up when he was released to join the Albion in May 1905 at the age of 22. A forward for the majority of his playing days, Billy was once described as 'a very clever dribbler who lacks a good knowledge of the geography of the goalposts,' a comment perhaps substantiated by his career haul of just eleven goals from 228 appearances in Southern League and Football League matches.

In his only season at the Goldstone Ground he missed just one Southern League game and was particularly effective in the club's F.A. Cup run that year, but in June 1906 he was transferred to Manchester United (together with Frank Buckley)

where he made only three First Division appearances before moving to Scotland with Heart of Midlothian in January 1907. Three months later he appeared in the Hearts team beaten 3–0 by Celtic in the Scottish Cup final. Billy returned to the South Coast with Portsmouth in January 1908, where he was converted into a half-back and played in 107 Southern League matches before being released in June 1911. After joining Coventry City, he made a further 106 Southern League appearances, many as skipper, but retired in May 1914 because of injury. Billy subsequently became landlord of the Dyers Arms in Coventry.

Season	SL	FAC	UL	Total
1905–06	33 (4)	5 (3)	13 (2)	51 (9)
Total	33 (4)	5 (3)	13 (2)	51 (9)

YOUNG, ALAN   1983–84

forward   Ht 5 11, Wt 13 04   29 apps, 12 goals
full name: Alex Forbes Young
born: Kirkcaldy, Fife, Scotland, 26.10.1955
debut: Chelsea (h), 3.9.1983 (FL D2)

A Scottish schoolboy international, 'Alan' Young played for Kirkcaldy Y.M.C.A. before joining Oldham Athletic as a professional in July 1974, and had scored 30 goals in 122 League outings at Boundary Park when he became one of the first players to move under the newly-won freedom-of-contract scheme in July 1979; he was transferred to Leicester City for a fee – set by a tribunal – of £250,000. Scoring twice on his debut, Alan performed well at Filbert Street and hit fourteen goals as City won the Second Division championship in 1979–80. In August 1982 the burly Scot was transferred to Sheffield United, and arrived at the Goldstone twelve months later as a replacement for Michael Robinson when Jimmy Melia paid £140,000 for him.

Though in and out of the side with injuries, Alan was a consistent scorer for the Albion when he did play, and opened his account with a spectacular overhead shot on his debut against Chelsea. Particularly strong in the air, he showed an excellent touch for such a big man and scored twelve times in 29 appearances. However, when Chris Cattlin took over, he didn't figure in the new manager's future plans, and, after a deal with Barnsley had fallen through, the 28-year-old striker eventually signed for Notts County for around £50,000 in September 1984.

Two seasons at Meadow Lane were followed by a term at Rochdale before Alan went non-League as player-coach at Shepshed Charterhouse in March 1988. He played for Ilkeston Town in 1989–90, and later had a spell on the coaching staff back at Notts County where he is now the Football in the Community Officer.

Season	FL	FAC	FLC	Total
1983–84	25+1 (12)	1	2	28+1 (12)
Total	25+1 (12)	1	2	28+1 (12)

YOUNG, ERIC   1982–87

central defender   Ht 6 2, Wt 13 00   148 apps, 11 goals
born: Changi, Singapore, 25.3.1960
debut: Blackburn Rovers (a), 24.9.1983 (FL D2)

Over the years, Albion have been fortunate to have had the services of many excellent centre-halves, and Eric Young must certainly be numbered among them. Playing a major part in the tightest Albion defence since the war, he made the transition from Isthmian League to Football League look very easy, and acquitted himself well in the top flight after leaving the club. Solid in the air and hard to pass on the ground, he was also comfortable with the ball at his feet and posed a considerable threat to opposition penalty-areas.

The son of West Indian parents, Eric was born in Singapore where they were stationed with the R.A.F., but was brought up in Staines, Middlesex, and played for Staines Town before joining Slough Town during the 1978–79 season. Developing his game rapidly at Wexham Park, he gained F.A. representative honours, but declined invitations to play for the Isthmian League XI and the England Semi-Professional side because of his studies to become a quantity surveyor.

After four seasons with Slough, Eric, described as 'the best centre-half in non-League football', was attracting attention from a number of clubs, but it was Albion manager Mike Bailey who signed the promising 22-year-old in November 1982 for £10,000. With a string of consistent performances in the reserves behind him, the lanky

defender also worked hard on his physique and made his Second Division debut in September 1983 in place of the injured Steve Foster; he also took a leaf out of his senior's book by wearing a headband to protect scar-tissue. By March 1984, Eric was playing so well that Foster was sold to Aston Villa, and the following season his solid defensive partnership with Gary O'Reilly was the corner stone of Albion's valiant attempt to regain a place in the First Division; just 34 goals were conceded, the club's lowest ever total in the Football League (equalling the figure of 1922–23).

After suffering serious eye injuries at the start of 1986–87, Eric was sold to First Division Wimbledon for a giveaway fee of £75,000 in July 1987 as Albion tumbled into Division Three, but it proved a good move for him as he won an F.A. Cup winner's medal in 1988 and gained his first cap for Wales in May 1990. (As a British passport holder he had the choice of the home countries). After 99 League games for the 'Dons', the 30-year-old defender moved to Crystal Palace for £850,000 in August 1990 and won a ZDS Full Members Cup winner's medal in 1991. He also brought his collection of Welsh caps up to 20, but was released in 1995 and joined Wolves in September after a trial. Indeed, Eric so impressed his new manager, Graham Taylor, that he was made acting captain and won one more cap, but at the end of 1996–97, at the age of 37, he was released by the First Division side to link up with Crystal Palace once again on a non-contract basis for 1997–98.

Season	FL	FAC	FLC	FMC	Total
1983–84	30 (4)	2	3	0	35 (4)
1984–85	35 (3)	2	2	0	39 (3)
1985–86	32 (2)	5 (1)	3	2	42 (3)
1986–87	29 (1)	2	0+1	0	31+1 (1)
Total	126 (10)	11 (1)	8+1	2	147+1 (11)

YOUNG, LEON   1948–49

centre-half   Ht 6 1, Wt 12 08   8 apps
full name: Leonard Archibald Young
born: East Ham, Essex, 23.2.1912
debut: Aldershot (h), 14.2.1948 (FL D3(S))

One of several players recruited by Albion manager Don Welsh during the 1947–48 campaign, in a vain bid to avert the threat of having to apply for re-election, Leon Young was a few days short of his 36th birthday when he arrived at the Goldstone to add some experience to a faltering defence in February 1948. Having represented Essex as a schoolboy, Leon played for non-League Colchester Town and Ilford before joining West Ham United as an amateur in May 1933. After signing professional forms the following April, the tall defender was immediately drafted into the first team and played in the "Hammers'" final three matches of the 1933–34 season, but was then forced to play second-fiddle to England international Jim Barrett and consequently made the Second Division side just nine more times over the next three seasons. In November 1937, Leon was transferred to Reading and spent a war-interrupted ten years at Elm Park, appearing in 83 peacetime Third Division (South) matches before arriving in Hove for a fee of £1,000.

With Albion propping up the rest of the Southern Section, he was introduced to the line-up immediately and his debut saw a 1–1 home draw with Aldershot, a result which heralded a tremendous improvement. The club lost only four of its remaining sixteen games and the veteran pivot played his part well with his strong and steady play – in his seven appearances the team was unbeaten and conceded just three goals – but a series of remarkable results on the last day of the campaign saw Albion finish bottom. Leon subsequently enjoyed only one more outing in the first team during the 1948–49 season, at the end of which he retired.

Season	FL	Total
1947–48	7	7
1948–49	1	1
Total	8	8

YOUNG, WILLIE   1984

central defender	Ht 6 3, Wt 14 03	4 apps

full name: William David Young
born: Heriot, Midlothian, Scotland, 21.11.1951
debut: Manchester City (h), 10.3.1984 (FL D2)

Willie Young arrived at the Goldstone on loan from Norwich City in March 1984 as a stand-in for the suspended Steve Gatting. The holder of five Scottish under-23 caps, the 32-year-old defender was coming to the end of a successful if somewhat controversial career.

Indeed, he would probably have won a number of full caps had he not been banned from the Scotland side for life, along with four others, following incidents in a Copenhagen night-club while a squad member in September 1975. Willie may also be remembered for being rather fortunate not to become the first player sent off in an F.A. Cup final when he brought down West Ham United's Paul Allen towards the end of the 1980 final.

The towering Scot had arrived at Carrow Road in August 1983 via an unsuccessful trial with Falkirk, the Scottish junior club Seton Athletic, Aberdeen (1969), Tottenham Hotspur (September 1975), Arsenal (March 1977), and Nottingham Forest (December 1981), and had commanded transfer fees totalling around £350,000. Norwich splashed out £40,000 for his services, but in July 1984 he was sacked for alleged misconduct and spent September and October 1984 at Darlington on a non-contract basis.

Easily distinguished by a mop of red hair, Willie appeared in three consecutive F.A. Cup Finals for Arsenal, gaining a winner's medal in 1979 and finishing on the losing side in 1978 and 1980. He also played in the "Gunners'" side which lost the European Cup-Winners' Cup final on penalties to Valencia in 1980. After leaving the game he took to running an equestrian centre near Newark.

Season	FL	Total
1983–84	4	4
Total	4	4

Albion Wartime Players

When the United Kingdom declared war on Hitler's Germany on 3 September 1939, the British Government banned the assembly of crowds and the Football League immediately suspended its normal competitions; Albion had played three games in the Third Division (South). As the position stabilised so the playing of friendly matches was allowed, and emergency regional competitions were established by the Football League in October 1939.

Unlike the First World War, when the club closed down from 1915 until 1919 and did not participate in emergency tournaments, Albion kept going throughout the conflict although it was a struggle at times.

Many players were called up for the Forces and other services, commitments that took them away from the area. With restrictions placed upon travelling it would have been almost impossible for clubs to field teams, so a 'guest player' system was established where a team could utilise any player, registered or not, who could travel to the ground and back within the same day.

Albion manager Charlie Webb made good use of guest players, particularly those Liverpool men who were stationed in Sussex during the conflict, but he also found it necessary to commandeer spectators on occasion, most notably at Norwich on Christmas Day 1940 when a scratch side lost 18–0!

Three of that side were Albion 'juniors'. In May 1940 the club had established a junior side to encourage the development of young players in Sussex, and the team did much to keep local football alive in the county. A number of junior players did get to turn out for the senior side.

In 1941 the club joined a breakaway group of London-based sides unhappy with the Football League's fixture arrangements and played in a London War League under the auspices of the London F.A., but at the end of the season they were all welcomed back into the Football League fold.

The emergency competitions continued until things returned to normal a year after the war ended, in 1946.

This section gives brief biographical details of the 213 players who only made appearances in these wartime competitions. The wartime careers of players who also made peacetime appearances are included in the main *Albion Players* section. Note that the 1945–46 F.A. Cup tournament did require the use of registered players and is therefore included in the main *Albion Players* section rather than this wartime section.

Specifically, the 243 wartime matches played by the Albion comprise:

- Football League south regional competitions 1939–41 & 1942–45
- Football League South 1940–41 (This league used the results from the Football League's south regional competition, but there was a separate challenge match on 31 May 1941.)
- Football League War Cup 1939–41
- London War League 1941–42
- London War Cup 1941–42
- Football League (South) Cup 1942–45
- Football League Division Three (South) South 1945–46
- Football League Division Three (South) Cup 1945–46

Note that the results of the matches at the Goldstone Ground on 18 September 1940 and 12 October 1940, which were abandoned because of possible air-raids, were allowed to stand and are included in all statistics. However, the Goldstone match on 21 September 1940 was abandoned after just three-and-a-half minutes and was not counted in any table; it is not, therefore, included in statistics within this book.

Note also that the complete line-ups for eleven matches during 1941–42 have yet to be confirmed; those players who were expected to play have been included in this volume. In addition, one player from the match on 1 January 1944 has not been identified at all and is included in this section as an *'unknown guest player'*.

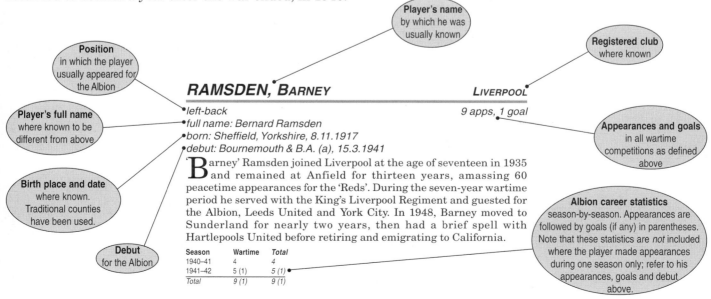

RAMSDEN, BARNEY — *LIVERPOOL*

left-back — 9 apps, 1 goal

full name: Bernard Ramsden
born: Sheffield, Yorkshire, 8.11.1917
debut: Bournemouth & B.A. (a), 15.3.1941

'Barney' Ramsden joined Liverpool at the age of seventeen in 1935 and remained at Anfield for thirteen years, amassing 60 peacetime appearances for the 'Reds'. During the seven-year wartime period he served with the King's Liverpool Regiment and guested for the Albion, Leeds United and York City. In 1948, Barney moved to Sunderland for nearly two years, then had a brief spell with Hartlepools United before retiring and emigrating to California.

Season	Wartime	Total
1940–41	4	4
1941–42	5 (1)	5 (1)
Total	9 (1)	9 (1)

Labels in diagram:
- Player's name — by which he was usually known
- Registered club — where known
- Position — in which the player usually appeared for the Albion
- Player's full name — where known to be different from above
- Appearances and goals — in all wartime competitions as defined above
- Birth place and date — where known. Traditional counties have been used.
- Albion career statistics — season-by-season. Appearances are followed by goals (if any) in parentheses. Note that these statistics are *not* included where the player made appearances during one season only; refer to his appearances, goals and debut above.
- Debut — for the Albion

ABEL, SAMMY QUEEN'S PARK RANGERS

right-back   1 app

born: Neston, Cheshire, 30.12.1908
debut: Southend United (h), 10.4.1940

Sammy Abel was a long-term servant of Queen's Park Rangers, remaining on the staff from 1934 until 1946. Previously with Bury (1929–30), Accrington Stanley (1930–31), Chesterfield (1931–33) and Fulham (1933–34), he was a centre-forward in his early days but was converted into a full-back during his time at Loftus Road. Sammy made around 170 wartime appearances for Q.P.R., and also guested for Chelsea, Crystal Palace and Fulham before retiring in 1946 at the age of 37.

ADAMS, BILLY TOTTENHAM HOTSPUR

outside-left   1 app

born: Arlecdon, Cumberland, 8.1.1919
debut: Reading (h), 21.10.1944

After joining Spurs in 1943, Billy Adams made only a handful of wartime appearances before returning to his native county with Carlisle United in 1946, where he spent one season before dropping into non-League football with Cheltenham and then Workington. He remained with the Cumberland side for their first season as a Football League club in 1951–52.

ALEXANDER, FRED QUEEN'S PARK RANGERS

centre-half   1 app

debut: Bristol Rovers (a), 15.9.1945

Fred Alexander first played for Q.P.R. during the 1943–44 season, but made only four appearances in the emergency competitions up to 1946. He also guested briefly for Luton Town and Millwall, but didn't play League football after the war.

ANDERSON, JOCK PORTSMOUTH

centre-forward   3 apps

born: Dundee, Angus, Scotland, 8.5.1915
debut: West Ham United (h), 20.11.1943

On the Fratton staff for thirteen years from 1933 until 1946, Jock Anderson led the Portsmouth attack in the 1939 F.A. Cup final, scoring once in the unexpected 4–1 victory over favourites Wolverhampton Wanderers. He played in almost 100 wartime games for 'Pompey', and made a single guest appearance for Luton Town before finishing his career with a short spell at Aldershot in 1946–47.

AUSTEN, BERT BRIGHTON & HOVE ALBION

full-back   6 apps

full name: Herbert Austen
debut: Watford (h), 1.6.1940

One of the original intake of Albion juniors, Bert Austen had previously played for Hove Penguins, and made his senior debut just a few weeks later, one of five youngsters drafted in for the 2–2 draw with Watford in June 1940. He also played during 1940–41 but then disappeared from the scene.

Season	Wartime	Total
1939–40	2	2
1940–41	2	4
Total	6	6

BALL

inside-left   1 app

debut: Clapton Orient (a), 1.1.1944

Ball was an eleventh-hour recruit who appeared in a 3–0 defeat at Orient on New Year's Day 1944.

BALMER, JACK LIVERPOOL

inside-forward   14 apps, 16 goals

born: Liverpool, Lancashire, 6.2.1916
debut: Bournemouth & B.A. (a), 15.3.1941

One of a whole host of Liverpool players to turn out for the Albion while stationed in Sussex, Jack Balmer spent his entire professional career with the Merseyside club, scoring 99 goals in 292 League games between 1935 and 1952. In 1947 he scored three consecutive hat-tricks as Liverpool won the League championship. Jack gained a wartime cap for England v. Wales in November 1939, and also guested for Newcastle United. His record with the Albion was outstanding, even by wartime standards: the 25-year-old hit sixteen goals in just fourteen games.

Season	Wartime	Total
1940–41	8 (9)	8 (9)
1941–42	6 (7)	6 (7)
Total	14 (16)	14 (16)

BARBER

inside-left   1 app

debut: Portsmouth (a), 29.3.1941

Barber was an inside-forward of unknown background. (It is possible that he was George Barber of Chelsea, but he was usually a full-back.)

BARLOW, K. SOUTHAMPTON

right-half   1 app

debut: Southampton (a), 23.12.1944

Barlow was a Southampton lad loaned to the Albion for a match against his own club.

BARTRAM, A.

goalkeeper   1 app

debut: Norwich City (a), 25.12.1940

One of the emergency players who turned out for the Albion when they arrived at Carrow Road with only four men on Christmas Day 1940, Bartram was the unfortunate goalkeeper on the receiving end of a sensational 18–0 defeat.

BENTLEY, GEORGE BRIGHTON & HOVE ALBION

outside-left   1 app

debut: Crystal Palace (a), 26.2.1944

George Bentley was an Albion youngster, but made very few appearances for either the senior or junior sides.

BIRD, S.

inside-right   1 app

debut: Norwich City (a), 25.12.1940

Bird was one of seven emergency players who made up the team in the infamous 18–0 defeat at Carrow Road.

BLACKMAN, JACK — CRYSTAL PALACE

left-half — *1 app*
born: Bermondsey, London, 1911
debut: Crystal Palace (h), 26.9.1942

Originally a centre-forward, Jack Blackman scored 52 goals in 100 Third Division matches for Crystal Palace during the four seasons before the war, having previously played for Queen's Park Rangers (1931–35). The Londoner turned out regularly for the 'Glaziers' throughout the hostilities, while also making fleeting appearances for Aldershot, Millwall, Charlton Athletic, Clapton Orient and Luton Town. In September 1942 he was loaned to the Albion for a match against his own club at the Goldstone in September 1942 which Palace won 8–1. Jack dropped into the Southern League with Guildford City in May 1946, but returned to Selhurst Park as assistant trainer on hanging up his boots. He was also a noted amateur boxer in his youth.

BOJAR, FELIX

utility player — *10 apps*
born: Poland, 26.12.1917
debut: Chelsea (h), 5.9.1942

A corporal P.T. instructor serving with the Polish Air Force, Felix Bojar was a 24-year-old former international full-back and the first foreigner ever to play for the Albion. Described as a brilliant, two-footed player with great ball-control, he appeared in defence and attack during his sojourn at the Goldstone, and also assisted the Albion juniors.

BOTT, WILF — QUEEN'S PARK RANGERS

winger — *15 apps, 3 goals*
born: Edlington, Yorkshire, 25.4.1907
debut: Reading (a), 13.1.1940

A lightning-fast winger who could also perform more than adequately in the inside roles, Wilf Bott joined Queen's Park Rangers in May 1936 having previously seen service with Doncaster Rovers (1927–31), Huddersfield Town (1931–34) and Newcastle United (1934–36). He guested for the Albion, Aldershot and Chelsea in the early part of the war, but when things returned to normal Wilf moved into non-League football with Lancaster Town.

BOWLES, REG — BRIGHTON & HOVE ALBION

full-back — *6 apps*
born: Ashford, Kent, 16.3.1926
debut: Millwall (h), 29.11.1941

Almost a legend in Sussex non-League circles, Reg Bowles attended Lancing Senior School and joined the Albion as a junior in 1940. In November 1941 he was called up as a last-minute replacement for the first team against Millwall at the tender age of just 15 years 258 days, and he remains, by some way, the youngest player ever to make a senior appearance for the club. In 1942–43, Reg gained winner's medals in the Sussex County Wartime League Cup and the R.U.R. Charity Cup with the Albion juniors, and subsequently served with the Royal Navy in the Far East.

After the war he was employed at the railway works in Lancing, and played for Lancing Athletic before joining Worthing whom he skippered to three Senior Cup finals, gaining winner's medals in 1952 and 1957. Also on Watford's books as an amateur for a short time, Reg represented Sussex on 52 occasions, many as captain, and was chosen for the Middlesex Wanderers' tour of the Netherlands in 1950–51.

Season	Wartime	Total
1941–42	2	2
1942–43	4	4
Total	6	6

BOYD, JIMMY — GRIMSBY TOWN

inside-right — *1 app*
born: Glasgow, Lanarkshire, Scotland, 29.4.1907
debut: Southampton (a), 29.4.1944

Jimmy Boyd celebrated his 37th birthday by turning out for the Albion in a 3–0 defeat at The Dell, but his main claim to fame was a ten-year spell (1925–35) playing for Newcastle United, where he gained an F.A. Cup winner's medal in 1932 and a Scottish cap *v.* Ireland in 1934. He was also a member of the "Magpies"' forward line which made short work of the Albion in the fifth-round F.A. Cup tie at St James's Park in February 1930, winning 3–0. Jimmy later had stints with Derby County, Bury and Dundee before joining Grimsby Town in 1938. He played virtually no senior football during the war, making just single appearances for the Albion and Clapton Orient in 1943–44.

BRATLEY, GEORGE — CRYSTAL PALACE

defender — *14 apps*
debut: Brentford (a), 26.8.1944

Although registered with Crystal Palace, George Bratley played in only two wartime matches for the 'Glaziers' and didn't appear in peacetime football, but he spent some considerable time guesting for the Albion during 1944–45.

BRIGGS, VIC — SOUTHWICK

wing-half — *6 apps*
born: Southwick, Sussex, 22.3.1910
debut: Portsmouth (a), 27.1.1940

Generally regarded as Southwick's finest-ever player, Vic Briggs appeared in five Sussex Senior Cup finals for the 'Wickers' between 1927 and 1948, gaining winner's medals on four occasions, and starred in three County League championship sides. He added two more Senior Cup winner's medals to his collection during a spell with Worthing immediately after the war before returning to his beloved Southwick. Vic was also a trialist for the England amateur team and appeared in 53 representative matches for Sussex, a total that would have been far greater but for the seven–year break during the Second World War.

When he died in 1980, the Southwick legend's ashes were scattered over the Old Barn Way pitch. Vic initially assisted Albion's reserve team in 1931–32, and was also associated briefly with Spurs during the war.

Season	Wartime	Total
1939–40	5	5
1940–41	1	1
Total	6	6

BRISCOE, JIMMY   HEART OF MIDLOTHIAN

outside-right   3 apps, 1 goal
born: Clock Face, St Helens, Lancashire, 23.4.1917
debut: Brentford (h), 2.12.1944

After starting out in his native Lancashire with Preston North End, Jimmy Briscoe moved north of the border in 1937 to sign for Scottish First Division side Heart of Midlothian. In addition to his wartime appearances for the Albion, he also guested for Blackburn Rovers, Arsenal, Crystal Palace, Fulham, Millwall and Southend United. After the war Jimmy had two seasons with Northampton Town in the Third Division (South)

BROWN, JIMMY   ROMFORD TOWN

left-back   15 apps
full name: James R. Brown
debut: Southampton (h), 26.12.1944

A young amateur full-back who was later registered by the Albion, Jimmy Brown was a Romford Town player who turned out for the Brighton junior side before being promoted to the first eleven for an extended run during the latter half of the 1944–45 campaign.

BROWN, JIMMY   MOTHERWELL

left-back   1 app
debut: Reading (h), 21.10.1944

Jimmy Brown's sole outing for the Albion came in a 9–3 home defeat at the hands of Reading, with a team containing no fewer than nine guest players.

BROWNING, CHARLIE   BRIGHTON & HOVE ALBION

wing-half   8 apps
debut: Clapton Orient (a), 13.9.1941

Charlie Browning was an Albion junior who assisted the first team during 1941–42.

BUCKELL

outside-right   1 app
debut: Millwall (a), 7.3.1942

Buckell was a spectator at the match with Millwall in March 1942 who was pressed into service when Albion arrived short of players. The game was lost 2–0.

BUNYON, W.   CLAPTON ORIENT

defender   1 app
debut: Clapton Orient (a), 25.12.1942

Bunyon was loaned to Albion for a Christmas Day fixture at Clapton Orient in 1942, but, despite the home club's generosity, Brighton were still forced to recruit members of the crowd to make up the numbers and lost 3–1 with a much-weakened side.

BURDETT

centre-forward   1 app
debut: Watford (a), 21.2.1942

Burdett's pedigree is unknown, but it is possible that he was Tom Burdett who had spells with Hull City, Fulham, Lincoln City and Bury before the war.

BURGESS, RON   TOTTENHAM HOTSPUR

outside-right   4 apps
born: Cwm, Ebbw Vale, Monmouthshire, Wales, 9.4.1917
debut: Queen's Park Rangers (a), 13.12.1941

In a superb career spanning the war with Spurs, Ron Burgess played in 327 League and Cup matches, mainly as a wing-half, and skippered the League championship-winning side of 1950–51. In addition to ten wartime international appearances, he gained 32 full caps for Wales, represented Great Britain against the Rest of Europe in 1947, and played for the Football League *v.* the Scottish League the same year. On leaving White Hart Lane, Ron became player-manager of Swansea Town (1955–58) and was boss at Watford (1959–63).

On the outbreak of war he joined the Police Reserve Force along with several of his Spurs team-mates, but soon volunteered for service with the R.A.F. and became a P.T. instructor. Ron also guested for Huddersfield Town, Millwall, Nottingham Forest, Notts County and Reading.

BURTENSHAW, CHARLIE   BRIGHTON & HOVE ALBION

forward   3 apps
born: Portslade-by-Sea, Sussex, 16.10.1922
debut: Portsmouth (a), 5.10.1940

The elder brother of Albion's Steve (see *Albion Players*), Charlie Burtenshaw started out with St Andrews F.C. and became a Brighton junior, assisting the first team as a teenager in 1940–41. He played for Southwick after the war before graduating into the Football League with Luton Town. In October 1949, Charlie, together with another brother Bill, signed for Gillingham and added a further 28 League games to his name after the Kent club were re-admitted to the Football League in 1950.

BUSH, TOM   LIVERPOOL

centre-half   3 apps
born: Hodnet, Shropshire, 22.2.1914
debut: Bournemouth & B.A. (a), 15.3.1941

After joining Liverpool in 1933, Tom Bush spent most of his fourteen war-interrupted years at Anfield as a reserve, although he

enjoyed extended runs in the League side during the two seasons prior to the conflict. After 64 First Division appearances for the Anfield side, he retired in 1947 to take up coaching. Tom also guested for Fulham and Leeds United during the war.

Season	Wartime	Total
1940–41	1	1
1941–42	2	2
Total	3	3

BUTLER, MALCOLM   BLACKPOOL

right-back   1 app
born: Belfast, Co. Antrim, Ireland, 6.8.1913
debut: Queen's Park Rangers (a), 20.4.1940

Malcolm Butler joined Blackpool from Belfast Celtic in 1935 and appeared for Northern Ireland against Wales in the final international match of 1938–39, but then war broke out and a promising career was virtually ended. He guested for the Albion, Chelsea, Grimsby Town, Millwall and Manchester City during the conflict while serving as a navigator in the R.A.F., eventually attaining the rank of flight-lieutenant, and ended his football days with a season at Accrington Stanley in 1947–48.

CAMERON, JOCK — BRIGHTON & HOVE ALBION

right-half — *1 app*
debut: Clapton Orient (a), 25.12.1942

Jock Cameron played for the Albion junior team which won the Sussex County Wartime League Cup and the R.U.R. Charity Cup in 1942–43. He was drafted into the first eleven for the Christmas Day fixture with Orient that season.

CATER, RON — WEST HAM UNITED

centre-half — *1 app*
born: Fulham, London, 2.2.1922
debut: West Ham United (a), 27.2.1943

Loaned to Albion for a match with his own club, West Ham United, Ron Cater joined the 'Hammers' at the age of fifteen in 1937 and had yet to make his Football League debut when war broke out. He served with the Essex Territorials and the Royal Artillery during the hostilities, and remained at Upton Park until 1951, making 63 Second Division appearances before ending his career with a spell at Leyton Orient.

CHAPMAN, A.

centre-forward — *1 app*
debut: Queen's Park Rangers (a), 13.12.1941

Chapman was a young London amateur drafted into Albion's team for a match with Q.P.R. which ended in a 3–0 defeat.

CHESTERS, ARTHUR — CRYSTAL PALACE

goalkeeper — *7 apps*
born: Salford, Lancashire, 14.2.1910
debut: Queen's Park Rangers (a), 20.4.1940

Arthur Chesters joined Crystal Palace in 1937 after previous service with Manchester United and Exeter City. In the two seasons leading up to the war he was Palace's regular custodian, and appeared for the 'Glaziers', Albion and Fulham during the initial wartime season. Arthur later played for Leicester City and guested extensively for Rochdale from 1944. He was officially transferred to the Lancashire club for the 1945-46 transitional season after which he hung up his gloves.

CHRISTIE

centre-half — *1 app*
debut: Portsmouth (h), 1.3.1941

Christie was an unidentified guest player who played in an excellent 4–0 Goldstone defeat of Portsmouth. (He could perhaps have been Norman Christie, formerly of Blackburn Rovers.)

CLARKSON, GEORGE — BLACKBURN ROVERS

inside-left/left-back — *2 apps*
debut: Brentford (h), 6.1.1940

Although registered with Blackburn Rovers, George Clarkson didn't play for their first team in either regular or wartime football.

CLATWORTHY, LES — CHELSEA

left-back — *1 app*
debut: Chelsea (a), 25.10.1941

Loaned to Albion by Chelsea for a fixture at Stamford Bridge (which Albion won 3–1), Les Clatworthy appeared for Chelsea as an amateur in 1940–41 and 1941–42, then concentrated on the more important task of flying planes for the R.A.F. as a flight-sergeant pilot. He was later awarded the Distinguished Flying Medal.

CLIFFORD, JOHN — NORTHAMPTON TOWN

goalkeeper — *1 app*
debut: Crystal Palace (a), 6.4.1940

With Albion a man short for a game at Selhurst Park during the first wartime season, John Clifford made up the numbers after ten minutes, taking over in goal from Gordon Mee who moved to the left wing. At half-time Palace led 5–0 and the pair swapped places, but the 'Glaziers' added five more to complete a 10–0 scoreline.

COCKER, JOE — ARSENAL

outside-left — *1 app*
debut: Arsenal (a), 10.4.1944

Joe Cocker was an Arsenal youngster who guested for the Albion in a 3–1 defeat against the 'Gunners' at White Hart Lane. He formerly played for the Arsenal nursery club, Margate.

COLBORN, HAROLD — BRIGHTON & HOVE ALBION

outside-right — *3 apps, 1 goal*
debut: Southampton (a), 31.8.1940

A youngster from the Hove Penguins club, Harold Colborn made four appearances in Albion's reserve side during 1938–39, the last season before the war, and subsequently played for the newly formed Albion junior team in the early days of the conflict.

COLLINS, JOHN — BRIGHTON & HOVE ALBION

centre-forward — *1 app, 1 goal*
debut: Aldershot (h), 13.5.1940

An Albion junior, John Collins was just sixteen when he scored the second goal in a 2–2 draw with Aldershot at the Goldstone.

COOK, P. R. — LUTON TOWN

left-back — *1 app*
debut: Luton Town (a), 3.10.1942

Cook was borrowed from Luton Town for a 5–2 defeat at Kenilworth Road.

COOK, R. — ST JOHNSTONE

centre-forward/outside-left — *9 apps, 3 goals*
debut: Brentford (a), 26.8.1944

A guest from St Johnstone, Cook was unfortunate to play for the Albion at the start of 1944–45, a period which saw some fearful hidings home and away. In fact, Albion won just one of his nine games.

CORNISH, DENNIS — BRIGHTON & HOVE ALBION

winger — *4 apps, 3 goals*
born: Newton Abbott, Devon, 1926
debut: Watford (h), 14.4.1945

An Albion youngster, Dennis Cornish played in the last four fixtures of the 1944–45 campaign and finished on the winning side on each occasion, scoring three goals in the process. In May 1945 he was in the Albion juniors' side which lost the R.U.R. Cup final to Worthing.

COTHLIFF, HAROLD   TORQUAY UNITED

inside-right   *1 app, 1 goal*
born: Liverpool, Lancashire, 24.3.1916
debut: Reading (a), 18.5.1940

A former Nottingham Forest reserve, Harold Cothliff joined Torquay United in 1938 and was ever-present in the last season before the war. The West Country club closed down after the initial season of regional competition, but Harold guested prolifically for Fulham, Portsmouth, Reading, Chelsea, Chester, Clapton Orient, Millwall and Bournemouth. He returned to Plainmoor when Torquay reorganised in 1945 and remained for three seasons, after which he departed from the first-class game.

COURT, DICK

inside-right   *1 app*
born: India
debut: Aldershot (a), 27.4.1940

D ick Court was seconded, along with his former Aldershot team-mate Laurie Kelly, when Albion arrived at the Recreation Ground two men short in April 1940. Dick had joined the 'Shots' in 1937, and appeared briefly up to the outbreak of war when he was released.

COWAN, SAM   BRIGHTON & HOVE ALBION

defender   *3 apps*
born: Chesterfield, Derbyshire, 10.5.1901
debut: Southampton (h), 30.12.1939

I n a long career with Doncaster Rovers, Manchester City and Bradford City, Sam Cowan won three England caps, represented the Football League in 1934, and skippered Manchester City's

victorious F.A. Cup final side in the same year; he also served on the Players' Union executive committee. A bulky centre-half, he was a natural attacker and a born leader, and was an excellent appointment when he came to Hove in 1938 as trainer. During the war Sam was pressed into service on three occasions: twice in 1939–40 and once in 1945–46. On 13 October 1945, at the age of 44 years 156 days, he became the oldest player ever to pull on an Albion shirt in a competitive match, a 3–0 defeat at Bourne-mouth.

After the war Sam briefly managed Manchester City during 1946–47, and subsequently became masseur to the Sussex and England cricket teams. He also managed Brighton Tigers Ice Hockey Club for some time. Sam died in October 1964 while refereeing a football match in aid of Sussex and England cricketer Jim Parks's testimonial fund at Haywards Heath.

Season	Wartime	Total
1939–40	2	2
1945–46	1	1
Total	3	3

CRAWFORD, TED   CLAPTON ORIENT

inside-left   *6 apps, 2 goals*
born: Filey, Yorkshire, 31.10.1906
debut: Fulham (h), 16.9.1944

T ed Crawford began his career with Halifax Town in 1931 and was transferred to Liverpool a year later. In July 1933 he joined

Clapton Orient and scored 68 goals in 199 League appearances up to the war, during which he also guested for Watford. After the war he turned to coaching on the Continent with Degerfors IF (Sweden) from 1945 until 1949, and then in Italy with Bologna. During his stint with the Albion, Ted was sent off for fighting in the 3–1 defeat at Aldershot in October 1944.

CROFT, CHARLIE   HUDDERSFIELD TOWN

left-half   *1 app*
born: Thornhill, Yorkshire, 26.11.1918
debut: Brentford (h), 2.12.1944

C harlie Croft joined Huddersfield Town as an amateur in 1938 and was signed as a professional just before the outbreak of hostilities a year later, but appeared only briefly in the emergency competitions. A sergeant P.T. instructor in the Army during the war, Charlie ended his Football League career with three seasons at Mansfield Town (1947–50) after which he had four seasons in the Midland League with Boston United.

CUNLIFFE, ARTHUR   HULL CITY

forward   *19 apps, 11 goals*
born: Blackrod, Lancashire, 5.2.1909
debut: Charlton Athletic (h), 1.11.1941

A n exceptionally fast winger, Arthur Cunliffe played for Blackburn Rovers (1928–33), Aston Villa (1933–35), Middlesbrough (1935–37), Burnley (1937–38) and Hull City, winning England caps against Ireland and Wales during 1932–33 while with Blackburn. An Army P.T. instructor during the war, he spent a lengthy spell with the Albion during 1941–42, helping to coach the youngsters and occasionally turning out for the junior team. Arthur guested for Aldershot throughout the war years, clocking up over 60 appearances, and also turned out for Reading, Fulham, Rochdale and Stoke City. He joined Rochdale on a permanent basis in 1946 and was subsequently involved with Bournemouth until 1974, as trainer and then physio.

A. CUNLIFFE
Blackburn Rovers

CURTIS, GEORGE   ARSENAL

inside-forward   *3 apps*
debut: Watford (h), 15.11.1941
See *Albion Managers*

CURTIS, J. W.

centre-half   *1 app*
debut: Aldershot (a), 4.5.1946

A sergeant in the Guards, Curtis played for an Army representative side in Germany. After returning to England he wrote to Albion manager Charlie Webb requesting a trial, and was chosen to play in the last of the wartime fixtures, impressing in a 2–2 draw at Aldershot. Webb was said to be hopeful of signing the soldier, but nothing was forthcoming.

DEVINE, JOHN   QUEEN'S PARK RANGERS

inside-right   *1 app*
born: Glasgow, Lanarkshire, Scotland
debut: Bournemouth & B.A. (h), 17.4.1940

J ohn Devine made fourteen appearances for Aberdeen between 1935 and 1938 before joining Queen's Park Rangers. He played briefly for the Londoners during the early part of the war, and also guested for Clapton Orient.

DEVONPORT, GEORGE — TORQUAY UNITED

inside/outside-right — 5 apps, 1 goal
debut: Southend United (a), 25.1.1941

Although registered with Torquay United, George Devonport never appeared in their first eleven.

DOOLEY, A.

inside-left — 1 app
debut: Millwall (a), 5.2.1944

Dooley was a young Scot of otherwise unknown credentials who was employed in a 7–4 defeat by Millwall in February 1944.

DRIVER, ALLENBY — SHEFFIELD WEDNESDAY

inside-left — 1 app, 1 goal
born: Mansfield, Nottinghamshire, 29.12.1918
debut: West Ham United (a), 6.5.1944

Allenby Driver started out as a professional with Sheffield Wednesday in 1936, but made the first team on just six occasions before the war. He turned out for the 'Owls' on occasion throughout the conflict while serving in the Royal Artillery, and also guested for Brentford, Crystal Palace, Fulham, Millwall, Watford and the Albion. In 1946, Allenby was transferred to Luton Town, and went on to play for Norwich City (1948–50), Ipswich Town (1950–52) and Walsall (1952–53) before dropping into non-League football with Corby Town and Frickley Athletic.

DUKE, GEORGE — LUTON TOWN

goalkeeper — 2 apps
born: Westhampnett, Sussex, 6.9.1920
debut: Southampton (a), 11.11.1939

A former pupil at Moulsecoomb School and a Brighton Boys representative, George Duke played for Southwick in the Sussex County League for two seasons before signing for Luton Town just before the war. He guested widely during the seven years of emergency competition, appearing for Aldershot, Arsenal, Brentford, Chelsea, Fulham, Queen's Park Rangers and Reading as well as the Albion. In fact he was the first guest player to turn out for Brighton. George remained on the Luton staff until signing for Bournemouth in 1949 where he saw out his League career.

DYE, DEREK — NORWICH CITY

left-half — 1 app
debut: Norwich City (a), 25.12.1940

Derek Dye was one of the Norwich City youngsters who helped make up Albion's team for the calamitous 18–0 Christmas Day defeat at Carrow Road in 1940.

EASDALE, JACK — LIVERPOOL

centre-half — 37 apps, 1 goal
born: Dumbarton, Dunbartonshire, Scotland, 16.1.1919
debut: Clapton Orient (a), 13.9.1941

Jack Easdale joined Liverpool in 1937, but had still to make his first-team debut when the war started. He gave Albion sterling service when Army commitments allowed, along with a number of his Liverpool team-mates, but struggled to make an impact at Anfield after the war, making the League side on just two occasions as the 'Reds' carried off the First Division championship in 1946–47. Jack was transferred to Stockport County in 1948 where he again appeared only briefly before departing from the Football League.

Season	Wartime	Total
1941–42	2 (1)	2 (1)
1942–43	20	20
1943–44	15	15
Total	37 (1)	37 (1)

EASTHAM, GEORGE — BLACKPOOL

inside-forward — 3 apps
born: Blackpool, Lancashire, 13.9.1913
debut: Portsmouth (a), 24.1.1942

George Eastham enjoyed a fine career as a clever inside-forward in the First Division before the war with Bolton Wanderers (1932–37), Brentford (1937–38) and Blackpool, playing for England in the 1–0 win over the Netherlands in Amsterdam in 1935. He also represented the Football League in a crushing 10–2 victory against an Ireland/Wales combination at Everton the same year, a match which was played to mark King George V's Silver Jubilee and experimentally officiated by two referees.

A schemer rather than a striker, George guested all over the country during the early war years, playing for Bolton Wanderers, Birmingham, Brentford, Mansfield Town, Millwall, Queen's Park Rangers and York City, but resumed his attachment with Blackpool in 1945 and went on to play for Swansea Town (1947–48), Rochdale (1948) and Lincoln City (1948–50). He subsequently tried his hand in management with Ards (Irish League), Accrington Stanley, Distillery (Irish League), Ards for a second spell, and the Hellenic club of Cape Town.

George's brother was Harry Eastham (see below). His son, George Eastham junior, won fame with Newcastle United, Arsenal, Stoke City and England.

EASTHAM, HARRY — LIVERPOOL

outside-right — 50 apps, 4 goals
born: Blackpool, Lancashire, 30.6.1917
debut: Southend United (h), 5.4.1941

One of the Liverpool contingent who served Albion so well during the war years, Harry Eastham joined the Anfield staff in 1936 and was making his presence felt when the closure of regular football came in 1939. He won the League title with the 'Reds' in 1946–47, but then played more than 150 games for Tranmere Rovers (1948–53) before ending his career at Accrington Stanley (1953–55). In addition to his wartime games for the Albion, Harry also guested for Bolton Wanderers, Blackpool, Leeds United, Newcastle United, New Brighton and Southport. His brother, George Eastham, also played for the Albion during the war (see above).

Season	Wartime	Total
1940–41	5	5
1941–42	7	7
1942–43	20 (3)	20 (3)
1943–44	18 (1)	18 (1)
Total	50 (4)	50 (4)

EDINGTON, JOHN — ARSENAL

right-half — 1 app
debut: West Ham United (h), 20.11.1943

John Edington made eight appearances for Arsenal in 1943–44, the season he guested for the Albion, and also appeared briefly for Halifax Town.

EVANS, TOMMY   BRIGHTON & HOVE ALBION

winger   25 apps
born: Merthyr Tydfil, Glamorgan, Wales
debut: Aldershot (h), 21.10.1939

Tommy Evans joined Cardiff City from Caerau Athletic in April 1938 and made a single appearance in their Third Division team before arriving at the Goldstone on trial in May 1939. He was signed during the summer, but war was declared in September before he had been given the opportunity to make his League debut. The tricky little winger – just 5' 4" and 9 stone – continued to play for Albion in the emergency competitions until the end of March 1940 when he departed from the area and disappeared from the football scene.

FAIRHURST, BILLY   BURY

goalkeeper   33 apps
born: St Helens, Lancashire
debut: Luton Town (h), 22.1.1944

A Liverpool junior who made his Football League debut with Wigan Borough in 1930, Billy Fairhurst then drifted into non-League football with Rhyl, and also had a spell in Rugby League as a full-back for St Helens Recreation before joining Bury in 1934. He played occasionally for the 'Shakers' during the early years of the war when he also guested for Manchester United, Liverpool and Bristol City. Billy had an extended run with the Albion, being more-or-less the regular goalkeeper from January 1943 to March 1945, but he didn't play League football after the war.

Season	Wartime	Total
1943–44	7	7
1944–45	26	26
Total	33	33

FARMER, ALEX   QUEEN'S PARK RANGERS

left-back   1 app
born: Lochgelly, Fife, Scotland, 1909
debut: Queen's Park Rangers (a), 28.10.1944

Alex Farmer joined Queen's Park Rangers in 1934 after previous experience with Kettering Town, Nottingham Forest (where he made sixteen League appearances) and Yeovil & Petters United. He played intermittently for Q.P.R. up to 1945, and was loaned to the Albion for a match against his own club as well as guesting for Charlton Athletic. When he retired Alex became assistant trainer at Loftus Road and was still involved with the club well into the 1950s.

FELTON, BOB   PORT VALE

left-back   1 app
born: Gateshead, Co. Durham, 12.8.1918
debut: Portsmouth (h), 14.9.1940

An Everton reserve-team player before joining Port Vale in 1938, Bob Felton didn't appear for Vale during the war until the 1945–46 transitional season, after which he was transferred to Crystal Palace where he made just one appearance before leaving the first-class game.

FLACK, DOUG   FULHAM

goalkeeper   1 app
born: Staines, Middlesex, 24.10.1920
debut: Reading (a), 13.1.1940

Doug Flack joined Fulham as an office-boy in 1935, but had to wait thirteen years until 1948 to make the "Cottagers'" Football

League team. He guested for Brentford, Clapton Orient, Portsmouth, Reading, Spurs and West Ham United in the early war years, then joined the Royal Air Force in 1942, serving in the Far East for the remainder of the conflict.

In 1948–49, Doug played in 29 matches of Fulham's Second Division championship success, but made only 25 more League appearances before being transferred to Walsall in 1953. A qualified coach, he was involved with Corinthian-Casuals and Tooting & Mitcham United after hanging up his gloves.

FORD, FRED   CHARLTON ATHLETIC

centre-half   12 apps
born: Belvedere, Erith, Kent, 10.2.1916
debut: Watford (a), 21.2.1942

Fred Ford joined Charlton Athletic in 1936 and appeared in their First Division team on 22 occasions up to the war. Initially guesting for the Albion in the two seasons 1941–43, he re-appeared during 1945–46 after recovering from a wound received while crossing the Rhine with the Royal Engineers. Fred also made guest appearances for Fulham, Millwall and Spurs, and was transferred to Millwall in November 1945. In 1947 he became player-coach with Carlisle United, but was forced into retirement through injury two years later. Fred went on to enjoy a long career in coaching and management, holding the reins at Bristol City (1960–67, winning promotion to Division Two in 1965), Bristol Rovers (1968–69), and Swindon Town (1969–71).

Season	Wartime	Total
1941–42	8	8
1942–43	1	1
1945–46	3	3
Total	12	12

FOX, DAN   BRIGHTON & HOVE ALBION

outside-left   4 apps
debut: Brentford (h), 25.3.1944

Don Fox was on Swansea Town's books in 1942–43, but was registered with the Albion the following season when he made his four appearances.

FRANCE, ERNIE   BRIGHTON & HOVE ALBION

left-half   2 apps
born: Eastleigh, Hampshire, 27.5.1924
debut: Clapton Orient (h), 26.12.1942

Formerly with Lancing Rovers as a centre-forward, Ernie France was an early recruit of the newly formed Albion junior team in 1940 and played fairly regularly for the youngsters throughout the war, winning medals for the Sussex County Wartime League Cup and R.U.R. Charity Cup in 1942–43. He also turned out briefly for Southampton's reserves.

Ernie joined Lancing Athletic in 1946 while employed at the local Southern Railway workshops, and skippered the County League side into the 1950s. He also represented Sussex at both junior and senior levels.

Season	Wartime	Total
1942–43	1	1
1943–44	1	1
Total	2	2

FRANCIS, VIC — HASTINGS & ST LEONARDS

inside-right — *1 app*
debut: Aldershot (h), 13.5.1940

A prominent player on the local scene either side of the war, Vic Francis won a hatful of honours in Sussex football, appearing in six Senior Cup finals and gaining five winner's medals: in 1932 and 1933 with Eastbourne, and in 1936, 1938 and 1940 with Hastings & St Leonards.

FROST, ARTHUR — NEW BRIGHTON

outside-right — *3 apps, 1 goal*
born: Liverpool, Lancashire, 1.12.1915
debut: Millwall (h), 17.2.1945

Arthur Frost joined New Brighton on his release from the Army in 1938 and was transferred to Newcastle United in March 1939, where he was to make just one appearance before the outbreak of war effectively ruined his blossoming career. During the conflict he guested for the Albion and Southport, and subsequently played for South Liverpool.

GILLESPIE, IAN — CRYSTAL PALACE

outside-right — *1 app*
born: Plymouth, Devon, 6.5.1913
debut: Crystal Palace (h), 26.9.1942

Ian Gillespie joined Crystal Palace from Harwich & Parkeston in February 1937 and scored four goals in 21 Third Division appearances up to the war. After playing for the 'Glaziers' fairly regularly during the war years (in addition to assisting the Albion, Millwall, Clapton Orient and West Ham United), he joined Ipswich Town for the 1945–46 transitional season and remained at Portman Road for the initial peacetime campaign, after which he left the League scene.

GORE, LES — CLAPTON ORIENT

outside-left — *2 apps, 1 goal*
born: Coventry, Warwickshire
debut: Watford (a), 19.9.1942

Les Gore joined Fulham in 1933, but failed to make the "Cottagers" first eleven and went on to play for Stockport County, Carlisle United and Bradford City before signing for Clapton Orient in 1939. He appeared for Orient in the first and last of the wartime seasons, but didn't resume his career when things returned to normal in 1946.

GRAINGER, JACK — SOUTHPORT

left-back — *2 apps*
born: South Elmsall, Yorkshire, 17.7.1912
debut: Charlton Athletic (a), 30.10.1943

Jack Grainger played for Barnsley before joining Southport in 1933 where he was a regular up to the war. He continued to play for the 'Sandgrounders' during the first two regional seasons, and returned to Haig Avenue in 1945. Famed for his sliding tackle on one knee, Jack had one more season with the Lancashire club after the war when he brought his total of Football League outings for them to 222 before going into non-League football with Prescot Cables, Hyde United, Clitheroe and Bangor City. He later returned to Southport to act as a gateman on match days.

GREGORY, FRED — CRYSTAL PALACE

centre-half — *1 app*
born: Mexborough, Yorkshire, 24.10.1911
debut: Watford (a), 21.2.1942

Described in the local Press as 'an old friend from Crystal Palace', Fred Gregory joined the Selhurst staff in December 1937 after service with Doncaster Rovers (1929–30), Manchester City (1930–34) and Reading (1934–37). Playing sporadically for Palace throughout the war, Fred guested for long periods with the Yorkshire clubs Barnsley, Bradford City, Doncaster Rovers and Rotherham United, and also appeared briefly for Portsmouth and Watford in the emergency competitions. On the restoration of peace he had short spells with Hartlepools United and Rotherham United during 1946–47 to bring his tally of League matches up to 227 before retiring.

GREGORY, JACK — SOUTHAMPTON

left-back — *1 app*
born: Southampton, Hampshire, 25.1.1925
debut: Southampton (a), 23.12.1944

Signed by Southampton as a professional in 1943, Jack Gregory was one of the players drafted at the last moment when Albion turned up with only nine men for a match against the 'Saints' at The Dell in 1944; he also played for the Albion in a friendly at Southampton in April 1945. Jack remained with Southampton until 1955, but failed to establish himself in the first team and subsequently played for Leyton Orient (1955–59), Bournemouth (1959–60), and for Ashford Town and Hastings United in the Southern League.

GRIER

left-half — *1 app*
debut: Clapton Orient (a), 1.1.1944

Grier was an unknown emergency recruit who played in the 3–0 defeat at Clapton Orient on New Year's Day 1944.

GRIFFIN, ALBERT — BRIGHTON & HOVE ALBION

outside-right — *4 apps, 1 goal*
born: Brighton, Sussex, 6.4.1925
debut: Clapton Orient (h), 6.4.1942

An Albion junior, Albert Griffin played his first senior match on his seventeenth birthday and scored in a 5–2 win over Clapton Orient. He assisted the juniors in winning the Sussex County Wartime League Cup in 1942–43, and also appeared in the R.U.R. Charity Cup-winning team the same season when the youngsters defeated Worthing 4–3 at Woodside Road. Albert had previously played for the Brighton club Elder Athletic.

Season	Wartime	Total
1941–42	2 (1)	2 (1)
1942–43	2	2
Total	4 (1)	4 (1)

GRIFFITHS, MAL — LEICESTER CITY

forward — *12 apps, 5 goals*
born: Merthyr Tydfil, Glamorgan, Wales, 8.3.1919
debut: Reading (h), 29.8.1942

Mal Griffiths joined Arsenal as an amateur at the age of sixteen in 1936 and, after turning professional, made his First Division debut during 1937–38 when the 'Gunners' carried off the Football League championship for the fifth time in eight seasons. In September 1938 he was transferred to Leicester City and went on to give terrific service at Filbert Street until 1956, appearing in 439 League and

Cup matches before moving into non-League fare with Burton Albion; he appeared on the right wing in the Leicester side defeated by Wolves in the 1949 F.A. Cup final. Mal was also capped by Wales on eleven occasions after the war. Although lost to Leicester for most of the conflict, he appeared for Aldershot, Bournemouth, Cardiff City, Chelsea and Fulham up to 1942.

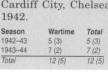

Season	Wartime	Total
1942–43	5 (3)	5 (3)
1943–44	7 (2)	7 (2)
Total	12 (5)	12 (5)

GROVES, KEN — PRESTON NORTH END

goalkeeper — *1 app*
debut: Arsenal (a), 7.10.1944

After joining Preston North End at the age of seventeen, Ken Groves had yet to make the first team when hostilities broke out. He played just three matches for the Lancashire club during their three seasons of wartime football, but appeared as a guest for Brentford, Lincoln City, Millwall and Southport in addition to the Albion. Ken had a brief spell with Reading in the initial post-war campaign.

GRUNDY, ARNOLD — NEWCASTLE UNITED

left-half — *1 app*
born: Gateshead, Co. Durham, 19.9.1919
debut: Queen's Park Rangers (h), 9.3.1940

Arnold Grundy joined Newcastle United in 1936, but made only one first-team appearance, at the age of seventeen, before the war brought his Football League career to an end. He guested for Albion, Fulham, Liverpool and Tranmere Rovers during the conflict, but, although retained on the St James's Park staff until 1944, did not appear in the "Magpies'" wartime ranks.

GUNN, ALFIE — BRIGHTON & HOVE ALBION

outside-right — *15 apps, 4 goals*
debut: Portsmouth (a), 5.10.1940

A member of the Albion junior team which carried off the Sussex County Wartime League Cup and the R.U.R. Charity Cup in 1942–43, Alfie Gunn played locally for Southwick Wednesday before joining the Albion, but was lost to the club for much of the war owing to more pressing duties in Italy.

Season	Wartime	Total
1940–41	10 (1)	10 (1)
1941–42	2 (1)	2 (1)
1945–46	3 (2)	3 (2)
Total	15 (4)	15 (4)

HANCOCK, JOHN — BRIGHTON & HOVE ALBION

left-back — *1 app*
debut: Charlton Athletic (h), 4.11.1944

Although registered with the Albion, John Hancock made just one senior appearance for the club, a 7–1 Goldstone annihilation at the hands of Charlton Athletic.

HARLOCK, DES — TRANMERE ROVERS

outside-right — *1 app*
born: Blaenau, Wales, 20.12.1922
debut: Queen's Park Rangers (h), 24.10.1942

Des Harlock first appeared for Tranmere Rovers during the 1941–42 season and remained at Prenton Park until 1954, making 151 peacetime League appearances for the Birkenhead club.

HARMAN, CHARLIE — BRIGHTON & HOVE ALBION

outside-left — *18 apps, 4 goals*
born: Uckfield, Sussex, 1924
debut: Watford (h), 1.6.1940

Charlie Harman represented Brighton Boys as a lad, and went on to become an outstanding member of the first intake of Albion juniors. At the tender age of sixteen he was one of five youngsters drafted into the senior side for a match with Watford at the Goldstone in June 1940, a game which ended in a creditable 2–2 draw. Charlie graduated as a fighter pilot in 1942 and saw action in Italy. He played for Worthing after the war.

Season	Wartime	Total
1939–40	2 (1)	2 (1)
1940–41	16 (3)	16 (3)
Total	18 (4)	18 (4)

HART, ARCHIE — THIRD LANARK

outside-right — *15 apps, 2 goals*
born: Glasgow, Lanarkshire, Scotland
debut: Portsmouth (h), 18.10.1941

Archie Hart was recruited by the Scottish League club Third Lanark in the late 1930s from Rutherglen Glencairn. During the 1941–42 season, while serving as a cadet-rating in the Royal Navy, he was available to the Albion for a lengthy period when he attended a course at *H.M.S. King Alfred*, the officers' training establishment in Hove. Archie later served overseas and was captured by the enemy, but returned to the Sussex area after the conflict and made a single appearance for Brighton during the 1945–46 transitional season.

Season	Wartime	Total
1941–42	14 (2)	14 (2)
1945–46	1	1
Total	15 (2)	15 (2)

HAWORTH

right-half — *3 apps*
debut: Watford (a), 21.2.1942

Haworth was an unknown player who assisted Albion in the latter stages of the 1941–42 season.

HENLEY, LES — ARSENAL

inside-left — *1 app*
born: Lambeth, London, 26.9.1922
debut: Arsenal (h), 6.12.1941

An England schoolboy international, Les Henley joined Arsenal as an amateur in 1939 and turned pro in 1941. Together with his team-mate Stan Morgan, Les was somewhat oddly loaned to Albion for a match with the 'Gunners' at Hove in 1941. Appearing for Arsenal throughout the war while serving in the Army, he guested all over the capital: for Brentford, Crystal Palace, Fulham, Queen's Park Rangers, Spurs and West Ham United. He also had a few games for Reading, and joined the Elm Park staff permanently in 1946, going on to play 181 League games before retiring in 1953.

Les then managed Bohemians (Dublin, 1953–54) and Wimbledon (1955–71), leading the 'Dons' to a hat-trick of Isthmian League titles and to an F.A. Amateur Cup final victory in 1963 before the club turned professional and entered the Southern League the following year.

HICKMAN, S.

goalkeeper — *1 app*
debut: Fulham (h), 8.1.1944

A goalkeeper of unknown credentials who appeared between the Albion posts in a 6–3 home defeat by Fulham, Hickman had represented the R.A.F. in a match at the Goldstone a few weeks earlier, and had also been for a trial with Aston Villa.

HICKMAN, STAN — BRIGHTON & HOVE ALBION

left-half   12 apps
born: Catford, Lewisham, London, 18.5.1922
debut: Watford (h), 1.6.1940

Stan Hickman has been associated with Lancing F.C. since its formation as part of the Lancing Athletic Club in 1938, and is now a vice-president of the football club. Towards the end of the first wartime season, 1939–40, Stan was one of the original intake of Albion juniors, and was drafted for first-team duty a few weeks later in June 1940 along with four other youngsters in a 2–2 draw with Watford at the Goldstone. Conscripted by the R.A.F., he served as a wireless-operator and air-gunner for the remainder of the war, and played representative football for the service, but on the cessation of hostilities he rejoined Lancing and was performing the duties of player-secretary at the time of their election to the Sussex County League in 1948. Stan later concentrated on his business interests and now lives near Arundel.

Season	Wartime	Total
1939–40	2	2
1940–41	10	10
Total	12	12

HILLMAN, DENNIS — BRIGHTON & HOVE ALBION

outside-right   12 apps, 3 goals
born: Southend-on-Sea, Essex, 27.11.1918
debut: Fulham (h), 8.1.1944

Dennis Hillman was with Southend United as a youngster, but became an Albion junior while in the Brighton area. After recovering from an arm wound sustained while serving in the Army, he was released to join Colchester United in the Southern League and remained at Layer Road for two seasons after their election to the Football League in 1950. Dennis subsequently played for Gillingham, Hastings United (assisting them to the F.A. Cup third round in 1954 and 1955) and Ramsgate.

Season	Wartime	Total
1943–44	9 (3)	9 (3)
1945–46	3	3
Total	12 (3)	12 (3)

HODGSON, SAM — GRIMSBY TOWN

centre-half   9 apps
born: Seaham, Co. Durham, 21.1.1919
debut: Chelsea (h), 18.11.1944

Sam Hodgson joined Grimsby Town at the age of seventeen in 1936, but had to wait until 1946 to make his debut in the regular Football League before finishing his career with Mansfield Town in 1948–49. He played for the 'Mariners' only fleetingly during the war years, but managed guest appearances for the Albion, Bradford (P.A.), Middlesbrough, Reading and Swansea Town. Sam's older brother Jack starred for Grimsby during their halcyon years as a First Division side in the 1930s, and was still turning out after the war.

HOLLIS, HARRY — CHESTER

left-half   1 app
born: Shotton, Flintshire, Wales, 12.12.1913
debut: Brentford (h), 25.3.1944

Harry Hollis first appeared for Chester in the initial wartime season and continued to turn out for them on occasion throughout the hostilities. He was transferred to Wrexham in 1946, but made just one League appearance before departing from the first-class game.

HOOPER, PERCY — TOTTENHAM HOTSPUR

goalkeeper   1 app
born: Lambeth, London, 17.12.1914
debut: Millwall (a), 5.2.1944

Percy Hooper joined Tottenham in 1933 and made 97 League appearances up to the war, becoming their regular custodian during the last two peacetime seasons. He continued to play for Spurs during the war, clocking up over 100 appearances in the various emergency competitions, and also turned out for Arsenal, Bath City, Crystal Palace, Gillingham and West Ham United in addition to assisting the Albion. In March 1947, Percy was transferred to Swansea Town, and later played for Chingford and King's Lynn.

HUGHES, HORACE — BRIGHTON & HOVE ALBION

inside/outside-left   2 apps
debut: Exeter City (a), 23.2.1946

A local amateur registered with the Albion in 1945–46, Horace Hughes left the Goldstone in 1947 to play at centre-half for the fine Horsham side of the late '40s. The 'Hornets' reached the first round proper of the F.A. Cup in 1947–48, only to be beaten 9–1 by a Tommy Lawton-inspired Notts County at Meadow Lane; shared the R.U.R. Cup in 1949, having drawn 1–1 with Worthing; and won the Sussex Senior Cup in 1950.

ISAAC, BILL — BRIGHTON & HOVE ALBION

inside-left   11 apps, 3 goals
born: East Cramlington, Northumberland
debut: Aldershot (h), 21.10.1939

Signed by Albion manager Charlie Webb from Newcastle United during the summer of 1939, Bill Isaac had been only a reserve-team player at St James's Park but made his first-team debut for Brighton in the third and final match of the aborted 1939–40 programme. He went on to make one wartime appearance that season and ten the following term. Having seen action with the Territorials during the early part of the war, he was among those evacuated from Dunkirk. Bill subsequently contracted meningitis and died on Easter Monday 1941, two months after his last game for the Albion.

Season	Wartime	Total
1939–40	1 (1)	1 (1)
1940–41	10 (2)	10 (2)
Total	11 (3)	11 (3)

Note: Isaac's first game for the Albion was Bristol City (h), 2.9.1939 (FL D3(S)), but this game was deleted from the record when the Football League competition was aborted on the outbreak of war.

ITHELL, JIMMY BOLTON WANDERERS

centre-half/centre-forward 2 apps
born: Hawarden, Flintshire, Wales, 7.2.1916
debut: Norwich City (a), 25.12.1940

Jimmy Ithell's first guest appearance for the Albion came at Carrow Road, Norwich, on Christmas Day 1940 when, along with several Norwich juniors and soldiers from the crowd, he made up the side which lost 18–0; Albion had arrived with just four players, and Jimmy scored an own-goal. His other appearance for the club came during 1943–44 in a 2–0 defeat at Tottenham.

Although Jimmy had joined Bolton in 1936, he was destined never to make a peacetime Football League appearance for the 'Trotters'. Serving with the Bolton Artillery in the early days of the war, together with most of his Wanderers team-mates, he soon saw action in France and was subsequently involved in the Dunkirk evacuation. Jimmy played only occasionally during the war, appearing on two occasions for Bolton in 1942–43 and guesting at various times for the Albion, Chester, Mansfield Town and Reading, but in 1946 he was transferred to Swindon Town and went on to play in 107 Third Division matches before joining Boston United as player-manager.

Season	Wartime	Total
1940–41	1	1
1943–44	1	1
Total	2	2

JACKSON, LES BRADFORD (PARK AVENUE)

centre-half 1 app
debut: Watford (a), 11.11.1944

Although registered with Bradford (P.A.), Les Jackson did not appear in their senior team before, during, or after the war.

JONES, LES BRIGHTON & HOVE ALBION

outside-right 1 app
debut: Watford (a), 8.2.1941

Les Jones was the son of Albion's groundsman and former star player Bill 'Bullet' Jones (see *Albion Players*). He was pressed into service for a match at Watford in February 1941, and was appointed manager of Albion's junior team two months later.

JONES, RON LIVERPOOL

inside-left 1 app, 1 goal
born: Mold, Flintshire, Wales
debut: Southampton (h), 19.4.1941

After starting out with Wrexham in 1935, where he quickly gained a reputation as a goalscoring winger, Ron Jones was transferred to Liverpool in 1938 and had five outings in the First Division side before the war, but he appeared just once for the 'Reds' during the seven seasons of emergency competition. Ron guested very briefly for Wrexham in 1945–46, but didn't resume his League career when things returned to normal.

JONES, SYD ARSENAL

utility player 21 apps, 1 goal
born: Rothwell, Yorkshire, 15.2.1921
debut: Portsmouth (h), 18.10.1941

Syd Jones signed for Arsenal in the early days of the Second World War, but did not appear in the "Gunners'" senior team until the transitional season of 1945–46. Available to the Albion for lengthy periods from 1941 to 1943, he proved a versatile player and appeared in a wide variety of positions. After the war Syd remained at Highbury as a reserve-team player until 1948 when he was transferred to Walsall,

and made 146 Third Division appearances for the 'Saddlers' before leaving the first-class game in 1952.

Season	Wartime	Total
1941–42	10 (1)	10 (1)
1942–43	11	11
Total	21 (1)	21 (1)

KAY, JOHN BRENTFORD

outside-left 3 apps, 1 goal
debut: Reading (h), 25.11.1939

John Kay made fleeting appearances for Brentford and the Albion during the first season of wartime football, then disappeared from the football scene.

KEEN, ERIC HEREFORD UNITED

left-half 1 app
full name: Errington Keen
born: Walker, Newcastle upon Tyne, Northumberland, 4.9.1910
debut: Southend United (h), 10.4.1940

A former Newcastle United defender, Eric Keen, also known as 'Ike', spent eight excellent years with Derby County during he which clocked up 237 League and Cup appearances and won four England caps. A good tackler and stylish passer, he was released in 1938 to join Chelmsford City, and was appointed player-manager of Hereford United just two months before the outbreak of war.

Eric enjoyed a second lease of life during the hostilities, guesting extensively for the Albion, Charlton Athletic, Everton, Fulham, Lincoln City, Liverpool, Millwall, Notts County and Rochdale. He joined Leeds United in 1945, and subsequently played for Bacup Borough before taking a coaching post in Sweden with IFK Norrkoping in 1949.

KELLY, JIMMY QUEEN'S PARK RANGERS

outside-left 1 app, 1 goal
debut: Southend United (h), 10.4.1940

Jimmy Kelly appeared for Queen's Park Rangers and the Albion during the opening season of wartime fare, then disappeared from the football scene.

KELLY, LAWRIE ALDERSHOT

right-back 3 apps
born: Bellshill, Lanarkshire, Scotland
debut: Aldershot (a), 27.4.1940

Lawrie Kelly played for Southend United, Bristol City and Aldershot in the 1930s, and appeared fairly frequently for the 'Shots' in the wartime emergency competitions up until 1944. Two of his three guest outings with the Albion were, in fact, against Aldershot.

Season	Wartime	Total
1939–40	1	1
1941–42	2	2
Total	3	3

KEMP, DIRK LIVERPOOL

goalkeeper 13 apps
born: Cape Town, South Africa
debut: Chelsea (h), 4.9.1943

One of several South Africans signed by Liverpool in the 1930s, Dirk Kemp joined the Anfield staff in 1936 and was soon drafted into the first team. He was serving with the King's Liverpool Regiment during the war, holding the rank of lieutenant, when he assisted the Albion during 1943–44. Dirk also guested for York City and Southport, and played briefly in Northern Ireland. In 1952 he was instrumental in the arrival of Denis Foreman (see *Albion Players*) at the Goldstone.

KINGHORN, BILL — LIVERPOOL

winger   20 apps, 7 goals
born: Strathblane, Stirlingshire, Scotland, 27.2.1912
debut: Southampton (h), 19.4.1941

Bill Kinghorn won four Scottish amateur caps with Queen's Park in the Scottish League before joining Liverpool as a pro in 1938, but after breaking into the first team in 1938–39 his promising career was thwarted by the war. One of the King's Liverpool Regiment contingent that proved so useful to the Albion, Bill guested all over the country during the conflict, appearing for Blackburn Rovers, Burnley, Leeds United, Leicester City, Manchester City and Newcastle United, and even managed to play for Liverpool on twelve occasions before hanging up his boots in 1945.

Season	Wartime	Total
1940–41	1	1
1942–43	17 (7)	17 (7)
1943–44	2	2
Total	20 (7)	20 (7)

KIRKMAN, NORMAN — BURNLEY

left-back   1 app
born: Bolton, Lancashire, 6.6.1920
debut: Portsmouth (h), 10.10.1942

Norman Kirkman first appeared in Burnley's ranks during 1940–41 and played occasionally throughout the rest of the war, but was fated never to appear in a regular Football League match at Turf Moor. He made a name for himself on transferring to Rochdale in 1946, and went on to play for Chesterfield (1947–49), Leicester City (1949–50) and Southampton (1950–52), followed by spells as player-manager at Exeter City (1952–53) and manager at Bradford (Park Avenue).

KYLE

goalkeeper   1 app
debut: Clapton Orient (a), 28.3.1942

Kyle was a goalkeeper of unknown credentials who played in a London War Cup defeat at Orient. Surprisingly, Albion's promising junior 'keeper, Jack Ball, was played on the left wing.

LANE, BILLY

inside-right   1 app, 1 goal
debut: Clapton Orient (a), 28.3.1942
See *Albion Managers*

LANEY, LES — SOUTHAMPTON

outside-left   1 app, 1 goal
debut: Bournemouth & B.A. (a), 15.3.1941

A Southampton youngster who appeared for the 'Saints' in each of the five wartime seasons up to 1944, Les Laney also guested for Bristol City and Portsmouth.

LAWRENCE

right-back   1 app
debut: Clapton Orient (a), 1.1.1944

Lawrence was one of several last-minute players recruited by the Albion for a game at Clapton Orient on New Year's Day 1944 which ended in a 3–0 defeat.

LAYTON, BILLY — READING

inside-left   1 app
born: Shirley, Birmingham, Warwickshire, 13.1.1915
debut: Southend United (h), 10.4.1940

Billy Layton played for Reading from 1937 until leaving for Bradford (Park Avenue) in 1947. He subsequently joined Colchester United for their initial season in the Football League in 1950. In addition to his one wartime outing with the Albion, Billy also appeared for Clapton Orient, Luton Town, Portsmouth and Walsall.

LEWIS, BILL — WEST HAM UNITED

left-back   1 app
born: West Ham, Essex, 23.11.1921
debut: West Ham United (a), 8.11.1941

A London and Essex Schools representative, Bill Lewis started out on his football career as an amateur with his local club, West Ham United, in 1938 and was a regular with the 'Hammers' until 1945 when he was transferred to Blackpool. Four seasons at Bloomfield Road were followed by six with Norwich City, where he appeared in 256 League and Cup matches before joining the coaching staff at Carrow Road.

Bill's sole game for the Albion came in a 4–0 defeat at the hands of his own club, West Ham, at Upton Park when he was lent to the visitors.

LEWIS, DOUG — SOUTHAMPTON

goalkeeper   1 app
debut: Crystal Palace (h), 16.12.1944

Although registered with the Football League for Southampton, Doug Lewis had only one outing with the 'Saints', during the 1943–44 season.

LOBB, FRED — BRIGHTON & HOVE ALBION

left-half   1 app
debut: Crystal Palace (a), 9.9.1944

Fred Lobb was registered with the Albion in 1944–45, but made just the one senior appearance, a 5–2 defeat against Crystal Palace at Selhurst Park.

LONDON, DERRY — BRIGHTON & HOVE ALBION

left-half   1 app
full name: Dermot London
debut: Reading (a), 25.8.1945

A late recruit to the ranks of Albion juniors, Derry London played in the young team which lost 3–1 to Worthing at Woodside Road in the Sussex (Royal Ulster Rifles) Charity Cup final in May 1945. (The R.U.R. Cup was then competed for by the winners and runners-up in the Sussex Wartime Cup, which was played on a league basis.) The splendidly-named youngster made his only senior appearance in the opening game of the following campaign, a 2–1 win at Elm Park, Reading.

LOWE, HENRY   QUEEN'S PARK RANGERS

inside-left   1 app
born: Kingskettle, Fife, Scotland
debut: Reading (a), 13.1.1940

Henry Lowe joined Watford in 1930 and was transferred to Queen's Park Rangers in 1935. In the four seasons leading up to the outbreak of the Second World War he hardly missed a match, and continued to play for Rangers on a fairly regular basis up to 1943. A nomadic wartime guest player, Henry appeared for Aldershot, Chelsea, Crystal Palace, Millwall, New Brighton, Watford and the Albion. His one appearance for Brighton was in a 1–0 defeat at Elm Park, Reading.

LOWRIE

centre-forward   1 app
debut: Clapton Orient (a), 1.1.1944

Lowrie was one of no fewer than six emergency players employed for the game at Clapton Orient on New Year's Day 1944, in which Orient, not surprisingly, triumphed 3–0.

LYLE

centre-half   1 app
debut: Fulham (h), 16.9.1944

Lyle was an amateur of otherwise unknown credentials who played in a 7–1 Goldstone defeat at the hands of Fulham.

McDERMOTT, JOE   GATESHEAD

outside-right   18 apps, 5 goals
born: Fendownes
debut: Portsmouth (h), 1.3.1941

Joe McDermott started out as a junior with Middlesbrough, but made his name with Gateshead, for whom he scored 29 goals in 102 Third Division (North) matches between 1933 and 1939. He made only one wartime appearance for Gateshead, during the 1945–46 season, but guested for the Albion, Fulham and Lincoln City. Joe initially played for the Albion in 1940–41, but returned to the area in 1944 when he was available for an extended period.

Season	Wartime	Total
1940–41	1	1
1944–45	16 (5)	16 (5)
1945–46	1	1
Total	18 (5)	18 (5)

McFARLANE, D. L.   CRYSTAL PALACE

goalkeeper   1 app
debut: Portsmouth (h), 28.4.1945

McFarlane played in goal for Crystal Palace during the last two wartime seasons, but did not appear in their first team subsequently. He was not unduly troubled in his only match with the Albion, maintaining a watching brief as 'Pompey' were demolished 8–0 at the Goldstone in the penultimate fixture of the 1944–45 campaign.

McINNES, JIMMY   LIVERPOOL

left-half   30 apps
born: Ayr, Ayrshire, Scotland
debut: Luton Town (h), 22.3.1941

One of the much-travelled Liverpool players who assisted Albion during the war years, Jimmy McInnes had played in the Third

Lanark side which lost the 1936 Scottish Cup final 1–0 to Rangers. After moving to Anfield in 1938, he was first-choice left-half until the war. In addition to his wartime appearances for Liverpool and the Albion, Jimmy also guested for Fulham, Leeds United, Luton Town, Manchester United, Millwall, Newcastle United, Queen's Park Rangers and York City. On retiring in 1946 he joined the Anfield administrative staff, serving as assistant secretary and secretary from 1955 until his death in 1965.

Season	Wartime	Total
1940–41	6	6
1941–42	5	5
1942–43	5	5
1943–44	14	14
Total	30	30

McKENZIE, DUNCAN   MIDDLESBROUGH

right-half   12 apps
born: Glasgow, Lanarkshire, Scotland, 10.8.1912
debut: Queen's Park Rangers (a), 12.2.1944

After joining Albion Rovers at the age of seventeen, Duncan McKenzie was transferred to Brentford in 1932, and was a member of the team which won rapid promotion from the Third Division to the First, appearing in more than 150 League matches and winning a Scottish cap v. Ireland before his transfer to Middlesbrough in 1938. During the war he made more than 100 guest appearances for Brentford, playing in the team which carried off the London War Cup in May 1942 by defeating Portsmouth at Wembley, and also turned out briefly for Southend United. Although his registration was retained until 1945, Duncan was lost to 'Boro during the hostilities and did not resume his career in 1946.

Season	Wartime	Total
1943–44	8	8
1944–45	4	4
Total	12	12

McNEILL, HAMILTON   BURY

centre-forward   2 apps, 3 goals
born: Glasgow, Lanarkshire, Scotland
debut: Luton Town (h), 22.1.1944

Hamilton McNeill was a feared goalscorer with Ayr United and Hull City before joining Bury in February 1939. Scoring six goals in fifteen Second Division matches during the remainder of 1938–39, he played briefly for the 'Shakers' in the first two wartime seasons before other commitments ended his football activities. On his Albion debut Hamilton grabbed a hat-trick in an 8–0 win over Luton Town.

MALONE, RON   BRIGHTON & HOVE ALBION

outside-left   1 app, 1 goal
debut: Crystal Palace (a), 27.12.1943

Registered with Albion in 1943–44, Ron Malone made his only senior outing in a 6–2 defeat at Selhurst Park.

MALPASS, SAM   FULHAM

defender   29 apps, 1 goal
born: Consett, Co. Durham, 12.9.1918
debut: Clapton Orient (h), 25.12.1941

Initially a junior with Huddersfield Town, Sam Malpass was transferred to Fulham in 1939 and played occasionally for the

'Cottagers' throughout the war. He also appeared for Bradford City, Chelsea, Crystal Palace, Halifax Town, Hartlepools United, Millwall and Watford, and was available to the Albion for a lengthy period from late 1941 until early 1943, playing in a number of defensive positions. Sam made his peacetime Football League debut for Fulham at the age of 28 in 1946, and ended his career with 41 games for Watford (1947–49). When Albion thrashed Wisbech Town 10–1 in a first-round F.A. Cup tie in November 1965, Sam was trainer of the Southern League club.

Season	Wartime	Total
1941–42	13	13
1942–43	16 (1)	16 (1)
Total	29 (1)	29 (1)

MARTINDALE, LEN — BURNLEY

inside-right — 4 apps
born: Bolton, Lancashire, 30.6.1920
debut: Crystal Palace (a), 19.1.1946

Signed by Burnley at the age of sixteen in 1937, Len Martindale made his League debut as a seventeen-year-old and looked set for a fine future, but then the war intervened. Despite service in India, he managed to turn out for Burnley when commitments allowed, and appeared as a guest for Bolton Wanderers, Blackburn Rovers, Manchester United, Watford and the Albion. Len remained at Turf Moor until December 1951 when he moved on to Accrington Stanley, his last Football League club.

MATTHEWSON, GEORGE — BURY

centre-half — 1 app
born: Gateshead, Co. Durham
debut: West Ham United (a), 6.5.1944

George Matthewson developed his football in the Army, but was snapped up by Bury in 1931 for whom he made more than 200 Second Division appearances up to the war. He then found himself back in the Army, but continued playing for the 'Shakers' until 1944 on the few occasions that he could be released from his service duties. George also appeared as a guest for Crystal Palace, Fulham, Grimsby Town, Millwall, Watford and the Albion.

MILES

outside-right — 1 app
debut: Bournemouth & B.A. (h), 6.10.1945

Miles was an unknown player who appeared in a 4–2 Goldstone defeat of Bournemouth in the last of the wartime seasons.

MILLBANK, JOE — CRYSTAL PALACE

centre-half — 1 app
born: Edmonton, Middlesex, 30.9.1919
debut: Aldershot (h), 3.11.1945

Joe Millbank was transferred from Wolves to Crystal Palace at the age of nineteen in August 1939, and appeared on and off throughout the Second World War, totalling around 70 matches. He made his peacetime League debut in 1946, and played in 38 Third Division games before moving to Queen's Park Rangers in July 1948, where he ended his career. Joe also guested for Millwall during the war.

MOORE, BERIAH — CARDIFF CITY

outside-left — 1 app
born: Cardiff, Glamorgan, Wales, 25.12.1919
debut: Bristol City (a), 5.9.1945

A left-winger with an amazing goalscoring record, Beriah Moore signed professional forms for his local club, Cardiff City, in 1941, and played regularly for the 'Bluebirds' during the war, scoring over

100 goals in the emergency competitions. He spent the first post-war season with Bangor City, but returned to Ninian Park in 1947 before rejoining Bangor. Beriah made a come-back in the Football League with Newport County in 1950 where he became a big favourite, scoring 58 goals in 137 League and Cup outings before returning to Bangor for a third spell. The Welsh winger also guested for Bristol City during the hostilities.

MOORES, PETER — PORTSMOUTH

outside-right — 1 app
debut: Portsmouth (a), 24.1.1942

A Royal Marine who was taken on the Fratton Park staff as a junior late in 1940–41, Peter Moores scored four goals on his debut, an 8–1 Hampshire Cup win over Southampton, but failed to live up to the early promise. He was loaned to the Albion by the home side for a match at Fratton Park in January 1942, a game which 'Pompey' won 5–3.

MORGAN, STAN — ARSENAL

forward — 31 apps, 16 goals
born: Abergwynfi, Glamorgan, Wales, 10.10.1920
debut: Watford (h), 15.11.1941

Stan Morgan joined Arsenal as an amateur in 1938 and turned professional in 1941, but made more appearances for the Albion than the 'Gunners' in the emergency competitions, being available for an extended spell from 1941 to 1943. Playing fairly regularly from November 1941 to the end of the season, Stan was missing from the line-ups in February 1942 when, together with his Arsenal colleague and regular Albion guest Cyril Tooze (see below), he was among the supporting troops for the daring commando raid on the German radar station at Bruneval on the Normandy coast; the pair received a terrific round of applause on their next appearance at the Goldstone Ground in March.

After guesting for Swindon Town during the 1945–46 transitional season, Stan played a reserve-team role for Arsenal when peace was restored and made just two first-team appearances. He met with greater success in subsequent stints with Walsall (1948), Millwall (1948–53) and Leyton Orient (1953–56), bringing his total of Football League outings to 264.

Season	Wartime	Total
1941–42	19 (7)	19 (7)
1942–43	12 (9)	12 (9)
Total	31 (16)	31 (16)

MOUNTFORD, GEORGE — STOKE CITY

inside-forward — 1 app
born: Stoke-on-Trent, Staffordshire, 30.3.1921
debut: Reading (h), 29.8.1942

George Mountford played for Stoke City's reserve team before the war and, despite being in transit during the early days of the conflict, appeared regularly for the Potteries club from 1942. He remained at the Victoria Ground until 1952, adding 147 Football League appearances to almost 100 wartime outings, and finished his career with a couple of seasons at Queen's Park Rangers. George's brother Frank also played for Stoke for many years.

MUIR, BOB — ROCHDALE

right-back — 2 apps
debut: Aldershot (a), 14.10.1944

Although registered with Rochdale, Bob Muir appeared only briefly for the Lancashire club toward the end of the war.

MULRANEY, JOCK — IPSWICH TOWN

inside-left — *1 app*
full name: Ambrose Mulraney
born: Wishaw, Lanarkshire, Scotland, 18.5.1916
debut: West Ham United (h), 14.2.1942

'Jock' Mulraney enjoyed a lengthy but somewhat chequered career. After a spell with Celtic in 1933–34 and trial periods with Hearts, Hamilton Academical, Blackpool and Clapton Orient, he dropped into the Southern League with Dartford. On joining Ipswich Town, also in the Southern League, he became a regular in the side which was elected to the Football League in 1938. However, being somewhat out on a limb geographically, Ipswich did not compete in the wartime competitions until 1945, so Jock made guest appearances all over the country while serving with the R.A.F.; he appeared for Birmingham City, Blackburn Rovers, Brentford, Charlton Athletic, Clapton Orient, Leicester City, Manchester City, Northampton Town, Norwich City, Sheffield Wednesday, Wolves and the Albion.

In October 1945, Jock was transferred to Birmingham City where he made 28 Second Division appearances in the initial peacetime campaign, after which he played non-League football for Shrewsbury Town and Kidderminster Harriers, only to return to the First Division for a season with Aston Villa in September 1948. He later managed the Midlands clubs Cradley Heath and Brierley Hill.

MUNRO, ALEX — BLACKPOOL

outside-right — *6 apps*
born: Carriden, Bo'ness, West Lothian, Scotland, 6.4.1912
debut: Reading (h), 1.9.1945

Alex Munro signed for Heart of Midlothian in 1932 and gained two Scottish caps before joining Blackpool's large north-of-the-border contingent in 1937 to strengthen their push towards Division One that season. During 1937–38 he won a further cap, and was a fixture in the "Seasiders'" line-ups until the war. In 1939–40 he continued to turn out on a regular basis, but was then virtually lost to Blackpool until the initial post-war campaign, although he guested for Middlesbrough in 1940–41.

In July 1942, Alex was reported as missing while serving in the Middle East, but turned up safely in an Italian P.O.W. camp two months later. He went on to play in the splendid 1948 F.A. Cup final, partnering Stanley Matthews on the right wing as Blackpool lost 4–2 to the emerging Manchester United. On hanging up his boots in 1950, Alex joined the Bloomfield Road coaching staff.

MUTTITT, ERNIE — BRENTFORD

left-back — *2 apps*
born: Middlesbrough, Yorkshire
debut: Brentford (a), 11.9.1943

Ernie Muttitt joined Middlesbrough as a left-winger in 1929 and had the distinction of scoring the decisive goal in a 2–1 victory over Arsenal at Highbury on his debut. Transferred to Brentford in 1932, he played his part in their rise from the Third Division to the First over three seasons in the mid 1930s, and remained at Griffin Park as a fringe player in the four seasons leading up to the war. Ernie managed to turn out for the 'Bees' on at least one occasion in each of the seven seasons of regional fare, and also guested for a profusion of clubs: Albion, Aldershot, Charlton Athletic, Chelsea, Clapton Orient, Crystal Palace, Fulham, Millwall, Reading, Southend United, Watford and West Ham United.

NEEDHAM, FRED — STOCKPORT COUNTY

right-half — *3 apps*
debut: Brentford (a), 26.8.1944

Fred Needham first played for Stockport County during 1942–43, but did not appear again after 1944. He guested for the Albion in the opening three fixtures of the 1944–45 campaign.

NIXON

left-back — *1 app*
debut: Fulham (h), 10.1.1942

Nixon was an otherwise unidentified player who turned out in a 7–3 defeat by Fulham at the Goldstone.

O'DONNELL, FRANK — ASTON VILLA

centre-forward/inside-left — *26 apps, 12 goals*
born: Buckhaven, Fife, Scotland, 31.8.1911
debut: Southampton (h), 20.2.1943

After joining Celtic in 1930, Frank O'Donnell was transferred to Preston North End in 1935 along with his brother Hugh for a combined fee of £5,000. While at Deepdale he gained five Scottish caps and scored North End's goal when they were beaten 3–1 by Sunderland in the 1937 F.A. Cup final, but by the time they won the competition twelve months later he had moved on to Blackpool where he added a sixth cap to his collection before signing for Aston Villa in November 1938.

Frank scored fourteen goals for Villa before war was declared, but the Midlanders did not take part in the first three seasons of regional competition, and his talents were consequently in great demand wherever he happened to be stationed; he guested for Blackpool, Brentford, Fulham, Heart of Midlothian, Liverpool, Preston North End, Spurs, Wolverhampton Wanderers and York City, and appeared for the Albion during the latter stages of the war.

In January 1946 he was transferred to Nottingham Forest, but left to become player-manager at Buxton in 1948. One of the finest forwards in Britain during the late 1930s, Frank died in 1952 at the age of 41.

Season	Wartime	Total
1942–43	1 (1)	1 (1)
1944–45	14 (3)	14 (3)
1945–46	11 (8)	11 (8)
Total	26 (12)	26 (12)

OFFORD, STAN — BRADFORD (PARK AVENUE)

inside-right — *1 app, 1 goal*
debut: Fulham (h), 16.9.1944

Stan Offord made the odd appearance for Bradford (Park Avenue) throughout the war years, but did not play when the football situation was restored to normal in 1946. He guested briefly for Halifax Town during 1941–42.

OHLENS, P. W. — SOUTHWICK

centre-forward — *1 app, 1 goal*
debut: Clapton Orient (a), 25.12.1942

Ohlens had appeared in Albion's junior team before being drafted into the first eleven for the Christmas Day fixture at Orient in

1942, when Albion were also forced to recruit two members of the crowd in order to field a full complement. He had played for Hove in the Sussex County League immediately before the war before joining Southwick.

OWENS

right-half   *1 app*
debut: Arsenal (a), 14.3.1942

Owens was an Army colleague of Blackpool's George Eastham who turned up at White Hart Lane to watch his friend guest for the Albion, but found himself playing against the might of Arsenal because of a shortfall in the Brighton side! (Arsenal's Highbury Stadium was commandeered by the War Office on the outbreak of hostilities and the 'Gunners' played their home matches at Tottenham Hotspur's headquarters.)

PACKHAM, WALLY   HASTINGS & ST LEONARDS

goalkeeper   *2 apps*
debut: Fulham (a), 2.12.1939

A young goalkeeper from the Hastings club who had a number of outings in Albion's reserves during the two seasons leading up to the war, Wally Packham turned out briefly for the first team during the hostilities, and continued to assist the second eleven when peace was restored in 1945.

PARR, CHARLIE   HAYWARDS HEATH

inside-right   *1 app*
debut: Crystal Palace (h), 12.1.1946

Charlie Parr appeared with the Albion juniors toward the end of the war while playing for the Haywards Heath club, but made the first team just once. He played for Heath in the 1947 Sussex Senior Cup final when they were beaten 1–0 by Worthing at the Dripping Pan in Lewes.

PATERSON, GEORGE   LIVERPOOL

left-half/inside-left   *2 apps*
born: Aberdeen, Aberdeenshire, Scotland, 19.12.1916
debut: Clapton Orient (a), 13.9.1941

One of the lesser-known Liverpool players to appear for the Albion during the war, George Paterson joined the Anfield staff as a left-winger from the Aberdeen works' team Hall-Russell in 1937, but made only two First Division appearances before the war. He guested for the Albion, Burnley, Leeds United, Queen's Park Rangers, Reading and York City in the regional competitions, but had only a handful of outings for Liverpool although he played for the 'Reds' at least once during each of the seven wartime seasons. George was transferred to Swindon Town in 1946 where he remained until retiring in 1950, subsequently joining Liverpool's coaching staff under Bill Shankly.

PEARSON, STAN   MANCHESTER UNITED

inside-left   *8 apps, 3 goals*
born: Salford, Lancashire, 11.1.1919
debut: Reading (a), 6.9.1941

One of the stars of Matt Busby's Manchester United side in the immediate aftermath of the Second World War, Stan Pearson joined the Old Trafford staff in 1935 and went on to enjoy an eighteen-year career with United, scoring 149 goals in 345 peacetime League and Cup appearances. In 1948 he scored in the F.A. Cup final win over Blackpool at Wembley (having hit a hat-trick in the semi-final), and gained a Football League championship medal in 1952 when he was top scorer. Blessed with excellent control and a lethal shot, he was also capped by England eight times and represented the Football League against the Irish League in 1951–52, scoring a hat-trick.

Stan left United for Bury in 1954 where he hit 56 goals in 122 League games. He then joined Chester, where he played into his 40th year before taking the post of manager from 1959 to 1961. On retiring from the professional ranks he became a newsagent in the Cheshire town of Prestbury while managing the local team. Stan died in February 1997 at the age of 78.

In addition to guesting for the Albion he also appeared with Middlesbrough and Queen's Park Rangers in the regional competitions. During the latter part of the war Stan served with the Army in India and Burma.

Season	Wartime	Total
1941–42	3 (1)	3 (1)
1942–43	5 (2)	5 (2)
Total	8 (3)	8 (3)

PETERS, BILL   BRIGHTON & HOVE ALBION

outside-left   *1 app, 1 goal*
full name: Cyril Peters
born: 1919
debut: Clapton Orient (h), 25.12.1941

The Reverend Bill Peters was recommended to the Albion following his graduation from Cambridge University by the club's former skipper Jack Jenkins. The Cambridge 'blue' played for the Brighton junior team, and was drafted into the first eleven for the Christmas Day fixture with Clapton Orient in 1941, scoring the opening goal in a 4–1 victory. Two months later, though, he broke his leg while playing for the juniors.

Appointed curate to St Michael's Church, Brighton, in 1942, Bill was later chaplain at Brighton College from 1950 until 1969 when he moved into the Sussex Weald to become Rector of Uckfield, Isfield and Little Horsted, a position he held until retiring in July 1996. An active pillar of the Uckfield community, he was a school governor, chairman of the local housing association, chairman of the local bowls club, and played cricket until 1990. On his retirement he was described as 'a man of few well-chosen and gently-spoken words'.

PINCHBECK, F.

left-back   *1 app*
debut: Norwich City (a), 25.12.1940

Pinchbeck was one of seven emergency recruits who played in the infamous 18–0 defeat by Norwich City at Carrow Road on Christmas Day 1940.

PINKERTON, HARRY   FALKIRK

right-half   *3 apps*
born: Glasgow, Lanarkshire, Scotland, 7.5.1915
died: Toronto, Ontario, Canada, c. 1986
debut: Reading (h), 21.10.1944

Harry Pinkerton most probably did not enjoy his brief spell with Albion, the three games in which he participated ending in heavy defeats with a goals-against tally of 21. After playing for Hull City (1933–35), Port Vale (1935–36) and Burnley, Harry joined Falkirk in 1938 and represented Scotland in the first wartime international against England in December 1939. He also played for Falkirk in the Scottish Southern League Cup final of 1943 when they were beaten on a corner-kick count after a 1–1 draw with Rangers at Hampden Park. Harry also made wartime guest appearances with Dundee United and Millwall, but dropped into Scottish junior football with Bo'ness United in 1946 before later coaching in Canada.

POINTON, BILL   PORT VALE

inside-left   *1 app*
born: Hanley, Staffordshire, 25.11.1920
debut: Portsmouth (h), 22.4.1944

Bill Pointon played regularly for Port Vale during the last two seasons of wartime fare and scored 26 goals in 74 outings in the first three peacetime campaigns. He subsequently had short spells with Queen's Park Rangers and Brentford.

POULTER, J.

outside-right   *1 app*
debut: Norwich City (a), 25.3.1940

Poulter was listed in the Press as a Wolverhampton Wanderers player, but no evidence of a connection with the Midlands club has been established. The Football League noted him as 'unattached'.

PRYDE, BOB   BLACKBURN ROVERS

left-back   *1 app*
born: Methil, Fife, Scotland, 25.4.1913
debut: Crystal Palace (a), 3.1.1942

Better known as a half-back, Bob Pryde enjoyed a long career with Blackburn Rovers following his transfer from St Johnstone in 1933, remaining at Ewood Park until 1949 and making 345 League and Cup appearances in addition to 180 wartime outings. In October 1941 he represented the Football League *v.* Scottish League, and three months later experienced the other side of the game when he assisted Albion in a 10–1 defeat at Selhurst Park. Bob served in the Army and thus guested widely: for Aldershot, Bolton Wanderers, Fulham, Liverpool, Southport, Spurs and West Ham United. He also played for a Central Mediterranean Forces representative side while in Italy.

After the war Bob made another appearance for the Football League in a 3–1 defeat of the League of Ireland at Dalymount Park in April 1947, and became player-manager of Wigan Athletic (1949–52) in the Lancashire Combination on leaving Blackburn. A fine entertainer in several senses, Bob was also a singer and violinist, and was well-known in Blackburn dramatic circles.

PUGH, JOHN   CARDIFF CITY

left-back   *1 app*
debut: Bristol City (a), 5.9.1945

John Pugh first appeared for Cardiff City in 1939–40 and played regularly until 1944, clocking up in excess of 80 wartime appearances for the 'Bluebirds'. He guested for the Albion and Torquay United during the transitional 1945–46 season, but did not play League football subsequently. His one appearance in a Brighton shirt came in a 3–1 defeat at Bristol City.

RAMSDEN, BARNEY   LIVERPOOL

left-back   *9 apps, 1 goal*
full name: Bernard Ramsden
born: Sheffield, Yorkshire, 8.11.1917
debut: Bournemouth & B.A. (a), 15.3.1941

'Barney' Ramsden joined Liverpool at the age of seventeen in 1935 and remained at Anfield for thirteen years, amassing 60

peacetime appearances for the 'Reds'. During the seven-year wartime period he served with the King's Liverpool Regiment and guested for the Albion, Leeds United and York City. In 1948, Barney moved to Sunderland for nearly two years, then had a brief spell with Hartlepools United before retiring and emigrating to California.

Season	Wartime	Total
1940–41	4	4
1941–42	5 (1)	5 (1)
Total	9 (1)	9 (1)

REECE, TOM   CRYSTAL PALACE

half-back   *30 apps, 2 goals*
born: Wolverhampton, Staffordshire, 17.5.1919
debut: Clapton Orient (h), 2.9.1944

Tom Reece was transferred from Wolves to Crystal Palace at the age of nineteen in September 1938, and made his Football League debut in the last season before the war. During the hostilities he played for Palace while also guesting for the Albion, Stockport County, Watford and Wolves. Tom remained at Selhurst Park until 1948 when he left for Kidderminster Harriers.

Season	Wartime	Total
1944–45	26 (1)	26 (1)
1945–46	4 (1)	4 (1)
Total	30 (2)	30 (2)

REID, ERNIE   NORWICH CITY

utility player   *87 apps, 13 goals*
born: Pentrebach, Merthyr Tydfil, Glamorgan, Wales, 25.3.1914
debut: Watford (a), 19.9.1942

Ernie Reid made more wartime appearances for the Albion than any other guest player and was a tremendous asset to the club during a difficult period; the versatile Welshman played in a wide variety of positions – including goalkeeper – and appeared on a regular basis between 1942 and 1945.

Ernie started out with Swansea Town in 1936, but made his Football League debut in the First Division after his transfer to Chelsea in 1937. He met with little success at Stamford Bridge, however, and was not retained on the completion of the 1938–39 campaign. At the time of his first outing with the Albion in September 1942, Ernie was registered with Norwich City, but he failed to make a senior appearance for the 'Canaries' until the 1945–46 transitional season. He remained at Carrow Road until joining Southern League side Bedford Town in 1947.

Season	Wartime	Total
1942–43	29 (2)	29 (2)
1943–44	25 (6)	25 (6)
1944–45	31 (5)	31 (5)
1945–46	2	2
Total	87 (13)	87 (13)

RICHARDSON, DAVE   BRADFORD CITY

centre-half   *1 app*
debut: Portsmouth (h), 22.4.1944

Dave Richardson initially played for Bradford City during the 1940–41 season and clocked up almost 50 wartime appearances up to 1945, but didn't figure when peace was restored.

RICHMOND

inside-right   *1 app*
debut: Clapton Orient (a), 25.12.1942

Richmond was one of several volunteers from the crowd employed to make up the numbers for the Christmas Day fixture against Clapton Orient at Brisbane Road in 1942. Albion put up a good show in losing only 3–1.

ROBSON, BERT — CRYSTAL PALACE

outside-right — 1 app, 1 goal
born: Crook, Co. Durham, 14.11.1916
debut: Cardiff City (h), 27.10.1945

One of three Palace players who assisted Albion in a 3–2 home defeat by Cardiff City in October 1945, Bert Robson spent some twelve years at Selhurst Park, joining the staff as an eighteen-year-old centre-forward from the Godalming club in December 1934 and making his League debut during the 1936–37 season. He scored prolifically for the 'Glaziers' throughout the war, netting well over 100 goals in some 170 appearances, and remained with the club until 1948 when he moved into the Kent League with Tunbridge Wells Rangers. Bert also guested for Chelsea and Clapton Orient during the 1945–46 transitional season.

ROSS, GEORGE — DUNDEE UNITED

outside-right — 1 app
born: Bonnyrigg, Midlothian, Scotland
debut: Aldershot (a), 14.10.1944

A free-scoring winger, George Ross started out with Dundee United, making his debut in 1928–29, the season that United won the Division Two championship. Transferred to Portsmouth in 1930, he failed to make his mark in the English First Division and returned to his former club in 1932. George remained at Tannadice until the war, bringing his total of goals to 65 from 151 League appearances before joining the Army.

ROWLEY, ARTHUR — WEST BROMWICH ALBION

left-back — 5 apps, 1 goal
born: Wolverhampton, Staffordshire, 21.4.1926
debut: Reading (a), 25.8.1945

Arthur Rowley was a virtually unknown eighteen-year-old when he first appeared in Albion's junior team during the latter part of the 1944–45 season, but he impressed the management and was selected at left-back in the senior side for the early matches the following term. The young lad from the Black Country was described in the local Press as 'the best defender seen in an Albion side since before the war', but, after changing to an inside-forward role, it was as the most prolific goalscorer in the history of the English professional game that Arthur went on to earn his place in the record books.

Having made his senior debut for Manchester United at the age of fifteen in 1941, he played alongside his elder brother Jack (who was to star for United and England after the war), and turned out for Wolves as an amateur during 1943–44 before joining West Bromwich Albion the following season.

It was not until signing for Fulham in 1948 that he began to show the goalscoring flare that was to see him through the rest of his career, though. His 27 goals for the 'Cottagers' were followed by 251 for Leicester City (1950–58) and

152 for Shrewsbury Town as player-manager (1958–65), bringing his total of goals to an amazing 434 from 619 League matches. These phenomenal feats, achieved mainly in the Second and Third Divisions, earned Arthur just one England B cap and a single appearance for the Football League.

On leaving Gay Meadow in 1968 he went on to manage Sheffield United (1968–69) and Southend United (1970–76). In 1994 it was revealed that he was having to sell his memorabilia to finance a knee operation, but his former clubs, Shrewsbury and Leicester, rallied to assist one of the all-time greats of the game.

SAGE, FRANK — CARDIFF CITY

left-back — 1 app
born: Chipping Sodbury, Gloucestershire, 31.5.1924
debut: Swindon Town (a), 12.9.1945

Although registered with Cardiff City in 1944, Frank Sage never appeared in the Welsh club's first team. In 1948 he moved on to Newport County, but made only three appearances before joining Chippenham Town in the Western League where he played for a number of years.

SANDERSON

right-half — 1 app
debut: Clapton Orient (a), 1.1.1944

Sanderson was one of the players recruited from the crowd for the 3–0 defeat at Clapton Orient on New Year's Day 1944.

SCRIMSHAW, STAN — BRADFORD CITY

centre-half — 2 apps
born: Hartlepool, Co. Durham, 7.8.1915
debut: Chelsea (h), 31.1.1942

Stan Scrimshaw's two appearances for the Albion were a real contrast: an 8–2 Goldstone defeat of Chelsea and an 8–2 thrashing at Charlton within the space of a week. Stan had joined his local club, Hartlepools United, in 1935, but was transferred to Bradford City two years later, playing for the Yorkshire side – mainly as a reserve – until 1947. He finished his League career with a couple of seasons at Halifax Town. Stan also made wartime guest appearances for Bristol City, Grimsby Town, Huddersfield Town, Millwall, Northampton Town and Norwich City as well as Hartlepools and the Albion.

SHAFTO, JOHN — LIVERPOOL

centre-forward — 28 apps, 23 goals
born: Humshaugh, Northumberland, 8.11.1918
debut: Queen's Park Rangers (h), 30.8.1941

John Shafto showed tremendous promise on joining Liverpool in 1936: he made his First Division debut at the age of eighteen and had scored seven goals in 20 outings when war was declared. John managed only a handful of appearances on Merseyside during the hostilities but guested for Bradford City and Brighton. Indeed, he played regularly for the Albion during 1942–43 and finished as top scorer with sixteen goals from eighteen games, including a hat-trick and a four-goal haul in an 8–0 win over Luton Town. John did not reappear in the Football League after the war.

Season	Wartime	Total
1941–42	1 (1)	1 (1)
1942–43	18 (16)	18 (16)
1943–44	9 (6)	9 (6)
Total	28 (23)	28 (23)

SHEPPARD, RICHARD — BRIGHTON & HOVE ALBION

winger 5 apps, 1 goal
debut: Reading (h), 1.9.1945

Richard Sheppard was an Albion junior who got his chance when Bert Stephens was unavailable in the final season of emergency competition.

SIMMONS, L.

outside-left 1 app
debut: Watford (a), 21.2.1942

The son of the Watford club secretary, Simmons made up the numbers for Albion in a 7–1 defeat at Vicarage Road.

SLATER

right-half 1 app
debut: Portsmouth (a), 29.3.1941

Slater was one of five guest players who turned out in a 3–2 defeat at Fratton Park.

SMITH, A.

outside-left 1 app
debut: Norwich City (a), 25.12.1940

Smith was one of seven unfortunate emergency players who made up Albion's team in the 18–0 defeat at Norwich.

SPERRIN, BILL — TOTTENHAM HOTSPUR

outside-right 2 apps
born: Wood Green, Middlesex, 9.4.1922
debut: Millwall (a), 5.2.1944

Bill Sperrin first appeared for Tottenham Hotspur in November 1940 as an eighteen-year-old amateur from the Athenian League club Finchley, and played for Spurs occasionally until 1944. He also guested for Albion, Bradford City, Chelsea, Clapton Orient, Fulham and Millwall, but returned to Finchley when peace broke out. Bill subsequently enjoyed a lengthy spell with Brentford (1949–55) before joining Tunbridge Wells Rangers. His elder brother Jimmy also played for Spurs during the war.

SPRY

outside-right 1 app
debut: Portsmouth (a), 29.3.1941

Spry was an emergency player enlisted to make up a depleted team for a match at Fratton Park in 1941. Albion performed well under the circumstances, restricting a strong 'Pompey' eleven to a 3–2 victory.

STACEY, W. A.

centre-forward 1 app
debut: Norwich City (a), 25.12.1940

An emergency recruit who led Albion's attack in the Christmas Day fixture at Carrow Road in 1940, Stacey held a watching brief as Albion sank 18–0.

STEAR, JIMMY — SOUTHAMPTON

left-back 1 app
debut: Crystal Palace (a), 9.9.1944

Jimmy Stear played briefly for Southampton in the last two wartime seasons, and appeared as a guest for the Albion in a 5–2 defeat at Selhurst Park.

SWINFEN, REG — QUEEN'S PARK RANGERS

outside-right 1 app
born: Battersea, London, 4.5.1915
debut: Southend United (h), 10.4.1940

Reg Swinfen started his professional career with Queen's Park Rangers in the mid 1930s, making his first-team debut during the 1936–37 season, and managed to turn out for Rangers on occasion during each of the seven wartime seasons. He also guested for Bournemouth, Clapton Orient and Huddersfield Town. After the war he had a single outing with Q.P.R. in 1946–47, his last Football League match, and subsequently played for Tonbridge before becoming player-coach at Crawley, a key figure in establishing the club in the Sussex County League during the early 1950s. A keen member of the Hawth Bowls Club, Reg lived in the Northgate area of the town and worked as a security guard at Gatwick Airport until his retirement. He died in October 1996.

SZAJNA-STANKOWSKI, BISHEK

goalkeeper 1 app
debut: Reading (h), 28.8.1943

A Polish airman, Bishek Stankowski kept goal in the opening match of the 1943–44 season and was on the receiving end of a 4–0 home defeat by Reading. He had previously appeared at the Goldstone for an R.A.F. XI under the pseudonym 'A. Pole' to avoid possible reprisals by the Germans against his family back home in Poland.

TAIT, TOMMY — TORQUAY UNITED

inside-right 1 app
born: Hetton-le-Hole, Co. Durham, 20.11.1908
debut: Reading (a), 13.1.1940

Though turning out at inside-right for the Albion, Tommy Tait was in fact a prolific centre-forward. An England Schools international, he joined Sunderland at the age of sixteen and had a brief spell with Middlesbrough before joining Southport on a free transfer in 1927 where his form quickly attracted the bigger clubs. He went on to play for Manchester City (1928–30), Bolton Wanderers (1930–31), Luton Town (1931–34), Bournemouth (1934) and Reading (1934–39), netting 181 goals in 325 League games. Transferred to Torquay United in 1939, Tommy played for the Devon side in the first wartime season, but the club then shut down until 1945 when he reappeared in their line-up. He guested for Reading and Southampton as well as Albion.

TAPKEN, NORMAN — MANCHESTER UNITED

goalkeeper 2 apps
born: Wallsend, Northumberland, 21.2.1914
debut: Southampton (a), 23.12.1944

A fine servant of Newcastle United during the 1930s, Norman Tapken joined the 'Magpies' as a nineteen-year-old in 1933 and became first-choice goalkeeper from 1934 to 1937, clocking up in excess of 100 Second Division outings. In 1938 he was transferred to Manchester United for £850 and was on the staff at Old Trafford until 1947, although he was lost to the club during the war years until the 1945–46 season. Apart from his two matches for the Albion, Norman made guest appearances for Aldershot, Chester, Darlington, Newcastle United and Sunderland. On leaving Manchester United he moved on to Darlington, and subsequently had a brief spell with Shelbourne in the League of Ireland before becoming assistant trainer at Stoke City in 1952.

TAYLOR, Phil — LIVERPOOL

half-back — 39 apps, 5 goals
born: Bristol, Gloucestershire, 18.9.1917
debut: Southampton (h), 14.4.1941

Phil Taylor skippered England Schoolboys and signed professional forms for his local club, Bristol Rovers, in 1935 where he quickly impressed. A year later he was transferred to Liverpool and became a great favourite of the Anfield crowd for eighteen years, playing at inside-right up to the war. However, it was as a right-half after the seven-year break that he really made his name, winning a League championship medal in 1946–47; collecting three England caps during 1947–48; representing the Football League on four occasions; and skippering the 1950 F.A. Cup final side which lost 2–0 to Arsenal.

An excellent passer of the ball, Phil played in 345 peacetime games for the 'Reds' (in addition to almost 100 outings in the emergency competitions) before retiring at the age of 36 in 1954. On hanging up his boots he joined the Anfield coaching staff and, between 1956 and 1959, was manager of the club, taking over from former Albion boss Don Welsh and handing over to the great Bill Shankly.

Phil guested for the Albion from 1941 to 1944, and also turned out for Bristol Rovers, Leeds United and Newcastle United while serving in the Army. He was also a professional cricketer and made one appearance for Gloucestershire in 1938.

Season	Wartime	Total
1940–41	4	4
1941–42	8 (1)	8 (1)
1942–43	11	11
1943–44	16 (4)	16 (4)
Total	39 (5)	39 (5)

THEW

inside-right — 1 app
debut: Crystal Palace (a), 3.1.1942

Thew was an emergency player who appeared in a crushing 10–1 defeat at Selhurst Park.

THORNE, Albert — BRIGHTON & HOVE ALBION

right-back/centre-forward — 3 apps, 1 goal
born: Brighton, Sussex, 22.7.1923
debut: Arsenal (h), 11.4.1942

Educated at Brighton's Coombe Road School, Albert Thorne played for Brighton Boys and was turning out for Elder Athletic when he was recruited for Albion's new junior team. He skippered the side for three seasons, but was then called into the Royal Navy and served with the Fleet Air Arm for three years, appearing briefly for Southampton's reserves. After the war, while working for the local Allen West engineering company, he played for Lancing Athletic and remained with them on their election to the Sussex County League in 1948.

Season	Wartime	Total
1941–42	1	1
1942–43	2 (1)	2 (1)
Total	3 (1)	3 (1)

TOOTILL, Alf — CRYSTAL PALACE

goalkeeper — 1 app
born: Ramsbottom, Lancashire, 12.11.1908
debut: Brentford (a), 11.9.1943

A vastly experienced goalkeeper by the time he guested for the Albion, Alf Tootill had joined Accrington Stanley in 1927, but quickly moved up a sphere when he was transferred to Wolves in 1929. A regular in the League team at Molineux for more than three seasons, he was ever-present in the Second Division championship side of 1931–32 before moving to Fulham. Alf subsequently made 203 League appearances for the 'Cottagers' (1932–38), after which he was transferred to Crystal Palace where he brought his total of League outings to 373 before the onset of war. He played for Palace on a regular basis in the emergency competitions, appearing in almost 150 matches, and also turned out as a guest for Ipswich Town before his retirement in 1945.

TOOZE, Cyril — ARSENAL

left-back — 17 apps
debut: Portsmouth (h), 18.10.1941

Although registered with Arsenal, Cyril Tooze was destined never to make a senior appearance for the 'Gunners' although he played for their nursery team, Margate. Along with his Arsenal club-mate Stan Morgan (see above), who also guested regularly for the Albion, he was among the supporting troops during the commando raid on the German radar station at Bruneval in Normandy in February 1942, and earned a terrific reception from the Goldstone crowd on his next appearance at Hove the following month. Sadly, Cyril was killed while serving in Italy with the Royal Fusiliers in February 1944, the victim of a sniper's bullet.

TOWNSEND, Len — BRENTFORD

centre-forward — 1 app, 1 goal
born: Brentford, Middlesex, 31.8.1917
debut: Southampton (h), 26.12.1944

Len Townsend started out with Isleworth Town and the Athenian League side Hayes, for whom he scored 72 goals in his only full season. After signing for his local League side, Brentford, Len made his First Division debut on Boxing Day 1938 and showed great promise. Serving as a light infantryman during the conflict, he hit 103 goals in nearly 150 wartime outings for the 'Bees', and took particular delight in scoring against the Albion, striking 24 times in fourteen games between the clubs during the period 1939–46. Indeed, in September 1942 he scored six goals in a 9–4 victory over Brighton to establish a Brentford record.

While stationed in Ulster in 1943 he played for Belfast Celtic, where he won an Irish Cup medal and represented the Northern Ireland Regional League in a 2–2 draw with the League of Ireland at Windsor Park. Len guested for Chelsea, Leeds United, Plymouth Argyle, Swansea Town and West Ham United, as well as making a solitary appearance for the Albion.

In 1947 he left Griffin Park for Bristol City, where he registered 43 goals in 74 Third Division (South) matches over two seasons before finishing his career with spells at Millwall and Guildford City in the Southern League. Len then did some coaching at Hayes and Maidenhead United. He now lives in retirement in Seaford, Sussex.

TULLY, FRED — CLAPTON ORIENT

outside-left — 1 app
born: St Pancras, London, 1907
debut: Clapton Orient (h), 26.12.1942

A diminutive winger, Fred Tully entered the senior ranks when he joined Aston Villa in 1926, but in seven years at Villa Park he made the first team on just seven occasions. On moving to Southampton in 1933 he met with wider opportunity, scoring nine goals in 97 Second Division appearances before dropping into Division Three with Clapton Orient in 1937, where he played regularly until hanging up his boots at the age of 39 in 1943. Fred was loaned to Brighton for a Boxing Day fixture with the Orient at the Goldstone which Albion won 1–0.

TUNNICLIFFE, BILL — BOURNEMOUTH & B.A.

outside-left — 5 apps, 2 goals
born: Stoke-on-Trent, Staffordshire, 5.1.1920
debut: Reading (a), 6.9.1941

After starting out with Port Vale, where he made his initial first-team appearance at the age of seventeen during the 1936–37 season, Bill Tunnicliffe was transferred to Bournemouth in 1938 and remained at Dean Court for a war-interrupted nine years. In 1947 he moved to Wrexham and scored 73 goals in 236 League outings for the Welsh side before ending his career with two seasons at Bradford City (1953–55). Bill also turned out as a guest for Brentford, Chester and Reading during the war.

WALKER, CYRIL — SHEFFIELD WEDNESDAY

inside-right — 2 apps
born: Pirton, Hertfordshire, 24.2.1914
debut: West Ham United (h), 14.2.1942

Cyril Walker started out as a Watford junior, but appeared with Gillingham and Sheffield Wednesday during 1937–38 before moving down to non-League football at the end of that season. During the war years he guested for Albion, Raith Rovers, Crystal Palace, Norwich City, Sheffield Wednesday and Watford while serving in the R.A.F., and had a brief spell with the 'Canaries' in their initial post-war campaign. He subsequently played for Dartford, and held coaching posts with Chatham, Snowdown Colliery and Dartford.

Season	Wartime	Total
1941–42	1	1
1942–43	1	1
Total	2	2

WALLER, HENRY — ARSENAL

half-back — 5 apps
born: Ashington, Northumberland, 20.8.1917
debut: Portsmouth (h), 18.10.1941

Henry Waller joined Arsenal from Ashington in 1937 at the age of 20 and was on the Highbury staff for ten years, but his career was ruined by the war. After making his first senior appearance for the 'Gunners' in 1941, he later saw service with the Army in Sicily and Italy, and his availability was severely curtailed (although he managed guest appearances for Clapton Orient, Reading, Sunderland, Watford and West Ham United). In 1947, Henry was transferred to the renamed Leyton Orient on a permanent basis, but after one season at Brisbane Road he returned to the Ashington club.

WALLIS, JOHNNY — TOTTENHAM HOTSPUR

left-back — 3 app
born: Finchley, Middlesex, 1922
debut: Chelsea (h), 18.11.1944

With an illustrious career as a schoolboy behind him – he represented London, Middlesex and England Schools – Johnny Wallis joined Spurs as an amateur in 1936 and was taken on the ground staff in 1938. Although the war inevitably affected his career, he was still able to turn out for Spurs, and also guested for the Albion and Enfield during the hostilities. Soon after making his third appearance for Brighton, Johnny was serving in Palestine when he suffered the severe shrapnel wounds which virtually ended his football career. After playing for non-League sides Chelmsford City and Wisbech Town, he joined the Tottenham coaching staff in 1948 and went on to serve as coach, reserve-team manager and physio. For many years Johnny was kit manager to the reserve and junior teams at White Hart Lane.

WARD, JACK — NOTTINGHAM FOREST

outside-right — 2 apps
debut: Southampton (a), 29.4.1944

Although registered with Nottingham Forest, Jack Ward appeared only briefly for them in the early part of the war. He guested for the Albion in the last two matches of the 1943–44 season.

WASSALL, JACK — MANCHESTER UNITED

inside-left — 4 apps
born: Shrewsbury, Shropshire, 11.2.1917
debut: Tottenham Hotspur (h), 29.1.1944

Jack Wassall was recruited by Manchester United from Wellington Town of the Birmingham League, and made his first-team debut at the age of eighteen in November 1935. In the four seasons before the war he totalled 48 appearances and was featured as one of the 'Young Players of 1939' by the *Topical Times*. Having played in one of the three First Division matches of the abandoned 1939–40 League season, Jack was then lost to Old Trafford for the duration. Two seasons with Stockport County from 1946 saw the end of his Football League career.

WATSON, JACK — BURY

centre-half — 2 apps
born: Hamilton, Lanarkshire, Scotland, 31.12.1917
debut: Arsenal (a), 27.3.1943

Jack Watson joined Bury in 1938 and appeared briefly in the Lancashire club's League team before the war. Playing for the 'Shakers' throughout the hostilities when his wartime duties allowed, he also had extended spells as a guest with Fulham and was transferred to the London club in 1946 where he was first-choice centre-half for two years. Jack then enjoyed a season in Spain as player-coach at Real Madrid before seeing out his football career with Crystal Palace (1949–51).

WATTS, ROY — BRIGHTON & HOVE ALBION

right-back — 6 apps
full name: Royston Watts
debut: Watford (h), 1.6.1940

Roy 'Snozzle' Watts was one of five youngsters who came into the first team in June 1940, just three weeks after the Albion junior side played its first match. Having played for Brighton Boys, he graduated though the Hove Penguins youth club to the Albion juniors. In December 1940, Roy turned out for Charlton Athletic *against* the Albion when the visitors arrived one man short.

Season	Wartime	Total
1939–40	2	2
1940–41	4	4
Total	6	6

WEAVER, SAM — CHELSEA

inside-left — 1 app
born: Pilsley, Derbyshire, 8.2.1909
debut: Queen's Park Rangers (a), 12.2.1944

Although appearing at inside-left for the Albion, Sam Weaver won fame as a wing-half and was an early exponent of the long throw-in. After starting out with Hull City in 1928, he was transferred to Newcastle United in 1929 and spent seven years at St James's Park, gaining Football League representative honours and three England caps. In 1932 he gained an F.A. Cup winner's medal when the 'Magpies' beat Arsenal 2–1 after the controversial 'over the line' goal incident. A good tackler and aggressive attacker, Sam moved on to Chelsea in 1936 and missed only a handful of games in the three seasons leading up to the war, skippering the team in 1938–39.

After guesting for the Albion, Clapton Orient, Derby County, Fulham, Leeds United, Notts County, Southampton, West Ham United and Wrexham at various times during the seven years of wartime fare, he joined Stockport County on a permanent basis in 1945 and, after retiring in 1947, held coaching posts at Leeds United and Millwall. He also coached at Mansfield Town where he was manager from 1958 to 1960. Sam played first-class cricket for Somerset in 1939 and was masseur to Derbyshire for many years from 1956.

WEIR, JOCK — HIBERNIAN

centre-forward/outside-right — 3 apps, 1 goal
born: Fauldhouse, West Lothian, Scotland, 20.10.1923
debut: Southampton (a), 23.12.1944

An ordinary seaman in the Fleet Air Arm, Jock Weir turned up for Albion's match at Southampton in 1944 and asked to play for either side. Charlie Webb accommodated the Scot and he was re-employed for the following two games. Jock had joined Hibernian in 1941 and also assisted Cardiff City during the war. He went on to play for Blackburn Rovers (January 1947), Celtic (February 1948), Falkirk (October 1952), Llanelly (July 1953) and Dumbarton (December 1953).

WELSH, DON — CHARLTON ATHLETIC

centre-forward — 9 apps, 17 goals
debut: Portsmouth (h), 1.3.1941
See *Albion Managers*

Season	Wartime	Total
1940–41	7 (15)	7 (15)
1941–42	2 (2)	2 (2)
Total	9 (17)	9 (17)

WESTBY, JACK — BLACKBURN ROVERS

defender — 16 apps
born: Aintree, Lancashire, 20.5.1916
debut: Aldershot (a), 2.11.1940

Jack Westby joined Blackburn Rovers at the age of 20 in 1937 and made two appearances for the Second Division club before the outbreak of war. He played for Rovers during the early part of the conflict while serving in the Army, and guested for Aldershot, Liverpool and the Albion. In May 1944 he was transferred to Liverpool and brought his total of wartime appearances for the 'Reds' to around 80 during the last two seasons before the return to regular League football in 1946. Jack ended his career with a season at Southport (1947–48) before moving into non-League circles with Runcorn.

Season	Wartime	Total
1940–41	4	4
1941–42	12	12
Total	16	16

WHARTON, F. — HIBERNIAN

right-back — 1 app
debut: Crystal Palace (a), 19.1.1946

Wharton's sole appearance for the Albion came in a 6–1 drubbing at Selhurst Park, one of a series of huge defeats suffered at the hands of Palace during the war.

WILLIAMS, S. — CARDIFF CITY

left-half/outside-right — 7 apps
debut: Aldershot (a), 22.11.1941

A versatile player, Williams appeared at left-half for the Albion on three occasions, then had an additional four outings on the right-wing. Although registered with Cardiff City, he did not appear in their senior team.

WILLIAMS, WALTER — CARDIFF CITY

centre-forward — 1 app
debut: Bristol City (a), 5.9.1945

Walter Williams appeared regularly for Cardiff City in the 1943–44 season, his only outings for the 'Bluebirds'. He made a guest appearance for the Albion in the third fixture of the 1945–46 transitional campaign.

WILSON, ALBERT — CRYSTAL PALACE

outside-left — 1 app
born: Rotherham, Yorkshire, 28.1.1915
debut: Cardiff City (h), 27.10.1945

Albert Wilson joined Derby County in 1936 but made only one League appearance for the 'Rams' before moving on to Mansfield

Town in 1938. In January 1939 he was transferred to Crystal Palace and remained at Selhurst Park throughout the war, appearing in around 180 regional matches. Albert subsequently had a season with his home-town club, Rotherham United (1946–47), and another with Grimsby Town (1947–48) before dropping into non-League football with Boston United. He was subsequently groundsman at Rotherham for many years.

WILSON, ALEC   HUDDERSFIELD TOWN

inside-left   *1 app*
debut: Clapton Orient (a), 2.3.1940

Alec Wilson was a Huddersfield Town junior who guested for the Albion in a 5–1 defeat at Clapton Orient in the initial wartime season.

WILSON, FRED   BOURNEMOUTH & B.A.

centre-half   *24 apps*
born: Nottingham, Nottinghamshire, 10.11.1918
debut: Southampton (h), 8.3.1941

On Wolves' books as a youngster, Fred Wilson had his first taste of League football following his transfer to Bournemouth in February 1939 where he made a single appearance before the outbreak of war. He played on occasion for the 'Cherries' until their closure for the remainder of the hostilities in 1942, and guested for the Albion, Crystal Palace and Leicester City. Fred returned to Dean Court during the 1945–46 transitional campaign and, when things returned to normal, brought his total of League appearances up to 98 before moving into the Southern League with Weymouth in 1951.

Season	Wartime	Total
1940–41	8	8
1941–42	4	4
1943–44	12	12
Total	24	24

WINNING, ALEX   CLYDE

defender   *17 apps*
born: Glasgow, Lanarkshire, Scotland
debut: Brentford (a), 26.8.1944

Alex Winning joined Glasgow Rangers from Shawfield Juniors in the late 1930s, but failed to make an impact at Ibrox and was transferred to Clyde just before the war. He guested extensively for the Albion during the 1944–45 season and played a variety of defensive roles, having also turned out briefly for Aldershot and Millwall earlier in the war.

WOODLEY, VIC   CHELSEA

goalkeeper   *1 app*
born: Cippenham, Buckinghamshire, 26.2.1911
debut: Arsenal (a), 18.4.1942

One of England's finest in the 1930s, Vic Woodley joined the Chelsea staff from Windsor & Eton in 1931 and went on to enjoy a splendid career as a classy goalkeeper at Stamford Bridge. Having rapidly established himself between the posts, he clocked up 272 League and Cup appearances up to 1939, represented the Football League on four occasions, and was also a regular in the England team, playing in nineteen consecutive international matches before the outbreak of war. He appeared for Chelsea throughout the conflict, playing in 106 wartime games, and added another cap to his collection, against Wales in the first of the wartime internationals.

Vic joined Southern League Bath City in December 1945, but Derby County, in the midst of an injury crisis, signed the experienced custodian to play in the initial post-war F.A. Cup ties. Thus it was that he gained a winner's medal at the age of 35 before returning to Bath as player-manager. Vic also guested for Brentford and Spurs during the first wartime season, but his only game for the Albion came in 1941–42, a 5–1 reverse against Arsenal.

WOODS

outside-left   *1 app*
debut: Aldershot (h), 28.2.1942

Nothing is known of Woods except that he played for Albion in a 5–1 defeat by Aldershot at the Goldstone in the 1941–42 season, in a team which included seven guest players. He was probably a serviceman stationed in the Sussex area.

WOODWARD, DAI   BOURNEMOUTH & B.A.

half-back   *6 apps*
full name: Laurie Woodward
born: Troedyrhiw, Merthyr Tydfil, Glamorgan, Wales, 5.7.1918
debut: Millwall (a), 17.10.1942

'Dai' Woodward made 275 League appearances for Bournemouth between 1946 and 1956, having joined the 'Cherries' from Wolves during the summer of 1939. On retiring he was appointed to the coaching staff at Dean Court and was later awarded the Football League's long service medal to commemorate 20 years with one club. For his testimonial in 1965, Arsenal sent a strong side down to the seaside to play Bournemouth.

At the time of his guest appearances for the Albion, Dai was employed as a driver with the Royal Welch Regiment. He came from a football-playing family: his father played for Merthyr Town and Aberdare Athletic; his Uncle Tom appeared with Chesterfield, Preston North End and Swansea Town; and brother Vivian played for Fulham, Millwall, Brentford and Aldershot.

Season	Wartime	Total
1942–43	2	2
1943–44	4	4
Total	6	6

WRIGHT, TOMMY   MANCHESTER CITY

left-half   *9 apps, 1 goal*
born: Glossop, Derbyshire, 11.1.1917
debut: Luton Town (h), 22.1.1944

Although he joined Manchester City in 1937, it was another ten years before Tommy Wright made his debut in the regular Football League — with Accrington Stanley. After playing briefly for City in the wartime competitions, Tommy drifted into non-League football with Altrincham. He had a fruitless spell with Hull City in 1947 and moved on to Accrington later that year, making 20 appearances in just over twelve months for the Third Division (North) side before being released to join non-League Stalybridge Celtic.

YOUNG

goalkeeper   *1 app*
debut: Clapton Orient (a), 1.1.1944

Young was an emergency goalkeeper who appeared in the 3–0 defeat at Clapton Orient on New Year's Day 1944.

UNKNOWN EMERGENCY PLAYER

centre-half   *1 app*
debut: Clapton Orient (a), 1.1.1944

Albion arrived for the match at Orient on New Year's Day 1944, with only four men and had to find seven emergency recruits. Six of these have been identified, but the seventh is, so far, untraced.

Albion's 'Nearly Men'

This section contains brief biographies of the 'nearly men', those players who nearly made it into the Albion first team for various reasons.

Ten of the twelve players here warmed the Albion bench without being called upon, but the other two were particularly unlucky, having played in the Football League's 1939–40 campaign for the club only for the competition to be aborted upon the outbreak of war in September 1939; they did not go on to play for the Albion in wartime matches.

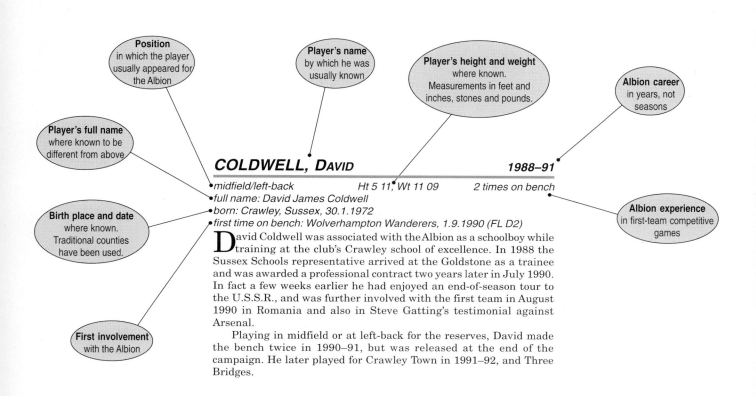

Position
in which the player usually appeared for the Albion

Player's name
by which he was usually known

Player's height and weight
where known.
Measurements in feet and inches, stones and pounds.

Albion career
in years, not seasons

Player's full name
where known to be different from above.

Birth place and date
where known.
Traditional counties have been used.

First involvement
with the Albion

Albion experience
in first-team competitive games

COLDWELL, DAVID   1988–91

• *midfield/left-back*   Ht 5 11, Wt 11 09   *2 times on bench*
• *full name: David James Coldwell*
• *born: Crawley, Sussex, 30.1.1972*
• *first time on bench: Wolverhampton Wanderers, 1.9.1990 (FL D2)*

David Coldwell was associated with the Albion as a schoolboy while training at the club's Crawley school of excellence. In 1988 the Sussex Schools representative arrived at the Goldstone as a trainee and was awarded a professional contract two years later in July 1990. In fact a few weeks earlier he had enjoyed an end-of-season tour to the U.S.S.R., and was further involved with the first team in August 1990 in Romania and also in Steve Gatting's testimonial against Arsenal.

Playing in midfield or at left-back for the reserves, David made the bench twice in 1990–91, but was released at the end of the campaign. He later played for Crawley Town in 1991–92, and Three Bridges.

BOOK, STEVE — 1993–94

goalkeeper — *19 times on bench*
full name: Steven Book
born: Bournemouth, Dorset, c. 1969
first time on bench: Reading (h), 20.11.1993 (FL D2)

The son of Kim Book, once a goalkeeper himself with Bournemouth, Northampton Town, Mansfield Town and Doncaster Rovers, and the nephew of Tony Book (ex-Manchester City), Steve Book came to the Goldstone on trial early in 1993–94, and signed as a professional in November 1993 as cover for Nicky Rust while young Mark Ormerod continued his apprenticeship. He went on to occupy the bench nineteen times without being called upon.

The 24-year-old 'keeper had had nomadic experience in the West Country with Tiverton Town, Taunton Town, Welton Rovers, Paulton Rovers, Weston-super-Mare and Frome Town while also spending time as a non-contract pro with Bath City. It was while with Frome in 1992–93 that he played alongside Bryan Wade, the ex-Albion forward, who arranged for the trial.

Released in March 1994, Steve joined Wycombe Wanderers briefly before returning to his native patch. In 1997 he left Forest Green Rovers to join up with Cheltenham Town in the Football Conference.

COLDWELL, DAVID — 1988–91

midfield/left-back — Ht 5 11, Wt 11 09 — *2 times on bench*
full name: David James Coldwell
born: Crawley, Sussex, 30.1.1972
first time on bench: Wolverhampton Wanderers, 1.9.1990 (FL D2)

David Coldwell was associated with the Albion as a schoolboy while training at the club's Crawley school of excellence. In 1988 the Sussex Schools representative arrived at the Goldstone as a trainee and was awarded a professional contract two years later in July 1990. In fact a few weeks earlier he had enjoyed an end-of-season tour to the U.S.S.R., and was further involved with the first team in August 1990 in Romania and also in Steve Gatting's testimonial against Arsenal.

Playing in midfield or at left-back for the reserves, David made the bench twice in 1990–91, but was released at the end of the campaign. He later played for Crawley Town in 1991–92, and Three Bridges.

CORMACK, LEE — 1989–90

striker — *7 times on bench*
full name: Lee Darin Daniel Cormack
born: Londonderry, Co. Londonderry, Northern Ireland, 14.10.1970
first time on bench: Oldham Athletic (h), 3.3.1990 (FL D2)

Although born in Londonderry, where his father was in the Army, Lee Cormack grew up in Hampshire and represented Eastleigh and Hampshire Schools. The talented youngster moved to the F.A.'s National School at Lilleshall and went on to play for England Schools. Taken on as a trainee by Southampton, he won England youth honours, but after two years at The Dell he was released in 1989 and arrived at the Goldstone on a three-month trial.

Lee impressed manager Barry Lloyd and he was taken on as a non-contract professional in October, allowing him to be farmed out to Bognor Regis Town for experience. The nineteen-year-old forward scored regularly for the 'Rocks' and also for the Albion reserves, and

was drafted into the first-team squad several times towards the end of 1989–90. After touring the U.S.S.R. with Albion at the end of the campaign, Lee warmed the bench twice more early the following season, but then returned to Bognor on a permanent basis where he established himself for several seasons while undertaking a sports studies course in Chichester. After 196 games and 56 goals for the Isthmian Leaguers, he moved to Worthing in January 1997.

DICK, ALLY — 1990

winger — Ht 5 9, Wt 10 07 — *1 time on bench*
full name: Alistair Dick
born: Stirling, Stirlingshire, Scotland, 25.4.1965
first time on bench: Blackburn Rovers (a), 5.5.1990 (FL D2)

Ally Dick was probably the most experienced of the Albion 'nearly' men. In five years on the staff at White Hart Lane the young winger played only seventeen League games, but he did pick up a UEFA Cup winner's medal in 1984 at the end of his best season with the club. The former Scottish Schools representative was a trainee with Spurs and turned pro in 1983, but he was never able to establish himself in the first team and was released in 1986.

Ally then tried his luck abroad, joining Ajax of Amsterdam, but he didn't figure in their European Cup-Winners' Cup triumph of 1987. After nearly four years in Holland he found himself for sale at £200,000, but there were no takers and he was eventually released to join up with the Albion in March 1990. Given a contract until the end of the season, Ally made the bench for the last game of the campaign but was not called upon and was then released. After a spell in South Africa he surfaced again in January 1997 with Alloa in the Scottish League.

DINEEN, JACK — 1987–89

forward — Ht 5 7, Wt 10 10 — *4 times on bench*
born: Brighton, Sussex, 23.9.1970
first time on bench: Southend United (h), 25.11.1987 (AMC group)

A promising young forward from Portslade who attended Hove's Cardinal Newman School, Jack Dineen played for the Sussex youth side, represented the British Catholic Schools against their Belgian counterparts in December 1987, and played for Eire's under-17 team. Associated as a schoolboy with the Albion, Jack signed a pro contract at the age of 17 in October 1987 and was quickly included in the senior squad. He won a Sussex Senior Cup medal at the end of his first season as a pro.

Released in 1990, Jack then pursued a nomadic career around Sussex, playing for Bognor Regis Town, Crawley, Town, Worthing, Southwick and Burgess Hill. For 1997–98 he linked up with Peacehaven & Telscombe.

FULLER, BOB — 1967–68

centre-forward — *1 time on bench*
first time on bench: Southport (h), 30.3.1968 (FL D3)

Signed from Newcastle United for £2,000 during the close season of 1967, Bob Fuller top-scored for the Albion reserves with ten goals from 31 games, but he was unable to dislodge either the prolific Kit Napier or his striking partner, Charlie Livesey, from their first-team berths. Bob made the bench just once in his year at the Goldstone and was released at the end of the campaign.

HARRIS, JOE — 1939 & 1945–46

left-half — 3 apps in aborted 1939–40 Football League
born: Sutton-in-Ashfield, Nottinghamshire
debut: Port Vale (h), 26.8.1939 (FL D3(S) aborted)

Joe Harris was signed as a youngster from Doncaster Rovers, where he had been a reserve, during the summer of 1939 and went straight into the Albion first team. He played in the three matches at the start of the aborted 1939–40 Third Division season, but the outbreak of war meant that he would never make an appearance in the regular Football League. Joe played no senior football during the conflict, but Albion retained his registration until 1946 and he returned to play in the London Combination side in the transitional 1945–46 season before leaving the scene. Nottinghamshire-born, he served with the Sherwood Foresters during the war.

HUGHES, ALAN — 1994–95

goalkeeper — 1 time on bench
full name: Alan David Hughes
born: Dublin, Co. Dublin, Republic of Ireland, 5.7.1978
first time on bench: Cardiff City (h), 15.3.1995 (FL D2)

Alan Hughes was one of a number of young Irishmen to join the Albion in recent times, but he survived only one year as a trainee with the club. During that time he represented his country at under-18 level and also played on loan for Crawley Town, but shortly after warming the bench in the absence of regular reserve Mark Ormerod, he was released in April 1995 and returned to Dublin.

McGUINNESS, PAUL — 1990

midfield — Ht 5 7, Wt 11 05 — 5 times on bench
born: Manchester, Lancashire, 2.3.1966
first time on bench: Hull City (h), 24.10.1990 (FL D2)

The son of the former Manchester United manager and England international Wilf McGuinness, Paul was unable to live up to his pedigree and failed to make a single League appearance in two spells with his father's club, 1984–86 and 1989–91. In between Paul turned out for Crewe Alexandra, making thirteen League appearances, but arrived at the Goldstone on loan from United in October 1990. Warming the bench on five consecutive occasions, he was unlucky not to get on the pitch, but after returning to Old Trafford he was released at the end of the season to join Chester City for whom he made another fourteen League appearances in two seasons. He is believed to have played for Derry City in the League of Ireland thereafter.

NORTON, TERRY — 1973–74

right-back — 1 time on bench
born: 11.1.1956
first time on bench: Watford (a), 22.12.1973 (FL D3)

An England Schools representative from Kent, Terry Norton arrived at the Goldstone as a seventeen-year-old in the latter half of the 1972–73 season and quickly impressed in his full-back

role. With a limited amount of Southern League experience under his belt with Canterbury City, he went on to gain a Sussex Professional Cup winner's medal in April 1973, and was a regular in both the reserves and the youth team. Following his involvement with the League side in December 1973, Terry turned professional the following month on his eighteenth birthday and looked set for a fine future.

However, together with Pat Hilton and Mick Brown, he was dismissed by assistant manager Peter Taylor as the trio, along with Steve Piper, celebrated Hilton's birthday a little too boisterously, resulting in a broken window at the Goldstone. Terry then disappeared from the League scene.

REED, PETER — 1991–92

defender — 1 time on bench
full name: Peter M. Reed
born: 1972
first time on bench: Southend United (a), 7.12.1991 (FL D2)

Peter Reed looked to have a promising career ahead of him when he joined West Ham United as a trainee following two years at the F.A.'s National School of Excellence at Lilleshall, but the 'Hammers' declined to offer him a professional contract and released in in 1991. Invited to the Goldstone by coach Larry May, the eighteen-year-old impressed in the friendly and reserve games, and was awarded a contract until the end of the season. Shortly afterwards he was included in the first-team squad, but after gaining a Sussex Senior Cup winner's medal in May 1992 he was released at the end of the season and went on to play for Chelmsford City.

SPENCER, GEOFF — 1939

outside-right — 3 apps in aborted 1939–40 Football League
full name: Geoffrey Spencer
born: Shavington, Cheshire, 9.11.1913
debut: Port Vale (h), 26.8.1939 (FL D3(S) aborted)

Signed by Charlie Webb from West Bromwich Albion (along with goalkeeper Harry Baldwin) in May 1939, Geoff Spencer played in the three matches of the aborted 1939–40 Third Division before the outbreak of war, but then completely disappeared from the football scene. Blessed with excellent control and a fine crosser of the ball, Geoff had joined West Brom. from Nantwich Victoria in March 1933 but had had to wait until 1938–39 to make his initial appearances in the first team, scoring twice in thirteen Second Division outings. He played regularly for the "Throstles'" reserves and was capped at junior level against Scotland in 1937, but he was plagued with injuries throughout his short career.

Albion Managers

This section includes full biographies of all 21 men who have managed Brighton & Hove Albion F.C. It also includes the six who have undertaken the job on a temporary, caretaker basis.

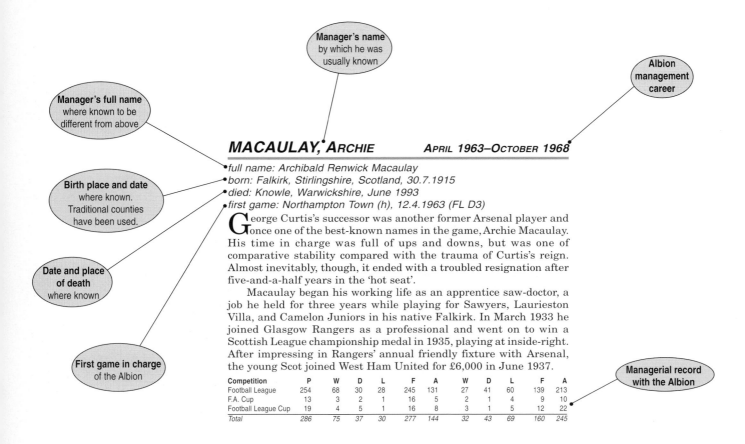

Manager's name
by which he was
usually known

Albion
management
career

Manager's full name
where known to be
different from above

Birth place and date
where known.
Traditional counties
have been used.

Date and place
of death
where known

First game in charge
of the Albion

Managerial record
with the Albion

MACAULAY, ARCHIE   *APRIL 1963–OCTOBER 1968*

full name: Archibald Renwick Macaulay
born: Falkirk, Stirlingshire, Scotland, 30.7.1915
died: Knowle, Warwickshire, June 1993
first game: Northampton Town (h), 12.4.1963 (FL D3)

George Curtis's successor was another former Arsenal player and once one of the best-known names in the game, Archie Macaulay. His time in charge was full of ups and downs, but was one of comparative stability compared with the trauma of Curtis's reign. Almost inevitably, though, it ended with a troubled resignation after five-and-a-half years in the 'hot seat'.

Macaulay began his working life as an apprentice saw-doctor, a job he held for three years while playing for Sawyers, Laurieston Villa, and Camelon Juniors in his native Falkirk. In March 1933 he joined Glasgow Rangers as a professional and went on to win a Scottish League championship medal in 1935, playing at inside-right. After impressing in Rangers' annual friendly fixture with Arsenal, the young Scot joined West Ham United for £6,000 in June 1937.

Competition	P	W	D	L	F	A	W	D	L	F	A
Football League	254	68	30	28	245	131	27	41	60	139	213
F.A. Cup	13	3	2	1	16	5	2	1	4	9	10
Football League Cup	19	4	5	1	16	8	3	1	5	12	22
Total	*286*	*75*	*37*	*30*	*277*	*144*	*32*	*43*	*69*	*160*	*245*

JACKSON, JOHN   JUNE 1901–MARCH 1905

born: Deritend, Birmingham, Warwickshire, 14.2.1861
died: Brighton, Sussex, 19.6.1931
first game: Brighton Athletic (h), 21.9.1901 (FAC Prelim.)

When the founders of Brighton United cast an eye for someone to organise and run the team, they opted for Leicester Fosse's 37-year-old trainer John Jackson. The son of a Birmingham master toolmaker, Jackson had spent his somewhat undistinguished playing days as a goalkeeper with Coventry Rovers, but, on retiring from the active side of the game, he became assistant trainer with Wolverhampton Wanderers and played his part in their F.A. Cup success of 1893 when they defeated Everton 1–0 in the final at Fallowfield, Manchester.

A year later he migrated to Leicestershire where he helped re-form the Loughborough club. The 'Luffs' carried off the championship of the Midland League at their first attempt in 1894–95, a success which brought them election to the Football League, but he moved

JACKSON

on to Liverpool as trainer. In his only season at Anfield, 1895–96, the club won promotion to the First Division, and for his part in the triumph Jackson received a 'purse of gold and a gold medal'. In 1896 he returned to the Midlands and the Second Division with Leicester Fosse, and arrived in Brighton two years later for the opening of the United episode.

During his time with Brighton United, Jackson was instrumental in bringing some fine players to the town. In its first season the team did well enough, easily finishing clear of the bottom two in the Southern League's First Division, but there were constant battles against poor weather and low attendances, and the club lost over £1,000. In 1899–1900, United lost their first eight Southern League matches and slumped to the bottom of the table. As the financial situation grew ever worse, the club was forced to give up the struggle in March 1900 and was wound up.

On the demise of United, Jackson entered the licensed trade as landlord of the Farm Tavern, Farm Road, Hove, helped no doubt by the proceeds of a benefit match – United beating the 2nd Scots Guards 5–2 – which had been staged in March 1899 probably as part of the deal to attract him to the South Coast.

After speaking at the inaugural meeting of the amateur Brighton & Hove Rangers club which rose from the ashes of United in July 1900, Jackson disappeared from the local football scene for a year, only to re-emerge in the spring of 1901 as an active promoter of Rangers' ambitions to join the Southern League. The plan went awry, though, and the amateur club also folded, leaving Jackson, the most experienced football man in the town, to pick up the pieces as the driving-force behind the formation of a new semi-professional club. He organised the meeting, held at the Seven Stars, Ship Street, on

24 June 1901, at which the new club was formed, and became its first team manager. John Jackson can, therefore, rightly be described as the founder of Brighton & Hove Albion Football Club.

As well as founding the Albion, 40-year-old Jackson – who continued to run the Farm Tavern for a time – played a huge part in its early success as manager and, on occasion, as secretary. His experience proved invaluable in keeping the club solvent within a very limited budget, and he led the team to promotion in its second season.

After struggling initially, Albion established themselves in the First Division of the Southern League and converted to a limited company, but Jackson was relieved of his duties in March 1905 because of irregular payments to players and because of the administrative chaos that had accrued in the club office. The situation led to an F.A. inquiry a couple of months later, as a result of which Jackson received a severe censure. Paid £75 in lieu of notice, he was, however, awarded a testimonial match, Albion taking on Tottenham Hotspur at Easter.

After leaving the Goldstone, Jackson became licensee of the Camden Arms in Kemp Street, Brighton, but he was enticed back into the game in 1907 for a short time as trainer at Blackpool, where he was also in charge of the ground arrangements.

John Jackson died in June 1931 at the age of 70. He had been landlord of the Running Horse in King Street, Brighton, since 1910. The founder of the Albion lies in a now-unmarked grave in the Brighton & Preston Cemetery.

Competition	P	W	D	L	F	A	W	D	L	F	A
Southern League	87	25	8	11	88	51	10	11	22	61	75
Southern League Test	1	0	0	0	0	0	1	0	0	5	3
F.A. Cup	15	6	1	2	48	17	4	0	2	18	6
South Eastern League	22	7	1	3	33	12	4	1	6	12	27
Total	*125*	*38*	*10*	*16*	*169*	*80*	*19*	*12*	*30*	*96*	*111*

SCOTT-WALFORD, FRANK   MARCH 1905–APRIL 1908

born: Perry Bar, Birmingham, Warwickshire, 1866
first game: West Ham United (h), 25.3.1905 (SL D1)

Frank Scott-Walford was appointed secretary-manager in March 1905 to clear up the administrative mess left by his predecessors, manager John Jackson and club secretary Charles Campbell, but he was soon to become embroiled in another scandal which rocked the club.

Despite bringing eighteen new players to the Goldstone during the summer of 1905, Frank Walford (as he was generally known) saw his team perform poorly in the Southern League, but it won through to the first round proper of the F.A. Cup (equivalent to the third round now) for the first time ever. In fact it was incidents at a qualifying-round tie with Glossop that landed the club in trouble. Walford was found guilty by the F.A. of making an irregular approach to one of the Glossop players and was suspended for fifteen weeks from 16 April 1906 until 1 August as a result.

Nevertheless, the situation on the field quickly improved and the following season saw Albion in third place in the Southern League. Indeed, during Scott-Walford's three years at the Goldstone the playing standard progressed considerably, particularly in the F.A. Cup where, in addition to 1905–06, another good run in 1907–08 brought in much-needed revenue.

Not for the last time, though, Albion found their manager attracting the attention of more-established clubs. In April 1908, Walford, who was then in his early 40s, was courted by Leeds City and the Albion board reluctantly agreed to his release. During the summer he returned to Hove to sign five Brighton players for his new club. Walford remained at Elland Road for four years, but a lack of funds hindered any real progress, and when the Yorkshire club was forced to seek re-election to the Second Division in May 1912 he resigned. (His successor was the immortal Herbert Chapman, who later led Huddersfield Town and Arsenal to multiple League championships.) Returning to the Southern League as manager of Coventry City in 1914, Walford stayed at Highfield Road until the First World War brought about the termination of regular League football in 1915.

In his youth Walford had been an amateur goalkeeper on Tottenham Hotspur's staff and also played for the London Caledonians, but a near-fatal kick on the head ushered in the end of his playing days. Throughout his career he was noted as an organiser. Prior to his arrival in Hove he was prominent in Middlesex, where he had been involved in the development of young talent, and was the leading light in the formation of the Enfield & District League which he served as president. Walford had also been a Southern League referee, a Football League linesman, and a contributor to several publications with news of Tottenham Hotspur.

Competition	P	W	D	L	F	A	W	D	L	F	A
Southern League	109	30	13	12	87	59	10	9	35	45	97
F.A. Cup	11	1	2	1	5	5	2	3	2	7	9
United League	32	9	4	3	40	22	3	6	7	21	32
Western League	12	5	1	0	12	4	1	1	4	7	15
Southern Charity Cup	4	1	1	0	3	1	0	1	1	3	4
Total	168	46	21	16	147	91	16	20	49	83	157

Note: Scott-Walford was suspended by the F.A. from 16.4.1906 until 1.8.1906. The five matches played during this period, probably under the direct control of the club directors, have been included above.

ROBSON, JACK — APRIL 1908–DECEMBER 1914

full name: John Robert Robson
born: Gainford, Co. Durham, 1854
died: Hull, Yorkshire, 11.1.1922
first game: Millwall (h), 4.4.1908 (SL D1)

Jack Robson was appointed manager on Scott-Walford's departure in April 1908 and, like his predecessor, immediately set about making wholesale changes. Over the next year or so he signed a number of players who were to give long and splendid service to the club – Charlie Webb, Billy Booth, Bob Whiting, Joe Leeming, Bullet Jones, Joe McGhie and Archie Needham – and built one of the best sides in the club's history which brought the first major success to the Goldstone. Under Robson's guidance Albion became one of the strongest and most respected teams in the Southern League, with the pinnacle of his six-and-a-half years in charge undoubtedly the triple triumph of Southern League championship, Southern Charity Cup, and F.A. Charity Shield in 1910.

Born in County Durham but brought up in Middlesbrough, Yorkshire, Robson played his football as a goalkeeper for Middlesbrough Swifts (the reserve team of the original Middlesbrough club), but his real talent lay in an ability to develop and blend the skills of others. In 1899 he took the post of secretary-manager at Middlesbrough on the club's election to the Football League, and led them to promotion to Division One in 1902. Having established 'Boro in the top flight over the next three seasons, he left Ayresome Park in 1905 after a seventeen-year association with the club to become secretary-manager at the newly formed Crystal Palace club.

In their first season Robson led Palace to the championship of the Southern League's Second Division, but they struggled in Division One and he left the club at the end of the season in 1907.

Robson was in his mid 50s when he arrived at the Goldstone in April 1908, but he transformed the Albion's fortunes. Although the club finished just two places above the relegation zone in 1908–09, they took the Southern League title the following season with a sustained display of attacking brilliance and defensive excellence, especially at home where 18 of the 21 matches were won. The goals-against total of just 28 remains a record to this day. For good measure Albion also won the Southern Charity Cup, but followed up with the greatest triumph when they took on the Football League champions, Aston Villa, in September 1910 for the F.A. Charity Shield. The 1–0 victory at Stamford Bridge led to Robson's team being dubbed 'Champions of England'.

Albion remained a force in the Southern League for the next few years, but were never quite able to repeat the outstanding feats of 1910. Nevertheless, Robson's considerable achievements at the Goldstone won the admiration of Manchester United and he was released in December 1914 to become manager of the First Division side. He remained at the helm until ill-health forced his retirement in October 1921, but was then retained as assistant to his successor, John Chapman.

Jack Robson died from the effects of pneumonia in January 1922. Such was the esteem in which he was held that the Football League played a trial representative match for his widow's benefit at Old Trafford on 8 March 1922.

Competition	P	W	D	L	F	A	W	D	L	F	A
Southern League	262	90	25	14	282	99	25	42	66	101	192
F.A. Cup	13	2	2	1	4	2	2	1	5	7	12
F.A. Charity Shield	1	0	0	0	0	0	1	0	0	1	0
Western League	12	5	0	1	16	5	2	2	2	7	8
Western League Champ.	2	0	0	0	0	0	0	1	1	2	3
Southern Alliance	32	11	4	1	45	11	8	3	5	22	23
Southern Charity Cup	23	6	0	2	19	9	7	4	4	15	18
Total	345	114	31	19	366	126	45	53	83	155	256

NELMES, ALF — CARETAKER DECEMBER 1914–MAY 1915

full name: Alfred Nelmes
born: Bristol, Gloucestershire, 1871
died: Cleveland, February 1940
first game: Gillingham (a), 2.1.1915 (SL D1)

When Jack Robson departed for Manchester United in December 1914 the First World War had been in progress for four months, and Albion saw out the remainder of the season with head trainer Alf Nelmes looking after team matters. The Bristol-born veteran had arrived at the Goldstone as a player during the summer of 1908 and took part in the pre-season public trial match, but he left for Ilkeston United without kicking a ball in anger. A year later he returned to Hove in the role of trainer.

Before coming to Sussex, Nelmes had enjoyed an illustrious playing career. Starting out as an amateur with Saltburn, he gained two F.A. Amateur Cup winner's medals with Middlesbrough (1895 and 1898) before turning professional with Grimsby Town in August 1898. Having assisted the 'Mariners' to the Second Division championship in 1901, and with well over 200 appearances to his name, he then moved to Second Division Burton United in May 1906 before arriving at the Goldstone.

When Albion closed down for the duration of the war Nelmes rejoined Jack Robson at Old Trafford, but returned to Hove in 1920 as trainer and remained with the club until retiring in May 1926.

Competition	P	W	D	L	F	A	W	D	L	F	A
Southern League	18	5	2	3	11	9	1	1	6	8	16
F.A. Cup	3	1	1	0	2	1	0	0	1	0	3
Total	21	6	3	3	13	10	1	1	7	8	19

WEBB, CHARLIE   JUNE 1919–MAY 1947

first game: Brentford (a), 30.8.1919 (SL D1)
See *Albion Players Who's Who*

Competition	P	W	D	L	F	A	W	D	L	F	A
Football League	840	266	85	69	889	411	95	106	219	440	717
Southern League	42	11	5	5	43	28	3	3	15	17	44
F.A. Cup	77	22	10	5	98	38	15	7	18	58	66
Division 3 (South) Cup	13	2	0	2	10	9	2	3	4	11	14
Wartime	243	48	21	55	308	304	22	12	85	193	436
Total	1215	349	121	136	1348	790	137	131	341	719	1277

COOK, TOMMY   MAY 1947–NOVEMBER 1947

first game: Watford (a), 23.8.1947 (FL D3(S))
See *Albion Players Who's Who*

Competition	P	W	D	L	F	A	W	D	L	F	A
Football League	17	2	1	6	6	18	1	2	5	7	17
Total	17	2	1	6	6	18	1	2	5	7	17

WELSH, DON   NOVEMBER 1947–MARCH 1951

full name: Donald Welsh
born: Manchester, Lancashire, 25.2.1911
died: Stevenage, Hertfordshire, 2.2.1990
first game: Exeter City (h), 15.11.1947 (FL D3(S))

With Albion's fortunes at a low ebb – culminating in an angry, on-pitch crowd demonstration in November 1947 – the directors turned to Don Welsh, the 36-year-old captain of Charlton Athletic who had lifted the F.A. Cup just a few months earlier. Coming to the Goldstone as secretary-manager in place of Tommy Cook and Charlie Webb, the former England international was a big capture for the Third Division club and soon brought about a transformation in the team's fortunes.

Back in his early days in Manchester, Welsh had shown considerable promise and represented both the city's and the county's schools. On leaving Prince's Road School he worked in an accountant's office, but then joined the Royal Navy as a sixteen-year-old boy seaman, which allowed him to play football for Valetta while stationed in Malta and also as an amateur for Torquay United while based at Devonport from 1932 to 1934. On his release from the service, Welsh turned professional with Torquay in July 1934. Such was his form as a half-back that he quickly won the admiration of bigger clubs, and in February 1935 he signed for Charlton Athletic for £3,250. He was destined to become one of their all-time 'greats'.

Welsh spent twelve years at The Valley and was involved in some of Charlton's greatest-ever successes. In the three seasons 1934–37 the Londoners were transformed from a Third Division side into runners-up for the Division One title, and they remained in the top flight until 1957. Welsh wielded a major influence during that spell, and won three England caps at left-half and inside-left just before the outbreak of war. Well-built and blessed with a powerful shot, he also represented the Football League in September 1938, and went on to gain a further nine wartime caps.

During the war he served as an Army physical training instructor, but was fortunate to play football on a regular basis. Indeed, he was at his peak during the emergency, scoring an incredible total of 164 goals in just 163 matches for both Charlton and the other clubs he guested with: Liverpool, Aldershot, Chester, Manchester City, Southend United and Millwall. The total also includes seventeen goals he scored for the Albion in only nine games in 1941 and 1942! In fact he hit six in a single game against Luton Town on 22 March 1941 to equal Arthur Attwood's Albion record.

After captaining Charlton in two wartime cup finals at Wembley – losing to Arsenal in 1943 but defeating Chelsea in 1944 – Welsh led his team to the first post-war F.A. Cup final in 1946, only to lose 4–1 to Derby County. The following year he was back again, this time lifting the Cup after a 1–0 triumph over Burnley before arriving at the Goldstone in November.

With the Albion just one place above the basement at the time, the new manager had intended to register himself as a player, but with Charlton demanding a transfer fee the idea was quickly dropped.

Welsh therefore gave the existing staff the chance to restore respectability, but when the win-less run grew to fifteen League games he was forced into the transfer market in February and March 1948, spending lavishly – for the Albion – to bring some experienced players to the Goldstone. The new blood brought about a big improvement, but in an incredibly tight finish Albion finished bottom and were forced to seek re-election to the Football League for the only time.

The first Brighton manager to coach the players himself – a genuine 'track-suit manager' – he threw himself at the task of improving the club's fortunes and continued the changes. In 1948, Welsh introduced a new strip of blue shirts with white sleeves, the first change since 1904, and, so the story goes, instructed the groundsman to burn the club's records in a somewhat futile, 'look-only-to-the-future' gesture. Back on the pitch he initiated a new defence-in-depth system, relying on swift counter-attacks to catch the opposition unawares, and brought in yet more reinforcements. As a result Albion climbed to sixth place in the Third Division (South) and gates soared amid a general post-war surge of interest for the game. An 'A' team to blood young players was also established.

Although sixth was the best position achieved during Welsh's reign, his considerable success in stabilising the Albion did not go unnoticed. There had been rumours that he would leave in 1949, and in March 1951 he accepted Liverpool's invitation to become their manager. In five years at Anfield he laid out a small fortune on players, but was unable to prevent a drop into the Second Division in 1954. The team narrowly missed promotion in 1955–56, but Welsh was dismissed and opted for a quieter life, running a hotel in Bovey Tracey, Devon, and managing the local side. In July 1958, though, he was tempted back into the Football League as manager of Bournemouth.

On leaving Dean Court in February 1961, Welsh then ran a youth centre in Camberwell, south London, and coached the Isthmian League side Wycombe Wanderers from July 1962 until November 1964. He also joined the administrative staff at Charlton Athletic for a brief period. In 1990, at the age of 78, he died of cancer at his daughter's home in Stevenage. A superb, all-round sportsman, Welsh at one time served as the professional with Torquay Cricket Club, and also played water-polo, hockey and rugby for the Royal Navy.

Competition	P	W	D	L	F	A	W	D	L	F	A
Football League	141	32	23	16	111	90	14	29	27	70	133
F.A. Cup	11	4	0	0	11	2	1	2	4	8	14
Total	152	36	23	16	122	92	15	31	31	78	147

LANE, BILLY   MARCH 1951–MAY 1961

full name: William Harry Charles Lane*
born: Tottenham, Middlesex, 23.10.1903
died: Chelmsford, Essex, 10.11.1985
first game: Bournemouth & B.A. (a), 10.3.1951 (FL D3(S))

When Don Welsh departed for Liverpool in March 1951, his assistant, Billy Lane, took charge of the team on a caretaker basis until the end of the season. Quickly scrapping the defensive style employed by his predecessor, the new man introduced a refreshing policy of all-out attack which reaped a swift reward and averted any re-election problems. Indeed, within a few weeks the team set a new club record in the League by crushing Newport County 9–1. There were more than 50 applicants for the vacant manager's position (which was separated from the role of secretary), but Lane's performance in lifting the club well-clear of the re-election zone won him the board's vote.

Attack came naturally to a man who, during his playing days, had been a tremendous goalscorer; he had netted 177 times in 317 League games for seven clubs. Lane began his career in north London with the junior clubs Gnome Athletic, London City Mission and Park Avondale. He then enjoyed an unsuccessful trial with Charlton Athletic before graduating into the Athenian League with Barnet. In 1923, at the age of eighteen, he joined Tottenham Hotspur and was farmed out to their Southern League nursery club, Northfleet United. On graduating to the senior ranks at Spurs, Lane scored seven goals in 25 First Division outings, prompting Leicester City to pay £2,250 for his signature in November 1926. However, with the prolific Arthur Chandler leading City's attack, he received scant opportunity to impress in nearly two years at Filbert Street and, after an equally unfruitful term with Second Division Reading, he moved into Division Three with Brentford in May 1929.

Lane's form with the 'Bees' was little short of astonishing. In his first season Brentford finished runners-up – they won all 21 home games – and he scored 33 times. Indeed, in three years with the Middlesex side he netted 84 times in 113 League games, but in 1932 he moved on to Watford. Once again Lane performed brilliantly, hitting 70 goals in 125 League outings which included a remarkable hat-trick in two-and-a-half minutes against Clapton Orient in December 1933. Transferred to Bristol City in December 1935, he finished his League career with a move to Clapton Orient in July 1937, and hung up his boots after a spell with Gravesend United in the Kent League.

On retiring as a player Lane became manager at Gravesend, but was soon appointed assistant to his old boss, Harry Curtis, at Brentford. The war saw him serve with the R.A.S.C. and the Army Physical Training Corps, and also allowed him to dust off his boots with a few guest appearances for the Albion, Clapton Orient, Reading and Watford. In 1947 he took over as manager of Southern League side Guildford City, and was brought to the Goldstone as assistant to Don Welsh in April 1950.

After being invited to take over permanently in August 1951, 47-year-old Lane went on to enjoy one of the most successful periods of any Albion manager, an era of sustained entertainment in front of large, adoring crowds. The players he signed – men such as Peter Harburn, Denis Foreman, Adrian Thorne, Eric Gill, Dennis Gordon, Albert Mundy and Jimmy Langley – are still remembered with great affection by older supporters. On taking over Lane immediately reintroduced the traditional blue-and-white stripes, and the club enjoyed its best season since the war, finishing fifth in the Third Division (South). Under his guidance Albion were runners-up twice, in 1953–54 and 1955–56. On the latter occasion the side narrowly lost out to Leyton Orient after registering 65 points (2 per win) and 112 goals, both still club records.

In 1957–58, Lane's hard work finally paid off when Albion won the Southern Section – at the 31st attempt – amid a tidal wave of euphoria, a triumph which he himself accepted with great modesty. The team struggled from day one in the Second Division, though – the first game was lost 9–0 at Middlesbrough – and the manager worked a minor miracle in lifting the club to a final placing of twelfth. The following season Albion struggled once again, and Lane, who by this time was among the longest-serving managers in the League, blamed himself for the club's inability to make an impact. He was, of course, starved of cash for any meaningful rebuilding of the side.

With Albion fighting against relegation again during 1960–61, Lane came under pressure from the board. Rather than be pushed, he jumped, tendering his resignation at the end of a season which saw the club finish five places clear of the drop. The 57-year-old left the Goldstone to become manager at Gravesend & Northfleet for two years, leading the Southern League club to the fourth round of the F.A. Cup in 1962–63 when they took First Division Sunderland to a replay. He later scouted for Arsenal and Spurs.

A devout churchman and occasional lay preacher, Billy Lane was well respected by his players and seldom had to take disciplinary action. He will long be remembered by Albion followers as the guiding light behind a vintage era, a ten-year period when attendances averaged over 16,000 and culminated in the club's first-ever Football League promotion campaign.

Note: Billy changed his surname from 'Lohn' to 'Lane', probably because of the German connotations at the time of the First World War.

Competition	P	W	D	L	F	A	W	D	L	F	A
Football League	462	137	55	38	531	275	72	55	105	319	425
F.A. Cup	29	7	5	4	41	21	3	4	6	22	22
Football League Cup	2	0	0	1	0	2	1	0	0	3	1
Total	493	144	60	43	572	298	76	59	111	344	448

CURTIS, GEORGE   JUNE 1961–FEBRUARY 1963

full name: George Frederick Curtis
born: Orsett, Essex, 3.12.1919
first game: Scunthorpe United (a), 19.8.1961 (FL D2)

George Curtis was a highly respected coach and tactician when he was brought to the Goldstone as Billy Lane's successor in June 1961, but he inherited a lowly Second Division team with a disgruntled support and dwindling gates. A passionate believer in giving youth its chance, Curtis's views on the game greatly impressed the board which was, as ever, strapped for cash. His stated philosophy was: 'You bring a youth up within the club. If the lad fails, it's the fault of a) the manager and b) the youngster.' Unfortunately, it proved to be a disastrous policy for the club, which slumped to a nadir during his time in charge.

As a youth, Curtis was playing for the Anglo club in Purfleet when he joined Arsenal in 1936. Farmed out to Margate, Arsenal's nursery side, he signed professional forms for the 'Gunners' in April 1937 and progressed through the reserves to make his First Division debut at inside-left in April 1939. Five months later, though, the outbreak of war brought about the closure of regular League football. Curtis served with the R.A.F. but played occasionally for the 'Gunners' throughout the conflict; he also turned out at various times for West Ham United, Norwich City, Clapton Orient, Wolverhampton Wanderers, Swansea Town, Chelsea, and, briefly in 1941–42, the

Albion. After playing eleven League games for Arsenal in the first post-war campaign, Curtis joined Second Division Southampton in August 1947 (as part of the transaction that saw Don Roper move to Highbury) and went on to enjoy the best part of his career, the 'Saints' missing out narrowly on promotion to Division One in three successive campaigns.

On leaving Southampton in 1952, Curtis had a spell with the French club Valenciennes, but returned to England a year later as player-coach to

Chelmsford City in the Southern League, and then took a coaching post with Grays Athletic. A qualified coach since 1947, he joined the F.A. staff in 1954, spending some time coaching in the Sudan, and was manager of the England youth team from 1955 until 1957 when he was appointed trainer-coach to Sunderland.

A tall, mild-mannered man of impeccable demeanour, Curtis was an extremely fit 41-year-old when he joined the Albion in 1961 and was an active 'track-suit manager', to be seen daily with his players in training sessions which quickly won him the respect of his staff. However, his period at the helm proved catastrophic. The introduction of the more defensive 4–2–4 system brought little success, and a lack of funds precluded the signing of proven players. Most of the club's senior staff were either released or transferred at the end of the 1961–62 campaign – which saw Albion drop back into the Third Division – and a clutch of youngsters ('Curtis's Cubs') was signed to be thrust in at the deep end against seasoned professionals.

The result was another struggle from the start of 1962–63. A reconstituted board soon came up with some spending money and demanded that Curtis bring in some more-experienced men, but by February the team was in very real danger of dropping straight through the Third Division and into the basement. Enough was enough for the directors, and in February 1963 the manager was released from his contract 'by mutual consent' with 20 months still to run.

After leaving the Goldstone, Curtis coached at Cambridge University and Hastings United, and became manager of Stevenage Town in January 1964 where he recruited several of his former Albion youngsters. The Southern League club gained promotion to the Premier Division in 1966–67, but folded a year later and Curtis moved on to coach briefly at Hull City. He subsequently coached San Diego Sockers (1968); managed Rosenborg in the Norwegian League (1968–71) and Hitchin Town (for two months); became manager-coach of the Norwegian national side (1971–76); coached in Qatar (1979–81); and now lives in his native Essex where he retained an involvement in the game for some years, passing on his knowledge to youngsters as part of a FIFA coaching scheme.

Although the results he produced during his time with the Albion were dire, George Curtis did, to his credit, make several excellent signings on a tight budget. Norman Gall, Jimmy Collins and Bill Cassidy all went on to give the club splendid service, as did young goalkeeper Brian Powney who was given his chance by Curtis.

Competition	P	W	D	L	F	A	W	D	L	F	A
Football League	71	10	13	13	41	56	6	7	22	38	84
F.A. Cup	2	0	0	1	0	3	0	0	1	1	2
Football League Cup	2	0	0	1	1	5	0	0	1	1	5
Total	75	10	13	15	42	64	6	7	24	40	91

WILSON, JOE   CARETAKER FEBRUARY 1963–APRIL 1963

first game: Bristol Rovers (a), 9.2.1963 (FL D3)
See *Albion Players Who's Who*

Competition	P	W	D	L	F	A	W	D	L	F	A
Football League	9	3	0	1	7	3	2	1	2	9	11
Total	9	3	0	1	7	3	2	1	2	9	11

MACAULAY, ARCHIE   APRIL 1963–OCTOBER 1968

full name: Archibald Renwick Macaulay
born: Falkirk, Stirlingshire, Scotland, 30.7.1915
died: Knowle, Warwickshire, June 1993
first game: Northampton Town (h), 12.4.1963 (FL D3)

George Curtis's successor was another former Arsenal player and once one of the best-known names in the game, Archie Macaulay. His time in charge was full of ups and downs, but was one of comparative stability compared with the trauma of Curtis's reign. Almost inevitably, though, it ended with a troubled resignation after five-and-a-half years in the 'hot seat'.

Macaulay began his working life as an apprentice saw-doctor, a job he held for three years while playing for Sawyers, Laurieston Villa, and Camelon Juniors in his native Falkirk. In March 1933 he joined Glasgow Rangers as a professional and went on to win a Scottish League championship medal in 1935, playing at inside-right.

After impressing in Rangers' annual friendly fixture with Arsenal, the young Scot joined West Ham United for £6,000 in June 1937.

The Second World War saw Macaulay serve with the Essex Regiment Territorials, with whom he reached the rank of sergeant-major P.T.I. He also appeared in the "Hammers'" victorious wartime cup team at Wembley in 1940; represented Scotland on five occasions in wartime internationals; and guested for Aldershot, Doncaster Rovers, Falkirk and Northampton Town. Developing into a wing-half during the hostilities, he was transferred to Brentford for £7,500 in October 1946, and although the 'Bees' were unceremoniously relegated from the First Division at the end of the season, Macaulay won the first of seven full caps in a 1–1 draw against England at Wembley. Indeed, such was his cultured performance at right-half during that match that he was selected for the Great Britain side which defeated the Rest of Europe 6–1 at Hampden Park a month later.

His relationship with Brentford soon deteriorated, though, as the 'Bees' demanded that all their players should be full-time. Macaulay also had a job as a sports-coach for a London college and consequently asked for a transfer, but his strong personality quickly saw the Press brand him, somewhat unfairly, the 'stormy petrel of London soccer'. Nevertheless, he secured a £10,000 move to Arsenal in July 1947 amid hot competition, and gained a First Division championship medal in his first season at Highbury at the age of 32. He went on to clock up 103 League outings for the 'Gunners' and was rewarded with further international honours, but after playing in an F.A. Cup semi-final replay against Chelsea in 1950 he was omitted from the team for the final and moved on to Fulham for £10,000 shortly afterwards.

After three seasons at Craven Cottage, Macaulay took his first step into management when he was appointed player-manager of Southern League Guildford City. In 1955 he became coach at Dundee, but received his biggest break when he took over the reins at near-bankrupt Norwich City in April 1957. In four years at Carrow Road he worked a near-miracle. In 1959, Macaulay guided the 'Canaries' to the F.A. Cup semi-finals, but with the whole country willing them to become the first Third Division side to reach Wembley they lost 1–0 in a replay to Luton Town. A year later he led the side to promotion to the Second Division.

His success at Norwich earned Macaulay the chance to manage First Division West Bromwich Albion in October 1961, but in April 1963 he asked to be released early from his £3,000 p.a. contract. Rumour had it that he felt restricted by the directors at The Hawthorns, but in fact it was because Mrs Macaulay had found it difficult to settle in the Midlands. With the West Brom. board reluctantly agreeing to his request, Brighton chairman Eric Courtney-King quickly contacted the 47-year-old Scot and a couple of weeks later secured him as the new manager.

Macaulay arrived at the Goldstone too late to save the club from the ignominy of relegation to the League's basement, but his first full season in charge saw Albion finish in a respectable eighth place in Division Four. Given a free hand at the Goldstone, he introduced a revolutionary new wage structure incorporating appearance payments and bonuses according to the team's League position, and brought in a tough new training regime befitting a former P.T.I. But his biggest coup was to sign the experienced Bobby Smith in May 1964 for a modest £5,000 from Spurs. The ex-England centre-forward proved an inspiration, and the team scored 102 goals on their way to the Fourth Division title before an average crowd of almost 18,000.

Macaulay's three campaigns in the Third Division were less than distinguished, though. Despite the acquisition of such excellent players as Dave Turner, Wally Gould, Charlie Livesey and Kit Napier, life was often a struggle. Indeed, the club narrowly avoided a return to the basement in 1966–67, although there were excellent runs to the fourth round of both the F.A. Cup and the League Cup that season.

The following term there was turmoil in the boardroom, performances on the field were generally unimpressive, attendances tumbled, and the reserve team was scrapped for financial reasons. As the manager came under increased pressure from directors and supporters alike, he felt it time to resign in October 1968, just 24 hours before the annual meeting of shareholders, although he took charge of the team for the last time the following day.

Archie Macaulay did a little scouting for Liverpool on leaving the Goldstone, but he largely forsook the game thereafter. He later worked as a traffic-warden in Chelsea before taking a local-government post in Norwich.

Competition	P	W	D	L	F	A	W	D	L	F	A
Football League	254	68	30	28	245	131	27	41	60	139	213
F.A. Cup	13	3	2	1	16	5	2	1	4	9	10
Football League Cup	19	4	5	1	16	8	3	1	5	12	22
Total	286	75	37	30	277	144	32	43	69	160	245

TEAM-SELECTION COMMITTEE CARETAKER NOVEMBER 1968

first game: Stockport County (a), 1.11.1968 (FL D3)

Following Archie Macaulay's resignation at the end of October 1968, the board took the unusual step of appointing a team-selection committee, including skipper Nobby Lawton, for games at Stockport and Crewe. Both matches were lost.

Competition	P	W	D	L	F	A	W	D	L	F	A
Football League	2	0	0	0	0	0	0	0	2	1	4
Total	2	0	0	0	0	0	0	0	2	1	4

GOODWIN, FREDDIE   NOVEMBER 1968–MAY 1970

full name: Frederick Goodwin
born: Heywood, Lancashire, 28.6.1933
first game: Bristol Rovers (h), 9.11.1968 (FL D3)

Freddie Goodwin was a quiet, introverted manager, somewhat in contrast to Archie Macaulay. His time at the Goldstone was brief, but it won him the admiration of a number of clubs and Albion eventually found themselves unable to hold on to their man.

He first came to prominence as a 'Busby Babe', signing professional forms for Manchester United in October 1953, but was overshadowed in his early days by the incomparable Duncan Edwards. Following the Munich air crash, though, Goodwin became a regular member of United's reorganised side and appeared in the team which lost the 1958 F.A. Cup final just three months after the disaster. He went on to appear in 106 League and Cup games for United before joining Leeds United for £10,000 in March 1960, but the Yorkshire side were relegated to Division Two at the end of the season.

Always a deep thinker on the tactical side of the game, Goodwin rubbed shoulders with the likes of Don Revie and Jack Charlton at Elland Road, and totalled 120 appearances, mainly under Revie as manager. Following Leeds' return to Division One in 1964, he was appointed player-manager of Third Division Scunthorpe United – upon Revie's recommendation – in December 1964 at the age of 31. Goodwin learned his trade in nearly two years at the Old Show Ground, then followed the lucrative path to the U.S.A. as manager-coach of the New York Generals.

When Archie Macaulay left the Goldstone in October 1968 there were some famous names among the applicants – John Bond, Don Howe, and two former Goldstone stars, Jack Mansell and Bobby Smith – but the successful candidate was Freddie Goodwin, recently returned from the States. The team was deep in relegation trouble when he took over and only 6,175 attended his first match in charge, but the new manager soon brought in new faces – his former Old Trafford colleague Alex Dawson from Bury, goalkeeper Geoff Sidebottom and Barrie Wright, both of whom had played for him in New York, and Eddie Spearritt from Ipswich Town – and by the end of the season the team was transformed into a unit that looked capable of winning promotion, with attendances almost doubled. That improvement, based on a sound defence, continued the following season, 1969–70, when Albion eventually missed out on promotion after leading the Third Division at Easter.

Goodwin's achievements in his short time at the Goldstone attracted the attention of Second Division Birmingham City, who had recently parted company with Stan Cullis. The lure of a big-city club proved too strong, and on the completion of the 1969–70 campaign Albion reluctantly released Goodwin from his contract. It was a somewhat acrimonious departure, though, as he took player-coach Willie Bell (with an illegal approach for which City were later fined £5,000) and George Dalton with him.

In just over five years at St Andrews he took Birmingham back to Division One and to two F.A. Cup semi-finals, in 1973 and 1975, but a calamitous opening to the 1975–76 season cost him his job. His successor at St Andrews was, ironically, Willie Bell. Goodwin subsequently returned to the United States as coach to the Minnesota Kicks. He still lives in Minnesota and is now a successful name in the travel business.

In addition to his football activities, the young Freddie Goodwin was also a professional cricketer, appearing in eleven matches for Lancashire as a fast/medium-pace bowler between 1955 and 1956.

Competition	P	W	D	L	F	A	W	D	L	F	A
Football League	74	26	9	4	74	28	9	9	17	33	48
F.A. Cup	8	1	2	1	6	6	1	2	1	3	3
Football League Cup	3	2	0	1	5	3	0	0	0	0	0
Total	85	29	11	6	85	37	10	11	18	36	51

SAWARD, PAT   JUNE 1970–OCTOBER 1973

full name: Patrick Saward
born: Cork, Co. Cork, Irish Free State, 17.8.1928
first game: Torquay United (h), 15.8.1970 (FL D3)

A deep-thinking former Eire international, Pat Saward produced one of the most outstanding achievements in the history of the Albion with the exhilarating promotion to Division Two in 1972, but he was unable to maintain that success as the club was ignominiously relegated. Subsequently dismissed, he must have considered himself somewhat unfortunate to have been largely forgotten amid the hullabaloo surrounding his successor.

A stylish wing-half or inside-forward, Saward began his senior career as an amateur with Crystal Palace but did not make the League side. In July 1951 he was taken on as a professional by Millwall and played in 120 Third Division (South) games for the 'Dockers', winning his first cap for the Republic of Ireland in March 1954 in a 1–0 World Cup qualifying win over Luxembourg. August 1955 saw Saward transferred to First Division Aston Villa, with whom he made a further 152 League appearances over the next five seasons and gained an F.A. Cup winner's medal in 1957. Although they were relegated in 1959, Villa bounced straight back as Second Division champions under the captaincy of the conscientious Irishman. In March 1961 he was transferred to Second Division Huddersfield Town where he played 59 League games and gained the last of eighteen international caps before moving on to Coventry City in October 1963.

Saward joined the Highfield Road coaching-staff under manager Jimmy Hill and met with considerable success, guiding City's youngsters to the runner's-up spot in the F.A. Youth Cup in 1968 and again in 1970. During his time at Coventry the 'Sky Blues' gained rapid promotion from the Third Division to the First.

The dapper Irishman – he had once been a male model – first applied for the Albion manager's job in 1968 when Freddie Goodwin was appointed, but when Goodwin moved on to Birmingham City in the summer of 1970, Saward successfully re-applied for the vacancy

and took up his post towards the end of June. An advocate of attacking, entertaining football, he brought a new zest to the Goldstone Ground and made his players feel really important; he smartened them up, kitted them out in new jackets and trousers, and gave them their own lounge to relax in. Saward gave the Albion total commitment; indeed, he had to be given oxygen on one occasion when he collapsed through exhaustion. An infectious personality, he caught the public's imagination in December 1970 by launching his celebrated 'Buy-a-Player Fund' which resulted in Bert Murray being tagged 'The People's Player'. The manager himself was branded 'The Loan Ranger' for the number of players he borrowed from other clubs.

Saward, 42, eventually steered the Albion clear of the relegation zone in 1971, and prepared for the 1971–72 season with a policy of all-out attack. In a fascinating, four-way struggle Albion finished runners-up to Aston Villa, and really caught the eye with a number of remarkable scorelines away from home – the side won twelve times on their travels – and for a never-say-die attitude that saw the side score many crucial late goals. The points total equalled the club record of 65 set in 1955–56.

But when it became time to defend, the club was found wanting and finished bottom of the Second Division in 1972–73. In October 1973, Albion were struggling near the foot of Division Three when the directors decided they had to make a change. Many supporters were opposed to the dismissal of the man who had given his all to the club and inspired such an unexpected and outstanding success, and there was a public demonstration demanding his reinstatement, but Saward was quickly forgotten when one of the biggest names in the game came to the Goldstone as his replacement.

After leaving the Albion, Saward spent most of his remaining career in football abroad, taking up posts in the Middle East and Nigeria. In the early 1980s he was back in England, in Lowestoft, but was unable to obtain a job in English football and turned to running a holiday business in Minorca, Spain.

Competition	P	W	D	L	F	A	W	D	L	F	A
Football League	146	31	23	19	103	77	21	20	32	84	113
F.A. Cup	7	2	1	1	12	4	1	0	2	3	4
Football League Cup	6	1	0	1	3	3	1	0	3	1	7
Total	159	34	24	21	118	84	23	20	37	88	124

WILSON, GLEN   CARETAKER OCTOBER 1973

first game: Southport (h), 24.10.1973 (FL D3)
See *Albion Players Who's Who*

Competition	P	W	D	L	F	A	W	D	L	F	A
Football League	2	1	0	0	4	0	0	0	1	0	3
Total	2	1	0	0	4	0	0	0	1	0	3

CLOUGH, BRIAN   NOVEMBER 1973–JULY 1974

full name: Brian Howard Clough
born: Grove Hill, Middlesbrough, Yorkshire, 21.3.1935
first game: York City (h), 3.11.1973 (FL D3)

The appointment of Brian Clough as manager of the Albion amazed not only the local fans, it stunned the whole world of football. The outspoken former manager of Derby County was perhaps the biggest name – many would say *mouth* – in the country at the time, and it

was a huge coup for ambitious chairman Mike Bamber. But while supporters welcomed the arrival of the 'Messiah' on the South Coast, Clough himself treated the appointment purely as a brief stop on the way to bigger and better things. Nevertheless, his arrival at the Goldstone ushered in a new, exciting era in the history of the Albion.

But not only was Clough a hugely successful manager over many years, he was also a record-breaking centre-forward in a career which was terminated by injury. It began on his native Teesside with the Great Broughton and Billingham Synthonia clubs while he worked as a clerk for I.C.I., but his prowess as a goal-poacher soon attracted the attention of Middlesbrough who took him on as a sixteen-year-old amateur. After signing as a professional in May 1952 his opportunities were limited by National Service with the R.A.F., but he made his first-team debut in September 1955 and quickly became a scoring phenomenon at Ayresome Park, netting 38, 40, 43, 39 and 34 Second Division goals over the next five seasons. Indeed, he twice finished top scorer in the Football League.

Clough's feats in an otherwise average 'Boro side brought international recognition, and he made his debut for England 'B' against Scotland in February 1957, scoring once in a 4–1 victory. Two goals in three under-23 internationals followed, but the England selectors preferred West Bromwich Albion's Derek Kevan in the full side, and the outspoken and somewhat arrogant young Clough was restricted to just two full caps. After knocking five goals past Dave Hollins in Albion's record 9–0 defeat at Ayresome Park in 1958, and going 'nap' again for the Football League against the League of Ireland, his two full internationals came against Wales and Sweden in October 1959, but the controversial centre-forward failed to hit the net and did not receive another opportunity.

Unhappy at the prospect of continual Second Division football with Middlesbrough, Clough was placed on the transfer list in the summer of 1961 and moved to more ambitious Sunderland for £45,000. The Wearsiders missed out by one point on promotion in 1961–62, but challenged again the following season. Clough had 28 goals to his name by Boxing Day, but he was then involved in a collision with Bury 'keeper Chris Harker which caused the ligament damage that was to finish his career. Sunderland eventually won promotion in 1964, and after nearly two years out of the game Clough made a brief, three-match come-back in the First Division, but at the age of just 29 his playing days were over.

His incredible record of 251 goals (all but one of them in Division Two) from 274 appearances set a goals-per-game ratio unequalled in the post-war era, but it was no consolation to a man who felt he had been denied ultimate playing success. Instead he had to look to the future and qualified as a coach. Put in charge of the youth side at Sunderland, he was also granted a testimonial match, but at the end of the 1964–65 season he was sacked along with the manager, George Hardwick.

After three months out of work Clough took the job of manager at Fourth Division Hartlepools United, where he immediately appointed an old friend from Middlesbrough, Peter Taylor, as trainer/assistant manager. Taylor had a profound influence on the younger Clough, and was the driving-force behind the assembly of a new team for the unfashionable County Durham club. Their two years at the Victoria Ground saw a reasonable side assembled, but the lure of bigger things proved too great and Clough and Taylor moved together to Second Division Derby County in 1967, leaving the 'Pool to win promotion for the first time in their history the following season.

After an initial eighteenth placing, Clough led the 'Rams' to the Second Division title in 1968–69 and, three years later, to their first-ever League championship. The Derby manager was now quite outspoken and his opinions were much sought after by the national media. The 'Rams', enjoying the most successful period in their history, reached the European Cup semi-finals in 1973, but there were signs of a rift between Clough and Taylor on one side, and the directors on the other. The showdown came in October 1973 when chairman Sam Longson delivered an ultimatum to his manager over his television and newspaper activities. Clough promptly resigned – together with Taylor – and despite a massive campaign in Derby to have them reinstated they arrived at the Goldstone Ground just over two weeks later on five-year contracts.

While recognising the club's undoubted potential, Clough really took the Albion job because of the freedom that Mike Bamber promised him over his media work. In fact, it always seemed that he was using Brighton merely as a stop-gap convenience; for instance, he always lived in a hotel. Towards the end of the season rumours abounded of his imminent departure for a variety of destinations – Iran, Aston Villa, Derby – and holidays taken at crucial times added to the speculation as Albion wallowed in the lower half of the Third Division. 'Of course I'm bigger than Brighton — I was bigger than Derby too,' ran one headline.

But although his commitment was often in doubt, there was no disputing the effect the 38-year-old had on the club, the team and the fans. His first match in charge added 10,000 to the Goldstone gate, and he kept the Albion firmly in the media spotlight, but embarrassing home defeats by non-League Walton & Hersham (4–0 in the F.A. Cup) and Bristol Rovers (8–2) led to a massive turnover in players. The changes, largely initiated by Taylor, lifted Albion clear of any relegation danger, but the players felt the full fury of the famous tongue: 'pathetic' and 'spineless' were some of the more public comments. Clough and Taylor were brutal with anyone they thought wasn't giving his all, and a number of long-serving players found themselves shown the door, but those that remained had a new belief in themselves.

At the end of the season Clough and Taylor were making great promises about the future, but all the rumours surrounding the manager came to a head in July 1974 when, after just nine months in charge, he left to take the reins at Leeds United following the appointment of Don Revie as England manager, thereby splitting his partnership with Peter Taylor – who stayed behind as Albion boss – for the first time since it was forged at Hartlepool. It was a bombshell at the time, but when the dust settled many supporters thought that perhaps Albion had got the best result; after all, Taylor had been the one who had signed all the new players and had showed that he was committed to the club.

Nevertheless, the Brighton board issued a writ against Leeds, claiming that Clough had broken his five-year contract under enticement from Elland Road and also alleged that the Yorkshire club had reneged on a compensation agreement. The Leeds chairman countered by claiming that Clough had applied for the post. The matter was eventually settled out of court in December 1975 with Leeds compensating Albion to the tune of £45,000, but Clough was later to admit that he had left the Goldstone too soon and let 'the best chairman I ever worked for' down badly.

However, his time with the reigning League champions lasted just 44 days before he was sacked; he made sweeping changes which apparently alienated the existing staff and created discontent in the dressing-room. After leaving Elland Road he spent a few months on the cabaret circuit before joining Second Division Nottingham Forest in January 1975 to take the dormant Midlands side into a new era as one of the country's most successful clubs. Rejoined by Taylor in 1976, the pair took Forest to promotion in 1977, and followed it up with the League championship at the first attempt, thus repeating their success

of six years earlier at nearby Derby. This time, though, Forest also clinched the League Cup in 1978 and 1979, and lifted the European Cup in 1979 and 1980. While the club finished consistently highly in the League, there was further success with the League Cup in 1989 and '90, and the Full Members (Simod/ZDS) Cup in 1989 and '92. In 1991 he was awarded the O.B.E.

After 28 years in the high-pressure world of football management, Brian Clough retired from the game following Forest's relegation in 1993 and has had little involvement with it since. In November 1994 his autobiography was published, dedicated to his late partner, Peter Taylor (see below).

Competition	P	W	D	L	F	A	W	D	L	F	A
Football League	32	8	3	5	23	23	4	5	7	16	19
F.A. Cup	2	0	0	1	0	4	0	1	0	0	0
Total	34	8	3	6	23	27	4	6	7	16	19

TAYLOR, Peter   JULY 1974–JULY 1976

full name: Peter Thomas Taylor
born: Nottingham, Nottinghamshire, 2.7.1928
died: Majorca, Spain, 4.10.1990
first game: Crystal Palace (h), 17.8.1974 (FL D3)

Although inextricably linked with Brian Clough (see above), Peter Taylor will be remembered more fondly in Brighton and Hove than his erstwhile partner for his undoubted commitment to the Albion. Indeed, it was when Clough left the Goldstone for Leeds that their partnership first split, but their subsequent outstanding success together at Nottingham Forest made Albion supporters wonder, 'What if … ?'

A goalkeeper by trade, Taylor signed professional forms for Coventry City at the age of seventeen in May 1946 and went on to make 87 League appearances in Divisions Two and Three (South) for the Warwickshire side, where he was profoundly influenced by manager Harry Storer. In August 1955, Middlesbrough paid £3,500 for his services and he played 140 League games for 'Boro. While at Ayresome Park, Taylor became friendly with the young centre-forward, Brian Clough; both 'loners' in their own way, their paths were to be intertwined for some 27 years. Taylor took the arrogant Clough under his wing, even to the detriment of his own career which finished with a single game for Port Vale in 1961–62.

His first job as a manager was with Burton Albion in the Southern League, but in 1965, with the Staffordshire club in contention for promotion to the Premier Division and a new contract on offer, he joined his old pal as trainer/assistant manager at Hartlepools United. Although Clough was the man in the limelight, Taylor was the driving-force behind their management team and was a major influence in their subsequent success with Derby County, whom they took to the League championship in 1972.

It was as a result of his partner's differences with the Derby board over his media work that the pair left the Baseball Ground and headed south for

Brian Clough (left) and Peter Taylor (right) with, in the middle, Albion chairman Mike Bamber

the Goldstone in a spectacular coup by Albion chairman Mike Bamber. But while Clough spent some of his time with the club on exotic holidays, Taylor got on with the job in hand and started to build a new team which steered the club clear of any relegation danger. The new players continued to sign, but when Clough left for Leeds in July 1974 after just nine months, his partner and confidante opted to remain at the Goldstone, honour his contract, and try to see the job through with his own team.

Now a League manager on his own for the first time, Taylor continued his dealing in the transfer market and brought some excellent players to Sussex, notably Brian Horton for a give-away £27,000 and the untried Peter Ward for just £4,000. A dour disciplinarian, he had predicted the club would win the Third Division championship in 1974–75 but Albion finished 19th. In 1975–76, though, the team challenged strongly for promotion only to miss out by three points.

Four weeks before the start of the new season in July 1976, Taylor resigned, out of the blue. He cited his failure to bring the club promotion within two seasons, but that seemed rather spurious in view of the timing and was also somewhat harsh on himself. Although shocked by his resignation, few were surprised when he rejoined his former partner Brian Clough, by then in charge at Nottingham Forest, just over a week later, leaving Alan Mullery to steer the team built by Taylor to promotion.

Reunited after two years, Clough and Taylor led Forest to unprecedented success over the next six years, including the European Cup in 1979 and 1980, but a rift started to grow between the two and Taylor left the City Ground in May 1982, apparently exhausted by his work. Fifteen years of managerial partnership ended in acrimony as he returned to Derby County, then back in Division Two, as manager in November 1982, but his second spell at the Baseball Ground was not a success and he was sacked by in April 1984 with the 'Rams' bound for Division Three.

Peter Taylor retired from football at the age of 55, and died while on holiday in Majorca in October 1990. Two days later Albion honoured their former manager with a minute's silence, while Brian Clough dedicated his 1994 autobiography to his late friend and partner.

the World Cup in Mexico in 1970, and went on to captain his country against Malta in February 1971. However, he also had the dubious distinction of being the first England player ever to be sent off, against Yugoslavia in June 1968.

After 308 League games for Tottenham, Mullery was forced out of the side by an injury and moved back to Fulham for six games on loan in March 1972, but he returned to White Hart Lane to skipper Spurs to victory over Wolves in the UEFA Cup final. Following that success he returned permanently to Craven Cottage for £65,000 – with expectations of eventually becoming manager – and made an additional 182 appearances before retiring. An unexpected bonus came in 1974–75 when he captained the Second Division side in the F.A. Cup final against West Ham United; Fulham lost 2–0, but he was further honoured with the Footballer of the Year award and was granted the M.B.E.

In July 1976, though, Mullery had left Fulham and was out of work when he received a telephone call from Mike Bamber. The Albion chairman had recalled the determination of the 34-year-old Londoner from a match against Fulham in January 1973 when Mullery was moved to strike one of his team mates to gee him up. Such an attitude would surely make a man a fine manager, mused Bamber, and so the former England international became Albion's boss just 24 hours after the departure of Peter Taylor. (It was also a temper that was to land him in trouble with the F.A. on a number of occasions as Albion manager.)

In fairness to his predecessor the new man took over a fine squad of players, but he renewed their confidence and self-belief, and was a breath of fresh air compared with the dour Taylor. Having just finished playing himself he quickly won their respect and proved an inspiration, although a tongue-lashing from Mullery was certainly something to be feared. Success came quickly as he won the Manager of the Month award in September 1976 – still the only occasion an Albion man has collected the accolade for the whole League – and the divisional award the following February. With the incomparable Peter Ward hitting 36 goals in the season, Mullery led his team to runner's-up spot in Division Three with some exhilarating football in front of huge, adoring crowds, then set his sights on Division One.

The flamboyant, cigar-smoking manager was given unprecedented spending power by Bamber, the ambitious chairman, and big-money signings such as Mark Lawrenson, Gary Williams, Peter Sayer and Teddy Maybank helped produce a second successive bid. Attendances grew to record levels as the club challenged for a place in the top flight, but Albion missed out on goal-difference on the final day of the campaign. On that day Mullery promised over 33,000 fans that the club would double its efforts the following season, and kept it by taking the team to second spot in 1979 to claim a place amongst the elite for the first time ever.

Although Albion struggled to find their feet in their first two seasons in Division One, the star names continued to arrive – John Gregory, Steve Foster, Neil McNab, Gordon Smith, Michael Robinson and Andy Ritchie – and Mullery seemed set to establish the club in the top flight after a narrow squeak in 1980–81. A new contract was agreed, but misunderstandings with Bamber, particularly over the sale of Lawrenson to Liverpool and proposed cuts to his staff, led to a showdown in June 1981 which prompted the resignation of the manager.

Quickly finding employment as boss of Charlton Athletic (1981–82) – thereby effectively swapping jobs with Mike Bailey (see below) – Mullery subsequently had spells in charge of Crystal Palace (1982–84) – where he also became a director – and Queen's Park Rangers (1984), but he was never able to reproduce the success he had brought to the Goldstone. On being dismissed after just a few months at Loftus Road, he moved into the printing trade, vowing

Competition	P	W	D	L	F	A	W	D	L	F	A
Football League	92	32	10	4	96	36	6	9	31	38	81
F.A. Cup	6	2	0	1	4	2	2	0	1	5	2
Football League Cup	6	0	2	1	5	6	0	2	1	1	2
Total	104	34	12	6	105	44	8	11	33	44	85

MULLERY, ALAN   JULY 1976–JUNE 1981

full name: Alan Patrick Mullery, M.B.E.
born : Notting Hill, Kensington, London, 23.11.1941
first game: Southend United (a), 14.8.1976 (FLC R1 Lg1)

When Alan Mullery followed Peter Taylor into the Goldstone 'hot seat' in 1976, he was the most accomplished footballer ever to take charge of the Albion, but was completely unproven as a manager. When he left Hove five years later he had built a reputation as one of the best young managers in the game and had led the club to undreamed-of heights. But he was never able to reproduce that success at a number of other clubs, and failed again when he returned to the Goldstone for a second, brief spell. Nevertheless, he will also be associated with the time when the 'Seagulls' really ruled the roost.

Mullery's career began when he joined the Fulham ground staff in June 1957 after representing West London, All-London and Middlesex schools. He made his first-team debut in February 1959, two months after signing professional forms, and held his place to the end of the season as the 'Cottagers' won promotion to Division One. The aggressive right-half went on to clock up 218 senior appearances for Fulham over six seasons, and also won three England under-23 caps while at Craven Cottage.

In March 1964, Tottenham Hotspur paid £72,500 for Mullery as a replacement for Danny Blanchflower and his career continued in spectacular fashion. Before the year was out he had represented the Football League twice and made his first appearance for the full England side. That cap, from a 1–1 draw with the Netherlands in Amsterdam, was the first of 35. In 1967 he helped Spurs win the F.A. Cup final against Chelsea, and gained a League Cup winner's trophy in 1971. He was a member of the England team which defended

315

never to work in football again, and wrote his life-story in 1985, *Alan Mullery: An Autobiography*.

In May 1986, though, he returned to Hove at the age of 44 to take charge of the Albion following the dismissal of Chris Cattlin, but he was unable to repeat his first miracle. With the club descending into financial turmoil, Mullery was ordered to sell players rather than buy, but was given very little chance to prove himself when, with Albion fifteenth in Division Two, he was sacked after just under nine months for an alleged lack of commitment. The board cited the fact that he hadn't moved house to the area and that he failed to attend local matches and Junior Seagulls functions, but it left supporters bewildered.

'The rats are winning. I've been stabbed in the back after being given five years to rebuild the club,' said a bitter Mullery, but he was soon back in the game as part-time manager of Southwick in the Isthmian League from August until November 1987. Thereafter, and somewhat disillusioned, he ran a sporting-goods shop in Banstead, Surrey, for a few years, but returned to football as a coach in Malaysia and as a media pundit. In October 1996 he was appointed Director of Football at Third Division Barnet, a position which effectively put him in charge of the team, but he stepped down to a scouting role the following March before leaving Underhill a few weeks later.

Competition	P	W	D	L	F	A	W	D	L	F	A
Football League	214	68	22	17	205	92	27	33	47	114	149
F.A. Cup	10	1	1	3	8	9	1	2	2	5	6
Football League Cup	25	7	4	1	16	7	5	4	4	18	18
Total	*249*	*76*	*27*	*21*	*229*	*108*	*33*	*39*	*53*	*137*	*173*

Note: The above figures refer only to Mullery's first spell in charge of the Albion. See below for his second spell.

BAILEY, MIKE   JUNE 1981–DECEMBER 1982

full name: Michael Alfred Bailey
born: Wisbech, Cambridgeshire, 27.2.1942
first game: West Ham United (a), 29.8.1981 (FL D1)

Alan Mullery was always going to be a tough act to follow as Albion manager, but 39-year-old Mike Bailey came with excellent credentials and did well enough in his first season to lead the club to its highest position ever in the Football League, thirteenth in Division One. Yet despite the apparent success, Bailey's tenure was marked by discontent among supporters who despaired at the nature of the football that was served up to them.

A tough-tackling wing-half, Bailey was brought up near Great Yarmouth, played for Precasters (Gorleston), and joined Charlton  Athletic on leaving school, signing professional forms in March 1959. He made 151 League appearances for the 'Valiants' in Division Two, scoring 20 goals, and also gained five England under-23 and two full international caps in 1964. In March 1966 he was transferred to Wolverhampton Wanderers for £35,000, the start of a glorious, eleven-year career at Molineux. In his first season Bailey helped Wolves back into Division One and went on to make 361 League appearances, most of them as skipper. He gained a UEFA Cup runner's-up medal in 1972; won a League Cup winner's trophy in 1974; and also represented the Football League.

Bailey played his last game for Wolves in October 1976 and enjoyed a very successful testimonial. Aged 34, he moved to the U.S.A. the following January as player/assistant coach to Minnesota Kicks under former Albion manager Freddie Goodwin, before returning to England as Hereford United's player-manager in August 1978. After stabilising the relegated club to fourteenth position in the Fourth Division, he left Edgar Street in October 1979 for a coaching post with his first club, Charlton Athletic. When he was appointed manager

in March 1980, the 'Valiants' were on the way to relegation, but Bailey successfully led them straight back to Division Two in 1980–81.

On Mullery's resignation in June 1981 the Albion board appointed Bailey as manager, but despite the high placing in his first season he did not enjoy the happiest of times. While the team gained excellent victories at Southampton, Tottenham and Liverpool, and challenged for a time for a UEFA Cup spot, the tactics employed were so defensive at times as to be tedious, and the public voted with their voices and their feet. While the plan may have produced dividends in the long term, the lack of entertainment produced a short-term fall in income which caused alarm in the boardroom. A poor end to the season was followed by a bad start to 1982–83, and with Albion struggling in front of low crowds Bailey left the club 'by mutual consent' in December 1982.

After leaving the Goldstone, Bailey had a spell managing a Greek club, then became player-manager at Bexley, Kent. He later ran the New Valley Club at Charlton's ground and was subsequently the leading light behind a successful property-developing company in south London. In November 1989, Bailey took over from Malcolm Allison as manager of Vauxhall Conference side Fisher Athletic, but left the club in January 1991 following a boardroom shake-up and joined Portsmouth's staff during the summer where he remained in charge of the reserve team until dismissed in February 1995. Later that year he became general manager of Leatherhead in the Isthmian League, and took over team affairs in March 1996.

Competition	P	W	D	L	F	A	W	D	L	F	A
Football League	59	13	9	7	41	31	5	7	18	17	57
F.A. Cup	3	1	0	1	3	4	0	1	0	0	0
Football League Cup	5	1	0	1	2	1	0	1	2	2	6
Total	*67*	*15*	*9*	*9*	*46*	*36*	*5*	*9*	*20*	*19*	*63*

AITKEN, GEORGE   JOINT CARETAKER
DECEMBER 1982–MARCH 1983

full name: George Bruce Aitken
born: Dalkeith, Midlothian, Scotland, 13.8.1928
first game: Norwich City (h), 11.12.1982 (FL D1)

When Mike Bailey left the Albion, the board turned to two existing employees to take charge of the team, chief scout Jimmy Melia and reserve-team coach George Aitken. The pair shared the duties for three months, but the 54-year-old Scot took a background role compared to that of the effervescent Melia.

In his time as a player, Aitken had been a constructive, dominating centre-half in the lower divisions. After turning out for Midlothian Schools, he played for the junior side Edinburgh Thistle and assisted Hibernian as an amateur, but signed as a professional for Middlesbrough in June 1946. After just eighteen games for the First Division club, Aitken joined Workington in July 1953 for £5,000 to become a stalwart in their Third Division (North) side. In six seasons he made 263 League appearances for the Cumberland club, and became a great admirer of his manager, the immortal Bill Shankly.

At the end of his playing days Aitken joined Workington's coaching staff under Joe Harvey, then assisted Harvey's successor, Ken Furphy, in taking the club to their only Football League promotion in 1963–64 when they achieved third place in Division Four. Furphy moved south to Watford soon after, and a year later Aitken followed him. The pair took the Hertfordshire club to the Third Division championship in 1968–69 and to an F.A. Cup semi-final appearance the following season.

After seven years at Vicarage Road, Aitken returned to Workington, back in Division Four, as manager in 1971 and remained in charge at Borough Park for nearly four years. Two moderate seasons were followed by two applications for re-election, and he resigned in 1975 to take up a post under manager Tom Casey at Grimsby Town.

Aitken arrived in Hove in the summer of 1976 to join Peter Taylor as trainer-coach, and he remained at the Goldstone for ten years in a variety of positions. Thrust into the spotlight together with Melia in December 1982, he returned to the background the following March when his colleague was appointed manager. He subsequently became chief scout, but lost his job when manager Chris Cattlin was dismissed in April 1986. Since then he has scouted for Graham Taylor at both Watford and Aston Villa, and continued to assist Taylor when he was England manager. In January 1988, Aitken's many friends organised a testimonial dinner for his benefit at Hove Town Hall, and he still lives in the town.

Competition	P	W	D	L	F	A	W	D	L	F	A
Football League	13	1	3	3	8	9	1	1	4	5	11
F.A. Cup	5	2	1	0	6	1	2	0	0	3	1
Total	18	3	4	3	14	10	3	1	4	8	12

Note: The figures above refer to the period 6.12.1982 until 17.3.1983 when Aitken and Melia were joint caretaker managers.

MELIA, JIMMY   DECEMBER 1982–OCTOBER 1983

full name: James John Melia
born: Liverpool, Lancashire, 1.11.1937
first game: Norwich City (h), 11.12.1982 (FL D1)

When Jimmy Melia was given the opportunity to manage the Albion, he grabbed it with both hands and produced a side which fought its way to Wembley for the first time. The ebullient 45-year-old will forever be associated with those incredible days, but in the League his team proved much less competent and was relegated after four seasons in the top flight. In fact the F.A. Cup final was the one highlight in an otherwise dismal managerial career with five Football League clubs.

One of eleven children, Melia represented England at schoolboy level before joining the Liverpool ground staff, and signed professional forms in November 1954. Scoring on his debut as an eighteen-year-old in December 1955, he went on to win England Youth honours and hit 78 goals in 287 League and Cup matches for the 'Reds'. Indeed, his intelligent play as an inside-forward was instrumental in securing the Second Division championship under Bill Shankly in 1961–62, and as Liverpool started their domination of the English game he gained a League championship medal in 1963–64, making 24 appearances before joining Wolverhampton Wanderers for £55,000 in March 1964. He also represented the Football League and won two full caps in 1963.

The prematurely balding Melia remained at Molineux for just nine months. Next stop was Southampton, whom he assisted into the First Division for the first time in 1966. After 139 League games at The Dell, Melia dropped into the Fourth Division in November 1968 as Aldershot's player-coach, and was appointed player-manager the following April. He made 135 League appearances for the 'Shots, but was unable to achieve promotion although the club enjoyed two good runs in the F.A. Cup during his period in charge.

Dismissed by the Hampshire club in February 1972, Melia accepted the post of player-coach at Crewe Alexandra, the Football League's bottom club that season, and played his final four League matches shortly after, bringing his total to 571. In May 1972 he graduated to team manager and the 'Railwaymen' improved slightly to 21st place in the next campaign, but he was then sacked again and on his way to Southport as assistant to Alan Ball (senior) after nearly two years at Gresty Road. At the end of July 1975, Melia was appointed manager, but, with the 'Sandgrounders' only one place off the foot of the table – without a win and playing before crowds of less than 1,000 – he resigned after just two months in charge.

Following seven years in the Fourth Division, Melia moved abroad and took up a coaching post in the Middle East before moving on to the U.S.A. to coach California Laser, Cleveland Cobras and New York Eagles. On his return to England, Albion manager Alan Mullery appointed him chief scout in April 1980, a post he retained under Mike Bailey.

Installed as joint acting manager with George Aitken on Bailey's departure, Melia quickly took the leading role and was appointed full-time in March 1983 on the strength of the club's run to the F.A. Cup semi-finals for the first time. The bubbly little figure with the white disco-dancing shoes and model girlfriend will always be remembered for bringing a smile back to the Goldstone with a totally

different style of play to Bailey, and for leading the team out at Wembley; but in the bread-and-butter fare of the Football League, Melia's team was less than competitive and finished the season bottom of Division One, eight points from safety.

In the summer of 1983, Albion chairman Mike Bamber appointed former player Chris Cattlin as coach. It was a move designed to instil some discipline into what had become a very relaxed regime under Melia, but as it was done in the manager's absence it was almost bound to cause friction. When Cattlin started to select the team, Melia had to consider his position and felt obliged to resign in October. It was not an amicable separation. With accusations flying in all directions, he showed up on the North Terrace at the next home game to be chaired on the shoulders of Albion's noisiest supporters as they chanted 'Melia in, Bamber out!' It was a sad, farcical departure for a man who had been so popular and yet, apart from that glorious run in the Cup, had achieved very little for the club with just seven wins from 35 League games.

Melia soon took up a post with Belenenses in the Portuguese League, but, after guiding the Second Division club to promotion, he left Portugal in November 1985 and returned some eight months later to the English game as manager of Fourth Division Stockport County. In November 1986, with only one win behind him, Melia resigned and departed for the Middle East, coaching and managing in Kuwait and the United Arab Emirates until the Gulf crisis of 1990–91 persuaded him to move to an indoor coaching post in Dallas, U.S.A., where he now runs Dallas Inter, a football development scheme with nine junior teams.

Competition	P	W	D	L	F	A	W	D	L	F	A
Football League	35	5	6	7	24	19	2	6	9	16	29
F.A. Cup	8	2	1	0	6	1	3	1	1	7	8
Football League Cup	1	1	0	0	4	2	0	0	0	0	0
Total	44	8	7	7	34	22	5	7	10	23	37

Note: The figures above refer to the period 6.12.1982 until 17.3.1983 when Melia and Aitken were joint caretaker managers, together with the period 17.3.1983 until 19.10.1983 when Melia was in sole charge.

CATTLIN, CHRIS   OCTOBER 1983–APRIL 1986

first game: Sheffield Wednesday (h), 22.10.1983 (FL D2)
See *Albion Players Who's Who*

Competition	P	W	D	L	F	A	W	D	L	F	A
Football League	115	32	16	10	105	54	18	11	28	65	86
F.A. Cup	10	4	0	1	6	2	2	1	2	9	9
Football League Cup	7	2	0	0	8	3	1	0	4	3	10
Full Members Cup	2	0	0	1	1	2	1	0	0	3	1
Total	134	38	16	12	120	61	22	12	34	80	106

PETCHEY, GEORGE WILLIAM   CARETAKER MAY 1986

born: Whitechapel, Stepney, London, 24.6.1931
first game: Hull City (a), 2.5.1986 (FL D2)

A quiet, dedicated professional, George Petchey took over as caretaker manager of the Albion on the dismissal of Chris Cattlin and oversaw just one match. Yet amazingly, at the age of 65, he was caretaker again briefly over ten years later.

Petchey began his football career as a junior with West Ham United, signing as a professional in August 1948, but he made only

two League appearances in five seasons. In July 1953 he was transferred to Queen's Park Rangers for £6,000 and went on to play 255 games for the west London side in the Third Division, mostly at left-half, before joining Crystal Palace in June 1960. In his first season at Selhurst the 'Glaziers' finished second in the Fourth Division. By the time an eye injury ended his career in 1964, he had 143 League games under his belt for Palace who had by then moved up to the Second Division.

Joining the coaching staff at Selhurst, Petchey had a spell as assistant to manager Bert Head. A progression to a managerial post was a natural course, and in 1968 he was interviewed for the vacancy at the Goldstone eventually filled by Freddie Goodwin, but it wasn't until July 1971 that he took over from Jimmy Bloomfield at Orient. The side occupied the middle and lower reaches of the Second Division in the six seasons Petchey spent at Brisbane Road, except for 1973–74 when they finished fourth, just one point from promotion. In 1977, however, Orient avoided relegation only on goal-difference and Petchey resigned just two weeks into the following season.

He was not off the London scene for long, though. Five months later he was in charge at Millwall, a club in desperate trouble with just three Second Division wins behind them, but they worked a miracle and won their last six games to escape relegation by a single point. It proved only a temporary delay, however, and the 'Lions' went down the following season. After a good start in Division Three, Millwall fell away to finish fourteenth in 1979-80 and the following season were in the relegation positions by December, forcing Petchey to leave The Den.

The 48-year-old, who had lived in Southwick since the late 1950s, then became a scout for Sunderland, but in November 1983 he first became involved with the Albion when Chris Cattlin asked him to look after the reserves and youth development. A year later he was promoted to chief coach in place of the more volatile Sammy Nelson, and was Cattlin's right-hand man until his boss was sacked in April 1986. Petchey was put in charge for the final game, but, although reported as being interested in the job, he left the club soon afterwards.

After scouting for Sunderland and Watford, Petchey retired from the game, but was tempted to return to the Goldstone at the age of 63 in January 1994 as youth development officer under Liam Brady. Following Brady's departure in November 1995 he was appointed assistant to new manager Jimmy Case, and took temporary charge again following Case's dismissal in December 1996, although no first-team matches were involved. When Steve Gritt was appointed Petchey was dismissed, but, having reached retirement age, he continued to assist the club by helping look after the under-14 boys for nothing.

Competition	P	W	D	L	F	A	W	D	L	F	A
Football League	1	0	0	0	0	0	0	0	1	0	2
Total	1	0	0	0	0	0	0	0	1	0	2

MULLERY, ALAN   MAY 1986–JANUARY 1987

first game: Portsmouth (h), 23.8.1986 (FL D2)
See above

Competition	P	W	D	L	F	A	W	D	L	F	A
Football League	24	5	4	3	14	9	2	3	7	11	20
Football League Cup	2	0	1	0	0	0	0	0	1	0	3
Full Members Cup	1	0	0	1	0	3	0	0	0	0	0
Total	27	5	5	4	14	12	2	3	8	11	23

Note: The above figures refer only to Mullery's second spell in charge of the Albion. See above for his first spell.

LLOYD, BARRY   JANUARY 1987–DECEMBER 1993

full name: Barry David Lloyd
born: Hillingdon, Middlesex, 19.2.1949
first game: Sheffield United (a), 10.1.1987 (FAC R3)

Although a large number of fans often doubted Barry Lloyd's abilities as Albion manager, there was rarely any question over his commitment to the club. His record in the 'hot seat' was mixed: relegation followed by immediate promotion, then nearly an unexpected return to the top flight, followed by another relegation; but the financial turmoil the club found itself in for much of the time certainly provided some mitigation. His talent in finding bargains on the transfer market was invaluable and he sowed the seeds of the best youth policy in Albion history, but his time at the Goldstone was plagued with troubles and unrest, and at the end of his near-seven years in charge there was absolutely no doubt that a change was necessary to get the club back on its feet.

Lloyd's early enthusiasm for the game was fuelled by helping in the club shop at Hayes while his father was playing for the Athenian League club. After representing Middlesex and the South of England as a schoolboy, he joined Chelsea, signing professional forms at seventeen in February 1966. He gained England Youth honours, but made just ten First Division appearances for the 'Pensioners' before moving to Fulham as the lesser half of an exchange deal with John Dempsey in January 1969.

A regular in Fulham's midfield for the next six years, Lloyd skippered the side that won promotion from Division Three in 1971, but he lost his place in December 1974 and played in only three matches on the "Cottagers'" marathon march to the F.A. Cup final in 1975. Though warming the bench on the big day, Lloyd did not get on as West Ham United triumphed 2–0. After one more season at Craven Cottage, and a total of 289 League and Cup games, he moved on to Hereford United in October 1976 and made fourteen appearances in their only Second Division campaign.

In the summer of 1977, Lloyd returned to the London area with Brentford, then managed by his former Fulham boss, Bill Dodgin, and helped the 'Bees' to promotion to the Third Division in his only season at Griffin Park. After a summer in the U.S.A. with the Houston Hurricanes, he took over as player-manager of Yeovil Town and led them to the Southern League Cup final at his first attempt, where they lost out to Bath City. Southern League performances were impressive enough for the 'Glovers' to be admitted as founder members of the Alliance Premier League in 1979, but the Somerset side struggled in the new national league and Lloyd was dismissed in January 1981.

Five months later he arrived in Sussex as the first full-time manager-coach of the ambitious Isthmian League club Worthing, and the next few years brought unprecedented success to the 'Rebels'. In his first season, 1981–82, the side ran away with the championship of the Second Division, and followed it with an equally convincing First Division title and a superb run to the second round of the F.A. Cup in 1982–83, the first time Worthing had reached the competition proper since 1936. The 1983–84 season saw the finest Worthing team in history just miss out on promotion to the Alliance (Gola) Premier League, finishing runners-up to Harrow Borough, and they repeated the feat in 1984–85, coming second to Sutton United.

In April 1986, Albion brought back Alan Mullery as manager with Peter Suddaby as his no.2. Lloyd, a former Fulham colleague of the new manager, was installed as reserve- and youth-team coach to re-shape the club's youth policy, and he remained largely in the background until January 1987 when, with the team fifteenth in Division Two, Mullery was sacked and Lloyd was installed as the new manager the following day.

Although successful in non-League circles, he was unproven in the high-pressure world of the Second Division and the supporters soon let him know it. It was fifteen games before the team secured a victory for the new manager, and as the club sank remorselessly towards the Third Division the personal abuse hurled at Lloyd was intense.

At the end of the season the 38-year-old rebuilt the team with a number of inspired signings, and guided the Albion to promotion at the first time of asking. Back in the Second Division, the club struggled for a couple of seasons and the unrest grew again, but in 1990–91, Albion, inspired by some Lloyd bargain-buys, unexpectedly made it to the Wembley play-off final only to miss out on promotion to Division One at the final hurdle to Notts County. The following season, though, the manager's hands were tied by ever-spiralling debts and Albion finished in the relegation zone.

Over the next eighteen months Lloyd became – if he wasn't already – the most unpopular manager in the club's history, yet nobody could have worked harder to save the club. While the manager lost any rapport he may have enjoyed with the fans, his workload was greatly increased in December 1991 when he was appointed managing director, responsible for the day-to-day running of all aspects of the club. Unfortunately, the appointment coincided with the worst financial crisis in Albion history, and as he became embroiled in money matters Lloyd grew more distanced from the players; coach Martin Hinshelwood was left largely in charge of team affairs except during matches.

As morale plummeted, disenchantment on the terraces reached new heights, and demonstrations against Lloyd peaked in October and November 1993 as the club struggled for its very existence in the High Court. Following the takeover by Bill Archer and Greg Stanley, David Bellotti was appointed chief executive, allowing Lloyd to return to matters football, but the new arrangement lasted just three weeks. With gates at their lowest level ever in the Football League and with intense cries on all sides for the manager's head, Lloyd left the club on 4 December 1993 'by mutual consent' with a year's salary to tide him over.

Thereafter he pursued a number of posts in football but without reward until he returned to Worthing as a consultant in September 1996.

Competition	P	W	D	L	F	A	W	D	L	F	A
Football League	312	71	40	45	225	181	39	31	86	166	264
Division 2 Play-offs	3	1	0	0	4	1	1	0	1	3	4
F.A. Cup	20	6	1	4	23	13	3	2	4	12	13
Football League Cup	18	4	1	4	10	12	0	3	6	4	17
Associate Members Cup	11	4	1	2	17	16	2	1	1	9	6
Full Members Cup	7	2	0	1	6	5	0	1	3	1	10
Total	*371*	*88*	*43*	*56*	*285*	*228*	*45*	*38*	*101*	*195*	*314*

HINSHELWOOD, MARTIN   CARETAKER DECEMBER 1993

born: Reading, Berkshire, 16.6.1953
first game: Hartlepool United (a), 11.12.1993 (FL D2)

Although Martin Hinshelwood was officially in charge of the Albion side for just one match following the departure of Barry Lloyd, he had had a profound influence on the team long before that while Lloyd's duties as managing director kept him away from the training ground for many months.

The son of Wally Hinshelwood, the Reading and Bristol City right-winger, Martin was raised in Deal, Kent, and New Addington, Surrey, where he became associated with Fulham. After representing Dover, Croydon and Surrey Schools, he was taken on as an apprentice by Crystal Palace in 1969, signing as a professional in August 1970. A few years later he was joined on the Selhurst Park staff by his brother Paul, a full-back.

Hinshelwood's best season was in 1975–76 when he played 28 times in the midfield as Palace just missed out on promotion to Division Two along with arch-rivals Brighton. However, after just 69 League games he was forced to retire from professional football in 1979 at the age of 27 following a severe knee injury.

That setback launched Hinshel-wood on a coaching career, initially as youth-team coach with Palace, but then with Leatherhead in the Isthmian League as player-manager before returning to Palace for a short spell. He then took employment outside the game in Croydon, but kept his hand in with part-time coaching in the Isthmian League at Barking, Dorking and Kingstonian before returning to League circles as reserve-team coach at Chelsea for two years.

In June 1987, Hinshelwood arrived at the Goldstone as chief coach under Barry Lloyd, and he played his part in seeing the Albion back into the Second Division in 1988, and to the Wembley play-off final in 1991. The following December, Lloyd was appointed managing director, and as his workload off the training field mounted so Hinshelwood increasingly took charge of team affairs. By 1993–94 he was virtually full-time in charge of the team — except on match days.

When Lloyd left the club at the start of December 1993, Hinshelwood took charge for a fixture at Hartlepool and was considered one of the favourites for the manager's post, but he lost out to Liam Brady and left the Goldstone in the New Year as the new man brought in his own coaching staff. (He later won compensation at an industrial tribunal for unfair dismissal.)

Finding employment as assistant to former Albion player Les Briley at Slough Town in February 1994, Hinshelwood lost out again as the Conference side were relegated in May 1994. He subsequently became youth-team coach at Portsmouth, where he was joined on the staff by his son, Danny, for a time, and he also coaches Selsey in the Sussex County League.

Competition	P	W	D	L	F	A	W	D	L	F	A
Football League	1	0	0	0	0	0	0	1	0	2	2
Total	*1*	*0*	*0*	*0*	*0*	*0*	*0*	*1*	*0*	*2*	*2*

BRADY, LIAM   DECEMBER 1993–NOVEMBER 1995

full name: William Liam Brady
born: Dublin, Co. Dublin, Republic of Ireland, 13.2.1956
first game: Bradford City (h), 18.12.1993 (FL D2)

Few supporters nominated ex-Celtic manager Liam Brady to take over at the Albion following the departure of Barry Lloyd in December 1993, but when the board announced the appointment it was greeted with almost universal delight by a Sussex public crying out for success. And success is something Brady knew all about, for he had been, quite simply, the most accomplished player to come out of the British Isles for many years and a star on the world stage. Sadly, though, the odds were stacked against him at both clubs he went on to manage.

The youngest of seven children – his brothers Pat and Ray (an Eire international) played for Millwall and Q.P.R. – Brady played Gaelic football at school but joined a soccer club at the age of nine. Four years later he was spotted by an Arsenal scout, and left home at fifteen to join the Highbury staff as an apprentice, signing as a professional in August 1973. A sparkling career in the "Gunners'" youth team promised much, and the young 'Chippie' Brady – so called because of his fondness for that food – made an excellent debut, coming on as a substitute at home to Birmingham City in October 1973 and changing the course of the match in Arsenal's favour.

If ever a single player transformed a club, that player was Brady and the club was Arsenal. Forsaking the dull, stereotyped play of the north London side, he produced a midfield exhibition of imaginative, exhilarating and skilful football over the next six years or so which made him the idol of the Highbury fans. His first cap for the Republic of Ireland came in October 1974 against the U.S.S.R in Dublin at the age of just eighteen, a match the Irish won 3–0. It was the first of a record number of appearances for his country.

The peak of Brady's success in England came in 1979, when he was voted P.F.A. Player of the Year and Arsenal beat Manchester

United 3–2 to win the F.A. Cup. It was the second of three successive appearances in the final for the 'Gunners'; he played in all three, but Arsenal lost twice, and also lost the 1980 European Cup Winners' Cup final to Valencia, his last competitive game for the club.

Attracted by the riches available in Italy, and by the experience such a move would offer, Brady was transferred to Juventus for £600,000, the maximum then allowable. After a slow start he found his feet in the Italian League halfway through his first season and became an enormous success, helping the club to two championships in his two years in Turin. However, the Juventus coach then brought in two more foreign stars and Brady found it was time to move on, to Sampdoria for £780,000. Two seasons in Genoa saw him play in virtually every match, but the club could only manage mid-table positions and in the summer of 1984 he joined Inter Milan for £1•75 million. Again he was almost ever-present as Inter finished third in 1984–85 and sixth the following term.

After two seasons in Milan, the talented Irishman moved to Ascoli for £500,000 but did not enjoy a great deal of success as the small-town club struggled in the top division. With 189 games in the Italian League to his credit, he returned to England with West Ham United in March 1987 for just £100,000 and went on bring his total of Football

League appearances to 324. In August 1987 he represented the League in the centenary match against the Rest of the World, but increasing injury problems saw him retire from full-time football in the summer of 1990 at the age of 34.

But while he was thrilling crowds in England and Italy, Brady also established a magnificent reputation on the international field with the Republic of Ireland. He became captain in 1980 and skippered the side thirteen times. In all he made 72 appearances – a record until beaten by Packie Bonner in June 1994 – and was a first choice for fifteen years from 1974 until 1989. It was most unfortunate that his one serious injury kept him out of the Republic's thrilling debut in the European Championship finals in West Germany in 1988. His last cap was his own testimonial game, a match against Finland in Dublin in May 1990.

After a tremendous playing career, Brady established a sports agency in Dublin, but the yearning for day-to-day involvement in the game proved too strong and in June 1991 he was appointed manager of Celtic. The task facing him was huge: to restore the fortunes of the fallen Glasgow giants. The 'Bhoys' finished third in both his seasons at Parkhead and qualified for Europe, but, living in the shadow of arch-rivals Rangers, it was not enough and the pressure mounted. Although the team played good football in his own mould, some of his signings did not come off and he resigned in October 1993.

The managerial post at the Goldstone became vacant in December 1993, but Brady could well have been installed at Barnet had it not been for the financial troubles at Underhill. He was, in the words of Albion chief executive David Bellotti, 'head and shoulders above the rest' of more than 20 applicants, and was appointed on a two-year contract. The new manager was an excellent signing if only because he gave the supporters hope once more, but he also brought a breath of fresh air throughout the club, and instilled some much-needed discipline and self-belief into the team who responded with some excellent performances.

Despite having little money to play with, Brady transformed the struggling club's playing fortunes in 1993–94, lifting the side to a final fourteenth place in Division Two, and deservedly won the

division's Manager of the Month award in February 1994. He won it again in September after an excellent start to the new campaign, and confirmed his commitment to the club in the face of rumours of a move to Arsenal. In May 1995 he launched 'Give Kids a Chance', a campaign to ensure that the best young players in Sussex sign for their local professional club.

In 1995–96, though, Albion descended into unprecedented turmoil when the board arranged the sale of the Goldstone Ground with no suitable alternative, and Brady suddenly found himself in the middle of a crisis. Although the team was at the foot of Division Three, the public was generally supportive as the manager left no one in any doubt where he stood: he was firmly on the side of the supporters and they looked up to him for it. In September he defused a half-time on-pitch demonstration, and later launched a number of thinly-veiled verbal attacks on the board.

Utterly frustrated by the club's suicidal policies, he called it a day in November 1995 and left the Goldstone with a damning condemnation ringing in the ears of his former employers. Although he was interviewed for manager of the Republic of Ireland side in January, the 40-year-old legend surfaced again in April 1996 when he fronted a consortium hoping to take control of the club. On the morning following the infamous abandoned game against York City, Brady appeared in Hove Park to announce that he had a group behind him ready and willing to invest in the Albion, and that he personally was prepared to pay the first instalment of the rent required by the new owners of the Goldstone for another season at the ground which had been home since 1902. It was just what desperate supporters wanted to hear: a genuine football man of impeccable credentials was looking to rescue their club from the clutches of Archer, Stanley and Bellotti.

The negotiations between the two rival sides proved fruitless during the summer of 1996, though, and Brady was forced to choose between a prolonged battle for the Albion or a post in charge of Arsenal's youth development. He chose the latter, but he still lives in Hove and follows the fortunes of his local club with much more than just a passing interest. Indeed, Liam Brady will go down in Albion history as one of the prime movers behind the group that eventually took over the club in 1997 to save it from probable oblivion.

Competition	P	W	D	L	F	A	W	D	L	F	A
Football League	90	20	14	12	64	47	9	13	22	46	70
F.A. Cup	2	0	0	0	0	0	0	1	1	3	4
Football League Cup	8	2	1	1	4	4	2	0	2	6	8
Associate Members Cup	4	0	0	2	0	3	1	1	0	5	2
Total	104	22	15	15	68	54	12	15	25	60	84

CASE, JIMMY   NOVEMBER 1995–DECEMBER 1996

first game: Canvey Island (h), 21.11.1995 (FAC R1 rep)
See *Albion Players Who's Who*

Competition	P	W	D	L	F	A	W	D	L	F	A
Football League	51	6	9	10	31	36	4	2	20	20	46
F.A. Cup	5	1	2	0	5	2	0	2	0	0	0
Football League Cup	2	0	0	1	0	1	0	0	1	0	2
Associate Members Cup	2	0	0	0	0	0	1	0	1	4	5
Total	60	7	11	11	36	39	5	4	22	24	53

GRITT, STEVE   DECEMBER 1996–

full name: Stephen J. Gritt
born: Bournemouth, Hampshire, 31.10.1957
first game: Hull City (h), 14.12.1996 (FL D3)

When Steve Gritt moved into the Goldstone 'hot seat' in December 1996 it had never been hotter. The club had just had two points deducted by the F.A. because of pitch invasions, leaving the team eleven points adrift at the bottom of the Football League and in severe danger of relegation to the Conference, while supporters were waging a bitter war against discredited but entrenched directors who had sold the club's home. That he was to emerge from such a disastrous situation a hero speaks volumes for his professionalism and dedication.

Gritt began his career with AFC Bournemouth, his home-town club which he joined as an apprentice in July 1974. Two years later he turned professional, but he had only six League outings at Dean

Court, and also had loan-spells with Hereford United and Dorchester Town. His big breakthrough came in July 1977 when he was released to join Second Division Charlton Athletic.

It was a free transfer made in heaven for both club and player. Gritt went on to make 347 League appearances for the 'Valiants' in every outfield position, although he was usually a full-back or midfielder. He was a stalwart of the side that won promotion to Division Two in 1981, and also figured in the team that brought First Division football back to The Valley in 1986. In July 1989, Gritt moved on to Walsall, but returned to Charlton seven months later and was appointed reserve-team coach in October 1990. The following summer he was promoted to joint manager with Alan Curbishley, the ex-Albion player, and the pair guided the 'Valiants' to some high positions in Division Two (which became Division One). He made his last League appearance in April 1993, but in June 1995 the Charlton board opted for Curbishley to take over the reins completely and Gritt left the club to start a long period of unemployment

He played briefly for Welling United and spent three months at Tooting & Mitcham United at the start of 1996–97, but he also scouted for Torquay United and Gillingham, and helped out a good deal at the latter where he looked after the under-14s. Nevertheless, Gritt was desperate to get back into the full-time game and successfully applied for the Albion manager's post, then the most unenvied job in football. As a man of proven experience he looked a good appointment, but he was seen by some supporters as an Archer/Bellotti stooge and was given a very cold reception at his first game. With offensive graffiti already adorning the Goldstone brickwork, the 39-year-old took the field to a disgraceful chorus of whistling and booing before Albion thumped Hull City 3–0. 'It wasn't the kind of welcome I was expecting so it was disappointing,' he said, but it left him in little doubt about the serious situation in Hove.

His first direct contact with embittered fans came a week later at Brisbane Road, Leyton, when he appealed to them to confine their protests to peaceful demonstrations – which was, in fact, what they were doing! But by the time he attended a public meeting in mid January, more reasonable voices among the fans' leadership were appealing for him to be given the chance to prove himself. Gritt himself was applauded when he told the audience that he now realised the passion that existed for Brighton & Hove Albion.

The holder of a full F.A. coaching badge, it was on the pitch and training ground that Gritt had to make his mark, and he did just that. He instilled confidence, discipline, organisation and strategy into his players who started to produce the results, while the supporters, with their enthusiasm renewed by the 5–0 'Fans United' thrashing of Hartlepool United, provided the inspiration and backing that had been lacking previously. As the team started to close the gap so the pressure intensified, but by now fans were singing the praises of Gritt who was rewarded with a divisional Manager of the Month award in February 1997. Home form, in front of large, passionate crowds, was superb and only two points were dropped after the New Year, but away from home the team failed to win once following his appointment.

Nevertheless, the team produced the results that mattered in the final days of the Goldstone Ground, and forced the draw at Hereford which sealed a remarkable escape and condemned their opponents to the obscurity of non-League football. It was a truly magnificent achievement by the new manager and his staff, and all Albion fans will be eternally grateful to the man who was treated init-ially with such puerile disdain. But after the great euphoria of League survival had died away, rumours that Gritt would be whisked away by

another club abounded. There were problems with the new playing budget imposed by the discredited board just hours before the showdown at Hereford, and there were greater troubles caused by the delayed takeover of the club by a popular consortium. After talks with chairman-to-be Dick Knight, Gritt pledged himself to the club – as long as the off-the-field problems were sorted out – but rarely can a manager have had to field a team in such adverse circumstances.

As well as being an excellent professional footballer, Gritt was also a fair cricketer, winning representative honours for the English Schools and playing for the Hampshire seconds. But it all pales into insignificance for a man who has raised thousands of pounds for the British Brain and Spine Foundation following the discovery that his daughter, Hayley, was suffering from a brain tumour from which she has happily recovered.

Competition	P	W	D	L	F	A	W	D	L	F	A
Football League	24	10	2	0	27	8	0	4	8	8	20
Associate Members Cup	2	1	0	0	3	2	0	0	1	0	1
Total	26	11	2	0	30	10	0	4	9	8	21

Note: The above figures include all matches up to the end of the 1996–97 season.

Brighton United

Brighton United was the first professional club in Sussex and the forerunner of today's Brighton & Hove Albion.

It was formed at a meeting at the Imperial Hotel, Queen's Road, Brighton, held on 26 November 1997, chiefly through the efforts of Sussex County F.A. men Edgar Everest and Charles Meaden, and played its first game on 1 September 1898, a friendly against Southwick. Two days later United played Southhampton in the Southern League's First Division, the first-ever game played at The Dell.

It was, however, a struggle to keep going. Bad weather affected attendances at the club's home ground, the County Cricket Ground in Hove, where there was no covered accommodation for spectators, and a loss of over £1,000 was made on the season.

In 1899–1900 things started badly for the club and got worse. Results were poor and United sunk to the bottom of the division. Attendances were poorer, and the club lived from day to day. Eventually, on 29 March 1900, a meeting of shareholders voted to wind the club up voluntarily. Brighton United withdrew from the Southern League and the Thames & Medway Combination and ceased trading.

The manager throughout the club's existence was John Jackson (see *Albion Managers*).

In 1900 some leading supporters promoted the formation of a high-class amateur side, Brighton & Hove Rangers, as 'compensation' for the loss of United, but that club also folded, leading to the establishment of Brighton & Hove Albion in June 1901 (principally by John Jackson).

This section give biographical details of the 37 players who represented Brighton United in first-team competitions, some of whom went on to play for the Albion. Specifically, these competitions were:

- Southern League (**SL**) 1898–1900
- Football Association Challenge Cup (**FAC**) 1898–1900
- United League (**UL**) 1898–99
- Thames & Medway Combination (**T&MC**) 1899–1900

Note that, for the purposes of this volume, all matches played by Brighton United have been counted towards players' totals except Warmley (h) 14.1.1899 and Cowes (h) 11.11.1899: Warmley withdrew from the Southern League in January 1899, and Cowes withdrew in December 1899 — before Brighton United in March 1900.

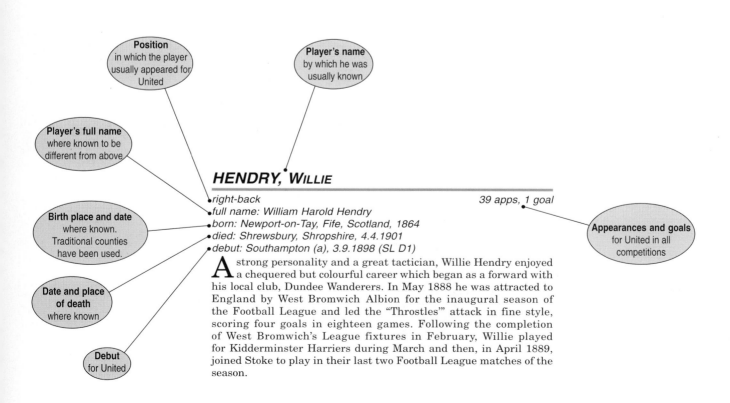

Position in which the player usually appeared for United

Player's name by which he was usually known

Player's full name where known to be different from above

Birth place and date where known. Traditional counties have been used.

Date and place of death where known

Debut for United

Appearances and goals for United in all competitions

HENDRY, WILLIE

right-back   *39 apps, 1 goal*
full name: William Harold Hendry
born: Newport-on-Tay, Fife, Scotland, 1864
died: Shrewsbury, Shropshire, 4.4.1901
debut: Southampton (a), 3.9.1898 (SL D1)

A strong personality and a great tactician, Willie Hendry enjoyed a chequered but colourful career which began as a forward with his local club, Dundee Wanderers. In May 1888 he was attracted to England by West Bromwich Albion for the inaugural season of the Football League and led the "Throstles'" attack in fine style, scoring four goals in eighteen games. Following the completion of West Bromwich's League fixtures in February, Willie played for Kidderminster Harriers during March and then, in April 1889, joined Stoke to play in their last two Football League matches of the season.

ASHBY, HARRY

right-back   *14 apps*
full name: Henry Radford Ashby
born: Derby, Derbyshire, 1875
debut: Queen's Park Rangers (a), 2.9.1899 (SL D1)

Harry Ashby joined Burton Swifts from Derby Athletic in 1896, and appeared in 88 Second Division games in three seasons for the Staffordshire club before being recruited by Brighton United in May 1899 at the age of 23. Although he was installed as team captain, Harry's stay in Sussex lasted just six months and he left the club in November 1899, later returning to Staffordshire with the newly formed Burton United. Three seasons and 91 League matches later, the Derby-born full-back moved to Plymouth Argyle in the Southern League, but moved back to the Football League in July 1905 with Leicester Fosse. A regular for nearly two seasons, Harry made 68 League and Cup appearances for Fosse until a badly-broken leg enforced his premature retirement in March 1907 at the age of 31; he was subsequently awarded a benefit match.

BAKER, BERT

outside-right   *7 apps, 2 goals*
debut: Chatham (h), 9.12.1899 (SL D1)
See *Albion Players Who's Who*

BULLIMER, LEO

goalkeeper   *33 apps*
full name: Leon Antonin L. Bullimer
born: Stoke-upon-Trent, Staffordshire, 1874
died: Northampton, Northamptonshire, 24.4.1954
debut: Southampton (a), 3.9.1898 (SL D1)

The son of Antonin Boullemier, the renowned French ceramic artist, Leo Bullimer (who used the anglicised form of the surname) grew up in Stoke-upon-Trent where his father had worked for the Minton company since 1865, and became a professional footballer with both Potteries clubs, Stoke and Burslem Port Vale. It was not until he joined Lincoln City in December 1895 that he made his League debut, though. The young goalkeeper became a regular for the 'Imps' and made 49 consecutive League appearances before moving into the Southern League with Reading during the close season of 1897.

In May 1898, Leo was one of the first players to be signed up by the Brighton United management, and he performed brilliantly in the new club's opening Southern League match at Southampton, keeping the champions-elect at bay for long periods when United were reduced to ten men early in the game before eventually losing 4–1. The regular 'keeper for the first half of United's initial campaign, he lost his place in the New Year to Tom Spicer and left for Lancashire League side Stockport County in May 1899, making his final move in 1901 to Northampton Town.

After hanging up his gloves in 1905, Leo took to refereeing and officiated several Albion matches before the Great War. He gained wide respect with the whistle, and took charge of the match between the Irish and Scottish Leagues in Belfast in November 1913. Granted special permission (as an ex-professional) to sit on the council of the Northants County Football Association, Leo lived in Northampton until his death at the age of 79, and was also a great servant of the county cricket club. The 1955 *Wisden Cricketers' Almanack* included this note in his obituary:

'Was for 51 years scorer for Northamptonshire until retiring in 1952. His efforts in raising funds did much to keep Northamptonshire going during some of their worst financial crises.'

CALDWELL, JOCK

left-back   *45 apps, 1 goal*
debut: Southampton (a), 3.9.1898 (SL D1)
See *Albion Players Who's Who*

CARTER, JOHN

right-back   *16 apps*
born: c. 1876
debut: Thames Ironworks (h), 15.10.1898 (FAC Q2)

John Carter arrived at the County Ground in 1898 at the age of 22 with a fine reputation from the Bristol-based Southern League club Warmley. However, he found it difficult to compete with the experience of Willie Hendry and struggled to make the team. John left Brighton United for junior football in May 1899 at the end of the club's first season, having made sixteen appearances.

CLARK, JOE

inside/outside-right   *11 apps*
full name: Joseph Carter
born: Dundee, Angus, Scotland
debut: Southampton (a), 3.9.1898 (SL D1)

A regular goalscorer for Dundee for two seasons before signing for Brighton United in May 1898, Joe Clark was unable to reproduce his form at the County Ground and failed to net a goal in eleven outings. He turned out on the right wing and at inside-right during the first half of 1898–99, but was released to rejoin Dundee in January.

At the start of the following campaign in September 1899, Joe again tried his luck south of the border, this time with Newton Heath

(later Manchester United) but, unable to score in nine Second Division matches, he met with little success and joined the Army at the end of 1899–1900, seeing action in South Africa during the Boer War. In October 1901 he returned to his native Dundee and joined the local junior club Lochee United. Joe went on to play for Dunfermline Athletic (August 1903) and East Fife (August 1905).

COLLINS, ROGER

centre-forward   *1 app, 2 goals*
full name: Arthur Collins
born: Brighton, Sussex, 1876
debut: Woolwich Arsenal (a), 31.10.1898 (UL)

'Roger' Collins was a prominent local amateur who netted both Brighton United goals in a 5–2 United League defeat at the hands of Woolwich Arsenal at Plumstead. A member of the Southwick side which won the Sussex Senior Cup in 1897 (beating Eastbourne 2–0 after two replays), he was playing for Brighton Athletic at the time of his United game, and helped them win both the East Sussex Senior League and the Royal Irish Rifles Charity Cup in successive seasons, 1897–98 and 1898–99. A fleet-footed centre-forward, Roger was the Southwick village 100-yard sprint champion in his youth.

COLLINS, NED

full-back — 4 apps
debut: New Brompton (a), 23.10.1899 (T&MC)
See *Albion Players Who's Who*

DAVIDSON, JIMMY

inside-forward — 49 apps, 7 goals
full name: James Wilkie Davidson
born: Edinburgh, Midlothian, Scotland, 25.10.1873
debut: New Brompton (a), 10.9.1898 (SL D1)

Jimmy Davidson joined Celtic from Leith Athletic in 1892, and gained a Scottish League championship medal while still in his teens when the 'Celts' carried off the first of their 35 titles in his first season in Glasgow. In three years at Celtic Park he scored ten goals in 22 League matches before joining Burnley in July 1895 where he made 20 First Division appearances. In March 1897 the tricky Scot was loaned to Lincoln City for two months before switching to the Southern League with Tottenham Hotspur, and signed for Brighton United at the age of 23 in May 1898.

Jimmy remained at the County Ground throughout the life of the club, but when United folded in March 1900 he rejoined Burnley and added a further 45 League games to his total. Noted for his creative talents, Jimmy represented the Southern League in a 6–0 defeat by the London F.A. at Leyton Cricket Ground in February 1898 while on Spurs' books. During his Celtic days he acquired the nickname 'Tooty'.

FARRELL, PADDY

half-back — 57 apps, 1 goal
debut: Southampton (a), 3.9.1898 (SL D1)
See *Albion Players Who's Who*

FREEMAN, STAN

left-back — 1 app
debut: Sheppey United (h), 1.3.1899 (SL D1)

A member of the Brighton Athletic team which won the East Sussex Senior League in 1897–98 and 1898–99, Stan Freeman was enlisted as a late stand-in for the injured Jock Caldwell in March 1899, but was not called upon subsequently. He went on to play for Brighton & Hove Rangers, and appeared in the side beaten 3–1 by Eastbourne in the 1901 Sussex Senior Cup final.

HADDEN, SID

inside/outside-right — 6 apps
full name: Sidney Hadden
born: Old Town, Hastings, Sussex, 26.8.1877
died: West Ham, Essex, 1934
debut: New Brompton (h), 27.1.1900 (SL D1)

Sid Hadden played for Hastings & St Leonards and Eastbourne Swifts during the 1890s, but was a professional on the books of Kent League Ashford United when he signed for Brighton United in November 1899. Following United's demise in March 1900, he was reinstated as an amateur and rejoined Hastings where he won East Sussex Senior League championship medals in 1901, 1902 and 1904.

Sid was suspended by the Football Association in October 1905 for a month when it was alleged that he was receiving payment (along with two colleagues) to turn out for Hastings; the club was expelled from the Amateur Cup and subsequently adopted professionalism.

In January 1908, with Sid unemployed and out of action following a cartilage operation, a fund-raising match, the Gaiety Theatre *v.* Hastings Hippodrome, was held at the Central Ground, Hastings, which raised £10 15*s*. 10*d*. for the Hadden family. In 1910 he was working for – and playing football for – the Beckton gasworks in Essex when he was drawn into the machinery, breaking an arm and suffering other severe injuries which effectively ended his football days.

As well as being the first Hastings footballer to gain representative honours for Sussex, Sid was also a noted cricketer: he played as a wicket-keeper/batsman for Hastings, Sussex Colts and Sussex Club & Ground, and subsequently held professional appointments with the Highbury House, Granville, and Haslingden clubs (appearing briefly for the latter town's football team in the Lancashire League early in 1904–05). Somewhat late in life he broke into first-class cricket, playing six matches for Essex between 1912 and 1920.

HALMAN, CHARLIE

outside-left — 1 app
full name: Charles William Halman
born: Brighton, Sussex, 1875
debut: Bristol City (h), 26.10.1898 (UL)

One of the Brighton Athletic amateurs who assisted the Brighton United club during its brief existence, Charlie Halman deputised for Jock Malloch on the left wing in a 2–1 United League victory over Bristol City at the County Ground in October 1898, and also turned out in a friendly match against a Southern Suburban League XI a few weeks later. He was a leading member of the Brighton Athletic team which annexed the championship of the East Sussex Senior League and R.I.R. Charity Cup in successive seasons, 1897–98 and 1898–99.

HARLAND, LOHMANN

wing-half — 5 apps
debut: Thames Ironworks (h), 29.11.1899 (T&MC)
See *Albion Players Who's Who*

HARRISON, JOHN

left-back — 2 apps
full name: John Archie H. Harrison
born: Brighton, Sussex, 1873
debut: Swindon Town (a), 3.3.1900 (SL D1)

John Harrison was playing for the Preston Park-based side North End Rangers when he was recruited by Brighton United a few weeks before the club's liquidation to take the place of the indisposed Andy Mills in two successive games. The following season John joined the newly formed amateur club Brighton & Hove Rangers and didn't miss a competitive match until he was sent off for kicking an opponent in the Sussex Senior Cup semi-final with Hove in February 1901, which resulted in him being suspended for six weeks and missing the final.

At the formation meeting of Brighton & Hove Albion Football Club, held on 24 June 1901 at the Seven Stars in Ship Street, Brighton, John concurred with the view of Rangers' founder, William Avenell, that the defunct club's committee had left something to be desired. Despite proposing George Hannan as secretary of the new club, he did not go on to play for the Albion.

HENDRY, WILLIE

right-back   *39 apps, 1 goal*
full name: William Harold Hendry
born: Newport-on-Tay, Fife, Scotland, 1864
died: Shrewsbury, Shropshire, 4.4.1901
debut: Southampton (a), 3.9.1898 (SL D1)

A strong personality and a great tactician, Willie Hendry enjoyed a chequered but colourful career which began as a forward with his local club, Dundee Wanderers. In May 1888 he was attracted to England by West Bromwich Albion for the inaugural season of the Football League and led the "Throstles'" attack in fine style, scoring four goals in eighteen games. Following the completion of West Bromwich's League fixtures in February, Willie played for Kidderminster Harriers during March and then, in April 1889, joined Stoke to play in their last two Football League matches of the season.

Converted into a centre-half with great success at Stoke, he was, nevertheless, soon on the move, joining Preston North End's 'Invincibles' for their final match of the 1889–90 campaign which saw them clinch the championship for the second season running with a 1–0 victory at Notts County. Willie was the regular centre-half at Deepdale during the 1890–91 season, but, shortly after North End lost interest in the F.A. Cup, he was released to join Sheffield United in February 1891.

United were competing in the Midland Counties League at the time, but, on becoming founder members of the Football League's Second Division in 1892, they finished runners-up to Small Heath and clinched promotion to the top flight in the subsequent 'test matches' with Willie an essential member of the team. Described as 'a neat, scientific player', he skippered the 'Blades' and was a major influence at Bramall Lane for four seasons. United's committee valued his opinions greatly, and he is credited as having been largely responsible for the early development of the Yorkshire club. Willie was also instrumental in honing the latent skills of the young Ernest 'Nudger' Needham, who was to become one of England's all-time great internationals.

On the completion of the 1894–95 campaign, the dominant Scot returned to his native city to play for Dundee for nearly three seasons. After a trial period with West Herts (forerunners of Watford) in March 1898, 34-year-old Willie was signed by the infant Brighton United in May 1898 and was a huge attraction, his experience proving invaluable during the club's first season. He performed admirably at right-back but was released in May 1899 to join Shrewsbury Town in the Birmingham League where he was still playing at the time of his death from a heart-attack at the age of 36. In 1945 a former Sheffield United stalwart reminisced: 'Willie Hendry was the best player Sheffield ever had' — praise indeed!

HILL, BOB

inside-right/centre-forward   *30 apps, 15 goals*
full name: Robert Hill
born: Scotland
debut: Queen's Park Rangers (a), 2.9.1899 (SL D1)

One of several vastly experienced players signed by the Brighton United club during its brief existence, Bob Hill had played for Linfield while serving in Ireland with a Scottish regiment, and gained two Irish Cup winner's medals, in 1891 and 1892. Joining Sheffield United as a professional towards the end of their first season as a Football League club in February 1893, he made his first appearance in a friendly match under the pseudonym 'Jones', but, more legitimately, scored 22 goals in 57 League appearances for the 'Blades' before moving to Manchester City in November 1895. However, Bob couldn't hold down a regular place in City's first team and appeared in only 21 Second Division matches before his release in May 1897.

Appointed player-coach of Watford St Mary's in February 1898, he subsequently appeared briefly with West Herts (forerunners of Watford) before moving on to Millwall in October 1898, and arrived in Sussex in May 1899 for the second and final season of Brighton United's existence. The versatile, fleet-footed Scot held a regular place in United's side, top-scoring with fifteen goals in all competitions, but when the club folded in March 1900 he returned to his native Scotland with Dundee.

HOWES, ARTHUR

goalkeeper   *11 apps*
debut: Queen's Park Rangers (a), 2.9.1899 (SL D1)
See *Albion Players Who's Who*

LONGAIR, BILL

centre-half   *44 apps, 3 goals*
full name: William Longair
born: Dundee, Angus, Scotland, 19.7.1870
died: Dundee, Angus, Scotland, 28.11.1926
debut: Southampton (a), 3.9.1898 (SL D1)

B righton United's skipper during their first season, Bill Longair began his career playing junior football in his home city with Rockwell and Dundee North End. After joining Dundee F.C. on their formation in 1893, he played in their opening Scottish League fixture, a 3–3 draw with Glasgow Rangers, and went on to represent Scotland against Ireland in Belfast in March 1894; he had also been selected for the game with Wales a week earlier but had had to withdraw because of an injury. After one appearance for Newton Heath (forerunners of Manchester United) in the Football League in April 1895, Bill signed for Sunderland in May 1896, but again made just

one appearance and was quickly on the move to Burnley who paid £50 for his transfer in November. In May 1897 he returned to Dundee, and arrived on the South Coast along with six of his team-mates twelve months later.

Originally a centre-forward noted for his heading ability, Bill performed admirably at centre-half for the 'Greenbacks' and became a great favourite with the Brighton public who were sorry to see him released in May 1899 to rejoin Dundee for a third spell.

United's loss was Dundee's gain, though. As the *Scottish Sport* put it, 'The well-beloved of all centre-halves in Scotland has returned to the fold.' When he retired in 1902, Bill became trainer at Dens Park until 1924, and was then appointed groundsman until his death two years later. In his early days at Dundee he was tagged with the somewhat strange nickname 'Plum'.

LOW, JOHN

wing-half   *54 apps*
full name: John Hamilton Low
born: Dundee, Angus, Scotland, 29.10.1874
debut: Bedminster (a), 14.9.1898 (SL D1)

One of seven men recruited from Dundee in May 1898, John Low had been a reserve-team player with the Scottish First Division side but found greater scope for his talents with Brighton United. Equally at home in either wing-half berth, he proved a great success at Hove and appeared in 54 matches. In March 1900, following the demise of United, John moved to Bolton Wanderers.

McARTHUR, WILLIE

utility player   69 apps, 23 goals
full name: William McArthur
born: Lintmill, Renfrewshire, Scotland, 17.8.1870
debut: Southampton (a), 3.9.1898 (SL D1)

Willie McArthur played for Renton and Sunderland Albion as a youngster, and assisted Middlesbrough Ironopolis to three successive Northern League championships before joining First Division Bolton Wanderers for the 1893–94 season. In April 1894 he signed for Leicester Fosse, then in the Midland League, and went on to score 27 goals in 55 Second Division matches for the club when they entered the Football League at the end of that season. Released to play for Dundee in May 1896, Willie joined the migration to the South Coast in May 1898 and proved a valuable acquisition; although his recognised spot was at centre-forward, he played in six different positions for Brighton United.

When the ill-fated club folded in March 1900, Willie enlisted with the Army and served as a private with the Royal Sussex Regiment during the South African Boer War, but on his return to England and Sussex he was reinstated as an amateur and became a dominant figure on the local scene with Worthing, where he was a team-mate of the future Albion star Charlie Webb. Before hanging up his boots in 1909, he skippered both the Sussex and the West Sussex League representative sides; triumphed in two Senior Cup finals; won three West Sussex Senior League titles; and gained three Royal Irish Rifles Charity Cup winner's medals.

McAVOY, FRANK

centre-half   69 apps, 1 goal
debut: Southampton (a), 3.9.1898 (SL D1)
See *Albion Players Who's Who*

McLEOD, RODDY

inside-right/centre-forward   41 apps, 29 goals
full name: Roderick McLeod
born: Kilsyth, Stirlingshire, Scotland, February 1871
died: Walworth, Southwark, London, 20.12.1931
debut: Southampton (a), 3.9.1898 (SL D1)

Roddy McLeod played for Westburn Juniors on leaving school and graduated via Partick Thistle to West Bromwich Albion in January 1891. In just over six years with the 'Throstles' he was an outstanding success, scoring 52 goals in 151 League matches and appearing in two F.A. Cup finals: in 1892 when West Brom. beat Aston Villa 3–0 at Kennington Oval, and in 1895 when Villa gained revenge over their great rivals, winning 1–0 at The Crystal Palace. Roddy was transferred to Leicester Fosse in August 1897 where he met up with trainer John Jackson, and when Brighton United were formed he was recruited along with Jackson in May 1898, the latter as trainer-manager. The star of the side during that first season, Roddy found the net on 29 occasions in all competitions, but moved along the coast to Southampton in April 1899. However, he fell out with the "Saints'" management after being omitted from the 1900 F.A. Cup final team and left for Brentford the following August where he helped the 'Bees' to top the Second Division of the Southern League in the first of two seasons with the club. Despite being rather frail, Roddy was a bundle of tricks and capable of filling any of the forward positions; he was tremendously popular wherever he played.

McWHIRTER, PETER

outside-right   33 apps, 5 goals
born: Glasgow, Lanarkshire, Scotland, 23.6.1871
died: 1943
debut: Bedminster (a), 14.9.1898 (SL D1)

Peter McWhirter emigrated to Canada at the age of sixteen and remained in North America for six years, during which time he played for the Toronto Scots and Chicago Thistles clubs, and also represented Canada v. Michigan in an inter-state match. On returning to Scotland at Christmas 1893, Peter joined Second Division Greenock Morton, then spent the 1894–95 season in Clyde's reserve team before signing for Leicester Fosse in October 1895. Eighteen first-team outings at Filbert Street were followed by a spell with the Southampton-based Southern League club Freemantle during the early part of the 1896–97 campaign, after which he briefly rejoined his emigrant family in Canada.

The itinerant Scot spent the 1897–98 season with the Bristol-based side Warmley, assisting them to promotion to the First Division of the Southern League. The summer of 1898 saw Peter join the staff of the newly formed Brighton United club. He started out at right-half in his spell at the County Ground, but soon resumed his usual role on the right wing. After appearing in 33 competitive games during United's first season, he was released to rejoin Leicester Fosse in August 1899, where he spent a year in the reserves before disappearing from the first-class scene.

MALLOCH, JOCK

inside/outside-left   66 apps, 13 goals
full name: John Malloch
born: Lochee, Dundee, Angus, Scotland, 2.11.1877
debut: Southampton (a), 3.9.1898 (SL D1)

One of the seven Dundee players signed by Brighton United in May 1898, Jock Malloch had joined Dundee from the local junior club East Craigie in 1897 and went on to enjoy a highly successful career. Just 20 years of age on his arrival at the County Ground, he was a remarkably consistent performer and developed a fine partnership with his erstwhile Dundee team-mate Davie Willocks down the "Greenbacks'" left wing. He remained with the club throughout its brief existence, playing in 66 competitive matches and missing only a few games through injury, but after United folded in March 1900 he signed for First Division Sheffield Wednesday.

In making 144 League appearances for the 'Owls', Jock won fame nationally and gained championship medals in two successive seasons, 1902–03 and 1903–04. In March 1908 he enjoyed a joint benefit together with goalkeeper Jack Lyall, a 2–1 First Division defeat of Nottingham Forest, before ending his League career with a spell at Barnsley from January 1909. Jock resided in the West Yorkshire village of South Elmsall and continued to play for the nearby Frickley Colliery side.

MERCER, TOBY

utility forward   28 apps, 4 goals
full name: John Thomas Mercer
born: Belfast, Co. Antrim, Ireland, 1877
died: January 1947
debut: Queen's Park Rangers (a), 2.9.1899 (SL D1)

After a trial with Preston North End, 'Toby' Mercer made his name with Belfast Distillery, where he won an Irish League championship medal in 1899 and played for Ireland against England (twice), Scotland and Wales. In May 1899 he signed for Brighton United and, though normally a right-winger, appeared in all the forward positions, but he was transferred to Leicester Fosse in February 1900. Toby made little impression at Filbert Street and returned to Ireland with Linfield during the close season of 1900 where he was a prominent member of the team which carried off the Irish League-and-Cup double in 1901–02. In February 1903, Toby rejoined Distillery and gained another Irish Cup winner's medal that season before crossing the Irish Sea once more to play for Derby County in the First Division in October 1903.

Described as 'a dashing player, though prone to over-enthusiasm at times', he won a total of eleven full international caps and also represented the Irish League on six occasions. After retiring in 1905, Toby became a successful businessman in his native city. A director of Linfield for 20 years and subsequently chairman of Distillery, he also ran a junior club called Belfast United and recommended a number of young players – including Albion's Jimmy Hopkins – to Arsenal in the early 1920s, several of whom went on to represent Ireland. Toby was chairman of the Irish League from 1941 to 1942.

MILLS, ANDY

left-back   33 apps, 1 goal
full name: Andrew Mills
born: Knighton, Radnor, Wales, 15.12.1877
debut: Queen's Park Rangers (a), 2.9.1899 (SL D1)

Andy Mills missed just one match during Brighton United's second – and curtailed – campaign in the Southern League, having joined the club from Swindon Town in June 1899; he had also had brief experience with Blackburn Rovers, making two appearances in their First Division side during the 1897–98 campaign. He left Hove when United folded in March 1900 and signed for Leicester Fosse in May, where he made 64 League appearances over three seasons. In February 1903, while playing in a Welsh international trial match, Andy received the injury which effectively ended his football career, although he did turn out briefly for Fosse after recovering.

NORMAN, WALTER

right-back   1 app
full name: Walter Oliver Norman
born: Cuckfield, Sussex, 1876
debut: Chatham (a), 22.11.1899 (T&MC)

Walter Norman gave tremendous service to the Burgess Hill club over many years, initially as a stalwart member of the playing staff and subsequently as a committee man. Also a referee of considerable note, he served on the councils of the Mid Sussex League and the Sussex County F.A., being vice-chairman of the latter in 1908–09 and chairman in 1909–10. Walter assisted Brighton United in a 2–1 defeat at Chatham in a Thames & Medway Combination fixture during the season of the club's liquidation, 1899–1900.

OAKDEN, HARRY

outside-right   18 apps, 5 goals
born: Derby, Derbyshire, 1877
debut: Queen's Park Rangers (a), 2.9.1899 (SL D1)

Harry Oakden joined Derby County from the local Alvaston & Boulton club in November 1898, and scored five goals in twelve League and Cup games for the 'Rams' during the remainder of the 1898–99 season. Brought to Sussex as a replacement for Peter McWhirter in May 1899, Harry was never an automatic choice in the Brighton United side and, when the club was wound up, left for Belfast-based Distillery together with Paddy Farrell.

On returning to England in September 1901 he joined Swindon Town, where he played in 87 Southern League matches before being forced into retirement through injury in 1906 (for which he was granted a benefit match in September). A cousin, F. Oakden, had a trial with Brighton United and partnered him on the right flank in two friendly fixtures.

Harry was inadvertently a major factor behind United's liquidation when he reported the club to the F.A. in order to obtain £23 in wages owing to him. The Association's Emergency Committee ordered the club to pay him or face suspension, a decision which helped convince United that they were unable to carry on.

PAIGE, JIMMY

inside-right   7 apps, 3 goals
full name: James Eden Paige
born: Shoreham-by-Sea, Sussex, 1875
debut: Swindon Town (h), 28.1.1899 (SL D1)

Jimmy Paige was an outstanding member of the Southwick team which appeared in four consecutive Sussex Senior Cup finals, finishing as runners-up in 1894, 1895 and 1896 before winning the county's premier trophy in 1897. Also a Sussex representative, Jimmy played in the Southwick side which played Brighton United in the latter's first-ever match in September 1898, and signed professional forms for United in January 1899.

However, when he turned out for Southwick against Worthing in a West Sussex Senior League match three months later, the 'Little Wickers' were reported to the Football Association for fielding a professional. As a result of its inquiries, an F.A. Commission suspended Paige for one month and fined Southwick £5, a huge sum for the village side at the time which brought about its demise. (Southwick Swifts emerged from the ashes, but it was 1906 before a Southwick Football Club reappeared on the scene.) Jimmy was subsequently reinstated as an amateur and played for Brighton Athletic.

PARRY, Maurice

wing-half   *37 apps, 1 goal*
full name: Maurice Pryce Parry
born: Trefonen, Shropshire, 1878
died: Bootle, Lancashire, 24.3.1935
debut: Queen's Park Rangers (a), 2.9.1899 (SL D1)

A superbly-built half-back – six feet tall and weighing in at thirteen stone – Maurice Parry played for Newtown, Long Eaton Rangers and Oswestry United before joining the Football League ranks with Leicester Fosse in August 1898. At this point he had no thoughts of making a career in the game and played just once in Fosse's senior team before moving on to nearby Loughborough in February 1899, but, after appearing in twelve Football League games during the remainder of the 1898–99 season (when the 'Luffs' finished next to bottom of the Second Division), Maurice was released in May to join Brighton United as a professional.

Just 20 years of age, he was one of the few successes in a calamitous campaign which saw the death of the club because of poor finances, but United's demise proved a boon for Maurice who then joined Liverpool where he quickly won fame. A regular member of the "Reds'" side for almost nine years, he amassed 207 League appearances, winning a Second Division winner's medal in 1904–05 and a Football League championship medal the following term. He was also selected for Wales against the other three home countries in his first season at Anfield and went on to win sixteen full caps.

In May 1909, Maurice moved to Partick Thistle where he retired in 1911. He subsequently coached in South Africa, and became manager of Second Division Rotherham County from 1921 to 1923 before moving abroad again as a coach in Barcelona, Frankfurt and Cologne; he also had spells coaching in Liverpool and Jersey. Badly gassed during the First World War, Maurice died of bronchitis at the age of 56 in 1935. His brother Tom was also a Welsh international with Oswestry, while his son Frank played for Everton, Grimsby Town, Accrington Stanley and Nelson.

SHARP, Alf

centre/inside-forward   *13 apps, 4 goals*
debut: Kettering Town (a), 18.2.1899 (UL)
See *Albion Players Who's Who*

SPICER, Tom

goalkeeper   *43 apps*
full name: Thomas Ashby Spicer
born: Brighton, Sussex, 1876
debut: Southampton (a), 18.1.1899 (UL)

An amateur from the Brighton-based Silver Star club, Tom Spicer came to the notice of the United management with a superb display when guesting for Brighton Athletic against the professionals in a friendly match at the County Ground on Boxing Day 1898. Invited to play for United against Eastbourne Swifts the following day, he made his debut in the Southern League team in February 1899 and quickly established himself between the posts to the exclusion of the more experienced Leo Bullimer.

Tom remained first-choice 'keeper the following term, impressing with a series of brilliant performances in a struggling side, and signed for Woolwich Arsenal following the club's demise in March 1900. However, with future England star Jimmy Ashcroft to contend with, Tom found his opportunities limited and was released to join Brentford in May 1901 where he remained until leaving the first-class game in 1906, having appeared in more than 50 Southern League games for the 'Bees'.

SUTHERLAND, Jim

left-half/outside-left   *2 apps*
debut: New Brompton (a), 17.2.1900 (SL D1)
See *Albion Players Who's Who*

TURNER, Bob

utility defender   *2 apps*
full name: Robert Turner
born: Manchester, Lancashire, c. 1877
debut: Sheppey United (a), 5.9.1899 (T&MC)

Bob Turner set out on a somewhat uncertain professional career with Southern League side Gravesend United in May 1897, but joined his home-town club Newton Heath (now Manchester United) twelve months later, appearing in two Second Division matches during the 1898–99 season before being released to join Brighton United in May 1899. He failed to settle at the County Ground, though, and made just three first-team appearances during a brief stay, the last of which, a 5-1 victory over Cowes, was subsequently deleted when the Isle of Wight club folded.

In December 1899 he signed for Southern League rivals Thames Ironworks (now West Ham United), then played for Fulham (1900–01) and the Irish League club Glentoran (1901–02). Bob returned to England with Watford in August 1902, but his time with the Hertfordshire club was even shorter than his spell with Brighton United as, a few weeks later, he was suspended for a breach of discipline and subsequently dismissed. A short time later, in October 1902, he was engaged by Rossendale United playing in the Lancashire Combination.

WILLIAMS, C.

centre-forward   *4 apps, 1 goal*
debut: Eastbourne (h), 30.9.1899 (FAC Q1)

Williams was a prominent player for both Worthing Athletic and Worthing in the West Sussex Senior League before joining Brighton United as a professional in June 1899. He made his first-team debut in the absence of Toby Mercer in an F.A. Cup qualifying tie against Eastbourne, and scored a goal in a 6–1 victory. Williams subsequently played in just three Southern League matches, although he appeared in a number of friendly games up to the time of the club's closure in March 1900.

WILLOCKS, Davie

inside/outside-left   *60 apps, 24 goals*
full name: David King Willocks
born: Arbroath, Angus, Scotland, 6.1.1871
debut: Southampton (a), 3.9.1898 (SL D1)

Davie Willocks started out with Bolton Wanderers at the age of 21 in 1892, and registered eight goals in 32 First Division appearances over two seasons with the 'Trotters'. A versatile forward, he played in every attacking position for Burton Swifts after moving to the Staffordshire club during the summer of 1894, and top-scored in both his seasons there, totalling 25 goals from 58 Second Division outings. After returning to his native Scotland with Dundee in May 1896, Davie was a regular member of their side until signing for Brighton United in May 1898.

He developed a great understanding on the left with Jock Malloch at the County Ground and scored 21 goals in all competitions in United's opening season, but departed for his home-town club, Arbroath, in the Scottish Northern League in December 1899, where he remained until retiring in 1905.

Records and Reference

This section contains reference material and club records relating to the personnel of Brighton & Hove Albion from 1901 until 1997. Records are to the end of the 1996–97 season, but the boardroom changes of September 1997 have also been recorded.

For records relating to the performances of the club, and for detailed match line-ups, results and season-by-season commentaries, the reader is referred to *Seagulls! The Story of Brighton & Hove Albion F.C.* by the same authors and publishers (ISBN 0 9521337 0 9)

Chairmen of The Brighton and Hove Albion Football Club, Limited

George Broadbridge (1904–05)
Chartered secretary, London

William Goodwin (1905–09 & 1930–40)
Fishmonger, Brighton

Peter Vey (1909–14)
Draper, Brighton

Henry Miles (1914–19)
Electrician, Brighton

Charles Brown (1919–30)
Tailor, Brighton

Albert Hillman (1940)
Contractor; Mayor of Hove 1936–40

Charles Wakeling (1940–51)
Accountant, director of greyhound stadium, Hove

Major Carlo Campbell DSO MC (1951–58)
Director of food companies and greyhound stadium, Hove

Alec Whitcher (1958–60)
Mechanical engineer, Haywards Heath

Gerald Paling (1960–62)
Civil servant, Hove

Eric Courtney-King (1962–68)
Company director, Shoreham-by-Sea

Tom Whiting (1968–72)
Solicitor, Hove

Len Stringer (joint 1972–73)
Funeral director, Hove

Mike Bamber (joint 1972–73 & 1973–84)
Farmer, property developer, Piddinghoe

Bryan Bedson (1984–87)
Printing company director, Patching

Dudley Sizen (1987–91)
Plastics company director, Lindfield

Greg Stanley (1991–95)
D.I.Y. company chairman, Arundel

Bill Archer (1995–97)
D.I.Y. company managing director, Blackburn

Dick Knight (1997–)
Advertising company chairman, Hove

Note that the club was run by a committee from 1901 until 1904 before it was incorporated as a limited company. The chairmen of the club committee were:
Daniel Bott (1901–02)
Harry Callaghan (1902–04)

Note also that Alderman Cyril Clarke (Mayor of Hove 1956–58) was acting chairman following the death of Alec Whitcher in 1960 and before the appointment of Gerald Paling.

Directors of The Brighton and Hove Albion Football Club, Limited

original member of the board

Director	Description	Service
ALDERTON, Reg*	Commercial traveller, Hove	1904–05
BROADBRIDGE, George*	Chartered secretary, London; later Lord Broadbridge of Brighton	1904–05 & 1905–06
BUNKER, Charles*	Fishmonger, Hove	1904
COOTER, Tom*	Tailor, Brighton	1904–05
GRINYER, Albert*	Landlord of Albion Inn, Hove	1904
PARKER, Ben*	Landlord of Cliftonville Hotel, Hove	1904–05 & 1905
STEVENS, Fred*	Jeweller and watchmaker, Hove	1904–05
BAKER, William	Landlord of Standard Hotel, Brighton	1904–05
GADD, Harry	Hotelier, Albion Hotel, Queenis Road, Brighton	1904–05
CLARK, Noah	Fishmonger, Brighton	1904–05 & 1906–30
COHEN, Meyer	Finanacier, Brighton	1904
MERRIMAN, Richard	Brighton	1904 & 1904–05
SMITH, Frank	Merchant, Hove Park Stores	1905
GOODWIN, William	Fishmonger, Brighton	1905–40
BLOGG, William	Printer, Hove	1905
CARDWELL, Charles	Ironmonger and engineer, Brighton	1905
BUTCHER, Cecil	Accountantis clerk, Hove	1905–29
MILES, Henry	Electrician, Brighton	1905–40
VEY, Peter	Draper, Brighton	1905–31
BROWN, Charles	Tailor, Brighton	1906–30 & 1931–36
BANFIELD, Tom	Ironmonger, Brighton	1906–12
STAFFORD, William	Store owner, Western Road, Brighton	1911–14
HARRINGTON, Tom	Coachbuilder, Brighton	1914–28
FARR, John	Tailor, Brighton	1923–35
BALL, Alfred	Tax collector, Hove	1923–39
BRAZIER, Henry	Builder and fruit grower, Worthing	1926–33
RIDGE, Herbert	Solicitor, Hove	1930–43
HILLMAN, Albert	Contractor; Mayor of Hove 1936–40	1933–40
BAYLIS, Charles	Retired gentleman, Hove; ex-director of Reading F.C.	1934–40
NEAL, William	Company director, Hove	1937–40
SERVICE, Hubert	Company director, Eastbourne	1939–40
WAKELING, Charles	Accountant; director of greyhound stadium, Hove	1940–51
CAMPBELL, Carlo	Director of food companies and of greyhound stadium, Hove	1940–58
WHITCHER, Alec	Mechanical engineer and company director, Haywards Heath	1943–60
PALING, Gerald	Civil servant, Hove	1946–62
HOLLIS, General Sir Leslie	Company director, Haywards Heath	1954–60
COVERDALE, Harry	Jeweller, Hove	1954–60
PEMBROKE, Arthur	Architect, Hove	1954–63
GREIG, Alexander	Medical practioner, Hove	1956–62
CLARKE, Cyril	Company director; Mayor of Hove 1956–58	1958–62
COURTNEY-KING, Eric	Company director, Shoreham-by-Sea	1960–68
WHITING, Tom	Solicitor, Hove	1960–73
BRAZIER, Anthony	Company director and son of Henry Brazier, Findon	1960–67
PARIS, Harold	Building company director, Hove	1962–71
DUPONT, Alfred	Business consultant and director of greyhound stadium, Hove	1962–65 & 1966–67
STRINGER, Len	Funeral company director, Hove	1962–73
ARNOLD, Fred	Company director, Brighton	1962–64
WISDOM, Norman	Company director and entertainer, West Chiltington	1964–70
STEVENS, Victor	Chartered accountant, Dorking	1968–70
DE BOER, Tony	Company director, Ditchling Common	1968–73
HUTCHISON, George	Farmer, Hove	1969–74
BAMBER, Mike	Farmer, estate agent and surveyor, property developer, Piddinghoe	1970–84
BLOOM, Harry	Car sales company director, Brighton	1970–80
APPLEBY, Tom	Cattle and general haulage contractor, Piltdown	1971–85 & 1990–91
HYAMS, Norman	Development and investment company director, Wimbledon	1972–83
SMITH, Bill	Building company director, Hove	1972–79
SIZEN, Dudley	Plastics company director,Lindfield	1973–83 & 1984–91 & 1993–96
WICKENDEN, Keith	Ferry company director; M.P. for Dorking 1979–83	1973–83
BEDSON, Bryan	Printing company director	1983–89
GREENWOOD, Ron	Former England manager, Hove	1983–84
CAMPBELL, John	Marine consultant, Chelwood Gate	1983–92 & 1992–94
KENT, Peter	Visual aids company director, Cuckfield	1984–90 & 1990–92 & 1993–96
CROWN, Richard	Computer company director, Hove	1985
BLOOM, Ray	Company director and hotelier; son of Harry Bloom	1985–96
APPLEBY, Gene	Wife of Tom Appleby, Little Horsted	1985–90
STANLEY, Greg	D.I.Y. company director, Angmering	1985–97
SHANNON, Frank	Motor company financial director, Hove	1985–89
CLARKE, Bernard	Accountant, Hove	1988–93 & 1993–96
SULLIVAN, Dennis	Advertising executive, Hove	1990–93 & 1994–96
ARCHER, Bill	D.I.Y. company director, Blackburn	1990–
LLOYD, Barry	Manager, Brighton and Hove Albion F.C.	1991–93
BELLOTTI, David	Chief executive, Brighton and Hove Albion; ex-M.P. for Eastbourne	1993–97
STANLEY, Diana	Midwife; wife of Greg Stanley	1993–97
KNIGHT, Dick	Advertising company chairman, Hove	1997–
PINNOCK, Bob	Accountant, Hassocks	1997–
PERRY, Martin	Director, Alfred McAlpine Special Projects, London	1997–
SMITH, Sir John	Former Deputy Commissioner, Metropolitan Police; consultant to F.A.	1997–
FAULKNER, Richard	Vice-chairman of Football Trust	1997–

Players with more than 100 appearances

Apps	Player	Apps	Player	Apps	Player	Apps	Player	Apps	Player
566	Wilson, Tug	255	Templeman, John	193	Curran, Jack	155	Wilson, Danny	123	O'Reilly, Gary
491	O'Sullivan, Peter	252	Burtenshaw, Steve	193	Gould, Wally	152	Stevens, Gary	122	Mansell, Jack
488	Gall, Norman	252	Chivers, Gary	192	Rollings, Andy	151	Dublin, Keith	121	Grealish, Tony
466	Farrell, Bobby	252	Horton, Brian	192	Rust, Nicky	151	Kent, Harry	121	Minton, Jeff
443	Longstaff, Bert	251	Risdon, Stan	191	Davie, Jock	151	Tiler, Ken	120	Nogan, Kurt
436	Wilson, Glen	247	Napier, John	191	Marsden, Harry	150	Mellor, Ian	120	Smith, Peter
424	Tennant, Des	246	Marriott, Ernie	191	Thomson, Charlie	150	Smith, Reg	119	Anthony, Walter
396	Wilkinson, Reg	245	Crumplin, John	190	Piper, Steve	149	Whent, Jack	115	Jennings, Sam
386	Powney, Brian	241	Woodhouse, Jack	186	Stevens, Jack	148	Young, Eric	115	Leadbetter, Jimmy
375	Wilkins, Dean	238	Leeming, Joe	185	Neil, Andy	147	Wilkinson, Howard	115	McNab, Neil
369	Booth, Billy	237	Martin, Ted	183	Case, Jimmy	146	Livesey, Charlie	115	Munday, Stuart
369	Gatting, Steve	234	Webb, Stan	183	Towner, Tony	146	Tiddy, Mike	114	Cattlin, Chris
366	Stephens, Bert	233	Hopkins, Jimmy	182	Whitfield, Ken	146	Wilson, Harry	114	Tawse, Brian
353	Wilson, Joe A.	232	Spearritt, Eddie	181	Kirkwood, Dan	143	Brett, Frank	113	Moore, Bernard
349	Walker, Dave	231	Jenkins, Jack	179	Jones, Bullet	142	Spencer, Frank	112	Joynes, Dick
341	Darling, Len	227	Ward, Peter	178	Langley, Jimmy	141	Bremner, Kevin	112	Miller, Bill
338	Turner, Dave	226	Henderson, Stewart	178	Mundy, Albert	136	Turner, Tom	110	Byrne, John
332	Foster, Steve	225	Hayes, Billy	177	Williams, Gary	134	Mee, Gordon	110	Longdon, Billy
332	Little, Wally	224	Moseley, Graham	176	Goodchild, Johnny	133	Harburn, Peter	110	Willemse, Stan
331	Chapman, Ian	221	Collins, Jimmy	175	Hutchings, Chris	133	Robinson, Michael	109	Murray, Bert
320	Whiting, Bob	220	Baxter, Bobby	174	Connor, Terry	132	Curbishley, Alan	109	Pearce, Graham
319	Smith, Potter	219	Foreman, Denis	174	Hulme, Arthur	132	Reed, Billy G.	107	Bennett, Ken
315	Codner, Robert	219	Howard, Frankie	174	Lawrenson, Mark	131	Needham, Archie	107	Williams, Reg
315	Mooney, Paul	217	King, Ernie	166	Nelson, Garry	130	Walker, Clive	106	Thompson, Jack
297	Jennings, Roy	217	McCarthy, Paul	165	McNichol, Johnny	129	Cassidy, Bill	105	Wood, Paul
296	Gill, Eric	215	Baldwin, Harry	164	Ball, Jack	128	McNeill, Ian	104	Attwood, Arthur
293	Gordon, Dennis	209	Cook, Tommy	162	Penney, Steve	127	Lawton, Nobby	104	Dutton, Harry
291	Napier, Kit	202	Willard, Jess	160	Keeley, John	125	Smith, Gordon	103	Allsopp, Tommy
279	Bertolini, Jack	201	Digweed, Perry	159	Higham, Gunner	124	Bissett, Nicky	102	MacDonald, Hugh
275	Webb, Charlie	199	Ryan, Gerry	158	Grummitt, Peter	124	McCoy, Tim	102	Ritchie, Andy
272	Coomber, George	195	Nightingale, Jack	156	McGhie, Joe	123	Bisset, Tommy	100	Hastings, Bill

Appearance record holders

Apps	Player	Date of record
65	Jock Caldwell	–
174	Arthur Hulme	14.1.1905
443	Bert Longstaff	1.4.1911
566	Tug Wilson	31.12.1932

Most appearances by competition

Totals include appearances as substitute

Competition	Apps	Player
FL (total)	509	Tug Wilson
FAPL / FL D1 (old)	156	Steve Foster
FL D1 (new) / D2 (old)	191	Steve Gatting
FL D2 (new) / D3 (old)	322	Norman Gall
FL D3 (new) / D4 (old)	91	Jimmy Collins
FL D3(S)	509	Tug Wilson
FAC	49	Tug Wilson
FAC (proper only)	45	Tug Wilson
FLC	31	Peter O'Sullivan
Wartime	216	Stan Risdon
SL D1	315	Bert Longstaff
SL D2	26	Jock Caldwell

Consecutive-appearance record holders

Apps	Player	Date of record
24	Jock Caldwell	–
35	Frank Scott	14.2.1903
73	Billy Roberts	3.9.1904
143	Billy Booth	12.2.1910
175	Billy Hayes	17.11.1923
247	Eric Gill	26.9.1956

Players with 100 or more consecutive appearances

The date given is the first game of the sequence

Apps	Player	Date
247	Eric Gill	21.2.1953
194	Peter O'Sullivan	16.10.1970
193	Jack Bertolini	25.4.1959
175	Billy Hayes	2.10.1920
146	Gary Williams	15.10.1977
143	Billy Booth	28.10.1908
139	Brian Horton	4.9.1976
124	Peter Grummitt	9.11.1974
123	Dean Wilkins	29.4.1989
115	Reg Wilkinson	9.10.1926
113	Jimmy Collins	2.10.1962
112	Johnny McNichol	22.10.1949
106	John Napier	7.2.1970
105	Bob Whiting	6.3.1909
104	George Coomber	30.8.1922
101	Jack Mansell	13.9.1950
100	Garry Nelson	12.9.1987

Players selected as sub on 40 or more occasions

88	Crumplin, John
84	Ormerod, Mark
73	Ryan, Gerry
49	Andrews, Phil
47	Funnell, Simon
46	Owers, Adrian
43	Chapman, Ian
43	Fox, Simon
42	Armstrong, Gerry

Most games in a season

Games	Player	Season
57	Norman Gall	1966–67
"	Keith Dublin	1987–88
"	John Keeley	1987–88
"	Dean Wilkins	1990–91
56	Bobby Baxter	1966–67
"	Dave Turner	1966–67
"	Graham Cross	1976–77
"	Steve Piper	1976–77
"	Peter Ward	1976–77
"	Steve Gatting	1987–88
"	Nicky Rust	1995–96
55	Billy Booth	1908–09
"	Dean Wilkins	1987–88
"	Clive Walker	1990–91

Players substituted on 20 or more occasions

35	Wilkins, Dean
32	Crumplin, John
28	O'Sullivan, Peter
24	Ryan, Gerry
23	Turner, Dave
21	Chapman, Ian
21	Towner, Tony
20	Codner, Robert
20	Wood, Paul

Players who came on as sub on 20 or more occasions

52	Ryan, Gerry
39	Crumplin, John
31	Andrews, Phil
24	Chapman, Ian
21	Munday, Stuart
20	Armstrong, Gerry

Player with careers of 10 years or more

Players whose last game for Albion was 10 years or more after their first. Spans in years and days. * played for Albion in more than one spell.

Player	Career span	Appearances
Foster, Steve*	16–047	332
Longstaff, Bert	14–349	443
Darling, Len	14–193	341
Case, Jimmy*	14–063	183
Burtenshaw, Steve	13–236	252
Wilson, Tug	13–175	566
McCoy, Tim*	13–077	124
Martin, Ted	13–033	237
Marriott, Ernie	13–018	246
Dugnolle, Jack*	12–181	74
Farrell, Bobby	12–167	466
Wilkins, Dean*	12–151	375
Moore, Bernard*	12–125	113
Higham, Gunner	12–116	159
Digweed, Perry	12–111	201
Stephens, Bert	12–090	366
Powney, Brian	11–364	386
Booth, Billy	11–242	369
Gall, Norman	11–182	488
Ball, Jack	11–021	164
Coomber, George	11–009	272
Jennings, Roy	10–352	297
Woodhouse, Jack	10–331	241
Wilson, Joe	10–261	353
O'Sullivan, Peter*	10–260	491
Risdon, Stan	10–236	251
Miller, Bill	10–234	112
Wilson, Glen	10–212	436
Jones, Bullet*	10–110	179
Beech, George*	10–081	8
Tennant, Des	10–068	424

The most and least successful players

Based on 1 point for a win, 0.5 points for a draw. Qualification is 100 appearances.

Most successful		Least successful	
Player	Average	Player	Average
Hastings, Bill	0.67	Longdon, Billy	0.33
Harburn, Peter	0.65	Risdon, Stan	0.39
Mundy, Albert	0.63	McNab, Neil	0.40
Cattlin, Chris	0.63	Rust, Nicky	0.41
Leadbetter, Jimmy	0.62	Minton, Jeff	0.41
McGhie, Joe	0.62	Mee, Gordon	0.41
Foreman, Denis	0.61	Smith, Peter	0.41
Gill, Eric	0.61	Tiddy, Mike	0.41
Gordon, Dennis	0.61	Stevens, Gary	0.42
Tiler, Ken	0.61	Smith, Gordon	0.43
Webb, Charlie	0.60	Robinson, Michael	0.43
Langley, Jimmy	0.60	Munday, Stuart	0.43
Jennings, Sam	0.59	Ritchie, Andy	0.44
Whitfield, Ken	0.59	McNeill, Ian	0.44
Whiting, Bob	0.59	Wood, Paul	0.44
Smith, Reg	0.59	Bertolini, Jack	0.44
Curran, Jack	0.59	Chapman, Ian	0.45
Dutton, Harry	0.58	Bissett, Nicky	0.45
Cook, Tommy	0.58	Marriott, Ernie	0.45
Tennant, Des	0.58	Byrne, John	0.45
Leeming, Joe	0.58	Grealish, Tony	0.45
Nightingale, Jack	0.58	Codner, Robert	0.46
Wilson, Glen	0.58	Wilson, Joe	0.46
Rollings, Andy	0.58	Darling, Len	0.46
Jones, Bullet	0.57	Willemse, Stan	0.46
McCoy, Tim	0.57		
Needham, Archie	0.57		
Horton, Brian	0.57		

Players with more than 20 goals

Goals	Goals/game	Player	Goals	Goals/game	Player	Goals	Goals/game	Player	Goals	Goals/game	Player
174	0.48	Stephens, Bert	54	0.58	Hall, Jack H.	36	0.11	Little, Wally	25	0.29	Saunders, Dean
123	0.59	Cook, Tommy	52	0.46	Miller, Bill	35	0.23	Mellor, Ian	25	0.20	Smith, Gordon
120	0.63	Davie, Jock	49	0.14	Wilson, Joe A.	34	0.68	Scott, Frank	25	0.14	Towner, Tony
99	0.34	Napier, Kit	48	0.22	Collins, Jimmy	34	0.68	Vallance, Hugh	25	0.11	Spearritt, Eddie
95	0.42	Ward, Peter	47	0.15	Codner, Robert	34	0.10	Turner, Dave	24	0.35	Gilliver, Alan
95	0.20	Farrell, Bobby	47	0.11	Tennant, Des	33	0.52	Addinall, Bert	24	0.12	Willard, Jess
90	0.51	Mundy, Albert	46	0.26	Goodchild, Johnny	33	0.29	Leadbetter, Jimmy	23	0.82	Shafto, John
86	0.19	Longstaff, Bert	46	0.24	Gould, Wally	33	0.17	Nightingale, Jack	23	0.72	Nicol, Geordie
82	0.45	Kirkwood, Dan	45	0.68	Brown, Buster	31	0.14	Howard, Frankie	23	0.33	Nicholas, Tony
79	0.29	Webb, Charlie	44	0.52	Thorne, Adrian	31	0.08	Wilkins, Dean	22	0.32	Laverick, Bobby
75	0.72	Attwood, Arthur	44	0.52	Binney, Fred	30	0.23	Cassidy, Bill	22	0.30	James, Tony
75	0.32	Hopkins, Jimmy	43	0.32	Robinson, Michael	30	0.16	Neil, Andy	22	0.23	McDougald, Junior
71	0.13	Wilson, Tug	43	0.09	O'Sullivan, Peter	30	0.09	Walker, Dave	22	0.20	Joynes, Dick
69	0.39	Jones, Bullet	41	0.38	Bennett, Ken	29	0.54	Curry, Bill	22	0.09	Woodhouse, Jack
69	0.32	Foreman, Denis	41	0.16	Horton, Brian	29	0.45	Garfield, Ben	22	0.07	Jennings, Roy
65	0.49	Harburn, Peter	40	0.62	Smith, Jimmy	29	0.45	Dawson, Alex	21	0.62	Smith, Bobby A.
64	0.22	Gordon, Dennis	40	0.54	Law, Alec	29	0.38	Irvine, Willie	21	0.42	Small, Mike
63	0.55	Jennings, Sam	40	0.28	Bremner, Kevin	28	0.53	Sexton, Dave	21	0.06	Gatting, Steve
60	0.50	Nogan, Kurt	39	0.25	Wilson, Danny	28	0.28	Beamish, Ken	20	0.34	Maskell, Craig
59	0.36	Nelson, Garry	39	0.24	McNichol, Johnny	28	0.25	Byrne, John	20	0.29	Cargill, Jimmy
59	0.34	Connor, Terry	39	0.20	Ryan, Gerry	28	0.06	Wilson, Glen	20	0.27	Thompson, Stan
58	0.51	Moore, Bernard	37	0.28	Reed, Billy G.	26	0.25	Ritchie, Andy	20	0.26	Fuller, Eddie
57	0.18	Smith, Potter	37	0.25	Livesey, Charlie	26	0.24	Murray, Bert	20	0.22	Fell, Gerry
55	0.65	Doran, Jack	36	0.38	Smith, Jack	25	0.48	Martin, Jack			

Aggregate goal record holders

Goals	Player	Date of record
3	Bert Baker	–
4	Clem Barker	5.10.1901
7	Frank McAvoy	26.10.1901
8	Clem Barker	21.12.1901
9	Frank McAvoy	8.2.1902
34	Frank Scott	1.11.1902
54	Jack Hall	23.10.1907
57	Bert Longstaff	23.12.1911
58	Charlie Webb	15.1.1913
66	Bert Longstaff	12.3.1913
79	Charlie Webb	4.2.1914
86	Bert Longstaff	7.2.1920
123	Tommy Cook	3.9.1927
174	Bert Stephens	9.1.1943

Goals in a season record holders

Goals	Player	Season
9	Frank McAvoy	1901–02
31	Frank Scott	1902–03
32	Hugh Vallance	1929–30
35	Arthur Attwood	1932–33
36	Peter Ward	1976–77

League goals in a season record holders

Southern League and Football League games only

Goals	Player	Season
6	Frank McAvoy	1901–02
11	Frank Scott	1902–03
22	Jack Hall	1906–07
25	Jimmy Smith	1911–12
"	Tommy Cook	1923–24
"	Sam Jennings	1926–27
"	Tommy Cook	1927–28
30	Hugh Vallance	1929–30
32	Peter Ward	1976–77

Most goals by competition

Competition	In a career		In a season			In a game			
	Goals	Player	Goals	Player	Season	Goals	Player	Opponents	Date
FL (total)	114	Tommy Cook	32	Peter Ward	1976–77	5	Jack Doran	Northampton Town	5.11.1921
						"	Adrian Thorne	Watford	30.4.1958
FAPL / FL D1 (old)	37	Michael Robinson	19	Michael Robinson	1980–81	3	Peter Ward	Wolverhampton W.	21.12.1979
						"	Gordon Smith	Coventry City	4.10.1980
FL D1 / FL D2 (old)	50	Terry Connor	23	Bill Curry	1959–60	4	Adrian Thorne	Bristol Rovers	27.8.1960
						"	Bryan Wade	Newcastle United	16.1.1991
FL D2 / FL D3 (old)	84	Kit Napier	32	Peter Ward	1976–77	4	Alex Dawson	Hartlepools United	22.2.1969
						"	Peter Ward	Walsall	5.10.1976
FL D3 / FL D4 (old)	29	Jimmy Collins	21	Wally Gould	1964–65	3	Keith Webber	York City	7.10.1963
						"	Craig Maskell	Hartlepool United	8.2.1997
FL D3(S)	114	Tommy Cook	30	Hugh Vallance	1929–30	5	Jack Doran	Northampton Town	5.11.1921
						"	Adrian Thorne	Watford	30.4.1958
FAC	19	Arthur Attwood	15	Arthur Attwood	1932–33	6	Arthur Attwood	Shoreham	1.10.1932
FAC (proper only)	18	Jock Davie	10*	Jock Davie	1945–46	4	Jock Davie	South Liverpool	15.12.1937
			7	Jock Davie	1937–38	"	Peter Harburn	Newport County	19.11.1955
FLC	11	Peter Ward	5	Kurt Nogan	1994–95	3	Danny Wilson	Bradford City	25.9.1985
Wartime	78	Bert Stephens	27	Jock Davie	1941–42	6	Don Welsh	Luton Town	22.3.1941
			27†	Bernard Moore	1945–46				
SL D1	64	Charlie Webb	25	Jimmy Smith	1911–12	4	Jimmy Smith	Stoke	30.12.1911
						"	Charlie Webb	Southampton	19.10.1912
SL D2	11	Frank Scott	11	Frank Scott	1902–03	5	Frank Scott	Southall	28.2.1903

* The 1945–46 F.A. Cup competition was a unique, two-legged affair. The record for the normal competition proper is therefore given as well.
† Bernard Moore also scored one goal in the 1945–46 F.A. Cup to total 28 for the season, but the F.A. Cup is not counted as a 'wartime' competition in this book.

Players scoring 20 or more goals in a season

36	Ward, Peter	1976–77	27	Binney, Fred	1975–76	25	Martin, Jack	1908–09	21	Kirkwood, Dan	1928–29
35	Attwood, Arthur	1932–33	27	Davie, Jock	1941–42	24	Davie, Jock	1937–38	21	Mundy, Albert	1954–55
32	Nelson, Garry	1987–88	27	Harburn, Peter	1955–56	23	Cook, Tommy	1926–27	21	Small, Mike	1990–91
32	Vallance, Hugh	1929–30	27	Jennings, Sam	1926–27	23	Doran, Jack	1921–22	21	Stephens, Bert	1935–36
31	Kirkwood, Dan	1929–30	27	Law, Alec	1935–36	23	Stephens, Bert	1937–38	20	Garfield, Ben	1902–03
31	Scott, Frank	1902–03	27	Smith, Jimmy	1911–12	22	Addinall, Bert	1953–54	20	Harburn, Peter	1957–58
29	Attwood, Arthur	1931–32	26	Brown, Buster	1934–35	22	Davie, Jock	1939–40	20	Hopkins, Jimmy	1923–24
28	Cook, Tommy	1923–24	26	Cook, Tommy	1927–28	22	Doran, Jack	1920–21	20	Jennings, Sam	1925–26
28	Hall, Jack H.	1906–07	26	Curry, Bill	1959–60	22	Jones, Bullet	1909–10	20	Miller, Bill	1913–14
28	Moore, Bernard	1945–46	26	Hall, Jack H.	1907–08	22	Nogan, Kurt	1992–93	20	Mundy, Albert	1956–57
28	Mundy, Albert	1955–56	26	Nogan, Kurt	1993–94	22	Robinson, Michael	1980–81	20	Sexton, Dave	1957–58
28	Napier, Kit	1967–68	26	Stephens, Bert	1936–37	21	Gould, Wally	1964–65	20	Smith, Bobby	1964–65

Top scorers each season

Season	Goals	Player	Season	Goals	Player	Season	Goals	Player
1901–02	9	Frank McAvoy	1938–39	17	Bert Stephens	1965–66	14	Charlie Livesey
1902–03	31	Frank Scott	1939–40	22	Jock Davie	1966–67	10	Kit Napier
1903–04	9	Billy Roberts	1940–41	15	Don Welsh	" "	"	Eric Whitington
1904–05	13	Andy Gardner	1941–42	27	Jock Davie	1967–68	28	Kit Napier
1905–06	9	Billy Yates	1942–43	16	John Shafto	1968–69	18	Kit Napier
" "	"	Dickie Joynes	1943–44	11	Bert Stephens	1969–70	16	Alan Gilliver
1906–07	28	Jack Hall	" "	"	Tommy Hassell	1970–71	13	Kit Napier
1907–08	26	Jack Hall	1944–45	15	Bert Stephens	1971–72	19	Kit Napier
1908–09	25	Jack Martin	" "	"	Cyril Hodges	1972–73	10	Ken Beamish
1909–10	22	Bullet Jones	1945–46	28	Bernard Moore	1973–74	12	Ken Beamish
1910–11	19	Bullet Jones	1946–47	10	George Chapman	1974–75	13	Fred Binney
1911–12	27	Jimmy Smith	1947–48	14	Tony James	1975–76	27	Fred Binney
1912–13	13	Charlie Webb	1948–49	11	Des Tennant	1976–77	36	Peter Ward
1913–14	20	Bill Miller	1949–50	9	Johnny McNichol	1977–78	17	Peter Ward
1914–15	13	Bullet Jones	1950–51	14	Johnny McNichol	1978–79	13	Peter Ward
1919–20	10	Jack Doran	1951–52	19	Billy Reed	1979–80	18	Peter Ward
1920–21	22	Jack Doran	" "	"	Ken Bennett	1980–81	22	Michael Robinson
1921–22	23	Jack Doran	1952–53	13	Ken Bennett	1981–82	14	Andy Ritchie
1922–23	13	Eddie Fuller	1953–54	22	Bert Addinall	1982–83	10	Michael Robinson
1923–24	28	Tommy Cook	1954–55	21	Albert Mundy	1983–84	17	Terry Connor
1924–25	18	Tommy Cook	1955–56	28	Albert Mundy	1984–85	16	Terry Connor
1925–26	20	Sam Jennings	1956–57	20	Albert Mundy	1985–86	19	Dean Saunders
1926–27	27	Sam Jennings	1957–58	20	Peter Harburn	1986–87	9	Terry Connor
1927–28	26	Tommy Cook	" "	"	Dave Sexton	1987–88	32	Garry Nelson
1928–29	21	Dan Kirkwood	1958–59	17	John Shepherd	1988–89	16	Garry Nelson
1929–30	32	Hugh Vallance	1959–60	26	Bill Curry	1989–90	12	Kevin Bremner
1930–31	19	Geordie Nicol	1960–61	14	Adrian Thorne	1990–91	21	Mike Small
1931–32	29	Arthur Attwood	1961–62	10	Johnny Goodchild	1991–92	14	Mark Gall
1932–33	35	Arthur Attwood	" "	"	Bobby Laverick	1992–93	22	Kurt Nogan
1933–34	15	Buster Brown	" "	"	Tony Nicholas	1993–94	26	Kurt Nogan
1934–35	26	Buster Brown	1962–63	11	Peter Donnelly	1994–95	13	Junior McDougald
1935–36	27	Alec Law	1963–64	15	Johnny Goodchild	1995–96	9	Junior McDougald
1936–37	26	Bert Stephens	1964–65	21	Wally Gould	1996–97	16	Craig Maskell
1937–38	24	Jock Davie						

Player who top-scored more than once

Player	
Napier, Kit	5
Stephens, Bert	4
Ward, Peter	4
Connor, Terry	3
Cook, Tommy	3
Davie, Jock	3
Doran, Jack	3
Jones, Bullet	3
Mundy, Albert	3
Attwood, Arthur	2
Beamish, Ken	2
Bennett, Ken	2
Binney, Fred	2
Brown, Buster	2
Goodchild, Johnny	2
Hall, Jack	2
Jennings, Sam	2
McDougald, Junior	2
McNichol, Johnny	2
Nelson, Garry	2
Nogan, Kurt	2
Robinson, Michael	2

Players who scored 5 or more penalties

	Player
26	Little, Wally
23	Tennant, Des
17	Horton, Brian
15	Wilson, Danny
13	Caldwell, Jock
13	Jennings, Roy
12	Wilkinson, Reg
10	Langley, Jimmy
9	Curbishley, Alan
8	Jones, Bullet
8	Miller, Bill
8	Wilson, Glen
7	Collins, Jimmy
7	Doran, Jack
6	Hulme, Arthur
6	Mundee, Denny
6	Murray, Bert
6	Small, Mike
6	Spearritt, Eddie
6	Ward, Peter
5	Howell, Ronnie
5	McAteer, Tom
5	Napier, Kit
5	Webb, Charlie

Players who scored 3 or more hat-tricks

	Player
8	Tommy Cook
"	Jock Davie
6	Bert Stephens
5	Arthur Attwood
4	Jimmy Smith
"	Jack Doran
"	Hugh Vallance
"	Bobby Farrell
"	Oliver Brown
3	Ben Garfield
"	Jimmy Hopkins
"	Sam Jennings
"	Dan Kirkwood
"	Alec Law
"	Albert Mundy
"	Bill Curry
"	Peter Ward

Players who scored hat-tricks

Player	Goals	Date	Opponents	Competition	Player	Goals	Date	Opponents	Competition
Baker, Bert	3	21.9.1901	Brighton Athletic (h)	FAC Prelim.	Brown, Buster	3	28.9.1935	Newport County (h)	FL D3(S)
Garfield, Ben	3	4.10.1902	Brighton Amateurs (h)	FAC Q1	Law, Alec	4	26.10.1935	Notts County (h)	FL D3(S)
Lee, Barney	3	4.10.1902	Brighton Amateurs (h)	FAC Q1	Law, Alec	3	4.12.1935	Cheltenham Town (a)	FAC R1 Rep
West, H. C.	3	4.10.1902	Brighton Amateurs (h)	FAC Q1	Law, Alec	3	25.12.1935	Bristol City (h)	FL D3(S)
Scott, Frank	4	18.10.1902	Shoreham (a)	FAC Q2	Davie, Jock	3	14.11.1936	Exeter City (a)	FL D3(S)
Thair, Sid	3	18.10.1902	Shoreham (a)	FAC Q2	Stephens, Bert	3	20.2.1937	Walsall (h)	FL D3(S)
Scott, Frank	5	28.2.1903	Southall (a)	SL D2	Davie, Jock	3	27.11.1937	Tunbridge Wells Rangers (h)	FAC R1
Garfield, Ben	3	25.3.1903	Hitchin Town (h)	SE League	Davie, Jock	4	15.12.1937	South Liverpool (h)	FAC R2 Rep
Ward, W,	3	11.4.1903	Bedford Queen's Eng. Wks (h)	SE League	Stephens, Bert	3	9.4.1938	Exeter City (h)	FL D3(S)
Garfield, Ben	4	27.4.1903	Watford (h)	SL Test	Farrell, Bobby	3	7.1.1939	Swindon Town (h)	FL D3(S)
Ward, Alf	3	29.10.1904	Shoreham (h)	FAC Q3	Farrell, Bobby	3	4.11.1939	Chelsea (h)	wartime
Fisher, Albert	3	30.4.1906	Grays United (h)	Utd League	Davie, Jock	3	30.12.1939	Southampton (h)	wartime
Joynes, Dick	3	30.4.1906	Grays United (h)	Utd League	Farrell, Bobby	3	30.12.1939	Southampton (h)	wartime
Hall, Jack H.	3	5.9.1906	Luton Town (h)	Utd League	Wilson, Joe A.	3	30.12.1939	Southampton (h)	wartime
Joynes, Dick	3	5.9.1906	Luton Town (h)	Utd League	Welsh, Don	6	22.3.1941	Luton Town (h)	wartime
Martin, Jack	3	9.4.1909	Reading (h)	SL D1	Stephens, Bert	3	14.4.1941	Southampton (h)	wartime
Featherstone, George	3	11.9.1909	Coventry City (h)	SL D1	Davie, Jock	3	25.10.1941	Chelsea (a)	wartime
Longstaff, Bert	3	8.1.1910	Brentford (h)	SL D1	Morgan, Stan	3	17.1.1942	Tottenham Hotspur (h)	wartime
Smith, Jimmy	3	28.10.1911	Watford (a)	SL D1	Davie, Jock	5	31.1.1942	Chelsea (h)	wartime
Needham, Archie	3	4.11.1911	New Brompton (h)	SL D1	Davie, Jock	3	6.4.1942	Clapton Orient (h)	wartime
Needham, Archie	3	15.11.1911	Southampton (h)	SCC R1 Rep	Shafto, John	3	12.12.1942	Brentford (h)	wartime
Smith, Jimmy	4	30.12.1911	Stoke (h)	SL D1	Shafto, John	4	9.1.1943	Luton Town (h)	wartime
Smith, Jimmy	3	2.3.1912	Watford (h)	SL D1	Stephens, Bert	3	2.10.1943	Luton Town (a)	wartime
Smith, Jimmy	3	30.3.1912	Queen's Park Rangers (h)	SL D1	McNeill, Hamilton	3	22.1.1944	Luton Town (h)	wartime
Webb, Charlie	4	19.10.1912	Southampton (h)	SL D1	Hodges, Cyril	4	17.2.1945	Millwall (h)	wartime
Flannery, Tom	3	10.4.1913	Reading (h)	SCC R2 Rep	Stephens, Bert	3	28.4.1945	Portsmouth (h)	wartime
Brown, Bill	3	19.11.1913	Croydon Common (h)	S Alliance	Stephens, Bert	3	5.5.1945	Aldershot (h)	wartime
Brown, Bill	3	18.2.1914	Brentford (h)	S Alliance	Moore, Bernard	4	22.9.1945	Crystal Palace (h)	wartime
Miller, Bill	3	22.4.1914	Southend United (a)	S Alliance	Davie, Jock	3	26.1.1946	Aldershot (h)	FAC R4 Lg1
Miller, Bill	3	21.11.1914	Croydon Common (h)	SL D1	Trainor, Peter	3	12.10.1946	Notts County (h)	FL D3(S)
March, Zach	3	6.12.1919	Watford (h)	SL D1	Chapman, George	3	14.12.1946	Mansfield Town (h)	FL D3(S)
Doran, Jack	3	2.4.1920	Southend United (h)	SL D1	Morrad, Frank	3	7.5.1949	Ipswich Town (h)	FL D3(S)
Doran, Jack	3	31.8.1921	Exeter City (a)	FL D3(S)	McNichol, Johnny	4	18.4.1951	Newport County (h)	FL D3(S)
Doran, Jack	3	7.9.1921	Exeter City (h)	FL D3(S)	Reed, Billy G.	3	12.9.1951	Ipswich Town (h)	FL D3(S)
Doran, Jack	5	5.11.1921	Northampton Town (h)	FL D3(S)	McNichol, Johnny	3	22.9.1951	Reading (a)	FL D3(S)
Hopkins, Jimmy	3	6.10.1923	Portsmouth (a)	FL D3(S)	Howard, Frankie	3	27.11.1954	Watford (h)	FL D3(S)
Cook, Tommy	3	3.11.1923	Aberdare Athletic (h)	FL D3(S)	Mundy, Albert	3	24.8.1955	Walsall (h)	FL D3(S)
Cook, Tommy	4	22.12.1923	Bournemouth & B.A. (h)	FL D3(S)	Foreman, Denis	3	19.11.1955	Newport County (h)	FAC R1
Cook, Tommy	3	5.1.1924	Reading (h)	FL D3(S)	Harburn, Peter	4	19.11.1955	Newport County (h)	FAC R1
Cook, Tommy	3	2.2.1924	Everton (h)	FAC R2	Stephens, Malcolm	3	14.1.1956	Crystal Palace (h)	FL D3(S)
Hopkins, Jimmy	3	29.3.1924	Norwich City (h)	FL D3(S)	Mundy, Albert	3	21.4.1956	Bournemouth & B.A. (h)	FL D3(S)
Dennison, Bob	3	6.9.1924	Millwall (h)	FL D3(S)	Mundy, Albert	3	27.4.1957	Reading (h)	FL D3(S)
Cook, Tommy	3	4.10.1924	Newport County (h)	FL D3(S)	Sexton, Dave	3	23.11.1957	Crystal Palace (a)	FL D3(S)
Cook, Tommy	3	8.10.1924	Merthyr Town (h)	FL D3(S)	Sexton, Dave	3	21.12.1957	Gillingham (h)	FL D3(S)
Dennison, Bob	3	14.1.1925	Watford (h)	FAC R1 Rep	Thorne, Adrian	5	30.4.1958	Watford (h)	FL D3(S)
Jennings, Sam	3	25.3.1925	Aberdare Athletic (h)	FL D3(S)	Curry, Bill	3	5.9.1959	Portsmouth (h)	FL D2
Fuller, Eddie	3	25.12.1925	Aberdare Athletic (h)	FL D3(S)	Curry, Bill	3	8.2.1960	Rotherham United (n)	FAC R4 2Rep
Nightingale, Jack	3	24.2.1926	Bournemouth & B.A. (a)	FL D3(S)	Curry, Bill	3	12.3.1960	Bristol City (h)	FL D2
Jennings, Sam	4	18.9.1926	Swindon Town (h)	FL D3(S)	Thorne, Adrian	4	27.8.1960	Bristol Rovers (h)	FL D2
Hopkins, Jimmy	3	29.1.1927	Bristol Rovers (h)	FL D3(S)	Webber, Keith	3	7.10.1963	York City (a)	FL D4
Jennings, Sam	3	27.8.1927	Brentford (h)	FL D3(S)	Livesey, Charlie	3	13.11.1965	Wisbech Town (h)	FAC R1
Cook, Tommy	3	10.9.1927	Millwall (h)	FL D3(S)	Smith, Jack	3	27.11.1965	Southend United (h)	FL D3
Kirkwood, Dan	4	7.9.1929	Norwich City (h)	FL D3(S)	Napier, Kit	3	9.11.1968	Bristol Rovers (h)	FL D3
Vallance, Hugh	3	28.9.1929	Merthyr Town (h)	FL D3(S)	Dawson, Alex	4	22.2.1969	Hartlepool (a)	FL D3
Vallance, Hugh	3	2.11.1929	Northampton Town (a)	FL D3(S)	Gilliver, Alan	3	11.3.1970	Halifax Town (h)	FL D3
Vallance, Hugh	3	23.11.1929	Luton Town (h)	FL D3(S)	Napier, Kit	3	28.8.1971	Mansfield Town (h)	FL D3
Vallance, Hugh	3	21.12.1929	Fulham (h)	FL D3(S)	Howell, Ronnie	3	12.1.1974	Charlton Athletic (a)	FL D3
Kirkwood, Dan	4	1.2.1930	Merthyr Town (a)	FL D3(S)	Mellor, Ian	3	5.10.1976	Walsall (h)	FL D3
Kirkwood, Dan	3	5.4.1930	Bournemouth & B.A. (h)	FL D3(S)	Ward, Peter	4	5.10.1976	Walsall (h)	FL D3
Carruthers, Jack	3	26.12.1930	Bristol Rovers (h)	FL D3(S)	Ward, Peter	3	21.1.1978	Mansfield Town (h)	FL D2
Nicol, Geordie	4	27.12.1930	Gillingham (h)	FL D3(S)	Poskett, Malcolm	3	18.4.1978	Bristol Rovers (h)	FL D2
Attwood, Arthur	3	5.12.1931	Coventry City (h)	FL D3(S)	Poskett, Malcolm	3	23.12.1978	Charlton Athletic (a)	FL D2
Attwood, Arthur	3	26.3.1932	Thames (h)	FL D3(S)	Maybank, Teddy	3	26.12.1978	Cardiff City (h)	FL D2
Attwood, Arthur	4	23.4.1932	Gillingham (h)	FL D3(S)	Ward, Peter	3	21.12.1979	Wolverhampton Wanderers (a)	FL D1
Attwood, Arthur	6	1.10.1932	Shoreham (h)	FAC Q1	Smith, Gordon	3	4.10.1980	Coventry City (a)	FL D1
Smith, Potter	3	1.10.1932	Shoreham (h)	FAC Q1	Case, Jimmy	3	1.10.1983	Charlton Athletic (h)	FL D2
Farrell, Bobby	3	29.10.1932	Hastings & St Leonards (a)	FAC Q3	Wilson, Danny	3	25.9.1985	Bradford City (h)	FLC R2 Lg1
Attwood, Arthur	3	6.5.1933	Bristol City (h)	FL D3(S)	Bremner, Kevin	3	31.12.1988	Birmingham City (h)	FL D2
Brown, Buster	3	21.4.1934	Bournemouth & B.A. (h)	FL D3(S)	Wade, Bryan	4	16.1.1991	Newcastle United (h)	FL D2
Brown, Buster	3	26.4.1934	Exeter City (h)	SSC SF 2Rep	Nogan, Kurt	3	1.1.1994	Cambridge United (h)	FL D2
Brown, Buster	3	29.9.1934	Swindon Town (a)	FL D3(S)	Maskell, Craig	3	8.2.1997	Hartlepool United (h)	FL D3

Players scoring 4 or more goals in a match

Goals	Player	Date	Score	Opponents	Comp.
6	Arthur Attwood	1.10.1932	12–0	Shoreham	FAC Q1
"	Don Welsh	22.3.1941	7–4	Luton Town	Wartime
5	Frank Scott	28.2.1903	8–0	Southall	SL D2
"	Jack Doran	5.11.1921	7–0	Northampton Town	FL D3(S)
"	Jock Davie	31.1.1942	8–2	Chelsea	Wartime
"	Adrian Thorne	30.4.1958	6–0	Watford	FL D3(S)
4	Frank Scott	18.10.1902	12–0	Shoreham	FAC Q2
"	Ben Garfield	27.4.1903	5–3	Watford	SL Test
"	Jimmy Smith	30.12.1911	4–0	Stoke	SL D1
"	Charlie Webb	19.10.1912	5–2	Southampton	SL D1
"	Tommy Cook	22.12.1923	5–0	Bournemouth & B.A.	FL D3(S)
"	Sam Jennings	18.9.1926	9–3	Swindon Town	FL D3(S)
"	Dan Kirkwood	7.9.1929	6–3	Norwich City	FL D3(S)
"	Dan Kirkwood	1.2.1930	8–2	Merthyr Town	FL D3(S)
"	Geordie Nicol	27.12.1930	5–0	Gillingham	FL D3(S)
"	Arthur Attwood	23.4.1932	7–0	Gillingham	FL D3(S)
"	Alec Law	26.10.1935	5–1	Notts County	FL D3(S)
"	Jock Davie	15.12.1937	6–0	South Liverpool	FAC R2 rep
"	John Shafto	9.1.1943	8–0	Luton Town	Wartime
"	Cyril Hodges	17.2.1945	6–2	Millwall	Wartime
"	Bernard Moore	22.9.1945	7–2	Crystal Palace	Wartime
"	Johnny McNichol	18.4.1951	9–1	Newport County	FL D3(S)
"	Peter Harburn	19.11.1955	8–1	Newport County	FAC R1
"	Adrian Thorne	27.8.1960	6–1	Bristol Rovers	FL D2
"	Alex Dawson	22.2.1969	5–2	Hartlepools United	FL D3
"	Peter Ward	5.10.1976	7–0	Walsall	FL D3
"	Bryan Wade	16.1.1991	4–2	Newcastle United	FL D2

Players scoring in 5 or more consecutive games

The date shown is the first game of the sequence

Games	Goals	Player	Date	Competitions		
8	14	Arthur Attwood	14.11.1931	6 FL	2 FAC	
"	13	Bernard Moore	25.8.1945	8 wartime		
"	12	Peter Harburn	15.10.1955	7 FL	1 FAC	
"	9	Arthur Attwood	29.10.1932	5 FL	3 FAC	
"	8	Cyril Thompson	13.9.1950	8 FL		
6	10	Jack Martin	22.3.1909	4 SL	1 WL	1 SCC
"	8	Bert Addinall	26.12.1953	6 FL		
"	7	Frank McAvoy	28.9.1901	3 FL	3 FAC	
5	7	Frank O'Donnell	15.9.1945	5 wartime		
"	"	Peter Ward	20.9.1977	4 FL	1 FLC	
"		Kurt Nogan	7.4.1993	5 FL		
"	6	Frank Scott	20.12.1902	3 SL	2 SEL	
"	"	Dan Kirkwood	15.12.1928	5 FL		
"	5	Andy Gardner	22.10.1904	3 SL	2 FAC	
"	"	Bert Stephens	29.12.1945	2 FAC	3 wartime	
"	"	Bert Addinall	11.4.1953	5 FL		
"	"	Wally Gould	28.9.1964	5 FL		

Players who scored on their Albion debut

* made debut in a wartime match

Player		Player		Player		Player		Player	
Baker, Bert	3	Williamson,	1	Welsh, Don*	2	Frost, Arthur*	1	Napier, Kit	2
Mendham, C. J.	1	Williams, D. H.	1	Balmer, Jack*	1	Robson, Bert*	1	Flood, Paul	1
Barker, Clem	2	Williams, Dave	1	Laney, Les*	1	Hindley, Frank*	1	Blackburn, Ken	1
Smith, Albert	1	Doran, Jack	1	Jones, Ron*	1	James, Tony	1	Duffy, Alan	1
Sear	1	Broadhead, Arnold	1	Shafto, John*	1	Ferrier, John	1	Irvine, Willie	1
Scott, Frank	1	Dennison, Bob	1	Pearson, Stan*	1	Redfern, Bob	1	Conway, Mick	1
Ward, W.	2	Smith, Jack	2	Tunnicliffe, Bill*	1	Thomas, Lyn	1	Mellor, Ian	1
Roberts, Billy	1	Goord, George	1	Easdale, Jack*	1	Lewis, George	1	Martin, Neil	1
Good, Mickey	1	Thomson, Norman	1	Jones, Syd*	1	Mansell, Jack	1	Ward, Peter	1
Gardner, Andy	1	Vallance, Hugh	1	Peters, Bill*	1	Thompson, Cyril	1	Maybank, Teddy	1
Buckley, Chris	1	Thompson, Stan	1	Lancelotte, Eric*	1	Owens, Les	1	Poskett, Malcolm	1
Hall, Jack H.	1	Townsend, Eric	1	Lane, Billy*	1	Leadbetter, Jimmy	1	Smith, Gordon	1
Ronaldson, Duncan	1	Eyres, Jack	1	Griffin, Albert*	1	Foreman, Denis	1	Howlett, Gary	1
Robertson, Jimmy	1	Law, Alec	1	Ohlens, P. W.*	1	Addinall, Bert	1	Young, Alan	1
Brennan, Jimmy	1	Richards, Billy	2	O'Donnell, Frank*	1	Mundy, Albert	1	Wilson, Danny	2
Webb, Charlie	1	Hurst, Stan	1	Malone, Ron*	1	Stephens, Malcolm	1	Nelson, Garry	1
Connor, Nat	1	Goffey, Bert	1	Wright, Tommy*	1	Sexton, Dave	1	Moulden, Paul	1
Smith, Jimmy	2	Isaac, Bill*	1	McNeill, Hamilton*	3	Thorne, Adrian	1	Cotterill, Steve	1
Stott, Tom	1	Kay, John*	1	Driver, Allenby*	1	Goodchild, Johnny	2	Chamberlain, Mark	1
Woodhouse, Jack	1	Kelly, Jimmy*	1	Cook, R.*	1	Smith, Bobby	2	Storer, Stuart	1
Simpson, Bobby	1	Collins, John*	1	Hodges, Cyril*	2	McQuarrie, Andy	1	Berry, Greg	1
Ault, Alfred	1	Cothliff, Harold*	1	Offord, Stan*	1	Kydd, David	1	Baird, Ian	1
Kitchen, Sid	1	Willemse, Stan*	1	Townsend, Len*	1	Wilkinson, Howard	1	Morris, Mark	1

Goalscoring substitutes

Player	Date	Opponents		Player	Date	Opponents		Player	Date	Opponents	
Livesey, Charlie	1.2.1967	Aldershot	1	Morgan, Sammy	18.12.1976	Chesterfield	1	Armstrong, Gerry	31.8.1987	Northampton Town	1
Flood, Paul	23.8.1967	Colchester United	1	Ruggiero, John	20.8.1977	Southampton	1	Armstrong, Gerry	10.2.1988	Hereford United	1
Wilkinson, Howard	16.9.1967	Tranmere Rovers	1	Fell, Gerry	27.9.1977	Luton Town	2	Jasper, Dale	17.2.1988	Chesterfield	1
Wilkinson, Howard	4.10.1967	Grimsby Town	1	Potts, Eric	25.2.1978	Sunderland	2	Crumplin, John	2.3.1988	Port Vale	1
Templeman, John	21.10.1967	Mansfield Town	1	Potts, Eric	15.4.1978	Tottenham Hotspur	1	Armstrong, Gerry	3.9.1988	Oxford United	1
Armstrong, Dave	21.10.1968	Orient	1	Sayer, Peter	28.10.1978	West Ham United	1	Crumplin, John	20.3.1990	Watford	1
Wilkinson, Howard	20.12.1968	Reading	1	Ward, Peter	3.2.1979	Leicester City	1	Wade, Bryan	20.2.1991	Leicester City	1
Napier, Kit	30.8.1969	Bury	1	Clark, Paul	24.2.1979	Fulham	1	Robinson, John	22.5.1991	Millwall	1
Gilliver, Alan	3.1.1970	Doncaster Rovers	1	Ryan, Gerry	15.9.1979	Ipswich Town	1	Bissett, Nicky	20.8.1991	Bristol City	1
Woffinden, Colin	21.11.1970	Cheltenham Town	1	Stevens, Gary	2.2.1980	Ipswich Town	1	Crumplin, John	16.12.1992	Woking	1
Irvine, Willie	5.2.1972	Wrexham	1	Ritchie, Andy	5.12.1981	Sunderland	1	Farrington, Mark	14.4.1993	Hull City	1
Lutton, Bertie	31.3.1972	Torquay United	1	Ryan, Gerry	20.11.1982	Watford	1	Chamberlain, Mark	20.8.1994	Plymouth Argyle	1
Irvine, Willie	8.4.1972	Wrexham	1	Ritchie, Andy	22.1.1983	Luton Town	1	McDougald, Junior	27.12.1994	Shrewsbury Town	1
Bridges, Barry	23.4.1973	Portsmouth	1	Ryan, Gerry	2.4.1983	Tottenham Hotspur	1	Fox, Mark	7.3.1995	Leyton Orient	1
Brown, Mick	27.1.1974	Cambridge United	1	Connor, Terry	23.4.1983	Coventry City	1	Munday, Stuart	6.5.1995	Bradford City	1
Welch, Ronnie	14.9.1974	Watford	1	Saunders, Dean	20.8.1985	Barnsley	1	McGarrigle, Kevin	6.3.1996	Wycombe Wand.	1
Mellor, Ian	4.9.1976	Rotherham United	1	Jacobs, Steve	15.2.1986	Peterborough Utd	1	Storer, Stuart	12.10.1996	Cambridge United	1
Fell, Gerry	18.9.1976	York City	1	O'Regan, Kieran	31.3.1986	Portsmouth	1	Reinelt, Robbie	3.5.1997	Hereford United	1
Burnett, Dennis	25.9.1976	Tranmere Rovers	1	Jasper, Dale	25.10.1986	Derby County	1				

Albion teenagers

* played as a teenager in wartime matches only. Ages given in years and days.

Name	Age	Name	Age	Name	Age	Name	Age	Name	Age
Bowles, Reg*	15-258	Johnson, Ross	17-291	Woolgar, Phil	18-234	Stemp, Wayne	19-049	Rollings, Andy	19-246
Willemse, Stan*	16-008	Blackburn, Ken	17-303	Standing, John	18-237	Flood, Paul	19-055	James, David	19-259
Chase, Charlie*	16-122	Cochrane, Johnny	17-303	Virgo, James	18-244	Mayo, Kerry	19-063	Geard, Glen	19-261
Fox, Simon	16-238	Lambert, Martin	17-339	Franks, Ken	18-246	Clark, Paul	19-066	Boorn, Alan	19-263
Chapman, Ian	16-259	Edwards, Sean	17-352	Thorne, Albert*	18-263	Duke, George*	19-066	Foreman, Denis	19-267
Collins, John*	16-???	Burtenshaw, Charlie*	17-355	South, Alex	18-268	Coughlan, Derek	19-070	Kydd, David	19-273
Harman, Charlie*	16-???	Elliott, Mark	17-360	McKenna, Brian	18-270	Henley, Les*	19-071	Webb, Stan	19-281
Griffin, Albert*	17-000	Langley, Ernie*	17-???	Hilton, Pat	18-285	Ferrier, John	19-076	Dillon, John	19-282
McGarrigle, Kevin	17-028	Austen, Bert*	17-???	Dovey, Alan	18-287	Flack, Doug*	19-081	Crumplin, John	19-299
Conway, Mick	17-048	Watts, Roy*	17-???	Simmonds, Danny	18-289	Templeman, John	19-097	Fitch, Barry	19-303
Busby, Dave	17-085	Hickman, Stan*	18-014	Rust, Nicky	18-323	Vessey, Tony	19-099	Harlock, Des*	19-308
Burtenshaw, Steve	17-139	Bailey, Craig	18-067	Henderson, Stewart	18-335	Rowley, Arthur*	19-126	Penney, Steve	19-314
Stevens, Gary	17-169	Broomfield, Des*	18-085	Buckley, Chris	18-336	Whitington, Eric	19-140	Goodwin, Ian	19-319
Wosahlo, Bradley	17-194	McGrath, Derek	18-091	Stanley, Terry	18-345	Bence, Paul	19-142	Ritchie, Andy	19-329
Massimo, Franco	17-201	Fox, Mark	18-098	Ramsey, Chris	18-355	Munday, Stuart	19-147	Gregory, Jack*	19-333
Powney, Brian	17-203	Hannam, Dave	18-138	Tuck, Stuart	18-362	O'Sullivan, Peter	19-164	Rodon, Chris	19-339
Andrews, Phil	17-207	Myall, Stuart	18-142	O'Dowd, Greg	19-005	Steele, Simon	19-182	Brophy, Harry	19-344
Townsend, Eric	17-210	Ball, Jack*	18-150	Moore, Bernard*	19-008	O'Regan, Kieran	19-186	Lewis, Bill*	19-350
Gilbert, Phil	17-229	Jest, Syd	18-188	Piper, Steve	19-016	Duncliffe, John	19-191	Howlett, Gary	19-354
Newman, Daren	17-241	France, Ernie*	18-213	Hickman, Mike	19-021	McDougald, Junior	19-213	Kerr, Stewart	19-354
Funnell, Simon	17-268	Keown, Martin	18-214	Thompson, Pat	19-027	McCoy, Tim*	19-215	Upton, Nobby	19-359
Towner, Tony	17-284	McCarthy, Paul	18-225	Brown, Gary	19-041	Howard, Frankie	19-217	Gall, Norman	19-364
Gipp, David	17-286	Robinson, John	18-230	Borthwick, Walter	19-042	Badminton, Roger	19-243		

Players known to have played aged 35 or older

* played at age 35 or more in wartime matches only. Age given in years and days.

Name	Age	Name	Age	Name	Age	Name	Age	Name	Age
Cowan, Sam*	44-156	Downs, Dickie	38-115	Gordon, Dennis	36-326	Longstaff, Bert	36-013	Corrigan, Joe	35-176
Case, Jimmy	41-166	Wilson, Joe	38-050	Jenkins, Jack	36-281	Leeming, Joe	36 or 37	Briley, Les	35-172
Williams, Skilly	38-357	Foster, Steve	38-020	Wilson, Ernie	36-277	Feebery, Jack	35-359	Martin, Neil	35-106
Wilson, Alex	38-319	Crawford, Ted*	37-356	Darling, Len	36-259	Walker, Clive	35-333	Byrne, John	35-098
Jones, Bullet	38-271	Jones, Les	37-296	Young, Leon	36-191	Martin, Ted	35-207	Marriott, Ernie	35-097
Stephens, Bert	38-200	Small, Sammy	37-195	Worthington, Frank	36-169	Barker, Don	35-194	Farrell, Bobby*	35-066
Lane, Billy*	38-156	Medhurst, Harry	37-009	Humphrey, John	36-092	Hawley, Fred	35-178	Wilkinson, Reg	35-040
Jones, Herbert	38-131	Boyd, Jimmy*	37-000	Brett, Frank	36-027	Lewis, George	35-178	Weaver, Sam*	35-004
Stapleton, Frank	38-118	Osman, Russell	36-343						

Teenage goalscorers

* scored in a wartime match

Name	Age
Willemse, Stan*	16-008
Griffin, Albert*	17-000
Conway, Mick	17-048
Townsend, Eric	17-210
Blackburn, Ken	17-303
Stevens, Gary	17-309
Towner, Tony	17-312
Chase, Charlie*	17-328
Bailey, Craig	18-081
Cochrane, Johnny	18-099
Hannam, Dave	18-152
Gilbert, Phil	18-228
McGarrigle, Kevin	18-332
Buckley, Chris	18-336
Funnell, Simon	19-027
Flood, Paul	19-055
Keown, Martin	19-063
Ferrier, John	19-076
Clark, Paul	19-094
Fox, Mark	19-110
Munday, Stuart	19-154
Rowley, Arthur*	19-154
Thorne, Albert*	19-157
Chapman, Ian	19-185
Hilton, Pat	19-196
McDougald, Junior	19-217
O'Sullivan, Peter	19-231
Rollings, Andy	19-257
Robinson, John	19-266
Foreman, Denis	19-267
Kydd, David	19-273
Dillon, John	19-289
Howlett, Gary	19-354
Ritchie, Andy	19-360
Virgo, James	19-362

Oldest known goalscorers

* scored in wartime match

Name	Age
Jones, Bullet	38-208
Lane, Billy*	38-156
Stephens, Bert	38-011
Foster, Steve	38-006
Crawford, Ted*	37-356
Wilson, Joe	36-262
Jenkins, Jack	36-242
Worthington, Frank	36-162
Wilson, Tug	36-149
Gordon, Dennis	35-300
Walker, Clive	35-281
Hawley, Fred	35-175
Barker, Don	35-145
Lewis, George	35-143
Longstaff, Bert	35-140
Darling, Len	35-113
Martin, Neil	35-047
Byrne, John	35-044

Oldest known debutants

* played in wartime matches only

Name	Age
Wilson, Alex	38-319
Cowan, Sam*	38-234
Lane, Billy*	38-156
Stapleton, Frank	38-115
Downs, Dickie	38-017
Crawford, Ted*	37-321
Jones, Herbert	37-265
Jones, Les	37-093
Boyd, Jimmy*	37-000
Medhurst, Harry	36-284
Williams, Skilly	36-236
Osman, Russell	36-224
Humphrey, John	36-032
Young, Leon	35-356
Small, Sammy	35-317
Worthington, Frank	35-276
Barker, Don	35-075
Weaver, Sam*	35-004
Briley, Les	34-348
Lewis, George	34-306
Hawley, Fred	34-305
Tootill, Alf*	34-303
Corrigan, Joe	34-303
Martin, Neil	34-300
McGrath, John	34-101
Morris, Mark	34-037
Martin, David	33-345
Chivers, Martin	33-338
Farrell, Bobby*	33-300
Holley, George	33-278
Munro, Alex*	33-148
Mortimer, Dennis	33-134
Feebery, Jack	33-109
Walker, Clive	33-091
Moffatt, Billy	33-068

Player age records by competition

Competition	Oldest known player			Youngest known player		
	Age	Player	Last game	Age	Player	First game
FL (total)	41–166	Jimmy Case	31.10.1995	16–238	Simon Fox	23.4.1994
FAPL / FL D1 (old)	34–183	Martin Chivers	27.10.1979	17–169	Gary Stevens	15.9.1979
FL D1 / FL D2 (old)	36–326	Dennis Gordon	29.4.1961	16–259	Ian Chapman	14.2.1987
FL D2 / FL D3 (old)	41–166	Jimmy Case	31.10.1995	16–238	Simon Fox	23.4.1994
FL D3 / FL D4 (old)	36–092	John Humphrey	3.5.1997	18–338	Brian Powney	10.9.1963
FL D3(S)	38–357	Skilly Williams	26.12.1928	17–139	Steve Burtenshaw	11.4.1953
FAC	38–325	Skilly Williams	24.11.1928	17–302	Gary Stevens	26.1.1980
FLC	40–140	Jimmy Case	5.10.1994	17–179	Gary Stevens	25.9.1979
Wartime	44–156	Sam Cowan	13.10.1945	15–258	Reg Bowles	29.11.1941
SL D1	38–250	Bullet Jones	29.11.1919	19–46	Chris Buckley	25.12.1905
SL D2	c. 31–230	Ned Collins	1.4.1902	c. 21–0	Bertie Blunden	25.1.1902

Players who were ever-present throughout a season

1901–02	Jock Caldwell	1923–24	George Coomber	1950–51	Johnny McNichol	1961–62	Jack Bertolini	1978–79	Gary Williams
	Paddy Farrell		Billy Hayes	1951–52	Jack Mansell		Steve Burtenshaw	1979–80	Brian Horton
1903–04	Billy Roberts		Jimmy Hopkins		Billy Reed	1962–63	Jack Bertolini		Gary Williams
1906–07	Hugh MacDonald	1924–25	Wally Little		Glen Wilson	1963–64	Jimmy Collins	1980–81	Steve Foster
1909–10	Fred Blackman		Ernie Wilson	1953–54	Eric Gill	1968–69	John Napier		Michael Robinson
	Billy Booth	1927–28	Reg Wilkinson		Eric Langley	1971–72	Norman Gall	1984–85	Chris Hutchings
	Joe Leeming		Reg Williams		Glen Wilson		Peter O'Sullivan		Graham Moseley
	Bob Whiting		Ernie Wilson	1954–55	Eric Gill		Eddie Spearritt	1987–88	Keith Dublin
1910–11	Billy Booth	1929–30	Jack Curran	1955–56	Eric Gill	1972–73	Peter O'Sullivan		John Keeley
1911–12	Charlie Webb	1931–32	Harry Marsden		Dennis Gordon	1973–74	Peter O'Sullivan	1988–89	Gary Chivers
	Bob Whiting		Potter Smith		Albert Mundy	1975–76	Peter Grummitt		Garry Nelson
1919–20	Billy Hayes	1934–35	Charlie Thomson	1956–57	Eric Gill		Harry Wilson	1989–90	Dean Wilkins
1920–21	Jack Woodhouse	1937–38	Joe Wilson	1958–59	Glen Wilson	1976–77	Graham Cross	1990–91	Dean Wilkins
1921–22	Jack Feebery	1939–40	Jack Stevens	1959–60	Jack Bertolini		Steve Piper	1993–94	Nicky Rust
	Billy Hayes	1942–43	Stan Risdon		Roy Jennings		Peter Ward	1995–96	Nicky Rust
1922–23	Billy Hayes	1945–46	Joe Wilson	1960–61	Jack Bertolini	1977–78	Brian Horton		
	Andy Neil	1947–48	Tony James		Bob McNicol				

Captains

The following list shows the players who were captains at the beginning of each season, and those who took over for lengthy periods throughout that season

1901–02	Frank McAvoy	1928–29	Skilly Williams	1950–51	Des Tennant	1967–68	Dave Turner	1984–85	Jimmy Case
	Jock Caldwell		Dan Kirkwood	1951–52	Johnny McNichol		Nobby Lawton		Danny Wilson
1902–03	Jock Caldwell	1929–30	Reg Smith	1952–53	Jess Willard		John Napier	1985–86	Danny Wilson
1903–04	Tom McAteer		Jack Curran		Des Tennant	1968–69	Nobby Lawton	1986–87	Danny Wilson
1904–05	Tom Robertson	1930–31	Frank Brett	1953–54	Des Tennant		Dave Turner	1987–88	Doug Rougvie
1905–06	Arthur Hulme	1931–32	Frank Brett	1954–55	Glen Wilson	1969–70	Nobby Lawton	1988–89	Steve Gatting
1906–07	Harry Kent	1932–33	Frank Brett		Jimmy Langley	1970–71	John Napier		Gary Chivers
1907–08	Harry Kent	1933–34	Frank Brett	1955–56	Jimmy Langley	1971–72	John Napier	1989–90	Steve Gatting
1908–09	Tom Stewart		Reg Wilkinson	1956–57	Jimmy Langley		Brian Bromley		Alan Curbishley
1909–10	Joe Leeming	1934–35	Herbert Jones		Ken Whitfield	1972–73	Brian Bromley	1990–91	Dean Wilkins
1910–11	Joe Leeming	1935–36	Potter Smith	1957–58	Ken Whitfield		Bert Murray	1991–92	Dean Wilkins
1911–12	Joe Leeming	1936–37	Potter Smith		Glen Wilson	1973–74	Eddie Spearritt		Gary Chivers
1912–13	Joe Leeming		Ernie King	1958–59	Glen Wilson		Norman Gall	1992–93	Gary Chivers
1913–14	Joe Leeming	1937–38	Dave Walker	1959–60	Glen Wilson	1974–75	Ernie Machin	1993–94	Dean Wilkins
1914–15	Billy Booth	1938–39	Dave Walker	1960–61	Roy Jennings		Billy McEwan		Robert Codner
1919–20	Billy Booth	1939–40	Len Darling	1961–62	Roy Jennings		Graham Winstanley		Steve Foster
1920–21	Jack Rutherford	1940–41	Stan Risdon	1962–63	Roy Jennings	1975–76	Graham Winstanley	1994–95	Steve Foster
	Jack Woodhouse	1941–42	Stan Risdon	1963–64	Roy Jennings		Ernie Machin		Paul McCarthy
1921–22	Jack Feebery	1942–43	Stan Risdon		Jimmy Collins	1976–77	Brian Horton	1995–96	Paul McCarthy
1922–23	Jack Feebery	1943–44	Stan Risdon	1964–65	Jimmy Collins	1977–78	Brian Horton		George Parris
	George Coomber	1944–45	Stan Risdon		Bobby Smith	1978–79	Brian Horton	1996–97	George Parris
1923–24	George Coomber	1945–46	Stan Risdon		Mel Hopkins	1979–80	Brian Horton		Mark Morris
1924–25	George Coomber	1946–47	Len Darling	1965–66	Jimmy Collins	1980–81	Brian Horton		Ian Baird
	Jack Jenkins	1947–48	Ernie Marriott		Jimmy Magill	1981–82	Steve Foster		
1925–26	Jack Jenkins	1948–49	Sammy Small	1966–67	Jimmy Magill	1982–83	Steve Foster		
1926–27	Skilly Williams		Jack Whent		Jimmy Collins	1983–84	Steve Foster		
1927–28	Skilly Williams	1949–50	Jack Whent		Dave Turner		Jimmy Case		

Incoming transfer records since 1919

Transfer fees are private between clubs. These figures are derived mainly from the Press

Fee	Player	Selling club	Date
£200	George Holley	Sunderland	July 1919
"	David Williams	Luton Town	Feb. 1920
£250	Harry Bentley	Sheffield Wed.	c.s. 1920
£500	Fred Groves	Arsenal	Aug. 1921
£650	Sam Jennings	West Ham United	March 1925
£3,250	Eric Lancelotte	Charlton Athletic	Feb. 1948
£5,000	Johnny McNichol	Newcastle United	Aug. 1948
£7,000	Matt McNeil	Barnsley	July 1953
"	Ian McNeill	Leciester City	March 1959
£13,000	Bill Curry	Newcastle United	July 1959
£15,000	Tony Nicholas	Chelsea	Nov. 1960
£25,000	John Napier	Bolton Wanderers	Aug. 1967
£25,000	Ken Beamish	Tranmere Rovers	March 1972
+ Alan Duffy			
£29,000	Barry Bridges	Millwall	Aug. 1972
£35,000‡	Ronnie Welch	Burnley	Dec. 1973
" ‡	Harry Wilson	Burnley	Dec. 1973
£40,000	Ian Mellor	Norwich City	April 1974
£45,000*	Ken Tiler	Chesterfield	Nov. 1974
£111,111	Mark Lawrenson	Preston North End	June 1977
£238,000	Teddy Maybank	Fulham	Nov. 1977
£250,000	John Gregory	Aston Villa	July 1979
£400,000	Gordon Smith	Rangers	June 1980
"	Michael Robinson	Manchester City	June 1980
£500,000	Andy Ritchie	Manchester United	Oct. 1980
" †	Terry Connor	Leeds United	March 1983

‡ *combined fee of £70,000*
* *£45,000-rated in swap for Ronnie Welch and Billy McEwan*
† *£500,000-rated in swap for Andy Ritchie*

Outgoing transfer records since 1908

Transfer fees are private between clubs. These figures are derived mainly from the Press

Fee	Player	Buying club	Date
£700*	Jack Hall	Middlesbrough	April 1908
£735	Jimmy Smith	Bradford (Park Avenue)	Nov. 1912
+ Bobby Simpson			
£1,500	David Parkes	Sheffield Wed.	March 1914
+ George Beech			
£3,000	Andy Neil	Arsenal	March 1924
£6,000	Stan Willemse	Chelsea	July 1949
£12,000	Johnny McNichol	Chelsea	Aug. 1952
+ Jimmy Leadbetter			
£15,000	Jack Mansell	Cardiff City	Oct. 1952
£16,000	Steve Govier	Grimsby Town	Dec. 1974
£26,000	Ken Beamish	Blackburn Rovers	May 1974
£30,000	Ian Mellor	Chester	Feb. 1978
£37,000	Eric Potts	Preston North End	Aug. 1978
£65,000	Tony Towner	Millwall	Oct. 1978
£100,000	Eric Steele	Watford	Oct. 1979
£150,000	Teddy Maybank	Fulham	Dec. 1979
£175,000	Ray Clarke	Newcastle United	July 1980
£450,000	Peter Ward	Nottingham Forest	Oct. 1980
£900,000	Mark Lawrenson	Liverpool	Aug. 1981

* *maximum fee at time of £350; Hall and 'makeweight' Harry Kent left for combined fee of £700*

Players of the Season

Voted for by the fans, this award was inaugurated in 1969 at the suggestion of two supporters, Ron and Winn Carr.

1968–69	John Napier	1974–75	not chosen	1980–81	Michael Robinson	1986–87	Terry Connor	1992–93	Steve Foster
1969–70	Stewart Henderson	1975–76	not chosen	1981–82	Andy Ritchie	1987–88	Garry Nelson	1993–94	Kurt Nogan
1970–71	Norman Gall	1976–77	Brian Horton	1982–83	Gary Stevens	1988–89	John Keeley	1994–95	Peter Smith
1971–72	Bert Murray	1977–78	Peter O'Sullivan	1983–84	Jimmy Case	1989–90	Keith Dublin	1995–96	Ian Chapman
1972–73	Eddie Spearritt	1978–79	Mark Lawrenson	1984–85	Graham Moseley	1990–91	Perry Digweed	1996–97	not chosen
1973–74	Norman Gall	1979–80	Steve Foster	1985–86	Dean Saunders	1991–92	Mark Gall		

Albion goalkeepers

* played in goal in wartime games only

Goalkeeper	Apps	Goals/game	Goalkeeper	Apps	Goals/game	Goalkeeper	Apps	Goals/game	Goalkeeper	Apps	Goals/game
Powney, Brian	386	1.29	Burns, Tony	67	1.58	Tustin, Bill	4	3.25	Groves, Ken*	1	6.00
Whiting, Bob	320	1.05	McGonigal, Bert	62	1.63	Downsborough, Peter	3	1.00	Hickman, S.*	1	6.00
Gill, Eric	296	1.39	Cook, Walter	55	1.38	Forster, Derek	3	3.00	Hooper, Percy*	1	7.00
Webb, Stan	234	1.39	Howes, Arthur	49	2.02	Hughes, Tommy	3	1.67	Kyle, *	1	3.00
Hayes, Billy	225	1.19	Sidebottom, Geoff	45	0.96	Seymour, Ian	3	1.33	Lewis, Doug*	1	3.00
Moseley, Graham	224	1.25	Corrigan, Joe	42	1.45	Sutherland, Jim	3	1.33	McFarlane, D. L.*	1	0.00
Baldwin, Harry	215	1.72	Duckworth, Joe	40	1.40	Collins, Glyn	2	1.50	McKenna, Brian	1	4.00
Digweed, Perry	201	1.47	Fairhurst, Billy*	33	3.30	Duke, George*	2	3.50	Martin, Ted*	1	0.00
Rust, Nicky	192	1.48	Whitehurst, Squire	32	1.31	Kelly, John	2	1.50	Newton, Jimmy	1	4.00
Thomson, Charlie	191	1.32	Ormerod, Mark	22	1.09	Kerr, Stewart	2	1.50	Phillips, John	1	2.00
Ball, Jack	163	1.89	Beale, Bob	21	1.67	Meola, Tony	2	1.00	Randall, Ossie	1	3.00
Keeley, John	160	1.39	Wilcock, George	21	1.48	Packham, Wally*	2	5.00	Reid, Ernie*	1	6.00
Grummitt, Peter	158	1.08	Medhurst, Harry	14	2.29	Risdon, Stan	2	4.00	Sommer, Juergen	1	0.00
Mee, Gordon	132	2.56	Wright, Joe	14	1.71	Robinson, G. L.	2	4.50	Steele, Simon	1	3.00
Williams, Skilly	107	1.54	Crinson, Bill	13	1.00	Tapken, Norman*	2	4.00	Szajna-Stankowski, Bishek*	1	4.00
MacDonald, Hugh	102	1.38	Kemp, Dirk*	13	2.00	Bartram, A.*	1	18.00	Telford, J.	1	1.00
Steele, Eric	98	1.02	Bunting, John	8	1.25	Callow, J. W.	1	1.00	Tootill, Alf*	1	2.00
Baker, Charlie	87	1.84	Dovey, Alan	8	1.88	Chivers, Gary †	1	0.00	Woodley, Vic*	1	5.00
Beeney, Mark	87	1.37	Chesters, Arthur*	7	2.43	Coles, David	1	1.00	Woolgar, Phil	1	1.00
Mellors, Mark	83	1.37	Fearon, Ron	7	1.29	Flack, Doug*	1	1.00	Young*	1	3.00
Hollins, Dave	73	2.01	Gardiner, J. J.	7	1.43						

† *Gary Chivers, normally an outfield defender, played in goal only for the first eight minutes at Millwall in September 1991 before being replaced by substitute Mark Beeney*

Most home-grown team

The teams for the following games contained 7 players who progressed from the youth team

22.8.1995	Fulham (a)	FLC R1 Lg2	0–2

Chapman, Myall, Tuck, McCarthy, McGarrigle, Andrews; subs. S. Fox, Virgo

Note that only 7 were on at any time as Fox was substitute for McGarrigle

9.10.1993	Stockport County (h)	FL D2	1–1

Myall, Tuck, Chapman, Munday, McCarthy, Simmonds, Funnell

Most players from Sussex

The teams for the following teams contained 6 players born in Sussex

6.10.1993	Middlesbrough (h)	FLC R2 Lg2	0–2

Myall, Tuck, Chapman, Simmonds, Funnell; sub. Geddes

23.10.1993	Rotherham United (h)	FL D2	0–2

Myall, Chapman, Tuck, Geddes; subs. Funnell, Simmonds

Most costly team

The following team cost about £2·6 million to assemble, around £13 million at 1997 prices

17.10.1981	Liverpool (h)	FL D1	3–3

Digweed (£150,000), Shanks (free), Williams (c. £100,000), Grealish (£100,000+),
Foster (£150,000), Gatting (£200,000), Case (£350,000), Ritchie (£500,000),
Robinson (£400,000), Smith (£400,000), McNab (£230,000)

Least costly team

These starting line-ups are believed to be the only ones since 1948 that cost nothing in transfers

3.1.1994	Plymouth Argyle (a)	FL D2	1–1

Rust, Simmonds, Pates, Chapman, Foster, McCarthy, Flatts, Case, Nogan, Funnell, Edwards

8.1.1994	Hull City (a)	FL D2	0–0

Rust, Simmonds, Pates, Chapman, Foster, McCarthy, Flatts, Case, Nogan, Funnell, Edwards

15.1.1994	AFC Bournemouth (h)	FL D2	3–3

Rust, Simmonds, Pates, Chapman, Foster, McCarthy, Flatts, Case, Nogan, Funnell, Edwards

22.1.1994	Stockport County (a)	FL D2	0–3

Rust, Munday, Pates, Chapman, Foster, McCarthy, Flatts, Case, Nogan, Funnell, Edwards

7.10.1995	Rotherham United (a)	FL D2	0–1

Rust, Smith, Chapman, Munday, Foster, McCarthy, Parris, McDougald, Bull, Minton, Osman

14.10.1995	Swindon Town (h)	FL D2	1–3

Rust, Smith, Chapman, Munday, Foster, McGarrigle, Parris, McDougald, McCarthy, Minton, Osman

9.12.1995	AFC Bournemouth (h)	FL D2	2–0

Rust, Smith, Myall, Parris, Johnson, Mundee, McDougald, Minton, Byrne, Chapman

14.12.1995	Fulham (h)	FAC R2 Rep 0–0 (lost on pens)	

Rust, Smith, Myall, Parris, Johnson, McCarthy, Mundee, McDougald, Minton, Andrews, Chapman

Most debutants

There were, of course, 11 debutants in the very first game, but 10 played in the game below

2.9.1908	Southampton (h)	SL D1	1–3

Atkinson, Booth, Hall, Jee, Leeming, Martin, Robertson, Stewart, Tustin, Wilson

In recent times the highest number of debutants has been 5

17.8.1974	Crystal Palace (h)	FL D3	1–0

Binney, Govier, Marlowe, Mellor, Rollings

Oldest and youngest teams

The following team had an average age of 32 years 152 days

7.9.1946	Bristol City (a)	FL D3(S)	0–0

Baldwin (26), Marriott (33), Green (29), Darling (35), Trainor (31), Dugnolle (32),
Stephens (37), Wilson (37), Hindley (30), Barker (35), Hanlon (26)

The following team had an average age of 21 years 153 days

9.10.1993	Stockport County (h)	FL D2	1–1

Rust (19), Myall (18), Tuck (19), Chapman (23), Munday (21), McCarthy (22),
Simmonds (18), Funnell (19), Nogan (23), Codner (28), Edwards (22)

Most games without a goal

The following outfield players all played more than 100 games without ever scoring a goal

Leeming, Joe	238
King, Ernie	217
Curran, Jack	193
Marsden, Harry	191
Stevens, Jack	186
Tiler, Ken	151
Brett, Frank	143
Spencer, Frank	142
Turner, Tom	136
McCoy, Tim	124
Thompson, Jack	106

Successive clean sheets

The goalkeepers below each kept 5 or more 'clean sheets' in succession.
The date given is the first game of the sequence.

	Goalkeeper	Date	Competitions	
7	Billy Hayes	22.12.1923	5 FL	2 FAC
5	Bob Whiting	1.10.1910	4 SL	1 SCC
5	Billy Hayes	8.3.1924	5 FL	
5	Peter Grummitt	29.1.1977	5 FL	
5	Nicky Rust	25.2.1995	5 FL	

Briefest Albion careers

The following players made only one appearance as a substitute

Minutes played	Player
8	Sean Edwards
13	Paul Bence
14	Ricardo Gabbiadini
15	Chris Rodon
17	Moshe Gariani
25	Greg O'Dowd

Most experienced team

The following team had an average of 212 previous appearances for the Albion

26.4.1934	Exeter City (h)	SSC SF 2Rep	3–4

Webb (231), Marsden (188), King (75), Wilkinson (393), Mooney (280), Walker (127),
Thompson (66), Farrell (253), Brown (7), Smith (203), Wilson (511)

Most unchanged team

The team below went 11 matches (8 FL, 3 FAC) unchanged from 17.11.1934 until 12.1.1935

Thomson, King, Jones, Darling, Mooney, Walker, Jepson, Farrell, Brown, Smith, Wilson

Managers of the Month

Pat Saward	April 1971
	December 1971
	April 1972
	March 1973
Alan Mullery	September 1976 (entire League)
	February 1977
	April 1978
	December 1978
Chris Cattlin	January 1984
	January 1986
Barry Lloyd	February 1988
	April 1988
Liam Brady	February 1994
	September 1994
Steve Gritt	February 1997

Full international appearances by Albion players

* Home International championship   † World Cup qualifier   ‡ World Cup finals   § European Championship qualifier   g goal scored

Charlie Webb (Ireland)
3 appearances

Date	Opponent	Score	Venue
15.3.1909	Scotland*	0–5	Glasgow
20.3.1909	Wales*	2–3	Belfast
18.3.1911	Scotland*	0–2	Glasgow

Jack Doran (Ireland)
3 appearances

Date	Opponent	Score	Venue
23.10.1920	England*	0–2	Sunderland
22.10.1921	England*	1–1	Belfast
1.4.1922	Wales*	1–1	Belfast

Jack Jenkins (Wales)
8 appearances

Date	Opponent	Score	Venue
16.2.1924	Scotland*	2–0	Cardiff
3.3.1924	England*	2–1	Blackburn
15.3.1924	Ireland*	1–0	Belfast
14.2.1925	Scotland*	1–3	Edinburgh
18.4.1925	Ireland*	0–0	Wrexham
31.10.1925	Scotland*	0–3	Cardiff
1.3.1926	England*	3–1	Selhurst Park
30.10.1926	Scotland*	0–3	Glasgow

Tommy Cook (England)
1 appearance

Date	Opponent	Score	Venue
28.2.1925	Wales*	2–1	Swansea

Jimmy Hopkins (Ireland)
1 appearance

Date	Opponent	Score	Venue
24.10.1925	England*	0–0	Belfast

Jimmy Magill (Northern Ireland)
5 appearances

Date	Opponent	Score	Venue
10.11.1965	England*	1–2	Wembley
24.11.1965	Albania†	1–1	Tirana
30.3.1966	Wales*	4–1	Cardiff
7.5.1966	West Germany	0–2	Belfast
22.6.1966	Mexico	4–1	Belfast

Willie Irvine (Northern Ireland)
3 appearances

Date	Opponent	Score	Venue
20.5.1972	Scotland*	0–2	Glasgow
23.5.1972	England*	1–0	Wembley
27.5.1972	Wales*	0–0	Wrexham

Peter O'Sullivan (Wales)
3 appearances, 1 goal

Date	Opponent	Score	Venue
12.5.1973	Scotland (sub.)*	0–2	Wrexham
6.5.1976	Scotland*	1–3	Glasgow
25.10.1978	Malta (sub.)§ (1 g)	7–0	Wrexham

Joe Kinnear (Republic of Ireland)
1 appearance

Date	Opponent	Score	Venue
29.10.1975	Turkey (sub.)§	4–0	Dublin

Sammy Morgan (Northern Ireland)
2 appearances

Date	Opponent	Score	Venue
8.5.1976	Scotland*	0–3	Glasgow
14.5.1976	Wales (sub.)*	0–1	Swansea

Mark Lawrenson (Republic of Ireland)
14 appearances, 2 goals

Date	Opponent	Score	Venue
12.10.1977	Bulgaria†	0–0	Dublin
12.4.1978	Poland	0–3	Lodz
21.5.1978	Norway (sub.)	0–0	Oslo
24.5.1978	Denmark§	3–3	Copenhagen
20.9.1978	Northern Ireland§	0–0	Dublin
25.10.1978	England§	1–1	Dublin
6.2.1980	England§	0–2	Wembley
26.3.1980	Cyprus† (1 g)	3–2	Nicosia
30.4.1980	Switzerland	2–0	Dublin
10.9.1980	Netherlands† (1 g)	2–1	Dublin
15.10.1980	Belgium†	1–1	Dublin
28.10.1980	France†	0–2	Paris
19.11.1980	Cyprus†	6–0	Dublin
23.5.1981	Poland	0–3	Bydgoszcz

Gerry Ryan (Republic of Ireland)
16 appearances, 1 goal

Date	Opponent	Score	Venue
25.10.1978	England§	1–1	Dublin
22.5.1979	West Germany (1 g)	1–3	Dublin
11.9.1979	Wales	1–2	Swansea
26.3.1980	Cyprus (sub.)†	3–2	Nicosia
30.4.1980	Switzerland	2–0	Dublin
16.5.1980	Argentina (sub.)	0–1	Dublin
28.10.1980	France (sub.)†	0–2	Paris
21.5.1981	West Germany 'B'	0–3	Bremen
23.5.1981	Poland (sub.)	0–3	Bydgoszcz
9.9.1981	Netherlands (sub.)†	2–2	Rotterdam
28.4.1982	Algeria (sub.)	0–2	Algiers
22.5.1982	Chile (sub.)	0–1	Santiago
30.5.1982	Trinidad & Tobago	1–2	Port of Spain
23.5.1984	Poland	0–0	Dublin
3.6.1984	China	1–0	Sapporo
8.8.1984	Mexico	0–0	Dublin

Peter Ward (England)
1 appearance

Date	Opponent	Score	Venue
31.5.1980	Australia (sub.)	2–1	Sydney

Moshe Gariani (Israel)
3 appearances

Date	Opponent	Score	Venue
18.6.1980	Sweden†	1–1	Stockholm
12.11.1980	Sweden†	0–0	Tel Aviv
17.12.1980	Portugal†	0–3	Lisbon

Michael Robinson (Republic of Ireland)
13 appearances, 3 goals

Date	Opponent	Score	Venue
28.10.1980	France†	0–2	Paris
19.11.1980	Cyprus† (1 g)	6–0	Dublin
25.3.1981	Belgium†	0–1	Brussels
21.5.1981	West Germany 'B'	0–3	Bremen
23.5.1981	Poland	0–3	Bydgoszcz
9.9.1981	Netherlands† (1 g)	2–2	Rotterdam
14.10.1981	France† (1 g)	3–2	Dublin
28.4.1982	Algeria	0–2	Algiers
22.5.1982	Chile	0–1	Santiago
22.9.1982	Netherlands§	1–2	Rotterdam
13.10.1982	Iceland§	2–0	Dublin
17.11.1982	Spain§	3–3	Dublin
30.3.1983	Malta§	1–0	Valletta

Jacob Cohen (Israel)
4 appearances

Date	Opponent	Score	Venue
12.11.1980	Sweden†	0–0	Tel Aviv
17.12.1980	Portugal†	0–3	Lisbon
25.2.1981	Scotland†	0–1	Tel Aviv
28.4.1981	Scotland†	1–3	Glasgow

Tony Grealish (Republic of Ireland)
11 appearances, 1 goal

Date	Opponent	Score	Venue
9.9.1981	Netherlands†	2–2	Rotterdam
28.4.1982	Algeria	0–2	Algiers
22.5.1982	Chile	0–1	Santiago
27.5.1982	Brazil	0–7	Uberlandia
30.5.1982	Trinidad & Tobago	1–2	Port of Spain
22.9.1982	Netherlands§	1–2	Rotterdam
13.10.1982	Iceland§ (1 g)	2–0	Dublin
17.11.1982	Spain§	3–3	Dublin
27.4.1983	Spain§	0–2	Zaragoza
21.9.1983	Iceland§	3–0	Reykjavik
12.10.1983	Netherlands§	2–3	Dublin

Micky Thomas (Wales)
5 appearances

Date	Opponent	Score	Venue
18.11.1981	U.S.S.R. (sub.)†	0–3	Tbilisi
24.3.1982	Spain	1–1	Valencia
27.4.1982	England*	0–1	Cardiff
24.5.1982	Scotland (sub.)*	0–1	Glasgow
27.5.1982	N. Ireland (sub.)*	3–0	Wrexham

Steve Foster (England)
3 appearances

Date	Opponent	Score	Venue
23.2.1982	Northern Ireland*	4–0	Wembley
25.5.1982	Netherlands	2–0	Wembley
25.6.1982	Kuwait‡	1–0	Bilbao

Sammy Nelson (Northern Ireland)
4 appearances

Date	Opponent	Score	Venue
23.2.1982	England*	0–4	Wembley
28.4.1982	Scotland*	1–1	Belfast
25.6.1982	Spain (sub.)‡	1–0	Valencia
1.7.1982	Austria‡	2–2	Madrid

Kieran O'Regan (Republic of Ireland)
4 appearances

Date	Opponent	Score	Venue
16.11.1983	Malta§	8–0	Dublin
23.5.1984	Poland	0–0	Dublin
8.8.1984	Mexico	0–0	Dublin
26.5.1985	Spain (sub.)	0–0	Cork

Gary Howlett (Republic of Ireland)
1 appearance

Date	Opponent	Score	Venue
3.6.1984	China (sub.)	1–0	Sapporo

Steve Penney (Northern Ireland)
17 appearances, 2 goals

Date	Opponent	Score	Venue
16.10.1984	Israel	3–0	Belfast
11.9.1985	Turkey†	0–0	Izmir
16.10.1985	Romania†	1–0	Bucharest
13.11.1985	England†	0–0	Wembley
26.2.1986	France	0–0	Paris
26.3.1986	Denmark	1–1	Belfast
23.4.1986	Morocco	2–1	Belfast
3.6.1986	Algeria‡	1–1	Guadalajara
7.6.1986	Spain‡	1–2	Guadalajara
15.10.1986	England§	0–3	Wembley
12.11.1986	Turkey§	0–0	Izmir
18.2.1987	Israel (1 g)	1–1	Tel Aviv
23.3.1988	Poland	1–1	Belfast
27.4.1988	France	0–0	Belfast
21.5.1988	Malta† (1 g)	3–0	Belfast
14.9.1988	Republic of Ireland†	0–0	Belfast
21.12.1988	Spain†	0–4	Seville

Dean Saunders (Wales)
5 appearances, 2 goals

Date	Opponent	Score	Venue
26.3.1986	Rep. of Ireland (sub.)	1–0	Dublin
10.5.1986	Canada	0–2	Toronto
20.5.1986	Canada (2 g)	3–0	Vancouver
10.9.1986	Finland	1–1	Helsinki
18.2.1987	U.S.S.R.	0–0	Swansea

Danny Wilson (Northern Ireland)
3 appearances

Date	Opponent	Score	Venue
12.12.1986	Turkey§	0–0	Izmir
18.2.1987	Israel	1–1	Tel Aviv
1.4.1987	England (sub.)§	0–2	Belfast

John Byrne (Republic of Ireland)
1 appearance, 1 goal

Date	Opponent	Score	Venue
6.2.1991	Wales (1 g)	3–0	Wrexham

'B' internationals

Jimmy Langley (England)
3 games

23.3.1955	West Germany	1–1	Sheffield
19.10.1955	Yugoslavia	5–1	Manchester
29.2.1956	Scotland	2–2	Dundee

Peter Ward (England)
1 game

14.10.1980	U.S.A. (sub.)	1–0	Manchester

Under-23 internationals

Freddie Jones (Wales)
1 game

25.11.1959	Scotland	1–1	Wrexham

Dave Hollins (Wales)
2 games

25.11.1959	Scotland	1–1	Wrexham
8.2.1961	England	0–2	Everton

John Napier (Northern Ireland)
1 game

20.3.1968	Wales	1–0	Cardiff

Peter O'Sullivan (Wales)
6 games

13.1.1971	Scotland (sub.)	1–0	Swansea
5.1.1972	England	0–2	Swindon
26.1.1972	Scotland	0–2	Aberdeen
29.11.1972	England	0–3	Wrexham
14.3.1973	Scotland	1–2	Swansea
4.2.1976	Scotland	2–3	Wrexham

England trialists

g goal scored

Fred Blackman

23.1.1911	Stripes v Whites	1–4	Tottenham

Billy Booth

25.11.1912	The South v England XI	2–1	Tottenham
20.1.1913	England XI v The North	0–5	Manchester

Tommy Cook

19.1.1925	The South v The North	3–1	Chelsea
9.2.1925	England XI v Rest (1g)	2–2	Manchester

Football League Division 3 (South) representatives

All matches v. Division 3 (North). g goal scored.

Jimmy Langley

16.3.1955		2–0	Reading
8.10.1956		2–1	Coventry

Glen Wilson

16.3.1955	(sub.)	2–0	Reading
2.4.1957		1–2	Stockport
20.10.1957		2–2	Selhurst Park

Peter Harburn

18.3.1958	(1 g)	1–0	Carlisle

Dave Sexton

18.3.1958		1–0	Carlisle

Frankie Howard

18.3.1958	(sub.)	1–0	Carlisle

Under-21 internationals

§ European Championship qualifier   g goal scored

Peter Ward (England)
2 games, 3 goals

6.9.1977	Norway§ (3 g)	6–0	Hove
23.4.1980	East Germany§	0–1	Jena

Steve Foster (England)
1 game

23.4.1980	East Germany (sub.)§	0–1	Jena

Andy Ritchie (England)
1 game

7.4.1982	Poland§	2–2	West Ham

Gary Stevens (England)
1 game

26.4.1983	Hungary§	1–0	Newcastle

Kieran O'Regan (Republic of Ireland)
5 games

5.6.1983	France	1–1	Toulon
7.6.1983	Argentina	0–1	Hyeres
9.6.1983	U.S.S.R.	0–1	Toulon
11.6.1983	China	5–1	Six-Fours
25.3.1985	England	2–3	Portsmouth

Gary Howlett (Republic of Ireland)
4 games, 1 goal

5.6.1983	France (1 g)	1–1	Toulon
7.6.1983	Argentina	0–1	Hyeres
9.6.1983	U.S.S.R.	0–1	Toulon
11.6.1983	China	5–1	Six-Fours

Gerry Ryan (Republic of Ireland)
1 game

25.3.1985	England	2–3	Portsmouth

Terry Connor (England)
1 game, 1 goal

11.11.1986	Yugoslavia§ (1 g)	1–1	Peterborough

Derek McGrath (Republic of Ireland)
3 games

30.5.1990	Malta	1–1	Valletta
26.3.1991	England§	0–3	Brentford
30.4.1991	Poland§	1–2	Dundalk

Paul McCarthy (Republic of Ireland)
10 games, 1 goal

30.5.1990	Malta (sub.)	1–1	Valetta
13.11.1990	England§	0–3	Cork
26.3.1991	England (sub.)§	0–3	Brentford
30.4.1991	Poland§	1–2	Dundalk
24.3.1992	Switzerland	1–1	Dublin
25.5.1992	Albania§	3–1	Dublin
17.11.1992	Spain§ (1 g)	1–2	Jerez
27.4.1993	Denmark§	0–2	Dublin
26.5.1993	Albania§	1–1	Tirana
12.10.1993	Spain§	0–2	Drogheda

John Robinson (Wales)
1 game

19.5.1992	Romania§	3–2	Bucharest

League representatives

Players representing first-team leagues only. g goal scored.

Fred Blackman (Southern Lge)
2 games

11.4.1910	Football League	2–2	Chelsea
14.11.1910	Football League	3–2	Tottenham

Billy Booth (Southern League)
7 games

24.10.1910	Scottish League	1–0	Millwall
14.11.1910	Football League	3–2	Tottenham
20.3.1911	Irish League	4–0	West Ham
30.9.1911	Irish League	2–1	Belfast
2.10.1911	Scottish League	2–3	Clyde
15.3.1913	Irish League	1–1	Millwall
9.2.1914	Football League	1–3	Millwall

Charlie Webb (Southern League)
1 game, 1 goal

30.9.1912	Football League (1 g)	1–2	Manchester

Charlie Webb (Southern Alliance)
1 game

8.10.1913	Croydon Common	2–1	Selhurst

Joe Leeming (Southern Alliance)
1 game

8.10.1913	Croydon Common	2–1	Selhurst

Gunner Higham (Southern League)
2 games

11.10.1913	Irish League	4–1	Dublin
13.10.1913	Scottish League	0–5	Glasgow

Bill Jones (Southern League)
1 game

12.10.1914	Scottish League	1–1	Millwall

Jimmy Langley (Football League)
1 game

31.10.1956	Irish League	3–2	Newcastle

Other miscellaneous representative appearances

Joe Leeming

1910 F.A. summer tour		South Africa

Jack Woodhouse

1920 F.A. summer tour		South Africa

Denis Foreman

27.11.1952	F.A. XI v Cambridge Univ.	8–0	Cambridge
12.3.1956	Springboks XI v Scotland XI	1–2	Glasgow

Jimmy Langley

3.11.1954	F.A. XI v The Army	1–1	Sheffield
1955	F.A. summer tour		West Indies
12.10.1955	F.A. XI v R.A.F.	9–0	Bristol
1956	F.A. summer tour		South Africa
10.10.1956	F.A. XI v R.A.F.	2–1	Sheffield
7.11.1956	F.A. XI v The Army	7–3	Manchester

Peter O'Sullivan

26.4.1976	Wales XI v London XI (1 g)	1–0	Highbury

Tony Grealish

1.6.1982	R. of Ireland XI v ASL	3–1	Port of Spain

Gerry Ryan

1.6.1982	R. of Ireland XI v ASL (1g)	3–1	Port of Spain

Steve Foster

9.2.1982	England XI v Man. City	2–1	Manchester
23.3.1982	England XI v Athletic Bilbao	1–1	Bilbao
18.5.1982	England XI v Aston Villa (1g)	2–3	Birmingham

John Byrne

11.8.1991	R. of Ireland XI v Man. Utd (sub.)	1–1	Manchester

Albion beneficiaries

The following players, ex-players and other employees have enjoyed benefit games or collections (for long service except where indicated).
Note that in earlier years it was the custom to grant the proceeds of a scheduled league game to the beneficiary.

Beneficiary	Date	Match	Type of match	Score	Attendance	Proceeds
John Jackson	25.4.1905	Albion v. Tottenham Hotspur	Testimonial	3–3		

Albion's former manager was awarded a testimonial match on Easter Tuesday which was played for the 'Jackson Souvenir Cup'. At a post-match social gathering, it was announced that the trophy was to be offered for competition annually between schoolboy teams representing Brighton and Tottenham.

Ben Garfield						

After moving to Tunbridge Wells Rangers in 1905, the former winger had to retire because of injury. Albion launched an appeal on his behalf in September 1905.

Arthur Hulme	27.11.1907	Albion v. Southampton	Western League	3–0	1,500	
Ralph Routledge	30.4.1913	Albion v. Millwall	Southern Alliance	2–2	1,000	£51 9s. 9d.

Ralph was forced into retirement by a knee injury received in the Southern League match with Coventry City in September 1912. A fund was set up for his benefit to which the receipts from the above fixture were donated. Routledge subsequently made a comeback in 1914–15.

Bert Longstaff	16.4.1913	Albion v. Portsmouth	Southern Alliance	3–0	2,000	£135 3s.
	5.5.1923	Albion v. Merthyr Town	Football League	0–0	5,000	

The Merthyr Town game was a joint benefit with Bill Miller.

Billy Booth	14.3.1914	Albion v. Exeter City	Southern League	2–1	3,000	
Joe Leeming	13.4.1914	Reserves v. Southampton	South Eastern League	3–2	3,500	£118

Club captain Joe stepped down to play for the Lambs in his benefit match on Easter Monday.

Bob Whiting	21.10.1914	Albion v. Chelsea	Testimonial			

Bob's benefit match against his former club was postponed indefinitely owing to the poor wartime attendances. Whiting unfortunately lost his life during the conflict and his benefit was therefore never realised.

Fred Bates	21.11.1914	Albion v. Croydon Common	Southern League	4–1	3,000	£3 2s. 9d.

Albion's groundsman was killed in the early days of the war while serving with the Royal Scots Fusiliers, and a collection was made on behalf of his widow at the above match.

Gunner Higham	24.4.1920	Albion v. Newport County	Southern League	3–1	10,500	£605 3s.
Charlie Webb	23.4.1921	Albion v. Watford	Football League	0–3	10,000	£495 15s. 11d.
	28.9.1949	Portsmouth v. Arsenal	Testimonial	2–1	13,000	

The two First Division sides met at the Goldstone in a splendid tribute to the man who was associated with the Albion as player and manager from 1908 until 1947.

Jack Bollington	30.11.1921	Albion v. Cardiff City	Testimonial	0–3	4,500	

Jack retired after breaking a leg in the F.A. Cup tie with Cardiff City at the Goldstone in January 1921, and the two clubs met the following November for his benefit.

Jack Woodhouse	22.4.1922	Albion v. Gillingham	Football League	0–1	6,000	
George Coomber	7.4.1923	Albion v. Reading	Football League	3–1	7,703	£480
Bill Miller	5.5.1923	Albion v. Merthyr Town	Football League	0–0	5,000	

A joint testimonial with Bert Longstaff.

Reg Phillips	2.4.1924	Reserves v. Southampton	Testimonial	2–1		£125

Reg died at the age of 23 in March 1924 and the receipts from the above match were donated to his family.

Wally Little	28.3.1925	Albion v. Queenis Park Rangers	Football League	5–0	6,500	
Jack Thompson	3.3.1926	Albion v. Portsmouth	Testimonial	4–4	1,124	
Tommy Cook	5.3.1927	Albion v. Gillingham	Football League	3–2	9,447	£437 15s. 1d.
Jack Nightingale	2.4.1927	Albion v. Charlton Athletic	Football League	3–2	7,823	£338
Tug Wilson	10.3.1928	Albion v. Gillingham	Football League	0–0	7,860	£326 15s. 2d.
	4.5.1933	Albion v. Birmingham	Testimonial	2–1	4,700	£323 6s. 9d.
Jack Jenkins	24.3.1928	Albion v. Merthyr Town	Football League	5–0	7,663	
Ernie Ison, Reg Smith	18.4.1930	Albion v. Coventry City	Football League	1–1	9,100	
and Reg Wilkinson	19.4.1930	Albion v. Queenis Park Rangers	Football League	2–3	6,411	
	21.4.1930	Reserves v. Coventry City	London Combination	3–1		

These three long-serving players were unfortunate that their benefit season coincided with a financial crisis at the Goldstone, which meant that they were not granted a game. Collections were made on their behalf at the above Eastertide matches.

Paul Mooney and Stan Webb	14.3.1931	Albion v. Notts County	Football League	1–3	14,037	

Mooney and Webb had to make do with the proceeds of a collection at the above fixture, attended by the biggest crowd of the season.

Jack Williams	27.4.1932	Albion v. Portsmouth	Testimonial	0–2	3,804	

Jack was forced to retire through injury.

Bobby Farrell	1.5.1935	Albion v. Portsmouth	Testimonial	2–3	3,200	

Bobby was due a benefit in 1934 but it was held over for a year because of the financial situation.

Potter Smith	29.4.1936	Albion v. Brentford	Testimonial	1–2	3,354	
Dave Walker	28.4.1937	Albion v. Southampton	Testimonial	1–1	2,617	
Albert Underwood	30.10.1937	Reserves v. Arsenal	London Combination	3–3	3,935	

Albion's long-serving secretary died in January 1937 and the gate receipts from the above match were donated to his widow.

Ernie King	4.5.1938	Albion v. Bolton Wanderers	Testimonial	1–5	3,022	
Ted Martin	19.4.1939	Albion v. West Ham United	Testimonial	2–0	794	
Dickie Meades	3.5.1939	Albion v. Brentford	Testimonial	0–1	752	

Dickie retired after nineteen years as Albion's trainer and was rewarded with a testimonial match.

Jack Carruthers	20.12.1947	Albion v. Hartlepools United	F.A. Cup	2–1	15,000	

Jack died in November 1947 at the age of 45 and a collection was made on behalf of his family at the above match.

Len Darling, Ernie Marriott,	26.4.1948	Notts County	Testimonial	1–7	6,068	
Stan Risdon and Bert Stephens	27.9.1948	Albion v. Wolverhampton Wanderers	Testimonial	1–4	5,128	
	25.4.1949	Albion v. Charlton Athletic	Testimonial	1–3	3,618	

All three games were joint testimonials with Joe Wilson.

Albion beneficiaries (cont.)

The following players, ex-players and other employees have enjoyed benefit games or collections (for long service except where indicated).
Note that in earlier years it was the custom to grant the proceeds of a scheduled league game to the beneficiary.

Beneficiary	Date	Match	Type of match	Score	Attendance	Proceeds
Joe Wilson	26.4.1948	Albion v. Notts County	Testimonial	1–7	6,068	
	27.9.1948	Albion v. Wolverhampton Wanderers	Testimonial	1–4	5,128	
	25.4.1949	Albion v. Charlton Athletic	Testimonial	1–3	3,618	
The above three games were joint testimonial matches with Len Darling, Ernie Marriott, Stan Risdon and Bert Stephens.						
	13.11.1961	Albion v. G. Gunn International XI	Testimonial	0–5	12,600	£1,530
	3.5.1974	Albion v. All-Star XI	Testimonial	2–2	4,464	c. £2,000
Reg Hipkin	14.1.1950	Albion v. Newport County	Football League	5–0	11,502	
A collection was made at the above match for Reg who had to give up the game because of a knee injury sustained at Bristol Rovers in November 1948.						
Harry Baldwin and Jack Ball	28.9.1950	Albion v. All-Star XI	Testimonial	4–3	7,965	
	30.4.1951	Albion v. Liverpool	Testimonial	1–1	11,254	
The Liverpool game was a joint testimonial with Jack Dugnolle.						
Jack Dugnolle	10.2.1951	'A' team v. Dagenham	Metropolitan League	0–3	1,065	
	30.4.1951	Albion v. Liverpool	Testimonial	1–1	11,254	
	5.5.1951	'A' team v. Southwick	Testimonial	5–4		
Jack first came to the Goldstone in 1933 and spent five years with the club. He returned in 1946 and two years later became coach of the newly formed 'A' team. The Liverpool game was a joint testimonial with Harry Baldwin and Jack Ball.						
Jess Willard	17.4.1952	Reserves v. Chichester Invitation XI	Testimonial	4–2	1,200	Over £50
		Played at Priory Park, Chichester.				
	2.5.1952	Albion v. Nottingham Forest	Testimonial	5–4	6,000	
Alex Wilson	29.9.1952	Arsenal v. All-Star XI	Testimonial	2–4	9,350	
When Alex decided to give up his job as Albion's trainer, his former club Arsenal brought their team to the Goldstone to play an All-Star team including many international players.						
Des Tennant	1.5.1954	Des Tennantis XI v. Brentford	Testimonial	6–1	3,500	
Tennant's XI consisted mainly of Albion and ex-Albion players.						
Albion Players' Benefit Fund	3.5.1957	Albion v. Liverpool	Testimonial	0–2	2,678	
	14.4.1959	Albion v. Kilmarnock	Testimonial	3–1	4,430	
	1.5.1959	Albion v. Newcastle United	Testimonial	1–1	6,682	
	30.3.1960	Albion v. Djurgarden (Sweden)	Testimonial	0–0	5,500	
In the late 1950s a general fund was set up for those long-serving players who were due a benefit. Eric Gill, Dennis Gordon, Roy Jennings, Don Bates and Tommy Bisset were among those to receive monies from the fund.						
Frankie Howard	12.11.1962	Albion v. G. Gunn International XI	Testimonial	5–5	5,827	
	3.3.1975	Albion v. Queenis Park Rangers	Testimonial	2–1	7,210	
Albion's groundsman enjoyed a third testimonial season in 1988–89 but did not have a benefit match.						
Steve Burtenshaw	11.11.1963	Albion v. G. Gunn International XI	Testimonial	3–7	5,500	£670
The match was abandoned after 85 minutes when the crowd invaded the pitch thinking the final whistle had been blown.						
Jack Bertolini and Cyril Hodges	13.11.1967	Albion v. All-Star XI	Testimonial	5–6	15,768	£3,500
Jack was forced to give up the game in 1965 after suffering a serious knee-ligament injury. Cyril first came to Hove in October 1946 but soon retired because of injury. He returned in 1957 as assistant trainer and remained at the Goldstone for eleven years.						
Norman Gall and Brian Powney	11.5.1971	Albion v. Wolverhampton Wanderers	Testimonial	0–2	6,385	£1,888
	16.5.1971	Albion v. International Club	Testimonial	9–1		
The above match was played at the greyhound stadium, Hove.						
	5.5.1972	Albion v. Chelsea	Testimonial	2–3	14,230	
Geoff Sidebottom	11.5.1972	Albion v. Birmingham City	Testimonial	2–2	8,886	
Geoff was forced into retirement because of serious head injuries.						
Joe Kinnear	23.3.1976	Albion v. Tottenham Hotspur	Testimonial	1–6	7,124	c. £4,000
Joe spent ten years as a professional at White Hart Lane before coming to the Goldstone.						
Chris Cattlin	9.8.1977	Albion v. Coventry City	Testimonial	3–1	8,918	
Chris had eight years with Coventry City prior to joining the Albion.						
Peter Grummitt	2.5.1978	Albion v. Alan Mulleryis All-Star XI	Testimonial	8–7	5,615	
Peter had to give up the game because of chronic injuries to his knee and hip.						
Peter O'Sullivan	22.4.1980	Albion v. Southampton	Testimonial	1–3	6,881	c. £10,000
Gary Williams	14.5.1984	Albion v. Ex-Albion XI	Testimonial	3–3	2,600	
Gary spent five years at the Goldstone before moving to Crystal Palace where he received the injury that cut short his League career. He was playing for Whitehawk when he was granted this testimonial match.						
Gerry Ryan	8.8.1986	Albion v. Tottenham Hotspur	Testimonial	0–4	10,759	c. £20,000
Gerry had to hang up his boots after suffering a severely broken leg at Crystal Palace in April 1985.						
Graham Moseley	3.4.1990	Albion 1983 v. Tottenham Hotspur	Testimonial	0–3	6,410	c. £18,000
Graham left the Goldstone for Cardiff City after almost nine years, but was forced into early retirement owing to injuries incurred in a car crash. The Albion 1983 side contained nine of the players who represented the club in the 1983 F.A. Cup final and replay.						
Steve Gatting	17.8.1990	Albion v. Arsenal	Testimonial	2–2	5,517	
	12.11.90	Albion v. Eastbourne Select XI	Testimonial	6–0	1,300	
Above match played at Priory Lane, Langney Sports F.C.						
Perry Digweed						
The long-serving goalkeeper had a testimonial season in 1991–92 but did not have a benefit match.						
Gary Chivers	7.8.1992	Albion v. Crystal Palace	Testimonial	0–1	3,273	
Albion's captain received a testimonial after just over four years at the club and fourteen as a professional.						
Gary O'Reilly						
The former defender, whose professional career was finished by injury, enjoyed a testimonial season in 1993–94 but did not have a benefit match.						
Jimmy Case	17.10.1994	Albion v. Liverpool	Testimonial	1–2	15,645	c. £75,000
After 21 years as a professional, Albion's player-coach was rewarded with a game that attracted the highest crowd of the season to the Goldstone Ground.						
Steve Foster	26.7.1996	Albion v. Sheffield Wednesday	Testimonial	1–7	3,831	
Albion's veteran defender retired at the end of the previous season after 669 League games for five clubs, and 332 senior games for the Albion.						

Albion players in debut order

Player	Debut	Last game	Player	Debut	Last game	Player	Debut	Last game
1901–02			Good, Mickey	3.9.1904	29.4.1905	Crump, Fred	5.9.1908	13.2.1909
			Hulse, Ben	3.9.1904	22.4.1905	Grierson, Tom	7.9.1908	3.3.1909
Baker, Bert	21.9.1901	31.1.1903	Livingstone, Archie	3.9.1904	18.3.1905	Lloyd, Arthur	12.9.1908	13.2.1909
Barker, Clem	21.9.1901	15.2.1902	Mellors, Mark	3.9.1904	28.4.1906	Whiting, Bob	12.9.1908	1.5.1915
Caldwell, Jock	21.9.1901	23.4.1904	O'Brien, Joe	3.9.1904	21.4.1905	Brennan, Jimmy	16.9.1908	7.12.1908
Colclough, Ephraim	21.9.1901	25.1.1902	Robertson, Tom	3.9.1904	29.4.1905	Dalton, Ted	7.10.1908	29.4.1909
Collins, Ned	21.9.1901	1.4.1902	Kelly, Willie	10.9.1904	29.4.1905	Isherwood, Bob	14.10.1908	21.10.1908
Farrell, Paddy	21.9.1901	13.4.1904	Lyon, Bertie	17.9.1904	29.4.1905	Elliott, Teddy	2.12.1908	28.12.1908
McAvoy, Frank	21.9.1901	15.2.1902	Millar, Arthur	17.9.1904	22.4.1905	Webb, Charlie	2.1.1909	5.4.1915
Mendham, C. J.	21.9.1901	21.12.1901	Ward, Alf	17.9.1904	12.11.1904	**1909–10**		
Russell, Jock	21.9.1901	5.4.1902	White, Tom	1.10.1904	23.4.1906			
Sutherland, Jim	21.9.1901	18.10.1902	Leach, George	8.10.1904	12.4.1909	Blackman, Fred	1.9.1909	29.4.1911
Whitehurst, Squire	21.9.1901	5.9.1903	Robinson, G. L.	22.4.1905	29.4.1905	Featherstone, George	1.9.1909	12.2.1910
Mitchell, F.	28.9.1901	1.10.1902	**1905–06**			Hastings, Bill	1.9.1909	24.1.1912
Sharp, Alf	28.9.1901	28.9.1901				Jones, Bullet	1.9.1909	20.12.1919
Smith, Albert	26.10.1901	27.4.1903	Allsopp, Tommy	2.9.1905	30.4.1907	McGhie, Joe	1.9.1909	30.4.1913
Coles, Donald	30.11.1901	18.4.1903	Buckley, Frank	2.9.1905	28.4.1906	Middleton, Harry	1.9.1909	4.4.1910
Thair, Sid	4.1.1902	12.12.1903	Clare, Edwin	2.9.1905	13.4.1906	Connor, Nat	18.9.1909	15.1.1910
Blunden, Bertie	25.1.1902	5.4.1902	Fisher, Albert	2.9.1905	30.4.1906	Haworth, Jack	7.10.1909	10.2.1912
Callow, J. W.	1.2.1902	15.2.1902	Innes, Bob	2.9.1905	30.4.1906	Armstrong, Arthur	16.10.1909	23.10.1909
Dollman, Frank	1.2.1902	5.4.1902	Kennedy, Jimmy	2.9.1905	23.4.1906	Coleman, Jimmy	22.1.1910	10.4.1915
Telford, J.	1.2.1902	1.2.1902	Kennedy, Willie	2.9.1905	23.4.1906	Eacock, Jack	2.4.1910	2.4.1910
Woodhams, Wilf	8.2.1902	5.4.1902	Mochan, Charlie	2.9.1905	23.4.1906	**1910–11**		
Gardiner, J. J.	15.2.1902	20.9.1902	Yates, Billy	2.9.1905	30.4.1906			
Hill, W.	1.3.1902	11.10.1902	Hall, Proctor	6.9.1905	21.4.1906	Miller, Bill	10.9.1910	2.5.1921
King, Eddie	1.3.1902	22.3.1902	Joynes, Dick	6.9.1905	25.4.1908	Thomas, Jack	14.9.1910	24.12.1910
Sear	1.3.1902	8.3.1902	Kent, Harry	6.9.1905	20.4.1908	Wake, Tom	14.9.1910	27.11.1912
Mansfield, W.	1.4.1902	18.10.1902	Lumley, Joe	6.9.1905	17.4.1912	Routledge, Ralph	26.11.1910	1.5.1915
King, P.	5.4.1902	5.4.1902	Turner, Tom	6.9.1905	9.1.1909	Smith, Jimmy	7.1.1911	20.11.1912
1902–03			Anthony, Walter	20.9.1905	8.2.1908	Sharpe, Ivan	4.2.1911	9.2.1911
			Wragg, Billy	20.9.1905	2.4.1906	Smart, Freddie	22.2.1911	28.4.1913
Broughton, F.	13.9.1902	18.4.1903	Rule, Arthur	30.9.1905	30.9.1905	Perkins, Bill	25.2.1911	25.2.1911
Garfield, Ben	13.9.1902	22.2.1905	Beale, Bob	11.10.1905	21.4.1908	Ford, G. W.	4.3.1911	4.3.1911
Harland, Lohmann	13.9.1902	14.4.1903	Buckley, Chris	11.10.1905	28.4.1906	Crinson, Bill	24.4.1911	17.4.1913
Hulme, Arthur	13.9.1902	14.11.1908	Graham, John	14.10.1905	14.10.1905	Stott, Tom	26.4.1911	27.4.1911
Lee, Barney	13.9.1902	25.4.1903	Langley, Ernie	28.10.1905	28.10.1905	**1911–12**		
Scott, Frank	13.9.1902	13.4.1904	Edwards, W. G.	31.1.1906	31.1.1906			
Lamb, Billy	17.9.1902	2.4.1904	Harding, F.	31.1.1906	31.1.1906	Needham, Archie	2.9.1911	1.5.1915
Howes, Arthur	24.9.1902	23.4.1904	Kitto, Dick	31.1.1906	31.1.1906	Henderson, Crosby	6.9.1911	20.4.1912
West, H. C.	24.9.1902	25.4.1903	Foster	2.4.1906	2.4.1906	Goodwin, Fred	9.9.1911	12.4.1913
Gooch, A. G.	27.9.1902	18.10.1902	**1906–07**			Parlett, Frank	17.2.1912	23.4.1914
Hardman, J.	4.10.1902	19.3.1904				Parker, J.	8.4.1912	8.4.1912
Craven, W.	18.10.1902	18.10.1902	Gregory, Julius	1.9.1906	25.4.1908	Piggin, Lionel	9.4.1912	13.4.1912
Reed, Walter	18.10.1902	18.10.1902	Hall, Jack H.	1.9.1906	18.4.1908	Sulston, Cecil	13.4.1912	13.4.1912
Starks, G. T.	18.10.1902	18.10.1902	Lewis, Jack	1.9.1906	30.4.1907	Matthews, Charlie	20.4.1912	18.2.1914
Wickham, Alf	18.10.1902	18.10.1902	MacDonald, Hugh	1.9.1906	25.4.1908	**1912–13**		
Lanham, Charlie	27.10.1902	27.10.1902	McDonald, Willie	1.9.1906	25.4.1908			
Owen, F.	22.11.1902	9.3.1903	Smith, Alec	1.9.1906	26.12.1906	Spencer, Frank	21.9.1912	1.5.1920
Goulding	6.12.1902	6.12.1902	Smith, Wally	1.9.1906	27.4.1907	Flannery, Tom	2.10.1912	28.4.1913
Taylor, A. J.	6.12.1902	27.4.1903	Schooley, Herbert	4.10.1906	4.10.1906	Woodhouse, Jack	2.10.1912	29.8.1923
Millard, A.	21.2.1903	21.2.1903	Woolven, Harold	4.10.1906	31.10.1906	Hodge, Billy	9.10.1912	12.11.1913
Grayer, S.	21.3.1903	11.4.1903	Longstaff, Bert	7.11.1906	22.10.1921	Middleton, Billy	9.10.1912	30.4.1913
Ward, W.	25.3.1903	25.4.1903	Harker, Frank	12.12.1906	12.12.1906	Longstaff, Harvey	16.10.1912	26.3.1913
Ffennell, Edgar	18.4.1903	18.4.1903	**1907–08**			Whittington, Dick	19.10.1912	3.12.1913
Smith, W.	18.4.1903	18.4.1903				Taylor, Joe	23.10.1912	23.10.1912
Allen, A.	25.4.1903	25.4.1903	Archer, Arthur	7.9.1907	25.4.1908	Houghton, F.	13.11.1912	13.11.1912
Hammond, Harry	25.4.1903	25.4.1903	Burnett, Jimmy	7.9.1907	11.4.1908	Nash, H.	4.12.1912	4.12.1912
Payne	25.4.1903	25.4.1903	Morris, Tom	7.9.1907	30.1.1909	Simpson, Bobby	14.12.1912	16.10.1913
Sweetman, George	25.4.1903	25.4.1903	Ronaldson, Duncan	7.9.1907	25.4.1908	Longhurst, G. R.	29.1.1913	29.1.1913
1903–04			Wombwell, Dick	7.9.1907	8.2.1908	Parkes, David	29.1.1913	7.3.1914
			Fitchie, Tom	2.10.1907	2.10.1907	Ault, Alfred	19.2.1913	19.2.1913
Boulton, Bill	5.9.1903	16.1.1904	Porter, Willie	16.10.1907	16.10.1907	Kitchen, Sid	19.2.1913	19.2.1913
Hyde, Len	5.9.1903	13.4.1904	Higham, Gunner	6.1.1908	1.5.1920	Brown, Bill	26.2.1913	18.3.1914
McAteer, Tom	5.9.1903	23.4.1904	Townshend, A.	6.1.1908	2.11.1908	Williamson	26.2.1913	17.4.1913
Paddington, Albert	5.9.1903	23.4.1904	Dougal, Dave	29.2.1908	25.4.1908	Williams, D. H.	12.3.1913	15.3.1913
Roberts, Billy	5.9.1903	22.4.1905	Rodger, Tom	29.2.1908	25.4.1908	Birdsall, George	10.4.1913	10.4.1913
Rushton, George	19.9.1903	23.4.1904	**1908–09**			Tyler, Alfie	16.4.1913	27.3.1915
Cameron, Duncan	10.10.1903	5.3.1904				Pinder, W.	23.4.1913	23.4.1913
Haig-Brown, Alan	31.10.1903	28.10.1905	Atkinson, Jimmy	2.9.1908	29.4.1909	Turner	23.4.1913	23.4.1913
Dennett, J. W.	14.11.1903	21.11.1903	Booth, Billy	2.9.1908	1.5.1920	**1913–14**		
Parsons, Ted	12.12.1903	29.4.1905	Hall, Jack E.	2.9.1908	29.4.1909			
Pryce, Jack	19.12.1903	24.9.1904	Jee, Joe	2.9.1908	29.4.1909	Batey, Ginger	3.9.1913	30.1.1915
McCairns, Tom	28.12.1903	23.4.1904	Leeming, Joe	2.9.1908	25.4.1914	Carter, William	2.10.1913	2.10.1913
1904–05			Martin, Jack	2.9.1908	29.4.1909	Lowe, Harry	2.10.1913	13.4.1914
			Robertson, Jimmy	2.9.1908	24.4.1909	Roberts, J.	2.10.1913	2.10.1913
Aspden, Tommy	3.9.1904	22.10.1904	Stewart, Tom	2.9.1908	24.4.1909	Spooner, Billy	8.10.1913	1.4.1914
Gardner, Andy	3.9.1904	29.4.1905	Tustin, Bill	2.9.1908	3.3.1909	Wilcock, George	8.10.1913	20.2.1915
Gilhooly, Paddy	3.9.1904	29.4.1905	Wilson, Joe	2.9.1908	29.4.1909	Bridge, Mick	16.10.1913	26.11.1913

Albion players in debut order (cont.)

* see Albion Wartime Players ‡ see Albion's Nearly Men † also played for Albion in aborted 1939–40 Football League Division Three (South) season

Player	Debut	Last game	Player	Debut	Last game	Player	Debut	Last game
Coomber, George	16.10.1913	25.10.1924	Wilkinson, Reg	1.11.1924	5.5.1934	Wright, Joe	26.12.1932	18.11.1933
March, Zach	19.11.1913	6.5.1922	Mulhall, John	6.12.1924	13.12.1924	Harrison, Jack	29.4.1933	2.9.1933
Regan, J.	19.11.1913	19.11.1913	McKenna, Harold	31.1.1925	21.3.1925	**1933–34**		
Dodd, George	13.12.1913	18.4.1914	Hoyland, Fred	28.2.1925	5.9.1925			
Whitehouse, W.	18.3.1914	18.3.1914	Bradford, Jack	7.3.1925	14.3.1925	Lumberg, Albert	26.8.1933	7.2.1934
Paterson, Henry	1.4.1914	1.4.1914	Jennings, Sam	14.3.1925	5.5.1928	Darling, Len	14.10.1933	24.4.1948
1914–15			**1925–26**			Jepson, Bert	28.10.1933	4.5.1935
						Short, Jimmy	4.11.1933	4.5.1935
Beech, George	2.9.1914	22.11.1924	Hawley, Fred	29.8.1925	24.4.1926	Egan, Harry	22.2.1934	22.2.1936
Dexter, Charlie	2.9.1914	1.5.1915	Curran, Jack	14.9.1925	8.9.1930	Brown, Buster	31.3.1934	10.10.1936
Reed, Billy F.	24.10.1914	1.5.1915	Gilgun, Pat	10.10.1925	2.12.1925	**1934–35**		
1919–20			Webb, Stan	14.10.1925	5.5.1934			
			Goord, George	17.10.1925	17.10.1925	Jones, Herbert	25.8.1934	13.4.1935
Best, Jack	30.8.1919	17.1.1920	Mackay, Tommy	24.10.1925	24.10.1925	Payne, John	25.8.1934	19.1.1935
Groves, Henry	30.8.1919	22.11.1919	Mooney, Paul	24.10.1925	31.8.1935	Stevens, Jack	25.8.1934	3.10.1942
Hayes, Billy	30.8.1919	3.5.1924	Gough, Arthur	7.11.1925	23.4.1927	Thomson, Charlie	25.8.1934	4.2.1939
Holley, George	30.8.1919	26.12.1919	Cheetham, Jack	13.2.1926	17.4.1926	Barber, Stan	26.9.1934	26.9.1934
Pugh, Jimmy	30.8.1919	1.5.1920	Edmonds, Eddie	24.2.1926	5.1.1929	Marriott, Ernie	13.4.1935	1.5.1948
Eacock, Fred	6.9.1919	21.2.1920	Kelly, John	17.4.1926	21.4.1926	**1935–36**		
Little, Wally	20.9.1919	19.1.1929	Ison, Ernie	21.4.1926	18.10.1930			
Osborne, Fred	24.9.1919	11.10.1919	**1926–27**			Law, Alec	31.8.1935	18.3.1939
Moorhouse, Ben	22.11.1919	13.12.1919				Stephens, Bert	31.8.1935	29.11.1947
Ritchie, George	25.12.1919	6.9.1920	O'Rawe, Frank	28.8.1926	28.8.1926	Bellamy, Walter	12.9.1935	18.9.1935
Henderson, Billy	17.1.1920	17.4.1920	Williams, Skilly	28.8.1926	26.12.1928	Mee, Gordon	12.9.1935	25.12.1943
Brown, Tom	24.1.1920	2.5.1921	Mellon, Jimmy	6.10.1926	6.10.1926	Prest, Tommy	28.9.1935	17.4.1937
Brand, Bill	14.2.1920	21.2.1920	James, Dai	15.1.1927	6.4.1929	Richards, Billy	28.9.1935	9.1.1937
Williams, Dave	28.2.1920	16.4.1921	Sykes, Albert	15.1.1927	14.4.1928	McCarthy, Tom	19.10.1935	23.10.1935
Doran, Jack	6.3.1920	6.5.1922	Oswald, Willie	12.3.1927	18.2.1928	Dugnolle, Jack	2.11.1935	1.5.1948
1920–21			**1927–28**			Clarke, Billy	18.4.1936	18.4.1936
						1936–37		
Bentley, Harry	28.8.1920	6.5.1922	Simpson, Tommy	27.8.1927	5.5.1928			
Hall, Fretwell	28.8.1920	5.3.1921	Thomson, Norman	27.8.1927	28.4.1928	Cargill, Jimmy	29.8.1936	15.4.1939
Rodgerson, Ted	28.8.1920	7.1.1922	Readman, Joe	1.10.1927	17.3.1928	Davie, Jock	29.8.1936	20.4.1946
Rutherford, Jack	4.9.1920	7.5.1921	Chamberlain, Bert	29.10.1927	26.1.1929	Wilson, Joe A.	29.8.1936	17.5.1947
Bollington, Jack	6.9.1920	29.1.1921	Mace, Stan	27.12.1927	21.1.1928	McNaughton, Jock	10.9.1936	19.12.1945
Randall, Ossie	29.9.1920	29.9.1920	**1928–29**			Burton, Billy	19.9.1936	27.3.1937
Burnham, Jack	9.10.1920	9.10.1920				Brophy, Harry	30.9.1936	30.9.1936
Wisden, Alan	23.10.1920	23.10.1920	Kirkwood, Dan	25.8.1928	4.3.1933	Risdon, Stan	30.9.1936	24.5.1947
Rutherford, Jim	27.11.1920	7.5.1921	Townley, Jimmy	25.8.1928	30.3.1929	**1937–38**		
Neil, Andy	25.12.1920	7.5.1927	Turnbull, Billy	25.8.1928	20.10.1928			
Broadhead, Arnold	26.2.1921	6.5.1922	Pointon, Joe	1.9.1928	27.4.1929	Murfin, Clarrie	25.9.1937	25.9.1937
1921–22			Farrell, Bobby	22.9.1928	8.3.1941	Hall, Ernie	29.9.1937	20.11.1937
			Osborne, Jack	29.9.1928	13.10.1928	Hurst, Stan	9.10.1937	26.4.1939
Feebery, Jack	27.8.1921	3.5.1924	Lawson, Hector	1.12.1928	2.2.1929	Bowden, Ossie	6.11.1937	6.11.1937
Groves, Freddie	27.8.1921	5.1.1924	Williams, Jack	1.12.1928	2.4.1930	Goffey, Bert	4.12.1937	11.4.1942
Salt, Harold	27.8.1921	15.4.1922	Carruthers, Jack	5.1.1929	4.3.1933	**1938–39**		
Thompson, Jack	27.8.1921	5.4.1924	Gordon, Les	26.1.1929	4.5.1929			
Nightingale, Jack	31.8.1921	9.4.1927	**1929–30**			Philbin, Jack	27.8.1938	27.4.1946
Phillips, Reg	3.9.1921	10.9.1921				Trainor, Peter	27.8.1938	25.12.1947
McAllister, Billy	22.10.1921	20.12.1924	Nicol, Geordie	31.8.1929	9.9.1931	Atherton, Jack	3.12.1938	8.4.1939
Fuller, Eddie	4.2.1922	28.12.1929	Sly, Harold	31.8.1929	19.10.1932	Vasey, Bob	10.12.1938	29.4.1939
Evans, Tom E.	1.4.1922	15.4.1922	Smith, Potter	31.8.1929	10.4.1937	Green, Freddie	26.4.1939	30.8.1947
Channon, Vic	14.4.1922	15.4.1922	Vallance, Hugh	14.9.1929	20.9.1930	**1939–40**		
1922–23			Dutton, Harry	19.10.1929	5.3.1932			
			Marsden, Harry	26.10.1929	5.5.1934	Hindley, Frank† (see below)	–	–
Jenkins, Jack	26.8.1922	26.12.1928	Walker, Dave	2.11.1929	29.4.1939	Isaac, Bill† (see below)	–	–
Jones, Abe	26.8.1922	16.9.1922	Thompson, Stan	14.12.1929	16.2.1935	Baldwin, Harry† (see below)	–	–
Jones, Jimmy	26.8.1922	12.4.1924	McDonald, Murdo	15.3.1930	28.3.1931	Harris, Joe‡	–	–
Moore, Jimmy	26.8.1922	16.9.1922	Newton, Jimmy	3.5.1930	3.5.1930	Spencer, Geoff‡	–	–
Moorhead, George	26.8.1922	26.8.1922	**1930–31**			Evans, Tommy*	21.10.1939	30.3.1940
Saunders, Edgar	26.8.1922	7.2.1923				Isaac, Bill*†	21.10.1939	22.2.1941
Cook, Tommy	23.9.1922	1.5.1929	Brett, Frank	6.9.1930	6.4.1935	Longdon, Billy	21.10.1939	27.4.1946
Wilson, Ernie	21.10.1922	13.4.1936	Moffatt, Billy	6.9.1930	9.9.1931	Day, Albert	28.10.1939	4.5.1946
Hopkins, Jimmy	10.2.1923	4.5.1929	Duckworth, Joe	7.3.1931	30.1.1932	Duke, George*	11.11.1939	18.11.1939
1923–24			**1931–32**			Kay, John*	25.11.1939	10.2.1940
						Packham, Wally*	2.12.1939	16.12.1939
Brown, Freddie	25.8.1923	3.5.1924	Townsend, Eric	12.9.1931	7.10.1933	Broomfield, Des	30.12.1939	25.12.1947
Wright, Steve	25.8.1923	8.9.1923	Brown, Sam	3.10.1931	2.4.1932	Cowan, Sam*	30.12.1939	13.10.1945
Smith, Reg	24.11.1923	8.2.1930	Attwood, Arthur	7.11.1931	13.4.1935	Clarkson, George*	6.1.1940	10.2.1940
1924–25			Eyres, Jack	6.2.1932	7.5.1932	Bott, Wilf*	13.1.1940	8.6.1940
			King, Ernie	19.3.1932	8.1.1938	Flack, Doug*	13.1.1940	13.1.1940
Cook, Walter	30.8.1924	13.2.1926	Watson, Harold	26.3.1932	22.10.1932	Lowe, Henry*	13.1.1940	13.1.1940
Dennison, Bob	30.8.1924	11.3.1925	Ansell, George	13.4.1932	19.10.1932	Tait, Tommy*	13.1.1940	13.1.1940
Downs, Dickie	30.8.1924	6.12.1924	**1932–33**			Briggs, Vic*	27.1.1940	1.2.1941
Smith, Jack W.	30.8.1924	2.5.1925				Wilson, Alec*	2.3.1940	2.3.1940
Bunting, John	20.9.1924	20.12.1924	Martin, Ted	5.11.1932	8.12.1945	Grundy, Arnold*	9.3.1940	9.3.1940
Bedford, Ginger	1.11.1924	18.4.1925	Varco, Percy	17.12.1932	17.12.1932	Poulter, J.*	25.3.1940	25.3.1940

Albion players in debut order (cont.)

* see Albion Wartime Players   ‡ see Albion's Nearly Men   † also played for Albion in aborted 1939–40 Football League Division Three (South) season

Player	Debut	Last game
Clifford, John*	6.4.1940	6.4.1940
Abel, Sammy*	10.4.1940	10.4.1940
Keen, Eric*	10.4.1940	10.4.1940
Kelly, Jimmy*	10.4.1940	10.4.1940
Layton, Billy*	10.4.1940	10.4.1940
Swinfen, Reg*	10.4.1940	10.4.1940
Devine, John*	17.4.1940	17.4.1940
Butler, Malcolm*	20.4.1940	20.4.1940
Chesters, Arthur*	20.4.1940	8.6.1940
Court, Dick*	27.4.1940	27.4.1940
Kelly, Lawrie*	27.4.1940	7.3.1942
Collins, John*	13.5.1940	13.5.1940
Francis, Vic*	13.5.1940	13.5.1940
Cothliff, Harold*	18.5.1940	18.5.1940
Austen, Herbert*	1.6.1940	19.4.1941
Chase, Charlie	1.6.1940	30.1.1946
Harman, Charlie*	1.6.1940	19.4.1941
Hickman, Stan L.*	1.6.1940	15.3.1941
Watts, Roy*	1.6.1940	25.12.1940

1940–41

Player	Debut	Last game
Colborn, Harold*	31.8.1940	12.10.1940
Willemse, Stan	31.8.1940	7.5.1949
Felton, Bob*	14.9.1940	14.9.1940
Burtenshaw, Charlie*	5.10.1940	2.11.1940
Gunn, Alfie*	5.10.1940	23.2.1946
McCoy, Tim	5.10.1940	21.12.1953
Westby, Jack*	2.11.1940	24.1.1942
Bartram, A.*	25.12.1940	25.12.1940
Bird, S.*	25.12.1940	25.12.1940
Dye, Derek*	25.12.1940	25.12.1940
Ithell, Jimmy*	25.12.1940	9.10.1943
Pinchbeck, F.*	25.12.1940	25.12.1940
Smith, A.*	25.12.1940	25.12.1940
Stacey, W. A.*	25.12.1940	25.12.1940
Devonport, George*	25.1.1941	22.2.1941
Jones, Les*	8.2.1941	8.2.1941
Christie*	1.3.1941	1.3.1941
McDermott, Joe*	1.3.1941	13.10.1945
Welsh, Don*	1.3.1941	28.2.1942
Wilson, Fred*	8.3.1941	29.4.1944
Balmer, Jack*	15.3.1941	11.10.1941
Bush, Tom*	15.3.1941	11.10.1941
Laney, Les*	15.3.1941	15.3.1941
Ramsden, Bernard*	15.3.1941	11.10.1941
McInnes, Jimmy*	22.3.1941	27.12.1943
Barber*	29.3.1941	29.3.1941
Slater*	29.3.1941	29.3.1941
Spry*	29.3.1941	29.3.1941
Eastham, Harry*	5.4.1941	27.12.1943
Taylor, Phil*	14.4.1941	27.12.1943
Jones, Ron*	19.4.1941	19.4.1941
Kinghorn, Bill*	19.4.1941	18.9.1943

1941–42

Player	Debut	Last game
Shafto, John*	30.8.1941	27.12.1943
Pearson, Stan*	6.9.1941	12.12.1942
Tunnicliffe, Bill*	6.9.1941	8.11.1941
Browning, Charlie*	13.9.1941	14.3.1942
Easdale, Jack*	13.9.1941	27.12.1943
Paterson, George*	13.9.1941	27.9.1941
Hart, Archie*	18.10.1941	25.8.1945
Jones, Syd*	18.10.1941	10.4.1943
Tooze, Cyril*	18.10.1941	18.4.1942
Waller, Henry*	18.10.1941	3.1.1942
Clatworthy, Les*	25.10.1941	25.10.1941
Cunliffe, Arthur*	1.11.1941	18.4.1942
Lewis, Bill*	8.11.1941	8.11.1941
Curtis, George*	15.11.1941	7.3.1942
Morgan, Stan*	15.11.1941	20.3.1943
Williams, S.*	22.11.1941	14.2.1942
Bowles, Reg*	29.11.1941	10.4.1943
Henley, Les*	6.12.1941	6.12.1941
Ball, Jack	13.12.1941	3.1.1953
Burgess, Ron*	13.12.1941	27.12.1941
Chapman, A.*	13.12.1941	13.12.1941
Malpass, Sam*	25.12.1941	27.2.1943

Player	Debut	Last game
Peters, Bill*	25.12.1941	25.12.1941
Pryde, Bob*	3.1.1942	3.1.1942
Thew*	3.1.1942	3.1.1942
Nixon*	10.1.1942	10.1.1942
Eastham, George*	24.1.1942	21.3.1942
Moores, Peter*	24.1.1942	24.1.1942
Scrimshaw, Stan*	31.1.1942	7.2.1942
Mulraney, Ambrose*	14.2.1942	14.2.1942
Walker, Cyril*	14.2.1942	19.9.1942
Burdett*	21.2.1942	21.2.1942
Ford, Fred*	21.2.1942	19.9.1945
Gregory, Fred*	21.2.1942	21.2.1942
Haworth*	21.2.1942	28.3.1942
Lancelotte, Eric	21.2.1942	11.3.1950
Simmons, L.*	21.2.1942	21.2.1942
Woods*	28.2.1942	28.2.1942
Buckell*	7.3.1942	7.3.1942
Owens*	14.3.1942	14.3.1942
Kyle*	28.3.1942	28.3.1942
Lane, Billy*	28.3.1942	28.3.1942
Griffin, Albert*	6.4.1942	10.4.1943
Thorne, Albert*	11.4.1942	6.3.1943
Woodley, Vic*	18.4.1942	18.4.1942

1942–43

Player	Debut	Last game
Griffiths, Mal*	29.8.1942	30.10.1943
Mountford, George*	29.8.1942	29.8.1942
Bojar, Felix*	5.9.1942	10.4.1943
Gore, Les*	19.9.1942	26.9.1942
Reid, Ernie*	19.9.1942	8.9.1945
Blackman, Jack*	26.9.1942	26.9.1942
Gillespie, Ian*	26.9.1942	26.9.1942
Cook, P. R.*	3.10.1942	3.10.1942
Kirkman, Norman*	10.10.1942	10.10.1942
Woodward, Laurie*	17.10.1942	30.10.1943
Harlock, Des*	24.10.1942	24.10.1942
Bunyon, W.*	25.12.1942	25.12.1942
Cameron, Jock*	25.12.1942	25.12.1942
Ohlens, P. W.*	25.12.1942	25.12.1942
Richmond*	25.12.1942	25.12.1942
France, Ernie*	26.12.1942	25.12.1943
Moore, Bernard	26.12.1942	30.4.1955
Tully, Fred*	26.12.1942	26.12.1942
O'Donnell, Frank*	20.2.1943	3.11.1945
Cater, Ron*	27.2.1943	27.2.1943
Watson, Jack*	27.3.1943	3.4.1943

1943–44

Player	Debut	Last game
Szajna-Stankowski, Bishek*	28.8.1943	28.8.1943
Kemp, Dirk*	4.9.1943	18.12.1943
Muttitt, Ernie*	11.9.1943	12.2.1944
Tootill, Alf*	11.9.1943	11.9.1943
Hassell, Tommy	2.10.1943	23.12.1950
Grainger, Jack*	30.10.1943	6.11.1943
Anderson, Jock*	20.11.1943	11.12.1943
Edington, John*	20.11.1943	20.11.1943
Malone, Ron*	27.12.1943	27.12.1943
Ball*	1.1.1944	1.1.1944
Grier*	1.1.1944	1.1.1944
Lawrence*	1.1.1944	1.1.1944
Lowrie*	1.1.1944	1.1.1944
Sanderson*	1.1.1944	1.1.1944
Young*	1.1.1944	1.1.1944
unknown guest*	1.1.1944	1.1.1944
Hickman, S.*	8.1.1944	8.1.1944
Hillman, Dennis*	8.1.1944	20.4.1946
Fairhurst, Billy*	22.1.1944	24.3.1945
McNeill, Hamilton*	22.1.1944	29.1.1944
Wright, Tommy*	22.1.1944	18.3.1944
Wassall, Jack*	29.1.1944	11.3.1944
Dooley, A.*	5.2.1944	5.2.1944
Hooper, Percy*	5.2.1944	5.2.1944
Sperrin, Bill*	5.2.1944	12.2.1944
McKenzie, Duncan*	12.2.1944	21.10.1944
Weaver, Sam*	12.2.1944	12.2.1944
Bentley, George*	26.2.1944	26.2.1944
Fox, Dan*	25.3.1944	29.4.1944

Player	Debut	Last game
Hollis, Harry*	25.3.1944	25.3.1944
Cocker, Joe*	10.4.1944	10.4.1944
Pointon, Bill*	22.4.1944	22.4.1944
Richardson, Dave*	22.4.1944	22.4.1944
Boyd, Jimmy*	29.4.1944	29.4.1944
Ward, Jack*	29.4.1944	6.5.1944
Driver, Allenby*	6.5.1944	6.5.1944
Matthewson, George*	6.5.1944	6.5.1944

1944–45

Player	Debut	Last game
Bratley, George*	26.8.1944	28.4.1945
Cook, R.*	26.8.1944	24.3.1945
Needham, Fred*	26.8.1944	9.9.1944
Winning, Alex*	26.8.1944	31.3.1945
Reece, Tom*	2.9.1944	29.12.1945
Hodges, Cyril	9.9.1944	1.3.1947
Lobb, Fred*	9.9.1944	9.9.1944
Stear, Jimmy*	9.9.1944	9.9.1944
Crawford, Ted*	16.9.1944	21.10.1944
Lyle*	16.9.1944	16.9.1944
Offord, Stan*	16.9.1944	16.9.1944
Groves, Ken*	7.10.1944	7.10.1944
Muir, Bob*	14.10.1944	28.10.1944
Ross, George*	14.10.1944	14.10.1944
Adams, Billy*	21.10.1944	21.10.1944
Brown, Jimmy*	21.10.1944	21.10.1944
Pinkerton, Harry*	21.10.1944	11.11.1944
Farmer, Alex*	28.10.1944	28.10.1944
Hancock, John*	4.11.1944	4.11.1944
Jackson, Les*	11.11.1944	11.11.1944
Hodgson, Sam*	18.11.1944	24.2.1945
Wallis, John*	18.11.1944	16.12.1944
Briscoe, Jimmy*	2.12.1944	16.12.1944
Croft, Charlie*	2.12.1944	2.12.1944
Lewis, Doug*	16.12.1944	16.12.1944
Barlow, K.*	23.12.1944	23.12.1944
Gregory, Jack*	23.12.1944	23.12.1944
Tapken, Norman*	23.12.1944	13.1.1945
Weir, Jock*	23.12.1944	30.12.1944
Brown, James R.*	26.12.1944	14.4.1945
Townsend, Len*	26.12.1944	26.12.1944
Frost, Arthur*	17.2.1945	17.3.1945
Cornish, Dennis*	14.4.1945	5.5.1945
Whent, Jack	21.4.1945	6.5.1950
McFarlane, D. L.*	28.4.1945	28.4.1945

1945–46

Player	Debut	Last game
London, Dermot*	25.8.1945	25.8.1945
Rowley, Arthur*	25.8.1945	22.9.1945
Munro, Alex*	1.9.1945	29.9.1945
Sheppard, Richard*	1.9.1945	1.12.1945
Moore, Beriah*	5.9.1945	5.9.1945
Pugh, John*	5.9.1945	5.9.1945
Williams, Walter*	5.9.1945	5.9.1945
Baldwin, Harry†	8.9.1945	29.12.1951
Sage, Frank*	12.9.1945	12.9.1945
Alexander, Fred*	15.9.1945	15.9.1945
Miles*	6.10.1945	6.10.1945
Robson, Bert*	27.10.1945	27.10.1945
Wilson, Albert*	27.10.1945	27.10.1945
Millbank, Joe*	3.11.1945	3.11.1945
Watson, Jimmy	3.11.1945	16.3.1946
Hindley, Frank†	17.11.1945	24.5.1947
Parr, Charlie*	12.1.1946	12.1.1946
Martindale, Len*	19.1.1946	9.3.1946
Wharton, F.*	19.1.1946	19.1.1946
Hughes, Horace*	23.2.1946	22.4.1946
Curtis, J. W.*	4.5.1946	4.5.1946

1946–47

Player	Debut	Last game
Barker, Don	31.8.1946	28.12.1946
Hanlon, Wally	31.8.1946	24.4.1948
Chapman, George	11.9.1946	14.2.1948
Bamford, Harry	18.9.1946	28.12.1946
Ridley, Dave	21.9.1946	17.5.1947
James, Tony	5.10.1946	9.10.1948
Sim, Johnny	16.11.1946	4.3.1950

Albion players in debut order (cont.)

‡ see Albion's Nearly Men

Player	Debut	Last game	Player	Debut	Last game	Player	Debut	Last game
Grant, Jimmy	7.12.1946	7.12.1946	Jennings, Roy	31.1.1953	18.1.1964	Powney, Brian	28.4.1962	27.4.1974
Ferrier, John	21.12.1946	21.12.1946	Moffatt, Johnny	14.2.1953	21.2.1953	Standing, John	28.4.1962	18.9.1962
Gotts, Jim	21.12.1946	28.12.1946	Bisset, Tommy	6.4.1953	22.10.1960	**1962–63**		
Liddell, John	29.3.1947	7.4.1947	Burtenshaw, Steve	11.4.1953	3.12.1966	Dillon, John	18.8.1962	20.4.1963
Willard, Jess	29.3.1947	15.4.1953	**1953–54**			Donnelly, Peter	18.8.1962	24.10.1964
1947–48			Langley, Jimmy	19.8.1953	9.2.1957	James, David	18.8.1962	25.9.1962
Nevins, Laurie	23.8.1947	27.9.1947	McNeil, Matt	19.8.1953	3.3.1956	McGonigal, Bert	18.8.1962	6.11.1965
Redfern, Bob	23.8.1947	22.11.1947	Bennett, Ron	26.8.1953	17.10.1953	Cooper, Jim	1.9.1962	30.3.1964
Thomas, Lyn	23.8.1947	14.2.1948	Mundy, Albert	28.11.1953	11.1.1958	Bailey, Craig	11.9.1962	6.10.1962
Booth, Sammy	30.8.1947	19.3.1949	**1954–55**			Walker, Bob	15.9.1962	17.11.1962
Hacking, Bob	30.8.1947	14.2.1948	Whitfield, Ken	21.8.1954	20.12.1958	Hannam, Dave	25.9.1962	17.11.1962
Wilson, Alex	13.9.1947	13.9.1947	Edwards, Len	16.10.1954	23.3.1955	Gall, Norman	29.9.1962	30.3.1974
Vickers, Wilf	17.9.1947	1.5.1948	Longland, Johnny	27.11.1954	26.3.1955	Collins, Jimmy	2.10.1962	13.5.1967
McLeod, Bob	15.11.1947	15.11.1947	Trusler, Johnny	29.1.1955	29.1.1955	Upton, Nobby	3.11.1962	20.8.1966
Clelland, Dave	3.1.1948	1.5.1948	Stephens, Malcolm	26.3.1955	13.4.1957	Cassidy, Bill	1.12.1962	31.12.1966
Morrad, Frank	14.2.1948	6.1.1951	Harburn, Peter	8.4.1955	30.4.1958	Jackson, Allan	1.12.1962	3.4.1964
Young, Leon	14.2.1948	1.9.1948	**1955–56**			Waites, George	1.12.1962	12.10.1963
Hipkin, Reg	6.3.1948	13.11.1948	Clarke, Nobby	3.9.1955	7.9.1955	Franks, Ken	26.12.1962	26.12.1962
Willis, George	6.3.1948	16.4.1949	Neate, Derek	18.4.1956	19.4.1957	Sanders, Allan	26.1.1963	5.2.1966
Small, Sammy	27.3.1948	26.11.1949	**1956–57**			Webber, Keith	13.4.1963	7.9.1964
1948–49			Thomas, Rees	6.10.1956	28.9.1957	**1963–64**		
Davies, Ken	21.8.1948	6.5.1950	Humphries, Bob	10.11.1956	30.4.1957	Fitch, Barry	18.9.1963	18.9.1963
Guttridge, Ron	21.8.1948	18.2.1950	Grant, Alan	24.11.1956	24.11.1956	Turner, Dave	7.12.1963	26.4.1972
Lewis, George	21.8.1948	16.4.1949	Johnson, Mick	1.12.1956	29.12.1956	Healer, Ernie	14.12.1963	26.12.1963
McNichol, Johnny	21.8.1948	1.5.1952	Darey, Jeff	22.4.1957	16.11.1960	Gould, Wally	11.1.1964	10.2.1968
Tennant, Des	25.8.1948	1.11.1958	**1957–58**			Smith, Jack	11.1.1964	10.9.1966
Taylor, Geoff	15.9.1948	18.9.1948	Small, Peter	24.8.1957	12.4.1958	Knight, Peter	18.1.1964	11.12.1965
Daniels, Harry	25.9.1948	27.12.1949	Champelovier, Les	2.10.1957	2.10.1957	**1964–65**		
Jones, Les J.	2.10.1948	23.4.1949	Hodge, Eric	2.10.1957	2.11.1957	Hennigan, Mike	22.8.1964	17.4.1965
Kavanagh, Micky	13.11.1948	18.2.1950	Sexton, Dave	2.10.1957	22.4.1959	Smith, Bobby A.	22.8.1964	7.9.1965
Brennan, Paddy	20.11.1948	10.3.1951	Bates, Don	12.10.1957	30.4.1958	McQuarrie, Andy	29.8.1964	31.10.1964
Reed, Billy G.	25.12.1948	28.2.1953	Brown, Irvin	9.11.1957	12.4.1958	Hopkins, Mel	10.10.1964	17.9.1966
Wilkins, Jack	29.1.1949	31.3.1951	Ellis, Syd	23.11.1957	25.4.1959	Rees, Barrie	9.1.1965	26.3.1965
Mansell, Jack	26.2.1949	27.9.1952	Thorne, Adrian	18.1.1958	8.4.1961	Oliver, Jim	13.3.1965	10.2.1968
Roberts, Gordon	19.3.1949	7.4.1950	Hollins, Dave	1.3.1958	11.3.1961	**1965–66**		
McCurley, Kevin	2.4.1949	5.5.1951	**1958–59**			Davies, Peter	28.8.1965	5.10.1965
1949–50			Bertolini, Jack	23.8.1958	5.10.1965	Leggett, Peter	28.8.1965	2.10.1965
Pinchbeck, Cliff	20.8.1949	5.11.1949	Shepherd, Johnny	23.8.1958	12.12.1959	Brown, Gary	1.9.1965	1.9.1965
Suttle, Ken	5.9.1949	14.9.1949	Clayton, Ronnie	10.9.1958	26.3.1960	Livesey, Charlie	18.9.1965	11.1.1969
Rees, Mal	10.9.1949	14.9.1949	Jones, Freddie	13.9.1958	16.11.1960	Kydd, David	21.9.1965	2.10.1965
Leamon, Fred	14.9.1949	4.2.1950	Dixon, Tommy	11.10.1958	21.11.1959	Hickman, Mike	23.10.1965	11.5.1968
Morris, Bill	17.9.1949	5.5.1951	Little, Doz	18.10.1958	4.2.1961	Magill, Jimmy	30.10.1965	9.3.1968
Wilson, Glen	24.9.1949	23.4.1960	Tiddy, Mike	25.10.1958	23.4.1962	Leck, Derek	27.11.1965	1.4.1967
Connelly, Eddie	22.10.1949	10.4.1950	McNeill, Ian	21.3.1959	23.4.1962	Tawse, Brian	27.12.1965	25.10.1969
Vitty, Jack	22.10.1949	22.12.1951	Stevens, Norman	18.4.1959	18.4.1959	Whitington, Eric	5.2.1966	11.5.1968
Thompson, Cyril	11.3.1950	10.3.1951	**1959–60**			Henderson, Stewart	6.5.1966	16.12.1972
South, Alex	1.4.1950	13.11.1954	Curry, Bill	22.8.1959	24.9.1960	Tranter, Wilf	6.5.1966	27.4.1968
1950–51			McNicol, Bob	22.8.1959	23.4.1962	Collins, Glyn	18.5.1966	28.5.1966
Bennett, Ken	19.8.1950	6.4.1953	Abbis, Keith	7.11.1959	3.12.1960	**1966–67**		
Keene, Doug	19.8.1950	7.3.1953	**1960–61**			Wilkinson, Howard	20.8.1966	6.2.1971
Mulvaney, Jim	26.8.1950	30.12.1950	Laverick, Bobby	31.8.1960	23.4.1962	Burns, Tony	10.9.1966	7.12.1968
Howard, Frankie	4.9.1950	13.12.1958	Baker, Charlie	20.10.1960	8.5.1963	Napier, Kit	1.10.1966	29.8.1972
Johnston, Ron	18.11.1950	18.11.1950	Sitford, Tony	20.10.1960	23.4.1962	Templeman, John	27.12.1966	27.4.1974
Thompson, Pat	10.3.1951	10.3.1951	Nicholas, Tony	5.11.1960	28.4.1962	Dear, Brian	17.3.1967	29.4.1967
Garbutt, Ray	27.3.1951	11.4.1952	Windross, Dennis	19.11.1960	1.4.1961	Duncliffe, John	27.3.1967	4.5.1968
1951–52			Carolan, Joe	10.12.1960	7.4.1962	Badminton, Roger	16.5.1967	23.8.1967
Wetton, Albert	12.9.1951	14.1.1953	Crowther, Stan	31.3.1961	18.4.1961	Borthwick, Walter	16.5.1967	16.5.1967
Sirrell, Jimmy	22.9.1951	17.4.1954	**1961–62**			Woolgar, Phil	16.5.1967	16.5.1967
Higgins, Ron	5.1.1952	14.4.1952	Goodchild, Johnny	19.8.1961	11.4.1966	**1967–68**		
McIlvenny, Paddy	5.4.1952	13.11.1954	Smith, Dave	19.8.1961	28.4.1962	Dalton, George	19.8.1967	27.1.1968
1952–53			Brown, Alan	12.9.1961	9.12.1961	Napier, John	19.8.1967	7.10.1972
Leadbetter, Jimmy	23.8.1952	7.5.1955	Baxter, Bobby	25.11.1961	13.5.1967	Flood, Paul	23.8.1967	5.12.1970
Owens, Les	23.8.1952	10.1.1953	Jest, Syd	9.12.1961	8.5.1963	Lawton, Nobby	23.9.1967	13.2.1971
Gill, Eric	20.9.1952	19.9.1959	Hudson, Colin	26.12.1961	26.12.1961	Fuller, Bob‡	–	–
Gordon, Dennis	24.9.1952	29.4.1961	Caven, Joe	3.3.1962	15.9.1962	Bence, Paul	11.5.1968	11.5.1968
Fox, Reg	1.10.1952	8.10.1955	Cochrane, Johnny	10.3.1962	29.9.1962	**1968–69**		
Foreman, Denis	25.10.1952	29.4.1961	Gilbert, Phil	28.4.1962	24.8.1963	Everitt, Mike	10.8.1968	13.12.1969
McLafferty, Maurice	25.10.1952	2.5.1953	Miller, Ally	28.4.1962	28.4.1962	Smith, Bobby W.	10.8.1968	3.4.1971
Medhurst, Harry	15.11.1952	14.2.1953				Armstrong, Dave	14.9.1968	7.3.1970
Addinall, Bert	17.1.1953	30.4.1954				Dawson, Alex	14.12.1968	15.3.1971
Gilberg, Harry	17.1.1953	27.8.1955						

Albion players in debut order (cont.)

‡ see Albion's Nearly Men

Player	Debut	Last game
Wright, Barrie	4.1.1969	13.12.1969
Sidebottom, Geoff	11.1.1969	9.1.1971
Spearritt, Eddie	25.1.1969	10.3.1974
Blackburn, Ken	12.3.1969	12.3.1969

1969–70

Player	Debut	Last game
Bell, Willie	9.8.1969	15.4.1970
Gilliver, Alan	9.8.1969	13.2.1971
Stanley, Terry	13.12.1969	24.3.1971
Duffy, Alan	17.1.1970	15.1.1972

1970–71

Player	Debut	Last game
O'Sullivan, Peter	15.8.1970	2.5.1981
Sheridan, Alex	15.8.1970	7.5.1971
Goodwin, Ian	29.9.1970	10.11.1973
Woffinden, Colin	14.11.1970	20.2.1971
Seymour, Ian	6.2.1971	20.2.1971
Murray, Bert	27.2.1971	6.10.1973
Irvine, Willie	10.3.1971	25.11.1972
Dovey, Alan	1.5.1971	6.1.1973

1971–72

Player	Debut	Last game
Lutton, Bertie	11.9.1971	26.12.1972
Bromley, Brian	27.11.1971	1.9.1973
Dobson, Colin	22.1.1972	12.2.1972
Beamish, Ken	15.3.1972	27.4.1974

1972–73

Player	Debut	Last game
Howell, Graham	26.8.1972	22.12.1973
Bridges, Barry	2.9.1972	15.4.1974
Ley, George	23.9.1972	8.12.1973
Brown, Stan	14.10.1972	9.12.1972
Moore, John	14.10.1972	11.11.1972
Piper, Steve	18.11.1972	12.11.1977
McGrath, John	2.12.1972	16.12.1972
Robertson, Lammie	23.12.1972	27.4.1974
Boorn, Alan	30.12.1972	6.1.1973
Hilton, Pat	10.2.1973	26.12.1973
Hughes, Tommy	10.2.1973	2.3.1973
Towner, Tony	10.2.1973	23.9.1978
Conway, Mick	28.4.1973	17.11.1973

1973–74

Player	Debut	Last game
Brown, Mick	25.8.1973	3.4.1974
Howell, Ronnie	29.8.1973	20.4.1974
Downsborough, Peter	8.9.1973	15.9.1973
Boyle, John	22.9.1973	10.11.1973
Busby, Dave	20.10.1973	18.9.1974
Goodeve, Ken	8.12.1973	30.3.1974
Grummitt, Peter	8.12.1973	5.3.1977
Norton, Terry‡	–	–
Welch, Ronnie	26.12.1973	19.10.1974
Wilson, Harry	26.12.1973	10.5.1977
Fuschillo, Paul	27.2.1974	26.10.1974
McEwan, Billy	27.2.1974	9.11.1974

1974–75

Player	Debut	Last game
Binney, Fred	17.8.1974	18.9.1976
Govier, Steve	17.8.1974	16.10.1974
Marlowe, Ricky	17.8.1974	28.4.1975
Mellor, Ian	17.8.1974	31.1.1978
Rollings, Andy	17.8.1974	3.11.1979
Machin, Ernie	28.8.1974	17.3.1976
Mason, Tommy	21.9.1974	28.4.1975
Walker, Jim	21.9.1974	10.9.1975
Forster, Derek	1.10.1974	2.11.1974
Smith, Wilf	16.10.1974	9.11.1974
Winstanley, Graham	26.10.1974	21.4.1979
Tiler, Ken	16.11.1974	25.11.1978
Fell, Gerry	25.1.1975	5.11.1977
Lewis, Allen	25.1.1975	8.2.1975

1975–76

Player	Debut	Last game
Beal, Phil	16.8.1975	7.9.1976
Martin, Neil	16.8.1975	3.2.1976
Kinnear, Joe	30.8.1975	19.4.1976
Burnett, Dennis	6.9.1975	13.11.1976

Player	Debut	Last game
Butlin, Barry	20.9.1975	11.10.1975
Morgan, Sammy	27.12.1975	14.5.1977
Horton, Brian	13.3.1976	2.5.1981
Ward, Peter	27.3.1976	26.2.1983

1976–77

Player	Debut	Last game
Cattlin, Chris	14.8.1976	13.11.1979
Cross, Graham	14.8.1976	14.5.1977
Steele, Eric	12.3.1977	13.10.1979
Elliott, Mark	15.3.1977	26.3.1977

1977–78

Player	Debut	Last game
Lawrenson, Mark	13.8.1977	2.5.1981
Potts, Eric	13.8.1977	29.4.1978
Ruggiero, John	13.8.1977	29.4.1978
Williams, Gary	13.8.1977	15.5.1982
Clark, Paul	19.11.1977	28.2.1981
Maybank, Teddy	26.11.1977	3.11.1979
Poskett, Malcolm	4.2.1978	13.11.1979
Sayer, Peter	25.2.1978	3.5.1980
Moseley, Graham	18.4.1978	7.12.1985

1978–79

Player	Debut	Last game
Ryan, Gerry	27.9.1978	2.4.1985
Chivers, Martin	31.3.1979	30.10.1979

1979–80

Player	Debut	Last game
Gregory, John	18.8.1979	2.5.1981
Foster, Steve	28.8.1979	14.10.1995
Stevens, Gary	15.9.1979	26.5.1983
Clarke, Ray	3.11.1979	3.5.1980
Geard, Glen	13.11.1979	13.11.1979
Suddaby, Peter	17.11.1979	3.5.1980
Stille, Giles	29.12.1979	15.10.1983
McNab, Neil	9.2.1980	30.4.1983

1980–81

Player	Debut	Last game
McHale, Ray	16.8.1980	25.10.1980
Robinson, Michael	16.8.1980	26.5.1983
Smith, Gordon	16.8.1980	17.3.1984
Gariani, Moshe	6.9.1980	6.9.1980
Cohen, Jacob	18.10.1980	6.12.1980
Ritchie, Andy	22.10.1980	19.3.1983
Phillips, John	27.12.1980	27.12.1980
Digweed, Perry	17.1.1981	8.5.1993
Vessey, Tony	7.3.1981	7.3.1981
Ramsey, Chris	18.4.1981	19.11.1983

1981–82

Player	Debut	Last game
Case, Jimmy	29.8.1981	31.10.1995
Grealish, Tony	29.8.1981	10.3.1984
Shanks, Don	29.8.1981	4.12.1982
Gatting, Steve	12.9.1981	2.6.1991
Ring, Mike	6.10.1981	19.11.1983
Nelson, Sammy	27.10.1981	28.12.1982
Thomas, Mickey	7.11.1981	15.5.1982

1982–83

Player	Debut	Last game
Pearce, Graham	28.8.1982	2.5.1986
Smillie, Neil	28.8.1982	11.5.1985
Howlett, Gary	22.3.1983	20.10.1984
Connor, Terry	26.3.1983	9.5.1987
O'Regan, Kieran	14.5.1983	9.5.1987
Rodon, Chris	14.5.1983	14.5.1983

1983–84

Player	Debut	Last game
Lambert, Martin	29.8.1983	21.10.1989
Steele, Simon	29.8.1983	29.8.1983
Young, Alan	3.9.1983	12.5.1984
Corrigan, Joe	17.9.1983	12.5.1984
Young, Eric	24.9.1983	2.5.1987
Hutchings, Chris	26.11.1983	28.11.1987
Penney, Steve	26.11.1983	2.1.1989
Wilson, Danny	3.12.1983	9.5.1987
Wilkins, Dean	10.12.1983	9.5.1996
Kraay, Hans	27.12.1983	11.5.1985
Young, Willie	10.3.1984	31.3.1984

Player	Debut	Last game
Muir, Ian	31.3.1984	10.11.1984
Jones, Mark	7.4.1984	15.9.1984

1984–85

Player	Debut	Last game
Clarke, Jeff	25.8.1984	29.9.1984
Jacobs, Steve	25.8.1984	2.5.1986
Worthington, Frank	25.8.1984	11.5.1985
O'Reilly, Gary	28.8.1984	29.2.1992
Ferguson, Mick	6.10.1984	8.3.1986
Keown, Martin	23.2.1985	2.11.1985
Biley, Alan	13.3.1985	12.4.1986

1985–86

Player	Debut	Last game
Fashanu, Justin	17.8.1985	15.2.1986
Mortimer, Dennis	17.8.1985	2.5.1986
Oliver, Gavin	17.8.1985	9.11.1985
Saunders, Dean	17.8.1985	7.3.1987
Edwards, Sean	16.10.1985	16.10.1985
Massimo, Franco	12.4.1986	24.9.1986
Newman, Daren	12.4.1986	12.4.1986

1986–87

Player	Debut	Last game
Armstrong, Gerry	23.8.1986	9.11.1988
Berry, Les	23.8.1986	21.1.1987
Jasper, Dale	23.8.1986	9.3.1988
Rowell, Gary	30.8.1986	26.9.1987
Hughes, Darren	1.10.1986	9.5.1987
Keeley, John	11.10.1986	20.3.1990
Tiltman, Richard	10.1.1987	26.8.1987
Brown, Kevan	14.2.1987	5.10.1988
Chapman, Ian	14.2.1987	23.4.1996
Isaac, Bob	21.2.1987	8.10.1988
Campbell, Greg	7.3.1987	21.3.1987
Crumplin, John	21.3.1987	7.5.1994
Gipp, David	25.4.1987	9.4.1988

1987–88

Player	Debut	Last game
Bremner, Kevin	15.8.1987	5.5.1990
Dublin, Keith	15.8.1987	5.5.1990
Nelson, Garry	15.8.1987	22.5.1991
Rougvie, Doug	15.8.1987	2.4.1988
Curbishley, Alan	22.8.1987	5.5.1990
Wood, Paul	29.8.1987	27.1.1990
Dineen, Jack‡	–	–
Trusson, Mike	5.12.1987	13.5.1989
Horscroft, Grant	19.12.1987	26.12.1987
Cooper, Geoff	20.1.1988	22.4.1989
Chivers, Gary	19.3.1988	8.5.1993
Owers, Adrian	26.3.1988	20.10.1990

1988–89

Player	Debut	Last game
Codner, Robert	10.9.1988	18.2.1995
Fearon, Ron	24.9.1988	26.10.1988
May, Larry	1.10.1988	1.4.1989
Bissett, Nicky	9.11.1988	2.11.1994
Coles, David	11.3.1989	11.3.1989

1989–90

Player	Debut	Last game
Stemp, Wayne	28.10.1989	23.2.1991
Edwards, Alistair	16.12.1989	16.12.1989
Barham, Mark	30.12.1989	2.5.1992
Gotsmanov, Sergei	24.2.1990	5.5.1990
Cormack, Lee‡	–	–
McCarthy, Paul	17.3.1990	9.3.1996
Gabbiadini, Ricardo	16.4.1990	16.4.1990
Robinson, John	16.4.1990	12.9.1992
McGrath, Derek	25.4.1990	30.3.1991
Dick, Ally‡	–	–

1990–91

Player	Debut	Last game
Bromage, Russel	25.8.1990	29.8.1990
Small, Mike	25.8.1990	2.6.1991
Walker, Clive	25.8.1990	24.4.1993
Meola, Tony	1.9.1990	4.9.1990
Coldwell, David‡	–	–
Byrne, John	15.9.1990	9.5.1996
McGuinness, Paul‡	–	–

Albion players in debut order (cont.)

‡ see Albion's Nearly Men

Player	Debut	Last game	Player	Debut	Last game	Player	Debut	Last game
McKenna, Brian	27.10.1990	27.10.1990	Nogan, Kurt	17.10.1992	4.2.1995	Storer, Stuart	29.4.1995	–
Wade, Bryan	27.10.1990	1.2.1992	Myall, Stuart	3.4.1993	9.5.1996			
Gurinovich, Igor	1.12.1990	5.1.1991				**1995–96**		
Pates, Colin	2.3.1991	19.11.1994	**1993–94**			Bull, Garry	19.8.1995	7.10.1995
Iovan, Stefan	16.4.1991	26.11.1991	Rust, Nicky	14.8.1993	–	Virgo, James	22.8.1995	17.12.1996
Beeney, Mark	20.4.1991	17.4.1993	Geddes, Gavin	1.9.1993	15.1.1994	Berry, Greg	26.8.1995	24.9.1995
			Tuck, Stuart	28.9.1993	–	Osman, Russell	26.9.1995	23.1.1996
1991–92			Simmonds, Danny	2.10.1993	19.10.1994	Mundee, Denny	21.10.1995	4.3.1997
Meade, Rafael	31.8.1991	1.10.1994	Johnson, Ross	20.10.1993	–	McDonald, Paul	17.2.1996	–
Briley, Les	14.9.1991	21.3.1992	Book, Steve‡	–	–	Maskell, Craig	2.3.1996	–
Farrington, Mark	14.9.1991	26.2.1994	Flatts, Mark	1.1.1994	26.2.1994	Coughlan, Derek	12.3.1996	12.3.1996
Clarkson, Dave	5.10.1991	28.3.1992	Fox, Mark	23.2.1994	8.2.1997	Hobson, Gary	30.3.1996	–
Gall, Mark	26.10.1991	2.5.1992	Dickov, Paul	26.3.1994	23.4.1994	Rowe, Zeke	30.3.1996	9.5.1996
Gallacher, Bernard	2.11.1991	1.5.1993	Andrews, Phil	9.4.1994	1.1.1997	Allan, Derek	3.4.1996	–
Sommer, Juergen	16.11.1991	16.11.1991	Fox, Simon	23.4.1994	4.3.1997			
Reed, Peter‡	–	–	McGarrigle, Kevin	7.5.1994	14.1.1997	**1996–97**		
Munday, Stuart	22.2.1992	6.4.1996				Baird, Ian	17.8.1996	–
O'Dowd, Greg	21.3.1992	21.3.1992	**1994–95**			Peake, Jason	17.8.1996	–
Funnell, Simon	2.5.1992	19.10.1994	McDougald, Junior	13.8.1994	9.5.1996	Ormerod, Mark	7.9.1996	–
			Minton, Jeff	13.8.1994	–	Neal, Ashley	28.9.1996	29.10.1996
1992–93			Smith, Peter	17.8.1994	–	Adekola, David	12.10.1996	12.10.1996
Cotterill, Steve	15.8.1992	10.10.1992	Chamberlain, Mark	20.8.1994	18.2.1995	Warren, Christer	12.10.1996	19.10.1996
Moulden, Paul	15.8.1992	10.10.1992	Kerr, Stewart	2.11.1994	5.11.1994	Morris, Mark	2.11.1996	–
Edwards, Matthew	18.8.1992	16.3.1994	Stapleton, Frank	2.11.1994	5.11.1994	Mayo, Kerry	23.11.1996	–
Wilkinson, Darron	26.8.1992	16.4.1994	Akinbiyi, Ade	26.11.1994	2.1.1995	Reinelt, Robbie	15.2.1997	–
Wosahlo, Bradley	26.8.1992	11.12.1993	Parris, George	11.2.1995	14.1.1997	Humphrey, John	4.3.1997	–
Macciochi, Dave	16.9.1992	19.9.1992	Byrne, Paul	11.3.1995	8.4.1995	Martin, David	5.4.1997	5.4.1997
Kennedy, Andy	23.9.1992	6.4.1994	Hughes, Alan‡	–	–			

Albion Connections

This section summarises links between the Albion and other prominent clubs. It includes players and managers of Brighton & Hove Albion and Brighton United who have played for, managed or coached other clubs, but not generally trialists, part-time coaches, scouts or schoolboys.

Players in italics made appearances for the named club in wartime matches only, while bold type indicates those men who have managed the named club.

In all cases consult the main entry for fuller details.

* see *Albion Managers*
† see *Albion Wartime Players*
‡ see *Brighton United*
$ see *Albion's 'Nearly Men'*

Aberdare Athletic

BOULTON, Bill
DUCKWORTH, Joe
HENDERSON, Billy
JAMES, Dai
JONES, Les

Aberdeen

BURNETT, Jimmy
DEVINE, John†
LAWSON, Hector
McNEILL, Ian
MIDDLETON, Billy
ROUGVIE, Doug
SIMPSON, Bobby
WARD, Alf
YOUNG, Willy

Accrington Stanley

ABEL, Sammy†
BUTLER, Malcolm†
CHEETHAM, Jack
CLARKE, Billy
DUCKWORTH, Joe
EASTHAM, George†
EASTHAM, Harry†
GRAHAM, John
HAYES, Billy
McNICOL, Bob
MARTINDALE, Len†
MOULDEN, Paul
ROBERTS, Doug
THOMAS, Lyn
TOOTILL, Alf†
WRAGG, Billy
WRIGHT, Tommy†

Airdrieonians

CAVEN, Joe
COOPER, Jim
FASHANU, Justin
GOOD, Micky
KIRKWOOD, Dan
LAWSON, Hector
McCARTHY, Paul
NAPIER, Kit

Albion Rovers

DILLON, John
McATEER, Tom
McKENZIE, Duncan†
McQUARRIE, Andy

Aldershot

ANDERSON, Jock†
BAKER, Charlie
BAMFORD, Harry
BEENEY, Mark
BLACKMAN, Jack†
BOTT, Wilf†
BRILEY, Les
BROWN, Kevan
CLARKE, Billy
COLES, David
COURT, Dick†
CUNLIFFE, Arthur†
DAVIE, John
DUKE, George†
EGAN, Harry
GRIFFITHS, Mal†
HASSELL, Tommy
HILTON, Pat
HODGE, Eric
HOLLINS, Dave
HOPKINS, Gary
HOWLETT, Gary
HURST, Stan
KELLY, Lawrie†
LOWE, Henry†
MACAULAY, Archie*
McILVENNY, Paddy

MARLOWE, Ricky
MELIA, Jimmy*
MORRIS, Mark
MUNDY, Albert
MUTTITT, Ernie†
O'SULLIVAN, Peter
PREST, Tommy
PRYDE, Bob†
REINELT, Robbie
RING, Mike
ROLLINGS, Andy
SIRRELL, Jimmy
STAPLETON, Frank
TAPKEN, Norman†
THOMAS, Rees
TURNER, Dave
*WELSH, Don**
WESTBY, Jack†
WILSON, Joe
WINNING, Alex†

Alloa

DICK, Ally$
GRAHAM, John
McKENNA, Harold
MARTIN, Neil
THOMSON, Charlie

Arbroath

BORTHWICK, Walter
WILLOCKS, Davie‡

Ards

COCHRANE, Johnny
EASTHAM, George†

Arsenal

BEALE, Bob
BLACKMAN, Fred
BRADY, Liam*
BRISCOE, Jimmy†
BROPHY, Harry
BUCKLEY, Chris
BURNS, Tony
BURTENSHAW, Steve
CALDWELL, Jock
CLAYTON, Ronnie
CLELLAND, Dave
COCKER, Joe†
CURTIS, George*
DAVIES, Peter
DICKOV, Paul
DUKE, George†
EDINGTON, John†
EVERITT, Mike
FARRELL, Paddy
FITCHIE, Tom
FLATTS, Mark
FUSCHILLO, Paul
GATTING, Steve
GRIFFITHS, Mal†
GROVES, Freddie
GROVES, Henry
HACKING, Bob
HENLEY, Les†
HODGES, Cyril
HOOPER, Percy†
HOPKINS, Jimmy
JONES, Freddie
JONES, Les
JONES, Syd†
KEOWN, Martin
MACAULAY, Archie*
McAVOY, Frank
MacDONALD, Hugh
MAGILL, Jimmy
MEADE, Raphael
MILLER, Bill
MORGAN, Stan†
MORRAD, Frank
NEIL, Andy
NELSON, Sammy

O'REILLY, Gary
PATES, Colin
RUSSELL, Jock
RUST, Nicky
SEXTON, Dave
SMITH, Dave
SPEARRITT, Eddie
SPICER, Tom‡
STAPLETON, Frank
TAWSE, Brian
TIDDY, Mike
TOOZE, Cyril†
TYLER, Alf
WALLER, Henry†
WILLIAMS, Dave
WILSON, Alex
YOUNG, Willy

Arundel

PIPER, Steve
SUTTLE, Ken
TEMPLEMAN, John

Ashford etc.

DAY, Albert
GREGORY, Jack†
HADDEN, Sid‡
LANCELOTTE, Eric
LAVERICK, Bobby
SHEPHERD, John
STEVENS, Norman
WALKER, Bob

Ashington

GOTTS, Jim
RUTHERFORD, Jim
RUTHERFORD, Jack
STEVENS, Jack
TURNBULL, Billy
WALLER, Henry†

Aston Villa

BRETT, Frank
BUCKLEY, Chris
BUCKLEY, Frank
CROWTHER, Stan
CUNLIFFE, Arthur†
CURBISHLEY, Alan
DOBSON, Colin
FEEBERY, Jack
FISHER, Albert
FOSTER, Steve
GALLACHER, Bernard
GREGORY, John
GUTTRIDGE, Ron
HALL, Proctor
HUGHES, Tommy
JONES, Mark
KEOWN, Martin
MILLAR, Arthur
MORGAN, Sammy
MORTIMER, Dennis
MOSELEY, Graham
MULRANEY, Jock†
O'DONNELL, Frank†
PHILLIPS, John
SAUNDERS, Dean
SAWARD, Pat*
SEXTON, Dave
SIDEBOTTOM, Geoff
THOMPSON, Jack
TULLY, Fred†
VALLANCE, Hugh
VARCO, Percy
WALKER, Jim
YATES, Billy

Ayr United

ALLAN, Derek
HODGE, Billy
McAVOY, Frank
McNAB, Neil

McNEILL, Hamilton†
MIDDLETON, Billy

Ballymena United

HOPKINS, Mel
PENNEY, Steve
RING, Mike

Bangor (NI)

ARMSTRONG, Gerry
BYRNE, Paul

Barnet

BISSETT, Nicky
BULL, Garry
CHIVERS, Martin
CODNER, Robert
COOPER, Geoff
GIPP, David
GROVES, Freddie
HOWELL, Ronnie
LANE, Billy*
LAWRENSON, Mark
MULLERY, Alan*
PEARCE, Graham
ROWE, Zeke
THORNE, Adrian

Barnsley

DAVIE, Jock
DOWNS, Dickie
GRAINGER, Jack†
GREGORY, Fred†
HALL, Jack E.
HOLLEY, George
McCAIRNS, Tom
McHALE, Ray
McNEIL, Matt
MALLOCH, Jock‡
MAY, Larry
MOORE, Jimmy
MURFIN, Clarrie
WILCOCK, George
WILSON, Danny

Barrow

ATKINSON, Jimmy
BUSBY, Dave
CARGILL, Jimmy
DIXON, Tommy
JOHNSON, Mick
LLOYD, Arthur
PIGGIN, Lionel
SHORT, Jimmy

Barry Town

HUDSON, Colin
JONES, Les
REES, Mal
TENNANT, Des
WEBBER, Keith

Bath City

ADEKOLA, David
BOOK, Steve$
BRENNAN, Jimmy
HOOPER, Percy†
HUDSON, Colin
JAMES, Tony
LEAMON, Fred
MULVANEY, Jimmy
PINCHBECK, Cliff
SMITH, Jack
WADE, Bryan
WOODLEY, Vic†

Bedford Town

GOODEVE, Ken
GRANT, Alan
MOORE, Bernard
MORRAD, Frank
REID, Ernie†

RIDLEY, David
WILKINS, Jack

Berwick Rangers

HEALER, Ernie
MILLER, Ali

Birmingham City

ARCHER, Arthur
BELL, Willie
BEST, Jack
BRADFORD, Jack
BREMNER, Kevin
BRIDGES, Barry
BUCKLEY, Chris
BUCKLEY, Frank
BULL, Garry
COLES, David
CURBISHLEY, Alan
DALTON, George
EASTHAM, George†
EVANS, Tom
FERGUSON, Mick
GOOD, Micky
GOODWIN, Freddie*
HALL, Jack H.
HASTINGS, Bill
HAWLEY, Fred
HENDERSON, Crosby
HOYLAND, Fred
JONES, Abe
JONES, Bill
JONES, Mark
KENNEDY, Andy
MORTIMER, Dennis
MUIR, Ian
MULRANEY, Jock†
MURRAY, Bert
O'REILLY, Gary
PARRIS, George
SLY, Harold
SMALL, Sammy
SMITH, Wally
STORER, Stuart
SYKES, Albert
WILSON, Alex
WORTHINGTON, Frank
WRAGG, Billy

Blackburn Rovers

ANTHONY, Walter
BEAMISH, Ken
BRISCOE, Jimmy†
CHRISTIE, Norman†
CLARKSON, George†
CUNLIFFE, Arthur†
DUCKWORTH, Joe
GALLACHER, Bernard
GILLIVER, Alan
HACKING, Bob
HICKMAN, Mike
HILTON, Pat
HULSE, Ben
JONES, Herbert
KENNEDY, Andy
KINGHORN, Bill†
LUMLEY, Joe
MARTIN, Jack
MARTINDALE, Len†
MILLS, Andy‡
MOSELEY, Graham
MULRANEY, Jock†
NAPIER, Kit
O'BRIEN, Joe
PRYDE, Bob†
ROBERTSON, Jimmy
RUSSELL, Jock
STAPLETON, Frank
TURNER, Dave
WALKER, Jim
WEIR, Jock.†
WESTBY, Jack†

WILSON, Joe
WOMBWELL, Dick

Blackpool

BUCKLEY, Frank
BUSBY, Dave
BUTLER, Malcolm†
EASTHAM, George†
EASTHAM, Harry†
FUSCHILLO, Paul
GABBIADINI, Ricardo
JACKSON, John*
JONES, Herbert
LEWIS, Bill†
LYON, Bertie
McEWAN, Billy
MUNRO, Alex†
NAPIER, Kit
O'DONNELL, Frank†
POTTS, Eric
SMITH, Bobby
SPENCER, Frank
STEELE, Simon
SUDDABY, Peter
THOMAS, Lyn
WATSON, Jimmy
WILSON, Alex

Bognor Regis Town

COOPER, Geoff
CORMACK, Lee$
CRUMPLIN, John
DINEEN, Jack$
HUMPHRIES, Bob
LAMBERT, Martin
NEATE, Derek
O'REILLY, Gary
STANDING, John
STEELE, Simon
STEMP, Wayne
TILTMAN, Richard
WILKINS, Dean

Bohemians

FLOOD, Paul
KAVANAGH, Micky
RYAN, Gerry
WEBB, Charlie
WRIGHT, Steve

Bolton Wanderers

ATKINSON, Jimmy
BROMLEY, Brian
EASTHAM, George†
EASTHAM, Harry†
FEEBERY, Jack
GARDNER, Andy
GREGORY, John
ITHELL, Jimmy†
JEE, Joe
KENNEDY, Andy
LIDDELL, John
LOW, John‡
McARTHUR, Willie‡
McATEER, Tom
McGRATH, John
McNAB, Neil
MARTINDALE, Len†
NAPIER, John
PRYDE, Bob†
READMAN, Joe
RING, Mike
STORER, Stuart
TAIT, Tommy†
WILLOCKS, Davie‡
WORTHINGTON, Frank
WRIGHT, Steve

Boston United

BUNTING, John
CROFT, Charlie†
CURRY, Bill

DORAN, Jack
GILLIVER, Alan
ITHELL, Billy†
TILER, Ken
WILKINSON, Howard
WILSON, Albert†

AFC Bournemouth

ADEKOLA, David
BENNETT, Ken
BROWN, Irvin
BROWN, Sam
CASE, Jimmy
CHIVERS, Gary
COTHLIFF, Harold†
COTTERILL, Steve
CUNLIFFE, Arthur†
DARLING, Len
DUKE, George†
ELLIOTT, Mark
GEDDES, Gavin
GREGORY, Jack†
GRIFFITHS, Mal†
GRITT, Steve*
HANLON, Wally
HOWLETT, Gary
LONGDON, Billy
MARTIN, Ted
MORRIS, Mark
MUNDEE, Denny
READMAN, Joe
REDFERN, Bob
SWINFEN, Reg†
TAIT, Tommy†
THOMAS, Rees
TOWNSEND, Eric
TRUSSON, Mike
TUNNICLIFFE, Bill†
WALKER, Bob
WELSH, Don*
WILSON, Fred†
WOOD, Paul
WOODWARD, Dai†

Bradford (Park Avenue)

BARKER, Don
BROPHY, Harry
FISHER, Albert
GABBIADINI, Ricardo
HODGSON, Sam†
HOPKINS, Mel
JACKSON, Les†
KIRKMAN, Norman†
LAYTON, Billy†
MacDONALD, Hugh
MURFIN, Clarrie
OFFORD, Stan†
SIMPSON, Bobby
SIRRELL, Jimmy
SMITH, Jimmy
WARD, Alf
WILCOCK, George

Bradford City

BUCKLEY, Frank
COWAN, Sam†
DONNELLY, Peter
DOWNSBOROUGH, Peter
GILLIVER, Alan
GORE, Les†
GREGORY, Fred†
HALL, Proctor
HOWELL, Graham
HUTCHINGS, Chris
KENNEDY, Willie
MALPASS, Sam†
MELLOR, Ian
MELLORS, Mark
MULVANEY, Jimmy
NAPIER, John
NEWTON, Jimmy
OLIVER, Gavin

RICHARDSON, Dave†
ROBERTSON, Lammie
SCRIMSHAW, Stan†
SHAFTO, John†
SPERRIN, Bill†
STAPLETON, Frank
TUNNICLIFFE, Bill†
WATSON, Jimmy

Brechin City

OSBORNE, Jack

Brentford

BAMFORD, Harry
BENCE, Paul
BROUGHTON, F.
BROWN, Mick
BURNS, Tony
DAVIE, Jock
DAWSON, Alex
DORAN, Jack
DRIVER, Allenby†
DUKE, George†
EASTHAM, George†
EVERITT, Mike
FLACK, Doug†
GOTTS, Jim
GROVES, Ken†
HARBURN, Peter
HENLEY, Les†
KAY, John†
KEENE, Doug
LANE, Billy*
LANGLEY, Jimmy
LANHAM
LLOYD, Barry*
LONGDON, Billy
MACAULAY, Archie*
McKENZIE, Duncan†
McLEOD, Roddy‡
MORRAD, Fred†
MULRANEY, Jock†
MUNDEE, Denny
MUTTITT, Ernie†
MYALL, Stuart
O'DONNELL, Frank†
PARRIS, George
PAYNE, John
PEARCE, Graham
PIGGIN, Lionel
POINTON, Bill†
ROLLINGS, Andy
RUSHTON, George
SALT, Harold
SIRRELL, Jimmy
SMILLIE, Neil
SPERRIN, Bill†
SPICER, Tom‡
STEPHENS, Bert
STEWART, Tom
TAWSE, Brian
THOMSON, Norman
TOWNSEND, Len†
TUNNICLIFFE, Bill†
WALKER, Clive
WILLARD, Jess
WOODLEY, Vic†

Bristol City

BAIRD, Ian
BARBER, Stan
BROMAGE, Russel
BROWN, Tom
CONNOR, Terry
FAIRHURST, Billy†
FISHER, Albert
FLATTS, Mark
FORD, Fred†
GOOD, Micky
HAWLEY, Fred
KELLY, Lawrie†
LANE, Billy*

LANEY, Les†
LONGDON, Billy
MARTIN, Dave
MASKELL, Craig
MOORE, Beriah†
OSMAN, Russell
PARRIS, George
RAMSEY, Chris
RUSSELL, Jock
SCRIMSHAW, Stan†
SMITH, Dave
TOWNSEND, Len†
WOMBWELL, Dick

Bristol Rovers

ATTWOOD, Arthur
CONNOR, Terry
COOK, Tommy
DOBSON, Colin
EYRES, Jack
FORD, Fred†
GOUGH, Tony
GRAHAM, John
HULME, Arthur
JAMES, Tony
LEAMON, Fred
LEWIS, Jack
McCAIRNS, Tom
MacDONALD, Hugh
PIGGIN, Lionel
POINTON, Joe
RICHARDS, Billy
RUTHERFORD, Jack
SMITH, Wilf
TAYLOR, Geoff
TAYLOR, Phil†
WATSON, Jimmy

Burgess Hill Town

BROWN, Stan
CALLOW, J. W.
COLES, Donald
DENNETT, J.W.
DINEEN, Jack$
GARDINER, J.J.
NEWMAN, Daren
NORMAN, Walter‡
STANLEY, Terry
VESSEY, Tony
WOFFINDEN, Colin

Burnley

ASPDEN, Tommy
CATTLIN, Chris
CUNLIFFE, Arthur†
DAVIDSON, Jimmy‡
IRVINE, Willie
JENNINGS, Sam
KINGHORN, Bill†
KIRKMAN, Norman†
LIVINGSTONE, Archie
LONGAIR, Bill‡
McDONALD, Paul
MARTINDALE, Len†
MUIR, Ian
NOGAN, Kurt
PATERSON, George†
PENNEY, Steve
PINKERTON, Harry†
POTTS, Eric
PREST, Tommy
ROBERTSON, Lammie
ROWELL, Gary
SMITH, Dave
TILTMAN, Richard
WELCH, Ronnie
WILSON, Harry

Burton Albion, Burton United, etc.

ARCHER, Arthur
ASHBY, Harry‡

BROWN, Buster
COTTERILL, Steve
GARFIELD, Ben
GRIFFITHS, Mal†
JACKSON, Allan
LEWIS, Jack
LIVINGSTONE, Archie
NELMES, Alf*
TAYLOR, Peter*
WARD, Peter
WILLOCKS, Davie‡

Bury

ABEL, Sammy†
ADEKOLA, David
BEAMISH, Ken
BOYD, Jimmy†
BRENNAN, Jack
BURDETT, Tom†
DAWSON, Alex
DUTTON, Harry
EDMONDS, Alf
FAIRHURST, Billy†
GREGORY, Julius
HOYLAND, Fred
JACKSON, Allan
LEE, Barney
LEEMING, Joe
McGRATH, John
McHALE, Ray
McNEILL, Hamilton†
MATTHEWSON, George†
PEARSON, Stan†
POTTS, Eric
ROBERTSON, Lammie
RODGERSON, Ted
RONALDSON, Duncan
SMITH, Bobby
WATSON, Jack†
WILSON, Danny

Cambridge United

ADEKOLA, David
BAILEY, Craig
BILEY, Alan
BULL, Garry
CASSIDY, Bill
CLARK, Paul
FARRINGTON, Mark
FLATTS, Mark
HOWELL, Graham
HOWELL, Ronnie
HUMPHRIES, Bob
JAMES, David
LEGGETT, Peter
McNEIL, Matt
MORGAN, Sammy
NICHOLAS, Tony
TOWNER, Tony
WOSAHLO, Bradley

Canterbury City

BOORN, Alan
CAROLAN, Joe
DONNELLY, Peter
HIGGINS, Ron
HILTON, Pat
HOPKINS, Mel
McCURLEY, Kevin
NORTON, Terry$

Cardiff City

BAIRD, Ian
BOOTH, Sammy
BROWN, Tom
CLARKE, Nobby
DONNELLY, Peter
EGAN, Harry
ELLIOTT, Mark
EVANS, Tommy†
FARRINGTON, Mark
GRIFFITHS, Mal†

HUDSON, Colin
JONES, Les
McILVENNY, Paddy
MANSELL, Jack
MOORE, Beriah†
MOSELEY, Graham
OSMAN, Russell
PUGH, John†
REED, Billy
RODON, Chris
RUTHERFORD, Jack
SAGE, Frank†
SAUNDERS, Dean
SAYER, Peter
SMITH, Bobby
SMITH, Potter
STEELE, Eric
TENNANT, Des
THOMAS, Rees
TIDDY, Mike
TURNBULL, Billy
WEIR, Jock.†
WHITFIELD, Ken
WILLIAMS, S.†
WILLIAMS, Walter†

Carlisle United

ADAMS, Billy†
FORD, Fred†
GABBIADINI, Riccardo
GARDNER, Andy
GORE, Les†
KELLY, John
LYON, Bertie
McATEER, Tom
McNICOL, Bob
POSKETT, Malcolm
ROWELL, Gary
SPEARRITT, Eddie
WHITE, Tom
WINSTANLEY, Graham

Celtic

BRADY, Liam*
BYRNE, Paul
DAVIDSON, Jimmy‡
FARRELL, Paddy
GILGUN, Pat
GILHOOLY, Paddy
GRAHAM, John
KELLY, John
KENNEDY, Jimmy
KERR, Stuart
McATEER, Tom
MULRANEY, Jock†
O'DONNELL, Frank†
SIRRELL, Jimmy
WEIR, Jock.†

Charlton Athletic

BAILEY, Mike*
BERRY, Les
BLACKMAN, Jack†
BURNS, Tony
CLARKE, Billy
CURBISHLEY, Alan
DAVIE, Jock
DIGWEED, Perry
DODD, George
ELLIS, Syd
FARMER, Alex†
FORD, Fred†
FORSTER, Derek
GATTING, Steve
GILBERG, Harry
GILL, Eric
GRITT, Steve*
GROVES, Freddie
HIPKIN, Reg
HUMPHREY, John
JACOBS, Steve
KEEN, Eric†

LANCELOTTE, Eric
MULLERY, Alan*
MULRANEY, Jock†
MUTTITT, Ernie†
NELSON, Garry
O'SULLIVAN, Peter
OWENS, Les
PATES, Colin
PHILLIPS, John
ROBINSON, John
SMALL, Mike
TOWNER, Tony
TYLER, Alf
VITTY, Jack
WATTS, Royston†
WELSH, Don*

Chelmsford City etc.

ABBIS, Keith
BEAL, Phil
CASSIDY, Bill
CLARK, Paul
CURTIS, George*
FEARON, Ron
GIPP, David
GOULD, Wally
GROVES, Henry
HARBURN, Peter
KEELEY, John
KEEN, Eric†
KYDD, David
LEGGETT, Peter
NICHOLAS, Tony
OWERS, Adrian
REED, Peter$
SEXTON, Dave
STEVENS, Norman
SUTTLE, Ken
WALLIS, John†

Chelsea

ABEL, Sammy†
BARBER, George†
BOTT, Wilf†
BOYLE, John
BRIDGES, Barry
BRILEY, Les
BUTLER, Malcolm†
CHIVERS, Gary
CLATWORTHY, Les†
COTHLIFF, Harold†
CROWTHER, Stan
*CURTIS, George***
DIGWEED, Perry
DODD, George
DOVEY, Alan
DUBLIN, Keith
DUKE, George†
GRIFFITHS, Mal†
HASSELL, Tommy
HENDERSON, Stewart
HINSHELWOOD, Martin*
HIPKIN, Reg
HUGHES, Tommy
HUTCHINGS, Chris
ISAAC, Robert
JASPER, Dale
LAVERICK, Bobby
LEADBETTER, Jimmy
LIVESEY, Charlie
LLOYD, Barry*
LOWE, Henry†
McNEILL, Ian
McNICHOL, Johnny
MALPASS, Sam†
MAYBANK, Teddy
MEDHURST, Harry
MURRAY, Bert
MUTTITT, Ernie†
NICHOLAS, Tony
PATES, Colin
PHILLIPS, John

PORTER, Willie
REID, Ernie†
RIDLEY, Dave
ROBSON, Bert†
ROUGVIE, Doug
ROWE, Zeke
SEXTON, Dave
SMITH, Bobby
SPERRIN, Bill†
SUTTLE, Ken
THOMAS, Mickey
TOWNSEND, Len†
WALKER, Clive
WALLIS, John†
WEAVER, Sam†
WHITING, Bob
WHITINGTON, Eric
WILLEMSE, Stan
WOODLEY, Vic†

Cheltenham Town

ADAMS, Billy†
BLACKBURN, Ken
BOOK, Steve$
COTTERILL, Steve
THORNE, Adrian
WARREN, Christer

Chester City

BROWN, Sam
COTHLIFF, Harold†
FLANNERY, John
HOLLIS, Harry†
HOWLETT, Gary
ITHELL, Jimmy†
KEELEY, John
LAW, Alec
McGRATH, John
McGUINNESS, Paul$
MELLOR, Ian
PEARSON, Stan†
RITCHIE, George
RUGGIERO, John
SAYER, Peter
SMITH, Bobby
TAPKEN, Norman†
TUNNICLIFFE, Bill†
VASEY, Bob
WALKER, Jim
WEBBER, Keith
*WELSH, Don***

Chesterfield

ABEL, Sammy†
ARMSTRONG, Gerry
CROSS, Graham
CURRY, Bill
DAVIE, Jock
DENNISON, Bob
EGAN, Harry
GABBIADINI, Ricardo
HALL, Proctor
KIRKMAN, Norman†
LONGDON, Billy
McEWAN, Billy
McHALE, Ray
McQUARRIE, Andy
SMITH, Wilf
TILER, Ken
TURNBULL, Billy
WELCH, Ronnie
WILSON, Danny
WRAGG, Billy

Chichester City

MARCH, Zach
WILLARD, Jess

Chippenham Town

DAVIES, Ken
LANCELOTTE, Eric
LEAMON, Fred

SAGE, Frank†
SIM, Jock

Clyde

CAMERON, Duncan
CONNOR, Nat
FERRIER, John
GARDNER, Andy
HANLON, Wally
KENNEDY, Willie
LAWSON, Hector
McATEER, Tom
McWHIRTER, Peter‡
WINNING, Alex†

Clydebank

HUGHES, Tommy
NEIL, Andy

Colchester United

BREMNER, Kevin
BROWN, Stan
COLES, David
DARLING, Len
FERGUSON, Mick
HILLMAN, Dennis†
KEENE, Doug
KEELEY, John
LAYTON, Billy†
McCURLEY, Kevin
MARTIN, Dave
OLIVER, Jim
REINELT, Robbie
WALKER, Bob

Corinthians/Casuals

ANSELL, George
FLACK, Doug†
HAIG-BROWN, Alan

Coventry City

BATEY, Ginger
BEST, Jack
BOORN, Alan
CATTLIN, Chris
DALTON, George
DOBSON, Colin
DORAN, Jack
FERGUSON, Mick
FISHER, Albert
FLOOD, Paul
GOODWIN, Ian
HAWLEY, Fred
HOWLETT, Gary
JACOBS, Steve
JONES, Les
LAVERICK, Bobby
MACHIN, Ernie
MARTIN, Neil
MORRIS, Tom
MORTIMER, Dennis
NEWTON, Jimmy
OSBORNE, Fred
OWENS, Les
PUGH, Jimmy
RICHARDS, Billy
SAWARD, Pat*
SCOTT-WALFORD, Frank*
SEXTON, Dave
SMALL, Sammy
SMITH, Wilf
TAYLOR, Peter*
YATES, Billy

Cowdenbeath

McDONALD, Murdo

Crawley Town

ARMSTRONG, Gerry
BAKER, Charlie
BISSETT, Nicky
BROWN, Alan

BROWN, Gary
BYRNE, John
CODNER, Robert
COLDWELL, David$
COLES, David
CRUMPLIN, John
DARLING, Len
DAY, Albert
DINEEN, Jack$
EDWARDS, Sean
GEARD, Glen
GEDDES, Gavin
HANNAM, Dave
HEALER, Ernie
JASPER, Dale
JENNINGS, Roy
LAMBERT, Martin
LECK, Derek
LIVESEY, Charlie
MASSIMO, Franco
MEADE, Raphael
O'SULLIVAN, Peter
PATES, Colin
RING, Mike
ROBINSON, John
SHERIDAN, Alex
STANDING, John
STILLE, Giles
SWINFEN, Reg†
TILTMAN, Richard
TOWNER, Tony
UPTON, Nobby
VESSEY, Tony
WHITINGTON, Eric
WILKINS, Dean

Crewe Alexandra

BEAL, Phil
CLARKE, Billy
DILLON, John
DORAN, Jack
EDWARDS, Len
GABBIADINI, Ricardo
JASPER, Dale
McGUINNESS, Paul$
MELIA, Jimmy*
MOORE, Jimmy
PHILLIPS, John
WETTON, Albert

Crystal Palace

ABEL, Sammy†
ADDINALL, Bert
BENNETT, Ken
BENNETT, Ron
BLACKMAN, Jack†
BRATLEY, George†
BRISCOE, Jimmy†
BROPHY, Harry
BROWN, Mick
BURNS, Tony
CHASE, Charlie
CHESTERS, Arthur†
COLES, David
DAVIE, Jock
DRIVER, Allenby†
ELLIS, Syd
FELTON, Bob†
GILLESPIE, Ian†
GREGORY, Fred†
HANLON, Wally
HENLEY, Les†
HINSHELWOOD, Martin*
HOOPER, Percy†
HUMPHREY, John
JONES, Jimmy
KELLY, John
LANGLEY, Jimmy
LITTLE, Doz
LOWE, Henry†
McFARLANE, D.L.†
McNICHOL, Johnny

MALPASS, Sam†	BOYD, Jimmy†	MULVANEY, Jimmy	**Enfield**	GOULD, Wally
MARTIN, Neil	BUCKLEY, Frank	ROBERTSON, Jimmy		HASSELL, Tommy
MATTHEWSON, George†	BUTLIN, Barry	THOMSON, Norman	EDWARDS, Matthew	HILTON, Pat
MILLBANK, Joe†	**CLOUGH, Brian***	WEIR, Jock.†	HOWELL, Ronnie	JAMES, Tony
MORRAD, Frank	CRUMP, Fred		**PEARCE, Graham**	LANCELOTTE, Eric
MULLERY, Alan*	CURRY, Bill	**Dundee**	*WALLIS, John†*	LONGDON, Billy
MUTTITT, Ernie†	*EGAN, Harry*			NICHOLAS, Tony
NEEDHAM, Archie	GREGORY, John	BREMNER, Kevin	**Everton**	RICHARDS, Billy
O'REILLY, Gary	*HAWLEY, Fred*	BOYD, Jimmy†		THOMAS, Lyn
PETCHEY, George*	KEEN, Eric†	BURNETT, Jimmy	ATTWOOD, Arthur	THOMPSON, Cyril
PHILLIPS, John	LEWIS, Allen	CLARK, Joe‡	BILEY, Alan	THOMSON, Norman
REDFERN, Bob	McEWAN, Billy	DAVIE, Jock	BURTENSHAW, Steve	WHITINGTON, Eric
REECE, Tom†	MANSFIELD, W.	DOUGAL, Dave	DOWNS, Dickie	
ROBSON, Bert†	MARLOWE, Ricky	FARRELL, Bobby	FARRINGTON, Mark	**Forfar Athletic**
ROBSON, Jack*	MASON, Tommy	HENDRY, Willie‡	FELTON, Bob†	
SALT, Harold	MERCER, Toby‡	HILL, Bob‡	FERGUSON, Mick	OSBORNE, Jack
SAWARD, Pat*	MOSELEY, Graham	HOWES, Arthur	HARBURN, Peter	
SEXTON, Dave	OAKDEN, Harry‡	LONGAIR, Bill‡	HUGHES, Darren	**Fulham**
SMILLIE, Neil	PHILBIN, Jack	LOW, John‡	KEOWN, Martin	
SMITH, Potter	RYAN, Gerry	McARTHUR, Willie‡	*KEEN, Eric†*	ABEL, Sammy†
TOOTILL, Alf†	SAUNDERS, Dean	McATEER, Tom	LAVERICK, Bobby	*BLACKMAN, Fred*
WALKER, Cyril†	SHARPE, Ivan	McCARTHY, Tom	PINCHBECK, Cliff	*BRISCOE, Jimmy†*
WATSON, Jack†	STEELE, Eric	MACAULAY, Archie*	REES, Barrie	*BROPHY, Harry*
WILLARD, Jess	**TAYLOR, Peter***	MALLOCH, Jock‡	SANDERS, Allan	BROWN, Stan
WILLIAMS, Gary	THOMAS, Micky	RODGER, Tom	STEELE, Simon	BURDETT, Tom†
WILSON, Albert†	THOMPSON, Cyril	ROWELL, Gary	STORER, Stuart	*BUSH, Tom†*
WILSON, Fred†	WALKER, Jim	**SMITH, Dave**	THOMAS, Mickey	*CHESTERS, Arthur†*
YOUNG, Eric	WEAVER, Sam†	THOMSON, Charlie	WEBBER, Keith	COLES, David
	WILSON, Albert†	WILLOCKS, Davie‡		*COTHLIFF, Harold†*
Dagenham &	WOMBWELL, Dick		**Exeter City**	*CUNLIFFE, Arthur†*
Redbridge etc.	WOODLEY, Vic†	**Dundee United**		*DAVIE, Jock*
ARMSTRONG, Dave			ADEKOLA, David	DEAR, Brian
BELLAMY, Walter	**Distillery**	BORTHWICK, Walter	ATKINSON, Jimmy	DIGWEED, Perry
BISSETT, Nicky		McCARTHY, Tom	BARBER, Stan	*DRIVER, Allenby†*
CHAMPELOVIER, Les	**EASTHAM, George†**	MEADE, Raphael	BINNEY, Fred	*DUKE, George†*
CODNER, Robert	FARRELL, Paddy	OSBORNE, Jack	BROWN, Alan	FITCHIE, Tom
GILBERG, Harry	McILVENNY, Paddy	OSWALD, Willie	CHAMBERLAIN, Mark	FLACK, Doug†
HOWELL, Ronnie	MERCER, Toby‡	*PINKERTON, Harry†*	CHESTERS, Arthur†	*FORD, Fred†*
OWERS, Adrian	NICOL, Geordie	ROSS, George†	COCHRANE, Johnny	FOX, Reg
PORTER, Willie	ROBERTSON, Jimmy	SIMPSON, Tommy	FEEBERY, Jack	GORE, Les†
YOUNG, Len	OAKDEN, Harry‡	*THOMSON, Charlie*	FERRIER, John	*GRIFFITHS, Mal†*
			GOODWIN, Fred	*GRUNDY, Arnold†*
Darlington	**Doncaster Rovers**	**Dunfermline Athletic**	GRANT, Alan	*HENLEY, Les†*
			HUGHES, Darren	*HOLLEY, George*
BAXTER, Bobby	BOTT, Wilf†	BORTHWICK, Walter	HURST, Stan	JEPSON, Albert
BROMLEY, Brian	COWAN, Sam†	**CLARK, Joe‡**	JOHNSTON, Ron	JOHNSON, Mick
CASE, Jimmy	DONNELLY, Peter	*CONNELLY, Eddie*	**KIRKMAN, Norman†**	JONES, Les
DODD, George	GALLACHER, Bernard	RONALDSON, Duncan	LAMBERT, Martin	KEEN, Eric†
DUFFY, Alan	GREGORY, Fred†	ROUGVIE, Doug	LEY, George	LANGLEY, Jimmy
GOODCHILD, John	HARRIS, Joe§		RANDALL, Ossie	LLOYD, Barry*
HEALER, Ernie	HYDE, Len	**Durham City**	RISDON, Stan	LOWE, Harry
McEWAN, Billy	JOHNSON, Mick		ROBERTSON, Lammie	MACAULAY, Archie*
McNAB, Neil	KINNEAR, Joe	BURNHAM, Jack	STORER, Stuart	*McDERMOTT, Joe†*
MIDDLETON, Harry	*MACAULAY, Archie*		TEMPLEMAN, John	MacDONALD, Hugh
MUIR, Ian	MARSDEN, Harry	**Eastbourne Town**	THOMPSON, Stan	*McINNES, Jimmy†*
POSKETT, Malcolm	OWENS, Les		THOMSON, Charlie	MALPASS, Sam†
TAPKEN, Norman†	RUSSELL, Jock	CARRUTHERS, Jack	THORNE, Adrian	MATTHEWSON, George†
WAKE, Tom	STEPHENS, Malcolm	FRANCIS, Vic†	VARCO, Percy	MAYBANK, Teddy
WILSON, Harry	WEBBER, Keith	GRANT, Jim	VICKERS, Wilf	MEADE, Raphael
WINDROSS, Dennis	WINDROSS, Dennis	KING, Eddie	WHITE, Tom	MORRAD, Frank
YOUNG, Willie	WRAGG, Billy	LEACH, George	WILLIS, George	MULLERY, Alan*
			WILSON, Glen	*MUTTITT, Ernie†*
Dartford	**Dover Athletic etc.**	**Eastbourne United**		*O'DONNELL, Frank†*
			Falkirk	O'SULLIVAN, Peter
BOORN, Alan	ARMSTRONG, Dave	BURNETT, Dennis		PORTER, Willie
BOYLE, John	BLACKBURN, Ken	FLOOD, Paul	*MACAULAY, Archie*	*PRYDE, Bob†*
BURNS, Tony	BOORN, Alan	GALL, Norman	MULHALL, John	*REDFERN, Bob*
CHAMBERLAIN, Bert	BRENNAN, Paddy	GEARD, Glen	OLIVER, Jim	RICHARDS, Billy
GROVES, Freddie	BROWN, Alan	GRANT, Alan	PINKERTON, Harry†	ROUGVIE, Doug
KEENE, Doug	DANIELS, Harry	**MANSELL, Jack**	ROBERTSON, Jimmy	ROWLEY, Arthur†
KYDD, David	FEARON, Ron	MARRIOTT, Ernie	THOMSON, Charlie	SEXTON, Dave
LEWIS, George	GRUMMITT, Peter	POWNEY, Brian	WEIR, Jock.†	SEYMOUR, Ian
McLAFFERTY, Maurice	HILTON, Pat	WHITINGTON, Eric		SHANKS, Don
MULRANEY, Jock†	**LITTLE, Doz**	WOFFINDEN, Colin	**Farnborough Town**	*SPERRIN, Bill†*
NICHOLAS, Tony	McCOY, Tim			TOOTILL, Alf†
OWENS, Les	McILVENNY, Paddy	**East Fife**	BROWN, Kevan	TRANTER, Wilf
SITFORD, Tony	McNEILL, Ian		COOPER, Geoff	TURNER, Bob‡
WALKER, Cyril†	MEADE, Raphael	BORTHWICK, Walter	RING, Mike	WALKER, Clive
	MUNDAY, Stuart	**CLARK, Joe‡**	STEMP, Wayne	WARREN, Christer
Derby County	TRANTER, Wilf			WATSON, Jack†
	WALKER, Bob	**East Stirlingshire**	**Folkestone Town**	*WEAVER, Sam†*
ARMSTRONG, Arthur				*WILSON, Joe*
BILEY, Alan	**Dumbarton**	BROWN, Sam	BARHAM, Mark	
BIRDSALL, George		GILGUN, Pat	BOORN, Alan	
BOWDEN, Ossie	MIDDLETON, Billy	MOONEY, Paul	BROWN, Gary	
	MILLER, Ali		DAY, Albert	
		Ebbw Vale	FOX, Reg	
		BEECH, George		
		CLARKE, Billy		
		McALLISTER, Billy		

Gainsborough Trinity
BROWN, Freddie
EYRES, Jack
GILLIVER, Alan
MELLOR, Ian
MURFIN, Clarrie

Gateshead/ South Shields
BATEY, Ginger
BROWN, Tom
CLARKE, Jeff
GALL, Norman
HALL, Fretwell
HALL, Jack E.
LAVERICK, Bobby
McDERMOT, Joe†
TURNBULL, Billy
VITTY, Jack
WALKER, Bob

Gillingham
AKINBIYI, Ade
ARCHER, Arthur
BEALE, Bob
BEENEY, Mark
BERRY, Les
BREMNER, Kevin
BROWN, Freddie
BURTENSHAW, Charlie†
CHAPMAN, Ian
CLARK, Paul
DARLING, Len
DOBSON, Colin
DORAN, Jack
HILLMAN, Dennis†
HILTON, Pat
HOOPER, Percy†
HULME, Arthur
HUMPHREY, John
INNES, Bob
JACOBS, Steve
KELLY, John
KENNEDY, Jimmy
LEY, George
LIVESEY, Charlie
MARSDEN, Harry
MARTIN, Dave
MORRIS, Mark
NICOL, Geordie
OSWALD, Willie
OWERS, Adrian
PEARCE, Graham
REINELT, Robbie
RULE, Arthur
RUTHERFORD, Jack
SCOTT, Frank
SHEPHERD, John
SLY, Harold
SMILLIE, Neil
SPEARRITT, Eddie
TRUSSON, Mike
VALLANCE, Hugh
WALKER, Cyril†
WATSON, Jimmy
WILLIAMS, Jack

Glenavon
ARMSTRONG, Gerry
CURRAN, Jack
MOORHEAD, George

Glentoran
COCHRANE, Johnny
JENNINGS, Sam
McGONIGAL, Bert
MARRIOTT, Ernie
TURNER, Bob‡

Glossop
CRUMP, Fred

FITCHIE, Tom
HOYLAND, Fred
MENDHAM, C.
NEEDHAM, Archie
PRYCE, Jack
SHARPE, Ivan
TUSTIN, Bill
WILLIAMS, Dave

Gloucester
BLACKBURN, Ken
JOHNSON, Mick
McQUARRIE, Andy

Gravesend & Northfleet etc.
ATTWOOD, Arthur
BURNS, Tony
BUSBY, Dave
COOK, Tommy
GILBERG, Harry
HULME, Arthur
INNES, Bob
JEST, Syd
LANE, Billy*
LIDDELL, John
McAVOY, Frank
McNICOL, Bob
NICHOLAS, Tony
SITFORD, Tony
TOWNER, Tony
TURNER, Bob‡
WAITES, George
WETTON, Albert

Grays Athletic, Grays United, etc.
CURTIS, George*
FEARON, Ron
O'REILLY, Gary
ROBERTS, Billy
SALT, Harold
TAYLOR, A. J.
WHITE, Tom

Greenock Morton
BORTHWICK, Walter
CAVEN, Joe
McNAB, Neil
McWHIRTER, Peter‡
RING, Mike
WILSON, Alex

Grimsby Town
AITKEN, George*
BOYD, Jimmy†
BURNETT, Jimmy
BUTLER, Malcolm†
DOUGAL, Dave
DUNCLIFFE, John
GABBIADINI, Ricardo
GARDNER, Andy
GOVIER, Steve
HENDERSON, Crosby
HICKMAN, Mike
HODGSON, Sam†
HYDE, Len
JONES, Freddie
McCAIRNS, Tom
MATTHEWSON, George†
MOCHAN, Charlie
MORRIS, Tom
NELMES, Alf*
RODGER, Tom
RONALDSON, Duncan
SCRIMSHAW, Stan†
SMITH, Bobby
WILSON, Albert†

Guildford City
BENNETT, Ken
BISSET, Tommy

BLACKMAN, Jack†
CLARKE, Nobby
DAREY, Jeff
ELLIS, Syd
GILL, Eric
GORDON, Dennis
HOWARD, Frankie
KEENE, Doug
LANE, Billy*
LANGLEY, Jimmy
MACAULAY, Archie*
MUNDY, Albert
TOWNSEND, Len†
WILKINS, Jack

Halifax Town
ADEKOLA, David
CASE, Jimmy
CRAWFORD, Ted†
DOWNSBOROUGH, Peter
EDINGTON, John†
HALL, Fretwell
IRVINE, Willie
McGRATH, John
MALPASS, Sam†
McHALE, Ray
MOORE, Jimmy
MULVANEY, Jimmy
NEWTON, Jimmy
OFFORD, Stan†
O'REGAN, Kieran
PEAKE, Jason
ROBERTSON, Lammie
SCRIMSHAW, Stan†
SOUTH, Alex
WORTHINGTON, Frank

Hamilton Academical
KELLY, Willie
McDONALD, Paul
MILLER, Alily

Harrow Borough
GIPP, David
HUTCHINGS, Chris
PEARCE, Graham

Hartlepool United
CLOUGH, Brian*
COOPER, Jim
GABBIADINI, Ricardo
GREGORY, Fred†
HASTINGS, Bill
HIPKIN, Reg
MALPASS, Sam†
NEVINS, Laurie
OWENS, Les
PEAKE, Jason
POSKETT, Malcolm
RAMSDEN, Bernard†
SCRIMSHAW, Stan†
SMITH, Bobby
SMITH, Jack
SMITH, Potter
TAYLOR, Peter*
THOMPSON, Stan
WALKER, Bob
WALKER, Jim
WILSON, Harry
WRIGHT, Barrie

Hastings Town
BLACKMAN, Fred
COLEMAN, Jimmy
DAY, Albert
EACOCK, Jack
FOX, Simon
FRANCIS, Vic†
HADDEN, Sid‡
LAMB, Billy
MYALL, Stuart
PACKHAM, Wally†

PERKINS, Bill
SIMMONDS, Danny
THAIR, Sid
WISDEN, Alan

Hastings United
BALL, Jack
BOOTH, Sammy
BROOMFIELD, Des
BROWN, Alan
BROWN, Gary
BURNS, Tony
CASSIDY, Bill
CLAYTON, Ronnie
CURTIS, George*
FOREMAN, Denis
FOX, Reg
GREGORY, Jack†
GUTTRIDGE, Ron
HANNAM, Dave
HILLMAN, Dennis†
HUMPHRIES, Bob
KNIGHT, Peter
LANCELOTTE, Eric
LECK, Derek
LIDDELL, John
McILVENNY, Paddy
McLAFFERTY, Maurice
MOORE, Bernard
RISDON, Stan
SHERIDAN, Alex
SMITH, Bobby
STANDING, John
THOMPSON, Pat

Hayes
CHAMPELOVIER, Les
LANGLEY, Jimmy
NEATE, Derek
SUDDABY, Peter
TOWNSEND, Len†
WILKINSON, Darron

Haywards Heath
BISSET, Tommy
BROWN, Stan
BURNETT, Dennis
HODGE, Eric
HODGES, Cyril
PARR, Charlie†
STANDING, John
WETTON, Albert
WILKINS, Jack

Heart of Midlothian
BAIRD, Ian
BORTHWICK, Walter
BRISCOE, Jimmy†
FASHANU, Justin
McALLISTER, Billy
MUNRO, Alex†
NOGAN, Kurt
O'DONNELL, Frank†
PENNEY, Steve
WOMBWELL, Dick
YATES, Billy

Hereford United
ADEKOLA, David
AKINBIYI, Ade
BAILEY, Mike*
BINNEY, Fred
BRILEY, Les
CLARKE, Billy
CLAYTON, Ronnie
COLLINS, Glyn
FARRINGTON, Mark
GRITT, Steve*
HUGHES, Tommy
JONES, Freddie
JONES, Mark
KEEN, Eric†

LLOYD, Barry*
SMITH, Bobby

Hibernian
CALDWELL, Jock
DAVIE, Jock
McEWAN, Billy
McNEIL, Matt
MARTIN, Neil
MELLON, Jimmy
PRYCE, Jack
ROBERTSON, Tom
THOMSON, Norman
WEIR, Jock.†
WHARTON, F.†

Hillingdon Borough
BISSET, Tommy
LANGLEY, Jimmy
PEARCE, Graham

Home Farm
CAROLAN, Joe
HOWLETT, Gary
McKENNA, Brian
O'DOWD, Greg

Horsham
BAKER, Charlie
BOORN, Alan
BURNETT, Dennis
CHANNON, Vic
DUGNOLLE, Jack
EDWARDS, Sean
FLOOD, Paul
GALL, Norman
GEARD, Glen
GEDDES, Gavin
HUGHES, Horace†
LUTTON, Bertie
MASON, Tommy
MASSIMO, Franco
MATTHEWS, Charlie
SMALL, Peter
STANLEY, Terry
WHITINGTON, Eric

Huddersfield Town
BARHAM, Mark
BLACKMAN, Fred
BOTT, Wilf†
BROPHY, Harry
BURGESS, Ron†
CATTLIN, Chris
CRINSON, Bill
CROFT, Charlie†
DOBSON, Colin
GILLIVER, Alan
HENNIGAN, Mike
HORTON, Brian
HUTCHINGS, Chris
JEE, Joe
JEPSON, Bert
McHALE, Ray
McNAB, Neil
MALPASS, Sam†
MASKELL, Craig
NEAL, Ashley
O'REGAN, Kieran
RODGERSON, Ted
SAWARD, Pat*
SCRIMSHAW, Stan†
STAPLETON, Frank
SWINFEN, Reg†
WILSON, Alec†
WORTHINGTON, Frank

Hull City
BUCKLEY, Frank
BURDETT, Tom†
BURNETT, Dennis
CRUMPLIN, John

CUNLIFFE, Arthur†
CURTIS, George*
HOBSON, Gary
HORTON, Brian
KAVANAGH, Micky
McNEILL, Hamilton†
PINKERTON, Harry†
RING, Mike
RUSHTON, George
SMITH, Potter
WEAVER, Sam†
WRIGHT, Tommy†

Inveress Caledonian Thistle etc.
McNICHOL, Johnny

Ipswich Town
DAY, Albert
DRIVER, Allenby†
FASHANU, Justin
FEARON, Ron
GILLESPIE, Ian†
LEADBETTER, Jimmy
MEADE, Raphael
MOSELEY, Graham
MULRANEY, Jock†
OSMAN, Russell
REED, Billy
SPEARRITT, Eddie
TOOTILL, Alf†
WRIGHT, Steve

Kettering Town
ASPDEN, Tommy
BALDWIN, Harry
CASSIDY, Bill
EDWARDS, Matthew
FARMER, Alex†
FLATTS, Mark
GARFIELD, Ben
HOWELL, Ronnie
McCAIRNS, Tom
MORTIMER, Dennis
SOMMER, Juergen
WHENT, Jack

Kidderminster Harriers
DAVIE, Jock
HENDRIE, Willie‡
HYDE, Len
MULRANEY, Jock†
REECE, Tom†
VALLANCE, Hugh

Kilmarnock
GRAHAM, John
McDONALD, Willie
NEIL, Andy
SMITH, Gordon

Lancing
BOWLES, Reg†
BROMAGE, Russel
BURNETT, Dennis
FRANCE, Ernie†
HICKMAN, Stan†
HOPKINS, Mel
MOFFATT, Johnny
THORNE, Albert†
WOOLGAR, Phil

Leeds City
BLACKMAN, Fred
BUCKLEY, Frank
BURNETT, Jimmy
COOK, Walter
DOUGAL, Dave
JOYNES, Dick
KENNEDY, Jimmy
McDONALD, Willie
MORRIS, Tom

RODGER, Tom
SCOTT-WALFORD, Frank*
SHARPE, Ivan

Leeds United
BAIRD, Ian
BEENEY, Mark
BELL, Willie
BUSH, Tom†
CLOUGH, Brian*
CONNOR, Terry
DAVIE, Jock
EASTHAM, Harry†
GOODWIN, Freddie*
HENNIGAN, Mike
KEEN, Eric†
KINGHORN, Bill†
LANGLEY, Jimmy
McINNES, Jimmy†
McNAB, Neil
MOORE, Jimmy
PATERSON, George†
RAMSDEN, Bernard†
RITCHIE, Andy
SHARPE, Ivan
TAYLOR, Phil†
THOMAS, Mickey
TOWNSEND, Len†
WEAVER, Sam†
WILKINSON, Howard
WORTHINGTON, Frank
WRIGHT, Barrie

Leicester City
ALLSOPP, Tommy
ASHBY, Harry‡
ATTWOOD, Arthur
BELL, Willie
BUNTING, John
CHESTERS, Arthur†
CODNER, Robert
COLES, Donald
CROSS, Graham
EVERITT, Mike
GREGORY, John
GRIFFITHS, Mal†
HALL, Jack H.
HICKMAN, Mike
HOWES, Arthur
JACKSON, John*
JONES, Les
KINGHORN, Bill†
KIRKMAN, Norman†
LANE, Billy*
LYON, Bertie
McARTHUR, Willie‡
McLEOD, Roddy‡
McNEILL, Ian
McWHIRTER, Peter‡
MAY, Larry
MERCER, Toby‡
MILLS, Andy‡
MULRANEY, Jock†
OSBORNE, Fred
OSMAN, Russell
PARRY, Maurice‡
PEAKE, Jason
ROBERTSON, Lammie
ROWLEY, Arthur†
SMALL, Peter
WILSON, Fred†
WORTHINGTON, Frank
WRAGG, Billy
WRIGHT, Joe
YOUNG, Alan

Lewes
BATES, Don
FOX, Reg
GEARD, Glen
GEDDES, Gavin
GRANT, Alan

GRUMMITT, Peter
HASSELL, Tommy
HORSCROFT, Grant
KNIGHT, Peter
LONGLAND, Johnny
RING, Mike
STANLEY, Terry
TOWNER, Tony
WOFFINDEN, Colin
WOOLVEN, Harold

Leyton
TAYLOR, A. J.

Leyton Orient
BERRY, Greg
BLACKMAN, Jack†
BOYD, Jimmy†
BOYLE, John
BUNYON, W.†
CATER, Ron†
CHAMPELOVIER, Les
CLARK, Paul
CONNELLY, Eddie
COTHLIFF, Harold†
CRAWFORD, Ted†
CURTIS, George*
DAVIE, Jock
DENNISON, Bob
DEVINE, John†
DOUGAL, Dave
EDMONDS, Eddie
FASHANU, Justin
FEARON, Ron
FLACK, Doug†
GILLESPIE, Ian†
GORE, Les†
GREALISH, Tony
GREGORY, Jack†
HAIG-BROWN, Alan
HIGGINS, Ronnie
*LANE, Billy**
LAYTON, Billy†
LIDDELL, John
LITTLE, Wally
LUMBERG, Albert
MARTIN, Dave
MORGAN, Stan†
MORRAD, Frank
MULRANEY, Jock†
MUTTITT, Ernie†
NICHOLAS, Tony
PETCHEY, George*
PUGH, Jimmy
ROBSON, Bert†
RAMSEY, Chris
RODGERSON, Ted
SEXTON, Dave
SPERRIN, Bill†
STEWART, Tom
SWINFEN, Reg†
THOMSON, Norman
THORNE, Adrian
TOWNLEY, Jimmy
TULLY, Fred†
WAITES, George
WALLER, Henry†
WEAVER, Sam†
WILKINS, Dean
WILLEMSE, Stan

Lincoln City
BELL, Willie
BULLIMER, Leo‡
BURDETT, Tom†
CROSS, Graham
DAVIDSON, Jimmy‡
DAY, Albert
EASTHAM, George†
GILLIVER, Alan
GORDON, Dennis
GROVES, Ken†

HULME, Arthur
JONES, Les
KEEN, Eric†
LAWTON, Nobby
LEGGETT, Peter
McCAIRNS, Tom
McDERMOTT, Joe†
MARTIN, Jack
OSBORNE, Fred
SCOTT, Frank
SMITH, Wally
SYKES, Albert
WRIGHT, Steve

Linfield
CURRAN, Jack
HILL, Bob‡
McGONIGAL, Bert
MERCER, Toby‡
MOORHEAD, George
PENNEY, Steve

Littlehampton Town
BROMAGE, Russel
BUSBY, Dave
GEARD, Glen
HIPKIN, Reg
KAVANAGH, Micky
KNIGHT, Peter
MANSELL, Jack
MYALL, Stuart
PIPER, Steve
TILTMAN, Richard
WOOLGAR, Phil
WOOLVEN, Harold

Liverpool
BALMER, Jack†
BUSH, Tom†
CASE, Jimmy
CRAWFORD, Ted†
EASDALE, Jack†
EASTHAM, Harry†
FAIRHURST, Billy†
GRUNDY, Arnold†
GUTTRIDGE, Ron
JACKSON, John*
JONES, Ron†
KEEN, Eric†
KEMP, Dirk†
KINGHORN, Bill†
LAWRENSON, Mark
LAWSON, Hector
LONGDON, Billy
McCURLEY, Kevin
McINNES, Jimmy†
MELIA, Jimmy*
NEAL, Ashley
O'DONNELL, Frank†
PARRY, Maurice‡
PATERSON, George†
PRYDE, Bob†
RAMSDEN, Barney†
RITCHIE, George
ROBERTSON, Tom
ROBINSON, Michael
RODON, Chris
SAUNDERS, Dean
SHAFTO, John†
SOUTH, Alex
TAYLOR, Phil†
WELSH, Don*
WESTBY, Jack†

Loughborough
JACKSON, John*
PARRY, Maurice‡

Luton Town
ALEXANDER, Fred†
ALLSOPP, Tommy
ANDERSON, Jock†

BEDFORD, Sid
BILEY, Alan
BLACKMAN, Jack†
BROWN, Tom
BURTENSHAW, Charlie†
BUTLIN, Barry
CONNELLY, Eddie
COOK, P. R.†
DICKOV, Paul
DODD, George
DRIVER, Allenby†
DUKE, George†
FOSTER, Steve
GOODEVE, Ken
GREALISH, Tony
GREGORY, Julius
HACKING, Bob
HALL, Proctor
HASSELL, Tommy
HENDERSON, Crosby
HORTON, Brian
JONES, Bill
KIRKWOOD, Dan
LAYTON, Billy†
McINNES, Jimmy†
MEADE, Raphael
MOORE, Bernard
MOORE, John
MULVANEY, Jimmy
NOGAN, Kurt
POINTON, Joe
PUGH, Jimmy
REDFERN, Bob
RUTHERFORD, Jack
SEXTON, Dave
SHANKS, Don
SHARPE, Ivan
SMALL, Mike
SMALL, Peter
SOMMER, Juergen
SYKES, Albert
TAIT, Tommy†
THOMSON, Norman
WHENT, Jack
WHITFIELD, Ken
WILLIAMS, Dave
WILSON, Danny

Macclesfield Town
PARKES, David

Maidstone United
BEALE, Bob
BEENEY, Mark
BERRY, Les
BROMAGE, Russel
GALL, Mark
O'SULLIVAN, Peter
OWERS, Adrian
PEARCE, Graham
ROLLINGS, Andy
SHERIDAN, Alex
SITFORD, Tony
TILTMAN, Richard
WILLIAMS, Dave

Manchester City
BUCKLEY, Chris
BUCKLEY, Frank
BUTLER, Malcolm†
CLARKE, Jeff
CORRIGAN, Joe
COWAN, Sam†
DENNISON, Bob
DICKOV, Paul
DORAN, Jack
FASHANU, Justin
FISHER, Albert
GARBUTT, Ray
GREALISH, Tony
GREGORY, Fred†
GREGORY, Julius

HARRISON, Jack	**SMITH, Dave**	*EASTHAM, George†*	BOTT, Wilf†	LECK, Derek
HILL, Bob‡	STEELE, Eric	EDWARDS, Alistair	BOYD, Jimmy†	LIVESEY, Charlie
HORTON, Brian	STORER, Stuart	FORD, Fred†	CLARKE, Jeff	*MACAULAY, Archie**
HOWELL, Graham	WEAVER, Sam†	*GILLESPIE, Ian†*	CLARKE, Ray	McCOY, Tim
JONES, Les	WILSON, Albert†	GRAHAM, John	CONNELLY, Eddie	MARTIN, Dave
KINGHORN, Bill†		*GROVES, Ken†*	CURRY, Bill	MOORE, John
LITTLE, Doz	**Margate**	*HASSELL, Tommy*	DALTON, George	*MULRANEY, Jock†*
McNAB, Neil		HILL, Bob‡	DIGWEED, Perry	PINCHBECK, Cliff
MELLOR, Ian	BENNETT, Ronnie	HOWELL, Ronnie	DIXON, Tommy	ROBERTS, Doug
MULRANEY, Jock†	BROPHY, Harry	HULSE, Ben	*DORAN, Jack*	*SCRIMSHAW, Stan†*
PAYNE, John	BROWN, Alan	HUMPHRIES, Bob	DUFFY, Alan	WATSON, Jimmy
ROBINSON, Michael	BROWN, Stan	*KEEN, Eric†*	*EASTHAM, Harry†*	
SANDERS, Allan	COCKER, Joe†	LANHAM	FASHANU, Justin	**Northwich Victoria**
SMITH, Gordon	CURTIS, George*	LECK, Derek	FROST, Arthur†	
STEVENS, Jack	DAVIE, Jock	*LOWE, Henry†*	FULLER, Bob$	LOWE, Harry
TAIT, Tommy†	DONNELLY, Peter	MACCIOCHI, David	GARDNER, Andy	**McNEILL, Ian**
TURNBULL, Billy	HILTON, Pat	*McINNES, Jimmy†*	GRUNDY, Arnold†	**ROBERTSON, Lammie**
*WELSH, Don**	JEST, Syd	McNEILL, Ian	HALL, Ernie	SAYER, Peter
WHITFIELD, Ken	KYDD, David	*MALPASS, Sam†*	HENDERSON, Crosby	WALKER, Jim
WRIGHT, Tommy†	SHEPHERD, John	MARTIN, Dave	HOLLINS, Dave	
	SMITH, Jack	MARTIN, Jack	ISAAC, Bill†	**Norwich City**
Manchester United	TOOZE, Cyril†	*MATTHEWSON, George†*	JOHNSON, Mick	
	WALKER, Bob	MEADE, Raphael	KEEN, Eric†	AKINBIYI, Ade
BEALE, Bob		MILLAR, Arthur	*KINGHORN, Bill†*	ALLSOPP, Tommy
BRETT, Frank	**Merthyr Tydfil,**	*MILLBANK, Joe†*	LAWRENSON, Mark	ANSELL, George
BUCKLEY, Frank	**Merthyr Town**	MORGAN, Stan†	LEE, Barney	ARCHER, Arthur
CAROLAN, Joe		*MUTTITT, Ernie†*	McGRATH, John	BARHAM, Mark
CHESTERS, Arthur†	DAVIES, Peter	PAYNE, John	*McINNES, Jimmy†*	BEALE, Bob
CLARK, Joe‡	**FISHER, Albert**	**PETCHEY, George**	McNEIL, Matt	BROWN, Oliver
CROWTHER, Stan	GOUGH, Tony	*PINKERTON, Harry†*	McNICHOL, Johnny	**BUCKLEY, Frank**
DALTON, Ted	JONES, Abe	READMAN, Joe	MIDDLETON, Harry	CHIVERS, Martin
DAVIE, Jock	JONES, Mark	RIDLEY, Dave	NAPIER, Kit	CORRIGAN, Joe
DAWSON, Alex	McILVENNY, Paddy	SAWARD, Pat*	NEVINS, Laurie	*CURTIS, George**
FAIRHURST, Billy†	RICHARDS, Billy	*SCRIMSHAW, Stan†*	SMITH, Dave	DENNISON, Bob
GOODEVE, Ken	SMITH, Potter	SHEPHERD, John	STEELE, Eric	DORAN, Jack
GOODWIN, Freddie*		SMITH, Wilf	TAPKEN, Norman†	DRIVER, Allenby†
HALL, Proctor	**Middlesbrough**	*SPERRIN, Bill†*	*TAYLOR, Phil†*	DYE, Derek†
LAWTON, Nobby		TOWNER, Tony	THOMAS, Jack	FARRINGTON, Mark
LONGAIR, Bill‡	AITKEN, George*	TOWNSEND, Len†	TURNER, Dave	FASHANU, Justin
McGUINNESS, Paul$	BAIRD, Ian	WAITES, George	WEAVER, Sam†	FITCHIE, Tom
McINNES, Jimmy†	BARHAM, Mark	WEAVER, Sam†	WILSON, Glen	GILGUN, Pat
MANSELL, Jack	CLOUGH, Brian*	*WELSH, Don**	WILSON, Joe	GOFFEY, Bert
MARTINDALE, Len†	CUNLIFFE, Arthur†	WILSON, Joe	WINSTANLEY, Graham	GOVIER, Steve
NELMES, Alf*	GARBUTT, Ray	*WINNING, Alex†*		HALL, Fretwell
NICOL, Geordie	HALL, Jack H.		**Newhaven**	HIPKIN, Reg
O'SULLIVAN, Peter	HAWORTH, Jack	**Montrose**		JENNINGS, Sam
PEARSON, Stan†	*HODGSON, Sam†*		HASSELL, Tommy	KENNEDY, Jimmy
PUGH, Jimmy	JENNINGS, Sam	CAMERON, Duncan	KNIGHT, Peter	LEWIS, Bill†
RITCHIE, Andy	KENT, Harry	DOUGAL, Dave	McLAFFERTY, Maurice	LIVINGSTONE, Archie
ROBSON, Jack	McALLISTER, Billy	McCARTHY, Tom	NEWMAN, Daren	**MACAULAY, Archie**
RODGER, Tom	McDERMOTT, Joe†	MILLAR, Arthur	O'SULLIVAN, Peter	McNEIL, Matt
ROWLEY, Arthur†	*McKENZIE, Duncan†*	OSBORNE, Jack	**POWNEY, Brian**	MELLOR, Ian
SEXTON, Dave	*MUNRO, Alex†*	**ROUGVIE, Doug**	RING, Mike	MILLER, Ali
SMITH, Bobby	MUTTITT, Ernie†	SIMPSON, Tommy	ROLLINGS, Andy	*MULRANEY, Jock†*
STAPLETON, Frank	NELMES, Alf*		**STANDING, John**	OLIVER, Jim
TAPKEN, Norman†	*NEVINS, Laurie*	**Motherwell**	SUTTLE, Ken	OWENS, Les
THOMAS, Mickey	*PEARSON, Stan†*		TOWNER, Tony	REES, Mal
TRANTER, Wilf	POSKETT, Malcolm	BAILEY, Craig		REID, Ernie†
TURNER, Bob‡	**ROBSON, Jack**	BROWN, Jimmy†	**Newport County**	RITCHIE, George
WASSALL, John†	ROWELL, Gary	KELLY, John		ROLLINGS, Andy
WOMBWELL, Dick	TAIT, Tommy	MOORE, John	CLARKE, Billy	RONALDSON, Duncan
WORTHINGTON, Frank	TAYLOR, Peter*	RUSSELL, Jock	COLES, David	ROWELL, Gary
YATES, Billy	WINDROSS, Dennis		HALL, Proctor	*SCRIMSHAW, Stan†*
		Nelson	HUDSON, Colin	SMITH, Wally
Mansfield Town	**Millwall**		LAWSON, Hector	TAYLOR, Geoff
		JEE, Joe	LEAMON, Fred	THOMSON, Norman
BUNTING, John	*ALEXANDER, Fred†*	LEE, Barney	MOORE, Beriah†	VARCO, Percy
CLARKE, Ray	ARCHER, Arthur	LIVINGSTONE, Archie	SAGE, Frank†	WAITES, George
COLES, David	ARMSTRONG, Dave	LYON, Bertie	**SMITH, Bobby**	WALKER, Cyril†
CROFT, Charlie†	ARMSTRONG, Gerry	MACHIN, Ernie	TURNBULL, Billy	WILKINSON, Reg
CURRY, Bill	BARKER, Don			WRIGHT, Steve
DAVIE, Jock	BERRY, Greg	**New Brighton etc.**	**Northampton Town**	YOUNG, Willie
EASTHAM, George†	*BLACKMAN, Jack†*			
EDMONDS, Eddie	BREMNER, Kevin	*EASTHAM, Harry†*	*BALDWIN, Harry*	**Nottingham Forest**
EGAN, Harry	BRIDGES, Barry	FROST, Arthur†	BEDFORD, Sid	
FOX, Reg	BRILEY, Les	*LONGDON, Billy*	BRETT, Frank	ANTHONY, Walter
HINDLEY, Frank	*BRISCOE, Jimmy†*	*LOWE, Henry†*	BRISCOE, Jimmy†	*BALDWIN, Harry*
HODGSON, Sam†	*BURGESS, Ron†*	LUMBERG, Albert	BULLIMER, Leo‡	BOWDEN, Ossie
HOLLINS, Dave	BURNETT, Dennis	POTTS, Eric	CAMPBELL, Greg	BROWN, Oliver
ITHELL, Jimmy†	*BUTLER, Malcolm†*		CLIFFORD, John†	BULL, Garry
JONES, Les	BYRNE, John	**Newcastle United**	CRUMP, Fred	BUNTING, John
LONGDON, Billy	*COTHLIFF, Harold†*		EVERITT, Mike	*BURGESS, Ron†*
McEWAN, Billy	*DAVIE, Jock*	BAIRD, Ian	GALLACHER, Bernard	BURTON, Billy
READMAN, Joe	DEAR, Brian	*BALMER, Jack†*	GREGORY, John	BUTLIN, Barry
	DODD, George	BARBER, Stan	HUGHES, Darren	CARGILL, Jimmy
	DRIVER, Allenby†	BIRDSALL, George		

CLOUGH, Brian*	**Oxford United**	CURRAN, Jack	STEWART, Tom	MILLBANK, Joe†
COTHLIFF, Harold†		DALTON, Ted	THOMAS, Rees	MOORE, Jimmy

CLOUGH, Brian*
COTHLIFF, Harold†
DAVIE, Jock
EGAN, Harry
FARMER, Alex†
FASHANU, Justin
GORDON, Les
GRUMMITT, Peter
GUTTRIDGE, Ron
HAWLEY, Fred
HINDLEY, Frank
HOLLINS, Dave
INNES, Bob
JENNINGS, Sam
JONES, Les
McNAUGHTON, Jock
MARSDEN, Harry
MARTIN, Neil
O'DONNELL, Frank†
SAUNDERS, Dean
SHARPE, Ivan
SMALL, Peter
TAYLOR, Peter*
VASEY, Bob
WARD, Jack†
WARD, Peter
WILSON, Danny
WRAGG, Billy
YOUNG, Willie

Notts County

BAKER, Bert
BUCKLEY, Frank
BURGESS, Ron†
BUTLIN, Barry
CLARE, Edwin
DAVIE, Jock
DODD, George
FASHANU, Justin
FISHER, Albert
GUTTRIDGE, Ron
HAWLEY, Fred
INNES, Bob
JENNINGS, Sam
JONES, Les
JOYNES, Dick
KEEN, Eric†
KELLY, Willie
KENT, Harry
McCAIRNS, Tom
MELLORS, Mark
MORRAD, Frank
NELSON, Garry
SIRRELL, Jimmy
SMITH, Jack
STEELE, Eric
VASEY, Bob
WARD, Alf
WATSON, Jimmy
WEAVER, Sam†
WILKINSON, Howard
WILLIAMS, Dave
YOUNG, Alan

Nuneaton

BROPHY, Harry
GOODWIN, Ian
ISON, Ernie
LAVERICK, Bobby

Oldham Athletic

BROMAGE, Russel
GOODWIN, Ian
KEELEY, John
McCURLEY, Kevin
MacDONALD, Hugh
MOULDEN, Paul
RITCHIE, Andy
SMITH, Gordon
TURNBULL, Billy
YOUNG, Alan

Oxford United

BENNETT, Ken
BYRNE, John
BYRNE, Paul
FOSTER, Steve
GORDON, Dennis
HORTON, Brian
JOHNSTON, Ron
KEELEY, John
LAWRENSON, Mark
SAUNDERS, Dean

Partick Thistle

CRUMPLIN, John
KENNEDY, Jimmy
McLEOD, Roddy‡
PARRY, Maurice‡

Peacehaven & Telscombe

DINEEN, Jack$
DOVEY, Alan
FLOOD, Paul
NEWMAN, Daren
O'SULLIVAN, Peter
POWNEY, Brian
RING, Mike
STANLEY, Terry
STEELE, Simon

Peterborough United etc.

BREMNER, Kevin
BUTLIN, Barry
CODNER, Robert
DUNCLIFFE, John
EDWARDS, Matthew
HALL, Fretwell
KEELEY, John
LAWRENSON, Mark
LEWIS, Allen
LIVINGSTONE, Archie
McEWAN, Billy
MURRAY, Bert
NEAL, Ashley
NOGAN, Kurt
PIGGIN, Lionel
ROBERTSON, Lammie
ROWE, Zeke
SALT, Harold
SAUNDERS, Edgar
SMALL, Mike
SYKES, Albert
STEELE, Eric
WALKER, Jim

Plymouth Argyle

ASHBY, Harry‡
BAIRD, Ian
BINNEY, Fred
BREMNER, Kevin
BURNS, Tony
CAMPBELL, Greg
COOK, Walter
DUGNOLLE, Jack
EVERITT, Mike
GREGORY, John
MACHIN, Ernie
MEADE, Raphael
NELSON, Garry
OSMAN, Russell
RANDALL, Ossie
SIM, Jock
SMITH, Dave
THORNE, Adrian
TOWNSEND, Len†
TRUSSON, Mike
WILLIS, George

Pontypridd

ARMSTRONG, Arthur

CURRAN, Jack
DALTON, Ted
DORAN, Jack
HALL, Jack E.
JENKINS, Jack
OSBORNE, Fred
SAUNDERS, Edgar

Portadown

MAGILL, Jimmy

Port Vale

BEAMISH, Ken
BOOTH, Sammy
BROMAGE, Russel
BULLIMER, Leo‡
DOBSON, Colin
FELTON, Bob†
HORTON, Brian
HUGHES, Darren
JENNINGS, Sam
McGRATH, John
MORGAN, Sammy
PINCHBECK, Cliff
PINKERTON, Harry†
POINTON, Bill†
POINTON, Joe
RUSHTON, George
SMITH, Bobby
SPOONER, Billy
TAYLOR, Peter*
TUNNICLIFFE, Bill†

Portsmouth

ANDERSON, Jock†
BAIRD, Ian
BAILEY, Mike*
BATEY, Ginger
BENNETT, Ron
BILEY, Alan
BROMLEY, Brian
BROWN, Kevan
BROWN, Tom
BURNETT, Jimmy
CLARKE, Billy
CONNOR, Terry
COTHLIFF, Harold†
CRUMPLIN, John
DAVIE, Jock
DEXTER, Charlie
FARRELL, Bobby
FLACK, Doug†
FOSTER, Steve
GREGORY, Fred†
GREGORY, John
HARBURN, Peter
HINSHELWOOD, Martin*
HOLLINS, Dave
KITTO, Dick
LANEY, Les†
LAYTON, Billy†
LEWIS, Jack
LEY, George
McCOY, Tim
McNAB, Neil
MANSELL, Jack
MARCH, Zach
MARTIN, Ted
MASON, Tommy
MAY, Larry
MILLER, Bill
MOFFATT, Billy
MOORES, Peter†
MUNDY, Albert
PIPER, Steve
ROLLINGS, Andy
ROSS, George†
RUGGIERO, John
RULE, Arthur
SIMMONDS, Danny
SMITH, Jack
STEVENS, Gary

Preston North End

ASPDEN, Tommy
ATHERTON, Jack
BRADFORD, Jack
BRISCOE, Jimmy†
CROSS, Graham
DAWSON, Alex
DOUGAL, Dave
GOOD, Micky
GROVES, Ken†
HALL, Jack E.
HAYES, Billy
HENDRY, Willie‡
IRVINE, Willie
LAWRENSON, Mark
LAWTON, Nobby
McGRATH, John
NAPIER, Kit
NOGAN, Kurt
O'DONNELL, Frank†
O'RAWE, Frank
POTTS, Eric
RITCHIE, George
ROBERTS, Billy
ROBINSON, Michael
RODGER, Tom
SAYER, Peter
TRAINOR, Peter
WILCOCK, George
WILLIAMS, Gary
WILSON, Harry
WORTHINGTON, Frank

Queen of the South

MARTIN, Neil

Queen's Park

BELL, Willie
FITCHIE, Tom
KINGHORN, Bill†
NEWTON, Jimmy
SHERIDAN, Alex

Queen's Park Rangers

ABEL, Sammy†
ADDINALL, Bert
ALEXANDER, Fred†
ARCHER, Arthur
BLACKMAN, Fred
BLACKMAN, Jack†
BOTT, Wilf†
BRIDGES, Barry
BURNHAM, Jack
BURTENSHAW, Steve
BYRNE, John
CHIVERS, Gary
DANIELS, Harry
DAVIE, Jock
DEVINE, John†
DUKE, George†
EASTHAM, George†
FARMER, Alex†
FEARON, Ron
GARDNER, Andy
GILBERG, Harry
GREGORY, John
HAWLEY, Fred
HENLEY, Les†
HIGGINS, Ron
HOWES, Arthur
KELLY, Jimmy†
LANGLEY, Jimmy
LOWE, Henry†
McALLISTER, Billy
McCAIRNS, Tom
McINNES, Jimmy†

MILLBANK, Joe†
MOORE, Jimmy
MOUNTFORD, George†
MUIR, Ian
MULLERY, Alan*
NEIL, Andy
NEVINS, Laurie
PATERSON, George†
PEARSON, Stan†
PETCHEY, George*
POINTON, Bill†
PRYCE, Jack
ROBERTS, Billy
ROBINSON, Michael
RONALDSON, Duncan
SALT, Harold
SEXTON, Dave
SHANKS, Don
SMITH, Jack
SOMMER, Juergen
STAPLETON, Frank
SWINFEN, Reg†
TAYLOR, Geoff
VALLANCE, Hugh
VARCO, Percy
WALKER, Clive
WHITFIELD, Ken
WILKINS, Dean

Raith Rovers

CAVEN, Joe
McALLISTER, Billy
WALKER, Cyril†

Ramsgate

CASSIDY, Bill
GILBERT, Phil
HILLMAN, Dennis†
ISON, Ernie
JEST, Sid
LAVERICK, Bobby
McCURLEY, Kevin
READMAN, Joe
SMITH, Jack
STANLEY, Terry

Rangers

CASSIDY, Bill
EDWARDS, Alistair
KENNEDY, Andy
KIRKWOOD, Dan
LAWSON, Hector
MACAULAY, Archie*
McDONALD, Murdo
McKENNA, Harold
SMITH, Gordon
WINNING, Alex†

Reading

BENCE, Paul
BREMNER, Kevin
BROMLEY, Brian
BULLIMER, Leo‡
BURGESS, Ron†
BUTLIN, Barry
CLARK, Paul
CODNER, Robert
COTHLIFF, Harold†
CUNLIFFE, Arthur†
DAVIE, Jock
DAY, Albert
DIXON, Tommy
DOUGAL, Dave
DUCKWORTH, Joe
DUKE, George†
EDWARDS, Matthew
FEARON, Ron
FLACK, Doug†
GOOD, Micky
GREGORY, Fred†
GROVES, Ken†
HENDERSON, Stewart

HENLEY, Les†
HICKMAN, Mike
HODGSON, Sam†
HOWES, Arthur
HUMPHREY, John
ITHELL, Jimmy†
JENNINGS, Sam
JONES, Abe
JONES, Freddie
KEELEY, John
LANE, Billy*
LAYTON, Billy†
LEWIS, Allen
LYON, Bertie
McDONALD, Murd
MANSELL, Jack
MASKELL, Craig
MUTTITT, Ernie†
O'BRIEN, Joe
O'SULLIVAN, Peter
OWENS, Les
PATERSON, George†
RANDALL, Ossie
RITCHIE, George
RODGER, Tom
SMILLIE, Neil
TAIT, Tommy†
TAYLOR, Geoff
TUNNICLIFFE, Bill†
WALLER, Henry†
WILSON, Joe
YOUNG, Len

Rochdale

CHESTERS, Arthur†
CUNLIFFE, Arthur†
EASTHAM, George†
HALL, Jack E.
JENNINGS, Sam
JOHNSTON, Ron
KEEN, Eric†
KIRKMAN, Norman†
LONGDON, Billy
McHALE, Ray
MOULDEN, Paul
MUIR, Bob†
MURFIN, Clarrie
PARKES, David
PEAKE, Jason
PREST, Tommy
TOWNER, Tony
WILSON, Joe
YOUNG, Alan

Romford

ABBIS, Keith
BROWN, Jimmy†
HOLLINS, Dave
LANCELOTTE, Eric

Ross County

CASSIDY, Bill
McNEILL, Ian

Rotherham United, Rotherham County

CASSIDY, Bill
GILLIVER, Alan
GOULD, Wally
GREALISH, Tony
GREGORY, Fred†
HENNIGAN, Mike
HUTCHINGS, Chris
McDOUGALD, Junior
McEWAN, Billy
MANSELL, Jack
PARRY, Maurice‡
STEPHENS, Malcolm
TILER, Ken
TOWNER, Tony
TRUSSON, Mike
WILSON, Albert†

St Johnstone

BORTHWICK, Walter
COOK, R†
KIRKWOOD, Dan
OSWALD, Willie
PRYDE, Bob†

St Leonards StamCroft

BISSETT, Nicky
CHIVERS, Gary
GATTING, Steve
NELSON, Garry
TILTMAN, Richard
TRUSSON, Mike

St Mirren

BORTHWICK, Walter
McALLISTER, Billy
McAVOY, Frank
MACKAY, Tommy
McKENNA, Harold
McLAFFERTY, Maurice
MILLER, Ali
RUSSELL, Jock
SMITH, Gordon
WILSON, Alex

Salisbury

FITCH, Barry
GILBERT, Phil
GRANT, Alan
PINCHBECK, Cliff
WALKER, Bob

Scarborough

GABBIADINI, Ricardo
McEWAN, Billy
McHALE, Ray
RITCHIE, Andy

Scunthorpe United

CLELLAND, Dave
DONNELLY, Peter
GOODWIN, Freddie*
HARBURN, Peter
JONES, Les
MORRIS, Tom
MURFIN, Clarrie
PINCHBECK, Cliff
REES, Mal
SIDEBOTTOM, Geoff
SMITH, Reg
SMITH, Bobby
STEELE, Simon
WILSON, Danny

Sheffield United

BOOTH, Billy
BROWN, Freddie
BUTLIN, Barry
FEATHERSTONE, George
GILHOOLY, Paddy
GORDON, Les
GOULD, Wally
HARRISON, Jack
HAWLEY, Fred
HENDRY, Willie‡
HILL, Bob‡
HUMPHRIES, Bob
KENNEDY, Andy
LUMLEY, Joe
MACE, Stan
McEWAN, Billy
McGHIE, Joe
McHALE, Ray
McLAFFERTY, Maurice
MELLORS, Mark
MORRIS, Mark
MORTIMER, Dennis
NEEDHAM, Archie
ROWLEY, Arthur†

SIRRELL, Jimmy
TOWNER, Tony
TRUSSON, Mike
TURNER, Dave
WOOD, Paul
YOUNG, Alan

Sheffield Wednesday

BEECH, George
BENTLEY, Harry
BURTENSHAW, Steve
CRINSON, Bill
DEXTER, Charlie
DOBSON, Colin
DRIVER, Allenby†
EDWARDS, Len
GRUMMITT, Peter
HENNIGAN, Mike
JONES, Les
KIRKWOOD, Dan
LAW, Alec
MALLOCH, Jock‡
MANSELL, Jack
MAY, Larry
MEDHURST, Harry
MELLOR, Ian
MULRANEY, Jock†
OLIVER, Gavin
PARKES, David
POTTS, Eric
PRYCE, Jack
SALT, Harold
SHORT, Jimmy
SMITH, Dave
SMITH, Wilf
WALKER, Cyril†
WILKINSON, Howard
WILSON, Danny

Shelbourne

BRENNAN, Paddy
DORAN, Jack
HOWLETT, Gary
O'DOWD, Greg

Shoreham

BROMAGE, Russel
BROOMFIELD, Des
BROWN, Gary
BYRNE, John
CHAMBERLAIN, Bert
CHANNON, Vic
COLLINS, Ned
COLLINS, Jimmy
DUTTON, Harry
EACOCK, Jack
FLOOD, Paul
FUNNELL, Simon
GEARD, Glen
GEDDES, Gavin
HAIG-BROWN, Alan
HANNAM, Dave
LANGLEY, Ernie
LONGSTAFF, Bert
LONGSTAFF, Harvey
MAYBANK, Teddy
MILLER, Bill
O'SULLIVAN, Peter
PARLETT, Frank
SHERIDAN, Alex
SMITH, Reg
TILTMAN, Richard
TOWNSEND, Eric
TRUSLER, Johnny

Shrewsbury Town

BARHAM, Mark
BREMNER, Kevin
HENDRY, Willie‡
HUGHES, Darren
JONES, Mark
McNEILL, Ian

MARLOWE, Ricky
MULRANEY, Jock†
NIGHTINGALE, Jack
PHILLIPS, John
ROUGVIE, Doug
ROWLEY, Arthur†
THOMAS, Mickey

Sittingbourne

BARHAM, Mark
CASE, Jimmy
CLARKE, Nobby
GILGUN, Pat
MEADE, Raphael

Slough Town

BRILEY, Les
YOUNG, Eric

Southall

FASHANU, Justin
HUTCHINGS, Chris
LANHAM
MORRAD, Frank
PAYNE, John
REED, Walter

Southampton

ALLAN, Derek
BAIRD, Ian
BARLOW, K.†
BOWDEN, Ossie
BROPHY, Harry
BROWN, Kevan
BULL, Garry
CASE, Jimmy
CHIVERS, Martin
CURTIS, George*
DAVIE, Jock
FASHANU, Justin
FRANCE, Ernie†
GOTSMANOV, Sergei
GREGORY, Jack†
HASSELL, Tommy
HENNIGAN, Mike
JEPSON, Bert
JONES, Les
KIRKMAN, Norman†
LANEY, Les†
LEWIS, Doug†
LEWIS, George
LEWIS, Jack
LIVESEY, Charlie
McDONALD, Paul
McGRATH, John
McLEOD, Roddy‡
MASKELL, Craig
*MELIA, Jimmy**
MOORE, Jimmy
MOORHEAD, George
OSMAN, Russell
PADDINGTON, Albert
PIGGIN, Lionel
ROBERTSON, Tom
STEAR, Jimmy†
TAIT, Tommy†
THORNE, Albert†
TULLY, Fred†
WARD, Alf
WARREN, Christer
WEAVER, Sam†
WILCOCK, George
WILKINS, Jack
WORTHINGTON, Frank

Southend United

BENNETT, Ken
BOLLINGTON, Jack
BRISCOE, Jimmy†
BYRNE, Paul
CLARK, Paul
CODNER, Robert

DUBLIN, Keith
EGAN, Harry
FEARON, Ron
FELL, Gerry
GILBERG, Harry
HAYES, Billy
HILLMAN, Dennis†
HUTCHINGS, Chris
KEELEY, John
KELLY, Lawrie†
KITTO, Dick
LONGSTAFF, Harvey
McKENZIE, Duncan†
McNEILL, Ian
MARTIN, Dave
MIDDLETON, Billy
MUTTITT, Ernie†
NELSON, Garry
O'RAWE, Frank
OWERS, Adrian
PARRIS, George
RAMSEY, Chris
RODGERSON, Ted
RONALDSON, Duncan
ROWLEY, Arthur†
SMITH, Dave
SMITH, Wally
STEELE, Eric
STOTT, T.
THOMPSON, Cyril
*WELSH, Don**

Southport

EASTHAM, Harry†
FROST, Arthur†
GRAINGER, Jack†
GROVES, Kent†
HACKING, Bob
HILTON, Pat
ISON, Ernie
KEMP, Dirk†
LONGDON, Billy
MELIA, Jimmy*
OWENS, Les
PRYDE, Bob†
TAIT, Tommy†
WESTBY, Jack†

Southwick etc.

ARMSTRONG, Gerry
BARHAM, Mark
BISSET, Tommy
BRIGGS, Vic†
BROMAGE, Russel
BROWN, Gary
BROWN, Stan
BURTENSHAW, Charlie†
CHASE, Charlie
COLLINS, Arthur‡
COLLINS, Jimmy
COLLINS, Ned
DINEEN, Jack$
DOVEY, Alan
DUGNOLLE, Jack
DUKE, George†
EACOCK, Fred
ELLIOTT, Teddy
FLOOD, Paul
GALL, Norman
GEARD, Glen
GIPP, David
HANNAM, Dave
HARLAND, Lohmann
LANGLEY, Ernie
McILVENNY, Paddy
MASSIMO, Franco
MEADE, Raphael
MULLERY, Alan*
NEATE, Derek
NEWMAN, Daren
OHLENS, P. W.†
PAIGE, Jimmy‡

PARLETT, Frank
PIPER, Steve
POWNEY, Brian
ROLLINGS, Andy
SHEPHERD, John
SMART, Freddie
STANLEY, Terry
STEVENS, Norman
WEBB, Stan
WILLEMSE, Stan
WOFFINDEN, Colin

Stalybridge Celtic

ANTHONY, Walter
CHEETHAM, Jack
HAYES, Billy
McGHIE, Joe
McNICOL, Bob
MOORHOUSE, Ben
WORTHINGTON, Frank
WRIGHT, Tommy†

Stenhousemuir

KENNEDY, Willie

Stevenage Borough

CODNER, Robert
COLLINS, Jimmy
CURTIS, George*
FRANKS, Ken
HARBURN, Peter
HENNIGAN, Mike
STANDING, John
SMALL, Mike

Steyning Town

BATES, Don
FOREMAN, Denis
LONGSTAFF, Harvey
MASSIMO, Franco
NEATE, Derek
PARLETT, Frank
PIPER, Steve
STANLEY, Terry
VESSEY, Tony

Stirling Albion

BERTOLINI, Jack
McNICOL, Bob
SMITH, Gordon

Stockport County

BULLIMER, Leo‡
CRUMP, Fred
DODD, George
EASDALE, Jack†
GILLIVER, Alan
GORE, Les†
HAYES, Billy
JONES, Les
KEELEY, John
KENNEDY, Jimmy
KENNEDY, Willie
LUMBERG, Albert
MELIA, Jimmy*
NEEDHAM, Fred†
POSKETT, Malcolm
REECE, Tom†
ROBERTS, Billy
STEVENS, Jack
WASSALL, John†
WEAVER, Sam†
WEBBER, Keith
WHITE, Tom
WORTHINGTON, Frank

Stoke City

BILEY, Alan
BULLIMER, Leo‡
COLCLOUGH, Ephraim
CORRIGAN, Joe
CUNLIFFE, Arthur†

EYRES, Jack
GOULD, Wally
HALL, Ernie
HALL, Jack H.
HENDRY, Willie‡
JONES, Abe
MOUNTFORD, George†
PARKES, David
PARSONS, Ted
ROBERTSON, Tom
RUGGIERO, John
TAPKEN, Norman†
THOMAS, Mickey
TRUSSON, Mike
WATSON, Harold

Sunderland

BOLLINGTON, Jack
BYRNE, John
CLARKE, Jeff
CLOUGH, Brian*
CURTIS, George*
DAVIE, Jock
DILLON, John
FERGUSON, Mick
FORSTER, Derek
GABBIADINI, Ricardo
GOODCHILD, Johnny
HODGES, Cyril
HOLLEY, George
LONGAIR, Bill‡
McGHIE, Joe
MARTIN, Neil
RAMSDEN, Bernard†
ROWELL, Gary
STEWART, Tom
TAIT, Tommy†
TAPKEN, Norman†
WALKER, Clive
WALLER, Henry†
WILKINSON, Reg
WILSON, Alex
WORTHINGTON, Frank

Sutton United

FEARON, Ron
HORSCROFT, Grant
STILLE, Giles
VIRGO, James
WOFFINDEN, Colin

Swansea City

BURGESS, Ron†
CHEETHAM, Jack
CHIVERS, Gary
COLEMAN, Jimmy
CONNOR, Terry
CONWAY, Mick
*CURTIS, George***
DAVIES, Peter
DONNELLY, Peter
EASTHAM, George†
FOX, Dan†
HODGSON, Sam†
HOOPER, Percy†
HOYLAND, Fred
JONES, Les
LONGDON, Billy
McHALE, Ray
MORRIS, Billy
PHILLIPS, John
REED, Billy
REES, Mal
REID, Ernie†
SANDERS, Allan
SAUNDERS, Dean
SMITH, Bobby
SMITH, Jack
THOMAS, Lyn
TOWNSEND, Len†
WADE, Bryan

Swindon Town

BEAMISH, Ken
BENTLEY, Harry
BROADHEAD, Arnold
BROWN, Sam
CLARKE, Ray
DOWNSBOROUGH, Peter
EGAN, Harry
FORD, Fred†
HARDING, F.
HAWLEY, Fred
HOWELL, Ronnie
INNES, Bob
ITHELL, Jimmy†
JONES, Freddie
KENNEDY, Jimmy
KERR, Stuart
KIRKWOOD, Dan
LEGGETT, Peter
LYON, Bertie
McHALE, Ray
MASKELL, Craig
MILLS, Andy‡
MORGAN, Stan†
MUIR, Ian
NELSON, Garry
O'BRIEN, Joe
O'REGAN, Kieran
OAKDEN, Harry‡
PATERSON, George†
PIGGIN, Lionel
RAMSEY, Chris
RANDALL, Ossie
ROLLINGS, Andy
ROWE, Zeke
RUSHTON, George
SMITH, Bobby
SMITH, Jack
TEMPLEMAN, John
THOMAS, Lyn
THOMSON, Norman
TRANTER, Wilf
WADE, Bryan

Telford

BALDWIN, Harry
WASSALL, John†

Thames

KELLY, John

Third Lanark

BROWN, Sam
CALDWELL, Jock
HART, Archie†
LAWSON, Hector
LIVINGSTONE, Archie
McINNES, Jimmy†
McKENNA, Harold
MILLER, Ali
NEIL, Andy
SMITH, Jack

Tonbridge

BENNETT, Ken
BENNETT, Ron
BOORN, Alan
BURNS, Tony
CAROLAN, Joe
CHAPMAN, George
ELLIS, Syd
FLOOD, Paul
GILL, Eric
HIGGINS, Ron
LAVERICK, Bobby
LONGDON, Billy
McCOY, Tim
McCURLEY, Kevin
MARRIOTT, Ernie
SEYMOUR, Ian
SUTTLE, Ken

SWINFEN, Reg†

Tooting & Mitcham United

BUSBY, Dave
FLACK, Doug†
GRITT, Steve*
HOWELL, Ronnie
WOFFINDEN, Colin

Torquay United

BAXTER, Bobby
BENCE, Paul
BINNEY, Fred
COTHLIFF, Harold†
DAVIE, Jock
DEVONPORT, George†
FASHANU, Justin
FELL, Gerry
GREEN, Freddie
HALL, Fretwell
HICKMAN, Mike
LAMBERT, Martin
NELSON, Garry
PHILBIN, Jack
POINTON, Joe
PUGH, John†
ROLLINGS, Andy
SMITH, Dave
SOMMER, Juergen
TAIT, Tommy†
THOMAS, Rees
TIDDY, Mike
UPTON, Nobby
VARCO, Percy
WELSH, Don*
WRIGHT, Joe

Tottenham Hotspur

ADAMS, Billy†
ARCHER, Arthur
ARMSTRONG, Gerry
BEAL, Phil
BELLAMY, Walter
BENNETT, Ken
BRIGGS, Vic†
BURGESS, Ron†
CHIVERS, Martin
CLARKE, Ray
COLLINS, Jimmy
COOMBER, George
DAVIDSON, Jimmy‡
DAVIE, Jock
DICK, Ally$
EDWARDS, Matthew
FITCHIE, Tom
FLACK, Doug†
FORD, Fred†
GILBERG, Harry
GILHOOLY, Paddy
HAIG-BROWN, Alan
HENLEY, Les†
HOOPER, Percy†
HOPKINS, Mel
HUMPHRIES, Bob
HYDE, Len
JENNINGS, Sam
KENNEDY, Jimmy
KINNEAR, Joe
LANE, Billy*
LANHAM
LEACH, George
LOWE, Harry
McNAB, Neil
MULLERY, Alan*
O'DONNELL, Frank†
O'REILLY, Gary
PRYDE, Bob†
ROBERTS, Billy
ROBINSON, G. L.
RULE, Arthur
RUTHERFORD, Jack

SCOTT-WALFORD, Frank*
SMITH, Bobby
SPERRIN, Bill†
STEVENS, Gary
TOWNLEY, Jimmy
WALLIS, John†
WETTON, Albert
WHENT, Jack
WILSON, Joe†
WOODLEY, Vic†
YOUNG, Willie

Tranmere Rovers

BEAMISH, Ken
DUFFY, Alan
EASTHAM, Harry†
GRUNDY, Arnold†
HARLOCK, Des†
McNAB, Neil
MUIR, Ian
OLIVER, Gavin
WORTHINGTON, Frank

Tunbridge Wells United/Rangers

BRETT, Frank
CHANNON, Vic
DUGNOLLE, Jack
EACOCK, Fred
GARFIELD, Ben
GORDON, Dennis
GRANT, Alan
HANNAM, Dave
HUMPHRIES, Bob
LAMB, Billy
LEACH, George
McNICHOL, Johnny
ROBSON, Bert†
SCHOOLEY, Herbert
SHEPHERD, John
SPERRIN, Bill†
STEVENS, Norman
THAIR, Sid
TRUSLER, Johnny
VALLANCE, Hugh
WATSON, Jimmy
WEBB, Stan
WHITING, Bob

Walsall

ATTWOOD, Arthur
BALDWIN, Harry
BOLLINGTON, Jack
BRADFORD, Jack
BUCKLEY, Frank
CRUMP, Fred
DAVIES, Ken
DRIVER, Allenby†
EYRES, Jack
FLACK, Doug†
GOUGH, Tony
GREALISH, Tony
GRITT, Steve*
HORTON, Brian
HUTCHINGS, Chris
JONES, Syd†
LAYTON, Billy†
LYON, Bertie
MARTIN, Neil
MORGAN, Stan†
MOSELEY, Graham
POINTON, Joe
SALT, Harold
THOMSON, Norman
WALKER, Dave

Watford

AITKEN, George*
ARCHER, Arthur
ARMSTRONG, Gerry
BOWLES, Reg†
BURGESS, Ron†

CHASE, Charlie
CHIVERS, Gary
COLCLOUGH, Ephraim
COOMBER, George
CRAWFORD, Ted†
DAY, Albert
DIGWEED, Perry
DRIVER, Allenby†
DUBLIN, Keith
FLATTS, Mark
FULLER, Eddie
GARBUTT, Ray
GOOD, Micky
GOODEVE, Ken
GREGORY, Fred†
HASTINGS, Bill
HENDRY, Willie‡
HIGHAM, Gunner
HILL, Bob‡
HIPKIN, Reg
HURST, Stan
ISON, Ernie
KENNEDY, Andy
KENNEDY, Jimmy
KENT, Harry
LANE, Billy*
LEWIS, George
LIVESEY, Charlie
LOWE, Henry†
LYON, Bertie
McAVOY, Frank
MALPASS, Sam†
MARTINDALE, Len†
MATTHEWSON, George†
MEE, Gordon
MEOLA, Tony
MIDDLETON, Harry
MILLER, Bill
MORRIS, Mark
MUTTITT, Ernie†
POSKETT, Malcolm
REECE, Tom†
ROUTLEDGE, Ralph
SHARPE, Ivan
SMILLIE, Neil
SMITH, Jack
SPENCER, Frank
STEELE, Eric
THOMPSON, Cyril
TURNER, Bob‡
TYLER, Alfie
WALKER, Cyril†
WALLER, Henry†
WHITE, Tom
WILLIAMS, Reg
WOODHOUSE, Jack
WRAGG, Billy

Wealdstone

FERGUSON, Mick
GIPP, David

Wellingborough Town

HILL, W.
HYDE, Len
McCAIRNS, Tom

Welling United

BERRY, Les
COOPER, Geoff
GRITT, Steve*
SITFORD, Tony

West Bromwich Albion

ARMSTRONG, Gerry
BALDWIN, Harry
BARHAM, Mark
CHAMBERLAIN, Bert
CHAPMAN, George
CONNELLY, Eddie
DIGWEED, Perry
DUTTON, Harry

GARFIELD, Ben
GORDON, Dennis
GREALISH, Tony
HENDRY, Willie‡
HILTON, Pat
KING, Ernie
MACAULAY, Archie*
McLEOD, Roddy‡
MORTIMER, Dennis
O'REGAN, Kieran
ROWLEY, Arthur†
SPENCER, Geoff§
THOMAS, Mickey
VICKERS, Wilf

West Ham United

BRADY, Liam*
BROWN, Oliver
BURNETT, Dennis
CAMPBELL, Greg
CATER, Ron†
CURBISHLEY, Alan
*CURTIS, George**
DEAR, Brian
DIXON, Tommy
FASHANU, Justin
FLACK, Doug†
GILLESPIE, Ian†
GOODWIN, Fred
HENDERSON, Billy
HENLEY, Les†
HOOPER, Percy†
JENNINGS, Sam
JONES, Les
KELLY, Willie
LEWIS, Bill†
LUTTON, Bertie
LYON, Bertie
McATEER, Tom
MACAULAY, Archie*
MEDHURST, Harry
MUTTITT, Ernie†
PARRIS, George
PAYNE, John
*PETCHEY, George**
PRYDE, Bob†
REED, Peter$
SEXTON, Dave
SMALL, Mike
SMALL, Sammy
STANLEY, Terry
TOWNSEND, Len†
TURNER, Bob‡
WALLER, Henry†
WEAVER, Sam†
WHITING, Bob
WILLIAMS, Reg
YOUNG, Len

Weymouth

BRENNAN, Paddy
CLELLAND, Dave
JOHNSTON, Ron
KING, Ernie
LEGGETT, Peter
OSBORNE, Fred
WILSON, Fred†
WORTHINGTON, Frank

Whitehawk

BERTOLINI, Jack
BROWN, Gary
FELL, Gerry
GEARD, Glen
MAYBANK, Teddy
STEELE, Simon
WILLIAMS, Gary

Wigan Athletic

ADEKOLA, David
BROMLEY, Brian
McNEILL, Ian

PRYDE, Bob†
STORER, Stuart
WILSON, Danny

Wigan Borough

FAIRHURST, Billy†

Wimbledon

ARMSTRONG, Dave
BERRY, Greg
BRILEY, Les
BROWN, Stan
COLLINS, Jimmy
COTTERILL, Steve
DAREY, Jeff
DIGWEED, Perry
ELLIOTT, Mark
EVERITT, Mike
HENLEY, Les†
HOPKINS, Mel
KINNEAR, Joe
MARLOWE, Ricky
MARTIN, Dave
MORRIS, Mark
SHANKS, Don
SUDDABY, Peter
YOUNG, Eric

Woking

BEAL, Phil
BROWN, Kevan
CODNER, Robert
CRUMPLIN, John
MEDHURST, Harry
STEMP, Wayne
WALKER, Clive

Wolverhampton Wanderers

BAILEY, Mike*
BENNETT, Ron
BUCKLEY, Frank
*CURTIS, George**
DAVIES, Ken
HICKMAN, Mike
HIPKIN, Reg
HOLLEY, George
HUMPHREY, John
JACKSON, Allan
JACKSON, John*
LLOYD, Arthur
LUMBERG, Albert
LUTTON, Bertie
MELIA, Jimmy*
MILLBANK, Joe†
MORRIS, Tom
MULRANEY, Jock†
NEEDHAM, Archie
NIGHTINGALE, Jack
O'DONNELL, Frank†
POULTER, J.†
REDFERN, Bob
REECE, Tom†
RICHARDS, Billy
ROBERTS, Doug
ROWLEY, Arthur†
SIDEBOTTOM, Geoff
SMALL, Mike
STEELE, Eric
TOOTILL, Alf†
TOWNER, Tony
WHITFIELD, Ken
WILLIAMS, Jack
WILLIS, George
WILSON, Fred†
WOODWARD, Dai†
YOUNG, Eric

Worcester City

BALDWIN, Harry
COLLINS, Glyn
HUDSON, Colin

JONES, Mark
McQUARRIE, Andy
OSBORNE, Fred
VALLANCE, Hugh

Workington

ADAMS, Billy†
AITKEN, George*
BERTOLINI, Jack
DIXON, Tommy
DODD, George
GARBUTT, Ray
HARBURN, Peter
NAPIER, Kit
RUGGIERO, John
TRAINOR, Peter
VITTY, Jack

Worthing

ANSELL, George
ARMSTRONG, Gerry
BOOTH, Billy
BOWLES, Reg†
BRIGGS, Vic†
BUSBY, Dave
CHIVERS, Gary
CORMACK, Lee$
DINEEN, Jack$
DOVEY, Alan
DUGNOLLE, Jack
FLOOD, Paul
FULLER, Eddie
FUNNELL, Simon
GALL, Norman
GEARD, Glen
GEDDES, Gavin
GRUMMITT, Peter
HAIG-BROWN, Alan
HARMAN, Charlie†
KEELEY, John
LAMBERT, Martin
LLOYD, Barry*
LONGSTAFF, Harvey
McARTHUR, Willie‡
McCURLEY, Kevin
MASSIMO, Franco
NEATE, Derek
O'SULLIVAN, Peter
OWERS, Adrian
PIPER, Steve
SANDERS, Allan
STANLEY, Terry
STEELE, Simon
STEMP, Wayne
SUTTLE, Ken
TAYLOR, Joe
TILTMAN, Richard
VESSEY, Tony
WEBB, Charlie
WILKINS, Dean
WILLIAMS, Conde‡
WILSON, Alex
WOFFINDEN, Colin

Wrexham

BREMNER, Kevin
CASE, Jimmy
HOLLIS, Harry†
JONES, Ron†
LUMBERG, Albert
PUGH, Jimmy
THOMAS, Lyn
THOMAS, Mickey
TUNNICLIFFE, Bill†
WEAVER, Sam†
WEBBER, Keith

Wycombe Wanderers

ABBIS, Keith
BENCE, Paul
BOOK, Steve$
COOPER, Geoff

FUSCHILLO, Paul
GIPP, David
GREGORY, John
LAMBERT, Martin
McCARTHY, Paul
SMILLIE, Neil
SOMMER, Juergen
SUDDABY, Peter
WELSH, Don*

Yeovil Town

BRENNAN, Paddy
COLES, David
CONNOR, Terry
FARMER, Alex†
FERRIER, John
LLOYD, Barry*
PAYNE, John
SALT, Harold

York City

BULL, Garry
BYRNE, John
DANIELS, Harry
DUCKWORTH, Joe
EASTHAM, George†
EYRES, Jack
FELL, Gerry
GABBIADINI, Ricardo
GOODCHILD, Johnny
GOULD, Wally
HOWLETT, Gary
KEMP, Dirk†
MARSDEN, Harry
McINNES, Jimmy†
O'DONNELL, Frank†
PATERSON, George†
RAMSDEN, Bernard†
REDFERN, Bob
RUTHERFORD, Jack

Photo Credits

A & BC Chewing Gum (trade card)   32a, 32d, 119c

Adventure comic "Football Stars" (trade card)   72c

Albert Wilkes & Son, West Bromwich   107a, 179a, 221b, 257c

Aldershot F.C.   57b

William Avenell, Brighton (postcard)   17a

Avenell, Brighton, postcard   91c, 94d, 96b, 120a, 132b, 146a, 149a, 150a, 170d, 186b, 193a, 199b, 205a, 206b, 252b

B.S.Wood, Portslade (postcard)   106a, 172b

Brighton Camera Exchange (postcard)   263c

BCE postcard (Brighton Camera Exchange, 26 Market Street, Brighton)   24a, 24b, 33a, 38a, 41b, 49c, 51c, 60c, 65b, 69c, 74a, 77a, 89a, 97a, 99a, 103a, 109a, 123c, 124b, 125d, 126b, 129c, 140b, 154c, 157d, 149b, 158b, 168d, 173a, 185b, 187c, 190b, 200b, 219c, 225a, 226b, 236b, 241b, 243b, 261a, 267a, 272b

Brighton & Hove Albion F.C.   13a, 13d, 16b, 18a, 20a, 20b, 23a, 23b, 24c, 25a, 26b, 26c, 27c, 28b, 29a, 29b, 31a, 33b, 36a, 38b, 38c, 43a, 43b, 46d, 48b, 49a, 50a, 52a, 54b, 54c, 55d, 58a, 59c, 61b, 61c, 62b, 64b, 65a, 66a, 68b, 68c, 70c, 72b, 73b, 74c, 75a, 75c, 77d, 79d, 81b, 83c, 85a, 85d, 86a, 86b, 88a, 89b, 90b, 90c, 91a, 91b, 92c, 93b, 94a, 94b, 95b, 95c, 97d, 98a, 98c, 99b, 102a, 103b, 110a, 111a, 111b, 111c, 111d, 112b, 115b, 115c, 116b, 117a, 122b, 122c, 123a, 123d, 126a, 127b, 129a, 131a, 131b, 131c, 132c, 136b, 137a, 137c, 138b, 139a, 141a, 141c, 142b, 143b, 145c, 157b, 161c, 163a, 165a, 166a, 167b, 152b, 156a, 156b, 157c, 158c, 159c, 160a, 160b, 161a, 161b, 168a, 169a, 172d, 177a, 179c, 180b, 181a, 183a, 184d, 186a, 188b, 190a, 187b, 191a, 191b, 193b, 195a, 197a, 198a, 198b, 201a, 202a, 206c, 208c, 213a, 217b, 217c, 218b, 219a, 219d, 220a, 220c, 222d, 223a, 223b, 224a, 224b, 227d, 228a, 229a, 229b, 230a, 231a, 235a, 236c, 237a, 238a, 240b, 242a, 242b, 243a, 244c, 245b, 246b, 247d, 250b, 250c, 251b, 252a, 253a, 255c, 256b, 258b, 260b, 260c, 261b, 265c, 267c, 268c, 271a, 271c, 303f, 318b, 319a

Brighton & Hove Herald   18b, 32c, 55a, 55c, 68a, 77c, 88c, 96a, 104a, 113b, 144a, 147a, 173b, 196c, 231b, 251a, 264a, 304a, 304f, 309a, 310b, 333m, 333o

Brighton Gazette   71c

Deane, Wiles & Millar, Brighton (postcard)   47a, 74d, 76a, 78b, 135b, 153b, 172c, 174b, 179b, 185a, 220b, 255b, 263b, 272a

Evening Argus   16c, 21b, 23d, 26a, 27b, 28a, 29a, 35a, 35b, 36b, 37b, 39a, 39b, 39d, 42a, 44a, 44b, 46b, 47c, 48c, 53b, 53d, 54a, 59b, 62a, 63b, 65c, 66a, 69b, 71b, 74b, 77b, 78a, 78c, 79b, 82a, 84a, 86c, 89c, 92b, 93a, 97b, 100a, 100c, 101a, 106d, 114a, 115a, 116a, 117b, 117c, 118b, 119b, 121b, 124a, 125b, 127c, 130b, 134a, 135a, 136c, 140a, 143c, 144c, 145a, 148d, 166b, 167a, 155a, 156c, 157a, 158a, 159a, 170a, 171a, 174a, 174c, 176b, 176c, 177b, 183b, 184b, 186c, 188a, 187a, 194b, 196a, 198a, 199d, 203b, 204a, 206a, 207a, 208b, 209b, 210c, 211a, 213a, 214b, 215a, 216b, 216c, 222a, 227b, 230b, 231c, 232a, 233a, 233c, 239a, 242c, 249a, 256a, 263a, 265a, 267b, 268a, 270a, 273a, 273b, 274d, 303a, 303b, 303c, 303d, 303e, 304c, 304d, 304e, 312a, 313a, 314a, 315a, 316a, 316b, 317a, 333k, 333l, 333n, 333o, 333q

Foster, Brighton (postcard)   14b, 15b, 42b, 102b, 105d, 107b, 133b, 133c, 136a, 144b, 148c, 176a, 215b, 222c, 227a, 257a

G.A. Wiles (postcard)   30b, 35c, 40a, 42c, 76b, 79b, 83b, 109c, 110b, 112a, 145b, 162b, 182c, 189a, 196b, 199c, 200a, 204b, 208a, 213b, 258c, 262b, 269a

Hawkins, Brighton   32b, 46a, 57c, 92a, 118a, 121c, 137b, 191c, 215c, 236a, 236d, 238b

Hills & Saunders, Oxford   15a

J.D. Hunt, Tonbridge   146c, 235b

John Sinclair Ltd "Well Known Footballers" (trade card)   58c

Lambert Jackson, London N7   55b

Lancing College   104c

Lancing F.C.   269b, 278c, 283c, 286a, 296b

Monitor Press Features Ltd, London NW1   49b, 71a

Panini Ltd (sticker)   229c

E. Pannell, Hove (postcard)   16a, 17c, 22a, 30a, 34d, 36c, 37c, 40b, 40c, 47b, 50d, 53a, 59a, 63a, 70a, 72a, 75b, 76c, 79d, 83a, 84c, 85c, 97c, 102c, 106c, 108d, 110c, 113d, 123b, 128d, 133a, 143a, 147b, 147c, 148a, 164c, 166c, 155c, 169b, 170b, 170c, 171b, 184a, 192a, 192b, 200c, 205c, 210a, 219b, 221c, 225b, 228b, 234b, 238c, 247b, 247c, 258a, 259a, 272c

Pinnace (cigarette card)   26d, 39c, 61a, 105b, 128c, 173c, 184c, 212b, 212c, 214c

R & J Hill Ltd "Famous Footballers" (cigarette card)   217a

R. Armitage, Hove   106b, 138a, 226c, 253b

Robert L. Nicholson, Glasgow   124c

Sawbridgeworth Town F.C.   152a

Smith's "Cup Tie Cigarettes" (cigarette card)   85b, 149c

Stewart Weir   41a, 333r

Stuart Ashby   45a, 53, 70b, 82b, 90a, 103c, 227c

Supporters' Club handbooks   19b, 21c, 56b, 58b, 80a, 108b, 142a, 169c, 172a, 211d, 216d, 222b, 235a, 254a, 257b, 333b, 333e

Frank T. Dobinson, Brighton   34b, 178a, 239c, 250a, 260a

Sussex Daily News   245a, 277c, 278d, 285b, 288c, 333a

Sussex Sport Annual 1949–50   66c, 202b, 205b, 218c

Taddy & Co. "County Cricketers" (cigarette card)   141b

Taddy & Co. "Prominent Footballers" (cigarette card)   3a, 64a, 66b, 73a, 105c, 125c, 146b, 207b, 211c, 233b, 266a

Tim Carder   13c, 14a, 14c, 19a, 27a, 44c, 48a, 51a, 62c, 87a, 87b, 88b, 113c, 120b, 128a, 164b, 165c, 167c, 151b, 153c, 154b, 155b, 171c, 175c, 178b, 178c, 180a, 181b, 188c, 189c, 192c, 194a, 202c, 210b, 212a, 225c, 234a, 245c, 249b, 253c, 259b, 304b, 318a, 320a, 321a, 333s

Tudor Press Agency   22b, 182a, 216a, 221a, 241c

West Sussex Gazette   52b

Other photographs come from sources unknown.